CONTENTS

Published by SportsBooks Limited, 9 St Aubyns Place, York, YO24 1EQ
First published in 1887

Copyright © Stuart Barnes and SportsBooks 2014
www.sportsbooks.ltd.uk

A CIP catalogue ~~record for this book is available from the British Library.~~

Editorial compil~~ation by Stuart Barnes~~

ISBN-13 9781907524431

Front cover photograph of Mario Gotze scoring the goal that won the World Cup and back
cover photograph of Arsenal celebrating their FA Cup triumph by PAphotos.

Printed and bound in the UK by CPI Group (UK) Ltd, Croydon CRO 4YY

ROCK BOTTOM – NOW WILL THINGS START TO CHANGE?

By Stuart Barnes

WHERE DO ENGLAND and Roy Hodgson go from here? The glib reply would be: towards a friendly against Norway on September 3, followed five days later by the opening Euro 2016 qualifier in Switzerland. The serious response to the question concerns the direction the flagging national team and their embattled manager will take after a miserable showing in the World Cup. Evolution or revolution? Tinkering at the edges or radical reform? It could be argued that Hodgson's problems pale against those of Brazil after their shattering semi-final defeat by Germany and the loss to Holland in an admittedly hollow play-off match for third place. But that would be a trite view of our continuing failure to make an impact at international level which is testing the patience of England supporters to the point where their loyalty could be severely stretched in the months ahead. Further Euro qualifiers against Slovenia, Estonia, Lithuania and San Marino may offer a comfortable passage to the finals in France when an unthinkable third place in that group would probably still be enough to qualify because of UEFA's misguided increase in the number of finalists from 16 to 24, a decision which can only dilute the quality of the tournament. Whether the fans will feel it worthwhile to turn up at Wembley to see such modest fare is questionable. Unless, of course, they feel that a new-look team with a genuine chance of maturing into a force to be reckoned with is worth supporting in the same numbers.

Everyone has their own opinion about what changes should be made; I suspect an overwhelming majority in favour of major surgery, knowing that qualification will still be virtually guaranteed while the process of reshaping the side is taking place. At the time of this publication going to press, Steven Gerrard had not yet announced whether to carry on or call time after 114 caps to concentrate on his club football at Liverpool. The latter choice seemed to be on the cards. If so, I would hand the captaincy to Wayne Rooney in the hope it refreshes and revitalises his own international career, as well as handing him the responsibility of overseeing the development of some of the younger players like Ross Barkley, Luke Shaw, Raheem Sterling and possibly John Stones and Jon Flanagan. Defensive changes are a priority, with Glenn Johnson, Leighton Baines and Phil Jagielka unimpressive in Brazil, while fringe players James Milner and Rickie Lambert also look to be on the way out. Phil Jones could have an influential role, in the centre of the defence or as a midfield anchor, once new Manchester United manager Louis van Gaal decides which is his best position. And Arsenal's Theo Walcott, Alex Oxlade-Chamberlain and Jack Wilshere could have important parts to play if they can stay clear of the injury problems which dogged them last season. With Joe Hart unchallenged in goal, England's emerging line-up could look something like this: Hart; Flanagan, Cahill, Stones, Shaw; Jones, Henderson; Barkley, Rooney, Lallana; Sturridge. Other squad members: Forster, Walker, Smalling, Wilshere, Walcott, Oxlade-Chamberlain, Sterling, Welbeck. Worryingly, we were in a similar situation four years ago. After the 4-1 defeat by Germany in the last World Cup, the FA's football development officer, Sir Trevor Brooking, said: 'I am acutely aware there are no quick fixes and no easy answers. We must have more and better coaches with more access to more kids an earlier age.' At least England then made it to the last 16 in South Africa. This time, bottom place in the group not only showed that little progress has been made but that our presence at major championships – once revered – has become something of an irrelevance. This alone demands that we should follow the lead of Germany, who restructured coaching and administration and are now top of the world again. Six of the team that won the 2009 European Under-21 title – Neuer, Howedes, Boateng, Hummels, Khedira and Ozil – progressed to be World Cup winners five years later. From the England side, who were the beaten finalists, only Milner and Walcott have advanced. Those statistics speak for themselves. Regaining international respect and laying the foundations for a measure of success in the future will, first of all, involve an acceptance of how far we have fallen behind. Then, FA chairman Greg Dyke's commission on improving our game should be embraced. It has its faults, but increasing the number of English players playing regularly in the Premier League and banning non-European Union players outside the top flight would seem to be a step in the right direction.

WORLD CUP FINALS – BRAZIL 2014

GROUP A

BRAZIL 3 CROATIA 1
Sao Paulo (62,103); Thursday, June 12

Brazil (4-2-3-1): Julio Cesar, Dani Alves, Thiago Silva, Luiz, Marcelo, Paulinho (Hernanes 63), Luis Gustavo, Oscar, Hulk (Bernard 68), Neymar (Ramires 88), Fred. **Scorers:** Neymar (29, 71 pen), Oscar (90). **Booked:** Neymar, Luis Gustavo.
Croatia (4-2-3-1): Pletikosa, Srna, Corluka, Lovren, Vrsalijko, Modric, Rakitic, Perisic, Kovacic (Brozovic 61), Olic, Jelavic (Rebic 78). **Scorer:** Marcelo (11 og). **Booked:** Corluka, Lovren
Referee: Y Nishimua (Japan). **Half-time:** 1-1

MEXICO 1 CAMEROON 0
Natal (39,216); Friday, June 13

Mexico (5-3-2): Ochoa, Aguilar, Rodriguez, Marquez, Moreno, Layun, Herrera (Salcido 90), Vazquez, Guardado (Fabian 69), Dos Santos, Peralta (Hernandez 74). **Scorer:** Peralta (61). **Booked:** Moreno
Cameroon (4-3-2-1): Itandje, Djeuoue (Nounkeu 46), Nkoulou, Chedjou, Assou-Ekotto, Mbia, Song (Webo 90), Enoh, Moukandjo, Choupo-Moting, Eto'o. **Booked:** Nounkeu
Referee: W Roldan (Colombia). **Half-time:** 0-0

BRAZIL 0 MEXICO 0
Fortaleza (60,342); Tuesday, June 17

Brazil (4-2-3-1): Julio Cesar, Dani Alves, Thiago Silva, Luiz, Marcelo, Paulinho, Luiz Gustavo, Ramires (Bernard 46), Neymar, Oscar (Willian 84), Fred (Jo 68). **Booked:** Ramires, Thiago Silva
Mexico (5-3-2): Ochoa, Aguilar, Rodriguez, Marquez, Moreno, Layun, Herrera (Fabian 76), Vazquez, Guardado, Dos Santos (Jimenez 84), Peralta (Hernandez 74). **Booked:** Aguilar, Vazquez
Referee: C Cakir (Turkey)

CAMEROON 0 CROATIA 4
Manaus (39,982); Wednesday, June 18

Cameroon (4-3-2-1): Itandje, M'bia, Nkoulou, Chedjou (Nounkeu 46), Assou-Ekotto, Song, Matip, Enoh, Choupo-Moting (Salli 75), Moukandjo, Aboubakar (Webo 70). **Sent off:** Song (40)
Croatia (4-2-3-1): Pletikosa, Srna, Corluka, Lovren, Pranjic, Modric, Rakitic, Perisic (Rebic 78), Sammir (Kovacic 72), Olic (Eduardo 69), Mandzukic. **Scorers:** Olic (11), Perisic (48), Mandzukic (61, 73). **Booked:** Eduardo
Referee: P Proenca (Portugal). **Half-time:** 0-1

CAMEROON 1 BRAZIL 4
Brasilia (69,112); Monday, June 23

Cameroon (4-3-2-1): Itandje, Nyom, N'Koulou, Matip, Bedimo, M'Bia, N'Guemo, Enoh, Choupo-Moting (Makoun 81), Moukandjo (Salli 58), Aboubakar (Webo 72). **Scorer:** Matip (26). **Booked:** Enoh, Salli, M'Bia
Brazil (4-3-2-1): Julio Cesar, Dani Alves, Thiago Silva, Luiz, Marcelo, Paulinho (Fernandinho 46), Luiz Gustavo, Oscar, Hulk (Ramires 63), Neymar (Willian 71), Fred. **Scorers:** Neymar (17, 34), Fred (49), Fernandinho (84)
Referee: J Eriksson (Sweden). **Half-time:** 1-2

CROATIA 1 MEXICO 3
Recife (41,212); Monday, June 23

Croatia (4-3-2-1): Pletikosa, Srna, Corluka, Lovren, Vrsalijko (Kovacic 58), Modric, Rakitic, Pranjic (Jelavic 74), Perisic, Olic (Rebic 69), Mandzukic. **Scorer:** Perisic (87). **Booked:**

Rakitic. **Sent off**: Rebic (89)
Mexico (5-3-1-1): Ochoa, Aguilar, Rodriguez, Marquez, Moreno, Layun, Herrera. Vazquez, Guardado (Fabian 79), Dos Santos (Hernandez 62), Peralta (Pena 79). **Scorers**: Marquez (72), Guardado (75), Hernandez (82). **Booked**: Marquez, Vazquez
Referee: R Irmatov (Uzbekistan). **Half-time**: 0-0

GROUP TABLE

	P	W	D	L	F	A	Pts
Brazil Q	3	2	1	0	7	2	7
Mexico Q	3	2	1	0	4	1	7
Croatia	3	1	0	2	6	6	3
Cameroon	3	0	0	3	1	9	0

GROUP B

SPAIN 1 HOLLAND 5
Salvador (48,173); Friday, June 13

Spain (4-2-3-1): Casillas, Azpilicueta, Pique, Sergio Ramos, Jordi Alba, Busquets, Xabi Alonso (Pedro 63), Xavi, Silva (Fabregas 78), Iniesta, Diego Costa (Torres 63). **Scorer**: Xabi Alonso (27 pen). **Booked**: Casillas
Holland (3-4-1-2): Cillessen, Vlaar, De Vrij (Veltman 77), Martins Indi, Janmaat, De Guzman (Wijnaldum 62), De Jong, Blind, Sneijder, Van Persie (Lens 79), Robben. **Scorers**: Van Persie (44, 72), Robben (53, 80), De Vrij (64). **Booked**: De Guzman, De Vrij, Van Persie
Referee: N Rizzoli (Italy). **Half-time**: 1-1

CHILE 3 AUSTRALIA 1
Cuiaba (40,275); Friday, June 13

Chile (4-3-1-2): Bravo, Isla, Medel, Jara, Mena, Aranguiz, Diaz, Vidal (Gutierrez 60), Valdivia (Beausejour 68), Vargas (Pinilla 88), Sanchez. **Scorers**: Sanchez (12), Valdivia (14), Beausejour (90). **Booked**: Aranguiz
Australia (4-3-2-1): Ryan, Franjic (McGowan 49), Wilkinson, Spiranovic, Davidson, Jedinak, Bresciano (Troisi 78), Milligan, Leckie, Oar (Halloran 69), Cahill. **Scorer**: Cahill (35).
Booked: Cahill, Jedinak, Milligan
Referee: N Doue (Ivory Coast). **Half-time**: 2-1

AUSTRALIA 2 HOLLAND 3
Porto Alegre (42,877); Wednesday, June 18

Australia (4-2-3-1): Ryan, McGowan, Wilkinson, Spiranovic, Davidson, Jedinak, Bresciano (Bozanic 51), McKay, Leckie, Oar (Taggart 77), Cahill (Halloran 69). **Scorers**: Cahill (21), Jedinak (54 pen). **Booked**: Cahill
Holland (3-4-1-2): Cillessen, Vlaar, De Vrij, Martins Indi (Depay 45), Janmaat, De Guzman (Wijnaldum 78), De Jong, Blind, Sneijder, Van Persie (Lens 87), Robben. **Scorers**: Robben (20), Van Persie (58), Depay (68). **Booked**: Van Persie
Referee: D Haimoudi (Algeria). **Half-time**: 1-1

SPAIN 0 CHILE 2
Rio de Janeiro (74,101); Wednesday, June 18

Spain (4-2-3-1): Casillas, Azpilicueta, Javi Martinez, Sergio Ramos, Jordi Alba, Busquets, Xabi Alonso (Koke 46), Silva, Iniesta, Pedro (Cazorla 77), Diego Costa (Torres 64). **Booked**: Xabi Alonso
Chile (3-4-1-2): Bravo, Medel, Silva, Jara, Isla, Aranguiz (Gutierrez 64), Diaz, Mena, Vidal (Carmona 88), Vargas (Valdivia 85), Sanchez. **Scorers**: Vargas (20), Aranguiz (43). **Booked**: Vidal, Mena
Referee: M Geiger (USA). **Half-time**: 0-2

AUSTRALIA 0 SPAIN 3
Curitiba (39,375); Monday, June 23

Australia (4-3-2-1): Ryan, McGowan, Wilkinson, Spiranovic, Davidson, McKay, Jedinak, Bozanic (Bresciano 72), Leckie, Oar (Troisi 61), Taggart (Halloran 46). **Booked**: Spiranovic, Jedinak
Spain (4-3-2-1): Reina, Juanfran, Albiol, Sergio Ramos, Jordi Alba, Xabi Alonso (Silva 84), Iniesta, Koke, Cazorla (Fabregas 68), Villa (Mata 57), Torres. **Scorers**: Villa (36), Torres (69), Mata (82). **Booked**: Sergio Ramos
Referee: N Shukralla (Bahrain). **Half-time**: 0-1

HOLLAND 2 CHILE 0
Sao Paulo (62,996); Monday, June 23

Holland (4-3-1-2): Cillessen, Janmaat, Vlar, De Vrij, Blind, Wijnaldum, De Jong, Kuyt, Sneijder (Fer 75), Robben, Lens (Depay 69). **Scorers**: Fer (77), Depay (90). **Booked**: Blind
Chile (3-4-1-2): Bravo, Medel, Silva (Valdivia 70), Jara, Isla, Aranguiz, Diaz, Mena, Gutierrez (Beausejour 46) Vargas (Pinilla 81), Sanchez. **Booked**: Silva
Referee: B Gassama (Gambia). **Half-time**: 0-0

GROUP TABLE

	P	W	D	L	F	A	Pts
Holland Q	3	3	0	0	10	3	9
Chile Q	3	2	0	1	5	3	6
Spain	3	1	0	2	4	7	3
Australia	3	0	0	3	3	9	0

GROUP C

COLOMBIA 3 GREECE 0
Belo Horizonte (57,174); Saturday, June 14

Colombia (4-2-3-1): Ospina, Zuniga, Zapata, Yepes, Armero (Arias 74), Sanchez, Aguilar (Mejia 69), Cuadrado, Rodriguez, Ibarbo, Gutierrez (Martinez 76). **Scorers**: Armero (5), Gutierrez (58), Rodriguez (90). **Booked**: Sanchez
Greece (4-4-2): Karnezis, Torosidis, Manolas, Papastathopoulos, Holebas, Salpingidis (Fetfatzidis 57), Maniatos, Katsouranis, Kone (Karagounis 78), Samaras, Gekas (Mitroglou 64). **Booked**: Papastathopoulos, Salpingis
Referee: M Gelger (USA). **Half-time**: 1-0

IVORY COAST 2 JAPAN 1
Recife (40,267); Sunday, June 15

Ivory Coast (4-3-2-1): Barry, Aurier, Zokora, Bamba, Boka (Djakpa 75), Tiote, Y Toure, Serey Die (Drogba 62), Kalou, Gervinho, Bony (Ya Konan 78). **Scorers**: Bony (64), Gervinho (66). **Booked**: Bamba, Zokora
Japan (4-2-3-1): Kawashima, Uchida, Yoshida, Morishige, Nagatomo, Yamaguchi, Hasebe (Endo 53), Okazaki, Honda, Kagawa (Kakitani 86), Osako (Okubo 68). **Scorer**: Honda (16). **Booked**: Yoshida, Morishige
Referee: E Osses (Chile). **Half-time**: 0-1

COLOMBIA 2 IVORY COAST 1
Brasilia (68,748); Thursday, June 19

Colombia (4-2-3-1) Ospina, Zuniga, Zapata, Yepes, Armero (Arias 72), Aguilar (Mejia 78), Sanchez, Cuadrado, Rodriguez, Ibarbo (Quintero 53), Gutierrez. **Scorers**: Rodriguez (64), Quintero (70)
Ivory Coast (4-3-2-1): Barry, Aurier, Zokora, Bamba, Boka, Tiote, Y Toure, Serey Die (Bolly 73), Gervinho, Gradel (Kalou 67), Bony (Drogba 60). **Scorer**: Gervinho (73). **Booked**: Zokora, Tiote
Referee: H Webb (England). **Half-time**: 0-0

JAPAN 0 GREECE 0
Natal (39,485); Thursday, June 19

Japan (4-4-1-1): Kawashima, Uchida, Yoshida, Konno, Nagatomo, Okazaki, Yamaguchi, Hasebe (Endo 46), Okubo, Honda, Osako (Kagawa 57). **Booked**: Hasebe
Greece (4-3-2-1): Karnezis, Torosidis, Manolas, Papastathopoulos, Holebas, Maniatis, Katsouranis, Kone (Salpingidis 81), Fetfatzidis (Karagounis 41), Samaras, Mitroglou (Gekas 35). **Booked**: Katsouranis, Samaras, Torosidis. **Sent off**: Katsouranis (38)
Referee: J Aguilar (El Salvador)

JAPAN 1 COLOMBIA 4
Cuiaba (40,340); Tuesday, June 24

Japan (4-3-2-1): Kawashima, Uchida, Yoshida, Konno, Nagatomo, Aoyama (Yamaguchi 62), Honda, Hasebe, Okazaki (Kakitani 69), Kagawa (Kiyotake 85), Okubo. **Scorer**: Okazaki (45). **Booked**: Konno
Colombia (4-4-1-1): Ospina (Mondragon 85), Arias, Valdes, Balanta, Armero, Cuadrado (Carbonero 46), Mejia, Guarin, Quintero (Rodriguez 46) Martinez, Ramos. **Scorers**: Cuadrado (17), Martinez (55, 82), Rodriguez (89). **Booked**: Guarin
Referee: P Proenca (Portugal). **Half-time**: 1-1

GREECE 2 IVORY COAST 1
Fortaleza (59,095); Tuesday, June 24

Greece (4-3-2-1): Karnezis (Glykos 24), Torosidis, Manolas, Papastathopoulos, Holebas, Maniatis, Karagounis (Gekas 78), Christodoulopoulos, Kone (Samaris 12), Samaras, Salpingidis. **Scorers**: Samaris (42), Samaras (90 pen)
Ivory Coast (4-3-2-1): Barry, Aurier, K Toure, Bamba, Boka, Tiote (Bony 61), Y Toure, Serey Die, Kalou, Gervinho (Sio 83), Drogba (Diomande 78). **Scorer**: Bony (74). **Booked**: Drogba, Kalou, Serey Die
Referee: C Vera (Ecuador). **Half-time**: 1-0

GROUP TABLE

	P	W	D	L	F	A	Pts
Colombia Q	3	3	0	0	9	2	9
Greece Q	3	1	1	1	2	4	4
Ivory Coast	3	1	0	2	4	5	3
Japan	3	0	1	2	2	6	1

GROUP D

URUGUAY 1 COSTA RICA 3
Fortaleza (58,679); Saturday, June 14

Uruguay (4-4-2): Muslera, Maxi Pereira, Lugano, Godin, Caceres, Stuani, Arevalo, Gargano (A Gonzalez 60), Rodriguez (Hernandez 76), Forlan (Lodeiro 60), Cavani. **Scorer**: Cavani (24 pen). **Booked**: Lugano, Gargano, Caceres. **Sent off**: Maxi Pereira (90).
Costa Rica (5-2-2-1): Navas, Gamboa, Duarte, G Gonzalez, Umana, Diaz, Borges, Tajeda (Cubero 75), Ruiz (Urena 83), Bolanos (Barantes 89). Campbell. **Scorers**: Campbell (54), Duarte (57), Urena (84)
Referee: F Brych (Germany). **Half-time**: 1-0

ENGLAND 1 ITALY 2
Manaus (39,800); Saturday, June 14

England (4-2-3-1): Hart, Johnson, Cahill, Jagielka, Baines, Gerrard, Henderson (Wilshere 72), Welbeck (Barkley 61), Sterling, Rooney, Sturridge (Lallana 79). **Scorer**: Sturridge (37). **Booked**: Sterling
Italy (4-3-2-1): Sirigu, Darmian, Barzagli, Paletta, Chiellini, De Rossi, Verratti (Motta 57), Marchisio, Pirlo, Candreva (Parolo 79), Balotelli (Immobile 72). **Scorers**: Marchisio (35), Balotelli (50)
Referee: B Kuipers (Holland). **Half-time**: 1-1

URUGUAY 2 ENGLAND 1
Sao Paulo (62,575); Thursday, June 19
England (4-2-3-1): Hart, Johnson, Cahill, Jagielka, Baines, Gerrard, Henderson (Lambert 87, Sterling (Barkley 64), Rooney, Welbeck (Lallana 71), Sturridge. **Scorer:** Rooney (75). **Booked:** Gerrard
Uruguay (4-3-1-2): Muslera, Caceres, Gimenez, Godin, Arevalo, Pereira, Gonzalez (Fucile 79), Arevalo, Rodriguez, Lodeiro (Stuani 67), Suarez (Coates 89), Cavani. **Scorer:** Suarez (39, 85). **Booked:** Godin
Referee: C Velasco (Spain). **Half-time:** 1-0

ITALY 0 COSTA RICA 1
Recife (40,285); Friday, June 20
Italy (4-3-2-1): Buffon, Darmian, Barzagli, Chiellini, Abate, De Rossi, Pirlo, Thiago Motta (Cassano 46), Candreva (Insigne 57), Marchisio (Cerci 69), Balotelli. **Booked:** Balotelli
Costa Rica (5-2-2-1): Navas, Gamboa, Duarte, Gonzalez, Umana, Diaz, Borges, Tejeda (Cubero 68), Ruiz (Brenes 81), Bolanos, Campbell (Urena 74). **Scorer:** Ruiz (44). **Booked:** Cubero
Referee: E Osses (Chile). **Half-time:** 0-1

ITALY 0 URUGUAY 1
Natal (39,706); Tuesday, June 24
Italy (3-4-1-2): Buffon, Barzagli, Bonucci, Chiellini, Darmian, Verratti (Thiago Motta 75), Marchisio, De Sciglio, Pirlo, Immobile (Cassano 71), Balotelli (Parolo 46). **Booked:** Balotelli, De Sciglio. **Sent off:** Marchisio (59)
Uruguay (4-3-1-2): Muslera, Caceres, Gimenez, Godin, Arevalo, Pereira (Stuani 63), Gonzalez, Arevalo, Rodriguez (Ramirez 78), Lodeiro (Maxi Pereira 46), Suarez, Cavani. **Scorer:** Godin (81). **Booked:** Arevalo, Muslera
Referee: M Rodriguez (Mexico). **Half-time:** 0-0

COSTA RICA 0 ENGLAND 0
Belo Horizonte (57,823); Tuesday, June 24
Costa Rica (5-2-2-1): Navas, Gamboa, Duarte, Gonzalez, Miller, Diaz, Ruiz, Borges (Barrantes 78), Tejeda, Brenes (Bolanos 59), Campbell (Urena 66). **Booked:** Gonzalez
England (4-4-1-1): Foster, Jones, Cahill, Smalling, Shaw, Milner (Rooney 76), Lampard, Wilshere (Gerrard 73), Lallana (Sterling 62), Barkley, Sturridge. **Booked:** Barkley, Lallana
Referee: D Haimoudi (Algeria)

GROUP TABLE

	P	W	D	L	F	A	Pts
Costa Rica Q	3	2	1	0	4	1	7
Uruguay Q	3	2	0	1	4	4	6
Italy	3	1	0	2	2	3	3
England	3	0	1	2	2	4	1

GROUP E

SWITZERLAND 2 ECUADOR 1
Brasilia (68,351); Sunday, June 15
Switzerland (4-3-2-1): Benaglio, Lichtsteiner, Djourou, Von Bergen, Rodriguez, Behrami, Inler, Shaqiri, Xhaka, Stocker (Mehmedi 46), Drmic (Seferovic 75). **Scorers:** Mehmedi (48), Seferovic (90). **Booked:** Djourou
Ecuador (4-4-2): Dominguez, Paredes, Erazo, Guagua, Ayovi, A Valencia, Gruezo, Noboa, Montero (Rojas 76), Caicedo (Arroyo 70), E Valencia. **Scorer:** E Valencia (22). **Booked:** Paredes
Referee: R Irmatov (Uzbekistan). **Half-time:** 0-1

FRANCE 3 HONDURAS 0
Porto Alegre (43,012); Sunday, June 15

France (4-3-2-1): Lloris, Debuchy, Varane, Sakho, Evra, Pogba (Sissoko 57), Cabaye (Mavuba 65), Matuidi, Valbuena (Giroud 78), Griezmann, Benzema. **Scorers**: Benzema (45 pen, 72), Valladares (48 og). **Booked**: Evra, Pogba, Cabaye
Honduras (4-4-2): Valladares, Beckeles, Bernardez (Chavez 46), Figueroa, Izaguirre, Najar (Claros 58), Garrido, W Palacios, Espinoza, Bengtson (B Garcia 46), Costly. **Booked**: Palacios, Garcia, Garrido. **Sent off**: W Palacios (43)
Referee: S Ricci (Brazil). **Half-time**: 1-0

SWITZERLAND 2 FRANCE 5
Salvador (51,003); Friday, June 20

Switzerland (4-3-2-1): Benaglio, Lichtsteiner, Djourou, Von Bergen (Senderos 9), Rodriguez, Behrami (Dzemaili 46), Xhaka, Inler, Shaqiri, Mehmedi, Seferovic (Drmic 69). **Scorers**: Dzemaili (81), Xhaka (87)
France (4-3-2-1): Lloris, Debuchy, Varane, Sakho (Koscielny 66), Evra, Sissoko, Cabaye, Matuidi, Valbuena (Griezmann 82), Benzema, Giroud (Pogba 63). **Scorers**: Giroud (17), Matuidi (18), Valbuena (40), Benzema (67), Sissoko (73). **Booked**: Cabaye
Referee: B Kuipers (Holland). **Half-time**: 0-3

HONDURAS 1 ECUADOR 2
Curitiba (39,224); Friday, June 20

Honduras (4-4-2): Valladares, Beckeles, Bernardez, Figueroa, Izaguirre (J Garcia 46), B Garcia (Chavez 82), Garrido (Martinez 71), Claros, Espinoza, Bengtson, Costly. **Scorer**: Costly (31). **Booked**: Bernardez, Bengtson
Ecuador (4-4-2): Dominguez, Paredes, Erazo, Guagua, Ayovi, A Valencia, Minda (Gruezo 83), Noboa, Montero (Achilier 90), Caicedo (Mendez 82), E Valencia. **Scorer**: E Valencia (34, 65). **Booked**: A Valencia, E Valencia, Montero
Referee: B Williams (Australia). **Half-time**: 1-1

HONDURAS 0 SWITZERLAND 3
Manaus (40,322); Wednesday, June 25

Honduras (4-4-2): Valladares, Beckeles, Bernardez, Figueroa, J Garcia, B Garcia (Najar 77), W Palacios, Claros, Espinoza (Chavez 46), Bengtson, Costly (J Palacios 40). **Booked**: J Palacios
Switzerland (4-2-3-1): Benaglio, Lichtsteiner, Djourou, Schaer, Rodriguez, Behrami, Inler, Shaqiri (Dzemaili 87), Xhaka (Lang 77), Mehmedi, Drmic (Seferovic 73). **Scorer**: Shaqiri (6, 31, 71)
Referee: N Pitana (Argentina). **Half-time**: 0-2

ECUADOR 0 FRANCE 0
Rio de Janeiro (73,749); Wednesday, June 25

Ecuador (4-4-2): Dominguez, Paredes, Erazo, Guagua, Ayovi, A Valencia, Minda, Noboa (Caicedo 90), Montero (Ibarra 63), Arroyo (Achilier 82), E Valencia. **Booked**: Erazo. **Sent off**: A Valencia (50)
France (4-3-2-1): Lloris, Sagna, Koscielny, Sakho (Varane 61), Digne, Pogba, Schneiderlin, Matuidi (Giroud 67), Griezmann (Remy 79), Sissoko, Benzema
Referee: N Doue (Ivory Coast)

GROUP TABLE

	P	W	D	L	F	A	Pts
France Q	3	2	1	0	8	2	7
Switzerland Q	3	2	0	1	7	6	6
Ecuador	3	1	1	1	3	3	4
Honduras	3	0	0	3	1	8	0

GROUP F

ARGENTINA 2 BOSNIA-HERZEGOVINA 1
Rio de Janeiro (74,738); Sunday, June 15
Argentina (5-3-2): Romero, Zabaleta, Campagnaro (Gago 46), Fernandez, Garay, Rojo, Rodriguez (Higuain 46), Mascherano, Di Maria, Messi, Aguero (Biglia 87). **Scorers**: Kolasinac (3 og, Messi 65). **Booked**: Rojo
Bosnia-Herzegovina (4-2-3-1): Begovic, Mujdza (Ibisevic 69), Bicakcic, Spahic, Kolasinac, Pjanic, Misimovic (Medunjanin 74), Besic, Hajrovic (Visca 71), Lulic, Dzeko. **Scorer**: Ibisevic (84). **Booked**: Spahic
Referee: J Aguila (El Salvador). **Half-time**: 1-0

IRAN 0 NIGERIA 0
Curitiba (39,081); Monday, June 16
Iran (4-3-2-1): A Haghighi, Hosseini, Sadeghi, Montazeri, Pouladi, Heydari (Shojaei 89), Nekounam, Teymourian, Dejagh (Jahanbakhsh 78), Hajsafi, Ghoochannejhad. **Booked**: Teymourian
Nigeria (4-3-2-1): Enyeama, Ambrose, Oshaniwa, Oboobona (Yobo 29), Omeruo, Onazi, Azeez (Odemwingie 69), Mikel, Moses (Ameobi 52), Musa, Emenike
Referee: C Vera (Ecuador)

ARGENTINA 1 IRAN 0
Belo Horizonte (57,698); Saturday, June 21
Argentina (4-3-1-2): Romero, Zabaleta, Fernandez, Garay, Rojo, Gago, Mascherano, Di Maria (Biglia 90), Messi, Aguero (Lavezzi 77), Higuain (Palacio 77). **Scorer**: Messi (90)
Iran (4-3-2-1): A Haghighi, Hosseini, Sadeghi, Montazeri, Pouladi, Shojaei (Heydari 77) Nekounam, Teymourian, Dejagh (Jahanbakhsh 85), Hajsafi (R Haghighi 88), Ghoochannejhad
Booked: Nekounam, Shojaei
Referee: M Mazic (Serbia). **Half-time**: 0-0

NIGERIA 1 BOSNIA-HERZEGOVINA 0
Cuiaba (40,499); Saturday, June 21
Nigeria (4-4-1-1): Enyeama, Ambrose, Yobo, Oshaniwa, Omeruo, Musa (Ameobi 65), Onazi, Mikel, Babatunde (Uzoenyi 75), Odemwingie, Emenike. **Scorer**: Odemwingie (29). **Booked**: Mikel
Bosnia-Herzegovina (4-3-2-1): Begovic, Mujdza, Sunjic, Spahic, Medunjanin (Susic 64), Pjanic, Misimovic, Besic, Hajrovic (Ibisevic 57), Lulic, (Salihovic 58), Dzeko. **Booked**: Medunjanin
Referee: P O'Leary (New Zealand). **Half-time**: 1-0

NIGERIA 2 ARGENTINA 3
Porto Alegre (43,285); Wednesday, June 25
Nigeria (4-4-1-1): Enyeama, Ambrose, Yobo, Oshaniwa, Omeruo, Musa, Onazi, Mikel, Babatunde (Uchebo 66), Odemwingie (Nwofor 80, Emenike. **Scorer**: Musa (4, 47). **Booked**: Omeruo, Oshaniwa
Argentina (4-3-1-2): Romero, Zabaleta, Fernandez, Garay, Rojo, Gago, Mascherano, Di Maria, Messi (Alvarez 63), Aguero (Lavezzi 38), Higuain (Biglia 90). **Scorers**: Messi (3, 45), Rojo (50)
Referee: N Rizzoli (Italy). **Half-time**: 1-2

BOSNIA-HERZEGOVINA 3 IRAN 1
Salvador (48,011); Wednesday, June 25
Bosnia-Herzegovina (4-4-2): Begovic, Vrsajevic, Sunjic, Spahic, Kolasinac, Hadzic (Vranjes 61), Pjanic, Besic, Susic (Salihovic 61), Dzeko (Visca 84), Ibisevic. **Scorers**: Dzeko (23), Pjanic (59), Vrsajevic (83). **Booked**: Besic
Iran (4-3-2-1): A Haghighi, Hosseini, Sadeghi, Montazeri, Pouladi, Shojaei (Heydari 46),

Nekounam, Teymourian, Dejagh (Ansarifard 68), Hajsafi (Jahanbakhsh 63), Gnoochannejhad.
Scorer: Ghoochannejhad (82)
Referee: C Velasco (Spain), **Half-time**: 1-0

GROUP TABLE

	P	W	D	L	F	A	Pts
Argentina Q	3	3	0	0	6	3	9
Nigeria Q	3	1	1	1	3	3	4
Bosnia-Herz	3	1	0	2	4	4	3
Iran	3	0	1	2	1	4	1

GROUP G

GERMANY 4 PORTUGAL 0
Salvador (51,081); Monday, June 16

Germany (4-3-2-1): Neuer, Boateng, Mertesacker, Hummels (Mustafi 73), Howedes, Khedira, Lahm, Kroos, Ozil (Schurrle 63), Gotze, Muller (Podolski 80). **Scorers**: Muller (12 pen, 43, 78), Hummels (32)
Portugal (4-3-2-1): Rui Patricio, Joao Pereira, Bruno Alves, Pepe, Fabio Coentrao (Andre Almeida 65), Joao Moutinho, Miguel Veloso (Ricardo Costa 46), Raul Meireles, Nani, Ronaldo, Hugo Almeida (Eder 23). **Booked**: Joao Pereira
Referee: M Mazic (Serbia). **Half-time**: 3-0

GHANA 1 USA 2
Natal (39,760); Monday, June 16

Ghana (4-3-2-1): Kwarasey, Opare, Mensah, Boye, Asamoah, Rabiu (Essien 71), A Ayew, Muntari, J Ayew (Boateng 59), Atsu (Adomah 78), Gyan. **Scorer**: A Ayew (82). **Booked**: Rabiu, Muntari
USA (4-3-1-2): Howard, Johnson, Cameron, Besler (Brooks 46), Beasley, Bedoya (Zusi 77), Beckerman, Jones, Bradley, Altidore (Johannsson 23), Dempsey. **Scorers**: Dempsey (1), Brooks (86)
Referee: J Eriksson (Sweden). **Half-time**: 0-1

GERMANY 2 GHANA 2
Fortaleza (59,621); Saturday, June 21

Germany (4-3-2-1): Neuer, J Boateng (Mustafi 46), Mertesacker, Hummels, Howedes, Khedira (Schweinsteiger 70), Lahm, Kroos, Ozil, Gotze (Klose 69), Muller. **Scorers**: Gotze (51), Klose (71)
Ghana (4-3-2-1): Dauda, Afful, Mensah, Boye, Asamoah, Muntari, K Boateng (J Ayew 52), Rabiu (Agyemang-Badu 78), Atsu (Mubarak 72), A Ayew, Gyan. **Scorers**: A Ayew (54), Gyan (63). **Booked**: Muntari
Referee: S Ricci (Brazil). **Half-time**: 0-0

USA 2 PORTUGAL 2
Manaus (40,123); Sunday, June 22

USA (4-3-2-1): Howard, Johnson, Cameron, Besler, Beasley, Beckerman, Bradley, Jones, Bedoya (Yedlin 72), Zusi (Gonzalez 90), Dempsey (Wondolowski 87). **Scorers**: Jones (64), Dempsey (81). **Booked**: Jones
Portugal (4-3-2-1): Beto, Joao Pereira, Ricardo Costa, Bruno Alves, Andre Almeida (William 46), Joao Moutinho, Miguel Veloso, Raul Meireles (Varela 69), Nani, Ronaldo, Helder Postiga (Eder 16). **Scorers**: Nani (5), Varela (90)
Referee: N Pitana (Argentina). **Half-time**: 0-1

USA 0 GERMANY 1
Recife (41,876); Thursday, June 26

USA (4-2-3-1): Howard, Johnson, Gonzalez, Besler, Beasley, Beckerman, Jones, Zusi (Yedlin 84), Bradley, Davis (Bedoya 59), Dempsey. **Booked**: Gonzalez, Beckerman

Germany (4-3-2-1): Neuer, Boateng, Mertesacker, Hummels, Howedes, Schweinsteiger (Gotze 76), Lahm, Kroos, Ozil (Schurrle 89), Podolski (Klose 46), Muller. **Scorer**: Muller (55). **Booked**: Howedes

Referee: R Irmatov (Uzbekistan). **Half-time**: 0-0

PORTUGAL 2 GHANA 1
Brasilia (67,540); Thursday, June 26

Portugal (4-3-2-1): Beto (Eduardo 89), Joao Pereira, Pepe, Bruno Alves, Miguel Veloso, Joao Moutinho, William, Ruben Amorim, Nani, Ronaldo, Eder (Vieirinha 69). **Scorers**: Boye (30 og), Ronaldo (80). **Booked**: Joao Moutinho

Ghana (4-4-2): Dauda, Afful, Boye, Mensah, Asamoah, Atsu, Rabiu (Acquah 76), Agyemang-Badu, A Ayew (Mubarak 82), Waris (J Ayew 71), Gyan. **Scorer**: Gyan 57. **Booked**: Afful, Waris, J Ayew

Referee: N Shukralla (Bahrain). **Half-time**: 1-0

GROUP TABLE

	P	W	D	L	F	A	Pts
Germany Q	3	2	1	0	7	2	7
USA Q	3	1	1	1	4	4	4
Portugal	3	1	1	1	4	7	4
Ghana	3	0	1	2	4	6	1

GROUP H

BELGIUM 2 ALGERIA 1
Belo Horizonte (56,800); Tuesday, June 17

Belgium (4-3-2-1): Courtois, Alderweireld, Van Buyten, Kompany, Vertonghen, Witsel, De Bruyne, Dembele (Fellaini 65), Chadli (Mertens 46), Hazard, Lukaku (Origi 58). **Scorers**: Fellaini (70), Mertens (80). **Booked**: Vertonghen

Algeria (4-3-2-1): Mbolhi, Mostefa, Bougherra, Halliche, Ghoulam, Taider, Medjani (Ghilas 84), Bentaleb, Feghouli, Mahrez (Lacen 71), Soudani (Slimani 66). **Scorer**: Feghouli (24 pen). **Booked**: Bentaleb

Referee: M Rodriguez (Mexico). **Half-time**: 0-1

RUSSIA 1 SOUTH KOREA 1
Cuiaba (37,603); Tuesday, June 17

Russia (4-3-2-1): Akinfeev, Eschenko, Ignashevich, Berezutskiy, Kombarov, Faizulin, Glushakov (Denisov 71), Zhirkov (Kerzhakov 71), Samedov, Shatov (Dragoev 59), Kokorin. **Scorer**: Kerzhakov 74. **Booked**: Shatov

South Korea (4-4-2): Jung Sung-ryong, Lee Yong, Kim Young-gwon, Hong Jeong-ho (Hwang Seo-ho 72), Yun Suk-young, Ki Sung-yeung, Han Kook-young, Lee Chung-yong, Koo Ja-cheol, Park Chu-young (Lee Keun-ho 56), Son Heung-min (Kim Bo-kyung 84). **Scorer**: Lee Keun-ho (68). **Booked**: Son Heung-min, Ki Sung-yeung, Koo Ja-cheol

Referee: N Pitana (Argentina). **Half-time**: 0-0

BELGIUM 1 RUSSIA 0
Rio de Janeiro (73,819); Sunday, June 22

Belgium (4-3-2-1): Courtois, Alderweireld, Van Buyten, Kompany, Vermaelen (Vertonghen 31), Witsel, De Bruyne, Fellaini, Mertens (Mirallas 75), Hazard, Lukaku (Origi 57). **Scorer**: Origi (88). **Booked**: Witsel, Alderweireld

Russia (5-3-1-1): Akinfeev, Kozlov (Eshchenko 62), Berezutskiy, Glushakov, Ignashevich, Kombarov, Samedov (Kerzhakov 90), Faizulin, Shatov (Dzagoev 83), Kanunnikov, Kokorin. **Booked**: Glushakov

Referee: F Brych (Germany). **Half-time**: 0-0

SOUTH KOREA 2 ALGERIA 4
Porto Alegre (42,732); Sunday, June 22

South Korea (4-4-1-1): Jung Sung-ryong, Lee Yong, Kim Young-gwon, Hong Jeong-ho, Yun Suk-young, Ki Sung-yeung, Han Kook-young (Ji Dong-won 78), Lee Chung-yong (Lee Keun-ho 64), Koo Ja-cheol, Park Chu-young (Kim Shin-wook 57), Son Heung-min. **Scorers:** Son Heung-min (50), Koo Ja-cheol (72). **Booked:** Lee Yong, Han Kook-young

Algeria (5-2-2-1): Mbolhi, Mandi, Medjani, Bougherra (Belkalem 89), Halliche, Mesbah, Brahimi (Lacen 77), Djabou (Ghilas 73), Feghouli, Bentaleb, Slimani. **Scorers:** Slimani (26), Halliche (28), Djabou (38), Brahimi (62). **Booked:** Bougherra

Referee: W Roldan (Colombia). **Half-time:** 0-3

SOUTH KOREA 0 BELGIUM 1
Sao Paulo (61,397); Thursday, June 26

South Korea (4-4-2): Kim Seung-gyu, Lee Yong, Kim Young-gwon, Hong Jeong-ho, Yun Suk-young, Ki Sung-yeung, Han Kook-young (Lee Keun-ho 46), Lee Chung-yong, Koo Ja-cheol, Son Heung-min (Ji Dong-won 73), Kim Shin-wook (Kim Bo-kyung 66). **Booked:** Hong Jeong-ho

Belgium (4-3-2-1): Courtois, Vanden Borre, Van Buyten, Lombaerts, Vertonghen, Defour, Fellaini, Dembele, Mertens (Origi 60), Januzaj (Chadli 60), Mirallas (Hazard 88). **Scorer:** Vertonghen (77). **Booked:** Dembele. **Sent off:** Defour (44)

Referee: B Williams (Australia). **Half-time:** 0-0

ALGERIA 1 RUSSIA 1
Curitiba (39,311); Thursday, June 26

Algeria (4-4-1-1): Mbolhi, Mandi, Belkalem, Halliche, Mesbah, Feghouli, Medjani, Bentaleb, Djabou (Ghilas 77), Brahimi (Yebda 71), Slimani. **Scorer:** Slimani (60). **Booked:** Mesbah, Ghilas

Russia (4-4-1-1): Akinfeev, Kozlov, Berezutskiy, Ignashevich, Kombarov, Samedov, Glushakov (Denisov 46), Faizulin, Shatov (Dragoev 67), Kokorin, Kerzhakov (Kanunnikov 81). **Scorer:** Kokorin (6). **Booked:** Kozlov, Kombarov

Referee: C Cakir (Turkey). **Half-time:** 0-1

GROUP TABLE

	P	W	D	L	F	A	Pts
Belgium Q	3	3	0	0	4	1	9
Algeria Q	3	1	1	1	6	5	4
Russia	3	0	2	1	2	3	2
South Korea	3	0	1	2	3	6	1

ROUND OF 16

BRAZIL 1 CHILE 1 (aet, Brazil won 3-2 on pens)
Belo Horizonte (57,714); Saturday, June 28

Brazil (4-3-2-1): Julio Cesar, Dani Alves, Thiago Silva, Luiz, Marcelo, Fernandinho (Ramires 72), Luiz Gustavo, Oscar (Willian 106), Hulk, Neymar, Fred (Jo 64). **Scorer:** Luiz (18). **Booked:** Hulk, Luiz Gustavo, Jo, Dani Alves

Chile (3-4-1-2): Bravo, Medel (Rojas 108), Silva, Jara, Isla, Aranguiz, Diaz, Mena, Vidal (Pinilla 87), Sanchez, Vargas (Gutierrez 57). **Scorer:** Sanchez (32). **Booked:** Mena, Silva, Pinilla

Referee: H Webb (England). **Half-time:** 1-1

COLOMBIA 2 URUGUAY 0
Rio de Janeiro (73,804); Saturday, June 28

Colombia (4-4-2): Ospina, Zuniga, Zapata, Yepes, Armero, Cuadrado (Guarin 81), Aguilar, Sanchez, J Rodriguez (Ramos 85), Gutierrez (Mejia 68), Martinez. **Scorer:** J Rodriguez (28, 58). **Booked:** Armero

Uruguay (4-4-1-1): Muslera, Caceres, Gimenez, Godin, Maxi Pereira, Alvaro Perrira (Ramirez

53), Gonzalez (Hernandez 67), Arevalo, C Rodriguez, Cavani, Forlan (Stuani 53). **Booked**: Gimenez
Referee: B Kuipers (Holland). **Half-time**: 1-0

HOLLAND 2 MEXICO 1
Fortaleza (58,817); Sunday, June 29

Holland (4-3-1-2): Cillessen, Verhaegh (Depay 56), Vlaar, De Vrij, Blind, Kuyt, De Jong (Martins Indi 9), Wijnaldum, Sneijder, Robben, Van Persie (Huntelaar 76). **Scorers**: Sneijder (88), Huntelaar (90 pen)
Mexico (5-3-2): Ochoa, Aguilar, Rodriguez, Marquez, Moreno (Reyes 46), Layun, Herrera, Salcido, Guardado, Dos Santos (Aquino 61), Peralta (Hernandez 75). **Scorer**: Dos Santos (48). **Booked**: Aguilar, Marquez, Guardado
Referee: P Proenca (Portugal). **Half-time**: 0-0

COSTA RICA 1 GREECE 1 (aet, Costa Rica won 5-3 on pens)
Recife (41,242); Sunday, June 29

Costa Rica (5-2-2-1): Navas, Gamboa (Acosta 77), Duarte, Gonzalez, Umana, Diaz, Borges, Tejeda (Cubero 66), Ruiz, Bolanos (Brenes 83), Campbell. **Scorer**: Ruiz (52). **Booked**: Duarte, Tejeda, Ruiz, Navas. **Sent off**: Duarte (66)
Greece (4-3-2-1): Karnezis, Torosidis, Manolas, Papastathopoulos, Holebas, Maniatis (Katsouranis 78), Karagounis, Samaris (Mitroglou 58), Salpingidis (Gekas 69), Christodoulopoulos, Samaras. **Scorer**: Papastathopoulos (90). **Booked**: Samaris, Manolas
Referee: B Williams (Australia). **Half-time**: 0-0

FRANCE 2 NIGERIA 0
Brasilia (67,882); Monday, June 30

France (4-3-2-1): Lloris, Debuchy, Varane, Koscielny, Evra, Pogba, Cabaye, Matuidi, Valbuena (Sissoko 90), Benzema, Giroud (Griezmann 62). **Scorers**: Pogba (79), Yobo (90 og). **Booked**: Matuidi
Nigeria (4-4-1-1): Enyeama, Ambrose, Yobo, Oshinawa, Omeruo, Musa, Onazi (Gabriel 59), Mikel, Moses (Nwofor 89), Odemwingie, Emenike
Referee: M Geiger (USA). **Half-time**: 0-0

GERMANY 2 ALGERIA 1 (aet)
Porto Alegre (43,063); Monday, June 30

Germany (4-3-2-1): Neuer, Mustafi (Khedira 70), Mertesacker, Boateng, Howedes, Schweinsteiger (Kramer 109), Lahm, Kroos, Ozil, Gotze (Schurrle 46), Muller. **Scorers**: Schurrle (92), Ozil (119). **Booked**: Lahm
Algeria (4-2-3-1): Mbolhi, Mandi, Mostefa, Belkalem, Halliche (Bougherra 97), Lacen, Ghoulam, Taider (Brahimi 78), Feghouli, Slimani, Soudani (Djabou 100). **Scorer**: Djabou (120). **Booked**: Halliche
Referee: S Ricci (Brazil). **Half-time**: 0-0

ARGENTINA 1 SWITZERLAND 0 (aet)
Sao Paulo (63,255); Tuesday, July 1

Argentina (4-3-1-2): Romero, Zabaleta, Fernandez, Garay, Rojo (Basanta 105), Gago (Biglia 106), Mascherano, Di Maria, Messi, Lavezzi (Palacio 74), Higuain. **Scorer**: Di Maria (118). **Booked**: Rojo, Di Maria, Garay
Switzerland (4-2-3-1): Benaglio, Lichtsteiner, Djourou, Schar, Rodriguez, Behrami, Inler, Shaqiri, Xhaka (Fernandes 66), Mehmedi (Dzemaili 113), Drmic (Seferovic 82). **Booked**: Xhaka, Fernandes
Referee: J Eriksson (Sweden). **Half-time**: 0-0

BELGIUM 2 USA 1 (aet)
Salvador (51,227); Tuesday, July 1

Belgium (4-3-2-1): Courtois, Alderweireld, Van Buyten, Kompany, Vertonghen, Witsel, De Bruyne, Fellaini, Mertens (Mirallas 60), Hazard (Chadli 111), Origi (Lukaku 91). **Scorers**: De

Bruyne (93), Lukaku (105). **Booked**: Kompany
USA (4-3-2-1): Howard, Cameron, Gonzalez, Besler, Beasley, Zusi (Wondolowski 72), Jones, Bradley, Johnson (Yedlin 32), Bedoya (Green 105), Dempsey. **Scorer**: Green (107)
Referee: D Haimoudi (Algeria). **Half-time**: 0-0

QUARTER-FINALS

FRANCE 0 GERMANY 1
Rio de Janeiro (74,240); Friday, July 4
France (4-3-2-1): Lloris, Debuchy, Varane, Sakho (Koscielny 71), Evra, Pogba, Cabaye (Remy 73), Matuidi, Valbuena (Giroud 85), Griezmann, Benzema
Germany (4-2-3-1): Neuer, Lahm, Boateng, Hummels, Howedes, Schweinsteiger, Khedira, Kroos (Kramer 90), Muller, Ozil (Gotze 83), Klose (Schurrle 69). **Scorer**: Hummels (12).
Booked: Khedira, Schweinsteiger
Referee: N Pitana (Argentina). **Half-time**: 0-1

BRAZIL 2 COLOMBIA 1
Fortaleza (60,342); Friday, July 4
Brazil (4-2-3-1): Julio Cesar, Maicon, Thiago Silva, Luiz, Marcelo, Fernandinho, Paulinho (Hernanes 85), Hulk (Ramires 81), Oscar, Neymar (Henrique 87), Fred. **Scorers**: Thiago Silva (7), Luiz (68). **Booked**: Thiago Silva, Julio Cesar
Colombia (4-4-2): Ospina, Zuniga, Zapata, Yepes, Armero, Cuadrado (Quintero 81), Guarin, Sanchez, Ibarbo (Ramos 46), Gutierrez (Bacca 70), Rodriguez. **Scorer**: Rodriguez (80 pen).
Booked: Rodriguez, Yepes
Referee: C Velasco (Spain). **Half-time**: 1-0

ARGENTINA 1 BELGIUM 0
Brasilia (68,551); Saturday, July 5
Argentina (4-4-1-1): Romero, Zabaleta, Demichelis, Garay, Basanta, Lavezzi (Palacio 71), Biglia, Mascherano, Di Maria (Perez 33), Messi, Higuain (Gago 81). **Scorer**: Higuain (8).
Booked: Biglia
Belgium (4-3-2-1): Courtois, Alderweireld, Van Buyten, Kompany, Vertonghen, Witsel, De Bruyne, Fellaini, Mirallas (Mertens 60), Hazard (Chadli 75), Origi (Lukaku 59). **Booked**: Hazard, Alderweireld
Referee: N Rizzoli (Italy). **Half-time**: 1-0

HOLLAND 0 COSTA RICA 0 (aet, Holland won 4-3 on pens)
Salvador (51,179); Saturday, July 5
Holland (3-4-3): Cillessen (Krul 120), De Vrij, Vlaar, Martins Indi (Huntelaar 106), Kuyt, Wijnaldum, Sneijder, Blind, Robben, Van Persie, Depay (Lens 76). **Booked**: Martins Indi, Huntelaar
Costa Rica (5-2-2-1): Navas, Gamboa (Myrie 79), Acosta, Gonzalez, Umana, Diaz, Tejeda (Cubero 97), Borges, Ruiz, Bolanos, Campbell (Urena 66). **Booked**: Diaz, Umana, Gonzalez, Acosta
Referee: R Irmatov (Uzbekistan)

SEMI-FINALS

BRAZIL 1 GERMANY 7
Belo Horizonte (58,141); Tuesday, July 8
Brazil (4-2-3-1): Julio Cesar, Maicon, Luiz, Dante, Marcelo, Luiz Gustavo, Fernandinho (Paulinho 46), Hulk (Ramires 46), Oscar, Bernard, Fred (Willian 70). **Scorer**: Oscar (90).
Booked: Dante
Germany (4-2-3-1): Neuer, Lahm, Boateng, Hummels (Mertesacker 46), Howedes, Khedira (Draxler 76), Schweinsteiger, Kroos, Muller, Ozil, Klose (Schurrle 58). **Scorers**: Muller (11), Klose (23), Kroos (24, 26), Khedira (29), Schurrle (69, 79)
Referee: M Rodriguez (Mexico). **Half-time**: 0-5

HOLLAND 0 ARGENTINA 0 (aet, Argentina won 4-2 on pens)
Sao Paulo (63,267); Wednesday, July 9

Holland (3-4-1-2): Cillessen, Vlaar, De Vrij, Martins Indi (Janmaat 46), Kuyt, Wijnaldum, De Jong (Clasie 61), Blind, Sneijder, Robben, Van Persie (Huntelaar 96). **Booked**: Martins Indi, Huntelaar

Argentina (4-3-1-2): Romero, Zabaleta, Demichelis, Garay, Rojo, Biglia, Mascherano, Perez (Palacio 81), Messi, Higuain (Aguero 82), Lavezzi (Rodriguez 101). **Booked**: Demichelis
Referee: C Cakir (Turkey)

THIRD/FOURTH PLACE PLAY-OFF

BRAZIL 0 HOLLAND 3
Brasilia (68,034); Saturday, July 12

Brazil (4-2-3-1): Julio Cesar, Maicon, Thiago Silva, Luiz, Maxwell, Paulinho (Hernanes 57), Luiz Gustavo (Fernandinho 46), Ramires (Hulk 73), Oscar, Willian, Jo. **Booked**: Thiago Silva, Fernandinho, Oscar

Holland (3-4-1-2): Cillessen (Vorm 90), Vlaar, De Vrij, Martins Indi, Kuyt, Wijnaldum, Clasie (Veltman 90), Blind (Janmaat 70), De Guzman, Van Persie, Robben. **Scorers**: Van Persie (3 pen), Blind (16), Wijnaldum (90). **Booked**: Robben, De Guzman
Referee: D Haimoudi (Algeria). **Half-time**: 0-2

FINAL

GERMANY 1 ARGENTINA 0 (aet)
Estadio Maracana, Rio de Janeiro; Sunday, July 13

Germany (4-2-3-1): Neuer, Lahm (capt), Boateng, Hummels, Howedes, Kramer (Schurrle 32), Schweinsteiger, Muller, Kroos, Ozil (Mertesacker 120), Klose (Gotze 88). **Subs not used**: Weidenfeller, Zieler, Grosskreutz, Ginter, Podolski, Draxler, Durm. **Scorer**: Gotze (113). **Booked**: Schweinsteiger, Howedes. **Coach**: Joachim Low

Argentina (4-2-3-1): Romero, Zabaleta, Demichelis, Garay, Rojo, Biglia, Mascherano, Perez (Gago 86), Messi (capt), Lavezzi (Aguero 46), Higuain (Palacio 78). **Subs not used**: Andujar, Orion, Campagnaro, Di Maria, Rodriguez, A Fernandez, F Fernandez, Alvarez, Basanta. **Booked**: Mascherano, Aguero. **Coach**: Alejandro Sabella
Referee: N Rizzoli (Italy). **Half-time**: 0-0

BRAZIL 2014 FACTS AND FIGURES

Glory for Germany: Germany became the first European side to lift the trophy in the Americas. It was their fourth success in all, the last in Italy in 1990 when an 85th minute penalty by Andreas Brehme delivered victory over Argentina, who had two players sent off.

Super sub: Mario Gotze became the first substitute to score the winner in a World Cup Final.

Klose record: When Miroslav Klose scored Germany's second goal in their 7-1 semi-final victory over Brazil he became the tournament's all-time record marksman with 16. Klose overtook Brazil's Ronaldo, who was commentating on the match for television.

Brazil woe: That defeat was the worst in the hosts' history and their first at home in a competitive match since 1975 when they lost to Peru in the Copa America, also in Belo Horizonte. The margin was the biggest in any World Cup semi-final.

Scoring spree: There were 171 goals scored in the 64 matches, equalling the record total in France in 1998.

Golden Ball: Lionel Messi, Argentina's captain, was named the outstanding player of the finals.

Golden Boot: Colombia's James Rodriguez was top scorer with six goals, followed by Germany's Thomas Muller on five and Lionel Messi, Neymar (Brazil) and Robin van Persie (Holland) with four.

Golden Glove: Manuel Neuer, of Germany, received the award for the best goalkeeper.

Best young player: France's Paul Pogba, 21-year-old Juventus and former Manchester United midfielder.

Fair Play award: Colombia, who collected only five yellow cards in their five matches.

Red cards: Ten players were sent off, the lowest number since the 1986 tournament in Mexico when there were eight red cards.

England squad: Foster (WBA), Forster (Celtic), Hart (Manchester City); Baines (Everton), Cahill (Chelsea), Jagielka (Everton), Johnson (Liverpool), Jones (Manchester Utd), Shaw (Southampton), Smalling (Manchester Utd); Barkley (Everton), Gerrard (Liverpool, capt), Henderson (Liverpool), Lallana (Southampton), Lampard (Chelsea), Milner (Manchester City), Oxlade-Chamberlain (Arsenal), Sterling (Liverpool), Wilshere (Arsenal); Lambert (Liverpool), Rooney (Manchester Utd), Sturridge (Liverpool), Welbeck (Manchester Utd)

THE THINGS THEY SAY...

'We have players at their peak, but we also have young players in the squad who can go on to play on top of the world for a good few years yet. Then there are others not here who have fantastic futures' – **Joachim Low**, Germany's coach.

'I told him to show to the world that you are better than Messi and you can decide the World Cup. I had a good feeling about him' – **Joachim Low** on sending on match-winning substitute Mario Gotze.

'The players are bitter and sad because we had a huge dream. We needed to be more clinical' – **Alejandro Sabella**, Argentina's coach.

I'm very low. So are the players. We had high hopes of making an impact. I'm proud of the way they approached the tournament, but results colour everything. I've realised that at this level it is unbelievably unforgiving' – **Roy Hodgson**, England manager.

'If you look at the teams who have won the tournament, you can see the nastiness in them. I think we need to get that in us. Maybe we're too honest' – **Wayne Rooney**.

'It always ends like this. Soon the anger and shock will fade as the Premier League returns as more millions are lavished on new foreign stars' – **Patrick Collins**, *Mail on Sunday* columnist.

'We're supportive of Roy Hodgson – we've asked him to stay as manager. Roy has done a good job and it was always an approach for four years. We do not see any value in changing. We hope to do better in the next European Championship' – **Greg Dyke**, chairman of the FA.

'It's probably the worst moment of my life. The catastrophic result can be shared by the whole group. But I decided the tactics, so the person responsible is me' – **Luiz Felipe Scolari**, Brazil coach, after the 7-1 semi-final defeat by Germany.

'He is from Jupiter' – **Stephen Keshi**, Nigeria coach, after a match-winning performance from Argentina's Lionel Messi.

'Such behaviour cannot be tolerated on any football pitch, particularly at a World Cup when the eyes of millions of people are on the stars on the field,' **Claudio Sulser**, chairman of FIFA's disciplinary committee, announcing the four-month ban for Luis Suarez for biting Italy's Giorgio Chiellini.

HOW THE TEAMS QUALIFIED FOR BRAZIL
EUROPE
(Group winners qualified, plus winners of play-off matches involving eight best runners-up)

GROUP A

	P	W	D	L	F	A	Pts
Belgium Q	10	8	2	0	18	4	26
Croatia Q	10	5	2	3	12	9	17
Serbia	10	4	2	4	18	11	14
Scotland	10	3	2	5	8	12	11
Wales	10	3	1	6	9	20	10
Macedonia	10	2	1	7	7	16	7

Results: Croatia 1 Macedonia 0, Wales 0 Belgium 2, Scotland 0 Serbia 0, Serbia 6 Wales 1, Belgium 1 Croatia 1, Scotland 1 Macedonia 1, Macedonia 1 Croatia 2, Serbia 0 Belgium 3, Wales 2 Scotland 1, Croatia 2 Wales 0, Macedonia 1 Serbia 0, Belgium 2 Scotland 0, Croatia 2 Serbia 0, Macedonia 0 Belgium 2, Scotland 1 Wales 2, Belgium 1 Macedonia 0, Serbia 2 Scotland 0, Wales 1 Croatia 2, Belgium 2 Serbia 1, Croatia 0 Scotland 1, Serbia 1 Croatia 1, Macedonia 2 Wales 1, Scotland 0 Belgium 2, Wales 0 Serbia 3, Macedonia 1 Scotland 2, Croatia 1 Belgium 2, Wales 1 Macedonia 0, Scotland 2 Croatia 0, Belgium 1 Wales 1, Serbia 5 Macedonia 1

GROUP B

	P	W	D	L	F	A	Pts
Italy Q	10	6	4	0	19	9	22
Denmark	10	4	4	2	17	12	16
Czech Rep	10	4	3	3	13	9	15
Bulgaria	10	3	4	3	14	9	13
Armenia	10	4	1	5	12	13	13
Malta	10	1	0	9	5	28	3

Results: Malta 0 Armenia 1, Bulgaria 2 Italy 2, Denmark 0 Czech Rep 0, Bulgaria 1 Armenia 0, Italy 2 Malta 0, Czech Rep 3 Malta 1, Armenia 1 Italy 3, Bulgaria 1 Denmark 1, Czech Rep 0 Bulgaria 0, Italy 3 Denmark 1, Bulgaria 6 Malta 0, Denmark 3, Armenia 0 Czech Rep 3, Denmark 1 Bulgaria 1, Malta 0 Italy 2, Armenia 0 Malta 1, Czech Rep 0 Italy 0, Denmark 0 Armenia 4, Malta 1 Denmark 2, Italy 1 Bulgaria 0, Czech Rep 1 Armenia 2, Italy 2 Czech Rep 1, Armenia 0 Denmark 1, Malta 1 Bulgaria 2, Armenia 2 Bulgaria 1, Malta 1 Czech Rep 4, Denmark 2 Italy 2, Bulgaria 0 Czech Rep 1, Denmark 6 Malta 0, Italy 2 Armenia 2

GROUP C

	P	W	D	L	F	A	Pts
Germany Q	10	9	1	0	36	10	28
Sweden	10	6	2	2	19	14	20
Austria	10	5	2	3	20	10	17
Rep of Ireland	10	4	2	4	16	17	14
Kazakhstan	10	1	2	7	6	21	5
Faroe Is	10	0	1	9	4	29	1

Results: Kazakhstan 1 Rep of Ireland 2, Germany 3 Faroe Is 0, Austria 1 Germany 2, Sweden 2 Kazakhstan 0, Faroe Is 1 Sweden 2, Kazakhstan 0 Austria 0, Rep of Ireland 1 Germany 6, Faroe Is 1 Rep of Ireland 4, Austria 4 Kazakhstan 0, Germany 4 Sweden 4, Austria 6 Faroe Is 0, Kazakhstan 0 Germany 3, Sweden 0 Rep of Ireland 0, Germany 4

Kazakhstan 1, Rep of Ireland 2 Austria 2, Austria 2 Sweden 1, Rep of Ireland 3 Faroe Is 0, Sweden 2 Faroe Is 0, Rep of Ireland 1 Sweden 2, Germany 3 Austria 0, Kazakhstan 2 Faroe Is 1, Kazakhstan 0 Sweden 1, Austria 1 Rep of Ireland 0, Faroe Is 0 Germany 3, Sweden 2 Austria 1, Faroe Is 1 Kazakhstan 1, Germany 3 Rep of Ireland 0, Faroe Is 0 Austria 3, Rep of Ireland 3 Kazakhstan 1, Sweden 3 Germany 5

GROUP D

	P	W	D	L	F	A	Pts
Holland Q	10	9	1	0	34	5	28
Romania	10	6	1	3	19	12	19
Hungary	10	5	2	3	21	20	17
Turkey	10	5	1	4	16	9	16
Estonia	10	2	1	7	6	20	7
Andorra	10	0	0	10	0	30	0

Results: Estonia 0 Romania 2, Andorra 0 Hungary 5, Holland 2 Turkey 0, Romania 4 Andorra 0, Turkey 3 Estonia 0, Hungary 1 Holland 4, Turkey 0 Romania 1, Estonia 0 Hungary 1, Holland 3 Andorra 0, Andorra 0 Estonia 1, Romania 1 Holland 4, Hungary 3 Turkey 1, Andorra 0 Turkey 2, Holland 3 Estonia 0, Hungary 2 Romania 2, Estonia 2 Andorra 0, Holland 4 Romania 0, Turkey 1 Hungary 1, Turkey 5 Andorra 0, Estonia 2 Holland 2, Romania 3 Hungary 0, Andorra 0 Holland 2, Hungary 5 Estonia 1, Romania 0 Turkey 2, Holland 8 Hungary 1, Andorra 0 Romania 4, Estonia 0 Turkey 2, Hungary 2 Andorra 0, Turkey 0 Holland 2, Romania 2 Estonia 0

GROUP E

	P	W	D	L	F	A	Pts
Switzerland Q	10	7	3	0	17	6	24
Iceland	10	5	2	3	17	15	17
Slovenia	10	5	0	5	14	11	15
Norway	10	3	3	4	10	13	12
Albania	10	3	2	5	9	11	11
Cyprus	10	1	2	7	4	15	5

Results: Albania 3 Cyprus 1, Slovenia 0 Switzerland 2, Iceland 1 Norway 0, Cyprus 1 Iceland 0, Norway 2 Slovenia 1, Switzerland 2 Albania 0, Albania 1 Iceland 2, Switzerland 1 Norway 1, Slovenia 2 Cyprus 1, Cyprus 1 Norway 3, Iceland 0 Switzerland 2, Albania 1 Slovenia 0, Norway 0 Albania 1, Slovenia 1 Iceland 2, Cyprus 0 Switzerland 0, Albania 1 Norway 1, Iceland 2 Slovenia 4, Switzerland 1 Cyprus 0, Norway 2 Cyprus 0, Slovenia 1 Albania 0, Switzerland 4 Iceland 4, Iceland 2 Albania 1, Norway 0 Switzerland 2, Cyprus 0 Slovenia 2, Slovenia 3 Norway 0, Iceland 2 Cyprus 0, Albania 1 Switzerland 2, Cyprus 0 Albania 0, Norway 1 Iceland 1, Switzerland 1 Slovenia 0

GROUP F

	P	W	D	L	F	A	Pts
Russia Q	10	7	1	2	20	5	22
Portugal Q	10	6	3	1	20	9	21
Israel	10	3	5	2	19	14	14
Azerbaijan	10	1	6	3	7	11	9
N Ireland	10	1	4	5	9	17	7
Luxembourg	10	1	3	6	7	26	6

Results: Russia 2 N Ireland 0, Azerbaijan 1 Israel 1, Luxembourg 1 Portugal 2, Israel 0 Russia 4, N Ireland 1 Luxembourg 1, Portugal 3 Azerbaijan 0, Russia 1 Portugal 0, Luxembourg 0 Israel 6, Russia 1 Azerbaijan 0, Israel 3 Luxembourg 0, Portugal 1 N Ireland 1, N Ireland 1 Azerbaijan 1, Israel 3 Portugal 3, Luxembourg 0 Azerbaijan 0, Azerbaijan 0 Portugal 2, Northern Ireland 0 Israel 2, Azerbaijan 1 Luxembourg 1, Portugal 1 Russia 0, N Ireland 1

Russia 0, Russia 4 Luxembourg 1, Israel 1 Azerbaijan 1, N Ireland 2 Portugal 4, Luxembourg 3 N Ireland 2, Russia 3 Israel 1, Portugal 1 Israel 1, Luxembourg 0 Russia 4, Azerbaijan 2 N Ireland 0, Azerbaijan 1 Russia 1, Israel 1 N Ireland 1, Portugal 3 Luxembourg 0

GROUP G

	P	W	D	L	F	A	Pts
Bosnia-Herz Q	10	8	1	1	30	6	25
Greece Q	10	8	1	1	12	4	25
Slovakia	10	3	4	3	11	10	13
Lithuania	10	3	2	5	9	11	11
Latvia	10	2	2	6	10	20	8
Liechtenstein	10	0	2	8	4	25	2

Results: Liechtenstein 1 Bosnia-Herz 8, Lithuania 1 Slovakia 1, Latvia 1 Greece 2, Bosnia-Herz 4 Latvia 1, Slovakia 2 Liechtenstein 0, Greece 2 Lithuania 0, Liechtenstein 0 Lithuania 2, Slovakia 2 Latvia 1, Greece 0 Bosnia-Herz 0, Latvia 2 Liechtenstein 0, Bosnia-Herz 3 Lithuania 0, Slovakia 0 Greece 1, Bosnia-Herz 3 Greece 1, Liechtenstein 1 Latvia 1, Slovakia 1 Lithuania 1, Latvia 0 Bosnia-Herz 5, Liechtenstein 1 Slovakia 1, Lithuania 0 Greece 1, Latvia 2 Lithuania 1, Liechtenstein 0 Greece 1, Bosnia-Herz 0 Slovakia 1, Slovakia 1 Bosnia-Herz 2, Greece 1 Latvia 0, Lithuania 2 Liechtenstein 0, Lithuania 2 Latvia 0, Bosnia-Herz 4 Liechtenstein 1, Greece 1 Slovakia 0, Greece 2 Liechtenstein 0, Lithuania 0 Bosnia-Herz 1, Latvia 2 Slovakia 2

GROUP H

	P	W	D	L	F	A	Pts
England Q	10	6	4	0	31	4	22
Ukraine	10	6	3	1	28	4	21
Montenegro	10	4	3	3	18	17	15
Poland	10	3	4	3	18	12	13
Moldova	10	3	2	5	12	17	11
San Marino	10	0	0	10	1	54	0

Results: Montenegro 2 Poland 2, Moldova 0 England 5, San Marino 0 Montenegro 6, Poland 2 Moldova 0, England 1 Ukraine 1, Moldova 0 Ukraine 0, England 5 San Marino 0, Ukraine 0 Montenegro 1, San Marino 0 Moldova 2, Poland 1 England 1, Montenegro 3 San Marino 0, Moldova 0 Montenegro 1, Poland 1 Ukraine 3, San Marino 0 England 8, Montenegro 1 England 1, Poland 5 San Marino 0, Ukraine 2 Moldova 1, Montenegro 0 Ukraine 4, Moldova 1 Poland 1, Poland 1 Montenegro 1, Ukraine 9 San Marino 0, England 4 Moldova 0, San Marino 1 Poland 5, Ukraine 0 England 0, Moldova 3 San Marino 0, England 4 Montenegro 1, Ukraine 1 Poland 0, San Marino 0 Ukraine 8, Montenegro 2 Moldova 5, England 2 Poland 0

GROUP I

	P	W	D	L	F	A	Pts
Spain Q	8	6	2	0	14	3	20
France Q	8	5	2	1	15	6	17
Finland	8	2	3	3	5	9	9
Georgia	8	1	2	5	3	10	5
Belarus	8	1	1	6	7	16	4

Results: Georgia 1 Belarus 0, Finland 0 France 1, Georgia 0 Spain 1, France 3 Belarus 1, Finland 1 Georgia 1, Belarus 0 Spain 4, Belarus 2 Georgia 0, Spain 1 France 1, France 3 Georgia 1, Spain 1 Finland 1, France 0 Spain 1, Finland 1 Belarus 0, Belarus 1 Finland 1, Finland 0 Spain 2, Georgia 0 France 0, Georgia 0 Finland 1, Belarus 2 France 4, Spain 2 Belarus 1, France 3 Finland 0, Spain 2 Georgia 0

SOUTH AMERICA

(Top four qualified, along with fifth-placed team after play-off with Asia group play-off winners)

	P	W	D	L	F	A	Pts
Argentina Q	16	9	5	2	35	15	32
Colombia Q	16	9	3	4	27	13	30
Chile Q	16	9	1	6	29	25	28
Ecuador Q	16	7	4	5	20	16	25
Uruguay Q	16	7	4	5	25	25	25
Venezuela	16	5	5	6	14	20	20
Peru	16	4	3	9	17	26	15
Bolivia	16	2	6	8	17	30	12
Paraguay	16	3	3	10	17	31	12

Results: Ecuador 2 Venezuela 0, Uruguay 4 Bolivia 2, Argentina 4 Chile 1, Peru 2 Paraguay 0, Bolivia 1 Colombia 2, Paraguay 1 Uruguay 1, Chile 4 Peru 2, Venezuela 1 Argentina 0, Argentina 1 Bolivia 1, Colombia 1 Venezuela 1, Uruguay 4 Chile 0, Paraguay 2 Ecuador 1, Colombia 1 Argentina 2, Ecuador 2 Peru 0, Venezuela 1 Bolivia 0, Chile 2 Paraguay 0, Uruguay 1 Venezuela 1, Bolivia 0 Chile 2, Argentina 4 Ecuador 0, Peru 0 Colombia 1, Bolivia 3 Paraguay 1, Venezuela 0 Chile 2, Uruguay 4 Peru 2, Ecuador 1 Colombia 0, Colombia 4 Uruguay 0, Ecuador 1 Bolivia 0, Argentina 3 Paraguay 1, Peru 2 Venezuela 1, Chile 1 Colombia 3, Uruguay 1 Ecuador 1, Paraguay 0 Venezuela 2, Peru 1 Argentina 1, Colombia 2 Paraguay 0, Bolivia 1 Peru 1, Ecuador 3 Chile 1, Argentina 3 Uruguay 0, Bolivia 4, Uruguay 1, Venezuela 1 Ecuador 1, Paraguay 1 Peru 0, Chile 1 Argentina 2, Colombia 5 Bolivia 0, Uruguay 1 Paraguay 1, Argentina 3 Venezuela 0, Peru 1 Chile 0, Ecuador 4 Paraguay 1, Bolivia 1 Argentina 1, Venezuela 1 Colombia 0, Chile 2 Uruguay 0, Bolivia 1 Venezuela 1, Argentina 0 Colombia 0, Paraguay 1 Chile 2, Peru 1 Ecuador 0, Colombia 2 Peru 0, Ecuador 1 Argentina 1, Venezuela 0 Uruguay 1, Chile 3 Bolivia 1, Chile 3 Venezuela 0, Colombia 1 Ecuador 0, Paraguay 4 Bolivia 0, Peru 1 Uruguay 2, Bolivia 1 Ecuador 1, Paraguay 2 Argentina 5, Uruguay 2 Colombia 0, Venezuela 3 Peru 2, Argentina 3 Peru 1, Colombia 3 Chile 3, Ecuador 1 Uruguay 0, Venezuela 1 Paraguay 1, Chile 2 Ecuador 1, Paraguay 1 Colombia 2, Peru 1 Bolivia 1, Uruguay 3 Argentina 2

AFRICA

(Group winners to play-offs – five teams qualified)

GROUP A

	P	W	D	L	F	A	Pts
Ethiopia	6	4	1	1	8	6	13
South Africa	6	3	2	1	12	5	11
Botswana	6	2	1	3	8	10	7
Cent Af Rep	6	1	0	5	5	12	3

GROUP B

	P	W	D	L	F	A	Pts
Tunisia	6	4	2	0	13	6	14
Cape Verde	6	3	0	3	9	7	9
Sierra Leone	6	2	2	2	10	10	8
Eq Guinea	6	0	2	4	6	15	2

GROUP C

	P	W	D	L	F	A	Pts
Ivory Coast Q	6	4	2	0	15	5	14
Morocco	6	2	3	1	9	8	9
Tanzania	6	2	0	4	8	12	6
Gambia	6	1	1	4	4	11	4

GROUP D

	P	W	D	L	F	A	Pts
Ghana Q	6	5	0	1	18	3	15
Zambia	6	3	2	1	11	4	11
Lesotho	6	1	2	3	4	15	5
Sudan	6	0	2	4	3	14	2

GROUP E

	P	W	D	L	F	A	Pts
Burkina Faso	6	4	0	2	7	4	12
Rep Congo	6	3	2	1	7	3	11
Gabon	6	2	1	3	5	6	7
Niger	6	1	1	4	6	12	4

GROUP F

	P	W	D	L	F	A	Pts
Nigeria Q	6	3	3	0	7	3	12
Malawi	6	1	4	1	4	5	7
Kenya	6	1	3	2	4	5	6
Namibia	6	1	2	3	2	4	5

GROUP G

	P	W	D	L	F	A	Pts
Egypt	6	6	0	0	16	7	18
Guinea	6	3	1	2	12	8	10
Mozambique	6	0	3	3	2	10	3
Zimbabwe	6	0	2	4	4	9	2

GROUP H

	P	W	D	L	F	A	Pts
Algeria Q	6	5	0	1	13	4	15
Mali	6	2	2	2	7	7	8
Benin	6	2	2	2	8	9	8
Rwanda	6	0	2	4	3	11	2

GROUP I

	P	W	D	L	F	A	Pts
Cameroon Q	6	4	1	1	8	3	13
Libya	6	2	3	1	5	3	9
DR Congo	6	1	3	2	3	3	6
Togo	6	1	1	4	4	11	4

GROUP J

	P	W	D	L	F	A	Pts
Senegal	6	3	3	0	9	4	12
Uganda	6	2	2	2	5	6	8
Angola	6	1	4	1	8	6	7
Liberia	6	1	1	4	4	10	4

ASIA

(Top two from each group qualified. Third-placed teams played off – winner meeting fifth-placed South American side)

GROUP A

	P	W	D	L	F	A	Pts
Iran Q	8	5	1	2	8	2	16
South Korea Q	8	4	2	2	13	7	14
Uzbekistan	8	4	2	2	11	6	14
Qatar	8	2	1	5	5	13	7
Lebanon	8	1	2	5	3	12	5

GROUP B

	P	W	D	L	F	A	Pts
Japan Q	8	5	2	1	16	5	17
Australia Q	8	3	4	1	12	7	13
Jordan	8	3	1	4	7	16	10
Oman	8	2	3	3	7	10	9
Iraq	8	1	2	5	4	8	5

Group play-off: Jordan 2 Uzbekistan 2 (1-1, 1-1 aet) – Jordan won 9-8 on pens

NORTH, CENTRAL AMERICA AND CARIBBEAN

(Top three qualified, fourth team met Oceania group winners in play-off)

	P	W	D	L	F	A	Pts
USA Q	10	7	1	2	15	8	22
Costa Rica Q	10	5	3	2	13	7	18
Honduras Q	10	4	3	3	13	12	15
Mexico Q	10	2	5	3	7	9	11
Panama	10	1	5	4	10	14	8
Jamaica	10	0	5	5	5	13	5

OCEANIA

(Top team played off against fourth-placed North, Central America and Caribbean team)

	P	W	D	L	F	A	Pts
New Zealand	6	6	0	0	17	2	18
New Caledonia	6	4	0	2	17	6	12
Tahiti	6	1	0	5	2	12	3
Solomon Is	6	1	0	5	5	21	3

PLAY-OFFS

Europe: Croatia beat Iceland 2-0 (0-0, 2-0); France beat Ukraine 3-2 (0-2, 3-0); Greece beat Romania 4-2 (3-1, 1-1); Portugal beat Sweden 4-2 (1-0, 3-2)

South America/Asia: Uruguay beat Jordan 5-0 (5-0, 0-0)

Africa: Algeria 3 Burkina Faso 3 (2-3, 1-0, Algeria won on away goals); Cameroon beat Tunisia 4-1 (0-0, 4-1); Ghana beat Egypt 7-3 (6-1, 1-2); Ivory Coast beat Senegal 4-2 (3-1,1-1); Nigeria beat Ethiopia 4-1 (2-1, 2-0)

North, Central America and Caribbean/Oceania: Mexico 9 New Zealand 3 (5-1, 4-2)

WORLD CUP SUMMARIES 1930–2010

1930 – URUGUAY
WINNERS: Uruguay RUNNERS-UP: Argentina THIRD: USA FOURTH: Yugoslavia
Other countries taking part: Belgium, Bolivia, Brazil, Chile, France, Mexico, Paraguay, Peru, Romania. **Total entries:** 13
Venue: All matches played in Montevideo
Top scorer: Stabile (Argentina) 8 goals
Final (30/7/30): **Uruguay 4** (Dorado 12, Cea 55, Iriarte 64, Castro 89) **Argentina 2** (Peucelle 29, Stabile 35). **Att:** 90,000
Uruguay: Ballesteros; Nasazzi (capt), Mascheroni, Andrade, Fernandez, Gestido, Dorado, Scarone, Castro, Cea, Iriarte
Argentina: Botasso; Della Torre, Paternoster, J Evaristo, Monti, Suarez, Peucelle, Varallo, Stabile, Ferreira (capt), M Evaristo
Referee: Langenus (Belgium). **Half-time:** 1-2

1934 – ITALY
WINNERS: Italy RUNNERS-UP: Czechoslovakia THIRD: Germany FOURTH: Austria
Other countries in finals: Argentina, Belgium, Brazil, Egypt, France, Holland, Hungary, Romania, Spain, Sweden, Switzerland, USA. **Total entries:** 29 (16 qualifiers)
Venues: Bologna, Florence, Genoa, Milan, Naples, Rome, Trieste, Turin
Top scorers: Conen (Germany), Nejedly (Czechoslovakia), Schiavio (Italy), each 4 goals. **Final** (Rome, 10/6/34): **Italy 2** (Orsi 82, Schiavio 97) **Czechoslovakia 1** (Puc 70) after extra-time. **Att:** 50,000
Italy: Combi (capt); Monzeglio, Allemandi, Ferraris, Monti, Bertolini, Guaita, Meazza, Schiavio, Ferrari, Orsi
Czechoslovakia: Planicka (capt); Zenisek, Ctyroky, Kostalek, Cambal, Krcil, Junek, Svoboda, Sobotka, Nejedly, Puc
Referee: Eklind (Sweden). **Half-time:** 0-0 (90 mins: 1-1)

1938 – FRANCE
WINNERS: Italy RUNNERS-UP: Hungary THIRD: Brazil FOURTH: Sweden
Other countries in finals: Belgium, Cuba, Czechoslovakia, Dutch East Indies, France, Germany, Holland, Norway, Poland, Romania, Switzerland. **Total entries:** 25 (15 qualifiers)
Venues: Antibes, Bordeaux, Le Havre, Lille, Marseille, Paris, Reims, Strasbourg, Toulouse
Top scorer: Leonidas (Brazil) 8 goals
Final (Paris, 19/6/38): **Italy 4** (Colaussi 6, 36, Piola 15, 81) **Hungary 2** (Titkos 7, Sarosi 65). **Att:** 45,000
Italy: Olivieri; Foni, Rava, Serantoni, Andreolo, Locatelli, Biavati, Meazza (capt), Piola, Ferrari, Colaussi
Hungary: Szabo; Polgar, Biro, Szalay, Szucs, Lazar, Sas, Vincze, Sarosi (capt), Szengeller, Titkos

1950 – BRAZIL

WINNERS: Uruguay RUNNERS-UP: Brazil THIRD: Sweden FOURTH: Spain
Other countries in finals: Bolivia, Chile, England, Italy, Mexico, Paraguay, Switzerland, USA, Yugoslavia. **Total entries:** 29 (13 qualifiers)
Venues: Belo Horizonte, Curitiba, Porto Alegre, Recife, Rio de Janeiro, Sao Paulo
Top scorer: Ademir (Brazil) 9 goals
Deciding Match (Rio de Janeiro, 16/7/50): **Uruguay 2** (Schiaffino 64, Ghiggia 79) **Brazil 1** (Friaca 47). **Att:** 199,850
(For the only time, the World Cup was decided on a final pool system, in which the winners of the four qualifying groups met in a six-match series So, unlike previous and subsequent tournaments, there was no official final as such, but Uruguay v Brazil was the deciding match in the final pool)
Uruguay: Maspoli; Gonzales, Tejera, Gambetta, Varela (capt), Andrade, Ghiggia, Perez, Miguez, Schiaffino, Moran
Brazil: Barbosa; Augusto (capt), Juvenal, Bauer, Danilo, Bigode, Friaca, Zizinho, Ademir, Jair, Chico
Referee: Reader (England). **Half-time:** 0-0

1954 – SWITZERLAND

WINNERS: West Germany RUNNERS-UP: Hungary THIRD: Austria FOURTH: Uruguay
Other countries in finals: Belgium, Brazil, Czechoslovakia, England, France, Italy, Korea, Mexico, Scotland, Switzerland, Turkey, Yugoslavia. **Total entries:** 35 (16 qualifiers)
Venues: Basle, Berne, Geneva, Lausanne, Lugano, Zurich
Top scorer: Kocsis (Hungary) 11 goals
Final (Berne, 4/7/54): **West Germany 3** (Morlock 12, Rahn 17, 84) **Hungary 2** (Puskas 4, Czibor 9). **Att:** 60,000
West Germany: Turek; Posipal, Kohlmeyer, Eckel, Liebrich, Mai, Rahn, Morlock, O Walter, F Walter (capt), Schaefer
Hungary: Grosics; Buzansky, Lantos, Bozsik, Lorant, Zakarias, Czibor, Kocsis, Hidegkuti, Puskas (capt), J Toth
Referee: Ling (England). **Half-time:** 2-2

1958 – SWEDEN

WINNERS: Brazil RUNNERS-UP: Sweden THIRD: France FOURTH: West Germany
Other countries in finals: Argentina, Austria, Czechoslovakia, England, Hungary, Mexico, Northern Ireland, Paraguay, Scotland, Soviet Union, Wales, Yugoslavia. **Total entries:** 47 (16 qualifiers)
Venues: Boras, Eskilstuna, Gothenburg, Halmstad, Helsingborgs, Malmo, Norrkoping, Orebro, Sandviken, Stockholm, Vasteras
Top scorer: Fontaine (France) 13 goals
Final (Stockholm, 29/6/58): **Brazil 5** (Vava 10, 32, Pele 55, 88, Zagalo 76) **Sweden 2** (Liedholm 4, Simonsson 83). **Att:** 49,737
Brazil: Gilmar; D Santos, N Santos, Zito, Bellini (capt), Orlando, Garrincha, Didi, Vava, Pele, Zagalo
Sweden: Svensson; Bergmark, Axbom, Boerjesson, Gustavsson, Parling, Hamrin, Gren, Simonsson, Liedholm (capt), Skoglund
Referee: Guigue (France). **Half-time:** 2-1

1962 – CHILE

WINNERS: Brazil RUNNERS-UP: Czechoslovakia THIRD: Chile FOURTH: Yugoslavia
Other countries in finals: Argentina, Bulgaria, Colombia, England, Hungary, Italy, Mexico, Soviet Union, Spain, Switzerland, Uruguay, West Germany. **Total entries:** 53 (16 qualifiers)
Venues: Arica, Rancagua, Santiago, Vina del Mar
Top scorer: Jerkovic (Yugoslavia) 5 goals

Final (Santiago, 17/6/62): **Brazil 3** (Amarildo 17, Zito 69, Vava 77) **Czechoslovakia 1** (Masopust 16). **Att:** 68,679
Brazil: Gilmar; D Santos, Mauro (capt), Zozimo, N Santos, Zito, Didi, Garrincha, Vava, Amarildo, Zagalo
Czechoslovakia: Schroiff; Tichy, Novak, Pluskal, Popluhar, Masopust (capt), Pospichal, Scherer, Kvasnak, Kadraba, Jelinek
Referee: Latychev (Soviet Union). **Half-time:** 1-1

1966 – ENGLAND

WINNERS: England RUNNERS-UP: West Germany THIRD: Portugal FOURTH: USSR
Other countries in finals: Argentina, Brazil, Bulgaria, Chile, France, Hungary, Italy, Mexico, North Korea, Spain, Switzerland, Uruguay. **Total entries:** 53 (16 qualifiers)
Venues: Birmingham (Villa Park), Liverpool (Goodison Park), London (Wembley and White City), Manchester (Old Trafford), Middlesbrough (Ayresome Park), Sheffield (Hillsborough), Sunderland (Roker Park)
Top scorer: Eusebio (Portugal) 9 goals
Final (Wembley, 30/7/66): **England 4** (Hurst 19, 100, 120, Peters 78) **West Germany 2** (Haller 13, Weber 89) after extra-time. **Att:** 93,802
England: Banks; Cohen, Wilson, Stiles, J Charlton, Moore (capt), Ball, Hurst, Hunt, R Charlton, Peters
West Germany: Tilkowski; Hottges, Schnellinger, Beckenbauer, Schulz, Weber, Haller, Held, Seeler (capt), Overath, Emmerich
Referee: Dienst (Switzerland). **Half-time:** 1-1 (90 mins: 2-2)

1970 – MEXICO

WINNERS: Brazil RUNNERS-UP: Italy THIRD: West Germany FOURTH: Uruguay
Other countries in finals: Belgium, Bulgaria, Czechoslovakia, El Salvador, England, Israel, Mexico, Morocco, Peru, Romania, Soviet Union, Sweden. **Total entries:** 68 (16 qualifiers)
Venues: Guadalajara, Leon, Mexico City, Puebla, Toluca
Top scorer: Muller (West Germany) 10 goals
Final (Mexico City, 21/6/70): **Brazil 4** (Pele 18, Gerson 66, Jairzinho 71, Carlos Alberto 87) **Italy 1** (Boninsegna 38). **Att:** 107,412
Brazil: Felix; Carlos Alberto (capt), Brito, Piazza, Everaldo, Clodoaldo, Gerson, Jairzinho, Tostao, Pele, Rivelino
Italy: Albertosi; Burgnich, Facchetti (capt), Cera, Rosato, Bertini (Juliano 72), Domenghini, De Sisti, Mazzola, Boninsegna (Rivera 84), Riva
Referee: Glockner (East Germany). **Half-time:** 1-1

1974 – WEST GERMANY

WINNERS: West Germany RUNNERS-UP: Holland THIRD: Poland FOURTH: Brazil
Other countries in finals: Argentina, Australia, Bulgaria, Chile, East Germany, Haiti, Italy, Scotland, Sweden, Uruguay, Yugoslavia, Zaire. **Total entries:** 98 (16 qualifiers)
Venues: Berlin, Dortmund, Dusseldorf, Frankfurt, Gelsenkirchen, Hamburg, Hanover, Munich, Stuttgart
Top scorer: Lato (Poland) 7 goals
Final (Munich, 7/7/74): **West Germany 2** (Breitner 25 pen, Muller 43) **Holland 1** (Neeskens 2 pen). **Att:** 77,833
West Germany: Maier; Vogts, Schwarzenbeck, Beckenbauer (capt), Breitner, Bonhof, Hoeness, Overath, Grabowski, Muller, Holzenbein
Holland: Jongbloed; Suurbier, Rijsbergen (De Jong 69), Haan, Krol, Jansen, Van Hanegem, Neeskens, Rep, Cruyff (capt), Rensenbrink (R Van der Kerkhof 46)
Referee: Taylor (England). **Half-time:** 2-1

1978 – ARGENTINA

WINNERS: Argentina RUNNERS-UP: Holland THIRD: Brazil FOURTH: Italy
Other countries in finals: Austria, France, Hungary, Iran, Mexico, Peru, Poland, Scotland, Spain, Sweden, Tunisia, West Germany. **Total entries:** 102 (16 qualifiers)
Venues: Buenos Aires, Cordoba, Mar del Plata, Mendoza, Rosario
Top scorer: Kempes (Argentina) 6 goals
Final (Buenos Aires, 25/6/78): **Argentina** 3 (Kempes 38, 104, Bertoni 115) **Holland** 1 (Nanninga 82) after extra-time. **Att:** 77,000
Argentina: Fillol; Passarella (capt), Olguin, Galvan, Tarantini, Ardiles (Larrosa 66), Gallego, Ortiz (Houseman 74), Bertoni, Luque, Kempes
Holland: Jongbloed; Krol (capt), Poortvliet, Brandts, Jansen (Suurbier 73), Haan, Neeskens, W Van der Kerkhof, Rep (Nanninga 58), R Van der Kerkhof, Rensenbrink
Referee: Gonella (Italy). **Half-time:** 1-0 (90 mins: 1-1)

1982 – SPAIN

WINNERS: Italy RUNNERS-UP: West Germany THIRD: Poland FOURTH: France
Other countries in finals: Algeria, Argentina, Austria, Belgium, Brazil, Cameroon, Chile, Czechoslovakia, El Salvador, England, Honduras, Hungary, Kuwait, New Zealand, Northern Ireland, Peru, Scotland, Soviet Union, Spain, Yugoslavia. **Total entries:** 109 (24 qualifiers)
Venues: Alicante, Barcelona, Bilbao, Coruna, Elche, Gijon, Madrid, Malaga, Oviedo, Seville, Valencia, Valladolid, Vigo, Zaragoza
Top scorer: Rossi (Italy) 6 goals
Final (Madrid, 11/7/82): **Italy** 3 (Rossi 57, Tardelli 69, Altobelli 81) **West Germany** 1 (Breitner 84). **Att:** 90,089
Italy: Zoff (capt); Bergomi, Scirea, Collovati, Cabrini, Oriali, Gentile, Tardelli, Conti, Rossi, Graziani (Altobelli 18 – Causio 88)
West Germany: Schumacher; Kaltz, Stielike, K-H Forster, B Forster, Dremmler (Hrubesch 63), Breitner, Briegel, Rummenigge (capt) (Muller 70), Fischer, Littbarski
Referee: Coelho (Brazil). **Half-time:** 0-0

1986 – MEXICO

WINNERS: Argentina RUNNERS-UP: West Germany THIRD: France FOURTH: Belgium
Other countries in finals: Algeria, Brazil, Bulgaria, Canada, Denmark, England, Hungary, Iraq, Italy, Mexico, Morocco, Northern Ireland, Paraguay, Poland, Portugal, Scotland, South Korea, Soviet Union, Spain, Uruguay. **Total entries:** 118 (24 qualifiers)
Venues: Guadalajara, Irapuato, Leon, Mexico City, Monterrey, Nezahualcoyotl, Puebla, Queretaro, Toluca
Top scorer: Lineker (England) 6 goals
Final (Mexico City, 29/6/86): **Argentina** 3 (Brown 23, Valdano 56, Burruchaga 85) **West Germany** 2 (Rummenigge 74, Voller 82). **Att:** 115,026
Argentina: Pumpido; Cuciuffo, Brown, Ruggeri, Olarticoechea, Batista, Giusti, Maradona (capt), Burruchaga (Trobbiani 89), Enrique, Valdano
West Germany: Schumacher; Berthold, K-H Forster, Jakobs, Brehme, Briegel, Eder, Matthaus, Magath (Hoeness 62), Allofs (Voller 45), Rummenigge (capt)
Referee: Filho (Brazil). **Half-time:** 1-0

1990 – ITALY

WINNERS: West Germany RUNNERS-UP: Argentina THIRD: Italy FOURTH: England
Other countries in finals: Austria, Belgium, Brazil, Cameroon, Colombia, Costa Rica, Czechoslovakia, Egypt, Holland, Republic of Ireland, Romania, Scotland, Spain, South Korea, Soviet Union, Sweden, United Arab Emirates, USA, Uruguay, Yugoslavia. **Total entries:** 103 (24 qualifiers)
Venues: Bari, Bologna, Cagliari, Florence, Genoa, Milan, Naples, Palermo, Rome, Turin, Udine, Verona
Top scorer: Schillaci (Italy) 6 goals

Final (Rome, 8/7/90): **Argentina** 0 **West Germany** 1 (Brehme 85 pen). **Att:** 73,603
Argentina: Goycochea; Ruggeri (Monzon 45), Simon, Serrizuela, Lorenzo, Basualdo, Troglio, Burruchaga (Calderon 53), Sensini, Maradona (capt), Dezotti **Sent-off:** Monzon (65), Dezotti (86) – first players ever to be sent off in World Cup Final
West Germany: Illgner; Berthold (Reuter 75), Buchwald, Augenthaler, Kohler, Brehme, Matthaus (capt), Littbarski, Hassler, Klinsmann, Voller
Referee: Codesal (Mexico). **Half-time:** 0-0

1994 – USA

WINNERS: Brazil RUNNERS-UP: Italy THIRD: Sweden FOURTH: Bulgaria
Other countries in finals: Argentina, Belgium, Bolivia, Cameroon, Colombia, Germany, Greece, Holland, Mexico, Morocco, Nigeria, Norway, Republic of Ireland, Romania, Russia, Saudi Arabia, South Korea, Spain, Switzerland, USA. **Total entries:** 144 (24 qualifiers)
Venues: Boston, Chicago, Dallas, Detroit, Los Angeles, New York City, Orlando, San Francisco, Washington
Top scorers: Salenko (Russia), Stoichkov (Bulgaria), each 6 goals
Final (Los Angeles, 17/7/94): **Brazil** 0 **Italy** 0 after extra-time; Brazil won 3-2 on pens
Att: 94,194
Brazil: Taffarel; Jorginho (Cafu 21), Aldair, Marcio Santos, Branco, Mazinho, Mauro Silva, Dunga (capt), Zinho (Viola 105), Romario, Bebeto
Italy: Pagliuca; Mussi (Apolloni 35), Baresi (capt), Maldini, Benarrivo, Berti, Albertini, D Baggio (Evani 95), Donadoni, R Baggio, Massaro
Referee: Puhl (Hungary)
Shoot-out: Baresi missed, Marco Santos saved, Albertini 1-0, Romario 1-1, Evani 2-1, Branco 2-2, Massaro saved, Dunga 2-3, R Baggio missed

1998 – FRANCE

WINNERS: France RUNNERS-UP: Brazil THIRD: Croatia FOURTH: Holland
Other countries in finals: Argentina, Austria, Belgium, Bulgaria, Cameroon, Chile, Colombia, Denmark, England, Germany, Iran, Italy, Jamaica, Japan, Mexico, Morocco, Nigeria, Norway, Paraguay, Romania, Saudi Arabia, Scotland, South Africa, South Korea, Spain, Tunisia, USA, Yugoslavia. **Total entries:** 172 (32 qualifiers)
Venues: Bordeaux, Lens, Lyon, Marseille, Montpellier, Nantes, Paris (St Denis, Parc des Princes), Saint-Etienne, Toulouse
Top scorer: Davor Suker (Croatia) 6 goals
Final (Paris St Denis, 12/7/98): **Brazil** 0 **France** 3 (Zidane 27, 45, Petit 90). **Att:** 75,000
Brazil: Taffarel; Cafu, Junior Baiano, Aldair, Roberto Carlos; Dunga (capt), Leonardo (Denilson 46), Cesar Sampaio (Edmundo 74), Rivaldo; Bebeto, Ronaldo
France: Barthez; Thuram, Leboeuf, Desailly, Lizarazu; Karembeu (Boghossian 56), Deschamps (capt), Petit, Zidane, Djorkaeff (Viera 75); Guivarc'h (Dugarry 66) **Sent-off:** Desailly (68)
Referee: Belqola (Morocco). **Half-time:** 0-2

2002 – JAPAN/SOUTH KOREA

WINNERS: Brazil RUNNERS-UP: Germany THIRD: Turkey FOURTH: South Korea
Other countries in finals: Argentina, Belgium, Cameroon, China, Costa Rica, Croatia, Denmark, Ecuador, England, France, Italy, Japan, Mexico, Nigeria, Paraguay, Poland, Portugal, Republic of Ireland, Russia, Saudi Arabia, Senegal, Slovenia, South Africa, Spain, Sweden, Tunisia, USA, Uruguay. **Total entries:** 195 (32 qualifiers)
Venues: Japan – Ibaraki, Kobe, Miyagi, Niigata, Oita, Osaka, Saitama, Sapporo, Shizuoka, Yokohama. **South Korea** – Daegu, Daejeon, Gwangju, Incheon, Jeonju, Busan, Seogwipo, Seoul, Suwon Ulsan
Top scorer: Ronaldo (Brazil) 8 goals
Final (Yokohama, 30/6/02): **Germany** 0, **Brazil** 2 (Ronaldo 67, 79). **Att:** 69,029
Germany: Kahn (capt), Linke, Ramelow, Metzelder, Frings, Jeremies (Asamoah 77), Hamann,

Schneider, Bode (Zeige 84), Klose (Bierhoff 74), Neuville
Brazil: Marcos, Lucio, Edmilson, Roque Junior, Cafu (capt) Kleberson, Gilberto Silva, Roberto Carlos, Ronaldinho (Juninho 85), Rivaldo, Ronaldo (Denilson 90)
Referee: Collina (Italy). **Half-time:** 0-0

2006 – GERMANY
WINNERS: Italy RUNNERS-UP: France THIRD: Germany FOURTH: Portugal
Other countries in finals: Angola, Argentina, Australia, Brazil, Costa Rica, Croatia, Czech Republic, Ecuador, England, Ghana, Holland, Iran, Ivory Coast, Japan, Mexico, Paraguay, Poland, Saudi Arabia, Serbia & Montenegro, South Korea, Spain, Sweden, Switzerland, Trinidad & Tobago, Togo, Tunisia, Ukraine, USA. **Total entries:** 198 (32 qualifiers)
Venues: Berlin, Cologne, Dortmund, Frankfurt, Gelsenkirchen, Hamburg, Hanover, Kaiserslautern, Leipzig, Munich, Nuremberg, Stuttgart
Top scorer: Klose (Germany) 5 goals
Final (Berlin, 9/7/06): **Italy** 1 (Materazzi 19) **France** 1 (Zidane 7 pen) after extra-time: Italy won 5-3 on pens. **Att:** 69,000
Italy: Buffon; Zambrotta, Cannavaro (capt), Materazzi, Grosso, Perrotta (De Rossi 61), Pirlo, Gattuso, Camoranesi (Del Piero 86), Totti (Iaquinta 61), Toni
France: Barthez; Sagnol, Thuram, Gallas, Abidal, Makelele, Vieira (Diarra 56), Ribery (Trezeguet 100), Malouda, Zidane (capt), Henry (Wiltord 107) **Sent-off:** Zidane (110)
Referee: Elizondo (Argentina). **Half-time:** 1-1 90 mins: 1-1
Shoot-out: Pirlo 1-0, Wiltord 1-1, Materazzi 2-1, Trezeguet missed, De Rossi 3-1, Abidal 3-2, Del Piero 4-2, Sagnol 4-3, Grosso 5-3

2010 – SOUTH AFRICA
WINNERS: Spain RUNNERS-UP: Holland THIRD: Germany FOURTH: Uruguay
Other countries in finals: Algeria, Argentina, Australia, Brazil, Cameroon, Chile, Denmark, England, France, Ghana, Greece, Honduras, Italy, Ivory Coast, Japan, Mexico, New Zealand, Nigeria, North Korea, Paraguay, Portugal, Serbia, Slovakia, Slovenia, South Africa, South Korea, Switzerland, USA. **Total entries:** 204 (32 qualifiers)
Venues: Bloemfontein, Cape Town, Durban, Johannesburg (Ellis Park), Johannesburg (Soccer City), Nelspruit, Polokwane, Port Elizabeth, Pretoria, Rustenburg
Top scorers: Forlan (Uruguay), Muller (Germany), Sneijder (Holland) 5 goals
Final (Johannesburg, Soccer City, 11/7/10): **Holland** 0 **Spain** 1 (Iniesta 116) after extra-time; **Att:** 84,490
Holland: Stekelenburg, Van der Wiel, Heitinga, Mathijsen, Van Bronckhorst (capt) (Braafheid 105), Van Bommel, De Jong (Van der Vaart 99), Robben, Sneijder, Kuyt (Elia 71), Van Persie. **Sent off:** Heitinga (109)
Spain: Casillas (capt), Sergio Ramos, Puyol, Piquet, Capdevila, Busquets, Xabi Alonso (Fabregas 87), Iniesta, Xavi, Pedro (Jesus Navas 60), Villa (Torres 106)
Referee: Webb (England). **Half-time:** 0-0

DAY BY DAY DIARY 2013–14

JULY 2013

10 Celtic midfielder Victor Wanyama becomes the most costly 'export' from Scottish football when joining Southampton in a £12m deal.

11 Swansea break their transfer record by signing Ivory Coast striker Wilfried Bony from Vitesse Arnhem for £12m.

12 Kevin MacDonald leaves Swindon by mutual consent after six months as manager. England lose 3-2 to Spain in their opening match at the Women's European Championship Finals in Sweden.

13 Mohamed Al Fayed, Fulham's owner for 16 years, sells the club to billionaire Shahid Khan, owner of the Jacksonville Jaguars American football team.

14 Steven Gerrard signs a new two-year contract with Liverpool, keeping him at the club beyond his 35th birthday.

15 Gus Poyet's appeal against his sacking as Brighton manager is rejected by the club. England's women draw 1-1 with Russia in their second group game.

16 The FA announce the continuation of a 5.15pm kick-off for the FA Cup Final as the BBC and BT Sport are chosen to screen the competition in a four-year shared deal starting in 2014.

17 Manchester United turn down an offer of £22m from Chelsea for the unsettled Wayne Rooney.

18 A fortnight before the start of the season, the Football League announce deals worth a reported £300m – an immediate title sponsorship for five years with Sky Bet and a three-year extension to their broadcasting deal with Sky Sports. England's women lose 3-0 to France and finish bottom of their group.

19 Manchester City sign two international strikers – Montenegro's Stevan Jovetic from Fiorentina for £22m and Spain's Alvaro Negredo from Sevilla for £20m. Christian Benteke withdraws a transfer request and signs an extended contract with Aston Villa through to 2017.

20 Five days before his 40th birthday, Kevin Phillips agrees a new one-year contract with promoted Crystal Palace.

23 The new Scottish Professional Football League unveil their divisional structure – Premiership, Championship, League One and League Two.

24 Liverpool reject Arsenal's offer of £40m, plus £1, for Luis Suarez, a bid triggering a clause in the player's Anfield contract requiring him to be informed about it.

25 Hibernian suffer the biggest-ever aggregate defeat by a Scottish team in Europe. They are beaten 9-0 by Malmo in a Europa League second qualifying round match, having been beaten 7-0 in the home leg.

26 Papiss Cisse returns to training with Newcastle after initially refusing to wear training kit and match-day shirt bearing the logo of the club's controversial sponsor, loans company Wonga.

28 Tottenham chairman Daniel Levy cuts short his holiday to return to London as Real Madrid prepare an official bid for Gareth Bale.

29 Manager David Moyes returns from Manchester United's tour of Australia and the Far East for talks with Wayne Rooney.

31 Cardiff break their transfer record for the second time in a month when paying £8.5m for Tottenham's Steven Caulker.

AUGUST 2013

1 Tottenham sign Valencia striker Roberto Soldado for £26m, breaking their club record for the second time in a month.

2 Coventry are deducted ten points on the eve of the new season after the owners of the Ricoh Arena, their former home, reject a plan to take the club out of administration.

3 Newport, back in the Football League after an absence of 25 years, start with a 4-1 win

over Accrington. Mansfield, the other promoted team, lose 2-0 at Scunthorpe. A record League Two crowd of 18,181 at Fratton Park see Portsmouth beaten 4-1 by Oxford.

5 Manchester United reject a second Chelsea bid of £25m for Wayne Rooney. Former Rangers manager Walter Smith, appointed chairman at the end of May, resigns amid a power struggle at Ibrox.

6 Luis Suarez is reprimanded by Liverpool after claiming the club misled him about being allowed to leave and has to train on his own.

7 Manchester United's pursuit of Cesc Fabregas ends when the midfielder says he wants to stay at Barcelona. Vauxhall complete a four-year extension to sponsorship deals with the England, Scotland, Wales and Northern Ireland FAs.

8 The England governing body ban Blackpool's Thomas Ince for two games after video evidence shows him making an offensive gesture towards a match official during the Capital One Cup defeat by Preston.

9 Greg Dyke, chairman of the FA, calls on FIFA to switch the 2022 World Cup in Qatar to the winter or change the venue.

10 Chairman Assem Allam announces his intention to change Hull City's name to Hull Tigers. Cardiff break their transfer record for the third time with the £11m signing of Chile midfielder Gary Medel from Sevilla.

11 David Moyes wins his first trophy with Manchester United, who beat Wigan 2-0 in the Community Shield at Wembley – a match which sees the introduction of goal-line technology to British football.

13 With the FA preparing to interview candidates to succeed Stuart Pearce, England manager Roy Hodgson takes charge of the Under-21 side in a 6-0 win over Scotland in a friendly international.

14 Martin Paterson's header gives Michael O'Neill his first victory in his tenth match as Northern Ireland manager. It also delivers the team's first World Cup qualifying success – 1-0 against Fabio Capello's Russia. England, playing Scotland for the first time for 14 years, win 3-2 with a header by Rickie Lambert, who marks his international debut at 31 by scoring with his first touch after coming on as a substitute. Stoke's Cameron Jerome is fined £50,000 by the FA for breaking the governing body's betting rules.

15 Hull break their transfer record when paying £5.25m for Tottenham's Tom Huddlestone.

16 Luis Suarez returns to training with Liverpool's senior squad after talks with manager Brendan Rodgers. Blackpool manager Paul Ince is fined £3,000 by the FA for accusing referee Andrew Madely of bias after the Capital One Cup defeat by Preston.

17 Manchester United begin their defence of the Premier League title under David Moyes with a 4-1 win at Swansea.

18 Southampton sign Italy striker Dani Osvaldo from Roma for £14.6m, a club record fee.

19 Everton dismiss as 'derisory' a £28m bid from Manchester United for Marouane Fellaini and Leighton Baines. The FA ban Accrington managing director Robert Heys from all football activity for 21 months for breaching betting regulations. Manchester City's Pablo Zabaleta signs a four-year contract extension.

20 Former Peterborough manager Mark Cooper takes charge permanently at Swindon after a spell as caretaker. Hope Powell, head coach of the England women's team for 15 years, is sacked after failing to qualify from the group stage of the European Championship.

21 Arsenal manager Arsene Wenger admits defeat in his bid to sign Luis Suarez, who is staying at Anfield.

22 Gareth Southgate, winner of 57 England caps, succeeds Stuart Pearce as manager of the national under-21 team.

23 Kenny Miller retires from international football after winning his 69th Scotland cap and scoring against England. Celtic manager Neil Lennon signs a new one-year rolling contract.

25 Brazil midfielder Willian changes his mind about signing for Tottenham and decides to join Chelsea from the Russian club Anzhi Makhachkala for £30m.

26 After weeks of speculation and negotiating, Tottenham agree to sell Gareth Bale to Real Madrid.

27 Arsenal reach the Champions League group stage for the 16th successive season, beating Fenerbahce 5-0 on aggregate in the play-off round.

28 Chelsea manager Jose Mourinho gives up on his pursuit of Wayne Rooney. Celtic retrieve a two-goal deficit to win their play-off 3-2 on aggregate against Shakhtyor Karagandy.

29 Gordon Taylor, chief executive of the PFA, is given 'full support' by the players' union's management committee following allegations in *The Sun* that he ran up large gambling debts. Swansea and Tottenham reach the group stage of the Europa League with aggregate play-off round wins over Petrolul Ploiesti (6-3) and Dinamo Tbilisi (8-0) respectively.

30 Tottenham spend £45.7m on three players – record signing Erik Lamela (Roma) for £30m, Christian Eriksen (Ajax) and Vlad Chiriches (Steaua Bucharest). Ten-man Chelsea, with Ramires sent off for two yellow cards, lose 5-4 on penalties to Bayern Munich after the European Super Cup game ends 2-2.

31 Gareth Bale completes his move to Real Madrid for £85.3m, a fee which overtakes the previous world record £80m, paid by the Spanish club to Manchester United for Cristiano Ronaldo in 2009.

SEPTEMBER 2013

1 Sheffield United owner Kevin McCabe sells a 50 per cent stake in the club to Saudi businessman Prince Abdullah.

2 Arsenal break their transfer record on deadline-day by signing Real Madrid midfielder Mesut Ozil for £42.4m. Manchester United pay £27.5m for Everton's Marouane Fellaini, while Liverpool sign France defender Mamadou Sakho from Paris St-Germain for £18m. West Bromwich Albion break their club record with the £6m acquisition of Sunderland's Stephane Sessegnon. Premier League clubs' outlay of £630m during the summer window is a record. Bournemouth chairman Eddie Mitchell sells his 50 per cent share of the club to co-owner Maxim Demin.

3 The Football League release figures showing that clubs spent £21.5m on agents' fees during the 2012-13 season, a drop of £170,000.

4 Crystal Palace manager Ian Holloway is given a two-match touchline ban and fined £18,000 by the FA for criticising referee Mark Clattenburg after the defeat by Tottenham.

5 Manchester United winger Nani, who fell out with Sir Alex Ferguson, signs a new five-year contract after impressing new manager David Moyes.

6 Danny Welbeck scores twice as England beat Moldova 4-0 in a World Cup qualifier. Elsewhere, it's a miserable night for British and Irish teams. Wales manager Chris Coleman leaves Real Madrid signing Gareth Bale on the bench in Macedonia, where a 2-1 defeat ends his side's faint chance of qualifying. Northern Ireland are out of contention after Chris Brunt is sent off for two yellow cards and Kyle Lafferty is shown a straight red in a 4-2 reversal against Portugal, for whom Cristiano Ronaldo scores a hat-trick in 15 second-half minutes. Jamie Ward scores his first goal for the Irish. Scotland, already out, lose 2-0 to Belgium, while the Republic of Ireland suffer a damaging 2-1 defeat by Sweden. Aston Villa manager Paul Lambert is fined £8,000 by the FA for comments about referee Kevin Friend after the defeat by Chelsea. Billy Davies, the Nottingham Forest manager, receives a one-match touchline ban and £2,000 fine for confronting referee Craig Pawson after the defeat by Wigan.

7 Kyle Walker, Tottenham and England full-back, apologises after a newspaper photograph shows him inhaling nitrous oxide – laughing gas – on a night out in June. The FA take no action.

8 A sell-out 60,000 crowd at Celtic Park watch a testimonial match launching the charitable foundation of former Celtic and Aston Villa midfielder Stiliyan Petrov, who was forced to retire with leukaemia.

9 Greg Abbott, appointed in November 2008 and the third longest-serving manager in English football after Arsenal's Arsene Wenger and Paul Tisdale (Exeter), is sacked after Carlisle take two points from their first six matches.

10 Frank Lampard wins his 100th cap as England share a goalless draw with Ukraine to stay

on top of their group. The Republic of Ireland's chances of qualifying are effectively ended by a 1-0 defeat by Austria. Gareth Bale's first appearance for Wales since his world record transfer is not enough to prevent a 3-0 home defeat by Serbia. Northern Ireland manager Michael O'Neill describes his side's performance as 'pathetic' after an embarrassing 3-2 defeat by Luxembourg. Scotland move off the bottom of their group by winning 2-1 in Macedonia, with Watford's Ikechi Anya marking his first international start by scoring the first goal. Celtic are fined £4,200 by UEFA after fans let off fireworks at the Champions League qualifier against Cliftonville.

11 Giovanni Trapatonni's five-year reign as the Republic of Ireland manager comes to an end by 'mutual consent' in a meeting with FAI chief executive John Delaney. A crowd of more than 50,000 watch a charity testimonial match for long-serving Newcastle goalkeeper Steve Harper at St James' Park.

12 Rangers midfielder Ian Black is banned for ten matches – seven of them suspended – and fined £7,500 for breaching Scottish FA betting regulations.

13 England drop to 17th in the latest FIFA world rankings, their lowest position since 2001.

14 Gareth Bale scores on his debut for Real Madrid in a 2-2 draw against Villarreal.

16 Sunderland manager Paolo Di Canio is fined £8,000 by the FA after being sent off by referee Martin Atkinson during the game against Arsenal.

17 Wayne Rooney scores his 200th goal for Manchester United in a 4-2 Champions League win over Bayer Leverkusen.

18 Arsenal beat Marseille 2-1 in their opening group match, extending a run of successive away victories in all competitions to a club record ten.

19 UEFA's 54 member countries vote to move the 2022 World Cup in Qatar from the summer to winter.

21 Jesse Lingard, 20-year-old Manchester United midfielder, scores all four goals on his loan debut for Birmingham in the 4-1 win over Sheffield Wednesday.

22 Paolo Di Canio is sacked after six turbulent months as Sunderland manager with his side bottom-of-the-table five matches into the new season.

24 Celtic are knocked out of the Scottish League Cup on their own ground by Morton in a third round tie.

25 Capital One Cup holders Swansea lose 3-1 at Birmingham in the third round.

28 Derby's Nigel Clough, appointed in December 2008 and the Championship's longest-serving manager, is sacked after three defeats in eight days.

29 Liverpool end Arsenal's nine-year dominance of women's football, by winning the FA Super League title.

30 Former England manager Steve McClaren is appointed Nigel Clough's successor at Pride Park. Roberto Mancini, sacked by Manchester City, is appointed coach of Turkish club Galatasaray.

OCTOBER 2013

1 Graham Kavanagh, previously a player, player-coach and assistant manager at the club, is appointed Carlisle's permanent manager after a spell as caretaker.

2 The FA come under fire for not punishing Chelsea's Fernando Torres for scratching the face of Tottenham's Jan Vertonghen.

3 FIFA announce a task force to investigate whether the 2022 World Cup in Qatar should be moved to the winter. Tottenham's Michael Dawson signs a contract extension to 2016.

4 Rangers manager Ally McCoist agrees a cut, reported to be around 50 per cent, in his salary of £825,000 after the club post an annual loss of £14.4m. Kenny Dalglish, former Liverpool player and manager, returns to Anfield as a director of the club.

5 Belgian-born Adnan Januzaj, 18, scores twice on his full Premier League debut for Manchester United against Sunderland – and manager David Moyes reveals interest from the FA in claiming the player for England.

7 Blackpool manager Paul Ince is given a five-match stadium ban and fined £4,000 by the FA for threatening behaviour and violent conduct towards match officials after the game at

Bournemouth.

8 Former Brighton manager Gus Poyet succeeds Paolo Di Canio at the Stadium of Light.

9 Former England manager Glenn Hoddle and ex-England full-back Danny Mills are named by FA chairman Greg Dyke on an eight-strong commission to look at ways of improving the national team.

10 David Weir is sacked by Sheffield United after a single victory in his 13 matches as manager.

11 Andros Townsend scores on his debut and helps set up a goal for Wayne Rooney as England move to the brink of the World Cup Finals by beating Montenegro 4-1. Jonny Evans is shown a straight red card in stoppage-time of Northern Ireland's 2-0 defeat by Azerbaijan. The Republic of Ireland, with Noel King as caretaker-manager, lose 3-0 to Germany. Wales defeat Macedonia 1-0.

12 Speculation about the future of Cardiff manager Malky Mackay follows the dismissal of his head of recruitment, Iain Moody, by owner Vincent Tan, who replaces him with a 23-year-old Kazakhstani with no known football experience.

13 Six months after leading Gillingham to the club's first title for nearly half a century, Martin Allen is sacked with his side one point above the League One relegation zone.

14 Bury dismiss manager Kevin Blackwell after a run of two points from six matches in League Two.

15 England confirm their place in Brazil 2014 by beating Poland 2-0 with goals from Wayne Rooney and Steven Gerrard to finish top of their group. Liverpool's Harry Wilson, aged 16 years and 207 days, becomes the youngest-ever senior Wales international when brought off the bench in a 1-1 draw against Belgium. Craig Bellamy retires from international football after winning his 78th cap. Scotland complete the double over Croatia with a 2-0 victory, Northern Ireland finish off with a 1-1 draw against Israel, while the Republic of Ireland beat Kazakhstan 3-1.

16 Everton's Darron Gibson is ruled out for the rest of the season with cruciate ligament damage sustained in the Republic of Ireland's win.

17 Roy Hodgson denies an accusation of making a racist comment during his team talk at half-time of the match against Poland and is backed by the FA and England players.

18 Adnan Januzaj signs a new five-year contract with Manchester United. Tottenham's Andros Townsend is rewarded for his sparkling form for club and country with a new four-year deal.

19 FA chairman Greg Dyke responds to criticism from board member Heather Rabbatts about a lack of diversity on his all-white England commission by adding former captain Rio Ferdinand, along with Roy Hodgson.

20 Assistant referee Dave Bryan is struck by a smoke bomb thrown from the crowd during the Aston Villa–Tottenham match.

21 Tony Mowbray, the Championship's longest-serving manager with three years at Middlesbrough, is sacked after their indifferent start to the season.

22 Sir Alex Ferguson settles some old scores with David Beckham, Roy Keane, Wayne Rooney and Rafael Benitez in a controversial autobiography.

23 Manager Ian Holloway parts company with Crystal Palace by mutual consent after seven defeats in the opening eight games. Nigel Clough makes a rapid return to management when taking over at Sheffield United.

24 Liverpool manager Brendan Rogers claims Sir Alex Ferguson has harmed his legacy with comments in his book about players and managers. Chelsea manager Jose Mourinho accepts an £8,000 fine from the FA after being sent to the stands during the game against Cardiff for arguing with referee Anthony Taylor.

26 The Duke of Cambridge, president of the FA, tells a gala dinner to mark the governing body's 150th anniversary that despite praiseworthy efforts to remove discrimination from the game there is 'sadly more work to do'.

27 Chris Kiwomya is sacked after seven months as Notts County manager with his side bottom

of the table.
28 Tottenham's Kyle Walker signs a new contract keeping him at White Hart Lane until 2019.
29 David Beckham chooses Miami as the city in which to establish a new Major League Soccer franchise.
30 UEFA order CSKA Moscow to close one end of the stadium for their next Champions League home game following racial abuse by supporters of Manchester City's Yaya Toure.
31 Ray Clemence, 65, retires after 47 years in football as a world-class goalkeeper, England goalkeeping coach and the FA's head of national teams. Cardiff's controversial new head of recruitment, Alisher Apsalyamov, is told to stand down temporarily by the Home Office while his work permit is investigated. John Ruddy signs a new four-year contract with Norwich.

NOVEMBER 2013

1 Seven months after being sacked by Sunderland, Martin O'Neill agrees to become the Republic of Ireland's new manager. Pat Fenlon resigns as manager of Hibernian following home defeats by Aberdeen and Hearts.
2 Stoke goalkeeper Asmir Begovic scores after 13 seconds, his clearance bouncing over Southampton's Artur Boruc.
3 Amid widespread criticism, Tottenham manager Andre Villas-Boas defends his decision to let goalkeeper Hugo Lloris play on after suffering suspected concussion in a collision with Everton's Romelu Lukaku.
4 Michael O'Neill signs a two-year extension to his contract as Northern Ireland's manager. The Scottish Professional Football League announce a deal for matches to be shown for the first time in China.
5 Martin O'Neill is confirmed as the Republic manager, with former captain Roy Keane as his No 2. Norwich are fined £20,000 by the FA for their players' involvement in a stoppage-time fracas against Cardiff. Blackpool and Blackburn are both fined £5,000 for a brawl involving rival players. Alvaro Negredo scores a hat-trick as Manchester City beat CSKA Moscow 5-2 to reach the knock-out stage of the Champions League for the first time with two group matches to spare.
6 Fulham's Sascha Riether is banned for three matches for stamping on Manchester United's Adnan Januzaj under a new FA disciplinary procedure in which a three-man panel of former elite referees review video evidence of incidents not spotted by match officials. Shaun Derry, Queens Park Rangers midfielder, is appointed player-manager of Notts County, returning to the club where he started his career.
7 Southampton have three players – Rickie Lambert, Adam Lallana and Jay Rodriguez – named in an England squad for the first time for 27 years. Jermain Defoe overtakes Martin Chivers as Tottenham's record scorer in Europe with his 23rd goal in a 2-1 win over Sheriff Tiraspol which takes his side into the Europa League knock-out stage with two group matches to spare.
8 Hull manager Steve Bruce is fined £10,000 by the FA for calling referee Michael Oliver's decision to award Tottenham a penalty 'a joke.'
9 BT Sport announce an £897m deal to show Champions League and Europa League matches for three years from 2015, outbidding current rights holders ITV and Sky. Amy Fearn becomes the first woman to referee a match in the main draw of the FA Cup when taking charge of Dover's first round victory at Corby.
10 Caretaker Peter Taylor is given the manager's job at Gillingham – his second spell at the club – until the end of the season.
11 Terry Butcher, manager of Inverness for nearly five years, takes charge at Hibernian. Bury rename their Gigg Lane ground the JD Stadium as part of a sponsorship deal with the Bury-based sportswear firm.
12 Aitor Karanka, former assistant to Jose Mourinho at Real Madrid, succeeds Tony Mowbray at Middlesbrough. Ajax are fined £21,000 by UEFA for an offensive banner displayed by supporters at their Champions League home game against Celtic.

13 Rene Meulensteen, former assistant manager to Sir Alex Ferguson at Manchester United, joins Fulham's coaching staff.

14 Derby rename Pride Park the iPro Stadium in a £7m sponsorship deal with the sports drink company. Gary Fraser, 19-year-old Partick player on loan from Bolton, is given a seven-match suspension, in addition to an automatic two-game ban, by the Scottish FA for violent conduct in an under-20 match against Dunfermline.

15 England suffer their first defeat for a year, losing a friendly international 2-0 to Chile at Wembley. Martin O'Neill makes a winning start as Republic of Ireland manager – 3-0 against Latvia. Scotland draw 0-0 with the USA in the last international at Hampden Park before work begins to prepare the stadium for the 2014 Commonwealth Games in Glasgow. Northern Ireland lose to Turkey by the only goal of the game. Wojciech Szczesny signs a new long-term contract with Arsenal, the length of which is not disclosed by the club.

16 Having ended speculation about his future by signing a new two-year contract, Wales manager Chris Coleman sees his side concede a stoppage-time goal which gives Finland a 1-1 draw.

19 England lose 1-0 to Germany, thus recording back-to-back Wembley defeats for the first time since 1977. Scotland win by the same margin in Norway, while the Republic of Ireland share a goalless draw with Poland. England's Under-21 side beat San Marino 9-0 in a European Championship qualifying game – the biggest-ever winning margin by this age group.

20 Scunthorpe manager Brian Laws is sacked after successive home defeats by Accrington and then Grimsby in the FA Cup.

21 Referees' chief Mike Riley apologises to West Bromwich Albion for the stoppage-time penalty decision by match official Andre Marriner which cost them victory over Chelsea.

23 Tony Pulis, formerly in charge of Stoke, is appointed the new manager of Crystal Palace.

25 Portsmouth manager Guy Whittingham is sacked with his team 18th in League Two.

26 Jack Wilshere scores the fastest-ever goal by an English player in the Champions League – after 29 seconds against Marseille. Chelsea qualify for the knockout stage, despite a second group defeat by Basle. Celtic fail to go through after losing to AC Milan and also miss out on the consolation of a place in the Europa League. Referee Andrew Madley sends off the wrong player in a League One match. He dismisses Preston's Neil Kilkenny for violent conduct in their 2-0 win over Port Vale instead of the offender, Joe Garner, scorer of both goals.

27 Manchester United progress with their biggest away win in the competition for 56 years – 5-0 against Bayer Leverkusen. Crawley sack manager Richie Barker after seven league games without a win.

28 Neil Kilkenny's red card is rescinded by the FA and Joe Garner banned retrospectively for three matches. Sean O'Driscoll is dismissed by third-from-bottom Bristol City after ten months in charge.

29 The Premier League release figures showing clubs paying £96.7m in agents' fees in the year ending September 30, with Chelsea the biggest spenders – £13.7m.

30 Barnsley terminate David Flitcroft's contract after a home defeat by Birmingham leaves his side bottom.

DECEMBER 2013

1 There are three more managerial sackings, taking the total to eight in 12 days. Martin Jol leaves Fulham after six successive league and cup defeats and is replaced by coach Rene Meulensteen. Sheffield Wednesday sack Dave Jones with his team second from bottom. Owen Coyle pays the price for three home defeats in nine days after less than six months with Wigan.

2 Northern Ireland's leading scorer, David Healy, 34, retires from international football after 36 goals in 95 appearances. Saido Berahino, West Bromwich Albion's England Under-21 striker, signs a new contract through to 2017.

3 Blackpool have three players sent off near the end of their defeat at Yeovil – Kirk Broadfoot

for a second yellow card in the 89th minute, followed by Ricardo Fuller (straight red) and Gary MacKenzie (second booking) in stoppage-time. John Gregory, out of management in England since leaving Queens Park Rangers in 2007, takes charge at Crawley. Bristol City appoint Steve Cotterill, his seventh league job. Swindon announce a takeover of the club by director of football Lee Power, a former Norwich striker.

4   John Hughes, former Hartlepool and Hibernian manager, is appointed Terry Butcher's successor at Inverness.

5   Mark Sampson, manager of the Bristol Academy club, is appointed the new head coach of the England women's team.

6   England are drawn in a group with Italy, Uruguay and Costa Rica for the World Cup Finals. Brentford manager Uwe Rosler steps up a division to take over at Wigan.

7   Clubs up and down the country stage a minute's applause for Nelson Mandela. Two more Blackpool players, Neal Bishop and Angel Martinez, are sent off, this time at Derby, bringing the club's total of red cards so far this season to eight.

8   Six present and past players are arrested by the National Crime Agency over spot-fixing allegations.

9   Celtic suspend 128 supporters from all their matches after seats are ripped out during a 5-0 win at Motherwell.

10 Two sacked managers make a rapid return to the game – Richie Barker at Portsmouth and David Flitcroft at Bury. Brentford's sporting director, Mark Warburton, is named their new manager.

11 Arsenal reach the knock-out stage of the Champions League, despite losing their last group match against Napoli. Mark Schwarzer, Chelsea's No 2 goalkeeper aged 41 years and 66 days, becomes the oldest player to make his debut in the competition when playing against Steaua Bucharest.

12 Swansea qualify from their Europa League group. Wigan finish bottom of their group.

13 Norwich captain Sebastien Bassong signs a new contract through to 2016.

14 West Bromwich Albion manager Steve Clarke is sacked hours after a fourth successive defeat – 1-0 by Cardiff.

15 Bolton post an annual loss of £50.7m. Sir Alex Ferguson receives a 'Diamond Award' at the BBC Sports Personality of the Year night. Cristian Montano, one of the players arrested over spot-fixing allegations, has his contract terminated by Oldham.

16 Tottenham dismiss manager Andre Villas-Boas in the wake of a 5-0 home defeat by Liverpool and the 6-0 drubbing by Manchester City. Gianfranco Zola resigns as Watford manager after five successive home defeats. Cardiff owner Vincent Tan publicly criticises manager Malky Mackay for suggesting he needs three new players in the January transfer window.

17 Danny Wilson, in charge at Oakwell from 1994–98, returns for a second spell as Barnsley manager. Jonny Howson signs a new four-and-a-half-year contract with Norwich. The Scottish FA turn down an appeal by Hibernian manager Terry Butcher against a two-match touchline ban – one of them suspended – for being sent to the stands in a League Cup tie against Dundee United while in charge of Inverness.

18 Giuseppe Sannino, sacked by Chievo in November, succeeds fellow-Italian Gianfranco Zola at Vicarage Road. Swansea and Hull are both fined £20,000 by the FA for a players' fracas.

19 The crisis at Cardiff comes to a head when Vincent Tan sends an e-mail to Malky Mackay ordering him to resign or be sacked. Arsenal's Jack Wilshere is banned for two matches by the FA for an abusive gesture towards Manchester City fans.

20 After scoring 17 goals in his first 11 Premier League games of the season, Luis Suarez signs a contract with Liverpool through to 2018. Malky Mackay insist he will not resign.

21 Northampton manager Aidy Boothroyd is sacked following a 4-1 home defeat by Wycombe leaves his side bottom.

23 Tim Sherwood, Tottenham's technical co-ordinator, succeeds Andre Villas-Boas after two games as caretaker manager.

24 Alan Curbishley, former Charlton and West Ham manager, returns to club football after an

absence of more than five years as Fulham's first-team technical director. Russ Wilcox, with 13 points from five matches as caretaker, is appointed Scunthorpe manager.

26 Steve Lomas, Millwall manager for six months, is sacked after a 4-0 defeat by Watford leaves his team fifth from bottom.

27 Vincent Tan carries out his threat to fire Malky Mackay, claiming overspending in the summer transfer market. Belgian businessman Roland Duchatelet, owner of Standard Liege, agrees a takeover of Charlton for a reported £14m.

30 David Bernstein, former chairman of the FA, Manchester City and Wembley Stadium, is awarded a CBE in the New Year Honours. Arsenal midfielder Rachel Yankey, the most capped England women's player with 129 appearances, receives an OBE. Sue Hough, head of the FA Women's Committee, gets an MBE.

31 Chelsea post an annual loss of £49.4m. Watford are fined £5,000 by the FA for players' protests over a penalty award at Ipswich. Coventry's Dan Seaborne is banned for three matches for violent conduct, caught on camera, against Oldham.

JANUARY 2014

1 Ole Gunnar Solskjaer, the successful manager of Norwegian club Molde and winner of six Premier League titles with Manchester United, takes charge at Cardiff.

2 West Ham fine captain Kevin Nolan two weeks' wages for two red cards in four matches. Stoke manager Mark Hughes is fined £8,000 by the FA after being sent to the stands during the game at Newcastle. Torquay, second from bottom in League Two, sack Alan Knill after eight months as manager.

3 Referees' chief Mike Riley dismisses a claim by Southampton that their England midfielder Adam Lallana was sworn at by match official Mark Clattenburg at Everton. Southampton's record signing, Dani Osvaldo, is banned for three games and fined £40,000 by the FA for violent conduct during a touchline fracas at Newcastle, whose goalkeeping coach Andy Woodman is fined £1,250.

5 Eusebio, leading scorer at the 1966 World Cup Finals in England and one of the greatest of all European players, dies aged 71.

6 Theo Walcott is ruled out of the rest of the season, and the World Cup Finals, with a cruciate ligament injury sustained in Arsenal's FA Cup win over Tottenham.

7 Ian Holloway takes charge at Millwall – his seventh managerial appointment. Former Torquay captain Chris Hargreaves becomes the club's new manager. The FA decide to take no action on Southampton's complaint regarding Adam Lallana. Blackpool fine Michael Chopra two weeks' wages for posting an offensive item on *Twitter* criticising the club's training arrangements.

8 Five weeks after being sacked by Real Betis, Pepe Mel succeeds Steve Clarke at West Bromwich Albion.

9 Yaya Toure, Manchester City's Ivory Coast midfielder, is named African Player of the Year for the third successive time. Manchester United's Chris Smalling is forced to apologise for attending a private party dressed as a suicide bomber.

10 Liverpool manager Brendan Rodgers is fined £8,000 by the FA for describing match officials as 'horrendous' after the defeat by Manchester City. Huddersfield break their club record by paying £1.3m for Bradford's Nahki Wells.

12 Cristiano Ronaldo is crowned the world's best player with FIFA's *Ballon D'Or* award. The Real Madrid star takes over from Barcelona's Lionel Messi, winner for the previous four years, with Bayern Munich's Franck Ribery third in the voting.

13 Kenwyne Jones is fined two weeks' wages by Stoke after failing to turn up for their match against Liverpool.

14 Howard Webb is named as England's World Cup referee for the second successive tournament, with Darren Cann and Mike Mullarkey again as his assistants.

15 Southampton's executive chairman, Nicola Cortese, resigns over disagreements with owner Katharina Liebherr, leading to speculation about the future of manager Mauricio Pochettino. Chelsea sign midfielder Nemanja Matic from Benfica for £20.7m, three years

after selling him as part of the deal bringing David Luiz to Stamford Bridge from the Portuguese club.

16 Hull pay a club record £7.5m for Everton's Nikica Jelavic and agree a £6.5m fee for another striker, West Bromwich Albion's Shane Long. Mauricio Pochettino decides to stay at Southampton until the end of the season, then consider his position. Rangers players reject a pay cut of 15 per cent as the club's board attempt to cut costs.

17 Manager David Moyes is fined £8,000 by the FA for criticising match officials after Manchester United's Capital One Cup semi-final against Sunderland. West Bromwich Albion are warned that property website Zoopla will end their sponsorship of the club if Nicolas Anelka is not dropped for making a controversial gesture after scoring against West Ham.

18 Edgar Davids, the former Holland star, resigns after 15 months as Barnet manager with his side tenth in the Conference.

19 Chelsea sell Kevin de Bruyne to the German club Wolfsburg for £16.7m.

20 West Bromwich Albion ignore the threat from Zoopla by fielding Nicolas Anelka against Everton and the company call time on their backing at the end of the season. Accrington are fined £20,000 by the Football League, with £15,000 of it suspended, because manager James Beattie does not hold the necessary coaching qualifications.

21 Blackpool manager Paul Ince is sacked after a run of nine matches produce a single point. Shrewsbury's Graham Turner resigns with his side a point off the relegation zone. Manchester City break the record margin of victory for a League Cup semi-final, beating West Ham 9-0 over two legs.

22 Manchester United, out of the FA Cup and left trailing in the Premier League, lose their last chance of domestic honours when beaten by Sunderland on penalties in the second Capital One Cup semi-final. Everton are fined £45,000 by the FA for an unauthorised approach for Nottingham Forest defender Jamaal Lascelles in 2010. His agent at the time, Andy Niedwiecki, is fined £10,000 and the player himself receives a warning.

23 Dani Osvaldo, Southampton's record signing, is suspended by the club after a training incident with Jose Fonte, which leaves his team-mate with a facial injury, and later joins Juventus on loan. Manchester City lead a consortium taking over Australian club Melbourne Heart.

24 Manchester United begin their rebuilding plans by signing Chelsea's Juan Mata for a club record fee of £37.1m.

25 Stuart Gray is appointed Sheffield Wednesday manager on a permanent basis after a successful two months as caretaker.

26 Chris Wilder, English football's third longest-serving manager behind Arsenal's Arsene Wenger and Exeter's Paul Tisdale, resigns after five years with Oxford.

27 Arsenal sign a five-year kit deal with Puma reported to be worth a record £150m over five years. Chris Wilder swops a promotion challenge for a relegation struggle by taking charge at bottom club Northampton. Leighton Baines signs a new four-year contract with Everton.

28 Newcastle's Yohan Cabaye joins Paris St-Germain for £19m.

30 Manchester City post an annual loss of £51.6m.

31 Leeds manager Brian McDermott is told he has been dismissed after ten months in charge. Fulham break their transfer record on transfer deadline day by paying £12.4m for Greece striker Konstantinos Mitroglou from Olympiacos. Total spending by Premier League clubs during the winter window is £130m.

FEBRUARY 2014

1 There is confusion at Elland Road as Brian McDermott takes a call from the Leeds owners saying he has not been sacked. Aberdeen reach the Scottish League Cup Final by beating St Johnstone 4-0.

2 Inverness reach a major final for the first time when their nine-man side beat Hearts on penalties, having played throughout extra-time with nine men after the dismissal of Gary Warren and Josh Meekings.

3 Brian McDermott returns to the Leeds training ground and tells a press conference he has been reinstated. Joe Kinnear resigns after eight months as Newcastle's director of football.

4 Michael Laudrup becomes the seventh Premier League managerial casualty of the season – sacked by Swansea after a single win in ten matches.

5 David Beckham confirms his £15m plans to establish a Major League Soccer side in Miami.

6 Manchester United captain Nemanja Vidic tells the club he leaving for 'a new challenge' at the end of the season.

7 The FA fine Norwich £30,000 and Newcastle £20,000 for a players' fracas at Carrow Road. Millwall and Sheffield Wednesday are both fined £10,000 for a brawl in their match. An independent arbitration tribunal dismisses a legal challenge from West Ham against the FA decision to uphold Andy Carroll's three-match ban for his red card against Swansea.

10 West Ham announce the sale of Upton Park to developers, paving the way for the club's move to the Olympic Stadium in 2016.

11 Cardiff's Craig Bellamy is banned for three games by the FA after being caught on camera striking Swansea's Jonathan de Guzman.

12 Gary Bowyer, Blackburn's manager, receives a one-match touchline ban and £3,000 fine from the FA for misconduct after the game at Barnsley.

13 Tottenham agree a five-year sponsorship deal, worth a reported £16m a year, with insurance company AIA.

14 Sir Tom Finney, one of the finest British players of all-time, dies aged 91. Rene Meulensteen, manager of bottom-of-the-table Fulham for 75 days, is replaced by former Bayern Munich coach Felix Magath. The FA fine Huddersfield £7,500 and Charlton £5,000 for a players' confrontation in their FA Cup tie.

15 Amid confusion at Craven Cottage, Rene Meulensteen insists he has been sacked, while Fulham say his contract has not been terminated.

16 Cardiff City Stadium is named as the venue for the European Super Cup match, between the winners of the Champions League and Europa League, on August 12.

17 Fulham dismiss technical director Alan Curbishley and assistant head coach Ray Wilkins and confirm that Rene Meulensteen has left the club.

18 Tranmere suspend their manager, Ronnie Moore, pending the conclusion of an FA investigation into a potential breach of betting rules.

19 Ben Watson, Wigan's FA Cup match-winner in 2013, is ruled out for the rest of the season, and misses a quarter-final 'rematch' with Manchester City, after sustaining a double fracture of his right leg against Barnsley.

20 Millwall are fined £6,000 by the FA for their players' misbehaviour against Burnley.

21 Wayne Rooney signs a new five-and-a-half-year contract with Manchester United for a reported record £250,000 a week, effectively committing the rest of his career to the club.

22 Former Shrewsbury defender Michael Jackson is appointed manager of the club until the end of the season after a spell as caretaker.

25 Wembley Stadium sign a six-year sponsorship deal, worth around £25m, with the communications company EE.

27 Nicolas Anelka is banned for five matches and fined £80,000 by the FA for a racially offensive 'quenelle' gesture during West Bromwich Albion's game against West Ham. Anelka is also suspended by his club. Tottenham win their Europa League first knock-out round tie against Dnipro 3-2 on aggregate. Swansea are beaten 3-1 by Napoli

28 Manchester City manager Manuel Pellegrini is given a two-match touchline ban by UEFA for criticising referee Jonas Eriksson after the Champions League home defeat by Barcelona. Aidy Boothroyd, former Watford, Colchester, Coventry and Northampton manager, is appointed coach to England's Under-20 team.

MARCH 2014

1 Newcastle manager Alan Pardew is fined £100,000 and reprimanded by the club for headbutting Hull midfielder David Meyler in a touchline confrontation. Pardew, sent to the

stands by referee Kevin Friend, apologies for his action during Newcastle's 4-1 victory at the KC Stadium.

2 Manchester City come from behind to beat Sunderland 3-1 in the Capital One Cup Final.

3 Former England defender Sol Campbell claims in his biography that he would have become an established captain of the national team had he been white. There is no response from the FA, but anti-racist campaigners accuse him of seeking publicity to sell the book.

4 Nottingham Forest manager Billy Davies is given a five-match touchline ban and a £9,000 fine by the FA for abusive language towards referee Anthony Taylor at half-time of the match with Leicester. Jason Puncheon, of Crystal Palace, receives a £15,000 fine for derogatory comments on Twitter about Neil Warnock, his former manager. Arsenal's Per Mertesacker and Tomas Rosicky sign new contracts.

5 In their final match before Roy Hodgson selects his World Cup squad, England defeat Denmark with an 82nd-minute goal from Daniel Sturridge. Scotland continue their improvement under Gordon Strachan by winning by the same 1-0 scoreline in Poland, while Gareth Bale scores one goal and sets up two more as Wales overcome Iceland 3-1. In other friendlies, Northern Ireland share a goalless draw with Cyprus and the Republic of Ireland lose 2-1 at home to Serbia.

6 Charlie Adam is banned for three matches by the FA after being caught on camera stamping on Olivier Giroud in Stoke's win over Arsenal.

7 Queens Park Rangers post an annual loss of £65.4m.

9 Wigan repeat their 2013 FA Cup Final victory over Manchester City by beating the Premier League side in the quarter-finals of this season's competition.

10 Chris Powell, the Championship's longest-serving manager, is sacked after three years in charge at Charlton, the day after his bottom-of-the-table side are knocked out of the FA Cup by Sheffield United. Powell is replaced by Jose Riga, director of AC Milan's academy.

11 The FA give Alan Pardew a three-match stadium ban, a four-game touchline suspension and a £60,000 fine – a record punishment for a Premier League manager. Arsenal lose 3-1 on aggregate to Bayern Munich in the Champion League's first knock-out round.

12 Manchester City also bow out, beaten 4-1 on aggregate by Barcelona. Torquay midfielder Joss Labadie is banned for ten matches and fined £2,000 for biting Chesterfield's Ollie Banks. Rangers continue their climb towards a return to the Scottish Premiership by winning the League One title with eight games still to play.

14 Nicolas Anelka is sacked by West Bromwich Albion for gross misconduct after announcing he is quitting the club.

16 Aberdeen win their first trophy for 19 years, beating Inverness 4-2 on penalties after the Scottish Communities League Cup Final ends goalless.

17 Hull City owner Assem Allam's proposal to change the name of the club to Hull Tigers is rejected by the FA's membership committee.

18 Chelsea reach the Champions League quarter-finals with a 3-1 aggregate win over Galatasaray.

19 A hat-trick by Robin van Persie enables Manchester United to overcome a two-goal deficit from the first leg and go through with a 3-2 aggregate win over Olympiacos. Newcastle's Dan Gosling is fined £30,000 by the FA for breaching betting rules.

20 George Boyd is banned for three matches by the FA after being caught on camera spitting at Joe Hart in Hull's game against Manchester City. Tottenham go out of the Europa League, defeated 5-3 on aggregate by Benfica in the second knock-out round.

21 Gary Waddock, former Queens Park Rangers, Aldershot and Wycombe manager, takes charge at Oxford.

22 Referee Andre Marriner apologises for sending off the wrong player in Chelsea's 6-0 win over Arsenal. Marriner shows a red card to Kieran Gibbs, instead of Alex Oxlade-Chamberlain, during Arsene Wenger's 1,000th match as Arsenal manager.

23 Cambridge United win the FA Trophy for the first time, beating Gosport 4-0 in the final.

24 Nottingham Forest manager Billy Davies is sacked after eight matches without a win, culminating in a 5-0 defeat by Derby. The Football League rule that Italian businessman Massimo Cellino cannot take over Leeds because of a tax offence conviction.

25 UEFA approve a new Nations League tournament to most replace most international friendly matches from 2018.

26 Celtic clinch a third successive title with seven Scottish Premiership matches still to play.

27 Richie Barker is sacked, after less than four months as Portsmouth manager, with his side third from bottom of League Two.

28 Another team fighting to retain their league status make a managerial change. Bristol Rovers, fifth from bottom, replace John Ward with his assistant Darrell Clarke and appoint Ward director of football.

29 Scunthorpe's Russ Wilcox breaks a 125-year-old English league record with a 24th unbeaten match from the start of his appointment as manager.

30 Peterborough beat Chesterfield 3-1 in the Johnstone's Paint Trophy Final.

31 New inquests begin into the deaths of the 96 Liverpool supporters who lost their lives in the Hillsborough disaster.

25 David Moyes reaches a settlement with Manchester United, reported to be £7m, over his dismissal.

26 Torquay are relegated from the Football League for the second time in eight seasons.

27 Liverpool's Luis Suarez is named PFA Player of the Year. Celtic's Kris Commons receives the PFA Scotland award. Aberdeen's Derek McInnes is voted Scottish Manager of the Year.

28 AFC Wimbledon are deducted three points and given a suspended £5,000 fine for fielding an ineligible player against Cheltenham. Blackpool coach Bob Malcolm receives a two-match touchline ban and £1,000 fine from the FA over an incident with his own player, substitute Stephen Dobbie, during the defeat by Burnley.

29 Cristiano Ronaldo overtakes Lionel Messi's Champions League record of 14 goals in a season in Real Madrid's 4-0 win over Bayern Munich in their semi-final second leg.

30 Chelsea lose 3-1 on aggregate to Atletico Madrid. Wigan are fined £40,000 for breaching FA regulations on agents.

APRIL 2014

1 Barcelona are banned from signing players in the next two transfer windows and fined £300,000 by UEFA for breaching rules on signing under-18 players.

2 Stuart Pearce is appointed the new manager of Nottingham Forest, the club he served as a player for 12 years. Christian Benteke, Aston Villa's Belgium striker, is ruled out of the rest of the season and the World Cup with a torn achilles tendon.

3 A Premier League fine imposed on Sunderland in December 2013 for fielding an ineligible player, Ji Dong-won, in four league matches early in the season, comes to light. The amount remains undisclosed. So does a Football League fine for not having international clearance for the South Korean to play in a Capital One Cup tie. Seven more Football League players are arrested in connection with alleged spot-fixing and another six re-arrested.

4 The Football League's decision to block Massimo Cellino's £35m takeover of Leeds is overturned by an independent QC.

5 Leicester become the first Football League side to be promoted, returning to the Premier League after a ten-year absence. In Scotland, Hearts are relegated from the Premiership, having started the season with 15 points deducted for entering administration. Southampton's Jay Rodriguez has his chance of a place in England's World Cup squad ended by a knee ligament injury.

6 Chris Hughton is sacked as Norwich manager and youth coach Neil Adams given the job of trying to keep the club in the Premier League. Rangers are beaten 1-0 by Raith Rovers in the Ramsdens Cup Final.

7 Tottenham manager Tim Sherwood is told by chairman Daniel Levy he will be replaced at the end of the season. Hull City season-ticket holders vote narrowly in favour of changing the club's name to Hull Tigers.

8 Chelsea, 3-1 down from the first leg, beat Paris St-Germain 2-0 at Stamford Bridge to reach the semi-finals of the Champions League.

9 Manchester United go out, beaten 4-2 on aggregate by defending champions Bayern

Munich. Tranmere manager Ronnie Moore is sacked for breach of contract after admitting breaching FA gambling rules.

10 Chelsea manager Jose Mourinho is fined £8,000 by the FA after being sent off at Villa Park for walking on to the pitch to speak to referee Chris Foy about the sending-off of Ramires.

11 UEFA tell Chelsea they cannot stop the club's on-loan goalkeeper Thibaut Courtois from playing against them for Atletico Madrid in the Champions League semi-finals. Jackie McNamara, Dundee United manager, is given a three-match touchline ban, with two more games suspended, for a touchline altercation with St Johnstone manager Tommy Wright, who receives a suspended one-match ban.

12 Grounds throughout the country hold a minute's silence to mark the 25th anniversary of the Hillsborough disaster. Arsenal beat Wigan on penalties to reach the FA Cup Final. Dundee United defeat Rangers 3-1 in the first Scottish Cup semi-final.

13 Hull reach the FA Cup Final for the first time with a 5-3 victory over Sheffield United. St Johnstone reach their first Scottish Cup Final, overcoming Aberdeen 2-1.

14 Manchester United manager David Moyes fines Tom Cleverley, Danny Welbeck and Ashley Young for a night out after the Champions League defeat by Bayern Munich. Stephen Ireland signs a new three-year contract with Stoke.

15 Everton manager Roberto Martinez joins Liverpool's Brendan Rodgers to address the memorial service at Anfield for the victims of Hillsborough. Luton return to the Football League, after an absence of five years, as champions of the Conference.

16 Gareth Bale scores a brilliant individual goal after 85 minutes to give Real Madrid a 2-1 win over Barcelona in the Spanish Cup Final. Crawley's Paul Connolly is banned for five matches after being caught on camera hitting a Brentford supporter.

17 Lee Probert is named as referee for the FA Cup Final. Everton's Tim Howard signs a new contract through to 2016.

18 Dylan Tombides, a 20-year-old Australian striker with West Ham, dies of testicular cancer. Six players are shortlisted for the PFA Player of the Year award – Steven Gerrard, Eden Hazard, Adam Lallana, Daniel Sturridge, Luis Suarez and Yaya Toure.

19 Jose Mourinho loses his 77-match unbeaten Premier League record at Stamford Bridge as Chelsea are beaten 2-1 by Sunderland.

21 Burnley, 16/1 outsiders at the start of the Championship season, are promoted to the Premier League. Wolves become League One champions.

22 David Moyes, 11 months into a six-year contract, is sacked as Manchester United manager after the club's worst season in the Premier League. Ryan Giggs is appointed interim manager. Leicester clinch the Championship title. Hull's Yannick Sagbo is fined £15,000 by the FA for showing support for Nicolas Anelka's 'quenelle' gesture.

23 The League Managers' Association claim Manchester United handled the dismissal in an 'unprofessional manner'. Moyes, in a statement, admits performances and results have not been good enough. United's Adnan Januzaj opts to play international football for Belgium, the country of his birth, rather than England. FIFA suspend the transfer ban imposed on Barcelona after an appeal by the club.

24 Chelsea's Ramires is banned for four games by the FA, and misses the rest of the season, after an off-the-ball incident with Sunderland's Seb Larsson is caught on camera.

MAY 2014

1 Rui Faria, Jose Mourinho's assistant at Chelsea, is given a six-match stadium ban and £30,000 fine by the FA for attempting to confront referee Mike Dean and fourth official Phil Dowd after Sunderland's match-winning penalty at Stamford Bridge. Andy Awford is given the Portsmouth's manager's job on a permanent basis after leading the team away from the threat of relegation in a caretaker role.

2 West Bromwich Albion supporters oppose a change of strip from the traditional blue and white stripes to a predominantly white shirt.

3 Fulham and Cardiff are relegated from the Premier League. Bristol Rovers drop into the Conference. Chesterfield win the League Two title. Peter Taylor agrees a two-year contract

to remain Gillingham manager.

4 Luis Suarez completes the double when winning the Football Writers' Association Footballer of the Year award.

6 Nottingham Forest's Dexter Blackstock is fined £60,000 and given a suspended three-month ban by the FA for breaches of betting rules.

7 Garry Monk is appointed Swansea manager on a three-year contract after three months as caretaker.

8 A new 'League Three' consisting of Premier League B teams and Conference clubs is proposed by FA chairman Greg Dyke's commission on improving English football. It also calls for a ban on non-European Union players outside the top flight. Jose Mourinho is fined £10,000 by the FA for bringing the game into disrepute with sarcastic comments about referee Mike Dean and referees' chief Mike Riley.

9 Malky Mackay drops legal action against Cardiff over his dismissal and apologises to owner Vincent Tan. Cardiff's Juan Cala is banned for three matches and fined £12,500 by the FA for his behaviour after being sent off against Sunderland.

10 Kris Commons completes the double with the Scottish Football Writers' Association Footballer of the Year award.

11 Manchester City become Premier League champions for the second time in three years. Ashley Cole, winner of 107 caps, retires from international football after Roy Hodgson tells him he is not in England's World Cup squad. Motherwell score a stoppage-time winner against Aberdeen at Pittodrie to overtake their rivals for the Scottish Premiership's runners-up spot. Oscar Garcia resigns as Brighton manager after their Play-off semi-final defeat by Derby

12 Roy Hodgson announces eight players under 24 in his 23-strong squad for Brazil, including Southampton's Luke Shaw, Everton's Ross Barkley and Liverpool's Raheem Sterling. Aston Villa owner Randy Lerner puts the club up for sale. Liverpool's Brendan Rodgers is named the League Managers' Association Manager of the Year. Tony Pulis, of Crystal Palace, wins the Premier League award. Pepe Mel parts company with West Bromwich Albion by mutual consent after a troubled four months as manager. Two Scottish Premiership managers leave their clubs. Gary Locke, of Hearts, is sacked by the club's new owner, Edinburgh businesswomen Ann Budge. Danny Lennon's four-years in charge at St Mirren comes to be end when his contract is not renewed. Lennon is replaced by his assistant, Tommy Craig. Former Fleetwood manager Micky Mellon takes over at relegated Shrewsbury.

13 Tim Sherwood has his sacking confirmed, less than six months into an 18-month contract, for being too outspoken for the club. Former manager Craig Levein becomes director of football and former player Robbie Neilson is appointed head coach at Hearts.

14 After a goalless 120 minutes, Sevilla beat Benfica 4-2 on penalties to win the Europa League – the Portuguese club's eighth successive defeat in a European final.

15 UEFA fine Manchester City £49m, with £32.6m suspended, and restrict the club's Champions League squad to 21 players for breaching Financial Fair Play rules.

16 Barcelona's Lionel Messi becomes the game's highest-paid player when signing a new contract worth £16.3m a season.

17 Arsenal come from two goals down to beat Hull 3-2 in extra-time in the FA Cup Final – the club's first trophy since 2005. St Johnstone win the Scottish Cup for the first time in their 130-year history, defeating Dundee United 2-0.

18 Cambridge United return to the Football League after a nine-year absence, beating Gateshead 2-1 in the Conference Play-off Final and completing a Wembley double following their FA Trophy success.

19 Louis van Gaal, Holland's World Cup coach, is named Manchester United's new manager on a three-year contract. Ryan Giggs becomes assistant manager and announces his retirement as a player after 963 appearances for the club. Premier League clubs decide to take no action against chief executive Richard Scudamore after he apologises over leaked, sexist e-mails sent to friends.

20 Jose Riga leaves Charlton after two months as manager. Wycombe are fined £10,000 for

breaching FA rules when selling Matt Phillips to Blackpool. Agent Phil Smith is banned for two years, with 18 months suspended.

21 England win the European Under-17 Championship, beating Holland 4-1 on penalties after the final in Ta'Qali, Malta, ends 1-1.

22 Neil Lennon stands down after nearly four years as Celtic manager. Norwich appoint caretaker Neil Adams their permanent manager. Craig Bellamy, who played for nine clubs and won 78 Wales caps, announces his retirement. Former Tranmere manager Ronnie Moore is given a suspended one-month ban and fined £2,000 by the FA for breaching betting rules.

23 Liverpool manager Brendan Rodgers signs an extension of his contract through to 2018. Rui Faria has two matches of his six-game ban suspended by the FA on appeal.

24 An 89th minute goal by Bobby Zamora gives ten-man Queens Park Rangers victory over Derby in the Championship Play-off Final and an immediate return to the Premier League. Real Madrid equalise in stoppage-time and go on to beat Atletico Madrid 4-1 in extra-time in the Champions League Final. Gareth Bale is among their scorers.

25 Hibernian are relegated from the Scottish Premiership after 15 years in the top division. They lose 4-3 on penalties to Hamilton in the play offs and join Edinburgh neighbours Hearts in the Championship. Rotherham are promoted for the second successive season, retrieving a two-goal deficit to draw 2-2 with Leyton Orient and winning 4-2 on penalties in the League One Play-off Final.

26 Fleetwood beat Burton 1-0 in the League Two Play-off Final, the club's sixth promotion in ten seasons.

27 Mauricio Pochettino resigns as Southampton manager to take over at Tottenham. Rob Edwards, former assistant at Exeter, begins his first managerial job, succeeding Ronnie Moore at Tranmere.

28 Manchester United owner Malcolm Glazer dies aged 85. Sunderland manager Gus Poyet signs a new contract through to 2016. Scotland concede a 90th minute equaliser and draw 2-2 with World Cup-bound Nigeria at Craven Cottage.

29 Arsene Wenger signs a new contract with Arsenal through to 2017, taking his tenure at the club to 21 years.

30 England are 3-0 winners over Peru in their final game at Wembley before the World Cup. Uruguay, one of their group opponents, struggle to beat Northern Ireland 1-0. Manager Brian McDermott leaves Leeds by mutual consent after a troubled season for the club. The FA fine Sunderland £100,000 for infringing agents' regulations. Agent Abu Mahfuz receives a two-year ban, with 18 months suspended.

31 Another of England's opponents, Italy, use some fringe players against the Republic of Ireland at Craven Cottage and are held to a goalless draw.

JUNE 2014

1 The first major move of the summer takes Southampton's Rickie Lambert to Liverpool for £4m. Arsenal win the FA Women's Cup for the 13th time, defeating Everton 2-0 in the final at Milton Keynes.

2 Frank Lampard, Chelsea's record scorer in all competitions, announces he is leaving the club after 13 years at Stamford Bridge.

4 Raheem Sterling, 19, becomes the youngest England player to be sent off as England draw 2-2 with Ecuador in Miami. The Liverpool player and Manchester United's Antonio Valencia are dismissed after a touchline clash. England's first opponents, Italy, can only draw 1-1 with Luxembourg, ranked 112th in the world. Wales lose 2-0 to Holland.

5 Northern Ireland go down 2-0 to another of the World Cup finalists, Chile. Jose Riga makes an immediate return to management, taking over at Blackpool. Celtic appoint Ronny Deila, manager of Norwegian champions Stromsgodset, as Neil Lennon's successor.

6 Former Liverpool defender Sami Hyypia, sacked by Bayer Leverkusen in April, is appointed Brighton's new manager. Sir Trevor Brooking announces his retirement after more than ten years as the FA's director of football development.

7 England's final match before the tournament, a goalless draw against Honduras in Miami, is interrupted for 45 minutes by an electrical storm. Their final group opponents, Costa Rica, draw 1-1 with the Republic of Ireland

8 Sepp Blatter comes under pressure over corruption allegations in *The Sunday Times* relating to Qatar's successful bid for the 2022 World Cup.

9 The FIFA president accuses the British media of being driven by 'racism and discrimination.'

10 Greg Dyke, chairman of the FA, adds his voice to widespread calls for Sepp Blatter to resign. Former England defender Terry Butcher is sacked as Hibernian manager following the club's relegation from the Scottish Premiership. Hereford are expelled from the Conference after missing a deadline to pay football creditors. Chester are reinstated to the Premier Division.

11 Milan Mandaric sells Sheffield Wednesday to Azerbaijan businessman Hafiz Mammadov, who also owns the French club Lens. Hearts come out of administration after a year and have their transfer embargo lifted.

12 Hosts Brazil beat Croatia 2-1 in the first match of the World Cup Finals. Chelsea sign Barcelona's Cesc Fabregas for £27m after Arsenal turn down the chance to bring him back to the Emirates. Everton manager Roberto Martinez is given a new five-year contract.

13 Chelsea's David Luiz joins Paris Saint-Germain for £40m – a world record fee for a defender. Alan Irvine, former Sheffield Wednesday and Preston manager, takes charge at West Bromwich Albion.

14 England are beaten 2-1 by Italy in their opening game. The teams physio, Gary Lewin, sustains a dislocated ankle while celebrating Daniel Sturridge's equaliser.

15 Ronald Koeman, scorer of one of the goals for Holland which denied England a place in the 1994 finals, is appointed Southampton's new manager.

17 Dave Hockaday, former manager of Conference club Forest Green, takes charge at Leeds.

18 Defending champions Spain are knocked out of the tournament after losing group games against Holland and Chile. Manager Sean Dyche and his coaching staff are given new contracts for taking Burnley into the Premier League.

19 England are left on the brink of being eliminated as two goals by Liverpool's Luis Suarez in his first game after a knee operation give Uruguay a 2-1 win.

20 England's elimination is confirmed when Chile defeat Italy. Roy Hodgson insists he will not resign.

21 FA chairman Greg Dyke says the manager will continue through to the 2016 European Championship.

22 Antonio Valencia signs a new three-year contract with Manchester United.

23 Alan Stubbs, former Bolton, Celtic and Everton defender, is appointed Hibernian's new manager.

24 England draw 0-0 in their final game against Costa Rica, resulting in the national team's worst-ever showing in the World Cup. Luis Suarez is caught on camera biting Italy defender Giorgio Chiellini in Uruguay's 1-0 victory which takes them through to the knock-out stage.

25 Louis van Gaal makes his first signing for Manchester United – midfielder Ander Herrara from Athletic Bilbao for £28.8m

26 For the third biting offence of his career, Luis Suarez is given an immediate four-month ban by FIFA, ruling him out nine internationals and Liverpool's first 13 matches of the new season – assuming he remains with the club. Manchester United sign Southampton's Luke Shaw for £30m – a world record fee for a teenager.

27 Everton's Seamus Coleman signs a five-year extension to his contract

29 Luis Suarez says sorry – belatedly – for his latest misdemeanour and apologises to Giorgio Chiellini.

30 Anthony Fry steps down as chairman of the Premier League because of illness.

JULY 2014

1 Chelsea pay £32m for striker Diego Costa from Champions League runners-up Atletico Madrid.

2 Roy Keane is appointed assistant manager of Aston Villa, while continuing as assistant to Republic of Ireland manager Martin O'Neill.

3 Swansea skipper Ashley Williams ends speculation about his future by signing a new four-year contract. Wes Morgan, captain of newly-promoted Leicester, signs a new three-year deal.

4 Brazil star Neymar is ruled out of the remainder of the World Cup after sustaining a fractured vertebra in the quarter-final win over Colombia. Gary Waddock, manager of Oxford for less than four months, is sacked after businessman Darryl Eales buys a majority share in the club from owner Ian Lenagan. Waddock is replaced by Michael Appleton, formerly in charge of Blackburn, Portsmouth and Blackpool.

5 Holland coach Louis van Gaal sends on substitute goalkeeper Tim Krul to face a penalty shoot-out against Costa Rica – and the Newcastle player saves two spot-kicks to put his side into the semi-finals.

6 Leyton Orient owner Barry Hearn sells the club to Italian businessman Francesco Becchetti.

7 Alfredo Di Stefano, a European Cup winner with Real Madrid in the first five European Cup Finals and one of the finest players of all-time, dies aged 88.

8 Germany deliver one of the most remarkable scorelines in the history of the World Cup – a 7-1 win over Brazil in the first semi-final, with four of the goals coming in a six-minute spell in the first half.

9 Brazil's woe is heightened when South American rivals Argentina reach the final by beating Holland 4-2 on penalties after a goalless 120 minutes.

10 FIFA reject an appeal by Luis Suarez and the Uruguay Federation against the player's four-month suspension. Manchester City's Samir Nasri and Tottenham's Hugo Lloris sign new five-year contracts.

11 Barcelona sign Luis Suarez for £75m. Liverpool manager Brendan Rodgers admits it's time for the player to leave Anfield. Arsenal sign Chile World Cup star Alexis Sanchez from Barcelona for £35m.

13 A goal by substitute Mario Gotze five minutes from the end of extra-time gives Germany a win over Argentina in the World Cup Final.

14 Manchester United announce a world-record kit sponsorship with adidas worth £750m over ten years.

THE THINGS THEY SAY...

'We need a miracle to stay up now' – **Gus Poyet**, Sunderland manager, when his side were seven points adrift at the bottom with six games left.

'I'm starting to believe in miracles now' – **Gus Poyet** after Sunderland beat the drop with four successive victories.

'There are different ways to win titles. I choose the one with attractive football. For me, the aesthetic part is very important' – **Manuel Pellegrini**, manager of champions Manchester City, in an apparent dig at the tactics of Chelsea's Jose Mourinho.

'The single biggest source of inspiration for me is when I arrive at the ground and see the memorial and the names of the 96 individuals who were loved, cherished and went all too soon' – **Brendan Rodgers**, Liverpool manager, addressing a memorial service at Anfield on the 25th anniversary of the Hillsborough disaster.

ENGLISH TABLES 2013–2014

BARCLAYS PREMIER LEAGUE

			Home					Away						
		P	W	D	L	F	A	W	D	L	F	A	GD	PTS
1	Manchester City	38	17	1	1	63	13	10	4	5	39	24	65	86
2	Liverpool	38	16	1	2	53	18	10	5	4	48	32	51	84
3	Chelsea	38	15	3	1	43	11	10	4	5	28	16	44	82
4	Arsenal	38	13	5	1	36	11	11	2	6	32	30	27	79
5	Everton	38	13	3	3	38	19	8	6	5	23	20	22	72
6	Tottenham	38	11	3	5	30	23	10	3	6	25	28	4	69
7	Manchester Utd	38	9	3	7	29	21	10	4	5	35	22	21	64
8	Southampton	38	8	6	5	32	23	7	5	7	22	23	8	56
9	Stoke	38	10	6	3	27	17	3	5	11	18	35	-7	50
10	Newcastle	38	8	3	8	23	28	7	1	11	20	31	-16	49
11	Crystal Palace	38	8	3	8	18	23	5	3	11	15	25	-15	45
12	Swansea	38	6	5	8	33	26	5	4	10	21	28	0	42
13	West Ham	38	7	3	9	25	26	6	4	11	15	25	-11	40
14	Sunderland	38	5	3	11	21	27	5	5	9	20	33	-19	38
15	Aston Villa	38	6	3	10	22	29	4	5	10	17	32	-22	38
16	Hull	38	7	4	8	20	21	3	3	13	18	32	-15	37
17	WBA	38	4	9	6	24	27	3	6	10	19	32	-16	36
18	Norwich	38	6	6	7	17	18	2	3	14	11	44	-34	33
19	Fulham	38	5	3	11	24	38	4	2	13	16	47	-45	32
20	Cardiff	38	5	5	9	20	35	2	4	13	12	39	-42	30

Manchester City, Liverpool and Chelsea go into Champions League group stage; Arsenal into play-off round. Everton (group), Tottenham (play-offs) and Hull (third qualifying round) into Europa League

TV/merit money (league position): 1 £96.6m 2 £97.5m, 3 £94.1m 4 £92.9m, 5 £85m 6 £89.7m, 7 £89.2m, 8 £76.9m, 9 £75.7m, 10 £77.4m, 11 £73.2m, 12 £74.2m, 13 £73.7m, 14 £71.7m, 15 £72.7m, 16 £67m, 17 £65.8m, 18 £64.5, 19 £63.3m, 20 £62.1m

Biggest win: Manchester City 7 Norwich 0

Highest aggregate score: Cardiff 3 Liverpool 6, Manchester City 6 Arsenal 3

Highest attendance: 75,368 (Manchester Utd v Aston Villa)

Lowest attendance: 19,242 (Swansea v Stoke)

Player of Year: Luis Suarez (Liverpool)

Manager of Year: Tony Pulis (Crystal Palace)

Golden Boot: 31 Luis Suarez

Golden Glove: 16 clean sheets Petr Cech (Chelsea), Wojciech Szczesny (Arsenal) – joint

PFA Team of Year: Cech (Chelsea), Coleman (Everton), Kompany (Manchester City), Cahill (Chelsea), Shaw (Southampton), Hazard (Chelsea), Toure (Manchester City), Gerrard (Liverpool), Lallana (Southampton), Suarez (Liverpool), Sturridge (Liverpool)

Leading scorers (all competitions): 31 Suarez (Liverpool); 28 Aguero (Manchester City); 26 Dzeko (Manchester City); 24 Bony (Swansea), Sturridge (Liverpool), Toure (Manchester City); 22 Giroud (Arsenal); 19 Rooney (Manchester Utd); 18 Van Persie (Manchester Utd); 17 Hazard (Chelsea), Rodriguez (Southampton); 16 Lukaku (Everton); 15 Ramsey (Arsenal); 14 Adebayor (Tottenham), Gerrard (Liverpool) Lambert (Southampton), Remy (Newcastle).

SKY BET CHAMPIONSHIP

				Home					Away					
		P	W	D	L	F	A	W	D	L	F	A	GD	PTS
1	Leicester	46	17	4	2	46	22	14	5	4	37	21	40	102
2	Burnley	46	15	6	2	37	14	11	9	3	35	23	35	93
3	Derby	46	14	4	5	46	25	11	6	6	38	27	32	85
4	QPR*	46	15	4	4	38	18	8	5	10	22	26	16	80
5	Wigan	46	12	7	4	35	23	9	3	11	26	25	13	73
6	Brighton	46	10	7	6	31	21	9	8	6	24	19	15	72
7	Reading	46	8	10	5	38	25	11	4	8	32	31	14	71
8	Blackburn	46	11	7	5	34	21	7	9	7	36	41	8	70
9	Ipswich	46	12	6	5	35	24	6	8	9	25	30	6	68
10	Bournemouth	46	11	5	7	40	27	7	7	9	27	39	1	66
11	Nottm Forest	46	10	7	6	38	29	6	10	7	29	35	3	65
12	Middlesbrough	46	10	9	4	35	20	6	7	10	27	30	12	64
13	Watford	46	11	5	7	39	25	4	10	9	35	39	10	60
14	Bolton	46	6	11	6	29	23	8	6	9	30	37	-1	59
15	Leeds	46	9	5	9	35	31	7	4	12	24	36	-8	57
16	Sheffield Wed	46	9	4	10	39	33	4	10	9	24	32	-2	53
17	Huddersfield	46	8	6	9	34	32	6	5	12	24	33	-7	53
18	Charlton	46	7	6	10	21	28	6	6	11	20	33	-20	51
19	Millwall	46	6	9	8	26	33	5	6	12	20	41	-28	48
20	Blackpool	46	7	6	10	20	27	4	7	12	18	39	-28	46
21	Birmingham	46	2	8	13	29	40	9	3	11	29	34	-16	44
22	Doncaster	46	9	4	10	27	32	2	7	14	12	38	-31	44
23	Barnsley	46	5	8	10	22	36	4	4	15	22	41	-33	39
24	Yeovil	46	4	6	13	19	32	4	7	12	25	43	-31	37

*also promoted

Biggest win: Reading 7 Bolton 1, Sheffield Wed 6 Leeds 0
Highest aggregate score: Derby 4 Ipswich 4, Leicester 5 Bolton 3, Reading 7 Bolton 1
Highest attendance: 33,432 (Leeds v Brighton)
Lowest attendance: 4,463 (Yeovil v Millwall)
Player of Year: Danny Ings (Burnley)
Manager of Year: Nigel Pearson (Leicester)
Top league scorer: 28 Ross McCormack (Leeds)
PFA Team of Year: Schmeichel (Leicester), Trippier (Burnley), Morgan (Leicester), Shackell (Burnley), Cresswell (Ipswich) Drinkwater (Leicester), Reid (Nottm Forest), Bryson (Derby), Hughes (Derby), Ings (Burnley), McCormack (Leeds)
Leading scorers (all competitions): 29 McCormack (Leeds); 26 Ings (Burnley); 25 Deeney (Watford), Martin (Derby), Rhodes (Blackburn); 22 Grabban (Bournemouth), Nugent (Leicester); 21 Vokes (Burnley); 20 Austin (QPR); 16 Bryson (Derby), McGoldrick (Ipswich); Ulloa (Brighton), Vardy (Leicester); 15 Le Fondre (Reading), O'Grady (Barnsley); 13 Murphy (Ipswich), Pogrebnyiak (Reading), Smith (Leeds)
Also: 25 Bamford (Derby – 17 for MK Dons); 22 Wells (Huddersfield – 15 for Bradford); 17 Kermorgant (Bournemouth – 8 for Charlton); 14 Gestede (Blackburn – 1 for Cardiff)

SKY BET LEAGUE ONE

			Home				Away						
		P	W	D	L	F	A	W	D	L	F	A	GD	PTS
1	Wolves	46	17	4	2	48	15	14	6	3	41	16	58	103
2	Brentford	46	19	1	3	44	17	9	9	5	28	26	29	94
3	Leyton Orient	46	13	3	7	43	23	12	8	3	42	22	40	86
4	Rotherham*	46	10	10	3	44	30	14	4	5	42	28	28	86
5	Preston	46	12	9	2	44	26	11	7	5	28	20	26	85
6	Peterborough	46	14	3	6	34	21	9	2	12	38	37	14	74
7	Sheffield Utd	46	12	7	4	31	18	6	6	11	17	28	2	67
8	Swindon	46	14	3	6	40	27	5	6	12	23	32	4	66
9	Port Vale	46	13	3	7	35	30	5	4	14	24	43	-14	61
10	MK Dons	46	8	5	10	29	30	9	4	10	34	35	-2	60
11	Bradford	46	8	9	6	35	27	6	8	9	22	27	3	59
12	Bristol City	46	7	10	6	34	28	6	9	8	36	39	3	58
13	Walsall	46	7	7	9	21	28	7	9	7	28	21	0	58
14	Crawley	46	10	7	6	24	23	4	8	11	24	31	-6	57
15	Oldham	46	7	8	8	23	28	7	6	10	27	31	-9	56
16	Colchester	46	8	5	10	29	29	5	9	9	24	32	-8	53
17	Gillingham	46	10	5	8	35	31	5	3	15	25	48	-19	53
18	Coventry**	46	9	8	6	41	39	7	5	11	33	38	-3	51
19	Crewe	46	7	7	9	26	34	6	5	12	28	46	-26	51
20	Notts Co	46	12	2	9	40	28	3	3	17	24	49	-13	50
21	Tranmere	46	6	8	9	30	39	6	3	14	22	40	-27	47
22	Carlisle	46	8	6	9	27	32	3	6	14	16	44	-33	45
23	Shrewsbury	46	6	7	10	22	28	3	8	12	22	37	-21	42
24	Stevenage	46	7	5	11	29	34	4	4	15	17	38	-26	42

*also promoted. ** Deducted 10 pts for administration

Biggest win: Rotherham 6 Notts Co 0
Highest aggregate score: Wolves 6 Rotherham 4
Highest attendance: 30,110 (Wolves v Rotherham)
Lowest attendance: 1,603 (Coventry v Carlisle)
Player of Year: Adam Forshaw (Brentford)
Manager of Year: Kenny Jackett (Wolves) and Russell Slade (Leyton Orient) - joint
Top league scorer: 24 Sam Baldock (Bristol City)
PFA Team of Year: Ikeme (Wolves), Ricketts (Wolves), Batth (Wolves), Maguire (Sheffield Utd), Bidwell (Brentford), Sako (Wolves), Forshaw (Brentford), McDonald (Wolves), Pringle (Rotherham), Assombalonga (Peterborough), Wilson (Coventry)
Leading scorers (all competitions): 33 Assombalonga (Peterborough); 26 Agard (Rotherham), Baldock (Bristol City); 24 Garner (Preston); 22 Wilson (Coventry); 21 Emmanuel-Thomas (Bristol City), Mooney (Leyton Orient); 20 Lowe (Tranmere); 18 Donaldson (Brentford), Lisbie (Leyton Orient); 17 Cox (Leyton Orient), McDonald (Gillingham); 16 Aneke (Crewe), Pope (Port Vale), Westcarr (Walsall), Zoko (Stevenage); 14 Trotta (Brentford)
Also: 19 Clarke (Wolves – 18 for Coventry), Dicko (Wolves – 6 for Rotherham)

SKY BET LEAGUE TWO

		P	Home					Away						
			W	D	L	F	A	W	D	L	F	A	GD	PTS
1	Chesterfield	46	12	9	2	36	16	11	6	6	35	24	31	84
2	Scunthorpe	46	10	11	2	32	19	10	10	3	36	25	24	81
3	Rochdale	46	15	3	5	42	22	9	6	8	27	26	21	81
4	Fleetwood*	46	11	6	6	41	30	11	4	8	25	22	14	76
5	Southend	46	11	7	5	29	16	8	8	7	27	23	17	72
6	Burton	46	11	6	6	27	22	8	9	6	20	20	5	72
7	York	46	10	9	4	23	15	8	8	7	29	26	11	71
8	Oxford	46	8	6	9	24	23	8	8	7	29	27	3	62
9	Dag & Red	46	8	7	8	25	25	7	8	8	28	34	-6	60
10	Plymouth	46	8	7	8	23	26	8	5	10	28	32	-7	60
11	Mansfield	46	7	6	10	27	32	8	9	6	22	26	-9	60
12	Bury	46	8	12	3	33	23	5	8	10	26	28	8	59
13	Portsmouth	46	9	6	8	26	25	5	11	7	30	41	-10	59
14	Newport	46	10	6	7	37	27	4	10	9	19	32	-3	58
15	Accrington	46	6	10	7	33	29	8	5	10	21	27	-2	57
16	Exeter	46	6	6	11	22	27	8	7	8	32	30	-3	55
17	Cheltenham	46	5	9	9	29	35	8	7	8	24	28	-10	55
18	Morecambe	46	7	10	6	30	26	6	5	12	22	38	-12	54
19	Hartlepool	46	10	3	10	30	27	4	8	11	20	29	-6	53
20	AFC Wimbledon**	46	8	7	8	27	29	6	7	10	22	28	-8	53
21	Northampton	46	7	7	9	24	32	6	7	10	18	25	-15	53
22	Wycombe	46	6	6	11	20	27	6	8	9	26	27	-8	50
23	Bristol Rov	46	10	6	7	28	21	2	8	13	15	33	-11	50
24	Torquay	46	4	8	11	18	31	8	1	14	24	35	-24	45

*Also promoted. **Deducted 3 pts for ineligible player

Biggest win: Plymouth 5 Morecambe 0
Highest aggregate score: Fleetwood 5 Mansfield 4
Highest attendance: 18,181 (Portsmouth v Oxford)
Lowest attendance: 1,101 (Accrington v Bristol Rov))
Player of Year: Gary Roberts (Chesterfield)
Manager of Year: Russ Wilcox (Scunthorpe)
Top league scorer: 23 Sam Winnall (Scunthorpe)
PFA Team of Year: Lee (Chesterfield), Rose (Rochdale), Cooper (Chesterfield), Evatt (Chesterfield), Smith (Bristol Rov), Sarcevic (Fleetwood), Roberts (Chesterfield)), O'Toole (Bristol Rov), Henderson (Rochdale), Hogan (Rochdale), Winnall (Scunthorpe)
Leading scorers (all competitions): 23 Winnall (Scunthorpe); 21 Reid (Plymouth); 19 Hogan (Rochdale); 16 James (Hartlepool); 15 Harrison (Cheltenham), O'Toole (Bristol Rov), Sarcevic (Fleetwood); 14 Kee (Burton); 13 Ball (Fleetwood), Clucas (Mansfield), Doyle (Chesterfield), Fletcher (York), Murphy (Dag & Red), Zebroski (Newport); 12 Corr (Southend), McGurk (Burton), Roberts (Chesterfield)
Also: 16 Nardiello (Bury – 5 for Rotherham)

BARCLAYS PREMIER LEAGUE RESULTS 2013–2014

	Arsenal	Aston Villa	Cardiff	Chelsea	Crystal Palace	Everton	Fulham	Hull	Liverpool	Manchester City	Manchester Utd	Newcastle	Norwich	Southampton	Stoke	Sunderland	Swansea	Tottenham	WBA	West Ham
Arsenal	–	1-3	2-0	0-0	2-0	1-1	2-0	2-0	2-0	1-1	0-0	3-0	4-1	2-0	3-1	4-1	2-2	1-0	1-0	3-1
Aston Villa	1-2	–	2-0	1-0	0-1	0-2	1-2	3-1	0-1	3-2	0-3	1-2	4-1	0-0	1-4	0-0	1-1	0-2	4-3	0-2
Cardiff	0-3	0-0	–	1-2	0-3	0-0	3-1	0-4	3-6	3-2	2-2	1-2	2-1	0-3	1-1	2-2	1-0	0-1	1-0	0-2
Chelsea	6-0	2-1	4-1	–	2-1	1-0	2-0	2-0	2-1	2-1	3-1	3-0	0-0	3-1	3-0	1-2	1-0	4-0	2-2	0-0
Crystal Palace	0-2	1-0	2-0	1-0	–	0-0	1-4	1-0	3-3	0-2	0-2	0-3	1-1	0-1	1-0	3-1	0-2	0-1	3-1	1-0
Everton	3-0	2-1	2-1	1-0	2-3	–	4-1	2-1	3-3	3-1	2-0	3-2	2-0	2-1	4-0	0-1	3-2	0-0	0-0	1-0
Fulham	1-3	2-0	1-2	1-3	2-2	1-3	–	2-2	2-3	2-4	1-3	1-0	1-0	0-3	1-0	1-4	1-2	1-2	1-1	2-1
Hull	0-3	0-0	1-1	0-2	0-1	0-2	6-0	–	3-1	0-2	2-3	1-4	1-0	0-1	0-0	1-0	1-1	1-1	2-0	1-0
Liverpool	5-1	2-2	3-1	1-2	3-1	4-0	4-0	2-0	–	3-2	0-3	2-1	5-1	0-1	1-0	2-1	4-3	4-0	4-1	2-0
Manchester City	6-3	4-0	4-2	0-1	3-1	3-1	5-0	2-0	2-1	–	4-1	4-0	7-0	4-1	1-0	2-2	3-0	6-0	3-1	2-0
Manchester Utd	1-0	4-1	2-0	0-0	2-0	0-1	2-2	3-1	0-3	0-3	–	0-1	4-1	1-1	3-2	0-1	2-0	1-2	1-2	3-1
Newcastle	0-1	1-0	3-0	2-0	0-1	0-3	1-0	2-3	2-3	0-2	0-4	–	2-1	1-1	5-1	0-3	1-2	0-4	0-1	0-0
Norwich	0-2	0-1	0-0	0-0	0-0	2-2	2-0	1-1	2-3	0-0	0-1	0-0	–	1-0	1-1	2-0	1-1	1-0	1-0	0-0
Southampton	2-2	2-3	0-0	1-3	2-0	2-0	0-1	0-1	0-1	1-1	1-1	1-0	4-2	–	1-0	2-2	0-0	2-3	0-0	3-1
Stoke	1-0	0-1	1-1	3-2	1-2	1-1	1-0	0-1	3-5	1-0	2-1	0-0	1-1	2-2	–	1-0	1-0	0-1	2-0	0-1
Sunderland	1-3	0-1	4-0	2-1	3-1	0-1	4-1	2-1	2-1	2-2	2-1	2-1	2-2	0-1	2-2	–	1-3	1-2	1-2	1-2
Swansea	1-2	4-1	3-0	0-1	2-0	1-2	3-0	1-0	2-3	2-3	1-1	3-0	1-1	1-1	1-0	4-0	–	1-3	1-1	0-0
Tottenham	0-1	3-0	1-0	1-1	2-0	1-0	3-1	1-0	0-5	1-5	2-3	4-0	1-0	0-1	3-3	5-1	1-0	–	1-3	0-3
WBA	1-1	2-2	3-3	1-1	2-0	1-1	1-1	1-1	1-1	2-3	0-3	0-1	0-2	3-1	3-0	3-0	0-2	3-3	–	3-3
West Ham	1-3	0-0	2-0	0-0	3-1	2-3	3-0	2-1	1-2	1-3	0-2	1-0	2-0	0-1	1-2	0-0	2-0	2-0	3-3	–

SKY BET CHAMPIONSHIP RESULTS 2013–2014

	Barnsley	Birmingham	Blackburn	Blackpool	Bolton	Bournemouth	Brighton	Burnley	Charlton	Derby	Doncaster	Huddersfield	Ipswich	Leeds	Leicester	Middlesbrough	Millwall	Nottm Forest	QPR	Reading	Sheffield Wed	Watford	Wigan	Yeovil
Barnsley	–	0-3	2-2	2-0	0-1	0-1	0-0	0-1	2-2	1-2	0-0	2-1	2-2	0-1	0-3	3-1	1-0	1-0	2-3	1-1	1-1	1-5	0-4	1-1
Birmingham	1-1	–	2-4	1-1	1-2	2-4	3-3	3-3	0-1	3-3	1-0	1-2	1-1	1-3	1-2	2-2	1-0	0-0	0-2	1-2	4-1	0-1	0-1	0-2
Blackburn	5-2	2-3	–	4-1	4-1	0-1	3-3	0-1	0-1	1-1	1-0	3-2	1-1	1-0	1-1	2-1	3-2	0-0	0-0	0-0	2-0	4-3	4-3	0-2
Blackpool	1-0	1-2	2-2	–	0-0	0-1	0-1	0-1	0-3	1-3	1-1	0-0	2-3	1-0	1-1	0-2	1-0	1-1	0-2	0-0	2-0	1-0	1-0	1-1
Bolton	1-0	0-2	4-0	1-0	–	2-2	0-2	1-1	1-1	2-2	3-0	0-1	1-1	0-1	0-1	2-2	3-1	1-1	0-1	3-1	2-0	2-0	1-0	3-0
Bournemouth	1-0	2-2	1-3	1-2	1-0	–	2-2	1-1	2-1	2-0	5-0	2-1	1-1	4-1	0-1	0-2	5-2	4-1	2-1	1-1	2-4	1-1	1-0	3-0
Brighton	1-2	1-0	3-0	1-2	0-2	1-1	–	2-0	3-0	1-2	1-0	0-1	0-2	4-1	3-1	0-2	3-0	1-3	2-0	1-1	1-0	1-0	1-2	2-0
Burnley	1-0	3-0	1-1	2-1	1-1	1-0	2-0	–	3-0	2-0	2-0	3-2	0-2	2-1	0-0	2-1	0-1	1-1	2-0	2-1	1-1	0-0	1-2	2-0
Charlton	1-2	0-2	1-3	0-0	1-1	1-0	0-3	2-0	–	0-2	3-1	0-0	1-0	2-4	3-1	0-1	3-1	1-1	1-0	0-1	3-0	1-2	0-0	3-2
Derby	1-2	1-3	1-1	2-0	0-0	0-2	0-2	0-3	0-2	–	3-1	3-0	3-2	2-4	0-2	0-1	0-2	1-3	1-0	1-3	3-0	4-2	2-0	3-2
Doncaster	2-1	2-1	2-0	1-2	1-2	1-0	1-3	0-3	0-3	0-2	–	2-2	4-4	3-1	1-0	0-0	0-0	1-1	1-0	2-3	1-3	0-0	3-0	0-1
Huddersfield	2-2	1-3	2-0	1-3	0-1	5-1	1-0	0-2	3-0	0-2	3-1	–	0-3	3-2	1-0	0-0	0-0	5-0	1-0	2-2	2-2	1-2	1-0	3-2
Ipswich	5-0	2-4	3-1	0-1	3-1	2-2	1-1	2-1	2-1	1-1	0-0	2-1	–	3-2	1-0	2-2	1-0	2-2	1-3	2-4	1-0	3-3	1-0	1-1
Leeds	1-1	4-0	1-2	0-0	1-5	1-0	0-1	1-0	1-0	2-1	2-1	5-1	1-1	–	0-0	2-0	1-0	2-1	1-0	0-0	2-1	1-1	2-0	1-0
Leicester	0-0	3-2	2-1	1-0	0-0	1-2	0-1	1-0	1-2	0-3	2-1	3-0	1-0	0-0	–	1-2	3-0	1-3	5-2	2-0	1-1	2-2	3-0	2-1
Middlesbrough	3-1	3-1	0-0	1-1	1-0	3-3	0-1	0-1	0-1	1-0	1-1	2-0	3-0	0-0	1-2	–	1-2	2-2	2-0	3-0	0-1	2-2	2-0	4-1
Millwall	1-0	2-3	2-2	3-1	1-1	2-2	0-1	2-2	0-0	1-1	0-0	1-1	1-0	2-0	1-2	0-2	–	1-2	2-2	2-3	3-3	2-2	0-0	0-1
Nottm Forest	3-2	1-0	4-1	0-1	3-0	0-0	1-1	1-2	1-0	1-0	1-1	1-0	2-2	0-0	1-3	2-0	5-2	–	2-0	2-3	0-2	4-2	1-2	3-1
QPR	2-0	2-0	0-0	1-1	1-1	3-0	0-0	3-0	2-0	1-3	1-0	4-0	1-3	1-1	5-2	2-0	1-1	5-2	–	2-0	1-0	0-0	1-0	2-1
Reading	1-0	4-1	3-3	0-1	7-1	5-1	0-1	1-0	0-0	1-0	2-3	2-2	3-0	1-0	1-1	0-1	2-1	1-0	3-0	–	0-2	4-2	1-1	1-1
Sheffield Wed	3-0	3-3	1-0	3-2	0-1	1-2	2-1	1-0	2-3	2-1	2-1	2-1	1-0	1-0	2-2	0-2	1-1	1-0	3-0	5-2	–	3-3	0-3	1-1
Watford	3-0	1-0	3-3	4-0	2-0	1-1	1-0	2-1	0-1	1-3	1-0	2-1	2-0	3-1	2-2	2-2	4-0	2-1	0-1	0-1	1-0	–	2-1	0-1
Wigan	2-0	0-0	2-1	3-2	1-0	3-0	2-1	1-2	2-1	2-2	3-0	2-2	2-0	2-1	3-0	2-2	0-1	2-1	0-0	1-0	3-0	1-0	–	0-1
Yeovil	1-4	0-1	0-1	1-0	2-2	2-1	0-0	1-2	2-2	0-1	0-1	1-4	0-1	1-0	2-1	1-4	2-0	3-1	2-1	2-0	2-0	0-0	0-1	–

SKY BET LEAGUE ONE RESULTS 2013–2014

	Bradford	Brentford	Bristol City	Carlisle	Colchester	Coventry	Crawley	Crewe	Gillingham	Leyton Orient	MK Dons	Notts Co	Oldham	Peterborough	Port Vale	Preston	Rotherham	Sheffield Utd	Shrewsbury	Stevenage	Swindon	Tranmere	Walsall	Wolves
Bradford	–	4-0	1-2	1-0	0-2	0-0	1-0	0-0	1-1	1-1	1-0	1-1	2-3	1-0	1-0	0-0	0-1	2-2	2-0	2-3	1-1	0-1	0-2	1-2
Brentford	2-0	–	1-2	0-0	4-1	5-4	0-1	5-0	2-1	2-2	2-2	3-1	1-1	3-2	2-0	2-0	1-0	3-0	1-1	4-1	3-2	0-3	0-3	0-3
Bristol City	2-2	1-2	–	2-1	1-1	1-1	1-1	0-0	2-1	2-2	2-2	2-1	1-1	0-3	5-0	1-1	1-2	3-0	1-1	1-0	0-0	2-2	1-0	1-2
Carlisle	1-0	0-0	2-1	–	2-4	1-1	0-0	2-1	1-2	2-5	3-0	2-1	0-1	1-0	1-0	0-1	1-2	0-0	0-0	0-4	1-2	4-1	1-1	2-2
Colchester	0-2	4-1	1-1	2-4	–	1-0	1-1	2-2	3-0	2-1	2-3	0-4	0-1	1-0	1-0	1-2	0-3	2-1	0-0	4-0	1-2	1-2	2-1	0-3
Coventry	0-0	5-4	1-1	1-1	1-0	–	3-2	2-2	2-1	2-0	1-0	3-0	1-1	1-0	2-2	4-4	1-2	1-3	1-1	1-0	1-2	1-5	0-0	1-1
Crawley	1-0	0-1	1-1	0-0	1-1	3-2	–	1-2	3-2	2-1	0-2	1-1	1-0	4-2	3-2	2-2	1-2	2-2	1-1	1-1	1-2	1-2	0-3	2-1
Crewe	0-0	1-3	1-0	2-1	0-1	1-2	1-0	–	0-3	1-2	2-0	2-1	1-1	2-2	0-3	2-1	3-3	4-1	0-1	0-3	0-3	1-2	2-2	0-2
Gillingham	0-1	1-1	1-3	0-1	2-1	4-2	0-1	1-3	–	0-3	2-1	5-1	1-1	3-2	3-2	2-1	3-4	2-0	3-0	1-2	2-0	2-0	1-0	0-2
Leyton Orient	0-1	1-3	4-0	4-0	2-0	2-0	2-3	0-1	5-1	–	1-3	3-1	2-1	1-2	2-1	0-1	1-1	3-1	3-2	3-2	2-0	2-0	1-0	1-3
MK Dons	2-3	2-2	2-2	2-2	0-0	3-0	0-2	2-1	0-1	1-3	–	3-1	1-1	0-2	0-0	0-0	3-2	2-1	2-3	4-1	1-1	2-0	1-5	0-1
Notts Co	3-0	0-1	2-1	4-1	0-2	1-0	1-0	4-0	3-1	2-1	2-1	–	2-1	2-2	0-3	1-3	2-0	2-1	1-2	0-1	2-1	2-0	0-0	0-1
Oldham	1-1	1-3	1-2	1-1	2-0	1-0	1-0	0-1	1-0	2-1	2-1	2-1	–	2-4	4-2	2-1	0-1	2-1	1-2	0-1	1-0	3-0	1-0	1-0
Peterborough	2-1	1-2	1-1	1-2	1-1	1-0	0-2	5-4	2-0	1-3	1-2	4-3	3-2	–	5-4	5-4	2-0	2-0	3-1	2-2	2-3	3-2	2-1	0-3
Port Vale	2-1	1-1	1-2	2-1	2-0	3-2	2-1	1-0	0-1	2-1	1-0	2-1	2-1	3-1	–	0-2	3-3	2-1	1-0	3-0	1-1	1-1	1-1	1-1
Preston	2-2	1-0	1-0	6-1	1-1	1-3	0-2	0-2	4-1	2-1	2-2	2-0	2-1	1-0	3-2	–	1-0	0-0	5-2	2-1	1-0	3-1	0-1	0-0
Rotherham	0-0	3-0	3-0	0-0	2-2	2-1	1-3	4-2	1-2	6-0	2-1	6-0	3-2	0-1	1-0	0-0	–	3-1	2-2	1-0	2-0	3-1	3-2	3-3
Sheffield Utd	2-2	3-0	2-3	0-0	2-1	2-1	2-2	4-1	2-0	3-1	2-1	2-1	2-1	2-0	2-1	0-0	3-1	–	2-0	1-0	0-4	0-1	1-3	0-2
Shrewsbury	2-1	1-1	2-3	0-0	1-1	1-1	1-3	0-1	1-1	3-1	1-2	1-0	1-2	2-4	2-4	2-2	2-0	2-0	–	1-3	1-3	3-1	1-1	0-1
Stevenage	1-1	2-3	1-3	1-3	2-3	1-1	0-1	5-0	1-2	0-4	2-3	2-0	3-4	0-1	1-0	1-2	0-3	0-3	1-3	–	2-0	1-0	0-1	3-1
Swindon	1-0	1-3	3-2	3-1	0-1	3-1	3-3	2-2	1-2	0-4	1-2	2-0	0-1	0-5	5-2	1-0	1-2	2-0	3-1	0-0	–	2-0	1-3	1-4
Tranmere	1-2	3-4	1-1	0-1	2-1	1-0	1-1	1-1	1-1	1-0	0-1	3-2	2-1	0-2	0-2	2-0	0-0	0-1	1-0	2-1	1-2	–	1-1	1-1
Walsall	0-2	1-1	0-1	3-0	1-1	0-1	1-2	1-1	4-0	1-3	3-2	1-0	1-1	0-0	3-0	0-3	1-1	1-1	0-0	2-0	1-1	3-1	–	0-3
Wolves	2-0	0-0	1-2	0-0	2-1	1-1	2-1	2-0	1-1	1-1	2-1	2-0	2-0	2-0	0-1	6-4	3-3	0-1	0-0	2-1	3-2	2-0	0-1	–

SKY BET LEAGUE TWO RESULTS 2013–2014

	Accrington	AFC Wimb	Bristol Rov	Burton	Bury	Cheltenham	Chesterfield	Dag & Red	Exeter	Fleetwood	Hartlepool	Mansfield	Morecambe	Newport	Northampton	Oxford	Plymouth	Portsmouth	Rochdale	Scunthorpe	Southend	Torquay	Wycombe	York
Accrington	–	3-2	0-1	2-1	3-0	1-2	1-0	0-0	0-1	3-1	2-1	2-3	1-2	4-1	1-0	1-2	0-0	1-0	2-1	2-3	0-1	2-1	0-0	1-1
AFC Wimb	1-1	–	3-0	2-2	2-1	4-3	1-1	1-1	2-1	3-1	3-1	1-1	1-0	0-2	1-1	0-2	1-0	3-2	1-0	3-2	0-1	0-2	0-3	0-1
Bristol Rov	0-1	3-0	–	2-0	0-1	2-1	0-0	1-2	2-1	1-3	2-2	0-1	1-0	3-1	1-0	1-1	1-1	2-0	1-2	0-0	0-0	1-2	0-1	3-2
Burton	2-1	2-0	1-0	–	2-2	2-1	0-2	1-2	2-1	2-4	3-0	1-0	0-1	1-0	1-0	2-1	2-3	2-0	0-2	2-2	0-0	2-0	0-1	1-1
Bury	3-0	2-1	2-1	2-1	–	4-1	0-2	1-1	2-0	2-2	3-0	0-0	0-2	0-0	1-1	1-1	4-0	4-4	1-2	0-2	1-1	1-3	1-0	2-1
Cheltenham	1-2	4-3	2-1	2-1	4-1	–	1-4	2-0	1-0	2-2	2-2	0-0	1-0	0-0	1-1	2-2	1-3	0-0	0-0	2-2	0-0	1-0	1-1	2-2
Chesterfield	1-0	1-1	0-0	0-2	0-2	1-1	–	2-1	0-0	0-1	0-0	0-1	1-1	3-0	2-0	3-0	2-3	1-1	2-2	0-2	1-1	3-1	2-0	2-2
Dag & Red	0-0	2-0	2-0	1-2	4-0	2-0	2-2	–	1-1	0-1	1-4	0-0	1-0	1-1	2-0	1-0	0-1	1-4	1-0	0-2	0-1	0-1	0-1	2-0
Exeter	0-1	2-0	2-1	2-1	1-1	2-0	1-0	1-1	–	3-0	0-1	0-1	1-1	1-1	2-0	3-1	1-2	1-2	0-0	3-3	1-1	1-2	1-0	2-0
Fleetwood	3-1	3-1	3-1	4-0	3-1	0-1	0-2	0-1	3-1	–	2-0	5-4	2-2	4-1	2-0	3-2	0-2	3-3	0-3	2-0	1-1	4-1	1-2	2-1
Hartlepool	2-1	3-1	4-0	1-1	0-3	0-1	1-2	0-2	0-0	1-1	–	2-1	2-1	3-0	0-0	1-3	1-0	0-0	3-0	0-1	1-1	3-0	2-0	1-2
Mansfield	2-3	1-1	1-1	2-0	1-4	0-2	1-2	0-1	1-1	1-2	3-0	–	0-0	3-0	3-0	1-3	1-0	1-4	3-2	0-2	3-3	1-3	0-1	2-0
Morecambe	1-2	1-1	2-1	0-1	0-2	0-1	0-1	1-1	1-1	2-3	0-0	1-1	–	3-1	0-0	1-0	2-3	1-1	1-2	2-1	1-1	2-1	1-1	0-1
Newport	4-1	1-2	2-1	0-0	0-0	0-1	0-1	0-2	4-1	0-1	4-1	0-1	0-1	–	1-1	2-1	2-1	1-1	1-0	2-1	2-1	2-1	2-0	0-0
Northampton	1-0	2-2	1-0	1-0	0-3	1-1	3-0	1-1	2-3	0-0	3-0	3-0	1-3	3-1	–	3-0	1-0	2-0	1-0	3-1	3-1	1-2	1-4	3-0
Oxford	1-2	0-1	1-0	1-0	0-1	1-1	1-1	1-2	0-0	2-2	1-1	2-0	0-0	2-0	2-0	–	3-1	0-0	1-1	1-1	0-2	1-0	0-2	0-2
Plymouth	0-0	1-2	1-0	1-0	3-2	1-1	0-2	1-2	1-2	0-1	1-0	1-0	2-3	0-2	1-0	2-3	–	3-3	3-0	0-2	0-2	1-0	2-2	0-4
Portsmouth	1-0	1-2	3-2	0-0	1-0	1-0	0-2	2-2	1-2	0-1	1-1	0-0	0-0	1-1	0-2	0-2	2-3	–	3-3	1-2	1-2	2-0	2-2	0-1
Rochdale	2-1	1-0	1-0	1-0	1-0	0-0	2-2	3-0	1-2	1-0	1-0	2-2	3-0	0-0	3-2	1-0	3-3	3-0	–	0-4	1-2	1-0	2-2	0-0
Scunthorpe	0-2	1-2	1-1	2-0	2-2	1-1	1-1	0-1	2-3	2-0	2-0	3-0	1-3	1-0	2-0	3-0	1-0	1-1	0-4	–	2-2	3-1	0-0	4-1
Southend	1-0	0-1	1-1	0-0	1-1	0-0	1-1	0-1	1-3	1-1	1-0	0-1	1-1	0-1	1-2	1-3	0-2	1-1	1-1	2-2	–	1-0	0-0	0-0
Torquay	0-1	1-1	1-1	2-1	2-1	4-2	0-2	1-2	1-3	2-0	1-1	1-3	2-1	1-1	1-3	1-1	0-1	1-1	0-2	1-1	1-0	–	0-3	3-2
Wycombe	0-0	1-0	1-1	1-2	1-2	1-2	0-2	1-2	1-1	0-3	0-1	2-1	1-2	1-0	0-1	1-3	0-1	0-1	0-2	1-1	2-1	1-0	–	0-3
York	1-1	0-2	0-0	0-0	1-2	1-0	0-0	4-1	2-1	1-2	1-2	0-0	0-1	1-0	1-0	0-0	1-1	4-2	0-0	4-1	0-0	1-0	2-0	–

THE THINGS THEY SAY...

'Performances and results have not been what Manchester United and the fans are used to or expect. I understand and share their frustration. Taking charge after such a long period of continuous stability and success was inevitably going to be a significant challenge, but it was one I relished' – **David Moyes** after being sacked as Manchester United manager.

'I genuinely believe that when you give a man a six-year contract he deserves the opportunity and time and professionally the respect. Football is a world of madness. The average manager gets sacked every 12 months. I've always felt Manchester United should be different and stand against what's happening in the game' – **Gary Neville**, former Old Trafford stalwart.

'Tom never won a Championship medal or an FA Cup winner's medal. But he won something much more important – the hearts of his team-mates, the supporters, opposing players even and the whole country. He didn't dive, he didn't feign injury; that wasn't part of his repertoire. He was the footballers' footballer' – **Jimmy Armfield**, England's former World Cup captain, paying tribute at the funeral of Sir Tom Finney.

'Maybe I should be a bit cleverer and do what other players have done. Perhaps then I could have got the penalty' – **Matt Jarvis**, West Ham winger, after staying on his feet when tackled heavily by Arsenal's Bacary Sagna.

'The sending-off is big ammunition for people like me who think that one little screen in front of the fourth official is a big help against this kind of mistake' – **Jose Mourinho**, Chelsea manager, on referee Andre Marriner's mistake in showing a red card to Arsenal's Kieran Gibbs instead of Alex Oxlade-Chamberlain.

'Andre is an experienced referee and is obviously disappointed. Incidents of mistaken identity are very rare and are often the result of a number of different technical factors' – **Professional Game Match Officials Ltd**, the referees' body, on the incident.

"It is the best decision I have seen from a referee in my life. If you really want to stop players going down easily this is the way' – **Gus Poyet**, Sunderland manager, applauding Phil Dowd, who delayed his decision to award a penalty against Cardiff to see if Connor Wickham gained any advantage by staying on his feet when tackled.

'It costs almost twice as much as I got for winning the World Cup' – **Martin Peters** on the price (£90) of England's new shirts for Brazil 2014.

'I take full responsibility. We got a good hiding. It's one of the worst days in my career. The best way is not to explain too much the mistakes' – **Arsene Wenger** after his side's 6-0 defeat by Chelsea in his 1,000th game as Arsenal manager.

'I was asked if we practised penalties and I said no. I'm German and normally we don't have to' – **Uwe Rosler**, Wigan manager, after his side lost a penalty shoot-out to Arsenal in their FA Cup semi-final.

'We've been brainwashed by (the idea that) this Premier League is the best league in the world. Nonsense. It's the best brand, but we've seen with the way the English teams have struggled that they are falling behind the top sides in Europe' – **Roy Keane**, former Manchester United captain and now the Republic of Ireland's assistant manager and no. 2 at Aston Villa.

HIGHLIGHTS OF THE PREMIER LEAGUE SEASON 2013–14

AUGUST 2013

17 Two goals by Robin van Persie and two from Danny Welbeck – scorer of just one in the whole of the previous league season – launch Manchester United's title defence under David Moyes with a 4-1 victory at Swansea. Unsettled Wayne Rooney comes off the bench to provide two assists, while Wilfried Bony replies on his debut for Swansea, watched by a record Liberty Stadium crowd of 20,733 Another record-signing, Ricky van Wolfswinkel, is on the scoresheet. He heads Norwich's second in a 2-2 draw with Everton, for whom Ross Barkley opens his account for the club in Roberto Martinez's first game in charge. Another scorer on his debut is Antonio Luna, who completes Aston Villa's 3-1 success at the Emirates after two goals from Christian Benteke, one direct from the penalty spot and one from the rebound after his spot-kick is saved by Wojciech Szczesny. A miserable afternoon for Arsenal is compounded by a second yellow card for Laurent Koscielny and a knee injury sustained by Alex Oxlade-Chamberlain. Simon Mignolet has a notable debut for Liverpool, saving a Jon Walters penalty in the 89th minute and enabling his side to maintain their 1-0 advantage over Stoke, who have Mark Hughes in charge for the first time. Rickie Lambert, England's match-winner against Scotland, rounds off a week to remember with a 90th minute penalty to give Southampton victory against West Bromwich Albion. His team field the youngest full-back pairing in Premier League history – 18-year-olds Calum Chambers and Luke Shaw. Fulham are also 1-0 winners, courtesy of Pajtim Kasami's first for the club at Sunderland, while West Ham account for promoted Cardiff 2-0.

18 Frank Lampard has a penalty saved by Allan McGregor, then fires in a 35-yard free-kick as Chelsea overcome Hull 2-0 in Jose Mourinho's first match back as manager. The third promoted side, Crystal Palace, are also beaten as Roberto Soldado marks his Tottenham debut with the only goal of the match from the penalty spot.

19 Manchester City treat their new manager, Manuel Pellegrini, to a 4-0 victory over Newcastle, who lose Steven Taylor to a straight red card.

21 Branislav Ivanovic escapes with a booking after catching Christian Benteke in the face with a flailing arm, then heads the goal to give Chelsea a 2-1 win over Aston Villa.

24 Three players are on the mark for the first time for new clubs. On-loan Darren Bent scores for his sixth Premier League team in Fulham's 3-1 defeat by Arsenal, for whom Lukas Podolski nets twice. Emanuele Giaccherini's third minute header for Sunderland is cancelled out after 88 minutes by Southampton's Jose Fonte, while Marouane Chamakh's strike for Crystal Palace comes in a 2-1 defeat at Stoke. Despite losing Yannick Sagbo to a straight red on his home debut, Hull hold on to the lead established by Robbie Brady's penalty for more than an hour to beat Norwich. Aston Villa lose 1-0 to Liverpool and are left with an unwanted club record of 25 league games without keeping a clean sheet. Daniel Sturridge's goal is his seventh in six matches while Luis Suarez serves his ban.

25 Cardiff open their account in some style, Fraizer Campbell scoring twice in a 3-2 victory over Manchester City in front of a record crowd for the Cardiff City Stadium of 27,068.

26 Chelsea set out their stall by playing without a recognised striker against Manchester United and the first 'heavyweight' match of the season ends goalless.

31 Record signing Dwight Gayle and substitute Stuart O'Keefe are on the mark for the first time for the club as Crystal Palace score their first win – 3-1 against Sunderland, who have John O'Shea sent off for conceding the penalty which Gayle converts. Nathan Redmond's first for Norwich, the only one of the game, brings victory over Southampton. Another record crowd for Cardiff, 27,344, see their team maintain a solid start to the season with a goalless draw against Everton.

SEPTEMBER 2013

1 Daniel Sturridge marks his 24th birthday with the only goal against Manchester United to give Liverpool a third successive win – the club's best start since 1994. Arsenal also celebrate a major victory, with Olivier Giroud's strike accounting for Tottenham.

14 Record-signing Mesut Ozil takes only 11 minutes to make his mark for Arsenal, laying on a goal for Olivier Giroud at the Stadium of Light. Aaron Ramsey then scores twice in the 3-1 win over Sunderland, who have manager Paolo Di Canio sent to the stands in an altercation with referee Martin Atkinson. Tottenham's Christian Eriksen also makes an impressive debut, setting up both goals for Gylfi Sigurdsson in a 2-0 success against Norwich. Another man-of-the-match performance is given by Hatem Ben Arfa, who opens the scoring for Newcastle and makes a second for Yoan Gouffran as Aston Villa are beaten 2-1. Everton's Steven Naismith celebrates his 27th birthday with the only goal against Chelsea, Curtis Davies opens his account for Hull against Cardiff, while Steve Sidwell scores for Fulham on his 400th career appearance against West Bromwich Albion in another 1-1 draw. Kagisho Dikgacoi receives a straight red card in Crystal Palace's 2-0 defeat by Manchester United.

16 In front of another record crowd for the Liberty Stadium – 20,752 – Swansea's Jonjo Shelvey has a bitter-sweet match against former club Liverpool. After the midfielder scores his first goal for the club, two misplaced passes are punished by goals from Daniel Sturridge and, on his debut on loan, Victor Moses. Then, Shelvey sets up the equaliser for Michu.

21 Paolo Di Canio is involved in a bizarre stand-off with fans of bottom-of-the-table Sunderland after a 3-0 defeat by West Bromwich Albion. Stephane Sessegnon, the player he sold on transfer deadline day, scores his first Albion goal and the manager's afternoon goes from bad to worse when Steven Fletcher, just back from a lengthy lay-off with ankle trouble, sustains a shoulder injury. The following day Di Canio is sacked. Southampton take pride of place on an eventful day by beating leaders Liverpool 1-0 at Anfield thanks to Dejan Lovren's first strike in English football. On-loan Romelu Lukaku nets his first for Everton, but remembers nothing of the 85th minute effort which earns a 3-2 victory over West Ham, having been concussed scoring it. Earlier, Leighton Baines finds the top corner with two 25-yard free-kicks and West Ham's Mark Noble is sent off for two yellow cards. Another loanee, Loic Remy, opens his account for Newcastle with a brace but they are not enough against Hull, who twice come from behind to prevail 3-2 with Sone Aluko's sweet volley. Earlier in the day, Aluko's sister Eniola is among the scorers for the England women's team in a World Cup qualifier against Belarus. Substitute Libor Kozak's first for Aston Villa comes less than two minutes after he leaves the bench and proves the only goal at Norwich, where Brad Guzan saves a penalty from Robert Snodgrass to help his side keep a clean sheet for the first time in 27 league matches. John Obi Mikel also has a day to remember, scoring his first league goal in seven years at the club as Chelsea return to winning ways by beating Fulham 2-0.

22 Sergio Aguero is on the mark twice as Manchester City outplay Manchester United 4-1. Mesut Ozil provides assists for all three Arsenal goals against Stoke, whose consolation from Geoff Cameron is his first for the club. Swansea, 3-0 winners in Valencia in the Europa League, complete a great week by winning 2-0 at Crystal Palace.

28 A revitalised Aaron Ramsey scores his eighth goal in nine matches and sets up 18-year-old Serge Gnabry for his first for the club as Arsenal overcome Swansea 2-1 to end the month as leaders. Tottenham are two points behind after a 1-1 draw with Chelsea, who have Fernando Torres sent off for two yellow cards. In contrast, Manchester United fall into the bottom half of the table after six matches – the club's worst start since 1986. They go down 2-1 to West Bromwich Albion, winners at Old Trafford for the first time since 1978. Manchester City also have a bad day, leading twice but losing 3-2 to Aston Villa, for whom Leandro Bacuna scores for the first time. Steven Caulker, with a header, and substitute Jordon Mutch, with a 25-yard winner in stoppage-time, deliver their first ones for Cardiff, who beat Fulham 2-1. So does Southampton's record signing, Dani Osvaldo, in the 2-0 victory over Crystal Palace.

29 Luis Suarez returns from a ten-match ban for biting Chelsea's Branislav Ivanovic, and scores twice in Liverpool's 3-1 victory at Sunderland.

30 Romelu Lukaku scores twice and fellow-loanee Gareth Barry makes his 500th Premier League appearance as Everton defeat Newcastle 3-2.

OCTOBER 2013

5 An 18-year-old Belgian-born midfield player making his full Premier League debut provides much-needed impetus to Manchester United's stuttering start to the season. Adnan Januzaj scores twice in the space of six second-half minutes – his second goal a stunning volley – to set up a 2-1 win at Sunderland. Newcastle also register a welcome victory by the same scoreline as Loic Remy twice finds the target in eight first-half minutes at Cardiff. A 'double' of a different kind helps Manchester City end the division's only unbeaten record. Sergio Aguero puts them 2-1 ahead against Everton, then sees his penalty palmed against a post by Tim Howard, with the ball rebounding from the goalkeeper into the net for an own goal. At Anfield, Steven Gerrard writes another chapter in his distinguished Liverpool career by scoring for the 15th successive season. His goal comes from the penalty spot in a 3-1 success against Crystal Palace and enables the captain to overtake Billy Liddell's club record.

6 Ravel Morrison runs half the length of the pitch to score as West Ham record one of the shock early-season results. His solo goal completes a 3-0 away win over Tottenham, who had previously conceded just twice in 11 games in all competitions. Argentinian Claudio Yacob heads his first goal for West Bromwich Albion in the 1-1 draw against Arsenal, while the Brazilian Willian gets his first for Chelsea, who beat Norwich 3-1.

19 Four days after leading England to the World Cup Finals, Steven Gerrard scores his 100th Premier League goal for Liverpool. But the captain's penalty – conceded by Mapou Yanga-Mbiwa who is sent off for the offence – is not enough to deny ten-man Newcastle, for whom Tyneside-born substitute Paul Dummett scores his first goal for the club in a 2-2 draw. Chelsea manager Jose Mourinho is ordered from the touchline for arguing with referee Anthony Taylor during the 4-1 victory over Cardiff on an afternoon of controversy at Stamford Bridge. One of Eden Hazard's two goals is wrongly allowed to stand by the official after Samuel Eto'o illegally 'steals' the ball while goalkeeper David Marshall is bouncing it. Sergio Aguero nets twice and sets up a third goal for David Silva in Manchester City's 3-1 win at West Ham. A brace, too, for Mesut Ozil, along with one of the team goals of the season from Jack Wilshere at the end of a sequence of nine passes, as Arsenal overcome Norwich 4-1. Meanwhile, Manchester United continue to find it hard going, conceding an 89th minute equaliser at Old Trafford to Adam Lallana which maintains Southampton's impressive start. Sunderland, under Gus Poyet for the first time, concede four second-half goals to lose 4-0 at Swansea, thus equalling the worst Premier League start to a season of one point from eight matches. Yannick Sagbo opens his account for Hull at Everton, but Steven Pienaar comes off the bench to score with his first touch and give the home side the verdict 2-1.

21 Pajtim Kasami scores with a 28-yard volley, echoing Marco van Basten's famous strike for Holland in Euro 88, as Fulham equal their biggest Premier League away victory. They come from behind after Adrian Mariappa's first goal for Crystal Palace to win 4-1 in what proves to be Ian Holloway's final match as Palace manager.

26 Luis Suarez records a fourth hat-trick for Liverpool, his first at Anfield, in a 4-1 victory over West Bromwich Albion. It features two headers, one from the edge of the penalty box. Southampton celebrate their best start to a season in the top flight – 18 points from nine matches – by beating Fulham 2-0, Rickie Lambert scoring from a Jay Rodriguez flick-on, then laying on the second goal for his strike partner. Mixed fortunes for Mikael Arteta, who puts Arsenal on the way to victory by the same scoreline against Crystal Palace with a penalty, but is then sent off for a professional foul. After escaping with a yellow card for a studs-up challenge, substitute Javier Hernandez is on the mark with an 80th minute header to give Manchester United a 3-2 win over Stoke, for whom Marko Arnautovic opens his account. Stoke have six players booked, incurring a £25,000 fine. Cardiff goalkeeper David Marshall is involved in more controversy, this time throwing the ball out of touch with seconds remaining to allow treatment for Norwich's Alex Tettey, then seeing Tettey's team-mate Leroy Fer collect the subsequent throw-in to put the ball in the net. Cardiff players round on Fer as referee Mike Jones orders the throw-in to be retaken before ending the goalless draw.

27 Fernando Torres scores his first Premier League goal of 2013, capitalising on a 90th minute mix-up between Joe Hart and Matija Nastasic to give Chelsea a 2-1 victory over Manchester City. Earlier, Torres sets up Andre Schurrle's first goal for the team, who finish the month alongside Liverpool on 20 points, two behind leaders Arsenal. On-loan Fabio Borini's first for Sunderland, after 84 minutes, delivers a 2-1 success against Newcastle – and the club's first back-to-back wins over their neighbours since 1967. Mathieu Debuchy's goal for Newcastle is his first for the club.

NOVEMBER 2013

2 Goalkeepers make the headlines. At the Britannia Stadium, Stoke's Asmir Begovic sees his wind-assisted clearance bounce over the head of opposite number Artur Boruc and into the Southampton net after 13 seconds. At the Etihad, Joe Hart, England's No 1, watches from the substitutes' bench as Manchester City put seven past Norwich's John Ruddy, his understudy for the national team. Hart is left out for City's biggest win (7-0) in the top flight since 1968 after a series of mistakes for club and country and replaced by Costel Pantilimon. The top-of-the-table meeting of Arsenal and Liverpool goes the way of the home side, for whom Santi Cazorla and Aaron Ramsey deliver a 2-0 victory. Wayne Rooney scores for both sides in Manchester United's 3-1 win at Fulham, while Loic Remy's 89th minute strike seals Newcastle's 2-0 success against Chelsea. Sunderland have a nightmare at Hull, going down 1-0 to a Carlos Cuellar own goal, losing goalkeeper Kieren Westwood to a bang on the head and finishing with nine man after Lee Cattermole and Andrea Dossena receive straight red cards.

3 Steven Caulker heads the only goal of the game for Cardiff against Swansea in the first south Wales derby to be played in the top flight.

9 The pressure eases on manager Chris Hughton as Norwich come from behind to defeat West Ham 3-1, with Gary Hooper (pen) and Leroy Fer scoring their first Premier League goals for the club. But it remains on Fulham's Martin Jol after a 4-0 reversal against Liverpool, for whom Luis Suarez scores twice after being given permission to play ahead of Uruguay's World Cup play-off against Jordan. West Bromwich Albion are seconds away from their first win at Stamford Bridge for 30 years when a disputed penalty, despatched by Eden Hazard, gives Chelsea a 2-2 draw. Rickie Lambert converts his 33rd successive penalty and Adam Lallana celebrates an England call-up with a brilliant solo goal in front of Roy Hodgson as Southampton see off Hull 4-1.

10 Robin van Persie heads the only goal of the game against Arsenal, maintaining Manchester United's momentum, and two other matches deliver 1-0 results. Sunderland beat Manchester City at home by that scoreline for the fourth successive season, courtesy of Phil Bardsley's goal. Newcastle win at Tottenham, thanks to Loic Remy's seventh in seven matches and the season's finest goalkeeping performance by Tim Krul, who makes 14 saves, some of them world-class. Wilfried Bony scores twice as Swansea retrieve a two-goal deficit to lead 3-2, only for another controversial stoppage-time penalty, from Charlie Adam, to give Stoke a point.

23 A pulsating Merseyside derby delivers six goals for the first time in a league match since 1935. Everton lead 3-2 at Goodison, with Romelu Lukaku scoring twice. But substitute Daniel Sturridge earns Liverpool a point in the 89th minute. Two by Olivier Giroud give leaders Arsenal a 2-0 victory over third-place Southampton. Giroud dispossesses goalkeeper Artur Boruc for the first, then converts a penalty won by Per Mertesacker, four days after the German defender's match-winner against England. Frank Lampard also nets one of his two from the spot to end a ten-match goal drought – his worst for a decade – as Chelsea win 3-0 at West Ham. Crystal Palace's new manager, Tony Pulis, watches from the stands as Barry Bannan registers his first for the club for a 1-0 success at Hull. It comes three minutes after team-mate Yannick Bolasie is sent off and there is another red card, for Sunderland's Wes Brown, in a 2-0 defeat by Stoke. This one is rescinded on appeal. Scott Parker's first for Fulham is not enough to prevent a fourth successive defeat – 2-1 at home against Swansea.

24 Manchester City swamp Tottenham 6-0 after Jesus Navas sets them on the way with a goal after 14 seconds. The Spaniard adds another, Sergio Aguero also gets two and Spurs concede as many as they have done all season. Manchester United look set for victory at Cardiff until Kim Bo-Kyung's stoppage-time strike earns a 2-2 draw in front of a record stadium crowd of 28,016.

25 Aston Villa trail to two Shane Long goals in the opening 11 minutes for West Bromwich Albion, but recover to gain a point, with Ashley Westwood opening his account for the club.

30 Arsenal open up a seven-point lead at the top from an extra game played by beating Cardiff 3-0, Aaron Ramsey scoring twice and Mathieu Flamini netting his first goal since beginning a second spell at the club. Ramsey shows respect for his former team by not celebrating and the City fans respond with a warm ovation. On-loan Gerard Deulofeu, 19, marks his first Premier League start for Everton with his first league goal. So does team-mate Bryan Oviedo in the 4-0 victory over Stoke. Newcastle also continue to climb the table with a fourth successive win against West Bromwich Albion (2-1). Fulham's fifth successive defeat, 3-0 at Upton Park, is followed by manager Martin Jol's sacking. For West Ham, it's their first home success since the opening day of the season.

DECEMBER 2013

1 Southampton's Jay Rodriguez scores after 13 seconds, but Chelsea reply with three second-half goals, one of them from John Terry on his 400th Premier League appearance. Hull record their first win over Liverpool (3-1), on-loan Jake Livermore opening the scoring with his first goal for the club. Samir Nasri is on the mark twice as Manchester City overcome Swansea 3-0, while Wayne Rooney registers both Manchester United goals – one a penalty – in a 2-2 draw with Tottenham.

3 Marouane Chamakh nets his first goal for more than three months to give Tony Pulis his first victory with Crystal Palace – 1-0 against West Ham.

4 On the night Manchester United's faltering defence of the title is again exposed, Luis Suarez delivers the season's finest individual performance. The Uruguayan scores four goals in Liverpool's 5-1 trouncing of Norwich – one a dipping volley from 40 yards – and sets up Raheem Sterling for the fifth. In doing so, he becomes the first Premier League player to score three hat-tricks against one team. United lose to Everton at Old Trafford for the first time in 21 years, Bryan Oviedo scoring the only goal after 86 minutes, and fall 12 points behind top spot. All the leading teams are successful, with Nicklas Bendtner setting Arsenal on the way to a 2-0 win over Hull by scoring inside two minutes on his first league start since March 2011. In one of the games of the season, Eden Hazard's brace helps Chelsea overcome Sunderland 4-3, their ninth straight success at the Stadium of Light. Yaya Toure also gets two, one a penalty, as Manchester City are 3-2 winners over West Bromwich Albion, for whom Victor Anichebe registers his first goal. Rene Meulensteen takes charge of Fulham for the first time and sees Ashkan Dejagah score his first for the club. But Vlad Chiriches chalks up his first for Tottenham, who prevail 2-1 with Lewis Holtby's first in the Premier League. Fabian Delph also nets his first in the top flight to give Aston Villa a 3-2 win at Southampton, achieved despite having just 23 per cent of possession.

7 The day after England are drawn with Uruguay in their World Cup group, Luis Suarez continues his impressive form in a 4-1 win over West Ham. He is twice on the mark – the second awarded to him by the Dubious Goals Panel – and has another shot deflected in for an own goal. The visitors have Kevin Nolan shown a straight red card. Newcastle defeat Manchester United at Old Trafford for the first time since 1972, Yohan Cabaye scoring the only goal. Stoke overcome Chelsea in a league game for the first time since 1975 as on-loan substitute Oussama Assaidi strikes in the 90th minute for a 3-2 success after Andre Schurrle nets twice for Jose Mourinho's side. Another borrowed player, Cameron Jerome, gives his former Stoke manager Tony Pulis another boost with his first goal for Crystal Palace, who master Cardiff 2-0. Sergio Aguero records his tenth goal in 11 league appearances as Manchester City draw 1-1 at Southampton, while Norwich beat West Bromwich Albion 2-0 after conceding 18 goals in their previous four away matches.

8 Five minutes after coming off the bench, Everton's Gerard Deulofeu denies Arsenal victory with an 84th minute equaliser. Rene Meulensteen has his first victory as Fulham manager – 2-0 over Aston Villa.

9 On-loan Danny Graham ends an 11-month goal drought to give Hull a 1-1 draw against Swansea – the last team he scored for.

14 Arsenal, boasting the division's best defensive record, are the latest victims of Manchester City's unstoppable form at the Etihad. City win 6-3 to take their tally to 35 from eight home games – matching Tottenham's start to the 1962-63 season. Fernandinho scores twice – his first goals for the club – while Theo Walcott nets a brace for Arsenal. Steve Clarke is sacked after West Bromwich Albion go down 1-0 to Cardiff, their fourth successive defeat. Leon Osman marks his 300th Premier League appearance by setting Everton on the way to a 4-1 victory over Fulham. At St James' Park, Newcastle goalkeeping coach Andy Woodman and his Southampton counterpart, Toni Jimenez, are sent to the stands after a touchline confrontation during the 1-1 draw.

15 Manager Andre Villas-Boas pays the price for another heavy defeat for Tottenham, who lose 5-0 at home to Liverpool and have Paulinho shown a straight red card. Luis Suarez, captain in the absence of the injured Steven Gerrard, scores twice, while Jon Flanagan nets his first for the club. Danny Welbeck is also on the mark twice, his first goals since the opening day of the season, as Manchester United win 3-0 away to Aston Villa.

21 Luis Suarez celebrates signing a contract through to 2018 with two more goals, and lays on a third for Raheem Sterling, as Liverpool go top by defeating Cardiff 3-1. Suarez becomes the first Premier League player to net ten times in a single month. Manchester City move up to second as Vincent Kompany scores for both sides in a 4-2 victory at Fulham. Peter Crouch puts Stoke on the way to a 2-1 success against Aston Villa, sets up their second goal for Charlie Adam, then sees his wife, Abbey Clancy, win BBC's *Strictly Come Dancing* final. On-loan Matej Vydra opens his account for West Bromwich Albion in a 1-1 draw with Hull, while Ashley Young is on the mark for Manchester United for the first time in the league since May 2012 as West Ham are beaten 3-1. Jake Livermore's goal for Hull proves a costly affair. He kicks a photographer's camera behind the net while celebrating and is landed with a £6,000 bill, plus a donation to team-mate Tom Huddlestone's charity fund-raising. Newcastle make it 19 points out of 24 with a 3-0 success away to Crystal Palace, but neighbours Sunderland stay bottom after a goalless draw with Norwich in which Wes Brown receives a straight red card.

22 Emmanuel Adebayor, sidelined by Andre Villas-Boas, makes his first start of the season under the manager's successor, Tim Sherwood, and scores twice in Tottenham's 3-2 victory at Southampton. Everton, in the thick of the leading group, also win away, 2-1 against Swansea, Ross Barkley underlining his immense potential with a 30-yard free-kick for the decider.

23 Arsenal and Chelsea are goalless in a dour affair at the Emirates, where Frank Lampard comes nearest to breaking the deadlock when volleying against the bar.

26 Five teams come from behind to win, four players are shown red cards and a manager is also sent off in an eventful Boxing Day programme. Manchester City are among them, edging out Liverpool 2-1 thanks to goals from Vincent Kompany and Alvaro Negredo, who scores for the ninth successive match at the Etihad. Manchester United trail 2-0 after 13 minutes at Hull, for whom James Chester nets for the first time in the top flight. But Wayne Rooney becomes the first United player to reach 150 Premier League goals and Chester's own goal completes their comeback for a 3-2 success, marred by a second yellow card for Antonio Valencia. A brace in the space of three minutes by Theo Walcott, including his first header for the club, and one by injury-dogged Lukas Podolski on his first appearance for four months enable Arsenal to turn the tables on West Ham with a 3-1 victory. Stoke run into all sorts of trouble after leading Newcastle at St James' Park, where Glenn Whelan is shown two yellows, Marc Wilson a straight red and Mark Hughes is sent to the stands by Martin Atkinson for a touchline tantrum. The home side take full advantage to win 5-1, with Loic Remy on the mark twice, as well as having a penalty saved by Thomas Sorensen. Fulham also fall behind

before prevailing 2-1 at Norwich, Scott Parker's sweet strike settling the issue. Bottom-of-the-table Sunderland deliver the day's big surprise, ending Everton's unbeaten home record as Ki Sung-Yeung delivers the only goal with a penalty conceded by goalkeeper Tim Howard, who is sent off for fouling the South Korean. Southampton score three times in the opening 27 minutes – two of them from Jay Rodriguez – to win 3-0 at Cardiff, whose manager Malky Mackay is sacked the following day.

28 Tom Huddlestone, Hull's record signing, enjoys a hair-raising 27th birthday in a 6-0 win over Fulham in which all their goals come in the second half. The former Tottenham midfielder scores for the first time for the club, then keeps his promise to have his bushy locks trimmed. Robert Koren is on the mark twice in Hull's biggest Premier League victory and Fulham's heaviest defeat. Much-travelled Nicolas Anelka scores for his sixth Premier League side, but a brace in West Bromwich Albion's 3-3 draw with West Ham is followed by accusations of an offensive gesture. Swansea's on-loan Roland Lamah also opens his account in a 1-1 draw against Aston Villa. Joe Hart, left out of Manchester City's side for two months, gives a man-of-the-match performance as they grind out a 1-0 victory over battling Crystal Palace with a strike by Edin Dzeko. Sunderland also show plenty of spirit to cancel out Cardiff's two-goal lead through Steven Fletcher (83) and Jack Colback in stoppage-time to gain a point.

29 Arsenal end 2013 on top after Olivier Giroud delivers the only goal at Newcastle. They are a point ahead of Manchester City and two clear of Chelsea, who come from behind to defeat Liverpool 2-1 on John Terry's 600th appearance for the club. Everton stay in touch as full-back Seamus Coleman paves the way for a 2-1 win over Southampton with his fifth goal of the season – more than his combined tally for the previous four campaigns.

JANUARY 2014

1 Manchester United's title defence looks to be over when a fourth defeat at Old Trafford and a sixth overall leaves them 11 points adrift of top spot. They lose 2-1 to Tottenham, for whom Emmanuel Adebayor takes his tally to four goals in five league and cup matches since returning to the side and Tim Sherwood makes it ten points out of 12 since assuming control. Incoming Cardiff manager Ole Gunnar Solskjaer sees his new team hold out for 88 minutes at the Emirates before Nicklas Bendtner and Theo Walcott break their resistance to give Arsenal a 2-0 victory. Wilfried Bony scores two goals for Swansea, but they are not enough to prevent Manchester City prevailing 3-2 as Yaya Toure nets his 12th in all competitions. Chelsea's heavy reliance on midfielders for goals is underlined when their opener by Fernando Torres in a 3-0 win at Southampton is the team's first away from home in the league by a striker for nearly 13 months. By contrast, Luis Suarez reaches 20 in 15 matches for the campaign, becoming the fastest-ever in the Premier League to that total, when completing Liverpool's 2-0 success against Hull. On-loan Jason Puncheon opens his account for Crystal Palace from the penalty spot in a 1-1 draw against Norwich, who have Leroy Fer sent off for a second yellow card. In another meeting of struggling sides, Kevin Nolan's second dismissal in four games is blamed by his angry West Ham manager Sam Allardyce for a 2-1 defeat by Fulham. Mathieu Debuchy is also shown a straight red card as Newcastle lose 1-0 to West Bromwich Albion, who take three points for the first time in ten games.

11 Adam Johnson, with only one league goal all season, fires a hat-trick as Sunderland climb off the bottom by winning 4-1 at Fulham. Johnson completes it from the penalty spot and supplies the free-kick for Ki Sung-Yeung's strike. Under-pressure Sam Allardyce also celebrates as his West Ham side, with 22 goals conceded in six league and cup games, beat fellow-strugglers Cardiff 2-0 away from home, despite the dismissal of James Tomkins for two yellow cards. Petr Cech overtakes Peter Bonetti's club record with his 209th clean sheet in all competitions as Chelsea prevail 2-0 at Hull. The day after completing a £6m move to Major League Soccer club Toronto in February, Jermain Defoe nets his first league goal of the season in Tottenham's 2-0 defeat of Crystal Palace. It comes after Palace's Jason Puncheon delivers the worst penalty of this – and many other seasons – by shooting high and wide. Struggling Manchester United, facing the prospect of losing four successive matches for the

first time in 53 years, also win 2-0 against Swansea, a week after losing to Michael Laudrup's team in the FA Cup.

12 Alan Pardew apologises for a foul-mouthed rant at Manuel Pellegrini on the touchline during Newcastle's 2-0 home defeat by Manchester City. It follows a controversial decision by referee Mike Jones to disallow for offside a 'goal' by Cheick Tiote with Newcastle trailing 1-0. Luis Suarez is on the mark twice and Daniel Sturridge makes a scoring return after missing nine matches with an ankle injury as Liverpool win 5-3 at Stoke.

13 Arsenal win 2-1 away to Aston Villa with two first-half goals in a minute – Jack Wilshere scoring the first and setting up Olivier Giroud for the second.

18 Edin Dzeko fires Manchester City's 100th goal of the season in their 34th game in all competitions – the fastest by nine matches in the Premier League era. After goal-line technology is used for the first time in the Premier League to confirm it, City go on to a 4-2 victory over Cardiff. Santi Cazorla nets both in the space of five second-half minutes as Arsenal overcome Fulham 2-0, but Liverpool drop off the pace when held 2-2 by Aston Villa at Anfield. They have to come from two down for a point and so do Sunderland, who share four goals with Southampton. Yohan Cabaye is on the mark twice in Newcastle's 3-1 win at West Ham, while Jason Puncheon makes amends for his penalty miss the previous week by scoring the only goal for Crystal Palace against Stoke. Hull's Tom Huddlestone is sent off for two yellow cards at the end of a 1-0 defeat by Norwich, whose 87th winner by Ryan Bennett is his first of the season.

19 Samuel Eto'o becomes the first Chelsea player to score a hat-trick against Manchester United since Seamus O'Connell in the club's title-winning season of 1954-55. United are beaten 3-1 and have captain Nemanja Vidic shown a straight red card. Emmanuel Adebayor gets two as Tottenham win 3-1 at Swansea and make it five successive away league victories for the club for the first time since the Double-winning season of 1960-61.

20 Diego Lugano, captain of England's World Cup opponents Uruguay, scores his first goal for West Bromwich Albion in a 1-1 draw with Everton.

28 Daniel Sturridge is on the mark twice as Liverpool crush Everton 4-0 – the biggest winning margin in a Merseyside derby since 1982. Sturridge also misses a penalty and later apologises for his reaction to being substituted. Mathieu Flamini is sent off as Arsenal are held 2-2 at Southampton and there are three other straight red cards for violent conduct. Norwich's Bradley Johnson and Newcastle's Loic Remy are dismissed after clashing in a goalless draw, with Johnson later winning his appeal to the FA against the decision. Hull goalkeeper Allan McGregor is sent off for kicking out at Stuart O'Keefe in stoppage-time of a 1-0 defeat by Crystal Palace, for whom Jason Puncheon is again their match-winner. Record-signing Juan Mata takes just six minutes to make his mark for Manchester United, helping to set up Robin van Persie for a scoring return after injury in a 2-0 victory over Cardiff.

29 Manchester City go top in fine style – 5-1 winners over a Tottenham side they defeated 6-0 at the Etihad earlier in the season. Stevan Jovetic opens his account for the club, while Etienne Capoue's consolation is his first for Spurs, who have Danny Rose shown a straight red card in a first league defeat in seven for manager Tim Sherwood. The sending-off is later rescinded. City move a point ahead of Arsenal and three points clear of Chelsea, who have 39 shots at goal but are frustrated by West Ham in a goalless draw at Stamford Bridge. Aston Villa go two down in nine minutes against West Bromwich Albion, but hit back to win 4-3, Christian Benteke's decider coming from the penalty spot. Adam Johnson continues to lead Sunderland's bid for safety with the only goal against Stoke, who have Steven Nzonzi sent off for a second yellow card.

FEBRUARY 2014

1 Craig Bellamy becomes the first player to score for seven Premier League clubs as Cardiff overcome Norwich 2-1. Kenwyne Jones marks his debut with their second goal, 73 seconds later, to give Ole Gunnar Solskjaer his first top-flight victory since taking charge. Rejuvenated Sunderland score a third successive win over Newcastle for the first time since 1923, beating their neighbours 3-0 at St James' Park with Adam Johnson netting for the sixth time

in four games on his 200th Premier League appearance. Southampton are also 3-0 away winners, at Fulham, courtesy of goals in 11 second-half minutes from World Cup hopefuls Adam Lallana, Rickie Lambert and Jay Rodriguez in front of England manager Roy Hodgson. Two Charlie Adam strikes give Stoke their first league success over Manchester United since 1984. The first is deflected in by Michael Carrick and given as an own goal by the Dubious Goals Panel. Andy Carroll sets up both goals for Kevin Nolan and is then shown a straight red card in West Ham's 2-0 victory over Swansea – a result followed by the sacking of the Welsh side's manager Michael Laudrup. Shane Long scores his first for Hull in a 1-1 draw with Tottenham.

2   Making his first league start since the opening day of the season, injury-hit Alex Oxlade-Chamberlain hits both goals as Arsenal defeat Crystal Palace 2-0.

3   Chelsea end Manchester City's 100 per cent home record as Branislav Ivanovic provides the only one of the game after 32 minutes.

8   A hat-trick by Eden Hazard, including a penalty, lifts Chelsea to top spot. They overcome Newcastle 3-0 to take over from Arsenal, victims of a devastating opening 20 minutes at Anfield. Liverpool score four times and go on to win 5-1, with Martin Skrtel and Raheem Sterling both on the mark twice. Manchester City, meanwhile, are held to a goalless draw by Norwich, the side they crushed 7-0 at home earlier in the season. Three players make scoring debuts at Selhurst Park – Joe Ledley and on-loan Tom Ince in Crystal Palace's 3-1 win over West Bromwich Albion, for whom Thievy Bifouma nets 36 seconds after coming on as a substitute, a Premier League record. Also scoring for the first time for new clubs are Nikica Jelavic, in Hull's 2-0 victory over Sunderland, and Peter Odemwingie in Stoke's 2-2 draw at Southampton. Wes Brown's straight red card at the Stadium of Light is his third dismissal of the season – one of which has been rescinded. Kevin Nolan continues to make amends for his two red cards earlier in the campaign with two more goals for West Ham, who win 2-0 at Villa Park. Local derby honours go to Swansea, who with Garry Monk in temporary charge see off Cardiff 3-0.

9   Manchester United fall nine points adrift of a Champions League place when Darren Bent's stoppage-time header gives bottom-of-the-table Fulham a 2-2 draw at Old Trafford.

11   Another late goal denies Chelsea victory, Victor Anichebe scoring in the 87th minute to give West Bromwich Albion a 1-1 draw. James Collins registers his first in the Premier League for the club since 2006 as West Ham record a third successive 2-0 victory, this time against Norwich, to climb into the top half of the table – three weeks after languishing in the bottom three.

12   With Arsenal held to a goalless draw by Manchester United and Manchester City's game against Sunderland postponed because of high winds, Liverpool close in on the top three. Steven Gerrard's stoppage-time penalty secures a 3-2 win at Craven Cottage in what proves to be Rene Meulensteen's last game in charge of Fulham. A brace by Emmanuel Adebayor points Tottenham to a 4-0 success at Newcastle, who are goalless for the seventh time in eight league matches.

22   A stoppage-time goal by Frank Lampard, the only one of the game against Everton, keeps Chelsea on top. They are a point ahead of Arsenal, for whom Olivier Giroud is on the mark twice in a 4-1 success against Sunderland, watched by Dennis Bergkamp after the club idol has a statue unveiled at the Emirates. Yaya Toure's 13th of the season – matching his combined tally for the two previous league campaigns – keeps Manchester City a further two points back, with a game in hand, after a 1-0 win over Stoke. Hull score four goals away from home for the first time in top-flight football, two of them coming from Nikica Jelavic in a 4-0 win at Cardiff. West Ham also pull further away from trouble, overcoming Southampton 3-1 with Kevin Nolan's strike extending his purple patch to five goals in four games. The day after signing a reported £250,000 a week new contract, Wayne Rooney completes Manchester United's 2-0 victory over Crystal Palace.

23   Liverpool overtake Manchester City as the division's highest scores by defeating Swansea 4-3 to reach 70 for the season. Daniel Sturridge takes his tally to 18 in 19 appearances and Jordan Henderson also nets twice. Newcastle are grateful for just one after their lean spell,

Loic Remy's effort in added time breaking the deadlock against Aston Villa. Norwich boost their survival chances, while damaging Tottenham's Champions League prospects, as Robert Snodgrass nets the only goal at Carrow Road.

MARCH 2014

1 Newcastle's biggest away win of the season, 4-1 at Hull, is overshadowed by the touchline behaviour of manager Alan Pardew, who is sent to the stands for headbutting Hull midfielder David Meyler and is later fined by his club and banned for seven games by the FA. Newcastle are leading 3-1 at the time, with Moussa Sissoko contributing two of the goals. Andre Schurrle's hat-trick in 16 second-half minutes delivers a 3-1 success for Chelsea away to Fulham, for whom Johnny Heitinga's consolation is his first for the club. Luis Suarez, on his 100th Premier League appearance, ends a run of five blank games in Liverpool's 3-0 victory at Southampton. Suarez nets their first, lays on a second for substitute Raheem Sterling to score with his first touch, then wins the penalty converted by Steven Gerrard. Arsenal lose ground when a Jon Walters spot-kick enables Stoke to move further away from relegation trouble. Romelu Lukaku, sidelined for a month with injury, also scores the only goal as Everton end West Ham's winning run.

2 Christian Benteke is on the mark twice for Aston Villa, who come from behind to score four times in 16 minutes for a 4-1 victory over Norwich to ease their relegation worries. Glenn Murray also has cause for celebration with his first goal for Crystal Palace since a cruciate ligament injury sustained in the previous season's Championship play-offs. Substitute Murray converts the penalty awarded after Swansea's Chico Flores brings him down and is sent off. After the 1-1 draw, Palace manager Tony Pulis promises to fine two of his players, Marouane Chamakh and Jerome Thomas, for diving.

8 With Arsenal and Manchester City involved in FA Cup ties and Liverpool not playing, Chelsea extend their lead at the top. They score four times in the second-half for a 4-0 victory over Tottenham, who have Younes Kaboul sent off, a decision later rescinded. Demba Ba completes the scoring in the 88th and 89th minutes. Also shown a straight red card is Jon Walters, four minutes after converting a penalty in Stoke's 1-1 draw at Norwich. In the meeting of the bottom two, a brace by captain Steven Caulker points Cardiff to a 3-1 victory over Fulham, for whom on-loan Lewis Holtby scores his first goal for the club. Two other threatened teams lose at home – West Bromwich Albion 3-0 to Manchester United and Crystal Palace 1-0 to Southampton.

15 Chelsea's charge is halted amid three sendings-off at Villa Park. They lose 1-0 to an 82nd minute goal from Fabian Delph, have Willian dismissed for two yellow cards, Ramires shown a straight red and manager Jose Mourinho ordered from the touchline following the midfielder's stoppage-time stamp on Karim El Ahmadi. Manchester City captain Vincent Kompany also receives a straight red, ten minutes into the game at Hull, but his side win 2-0, with David Silva opening the scoring and laying on a second for Edin Dzeko. Two new managers win for the first time. Youssouf Mulumbu's 85th minute strike gives West Bromwich Albion a 2-1 success at Swansea in Pepe Mel's eighth game in charge. Felix Magath's fourth match at Fulham brings a 1-0 victory over Newcastle, earned by Ashkan Dejagah's goal. Elsewhere in the relegation struggle, Cardiff go down 2-1 at Everton to a mishit, stoppage-time shot from Seamus Coleman, Sunderland and Crystal Palace share a goalless draw, while Norwich are beaten 4-2 at Southampton, for whom 18-year-old Sam Gallagher scores for the first time. Stoke's Peter Odemwingie is on the mark twice in their 3-1 win over West Ham.

16 Steven Gerrard converts two penalties – and hits the post with a third – as Liverpool win 3-0 at Old Trafford. Luis Suarez completes another bad day for Manchester United, who have Nemanja Vidic sent off for two yellow cards. At White Hart Lane, Tomas Rosicky's strike after 72 seconds gives Arsenal victory over Tottenham.

22 One of the most eventful days in the history of the Premier League begins at lunch-time at Stamford Bridge as Arsene Wenger, in charge of his 1,000th match as Arsenal manager, sees his side torn apart 6-0 by Chelsea and one of his players mistakenly sent off. Andre Marriner

shows a red card to Kieran Gibbs, despite team-mate Alex Oxlade-Chamberlain admitting to the referee that he handled Eden Hazard's shot. Oscar scores two of the goals and Mohamed Salah records his first for the club in Chelsea's biggest win over their rivals. Liverpool also score six, taking their tally for the season to 82, a club record in the Premier League. A Luis Suarez hat-trick and two from Martin Skrtel set up the 6-3 scoreline at Cardiff, for whom Jordon Mutch gets two. Not to be outdone, Yaya Toure hits three in Manchester City's 5-0 victory over Fulham, two of them from the penalty spot, to take his tally in all competitions to 20 for the season. Martin Demichelis chips in with his first for the team, while Fernando Amorebieta is sent off for the second of the spot-kicks he concedes. Liam Rosenior heads his first for Hull after Nikica Jelavic's penalty is saved by West Bromwich Albion's Ben Foster. Shane Long wins it, then scores against his former club for a 2-0 victory. Norwich improve their positiion with the help of a spectacular volley from Alex Tettey, his first in the Premier League, in the 2-0 win over Sunderland, who have Marcos Alonso dismissed for two yellow cards. Everton record their eighth successive home victory in all competitions for the first time since 1986, overcoming faltering Swansea 3-2. Crystal Palace also stay in trouble after conceding a stoppage-time goal to Papiss Cisse, the only one of the game, at Newcastle. The day ends with Wayne Rooney volleying the first of his two in Manchester United's 2-0 success at Upton Park from just inside the West Ham half. It mirrors David Beckham's goal against Wimbledon in 1996 – and Beckham is there to see it.

23 Tottenham retrieve a 2-0 deficit to defeat Southampton with a brace from Christian Eriksen and a third in stoppage-time by Gylfi Sigurdsson. Stoke also come from behind to beat Aston Villa 4-1 – scoring four times away from home for the first time in the Premier League as Peter Crouch lays on the equaliser for Peter Odemwingie and scores the second himself.

25 Edin Dzeko finds the net after 43 seconds – the fastest goal by an away team at Old Trafford in the Premier League – and adds a second as Manchester City sweep past Manchester United 3-0. Arsene Wenger admits Arsenal are effectively out of the title running after Mathieu Flamini concedes a 90th minute own goal to give Swansea a 2-2 draw at the Emirates. They also face a challenge for the fourth Champions League place after Everton's 3-0 victory at Newcastle.

26 Hull goalkeeper Allan McGregor is sent off for the second time in two months, this time for bringing down Mohamed Diame and conceding a penalty in the 2-1 defeat at West Ham. McGregor is taken to hospital with kidney damage, but the red card is later rescinded. Daniel Sturridge scores his 20th league goal of the season in Liverpool's 2-1 victory over Sunderland.

29 Jose Mourinho writes off Chelsea's title chances after a second successive 1-0 away defeat, this time inflicted by a John Terry own goal against Crystal Palace – a huge result for Tony Pulis's side. Arsenal and Manchester City finish all square, with David Silva putting City ahead and Mathieu Flamini equalising. So do two relegation-threatened sides after a dramatic finish. West Bromwich Albion, having surrendered a two-goal lead to Cardiff, look to have won it with Thievy Bifouma's effort in the fourth minute of stoppage-time. But a minute later another substitute, Mats Daehli, levels at 3-3 with his first for the club. Swansea move clear of trouble as Jonathan de Guzman scores two in a 3-0 win over Norwich, while two other players are on the mark twice. Wayne Rooney's goals, one a penalty, and Juan Mata's first for the team, point Manchester United to a 4-1 success over Aston Villa. Southampton score four without replay against Newcastle, Jay Rodriguez opening and closing the scoring.

30 Liverpool go top by crushing Tottenham 4-0 and Luis Suarez overtakes Robbie Fowler's club record of 28 goals in a Premier League season. They lead Chelsea by two points from the same number of games, with Manchester City a further two behind from two fewer matches. Fulham look doomed after a 3-1 home defeat by Everton, for whom substitute Steven Naismith forces David Stockdale into conceding an own goal and rounds off the scoring himself.

31 Sunderland, second from bottom, miss the chance to boost their chances of staying up, losing 2-1 at home to West Ham.

5   Mohamed Salah has an impressive first league start for Chelsea in a 3-0 victory over Stoke. The Egypt winger opens the scoring, then wins the penalty which provides Frank Lampard with his 250th career goal from the rebound after his spot-kick is saved by Asmir Begovic. Manchester City score twice in first-half stoppage-time on the way to a 4-1 win over Southampton, who protest, justifiably, that David Silva is three yards offside when setting up Samir Nasri for the first one. Earlier, Southampton's Jay Rodriguez sustains knee ligament damage, ruling him out for up to six months. Crystal Palace, with only six away goals all season, move to within sight of safety when Jason Puncheon scores twice in a 3-0 success against Cardiff. Substitute Hugo Rodallega offers Fulham a lifeline with an 86th minute strike – his first of the campaign in the league – for a 2-1 win away to Aston Villa, for whom on-loan Grant Holt nets his first for the club. West Bromwich Albion also do their chances of staying up a power of good at fellow-strugglers Norwich, where one loanee, Morgan Amalfitano, scores the only goal of the game – a result which is followed by the dismissal of Norwich manager Chris Hughton. Also winners away from home are Manchester United. They defeat Newcastle 4-0 as Juan Mata nets twice and sets up Adnan Januzaj for another.

6   Two Steven Gerrard penalties, taking his tally from the spot for the season to 11 in all competitions, earn Liverpool a 2-1 win at West Ham, whose reply from Guy Demel is his first goal for the club. Also among the goals are Everton, who score three for the fourth successive match for the first time since 1987. They outplay Arsenal 3-0 to move to within a point of their rivals for a Champions League spot with a game in hand.

7   A brace by Emmanuel Adebayor, and a first for Harry Kane on his first Premier League start, for Tottenham push Sunderland deeper into trouble. They lose 5-1 after scoring first at White Hart Lane and are seven points from safety with two games in hand.

12   Five of the six matches played produce 1-0 scorelines. Hugo Rodallega is again Fulham's match-winner, this time against Norwich, who now face the toughest run-in of the sides bidding to beat the drop. Juan Cala gives Cardiff a measure of hope with the only goal at Southampton, while Jason Puncheon is again on the mark for Crystal Palace, inflicting a fourth successive defeat on Aston Villa. A Wes Brown own goal, Sunderland's sixth of the season, enables Everton to overtake Arsenal and set two Premier League records for the club – a seventh straight win and their highest points total (66). Stoke's Erik Pieters also enjoys a landmark against Newcastle – his first club goal since scoring for Utrecht in 2008. In the game which does produce goals, West Bromwich Albion surrender a 3-0 lead against Tottenham and concede a stoppage-time equaliser for the second successive home game. Christian Eriksen scores it for a 3-3 scoreline.

13   On an emotional afternoon at Anfield, with the 25th anniversary of the Hillsborough disaster approaching, Liverpool defeat Manchester City 3-2. Raheem Sterling and Martin Skrtel establish a 2-0 lead inside 26 minutes, City hit back through David Silva and a Glen Johnson own goal, then Philippe Coutinho strikes the winner after 78 minutes. In stoppage time, Liverpool's Jordan Henderson is sent off for a second yellow card. Chelsea keep alive their chances as Demba Ba follows up his decisive Champions League goal against Paris St-Germain with the only one against Swansea, who have Chico Flores shown two yellow cards – his second dismissal in six matches.

15   Arsenal regain fourth place by defeating West Ham 3-1, Lukas Podolski scoring twice.

16   A night of shocks for Manchester City and Everton. City's title chances are dealt another blow when Sunderland draw 2-2 at the Etihad with two goals from Connor Wickham, his first in the Premier League since October 2011. Everton lose 3-2 at home to Crystal Palace, for whom Scott Dann opens his account for the club.

19   Jose Mourinho loses his 77-match unbeaten Premier League record at Stamford Bridge as Chelsea are beaten 2-1 by Sunderland. Connor Wickham is again on the mark and Sunderland's winner is an 82nd minute penalty by Fabio Borini. On the touchline, Mourinho has to restrain his assistant, Rui Faria, from confronting referee Mike Dean about the decision to award it. Sunderland, although still bottom, close the gap on Fulham, beaten 3-1 at

Tottenham after Steve Sidwell has a penalty saved by Hugo Lloris, and Cardiff, who draw 1-1 with Stoke. Wilfried Bony eases the pressure on Swansea by scoring both goals in a 2-1 success at Newcastle, his second a penalty in stoppage-time. Referee Chris Foy is replaced by fourth official Anthony Taylor in this match after being struck in the face by a Jonjo Shelvey shot. Mile Jedinak's spot-kick brings Crystal Palace their fifth successive victory – 1-0 at West Ham. Aston Villa end their losing run in a goalless draw with Southampton at the end of a troubled week in which Paul Lambert's assistants Ian Culverhouse and Gary Karsa are suspended by the club.

20 Liverpool record a Premier League club record 11th successive win when beating Norwich 3-2. Raheem Sterling nets twice and sets up Luis Suarez to become the first Liverpool striker since Ian Rush in the 1986-87 season to score 30 league goals. Lukas Podolski also gets two and injury-dogged Aaron Ramsey is on the mark on his first start since Boxing Day as Arsenal win 3-0 at Hull – a month before the teams meet in the FA Cup Final. Everton complete the double over Manchester United for the first time since 1969, adding a 2-0 win to their single-goal success at Old Trafford. Leighton Baines extends his Premier League record of successful penalties to 13 in what proves to be David Moyes's last match as United manager.

21 Manchester City keep alive their title chances with a 3-1 victory over West Bromwich Albion, who come under more relegation pressure.

26 Ryan Giggs, appointed Manchester United's interim manager, enjoys a successful start, a 4-0 victory over against Norwich achieved by two goals each from Wayne Rooney and substitute Juan Mata. Everton miss the chance to regain fourth place, gifting Southampton a 2-0 victory with own goals conceded by Antolin Alcaraz, in the first minute, and Seamus Coleman. Fulham also waste an opportunity. Fernando Amorebieta, with their second goal, becomes the first Venezuelan to score in the Premier League, but Hull retrieve the deficit for a point. Two more for Wilfried Bony, one a penalty, along with a spectacular volley from the edge of the centre circle by Jonjo Shelvey, leave Swansea safe after the 4-1 defeat of an increasingly worried Aston Villa. West Bromwich Albion also climb, Pepe Mel's first Hawthorns success coming from the only goal of the game against West Ham by Saido Berahino. Stoke's Ryan Shawcross is sent off for a second bookable offence in the 1-0 home defeat by Tottenham.

27 The title race takes another twist as Liverpool lose 2-0 at home to Chelsea. Jose Mourinho rests key players ahead of the Champions League semi-final against Atletico Madrid, but sets up his side shrewdly and is rewarded with goals by Demba Ba and Willian. Manchester City win 2-0 at Crystal Palace, with Yaya Toure providing the cross for Edin Dzeko to open the scoring and netting the second himself. At the bottom, a brace by Connor Wickham takes his tally to five in three games for revitalised Sunderland, having been on the mark just once in 37 previous Premier League games. He also wins the penalty for their third goal in a 4-0 victory over Cardiff. Phil Dowd awards it – and sends off Juan Cala for the foul – after waiting to see if Wickham gains any advantage by staying on his feet. At the end of the month, Liverpool have 80 points, Chelsea 78 and City 77 with a game in hand and a superior goal difference.

28 Arsenal take a firm grip on fourth place after a 3-0 victory over Newcastle.

MAY 2014

3 Edin Dzeko is on the mark twice as Manchester City negotiate their biggest remaining hurdle, coming from behind to win 3-2 at Goodison Park, a result which ends Everton's Champions League chances. Two sides are relegated. Fulham are beaten 4-1 at Stoke and go down after 13 years in the Premier League. Cardiff make an immediate return to the Championship when losing 3-0 at Newcastle, who end a run of six successive defeats. Sunderland's revival continues. They beat Manchester United at Old Trafford for the first time since 1968, Seb Larsson scoring the only goal, while Aston Villa effectively ensure survival with a brace from Andreas Weimann in a 3-1 success against Hull. Stewart Downing's first goal for West Ham comes in a 2-0 victory over Tottenham, who have Younes Kaboul shown a straight red card.

4 Chelsea are virtually ruled out of contention when held to a goalless draw at home by Norwich.

5 Liverpool look certain to keep alive their chances when Joe Allen, Luis Suarez and a Damien Delaney own goal establish a 3-0 lead at Crystal Palace. But in a remarkable collapse, they concede three in ten minutes to Delaney and Dwight Gayle (2) and the game ends 3-3.

6 James Wilson, 18, makes a dream debut for Manchester United, scoring twice in a 3-1 victory over Hull.

7 Manchester City move to within touching distance of the title, and reach 100 goals for the season, by beating Aston Villa 4-0 with two more from Edin Dzeko. City lead Liverpool by two points going into the final round of matches. Sunderland complete their great escape with a fourth successive victory – 2-0 against West Bromwich Albion thanks to goals from Jack Colback and Fabio Borini. The result all but confirms that Norwich are relegated.

11 On the final day of the season, Manuel Pellegrini becomes the first manager from outside Europe to win the Premier League as goals by Samir Nasri and captain Vincent Kompany give Manchester City a 2-0 victory over West Ham and their second title in three years. Liverpool top a century of goals after a 2-1 win over Newcastle, who finish with nine men when Shola Ameobi is sent off for persistent dissent and Paul Dummett receives a straight red card. Dummett's is later rescinded. Tim Sherwood bows out as Tottenham manager with another Europa League place confirmed by the 3-0 defeat of Aston Villa. It's also the final match for Pepe Mel as West Bromwich Albion go down 2-1 to Stoke, whose ninth place is the club's highest in the Premier League. Four players score for the first time for their clubs, including Fulham's Cauley Woodrow (19) and 21-year-old Chris David on his debut. They are on the mark in a 2-2 draw with Crystal Palace, for whom Dwight Gayle nets two for the second time in a week. Carl Jenkinson gets his first as Arsenal confirm Norwich's relegation, while James McCarthy opens his account for Everton, who overcome Hull by the same 2-0 scoreline.

HOW MANCHESTER CITY REGAINED THE TITLE

AUGUST 2013

19 Manchester City 4 (Silva 6, Aguero 22, Toure 50, Nasri 75) Newcastle 0. Att: 46,842

25 Cardiff 3 (Gunnarsson 60, Campbell 79, 87) Manchester City 2 (Dzeko 52, Negredo 90). Att: 27,068

31 Manchester City 2 (Negredo 65, Toure 90) Hull 0. Att: 46,903

SEPTEMBER 2013

14 Stoke 0 Manchester City 0. Att: 25,052

22 Manchester City 4 (Aguero 16, 47, Toure 45, Nasri 50) Manchester Utd 1 (Rooney 87). Att: 47,156

28 Aston Villa 3 (El Ahmadi 51, Bacuna 73, Weimann 75) Manchester City 2 (Toure 45, Dzeko 56). Att: 34,063

OCTOBER 2013

5 Manchester City 3 (Negredo 17, Aguero 45, Howard 69 og) Everton 1 (Lukaku 16). Att: 47,267

19 West Ham 1 (Vaz Te 58) Manchester City 3 (Aguero 16, 51, Silva 80). Att: 34,507

27 Chelsea 2 (Schurrle 33, Torres 90) Manchester City 1 (Aguero 49). Att: 41,495

NOVEMBER 2013

2 Manchester City 7 (Johnson 16 og, Silva 20, Martin 25 og, Negredo 36, Toure 60, Aguero 71, Dzeko 86) Norwich 0. Att: 47,066

10 Sunderland 1 (Bardsley 21) Manchester City 0. Att: 40,137

24 Manchester City 6 (Jesus Navas 1, 90, Sandro 34 og, Aguero 41, 50, Negredo 55) Tottenham 0. Att: 47,228

DECEMBER 2013

1	Manchester City 3 (Negredo 8, Nasri 58, 77) Swansea 0. Att: 46,559 Att: 22,943
4	WBA 2 (Pantilimon 85 og, Anichebe 90) Manchester City 3 (Aguero 9, Toure 24, 74 pen). Att: 22,943
7	Southampton 1 (Osvaldo 42) Manchester City 1 (Aguero 10). Att: 31,229
14	Manchester City 6 (Aguero 14, Negredo 39, Fernandinho 50, 88, Silva 66, Toure 90 pen) Arsenal 3 (Walcott 31, 63, Mertesacker 90). Att: 47,229
21	Fulham 2 (Richardson 50, Kompany 69 og) Manchester City 4 (Toure 23, Kompany 43, Jesus Navas 78, Milner 83). Att: 25,509
26	Manchester City 2 (Kompany 31, Negredo 45) Liverpool 1 (Coutinho 24). Att: 47,351
28	Manchester City 1 (Dzeko 66) Crystal Palace 0. Att: 47,107

JANUARY 2014

1	Swansea 2 (Bony 45, 90) Manchester City 3 (Fernandinho 14, Toure 58, Kolarov 66). Att: 20,498
12	Newcastle 0 Manchester City 2 (Dzeko 8, Negredo 90). Att: 49,423
18	Manchester City 4 (Dzeko 14, Jesus Navas 33, Toure 76, Aguero 79) Cardiff 2 (Noone 29, Campbell 90). Att: 47,213
29	Tottenham 1 (Capoue 59) Manchester City 5 (Aguero 15, Toure 51 pen, Dzeko 53, Jovetic 78, Kompany 89). Att: 36,071

FEBRUARY 2014

3	Manchester City 0 Chelsea 1 (Ivanovic 32). Att: 47,364
8	Norwich 0 Manchester City 0. Att: 26,832
22	Manchester City 1 (Toure 70) Stoke 0. Att: 47,038

MARCH 2014

15	Hull 0 Manchester City 2 (Silva 14, Dzeko 90). Att: 24,895
22	Manchester City 5 (Toure 26 pen, 54 pen, 65, Fernandinho 84, Demichelis 88) Fulham 0. Att: 47,262
25	Manchester Utd 0 Manchester City 3 (Dzeko 1, 56, Toure 90). Att: 75,203
29	Arsenal 1 (Flamini 53) Manchester City 1 (Silva 18). Att: 60,060

APRIL 2014

5	Manchester City 4 (Toure 3 pen, Nasri 45, Dzeko 45, Jovetic 81) Southampton 1 (Lambert 37 pen). Att: 47,009
13	Liverpool 3 (Sterling 6, Skrtel 26, Coutinho 78) Manchester City 2 (Silva 57, Johnson 62 og). Att: 44,601
16	Manchester City 2 (Fernandinho 2, Nasri 88) Sunderland 2 (Wickham 73, 83). Att: 47,046
21	Manchester City 3 (Zabaleta 3, Aguero 10, Demichelis 36) WBA 1 (Dorrans 16). Att: 46,564
27	Crystal Palace 0 Manchester City 2 (Dzeko 4, Toure 43). Att: 24,769

MAY 2014

3	Everton 2 (Barkley 11, Lukaku 65) Manchester City 3 (Aguero 22, Dzeko 43, 48). Att: 39,454
7	Manchester City 4 (Dzeko 64, 72, Jovetic 89, Toure 90) Aston Villa 0. Att: 47,023
11	Manchester City 2 (Nasri 39, Kompany 49) West Ham 0. Att: 47,300 (clinched title)

FOOTBALL LEAGUE PLAY-OFFS 2014

With so much at stake and so little room for error, Football League play-offs rarely fail to deliver incident and drama. This year was no exception. If anything, the three matches captured the headlines even more. For Harry Redknapp and **Queens Park Rangers**, an immediate return to the Premier League looked unlikely when Gary O'Neil was sent off for bringing down Johnny Russell and denying the Derby County player a goal-scoring opportunity. There was more than half-an-hour still to play, Derby had been on top for most of the match and it was odds-on that they would now make that superiority count. Instead, Rangers successfully defended even deeper, with Rob Green standing firm in goal. Then, with the clock reaching 90 minutes, Derby captain Richard Keogh mistimed a clearance and substitute Bobby Zamora punished the mistake. with a classy finish which echoed his winner for West Ham against Preston in 2005. There was no time for Steve McClaren's players to respond, so it was another bitter Wembley disappointment for the manager on his return to the national stadium where his England side failed to qualify for Euro 2008 when losing to Croatia. Like Rangers, **Rotherham United** were staring at defeat when Moses Odubajo put Leyton Orient ahead with a superb volley and set up a second goal for Dean Cox. But they too responded to the challenge. Alex Revell pulled one back against his former club and equalised with an eye-catching, long-distance strike of his own. Again, in the penalty shoot-out, Rotherham trailed before Adam Collin saved from Mathieu Baudry and Chris Dagnall to give his team a second successive promotion, this time to the Championship. **Fleetwood Town** continued their remarkable rise when a 75th minute free-kick by Antoni Sarcevic was misjudged by Burton Albion goalkeeper Dean Lyness and settled the League Two Final. It was the club's sixth promotion in ten seasons – a climb which started in North West Counties football. **Cambridge United** returned to the league after a nine-year absence, beating Gateshead 2-1 in the Conference Final to complete a Wembley double after winning the FA Trophy. Ryan Donaldson crossed for Liam Hughes to score and got the second goal himself against his former club.

SEMI-FINALS, FIRST LEG

CHAMPIONSHIP

Brighton 1 (Lingard 18) **Derby** 2 (Martin 29 pen, Kuszczak 45 og). Att: 27,118. **Wigan** 0 **QPR** 0. Att: 14,560

LEAGUE ONE

Peterborough 1 (Assombalonga 16) **Leyton Orient** 1 (Odubajo 72). Att: 9,519. **Preston** 1 (Garner 49) **Rotherham** 1 (Revell 21). Att: 17,221

LEAGUE TWO

Burton 1 (McGurk 45) **Southend** 0. Att: 4,581. **York** 0 **Fleetwood** 1 (Blair 50). Att: 5,124

CONFERENCE

Grimsby 1 (Disley 24) **Gateshead** 1 (Larkin 7). Att: 5,234. **Halifax** 1 (Gregory 83 pen) **Cambridge Utd** 0. Att: 3,668.

SEMI-FINALS, SECOND LEG

CHAMPIONSHIP

Derby 4 (Hughes 34, Martin 56, Thorne 76, Hendrick 87) **Brighton** 1 (LuaLua 89). Att: 32,060 (Derby won 6-2 on agg). **QPR** 2 (Austin 73 pen, 96) **Wigan** 1 (Perch 9). Att: 17,061 (aet, QPR won 2-1 on agg)

LEAGUE ONE

Leyton Orient 2 (Cox 60, Dagnall 88) **Peterborough** 1 (Washington 90). Att: 8,545 (Leyton Orient won 3-2 on agg). **Rotherham** 3 (Thomas 24, Frecklington 34, Agard 67) **Preston** 1 (Gallagher 16). Att: 11,576 (Rotherham won 4-2 on agg)

LEAGUE TWO

Fleetwood 0 **York** 0. Att: 5,194 (Fleetwood won 1-0 on agg). **Southend** 2 (Leonard 32, Straker 39) **Burton** 2 (Holness 21, McGurk 69). Att: 9,696 (Burton won 3-2 on agg)

CONFERENCE

Cambridge Utd 2 (Sam-Yorke 11, 38) **Halifax** 0. Att: 6,262 (Cambridge Utd won 2-1 on agg). **Gateshead** 3 (Marwood 22, 84, O'Donnell 90) **Grimsby** 1 (Disley 60). Att: 8,144 (Gateshead won 4-2 on agg)

FINALS

CHAMPIONSHIP – SATURDAY, MAY 24, 2014

Derby County 0 **Queens Park Rangers** 1 (Zamora 90). Att: 87,348 (Wembley)
Derby County (4-3-3): Grant, Wisdom, Keogh (capt), Buxton, Forsyth, Hendrick, Thorne, W Hughes (Bryson 67), Russell (Dawkins 67), Martin, Ward (Bamford 90). **Subs not used:** Legzdins, Eustace, Sammon, Whitbread. **Manager:** Steve McClaren
Queens Park Rangers (4-4-2): Green, Simpson, Onuoha, Dunne, Hill (capt) (Henry 67), Hoilett, O'Neil, Barton, Kranjcar (Traore 33), Doyle (Zamora 57), Austin. **Subs not used:** Murphy, Morrison, Yun Suk-Young, A Hughes. **Booked:** Zamora. **Sent off:** O'Neil (60). **Manager:** Harry Redknapp
Referee: L Mason (Lancs). **Half-time:** 0-0

LEAGUE ONE – SUNDAY, MAY 25, 2014

Leyton Orient 2 (Odubajo 34, Cox 39) **Rotherham United** 2 (Revell 55, 60) – aet, Rotherham United won 4-3 on pens. Att: 43,401 (Wembley)
Leyton Orient (4-4-2): Jones, Cuthbert, Baudry, Clarke (capt), Omozusi, Odubajo, Vincelot, James, Cox (Batt 74), Mooney (Lundstram 105), Lisbie (Dagnall 75). **Subs not used:** Larkins, Sawyer, Bartley, Simpson. **Booked:** Cuthbert, Odubajo, Clarke, Mooney. **Manager:** Russell Slade
Rotherham United (4-4-2): Collin, Tavernier, Arnason, Morgan (capt), Skarz (Milsom 77), Pringle, Smallwood, Frecklington, Agard, Thomas (Brindley 54). Revell (Vuckic 105). **Subs not used:** Shearer, Davis, O'Connor, Hitchcock. **Booked:** Morgan, Tavernier, Pringle. **Manager:** Steve Evans
Referee: D Coote (Notts). **Half-time:** 2-0

LEAGUE TWO – MONDAY, MAY 26, 2014

Burton Albion 0 **Fleetwood Town** 1 (Sarcevic 75). Att: 14,007 (Wembley)
Burton Albion (4-4-2): Lyness, Edwards, Holness (Diamond 64), Cansdell-Sheriff, Hussey, MacDonald (Ismail 73), Weir, Bell (capt) (Palmer 78), McFadzean, Kee, McGurk. **Subs not used:** Hall, Gray, Alexander, Knowles. **Booked:** Edwards. **Manager:** Gary Rowett
Fleetwood Town (4-4-2): Maxwell, McLaughlin, Pond, Roberts (capt), Taylor, Goodall, Blair (Parkin 74), Sarcevic, Morris, Hume (Murdoch 85), Ball. **Subs not used:** Lucas, Evans, Schumacher, Matt, Jordan. **Manager:** Graham Alexander
Referee: M Naylor (Yorks). **Half-time:** 0-0

CONFERENCE – SUNDAY, MAY 18, 2014

Cambridge United 2 (Hughes 51, Donaldson 71) **Gateshead** 1 (Lester 80). Att: 19,613 (Wembley)

Cambridge United (4-4-2): Smith, Roberts, Miller (capt), Coulson, Taylor, Champion, Berry (Chadwick 65), Donaldson, Elliott (Cunnington 76), Sam-Yorke (Dunk 46), Hughes. **Subs not used**: Bonner, Chambers. **Booked**: Champion, Cunnington. **Manager**: Richard Money
Gateshead (4-4-2): Bartlett, Magnay, Curtis, Clark (capt), Baxter, Chandler (Lester 69), Turnbull, Maddison (O'Donnell 58), Marwood, Oster, Larkin (Hatch 58). **Subs not used**: Walker, Ramshaw. **Booked**: Maddison, Oster, Clark. **Manager**: Gary Mills
Referee: P Bankes (Merseyside). **Half-time**: 0-0

PLAY-OFF FINALS – HOME & AWAY

1987: Divs 1/2: Charlton beat Leeds 2-1 in replay (Birmingham) after 1-1 agg (1-0h, 0-1a). Charlton remained in Div 1 Losing semi-finalists: Ipswich and Oldham. **Divs 2/3: Swindon** beat Gillingham 2-0 in replay (Crystal Palace) after 2-2 agg (0-1a, 2-1h). Swindon promoted to Div 2. Losing semi-finalists: Sunderland and Wigan; Sunderland relegated to Div 3. **Divs 3/4: Aldershot** beat Wolves 3-0 on agg (2-0h, 1-0a) and promoted to Div 3. Losing semi-finalists: Bolton and Colchester; Bolton relegated to Div 4

1988: Divs 1/2: Middlesbrough beat Chelsea 2-1 on agg (2-0h, 0-1a) and promoted to Div 1; Chelsea relegated to Div 2. Losing semi-finalists: Blackburn and Bradford City. **Divs 2/3: Walsall** beat Bristol City 4-0 in replay (h) after 3-3 agg (3-1a, 0-2h) and promoted to Div 2. Losing semi-finalists: Sheffield Utd and Notts County; Sheffield Utd relegated to Div 3. **Divs 3/4: Swansea** beat Torquay 5-4 on agg (2-1h, 3-3a) and promoted to Div 3. Losing semi-finalists: Rotherham and Scunthorpe.; Rotherham relegated to Div 4

1989: Div 2: Crystal Palace beat Blackburn 4-3 on agg (1-3a, 3-0h). Losing semi-finalists: Watford and Swindon. **Div 3: Port Vale** beat Bristol Rovers 2-1 on agg (1-1a, 1-0h). Losing semi-finalists: Fulham and Preston **Div.4: Leyton Orient** beat Wrexham 2-1 on agg (0-0a, 2-1h). Losing semi-finalists: Scarborough and Scunthorpe

PLAY-OFF FINALS AT WEMBLEY

1990: Div 2: Swindon 1 Sunderland 0 (att: 72,873). Swindon promoted, then demoted for financial irregularities; Sunderland promoted. Losing semi-finalists: Blackburn and Newcastle Utd **Div 3: Notts County** 2 Tranmere 0 (att: 29,252). Losing semi-finalists: Bolton and Bury. **Div 4: Cambridge Utd** 1 Chesterfield 0 (att: 26,404). Losing semi-finalists: Maidstone and Stockport County

1991: Div 2: Notts County 3 Brighton 1 (att: 59,940). Losing semi-finalists: Middlesbrough and Millwall. **Div 3: Tranmere** 1 Bolton 0 (att: 30,217). Losing semi-finalists: Brentford and Bury. **Div 4: Torquay 2** Blackpool 2 – Torquay won 5-4 on pens (att: 21,615). Losing semi-finalists: Burnley and Scunthorpe

1992: Div 2: Blackburn 1 Leicester 0 (att: 68,147). Losing semi-finalists: Derby and Cambridge Utd. **Div 3: Peterborough** 2 Stockport 1 (att: 35,087). Losing semi-finalists: Huddersfield and Stoke. **Div 4: Blackpool** 1 Scunthorpe 1 aet, Blackpool won 4-3 on pens (att: 22,741). Losing semi-finalists: Barnet and Crewe

1993: Div 1: Swindon 4 Leicester 3 (att: 73,802). Losing semi-finalists: Portsmouth and Tranmere. **Div 2: WBA** 3 Port Vale 0 (att: 53,471). Losing semi-finalists: Stockport and Swansea. **Div 3: York** 1 Crewe 1 aet, York won 5-3 on pens (att: 22,416). Losing semi-finalists: Bury and Walsall

1994: Div 1: Leicester 2 Derby 1 (att: 73,671). Losing semi-finalists: Millwall and Tranmere. **Div 2: Burnley** 2 Stockport 1 (att: 44,806). Losing semi-finalists: Plymouth Argyle and York. **Div 3: Wycombe** 4 Preston 2 (att: 40,109). Losing semi-finalists: Carlisle and Torquay

1995: Div 1: Bolton 4 Reading 3 (att: 64,107). Losing semi-finalists: Tranmere and Wolves. **Div 2: Huddersfield** 2 Bristol Rov 1 (att: 59,175). Losing semi-finalists: Brentford and Crewe. **Div 3: Chesterfield** 2 Bury 0 (att: 22,814). Losing semi-finalists: Mansfield and Preston

1996: Div 1: Leicester 2 Crystal Palace 1 aet (att: 73,573). Losing semi-finalists: Charlton and Stoke. **Div 2: Bradford City** 2 Notts Co 0 (att: 39,972). Losing semi-finalists: Blackpool and Crewe. **Div 3: Plymouth Argyle** 1 Darlington 0 (att: 43,431). Losing semi-finalists: Colchester and Hereford

1997: Div 1: Crystal Palace 1 Sheffield Utd 0 (att: 64,383). Losing semi-finalists: Ipswich and Wolves. **Div 2: Crewe** 1 Brentford 0 (att: 34,149). Losing semi-finalists: Bristol City and Luton. **Div 3: Northampton** 1 Swansea 0 (att: 46,804). Losing semi-finalists: Cardiff and Chester

1998: Div 1: Charlton 4 Sunderland 4 aet, Charlton won 7-6 on pens (att: 77, 739). Losing semi-finalists: Ipswich and Sheffield Utd. **Div 2: Grimsby** 1 Northampton 0 (att: 62,988). Losing semi-finalists: Bristol Rov and Fulham. **Div 3: Colchester** 1 Torquay 0 (att: 19,486). Losing semi-finalists: Barnet and Scarborough

1999: Div 1: Watford 2 Bolton 0 (att: 70,343). Losing semi-finalists: Ipswich and Birmingham. **Div 2: Manchester City** 2 Gillingham 2 aet, Manchester City won 3-1 on pens (att: 76,935). Losing semi-finalists: Preston and Wigan. **Div 3: Scunthorpe** 1 Leyton Orient 0 (att: 36,985). Losing semi-finalists: Rotherham and Swansea

2000: Div 1: Ipswich 4 Barnsley 2 (att: 73,427). Losing semi-finalists: Birmingham and Bolton. **Div 2: Gillingham** 3 Wigan 2 aet (att: 53,764). Losing semi-finalists: Millwall and Stoke. **Div 3: Peterborough** 1 Darlington 0 (att: 33,383). Losing semi-finalists: Barnet and Hartlepool

PLAY-OFF FINALS AT MILLENNIUM STADIUM

2001: Div 1: Bolton 3 Preston 0 (att: 54,328). Losing semi-finalists: Birmingham and WBA. **Div 2: Walsall** 3 Reading 2 aet (att: 50,496). Losing semi-finalists: Stoke and Wigan. **Div 3: Blackpool** 4 Leyton Orient 2 (att: 23,600). Losing semi-finalists: Hartlepool and Hull.

2002: Div 1: Birmingham 1 Norwich 1 aet, Birmingham won 4-2 on pens, (att: 71,597). Losing semi-finalists: Millwall and Wolves. **Div 2: Stoke** 2 Brentford 0 (att: 42,523). Losing semi-finalists: Cardiff and Huddersfield. **Div 3: Cheltenham** 3 Rushden & Diamonds 1 (att: 24,368). Losing semi-finalists: Hartlepool and Rochdale

2003: Div 1: Wolves 3 Sheffield Utd 0 (att: 69,473). Losing semi-finalists: Nott'm Forest and Reading. **Div 2: Cardiff** 1 QPR. 0 aet (att: 66,096). Losing semi-finalists: Bristol City and Oldham. **Div 3: Bournemouth** 5 Lincoln 2 (att: 32,148). Losing semi-finalists: Bury and Scunthorpe

2004: Div 1: Crystal Palace 1 West Ham 0 (att: 72,523). Losing semi-finalists: Ipswich and Sunderland. **Div 2: Brighton** 1 Bristol City 0 (att: 65,167). Losing semi-finalists: Hartlepool and Swindon. **Div 3: Huddersfield** 0 Mansfield 0 aet, Huddersfield won 4-1 on pens (att: 37,298). Losing semi-finalists: Lincoln and Northampton

2005: Championship: West Ham 1 Preston 0 (att: 70,275). Losing semifinalists: Derby Co and Ipswich. **League 1: Sheffield Wed** 4 Hartlepool 2 aet (att: 59,808). Losing semi-finalists: Brentford and Tranmere **League 2: Southend** 2 Lincoln 0 aet (att: 19532). Losing semi-finalists: Macclesfield and Northampton

2006: Championship: Watford 3 Leeds 0 (att: 64,736). Losing semi-finalists: Crystal Palace and Preston. **League 1: Barnsley** 2 Swansea 2 act (att: 55,419), Barnsley won 4-3 on pens. Losing semi-finalists: Huddersfield and Brentford. **League 2: Cheltenham** 1 Grimsby 0 (att: 29,196). Losing semi-finalists: Wycombe and Lincoln

PLAY-OFF FINALS AT WEMBLEY

2007: Championship: Derby 1 WBA 0 (att: 74,993). Losing semi-finalists: Southampton and Wolves. **League 1: Blackpool** 2 Yeovil 0 (att: 59,313). Losing semi-finalists: Nottm Forest and Oldham. **League 2: Bristol Rov** 3 Shrewsbury 1 (att: 61,589). Losing semi-finalists: Lincoln and MK Dons

2008: Championship: Hull 1 Bristol City 0 (att: 86,703). Losing semi-finalists: Crystal Palace and Watford. **League 1: Doncaster** 1 Leeds 0 (att: 75,132). Losing semi-finalists: Carlisle and Southend. **League 2: Stockport** 3 Rochdale 2 (att: 35,715). Losing semi-finalists: Darlington and Wycombe

2009: Championship: Burnley 1 Sheffield Utd 0 (att: 80,518). Losing semi-finalists: Preston and Reading. **League 1: Scunthorpe** 3 Millwall 2 (att: 59,661). Losing semi-finalists: Leeds and MK Dons. **League 2: Gillingham** 1 Shrewsbury 0 (att: 53,706). Losing semi-finalists: Bury and Rochdale

2010: Championship: Blackpool 3 Cardiff 2 (att: 82,244). Losing semi-finalists: Leicester and Nottm Forest. **League 1: Millwall** 1 Swindon 0 (att:73,108). Losing semi-finalists: Charlton and Huddersfield. **League 2: Dagenham & Redbridge** 3 Rotherham 2 (att: 32,054). Losing semi-finalists: Aldershot and Morecambe

2011: Championship: Swansea 4 Reading 2 (att: 86,581). Losing semi-finalists: Cardiff and Nottm Forest. **League 1: Peterborough** 3 Huddersfield 0 (Old Trafford, att:48,410). Losing semi-finalists: Bournemouth and MK Dons. **League 2: Stevenage** 1 Torquay 0 (Old Trafford, att: 11,484. Losing semi-finalists: Accrington and Shrewsbury

2012: Championship: West Ham 2 Blackpool 1 (att: 78,523). Losing semi-finalists: Birmingham and Cardiff. **League 1: Huddersfield** 0 Sheffield Utd 0 aet, Huddersfield won 8-7 on pens (att: 52,100). Losing semi-finalists: MK Dons and Stevenage. **League 2: Crewe** 2 Cheltenham 0 (att: 24,029). Losing semi-finalists: Southend and Torquay

2013: Championship: Crystal Palace 1 Watford 0 (att: 82,025). Losing semi-finalists: Brighton and Leicester. **League 1: Yeovil** 2 Brentford 1 (att: 41,955). Losing semi-finalists: Sheffield Utd and Swindon. **League 2: Bradford** 3 Northampton 0 (att: 47,127). Losing semi-finalists: Burton and Cheltenham

HISTORY OF THE PLAY-OFFS

Play-off matches were introduced by the Football League to decide final promotion and relegation issues at the end of season 1986-87. A similar series styled 'Test Matches' had operated between Divisions One and Two for six seasons from 1893-98, and was abolished when both divisions were increased from 16 to 18 clubs.

Eighty-eight years later, the play-offs were back in vogue. In the first three seasons (1987-88-89), the Finals were played home-and-away, and since they were made one-off matches in 1990, they have featured regularly in Wembley's spring calendar, until the old stadium closed its doors and the action switched to the Millennium Stadium in Cardiff in 2001.

Through the years, these have been the ups and downs of the play-offs:

1987: Initially, the 12 clubs involved comprised the one that finished directly above those relegated in Divisions One, Two and Three and the three who followed the sides automatically promoted in each section. Two of the home-and-away Finals went to neutral-ground replays, in which **Charlton** clung to First Division status by denying Leeds promotion while **Swindon** beat Gillingham to complete their climb from Fourth Division to Second in successive seasons, via the play-offs, Sunderland fell into the Third and Bolton into Division Four, both for the first time. **Aldershot** went up after finishing only sixth in Division Four; in their Final, they beat Wolves, who had finished nine points higher and missed automatic promotion by one point.

1988: Chelsea were relegated from the First Division after losing on aggregate to **Middlesbrough**, who had finished third in Division Two. So Middlesbrough, managed by Bruce Rioch, completed the rise from Third Division to First in successive seasons, only two years after their very existence had been threatened by the bailiffs. Also promoted via the play-offs: **Walsall** from Division Three and **Swansea** from the Fourth. Relegated, besides Chelsea: Sheffield Utd (to Division Three) and Rotherham (to Division Four).

1989: After two seasons of promotion-relegation play-offs, the system was changed to involve the four clubs who had just missed automatic promotion. That format has remained. Steve Coppell's **Crystal Palace**, third in Division Two, returned to the top flight after eight years, beating Blackburn 4-3 on aggregate after extra time. Similarly, **Port Vale** confirmed third place in Division Three with promotion via the play-offs. For **Leyton Orient**, promotion seemed out of the question in Division Four when they stood 15th on March 1. But eight wins and a draw in the last nine home games swept them to sixth in the final table, and two more home victories in the play-offs completed their season in triumph.

1990: The play-off Finals now moved to Wembley over three days of the Spring Holiday weekend. On successive afternoons, **Cambridge Utd** won promotion from Division Four and **Notts Co** from the Third. Then, on Bank Holiday Monday, the biggest crowd for years at a Football League fixture (72,873) saw Ossie Ardiles' **Swindon** beat Sunderland 1-0 to reach the First Division for the first time. A few weeks later, however, Wembley losers **Sunderland** were promoted instead, by default; Swindon were found guilty of "financial irregularities" and stayed in Division Two.

1991: Again, the season's biggest League crowd (59,940) gathered at Wembley for the First Division Final in which **Notts Co** (having missed promotion by one point) still fulfilled their ambition, beating Brighton 3-1. In successive years, County had climbed from Third Division to First via the play-offs – the first club to achieve double promotion by this route. Bolton were denied automatic promotion in Division Three on goal difference, and lost at Wembley to an extra-time goal by **Tranmere**. The Fourth Division Final made history, with Blackpool beaten 5-4 on penalties by **Torquay** – first instance of promotion being decided by a shoot-out. In the table, Blackpool had finished seven points ahead of Torquay.

1992: Wembley that Spring Bank Holiday was the turning point in the history of **Blackburn**. Bolstered by Kenny Dalglish's return to management and owner Jack Walker's millions, they beat Leicester 1-0 by Mike Newell's 45th-minute penalty to achieve their objective – a place in the new Premier League. Newell, who also missed a second-half penalty, had recovered from a broken leg just in time for the play-offs. In the Fourth Division Final **Blackpool** (denied by penalties the previous year) this time won a shoot-out 4-3 against Scunthorpe., who were unlucky in the play-offs for the fourth time in five years. **Peterborough** climbed out of the Third Division for the first time, beating Stockport County 2-1 at Wembley.

1993: The crowd of 73,802 at Wembley to see **Swindon** beat Leicester 4-3 in the First Division Final was 11,000 bigger than that for the FA Cup Final replay between Arsenal and Sheffield Wed Leicester rallied from three down to 3-3 before Paul Bodin's late penalty wiped away **Swindon**'s bitter memories of three years earlier, when they were denied promotion after winning at Wembley. In the Third Division Final, **York** beat Crewe 5-3 in a shoot-out after a 1-1 draw, and in the Second Division decider, **WBA** beat Port Vale 3-0. That was tough on Vale, who had finished third in the table with 89 points – the highest total never to earn promotion in any division. They had beaten Albion twice in the League, too.

1994: Wembley's record turn-out of 158,586 spectators at the three Finals started with a crowd of 40,109 to see Martin O'Neill's **Wycombe** beat Preston 4-2. They thus climbed from Conference to Second Division with successive promotions. **Burnley**'s 2-1 victory in the Second Division Final was marred by the sending-off of two Stockport players, and in the First Division decider **Leicester** came from behind to beat Derby Co and end the worst Wembley record of any club. They had lost on all six previous appearances there – four times in the FA Cup Final and in the play-offs of 1992 and 1993.

1995: Two months after losing the Coca-Cola Cup Final to Liverpool, Bruce Rioch's **Bolton** were back at Wembley for the First Division play-off Final. From two goals down to Reading in front of a crowd of 64,107, they returned to the top company after 15 years, winning 4-3 with two extra-time goals. **Huddersfield** ended the first season at their new £15m. home with promotion to the First Division via a 2-1 victory against Bristol Rov – manager Neil Warnock's third play-off success (after two with Notts Co). Of the three clubs who missed automatic promotion by one place, only **Chesterfield** achieved it in the play-offs, comfortably beating Bury 2-0.

1996: Under new manager Martin O'Neill (a Wembley play-off winner with Wycombe in 1994), **Leicester** returned to the Premiership a year after leaving it. They had finished fifth in the table, but in the Final came from behind to beat third-placed Crystal Palace by Steve Claridge's shot in the last seconds of extra time. In the Second Division **Bradford City** came sixth, nine points behind Blackpool (3rd), but beat them (from two down in the semi-final first leg) and then clinched promotion by 2-0 v Notts County at Wembley. It was City's greatest day since they won the Cup in 1911. **Plymouth Argyle** beat Darlington in the Third Division Final to earn promotion a year after being relegated. It was manager Neil Warnock's fourth play-off triumph in seven seasons after two with Notts County (1990 and 1991) and a third with Huddersfield in 1995.

1997: High drama at Wembley as **Crystal Palace** left it late against Sheffield Utd in the First Division play-off final. The match was scoreless until the last 10 seconds when David Hopkin lobbed Blades' keeper Simon Tracey from 25 yards to send the Eagles back to the Premiership after two seasons of Nationwide action. In the Second Division play-off final, **Crewe** beat Brentford 1-0 courtesy of a Shaun Smith goal. **Northampton** celebrated their first Wembley appearance with a 1-0 victory over Swansea thanks to John Frain's injury-time free-kick in the Third Division play-off final.

1998: In one of the finest games ever seen at Wembley, **Charlton** eventually triumphed 7-6 on penalties over Sunderland. For Charlton, Wearside-born Clive Mendonca scored a hat-trick and Richard Rufus his first career goal in a match that lurched between joy and despair for both sides as it ended 4-4. Sunderland defender Michael Gray's superb performance ill deserved to end with his weakly struck spot kick being saved by Sasa Ilic. In the Third Division, the penalty spot also had a role to play, as **Colchester**'s David Gregory scored the only goal to defeat Torquay, while in the Second Division a Kevin Donovan goal gave **Grimsby** victory over Northampton.

1999: Elton John, watching via a personal satellite link in Seattle, saw his **Watford** side overcome Bolton 2-0 to reach the Premiership. Against technically superior opponents, Watford prevailed with application and teamwork. They also gave Bolton a lesson in finishing through match-winners by Nick Wright and Allan Smart. **Manchester City** staged a remarkable comeback to win the Second Division Final after trailing to goals by Carl Asaba and Robert Taylor for Gillingham. Kevin Horlock and Paul Dickov scored in stoppage time and City went on to win on penalties. A goal by Spaniard Alex Calvo-Garcia earned **Scunthorpe** a 1-0 success against Leyton Orient in the Third Division Final.

2000: After three successive play-off failures, **Ipswich** finally secured a place in the Premiership. They overcame the injury loss of leading scorer David Johnson to beat Barnsley 4-2 with goals by 36-year-old Tony Mowbray, Marcus Stewart and substitutes Richard Naylor and Martijn Reuser. With six minutes left of extra-time in the Second Division Final, **Gillingham** trailed Wigan 2-1. But headers by 38-year-old player-coach Steve Butler and fellow substitute Andy Thomson gave them a 3-2 victory. Andy Clarke, approaching his 33rd birthday, scored the only goal of the Third Division decider for **Peterborough** against Darlington.

2001: Bolton, unsuccessful play-off contenders in the two previous seasons, made no mistake at the third attempt. They flourished in the new surroundings of the Millennium Stadium to beat Preston 3-0 with goals by Gareth Farrelly, Michael Ricketts – his 24th of the season – and Ricardo Gardner to reach the Premiership. **Walsall**, relegated 12 months earlier, scored twice in a three-minute spell of extra time to win 3-2 against Reading in the Second Division Final, while **Blackpool** capped a marked improvement in the second half of the season by overcoming Leyton Orient 4-2 in the Third Division Final.

2002: Holding their nerve to win a penalties shoot-out 4-2, **Birmingham** wiped away the memory of three successive defeats in the semi-finals of the play-offs to return to the top division after an absence of 16 years. Substitute Darren Carter completed a fairy-tale first season as a professional by scoring the fourth spot-kick against Norwich. **Stoke** became the first successful team to come from the south dressing room in 12 finals since football was adopted by the home of Welsh rugby, beating Brentford 2-0 in the Second Division Final with Deon Burton's strike and a Ben Burgess own goal. Julian Alsop's 26th goal of the season helped **Cheltenham** defeat

League newcomers Rushden & Diamonds 3-1 in the Third Division decider.

2003: Wolves benefactor Sir Jack Hayward finally saw his £60m investment pay dividends when the club he first supported as a boy returned to the top flight after an absence of 19 years by beating Sheffield Utd 3-0. It was also a moment to savour for manager Dave Jones, who was forced to leave his previous club Southampton because of child abuse allegations, which were later found to be groundless. **Cardiff**, away from the game's second tier for 18 years, returned with an extra-time winner from substitute Andy Campbell against QPR after a goalless 90 minutes in the Division Two Final. **Bournemouth**, relegated 12 months earlier, became the first team to score five in the end-of-season deciders, beating Lincoln 5-2 in the Division Three Final.

2004: Three tight, tense Finals produced only two goals, the lowest number since the Play-offs were introduced. One of them, scored by Neil Shipperley, gave **Crystal Palace** victory over West Ham, the much-travelled striker tapping in a rebound after Stephen Bywater parried Andy Johnson's shot. It completed a remarkable transformation for Crystal Palace, who were 19th in the table when Iain Dowie left Oldham to become their manager. **Brighton** made an immediate return to Division One in a poor game against Bristol City which looked set for extra-time until Leon Knight netted his 27th goal of the campaign from the penalty spot after 84 minutes. **Huddersfield** also went back up at the first attempt, winning the Division Three Final in a penalty shoot-out after a goalless 120 minutes against Mansfield.

2005: Goals were few and far between for Bobby Zamora during **West Ham**'s Championship season – but what a difference in the Play-offs. The former Brighton and Tottenham striker scored three times in the 4-2 aggregate win over Ipswich in the semi-finals and was on the mark again with the only goal against Preston at the Millennium Stadium. **Sheffield Wed** were eight minute away from defeat against Hartlepool in the League One decider when Steven MacLean made it 2-2 from the penalty spot and they went on to win 4-2 in extra-time. **Southend**, edged out of an automatic promotion place, won the League Two Final 2-0 against Lincoln, Freddy Eastwood scoring their first in extra-time and making the second for Duncan Jupp. **Carlisle** beat Stevenage 1-0 with a goal by Peter Murphy in the Conference Final to regain their League place 12 months after being relegated.

2006: From the moment Marlon King scored his 22nd goal of the season to set up a 3-0 win over Crystal Palace in the semi-final first leg, **Watford** had the conviction of a team going places. Sure enough, they went on to beat Leeds just as comfortably in the final. Jay DeMerit, who was playing non-league football 18 months earlier, headed his side in front. James Chambers fired in a shot that hit a post and went in off goalkeeper Neil Sullivan. Then Darius Henderson put away a penalty after King was brought down by Shaun Derry, the man whose tackle had ended Boothroyd's playing career at the age of 26. **Barnsley** beat Swansea on penalties in the League One Final, Nick Colgan making the vital save from Alan Tate, while Steve Guinan's goal earned **Cheltenham** a 1-0 win over Grimsby in the League Two Final. **Hereford** returned to the Football League after a nine-year absence with Ryan Green's extra-time winner against Halifax in the Conference Final.

2007: Record crowds, plenty of goals and a return to Wembley for the finals made for some eventful and entertaining matches. Stephen Pearson, signed from Celtic for £650,000 in the January transfer window, took **Derby** back to the Premier League after an absence of five seasons with a 61st minute winner, his first goal for the club, against accumulated West Bromwich Albion. It was third time lucky for manager Billy Davies, who had led Preston into the play-offs, without success, in the two previous seasons. **Blackpool** claimed a place in the game's second tier for the first time for 30 years by beating Yeovil 2-0 – their tenth successive victory in a remarkable end-of-season run. Richard Walker took his tally for the season to 23 with two goals for **Bristol Rov**, who beat Shrewsbury 3-1 in the League Two Final. Sammy McIlroy, who led Macclesfield into the league in 1997, saw his Morecambe side fall behind in the Conference Final against Exeter, but they recovered to win 2-1.

2008: Wembley has produced some unlikely heroes down the years, but rarely one to match 39-year-old Dean Windass. The **Hull** striker took his home-town club into the top-flight for the

first time with the only goal of the Championship Final against Bristol City – and it was a goal fit to grace any game. In front of a record crowd for the final of 86,703, Fraizer Campbell, his 20-year-old partner up front, picked out Windass on the edge of the penalty box and a sweetly-struck volley flew into the net. **Doncaster**, who like Hull faced an uncertain future a few years earlier, beat Leeds 1-0 in the League One Final with a header by James Hayer from Brian Stock's corner. Jim Gannon had lost four Wembley finals with **Stockport** as a player, but his first as manager brought a 3-2 win against Rochdale in the League Two Final with goals by Anthony Pilkington and Liam Dickinson and a Nathan Stanton own goal. Exeter's 1-0 win over Cambridge United in the Conference Final took them back into the Football League after an absence of five years.

2009: Delight for Burnley, back in the big time after 33 years thanks to a fine goal from 20 yards by Wade Elliott, and for their town which became the smallest to host Premier League football. Despair for Sheffield Utd, whose bid to regain a top-flight place ended with two players, Jamie Ward and Lee Hendrie, sent off by referee Mike Dean. Martyn Woolford capped a man-of-the-match performance with an 85th minute winner for Scunthorpe, who beat Millwall 3-2 to make an immediate return to the Championship, Matt Sparrow having scored their first two goals. Gillingham also went back up at the first attempt, beating Shrewsbury with Simeon Jackson's header seconds from the end of normal time in the League Two Final. Torquay returned to the Football League after a two-year absence by beating Cambridge United 2-0 in the Conference Final.

2010: Blackpool, under the eccentric yet shrewd Ian Holloway, claimed the big prize two years almost to the day after the manager was sacked from his previous job at Leicester. On a scorching afternoon, with temperatures reaching 106 degrees, they twice came back from a goal down to draw level against Cardiff through Charlie Adam and Gary Taylor-Fletcher, then scored what proved to be the winner through Brett Ormerod at the end of a pulsating first half. **Millwall**, beaten in five previous play-offs, reached the Championship with the only goal of the game against Swindon from captain Paul Robinson. **Dagenham & Redbridge** defeated Rotherham 3-2 in the League Two Final, Jon Nurse scoring the winner 20 minutes from the end. **Oxford** returned to the Football League after an absence of four years with a 3-1 over York in the Conference Final.

2011: Scott Sinclair scored a hat-trick as **Swansea** reached the top flight, just eight years after almost going out of the Football League. Two of his goals came from the penalty spot as Reading were beaten 4-2 in the Championship Final, with Stephen Dobbie netting their other goal. The day after his father's side lost to Barcelona in the Champions League Final, Darren Ferguson led **Peterborough** back to the Championship at the first attempt with goals by Tommy Rowe, Craig Mackail-Smith and Grant McCann in the final 12 minutes against Huddersfield. John Mousinho scored the only one of the League Two Final for **Stevenage**, who won a second successive promotion by beating Torquay. **AFC Wimbledon**, formed by supporters in 2002 after the former FA Cup-winning club relocated to Milton Keynes, completed their rise from the Combined Counties to the Football League by winning a penalty shoot-out against Luton after a goalless draw in the Conference Final.

2012: West Ham were third in the Championship and second best to Blackpool in the final. But they passed the post first at Wembley, thanks to an 87th minute goal from Ricardo Vaz Te which gave Sam Allardyce's side a 2-1 victory. Allardyce brought the Portuguese striker to Upton Park from Barnsley for £500,000 – a fee dwarfed by the millions his goal was worth to the club. Goalkeepers took centre stage in the League One Final, with **Huddersfield** and Sheffield United still locked in a marathon shoot-out after a goalless 120 minutes. Alex Smithies put the 21st penalty past his opposite number Steve Simonsen, who then drove over the crossbar to give Huddersfield victory by 8-7. Nick Powell, 18, lit up the League Two Final with a spectacular volley as **Crewe** beat Cheltenham 2-0. **York** regained a Football League place after an absence of eight years by beating Luton 2-1 in the Conference decider.

2013: Veteran Kevin Phillips, a loser in three previous finals, came off the bench to fire **Crystal Palace** into the Premier League with an extra-time penalty. Wilfried Zaha was brought

down by Marco Cassetti and 39-year-old Phillips showed nerves of steel to convert the spot-kick. A goalline clearance by Joel Ward then denied Fernando Forestieri as Watford sought an equaliser. **Yeovil** upset the odds by reaching the Championship for the first time. They defeated Brentford 2-1, Paddy Madden scoring his 23rd goal of the season and on-loan Dan Burn adding the second. **Bradford**, back at Wembley three months after their Capital One Cup adventure, swept aside Northampton 3-0 in the League Two Final with goals from James Hanson, Rory McArdle and Nahki Wells. **Newport** returned to the Football League after a 25-year absence by defeating Wrexham 2-0 in the Conference Final.

Year	Matches	Agg. Att
1987	20	310,000
1988	19	305,817
1989	18	234,393
1990	15	291,428
1991	15	266,442
1992	15	277,684
1993	15	319,907
1994	15	314,817
1995	15	295,317
1996	15	308,515
1997	15	309,085
1998	15	320,795
1999	15	372,969
2000	15	333,999
2001	15	317,745
2002	15	327,894
2003	15	374,461
2004	15	388,675
2005	15	353,330
2006	15	340,804
2007	15	405,278 (record)
2008	15	382,032
2009	15	380,329
2010	15	370,055
2011	15	310,998
2012	15	332,930
2013	15	346,062
2014	15	307,011

THE THINGS THEY SAY...

'English football is an oil tanker that needs turning. We have gone from 70 per cent English players in the Premier League to 30% and it's still falling. If that continues, we won't have a chance in hell in future tournaments. We have got to stop that decline' – **Greg Dyke**, chairman of the FA.

'It was a heat-of-the-moment thing and I massively regret it. I apologised to him, to everyone at Hull and in particular to our own fans' – **Alan Pardew**, Newcastle manager, after headbutting Hull midfielder David Meyler in a touchline confrontation.

'People tell me this is the business end of the season, but the business end is every game' – **Sean Dyche**, Burnley manager, as his team closed in on promotion to the Premier League.

ENGLISH HONOURS LIST

PREMIER LEAGUE

	First	Pts	Second	Pts	Third	Pts
1992–3a	Manchester Utd	84	Aston Villa	74	Norwich	72
1993–4a	Manchester Utd	92	Blackburn	84	Newcastle	77
1994–5a	Blackburn	89	Manchester Utd	88	Nottm Forest	77
1995–6b	Manchester Utd	82	Newcastle	78	Liverpool	71
1996–7b	Manchester Utd	75	Newcastle	68	Arsenal	68
1997–8b	Arsenal	78	Manchester Utd	77	Liverpool	65
1998–9b	Manchester Utd	79	Arsenal	78	Chelsea	75
1999–00b	Manchester Utd	91	Arsenal	73	Leeds	69
2000–01b	Manchester Utd	80	Arsenal	70	Liverpool	69
2001–02b	Arsenal	87	Liverpool	80	Manchester Utd	77
2002–03b	Manchester Utd	83	Arsenal	78	Newcastle	69
2003–04b	Arsenal	90	Chelsea	79	Manchester Utd	75
2004–05b	Chelsea	95	Arsenal	83	Manchester Utd	77
2005–06b	Chelsea	91	Manchester Utd	83	Liverpool	82
2006–07b	Manchester Utd	89	Chelsea	83	Liverpool	68
2007–08b	Manchester Utd	87	Chelsea	85	Arsenal	83
2008-09b	Manchester Utd	90	Liverpool	86	Chelsea	83
2009–10b	Chelsea	86	Manchester Utd	85	Arsenal	75
2010–11b	Manchester Utd	80	Chelsea	71	Manchester City	71
2011–12b	*Manchester City	89	Manchester Ud	89	Arsenal	70
2012–13b	Manchester Utd	89	Manchester City	78	Chelsea	75
2013–14b	Manchester City	86	Liverpool	84	Chelsea	82

* won on goal difference. Maximum points: a, 126; b, 114

FOOTBALL LEAGUE

FIRST DIVISION

1992–3	Newcastle	96	West Ham	88	††Portsmouth	88
1993–4	Crystal Palace	90	Nottm Forest	83	††Millwall	74
1994–5	Middlesbrough	82	††Reading	79	Bolton	77
1995–6	Sunderland	83	Derby	79	††Crystal Palace	75
1996–7	Bolton	98	Barnsley	80	††Wolves	76
1997–8	Nottm Forest	94	Middlesbrough	91	††Sunderland	90
1998–9	Sunderland	105	Bradford City	87	††Ipswich	86
1999–00	Charlton	91	Manchester City	89	Ipswich	87
2000–01	Fulham	101	Blackburn	91	Bolton	87
2001–02	Manchester City	99	WBA	89	††Wolves	86
2002–03	Portsmouth	98	Leicester	92	††Sheffield Utd	80
2003–04	Norwich	94	WBA	86	††Sunderland	79

CHAMPIONSHIP

2004–05	Sunderland	94	Wigan	87	††Ipswich	85
2005–06	Reading	106	Sheffield Utd	90	Watford	81
2006–07	Sunderland	88	Birmingham	86	Derby	84
2007–08	WBA	81	Stoke	79	Hull	75
2008–09	Wolves	90	Birmingham	83	††Sheffield Utd	80
2009–10	Newcastle	102	WBA	91	††Nottm Forest	79
2010–11	QPR	88	Norwich	84	Swansea	80
2011–12	Reading	89	Southampton	88	West Ham	86
2012–13	Cardiff	87	Hull	79	††Watford	77
2013-14	Leicester	102	Burnley	93	††Derby	85

Maximum points: 138 ††Not promoted after play-offs

SECOND DIVISION

Year						
1992–3	Stoke	93	Bolton	90	††Port Vale	89
1993–4	Reading	89	Port Vale	88	††Plymouth Argyle	85
1994–5	Birmingham	89	††Brentford	85	††Crewe	83
1995–6	Swindon	92	Oxford Utd	83	††Blackpool	82
1996–7	Bury	84	Stockport	82	††Luton	78
1997–8	Watford	88	Bristol City	85	Grimsby	72
1998–9	Fulham	101	Walsall	87	Manchester City	82
1999–00	Preston	95	Burnley	88	Gillingham	85
2000–01	Millwall	93	Rotherham	91	††Reading	86
2001–02	Brighton	90	Reading	84	††Brentford	83
2002–03	Wigan	100	Crewe	86	††Bristol City	83
2003–04	Plymouth Argyle	90	QPR	83	††Bristol City	82

LEAGUE ONE

Year						
2004–05	Luton	98	Hull	86	††Tranmere	79
2005–06	Southend	82	Colchester	79	††Brentford	76
2006–07	Scunthorpe	91	Bristol City	85	Blackpool	83
2007–08	Swansea	92	Nottm Forest	82	Doncaster	80
2008–09	Leicester	96	Peterborough	89	††MK Dons	87
2009–10	Norwich	95	Leeds	86	Millwall	85
2010–11	Brighton	95	Southampton	92	††Huddersfield	87
2011–12	Charlton	101	Sheffield Wed	93	††Sheffield Utd	90
2012–13	Doncaster	84	Bournemouth	83	††Brentford	79
2013–14	Wolves	103	Brentford	94	††Leyton Orient	86

Maximum points: 138 †† Not promoted after play–offs

THIRD DIVISION

Year						
1992–3a	Cardiff	83	Wrexham	80	Barnet	79
1993–4a	Shrewsbury	79	Chester	74	Crewe	73
1994–5a	Carlisle	91	Walsall	83	Chesterfield	81
1995–6b	Preston	86	Gillingham	83	Bury	79
1996–7b	Wigan	87	Fulham	87	Carlisle	84
1997–8b	Notts Co	99	Macclesfield	82	Lincoln	75
1998–9b	Brentford	85	Cambridge Utd	81	Cardiff	80
1999–00b	Swansea	85	Rotherham	84	Northampton	82
2000–01b	Brighton	92	Cardiff	82	*Chesterfield	80
2001–02b	Plymouth Argyle	102	Luton	97	Mansfield	79
2002–03b	Rushden & D	87	Hartlepool Utd	85	Wrexham	84
2003–04b	Doncaster	92	Hull	88	Torquay	81

* Deducted 9 points for financial irregularities

LEAGUE TWO

Year						
2004–05b	Yeovil	83	Scunthorpe	80	Swansea	80
2005–06b	Carlisle	86	Northampton	83	Leyton Orient	81
2006–07b	Walsall	89	Hartlepool	88	Swindon	85
2007–08b	MK Dons	97	Peterborough	92	Hereford	88
2008–09b	Brentford	85	Exeter	79	Wycombe	78
2009–10b	Notts Co	93	Bournemouth	83	Rochdale	82
2010–11b	Chesterfield	86	Bury	81	Wycombe	80
2011–12b	Swindon	93	Shrewsbury	88	Crawley	84
2012–13b	Gillingham	83	Rotherham	79	Port Vale	78
2013–14b	Chesterfield	84	Scunthorpe	81	Rochdale	81

Maximum points: a, 126; b, 138;

FOOTBALL LEAGUE 1888–1992

1888–89*a*	Preston	40	Aston Villa	29	Wolves	28
1889–90*a*	Preston	33	Everton	31	Blackburn	27
1890–1*a*	Everton	29	Preston	27	Notts Co	26
1891–2*b*	Sunderland	42	Preston	37	Bolton	36

OLD FIRST DIVISION

1892–3*c*	Sunderland	48	Preston	37	Everton	36
1893–4*c*	Aston Villa	44	Sunderland	38	Derby	36
1894–5*c*	Sunderland	47	Everton	42	Aston Villa	39
1895–6*c*	Aston Villa	45	Derby	41	Everton	39
1896–7*c*	Aston Villa	47	Sheffield Utd	36	Derby	36
1897–8*c*	Sheffield Utd	42	Sunderland	39	Wolves	35
1898–9*d*	Aston Villa	45	Liverpool	43	Burnley	39
1899–1900*d*	Aston Villa	50	Sheffield Utd	48	Sunderland	41
1900–1*d*	Liverpool	45	Sunderland	43	Notts Co	40
1901–2*d*	Sunderland	44	Everton	41	Newcastle	37
1902–3*d*	The Wednesday	42	Aston Villa	41	Sunderland	41
1903–4*d*	The Wednesday	47	Manchester City	44	Everton	43
1904–5*d*	Newcastle	48	Everton	47	Manchester City	46
1905–6*e*	Liverpool	51	Preston	47	The Wednesday	44
1906–7*e*	Newcastle	51	Bristol City	48	Everton	45
1907–8*e*	Manchester Utd	52	Aston Villa	43	Manchester City	43
1908–9*e*	Newcastle	53	Everton	46	Sunderland	44
1909–10*e*	Aston Villa	53	Liverpool	48	Blackburn	45
1910–11*e*	Manchester Utd	52	Aston Villa	51	Sunderland	45
1911–12*e*	Blackburn	49	Everton	46	Newcastle	44
1912–13*e*	Sunderland	54	Aston Villa	50	Sheffield Wed	49
1913–14*e*	Blackburn	51	Aston Villa	44	Middlesbrough	43
1914–15*e*	Everton	46	Oldham	45	Blackburn	43
1919–20*f*	WBA	60	Burnley	51	Chelsea	49
1920–1*f*	Burnley	59	Manchester City	54	Bolton	52
1921–2*f*	Liverpool	57	Tottenham	51	Burnley	49
1922–3*f*	Liverpool	60	Sunderland	54	Huddersfield	53
1923–4*f*	*Huddersfield	57	Cardiff	57	Sunderland	53
1924–5*f*	Huddersfield	58	WBA	56	Bolton	55
1925–6*f*	Huddersfield	57	Arsenal	52	Sunderland	48
1926–7*f*	Newcastle	56	Huddersfield	51	Sunderland	49
1927–8*f*	Everton	53	Huddersfield	51	Leicester	48
1928–9*f*	Sheffield Wed	52	Leicester	51	Aston Villa	50
1929–30*f*	Sheffield Wed	60	Derby	50	Manchester City	47
1930–1*f*	Arsenal	66	Aston Villa	59	Sheffield Wed	52
1931–2*f*	Everton	56	Arsenal	54	Sheffield Wed	50
1932–3*f*	Arsenal	58	Aston Villa	54	Sheffield Wed	51
1933–4*f*	Arsenal	59	Huddersfield	56	Tottenham	49
1934–5*f*	Arsenal	58	Sunderland	54	Sheffield Wed	49
1935–6*f*	Sunderland	56	Derby	48	Huddersfield	48
1936–7*f*	Manchester City	57	Charlton	54	Arsenal	52
1937–8*f*	Arsenal	52	Wolves	51	Preston	49
1938–9*f*	Everton	59	Wolves	55	Charlton	50
1946–7*f*	Liverpool	57	Manchester Utd	56	Wolves	56
1947–8*f*	Arsenal	59	Manchester Utd	52	Burnley	52
1948–9*f*	Portsmouth	58	Manchester Utd	53	Derby	53

1949–50*f*	*Portsmouth	53	Wolves	53	Sunderland	52
1950–1*f*	Tottenham	60	Manchester Utd	56	Blackpool	50
1951–2*f*	Manchester Utd	57	Tottenham	53	Arsenal	53
1952–3*f*	*Arsenal	54	Preston	54	Wolves	51
1953–4*f*	Wolves	57	WBA	53	Huddersfield	51
1954–5*f*	Chelsea	52	Wolves	48	Portsmouth	48
1955–6*f*	Manchester Utd	60	Blackpool	49	Wolves	49
1956–7*f*	Manchester Utd	64	Tottenham	56	Preston	56
1957–8*f*	Wolves	64	Preston	59	Tottenham	51
1958–9*f*	Wolves	61	Manchester Utd	55	Arsenal	50
1959–60*f*	Burnley	55	Wolves	54	Tottenham	53
1960–1*f*	Tottenham	66	Sheffield Wed	58	Wolves	57
1961–2*f*	Ipswich	56	Burnley	53	Tottenham	52
1962–3*f*	Everton	61	Tottenham	55	Burnley	54
1963–4*f*	Liverpool	57	Manchester Utd	53	Everton	52
1964–5*f*	*Manchester Utd	61	Leeds	61	Chelsea	56
1965–6*f*	Liverpool	61	Leeds	55	Burnley	55
1966–7*f*	Manchester Utd	60	Nottm Forest	56	Tottenham	56
1967–8*f*	Manchester City	58	Manchester Utd	56	Liverpool	55
1968–9*f*	Leeds	67	Liverpool	61	Everton	57
1969–70*f*	Everton	66	Leeds	57	Chelsea	55
1970–1*f*	Arsenal	65	Leeds	64	Tottenham	52
1971–2*f*	Derby	58	Leeds	57	Liverpool	57
1972–3*f*	Liverpool	60	Arsenal	57	Leeds	53
1973–4*f*	Leeds	62	Liverpool	57	Derby	48
1974–5*f*	Derby	53	Liverpool	51	Ipswich	51
1975–6*f*	Liverpool	60	QPR	59	Manchester Utd	56
1976–7*f*	Liverpool	57	Manchester City	56	Ipswich	52
1977–8*f*	Nottm Forest	64	Liverpool	57	Everton	55
1978–9*f*	Liverpool	68	Nottm Forest	60	WBA	59
1979–80*f*	Liverpool	60	Manchester Utd	58	Ipswich	53
1980–1*f*	Aston Villa	60	Ipswich	56	Arsenal	53
1981–2*g*	Liverpool	87	Ipswich	83	Manchester Utd	78
1982–3*g*	Liverpool	82	Watford	71	Manchester Utd	70
1983–4*g*	Liverpool	80	Southampton	77	Nottm Forest	74
1984–5*g*	Everton	90	Liverpool	77	Tottenham	77
1985–6*g*	Liverpool	88	Everton	86	West Ham	84
1986–7*g*	Everton	86	Liverpool	77	Tottenham	71
1987–8*h*	Liverpool	90	Manchester Utd	81	Nottm Forest	73
1988–9*j*	††Arsenal	76	Liverpool	76	Nottm Forest	64
1989–90*j*	Liverpool	79	Aston Villa	70	Tottenham	63
1990–1*j*	Arsenal	83	Liverpool	76	Crystal Palace	69
1991–2*g*	Leeds	82	Manchester Utd	78	Sheffield Wed	75

Maximum points: *a*, 44; *b*, 52; *c*, 60; *d*, 68; *e*, 76; *f*, 84; *g*, 126; *h*, 120; *j*, 114

*Won on goal average †Won on goal diff ††Won on goals scored No comp 1915–19 –1939–46

OLD SECOND DIVISION 1892–1992

1892–3*a*	Small Heath	36	Sheffield Utd	35	Darwen	30
1893–4*b*	Liverpool	50	Small Heath	42	Notts Co	39
1894–5*c*	Bury	48	Notts Co	39	Newton Heath	38
1895–6*c*	*Liverpool	46	Manchester City	46	Grimsby	42
1896–7*c*	Notts Co	42	Newton Heath	39	Grimsby	38
1897–8*c*	Burnley	48	Newcastle	45	Manchester City	39
1898–9*d*	Manchester City	52	Glossop	46	Leicester Fosse	45

Season						
1899–1900d	The Wednesday	54	Bolton	52	Small Heath	46
1900–1d	Grimsby	49	Small Heath	48	Burnley	44
1901–2d	WBA	55	Middlesbrough	51	Preston	42
1902–3d	Manchester City	54	Small Heath	51	Woolwich Arsenal	48
1903–4d	Preston	50	Woolwich Arsenal	49	Manchester Utd	48
1904–5d	Liverpool	58	Bolton	56	Manchester Utd	53
1905–6e	Bristol City	66	Manchester Utd	62	Chelsea	53
1906–7e	Nottm Forest	60	Chelsea	57	Leicester Fosse	48
1907–8e	Bradford City	54	Leicester Fosse	52	Oldham	50
1908–9e	Bolton	52	Tottenham	51	WBA	51
1909–10e	Manchester City	54	Oldham	53	Hull	53
1910–11e	WBA	53	Bolton	51	Chelsea	49
1911–12e	*Derby	54	Chelsea	54	Burnley	52
1912–13e	Preston	53	Burnley	50	Birmingham	46
1913–14e	Notts Co	53	Bradford PA	49	Woolwich Arsenal	49
1914–15e	Derby	53	Preston	50	Barnsley	47
1919–20f	Tottenham	70	Huddersfield	64	Birmingham	56
1920–1f	*Birmingham	58	Cardiff	58	Bristol City	51
1921–2f	Nottm Forest	56	Stoke	52	Barnsley	52
1922–3f	Notts Co	53	West Ham	51	Leicester	51
1923–4f	Leeds	54	Bury	51	Derby	51
1924–5f	Leicester	59	Manchester Utd	57	Derby	55
1925–6f	Sheffield Wed	60	Derby	57	Chelsea	52
1926–7f	Middlesbrough	62	Portsmouth	54	Manchester City	54
1927–8f	Manchester City	59	Leeds	57	Chelsea	54
1928–9f	Middlesbrough	55	Grimsby	53	Bradford City	48
1929–30f	Blackpool	58	Chelsea	55	Oldham	53
1930–1f	Everton	61	WBA	54	Tottenham	51
1931–2f	Wolves	56	Leeds	54	Stoke	52
1932–3f	Stoke	56	Tottenham	55	Fulham	50
1933–4f	Grimsby	59	Preston	52	Bolton	51
1934–5f	Brentford	61	Bolton	56	West Ham	56
1935–6f	Manchester Utd	56	Charlton	55	Sheffield Utd	52
1936–7f	Leicester	56	Blackpool	55	Bury	52
1937–8f	Aston Villa	57	Manchester Utd	53	Sheffield Utd	53
1938–9f	Blackburn	55	Sheffield Utd	54	Sheffield Wed	53
1946–7f	Manchester City	62	Burnley	58	Birmingham	55
1947–8f	Birmingham	59	Newcastle	56	Southampton	52
1948–9f	Fulham	57	WBA	56	Southampton	55
1949–50f	Tottenham	61	Sheffield Wed	52	Sheffield Utd	52
1950–1f	Preston	57	Manchester City	52	Cardiff	50
1951–2f	Sheffield Wed	53	Cardiff	51	Birmingham	51
1952–3f	Sheffield Utd	60	Huddersfield	58	Luton	52
1953–4f	*Leicester	56	Everton	56	Blackburn	55
1954–5f	*Birmingham	54	Luton	54	Rotherham	54
1955–6f	Sheffield Wed	55	Leeds	52	Liverpool	48
1956–7f	Leicester	61	Nottm Forest	54	Liverpool	53
1957–8f	West Ham	57	Blackburn	56	Charlton	55
1958–9f	Sheffield Wed	62	Fulham	60	Sheffield Utd	53
1959–60f	Aston Villa	59	Cardiff	58	Liverpool	50
1960–1f	Ipswich	59	Sheffield Utd	58	Liverpool	52
1961–2f	Liverpool	62	Leyton Orient	54	Sunderland	53
1962–3f	Stoke	53	Chelsea	52	Sunderland	52
1963–4f	Leeds	63	Sunderland	61	Preston	56

1964–5f	Newcastle	57	Northampton	56	Bolton	50
1965–6f	Manchester City	59	Southampton	54	Coventry	53
1966–7f	Coventry	59	Wolves	58	Carlisle	52
1967–8f	Ipswich	59	QPR	58	Blackpool	58
1968–9f	Derby	63	Crystal Palace	56	Charlton	50
1969–70f	Huddersfield	60	Blackpool	53	Leicester	51
1970–1f	Leicester	59	Sheffield Utd	56	Cardiff	53
1971–2f	Norwich	57	Birmingham	56	Millwall	55
1972–3f	Burnley	62	QPR	61	Aston Villa	50
1973–4f	Middlesbrough	65	Luton	50	Carlisle	49
1974–5f	Manchester Utd	61	Aston Villa	58	Norwich	53
1975–6f	Sunderland	56	Bristol City	53	WBA	53
1976–7f	Wolves	57	Chelsea	55	Nottm Forest	52
1977–8f	Bolton	58	Southampton	57	Tottenham	56
1978–9f	Crystal Palace	57	Brighton	56	Stoke	56
1979–80f	Leicester	55	Sunderland	54	Birmingham	53
1980–1f	West Ham	66	Notts Co	53	Swansea	50
1981–2g	Luton	88	Watford	80	Norwich	71
1982–3g	QPR	85	Wolves	75	Leicester	70
1983–4g	†Chelsea	88	Sheffield Wed	88	Newcastle	80
1984–5g	Oxford Utd	84	Birmingham	82	Manchester City	74
1985–6g	Norwich	84	Charlton	77	Wimbledon	76
1986–7g	Derby	84	Portsmouth	78	††Oldham	75
1987–8h	Millwall	82	Aston Villa	78	Middlesbrough	78
1988–9j	Chelsea	99	Manchester City	82	Crystal Palace	81
1989–90j	†Leeds	85	Sheffield Utd	85	†† Newcastle	80
1990–1j	Oldham	88	West Ham	87	Sheffield Wed	82
1991–2j	Ipswich	84	Middlesbrough	80	†† Derby	78

Maximum points: *a*, 44; *b*, 56; *c*, 60; *d*, 68; *e*, 76; *f*, 84; *g*, 126; *h*, 132; *j*, 138 * Won on goal average † Won on goal difference †† Not promoted after play–offs

THIRD DIVISION 1958–92

1958–9	Plymouth Argyle	62	Hull	61	Brentford	57
1959–60	Southampton	61	Norwich	59	Shrewsbury	52
1960–1	Bury	68	Walsall	62	QPR	60
1961–2	Portsmouth	65	Grimsby	62	Bournemouth	59
1962–3	Northampton	62	Swindon	58	Port Vale	54
1963–4	*Coventry	60	Crystal Palace	60	Watford	58
1964–5	Carlisle	60	Bristol City	59	Mansfield	59
1965–6	Hull	69	Millwall	65	QPR	57
1966–7	QPR	67	Middlesbrough	55	Watford	54
1967–8	Oxford Utd	57	Bury	56	Shrewsbury	55
1968–9	*Watford	64	Swindon	64	Luton	61
1969–70	Orient	62	Luton	60	Bristol Rov	56
1970–1	Preston	61	Fulham	60	Halifax	56
1971–2	Aston Villa	70	Brighton	65	Bournemouth	62
1972–3	Bolton	61	Notts Co	57	Blackburn	55
1973–4	Oldham	62	Bristol Rov	61	York	61
1974–5	Blackburn	60	Plymouth Argyle	59	Charlton	55
1975–6	Hereford	63	Cardiff	57	Millwall	56
1976–7	Mansfield	64	Brighton	61	Crystal Palace	59
1977–8	Wrexham	61	Cambridge Utd	58	Preston	56
1978–9	Shrewsbury	61	Watford	60	Swansea	60
1979–80	Grimsby	62	Blackburn	59	Sheffield Wed	58
1980–1	Rotherham	61	Barnsley	59	Charlton	59
†1981–2	**Burnley	80	Carlisle	80	Fulham	78

†1982–3	Portsmouth	91	Cardiff	86	Huddersfield	82
†1983–4	Oxford Utd	95	Wimbledon	87	Sheffield Utd	83
†1984–5	Bradford City	94	Millwall	90	Hull	87
†1985–6	Reading	94	Plymouth Argyle	87	Derby	84
†1986–7	Bournemouth	97	Middlesbrough	94	Swindon	87
†1987–8	Sunderland	93	Brighton	84	Walsall	82
†1988–9	Wolves	92	Sheffield Utd	84	Port Vale	84
†1989–90	Bristol Rov	93	Bristol City	91	Notts Co	87
†1990–1	Cambridge Utd	86	Southend	85	Grimsby	83
†1991–2	Brentford	82	Birmingham	81	††Huddersfield	78

* Won on goal average ** Won on goal difference † Maximum points 138 (previously 92) †† Not promoted after play–offs

FOURTH DIVISION 1958–92

1958–9	Port Vale	64	Coventry	60	York	60	Shrewsbury	58
1959–60	Walsall	65	Notts Co	60	Torquay	60	Watford	57
1960–1	Peterborough	66	Crystal Palace	64	Northampton	60	Bradford PA	60
1961–2	Millwall	56	Colchester	55	Wrexham	53	Carlisle	52
1962–3	Brentford	62	Oldham	59	Crewe	59	Mansfield	57
1963–4	*Gillingham	60	Carlisle	60	Workington	59	Exeter	58
1964–5	Brighton	63	Millwall	62	York	62	Oxford Utd	61
1965–6	*Doncaster	59	Darlington	59	Torquay	58	Colchester	58
1966–7	Stockport	64	Southport	59	Barrow	59	Tranmere	58
1967–8	Luton	66	Barnsley	61	Hartlepool Utd	60	Crewe	58
1968–9	Doncaster	59	Halifax	57	Rochdale	56	Bradford City	56
1969–70	Chesterfield	64	Wrexham	61	Swansea	60	Port Vale	59
1970–1	Notts Co	69	Bournemouth	60	Oldham	59	York	56
1971–2	Grimsby	63	Southend	60	Brentford	59	Scunthorpe	57
1972–3	Southport	62	Hereford	58	Cambridge Utd	57	Aldershot	56
1973–4	Peterborough	65	Gillingham	62	Colchester	60	Bury	59
1974–5	Mansfield	68	Shrewsbury	62	Rotherham	58	Chester	57
1975–6	Lincoln	74	Northampton	68	Reading	60	Tranmere	58
1976–7	Cambridge Utd	65	Exeter	62	Colchester	59	Bradford City	59
1977–8	Watford	71	Southend	60	Swansea	56	Brentford	59
1978–9	Reading	65	Grimsby	61	Wimbledon	61	Barnsley	61
1979–80	Huddersfield	66	Walsall	64	Newport	61	Portsmouth	60
1980–1	Southend	67	Lincoln	65	Doncaster	56	Wimbledon	55
†1981–2	Sheffield Utd	96	Bradford City	91	Wigan	91	Bournemouth	88
†1982–3	Wimbledon	98	Hull	90	Port Vale	88	Scunthorpe	83
†1983–4	York	101	Doncaster	85	Reading	82	Bristol City	82
†1984–5	Chesterfield	91	Blackpool	86	Darlington	85	Bury	84
†1985–6	Swindon	102	Chester	84	Mansfield	81	Port Vale	79
†1986–7	Northampton	99	Preston	90	Southend	80	††Wolves	79
†1987–8	Wolves	90	Cardiff	85	Bolton	78	††Scunthorpe	77
†1988–9	Rotherham	82	Tranmere	80	Crewe	78	††Scunthorpe	77
†1989–90	Exeter	89	Grimsby	79	Southend	75	††Stockport	74
†1990–1	Darlington	83	Stockport	82	Hartlepool Utd	82	Peterborough	80
1991–2a	Burnley	83	Rotherham	77	Mansfield	77	Blackpool	76

* Won on goal average Maximum points: †, 138; a, 126; previously 92 †† Not promoted after play–offs

THIRD DIVISION – SOUTH 1920–58

1920–1a	Crystal Palace	59	Southampton	54	QPR	53
1921–2a	*Southampton	61	Plymouth Argyle	61	Portsmouth	53
1922–3a	Bristol City	59	Plymouth Argyle	53	Swansea	53
1923–4a	Portsmouth	59	Plymouth Argyle	55	Millwall	54
1924–5a	Swansea	57	Plymouth Argyle	56	Bristol City	53
1925–6a	Reading	57	Plymouth Argyle	56	Millwall	53

1926–7a	Bristol City	62	Plymouth Argyle	60	Millwall	56
1927–8a	Millwall	65	Northampton	55	Plymouth Argyle	53
1928–9a	*Charlton	54	Crystal Palace	54	Northampton	52
1929–30a	Plymouth Argyle	68	Brentford	61	QPR	51
1930–31a	Notts Co	59	Crystal Palace	51	Brentford	50
1931–2a	Fulham	57	Reading	55	Southend	53
1932–3a	Brentford	62	Exeter	58	Norwich	57
1933–4a	Norwich	61	Coventry	54	Reading	54
1934–5a	Charlton	61	Reading	53	Coventry	51
1935–6a	Coventry	57	Luton	56	Reading	54
1936–7a	Luton	58	Notts Co	56	Brighton	53
1937–8a	Millwall	56	Bristol City	55	QPR	53
1938–9a	Newport	55	Crystal Palace	52	Brighton	49
1946–7a	Cardiff	66	QPR	57	Bristol City	51
1947–8a	QPR	61	Bournemouth	57	Walsall	51
1948–9a	Swansea	62	Reading	55	Bournemouth	52
1949–50a	Notts Co	58	Northampton	51	Southend	51
1950–1d	Nottm Forest	70	Norwich	64	Reading	57
1951–2d	Plymouth Argyle	66	Reading	61	Norwich	61
1952–3d	Bristol Rov	64	Millwall	62	Northampton	62
1953–4d	Ipswich	64	Brighton	61	Bristol City	56
1954–5d	Bristol City	70	Leyton Orient	61	Southampton	59
1955–6d	Leyton Orient	66	Brighton	65	Ipswich	64
1956–7d	*Ipswich	59	Torquay	59	Colchester	58
1957–8d	Brighton	60	Brentford	58	Plymouth Argyle	58

THIRD DIVISION – NORTH 1921–58

1921–2b	Stockport	56	Darlington	50	Grimsby	50
1922–3b	Nelson	51	Bradford PA	47	Walsall	46
1923–4a	Wolves	63	Rochdale	62	Chesterfield	54
1924–5a	Darlington	58	Nelson	53	New Brighton	53
1925–6a	Grimsby	61	Bradford PA	60	Rochdale	59
1926–7a	Stoke	63	Rochdale	58	Bradford PA	57
1927–8a	Bradford PA	63	Lincoln	55	Stockport	54
1928–9a	Bradford City	63	Stockport	62	Wrexham	52
1929–30a	Port Vale	67	Stockport	63	Darlington	50
1930–1a	Chesterfield	58	Lincoln	57	Wrexham	54
1931–2c	*Lincoln	57	Gateshead	57	Chester	50
1932–3a	Hull	59	Wrexham	57	Stockport	54
1933–4a	Barnsley	62	Chesterfield	61	Stockport	59
1934–5a	Doncaster	57	Halifax	55	Chester	54
1935–6a	Chesterfield	60	Chester	55	Tranmere	54
1936–7a	Stockport	60	Lincoln	57	Chester	53
1937–8a	Tranmere	56	Doncaster	54	Hull	53
1938–9a	Barnsley	67	Doncaster	56	Bradford City	52
1946–7a	Doncaster	72	Rotherham	64	Chester	56
1947–8a	Lincoln	60	Rotherham	59	Wrexham	50
1948–9a	Hull	65	Rotherham	62	Doncaster	50
1949–50a	Doncaster	55	Gateshead	53	Rochdale	51
1950–1d	Rotherham	71	Mansfield	64	Carlisle	62
1951–2d	Lincoln	69	Grimsby	66	Stockport	59
1952–3d	Oldham	59	Port Vale	58	Wrexham	56
1953–4d	Port Vale	69	Barnsley	58	Scunthorpe	57
1954–5d	Barnsley	65	Accrington	61	Scunthorpe	58
1955–6d	Grimsby	68	Derby	63	Accrington	59
1956–7d	Derby	63	Hartlepool Utd	59	Accrington	58
1957–8d	Scunthorpe	66	Accrington	59	Bradford City	57

Maximum points: a, 84; b, 76; c, 80; d, 92 * Won on goal average

TITLE WINNERS

PREMIER LEAGUE

Manchester Utd............... 13
Arsenal 3
Chelsea 3
Manchester City................. 2
Blackburn 1

FOOTBALL LEAGUE CHAMPIONSHIP

Reading............................. 2
Sunderland 2
Cardiff............................... 1
Leicester........................... 1
Newcastle 1
QPR 1
WBA.................................. 1
Wolves............................... 1

DIV 1 (NEW)

Sunderland 2
Bolton 1
Brighton 1
Charlton............................ 1
Crystal Palace 1
Fulham.............................. 1
Manchester City................ 1
Middlesbrough 1
Newcastle 1
Norwich............................. 1
Nottm Forest 1
Portsmouth 1

DIV 1 (ORIGINAL)

Liverpool........................... 18
Arsenal 10
Everton.............................. 9
Aston Villa 7
Manchester Utd................. 7
Sunderland 6
Newcastle 4
Sheffield Wed.................... 4
Huddersfield 3
Leeds 3
Wolves.............................. 3
Blackburn 2
Burnley.............................. 2

Derby 2
Manchester City................. 2
Portsmouth 2
Preston 2
Tottenham......................... 2
Chelsea 1
Ipswich.............................. 1
Nottm Forest 1
Sheffield Utd...................... 1
WBA.................................. 1

LEAGUE ONE

Brighton 1
Charlton............................ 1
Doncaster 1
Leicester........................... 1
Luton 1
Norwich............................. 1
Scunthorpe 1
Southend 1
Swansea 1
Wolves.............................. 1

DIV 2 (NEW)

Birmingham 1
Brighton 1
Bury 1
Chesterfield....................... 1
Fulham.............................. 1
Millwall.............................. 1
Plymouth Argyle 1
Preston 1
Reading............................. 1
Stoke 1
Swindon 1
Watford 1
Wigan 1
Notts Co 1

DIV 2 (ORIGINAL)

Leicester........................... 6
Manchester City................. 6
Sheffield Wed.................... 5
Birmingham 4
Derby 4
Liverpool........................... 4
Ipswich.............................. 3
Leeds 3

Middlesbrough 3
Notts County 3
Preston 3
Aston Villa 2
Bolton 2
Burnley.............................. 2
Chelsea 2
Grimsby............................. 2
Manchester Utd................. 2
Norwich............................. 2
Nottm Forest 2
Stoke 2
Tottenham......................... 2
WBA.................................. 2
West Ham 2
Wolves.............................. 2
Blackburn 1
Blackpool.......................... 1
Bradford City..................... 1
Brentford 1
Bristol City 1
Bury 1
Coventry 1
Crystal Palace 1
Everton.............................. 1
Fulham.............................. 1
Huddersfield 1
Luton 1
Millwall.............................. 1
Newcastle 1
Oldham 1
Oxford Utd 1
QPR 1
Sheffield Utd...................... 1
Sunderland 1

LEAGUE TWO

Chesterfield....................... 2
Brentford 1
Carlisle 1
Gillingham 1
MK Dons 1
Notts County 1
Swindon 1
Walsall 1
Yeovil 1

APPLICATIONS FOR RE–ELECTION (System discontinued 1987)

14	Hartlepool	7	Walsall	4	Norwich
12	Halifax	7	Workington	3	Aldershot
11	Barrow	7	York	3	Bradford City
11	Southport	6	Stockport	3	Crystal Palace
10	Crewe	5	Accrington	3	Doncaster
10	Newport	5	Gillingham	3	Hereford
10	Rochdale	5	Lincoln	3	Merthyr
8	Darlington	5	New Brighton	3	Swindon
8	Exeter	4	Bradford PA	3	Torquay
7	Chester	4	Northampton	3	Tranmere

2	Aberdare	2	Oldham	1	Cardiff
2	Ashington	2	QPR	1	Carlisle
2	Bournemouth	2	Rotherham	1	Charlton
2	Brentford	2	Scunthorpe	1	Mansfield
2	Colchester	2	Southend	1	Port Vale
2	Durham	2	Watford	1	Preston
2	Gateshead	1	Blackpool	1	Shrewsbury
2	Grimsby	1	Brighton	1	Swansea
2	Millwall	1	Bristol Rov	1	Thames
2	Nelson	1	Cambridge Utd	1	Wrexham

RELEGATED CLUBS (TO 1992)

1892–3	In Test matches, Darwen and Sheffield Utd won promotion in place of Accrington and Notts Co
1893–4	Tests, Liverpool and Small Heath won promotion Darwen and Newton Heath relegated
1894–5	After Tests, Bury promoted, Liverpool relegated
1895–6	After Tests, Liverpool promoted, Small Heath relegated
1896–7	After Tests, Notts Co promoted, Burnley relegated
1897–8	Test system abolished after success of Burnley and Stoke, League extended Blackburn and Newcastle elected to First Division

Automatic promotion and relegation introduced

FIRST DIVISION TO SECOND DIVISION

1898–9	Bolton, Sheffield Wed
1899–00	Burnley, Glossop
1900–1	Preston, WBA
1901–2	Small Heath, Manchester City
1902–3	Grimsby, Bolton
1903–4	Liverpool, WBA
1904–5	League extended Bury and Notts Co, two bottom clubs in First Division, re–elected
1905–6	Nottm Forest, Wolves
1906–7	Derby, Stoke
1907–8	Bolton, Birmingham
1908–9	Manchester City, Leicester Fosse
1909–10	Bolton, Chelsea
1910–11	Bristol City, Nottm Forest
1911–12	Preston, Bury
1912–13	Notts Co, Woolwich Arsenal
1913–14	Preston, Derby
1914–15	Tottenham, *Chelsea
1919–20	Notts Co, Sheffield Wed
1920–1	Derby, Bradford PA
1921–2	Bradford City, Manchester Utd
1922–3	Stoke, Oldham
1923–4	Chelsea, Middlesbrough
1924–5	Preston, Nottm Forest
1925–6	Manchester City, Notts Co
1926–7	Leeds, WBA
1927–8	Tottenham, Middlesbrough
1928–9	Bury, Cardiff
1929–30	Burnley, Everton
1930–1	Leeds, Manchester Utd
1931–2	Grimsby, West Ham
1932–3	Bolton, Blackpool
1933–4	Newcastle, Sheffield Utd
1934–5	Leicester, Tottenham
1935–6	Aston Villa, Blackburn
1936–7	Manchester Utd, Sheffield Wed
1937–8	Manchester City, WBA

1938–9	Birmingham, Leicester
1946–7	Brentford, Leeds
1947–8	Blackburn, Grimsby
1948–9	Preston, Sheffield Utd
1949–50	Manchester City, Birmingham
1950–1	Sheffield Wed, Everton
1951–2	Huddersfield, Fulham
1952–3	Stoke, Derby
1953–4	Middlesbrough, Liverpool
1954–5	Leicester, Sheffield Wed
1955–6	Huddersfield, Sheffield Utd
1956–7	Charlton, Cardiff
1957–8	Sheffield Wed, Sunderland
1958–9	Portsmouth, Aston Villa
1959–60	Luton, Leeds
1960–61	Preston, Newcastle
1961–2	Chelsea, Cardiff
1962–3	Manchester City, Leyton Orient
1963–4	Bolton, Ipswich
1964–5	Wolves, Birmingham
1965–6	Northampton, Blackburn
1966–7	Aston Villa, Blackpool
1967–8	Fulham, Sheffield Utd
1968–9	Leicester, QPR
1969–70	Sheffield Wed, Sunderland
1970–1	Burnley, Blackpool
1971–2	Nottm Forest, Huddersfield
1972–3	WBA, Crystal Palace
1973–4	Norwich, Manchester Utd, Southampton
1974–5	Chelsea, Luton, Carlisle
1975–6	Sheffield Utd, Burnley, Wolves
1976–7	Tottenham, Stoke, Sunderland
1977–8	Leicester, West Ham, Newcastle
1978–9	QPR, Birmingham, Chelsea
1979–80	Bristol City, Derby, Bolton
1980–1	Norwich, Leicester, Crystal Palace
1981–2	Leeds, Wolves, Middlesbrough
1982–3	Manchester City, Swansea, Brighton
1983–4	Birmingham, Notts Co, Wolves
1984–5	Norwich, Sunderland, Stoke
1985–6	Ipswich, Birmingham, WBA
1986–7	Leicester, Manchester City, Aston Villa
1987–8	Chelsea**, Portsmouth, Watford, Oxford Utd
1988–9	Middlesbrough, West Ham, Newcastle
1989–90	Sheffield Wed, Charlton, Millwall
1990–1	Sunderland, Derby
1991–2	Luton, Notts Co, West Ham

* Subsequently re–elected to First Division when League extended after the war
** Relegated after play–offs

SECOND DIVISION TO THIRD DIVISION

1920–1	Stockport
1921–2	Bradford City, Bristol City
1922–3	Rotherham, Wolves
1923–4	Nelson, Bristol City
1924–5	Crystal Palace, Coventry
1925–6	Stoke, Stockport
1926–7	Darlington, Bradford City
1927–8	Fulham, South Shields
1928–9	Port Vale, Clapton Orient

1929–30	Hull, Notts County
1930–1	Reading, Cardiff
1931–2	Barnsley, Bristol City
1932–3	Chesterfield, Charlton
1933–4	Millwall, Lincoln
1934–5	Oldham, Notts Co
1935–6	Port Vale, Hull
1936–7	Doncaster, Bradford City
1937–8	Barnsley, Stockport
1938–9	Norwich, Tranmere
1946–7	Swansea, Newport
1947–8	Doncaster, Millwall
1948–9	Nottm Forest, Lincoln
1949–50	Plymouth Argyle, Bradford PA
1950–1	Grimsby, Chesterfield
1951–2	Coventry, QPR
1952–3	Southampton, Barnsley
1953–4	Brentford, Oldham
1954–5	Ipswich, Derby
1955–6	Plymouth Argyle, Hull
1956–7	Port Vale, Bury
1957–8	Doncaster, Notts Co
1958–9	Barnsley, Grimsby
1959–60	Bristol City, Hull
1960–1	Lincoln, Portsmouth
1961–2	Brighton, Bristol Rov
1962–3	Walsall, Luton
1963–4	Grimsby, Scunthorpe
1964–5	Swindon, Swansea
1965–6	Middlesbrough, Leyton Orient
1966–7	Northampton, Bury
1967–8	Plymouth Argyle, Rotherham
1968–9	Fulham, Bury
1969–70	Preston, Aston Villa
1970–1	Blackburn, Bolton
1971–2	Charlton, Watford
1972–3	Huddersfield, Brighton
1973–4	Crystal Palace, Preston, Swindon
1974–5	Millwall, Cardiff, Sheffield Wed
1975–6	Portsmouth, Oxford Utd, York
1976–7	Carlisle, Plymouth Argyle, Hereford
1977–8	Hull, Mansfield, Blackpool
1978–9	Sheffield Utd, Millwall, Blackburn
1979–80	Fulham, Burnley, Charlton
1980–1	Preston, Bristol City, Bristol Rov
1981–2	Cardiff, Wrexham, Orient
1982–3	Rotherham, Burnley, Bolton
1983–4	Derby, Swansea, Cambridge Utd
1984–5	Notts Co, Cardiff, Wolves
1985–6	Carlisle, Middlesbrough, Fulham
1986–7	Sunderland**, Grimsby, Brighton
1987–8	Sheffield Utd**, Reading, Huddersfield
1988–9	Shrewsbury, Birmingham, Walsall
1989–90	Bournemouth, Bradford City, Stoke
1990–1	WBA, Hull
1991–2	Plymouth Argyle, Brighton, Port Vale

** Relegated after play-offs

THIRD DIVISION TO FOURTH DIVISION

| 1958–9 | Rochdale, Notts Co, Doncaster, Stockport |
| 1959–60 | Accrington, Wrexham, Mansfield, York |

1960–1	Chesterfield, Colchester, Bradford City, Tranmere
1961–2	Newport, Brentford, Lincoln, Torquay
1962–3	Bradford PA, Brighton, Carlisle, Halifax
1963–4	Millwall, Crewe, Wrexham, Notts Co
1964–5	Luton, Port Vale, Colchester, Barnsley
1965–6	Southend, Exeter, Brentford, York
1966–7	Doncaster, Workington, Darlington, Swansea
1967–8	Scunthorpe, Colchester, Grimsby, Peterborough (demoted)
1968–9	Oldham, Crewe, Hartlepool Utd, Northampton
1969–70	Bournemouth, Southport, Barrow, Stockport
1970–1	Gillingham, Doncaster, Bury, Reading
1971–2	Mansfield, Barnsley, Torquay, Bradford City
1972–3	Scunthorpe, Swansea, Brentford, Rotherham
1973–4	Cambridge Utd, Shrewsbury, Rochdale, Southport
1974–5	Bournemouth, Watford, Tranmere, Huddersfield
1975–6	Aldershot, Colchester, Southend, Halifax
1976–7	Reading, Northampton, Grimsby, York
1977–8	Port Vale, Bradford City, Hereford, Portsmouth
1978–9	Peterborough, Walsall, Tranmere, Lincoln
1979–80	Bury, Southend, Mansfield, Wimbledon
1980–1	Sheffield Utd, Colchester, Blackpool, Hull
1981–2	Wimbledon, Swindon, Bristol City, Chester
1982–3	Reading, Wrexham, Doncaster, Chesterfield
1983–4	Scunthorpe, Southend, Port Vale, Exeter
1984–5	Burnley, Orient, Preston, Cambridge Utd
1985–6	Lincoln, Cardiff, Wolves, Swansea
1986–7	Bolton**, Carlisle, Darlington, Newport
1987–8	Doncaster, York, Grimsby, Rotherham**
1988–9	Southend, Chesterfield, Gillingham, Aldershot
1989–90	Cardiff, Northampton, Blackpool, Walsall
1990–1	Crewe, Rotherham, Mansfield
1991–2	Bury, Shrewsbury, Torquay, Darlington

** Relegated after plays–offs

DEMOTED FROM FOURTH DIVISION TO CONFERENCE

1987	Lincoln
1988	Newport
1989	Darlington
1990	Colchester
1991	No demotion
1992	No demotion

DEMOTED FROM THIRD DIVISION TO CONFERENCE

1993	Halifax
1994–6	No demotion
1997	Hereford
1998	Doncaster
1999	Scarborough
2000	Chester
2001	Barnet
2002	Halifax
2003	Exeter, Shrewsbury
2004	Carlisle, York

DEMOTED FROM LEAGUE TWO TO CONFERENCE

2005	Kidderminster, Cambridge Utd
2006	Oxford Utd, Rushden & Diamonds
2007	Boston, Torquay

2008	Mansfield, Wrexham
2009	Chester Luton
2010	Grimsby, Darlington
2011	Lincoln, Stockport
2012	Hereford, Macclesfield
2013	Barnet, Aldershot
2014	Bristol Rov, Torquay

RELEGATED CLUBS (SINCE 1993)

1993
Premier League to Div 1: Crystal Palace, Middlesbrough, Nottm Forest
Div 1 to Div 2: Brentford, Cambridge Utd, Bristol Rov
Div 2 to Div 3: Preston, Mansfield, Wigan, Chester

1994
Premier League to Div 1: Sheffield Utd, Oldham, Swindon
Div 1 to Div 2: Birmingham, Oxford Utd, Peterborough
Div 2 to Div 3: Fulham, Exeter, Hartlepool Utd, Barnet

1995
Premier League to Div 1: Crystal Palace, Norwich, Leicester, Ipswich
Div 1 to Div 2: Swindon, Burnley, Bristol City, Notts Co
Div 2 to Div 3: Cambridge Utd, Plymouth Argyle, Cardiff, Chester, Leyton Orient

1996
Premier League to Div 1: Manchester City, QPR, Bolton
Div 1 to Div 2: Millwall, Watford, Luton
Div 2 to Div 3: Carlisle, Swansea, Brighton, Hull

1997
Premier League to Div 1: Sunderland, Middlesbrough, Nottm Forest
Div 1 to Div 2: Grimsby, Oldham, Southend
Div 2 to Div 3: Peterborough, Shrewsbury, Rotherham, Notts Co

1998
Premier League to Div 1: Bolton, Barnsley, Crystal Palace
Div 1 to Div 2: Manchester City, Stoke, Reading
Div 2 to Div 3: Brentford, Plymouth Argyle, Carlisle, Southend

1999
Premier League to Div 1: Charlton, Blackburn, Nottm Forest
Div 1 to Div 2: Bury, Oxford Utd, Bristol City
Div 2 to Div 3: York, Northampton, Lincoln, Macclesfield

2000
Premier League to Div 1: Wimbledon, Sheffield Wed, Watford
Div 1 to Div 2: Walsall, Port Vale, Swindon
Div 2 to Div 3. Cardiff, Blackpool, Scunthorpe, Chesterfield

2001
Premier League to Div 1: Manchester City, Coventry, Bradford City
Div 1 to Div 2: Huddersfield, QPR, Tranmere
Div 2 to Div 3: Bristol Rov, Luton, Swansea, Oxford Utd

2002
Premier League to Div 1: Ipswich, Derby, Leicester
Div 1 to Div 2: Crewe, Barnsley, Stockport

Div 2 to Div 3: Bournemouth, Bury, Wrexham, Cambridge Utd

2003
Premier League to Div 1: West Ham, WBA, Sunderland
Div 1 to Div 2: Sheffield Wed, Brighton, Grimsby
Div 2 to Div 3: Cheltenham, Huddersfield, Mansfield, Northampton

2004
Premier League to Div 1: Leicester, Leeds, Wolves
Div 1 to Div 2: Walsall, Bradford City, Wimbledon
Div 2 to Div 3: Grimsby, Rushden & Diamonds, Notts Co, Wycombe

2005
Premier League to Championship: Crystal Palace, Norwich, Southampton
Championship to League 1: Gillingham, Nottm Forest, Rotherham
League 1 to League 2: Torquay, Wrexham, Peterborough, Stockport

2006
Premier League to Championship: Birmingham, WBA, Sunderland
Championship to League 1: Crewe, Millwall, Brighton
League 1 to League 2: Hartlepool Utd, MK Dons, Swindon, Walsall

2007
Premier League to Championship: Sheffield Utd, Charlton, Watford
Championship to League 1: Southend, Luton, Leeds
League 1 to League 2: Chesterfield, Bradford City, Rotherham, Brentford

2008
Premier League to Championship: Reading, Birmingham, Derby
Championship to League 1: Leicester, Scunthorpe, Colchester
League 1 to League 2: Bournemouth, Gillingham, Port Vale, Luton

2009
Premier League to Championship: Newcastle, Middlesbrough, WBA
Championship to League 1: Norwich, Southampton, Charlton
League 1 to League 2: Northampton, Crewe, Cheltenham, Hereford

2010
Premier League to Championship: Burnley, Hull, Portsmouth
Championship to League 1: Sheffield Wed, Plymouth, Peterborough
League 1 to League 2: Gillingham, Wycombe, Southend, Stockport

2011
Premier League to Championship: Birmingham, Blackpool, West Ham
Championship to League 1: Preston, Sheffield Utd, Scunthorpe
League 1 to League 2: Dagenham & Redbridge, Bristol Rov, Plymouth, Swindon

2012
Premier League to Championship: Bolton, Blackburn, Wolves
Championship to League 1: Portsmouth, Coventry, Doncaster
League 1 to League 2: Wycombe, Chesterfield, Exeter, Rochdale

2013
Premier League to Championship: Wigan, Reading, QPR
Championship to League 1: Peterborough, Wolves, Bristol City
League 1 to League 2: Scunthorpe, Bury, Hartlepool, Portsmouth

2014
Premier League to Championship: Norwich, Fulham, Cardiff
Championship to League 1: Doncaster, Barnsley, Yeovil
League 1 to League 2: Tranmere, Carlisle, Shrewsbury, Stevenage

ANNUAL AWARDS

FOOTBALL WRITERS' ASSOCIATION

Footballer of the Year: 1948 Stanley Matthews (Blackpool); **1949** Johnny Carey (Manchester Utd); **1950** Joe Mercer (Arsenal); **1951** Harry Johnston (Blackpool); **1952** Billy Wright (Wolves); **1953** Nat Lofthouse (Bolton); **1954** Tom Finney (Preston); **1955** Don Revie (Manchester City); **1956** Bert Trautmann (Manchester City); **1957** Tom Finney (Preston); **1958** Danny Blanchflower (Tottenham); **1959** Syd Owen (Luton); **1960** Bill Slater (Wolves); **1961** Danny Blanchflower (Tottenham); **1962** Jimmy Adamson (Burnley); **1963** Stanley Matthews (Stoke); **1964** Bobby Moore (West Ham); **1965** Bobby Collins (Leeds); **1966** Bobby Charlton (Manchester Utd); **1967** Jack Charlton (Leeds); **1968** George Best (Manchester Utd); **1969** Tony Book (Manchester City) & Dave Mackay (Derby) – shared; **1970** Billy Bremner (Leeds); **1971** Frank McLintock (Arsenal); **1972** Gordon Banks (Stoke); **1973** Pat Jennings (Tottenham); **1974** Ian Callaghan (Liverpool); **1975** Alan Mullery (Fulham); **1976** Kevin Keegan (Liverpool); **1977** Emlyn Hughes (Liverpool); **1978** Kenny Burns (Nott'm Forest); **1979** Kenny Dalglish (Liverpool); **1980** Terry McDermott (Liverpool); **1981** Frans Thijssen (Ipswich); **1982** Steve Perryman (Tottenham); **1983** Kenny Dalglish (Liverpool); **1984** Ian Rush (Liverpool); **1985** Neville Southall (Everton); **1986** Gary Lineker (Everton); **1987** Clive Allen (Tottenham); **1988** John Barnes (Liverpool); **1989** Steve Nicol (Liverpool); Special award to the Liverpool players for the compassion shown to bereaved families after the Hillsborough Disaster; **1990** John Barnes (Liverpool); **1991** Gordon Strachan (Leeds); **1992** Gary Lineker (Tottenham); **1993** Chris Waddle (Sheffield Wed); **1994** Alan Shearer (Blackburn); **1995** Jurgen Klinsmann (Tottenham); **1996** Eric Cantona (Manchester Utd); **1997** Gianfranco Zola (Chelsea); **1998** Dennis Bergkamp (Arsenal); **1999** David Ginola (Tottenham); **2000** Roy Keane (Manchester Utd); **2001** Teddy Sheringham (Manchester Utd); **2002** Robert Pires (Arsenal); **2003** Thierry Henry (Arsenal); **2004** Thierry Henry (Arsenal); **2005** Frank Lampard (Chelsea); **2006** Thierry Henry (Arsenal); **2007** Cristiano Ronaldo (Manchester Utd); **2008** Cristiano Ronaldo (Manchester Utd), **2009** Steven Gerrard (Liverpool), **2010** Wayne Rooney (Manchester Utd), **2011** Scott Parker (West Ham), **2012** Robin van Persie (Arsenal), **2013** Gareth Bale (Tottenham), **2014** Luis Suarez (Liverpool)

PROFESSIONAL FOOTBALLERS' ASSOCIATION

Player of the Year: 1974 Norman Hunter (Leeds); **1975** Colin Todd (Derby); **1976** Pat Jennings (Tottenham); **1977** Andy Gray (Aston Villa); **1978** Peter Shilton (Nott'm Forest); **1979** Liam Brady (Arsenal); **1980** Terry McDermott (Liverpool); **1981** John Wark (Ipswich); **1982** Kevin Keegan (Southampton); **1983** Kenny Dalglish (Liverpool); **1984** Ian Rush (Liverpool); **1985** Peter Reid (Everton); **1986** Gary Lineker (Everton); **1987** Clive Allen (Tottenham); **1988** John Barnes (Liverpool); **1989** Mark Hughes (Manchester Utd); **1990** David Platt (Aston Villa); **1991** Mark Hughes (Manchester Utd); **1992** Gary Pallister (Manchester Utd); **1993** Paul McGrath (Aston Villa); **1994** Eric Cantona (Manchester Utd); **1995** Alan Shearer (Blackburn); **1996** Les Ferdinand (Newcastle); **1997** Alan Shearer (Newcastle); **1998** Dennis Bergkamp (Arsenal); **1999** David Ginola (Tottenham); **2000** Roy Keane (Manchester Utd); **2001** Teddy Sheringham (Manchester Utd); **2002** Ruud van Nistelrooy (Manchester Utd); **2003** Thierry Henry (Arsenal); **2004** Thierry Henry (Arsenal); **2005** John Terry (Chelsea); **2006** Steven Gerrard (Liverpool); **2007** Cristiano Ronaldo (Manchester Utd); **2008** Cristiano Ronaldo (Manchester Utd), **2009** Ryan Giggs (Manchester Utd), **2010** Wayne Rooney (Manchester Utd), **2011** Gareth Bale (Tottenham), **2012** Robin van Persie (Arsenal), **2013** Gareth Bale (Tottenham), **2014** Luis Suarez (Liverpool)

Young Player of the Year: 1974 Kevin Beattie (Ipswich); **1975** Mervyn Day (West Ham); **1976** Peter Barnes (Manchester City); **1977** Andy Gray (Aston Villa); **1978** Tony Woodcock (Nott'm Forest); **1979** Cyrille Regis (WBA); **1980** Glenn Hoddle (Tottenham); **1981** Gary Shaw (Aston Villa); **1982** Steve Moran (Southampton); **1983** Ian Rush (Liverpool); **1984** Paul Walsh (Luton); **1985** Mark Hughes (Manchester Utd); **1986** Tony Cottee (West Ham); **1987** Tony

Adams (Arsenal); **1988** Paul Gascoigne (Newcastle); **1989** Paul Merson (Arsenal); **1990** Matthew Le Tissier (Southampton); **1991** Lee Sharpe (Manchester Utd); **1992** Ryan Giggs (Manchester Utd); **1993** Ryan Giggs (Manchester Utd); **1994** Andy Cole (Newcastle); **1995** Robbie Fowler (Liverpool); **1996** Robbie Fowler (Liverpool); **1997** David Beckham (Manchester Utd); **1998** Michael Owen (Liverpool); **1999** Nicolas Anelka (Arsenal); **2000** Harry Kewell (Leeds); **2001** Steven Gerrard (Liverpool); **2002** Craig Bellamy (Newcastle); **2003** Jermaine Jenas (Newcastle); **2004** Scott Parker (Chelsea); **2005** Wayne Rooney (Manchester Utd); **2006** Wayne Rooney (Manchester Utd); **2007** Cristiano Ronaldo (Manchester Utd); **2008** Cesc Fabregas (Arsenal); **2009** Ashley Young (Aston Villa); **2010** James Milner (Aston Villa); **2011** Jack Wilshere (Arsenal), **2012** Kyle Walker (Tottenham), **2013** Gareth Bale (Tottenham), **2014** Eden Hazard (Chelsea)

Merit Awards: 1974 Bobby Charlton & Cliff Lloyd; **1975** Denis Law; **1976** George Eastham; **1977** Jack Taylor; **1978** Bill Shankly; **1979** Tom Finney; **1980** Sir Matt Busby; **1981** John Trollope; **1982** Joe Mercer; **1983** Bob Paisley; **1984** Bill Nicholson; **1985** Ron Greenwood; **1986** England 1966 World Cup-winning team; **1987** Sir Stanley Matthews; **1988** Billy Bonds; **1989** Nat Lofthouse; **1990** Peter Shilton; **1991** Tommy Hutchison; **1992** Brian Clough; **1993** Manchester Utd, 1968 European Champions; Eusebio; **1994** Billy Bingham; **1995** Gordon Strachan; **1996** Pele; **1997** Peter Beardsley; **1998** Steve Ogrizovic; **1999** Tony Ford; **2000** Gary Mabbutt; **2001** Jimmy Hill; **2002** Niall Quinn; **2003** Sir Bobby Robson; **2004** Dario Gradi; **2005** Shaka Hislop; **2006** George Best; **2007** Sir Alex Ferguson; **2008** Jimmy Armfield; **2009** John McDermott, **2010** Lucas Radebe, **2011** Howard Webb, **2012** Graham Alexander, **2013** Eric Harrison/Manchester Utd Class of '92, **2014** Donald Bell (posthumously; only footballer to win Victoria Cross, World War 1)

MANAGER OF THE YEAR (1)

(Chosen by a panel from the governing bodies, media and fans)
1966 Jock Stein (Celtic); **1967** Jock Stein (Celtic); **1968** Matt Busby (Manchester Utd); **1969** Don Revie (Leeds); **1970** Don Revie (Leeds); **1971** Bertie Mee (Arsenal); **1972** Don Revie (Leeds); **1973** Bill Shankly (Liverpool); **1974** Jack Charlton (Middlesbrough); **1975** Ron Saunders (Aston Villa); **1976** Bob Paisley (Liverpool); **1977** Bob Paisley (Liverpool); **1978** Brian Clough (Nott'm Forest); **1979** Bob Paisley (Liverpool); **1980** Bob Paisley (Liverpool); **1981** Ron Saunders (Aston Villa); **1982** Bob Paisley (Liverpool); **1983** Bob Paisley (Liverpool); **1984** Joe Fagan (Liverpool); **1985** Howard Kendall (Everton); **1986** Kenny Dalglish (Liverpool); **1987** Howard Kendall (Everton); **1988** Kenny Dalglish (Liverpool); **1989** George Graham (Arsenal); **1990** Kenny Dalglish (Liverpool); **1991** George Graham (Arsenal); **1992** Howard Wilkinson (Leeds); **1993** Alex Ferguson (Manchester Utd); **1994** Alex Ferguson (Manchester Utd); **1995** Kenny Dalglish (Blackburn); **1996** Alex Ferguson (Manchester Utd); **1997** Alex Ferguson (Manchester Utd); **1998** Arsene Wenger (Arsenal); **1999** Alex Ferguson (Manchester Utd); **2000** Sir Alex Ferguson (Manchester Utd); **2001** George Burley (Ipswich); **2002** Arsene Wenger (Arsenal); **2003** Sir Alex Ferguson (Manchester Utd); **2004** Arsene Wenger (Arsenal); **2005** Jose Mourinho (Chelsea); **2006** Jose Mourinho (Chelsea); **2007** Sir Alex Ferguson (Manchester Utd); **2008** Sir Alex Ferguson (Manchester Utd); **2009** Sir Alex Ferguson (Manchester Utd), **2010** Harry Redknapp (Tottenham), **2011** Sir Alex Ferguson (Manchester Utd), **2012:** Alan Pardew (Newcastle), **2013** Sir Alex Ferguson (Manchester Utd), **2014** Tony Pulis (Crystal Palace)

MANAGER OF THE YEAR (2)

(Chosen by the League Managers' Association)
1993 Dave Bassett (Sheffield Utd); **1994** Joe Kinnear (Wimbledon); **1995** Frank Clark (Nott'm Forest); **1996** Peter Reid (Sunderland); **1997** Danny Wilson (Barnsley); **1998** David Jones (Southampton); **1999** Alex Ferguson (Manchester Utd); **2000** Alan Curbishley (Charlton Athletic); **2001** George Burley (Ipswich); **2002** Arsene Wenger (Arsenal); **2003** David Moyes (Everton); **2004** Arsene Wenger (Arsenal); **2005** David Moyes (Everton); **2006** Steve Coppell (Reading); **2007** Steve Coppell (Reading); **2008** Sir Alex Ferguson (Manchester Utd); **2009**

David Moyes (Everton), **2010** Roy Hodgson (Fulham), **2011** Sir Alex Ferguson (Manchester Utd), **2012**: Alan Pardew (Newcastle), **2013** Sir Alex Ferguson (Manchester Utd), **2014** Brendan Rodgers (Liverpool)

SCOTTISH FOOTBALL WRITERS' ASSOCIATION

Footballer of the Year: 1965 Billy McNeill (Celtic); **1966** John Greig (Rangers); **1967** Ronnie Simpson (Celtic); **1968** Gordon Wallace (Raith); **1969** Bobby Murdoch (Celtic); **1970** Pat Stanton (Hibernian); **1971** Martin Buchan (Aberdeen); **1972** David Smith (Rangers); **1973** George Connelly (Celtic); **1974** World Cup Squad; **1975** Sandy Jardine (Rangers); **1976** John Greig (Rangers); **1977** Danny McGrain (Celtic); **1978** Derek Johnstone (Rangers); **1979** Andy Ritchie (Morton); **1980** Gordon Strachan (Aberdeen); **1981** Alan Rough (Partick Thistle); **1982** Paul Sturrock (Dundee Utd); **1983** Charlie Nicholas (Celtic); **1984** Willie Miller (Aberdeen); **1985** Hamish McAlpine (Dundee Utd); **1986** Sandy Jardine (Hearts); **1987** Brian McClair (Celtic); **1988** Paul McStay (Celtic); **1989** Richard Gough (Rangers); **1990** Alex McLeish (Aberdeen); **1991** Maurice Malpas (Dundee Utd); **1992** Ally McCoist (Rangers); **1993** Andy Goram (Rangers); **1994** Mark Hateley (Rangers); **1995** Brian Laudrup (Rangers); **1996** Paul Gascoigne (Rangers); **1997** Brian Laudrup (Rangers); **1998** Craig Burley (Celtic); **1999** Henrik Larsson (Celtic); **2000** Barry Ferguson (Rangers); **2001** Henrik Larsson (Celtic); **2002** Paul Lambert (Celtic); **2003** Barry Ferguson (Rangers); **2004** Jackie McNamara (Celtic); **2005** John Hartson (Celtic); **2006** Craig Gordon (Hearts); **2007** Shunsuke Nakamura (Celtic); **2008** Carlos Cuellar (Rangers); **2009** Gary Caldwell (Celtic); **2010** David Weir (Rangers), **2011** Emilio Izaguirre (Celtic), **2012** Charlie Mulgrew (Celtic), **2013** Leigh Griffiths (Hibernian), **2014** Kris Commons (Celtic)

PROFESSIONAL FOOTBALLERS' ASSOCIATION SCOTLAND

Player of the Year: 1978 Derek Johnstone (Rangers); **1979** Paul Hegarty (Dundee Utd); **1980** Davie Provan (Celtic); **1981** Mark McGhee (Aberdeen); **1982** Sandy Clarke (Airdrieonians); **1983** Charlie Nicholas (Celtic); **1984** Willie Miller (Aberdeen); **1985** Jim Duffy (Morton); **1986** Richard Gough (Dundee Utd); **1987** Brian McClair (Celtic); **1988** Paul McStay (Celtic); **1989** Theo Snelders (Aberdeen); **1990** Jim Bett (Aberdeen); **1991** Paul Elliott (Celtic); **1992** Ally McCoist (Rangers); **1993** Andy Goram (Rangers); **1994** Mark Hateley (Rangers); **1995** Brian Laudrup (Rangers); **1996** Paul Gascoigne (Rangers); **1997** Paolo Di Canio (Celtic) **1998** Jackie McNamara (Celtic); **1999** Henrik Larsson (Celtic); **2000** Mark Viduka (Celtic); **2001** Henrik Larsson (Celtic); **2002** Lorenzo Amoruso (Rangers); **2003** Barry Ferguson (Rangers); **2004** Chris Sutton (Celtic); **2005** John Hartson (Celtic) and Fernando Ricksen (Rangers); **2006** Shaun Maloney (Celtic); **2007** Shunsuke Nakamura (Celtic); **2008** Aiden McGeady (Celtic); **2009** Scott Brown (Celtic), **2010** Steven Davis (Rangers), **2011** Emilio Izaguirre (Celtic), **2012** Charlie Mulgrew (Celtic), **2013** Michael Higdon (Motherwell), **2014** Kris Commons (Celtic)

Young Player of the Year: 1978 Graeme Payne (Dundee Utd); **1979** Ray Stewart (Dundee Utd); **1980** John McDonald (Rangers); **1981** Charlie Nicholas (Celtic); **1982** Frank McAvennie (St Mirren); **1983** Paul McStay (Celtic); **1984** John Robertson (Hearts); **1985** Craig Levein (Hearts); **1986** Craig Levein (Hearts); **1987** Robert Fleck (Rangers); **1988** John Collins (Hibernian); **1989** Billy McKinlay (Dundee Utd); **1990** Scott Crabbe (Hearts); **1991** Eoin Jess (Aberdeen); **1992** Phil O'Donnell (Motherwell); **1993** Eoin Jess (Aberdeen); **1994** Phil O'Donnell (Motherwell); **1995** Charlie Miller (Rangers); **1996** Jackie McNamara (Celtic); **1997** Robbie Winters (Dundee Utd); **1998** Gary Naysmith (Hearts); **1999** Barry Ferguson (Rangers); **2000** Kenny Miller (Hibernian); **2001** Stilian Petrov (Celtic); **2002** Kevin McNaughton (Aberdeen); **2003** James McFadden (Motherwell); **2004** Stephen Pearson (Celtic); **2005** Derek Riordan (Hibernian); **2006** Shaun Maloney (Celtic); **2007** Steven Naismith (Kilmarnock); **2008** Aiden McGeady (Celtic); **2009** James McCarthy (Hamilton), **2010** Danny Wilson (Rangers), **2011**: David Goodwillie (Dundee Utd), **2012** James Forrest (Celtic), **2013** Leigh Griffiths (Hibernian), **2014** Andy Robertson (Dundee Utd)

SCOTTISH MANAGER OF THE YEAR

1987 Jim McLean (Dundee Utd); **1988** Billy McNeill (Celtic); **1989** Graeme Souness (Rangers); **1990** Andy Roxburgh (Scotland); **1991** Alex Totten (St Johnstone); **1992** Walter Smith (Rangers); **1993** Walter Smith (Rangers); **1994** Walter Smith (Rangers); **1995** Jimmy Nicholl (Raith); **1996** Walter Smith (Rangers); **1997** Walter Smith (Rangers); **1998** Wim Jansen (Celtic); **1999** Dick Advocaat (Rangers); **2000** Dick Advocaat (Rangers); **2001** Martin O'Neill (Celtic); **2002** John Lambie (Partick Thistle); **2003** Alex McLeish (Rangers); **2004** Martin O'Neill (Celtic); **2005** Alex McLeish (Rangers); **2006** Gordon Strachan (Celtic); **2007** Gordon Strachan (Celtic); **2008** Billy Reid (Hamilton); **2009** Csaba Laszlo (Hearts), **2010** Walter Smith (Rangers), **2011:** Mixu Paatelainen (Kilmarnock), **2012** Neil Lennon (Celtic), **2013** Neil Lennon (Celtic), **2014** Derek McInnes (Aberdeen)

EUROPEAN FOOTBALLER OF THE YEAR

1956 Stanley Matthews (Blackpool); **1957** Alfredo di Stefano (Real Madrid); **1958** Raymond Kopa (Real Madrid); **1959** Alfredo di Stefano (Real Madrid); **1960** Luis Suarez (Barcelona); **1961** Omar Sivori (Juventus); **1962** Josef Masopust (Dukla Prague); **1963** Lev Yashin (Moscow Dynamo); **1964** Denis Law (Manchester Utd); **1965** Eusebio (Benfica); **1966** Bobby Charlton (Manchester Utd); **1967** Florian Albert (Ferencvaros); **1968** George Best (Manchester Utd); **1969** Gianni Rivera (AC Milan); **1970** Gerd Muller (Bayern Munich); **1971** Johan Cruyff (Ajax); **1972** Franz Beckenbauer (Bayern Munich); **1973** Johan Cruyff (Barcelona); **1974** Johan Cruyff (Barcelona); **1975** Oleg Blokhin (Dynamo Kiev); **1976** Franz Beckenbauer (Bayern Munich); **1977** Allan Simonsen (Borussia Moenchengladbach); **1978** Kevin Keegan (SV Hamburg); **1979** Kevin Keegan (SV Hamburg); **1980** Karl-Heinz Rummenigge (Bayern Munich); **1981** Karl-Heinz Rummenigge (Bayern Munich); **1982** Paolo Rossi (Juventus); **1983** Michel Platini (Juventus); **1984** Michel Platini (Juventus); **1985** Michel Platini (Juventus); **1986** Igor Belanov (Dynamo Kiev); **1987** Ruud Gullit (AC Milan); **1988** Marco van Basten (AC Milan); **1989** Marco van Basten (AC Milan); **1990** Lothar Matthaus (Inter Milan); **1991** Jean-Pierre Papin (Marseille); **1992** Marco van Basten (AC Milan); **1993** Roberto Baggio (Juventus); **1994** Hristo Stoichkov (Barcelona); **1995** George Weah (AC Milan); **1996** Matthias Sammer (Borussia Dortmund); **1997** Ronaldo (Inter Milan); **1998** Zinedine Zidane (Juventus); **1999** Rivaldo (Barcelona); **2000** Luis Figo (Real Madrid); **2001** Michael Owen (Liverpool); **2002** Ronaldo (Real Madrid); **2003** Pavel Nedved (Juventus); **2004** Andriy Shevchenko (AC Milan); **2005** Ronaldinho (Barcelona); **2006** Fabio Cannavaro (Real Madrid); **2007** Kaka (AC Milan); **2008** Cristiano Ronaldo (Manchester United), **2009** Lionel Messi (Barcelona)

WORLD FOOTBALLER OF YEAR

1991 Lothar Matthaus (Inter Milan and Germany); **1992** Marco van Basten (AC Milan and Holland); **1993** Roberto Baggio (Juventus and Italy); **1994** Romario (Barcelona and Brazil); **1995** George Weah (AC Milan and Liberia); **1996** Ronaldo (Barcelona and Brazil); **1997** Ronaldo (Inter Milan and Brazil); **1998** Zinedine Zidane (Juventus and France); **1999** Rivaldo (Barcelona and Brazil); **2000** Zinedine Zidane (Juventus and France); **2001** Luis Figo (Real Madrid and Portugal); **2002** Ronaldo (Real Madrid and Brazil); **2003** Zinedine Zidane (Real Madrid and France); **2004** Ronaldinho (Barcelona and Brazil); **2005** Ronaldinho (Barcelona and Brazil); **2006** Fabio Cannavaro (Real Madrid and Italy); **2007** Kaka (AC Milan and Brazil); **2008** Cristiano Ronaldo (Manchester United and Portugal), **2009** Lionel Messi (Barcelona and Argentina)

FIFA BALLON D'OR

(replaces European and World Footballer of the Year)
2010: Lionel Messi (Barcelona). **2011** Lionel Messi (Barcelona), **2012** Lionel Messi (Barcelona), **2013** Cristiano Ronaldo (Real Madrid)

FIFA WORLD COACH OF THE YEAR

2010: Jose Mourinho (Inter Milan). **2011** Pep Guardiola (Barcelona), **2012** Vicente del Bosque (Spain), **2013** Jupp Heynckes (Bayern Munich)

PREMIER LEAGUE

REVIEWS, APPEARANCES, SCORERS 2013–14

(Figures in brackets denote appearances as substitute)

ARSENAL

A season which opened on a gloomy note with a home defeat by Aston Villa closed on a high with the club's first trophy for nine years. Aaron Ramsey's goal completed a comeback from 2-0 down against Hull in the FA Cup Final – and begged the question: What else might they have won had the Welshman not missed more than three months of the season with a thigh injury and been joined on the injury list by Theo Walcott and Jack Wilshere? When Ramsey limped out of the Boxing Day victory over West Ham, he had scored 13 times and was the team's most influential player. Six days later, Walcott sustained a cruciate ligament injury, missing the rest of the campaign and the World Cup. Arsenal, who had been top since mid-September, remained there for another month until losing 5-1 to Liverpool. Then, they dropped out of the running when beaten 6-0 by Chelsea. A 17th successive season in the Champions League also came under threat after a 3-0 defeat by Everton, their rivals for fourth place. But, with Ramsey back in action, five straight victories to end the campaign proved decisive. There was also a penalty shoot-out victory over Wigan in an FA Cup semi-final that turned out to be much more demanding than expected. The latest European campaign ended against defending champions Bayern Munich in the first knock-out round, a 2-0 defeat at the Emirates doing the damage.

Akpom C	- (1)	Gnabry S	5 (4)	Podolski L	14 (6)
Arteta M	27 (4)	Jenkinson C	7 (7)	Ramsey A	20 (3)
Bendtner N	1 (8)	Kallstrom K	1 (2)	Rosicky T	17 (10)
Cazorla S	30 (1)	Koscielny L	32	Sagna B	34 (1)
Diaby A	- (1)	Mertesacker P	35	Sanogo Y	- (8)
Fabianski L	1	Miyaichi R	- (1)	Szczesny W	37
Flamini M	18 (9)	Monreal N	13 (10)	Vermaelen T	7 (7)
Gibbs K	24 (4)	Oxlade-Chamberlain A	6 (8)	Walcott T	9 (4)
Giroud O	36	Ozil M	25 (1)	Wilshere J	19 (5)

League goals (68): Giroud 16, Ramsey 10, Podolski 8, Ozil 5, Walcott 5, Cazorla 4, Wilshere 3, Arteta 2, Bendtner 2, Flamini 2, Koscielny 2, Mertesacker 2, Oxlade-Chamberlain 2, Rosicky 2, Gnabry 1, Jenkinson 1, Sagna 1
FA Cup goals (16): Giroud 3, Cazorla 3, Podolski 3, Arteta 1, Koscielny 1, Mertesacker 1, Oxlade-Chamberlain 1, Ozil 1, Ramsey 1, Rosicky 1. **Capital One Cup goals** (1): Eisfeld T 1
Champions League goals (14): Ramsey 5, Giroud 3, Wilshere 2, Gibbs 1, Ozil 1, Podolski 1, Walcott 1
Average home league attendance: 60,013. **Player of Year**: Aaron Ramsey

ASTON VILLA

Villa put an end to one unwanted record but another condemned them to a third successive season spent trying to avoid being dragged into a full-blown relegation struggle. They suffered ten home defeats, the club's worst ever, and an 11th in the final game there could have had serious consequences, with visits to Manchester City and Tottenham to follow. As it was, Ashley Westwood scored the 1,000th Premier League goal at Villa Park and Andreas Weimann added two more for a 3-1 victory over a Hull side with one eye on the FA Cup Final against Arsenal. The win effectively ensured survival, although there remained speculation over owner Randy Lerner's intentions and the future of manager Paul Lambert. Villa's problems had been compounded by a four-month goal drought for Christian Benteke, the previous season's leading scorer, who then missed the last six weeks of the season with a torn achilles tendon. His side did break a sequence of 68 home matches without back-to-back wins, dating back to the start of the 2010-11 season, by beating Norwich 4-1 and Chelsea 1-0. But they slipped back when conceding four goals to

Stoke, Manchester United and Swansesa during a run of six matches without a win. Further conclusive defeats by City and Spurs was followed by Lerner's announcement of his intention to put the club up for sale.

Agbonlahor G 29 (1)	Delph F 33 (1)	Luna A 16 (1)
Albrighton M 9 (10)	El Ahmadi K............. 26 (5)	Okore J 2 (1)
Bacuna L 28 (7)	Grealish J .... - (1)	Robinson C .... - (4)
Baker N 29 (1)	Guzan B 38	Sylla Y 5 (6)
Bennett J 3 (2)	Helenius N .... - (3)	Tonev A 6 (11)
Benteke C 24 (2)	Herd C..........................2	Vlaar R 32
Bertrand R 16	Holt G 3 (7)	Weimann A 31 (6)
Bowery J 2 (7)	Kozak L 8 (6)	Westwood A 35
Clark C 23 (4)	Lowton M................ 18 (5)	

League goals (39): Benteke 10, Bacuna 5, Weimann 5, Agbonlahor 4, Kozak 4, Delph 3, Westwood 3, El Ahmadi 2, Holt 1, Luna 1, Opponents 1
FA Cup goals (1): Helenius 1. **Capital One Cup goals** (3): Benteke 1, Delph 1, Weimann 1.
Average home league attendance: 36,080. **Player of Year**: Fabian Delph

CARDIFF CITY

A season which opened full of optimism gradually turned sour and finished with an immediate return to the Championship. Cardiff broke their transfer record three times during the summer window – striker Andreas Cornelius, central defender Steven Caulker and midfielder Gary Medel. And when Manchester City were beaten 3-2 in the opening home game, hopes were high.

Instead, speculation about the future of Malky Mackay followed the dismissal of his head of recruitment, Iain Moody, by owner Vincent Tan, who replaced him with a 23-year-old Kazakhstani with no known football experience. Tan sacked the manager for overspending, particularly on Cornelius, who failed to make a single start and was sold back to FC Copenhagen at a big loss. Mackay's successor, Ole Gunnar Solskjaer, the successful manager of Norwegian club Molde and winner of six Premier League titles with Manchester United, started with an FA Cup win at Newcastle. However, defeat at West Ham in his first league match left Cardiff in the bottom four and it was a position from which they never recovered, with season-long heroics from goalkeeper David Marshall not nearly enough to counter wide-ranging deficiencies. Solskjaer, who brought in players from his former club with little impact, was boosted when two goals by Caulker brought a 3-1 victory over Fulham. His side also retrieved a 2-0 deficit for a point away to West Bromwich Albion. But despite another determined performance at Southampton, they were crushed 4-0 at Sunderland and a return to St James Park ended their chances of staying up with a 3-0 beating.

Bellamy C 13 (9)	Gestede R .... - (3)	McNaughton K 3 (2)
Berget J I .... - (1)	Gunnarsson A........... 17 (6)	Medel G.........................34
Cala 7	Healey R..................... - (1)	Mutch J 26 (9)
Campbell F 32 (5)	Hudson M .... - (2)	Noone C 13 (4)
Caulker S 38	James T....................... - (1)	Odemwingie P 11 (4)
Connolly M.....................3	John D.................... 16 (4)	Taylor A 18
Cornelius A .... - (8)	Jones K 6 (5)	Theophile-Catherine K26 (2)
Cowie D 10 (8)	Kim Bo-Kyung... 21 (7)	Turner B 30 (1)
Daehli M.................... 5 (8)	Lewis J 1	Whittingham P 30 (2)
Eikrem M 1 (5)	Marshall D 37	Zaha W 5 (7)
Fabio........................13	Maynard N .... - (8)	

League goals (32): Mutch 7, Campbell 6, Caulker 5, Whittingham 3, Bellamy 2, Cala 2, Daehli 1, Gunnarsson 1, Jones 1, Kim Bo-Kyung 1, Noone 1, Odemwingie 1, Opponents 1
FA Cup goals (4): Campbell 3, Noone 1. **Capital One Cup goals** (4): Gestede 1, Maynard 1, Noone 1, Odemwingie 1
Average home league attendance: 27,429. **Player of Year**: David Marshall

CHELSEA

If the outcome of the title race had been decided on how the top four fared against each other, Chelsea would have been undisputed winners. They beat Manchester City and Liverpool home and away, put six past Arsenal and took a point at the Emirates. But, to Jose Mourinho's annoyance, his team dropped crucial points against some of the division's lesser lights and this failure meant they had to settle for third place, four points behind champions City. In successive away games, 1-0 defeats to Aston Villa and Crystal Palace ended their six-week stay at the head of the table. Mourinho's 77-match unbeaten Premier League record at Stamford Bridge was brought down by Sunderland. The final straw was a goalless draw against Norwich in the last home game. All the manager's tactical acumen in securing victories at the Etihad and Anfield had counted for little and it was easy to see what his summer transfer targets would be. Between them, strikers Fernando Torres, Samuel Eto'o and Demba Ba scored just 19 league goals. That Chelsea retained an interest in top spot was down to his midfielders, notably Eden Hazard who netted 14 times, including a hat-trick against Newcastle. Disappointment, too, in the Champions League, with a superior Atletico Madrid side winning 3-1 at Stamford Bridge after the first leg of the semi-final ended goalless.

Ake N	- (1)	Hazard E	32 (3)	Ramires	29 (1)
Azpilicueta C	26 (3)	Ivanovic B	36	Salah M	6 (4)
Bertrand R	1	Kalas T	2	Schurrle A	15 (15)
Cahill G	29 (1)	Lampard F	20 (6)	Schwarzer M	4
Cech P	34	Luiz D	15 (4)	Swift J	- (1)
Cole A	15 (2)	Lukaku R	- (2)	Terry J	34
De Bruyne K	2 (1)	Mata J	11 (2)	Torres F	16 (12)
Demba Ba	5 (14)	Matic N	15 (2)	Van Ginkel M	- (2)
Essien M	2 (3)	Mikel J O	11 (13)	Willian	18 (7)
Eto'o S	16 (5)	Oscar	24 (9)		

League goals (71): Hazard 14, Eto'o 9, Oscar 8, Schurrle 8, Lampard 6, Demba Ba 5, Torres 5, Willian 4, Ivanovic 3, Salah 2, Terry 2, Cahill 1, Mikel 1, Ramires 1, Opponents 2
FA Cup goals (3): Oscar 2, Mikel 1. **Capital One Cup goals (5):** Azpilicueta 1, Lampard 1, Mata 1, Ramires 1, Torres 1
Champions League goals (19): Torres 4, Demba Ba 3, Eto'o 3, Hazard 2, Ramires 2, Cahill 1, Lampard 1, Oscar 1, Schurrle 1, Opponents 1. **European Super Cup goals (2):** Hazard 1, Torres 1
Average home league attendance: 41,481. **Player of Year:** Eden Hazard

CRYSTAL PALACE

Tony Pulis put his record of never having been relegated in a 21-year managerial career on the line when he replaced Ian Holloway to take over a side with just four points from the opening 11 matches. Pulis, who secured six seasons of Premier League football for his previous club Stoke, quickly made an impression – back-to-back wins over West Ham and Cardiff, and a strong performance at Chelsea which should have produced a point. But he knew the squad had to be strengthened to survive and signed five players on winter transfer deadline day. Two of them, Joe Ledley and on-loan Tom Ince, made scoring debuts in a 3-1 success against West Bromwich Albion which took them away from the danger zone. But it was followed by five matches with a single goal scored and more worries. Then came the season's defining spell – five successive victories as key man Jason Puncheon scored twice at Cardiff, delivered the winner against Aston Villa and was on the mark again at Everton. By then, Palace were looking to cement a mid-table finish. It came with 11th place, along with one of the Manager of the Year awards for Pulis, who built the recovery by tightening up what had been a suspect defence. Along the way, he also received praise for promising to fine two of his players, Marouane Chamakh and Jerome Thomas, for diving during the game against Swansea.

Bannan B	13 (2)	Chamakh M	27 (5)	Delaney D	37
Bolasie Y	23 (6)	Dann S	14	Dikgacoi K	25 (1)

Dobbie S	1	Jerome C	20 (8)	Phillips K	- (4)
Gabbidon D	22 (1)	Kebe J	2 (4)	Puncheon J	29 (5)
Garvan O	1 (1)	Ledley J	14	Speroni J	37
Gayle D	8 (15)	Mariappa A	23 (1)	Thomas J	3 (6)
Campana J	4 (2)	McCarthy P	- (1)	Ward J	36
Guedioura A	4 (4)	Moxey D	18 (2)	Wilbraham A	1 (3)
Hennessey W	1	Murray G	3 (11)	Williams J	- (9)
Ince T	5 (3)	O'Keefe S	2 (10)		
Jedinak M	38	Parr J	7 (8)		

League goals (33): Gayle 7, Puncheon 7, Chamakh 5, Jerome 2, Ledley 2, Bannan 1, Dann 1, Delaney 1, Gabbidon 1, Ince 1, Jedinak 1, Mariappa 1, Murray 1, O'Keefe 1, Opponents 1
FA Cup goals (3): Chamakh 1, Gayle 1, Wilbraham 1. **Capital One Cup goals (1):** Garvan 1
Average home league attendance: 24,114. **Player of Year:** Julian Speroni

EVERTON

Goodison Park acclaimed an impressive 3-0 victory over Arsenal and was awash with the prospect of Champions League football as the season entered its closing stages. The win took Roberto Martinez and his team to within a point of their rivals and was followed by an own goal by Sunderland's Wes Brown which lifted them into the prized fourth place. Then, as neighbours Liverpool did in the race for the title, they found the expectancy and pressure too much, handing back the initiative when losing at home to Crystal Palace. Everton recovered to beat Manchester United, ending former manager David Moyes's time at Old Trafford in the process, but stumbled again by conceding two own goals at Southampton. That defeat left them trailing by four points and another 3-2 home defeat followed, this time against Manchester City, despite the boost of a spectacular opening goal from Ross Barkley. So Martinez, who succeeded Moyes after leading Wigan to the FA Cup, had to be satisfied with bringing two Premier League records to the club – the highest points total and a run of seven successive wins. The manager could also reflect with great satisfaction on the impact made by Barkley, the country's most exciting young talent, which brought him a place in England's World Cup squad.

Alcaraz A	5 (1)	Gibson D	- (1)	Mirallas K	28 (4)
Anichebe V	- (1)	Heitinga J	- (1)	Naismith S	13 (18)
Baines L	32	Hibbert T	- (1)	Osman L	27 (11)
Barkley R	25 (9)	Howard T	37	Oviedo B	8 (1)
Barry G	32	Jagielka P	26	Pienaar S	19 (4)
Coleman S	36	Jelavic N	5 (4)	Robles J	1 (1)
Deulofeu G	9 (16)	Kone A	- (5)	Stones J	15 (6)
Distin S	33	Lukaku R	29 (2)	Traore L	- (1)
Fellaini M	3	McCarthy J	31 (3)		
Garbutt L	- (1)	McGeady A	4 (12)		

League goals (61): Lukaku 15, Mirallas 8, Barkley 6, Coleman 6, Baines 5, Naismith 5, Barry 3, Deulofeu 3, Osman 3, Oviedo 2, McCarthy 1, Pienaar 1, Opponents 3
FA Cup goals: (12): Naismith 3, Jelavic 2, Baines 1, Barkley 1, Coleman 1, Gueye M 1, Heitinga 1, Lukaku 1, Traore 1. **Capital One Cup goals (3):** Deulofeu 1, Fellaini 1, Naismith 1
Average home league attendance: 37,731. **Player of Year:** Seamus Coleman

FULHAM

Thirteen seasons of Premier League football came to an end at Craven Cottage. So did Felix Magrath's record of never having been relegated as a coach or manager. Fulham's problems were season-long – 85 goals conceded, a record 39 players used in efforts to find the right formula and questionable signings. For Magath, it was a case of trying to pick up the pieces with two thirds of the campaign gone and the malaise ingrained. He started with a point away to fellow-strugglers West Bromwich Albion, lost the next two games, then claimed his first victory – at Newcastle. A 5-0 defeat by Manchester City kept them bottom before a chink of light appeared.

Hugo Rodallega's 86th minute goal brought victory at Villa Park. A week later, the Colombian scored the only goal against Norwich. But Fulham surrendered a two-goal lead against Hull and a 4-1 defeat at Stoke in their penultimate match confirmed the drop, the team having conceded more than 30 goals from set pieces over the course of the season. Previously, Rene Meulensteen, former assistant manager to Sir Alex Ferguson at Manchester United, had joined the coaching staff to help out under-pressure Martin Jol, who was then fired after six successive league and cup defeats. Meulensteen took over and brought in five players on deadline day – including £12.4m record-signing Konstantinos Mitroglou, who made just one start. Meulensteen lasted just for 75 days, with technical director Alan Curbishley and assistant head coach Ray Wilkins also going.

Amorebieta F............ 20 (3)	Hangeland B 23	Riise J A 17 (3)
Bent D.................... 11 (13)	Heitinga J 14	Roberts P..................... - (2)
Berbatov D.....................18	Holtby L 11 (2)	Rodallega H 6 (7)
Boateng D................... 2 (1)	Hughes A.................. 11 (2)	Ruiz B 8 (4)
Briggs M .... - (2)	Kacaniklic A............ 15 (8)	Senderos P 12
Burn D 6 (3)	Karagounis G............. 6 (8)	Sidwell S 36 (2)
Cole L........................ - (1)	Kasami P 20 (9)	Stekelenburg M 19
David C...................... - (1)	Kvist W 7 (1)	Stockdale D 19 (2)
Dejagh A.................. 13 (9)	Mesca .... - (1)	Taarabt A 7 (5)
Dembele M 1 (1)	Mitroglou K.............. 1 (2)	Tankovic M.............. 1 (2)
Dempsey C................. 4 (1)	Parker S 27 (2)	Tunnicliffe R 2 (1)
Diarra M 4	Richardson K 28 (3)	Woodrow C 5 (1)
Duff D 9 (6)	Riether S 30 (1)	Zverotic E 5 (1)

League goals (40): Sidwell 7, Dejagh 5, Berbatov 4, Richardson 4, Bent 3, Kasami 3, Parker 2, Rodallega 2, Amorebieta 1, David 1, Heitinga 1, Holtby 1, Kacaniklic 1, Ruiz 1, Senderos 1, Woodrow 1, Opponents 2
FA Cup goals (5): Bent 2, Dejagh 1, Rodallega 1, Sidwell 1. **Capital One Cup goals (7)**: Rodallega 3, Bent 1, Berbatov 1, Karagounis 1, Taarabt 1
Average home league attendance: 24,977. **Player of Year**: Ashkan Dejagah

HULL CITY

Delight turned to despair when a two-goal lead was lost at Wembley and it was Arsenal who lifted the FA Cup. But amid the disappointment, Steve Bruce and his players were applauded, not just for going so close to upsetting the odds but for having previously secured their Premier League place, effectively with five weeks of the season remaining. Bruce made important signings in the summer and winter transfer windows. He brought in midfielders Tom Huddlestone and Jake Livermore from Tottenham – the latter on loan. Then, after three successive New Year defeats followed a 6-0 win over Fulham, in which Huddlestone scored his first goal for the club, the manager acted again. He brought in a new striker partnership, Everton's Nikica Jelavic and West Bromwich Albion's Shane Long, whose goals halted the slide. Hull kept the relegation zone at arms length and went into their semi-final against Sheffield United with George Boyd's winner against Swansea having established a nine-point cushion. Although Jelavic and Long were both cup-tied, a 5-3 victory delivered the club's first major final, along with a guaranteed place in the Europa League. This clearly had an effect on the remaining league programme, with a single point gained from the final five fixtures. Despite this, they still finished four points clear.

Aluko S................... 10 (7)	Fryatt M.................... - (10)	Long S...........................15
Boyd G 9 (20)	Gedo .... - (2)	McGregor A....................26
Brady R 11 (5)	Graham D 12 (6)	Mclean A .... - (1)
Bruce A 19 (1)	Harper S 11 (2)	McShane P 9 (11)
Chester J 22 (2)	Huddlestone T........ 35 (1)	Meyler D 27 (3)
Davies C 37	Jakupovic E.......................1	Proschwitz N............... - (2)
Elmohamady A................38	Jelavic N.........................16	Quinn S 4 (11)
Faye A 3	Koren R 10 (12)	Rosenior L 22 (7)
Figueroa M 31 (1)	Livermore J 34 (2)	Sagbo Y 16 (12)

League goals (38): Jelavic 4, Long 4, Brady 3, Huddlestone 3, Livermore 3, Boyd 2, Davies 2, Elmohamady 2, Fryatt 2, Koren 2, Meyler 2, Sagbo 2, Aluko 1, Chester 1, Graham 1, Rosenior 1, Opponents 3
FA Cup goals (15): Fryatt 4, Davies 2, Meyler 2, Sagbo 2, Huddlestone 1, Koren 1, Mclean 1, Proschwitz 1, Quinn 1. **Capital One Cup goals** (4): Brady 1, McShane 1, Proschwitz 1, Opponents 1
Average home league attendance: 24,116. **Player of Year**: Curtis Davies

LIVERPOOL

Just when it seemed that the title was on its way to Anfield for the first title since 1990, Brendan Rodgers's side cracked under the pressure and were left counting the cost. Eleven straight victories, along with 38 goals scored, had taken Liverpool to the summit, seven points clear of Manchester City from two extra games played. Chelsea were still in with a shout and they inflicted the first blow as Jose Mourinho set up his side shrewdly for a 2-0 win on Merseyside. A week later, Liverpool looked to be coasting as Luis Suarez, fresh from winning the two major Player of the Year awards, extended his side's lead to 3-0 at Selhurst Park. Instead, Crystal Palace scored three times in the final 11 minutes for a result which cleared the way for City to finish on top. The runners-up spot was little consolation, particularly for captain Steven Gerrard, who had set his heart on his first title, together with the club's return to the Champions League. While City, Chelsea and Arsenal all faced the extra demands of European competition, Liverpool had a single focus. As Suarez and Daniel Sturridge formed a lethal partnership and Raheem Sterling blossomed with every game, they scored 101 goals. But in the end it was not enough to offset a suspect defence . No team had ever won the Premier League when conceding 50 goals, as Liverpool did. Rodgers was a winner, however, voted Manager of the Year by the League Managers' Association.

Agger D 16 (4)	Johnson G.....................29	Smith B...................... - (1)
Allen J...................... 15 (9)	Jose Enrique 6 (2)	Sterling R 24 (9)
Aspas I 5 (9)	Kelly M........................ - (5)	Sturridge D 26 (3)
Cissokho A................ 12 (3)	Lucas Leiva............. 20 (7)	Suarez L 33
Coutinho P............... 28 (5)	Luis Alberto .... - (9)	Teixeira J .... - (1)
Flanagan J 23	Mignolet S 38	Toure K.................... 15 (5)
Gerrard S 33 (1)	Moses V................. 6 (13)	Wisdom A 1 (1)
Henderson J...................35	Sakho M 17 (1)	
Ibe J............................ - (1)	Skrtel M 36	

League goals (101): Suarez 31, Sturridge 21, Gerrard 13, Sterling 9, Skrtel 7, Coutinho 5, Henderson 4, Agger 2, Allen 1, Flanagan 1, Moses 1, Sakho 1, Opponents 5
FA Cup goals (5): Aspas 1, Gerrard 1, Moses 1, Sturridge 1, Opponents 1. **Capital One Cup goals** (4): Sturridge 2, Henderson 1, Sterling 1
Average home league attendance: 44,671. **Player of Year**: Luis Suarez

MANCHESTER CITY

A perfectly-timed run at the most important stage of the season took City past their rivals and over the finishing line as champions for the second time in three years. It went down to another last-day decider, but compared to the stoppage-time drama of 2012, a 2-0 victory over West Ham proved relatively stress-free. Samir Nasri and captain Vincent Kompany scored the goals to give manager Manuel Pellegrini his first title in Europe in his first season at the club. Five straight wins took his side past Chelsea and Liverpool after a mid-April stumble looked is if it might prove costly. They lost 3-2 at Anfield and were held at home by Sunderland, leaving them six points behind Liverpool with a single game in hand. Brendan Rodgers's side then succumbed to the pressure, leaving City two points clear, with 102 goals scored, one short of Chelsea's record. They had overcome an indifferent start to the campaign, particularly away from home, and the intermittent absence through injury of Sergio Aguero. Such was the firepower from other areas that he was rarely missed. Yaya Toure scored 20 goals from midfield, while Edin Dzeko's five in

three matches at the end proved crucial. Their team beat Norwich 7-0, hit Tottenham for 11 in two games, put six past Arsenal and netted four or more in seven other games. Toure was also on the mark in a 3-1 victory over Sunderland in the Capital One Cup Final. But City are still to make an impact in the Champions League, losing out this time to Barcelona in the first knock-out round.

Aguero S................. 20 (3)	Jesus Navas 18 (12)	Negredo A............. 21 (11)
Boyata D..........................1	Jovetic S.................. 2 (11)	Pantilimon C 7
Clichy G.................. 18 (2)	Kolarov A 21 (9)	Richards M 2
Demichelis M 27	Kompany V 28	Rodwell J 1 (4)
Dzeko E 23 (8)	Lescott J 8 (2)	Silva D 26 (1)
Fernandinho............. 29 (4)	Milner J 12 (19)	Toure Y 35
Hart J.............................31	Nasri S 29 (5)	Zabaleta P 34 (1)
Javi Garcia 14 (15)	Nastasic M 11 (2)	

League goals (102): Toure 20, Aguero 17, Dzeko 16, Negredo 9, Nasri 7, Silva 7, Fernandinho 5, Jesus Navas 4, Kompany 4, Jovetic 3, Demichelis 2, Kolarov 1, Milner 1, Zabaleta 1, Opponents 5
FA Cup goals (13): Aguero 4, Negredo 3, Dzeko 2, Nasri 2, Jovetic 1, Kolarov 1. **Capital One Cup goals (22)**: Dzeko 6, Negredo 6, Toure 3, Jesus Navas 2, Jovetic 2, Aguero 1, Kolarov 1, Nasri 1
Champions League goals (19): Aguero 6, Negredo 5, Dzeko 2, Kolarov 1, Kompany 1, Milner 1, Nasri 1, Silva 1, Toure 1
Average home league attendance: 47,080. **Player of Year**: Yaya Toure

MANCHESTER UNITED

All good things come to an end. For some clubs the slide is gradual, manageable and relatively stress-free. For others, the shock to the system is severe and played out in the full glare of publicity. For Manchester United and David Moyes it was even worse that that, a nightmare time for a club accustomed to being the dominant presence in the Premier League Following Sir Alex Ferguson, the architect of that success, would have tested any manager. Moyes, with his track record at Everton, seemed best suited as anyone to meet a challenge which turned out to be even bigger than expected. Despite regaining the title by an 11-point margin in 2013, the team needed refreshing in some areas. The new manager was unable to achieve that and the outcome was painful. United finished out of the top six in the top flight for the first time since 1989-90. They lost seven times at Old Trafford, were beaten home and away by arch-rivals Liverpool and Manchester City and couldn't even find the consolation of a place in the Europa League for missing out on the customary Champions League spot. There was also an FA Cup third round defeat by Swansea and a League Cup semi-final lost to Sunderland. Moyes paid the price, sacked 11 months into a six-year contract after a 2-0 defeat by his old club. Ryan Giggs took over temporarily, winning his first match 4-0 against Norwich, before the appointment of Louis van Gaal, Holland's World Cup coach and a former a title winner with Bayern Munich – who ended United's Champions League hopes at the quarter-final stage – and Barcelona.

Anderson 2 (2)	Fletcher D................. 9 (3)	Rafael 18 (1)
Buttner A.................. 5 (3)	Giggs R..................... 6 (6)	Rooney W 27 (2)
Carrick M 26 (3)	Hernandez J 6 (18)	Smalling C 21 (4)
Cleverley T 18 (4)	Januzaj A 15 (12)	Valencia A 20 (9)
De Gea D 37	Jones P.........................26	Van Persie R 18 (3)
Evans J........................17	Kagawa S 14 (4)	Vidic N 23 (2)
Evra P...........................33	Lawrence T 1	Welbeck D 15 (10)
Fabio...............................1	Lindegaard A 1	Wilson J...........................1
Fellaini M 12 (4)	Mata J 14 (1)	Young A 13 (7)
Ferdinand R 12 (2)	Nani 7 (4)	Zaha W.......................- (2)

League goals (64): Rooney 17, Van Persie 12, Welbeck 9, Mata 6, Hernandez 4, Januzaj 4, Valencia 2, Wilson 2, Young 2, Carrick 1, Cleverley 1, Evra 1, Jones 1, Smalling 1, Opponents 1
FA Cup goals (1): Hernandez 1. **Capital One Cup goals (10)**: Hernandez 4, Evans 1, Evra 1, Fabio

1, Jones 1, Vidic 1, Young 1
Champions League goals (17): Van Persie 4, Rooney 2, Valencia 2, Evans 1, Evra 1, Jones 1, Nani 1, Smalling 1, Vidic 1, Welbeck 1, Opponents 2. **Community Shield goals** (2): Van Persie 2
Average home league attendance: 75,206. **Player of Year**: David de Gea

NEWCASTLE UNITED

The wheels came off for Alan Pardew's side after an outstanding run had left them riding high approaching the half-way point of the season. They were up to sixth on the back of 22 points accumulated from nine matches – and looking to go higher. The run included wins over Chelsea and Tottenham, followed by the club's first victory over Manchester United at Old Trafford since 1972. Yohan Cabaye scored the only goal of that game and was at the heart of his team's purple patch. But the £19m sale of the France midfielder player to Paris Saint-Germain – a move he wanted – along with the loss of leading scorer Loic Remy, first through suspension, then with a calf injury, had a dramatic effect on Newcastle's fortunes. They lost six successive Premier League games for the first time and failed to score nine times out of 12. They also lost Pardew to a seven-match ban, three from the ground and four from the touchline, for headbutting Hull midfielder David Meyler in a touchline confrontation which left the manager's future at the club open to question. A 3-0 win over Cardiff offered some respite, although the campaign finished on a low note with Shola Ameobi and Paul Dummett both sent off in the defeat at Liverpool. Dummett's red card was later resccinded, while Pardew kept his job and was promised reinforcements in the summer transfer market.

Ameobi Sammy	4 (6)	De Jong L	8 (4)	Obertan G	- (3)
Ameobi Shola	14 (2)	Dummett P	11 (7)	Remy L	24 (2)
Anita V	28 (6)	Elliot R	2	Santon D	26 (1)
Armstrong A	- (4)	Gosling D	4 (4)	Sissoko M	35
Ben Arfa H	13 (14)	Gouffran Y	31 (4)	Taylor S	9 (1)
Cabaye Y	17 (2)	Gutierrez J	1 (1)	Tiote C	31 (2)
Cisse P	15 (9)	Haidara M	3 (8)	Williamson M	32 (1)
Coloccini F	27	Krul T	36	Yanga-Mbiwa M	17 (6)
Debuchy M	28 (1)	Marveaux S	2 (7)		

League goals (43): Remy 14, Cabaye 7, Gouffran 6, Ben Arfa 3, Sissoko 3, Ameobi Shola 2, Cisse 2, Anita 1, Debuchy 1, Dummett 1, Taylor 1, Opponents 2
FA Cup goals (1): Cisse 1. **Capital One Cup goals** (4): Ameobi Sammy 1, Ameobi Shola 1, Cisse 1, Gouffran 1
Average home league attendance: 50,395. **Player of Year**: Loic Remy

NORWICH CITY

Was it a mistake sacking Chris Hughton and giving youth coach Neil Adams five games to preserve their Premier League status? The club thought it was the right move, even though they were five points clear of the bottom three at the time, with a superior goal difference. A season-long struggle, along with the division's worst scoring record, and one win in six matches at a crucial time were the obvious reasons. But it was still a contentious decision, with Norwich facing the most difficult run-in of all the teams facing relegation and, some thought, needing Hughton's experience to see them through it. In the event, Adams was not the saviour. He started with a single-goal defeat at Fulham, where his side paid the price for missed chances. They stretched Liverpool before losing 3-2, then lost 4-0 without much resistance at Old Trafford – a defeat which dropped them into the bottom three. A goalless draw at Chelsea offered a glimmer of hope, but that was extinguished four days later when Sunderland completed their great escape. Hughton achieved an 11th place finish in his first season, but failed to record any back-to-back victories this time. His side conceded three or more goals in nine league and cup matches, including a 7-0 defeat by Manchester City. Adams was later given the job permanently.

Bassong S	27	Bennett R	14 (2)	Elmander J	16 (13)
Becchio L	- (5)	Bennett E	1 (1)	Fer L	28 (1)

Garrido J.........................6	Martin R 29 (2)	Tettey A 17 (4)
Gutierrez J 2 (2)	Murphy J .... - (9)	Turner M 22
Hoolahan W 10 (6)	Olsson M 33 (1)	Van Wolfswinkel 16 (9)
Hooper G 22 (10)	Pilkington A 10 (5)	Whittaker S 16 (4)
Howson J 23 (4)	Redmond N............ 23 (11)	Yobo J 8
Johnson B................ 28 (4)	Ruddy J 38	
Loza J......................... - (1)	Snodgrass R 29 (1)	

League goals (28): Hooper 6, Snodgrass 6, Fer 3, Johnson 3, Howson 2, Bennett R 1, Elmander 1, Hoolahan 1, Pilkington 1, Redmond 1, Tettey 1, Whittaker 1, Van Wolfswinkel 1
FA Cup goals (1): Snodgrass 1. **Capital One Cup goals** (9): Elmander 2, Hooper 2, Fer 1, Murphy 1, Olsson 1, Pilkington 1, Whittaker 1
Average home league attendance: 26,805. **Player of Year**: Robert Snodgrass

SOUTHAMPTON

Southampton started the season by accumulating 18 points from nine matches – the club's best start in top flight football. They finished it with the highest points total (56) in the Premier League. It was a commendable performance under Mauricio Pochettino, but one that came at a cost. Adam Lallana developed into one of the country's most effective midfield players and became the target for top clubs. So did teenage left-back Luke Shaw, also capped by England for the first time and also named in Roy Hodgson's World Cup squad. Both moved for big-money fees. And the manager himself was the subject of speculation from the moment he declared he would consider his future at the end of the campaign following the resignation of executive chairman Nicola Cortese over disagreements with owner Katharina Liebherr. Strike pair Rickie Lambert – who also moved – and Jay Rodriguez gained recognition for their part with England debuts, although leading scorer Rodriguez was ruled out of contention for a place in the squad for Brazil by a knee ligament injury which kept him out of the team's final five games. Southampton were up to third behind Arsenal and Liverpool in early November before a tough six-match run, which included fixtures against Arsenal, Chelsea, Manchester City and Tottenham and which did not produce a win. They dropped into mid-table, but regrouped and went on to finish eighth. Pochettino left for Tottenham to be replaced by Dutchman Ronald Koeman.

Boruc A 29	Fox D 3	Ramirez G................. 3 (15)
Chambers C 18 (4)	Gallagher S 3 (15)	Reed H........................ - (4)
Clyne N 20 (5)	Gazzaniga P 7 (1)	Rodriguez J............... 30 (3)
Cork J..................... 21 (7)	Hooiveld J.........................3	Schneiderlin M......... 31 (2)
Davis S 28 (6)	Lallana A 37 (1)	Shaw L...........................35
Davis K.............................2	Lambert R 31 (6)	Wanyama V 19 (4)
Do Prado G .... - (9)	Lovren D 31	Ward-Prowse J........ 16 (18)
Fonte J 35 (1)	Osvaldo P 9 (4)	Yoshida M 7 (1)

League goals (54): Rodriguez 15, Lambert 13, Lallana 9, Fonte 3, Osvaldo 3, Davis S 2, Lovren 2, Schneiderlin 2, Gallagher 1, Ramirez 1, Yoshida 1, Opponents 2
FA Cup goals (6): Clyne 1, Do Prado 1, Gallagher 1, Lallana 1, Lambert 1, Rodriguez 1. **Capital One Cup goals** (8): Davis S 2, Ramirez 2, Hooiveld 1, Mayuka 1, Rodriguez 1, Yoshida 1
Average home league attendance: 30,211. **Player of Year**: Adam Lallana

STOKE CITY

Tony Pulis chartered a course through the middle reaches of the Premier League for five successive seasons. Mark Hughes, his successor as manager, went one better in his first one in charge with the club's first top-ten finish. It was testament to the way Hughes maintained the team's strength and directness, while at the same time introducing levels of skill and subtlety. They were in a spot of bother in mid-winter, conceding five goals to Newcastle and Liverpool, going six games without a win and falling to ninth from bottom. But two Charlie Adam strikes, the first deflected in by Michael Carrick and given as an own goal by the Dubious Goals Panel, delivered Stoke's first league success over Manchester United since 1984. A Jon Walters goal

brought victory over Arsenal and there was a run of four wins in five games, against West Ham, Aston Villa, Hull and Newcastle. Then, a victory over West Bromwich Albion in the final round of fixtures lifted them above Newcastle into ninth place. Other achievements during the course of the campaign were a first success against Chelsea in a league game since 1975 and a moment to remember for goalkeeper Asmir Begovic, who scored one of the Premier League's fastest-ever goals, his clearance bouncing over Southampton's Artur Boruc after 13 seconds.

Adam C 20 (11)	Huth R 12	Pieters E.................. 34 (2)
Arnautovic M............. 27 (3)	Ireland S................ 14 (11)	Shawcross R 37
Assaidi O 12 (7)	Jerome C .... - (1)	Shea B .... - (1)
Begovic A 32	Jones K 4 (3)	Sorensen T........................4
Butland J................... 2 (1)	Muniesa M 7 (6)	Walters J.............. 27 (5)
Cameron G.....................37	Nzonzi S 34 (2)	Whelan G.............. 28 (4)
Crouch P.............. 30 (4)	Odemwingie P 15	Wilkinson A................ 2 (3)
Etherington M 5 (6)	Palacios W 5 (11)	Wilson M 30 (3)
Guidetti J..................... - (6)	Pennant J .... - (8)	

League goals (45): Crouch 8, Adam 7, Odemwingie 5, Walters 5, Arnautovic 4, Assaidi 4, Cameron 2, Ireland 2, Nzonzi 2, Begovic 1, Pennant 1, Pieters 1, Shawcross 1, Opponents 2
FA Cup goals (2): Adam 1, Jones 1. **Capital One Cup goals** (9): Jones 4, Crouch 2, Arnautovic 1, Assaidi 1, Ireland 1
Average home league attendance: 26,137. **Player of Year**: Ryan Shawcross

SUNDERLAND

Gus Poyet admitted needing a 'miracle' with his side anchored to the bottom of the table – seemingly without a prayer – after five successive defeats. They had slipped seven points from safety in the wake of losing to Manchester City in the League Cup Final and to Hull in the sixth round of the FA Cup. Less than a month later, the manager was celebrating just that after Sunderland turned the form book upside down with the aid of a scoring burst out of the blue from Connor Wickham, a player who had spent much of the season out on loan. Wickham, with a single goal to his credit in 37 previous Premier League appearances, netted twice to earn a 2-2 away against Manchester City. Three days later, he was on the mark as Sunderland overcame Chelsea 2-1, a result which ended Jose Mourinho's 77-game unbeaten league record at Stamford Bridge. That was followed by another brace in the 4 0 victory over Cardiff. Then, a victory at Old Trafford for the first time since 1968, courtesy of the only goal of the game from Seb Larsson, left them within touching distance of survival. That was achieved as Jack Colback and Fabio Borini were on the mark to deliver a 2-0 success against West Bromwich Albion. It was a stunning recovery, contrasting sharply with turbulent times under Paolo Di Canio, who had signed 14 players in the summer transfer window. Di Canio was sacked after six months in charge and replaced by Poyet, himself the subject of an acrimonious dismissal by his former club, Brighton.

Alonso M 16	Diakite M.........................7	Mavrias C..................... 1 (3)
Altidore J 19 (12)	Dossena A................. 6 (1)	O'Shea J.........................33
Bardsley P 26	El Hadji Ba .... - (1)	Roberge V 7 (2)
Borini F 25 (7)	Fletcher S 13 (7)	Scocco I .... - (6)
Bridcutt L 9 (3)	Gardner C 7 (11)	Sessegnon S 2
Brown W 24 (1)	Giaccherini E 16 (8)	Vaughan D 2 (1)
Cabral A 1	Ji Dong-Won............... 2 (3)	Vergini S 10 (1)
Cattermole L 21 (7)	Johnson A 28 (8)	Westwood K 10
Celustka O 14 (7)	Ki Sung-Yueng ... 25 (2)	Wickham C 10 (5)
Colback J 28 (5)	Larsson S 24 (7)	
Cuellar C..........................4	Mannone V................. 28 (1)	

League goals (41): Johnson 8, Borini 7, Wickham 5, Giaccherini 4, Colback 3, Fletcher 3, Ki Sung-Yeung 3, Bardsley 2, Gardner 2, Altidore 1, Cattermole 1, Larsson 1, O'Shea 1
FA Cup goals (5): El Hadji Ba 1, Gardner 1, Johnson 1, Mavrias 1, Opponents 1. **Capital One**

Cup goals (14): Borini 3, Bardsley 2, Wickham 2, Altidore 1, Giaccherini 1, Johnson 1, Ki Sung-Yeung 1, Larsson 1, Roberge 1, Opponents 1
Average home league attendance: 41,090. **Player of Year**: Vito Mannone

SWANSEA CITY

Record-signing Wilfried Bony played a key role in Swansea resisting the threat of relegation at the end of a difficult season for the club, on and off the field. The £12m Ivory Coast striker scored 16 goals to keep them afloat in the absence of the previous campaign's leading marksman, Michu, who missed more than half the games through injury. Five of his goals came in the final three weeks when they were three points away from the bottom three and teams below them were mounting a late rally for survival. Caretaker-manager Garry Monk also had to deal with a potentially damaging training ground incident involving some of his players. But after helping earn a surprise point away to Arsenal, Bony netted twice at Newcastle – one in first-half stoppage time and a penalty in added time at the end – got two more against Aston Villa to ensure survival and for good measure scored again when Swansea also beat Sunderland in the final fixture. Monk, a former club captain, took over when Michael Laudrup was sacked after a previous lean spell of one win in ten. Results continued to be disappointing – defeats by Everton in the FA Cup fifth round and Napoli in the Europa League's first knock-out round. But, by the close, Monk had done enough to be given a three-year contract.

Vazquez A	5 (7)	Emnes M	2 (5)	Pozuelo A	7 (15)
Amat J	13 (4)	Flores J M	30 (1)	Rangel A	29 (1)
Bartley K	1 (1)	Fulton J	1 (1)	Routledge W	32 (3)
Bony W	27 (7)	Hernandez P	17 (1)	Shelvey J	29 (3)
Britton L	23 (2)	Ki Sung-Yeung	- (1)	Taylor N	6 (4)
Canas J	19 (4)	Lamah R	4 (5)	Tiendalli D	9 (1)
Davies B	32 (1)	Lita L	- (2)	Tremmel G	12
De Guzman J	26 (8)	Michu	15 (2)	Vorm M	26
Dyer N	19 (8)	Ngog D	- (3)	Williams A	34

League goals (54): Bony 16, Dyer 6, Shelvey 6, De Guzman 4, Davies 2, Flores 2, Hernandez 2, Lamah 2, Michu 2, Routledge 2, Emnes 1, Williams 1, Opponents 8
FA Cup goals (5): Bony 3, De Guzman 1, Routledge 1. **Capital One Cup goals** (1): Bony 1
Europa League goals (17): Bony 4, Michu 4, Routledge 3, De Guzman 2, Pozuelo 2, Lamah 1, Opponents 1
Average home league attendance: 20,406. **Player of Year**: Wilfried Bony

TOTTENHAM HOTSPUR

The sale of Gareth Bale to Real Madrid for a world record £85.3m, accompanied by the signing of seven players at a combined cost of £107m, meant a new-look line up at White Hart Lane. But it was the same old story in the search for Champions League football, with Tottenham left looking in from the outside as the big four dominated the division. The gulf was underlined by their results against that quartet of teams – seven defeats, a draw against Chelsea, 27 goals conceded, two scored. Two of those heavy losses, 6-0 against Manchester City and 5-0 at home to Liverpool, led to the sacking of manager Andre Villas-Boas a week before Christmas. He was succeeded by the club's technical co-ordinator, Tim Sherwood, who immediately led a revival of five wins and a draw in his first six matches, sparked by goals from a revitalised Emmanuel Adebayor. The purple patch ended with a 5-1 home defeat by City and although Spurs made further progress in the Europa League, it continued to have an effect on their Premier League form. By the time they went out to Benfica after reaching the last 16, Spurs had lost six matches in the wake of Thursday matches in that competition. They try again in the new season after a last-day 3-0 win over Aston Villa guaranteed sixth place – but with a new manager. Sherwood, who claimed he would have qualified for the Champions League had he been in charge for the entire season, was sacked five months into an 18-month contract, accused of being too outspoken, and replaced by Southampton's Mauricio Pochettino.

Adebayor E 20 (1)	Fryers E 3 (4)	Rose D 22
Bentaleb N 11 (4)	Holtby L 6 (7)	Sandro.................... 10 (7)
Capoue E 8 (4)	Kaboul Y 11 (2)	Sigurdsson G......... 14 (11)
Chadli N 15 (9)	Kane H...................... 6 (4)	Soldado R 22 (6)
Chiriches V 16 (1)	Lamela E 3 (6)	Townsend A........... 12 (13)
Dawson M 31 (1)	Lennon A 26 (1)	Veljkovic M .... - (2)
Defoe J 3 (11)	Lloris H 37	Vertonghen J................23
Dembele M 22 (6)	Naughton K 19 (3)	Walker K 26
Eriksen C 23 (2)	Paulinho 28 (2)	
Friedel B..........................1	Pritchard A .... - (1)	

League goals (55): Adebayor 11, Eriksen 7, Paulinho 6, Soldado 6, Sigurdsson 5, Kane 3, Capoue 1, Chadli 1, Chiriches 1, Defoe 1, Dembele 1, Holtby 1, Kaboul 1, Lennon 1, Rose 1, Sandro 1, Townsend 1, Walker 1, Opponents 5
FA Cup goals: None. **Capital One Cup goals** (7): Defoe 2, Adebayor 1, Chadli 1, Kane 1, Paulinho 1, Sigurdsson 1
Europa League goals (29): Defoe 7, Soldado 5, Chadli 3, Eriksen 3, Adebayor 2, Holtby 2, Dembele 1, Lamela 1, Paulinho 1, Rose 1, Townsend 1, Vertonghen 1, Opponents 1
Average home league attendance: 35,808. **Player of Year**: Christian Eriksen

WEST BROMWICH ALBION

Albion started poorly, never got into their stride, flirted with the relegation zone for much of the time and finished a season to forget fourth from bottom. Steve Clarke and his successor, Pepe Mel, struggled to make much impact on a side whose habit of wasting winning leads could have proved costly. Three times they conceded a 2-0 advantage established in the opening 11 minutes – twice against Aston Villa, once against Cardiff. A 3-0 lead against Tottenham was also squandered, with an equaliser in that game surrendered in stoppage-time. Clarke, who the previous season had led the club to their highest Premier League finish of eighth after taking over from Roy Hodgson, was sacked in mid-December in the wake of four successive defeats and replaced by Mel, himself dismissed by Real Betis five weeks earlier. The Spaniard had to contend with the Nicolas Anelka affair, with the striker banned and fined by the FA for a racially offensive 'quenelle' gesture during the game against West Ham and later fired by the club for gross misconduct. Mel's first win, 2-1 at Swansea and achieved by Youssouf Mulumbu's 85th minute goal, came in his eighth game. Albion went on to beat Norwich and West Ham, but these were only his only successes in 17 games in charge. Albion lost their last three games, surviving by three points, and Mel left by mutual consent after four months in charge. He was replaced by Alan Irvine, head of Everton's Academy.

Amalfitano M............ 26 (2)	Jones B 21	Reid S 16
Anelka N................ 11 (1)	Long S................. 11 (4)	Ridgewell L....................33
Anichebe V 11 (13)	Lugano D................. 7 (2)	Rosenberg M............ 1 (3)
Berahino S............. 11 (21)	McAuley G 32	Sessegnon S 23 (3)
Brunt C.................... 25 (3)	Morrison J............. 23 (9)	Sinclair S.................... 4 (4)
Daniels L .... - (1)	Mulumbu Y 33 (4)	Thievy 3 (3)
Dawson C................. 10 (2)	Myhill B.........................14	Vydra M 7 (16)
Dorrans G 12 (2)	O'Neil L .... - (3)	Yacob C 22 (5)
Foster B..........................24	Olsson J.........................32	
Gera Z 5 (9)	Popov G...................... 1 (1)	

League goals (43): Berahino 5, Sessegnon 5, Amalfitano 4, Anichebe 3, Brunt 3, Long 3, Vydra 3, Anelka 2, Dorrans 2, McAuley 2, Mulumbu 2, Thievy 2, Lugano 1, Morrison 1, Olsson 1, Ridgewell 1, Yacob 1, Opponents 2
FA Cup goals: None. **Capital One Cup goals** (4): Berahino 4
Average home league attendance: 25,193. **Player of Year**: Ben Foster

WEST HAM UNITED

Sam Allardyce had an uneasy relationship with sections of the Upton Park crowd, unhappy about what they maintained was a negative style of play and worried about the threat to their Premier League status. While some clubs under pressure changed managers in an effort to get out of trouble, West Ham kept faith. The immediate result was a move out of the bottom three with consecutive victories over Swansea, Aston Villa, Norwich and Southampton. Kevin Nolan played a key role, scoring five goals to make amends for two previous red cards in quick succession for which he came in for strong criticism. These victories were rewarded with a place in mid-table and suggested it could be maintained. Instead, there were more mixed results, with the fans again voicing their feelings, particularly during a run of four straight defeats which could have left the team vulnerable to those below them. A 2-0 win over Tottenham in the final home game ensured there would be no last-day pressure and although there remained speculation about the future, Allardyce kept his job. His target was to build a bigger, better squad, with the priority to introduce more attacking options after Andy Carroll's return of two goals in 15 appearances since returning from injury.

Adrian 20	Diarra A..................... 1 (2)	Nocerino A................. 2 (8)
Armero P 3 (2)	Downing S 29 (3)	Nolan K 33
Borriello M.................. - (2)	Jaaskelainen J.............18	O'Brien J 13 (4)
Carroll A 12 (3)	Jarvis M.................. 23 (9)	Petric M .... - (3)
Cole J 6 (14)	Johnson R.................. 2 (2)	Rat R 11 (4)
Cole C 9 (17)	Lee E .... - (1)	Reid W 18 (4)
Collins J 22 (2)	Maiga M 11 (3)	Taylor M.................. 16 (4)
Collison J................... 6 (4)	McCartney G 20 (2)	Tomkins J 31
Demel G 30 (2)	Morrison R 12 (4)	Vaz Te R 3 (5)
Diame M.................. 29 (6)	Noble M 38	

League goals (40): Nolan 7, Cole C 6, Diame 4, Cole J 3, Morrison 3, Noble 3, Carroll 2, Jarvis 2, Vaz Te 2, Collins 1, Demel 1, Downing 1, Maiga 1, Reid 1, Opponents 3
FA Cup goals: None. **Capital One Cup goals (9):** Jarvis 2, Morrison 2, Vaz Te 2, Collins 1, Maiga 1, Taylor 1
Average home league attendance: 34,196. **Player of Year:** Mark Noble

CHAMPIONSHIP

BARNSLEY

Danny Wilson's return to Oakwell for a second spell as manager failed to spark the revival needed to beat the drop. Barnsley were marooned in the bottom three for virtually the whole season and a late surge was not enough to prevent an end to eight seasons in the Championship. They conceded more goals (77) than any other team – a pattern set early on with five conceded against Blackburn and Watford and four against Wigan in the opening 11 matches which yielded a single victory. Wilson, previously in charge from 1994–98, took over following the sacking of David Flitcroft, who had kept them up by a point in 2013, and a brief spell with Micky Mellon as caretaker. After winning only one of his first ten matches, there were two convincing away victories in the space of five days to offer an escape route. Barnsley overcame promotion-chasing Reading 3-1 and Yeovil 4-1 to close within a point of moving out of the relegation zone. Another team in trouble, Charlton, were defeated on their own ground, but Easter setbacks against Leeds and Derby, left them needing to win at Middlesbrough to go into the final fixture against Queens Park Rangers still with a chance of staying up. They led at the Riverside, but were pegged back within a minute and conceded twice in stoppage time.

Bree J .... - (1)	Cywka T.................. 15 (15)	Digby P....................... 2 (3)
Butland J.......................13	Dagnall C................... 5 (3)	Etuhu K.................... 16 (4)
Crainie M................. 34 (1)	Dawson S.................. 29 (8)	Fox D 7

Frimpong E	6 (3)	
Goulbourne S	4	
Hassell B	2 (2)	
Hunt J	9 (2)	
Jennings D	24 (3)	
Kennedy T	44	
Lawrence L	10 (4)	
McCourt P	15 (8)	
McLaughlin R	9	
Mellis J	24 (6)	
Mvoto J-Y	25 (3)	
Noble-Lazarus R	2 (10)	
Nyatanga L	10 (2)	
O'Brien J	19 (10)	
O'Grady C	39 (1)	
Pedersen M	12 (6)	
Perkins D	22 (1)	
Pollitt M	2	
Proschwitz N	8 (6)	
Ramage P	24	
Rose D	1 (2)	
Scotland J	4 (16)	
Shea B	5 (3)	
Steele J	31	
Tudgay M	5	
Wiseman S	23	
Woods M	6 (2)	

League goals (44): O'Grady 15, Cywka 4, Proschwitz 4, Jennings 3, McCourt 2, Mellis 2, Mvoto 2, O'Brien 2, Pedersen 2, Scotland 2, Dagnall 1, Dawson 1, Kennedy 1, Lawrence 1, Noble-Lazarus 1, Tudgay 1
FA Cup goals (1): O'Brien 1. **Capital One Cup goals** (1): Dawson 1
Average home league attendance: 11,557. **Player of Year**: Chris O'Grady

BIRMINGHAM CITY

Great escapes don't come much more dramatic than the one Birmingham delivered on the final day of the season. A point adrift in the bottom three, they were two goals down after 76 minutes at Bolton and a fall into the third tier of English football for the first time in 20 years looked on the cards. Instead, the 6ft 8in Serbian Nikola Zigic pulled one back, Paul Caddis equalised in stoppage time and Doncaster's defeat at Leicester meant they survived with a superior goal difference. It had been a turbulent campaign for the cash-strapped club, whose owner Carson Yeung was jailed for six years in Hong Kong for money laundering. Manager Lee Clark's team, built largely on free transfers and loan signings, won just two of their 23 home games. The first, 4-1 against Sheffield Wednesday, was notable for 20-year-old Jesse Lingard, on loan from Manchester United, scoring all four goals on his debut. Ten days later, Millwall were beaten 4-0. There followed a run of ten games unbeaten, largely the result of away form, accompanied by a move eight points clear of trouble. But with loanees coming and going and Clark bemoaning the 'spine being ripped out of the team', Birmingham began sinking. They dropped into the relegation zone when losing to Leeds and a 13th home defeat, against Wigan, came in the penultimate game.

Adeyemi T	32 (3)	
Allan S	2 (3)	
Ambrose D	1	
Arthur K	- (1)	
Bartley K	14 (3)	
Bell A	1	
Blackett T	6 (2)	
Brown R	3 (3)	
Burke C	37 (7)	
Burn D	23 (1)	
Caddis P	35 (3)	
Dudka D	1 (1)	
Eardley N	5	
Elliott W	10 (5)	
Ferguson S	9 (9)	
Gray D	1 (6)	
Green M	7 (3)	
Hancox M	11 (3)	
Howard B	4 (1)	
Huws E	17	
Ibe J	4 (7)	
Lee O	14 (2)	
Lingard J	13	
Lovenkrands P	3 (12)	
Macheda F	10 (8)	
Martin A	6 (2)	
Mclean A	2 (5)	
Mullins H	7 (1)	
Murphy D	6	
Novak L	33 (5)	
Packwood W	12	
Randolph D	46	
Reilly C	21 (4)	
Robinson P	40	
Rusnak A	3	
Shinnie A	18 (8)	
Spector J	22	
Thorpe T	6	
Zigic N	21 (12)	

League goals (58): Macheda 10, Novak 8, Zigic 8, Lingard 6, Caddis 5, Burke 4, Bartley 3, Huws 2, Murphy 2, Shinnie 2, Adeyemi 1, Gray 1, Green 1, Howard 1, Ibe 1, Lee 1, Lovenkrands 1, Opponents 1
FA Cup goals (4): Burke 2, Novak 1, Robinson 1. **Capital One Cup goals** (13): Adeyemi 2, Allan 2, Bartley 2, Lovenkrands 2, Burn 1, Green 1, Lee 1, Novak 1, Shinnie 1
Average home league attendance: 15,457. **Player of Year**: Paul Robinson

BLACKBURN ROVERS

Jordan Rhodes enjoyed another productive season after saving Rovers from relegation in 2013. But his 25 goals, a total second only to Ross McCormack, of Leeds, along with his team's strong finish, were not quite enough for a place in the play-offs. Victory at Reading, earned by a goal

from Craig Conway on his first start for the club, took them within four points of the top-six. Then, three defeats in the space of 11 days proved costly. They were beaten in local derbies by Bolton and Burnley, and by Bournemouth, to lose touch with the leading group. A hat-trick by Rhodes against his former club, Huddersfield, next time out proved the start of an 11-match unbeaten run which produced 27 goals and took his side back into contention. It included a hat-trick by Rudy Gestede against Charlton which helped the former Cardiff striker win the division's Player of the Month award for April. Rovers, however, went into the last match at home still three points behind, and with an inferior goal difference. They defeated Wigan 4-3, but had to settle for eighth place.

Best L 5 (3)	Gestede R 21 (6)	Marshall B 13 (5)
Cairney T 36 (1)	Hanley G........................38	Morris J .... - (4)
Campbell D J 2 (5)	Henley A............... 13 (1)	Olsson M 4 (4)
Conway C.............. 16 (2)	Judge A 7 (4)	Rhodes J.................. 45 (1)
Dann S........................25	Kane T 23 (4)	Robinson P 21
Dunn D 14 (9)	Kean J........................18	Rochina 2 (3)
Eastwood S................7	Keane M......................13	Spurr T 43
Etuhu D.................. - (3)	Kilgallon M 23 (2)	Taylor C 14 (20)
Evans C 17 (4)	King J................. 20 (12)	Varney L 3 (5)
Fabio Nunes.............. - (1)	Lowe J.................... 38 (1)	Williamson L 22 (10)
Feeney L 1 (5)	Marrow A 2 (1)	

League goals (70): Rhodes 25, Gestede 13, Cairney 5, Conway 4, Dunn 4, Keane 3, Spurr 3, Best 2, Kane 2, King 2, Marshall 2, Evans 1, Hanley 1, Kilgallon 1, Lowe 1, Opponents 1
FA Cup goals (1) Dann 1. **Capital One Cup goals** (3): Cairney 1, Judge 1, Taylor 1
Average home league attendance: 14,961. **Player of Year**: Tom Cairney

BLACKPOOL

A flying start, a potentially disastrous slump and a nervous finish made it a roller-coaster season at Bloomfield Road. Blackpool were top with 16 points from the first six matches and looking good. Instead, they went into reverse, accompanied by a serious disciplinary problem with nine players sent off in the first half of the campaign. Three were dismissed near the end of their defeat at Yeovil – Kirk Broadfoot for a second yellow card in the 89th minute, followed by Ricardo Fuller (straight red) and Gary MacKenzie (second booking) in stoppage-time. Four days later, Neal Bishop and Angel Martinez saw red at Derby. Manager Paul Ince was sacked in late January after a run of nine matches produced a single point, with Scotland midfielder Barry Ferguson taking over as caretaker – a position he retained to the end of the campaign. Ferguson stopped playing to concentrate on managing, but brought himself back for matches against Leeds and Burnley, both of which added to the list of defeats and resulted in a drop into the bottom three. Finally, in the penultimate match, came salvation in the form of a 2-0 win at Wigan – only the third in 28 matches – achieved by goals from Andy Keogh and Stephen Dobbie. Blackpool were still in danger, but despite a 3-0 home defeat by Charlton, results elsewhere meant they survived. Former Charlton manager Jose Riga was then brought in.

Almond L.................... - (1)	Earnshaw R................... - (1)	Ince T..................... 22 (1)
Angel Martinez 18 (8)	Eccleston N 2 (2)	Keogh A.................. 9 (5)
Barkhuizen T............. 2 (12)	Ferguson B 18 (1)	MacKenzie G................35
Basham C 37 (3)	Foley K 4 (1)	McGahey H 4
Bishop N 29 (6)	Fuller R 22 (5)	McMahon T.................18
Blackett T.......................5	Gilks M........................46	Orr B 3 (1)
Broadfoot K...................33	Goodwillie D............ 8 (5)	Osbourne I 23 (1)
Cathcart C 29 (1)	Gosling D 13 (1)	Perkins D.......................20
Caton J...................... - (2)	Grandin E 3 (4)	Robinson J............. 33 (1)
Chopra M................. 5 (13)	Grant R 5 (1)	Tyson N .... - (10)
Davies S 13 (15)	Halliday A 12 (6)	Vellios A 2
Delfouneso N 3 (8)	Haroun F 5 (4)	Zeegelaar M .... - (2)
Dobbie S................. 23 (4)	Harris R 2 (2)	

League goals (38): Ince 7, Fuller 6, Dobbie 4, Davies 3, Goodwillie 3, Keogh 3, Basham 2, Gosling 2, Barkhuizen 1, Bishop 1, Cathcart 1, Grandin 1, Halliday 1, MacKenzie 1, Osbourne 1, Opponents 1
FA Cup goals (1): Barkhuizen 1. **Capital One Cup goals:** None
Average home league attendance: 14,216. **Player of Year**: Matt Gilks

BOLTON WANDERERS

A wretched start to the season effectively ruled out any prospect of another bid for a return to the Premier League. Bolton missed out on the play-offs on goal difference in 2013, but this time failed to win any of the opening ten matches. Five draws and five defeats represented the club's worst league start for 111 years before a 2-1 victory at Birmingham offered some welcome relief. Another lean run, this time a mid-season nine games without a victory, kept them in the bottom half of the table. It included a 7-1 beating at Reading, but the threat of being sucked into a relegation struggle was averted by successive wins over Watford (2-0), Blackburn (4-0) and Leeds (5-1). Bolton went on to put together a late run of seven undefeated matches, only to have more indifferent home form exposed. They won only six times on their own ground, one of the poorest records in the division, and finished with a defeat by Leicester and a draw against Birmingham, who retrieved a two-goal lead for the point which prevented relegation.

Andrews K 1	Jutkiewicz L 16 (4)	Odelusi S .... - (5)
Baptiste A................ 37 (2)	Kellett A .... - (3)	Pratley D................ 19 (1)
Beckford J 20 (13)	Knight Z 24 (7)	Ream T...........................42
Bogdan A.....................29	Lester C .... - (1)	Spearing J.....................45
Chung-Yong Lee...... 32 (13)	Lonergan A..................17	Threlkeld O 2
Danns N 26 (7)	Mason J.................. 12 (4)	Tierney M........................8
Davies C 2 (6)	McNaughton K 13	Trotter L.................. 10 (6)
Davies M 14 (4)	Mears T...........................1	Wheater D............... 21 (2)
Eagles C 13 (3)	Medo....................... 30 (5)	White H...................... 1 (1)
Feeney L.................... 3 (1)	Mills M 31 (11)	Youngs T .... - (1)
Hall R.................. 11 (11)	Moritz A.................. 7 (16)	
Hutton A..........................9	Ngog D 10 (7)	

League goals (59): Beckford 7, Jutkiewicz 7, Moritz 7, Danns 6, Mason 6, Baptiste 4, Chung-Yong Lee 3, Ngog 3, Knight 2, Medo 2, Pratley 2, Spearing 2, Davies M 1, Eagles 1, Hall 1, McNaughton 1, Mills 1, Trotter 1, Wheater 1, Opponents 1
FA Cup goals (2): Beckford 1, Ngog 1. **Capital One Cup goals** (4): Odelusi 2, Beckford 1, Hall 1
Average home league attendance: 16,140. **Player of Year**: Tim Ream

BOURNEMOUTH

Another season to savour at the Goldsands Stadium, where they were dreaming of place in the play-offs until the penultimate round of matches. Eddie Howe's promoted team had been locked into a secure lower mid-table position, with no relegation worries barring a complete collapse, when the campaign took on a whole new meaning. Yann Kermorgant, on his first start after a winter transfer move from Charlton, scored a hat-trick in a 5-0 win over Doncaster to launch a run of eight wins in ten matches. Kermorgant netted two more in a 4-1 victory over Leeds, his side scored another four against Birmingham and put three past Reading, with leading marksman Lewis Grabban again to the fore. This purple patch took Bournemouth to within two points of sixth-place Reading. But they conceded two goals in the final few minutes to lose 4-2 at home to Sheffield Wednesday and had to be satisfied with a point at Ipswich. And although two goals each from Grabban and Kermorgant accounted for Nottingham Forest 4-1, this success was not enough to keep the dream alive going into the final fixture at Millwall. Even so, it was an excellent effort, with Grabban finishing on 22 goals, all in the league.

Allsop R 11 (1)	Collison J..........................4	Daniels C 22 (1)
Arter H 31	Cook S..........................38	Elphick T................. 34 (4)
Camp L..........................33	Coulibaly M................ 2 (5)	Flahavan D.................. - (1)

Francis S 45 (1)	Kermorgant Y 11 (5)	Rantie T 14 (15)
Fraser R................ 23 (14)	MacDonald S......... 11 (12)	Ritchie M 28 (2)
Grabban L................ 43 (1)	McQuoid J 1	Smith A 1 (4)
Harte I.................... 22 (2)	O'Kane E 32 (5)	Surman A 30 (5)
Henderson S 2	Pitman B 12 (22)	Thomas W 1 (9)
Hughes R................. 1 (4)	Pugh M................ 32 (10)	Ward E 22 (11)

League goals (67): Grabban 22, Kermorgant 9, Ritchie 9, Pitman 5, Pugh 5, Arter 3, Cook 3, Fraser 3, Rantie 3, Elphick 1, Francis 1, Harte 1, O'Kane 1, Opponents 1
FA Cup goals (4): Pitman 2, Elphick 1, Fraser 1. **Capital One Cup goals** (1): O'Kane 1.
Average home league attendance: 9,951. **Player of Year**: Lewis Grabban

BRIGHTON AND HOVE ALBION

Brighton overcame injury problems during the season to reach the play-offs in a dramatic final match. But a double blow undermined their bid to go further. Ankle trouble ruled out Matthew Upson from the second leg of the semi-final at Derby, where his side had to overcome a 2-1 deficit. Then, with the return game still goalless, captain Gordon Greer, his partner in one the most settled and secure central defensive partnerships in the division, went off with a damaged hamstring. Brighton eventually went down 4-1 and also lost manager Oscar Garcia, who resigned afterwards, having been at the club for less than a year. The Spaniard was forced to bring in youngsters in the early part of the campaign when his side, with eight players sidelined, won only three of the opening 13 fixtures. By the midway point, Brighton had moved up and were right in the thick of it after a 4-1 victory away to champions-elect Leicester, followed by a 3-0 win over Charlton. Going into the final day of the regular campaign, Brighton were a point behind sixth-place Reading, with the two sides having identical goal differences. They ended it with a 2-1 win at Nottingham Forest, delivered by Leonardo Ulloa's stoppage-time goal, while Reading drew 2-2 against Burnley. Former Liverpool defender Sami Hyypia suceeded Garcia.

Agustien K 5 (6)	Chicksen A................. - (1)	LuaLua K 11 (21)
Andrews K 28 (3)	Conway C 11 (2)	Mackail-Smith C........ - (5)
Ankergren C 1	Crofts A 23	Maksimenko V.................1
Barker G .... - (1)	Dunk L 4 (2)	March S................... 7 (16)
Barnes A 17 (5)	El-Abd A 5 (4)	Obika A .... - (5)
Brezovan P....................4	Greer G....................40	Orlandi A 9 (5)
Bridcutt L 8 (3)	Ince R 26 (2)	Rodriguez D 6 (4)
Bruno 31 (2)	Kuszczak T 41	Stephens D 12 (2)
Buckley W 20 (10)	Lingard J 15	Ulloa L 31 (2)
Calderon I 18 (5)	Lita L .... - (5)	Upson M.......................43
Caskey J 19 (9)	Lopez D 26 (8)	Ward S.......................44

Play-offs – appearances: Andrews 2, Buckley 2, Calderon 2, Greer 2, Kuszczak 2, Lingard 2, Orlandi 2, Ulloa 2, Ward 2, Dunk 1, Ince 1, Forster-Caskey 1, Upson 1, LuaLua – (2), Mackail-Smith – (2), March – (1), Chicksen – (1)
League goals (55): Ulloa 14, Barnes 5, Crofts 5, Ward 4, Buckley 3, Caskey 3, Lingard 3, Lopez 3, Calderon 2, Stephens 2, Upson 2, Andrews 1, Bruno 1, Conway 1, Greer 1, Lita 1, LuaLua 1, Rodriguez 1, Opponents 2. **Play-offs – goals** (2): Lingard 1, LuaLua 1
FA Cup goals (6): Ulloa 2, Crofts 1, Ince 1, March 1, Obika 1. **Capital One Cup goals** (1): Barnes 1
Average home league attendance: 27,283. **Player of Year**: Matthew Upson

BURNLEY

Burnley started the season as rank outsiders for promotion. They finished it as runners-up to Leicester – a tremendous achievement for a club limited in part to free transfers and loan signings and managed by the impressive Sean Dyche on a budget dwarfed by some of their rivals. Dyche, controversially sacked by Watford's new owners in 2010 to make way for Gianfranco Zola as manager, had to sell top scorer Charlie Austin to Queens Park Rangers through economic

necessity. But in Danny Ings, voted the Championship's Player of the Year, and Sam Vokes, he had a pair of strikers who never stopped scoring until Vokes sustained a cruciate ligament injury and was ruled out of the final seven matches of the season. By then, Burnley had a nine-point cushion, having gone 16 matches unbeaten before a 2-0 reversal against Leicester in which they could have drawn level at the top. They safely negotiated the run-in to finish with a club record total of 93 points, making sure of a place in the Premier League by beating Wigan 2-0 with goals by Ashley Barnes and Michael Kightly in front of a season's best crowd of more than 19,000. Dyche, who captained Chesterfield to the semi-finals of the FA Cup in 1997, called his team's performance 'unbelievable' in a division widely regarded as becoming tougher by the year.

Arfield S 42 (3)	Ings D 40	Shackell J.......................46
Baird C...................... 5 (2)	Jones D 46	Stanislas J 7 (20)
Barnes A............... 11 (10)	Kightly M 32 (4)	Stock B 2 (7)
Cisak A .... - (1)	Lafferty D 8 (2)	Treacy K 9 (18)
Duff M...........................41	Long K 5 (2)	Trippier K.......................41
Edgar D 5 (12)	Marney D 38	Vokes S 39
Heaton T.......................46	Mee B 38	Wallace R 5 (9)
Hewitt S .... - (1)	Noble R .... - (1)	

League goals (72): Ings 21, Vokes 20, Arfield 8, Kightly 5, Barnes 3, Marney 3, Shackell 2, Stanislas 2, Treacy 2, Trippier 1, Duff 1, Jones 1, Opponents 3
FA Cup goals (3): Ings 1, Long 1, Vokes 1. **Capital One Cup goals** (8): Ings 4, Arfield 1, Jones 1, Stanislas 1, Trippier 1
Average home league attendance: 13,719. **Player of Year**: Sam Vokes

CHARLTON ATHLETIC:

The shadow of relegation hung over The Valley for much of a troubled season. Chris Powell, the Championship's longest-serving manager with three years in charge, bore the brunt of it, ironically at the same time as supervising a run to the quarter-finals of the FA Cup. He was sacked by new owner Roland Duchatelet in early March with his side bottom, having had to contend with the sale of key men Dale Stephens and Yann Kermorgant in the winter transfer window, alongside the introduction of players on loan from another club owned by the Belgian businessman, Standard Liege. Powell was replaced by Jose Riga, former director of AC Milan's academy, who also found league goals hard to come by until Charlton put three past Yeovil and Sheffield Wednesday, on-loan Marvin Sordell scoring a hat-trick at Hillsborough. Defeat by fellow-strugglers Barnsley prompted more concern and survival was still in the balance after the penultimate home game which Charlton lost 3-1 to Blackburn. Three days later, there was relief when they made use of a game in hand to defeat Watford by the same scoreline, thanks to Callum Harriott's first league goals of the campaign and one by captain Johnnie Jackson. The win provided a five-point cushion and no worries about a last-day visit to Blackpool. With the pressure off, Harriott netted all three goals in a 3-0 success. Riga left at the end of his short-term contract, replaced by another Belgian Bob Peeters.

Ajdarevic A 13 (6)	Hamer B 32	Poyet D..........................20
Alnwick B 10	Harriott C 17 (11)	Pritchard B 12 (5)
Church S 28 (10)	Hughes A.................... 1 (6)	Solly C..................... 10 (2)
Cook J 1 (2)	Jackson J............... 34 (4)	Sordell M................. 20 (11)
Cort L.......................1(2)_	Kermorgant Y 17 (4)	Stephens D 24 (2)
Cousins J 37 (5)	Lennon M 1 (1)	Stewart C 15 (3)
Dervite D 33 (7)	Morrison M 45	Thuram-Ulien Y 4
Evina C 4 (4)	Nego L 1	Tudgay M .... - (2)
Fox M 5 (1)	Obika J 3 (9)	Wiggins R 38
Ghoochanneijhad R... 10 (5)	Parzyszek P................. - (1)	Wilson L 39 (3)
Gower M 6 (1)	Petrucci D................... - (5)	Wood R..................... 18 (3)
Green D 5 (8)	Pigott J 2 (9)	

League goals (41): Sordell 7, Harriott 5, Jackson 5, Kermorgant 5, Church 3, Stephens 3, Stewart 3, Ajdarevic 2, Cousins 2, Dervite 2, Wilson 2, Ghoochanneijhad 1, Morrison 1
FA Cup goals (8): Kermorgant 3, Church 2, Green 1, Harriott 1, Morrison 1. **Capital One Cup goals** (6): Church 2, Green 1, Pigott 1, Sordell 1, Stephens 1
Average home league attendance: 16,134. **Player of Year**: Diego Poyet

DERBY COUNTY

For Steve McClaren, it was another crushing Wembley disappointment; for Derby's players, a heartbreaking end to their bid for a place in the Premier League. They dominated the Play-off Final, but failed to turn superiority into goals and paid the price when Bobby Zamora scored a last-minute winner for Queens Park Rangers. A club record points total of 85 and top place in the division's scoring charts with 84 goals proved scant consolation. They finished third, five points ahead of Rangers, and had swept aside Brighton 6-2 on aggregate in the semi-finals. McClaren, England's manager when defeat by Croatia meant failure to qualify for Euro 2008, was charged with reaching the play-offs when appointed at Pride Park at the end of September. He replaced Nigel Clough, the Championship's longest-serving manager, who was sacked after three defeats in eight plays with his side in the bottom half of the table. The new man made an immediate impact, a 3-1 victory over Leeds and not long after the start of a seven-match winning run. By the end of February, Derby were two points behind second-place Burnley, but lost touch after failing to score in four successive games. That sequence ended with Craig Bryson scoring a hat-trick in a 5-0 victory over Nottingham Forest, the biggest against their rivals for 116 years.

Bailey J .... - (1)	Eustace J................ 28 (7)	Martin C 44
Bamford P 14 (7)	Forsyth C 46	Naylor L........................ - (4)
Bennett M................ 1 (12)	Freeman K 5 (1)	Russell J 23 (16)
Bryson C 43 (2)	Grant L..........................46	Sammon C 3 (34)
Buxton J 43 (2)	Hendrick J 18 (12)	Smith A 7 (1)
Cisse K..................... 1 (2)	Hughes W 37 (4)	Thorne G.........................9
Coutts P 3 (5)	Jacobs M .... - (3)	Ward J 31 (7)
Davies B 1 (3)	Keane M 4 (3)	Whitbread Z 4
Dawkins S................ 20 (6)	Keogh R 41	Wisdom A 34

Play-offs – appearances: Buxton 3, Forsyth 3, Grant 3, Hendrick 3, Keogh 3, Martin 3, Russell 3, Thorne 3, Ward 3, Wisdom 3, Hughes 2 (1), Bryson 1 (1), Dawkins – (3), Bamford – (2), Eustace – (1), Sammon – (1)
League goals (84): Martin 20, Bryson 16, Russell 9, Bamford 8, Ward 7, Dawkins 4, Hendrick 4, Hughes 3, Buxton 2, Forsyth 2, Sammon 2, Bennett 1, Eustace 1, Keogh 1, Thorne 1, Whitbread 1, Opponents 2. **Play-offs – goals** (6): Martin 2, Hendrick 1, Hughes 1, Thorne 1, Opponents 1
FA Cup goals: None. **Capital One Cup goals** (7): Martin 3, Sammon 2, Hughes 1, Jacobs 1
Average home league attendance: 24,933. **Player of Year**: Craig Byson

DONCASTER ROVERS

Relegation is hard for any club to take. When it comes as the result of a stoppage-time goal, it's a desperate moment. Such was the fate of Paul Dickov's side, who went into the final day of the regular season a point above the drop zone. They held out for 75 minutes away to champions Leicester before conceding a penalty which settled the match. But with Birmingham, the team below them, trailing 2-0 at Bolton, their position looked secure. Instead, Birmingham pulled one back and levelled in the third minute of stoppage-time. Rovers went down with an inferior goal difference and made an immediate return to League One, having gone up as champions on an equally dramatic last day in 2013. In truth, much of the damage was done previously. After a 5-0 defeat at Bournemouth, they won four of the next six matches – against Huddersfield, Watford, Sheffield Wednesday and Leeds – to move eight points clear of the bottom three. That should have been enough. Instead, four successive home defeats, another reversal at Ipswich and a goalless draw against Millwall in which Abdoulaye Meite was sent off – a decision rescinded on appeal – left them hanging on.

Bennett K .... - (3)
Bowery J 3
Brown C 38 (2)
Coppinger J 34 (7)
Cotterill D 25 (15)
De Val Fernandez M 2 (3)
Duffy M 28 (8)
Forrester H 3 (4)
Furman D 25 (7)
Husband J 28
Johnstone S 18

Jones R 12
Keegan P 34
Khumalo B 30
Macheda F 12 (3)
McCombe J .... - (2)
McCullough L 13 (1)
Meite A 21
Neill L 4
Paynter B 1 (8)
Petersen A 1 (4)
Quinn P 31 (4)

Robinson T 19 (12)
Sharp B 15 (1)
Stevens E 11 (2)
Syers D .... - (2)
Tamas G 13 (1)
Turnbull R 28
Wabara R 13
Wakefield L 3 (1)
Wellens R 36 (1)
Woods M 3 (1)
Yun Suk-Young 2 (1)

League goals (39): Brown 9, Robinson 5, Coppinger 4, Cotterill 4, Sharp 4, Macheda 3, Duffy 2, Quinn 2, Furman 1, Husband 1, Jones 1, Meite 1, Opponents 2
FA Cup goals (2): Forrester 1, Wakefield 1. **Capital One Cup goals (2):** Khumalo 1, Paynter 1
Average home league attendance: 9,040. **Player of Year:** Chris Brown

HUDDERSFIELD TOWN

Huddersfield looked set to challenge for a position in the top half of the table after a 5-0 win over Barnsley, inspired by record-signing Nahki Wells. The £1.3m buy from Bradford in the January transfer window, provided assists for four of the goals. It was the third five-goal performance of the season for Mark Robins's side after victories over Bournemouth and Yeovil. But it was followed by the failure to score against three relegation-threatened teams, Doncaster, Charlton and Blackpool, and a worrying slide continued into the back end of the season. They went 10 matches without a victory and needed the points already accumulated as a safeguard against being overtaken by a bunch of teams below them. Even so, a 2-1 success at Yeovil came as a welcome relief and again Wells played a key role. The Bermudan striker opened the scoring with his seventh goal since moving and Adam Clayton netted the winner in stoppage-time. Huddersfield then had a final flourish – a 4-1 win at Watford featuring a second-half hat-trick from substitute Danny Ward – to finish two places higher than in 2013.

Billing P .... - (1)
Bunn H .... - (3)
Carr D .... - (2)
Carroll J 4
Clarke P 24 (2)
Clayton A 41 (1)
Lopez C .... - (2)
Dixon P 37
Gerrard A 39 (1)
Gobern O 12 (11)

Hammill A 42 (2)
Hogg J 34
Holmes D 2 (14)
Hunt J 1 (1)
Lolley J 1 (5)
Lynch J 27 (2)
Norwood O 37 (3)
Paterson M 13 (9)
Richards A 7 (2)
Scannell S 8 (30)

Smith T 23 (1)
Smithies A 46
Southern K 8 (2)
Stead J 6 (6)
Vaughan J 20 (3)
Wallace M 15 (2)
Ward D 27 (11)
Wells N 21 (1)
Woods C 11 (8)

League goals (58): Vaughan 10, Ward 10, Clayton 7, Wells 7, Norwood 5, Paterson 5, Hammill 4, Lynch 2, Gerrard 1, Lolley 1, Scannell 1, Southern 1, Stead 1, Woods 1, Opponents 2
FA Cup goals (3): Norwood 1, Paterson 1, Opponents 1. **Capital One Cup goals (5):** Vaughan 2, Hammill 1, Hogg 1, Lynch 1
Average home league attendance: 14,212. **Player of Year:** Adam Clayton

IPSWICH TOWN

After flirting with a play-off position for long spells, Ipswich went into the final fortnight of the season well placed to make the breakthrough. Successive wins over Huddersfield and Doncaster had lifted them to within goal difference of sixth place. They were level on 64 points with Reading and Brighton and Mick McCarthy sensed the momentum was there to maintain the challenge. But his side faltered when it mattered most, conceding two goals in three second-half minutes to lose 3-1 at Watford and twice surrendering the lead to drop points at home to Bournemouth. Then, in the final away game against promoted Burnley, their hopes were ended when McCarthy's

former Wolves player, Michael Kightly, scored the only goal. The manager acknowledged an overall improvement on the previous campaign when he took over a side bottom of the table, but expressed disappointment at missing out with players he felt were capable of going the distance. Ipswich defeated Sheffield Wednesday in the last match to finish ninth.

Anderson P 22 (9)	Hewitt E 4	Richardson F.............. 3 (4)
Berra C 41 (1)	Hunt S 15 (8)	Skuse C 43
Chambers L.....................46	Hyam L 33 (2)	Smith T 45
Cresswell A 42	Loach S 5 (1)	Tabb J 14 (13)
Ebanks-Blake S 1 (8)	Marriott J.................. - (1)	Taylor P 4 (14)
Edwards C.................. 9 (6)	McGoldrick D 30 (1)	Tunnicliffe R 23 (4)
Gerken D 41	Mings T 4 (12)	Williams J............... 11 (2)
Graham J .... - (2)	Murphy D............. 42 (3)	Wordsworth A 6 (4)
Green P 6 (8)	Nouble F............. 16 (22)	

League goals (60): McGoldrick 14, Murphy 13, Smith 6, Anderson 5, Berra 5, Chambers 3, Cresswell 2, Green 2, Nouble 2, Edwards 1, Hyam 1, Tabb 1, Taylor 1, Williams 1, Wordsworth 1, Opponents 2
FA Cup goals (3): McGoldrick 2, Nouble 1. **Capital One Cup goals:** None
Average home league attendance: 17,110. **Player of Year:** Christophe Berra

LEEDS UNITED

A bizarre sequence of events off the field captured most of the headlines at Elland Road. On the pitch, Leeds were less newsworthy, again falling short of the quality needed to challenge for a return to the top flight. Despite an outstanding contribution from Ross McCormack, they finished in the bottom half of the table, falling away in the second part of the season. When McCormack scored all four goals against Charlton, helping to establish a foothold in the play-off spots going into Christmas programme, they looked to be on the right track. But successive defeats by Nottingham Forest, Blackburn, Sheffield Wednesday (0-6) and Leicester, along with an FA Cup loss to Rochdale, cut short the optimism. Brian McDermott was sacked after ten months as manager as a £35m takeover of the club by an Italian consortium moved closer. Next day, McDermott took a call saying he had not been dismissed. The chaos continued with the Football League ruling that businessman Massimo Cellino could not assume control because of a tax offence. A fortnight later, that decision was overturned by an independent QC. McCormack, meanwhile, had netted a hat-trick against Huddersfield and went on to top the Championship's scoring charts with 28 goals. His team, however, lost five straight games to fall to 15th place. McDermott was replaced by David Hockaday, the former Forest Green manager.

Ariyibi G .... - (2)	Kebe J............................9	Smith M 20 (19)
Austin R 40	Kenny P.........................30	Stewart C................... 9 (2)
Blackstock D 2 (2)	Lees T 40 (1)	Tonge M................. 16 (7)
Brown M 12 (6)	McCormack R...............46	Varney L 11
Butland J.......................16	Mowatt A 24 (5)	Warnock S 27
Byram S 17 (8)	Murphy L........................37	White A 2 (7)
Drury A .... - (1)	Pearce J 45	Wickham C 5
El Hadji Diouf 2 (4)	Peltier L 23 (2)	Wootton S 19 (1)
Green P 7 (2)	Poleon D............. 2 (17)	Zaliukas M 13 (2)
Hunt N 13 (6)	Pugh D................. 19 (1)	

League goals (59): McCormack 28, Smith 12, Austin 3, Murphy 3, Pearce 2, Pugh 2, Varney 2, Blackstock 1, Kebe 1, Mowatt 1, Peltier 1, Poleon 1, Warnock 1, Opponents 1
FA Cup goals: None. **Capital One Cup goals** (5): Brown 1, McCormack 1, Poleon 1, Smith 1, Wootton 1
Average home league attendance: 25,088. **Player of Year:** Ross McCormack

LEICESTER CITY

Nigel Pearson led Leicester back to the Premier League after a ten-year absence and no-one could argue about their right to be there. They were the outstanding team, shadowing Queens Park Rangers and Burnley for the first half of the season, then taking a grip on top spot over Christmas and New Year. A club record run of nine successive wins swept them ten points clear. When that advantage was threatened by the consistency of second-place Burnley, a 2-0 victory at Turf Moor re-established control. Leicester went on to extend their unbeaten run to 21 games with a Friday night 2-1 win over Sheffield Wednesday, the winner coming from Frenchman Anthony Knockaert, whose penalty miss against Watford in 2013 cost his side a place in the play-off final. The following day, a combination of results ensured promotion with six games still to play. This run was ended by a 4-1 home defeat by Brighton, but substitute Lloyd Dyer's spectacular winner at Bolton a fortnight later proved a fitting title-clincher. David Nugent's tenth successful spot-kick in all competitions earned victory over Doncaster in the final game and raised the season's points tally to 102 points – another record for the club. Pearson was named the Championship's Manager of the Year.

De Laet R 35 (1)	Mahrez R 12 (7)	St Ledger S 1
Drinkwater D 43 (2)	Miquel I 6 (1)	Taylor-Fletcher G 2 (19)
Dyer L 31 (9)	Moore L 26 (4)	Vardy J 36 (1)
Hammond D.............. 7 (22)	Morgan W.....................45	Waghorn M................. - (2)
James M 28 (7)	Nugent D 44 (2)	Wasilewski M 26 (5)
King A 24 (6)	Phillips K 2 (10)	Whitbread Z 3
Knockaert A 36 (6)	Schlupp J 15 (11)	Wood C 7 (19)
Konchesky P 31	Schmeichel K.............46	

League goals (83): Nugent 20, Vardy 16, Drinkwater 7, Dyer 7, Knockaert 5, King 4, Wood 4, Mahrez 3, Taylor-Fletcher 3, Morgan 2, Phillips 2, De Laet 2, Hammond 1, James 1, Konchesky 1, Moore 1, Schlupp 1, Opponents 3
FA Cup goals (1): Nugent 1. **Capital One Cup goals** (14): Wood 4, Dyer 3, Knockaert 2, Drinkwater 1, Miquel 1, Morgan 1, Nugent 1, St Ledger 1
Average home league attendance: 24,994. **Player of Year**: Danny Drinkwater

MIDDLESBROUGH

Two unwanted club records contributed to another indifferent season on Teesside. Seven successive matches without scoring effectively ended their chances of reaching the play-offs. Nine sendings-off underlined the disappointment, seven of them coming under new manager Aitor Karanka. The Spaniard, former assistant to Jose Mourinho at Real Madrid, came in when Tony Mowbray, then the Championship's longest-serving manager with three years at the Riverside, was sacked after two wins in the opening 12 matches. Karanka enjoyed some success when a mid-winter run of five wins and a draw in six matches took his side to within five points of a place-off place. Then, the goals dried up completely, four goalless draws and three defeats sending them into the bottom half of the table 12 points adrift. The sequence was broken when on-loan Danny Graham netted twice for a 2-0 success against Ipswich. Later, there were wins over promotion-chasing Brighton, Derby and Burnley, but they were not enough and Middlesbrough finished 12th.

Adomah A................. 38 (4)	Graham D 17 (1)	Ledesman E 16 (11)
Ayala D.................... 17 (2)	Halliday A .... - (4)	Leutwiler J 1 (2)
Butterfield J 20 (11)	Haroun F .... - (1)	Main C 7 (16)
Carayol M 24 (8)	Hines S 3 (1)	Mejias T 1
Chalobah N.............. 15 (4)	Hoyte J 1 (2)	Morris B .... - (1)
Emnes M 14 (8)	Jutkiewicz L 12 (10)	Omeruo K 14
Friend G 39 (2)	Kamara K 16 (9)	Parnaby S 1 (2)
Gibson B.................. 26 (5)	Konstantopoulos D..........12	Reach A..................... 1 (1)
Given S....................16	Leadbitter G 37 (2)	Richardson F..................11

Smallwood R 9 (4)	Varga J 29 (5)	Williams R 22
Steele J 16	Whitehead D 34 (3)	Woodgate J 24 (1)
Tomlin L 9 (5)	Williams L 4 (5)	

League goals (62): Adomah 12, Carayol 8, Graham 6, Leadbitter 6, Ledesma 6, Kamara 4, Tomlin 4, Ayala 3, Butterfield 3, Friend 3, Chalobah 1, Emnes 1, Gibson 1, Jutkiewicz 1, Main 1, Whitehead 1, Opponents 1
FA Cup goals: None. **Capital One Cup goals (1):** Jutkiewicz
Average home league attendance: 15,748. **Player of Year:** George Friend

MILLWALL

Ian Holloway has been involved in some nail-biting finishes, at both ends of the table, and this was another to test the nerves of the much-travelled manager. It ended successfully with Millwall retaining their Championship place on the final day of the season when a header by Martyn Woolford brought a 1-0 victory over Bournemouth. Holloway, in his seventh job after leaving Crystal Palace by mutual consent in October, rated it his finest achievement. He took over from Steve Lomas, sacked after just six months in charge in the wake of a 4-0 defeat by Watford on Boxing Day with Millwall fourth from bottom. They stayed there for the next two months, then slipped into the relegation zone and were in serious trouble five points from safety. But a 2-1 win over Nottingham Forest was followed three days later by a 1-0 victory over Wigan – and the momentum was maintained. Two headed goals against Middlesbrough by 6ft 7in Austrian Stefan Maierhofer, on a short-term deal until end of season, took them out of the bottom three, Scott Malone came up with a stoppage-time equaliser for a point away to Queens Park Rangers and Woolford's winner stretched their unbeaten run at the most critical time of the campaign to eight matches.

Abdou N 21 (3)	Fredericks R............. 11 (3)	N'Guessan D .... - (1)
Bailey N 26 (2)	Garvan O........................ 13	Onyedinma K 3 (1)
Beevers M 27 (1)	Henry J 4 (1)	Osborne K............................ 1
Bessone F 1 (1)	Hoyte J 4 (1)	Robinson P 20 (5)
Bywater S 6 (1)	Jackson S 3 (11)	Shittu D.......................... 22
Campbell D J 6 (3)	Keogh A 6 (9)	Smith J...................... 3 (3)
Chaplow R 12 (7)	Lowry S 21 (1)	Trotter L 16 (3)
Connolly P 3 (1)	Maierhofer S 7 (4)	Upson E 10
Derry S........................ 7	Malone S 32 (1)	Waghorn M 13 (1)
Dunne A 28 (1)	Marquis J.................... 1 (1)	Williams S 15 (2)
Easter J 6 (14)	Martin L 16 (10)	Woolford M 38 (2)
Edwards C........................ 8	McDonald S 21 (11)	Wright J 2 (1)
Feeney L 5 (12)	Morison S 25 (16)	
Forde D 40	Moussi G 3	

League goals (46): Morison 8, Woolford 3, Easter 3, Malone 3, McDonald 3, Trotter 3, Waghorn 3, Campbell 2, Jackson 2, Maierhofer 2, Bailey 1, Chaplow 1, Edwards 1, Fredericks 1, Keogh 1, Martin 1, Shittu 1, Williams 1, Opponents 2
FA Cup goals (1): Woolford 1. **Capital One Cup goals (3):** Feeney 1, Keogh 1, Woolford 1
Average home league attendance: 11,062. **Player of Year:** David Forde

NOTTINGHAM FOREST

Forest's season fell apart after an FA Cup fifth round defeat by Sheffield United. They were established in a play-off position, with an eight-point cushion, and looked a good bet to make up for the disappointment of 2013 when missing out though a last-day defeat by Leicester. Instead, 12 matches failed to yield a single victory and a 5-0 defeat at Derby – the biggest defeat by their rivals for 116 years – pushed them out of the top six. Manager Billy Davies, five months into a four-year contract extension, was sacked, having previously been given a five-match touchline ban by the FA for abusive language towards referee Anthony Taylor at half-time of the match against Leicester. Gary Brazil was left to pick up the pieces as caretaker, with Stuart Pearce's

appointment as manager of the club he served as a player for 12 years not taking effect until the summer. The run continued with a 5-2 defeat by Queens Park Rangers before successive victories over Birmingham and Leeds, both earned by goals from Matt Derbyshire, offered the prospect of a revival. But another heavy defeat, 4-1 at Bournemouth, ruled that out and a last-day reversal at home to Brighton left them 11th, seven points adrift.

Abdoun D 15 (7)	Gomis K 1	Majewski R 23 (1)
Blackstock D...................1	Greening J 7 (6)	McLaughlin S...................3
Chalobah N.............. 7 (5)	Guedioura A 5	Miller I .... - (4)
Cohen C.........................16	Halford G 28 (8)	Moussi G 9 (2)
Collins D.................. 21 (2)	Harding D 13 (6)	Osborn B 6 (2)
Cox S 25 (9)	Henderson D 9 (25)	Paterson J.............. 22 (10)
Darlow K.........................43	Hobbs J.........................27	Peltier L 7
De Vries D.......................3	Jara G..................... 28 (4)	Rees J .... - (1)
Derbyshire M............ 8 (21)	Lansbury H 28 (1)	Reid A 29 (3)
Djebbour R 3 (4)	Lascelles J.....................29	Tudgay M 1 (1)
Evtimov D .... - (1)	Lichaj E 21 (3)	Vaughan D 9
Fox D 14	Mackie J 38 (7)	Wilson K 7 (2)

League goals (67): Reid 9, Cox 8, Henderson 8, Paterson 8, Derbyshire 7, Lansbury 7, Halford 4, Mackie 4, Chalobah 2, Lascelles 2, Abdoun 1, Cohen 1, Collins 1, Djebbour 1, Hobbs 1, Tudgay 1, Opponents 2
FA Cup goals (8): Paterson 4, Abdoun 1, Henderson 1, Mackie 1, Reid 1. **Capital One Cup goals** (6): Derbyshire 3, Halford 1, Lascelles 1, Majewski 1
Average home league attendance: 22,629. **Player of Year**: Andy Reid

QUEENS PARK RANGERS

Harry Redknapp was honest enough to admit that his side hardly deserved their Play-off Final victory over Derby. They were outplayed for much of the match and were hanging on when Bobby Zamora delivered a last-minute winner out of the blue. Nevertheless, it meant an immediate return to the Premier League, along with a much-needed windfall to ease the club's precarious financial position. Redknapp, who made wholesale changes to the squad relegated in 2013, also conceded that he went into the season uncertain of Rangers' prospects. His worries proved unfounded. They won eight of the opening ten fixtures and set a club record by keeping a clean sheet in eight in succession, with the evergreen Richard Dunne proving a key player in the centre of the defence. The manager made five more signings on winter transfer deadline day and the prospects of automatic promotion were maintained until three successive defeats were inflicted by Derby, Reading and Charlton. The defeats came in a run of five fixtures producing only two points and Rangers lost touch with second-place Burnley as a result. Such was the consistency of their rivals that a sizeable gap remained and they finished the regular campaign in fourth place, five points behind Derby.

Assou-Ekotto B 30 (1)	Green R 45	Murphy B.................... 1 (1)
Austin C 28 (3)	Henry K 17 (10)	O'Neil G 23 (6)
Barton J.................. 33 (1)	Hill C 40	Onuoha N 24 (2)
Benayoun Y.............. 10 (6)	Hitchcock T .... - (1)	Petrasso M................ - (1)
Carroll T 23 (3)	Hoilett J 23 (12)	Phillips M 13 (8)
Chevanton J .... - (2)	Hughes A.........................11	Simpson D 32 (1)
Donaldson C...................1	Jenas J 15 (11)	Traore A 13 (9)
Doyle K...................... 8 (1)	Johnson A 10 (7)	Wright-Phillips S 4 (7)
Dunne R 41	Keane W 6 (4)	Young L 1
Ehmer M........................ - (1)	Kranjcar N 21 (8)	Yun Suk-Young 4 (3)
Faurlin A.................. 5 (2)	Maiga M 2 (6)	Zamora R 7 (10)
Granero E 1	Morrison R 14 (1)	

Play-offs – appearances: Austin 3, Barton 3, Dunne 3, Green 3, Hill 3, Hoilett 3, O'Neil 3,

Onuoha 3, Simpson 3, Doyle 2 (1), Kranjcar 2 (1), Morrison 1 (1), Traore 1 (1), Zamora – (2), Henry – (1), Yun Suk-Young – 1
League goals (60): Austin 17, Morrison 6, Hoilett 4, Barton 3, Benayoun 3, Phillips 3, Zamora 3, Doyle 2, Jenas 2, Johnson 2, Kranjcar 2, Onuoha 2, Traore 2, Dunne 1, Henry 1, Hill 1, Hitchcock 1, Maiga 1, O'Neil 1, Yun Suk-Young 1, Opponents 2. **Play-offs – goals** (3): Austin 2, Zamora 1
FA Cup goals: None. **Capital One Cup goals** (2): Austin 1, Simpson 1
Average home league attendance: 16,655. **Player of Year**: Charlie Austin

READING

So near, yet so far for Reading, who were denied the chance of challenging for an immediate return to the Premier League by a stoppage-time goal. It was scored by Argentine striker Leonardo Ulloa, gave Brighton a 2-1 win over Nottingham Forest and put them into the play-offs. Reading, who had gone into the final day of the regular season a point ahead of their rivals, were left frustrated after drawing 2-2 with promoted Burnley. They had been in and out of the top six for most of the season before establishing what looked like a comfortable lead of five points over Brighton with six games to play. Nigel Adkins' injury-hit side were then beaten at Bournemouth and went down at Wigan to lose that advantage. But they rallied, regaining sixth place by defeating Middlesbrough and winning the penultimate fixture 3-1 at Doncaster with Adam Le Fondre's penalty and two goals in the final five minutes by Russian striker Pavel Pogrebnyak. Le Fondre had previously scored hat-tricks in successive home matches – 7-1 against Bolton and 5-1 against Blackpool.

Akpan H 17 (12)	Guthrie D................ 29 (3)	Morrison S 21
Baird C............................9	Hector M 4 (5)	Obita J 32 (2)
Blackman N 9 (21)	Karacan J 7	Pearce A 45
Bridge W............... 11 (1)	Kelly S 10 (5)	Pogrebnyak P 34 (5)
Cummings S 8 (3)	Le Fondre A 25 (13)	Robson-Kanu H 19 (17)
Drenthe R 17 (6)	Leigertwood M 2 (2)	Sharp B 6 (4)
Federici A.....................2	McAnuff J 28 (7)	Taylor J .... - (8)
Gorkss K 24 (1)	McCarthy A 44	Williams D 24 (6)
Gunter C...................44	McCleary G 35 (7)	

League goals (70): Le Fondre 15, Pogrebnyak 13, McCleary 5, Blackman 4, Guthrie 4, Robson-Kanu 4, Gorkss 3, Pearce 3, Williams 3, Drenthe 2, Karacan 2, McAnuff 2, Sharp 2, Akpan 1, Kelly 1, Morrison 1, Obita 1, Opponents 4
FA Cup goals: None. **Capital One Cup goals**: None
Average home league attendance: 19,166. **Player of Year**: Jordan Obita

SHEFFIELD WEDNESDAY

Stuart Gray guided Wednesday to relative respectability after a wretched start threatened to develop into a second successive battle to beat the drop. Under Dave Jones, they were the last of the 92 clubs to win to win in the league – drawing eight and losing four of their opening dozen matches. The victory came in some style, 5-2 against Reading, but three defeats immediately after kept them in the bottom three and Jones was sacked. Coach Gray was installed as caretaker and in his first game took two goals by on-loan Connor Wickham secured victory over leaders Leicester. Further wins over Watford and Blackpool, followed by the 6-0 defeat of Leeds, took Wednesday clear, earning Gray the job on a permanent basis. By the end of the season they were nine points clear of trouble in 16th place and would have gone higher with a better finish. The season's major disappointment came in the FA Cup when a 2-1 defeat by Charlton at Hillsborough ruled out a much-anticipated quarter-final tie against Sheffield United.

Afobe B 4 (8)	Coke G 20 (8)	Gardner A 5
Antonio M 24 (3)	Corry P .... - (1)	Gardner G 3
Best L 12 (3)	Floro R 1	Helan J 33 (10)
Buxton L........................20	Fryatt M.................... 7 (2)	Hutchinson S 8 (2)

Johnson J 5 (22)	Maghoma J 18 (7)	Oshilaja A 2
Johnson Reda.......... 17 (2)	Maguire C 23 (4)	Palmer L 33 (6)
Johnson Roger................17	Martinez D 11	Prutton D................... 7 (2)
Kirkland C....................35	Mattock J................ 20 (3)	Savic A .... - (1)
Lavery C 9 (12)	McCabe R 2 (5)	Semedo J 17 (5)
Lee K 26	McPhail S 13	Spence J 4
Llera M.................. 18 (4)	Nuhiu A................. 25 (13)	Stobbs J .... - (1)
Loovens G 21 (1)	Olofinjana S 6 (1)	Wickham C 11
Madine G .... - (1)	Onyewu O 18	Zayatte K 11

League goals (63): Maguire 9, Nuhiu 8, Wickham 8, Antonio 4, Best 4, Fryatt 4, Lavery 4, Buxton 3, Afobe 2, Helan 2, Johnson Reda 2, Maghoma 2, Mattock 2, Zayatte 2, Coke 1, Hutchinson 1, Lee 1, Prutton 1, Opponents 3
FA Cup goals (8): Best 1, Johnson J 1, Johnson Reda 1, Llera 1, Maghoma 1, Maguire 1, Mattock 1, Onyewu 1. **Capital One Cup goals** (1): McCabe 1
Average home league attendance: 21,238. **Player of Year**: Liam Palmer

WATFORD

Watford surrendered the chance of reaching the play-offs for the second successive year by conceding a host of late goals. They dropped points in the final ten minutes of ten matches, half of them during the run-in while attempting to close the gap on the top six. During that period they conceded equalisers to Blackburn, Burnley and Millwall and winners to Doncaster and Queens Park Rangers. That defeat at Loftus Road was followed by three further reversals, in which 11 goals were shipped, resulting in a bottom-half-of-the-table finish, 12 points adrift. These lapses overshadowed a club record run of six successive home wins, five of them in the league, without conceding a goal. Gianfranco Zola had made 13 summers signings – several of them loanees in the previous campaign – and his team beat promoted Bournemouth 6-1 in the first home game, with Troy Deeney scoring the club's first hat-trick for ten years. But five successive defeats at Vicarage Road resulted in Zola's dismissal in December and the appointment of fellow-Italian Giuseppe Sannino. Deeney enjoyed another prolific season – 24 Championship goals and another in an eventful FA Cup fourth round tie against Manchester City at the Etihad in which Watford led 2-0 before losing 4-2.

Abdi A 9 (4)	Doherty J .... - (1)	Merkel A 7 (4)
Acuna J 3 (6)	Doyley L 23 (1)	Murray S................ 22 (12)
Almunia M 37	Ekstrand J................ 31 (2)	Neill L .... - (1)
Angella G................. 39 (1)	Fabbrini D 8 (13)	Nosworthy N 5
Anya I..................... 29 (6)	Faraoni M D 26 (12)	O'Nien A .... - (1)
Battocchio C 21 (14)	Forestieri F 19 (9)	Park Chu-Young.......... 1 (1)
Belkalem E 5 (3)	Hall F 3 (2)	Pudil D 29 (8)
Bellerin H 6 (2)	Hoban T 5 (2)	Ranegie M 8 (2)
Bond J 9 (1)	Iriney....................... 12 (3)	Riera A 6 (2)
Brown R .... - (1)	Jakubiak A 1	Smith C 1
Cassetti M............... 32 (3)	McEachran J 5 (2)	Thorne G..........................8
Deeney T 44	McGugan L 31 (3)	Tozser D........................20
Diakite S................... 1 (5)	Mensah B .... - (1)	

League goals (74): Deeney 24, McGugan 10, Angella 7, Forestieri 7, Anya 5, Battocchio 4, Ranegie 4, Murray 3, Abdi 2, Faraoni 2, Pudil 2, Cassetti 1, Fabbrini 1, Merkel 1, Riera 1
FA Cup goals (5): Deeney 1, Faraoni 1, Forestieri 1, McGugan 1, Murray 1. **Capital One Cup goals** (7): Murray 2, Acuna 1, Angella 1, Battocchio 1, Faraoni 1, Opponents 1
Average home league attendance: 15,511. **Player of Year**: Troy Deeney

WIGAN ATHLETIC

A marathon season caught up with Wigan in the second of two crushing semi-final defeats. They went ahead through James Perch in the second leg of the play-off match at Loftus Road, the first

having finished goalless. The lead was held for more than an hour before Charlie Austin equalised from the penalty spot, then scored again in extra-time to send Queens Park Rangers through. It was Wigan's 62nd game of a season which had started with a 4-0 win at Barnsley under Owen Coyle, who succeeded Wembley winner Roberto Martinez when the Spaniard took over at Everton. Coyle was sacked after less than six months, his side suffering three home defeats in nine days and falling into bottom half of the table. Brentford's Uwe Rosler came in at the end of the club's first taste of European football – bottom of their Europa League group – and took them back up the domestic table. His new side retrieved a seven-point deficit to break into the top six by winning six successive matches. They also knocked out Crystal Palace and Cardiff in the FA Cup, followed by a repeat of the previous season's Wembley triumph over Manchester City in round six. Returning to the national scene, Wigan led Arsenal through a Jordi Gomez penalty, held the lead until the 82nd minute but lost a penalty shoot-out.

Al Habsi A 24	Gomez J 22 (9)	McManaman C 17 (13)
Albrighton M 2 (2)	Holgersson M .... - (1)	Nicholls L 6
Barnett L 39 (2)	Holt G 9 (7)	Perch J 38 (2)
Beausejour J 30 (3)	Keane W 2 (2)	Powell N 23 (8)
Boyce E 39 (3)	Kiernan R 7 (5)	Ramis I..........................15
Browning T 1 (1)	Maloney S 9 (1)	Rogne T 10 (2)
Caldwell G 2	Maynard N 11 (5)	Shotton R 7 (2)
Carson S 16	McArthur J.............. 37 (4)	Tunnicliffe R 3 (2)
Collison J................... 5 (4)	McCann C 22 (5)	Waghorn M..................15
Crainey S 14 (6)	McCarthy J.......................5	Watson B 25
Espinoza R.............. 7 (11)	McClean J................ 23 (14)	
Fortune M-A........... 16 (20)	McEachran J.............. 5 (3)	

Play-offs – appearances: Beausejour 2, Boyce 2, Caldwell 2, Carson 2, Gomez 2, Kiernan 2, Maloney 2, McArthur 2, McManaman 2, Perch 2, Fortune 1, McClean 1, Waghorn – (2), Barnett - (1), Espinoza – (1), Maynard – (1)
League goals (61): Gomez 7, Powell 7, Waghorn 5, Barnett 4, Fortune 4, Maynard 4, McArthur 4, Maloney 3, McClean 3, McManaman 3, Beausejour 2, Boyce 2, Holt 2, McCann 2, Ramis 2, Watson 2, Kiernan 1, Shotton 1, Opponents 3. **Play-offs – goals** (1): Perch 1
FA Cup goals (13): Gomez 3, Powell 2, Watson 2, Espinoza 1, Fortune 1, McCann 1, McClean 1, McManaman 1, Perch 1. **Capital One Cup goals:** None. **Community Shield goals:** None.
Average home league attendance: 15,176. **Player of Year:** Jordi Gomez

YEOVIL TOWN

The Championship is an unforgiving division. Even those clubs with money to spend on big squads are regularly caught out by its fierce competitive nature and struggle to cope. For one like Yeovil, with small crowds and limited resources, following up a momentous promotion via the Play-off Final presented a massive challenge, with the odds stacked heavily against them. So it proved, with an immediate return to League One, albeit after a brave bid which extended to the penultimate match of the campaign. Gary Johnson's side made a successful start, Ed Upson's 88th minute goal bringing victory at Millwall. But it was not until the 13th fixture that another win came – Upson's brace accounting for Nottingham Forest 3-1 and briefly lifting his side off the bottom. Johnson, restricted largely to free transfers and loan signings, added players in the winter transfer window and there was a glimmer of hope when back-to-back home wins, over Doncaster and Sheffield Wednesday, were recorded for the first time. With a month of the season remaining, Yeovil still had a chance of surviving – three points adrift. Then, a 3-2 defeat by fellow-strugglers Charlton proved pivotal and defeat at Brighton confirmed the drop.

Ayling L 41 (1)	Dunn C........................ 7 (1)	Grant J 27 (7)
Bakayogo Z 1	Edwards J 46	Hayter J 24 (13)
Davis L 18 (9)	Foley S 4 (3)	Hennessey W...................12
Dawson K 17 (18)	Fontaine L 4 (1)	Holmes D..........................5
Duffy S...........................37	Fyvie F 2	Hoskins S 6 (13)

Johnstone S 1	Moore K................. 10 (10)	Stech M..........................26
Lanzoni M................... 2 (4)	Morgan A 3 (9)	Stewart G..................- (1)
Lawrence T 17 (2)	Ngoo M 1 (5)	Tate A................................4
Lundstram J............. 13 (1)	Ofori-Twumasi N .... - (3)	Upson E 21 (3)
Madden P 7 (2)	Palazuelos R 6 (3)	Webster B 40 (1)
McAllister J.............. 35 (3)	Ralls J 33 (4)	Williams A 7 (2)
Miller I 19	Seaborne D 10	

League goals (44): Miller 10, Hayter 6, Moore 4, Upson 4, Grant 3, Ralls 3, Webster 3, Ayling 2, Lawrence 2, Lundstram 2, Davis 1, Dawson 1, Duffy 1, Edwards 1, Opponents 1
FA Cup goals (4): Hayter 2, Grant 1, Moore 1. **Capital One Cup goals (4):** Ayling 1, Dawson 1, Upson 1, Webster 1
Average home league attendance: 6,616. **Player of Year:** Luke Ayling

LEAGUE ONE

BRADFORD CITY

When Nahki Wells continued his own hot streak and his side quickly picked up the threads of the previous momentous season when they won promotion and reached the League Cup Final, there was an air of expectancy at Valley Parade that this might be another one to remember. Wells followed up his goals in the 2013 play-offs by netting in the opening five fixtures for a unbroken, club record scoring sequence of eight matches. It helped Bradford figure among the early pacemakers and the Bermudan went on to accumulate 15 in the first half of the campaign, including a hat-trick against Coventry. But they went off the boil during a barren mid-winter run of 13 matches without a win. The run was accompanied by the loss of Wells, who stepped up a division to join Huddersfield for a fee of around £1.3m during the January transfer window. City regained the winning touch with single goal successes against Port Vale and MK Dons and went on to consolidate a position in the middle reaches of the table. Three wins in the final four matches meant a top-half finish and a solid platform for the new campaign.

Atkinson C 1 (3)	Folan C........................ - (6)	Meredith J 24 (2)
Bates M................... 20 (2)	Graham J .... - (1)	Oliver L........................ 3 (1)
Bennett K 14 (4)	Gray A 2 (6)	Ravenhill R 3 (4)
Clarkson L.................... - (1)	Hanson J 34 (1)	Reach A..........................18
Connell A.................. - (13)	Jones G 43 (2)	Reid K 21 (5)
Darby S 46	Kennedy J 5 (3)	Stead J................................8
Davies A 28	McArdle R.....................41	Taylor M..................... 1 (1)
De Vita R 6 (14)	McBurnie O................ 2 (6)	Thompson G 29 (15)
Dolan M 9 (2)	McHugh C 11 (3)	Wells N 18 (1)
Doyle N 34 (5)	McLaughlan J.................46	Yeates M................. 10 (19)
Drury A 11 (1)	Mclean A 18 (2)	

League goals (57): Wells 14, Hanson 12, Jones 6, Mclean 4, Reid 4, McArdle 3, Reach 3, Thompson 2, Yeates 2, Bennett 1, Davies 1, De Vita 1, Gray 1, Kennedy 1, McHugh 1, Stead 1
FA Cup goals: None. **Capital One Cup goals (1):** Wells 1. **Johnstone's Paint Trophy goals:** None
Average home league attendance: 14,120. **Player of Year:** Stephen Darby

BRENTFORD

Brentford reflected on a tale of two penalties when finishing runners-up to Wolves and securing Championship football. In 2013, they were denied promotion on the final day of the regular season by Marcello Trotta's stoppage-time miss against Doncaster, then by defeat against Yeovil in the Play-off Final. This time, Alan Judge made no mistake from the spot for a 1-0 victory over Preston which made sure of second place with three matches remaining. It was a successful managerial debut for Mark Warburton, the club's sporting director, who stepped up when Uwe Rosler took charge of Wigan a few hours after being named League One's Manager of the

Month for November. Warburton started with six successive victories and the team's overall run continued through to 19 unbeaten league games – 16 wins and three draws – before a 3-0 home defeat by Wolves cost them the leadership. Brentford, left to dispute second place with Leyton Orient, began to gain the upper hand when Trotta scored in first-half stoppage time against their rivals and his side protected the lead despite the sending-off of James Tarkowski. As Orient continued to fade, they finished the campaign with a club record 94 points, eight clear, and midfielder Adam Forshaw was voted League One's Player of the Year.

Adams C .... - (3)	Douglas J 35	Norris L .... - (1)
Akpom C .... - (4)	El Alagui F 1 (11)	O'Connor K 6 (3)
Barron S 2	Fillo M 4 (3)	Reeves J 6 (14)
Bidwell J 38	Forshaw A 36 (3)	Saunders S 6 (11)
Bonham J .... - (1)	Grigg W 16 (18)	Saville G 33 (7)
Button D 42	Harris K 9 (1)	Tarkowski J 13
Clarke J .... - (1)	Teixeira J .... - (2)	Taylor M 5
Craig T 43 (1)	Judge A 22	Trotta M 28 (9)
Dallas S 6 (12)	Lee R 4	Venta J .... - (1)
Dean H 30 (2)	Logan S 14 (4)	Yennaris N 5 (3)
Diagouraga T 10 (9)	McAleny C 3 (1)	
Donaldson C 46	McCormack A 43	

League goals (72): Donaldson 17, Trotta 13, Forshaw 8, Judge 7, Saunders 5, Grigg 4, Saville 4, Douglas 3, Tarkowski 2, Taylor 2, Dallas 1, El Alagui 1, Harris 1, Logan 1, McCormack 1, Opponents 2
FA Cup goals: (7). Donaldson 1, El Alagui 1, Harris 1, McCormack 1, Reeves 1, Trotta 1, Opponents 1. **Capital One Cup goals** (3): El Alagui 2, Fillo 1. **Johnstone's Paint Trophy goals** (6): El Alagui 2, Nugent 2, Norris 1, Venta 1
Average home league attendance: 7,715. **Player of Year**: Tony Craig

BRISTOL CITY

Steve Cotterill faced a major rehabilitation job at his seventh league club when replacing Sean O'Driscoll, sacked after ten months as manager approaching the midway point of the season. City were second from bottom, low in confidence and facing a relegation battle. Two months later, their position had scarcely improved. Then, Cotterill began to effect a transformation in fortunes, with the help of the winter transfer window, some shrewd loan signings and Sam Baldock's goals. The former West Ham striker set up a 3-1 victory over promotion-minded Leyton Orient which proved a key turning point. They were still in the bottom four by the end of February. But the next 11 games netted 24 points, with a single defeat, as Baldock netted twice against Peterborough, Port Vale and Notts County. The result was an impressive rise into the top half of the table, with Baldock finishing the division's leading marksman on 24 goals, well supported by Jay Emmanuel-Thomas, whose tally of 15 included a hat-trick against Carlisle.

Baldock S 44 (1)	Flint A 32 (2)	Pack M 34 (9)
Barnett T 7 (10)	Fontaine L 2 (1)	Parish E 19
Bryan J 11 (10)	Gillett S 21 (2)	Paterson M 6 (2)
Burns W 1 (19)	Harewood M .... - (12)	Pearson S 2 (4)
Carey L 1 (1)	Kelly L .... - (2)	Reid B 19 (5)
Cunningham G 32 (5)	Kilkenny N 3	Shorey N 11 (3)
Dunk L 2	McLaughlin S .... - (5)	Taylor R 2 (5)
El-Abd A 13 (1)	Moloney B 27 (5)	Wagstaff S 35 (2)
Elliott M 16 (8)	Moore S 11	Williams D 40 (3)
Elliott W 17 (2)	Nosworthy N 10	Wynter J 2 (1)
Emmanuel-Thomas J. 42 (4)	O'Connor J 3	
Fielding F 16	Osborne K 25 (2)	

League goals (70): Baldock 24, Emmanuel-Thomas 15, Wagstaff 5, Elliott M 4, Elliott W 3, Flint 3, Bryan 2, Gillett 2, Barnett 1, Burns 1, Cunningham 1, Harewood 1, Nosworthy 1, Osborne 1, Paterson 1, Pearson 1, Reid 1, Williams 1, Opponents 2
FA Cup goals (6): Emmanuel-Thomas 4, Baldock 1, Elliott M 1. **Capital One Cup goals** (4): Baldock 1, Emmanuel-Thomas 1, Wagstaff 1, Wynter 1. **Johnstone's Paint Trophy goals** (3): Bryan 1, Emmanuel-Thomas 1, Moloney 1
Average home league attendance: 11,928. **Player of Year**: Sam Baldock

CARLISLE UNITED

Graham Kavanagh's first taste of management was an unhappy one. The former Republic of Ireland midfielder took over a side that conceded 13 goals in their first three league games – and were relegated after winning just one of their last 15. Kavanagh, assistant to Greg Abbott, stepped up to the job when the third longest-serving manager in English football after Arsenal's Arsene Wenger and Paul Tisdale (Exeter), was sacked after five years in the job when the first six games brought just two points. He made a successful start as caretaker and was appointed on a permanent basis following consecutive wins over Sheffield United, Stevenage and Notts County. Carlisle went into the New Year on the back of a win over promotion-chasing Peterborough and looking to cement a position in mid-table. Instead, they went downhill, falling into the bottom four after a 4-1 defeat by Notts County, losing 6-1 to Preston and needing to beat champions Wolves at Molineux in the final fixture to stand any chance of surviving. In the event, a 3-0 defeat proved irrelevant because of results elsewhere which left them five points adrift.

Amoo D 39 (4)	Drennan M 3 (3)	Meppen-Walters C 16 (4)
Amos B 9	Eccleston N .... - (2)	Miller L 28 (6)
Archibald-Henville T 4	Edwards M 1	Morris J 1 (5)
Beck M 5 (5)	Ehmer M 12	Noble L 31 (3)
Berrett J 38 (2)	Ekangamene C 4	Novo N 2 (4)
Black P 3 (1)	Feely K 1 (1)	O'Hanlon S 33
Brough P 1 (2)	Fleming G 4	Pearson J 3
Brown R 9 (3)	Gillespie M 15	Pickford J 18
Buaben P 10 (2)	Gillies J 3 (3)	Potts B 32 (5)
Butterfield D 1	Guy L .... `13 (10)	Redmond D 12 (3)
Byrne S 4 (13)	James R 1	Robson M 29 (3)
Campbell A .... - (1)	Lawrence T 8 (1)	Roddan C .... - (1)
Chantler C 15 (2)	Livesey D 8 (1)	Symington D 14 (17)
Chimbonda P 25 (1)	Lynch J .... - (1)	Thirlwell P 27
Dawson L 1	Madine G 5	Townsend C 10 (2)
Dempsey K .... - (4)	McSweeney J 8	

League goals (43): Amoo 8, Miller 5, Noble 5, Robson 5, O'Hanlon 4, Lawrence 3, Berrett 2, Madine 2, Potts 2, Buaben 1, Byrne 1, Ehmer 1, Guy 1, Meppen-Walters 1, Opponents 2
FA Cup goals (6): Miller 3, Beck 1, Berrett 1, Robson 1. **Capital One Cup goals** (5): Amoo 3, Berrett 1, Guy 1. **Johnstone's Paint Trophy goals**: None
Average home league attendance: 4,243. **Player of Year**: David Amoo

COLCHESTER UNITED

Freddie Sears scored vital goals as Colchester resisted the threat of relegation for the second successive season. It wasn't as tight as the previous campaign when they were still sweating going into the final fixture. But a run of five matches producing a single point and including defeats by fellow-strugglers Notts County and Tranmere, was worrying. It left them avoiding a place in the bottom four only on goal difference. Sears eased the pressure by netting twice in a 3-2 away win over another team in trouble, Stevenage, to provide a three-point cushion. Then, after a home defeat against Oldham, the former West Ham striker got two more, one from the penalty spot, as a handsome 4-1 home victory over promoted Brentford effectively ensured safety. Colchester had previously set their sights set on a place in the top half of the table after

scoring seven times against Gillingham and Carlisle in successive matches early in the New Year. But they slipped when the next six games yielded just two goals. At the end of the campaign, veteran midfielder Karl Duguid made the last of his 400-plus appearance for the club.

Bean M..................... 31 (4)	Kent F........................ - (1)	Spence M................... - (1)
Bolger C 4	Ladapo F .... - (2)	Szmodics S................ - (7)
Bond A.................... - (8)	Lee E 4	Taylor M.....................5
Bonne M............... 2 (12)	Massey G............. 22 (8)	Tozer B 1
Dickson R 28 (4)	Monakana J............. 6 (3)	Turgott B 3 (1)
Duguid K................. - (1)	Morrison C 17 (16)	Vose D.................. 19 (8)
Eastman T..................36	Okuonghae M..............44	Walker A.....................46
Eastmond C 32 (7)	Olufemi T 5 (8)	Watt S 19 (3)
Garbutt L..................19	Pappoe D.................. - (2)	Wilson B....................38
Gilbey A............. 26 (10)	Sanderson J .... - (1)	Wright David 33 (2)
Hubble C................... - (1)	Sears F................ 25 (7)	Wright, Drey 2 (10)
Ibehre J................ 32 (5)	Sesay A 2 (1)	Wynter A.................. 5 (1)

League goals (53): Sears 12, Ibehre 8, Bean 5, Eastmond 4, Massey 3, Watt 3, Bonne 2, Garbutt 2, Morrison 2, Okuonghae 2, Bond 1, Gilbey 1, Lee 1, Monakana 1, Taylor 1, Turgott 1, Wright David 1, Wynter 1, Opponents 2
FA Cup goals (2): Bonne 1, Garbutt 1. **Capital One Cup goals** (1): Ibehre 1. **Johnstone's Paint Trophy goals** (1): Wilson 1
Average home league attendance: 3,735. **Player of Year**: Tom Eastman

COVENTRY CITY

Manager Steven Pressley praised his players for the way they dealt with a season which delivered huge challenges before a ball had even been kicked. They had to contend with a ten-point penalty after the owners of the Ricoh Arena rejected a plan to take the club out of administration. And with the announcement that there would be no return to the stadium after a long-running dispute over rent, home matches had to be played at Northampton's Sixfields ground. It was first of three seasons planned there while a new stadium is built and many protesting supporters refused to travel the 34 miles. Just 2,204 watched the first game against Bristol City in which their team defeated Bristol City 5-4 with an 87th minute goal from Billy Daniels, his second. Callum Wilson also netted twice and got two more in a 4-4 draw against Preston soon after. It took just six matches to wipe out the deficit and move off the bottom of the table. Coventry scored three or more goals in eight other games and their combined for and against tally of 151 was unrivalled from an entertainment point of view. They were up to mid-table at the half-way stage, but hopes of finishing in the top half were ended by a run of seven matches without a victory during the run-in.

Adams B.................. 34 (2)	Fleck J 41 (2)	Phillips A.................. 3 (8)
Akpon C.................... 5 (1)	Garner L .... - (3)	Prutton D...................8
Baker C................ 31 (6)	Haynes R 1 (1)	Robinson A 5 (1)
Barton A................ 5 (9)	Loza J.................... - (1)	Seaborne D.............. 18 (3)
Christie C................ 33 (1)	Maguire C 1 (2)	Slager D .... - (3)
Clarke J................ 39 (1)	Manset M .... - (9)	Thomas C 40 (3)
Clarke L................ 22 (1)	Marshall M............. 6 (8)	Thomas G....................1
Dagnall C............. 4 (2)	McGeouch D .... -(8)	Webster A 40 (1)
Daniels B................ 10 (8)	Moussa F............. 36 (3)	Willis J................ 21 (7)
Delfouneso N 8 (6)	Murphy J 46	Wilson C 37
Eccleston N 4 (4)	Petrasso M...................7	

League goals (74): Wilson 21, Clarke L 15, Moussa 12, Baker 7, Daniels 3, Delfouneso 3, Webster 3, Maguire 2, Clarke J 1, Dagnall 1, Fleck 1, Manset 1, Petrasso 1, Phillips 1, Seaborne 1, Opponents 1
FA Cup goals (8): Clarke L 3, Baker 2, Moussa 1, Wilson 1, Opponents 1. **Capital One Cup goals**

(2): Baker 1, Moussa 1. **Johnstone's Paint Trophy goals**: None
Average home league attendance: 3,735. **Player of Year**: Callum Wilson

CRAWLEY TOWN

No club suffered more from the winter floods than Crawley. Wholesale postponements meant that at one stage they had completed seven fewer fixtures than some teams in the lower reaches of the division. To catch up, nine matches had to be fitted in during both March and April – and for a spell it looked like the demands on the players would prove too much. After beating leaders and eventually champions Wolves, they suffered six straight defeats to drop to within three points of the bottom four. Then, successive victories over Tranmere, Leyton Orient and Notts County eased the pressure and brought praise from manager John Gregory. The season then tailed off, but Crawley still finished in a respectable mid-table position and Gregory signed a two-year contract extension. Out of English management since leaving Queens Park Rangers in 2007, he took over when Richie Barker was sacked after a solid start to the season gave way to seven games without a win.

Adams N..........................24	Drury A.................... 36 (5)	Monakana J................. - (4)
Alexander G 9 (12)	Edwards G 5 (1)	Proctor J................ 21 (23)
Bennett K.........................4	Essam C .... - (2)	Rooney L .... - (4)
Boateng H.........................1	Fallon R..................... 3 (5)	Sadler M..........................46
Bulman D 34 (5)	Hurst J 11 (7)	Simpson J................. 37 (1)
Clarke B 28 (1)	Jones M 40 (2)	Sinclair E..................... 9 (6)
Connolly M............... 32 (4)	Jones P..........................46	Torres S 6 (16)
Connolly P 5 (2)	Kaiki S 2 (3)	Tubbs M..........................18
Dicker G 9 (2)	McFadzean K 41 (1)	Walsh J..........................39

League goals (48): Tubbs 8, Clarke 7, Proctor 6, Drury 5, Walsh 5, Alexander 4, Jones M 3, Edwards 2, Simpson 2, Sinclair 2, Adams 1, Connolly M 1, McFadzean 1, Sadler 1
FA Cup goals (3): Proctor 1, Sinclair 1, Opponents 1. **Capital One Cup goals** (3): Adams 2, Alexander 1. **Johnstone's Paint Trophy goals** (2): Jones M 1, Sinclair 1
Average home league attendance: 3,486. **Player of Year**: Joe Walsh

CREWE ALEXANDRA

Manager Steve Davis admitted the season had been a struggle from start to finish after his side emerged from a tense final day with their League One place intact. They went into it a single point clear of the bottom four and without a home victory for three months. Only successive away wins over Gillingham, Crawley and fellow-strugglers Shrewsbury had kept them in touch. But Crewe responded to a big crowd by beating Preston 2-1 thanks to goals from Adam Dugdale and Mathias Pogba. As it was, Tranmere's home defeat by Bradford meant they would have been safe anyway. But it was still a relief to finish on a high note, their fortunes having contrasted sharply with the previous campaign which brought mid-table security, along with the Johnstone's Paint Trophy. One victory in the opening ten matches – 2-1 against Tranmere – set the pattern. A Boxing Day defeat by Wolves left them bottom-of-the-table, although maximum points against Colchester and Carlisle in the two other holiday fixtures meant it was a brief stay.

Aneke C.................... 34 (6)	Guthrie J......................23	Oliver V................. 10 (15)
Audel T...................... 1 (1)	Hitchcock T 6	Osman A.................. 26 (5)
Clayton M 9 (4)	Ikpeazu U 10 (5)	Park C 3 (1)
Cloclough R 5 (3)	Inman B 28 (8)	Phillips S.........................9
Davis H..........................32	Leitch-Smith A J....... 13 (7)	Pogba M 17 (5)
Dugdale A....................21	Martin A 7	Ray G 5 (4)
Ellis M..................... 36 (1)	Mellor K 23 (5)	Robertson G 2 (1)
Etheridge N....................4	Mesca 6	Tootle M..........................43
Evans G 22 (1)	Molyneux L 4 (3)	Turton G 8 (4)
Garratt B......................26	Moore B 30 (10)	Waters B 1 (8)
Grant A.................... 34 (4)	Nolan L 8 (5)	West M .... - (2)

League goals (54): Aneke 14, Pogba 5, Ikpeazu 4, Inman 4, Moore 4, Davis 3, Hitchcock 3, Clayton 2, Colclough 2, Grant 2, Leitch-Smith 2, Oliver 2, Dugdale 1, Ellis 1, Evans 1, Mellor 1, Mesca 1, Turton 1,Opponents 1.
FA Cup goals (1): Grant 1. **Capital One Cup goals** (2): Aneke 1, Davis 1. **Johnstone's Paint Trophy goals** (1): Aneke 1
Average home league attendance: 4,932. **Player of Year**: Matt Tootle

GILLINGHAM

Six months after securing the club's first title for nearly half a century, Martin Allen was sacked with Gillingham on nine points from their opening 11 League One games and out of the League Cup and Johnstone's Paint Trophy. Peter Taylor returned to Priestfield for his second spell in charge, initially as caretaker, then given the job until the end of the campaign. Taylor, last in charge in 2000, took over a side leaking goals and it was a problem which never went away. They conceded three or more in 11 matches and finished with the second worst defensive record in the division. On the plus side, Danny Kedwell scored seven goals in seven games before injuries ruled him out for three months, while Cody McDonald had a run of seven in eight on the way to 17 for the season. Gillingham conceded 11 in three fixtures against promotion-seeking Rotherham, Peterborough and Leyton Orient at the beginning of April. But McDonald was on the mark again in a 2-0 victory over struggling Tranmere to effectively make them safe. Afterwards, Taylor agreed a two-year contract to remain in charge.

Akinfenwa A	17 (17)	Gregory S	35 (4)	Martin J	46
Allen C	2 (3)	Harriman M	33 (1)	McDonald C	35 (9)
Barrett A	45	Hessenthaler J	18 (1)	McKain D	- (1)
Birchall A	- (2)	Hewitt E	20	Millbank A	- (1)
Butcher S	- (1)	Hollands D	16 (1)	Mousinho J	4
Dack B	15 (13)	Inniss R	3	Muggleton S	- (1)
Daniels D	3	Kedwell D	23 (4)	Nelson S	46
Davies C	4 (3)	Lee C	22 (9)	Pigott J	4 (3)
Fagan C	12 (6)	Legge L	36 (1)	Smith C	6 (4)
Fish M	1 (1)	Linganzi A	16 (4)	Weston M	23 (16)
German A	- (9)	Marriott J	- (1)	Whelpdale C	21 (3)

League goals (60): McDonald 17, Akinfenwa 10, Kedwell 10, Dack 3, Barrett 2, Fagan 2, Lee 2, Legge 2, Martin 2, Weston 2, Daniels 1, Harriman 1, Hessenthaler 1, Hollands 1, Linganzi 1, Mousinho 1, Pigott 1, Whelpdale 1
FA Cup goals (1): Dack 1. **Capital One Cup goals**: None. **Johnstone's Paint Trophy goals** (1): Dack 1
Average home league attendance: 6,219. **Player of Year**: Stuart Nelson

LEYTON ORIENT

A season that started in record-breaking fashion ended in bitter disappointment at Wembley. Goals by Moses Odubajo and Dean Cox in the space of five first-half minutes looked to have paved the way for victory in the Play-Off Final. Instead, Alex Revell scored twice against his former team and Rotherham went on to win a penalty shoot-out 4-3. The consolation for Orient was a fine campaign in which an opening run of eight successive league wins, along with 23 goals scored, was the best in the club's 131-year history. So, too, was a total of 86 points accumulated. There was also personal recognition for Russell Slade, joint winner of the League Managers' Association's Manager of the Year award for League One with Kenny Jackett of Wolves. Slade's team led the division for more than four months before giving way to Brentford's own purple patch. Three successive defeats in February pushed them down to third; three straight victories restored the prospect of automatic promotion. After that, they were unable to match the greater consistency of their London rivals and Wolves, finishing eight points adrift of the runners-up spot.

Alnwick B	1	
Bartley M	9 (16)	
Batt S	7 (28)	
Baudry M	38 (1)	
Clarke N	46	
Coulthirst S	- (1)	
Cox D	44 (1)	
Cuthbert S	44	
Dagnall C	11 (9)	
Gorman J	- (2)	
Jakupovic E	13	
Jalal S	2	
James L	38 (4)	
Jones J	28	
Larkins J	2	
Lasimant Y	1 (10)	
Lisbie K	35 (4)	
Loza J	1 (2)	
Lundstram J	6 (1)	
Mooney D	34 (4)	
Ness J	3 (10)	
Odubajo M	46	
Omozusi E	38 (1)	
Sawyer G	16 (6)	
Simpson R	5 (9)	
Stockley J	- (8)	
Vincelot R	38 (1)	
Wright J	- (2)	

Play-offs – appearances: Baudry 3, Clarke 3, Cox 3, Cuthbert 3, Jones 3, Lisbie 3, Mooney 3, Odubajo 3, Omuzusi 3, Vincelot 3, James 2 (1), Lundstram 1 (1), Batt – (3), Dagnall – (2)
League goals (85): Mooney 19, Lisbie 16, Cox 12, Odubajo 10, Dagnall 6, Batt 4, Cuthbert 4, James 3, Bartley 2, Baudry 2, Clarke 2, Lasimant 2, Coulthirst 1, Ness 1, Stockley 1. **Play-offs – goals**: Cox 2, Odubajo 2, Dagnall 1
FA Cup goals (6): Batt 2, Cox 2, James 1, Mooney 1. **Capital One Cup goals** (3): Lisbie 2, Cox 1.
Johnstone's Paint Trophy goals (5): Batt 3, James 1, Mooney 1
Average home league attendance: 5,467. **Player of Year**: Nathan Clarke

MILTON KEYNES DONS

Patrick Bamford's productive loan spell and a string of penalties by Shaun Williams offered the platform for a bid for a play-off place for the third time in four years. Bamford scored 14 league goals, while Williams struck five successful spot-kicks, plus two more in cup ties. But after the Chelsea player's spell ended and he moved on to join Derby, Dons home form – at best indifferent throughout the first part of the campaign – deteriorated. They went eight matches without winning in front of their own supporters and needed five successive away victories to stay in with a chance. It came in a match against sixth-placed Peterborough, who at the time were just three points ahead. But they were unable to break that costly sequence, conceded twice in three second-half minutes and went down 2-0. A record crowd of 20,516 saw champions-elect Wolves come away with a 1-0 success. Then, when Dons were finally beaten on their travels, at Port Vale, they were nine points adrift with no chance of making up the ground. They finished tenth, with captain Dean Lewington having made his 500th appearance for the club.

Alli D	24 (9)	
Baldock G	20 (18)	
Bamford P	22 (1)	
Banton J	10 (1)	
Bowditch D	3 (9)	
Burns C	- (1)	
Carruthers S	19 (4)	
Chadwick L	14 (8)	
Cole L	2 (1)	
Flanagan T	6 (1)	
Galloway B	3 (5)	
Gleeson S	35	
Green D	5	
Hall R	4 (7)	
Hodson L	23	
Jennings D	6	
Kay A	28 (2)	
Kennedy M	7	
Lewington D	43	
Long C	4	
Loveridge J	2 (5)	
Martin D	40	
McLeod I	18 (18)	
McLoughlin L	6 (2)	
Odelusi S	6 (4)	
Otsemobor J	9	
Potter D	29	
Powell D	22 (10)	
Randall M	1 (3)	
Rasulo G	1 (6)	
Reeves B	26 (2)	
Smith A	14 (10)	
Spence J	29	
Williams S	25	

League goals (63): Bamford 14, Williams 8, McLeod 7, Reeves 7, Alli 6, Gleeson 3, Baldock 2, Banton 2, Carruthers 2, Kay 2, Spence 2, Bowditch 1, Chadwick 1, Hall 1, Hodson 1, Kennedy 1, Lewington 1, Long 1, Powell 1
FA Cup goals (9): Reeves 3, McLeod 2, Bamford 1, Chadwick 1, Galloway 1, Williams 1. **Capital One Cup goals** (4): Bamford 1, Banton 1, McLeod 1, Reeves 1. **Johnstone's Paint Trophy goals** (3): Alli 1, Bamford 1, Williams 1
Average home league attendance: 9,032. **Player of Year**: Ben Reeves

NOTTS COUNTY

Shaun Derry returned to the club where he started his career to engineer an escape from relegation against all the odds. The Queens Park Rangers midfielder took over when Chris Kiwomya was sacked after seven months as manager with his side bottom. The New Year brought some cheer with successive victories over Bradford, Sheffield United and Stevenage, accompanied by a move out of the bottom four. The respite was brief and a 6-0 beating at Rotherham, followed by defeats against MK Dons and Tranmere, left them seven points adrift with nine matches remaining. But three wins in eight days and nine goals scored against Carlisle, Crewe and Colchester transformed their fortunes. Then, a 2-0 deficit was turned into a 4-2 victory over Port Vale by two goals each from Jimmy Spencer and Jamal Campbell-Ryce. There were further wins over Crawley and Swindon and County went into the final fixture at Oldham two points clear of the bottom four, with a superior goal difference. Alan Sheehan's penalty earned a point and Derry hailed his team's achievement as 'fantastic'.

Appiah K	1 (6)	Grealish J	32 (5)	Roberts G	6
Arquin Y	4 (8)	Haber M	5 (6)	Sheehan A	42
Ball C	2 (4)	Haworth A	- (2)	Showunmi E	9 (5)
Balmy J	- (1)	Haynes D	15 (6)	Smith E	20 (4)
Bell D	4 (6)	Hollis H	9 (1)	Speiss F	1
Bialkowski B	44	Holt J	2	Spencer J	13
Boucaud A	26 (3)	Labadie J	15	Stevens E	2
Campbell-Ryce J	36	Leacock D	25 (1)	Tempest G	8 (6)
Coombes A	3 (3)	Liddle G	32	Thompson C	8 (3)
Dixon K	- (1)	McGregor C	32 (5)	Tyson N	4 (6)
Dumbuya M	23 (1)	Mullins H	15 (1)	Vela J	7
Fotheringham M	23 (5)	Murray R	15 (9)	Waite T	- (1)
Fox M	6 (1)	Nangle R	- (1)	Zoko F	- (1)
Freeman K	14	Pilkington K	1		

League goals (64): McGregor 12, Murray 7, Sheehan 7, Grealish 5, Spencer 5, Hollis 4, Liddle 4, Arquin 3, Campbell-Ryce 3, Haynes 3, Showunmi 3, Haber 2, Ball 1, Fotheringham 1, Fox 1, Labadie 1, Leacock 1, Mullins 1
FA Cup goals (2): Leacock 1, Murray 1. **Capital One Cup goals (5):** Arquin 1 Coombes 1, Haynes 1, McGregor 1, Showunmi 1. **Johnstone's Paint Trophy goals (2):** McGregor 1, Murray 1
Average home league attendance: 5,508. **Player of Year:** Alan Sheehan

OLDHAM ATHLETIC

Oldham were among much of the season on the fringes of the bottom four and attempting to avoid being sucked into a full-blown relegation struggle. They were successful, helped by a stirring comeback and some disciplined defensive performances. Defeats by Walsall and Port Vale in the space of four days early in the New Year left Lee Johnson's side with little breathing space. They looked to be heading for another reversal when trailing promotion-chasing Peterborough 3-0 at half-time, then falling 4-2 behind. But Gary Harkins equalised from the penalty spot in the 89th minute and Swiss defender Genseric Kusunga came up with a stoppage-time winner for a 5-4 scoreline which provided a four-point cushion. That was cut to two in the following weeks as the scramble for safety intensified. Then, five clean sheets in a run of seven matches proved crucial. So did a 3-2 away win over Bradford, in which 19-year-old striker Jonson Clarke-Harris scored twice, followed by more solid defensive work to leave Oldham well clear of trouble.

Baxter J	3 (1)	Dayton J	24 (10)	Kissock J P	2 (2)
Brown C	24 (3)	Dunfield T	1 (1)	Kusunga G	18
Byrne C	- (3)	Gafaiti A	- (1)	Lanzoni M	10
Byrom J	2 (2)	Grounds J	45	Lockwood A	18 (1)
Clarke-Harris J	23 (17)	Harkins G	22 (1)	MacDonald C	15 (15)

Mellor D 16 (4)	Pritchard J .... - (1)	Tarkowski J 26
Millar K 2 (9)	Rachubka P 10	Turner R 1 (1)
Mills J 11	Rodgers A 2 (5)	Wesolowski J 37 (2)
Montano C 6 (4)	Rooney A 16 (8)	Wilson J........................16
Oxley M 36	Rusnak A .... - (2)	Winchester C.............. 7 (5)
Petrasso M 9 (2)	Schmeltz S 5 (12)	Worrall D 17 (1)
Philliskirk D 33 (5)	Smith K 42	
Plummer E........................3	Stead J 4 (1)	

League goals (50): Clarke-Harris 6, Harkins 5, MacDonald 5, Philliskirk 4, Rooney 4, Wesolowski 4, Dayton 3, Baxter 2, Grounds 2, Lockwood 2, Montano 2, Tarkowski 2, Brown 1, Kusunga 1, Lanzoni 1, Petrasso 1, Smith 1, Wilson 1, Winchester 1, Worrall 1, Opponents 1
FA Cup goals (8): Philliskirk 2, Rooney 2, Kusunga 1, Clarke-Harris 1, Lanzoni 1, Smith 1.
Capital One Cup goals: None. **Johnstone's Paint Trophy goals (12):** Philliskirk 6, Clarke-Harris 1, Dayton 1, Rooney 1, Schmeltz 1, Tarkowski 1, Wesolowski 1
Average home league attendance: 4,415. **Player of Year:** James Wesolowski

PETERBOROUGH UNITED

Darren Ferguson led his side to victory in the Johnstone's Paint Trophy and then into the play-offs. But there was to be no second appearance at Wembley. His side lost to Leyton Orient in the semi-finals after scoring first through record-signing Britt Assombalonga's 33rd goal of the season in all competitions. They led for nearly an hour at London Road, then conceded an equaliser and went down 2-1 in the second leg. Assombalonga, signed from Watford during the summer, netted in his first four league games, all of which Peterborough won. After contesting the early leadership with Leyton Orient, they had a spell of six matches yielding a single point and were always trailing the top two from then on. There was a brief spell out of the top six when losing 5-4 to a stoppage-time goal at Oldham after leading 3-0, then 4-2. But Assombalonga's brace accounted for rivals MK Dons in a vital game and successive four-goal victories over Carlisle and Shrewsbury confirmed sixth place. Peterborough overcame the dismissal of Joe Newell to beat Chesterfield 3-1 in the Trophy final, with goals from Josh McQuoid, Shaun Brisley and Assombalonga's penalty giving Ferguson success in the competition as a player – with Wrexham in 2005 – and manager.

Ajose N.................. 19 (3)	Gordon J .... - (1)	Olejnik B 42
Alcock C 24 (4)	Isgrove L 3 (5)	Payne J.................. 29 (3)
Anderson J.................. 9 (4)	Jeffers S 3 (5)	Rowe T 33 (1)
Assombalonga B 41 (2)	Kearns D.................. 5 (6)	Santos R 1
Baldwin J.................. 10 (1)	Knight-Percival N 12 (3)	Swanson D.......... 25 (10)
Barnett T 16 (5)	Little M 34 (4)	Taylor P 6
Bostwick M 40 (2)	McCann G 26 (9)	Tomlin L 19
Brisley S 20 (2)	McQuoid J 8 (6)	Vassell K 3 (3)
Conlon T .... - (1)	Mendez-Laing N 3 (13)	Washington C 12 (5)
Day J.........Mendez-Laing 1......4	Newell J 6 (5)	Zakuani G 14 (1)
Ephraim H 6 (2)	Ntlhe K.................. 22 (5)	
Ferdinand K .... - (2)	Nugent B 11	

Play-offs – appearances: Ajose 2, Alcock 2, Assombalonga 2, Baldwin 2, Bostwick 2, Little 2, Olejnik 2, Payne 2, Rowe 2, Swanson 2, Knight-Percival 1, Ntlhe 1, Isgrove – (2), McCann – (2), Washington – (2)
League goals (72): Assombalonga 23, Ajose 7, Rowe 7, Barnett 6, Tomlin 5, Bostwick 4, McCann 4, Washington 4, Ntlhe 2, Payne 2, Swanson 2, Isgrove 1, Jeffers 1, Knight-Percival 1, Little 1, McQuoid 1, Mendez-Laing 1. **Play-off – goals:** Assombalonga 1, Washington 1
FA Cup goals (9): Assombalonga 5, Jeffers 2, Mendez-Laing 1, Rowe 1. **Capital One Cup goals (11):** Tomlin 5, Assombalonga 1, Barnett 1, Payne 1, Rowe 1, Swanson 1, Zakuani 1. **Johnstone's Paint Trophy goals (12):** Assombalonga 3, McCann 2, Brisley 1, McQuoid 1, Mendez-Laing 1, Ntlhe 1, Vassell 1, Opponents 2
Average home league attendance: 6,339. **Player of Year:** Britt Assombalonga

PORT VALE

Micky Adams and his promoted side were among the favourites to go down. Instead, they beat the odds and for good measure recorded the club's highest position for ten years. Vale secured ninth place after a solid season's work and it could have been higher. For the first time for 114 years they completed a league double over old rivals Walsall, a penalty from Jennison Myrie-Williams proving the only goal of the game. It lifted them to within four points of Peterborough in the final play-off position, albeit from an extra fixture played. But a training ground incident involving club captain Doug Loft and defender Daniel Jones had repercussions on and off the field. Loft sustained facial injuries, missing the remainder of the season. Jones was sacked. In their next game, Vale went down 4-2 at Notts County after establishing a 2-0 lead through Gavin Tomlin and an own goal. They returned to winning ways by beating MK Dons, but managed only one point from the final three games against Rotherham, Sheffield United and Peterborough.

Birchall C 14 (13)	Hughes L 6 (7)	Myrie-Williams J 26 (12)
Chilvers L 14	Hugill L 7 (13)	Neal C 31
Cuvelier F 1	Johnson S 15 (1)	Pope T............................ 41 (2)
Davis J 11	Jones D 17 (3)	Robertson C 36 (1)
Dickinson C....................40	Knott B 13 (5)	Shuker C...................... 1 (9)
Dodds L 16 (13)	Lines C 33 (1)	Taylor R 1 (5)
Duffy R.................... 26 (2)	Lloyd R 2 (1)	Tomlin G.................... 17 (7)
Griffith A............... 34 (4)	Loft D........................37	Williamson B.......... 18 (20)
Grimmer J......................13	Mohamed K 3 (3)	Yates A 33 (1)

League goals (59): Pope 12, Loft 9, Myrie-Williams 7, Tomlin 5, Dodds 4, Hugill 4, Williamson 4, Hughes 3, Robertson 3, Knott 2, Birchall 1, Grimmer 1, Lines 1, Taylor 1, Yates 1, Opponents 1
FA Cup goals (14): Myrie-Williams 3, Pope 2, Robertson 2, Williamson 2, Birchall 1, Hugill 1, Lines 1, Taylor 1, Tomlin 1. **Capital One Cup goals (1):** Robertson 1. **Johnstone's Paint Trophy goals (2):** Pope 2
Average home league attendance: 6,249. **Player of Year:** Tom Pope

PRESTON NORTH END

Preston's play-off hoodoo struck again. For the ninth time they were unsuccessful in the end-of-season lottery – this time after being tipped by many to deliver the winning number. They were held 1-1 by Rotherham at Deepdale, where leading marksman Joe Garner's equaliser, a 25-yard volley, was one of the goals of the season. Paul Gallagher, who scored two hat-tricks in the regular season, put them ahead in the return leg, but the lead lasted only eight minutes and his side eventually went down 3-1 after twice hitting the woodwork. Manager Simon Grayson, who won promotion from the third tier with three other clubs, described the record as a 'quirk' and maintained that the progress Preston had made augured well for the new season. They were in the top six for most of this campaign – without ever threatening to match the pace set by the top two – and looked to be in good shape for the knock-out stage when Craig Davies scored three in a 6-1 win over Carlisle and Gallagher's second treble highlighted a 5-2 victory over Shrewsbury. His first came in an FA Cup third round tie against Barnet, while Garner also got three, in the third round victory over Ipswich.

Beavon S 19 (8)	Garner J.................... 27 (8)	Laird S 31 (3)
Browne A.................... 4 (4)	Hayhurst W 2 (4)	Monakana J.................. - (2)
Brownhill J............. 11 (13)	Holmes L 17 (15)	Mousinho J .... - (2)
Buchanan D............. 16 (3)	Hume I 8 (8)	Rudd D............................46
Byrom J 7 (4)	Humphrey C........... 30 (12)	Welsh J.................... 30 (6)
Clarke T..........................42	Huntington P........... 19 (4)	Wiseman S................. 13 (2)
Davies C 12 (13)	Keane N 31 (7)	Wright B 43
Davies K 26 (12)	Kilkenny N 24 (3)	Wroe N 1 (4)
Gallagher P 26 (2)	King J....................... 21 (3)	

Play-offs – appearances: Clarke 2, Gallagher 2, Garner 2, King 2, Rudd 2, Welsh 2, Wright 2, Buchanan 1, Davies K 1 (1), Browne 1, Davies C 1, Holmes 1, Kilkenny 1, Laird 1, Wiseman 1, Humphrey – (2), Beavon – (1), Brownhill – (1), Keane 1
League goals (72): Garner 18, Gallagher 6, Davies C 5, Clarke 4, Wright 4, Beavon 3, Brownhill 3, Davies K 3, Holmes 3, Humphrey 3, Byrom 2, Hume 2, Huntington 2, Kilkenny 2, King 2, Welsh 2, Browne 1, Keane 1, Laird 1, Opponents 5. **Play-offs – goals (2)**: Gallagher 1, Garner 1
FA Cup goals (11): Garner 5, Gallagher 3, Davies K 2, Clarke 1. **Capital One Cup goals (1)**: Clarke 1. **Johnstone's Paint Trophy goals**: None
Average home league attendance: 10,234. **Player of Year**: Joe Garner

ROTHERHAM UNITED

Rotherham's powers of recovery were evident on the day a place in the play-offs was confirmed. They twice came from behind to win 4-3 at Gillingham, with Tom Hitchcock scoring a hat-trick. An even bigger test came in the Wembley final as Leyton Orient established a two-goal lead by half-time. And once again Steve Evans' team rose to the occasion as former Orient striker Alex Revell replied twice in the space of five minutes. Then, it was Adam Collin's turn to take centre stage, the goalkeeper saving two spot-kicks to give his side a 4-3 victory in the penalty shoot-out. The result was a second successive promotion for a club who had marked their first season in a new stadium with the runners-up spot in League Two. This time, Rotherham were in or around the play-off positions for the first half of the season, then cemented a place in the top six with an unbeaten run of 16 matches – 12 victories and four draws. It included a 6-0 success against Notts County and they went on to defeat a fancied Preston side in the semi-finals, drawing 1-1 at Deepdale and winning the return leg 3-1. Kieran Agard continued a productive season in that match, finishing with 26 goals in all competitions, including a hat-trick in a 6-4 defeat by champions Wolves.

Adams N.................... 7 (8)	Frecklington L 39	Shearer S........................12
Addison M 4 (2)	Hitchcock T 4 (7)	Skarz J 39 (2)
Agard K 43 (3)	Hylton D .... - (1)	Smallwood R............ 17 (1)
Arnason K 40	Mills P..................... 4 (6)	Tavernier J 27
Bradley M 20 (2)	Milsom R 18 (9)	Thomas W................. 8 (5)
Brindley R................ 11 (5)	Morgan C.......................35	Tidser M 2 (8)
Collin A 34	Nardiello D 5 (4)	Tubbs M 7 (10)
Davis C 14 (2)	O'Connor M 15 (14)	Turgott B ....- (1)
Dicko N 4 (1)	Pringle B 44 (1)	Vuckic H................... 9 (13)
Eaves T..................... 1 (7)	Revell A................ 42 (3)	Worrall D 1 (2)

Play-offs – appearances: Arnason 3, Collin 3, Frecklington 3, Morgan 3, Pringle 3, Revell 3, Skarz 3, Tavernier 3, Thomas 3, Agard 2, Smallwood 2, Milsom 1 (2), Brindley 1 (1), Vuckic – (3), O'Connor – (2), Davis – (1)
League goals (86): Agard 21, Frecklington 10, Revell 8, Dicko 5, Hitchcock 5, Nardiello 5, Pringle 5, Tavernier 5, Thomas 5, Vuckic 4, Bradley 2, O'Connor 2, Skarz 2, Adams 1, Davis 1, Milsom 1, Tubbs 1, Worrall 1, Opponents 2. **Play-offs – goals (6)**: Revell 3, Agard 1, Frecklington 1, Thomas 1
FA Cup goals (4): Agard 2, Frecklington 1, Revell 1. **Capital One Cup goals (2)**: Frecklington 1, Pringle 1. **Johnstone's Paint Trophy goals (6)**: Agard 2, Dicko 1, Eaves 1, Revell 1, Opponents 1.
Average home league attendance: 8,450. **Player of Year**: Lee Frecklington

SHEFFIELD UNITED

A wretched start, a momentous FA Cup run and a good finish were the ingredients of an eventful season at Bramall Lane. David Weir was sacked after a single victory in his 13 matches in charge in all competitions and replaced by Nigel Clough, making a rapid return to management after himself being dismissed by Derby. United were then fourth from bottom with nine points from 13 games. Three months later, their position in the table was just as precarious. By then, however, they had accounted for Colchester, Cambridge, Aston Villa and Fulham in the Cup. And while

for some teams juggling both competitions is a step too far, United prospered. Seven straight victories, without conceding a goal, took them out of trouble and into the top half of the table. In between were wins over Nottingham Forest and Charlton – and a Wembley semi-final. The dream ended there, although Hull were pushed all the way before prevailing 5-3. Back in the league, an eighth successive clean sheet, 0-0 with Preston, represented a club record. And the campaign ended with a move up to seventh as United came from behind to beat Coventry with goals from Ryan Flynn and Ben Davies.

Baxter J 29 (6)	Harris R 9 (2)	McGinn S 23 (7)
Brandy F................. 10 (4)	Hill M 24 (8)	McGinty S.......................2
Brayford J 15	Howard M 19	McMahon T......................23
Bunn H...................... - (2)	Ironside J.................. 1 (3)	Miller S 5 (8)
Coady C 32 (7)	Johns C .... - (1)	Murphy J 25 (9)
Collins N.......................44	Kennedy T 3 (2)	Paynter B.................. 6 (7)
Cuvelier F 5 (2)	Khan O...................... - (2)	Porter C 16 (16)
Davies B 8 (10)	King M 7 (1)	Reed L .... - (1)
Dimaio C................... 2 (1)	Lappin S 7 (2)	Scougall S 13 (2)
Doyle M 42 (1)	Long G 27	Taylor L 9 (11)
Flynn R 28 (4)	Maguire H......................41	Westlake D................. 4 (3)
Freeman K............... 10 (2)	McDonald K 1	White A 8
Hall R...................... 3 (1)	McFadzean C 3 (4)	Williams M......................2

League goals (48): Porter 7, Baxter 6, Coady 5, Flynn 5, Maguire 5, Murphy 4, Davies 3, Collins 2, Doyle 2, Scougall 2, Taylor 2, Brayford 1, King 1, McDonald 1, Opponents 2
FA Cup goals (17): Porter 4, Murphy 3, Baxter 2, Flynn 2, Brayford 1, Coady 1, Maguire 1, Miller 1, Scougall 1, Opponents 1. **Capital One Cup goals** (1): Doyle 1. **Johnstone's Paint Trophy goals**: None
Average home league attendance: 17,506. **Player of Year**: Harry Maguire

SHREWSBURY TOWN

After steering Shrewsbury away from the relegation zone in the previous season, Graham Turner warned that the new one would be tougher because of the strength of the relegated and promoted clubs coming into the division. Turrner's warning was borne out, although he was no longer manager when they went down. A sixth successive home defeat early in the New Year prompted his resignation and the appointment of former defender Michael Jackson until the end of the campaign. Amid further struggles at Greenhous Meadow, there was a notable victory at Notts County, where a 2-0 deficit in 13 minutes was transformed into a 3-2 success. Jon Taylor scored two of the goals and he was on the mark again in a 2-1 victory over Bradford, with debutant Shaun Miller netting in stoppage-time. Then, Taylor delivered the only goal against relegation rivals Stevenage to leave Shrewsbury within two points of safety. But successive defeats by two more strugglers, Tranmere and Crewe, followed by a 5-2 defeat away to promotion-chasing Preston, virtually put paid to their survival hopes. The drop was confirmed by a 4-2 home loss to Peterborough, Jackson reverted to assistant manager and former Fleetwood manager Micky Mellon took charge.

Anyon J 11	Grandison J................. 6 (8)	Miller S 5 (3)
Asante A........................1	Hall A 14 (3)	Mills J 12 (1)
Atajic B 3 (10)	Iorfa D 6 (1)	Mkandawire T........... 38 (1)
Bradshaw T............ 17 (11)	Jacobson J 40 (1)	Parry P 31 (8)
Burke G 1 (2)	Jones D 14 (1)	Reach A 17 (5)
Lopez C 4 (1)	Main C 4 (1)	Schmeltz S 2 (2)
Eaves T 20 (5)	Marsden J 1 (2)	Storey M 4 (2)
Foley S 6 (3)	McAlinden L 5 (2)	Summerfield L........ 24 (4)
Fyvie F 4	McAllister D 16 (10)	Tavernier J 1
Gayle C 2 (1)	McQuade A .... - (1)	Taylor J 36 (5)
Goldson C 30 (6)	Mendez-Laing N 3 (3)	Ugwu G 7

| Weale C ....35 | Winfield D .... 15 (2) | Wroe N .... 7 (3) |
| Wildig A................... 27 (3) | Woods R .... 37 (4) | |

League goals (44): Taylor 9, Bradshaw 7, Parry 5, Jacobson 4, McAlinden 3, Miller 3, Reach 3, Eaves 2, Wildig 2, Lopez 1, McAllister 1, Mkandawire 1, Summerfield 1, Ugwu 1, Woods 1
FA Cup goals: None. **Capital One Cup goals** (1): Wildig 1. **Johnstone's Paint Trophy goals** (1): Burke
Average home league attendance: 5,580.

STEVENAGE

The Stevenage success story of two promotions and one play-off semi-final in four seasons came to a halt, with manager Graham Westley admitting that his side were not good enough to avoid the drop. They were under pressure from the start when failing to win any of their first five games at the Lamex Stadium. And during the crucial run-in, home results dipped again – after the signing of Francis Zoko had suggested an escape route. Zoko, who initially penned a short-term contract, netted both goals on his league debut – a 2-1 win over promotion-minded Brentford. The Ivory Coast striker continued to score regularly, although a lack of support from other areas left Stevenage nine points from safety, albeit with games in hand over teams immediately above them. Then, in space of three weeks, six matches yielded 12 points, along with a move out of bottom four. But losing 3-2 at home to MK Dons, after leading 2-0 with ten minutes to go, proved a pivotal moment. With Zoko's goals drying up, they went another seven games without winning, culminating in a 3-1 home defeat by Bristol City which confirmed a return to League Two.

Akins L..................... 25 (6)	Doughty M 28 (8)	Morais F 18 (9)
Andrade B............... 3 (10)	Dunne J 6 (7)	Mousinho J 15 (1)
Arnold S 2 (1)	Flanagan T................. 1 (1)	N'Guessan J 2 (3)
Ashton J.....................40	Freeman L....................45	Obeng C 15
Banvo A..................... - (1)	Gordon R 1 (2)	Okenabirhie F............ 1 (2)
Burrow J 9 (11)	Gray D 9 (2)	Parrett D 8 (4)
Charles D 17 (5)	Haber M 1 (2)	Reid C 1 (3)
Chorley B.........................4	Hartley P 29 (2)	Shroot R 6 (4)
Cowan D .... - (1)	Henderson C 3	Smith J................... 40 (2)
Lopez D 1 (3)	Heslop S 23 (4)	Tansey G................. 14 (5)
Day C.........................44	Hills L 3 (1)	Tounkara O............... 6 (9)
Deacon R............... 12 (11)	Johnson R........................1	Wedgbury S............... 6 (8)
Dembele B.....................13	Jones L 21 (5)	Zoko F 33

League goals (46): Zoko 10, Freeman 6, Charles 4, Morais 4, Akins 3, Smith 3, Tansey 3, Burrow 2, Doughty 2, Hartley 2, Dembele 1, Dunne 1, Heslop 1, Mousinho 1, N'Guessan 1, Parrett 1, Opponents 1
FA Cup goals (9): Zoko 4, Akins 1, Charles 1, Freeman 1, Hartley 1, Morais 1. **Capital One Cup goals** (3): Burrow 1, Freeman 1, Morais 1. **Johnstone's Paint Trophy goals** (6): Morais 2, Zoko 2, Akins 1, Andrade 1
Average home league attendance: 2,963. **Player of Year**: Luke Freeman.

SWINDON TOWN

A late run of success was not enough to carry Swindon into the play-offs for the second successive year. After spending much of the season knocking on the door, they looked to have lost the chance when a run of seven matches failed to deliver a win. It included back-to-back home defeats by MK Dons and Wolves and left Mark Cooper's side ten points adrift. Then, a run of six hard-earned victories in the next seven games – all of which were settled by a one-goal margin – enabled them to overtake Dons and Walsall and close in on sixth-place Peterborough. The gap was four points as the teams went into their penultimate matches in which Swindon's 2-0 defeat by relegation-threatened Notts County was accompanied by red cards for Troy Archibald-Henville and Nathan Thompson. They were then overtaken by Sheffield United after losing at home to Rotherham and finished eight points adrift in eighth place. Former Peterborough manager Cooper

took over as caretaker when Kevin MacDonald left by mutual consent during pre-season after six months in the job. He was then appointed on a permanent basis.

Ajose N.................... 12 (4)	Jones M...................... - (1)	Reis T....................... 2 (4)
Archibald-Henville T . 13 (1)	Kasim Y.................... 34 (3)	Smith A................... 5 (3)
Barker G 2 (6)	Luongo M 44	Smith M 20
Barthram J................. 3 (8)	Mason H 13 (5)	Stephens J.....................10
Belford T......................5	McEveley J................ 31 (1)	Storey M 7 (11)
Byrne N 30 (6)	Murphy J 2 (4)	Thompson L 17 (11)
Cox L....................... 4 (1)	N'Guessan D 14 (10)	Thompson N 41
El-Gabbas M .... - (6)	Pritchard J............. 33 (3)	Waldon C 1 (2)
Foderingham W 41	Randall W.................. - (1)	Ward D 36
Gladwin B 6 (7)	Ranger N 19 (4)	Williams A 3
Hall G..................... 26 (1)	Raphael 13 (2)	
Harley R 16 (5)	Reckord J 3 (2)	

League goals (63): N'Guessan 8, Ranger 8, Smith M 8, Ajose 6, Luongo 6, Pritchard 6, Mason 5, Byrne 4, Storey 3, Kasim 2, Thompson L 2, Cox 1, Harley 1, Smith A 1, Thompson N 1, Opponents 1
FA Cup goals: None. **Capital One Cup goals (3):** Ranger 1, Pritchard 1, Williams 1. **Johnstone's Paint Trophy goals (8):** Ajose 4, Barthram 1, Pritchard 1, Ranger 1, Opponents 1
Average home league attendance: 8,129. **Player of Year:** Nathan Thompson

TRANMERE ROVERS

A continuous struggle to avoid the relegation zone and the sacking of Ronnie Moore for breaches of betting rules made this a turbulent season at Prenton Park. It started with 13 goals conceded in the opening four matches, defensive frailties which never went away. Veteran Ryan Lowe did his best at the other end, with the 35-year-old striker scoring ten times in one nine-match run, including a hat-trick in a 5-1 victory over Coventry. But his side were never clear of the bottom four and lost their manager, who was suspended by the club in mid-February pending an FA investigation and later dismissed for breach of contract after admitting the offences. Under caretaker John McMahon, Rovers moved three points clear of trouble by beating Colchester and Shrewsbury. But a failure to score in the next four games meant they were a point adrift of Crewe and two behind Notts County going into their own final fixture at home to Bradford. Two goals conceded in the last ten minutes resulted in a 2-1 defeat and the end of 13 seasons in League One. Rob Edwards was appointed the new manager.

Akpa Akpro J-L.......... 21 (4)	Holmes D................ 25 (3)	Peterson K 6
Ariyibi G .... - (2)	Horwood E 12 (6)	Power M 27 (6)
Arthurworrey S.......... 15 (2)	Jennings S 23 (2)	Ridehalgh L 36
Atkinson C 22	Jones A...................... 1 (1)	Robinson A 9 (10)
Bell-Baggie A 4 (8)	Kennedy M 8	Rowe J 7 (12)
Brown J 8 (1)	Kirby J 19 (12)	Sodje A................... 3 (6)
Cassidy J 19	Koumas J............... 24 (7)	Stockton C 2 (19)
Dugdale A........................4	Lowe R 44 (1)	Taylor A 41 (1)
Fon Williams O 43	McNulty J....................12	Thompson J 6
Foster S...........................4	Mooney J 3	Wallace J 16 (2)
Goodison I 15 (3)	Otsemobor J......................2	
Hateley T.........................8	Pennington M................17	

League goals (52): Lowe 19, Koumas 4, Robinson 3, Taylor 3, Akpa Akpro 2, Atkinson 2, Kirby 2, Pennington 2, Power 2, Stockton 2, Thompson 2, Wallace 2, Brown 1, Cassidy 1, Dugdale 1, Jennings 1, Ridehalgh 1, Rowe 1, Opponents 1
FA Cup goals (1) Lowe 1. **Capital One Cup goals (3):** Atkinson 1, Robinson 1, Stockton 1. **Johnstone's Paint Trophy goals (1):** Horwood 1
Average home league attendance: 5,113. **Player of Year:** Ryan Lowe

WALSALL

Walsall flattered to deceive, laying the foundation for a promotion challenge, failing to build on it and finally fading right out of the picture. A first-half hat-trick by Febian Brandy in a 5-1 away win over Notts County lifted his side into a play-off place early in the New Year. They stayed there for a fortnight before ten matches without a victory cast them eight points adrift. Two goals by leading scorer Craig Westcarr delivered a 2-0 success at Bradford to end that lean run and he was again on the mark with the only goal against Shrewsbury as Walsall moved to within two points of regaining a top-six spot. But Westcarr was sent off later in that game, banned for three matches and in his absence they fell away again. Although he was back on the mark at Stevenage, another defeat there meant they had taken just two points from five games at the most important stage of the season. Defeat in the final fixture by Colchester brought a fall into the bottom half of the table, accompanied by the club's lowest-ever goals tally at home – 21 in 23 matches.

Bakayoko A .... - (6)
Baxendale J 25 (15)
Benning M 14 (2)
Brandy F........................20
Butler A.........................45
Chambers A....................45
Chambers J....................40
Downing P 43 (1)

Featherstone N....... 15 (10)
Gray J..................... - (12)
Hemmings A 14 (13)
Hewitt T 8 (19)
Lalkovic M 30 (8)
Mantom S 43
McQuilkin J................ 2 (7)
Morris K 1 (1)

Ngoo M..................... 4 (10)
O'Donnell R 46
Purkiss B 10 (4)
Sawyers R 29 (15)
Taylor A 32 (1)
Westcarr C 40 (3)

League goals (49): Westcarr 14, Lalkovic 6, Sawyers 6, Mantom 5, Brandy 4, Baxendale 2, Benning 2, Butler 2, Hemmings 2, Chambers J 1, Downing 1, Gray 1, Ngoo 1, Taylor 1, Opponents 1
FA Cup goals (3): Westcarr 2, Sawyers 1. **Capital One Cup goals** (3): Hemmings 2, Baxendale 1.
Johnstone's Paint Trophy goals (2): Hemmings 1, Hewitt 1
Average home league attendance: 4,806. **Player of Year**: Sam Mantom

WOLVERHAMPTON WANDERERS

The good times returned to Molineux under Kenny Jackett after successive relegations cast a shadow over the one of the country's most famous old clubs. As the crowds flocked back, his side became champions with a record 103 points for the game's third tier, scoring 89 goals in the process. For more than half the season they were tucked in behind as Leyton Orient and Brentford monopolised top spot, then surged as Jackett's winter transfer window signings began to make a big impact, notably Nouha Dicko from Wigan. Nine successive wins, with 25 goals for and just two against, represented a club record, eclipsing the achievement of teams in 1915, 1967, 1987 and 1988. There was a minor stumble with a goalless draw against relegation-threatened Shrewsbury and defeat by Crawley in the space of four days when Brentford closed to within a point. But Wolves recovered the initiative and made sure of promotion with goals from Kevin McDonald and Dave Edwards for a 2-0 win over Crewe. Dicko scored a hat-trick in a 6-4 victory over Rotherham in front of a 30,000 crowd. Then, the title was secured with a 3-1 away success against Leyton Orient, followed later in the day by a stoppage-time equaliser conceded by Brentford against MK Dons.

Batth D.........................46
Cassidy J 4 (10)
Clarke L...................... 4 (9)
Davis D 12 (6)
Dicko N 16 (3)
Doherty M 15 (3)
Doyle K 16 (7)
Ebanks-Landell E 4 (3)
Edwards D 22 (8)
Elokobi G 1 (5)

Evans L 19 (7)
Foley K .... - (5)
Forde A...................... - (3)
Golbourne S 39 (1)
Griffiths L 18 (8)
Henry J................... 26 (6)
Ikeme C.........................41
Ismail Z 5 (4)
Jacobs M 28 (2)
McAlinden L 2 (5)

McCarey A 5
McDonald K 39 (2)
O'Hara J .... - (2)
Price J.................... 20 (6)
Ricketts S 42 (2)
Sako B 36 (4)
Sigurdarson B 7 (11)
Stearman R.............. 39 (1)

League goals (89): Dicko 13, Griffiths 12, Sako 12, Henry 10, Edwards 9, Jacobs 8, McDonald 5, Doyle 3, Batth 2, Ebanks-Landell 2, Evans 2, Ricketts 2, Sigurdarson 2, Stearman 2, Clarke 1, Doherty 1, Foley 1, Golbourne 1, McAlinden 1
FA Cup goals (2): Golbourne 1, Griffiths 1. **Capital One Cup goals**: None. **Johnstone's Paint Trophy goals** (2): McAlinden 1, Sako 1
Average home league attendance: 20,878. **Player of Year**: Kevin McDonald

LEAGUE TWO

ACCRINGTON STANLEY

Lee Molyneux's goals a played a major part in Accrington staving off the threat of relegation the previous season – including a hat-trick against Barnet. This time, returning to the club on loan from Crewe during the winter transfer window, he scored three in a 3-1 win over leaders Chesterfield, despite his team playing with ten men after Peter Murphy was sent off. They climbed six points clear of the bottom two as a result. Then, after that cushion was cut to three points, Molyneux netted twice in a 5-1 victory over Morecambe to give them more breathing space. There was still some work to do, particularly after a home defeat by second-from-bottom Northampton. But goals from Kayode Odejayi and James Gray earned maximum points in the penultimate match at Oxford to guarantee survival. Afterwards, manager James Beattie, the former England striker, thanked all his players for the way they responded after what he called a 'horrific' start to the campaign when the opening 12 games yielded just four points. They moved off the bottom with a run of five wins in six matches, but remained among a group of teams jostling to make a clean break from trouble.

Aldred T	46	Gray J	21 (14)	Murphy P	43 (1)
Atkinson R	11 (4)	Hatfield W	17 (14)	Naismith K	29 (9)
Bettinelli M	39	Hunt N	36 (1)	Naylor L	13
Bowerman G	10 (4)	Joyce L	45 (1)	Odejayi K	26 (6)
Buxton A	11	Liddle M	16 (3)	Richardson M	10 (5)
Carver M	1 (5)	Mahoney C	1 (3)	Webber D	14 (8)
Caton J	1 (1)	McCartan S	6 (12)	Wilson L	13 (2)
Clark L	- (1)	Miller G	4	Windass J	4 (6)
Dawber A	3	Mingoia P	31 (6)	Winnard D	37 (2)
Dunbavin I	4	Molyneux L	14 (3)		

League goals (54): Naismith 10, Murphy 9, Odejayi 8, Gray 7, Molyneux 6, Bowerman 3, Webber 3, Aldred 2, Winnard 2, Joyce 1, McCartan 1, Mingoia 1, Opponents 1
FA Cup goals: None. **Capital One Cup goals** (2): Carver 1, Mingoia 1. **Johnstone's Paint Trophy goals**: None
Average home league attendance: 1,605. **Player of Year**: Tom Aldred

AFC WIMBLEDON

A three-point deduction for fielding an ineligible player cast a shadow over the end of the season. The club also received a suspended £5,000 fine from the Football League for including midfielder Jake Nicholson in the 4-3 home win over Cheltenham. Nicholson, a second-half substitute, scored the second of his team's three goals in three minutes, with Jack Midson netting the winner in stoppage-time. Wimbledon dropped four places to 18th as a result of the deduction, but it had no impact on relegation issues because of sufficient points previously accumulated. So there was no repeat of the last-day drama in 2013 when Midson's late penalty kept them up. This time, Wimbledon won five of their opening eight fixtures to go third in the table. They dropped into the bottom half after a run of seven games without a win and continued to experience mixed fortunes, having to play catch-up in several games because of poor starts. There were first round defeats in all three cup competitions and manager Neal Ardley set out to build a new-look side in the summer in an effort for greater consistency.

143

Antwi W 14 (4)	Hylton D 10 (7)	Porter G 17 (4)
Appiah K 6 (1)	Jones D 17 (1)	Richards T 9 (1)
Arthur C 2 (24)	Kennedy C 21 (1)	Sainte-Luce K 3 (20)
Bennett A 32	Midson J................. 19 (18)	Sheringham C 8 (7)
Brown S 1	Mohamed K 5	Smith M 23
Collins M 9	Moore L 25 (8)	Strutton C 1 (2)
Fenlon J 15 (4)	Moore S 40	Sweeney P 18 (4)
Frampton A.....................31	Morris A 15 (2)	Weston R 6 (1)
Francomb G 28 (5)	Nicholson J............... 3 (1)	Worner R 45
Fuller B 45	Pell H 27 (6)	Wyke C 11 (6)

League goals (49): Smith 9, Midson 7, Frampton 4, Moore S 4, Pell 4, Appiah 3, Francomb 3, Hylton 3, Moore L 3, Wyke 2, Antwi 1, Arthur 1, Bennett 1, Jones 1, Nicholson 1, Sainte-Luce 1, Sheringham 1
FA Cup goals (1): Smith 1. **Capital One Cup goals** (1): Moore L 1. **Johnstone's Paint Trophy goals** (3): Fenlon 1, Francomb 1, Sweeney 1
Average home league attendance: 4,134. **Player of Year**: Barry Fuller

BRISTOL ROVERS

Ninety four years of league football came to an end in front of a shocked crowd of more than 10,000 at the Memorial Stadium on the final day of the season. Rovers went into the match against mid-table Mansfield three points clear after winning what looked like a make-or-break game at Wycombe with goals from Lee Brown and David Clarkson. They still needed a point to make sure of staying up without relying on the results of Wycombe and Northampton. But on a tense afternoon, Clarkson and Mark McChrystal hit the woodwork and their side were unable to retrieve a 36th minute goal scored by Colin Daniel. Both rivals won, Rovers went down on goal difference and angry fans on the pitch directed their anger at club directors. It was a traumatic introduction to management for Darrell Clarke, John Ward's assistant who took over little more than a month earlier with Ward becoming director of football. Clarke made a winning start against Morecambe, but a home defeat by basement team Torquay piled on the pressure. Under Ward – who was dismissed following the drop – Rovers had been in trouble for much of the campaign, before a five-match unbeaten run took them eight points clear and suggested a mid-table finish was a possibility.

Beardsley C............... 16 (8)	Gow A.............................4	Mildenhall S 46
Bond A 5	Harding M.................. 5 (6)	Mohamed K 20 (1)
Broghamber F........... 1 (3)	Harrison E.............. 9 (16)	Norburn O.......................16
Brown L 41	Harrold M 22 (8)	O'Toole J.........................41
Brunt R 9 (2)	Henshall A 1 (1)	Packwood W.....................8
Clarke O 29 (3)	Hunter S................... - (3)	Parkes T 44
Clarkson D 28 (6)	Keary P................... - (1)	Richards E 18 (4)
Clucas S 11 (6)	Lockyer T................. 38 (3)	Santos A.................. 7 (16)
Gill M .... - (1)	Lucas J................... - (1)	Smith M 43
Gillespie S 3 (10)	McChrystal M 35	Woodards D.............. 6 (3)

League goals (43): O'Toole 13, Clarkson 6, Harrold 6, Mohamed 4, Brown 2, Clarke 2, Richards 2, Beardsley 1, Gillespie 1, Harrison 1, Henshall 1, Lockyer 1, Parkes 1, Santos 1, Woodards 1
FA Cup goals (8): Beardsley 2, O'Toole 2, Richards 2, Harrold 1, Norburn 1. **Capital One Cup goals** (1): Richards 1. **Johnstone's Paint Trophy goals** (1): McChrystal 1.
Average home league attendance: 6,420. **Player of Year**: Michael Smith

BURTON ALBION

Manager Gary Rowett began planning for a third successive promotion bid immediately after the club's latest disappointment. In 2013, they lost to Bradford in the semi-finals of the play-offs. This time, a goal 15 minutes from the end brought a 1-0 defeat by Fleetwood in a closely-contested final which could have gone either way. Rowett's summer transfer targets were likely

to be players to improve his side's scoring record, with their total of 47 one of the poorest in the division. After an indifferent start, Burton established a place among the leading group in late October and stayed there. At the half-way point of the season they were level on points with the top two, Chesterfield and Scunthorpe, and still had a chance of automatic promotion after beating Hartlepool 3-0 in the penultimate home match. But points dropped against Newport, Chesterfield and Southend meant a sixth-place finish. In the semi-finals against Southend, they overcame the sending-off of Ian Sharps to win the home leg with a goal from Adam McGurk and went through after a 2-2 draw in the return when McGurk and Marcus Holness were on the mark.

Alexander G 7 (4)	Holness M................ 14 (3)	McFadzean C 7
Bell L 26 (8)	Renee-Howe J 7 (8)	McGurk A 31 (3)
Cansdell-Sherriff S..........32	Hussey C 22 (5)	Palmer M................. 31 (9)
Delap R 6	Ismail Z.................. 10 (5)	Phillips J 27 (6)
Diamond Z 6 (4)	Kee B 29 (8)	Pickford J 12
Dyer J .... - (4)	Knowles D............. 11 (17)	Reed A 3 (2)
Edwards P................ 39 (2)	Lainton R....................14	Sharps I.........................39
Gray D 7 (5)	Lyness D 20 (1)	Symes M 7 (6)
Harness M 1 (2)	MacDonald A......... 16 (19)	Weir R 40 (1)
Hemmings A 2 (3)	McCrory D.....................40	

Play-offs – appearances: Bell 3, Edwards 3, Holness 3, Hussey 3, Lyness 3, McFadzean 3, McGurk 3, Weir 3, Kee 2 (1), Cansdell-Sherriff 2, Gray 1 (1), Ismail 1 (1), Knowles 1 (1), MacDonald 1 (1), Sharps 1, Palmer – (2), Diamond – (1).
League goals (47): Kee 12, McGurk 9, Ismail 3, Knowles 3, Edwards 2, Phillips 2, Symes 2, Weir 2, Bell 1, Delap 1, Diamond 1, Howe 1, Hussey 1, McCrory 1, McFadzean 1, Reed 1, Sharps 1, Opponents 3. **Play-offs – goals** (3): McGurk 2, Holness 1
FA Cup goals (5): Kee 2, McGurk 1, Palmer 1, Phillips 1. **Capital One Cup goals** (4): Hussey 2, Dyer 1, Symes 1. **Johnstone's Paint Trophy goals:** None.
Average home league attendance: 2,720. **Player of Year:** Ian Sharps

BURY

A new team, a change of manager and a late run of success made for a lively campaign. Kevin Blackwell had to put together a fresh squad after the departure of most of his players in the wake of the previous season's financial crisis and relegation. He was sacked after a run of two points from six matches, to be replaced initially by his assistant, Ronnie Jepson, and eventually on a permanent basis by David Flitcroft, himself dismissed by Barnsley. Bury were then 20th in the table and Flitcroft signed a further eight players during the winter transfer window. Two away wins in five days against Wimbledon and Mansfield left them seven points clear of the relegation zone. Then, there were seven games without a win. But 13 points were secured from the next five, along with 13 goals scored, paving the way for a top-half finish. Hallam Hope scored a hat-trick in the first home game, although his side surrendered 3-0 and 4-2 leads to draw 4-4 against Portsmouth. The club renamed their Gigg Lane ground the JD Stadium as part of a sponsorship deal with the Bury-based sportswear firm.

Akpa-Akpro J-L... 5 (5)	Harrad S 10 (8)	Lockwood A....................1
Beeley S 20	Harrison S................... - (1)	Mayor D 30 (9)
Burgess S 1	Hinds R 8 (2)	McNulty J 21
Burke J..........................2	Holden E 2	Miller T 25 (3)
Cameron N................ 25 (2)	Hope H.........................8	Mills P............................21
Carroll J..................... 5 (1)	Howell D........................8	Mustoe J.........................6
Carson T.........................5	Hussey C 10 (1)	Nardiello D 25 (2)
Charles-Cook R........... 1 (1)	Hylton D 7	Navas M 1 (1)
Dudley A..................... - (2)	Jackson M 2 (6)	Obadeyi T .... - (7)
Edjenguele W 18 (1)	Jensen B......................36	Platt C 8 (9)
Forrester A............. 18 (10)	Jones C................. 33 (4)	Poscha M .... - (1)
Grimes A.................... 6 (9)	Lainton R....................4	Procter A 23 (9)

Reindorf J 1 (3)	Sedgwick C 32 (5)	Veseli F 18
Roberts G 11	Sinnott J 5 (4)	Walker R .... - (3)
Rooney J 1 (2)	Soares T 24 (6)	Young L .... - (4)
Rose D .... - (6)	Tutte A 19	

League goals (59): Nardiello 11, Forrester 6, Soares 6, Hope 5, Mayor 5, Cameron 4, Rose 3, Edjenguele 2, Hussey 2, Hylton 2, Platt 2, Procter 2, Sedgwick 2, Carroll 1, Hinds 1, Jackson 1, Jones 1, Reindorf 1, Sinnott 1, Tutte 1
FA Cup goals (1): Harrad 1. **Capital One Cup goals** (6): Beeley 1, Edjenguele 1, Forrester 1, Harrad 1, Hines 1, Reindorf 1. **Johnstone's Paint Trophy goals** (1): Sedgwick 1
Average home league attendance: 3,138. **Player of Year**: Brian Jensen

CHELTENHAM TOWN

After reaching the play-offs in two successive years, Cheltenham experienced an indifferent season this time. The root of the problem was home form and in particular the failure to hold on to winning leads. It happened in ten matches, six of which were drawn and four lost. As a result, just five games were won at Whaddon Road – only bottom club Torquay had fewer victories – and the team fared better on their travels. They started poorly, one win in the first eight matches. Things improved with a move into the top half of the table on the back of a run of 11 fixtures without defeat. Then came another lean spell and this was how it continued through to the final day when a fourth successive home defeat was inflicted by Dagenham and Redbridge. There was disappointment, too, in the FA Cup. After two money-spinning runs, Cheltenham went out in the first round to non-league Tamworth. A much better showing came in the Capital One Cup at Upton Park, where West Ham were pushed all the way before prevailing 2-1.

Braham-Barrett C 29	Goldson C 3 (1)	McGlashan J 38 (5)
Brown S 45	Gornell T 21 (13)	Noble D 25 (4)
Brown T 39	Hanks J 1 (1)	Penn R 13 (6)
Brundle M 7	Harrison B 35 (11)	Richards M 46
Cureton J 23 (12)	Ihiekwe M 13	Roberts C 1
Dale B .... - (1)	Inniss R 2	Roofe K 7 (2)
Daniels B 2	Jombati S 38 (5)	Taylor J 25 (8)
Deering S 29 (6)	Kotwica Z 1 (17)	Vincent A 7 (11)
Elliott S 32	Lowe K 12 (1)	Williams H 3 (2)
Gillespie S 3 (1)	Lucas L 2	Wilson J 4

League goals (53): Harrison 13, Cureton 11, McGlashan 6, Richards 6, Brown T 4, Gornell 3, Taylor 2, Vincent 2, Elliott 1, Jombati 1, Lowe 1, Roofe 1, Opponents 2
FA Cup goals: None. **Capital One Cup goals** (5): Harrison 2, Richards 2, Gornell 1. **Johnstone's Paint Trophy goals** (3): Gillespie 2, Taylor 1
Average home league attendance: 2,988. **Player of Year**: Byron Harrison

CHESTERFIELD

Paul Cook led Chesterfield to the title in his first full season in charge. A rousing finish in 2013 was not quite enough for a chance of honours via the play-offs. This time, they saw off strong challenges from two rivals to prove worthy champions. There was more recognition for the club when winger Gary Roberts was voted League Two's Player of the Year and was joined in the PFA Team of the Year by goalkeeper Tommy Lee and defenders Ian Evatt and Liam Cooper. Roberts's 11th goal was his most important – the championship clincher against Fleetwood in the final game, four minutes after Sam Hird had netted the equaliser. A week earlier, two by Jay O'Shea in a 2-0 victory at Burton had ensured promotion. Those goals left them three points ahead of Scunthorpe and Rochdale, who had both led the division during a highly competitive run-in. Chesterfield had signalled their intentions from the start, winning seven of the opening eight fixtures and drawing the other. They saw off the challenge of Oxford, the other side to lead the division, while at the same time progressing to the Johnstone's Paint Trophy Final. There was

disappointment at Wembley, with a 3-1 defeat by Peterborough, but not enough to prevent a subsequent five-match unbeaten run which proved decisive in the league.

Banks O 23 (2)	Gardner D 11 (5)	O'Shea J 27 (13)
Bennett M 1 (4)	Gnandullet A 10 (24)	Porter C 2 (1)
Brown M 2 (1)	Hird S 27 (8)	Richards M 21 (17)
Cooper L 38 (3)	Humphreys R 38 (4)	Roberts G 36 (4)
Darikwa T 32 (9)	Kearns D 6 (4)	Ryan J 39
Devitt J 3 (4)	Lee T 46	Smith N 12 (2)
Doyle E 26 (17)	McFadzean C 2 (2)	Talbot D 24 (1)
Edwards R 4 (1)	McSheffrey G 2 (7)	Togwell S 5 (5)
Evatt I 35	Morsy S 34	

League goals (71): Doyle 11, Roberts 11, O'Shea 9, Richards 8, Banks 7, Gnandullet 5, Cooper 3, Darikwa 3, Gardner 3, Hird 2, Humphreys 2, Ryan 2, Brown 1, Evatt 1, McSheffrey 1, Morsy 1, Opponents 1
FA Cup goals (3): Darikwa 1, Roberts 1, Ryan 1. **Capital One Cup goals** (1): Doyle 1. **Johnstone's Paint Trophy goals** (9): Banks 2, Darikwa 1, Doyle 1, Evatt 1, Gnandullet 1, McSheffrey 1, Morsy 1, Ryan 1
Average home league attendance: 6,317. **Player of Year**: Sam Morsy

DAGENHAM AND REDBRIDGE

After a tense climax to the previous season, Dagenham enjoyed the security of a place in the top half of the table. They could even have gone close to reaching the play-off places had it not been for some poor results in the final few weeks. Wayne Burnett's young side lost four out of five matches, two of them to relegation-threatened Wycombe and Northampton, before finishing on a high at Cheltenham. There, they twice came from behind and went on to win 3-2 with a goal from Adebayo Azeez. The result lifted them back up to ninth – a sharp contrast to 2013 when only a superior goal difference prevented a drop into the Conference. Dagenham's powers of recovery had been evident previously, notably in a dramatic match against promotion-bound Scunthorpe. Trailing 3-0, they pulled two goals back through Abu Ogogo and Chris Dixon. Then, after the game was halted for ten minutes when heavy rain left puddles on the pitch, Luke Norris marked his debut with an 89th minute equaliser.

Azeez A 10 (5)	Hines Z.................... 26 (1)	Saah B 41 (2)
Bingham B 23 (7)	Howell L 36 (4)	Samuel D 1
Chambers A 4 (2)	Hoyte G 42	Saunders M 2 (2)
Connors J 23	Ilesanmi F 23 (6)	Scott J 6 (5)
D'Ath L 17 (4)	Lewington C 42	Seabright J 4
Dennis L .... - (2)	Murphy R 32	Shields S 2 (10)
Dickson C 3 (22)	Norris L 16 (3)	Turgott B 3 (2)
Doe S 36 (1)	Nouble L .... - (1)	Wilkinson L 18 (4)
Edgar A .... - (7)	Obafemi A 9 (13)	Woodall B 4 (4)
Elito M 36 (9)	Ogogo A 44	
Gayle I 3 (1)	Reed J .... - (2)	

League goals (53): Murphy 13, Ogogo 8, Elito 7, Hines 6, Howell 4, Norris 4, Azeez 3, Obafemi 2, D'Ath 1, Dickson 1, Doe 1, Scott 1, Woodall 1, Opponents 1
FA Cup goals: None. **Capital One Cup goals** (2): Scott 1, Opponents 1. **Johnstone's Paint Trophy goals** (9): Hines 2, Saah 2, Dennis 1, Dickson 1, Elito 1, Obafemi 1, Ogogo 1
Average home league attendance: **Player of Year**: Abu Ogogo

EXETER CITY

Exeter reserved one of their best performances for the penultimate game of the season – and it was just as well. They were just two points clear of the relegation zone, with teams around them all jostling for safety, when a poor home record was exposed to leaders Scunthorpe, a

side unbeaten in a record-breaking 28 matches. The challenge was met by goals from Craig Woodman and Jimmy Keohane, an impressive 2-0 victory and a position of safety. It followed October's 4-0 away success at Glanford Park which had lifted them to third in the table and hinted at a sustained promotion challenge to follow. Instead, the next seven games failed to produce a victory and lost ground was never made up. Exeter were still in the top half going into the New Year after beating Torquay 3-1 in a local derby at Plainmoor. But there was only one win in the next three months and a 1-0 defeat by struggling Northampton was the team's 13th successive game at St James Park without a victory. That run ended when Fleetwood were seen off 3-0. But another defeat, this time in the return against Torquay, meant the pressure was back on.

Baldwin P 24 (1)	Gow A 18 (7)	Parkin S 17 (9)
Bennett S 44 (1)	Grimes M 23 (12)	Pym C 9
Butterfield D 26 (3)	Jay M 1 (1)	Reid J 1 (5)
Coles D.........................37	Keohane J 12 (9)	Richards E 11 (6)
Davies A 27 (5)	Krysiak A 37	Sercombe L.............. 42 (2)
Dawson A.................. 4 (1)	Moore-Taylor J 25 (4)	Tillson J 1
Doherty T 8 (2)	Nicholls T 19 (9)	Watkins O .... - (1)
Gill M...................... 19 (5)	O'Flynn J 18 (15)	Wheeler D 20 (15)
Gosling J.................... - (3)	Oakley M 22 (2)	Woodman C....................41

League goals (54): Gow 7, Bennett 6, Nicholls 6, Richards 5, Sercombe 5, O'Flynn 4, Keohane 3, Parkin 3, Wheeler 3, Coles 2, Davies 2, Grimes 1, Moore-Taylor 1, Woodman 1, Opponents 5
FA Cup goals: None. **Capital One Cup goals**: None. **Johnstone's Paint Trophy goals**: None
Average home league attendance: 3,700. **Player of Year**: Matt Grimes

FLEETWOOD TOWN

The remarkable rise of one of the smallest clubs in the league continued on its biggest stage. Leading marksman Antoni Sarcevic scored the only goal of a tense Play-off Final against Burton at Wembley to deliver a place in the game's third tier. It was the club's sixth promotion in ten seasons – a climb that started in North West Counties football, continued through the Northern Premier and Conference divisions and brought a place in League Two in 2012. This latest one was a fitting 44th birthday present for chairman Andy Pilley, who has bankrolled the success, and came in Graham Alexander's first full season as a manager. Alexander, who made more than 1,000 appearances during a 20-year playing career, brought in several new players during the summer, including former Manchester City youth product Sarcevic and Mark Roberts, a promotion winner with Stevenage. Roberts, the new captain, scored on his debut against Dagenham and Redbridge when a 3-1 victory launched Fleetwood's season. They were in the top seven for virtually the whole campaign – Sarcevic scoring a hat-trick in a 5-4 win over Mansfield – and were in with a chance of automatic promotion until dropping points in the final two games against Southend and Chesterfield. Like the Wembley win, their semi-final was a tight affair, settled by Matty Blair's goal in the away leg against his former club York.

Allen J...................... - (1)	Grant R............................1	McLaughlin C.......... 32 (3)
Ball D...................... 24 (6)	Hogan L.............. 14 (2)	Morris J 11 (3
Blair M 13 (11)	Howell D.................... 6 (2)	Murdoch S............. 25 (13)
Brown J 11 (10)	Hughes J 25	Parkin J.............. 14 (17)
Carr J 1 (3)	Hughes M 1 (4)	Pond N.............. 40 (1)
Cresswell R 18 (2)	Hume I 7 (1)	Roberts M......................33
Crowther R 5 (2)	Jordan S 10	Sarcevic A 39 (3)
Davies S........................28	Mandron M 4 (7)	Schumacher S.......... 31 (1)
Dieseruvwe E.............. - (4)	Marrow A 6 (1)	Taylor C 31 (1)
Evans G 22 (12)	Matt J.............. 14 (11)	Tyson N 4
Goodall A.............. 18 (1)	Maxwell C 18	

Play-offs – appearances: Ball 3, Blair 3, Hume 3, Maxwell 3, McLaughlin 3, Morris 3, Pond

3, Roberts 3, Sarcevic 3, Taylor 3, Schumacher 2, Goodall 1 (1), **Murdoch** – (2), **Parkin** – (2), Cresswell – (1)
League goals (66): Sarcevic 13, Ball 8, Matt 8, Parkin 7, Evans 6, Schumacher 5, Blair 3, Hughes 3, Roberts 3, Morris 2, Brown 1, Carr 1, Cresswell 1, Hume 1, Mandron 1, Marrow 1, Pond 1, Opponents 1. **Play-offs – goals** (2): Blair 1, Sarcevic 1
FA Cup goals (3): Ball 1, Hughes 1, Parkin 1. **Capital One Cup goals** (2): Ball 1, Evans 1.
Johnstone's Paint Trophy goals (12): Ball 3, Matt 2, Parkin 2, Blair 1, Hughes 1, McLaughlin 1, Pond 1, Sarcevic 1
Average home league attendance 2,819: **Player of Year:** Conor McLaughlin

HARTLEPOOL UNITED

Colin Cooper's first season as manager was a rollercoaster affair. The former Middlesbrough and Nottingham Forest defender, who took over from John Hughes after the club's relegation from League One, secured just one victory in his first nine matches. He then won October's Manager of the Month award – with Academy graduate striker Luke James collecting the players' award –for four straight wins. Mid-table consolidation gave way to a poor start to the New Year, followed by a move to within three points of a play-off place in the wake of a 4-0 victory over Bristol Rovers. Again the tide turned as six successive defeats resulted in a worrying slide to within two points of a relegation place. When Simon Walton was sent off with his side trailing to Morecambe, things looked bleak. But Jack Compton came off the bench to equalise, Jack Barmby scored the winner nine minutes from the end of normal time and results elsewhere meant they were virtually safe with two matches remaining.

Austin N 29	Harewood M 16 (3)	Poole J 21 (12)
Baldwin J......................28	Harrison S.................. 5 (1)	Rafferty A 3
Barmby J 12 (5)	Hartley P 1	Richards J.............. 11 (8)
Burgess C 41	Hawkins L.................. - (5)	Rodney N.............. 1 (11)
Collins C.................. 20 (4)	Holden D 23 (3)	Rutherford G .... - (1)
Compton J 25 (9)	Howard S 3 (5)	Smith C .... - (1)
Dolan M........................20	James L.................. 38 (4)	Sweeney A 3 (16)
Duckworth M..................30	Jones D .... - (1)	Walker B 31 (5)
Flinders S......................43	Monkhouse A 34 (2)	Walton S.............. 37 (2)
Franks J.................. 22 (17)	Oliver C 2 (1)	Williams L..........................7

League goals (50): James 13, Barmby 5, Franks 5, Compton 4, Monkhouse 4, Harewood 3, Poole 3, Walker 3, Walton 3, Baldwin 2, Dolan 2, Williams 2, Opponents 1
FA Cup goals (5): Baldwin 2, James 2, Monkhouse 1. **Capital One Cup goals** (1): Austin 1.
Johnstone's Paint Trophy goals (7): Burgess 1, Compton 1, Franks 1, James 1, Monkhouse 1, Poole 1, Rodney 1
Average home league attendance: 3,723. **Player of Year:** Luke James

MANSFIELD TOWN

Mansfield could feel well satisfied with their return to the Football League after a five-year absence. They surprised many who had forecast an immediate return to the Conference by finishing 11th and would have gone higher had it not been for late lapses against teams below them in the table. The first half of the season proved a topsy-turvy affair – eight matches unbeaten followed by a run of 13 without a victory. That included a 5-4 defeat at Fleetwood, where a stoppage-time penalty was conceded after Ross Dyer had equalised in the 89th minute. Boxing Day's 3-0 defeat at Rochdale was one of their poorest performances, but the tide turned after that, with improved defensive work a major factor. Mansfield worked their way out of trouble and went on to record four successive victories to move within six points of the top seven. Then some of the shine came off as matches against Accrington, Cheltenham and Torquay netted a single point. The campaign closed with Colin Daniel's winner against Bristol Rovers sending their opponents down.

Alabi J..............................1	Hutchinson B..........11 (5)	Poku G 1 (3)
Andrew C................11 (4)	Jennings J.................32 (1)	Price L 5
Beevers L................24 (2)	Marriott A 40	Rhead M................28 (12)
Blake J 3	Marsden L.......................2	Riley M.........................31
Briscoe L ....- (2)	McCombe J.....................5	Speight J 1 (7)
Cain M ....- (2)	McGuire J 25 (2)	Stevenson L 19 (2)
Clements C 23	Meikle L 2 (26)	Sutton R 35 (1)
Clucas S 29 (9)	Mitchell L 1	Tafazoli R.....................24
Daniel C 18 (10)	Murray A..................16 (2)	Thomas J ....- (1)
Dempster J 35 (1)	Murtagh K................2 (1)	Westlake D....................23
Dyer R 7 (5)	Palmer O 20 (18)	
Howell A...............30 (3)	Pilkington G....................2	

League goals (49): Clucas 8, Rhead 6, Stevenson 5, Jennings 4, Palmer 4, Howell 3, Daniel 2, Dyer 2, Hutchinson 2, McCombe 2, McGuire 2, Tafazoli 2, Andrew 1, Clements 1, Meikle 1, Murray 1, Riley 1, Speight 1, Opponents 1
FA Cup goals (10): Clucas 5, Daniel 1, Dyer 1, Howell 1, Palmer 1, Stevenson 1. **Capital One Cup goals:** None. **Johnstone's Paint Trophy goals:** None
Average home league attendance: 3,385. **Player of Year:** Matt Rhead

MORECAMBE

Morecambe's powers of recovery took them to the brink of a play-off place – and later helped keep at bay the threat of being sucked into a relegation battle. Over the course of the season, 34 points were accumulated from matches in which they conceded the first goal – eight victories and ten draws. Highlight came when Chesterfield established a 3-0 lead and looked a safe bet to consolidate their position at the top of the table. Instead, Kevin Ellison (47), Mark Hughes (62), Jack Sampson (71) and Padraig Amond (86) turned the game on its head for the home side. Victory over Fleetwood on Boxing Day left Morecambe two points away from a top-seven spot. Then, a run of ten matches without a win, culminating in a 5-0 beating at Plymouth, sent them sliding. They also conceded five at Accrington. But there were further comebacks in the return with Fleetwood and against another promotion-minded side, Scunthorpe, while a 3-0 win in the penultimate match at Wimbledon, achieved by goals from Jack Redshaw, Jamie Devitt and Amond from the penalty spot ensured safety.

Amond P..............33 (12)	Fleming A 33 (2)	Parrish A.................38 (1)
Arestidou A 1	Hughes M 43 (1)	Redshaw J 14 (15)
Beeley S 11 (1)	Kenyon A 33 (6)	Roche B 45
Devitt J.........................14	Marshall M 6 (9)	Sampson J 31 (11)
Diagne T 15 (12)	McCready C 20 (2)	Threlfall R...............31 (3)
Doyle C 1 (2)	McGee J 3 (8)	Williams R 21 (4)
Drummond S...........31 (4)	McGowan A ....- (2)	Wright A 30 (5)
Edwards R 8 (1)	Mustoe J...................4 (1)	
Ellison K...............38 (4)	Mwasilie J...........2 (17)	

League goals (52): Amond 11, Ellison 10, Redshaw 8, Hughes 5, Sampson 5, Williams 3, Devitt 2, Diagne 2, Fleming 2, Threlfall 1, Opponents 3
FA Cup goals: None. **Capital One Cup goals** (1): Williams 1. **Johnstone's Paint Trophy goals:** None
Average home league attendance: 1,939. **Player of Year:** Andy Fleming

NEWPORT COUNTY

A solid and satisfactory return to the Football League after an absence of 25 years might have even better had the weather not played havoc with the Rodney Parade pitch. January and February downpours caused six out of seven home games to be postponed, forced a succession of away matches to be played and resulted in a fixture backlog. Newport, managed by former Tottenham defender Justin Edinburgh, had made a flying start with a 4-1 win over Accrington. They climbed as high as third behind Oxford and Chesterfield approaching the half-way point

of the season and were still in touch with the leading group after a 3-2 victory over Oxford in their first home appearance for more than five weeks. But a crowded schedule took its toll, eight games in 26 days yielding just three points and a corresponding fall in the table. Wins over two struggling sides, Torquay and Wycombe, eased the pressure and there was a good finish with 10 men – Kevin Feely's 88th minute header accounting for promoted Rochdale after the dismissal of Ryan Jacksoon. The statistics showed Newport accumulating 37 points from the first 23 fixtures and 21 in the second half of the campaign.

Anthony B..............7	James T............. 5 (1)	Pipe D 22 (3)
Barker G .... - (2)	Jeffers S 4 (10)	Porter M 15 (7)
Blake D 8	Jolley C............. 20 (12)	Renee-Howe J 12 (3)
Burge R 12 (5)	Jones B 6 (1)	Sandell A 21 (2)
Chapman A 35 (4)	McLoughlin I............12	Stephens J.................2
Crow D 13 (14)	Minshull L 34 (6)	Washington C 16 (8)
Feely K 10	Naylor T........... 24 (9)	Willmott R 40 (6)
Flynn M 18 (14)	O'Connor A 1 (3)	Worley H..............26
Holloway A............ - (4)	Oshilaja A..............8	Yakubu I 22 (3)
Hughes A 23 (3)	Parish E..............7	Zebroski C......... 32 (3)
Jackson R 26 (3)	Pidgeley L...........25	

League goals (56): Zebroski 12, Minshull 4, Washington 4, Worley 4, Crow 3, Flynn 3, Renee-Howe 3, Sandell 3, Willmott 3, Yakubu 3, Burge 2, Chapman 2, Hughes 2, Jolley 2, Feely 1, Jones 1, Naylor 1, O'Connor 1, Porter 1, Opponents 1
FA Cup goals (4): Willmott 3, Naylor 1. **Capital One Cup goals (3):** Crow 2, Washington 1. **Johnstone's Paint Trophy goals (6):** Washington 2, Chapman 1, Oshilaja 1, Zebroski 1, Opponents 1
Average home league attendance: 3,453. **Player of Year:** Chris Zebroski

NORTHAMPTON TOWN

Chris Wilder gambled heavily when swopping a promotion challenge with Oxford for a relegation struggle at Sixfields. He took charge of a side rooted in the bottom two for four months and looking like staying there. But the gamble paid off thanks to shrewd work in the transfer market and the strongest finish of all the sides struggling to beat the drop. Wilder, who came in a month after Aidy Boothroyd was sacked four days before Christmas, provided much-needed momentum with the players he brought in. Northampton were still in trouble going into the final month of the season – until successive 1-0 victories over Accrington and Burton finally closed the gap. Then, their youngest-ever player took centre stage. Local boy Ivan Toney, who made his debut aged 16 in 2012, scored his first two goals in a 3-0 away win over Dagenham and Redbridge to lift his team out of the relegation places. In the final fixture, which brought Wilder up against his former club, Toney was on the mark again, along with John Marquis and Mathias Doumbe, in a 3-1 win which ensured safety.

Amankwaah K 21	Emerton D 11 (5)	McSweeney L 16 (2)
Blair M 3	Ferdinand K............4	Morris I.............. 23 (10)
Blyth J................ 8 (3)	German A 5 (2)	Moyo D.................. - (6)
Carter D..............37	Hackett C 35 (2)	Norris L 8 (2)
Collins L 21 (1)	Harrlott M 2 (3)	O'Donovan R 10 (5)
Connell A 11 (5)	Heath M 5	Platt C 7 (4)
Lopez C .... - (3)	Hooper J J .... - (3)	Ravenhill R.............25
Dallas S 10 (2)	Hope H..............3	Reid P..............16
Deegan G 22 (5)	Horwood E 7 (1)	Robertson G 14 (1)
Demontagnac I 2 (8)	Hurst J..............1	Sinclair E.......... 15 (5)
Diamond Z............14	Langmead K........... - (3)	Toney I 3 (10)
Dickenson B......... 8 (5)	Marquis J.......... 12 (2)	Tozer B 21 (8)
Doumbe M 30 (2)	McGinty S..............2	Widdowson J 24 (1)
Duke M...........46	McLeod I.............4	

League goals (42): Carter 5, Norris 4, Blyth 3, Dallas 3, Doumbe 3, Morris 3, Toney 3, Hackett 2, Marquis 2, Sinclair 2, Blair 1, Collins 1, Deegan 1, Diamond 1, Dickenson 1, Hope 1, McLeod 1, O'Donovan 1, Platt 1, Opponents 3

FA Cup goals (2): Emerton 1, Norris 1. **Capital One Cup goals** (1): O'Donovan 1. **Johnstone's Paint Trophy goals**: None

Average home league attendance: 4,548. **Player of Year**: Darren Carter

OXFORD UNITED

Oxford's season fell apart when Chris Wilder, English football's third longest-serving manager behind Arsenal's Arsene Wenger and Exeter's Paul Tisdale, resigned after five years with the club. Wilder exchanged a promotion challenge for a relegation battle, with his old team two points away from a top-three place and his new one bottom-of-the-table six points adrift. Mickey Lewis managed two victories during two months as caretaker before Gary Waddock, former Queens Park Rangers, Aldershot and Wycombe manager, took over on a permanent basis. His side were still in a play-off position, but three successive defeats pushed them down. Then, after a win over Plymouth revived hopes, single-goal losses to promotion-chasing Scunthorpe and York, followed by a home defeat by Accrington, left Waddock with that sinking feeling. There was another reversal in the final match, ironically against Northampton who stayed up as a result. Oxford were left nine points adrift of the top-seven.

Bevans M 9 (1)	Long S 3	Rose D 38 (2)
Clarke R 46	Marsh T .... - (5)	Ruffles J 21 (8)
Connolly D 8 (8)	Mullins J 35	Smalley D 23 (9)
Constable J 32 (12)	Newey T 40	Whing A 17 (1)
Davies S 7 (15)	O'Dowda C 4 (6)	Williams J 27 (9)
Hall A 15 (4)	Potter A 16 (8)	Wright J 31
Hunt D 46	Raynes M 25 (2)	Wroe N 16 (2)
Kitson D 27 (5)	Rigg S 20 (8)	

League goals (53): Constable 10, Smalley 7, Williams 7, Connolly 4, Kitson 4, Potter 4, Rose 4, Hall 3, Mullins 3, Rigg 2, Wroe 2, Newey 1, Ruffles 1, Opponents 1

FA Cup goals (7): Smalley 2, Constable 1, Davies 1, Mullins 1, Rose 1, Williams 1. **Capital One Cup goals**: None. **Johnstone's Paint Trophy goals** (1): Constable 1

Average home league attendance: 5,923. **Player of Year**: Ryan Clarke

PLYMOUTH ARGYLE

A place in the top half of the table contrasted sharply with the struggle to maintain a Football League place experienced in the two previous seasons. But Plymouth's bid to go a step further by reaching the play-offs came to nothing after some damaging home defeats during the run-in. After spending most of the first half of the campaign in the bottom half, they effected a modest improvement in the opening weeks of the New Year. The momentum built in the wake of a 4-0 defeat by York, with wins over Dagenham and Redbridge, Fleetwood and Morecambe yielding 11 goals. Then, two strikes by Reuben Reid brought 2-1 success against league leaders Chesterfield and a place in the top-seven. It was a brief stay. Although Reid was on the mark again in the next two games, a 1-1 draw at Accrington and a 2-1 home defeat by Exeter in front of a 13,000-plus crowd, cast his side three points adrift. Plymouth fell right away as Oxford and Wimbledon also prevailed at Home Park – and there was another 4-0 beating, this time at Bury. Reid finished with 21 goals to his credit, including a hat-trick in the FA Cup against Lincoln.

Alessandra L 39 (3)	Boco R 22 (5)	Lavery C 4 (4)
Banton J 11 (2)	Branston G 11 (1)	McCormick L 27
Bencherif H 5 (2)	Cole J 19 (1)	Morgan M 11 (10)
Berry D 27 (5)	Gurrieri A 19 (13)	Nelson C 43 (1)
Blackman A 3 (3)	Harvey T 3 (18)	Obadeyi T 5 (9)
Blanchaard M 34 (2)	Hayes P 4 (2)	Parsons M 10
Blizzard D 21 (5)	Hourihane C 45	Purrington B 11 (1)

Reckord J 11 (1)	Showunmi E............. 2 (5)	Wotton P.................. 12 (3)
Reid R 44 (2)	Thomas N 2 (8)	Young L 20 (14)
Richards J.............. - (1)	Trotman N.................41	

League goals (51): Reid 17, Hourihane 8, Alessandra 7, Young 4, Lavery 3, Trotman 2, Banton 1, Berry 1, Blanchard 1, Blizzard 1, Boco 1, Gurrieri 1, Harvey 1, Morgan 1, Nelson 1, Obadeyi 1
FA Cup goals (12): Reid 4, Alessandra 2, Gurrieri 2, Hourihane 1, Nelson 1, Purrington 1, Opponents - 1. **Capital One Cup goals (2):** Alessandra 2. **Johnstone's Paint Trophy goals (4):** Alessandra 1, Bencheri 1, Blackman 1, Boco 1
Average home league attendance: 7,304. **Player of Year:** Reuben Reid

PORTSMOUTH

Andy Awford won respect as a player at Fratton Park with more than 300 appearances over 11 years. He will now go down in the club's annals as the fledgling manager who removed the nightmare prospect of Conference football. With seven matches left of another troubled season, Portsmouth were two points away from a relegation place when Richie Barker was sacked and Awford installed as caretaker. He began a massive transformation in fortunes by securing maximum points against Newport and Hartlepool which took them clear of trouble. Then, wins over Dagenham and Redbridge, Bristol Rovers and Northampton established mid-table security. The 100% record was ended in a 4-4 draw at Bury, followed by a 3-3 scoreline against Plymouth in which Danny Hollamds scored all three goals. But Awford had done more than enough to land the job permanently – along with the grateful thanks of supporters who had continued to back the team through this latest trauma. Barker, who lasted less than four months, had fared no better than Guy Whittingham, whose problems began in the opening match – a 4-1 home defeat by Oxford in front in front of a record League Two crowd of 18,181.

Agyemang P 24 (17)	Drennan M................. 5 (5)	Moutaouakil Y 11 (2)
Alfei D............................15	East D 12 (3)	N'Gala B.................. 24 (3)
Barcham A........ 18 (8)	Ertl J 20 (9)	Padovani R 11 (7)
Bird R 5 (13)	Ferry S 19 (1)	Painter M.......................17
Bradley S................ 29 (4)	Fogden W 16 (3)	Potts D 5
Butler D.........................1	Harris A .... - (1)	Racon T................. 12 (4)
Carson T 36	Hollands D................. 6 (1)	Shorey N.......................21
Chorley B....................12	Holmes R 31 (9)	Smith P.........................4
Connolly D 11 (7)	Jervis J 12 (3)	Sullivan J.........................6
Cooper S.................. 7 (2)	Mahon G.................. - (1)	Taylor R 15 (3)
Craddock T 2 (6)	Maloney J .... - (1)	Wallace A 38 (6)
Devera J........................33	Marquis J 4 (1)	Webster A 3 (1)
Diagouraga T...................8	McCabe R 2 (2)	Whatmaugh J 11 (1)

League goals (56): Wallace 7, Taylor 6, Hollands 5, Agyemang 4, Connolly 4, Jervis 4, Barcham 3, Bird 3, Drennan 3, N'Gala 3, Bradley 2, Fogden 2, Holmes 2, Webster 2, Craddock 1, East 1, Ertl 1, Ferry 1, Marquis 1, Padovani 1
FA Cup goals (1): Connolly 1. **Capital One Cup goals:** None. **Johnstone's Paint Trophy goals (2):** Agyemang 1, Marquis 1
Average home league attendance: 15,460. **Player of Year:** Ricky Holmes

ROCHDALE

Keith Hill achieved a notable double by leading Rochdale to third place at the end of a competitive season at the top of League Two. He became the first manager in the club's history to achieve a second promotion, having taken them up in 2010. And Hill, who returned to Spotland in 2013 after a spell with Barnsley, would probably have been celebrating a title win had it not been for late lapses. Despite a poor disciplinary record, they took over at the top with a 3-0 win at Northampton – one which brought a ninth red card – and looked a sound bet to stay there. A run of four straight victories delivered ten goals, but it was followed by four games without a single one. Victory over Bristol Rovers restored some order, while Peter Vincenti and Ian Henderson

netted in the opening 16 minutes against Cheltenham to make sure of going up. Rochdale closed with a 2-1 defeat at Newport and were overtaken for the runners-spot, on goal difference, by Scunthorpe, the teams finishing three points behind Chesterfield. Leading scorer Scott Hogan included hat-tricks against Wimbledon and Oxford in his 17-goal haul.

Allen J.....................22 (3)	Gray R .... - (3)	Molyneux L ....- (3)
Barry-Murphy B 3	Henderson I 45	O'Connell J 38
Bennett R 18 (4)	Hery B...................... 4 (8)	Porter G......................1 (1)
Bunney J 7 (14)	Hogan S 29 (4)	Rafferty J.....................31
Cavanagh P..............17 (3)	Kennedy J...................4 (3)	Rose M..........................42
Cummins G...........15 (12)	Lancashire O.................38	Thomson R 1
Dicker G 10 (2)	Lillis J.........................45	Tutte A 7 (4)
Done M.................25 (13)	Lund M.........................40	Vidal J.........................2
Donnelly G.........16 (16)	Lynch C .... - (1)	Vincenti 31 (11)
Eastham A 15	McGinty S .... - (1)	

League goals (69): Hogan 17, Henderson 11, Lund 8, Allen 6, Donnelly 5, Vincenti 5, Cummins 4, Rose 4, Bunney 3, Tutte 2, Cavanagh 1, Dicker 1, Hery 1, Opponents 1
FA Cup goals (7): Hogan 2, Vincenti 2, Henderson 1, Lund 1, Rose 1. **Capital One Cup goals**: None. **Johnstone's Paint Trophy goals** (1): Rafferty 1
Average home league attendance: 2,900. **Player of Year**: Josh Lillis

SCUNTHORPE UNITED

However much Russ Wilcox applauded his players for finishing runners-up, it was the manager himself who captured the headlines. First, he broke a 125-year-old league record with a 24th unbeaten match from the start of his managerial reign. Two games later, the 50-year-old was credited with an unofficial world record. Then, he was named the division's Manager of the Year by the League Managers' Association and given a special merit award. The run came to an end in his 29th match – a 2-0 defeat by Exeter in which, ironically, Scunthorpe made sure of going up because of points dropped by Fleetwood. Wilcox, who also won promotion as a player and assistant manager at Glanford Park, stepped up when Brian Laws was sacked in November after successive home defeats by second-from-bottom Accrington and then by Grimsby in the FA Cup in the space of four days. It was not all plain sailing. Over the course of the season, his side gave up a winning lead in 14 of the 21 games that were drawn, conceding stoppage-time equalisers in six of them. But their sheer refusal to be beaten under the new man, which also resulted in a club record, was unrivalled. Sam Winnall, with 23, goals was the division's leading marksman, while Sam Slocombe saved five penalties.

Adelakun H.............8 (20)	Godden M................... - (4)	Ribeiro C 19 (2)
Alabi J......................- (1)	Hawkridge T 37 (8)	Slocombe S...................46
Boyce A......................- (2)	Hayes P...................5 (11)	Sparrow M 20 (6)
Burton D 19 (10)	Iwelumo C.................4 (8)	Spencer J 5 (8)
Byrne C 7 (3)	Madden P 17 (4)	Syers D........................37
Canavan N 45	McAllister S 37 (2)	Waterfall L 2 (7)
Clark J.......................- (1)	McSheffrey G 9 (4)	Welsh A 2 (2)
Collins M 9 (8)	Mirfin D.......................45	Williams M 25 (1)
Dawson A....................18	Noble-Lazarus R 2 (2)	Winnall S................43 (2)
Esajas E 8 (5)	Nolan E 37 (2)	Wootton J...............- (1)

League goals (68): Winnall 23, Syers 10, Burton 6, Madden 5, Canavan 4, Hayes 4, Sparrow 3, Adelakun 2, Esajas 2, Iwelumo 2, Mirfin 2, Hawkridge 1, Spencer 1, Waterfall 1, Opponents 2
FA Cup goals (1): Hawkridge 1. **Capital One Cup goals**: None. **Johnstone's Paint Trophy goals**: None
Average home league attendance: 4,012. **Player of Year**: Sam Slocombe

SOUTHEND UNITED

Barry Corr's fifth goal in six games brought victory over Burton in the regular season's final fixture, which proved to be a dress rehearsal for the teams' meeting in the play-offs. It also delivered a league double and Phil Brown's side had high hopes of going through to a Wembley final. Instead, they trailed 1-0 from the first leg and a second conceded at Roots Hall left them up against it. Goals by Ryan Leonard and Anthony Straker, in the space of seven minutes, levelled the aggregate score, but a third conceded 20 minutes from the end resulted in the club's third defeat at this stage in seven seasons. Southend's bid for an automatic promotion place was looking good early in the New Year, a 3-0 success against the eventual champions Chesterfield leaving them a point outside the top three. Then came a costly, barren run of 12 matches yielding just eight points – and a lost opportunity. They were back on track when beating Oxford 3-0 and gained maximum points from six of the final eight games, although these were not enough to make up lost ground.

Atkinson W 43 (2)	Egan J...........................13	Phillips M 23 (4)
Auger R 1	Gomis B .... - (2)	Prosser L 23 (2)
Barnard L 9 (4)	Hurst K.................... 39 (3)	Reid C .... - (6)
Bentley D......................46	Kiernan R 11 (1)	Sokolik J.........................10
Bolger C 1	Laird M................... 9 (10)	Straker A 27 (12)
Clifford C.............. 13 (10)	Leonard R................ 42 (1)	Thompson A 13 (3)
Coker B.........................45	Loza J...................... 4 (3)	Timlin M 32 (4)
Corr B..................... 35 (8)	Murphy J 4 (3)	White J...........................41
Cowan D .... - (2)	O'Neill L.........................1	Williams J................... - (2)
Eastwood F 11 (20)	Payne J.................... - (11)	Woodrow C.............. 10 (9)

Play-offs – appearances: Atkinson 2, Bentley 2, Coker 2, Corr 2, Egan 2, Hurst 2, Leonard 2, Sokolik 2, Timlin 2, White 2, Straker 1 (1), Murphy 1, Eastwood – (2), Barnard – (1), Clifford – (1), Payne – (1)
League goals (56): Corr 12, Hurst 11, Eastwood 6, Leonard 5, Prosser 3, Atkinson 2, Coker 2, Phillips 2, Straker 2, Timlin 2, Woodrow 2, Barnard 1, Clifford 1, Egan 1, Loza 1, Murphy 1, White 1, Opponents 1. **Play-offs – goals** (2): Leonard 1, Straker 1
FA Cup goals (10): Straker 3, Leonard 2, Atkinson 1, Corr 1, Hurst 1, Laird 1, Timlin 1. **Capital One Cup goals:** None. **Johnstone's Paint Trophy goals** (2): Woodrow 2
Average home league attendance: 5,959. **Player of Year:** Ben Coker

TORQUAY UNITED

A change of manager failed to save Torquay from relegation to the Conference for the second time in eight seasons. Alan Knill, who beat the drop in 2013, was sacked after defeats by Devon rivals Exeter and Plymouth over the Christmas and New Year programme left his side in the bottom two. Former club captain Chris Hargreaves succeeded him and made a successful start with victories over Wimbledon and Portsmouth in two of his first three games to stay within striking distance of a cluster of teams directly above them. But it was an uphill struggle. Torquay picked up a single point from next six games and were left ten points from safety. That gap was halved by away wins over fellow-strugglers Bristol Rovers and Exeter, achieved by performances which Hargreaves felt were more indicative of a team higher in the table. Even so, they went into the penultimate match at Mansfield knowing that their fate was largely in the hands of others. Northampton and Bristol Rovers both won, so their own 3-1 victory proved academic. A last-day home defeat by Wycombe, who survived as a result, left them five points from safety.

Azeez A 6 (3)	Chappell J............... 23 (13)	Harding B 16 (1)
Ball C..............................9	Coulthirst S.............. 5 (1)	Hawley K 22 (5)
Benyon E 23 (14)	Craig N...................... 6 (7)	Labadie J.........................10
Bodin B 23 (4)	Cruise T................... 18 (3)	Larthrope D............ 19 (4)
Cameron C............... 15 (9)	Downes S................. 30 (2)	Mansell L................ 41 (2)
Cargill B 5	Goodwin S 11 (1)	Marquis J.........................5

McCallum P 4 (1)	Pearce K 35	Sullivan D .... - (4)
McCourt J 10 (1)	Poke M 14	Thompson N 1 (2)
Mozika D 9 (3)	Rice M 32	Tonge D 36
Nicholson K 28 (1)	Showunmi E 7	Wilkinson C 2 (1)
O'Brien A .... - (3)	Stevens D 2 (4)	Yeoman A 2 (7)
O'Connor A 30 (1)	Stockley J 7 (12)	

League goals (42): Chappell 5, Downes 4, Pearce 4, Benyon 3, Hawley 3, Marquis 3, McCallum 3, Yeoman 3, Azeez 2, Ball 2, Coulthirst 2, Mansell 2, Bodin 1, Cameron 1, Goodwin 1, Labadie 1, Stockley 1, Opponents 1
FA Cup goals: None. **Capital One Cup goals**: None. **Johnstone's Paint Trophy goals**: None
Average home league attendance: 2,641. **Player of Year**: Krystian Pearce

WYCOMBE WANDERERS

Wycombe faced the end of 21 years of league football going into their final match at Torquay. A must-win home game against Bristol Rovers had resulted in a crushing 2-1 defeat and left them second from bottom, three points adrift. But on a dramatic afternoon, goals by Sam Wood, Steven Craig from the penalty spot and Matt McClure brought a 3-0 success at Plainmoor against a side already doomed. And although Northampton completed their own great escape, Rovers lost at home to Mansfield and went down with an inferior goal difference. Wycombe survived, reflecting how close they came to paying the price for a mid-season slump. There was no hint of the drop when a bright start to the campaign was rewarded with a place in the top seven after a dozen games. But a run of 18 matches produced a solitary victory – 4-1 against Northampton – and an alarming slide. It was arrested by a win over leaders Chesterfield, followed by maximum points gained against Exeter and Hartlepool, along with a move seven points clear. But Gareth Ainsworth's team let that advantage slip when the next six games yielded a single goal and they were back in trouble.

Arnold N 30 (1)	Kewley-Graham J 1	Pierre A 8
Bloomfield M 25 (7)	Knott B 15 (2)	Pittman J-P 2 (8)
Cowan-Hall P 20 (5)	Kretzschmar M 21 (14)	Rowe D 7
Craig S 17 (10)	Kuffour J 11 (13)	Scowen J 36 (1)
Doherty G 19 (1)	Lewis S 36	Spring M 2 (3)
Dunne C 9	McClure M 24 (12)	Stewart A 26 (7)
Hause K 13 (1)	McCoy M 32 (1)	Styche R 8 (6)
Ingram M 46	Morgan D 19 (10)	Togwell S 3 (1)
Jeffrey A 1 (10)	Morias J .... - (8)	Wood S 42 (1)
Johnson L 30	Mustoe J 3	

League goals (46): Morgan 8, McClure 7, Kretzschmar 6, Cowan-Hall 4, Craig 4, Kuffour 3, Lewis 3, Stewart 3, Wood 2, Hause 1, Johnson 1, Knott 1, Pierre 1, Scowen 1, Opponents 1
FA Cup goals (3): Cowan-Hall 1, Craig 1, Doherty 1. **Capital One Cup goals** (1): Kuffour 1.
Johnstone's Paint Trophy goals (5): McClure 2, Bloomfield 1, Knott 1, Stewart 1
Average home league attendance: 3,680. **Player of Year**: Josh Scowen

YORK CITY

York were the form team going into the play-offs. They finished the regular season with 17 successive unbeaten games under their belt, 13 without conceding a goal. But knock-out football at this level is rarely predictable and it was Nigel Worthington's team who conceded the only goal of the semi-final against Fleetwood. It was scored by Matty Blair, whose winner against Luton in the 2012 Conference Final took York back into the Football League. Blair was on the mark five minutes into the second half and Fleetwood protected the advantage in the second leg on their own ground to go through. Worthington, the former Northern Ireland manager, praised his side for going so far after struggling throughout the first half of the regular season when only goal difference kept them out of the bottom two. Winter transfer window signings transformed

their fortunes, including a run of six successive victories for the first time in the league since the 1983-84 season. York accumulated 49 points from New Year onwards, making sure of a place in the top seven with Michael Coulson's 25-yard free-kick in the penultimate fixture against Newport.

Allen T 4 (1)
Andrew C 5 (3)
Bowman R 22 (15)
Brobbel R 16 (3)
Carson J 29 (2)
Chamberlain T............. - (2)
Chambers A 8 (7)
Clay C...................... 6 (2)
Coulson M.............. 22 (11)
Cresswell R 3 (3)
Davies B 44

Dickinson C................ - (2)
Fletcher W 24 (8)
Fyfield J.................... 1 (1)
Hayhurst W 14 (4)
Ingham M 19
Jarvis R 21 (14)
Lowe K 30
McCarey A 5
McCombe J.............. 18 (1)
McGurk D 21 (2)
Montrose L.............. 26 (7)

O'Neill L 15
Oyebanjo L...................41
Parslow D 13
Penn R 21
Platt T 11 (9)
Pope N 22
Puri S............... 3 (5)
Reed A 17 (2)
Smith C 8 (1)
Taft G 2 (1)
Whitehouse E.................15

Play-offs – appearances: Andrew 2, Coulson 2, Davies 2, Hayhurst 2, Lowe 2, McCombe 2, Oyebanjo 2, Penn 2, Pope 2, Reed 2, Bowman 1 (1), Brobbel 1, Allan - (1), Jarvis – (1), Montrose – (1)
League goals (52): Fletcher 10, Bowman 8, Jarvis 8, Coulson 7, Brobbel 4, Carson 4, McCombe 3, Hayhurst 2, Lowe 1, McGurk 1, Montrose 1, O'Neill 1, Opponents 2. **Play-offs – goals:** None
FA Cup goals (5): Fletcher 3, Carson 1, Jarvis 1. **Capital One Cup goals:** None. **Johnstone's Paint Trophy goals:** None
Average home league attendance: 3,773. **Player of Year:** Lanre Oyebanjo

THE THINGS THEY SAY...

'It's a disease. I hope it's a disease we're almost rid of, but if people do it they've got to be reminded it's not right' – **Tony Pulis**, Crystal Palace manager, promising to fine Marouane Chamakh and Jerome Thomas for diving against Swansea.

'I wanted to come here, even if it was for a penny. This is my dream come true' – **Gareth Bale** after joining Real Madrid from Tottenham for a world record £85.3m and trebling his salary to around £13m a year.

'We sold Elvis and signed the Beatles' – **Erik Thorstvedt**, former Tottenham goalkeeper, on the sale of Gareth Bale and the club's signing of seven players for a total of £107m.

'I think there is sadness to it as this is something that will probably stay with people for a long while' – **Brendan Rodgers**, Liverpool manager, maintains Sir Alex Ferguson has damaged his legacy by criticising several players and managers, including Anfield figures Steven Gerrard, Jordan Henderson and Kenny Dalglish, in his autobiography.

'I'm not going to be negative about a man who gave me the chance to play for my boyhood team and believed in me' – **David Beckham** refusing to respond to criticism in the book that his football at Old Trafford was affected by a celebrity lifestyle.

'I dreamed of this all my life' – **Rickie Lambert**, Southampton, and now Liverpool, striker, after scoring the winner against Scotland with his first touch as an England player.

LEAGUE CLUB MANAGERS

Figure in brackets = number of managerial changes at club since the War

PREMIER LEAGUE

Arsenal (11)	Arsene Wenger	October 1996
Aston Villa (22)	Paul Lambert	June 2012
Burnley (24)	Sean Dyche	October 2012
Chelsea (27)	Jose Mourinho†	June 2013
Crystal Palace (38)	Tony Pulis	November 2013
Everton (17)	Roberto Martinez	June 2013
Hull (26)	Steve Bruce	June 2012
Leicester (27)	Nigel Pearson†	November 2011
Liverpool (13)	Brendan Rodgers	May 2012
Manchester City (29)	Manuel Pellegrini	June 2013
Manchester Utd (10)	Louis van Gaal	May 2014
Newcastle (25)	Alan Pardew	December 2010
QPR (31)	Harry Redknapp	November 2012
Southampton (25)	Ronald Koeman	June 2014
Stoke (23)	Mark Hughes	May 2013
Sunderland (26)	Gus Poyet	October 2013
Swansea (32)	Garry Monk	May 2014
Tottenham (23)	Mauricio Pochettino	May 2014
WBA (31)	Alan Irvine	June 2014
West Ham (13)	Sam Allardyce	June 2011

† Second spell at club

CHAMPIONSHIP

Birmingham (24)	Lee Clark	June 2012
Blackburn (28)	Gary Bowyer	May 2013
Blackpool (28)	Jose Riga	June 2014
Bolton (21)	Dougie Freedman	October 2012
Bournemouth (24)	Eddie Howe†	October 2012
Brentford (31)	Mark Warburton	December 2013
Brighton (32)	Sami Hyypia	June 2014
Cardiff (28)	Ole Gunnar Solskjaer	January 2014
Charlton (19)	Bob Peeters	May 2014
Derby (22)	Steve McClaren	September 2013
Fulham (30)	Felix Magath	February 2014
Huddersfield (26)	Mark Robins	February 2013
Ipswich (13)	Mick McCarthy	November 2012
Leeds (25)	David Hockaday	June 2014
Middlesbrough (20)	Aitor Karanka	November 2013
Millwall (30)	Ian Holloway	January 2014
Norwich (27)	Neil Adams	May 2014
Nottm Forest (21)	Stuart Pearce	April 2014
Reading (19)	Nigel Adkins	March 2013
Rotherham (23)	Steve Evans	April 2012
Sheffield Wed (28)	Stuart Gray	January 2014
Watford (29)	Giuseppe Sannino	December 2013
Wigan (20)	Uwe Rosler	December 2013
Wolves (23)	Kenny Jackett	May 2013

† Second spell at club. Number of changes since elected to Football League: Wigan 1978

LEAGUE ONE

Barnsley (23)	Danny Wilson†	December 2013
Bradford (33)	Phil Parkinson	August 2011

Bristol City (25)	Steve Cotterill	December 2013
Chesterfield (19)	Paul Cook	October 2012
Colchester (25)	Joe Dunne	September 2012
Coventry (32)	Steven Pressley	March 2013
Crawley (3)	John Gregory	December 2013
Crewe (21)	Steve Davis	November 2011
Doncaster (2)	Paul Dickov	May 2013
Fleetwood (1)	Graham Alexander	December 2012
Gillingham (23)	Peter Taylor†	November 2013
Leyton Orient (22)	Russell Slade	April 2010
MK Dons (15)	Karl Robinson	April 2010
Notts Co (38)	Shaun Derry	November 2013
Oldham (26)	Lee Johnson	March 2013
Peterborough (27)	Darren Ferguson†	January 2011
Port Vale (23)	Micky Adams†	May 2011
Preston (28)	Simon Grayson	February 2013
Rochdale (32)	Keith Hill†	January 2013
Scunthorpe (26)	Russ Wilcox	December 2013
Sheffield Utd (36)	Nigel Clough	October 2013
Swindon (28)	Mark Cooper	August 2013
Walsall (33)	Dean Smith	January 2011
Yeovil (4)	Gary Johnson†	January 2012

† Second spell at club. Number of changes since elected to Football League: Peterborough 1960, Yeovil 2003, Crawley 2011, Fleetwood 2012

LEAGUE TWO

AFC Wimbledon (1)	Neal Ardley	October 2012
Accrington (3)	James Beattie	May 2013
Burton (1)	Gary Rowett	May 2012
Bury (25)	David Flitcroft	December 2013
Cambridge Utd (-)	Richard Money	October 2012
Carlisle (4)	Graham Kavanagh	September 2013
Cheltenham (6)	Mark Yates	December 2009
Dag & Red (1)	Wayne Burnett	May 2013
Exeter (-)	Paul Tisdale	June 2006
Hartlepool (34)	Colin Cooper	May 2013
Luton (-)	John Still	February 2013
Mansfield (-)	Paul Cox	May 2011
Morecambe (1)	Jim Bentley	May 2011
Newport (-)	Justin Edinburgh	October 2011
Northampton (31)	Chris Wilder	January 2014
Oxford Utd (2)	Michael Appleton	July 2014
Plymouth (33)	John Sheridan	January 2013
Portsmouth (32)	Andy Awford	May 2014
Shrewsbury (4)	Micky Mellon	May 2014
Southend (28)	Phil Brown	March 2013
Stevenage (2)	Graham Westley†	March 2013
Tranmere (21)	Rob Edwards	May 2014
Wycombe (10)	Gareth Ainsworth	November 2012
York (1)	Nigel Worthington	March 2013

† Third spell at club. Number of changes since elected to Football League: Wycombe 1993, Cheltenham 1999, Dag & Red 2007, Morecambe 2007, Burton 2009, Stevenage 2010, AFC Wimbledon 2011. Since returning: Shrewsbury 2004, Carlisle 2005, Accrington 2006, Exeter 2008, Oxford Utd 2010, York 2012, Mansfield 2013, Newport 2013, Cambridge Utd 2014, Luton 2014

MANAGERIAL INS AND OUTS 2013–14

PREMIER LEAGUE

Cardiff   Out – Malky Mackay (Dec 2013); In – Ole Gunnar Solskjaer
Crystal Palace Out – Ian Holloway (Oct 2013); In – Tony Pulis
Fulham   Out – Martin Jol (Dec 2013); In – Rene Meulensteen; Out – (Feb 2014); In – Felix Magath
Manchester Utd Out – David Moyes (Apr 2014); In Louis van Gaal
Norwich   Out – Chris Hughton (Apr 2014); In – Neil Adams
Southampton   Out – Mauricio Pochettino (May 2014); In Ronald Koeman
Sunderland   Out – Paolo Di Canio (Sep 2013); In – Gus Poyet
Swansea   Out – Michael Laudrup (Feb 2014); In – Garry Monk
Tottenham   Out – Andre Villas-Boas (Dec 2013); In – Tim Sherwood; Out – (May 2014); In – Mauricio Pochettino
WBA   Out – Steve Clarke (Dec 2013); In – Pepe Mel; Out – (May 2014); In Alan Irvine

CHAMPIONSHIP

Barnsley   Out – David Flicroft (Dec 2013); In – Danny Wilson
Blackpool   Out – Paul Ince (Jan 2014); In – Jose Riga
Brighton   Out – Oscar Garcia (May 2014); In – Sami Hyypia
Charlton   Out – Chris Powell (Mar 2014); In – Jose Riga; Out – (May 2014); In – Bob Peeters
Derby   Out – Nigel Clough (Sep 2013); In – Steve McClaren
Leeds   Out – Brian McDermott (May 2014); In – David Hockaday
Middlesbrough Out – Tony Mowbray (Oct 2013); In – Aitor Karanka
Millwall   Out – Steve Lomas (Dec 2013); In – Ian Holloway
Nottm Forest   Out – Billy Davies (Mar 2014); In – Stuart Pearce
Sheffield Wed Out – Dave Jones (Dec 2013); In – Stuart Gray
Watford   Out – Gianfranco Zola (Dec 2013); In – Giuseppe Sannino
Wigan   Out – Owen Coyle (Dec 2013); In – Uwe Rosler

LEAGUE ONE

Brentford   Out – Uwe Rosler (Dec 2013); In – Mark Warburton
Bristol City   Out – Sean O'Driscoll (Nov 2013); In – Steve Cotterill
Carlisle   Out – Greg Abbott (Sep 2013); In – Graham Kavanagh
Crawley   Out – Richie Barker (Nov 2013); In – John Gregory
Gillingham   Out – Martin Allen (Oct 2013); In – Peter Taylor
Notts Co   Out – Chris Kiwomya (Oct 2013); In – Shaun Derry
Sheffield Utd Out – David Weir (Oct 2013); In – Nigel Clough
Shrewsbury   Out – Graham Turner (Jan 2014); In – Micky Mellon
Swindon   Out – Kevin MacDonald (Jul 2013); In – Mark Cooper
Tranmere   Out – Ronnie Moore (Apr 2014); In – Rob Edwards

LEAGUE TWO

Bristol Rov   Out – John Ward (Mar 2014); In – Darrell Clarke
Bury   Out – Kevin Blackwell (Oct 2013); In – David Flitcroft
Northampton   Out – Aidy Boothroyd (Dec 2013); In – Chris Wilder
Oxford   Out – Chris Wilder (Jan 2014); In – Gary Waddock; Out – (Jul 2014; In – Michael Appleton
Portsmouth   Out – Guy Whittingham (Nov 2013); In – Richie Barker; Out – (Mar 2014); In – Andy Awford
Scunthorpe   Out – Brian Laws (Nov 2013); In – Russ Wilcox
Torquay   Out – Alan Knill (Jan 2014); In – Chris Hargreaves

FA CUP 2013–14
(with Budweiser)

FIRST ROUND

Accrington 0 Tranmere 1
AFC Wimbledon 1 Coventry 3
Bishop's Stortford 1 Northampton 2
Boreham Wood 0 Carlisle 0
Braintree 1 Newport 1
Brentford 5 Staines 0
Bristol City 3 Dag & Red 0
Bristol Rov 3 York 3
Burton 2 Hereford 0
Bury 0 Cambridge Utd 0
Chesterfield 2 Daventry 0
Colchester 2 Sheffield Utd 3
Corby 1 Dover 2
Gillingham 1 Brackley 1
Gloucester 0 Fleetwood 2
Grimsby 0 Scunthorpe 0
Hartlepool 3 Notts Co 2
Hednesford 1 Crawley 2
Kidderminster 4 Sutton 1
Leyton Orient 5 Southport 2
Lincoln 0 Plymouth 0
Macclesfield 4 Swindon 0
MK Dons 4 Halifax 1
Morecambe 0 Southend 3
Oldham 1 Wolves 1
Oxford 2 Gateshead 2
Peterborough 2 Exeter 0
Preston 6 Barnet 0
Rotherham 3 Bradford 0
Salisbury 4 Dartford 2
Shortwood 0 Port Vale 4
St Albans 1 Mansfield 8
Stevenage 2 Portsmouth 1
Stourbridge 4 Biggleswade 1
Tamworth 1 Cheltenham 0
Torquay 0 Rochdale 2
Walsall 3 Shrewsbury 0
Welling 2 Luton 1
Wrexham 3 Alfreton 1
Wycombe 1 Crewe 1

FIRST ROUND REPLAYS

Brackley 1 Gillingham 0
Cambridge Utd 2 Bury 1
Carlisle 2 Boreham Wood 1
Crewe 0 Wycombe 2
Gateshead 0 Oxford 1 (aet)

Newport 1 Braintree 0
Plymouth 5 Lincoln 0
Scunthorpe 1 Grimsby 2
Wolves 1 Oldham 2
York 2 Bristol Rov 3

SECOND ROUND

Bristol Rov 0 Crawley 0
Cambridge Utd 0 Sheffield Utd 2
Carlisle 3 Brentford 2
Chesterfield 1 Southend 3
Fleetwood 1 Burton 1
Grimsby 2 Northampton 0
Hartlepool 1 Coventry 1
Kidderminster 4 Newport 2
Leyton Orient 1 Walsall 0
Macclesfield 3 Brackley 2
MK Dons 1 Dover 0
Oldham 1 Mansfield 1
Peterborough 5 Tranmere 0
Plymouth 3 Welling 1
Port Vale 4 Salisbury 1
Rotherham 1 Rochdale 2
Stevenage 4 Stourbridge 0
Tamworth 1 Bristol City 2
Wrexham 1 Oxford 2
Wycombe 0 Preston 1

SECOND ROUND REPLAYS

Burton 1 Fleetwood 0
Coventry 2 Hartlepool 1
Crawley 1 Bristol Rov 2
Mansfield 1 Oldham 4

TWO DOWN – BUT ARSENAL WIN FIRST TROPHY SINCE 2005

THIRD ROUND	FOURTH ROUND	FIFTH ROUND	SIXTH ROUND	SEMI-FINALS	FINAL
Hull.....2	Hull.....2	Hull.....1:2	*Hull.....3	Hull.....5	Hull.....2
*Middlesbrough.....0					
*Southend.....4	*Southend.....0				
Millwall.....1					
*Port Vale.....2:3	*Port Vale.....1	*Brighton.....1:1			
Plymouth.....2:2					
*Brighton.....1	Brighton.....3				
Reading.....0					
*Sunderland.....3	*Sunderland.....1	*Sunderland.....1	Sunderland.....0		
Carlisle.....1					
*Kidderminster.....0:3	Kidderminster.....0				
Peterborough.....0:2					
*Southampton.....4	*Southampton.....2	Southampton.....0			
Burnley.....3					
*Yeovil.....4	Yeovil.....0				
Leyton Orient.....0					
*Aston Villa.....1	*Sheffield Utd.....1:t1	*Sheffield Utd.....3	*Sheffield Utd.....2	Sheffield Utd.....3	
Sheffield Utd.....2					
*Norwich.....1:0	Fulham.....3				
Fulham.....1:3					
*Nottm Forest.....5	*Nottm Forest.....0:2	Nottm Forest.....1			
West Ham.....0					
*Ipswich.....1:2	Preston.....0:0				
Preston.....1:3					
*Rochdale.....2	*Rochdale.....1	*Sheffield Wed.....1	Charlton.....0		
Leeds.....0					
*Macclesfield.....1:1	Sheffield Wed.....2				
Sheffield Wed.....1:4					
*Grimsby.....2	*Huddersfield.....0	Charlton.....2			
Huddersfield.....3					

*Charlton 2:3
Oxford 2:0

*Blackburn 1:0
Manchester City........1:5

*Bristol City 1:0
Watford....................1:2

*Derby........................0
Chelsea 2

*Stoke.........................2
Leicester......................1

*Bolton........................2
Blackpool......................1

*Newcastle 1
Cardiff..........................2

*Wigan .... 3:†3
MK Dons..................3:1

*WBA...........................0
Crystal Palace 2

*Doncaster...................2
Stevenage.....................3

*Everton 4
QPR 0

*Birmingham 3
Bristol Rov 0

*Manchester Utd 1
Swansea 2

*Bournemouth.............4
Burton 1

*Liverpool 2
Oldham 0

*Barnsley.....................1
Coventry 2

Tottenham...................0
*__Arsenal__ 2

Charlton.......................1
*Manchester City.........4
Watford........................2
*Chelsea.......................1
Stoke............................0
*Bolton.........................0
Cardiff...........................1
*Wigan 2
Crystal Palace 1
*Stevenage 0
Everton.........................4
*Birmingham 1
Swansea 2
*Bournemouth.............0
Liverpool......................2
Coventry 0
*__Arsenal__ 4

*Manchester City.........2
Chelsea 0
*Cardiff 1
Wigan..........................2
*Everton 3
Swansea 1
Liverpool......................1
*__Arsenal__ 2

*Manchester City.........1
Wigan..........................2
Everton........................1
*__Arsenal__ 4

Wigan..........................1
__Arsenal__ ....†A:1

__Arsenal__ ....†3

*Drawn at home. † After extra-time. A – Arsenal won 4-2 on pens. Both semi-finals at Wembley

ROUND BY ROUND HIGHLIGHTS

FIRST ROUND

On-loan Connor Jennings scores twice as Macclesfield knock out Swindon for the second successive season. They win 4-0, with Scott Boden and Peter Winn also on the mark. Four other teams lose to non-league opposition. Brackley are denied by Bradley Dack's equaliser for Gillingham in the seventh minute of added time, but Glenn Walker's 20-yard drive in the replay puts them into the second round for the first time in the club's history. Former Everton striker Nick Chadwick also scores the only goal of the game as Tamworth overcome Cheltenham. Luke Berry nets both goals for Cambridge United, who defeat Bury 2-1 in a replay, while Grimsby put out Scunthorpe 2-1 at the second attempt with strikes from Lenell John-Lewis and Clayton McDonald. Gateshead are denied by Danny Rose's 90th minute equaliser for 2-2 at Oxford and are beaten 1-0 in extra-time in the replay. Boreham Wood also go close, losing 2-1 to Mark Beck's goal in the fifth minute of added time for Carlisle in another replay. Luke Garrard puts the Conference South side ahead with a penalty, then has a second spot kick saved. St Albans open the scoring against Mansfield, but are overwhelmed 8-1 as Sam Clucas scores four times. Preston are also big winners, 6-0 against Barnet, with Paul Gallagher netting a hat-trick.

SECOND ROUND

Three teams keep the non-league flag flying. Two goals each from Callum Gittings and Michael Gash point Kidderminster to a 4-2 success against Newport. Grimsby master Northampton 2-0 (Shaun Pearson and Patrick McLaughlin), while the meeting of two first-round surprise packets ends with Macclesfield beating Brackley 3-2 thanks to Jack Mackreth's 81st minute goal. Peterborough's Britt Assombalonga registers a hat-trick in the 5-0 defeat of Tranmere.

THIRD ROUND

Arsenal prevail in the tie of the round, defeating Tottenham 2-0 through goals from Santi Cazorla and Tomas Rosicky. Manchester United's troubled season under David Moyes continues with a 2-1 home defeat by Swansea, for whom Wilfried Bony's 90th minute header proves decisive. Paul Lambert, already under fire for claiming that Premier League sides 'could do without' the competition, also suffers a home defeat as Jamie Murphy and Ryan Flynn deliver a 2-1 success for Sheffield United. And Sam Allardyce sees his makeshift West Ham side humbled 5-0 by Nottingham Forest, Jamie Paterson netting a hat-trick in 14 second-half minutes. Also on the mark three times is substitute Joe Garner in Preston's 3-2 victory over Ipswich in a replay. Two Championship teams lose to League Two opposition. Leeds go down 2-0 at Rochdale, for whom Scott Hogan and Ian Henderson are on the mark, and Millwall lose 4-1 at Southend to goals from Barry Corr, Will Atkinson, Michael Timlin and Ryan Leonard in a match halted for 15 minutes by a floodlight failure. Joe Lolley signs off in style for Kidderminster before his £250,000 move to Huddersfield with the winner in a replay at Peterborough. His side win 3-2, with Michael Gash and Jack Byrne also on the scoresheet. Grimsby concede two goals in the final five minutes after leading Huddersfield 2-1, while Macclesfield go down 4-1 to Sheffield Wednesday in a replay. Liverpool defeat Oldham 2-0 in the teams' third meeting in successive seasons, one in which manager Brendan Rodgers' son Anton comes on as a 54th minute substitute for the League One side.

FOURTH ROUND

Watford look to be on course for an upset when leading Manchester City at the Etihad with goals from Fernando Forestieri and Troy Deeney. But a second-half hat-trick by Sergio Aguero proves decisive and his side come out on top 4-2. There is a shock in a replay at Craven Cottage, where Sheffield United substitute Shaun Miller breaks the deadlock in the last minute of extra-time to put out Fulham. Kidderminster, the last surviving non-leaguers, do themselves proud at Sunderland, who need a fifth minute goal from Charis Mavrias, his first for the club, to go

through. Everton's 4-0 success at Stevenage is marred by Bryan Oviedo's double fracture of the left leg, an injury which ruled him out of Costa Rica's World Cup squad.

FIFTH ROUND

Arsenal and Manchester City turn the tables on top-four rivals following defeats in Premier League matches. Arsene Wenger's side, crushed 5-1 at Anfield, overcome Liverpool 2-1, Alex Oxlade-Chamberlain opening the scoring and setting up their second goal for Lukas Podolski. City, beaten by Chelsea at the Etihad, go through 2-0 with goals from Stevan Jovetic and Samir Nasri on his return from injury. On-loan Lacina Traore is on the mark four minutes into his Everton debut, then substitute Steven Naismith wraps up a 3-1 victory over Swansea by scoring the second goal himself and winning a penalty, converted by Leighton Baines. At Bramall Lane, two in stoppage-time by Chris Porter follows Conor Coady's earlier strike as Sheffield United come from behind to see off Nottingham Forest 3-1. Ben Watson, Wigan's match-winner at Wembley the previous season, adds to Chris McCann's opener as they win 2-1 at Cardiff. But Watson's delight turns to despair three days later when he is ruled out for the rest of the season after sustaining a double fracture of his right leg in a league match against Barnsley.

SIXTH ROUND

Wigan repeat their victory over Manchester City in the 2013 final, with this upset coming at the Etihad. Jordi Gomez opens the scoring from the penalty spot, James Perch increases the lead and Samir Nasri's reply is not enough for the favourites. For the third time this season, Hull manager Steve Bruce savours victory over former club Sunderland as Curtis Davies, David Meyler and Matty Fryatt are on the mark in the second-half for a 3-0 victory. Two goals in the final ten minutes by Olivier Giroud confirm Arsenal's passage against Everton, Mesut Ozil and Mikael Arteta (pen) having put them on the way to a 4-1 success. Two in the space of three second-half minutes by Ryan Flynn and John Brayford enable Sheffield United to continue flying the flag for League One with a 2-0 win over Charlton.

SEMI-FINALS

Wigan, returning to Wembley, threaten another shock when Jordi Gomez converts a 63rd minute penalty after Per Mertesacker brings down Callum McManaman. But Mertesacker equalises eight minutes from the end of normal time and after the teams remain deadlocked in extra-time, Lukasz Fabianski saves penalties from Gary Caldwell and Jack Collison to give Arsenal a 4-2 shoot-out success. The second-semi-final produces eight goals for the first time since Manchester United's 5-3 win over Fulham in 1958. Hull end Sheffield United's splendid campaign by that scoreline, but only after United twice lead through Jose Baxter and Stefan Scougall. Yannick Sagbo and Matty Fryatt deliver equalisers, then Tom Huddlestone and Stephen Quinn make it 4-2. Jamie Murphy pulls one back, but David Meyler seals victory in stoppage-time

FINAL

'The FA Cup is alive and well' declared Clive Tyldesley as a gripping final remained in the balance. For those of us who still cherish the tournament's tradition, the dreams it evokes and its sheer unpredictability, the thoughts of the ITV commentator seemed spot-on. Past its sell-by date, insist some of the detractors. Not worth risking the next Premier League points for, according to some managers. Not bothered if we don't do well in it, Newcastle's directors told supporters days before this year's showpiece. Even the FA, by scrapping replays, having both semi-finals at Wembley and now changing the kick-off time of the final, have alienated the traditionalists. Wigan's win over Manchester City in 2013 embraced all the romance of the competition. So did their repeat victory over City in this season's sixth round, along with League One Sheffield United's progress to the last four. When Hull established a two-goal lead through James Chester and Curtis Davies in eight minutes, another eye-catching upset was on the cards. Had a header from the manager's son, Alex Bruce, gone in soon after, instead of being cleared off the line by Kieran Gibbs, they would surely have lifted the trophy for the

first time. Instead, Santi Cazorla and Laurent Koscielny levelled matters and Aaron Ramsey's sweet extra-time strike tilted the balance Arsenal's way. Even then it was not over as goalkeeper Lukasz Fabianksi's rush of blood offered a chance to substitute Sone Aluko, whose effort from a difficult angle drifted just wide. Overall, Arsene Wenger's side just about deserved their first trophy since 2005. But the real winner was the FA Cup itself – **STUART BARNES**

HULL CITY 2 ARSENAL 3 (aet)
Wembley (89,345); Saturday, May 17 2014

Hull (3-5-1-1): McGregor, Davies (capt), Bruce (McShane 67), Chester, Elmohamady, Livermore, Huddlestone, Meyler, Rosenior (Boyd 102), Quinn (Aluko 75), Fryatt. **Subs not used**: Harper, Figueroa, Koren, Sagbo. **Scorers**: Chester (4), Davies (8). **Booked**: Huddlestone, Meyler, Davies. **Manager**: Steve Bruce

Arsenal (4-2-3-1): Fabianski, Sagna, Koscielny, Mertesacker (capt), Gibbs, Arteta, Ramsey, Cazorla (Rosicky 106), Ozil (Wilshere 106), Podolski (Sanogo 61), Giroud. **Subs not used**: Szczesny, Vermaelen, Monreal, Flamini. **Scorers**: Cazorla (17), Koscielny (71), Ramsey (109). **Booked**: Giroud. **Manager**: Arsenal Wenger

Referee: L Probert (Wiltshire): **Half-time**: 2-1

HOW THEY REACHED THE FINAL

Hull City
Round 3: 2-0 away to Middlesbrough (Mclean, Proschwitz)
Round 4: 2-0 away to Southend (Fryatt 2)
Round 5: 1-1 away to Brighton (Sagbo); 2-1 home to Brighton (Davies, Koren)
Round 6: 3-0 home to Sunderland (Davies, Meyler, Fryatt)
Semi-finals: 5-3 v Sheffield Utd (Sagbo, Fryatt, Huddlestone, Quinn, Meyler)

Arsenal
Round 3: 2-0 home to Tottenham (Cazorla, Rosicky)
Round 4: 4-0 home to Coventry (Podolski 2, Giroud, Cazorla)
Round 5: 2-1 home to Liverpool (Oxlade-Chamberlain, Podolski)
Round 6: 4-1 home to Everton (Giroud 2, Ozil, Arteta pen)
Semi-finals: 1-1 v Wigan (Mertesacker) – aet, won 4-2 on pens

Leading scorers (from first round): 5 Assombalonga (Peterborough), Clucas (Mansfield), Garner (Preston); 4 Aguero (Manchester City), Emmanuel-Thomas (Bristol City), Fryatt (Hull), Paterson (Nottm Forest), Porter (Sheffield Utd), Reid (Plymouth), Zoko (Stevenage)

FINAL FACTS AND FIGURES

● Arsenal competed in their 18th FA Cup Final, equalling Manchester United's record. They also matched United's record of 11 victories.

● Arsene Wenger equalled another record – Sir Alex Ferguson's five wins with United.

● Hull were appearing in their first final. They reached the semi-finals once before, in 1930 when drawing 2-2 with Arsenal at Elland Road and losing the replay 1-0 at Villa Park.

● Arsenal conceded the same number of goals in eight minutes as they had in their previous five finals in the tournament.

● The last time a team came back from a two-goal deficit to win the trophy at Wembley was in 1966 when Jim McCalliog and David Ford put Sheffield Wednesday ahead and Mike Trebilcock (2) and Derek Temple replied for Everton.

● When the final was held in Cardiff while the national stadium was being rebuilt, Liverpool were two down to West Ham in 2006 and came back to win on penalties after a 3-3 scoreline.

- The last time two goals were scored so quickly was in 1987 when Clive Allen put Tottenham ahead in the second minute and Dave Bennett equalised six minutes later, with Coventry going to a 3-2 victory.

- Pre-match odds were being quoted of 100-1 against Hull's James Chester scoring the first goal.

- Match-winner Aaron Ramsey, then 17, was in the Cardiff team beaten by Portsmouth in the 2008 final, coming on as a 62nd minute substitute for Peter Whittinghm.

- This was the eighth FA Cup Final at the new Wembley and every one has been decided by a single-goal margin

WOMEN'S FOOTBALL

FA SUPER LEAGUE 2013

	P	W	D	L	F	A	GD	Pts
Liverpool	14	12	0	2	46	19	27	36
Bristol Acad	14	10	1	3	30	20	10	31
Arsenal*	14	10	3	1	31	11	20	30
Birmingham	14	5	3	6	16	21	-5	18
Everton	14	4	3	7	23	30	-7	15
Lincoln	14	2	4	8	10	15	-5	10
Chelsea	14	3	1	10	20	27	-7	10
Doncaster	14	1	3	10	9	42	-33	6

*Deducted 3 pts. Continental Cup Final: Arsenal 2 Lincoln 0

FA PREMIER LEAGUE NORTH

	P	W	D	L	F	A	GD	Pts
Sheffield	20	17	2	1	74	15	59	53
Preston	20	12	1	7	49	39	10	37
Bradford	20	11	2	7	36	33	3	35
Nottm Forest	20	10	3	7	44	24	20	33
Stoke	20	10	3	7	51	45	6	33
Sporting Club	20	8	4	8	36	34	2	28
Derby	20	7	4	9	45	51	-6	25
Wolves	20	6	2	12	28	48	-20	20
Blackburn	20	5	3	12	29	51	-22	18
Newcastle	20	5	2	13	33	66	-33	17
Leeds	20	4	4	12	37	56	-19	16

FA PREMIER LEAGUE SOUTH

	P	W	D	L	F	A	GD	Pts
Coventry	20	14	4	2	42	14	28	46
Gillingham	20	14	2	4	58	21	37	44
Cardiff	20	12	4	4	55	24	31	40
Portsmouth	20	12	1	7	42	29	13	37
Charlton	20	9	5	6	39	35	4	32
Lewes	20	9	4	7	31	32	-1	31
Brighton	20	7	2	11	32	31	1	23
Tottenham	20	6	4	10	27	36	-9	22
Keynsham	20	6	1	13	40	52	-12	19
West Ham	20	4	3	13	25	48	-23	15
Chesham	20	2	0	18	15	84	-69	6

FA CUP FINAL SCORES & TEAMS

1872 **Wanderers 1** (Betts) Bowen, Alcock, Bonsor, Welch; Betts, Crake, Hooman, Lubbock, Thompson, Vidal, Wollaston. Note: Betts played under the pseudonym 'AH Chequer' on the day of the match **Royal Engineers 0** Capt Merriman; Capt Marindin, Lieut Addison, Lieut Cresswell, Lieut Mitchell, Lieut Renny-Tailyour, Lieut Rich, Lieut George Goodwyn, Lieut Muirhead, Lieut Cotter, Lieut Bogle

1873 **Wanderers 2** (Wollaston, Kinnaird) Bowen; Thompson, Welch, Kinnaird, Howell, Wollaston, Sturgis, Rev Stewart, Kenyon-Slaney, Kingsford, Bonsor **Oxford University 0** Kirke-Smith; Leach, Mackarness, Birley, Longman, Chappell-Maddison, Dixon, Paton, Vidal, Sumner, Ottaway. March 29; 3,000; A Stair

1874 **Oxford University 2** (Mackarness, Patton) Neapean; Mackarness, Birley, Green, Vidal, Ottaway, Benson, Patton, Rawson, Chappell-Maddison, Rev Johnson **Royal Engineers 0** Capt Merriman; Major Marindin, Lieut W Addison, Gerald Onslow, Lieut Oliver, Lieut Digby, Lieut Renny-Tailyour, Lieut Rawson, Lieut Blackman Lieut Wood, Lieut von Donop. March 14; 2,000; A Stair

1875 **Royal Engineers 1** (Renny-Tailyour) Capt Merriman; Lieut Sim, Lieut Onslow, Lieut (later Sir) Ruck, Lieut Von Donop, Lieut Wood, Lieut Rawson, Lieut Stafford, Capt Renny-Tailyour, Lieut Mein, Lieut Wingfield-Stratford **Old Etonians 1** (Bonsor) Thompson; Benson, Lubbock, Wilson, Kinnaird, (Sir) Stronge, Patton, Farmer, Bonsor, Ottaway, Kenyon-Slaney. March 13; 2,000; CW Alcock. aet **Replay – Royal Engineers 2** (Renny-Tailyour, Stafford) Capt Merriman; Lieut Sim, Lieut Onslow, Lieut (later Sir) Ruck, Lieut Von Donop, Lieut Wood, Lieut Rawson, Lieut Stafford, Capt Renny-Tailyour, Lieut Mein, Lieut Wingfield-Stratford **Old Etonians 0** Capt Drummond-Moray; Kinnaird, (Sir) Stronge, Hammond, Lubbock, Patton, Farrer, Bonsor, Lubbock, Wilson, Farmer. March 16; 3,000; CW Alcock

1876 **Wanderers 1** (Edwards) Greig; Stratford, Lindsay, Chappell-Maddison, Birley, Wollaston, C Heron, G Heron, Edwards, Kenrick, Hughes **Old Etonians 1** (Bonsor) Hogg; Rev Welldon, Lyttleton, Thompson, Kinnaird, Meysey, Kenyon-Slaney, Lyttleton, Sturgis, Bonsor, Allene. March 11; 3,500; WS Rawson aet **Replay – Wanderers 3** (Wollaston, Hughes 2) Greig, Stratford, Lindsay, Chappell-Maddison, Birley, Wollaston, C Heron, G Heron, Edwards, Kenrick, Hughes **Old Etonians 0** Hogg, Lubbock, Lyttleton, Farrer, Kinnaird, (Sir) Stronge, Kenyon-Slaney, Lyttleton, Sturgis, Bonsor, Allene. March 18; 1,500; WS Rawson

1877 **Wanderers 2** (Kenrick, Lindsay) Kinnaird; Birley, Denton, Green, Heron, Hughes, Kenrick, Lindsay, Stratford, Wace, Wollaston **Oxford University 1** (Kinnaird og) Allington; Bain, Dunnell, Rev Savory, Todd, Waddington, Rev Fernandez, Otter, Parry, Rawson. March 24; 3,000; SH Wright, aet

1878 **Wanderers 3** (Kinnaird, Kenrick 2) (Sir) Kirkpatrick; Stratford, Lindsay, Kinnaird, Green, Wollaston, Heron, Wylie, Wace, Denton, Kenrick **Royal Engineers 1** (Morris) Friend; Cowan, (Sir) Morris, Mayne, Heath, Haynes, Lindsay, Hedley, (Sir) Bond, Barnet, Ruck. March 23; 4,500; SR Bastard

1879 **Old Etonians 1** (Clerke) Hawtrey; Edward, Bury, Kinnaird, Lubbock, Clerke, Pares, Goodhart, Whitfield, Chevalier, Beaufoy **Clapham Rovers 0** Birkett; Ogilvie, Field, Bailey, Prinsep, Rawson, Stanley, Scott, Bevington, Growse, Keith-Falconer. March 29; 5,000; CW Alcock

1880 **Clapham Rovers 1** (Lloyd-Jones) Birkett; Ogilvie, Field, Weston, Bailey, Stanley, Brougham, Sparkes, Barry, Ram, Lloyd-Jones **Oxford University 0** Parr; Wilson, King, Phillips, Rogers, Heygate, Rev Childs, Eyre, (Dr) Crowdy, Hill, Lubbock. April 10; 6,000; Major Marindin

1881 **Old Carthusians 3** (Page, Wynyard, Parry) Gillett; Norris, (Sir) Colvin, Prinsep, (Sir) Vintcent, Hansell, Richards, Page, Wynyard, Parry, Todd **Old Etonians 0** Rawlinson; Foley, French, Kinnaird, Farrer, Macauley, Goodhart, Whitfield, Novelli, Anderson, Chevallier. April 9; 4,000; W Pierce-Dix

1882 **Old Etonians 1** (Macauley) Rawlinson; French, de Paravicini, Kinnaird, Foley, Novelli, Dunn, Macauley, Goodhart, Chevallier, Anderson **Blackburn Rov 0** Howarth; McIntyre, Suter, Hargreaves, Sharples, Hargreaves, Avery, Brown, Strachan, Douglas, Duckworth. March 25; 6,500; JC Clegg

1883 **Blackburn Olympic 2** (Matthews, Costley) Hacking; Ward, Warburton, Gibson, Astley, Hunter, Dewhurst, Matthews, Wilson, Costley, Yates **Old Etonians 1** (Goodhart) Rawlinson; French, de Paravicini, Kinnaird, Foley, Dunn, Bainbridge, Chevallier, Anderson, Goodhart, Macauley. March 31; 8,000; Major Marindin, aet

1884 **Blackburn Rov 2** (Sowerbutts, Forrest) Arthur; Suter, Beverley, McIntyre, Forrest, Hargreaves, Brown, Inglis Sowerbutts, Douglas, Lofthouse **Queen's Park 1** (Christie) Gillespie; MacDonald, Arnott, Gow, Campbell, Allan, Harrower, (Dr) Smith, Anderson, Watt, Christie. March 29; 4,000; Major Marindin

1885 **Blackburn Rov 2** (Forrest, Brown) Arthur; Turner, Suter, Haworth, McIntyre, Forresl, Sowerbutts, Lofthouse, Douglas, Brown, Fecitt **Queen's Park 0** Gillespie; Arnott, MacLeod, MacDonald, Campbell, Sellar, Anderson, McWhammel, Hamilton, Allan, Gray. April 4; 12,500; Major Marindin

1886 **Blackburn Rov 0** Arthur; Turner, Suter, Heyes, Forrest, McIntyre, Douglas, Strachan, Sowerbutts, Fecitt, Brown **WBA 0** Roberts; Green, Bell, Horton, Perry, Timmins, Woodhall, Green, Bayliss, Loach, Bell. April 3; 15,000; Major Marindin **Replay – Blackburn Rov 2** (Sowerbutts, Brown) Arthur; Turner, Suter, Walton, Forrest, McIntyre, Douglas, Strachan, Sowerbutts, Fecitt, Brown **WBA 0** Roberts; Green, Bell, Horton, Perry, Timmins, Woodhall, Green, Bayliss, Loach, Bell. April 10; 12,000; Major Marindin

1887 **Aston Villa 2** (Hodgetts, Hunter) Warner; Coulton, Simmonds, Yates, Dawson, Burton, Davis, Albert Brown, Hunter, Vaughton, Hodgetts **WBA 0** Roberts; Green, Aldridge, Horton, Perry, Timmins, Woodhall, Green, Bayliss, Paddock, Pearson. April 2; 15,500; Major Marindin

1888 **WBA 2** (Bayliss), Woodhall) Roberts; Aldridge, Green, Horton, Perry, Timmins, Woodhall, Bassett, Bayliss, Wilson, Pearson **Preston 1** (Dewhurst) Mills-Roberts; Howarth, Holmes, Ross, Russell, Gordon, Ross, Goodall, Dewhurst, Drummond, Graham. March 24; 19,000; Major Marindin

1889 **Preston 3** (Dewhurst, Ross, Thomson) Mills-Roberts; Howarth, Holmes, Drummond, Russell, Graham, Gordon, Goodall, Dewhurst, Thompson, Ross **Wolves 0** Baynton; Baugh, Mason, Fletcher, Allen, Lowder, Hunter, Wykes, Brodie, Wood, Knight. March 30; 22,000; Major Marindin

1890 **Blackburn Rov 6** (Lofthouse, Jack Southworth, Walton, Townley 3) Horne; James Southworth, Forbes, Barton, Dewar, Forrest, Lofthouse, Campbell, Jack Southworth, Walton, Townley **Sheffield Wed 1** (Bennett) Smith; Morley, Brayshaw, Dungworth, Betts, Waller, Ingram, Woolhouse, Bennett, Mumford, Cawley. March 29; 20,000; Major Marindin

1891 **Blackburn Rov 3** (Dewar, Jack Southworth, Townley) Pennington; Brandon, Forbes, Barton, Dewar, Forrest, Lofthouse, Walton, Southworth, Hall, Townley **Notts Co 1** (Oswald) Thraves; Ferguson, Hendry, Osborne, Calderhead, Shelton, McGregror, McInnes Oswald, Locker, Daft. March 21; 23,000; CJ Hughes

1892 **WBA 3** (Geddes, Nicholls, Reynolds) Reader; Nicholson, McCulloch, Reynolds, Perry, Groves, Bassett, McLeod, Nicholls, Pearson, Geddes **Aston Villa 0** Warner; Evans, Cox, Devey, Cowan, Baird, Athersmith, Devey, Dickson, Hodgetts, Campbell. March 19; 32,810; JC Clegg

1893 **Wolves 1** (Allen) Rose; Baugh, Swift, Malpass, Allen, Kinsey, Topham, Wykes, Butcher, Griffin, Wood **Everton 0** Williams; Kelso, Howarth, Boyle, Holt, Stewart, Latta, Gordon, Maxwell, Chadwick, Milward. March 25; 45,000; CJ Hughes

1894 **Notts Co 4** (Watson, Logan 3) Toone; Harper, Hendry, Bramley, Calderhead, Shelton, Watson, Donnelly, Logan Bruce, Daft **Bolton 1** (Cassidy) Sutcliffe; Somerville, Jones , Gardiner, Paton, Hughes, Tannahill, Wilson, Cassidy, Bentley, Dickenson. March 31; 37,000; CJ Hughes

1895 **Aston Villa 1** (Chatt) Wilkes; Spencer, Welford, Reynolds, Cowan, Russell, Athersmith Chatt, Devey, Hodgetts, Smith **WBA 0** Reader; Williams, Horton, Perry, Higgins, Taggart, Bassett, McLeod, Richards, Hutchinson, Banks. April 20; 42,560; J Lewis

1896 **Sheffield Wed 2** (Spikesley 2) Massey; Earp, Langley, Brandon, Crawshaw, Petrie, Brash, Brady, Bell, Davis, Spikesley **Wolves 1** (Black) Tennant; Baugh, Dunn, Owen, Malpass, Griffiths, Tonks, Henderson, Beats, Wood, Black. April 18; 48,836; Lieut Simpson

1897 **Aston Villa 3** (Campbell, Wheldon, Crabtree) Whitehouse; Spencer, Reynolds, Evans, Cowan, Crabtree, Athersmith, Devey, Campbell, Wheldon, Cowan **Everton 2** (Bell, Boyle) Menham; Meechan, Storrier, Boyle, Holt, Stewart, Taylor, Bell, Hartley, Chadwick, Milward. April 10; 65,891; J Lewis

1898 **Nottm Forest 3** (Capes 2, McPherson) Allsop; Ritchie, Scott, Forman, McPherson, Wragg, McInnes, Richards, Benbow, Capes, Spouncer **Derby 1** (Bloomer) Fryer; Methven, Leiper, Cox, Goodall, Bloomer, Boag, Stevenson, McQueen. April 16; 62,017; J Lewis

1899 **Sheffield Utd 4** (Bennett, Beers, Almond, Priest) Foulke; Thickett, Boyle, Johnson, Morren, Needham, Bennett, Beers, Hedley, Almond, Priest **Derby 1** (Boag) Fryer; Methven, Staley, Cox,

169

Paterson, May, Arkesden, Bloomer, Boag, McDonald, Allen. April 15; 73,833; A Scragg

1900 **Bury 4** (McLuckie 2, Wood, Plant) Thompson; Darroch, Davidson, Pray, Leeming, Ross, Richards, Wood, McLuckie, Sagar, Plant **Southampton 0** Robinson; Meechan, Durber, Meston, Chadwick, Petrie, Turner, Yates, Farrell, Wood, Milward. April 21; 68,945; A Kingscott

1901 **Tottenham 2** (Brown 2) Clawley; Erentz, Tait, Morris, Hughes, Jones, Smith, Cameron, Brown, Copeland, Kirwan **Sheffield Utd 2** (Priest, Bennett) Foulke; Thickett, Boyle, Johnson, Morren, Needham, Bennett, Field, Hedley, Priest, Lipsham. April 20; 110,820; A Kingscott **Replay – Tottenham 3** (Cameron, Smith, Brown) Clawley; Erentz, Tait, Morris, Hughes, Jones, Smith, Cameron, Brown, Copeland, Kirwan. **Sheffield Utd 1** (Priest) Foulke; Thickett, Boyle, Johnson, Morren, Needham, Bennett, Field, Hedley, Priest, Lipsham. April 27; 20,470; A Kingscott

1902 **Sheffield Utd 1** (Common) Foulke; Thickett, Boyle, Needham, Wilkinson, Johnson, Bennett, Common, Hedley, Priest, Lipsham **Southampton 1** (Wood) Robinson; Fry, Molyneux, Meston, Bowman, Lee, Turner, Wood Brown, Chadwick, Turner. April 19; 76,914; T Kirkham. **Replay – Sheffield Utd 2** (Hedley, Barnes) Foulke; Thickett, Boyle, Needham, Wilkinson, Johnson, Barnes, Common, Hedley, Priest, Lipsham **Southampton 1** (Brown) Robinson; Fry, Molyneux, Meston, Bowman, Lee, Turner, Wood, Brown, Chadwick, Turner. April 26; 33,068; T Kirkham

1903 **Bury 6** (Leeming 2, Ross, Sagar, Wood, Plant) Monteith; Lindsey, McEwen, Johnston, Thorpe, Ross, Richards, Wood, Sagar Leeming, Plant **Derby 0** Fryer; Methven, Morris, Warren, Goodall, May, Warrington, York, Boag, Richards, Davis. April 18; 63,102; J Adams

1904 **Manchester City 1** (Meredith) Hillman; McMahon, Burgess, Frost, Hynds, Ashworth, Meredith, Livingstone, Gillespie, Turnbull, Booth **Bolton 0** Davies; Brown, Struthers, Clifford, Greenhalgh, Freebairn, Stokes, Marsh, Yenson, White, Taylor. April 23; 61,374; AJ Barker

1905 **Aston Villa 2** (Hampton 2) George; Spencer, Miles, Pearson, Leake, Windmill, Brawn, Garratty, Hampton, Bache, Hall **Newcastle 0** Lawrence; McCombie, Carr, Gardner, Aitken, McWilliam, Rutherford, Howie, Appleyard, Veitch, Gosnell. April 15; 101,117; PR Harrower

1906 **Everton 1** (Young) Scott; Crelley, W Balmer, Makepeace, Taylor, Abbott, Sharp, Bolton, Young, Settle, Hardman **Newcastle 0** Lawrence; McCombie, Carr, Gardner, Aitken, McWilliam, Rutherford, Howie, Orr, Veitch, Gosnell. April 21; 75,609; F Kirkham

1907 **Sheffield Wed 2** (Stewart, Simpson) Lyall; Layton, Burton, Brittleton, Crawshaw, Bartlett, Chapman, Bradshaw, Wilson, Stewart, Simpson **Everton 1** (Sharp) Scott; W Balmer, B Balmer, Makepeace, Taylor, Abbott, Sharp, Bolton, Young, Settle, Hardman. April 20; 84,594; N Whittaker

1908 **Wolves 3** (Hunt, Hedley, Harrison) Lunn; Jones, Collins, Rev Hunt, Wooldridge, Bishop, Harrison, Shelton, Hedley, Radford, Pedley **Newcastle 1** (Howie) Lawrence; McCracken, Pudan, Gardner, Veitch, McWilliam, Rutherford, Howie, Appleyard, Speedie, Wilson. April 25; 74,697; TP Campbell

1909 **Manchester Utd 1** (Sandy Turnbull) Moger; Stacey, Hayes, Duckworth, Roberts, Bell, Meredith, Halse, J Turnbull, S Turnbull, Wall **Bristol City 0** Clay; Annan, Cottle, Hanlin, Wedlock, Spear, Staniforth, Hardy, Gilligan, Burton, Hilton. April 24; 71,401; J Mason

1910 **Newcastle 1** (Rutherford) Lawrence; McCracken, Whitson, Veitch, Low, McWilliam, Rutherford, Howie, Higgins, Shepherd, Wilson **Barnsley 1** (Tufnell) Mearns; Downs, Ness, Glendinning, Boyle, Utley, Tufnell, Lillycrop, Gadsby, Forman, Bartrop. April 23; 77,747; JT Ibbotson **Replay – Newcastle 2** (Shepherd 2, 1pen) Lawrence; McCracken, Carr, Veitch, Low, McWilliam, Rutherford, Howie, Higgins, Shepherd, Wilson **Barnsley 0** Mearns; Downs, Ness, Glendinning, Boyle, Utley, Tufnell, Lillycrop, Gadsby, Forman, Bartrop. April 28; 69,000; JT Ibbotson.

1911 **Bradford City 0** Mellors; Campbell, Taylor, Robinson, Gildea, McDonald, Logan, Speirs, O'Rourke, Devine, Thompson **Newcastle 0** Lawrence; McCracken, Whitson, Veitch, Low, Willis, Rutherford, Jobey, Stewart, Higgins, Wilson. April 22; 69,068; JH Pearson **Replay – Bradford City 1** (Speirs) Mellors; Campbell, Taylor, Robinson, Torrance, McDonald, Logan, Speirs, O'Rourke, Devine, Thompson **Newcastle 0** Lawrence; McCracken, Whitson, Veitch, Low, Willis, Rutherford, Jobey, Stewart, Higgins, Wilson. April 26; 58,000; JH Pearson

1912 **Barnsley 0** Cooper; Downs, Taylor, Glendinning, Bratley, Utley, Bartrop, Tufnell, Lillycrop, Travers, Moore **WBA 0** Pearson; Cook, Pennington, Baddeley, Buck, McNeal, Jephcott, Wright, Pailor, Bowser, Shearman. April 20; 54,556; JR Schumacher **Replay – Barnsley 1** (Tufnell) Cooper; Downs, Taylor, Glendinning, Bratley, Utley, Bartrop, Harry, Lillycrop, Travers, Jimmy Moore **WBA 0** Pearson; Cook,

Pennington, Baddeley, Buck, McNeal, Jephcott, Wright, Pailor, Bowser, Shearman. April 24; 38,555; JR Schumacher. aet

1913 **Aston Villa 1** (Barber) Hardy; Lyons, Weston, Barber, Harrop, Leach, Wallace, Halse, Hampton, Stephenson, Bache **Sunderland 0** Butler; Gladwin, Ness, Cuggy, Thomson, Low, Mordue, Buchan, Richardson, Holley, Martin. April 19; 120,081; A Adams

1914 **Burnley 1** (Freeman) Sewell; Bamford, Taylor, Halley, Boyle, Watson, Nesbit, Lindley, Freeman, Hodgson, Mosscrop **Liverpool 0** Campbell; Longworth, Pursell, Fairfoul, Ferguson, McKinley, Sheldon, Metcalfe, Miller, Lacey, Nicholl. April 25; 72,778; HS Bamlett

1915 **Sheffield Utd 3** (Simmons, Fazackerly, Kitchen) Gough; Cook, English, Sturgess, Brelsford, Utley, Simmons, Fazackerly, Kitchen, Masterman, Evans **Chelsea 0** Molyneux; Bettridge, Harrow, Taylor, Logan, Walker, Ford, Halse, Thomson, Croal, McNeil. April 24; 49,557; HH Taylor

1920 **Aston Villa 1** (Kirton) Hardy; Smart, Weston, Ducat, Barson, Moss, Wallace, Kirton, Walker, Stephenson, Dorrell **Huddersfield 0** Mutch; Wood, Bullock, Slade, Wilson, Watson, Richardson, Mann, Taylor, Swann, Islip. April 24; 50,018; JT Howcroft. aet

1921 **Tottenham 1** (Dimmock) Hunter; Clay, McDonald, Smith, Walters, Grimsdell, Banks, Seed, Cantrell, Bliss, Dimmock **Wolves 0** George; Woodward, Marshall, Gregory, Hodnett, Riley, Lea, Burrill, Edmonds, Potts, Brooks. April 23; 72,805; S Davies

1922 **Huddersfield 1** (Smith pen) Mutch; Wood, Wadsworth, Slade, Wilson, Watson, Richardson, Mann, Islip, Stephenson, Billy Smith **Preston 0** Mitchell; Hamilton, Doolan, Duxbury, McCall, Williamson, Rawlings, Jefferis, Roberts, Woodhouse, Quinn. April 29; 53,000; JWP Fowler

1923 **Bolton 2** (Jack, JR Smith) Pym; Haworth, Finney, Nuttall, Seddon, Jennings, Butler, Jack, JR Smith, Joe Smith, Vizard **West Ham 0** Hufton; Henderson, Young, Bishop, Kay, Tresadern, Richards, Brown, Watson, Moore, Ruffell. April 28; 126,047; DH Asson

1924 **Newcastle 2** (Harris, Seymour) Bradley; Hampson, Hudspeth, Mooney, Spencer, Gibson, Low, Cowan, Harris, McDonald, Seymour **Aston Villa 0** Jackson; Smart, Mort, Moss, Milne, Blackburn, York, Kirton, Capewell, Walker, Dorrell. April 26; 91,695; WE Russell

1925 **Sheffield Utd 1** (Tunstall) Sutcliffe; Cook, Milton, Pantling, King, Green, Mercer, Boyle, Johnson, Gillespie, Tunstall **Cardiff 0** Farquharson; Nelson, Blair, Wake, Keenor, Hardy, Davies, Gill, Nicholson, Beadles, Evans. April 25; 91,763; GN Watson

1926 **Bolton 1** (Jack) Pym; Haworth, Greenhalgh, Nuttall, Seddon, Jennings, Butler, JR Smith, Jack, Joe Smith, Vizard **Manchester City 0** Goodchild; Cookson, McCloy, Pringle, Cowan, McMullan, Austin, Browell, Roberts, Johnson, Hicks. April 24; 91,447; I Baker

1927 **Cardiff 1** (Ferguson) Farquharson; Nelson, Watson, Keenor, Sloan, Hardy, Curtis, Irving, Ferguson, Davies, McLachlan **Arsenal 0** Lewis; Parker, Kennedy, Baker, Butler, John, Hulme, Buchan, Brain, Blythe, Hoar. April 23; 91,206; WF Bunnell

1928 **Blackburn 3** (Roscamp 2, McLean) Crawford; Hutton, Jones, Healless, Rankin, Campbell, Thornewell, Puddefoot, Roscamp, McLean, Rigby **Huddersfield 1** (Jackson) Mercer; Goodall, Barkas, Redfern, Wilson, Steele, Jackson, Kelly, Brown, Stephenson, Smith. April 21; 92,041; TG Bryan

1929 **Bolton 2** (Butler, Blackmore) Pym; Haworth, Finney, Kean, Seddon, Nuttall, Butler, McClelland, Blackmore, Gibson, Cook **Portsmouth 0** Gilfillan; Mackie, Bell, Nichol, McIlwaine, Thackeray, Forward, Smith, Weddle, Watson, Cook. April 27; 92,576; A Josephs

1930 **Arsenal 2** (James, Lambert) Preedy; Parker, Hapgood, Baker, Seddon, John, Hulme, Jack, Lambert, James, Bastin **Huddersfield 0** Turner; Goodall, Spence, Naylor, Wilson, Campbell, Jackson, Kelly, Davies, Raw, Smith. April 26; 92,488; T Crew

1931 **WBA 2** (WG Richardson 2) Pearson; Shaw, Trentham, Magee, Bill Richardson, Edwards, Glidden, Carter, WG Richardson, Sandford, Wood **Birmingham 1** (Bradford) Hibbs; Liddell, Barkas, Cringan, Morrall, Leslie, Briggs, Crosbie, Bradford, Gregg, Curtis. April 25; 92,406; AH Kingscott

1932 **Newcastle 2** (Allen 2) McInroy; Nelson, Fairhurst, McKenzie, Davidson, Weaver, Boyd, Richardson, Allen, McMenemy, Lang **Arsenal 1** (John) Moss; Parker, Hapgood, Jones, Roberts, Male, Hulme, Jack, Lambert, Bastin, John. April 23; 92,298; WP Harper

1933 **Everton 3** (Stein, Dean, Dunn) Sagar; Cook, Cresswell, Britton, White, Thomson, Geldard, Dunn, Dean, Johnson, Stein **Manchester City 0** Langford; Cann, Dale, Busby, Cowan, Bray, Toseland, Marshall, Herd, McMullan, Eric Brook. April 29; 92,950; E Wood

1934 **Manchester City 2** (Tilson 2) Swift; Barnett, Dale, Busby, Cowan, Bray, Toseland, Marshall, Tilson, Herd, Brook **Portsmouth 1** (Rutherford) Gilfillan; Mackie, Smith, Nichol, Allen, Thackeray, Worrall, Smith, Weddle, Easson, Rutherford. April 28; 93,258; Stanley Rous

1935 **Sheffield Wed 4** (Rimmer 2, Palethorpe, Hooper) Brown; Nibloe, Catlin, Sharp, Millership, Burrows, Hooper, Surtees, Palethorpe, Starling, Rimmer **WBA 2** (Boyes, Sandford) Pearson; Shaw, Trentham, Murphy, Bill Richardson, Edwards, Glidden, Carter, WG Richardson, Sandford, Wally. April 27; 93,204; AE Fogg

1936 **Arsenal 1** (Drake) Wilson; Male, Hapgood, Crayston, Roberts, Copping, Hulme, Bowden, Drake, James, Bastin **Sheffield Utd 0** Smith; Hooper, Wilkinson, Jackson, Johnson, McPherson, Barton, Barclay, Dodds, Pickering, Williams. April 25; 93,384; H Nattrass

1937 **Sunderland 3** (Gurney, Carter, Burbanks) Mapson; Gorman, Hall, Thomson, Johnston, McNab, Duns, Carter, Gurney, Gallacher, Burbanks **Preston 1** (Frank O'Donnell) Burns; Gallimore, Beattie, Shankly, Tremelling, Milne, Dougal, Beresford, O'Donnell, Fagan, O'Donnell. May 1; 93,495; RG Rudd

1938 **Preston 1** (Mutch pen) Holdcroft; Gallimore, Beattie, Shankly, Smith, Batey, Watmough, Mutch, Maxwell, Beattie, O'Donnell **Huddersfield 0** Hesford; Craig, Mountford, Willingham, Young, Boot, Hulme, Issac, MacFadyen, Barclay, Beasley. April 30; 93,497; AJ Jewell. aet

1939 **Portsmouth 4** (Parker 2, Barlow, Anderson) Walker; Morgan, Rochford, Guthrie, Rowe, Wharton, Worrall, McAlinden, Anderson, Barlow, Parker **Wolves 1** (Dorsett) Scott; Morris, Taylor, Galley, Cullis, Gardiner, Burton, McIntosh, Westcott, Dorsett, Maguire. April 29; 99,370; T Thompson

1946 **Derby 4** (Stamps 2. Doherty, B Turner og) Woodley; Nicholas, Howe, Bullions, Leuty, Musson, Harrison, Carter, Stamps, Doherty, Duncan **Charlton Athletic 1** (B Turner) Bartram; Phipps, Shreeve, Turner, Oakes, Johnson, Fell, Brown, Turner, Welsh, Duffy. April 27; 98,000; ED Smith. aet

1947 **Charlton Athletic 1** (Duffy) Bartram; Croker, Shreeve, Johnson, Phipps, Whittaker, Hurst, Dawson, Robinson, Welsh, Duffy **Burnley 0** Strong; Woodruff, Mather, Attwell, Brown, Bray, Chew, Morris, Harrison, Potts, Kippax. April 26; 99,000; JM Wiltshire. aet

1948 **Manchester Utd 4** (Rowley 2, Pearson, Anderson) Crompton; Carey, Aston, Anderson, Chilton, Cockburn, Delaney, Morris, Rowley, Pearson, Mitten **Blackpool 2** (Shimwell pen, Mortensen) Robinson; Shimwell, Crosland, Johnston, Hayward, Kelly, Matthews, Munro, Mortensen, Dick, Rickett. April 24; 99,000; CJ Barrick

1949 **Wolves 3** (Pye 2, Smyth) Williams; Pritchard, Springthorpe Crook, Shorthouse, Wright, Hancocks, Smyth, Pye, Dunn, Mullen **Leicester 1** (Griffiths) Bradley; Jelly, Scott, Harrison, Plummer, King, Griffiths, Lee, Harrison, Chisholm, Adam. April 30; 99,500; RA Mortimer

1950 **Arsenal 2** (Lewis 2) Swindin; Scott, Barnes, Forbes, L Compton, Mercer, Cox, Logie, Goring, Lewis, D Compton **Liverpool 0** Sidlow; Lambert, Spicer, Taylor, Hughes, Jones, Payne, Baron, Stubbins, Fagan, Liddell. April 29; 100,000; H Pearce

1951 **Newcastle 2** (Milburn 2) Fairbrother; Cowell, Corbett, Harvey, Brennan, Crowe, Walker, Taylor, Milburn, Jorge Robledo, Mitchell **Blackpool 0** Farm; Shimwell, Garrett, Johnston, Hayward, Kelly, Matthews, Mudie, Mortensen, Slater, Perry. April 28; 100,000; W Ling

1952 **Newcastle 1** (G Robledo) Simpson; Cowell, McMichael, Harvey, Brennan, Eduardo Robledo, Walker, Foulkes, Milburn, Jorge Robledo, Mitchell **Arsenal 0** Swindin; Barnes, Smith, Forbes, Daniel Mercer, Cox, Logie, Holton, Lishman, Roper. May 3; 100,000; A Ellis

1953 **Blackpool 4** (Mortensen 3, Perry) Farm; Shimwell, Garrett, Fenton, Johnston, Robinson, Matthews, Taylor, Mortensen, Mudie, Perry **Bolton 3** (Lofthouse, Moir, Bell) Hanson; Ball, Banks, Wheeler, Barrass, Bell, Holden, Moir, Lofthouse, Hassall, Langton. May 2; 100,000; M Griffiths

1954 **WBA 3** (Allen 2 [1pen], Griffin) Sanders; Kennedy, Millard, Dudley, Dugdale, Barlow, Griffin, Ryan, Allen, Nicholls, Lee **Preston 2** (Morrison, Wayman) Thompson; Cunningham, Walton, Docherty, Marston, Forbes, Finney, Foster, Wayman, Baxter, Morrison. May 1; 100,000; A Luty

1955 **Newcastle 3** (Milburn, Mitchell, Hannah) Simpson; Cowell, Batty, Scoular, Stokoe, Casey, White,

Milburn, Keeble, Hannah, Mitchell **Manchester City 1** (Johnstone) Trautmann; Meadows, Little, Barnes, Ewing, Paul, Spurdle, Hayes, Revie, Johnstone, Fagan. May 7; 100,000; R Leafe

1956 **Manchester City 3** (Hayes, Dyson, Johnstone) Trautmann; Leivers, Little, Barnes, Ewing, Paul, Johnstone, Hayes, Revie, Dyson, Clarke **Birmingham 1** (Kinsey) Merrick; Hall, Green, Newman, Smith, Boyd, Astall, Kinsey, Brown, Murphy, Govan. May 5; 100,000; A Bond

1957 **Aston Villa 2** (McParland 2) Sims; Lynn, Aldis, Crowther, Dugdale, Saward, Smith, Sewell, Myerscough, Dixon, McParland **Manchester Utd 1** (Taylor) Wood; Foulkes, Byrne, Colman, Blanchflower, Edwards, Berry, Whelan, Taylor, Charlton, Pegg. May 4; 100,000; F Coultas

1958 **Bolton 2** (Lofthouse 2) Hopkinson; Hartle, Banks, Hennin, Higgins, Edwards, Birch, Stevens, Lofthouse, Parry, Holden **Manchester Utd 0** Gregg; Foulkes, Greaves, Goodwin, Cope, Crowther, Dawson, Taylor, Charlton, Viollet, Webster. May 3; 100,000; J Sherlock

1959 **Nottingham Forest 2** (Dwight, Wilson) Thomson; Whare, McDonald, Whitefoot, McKinlay, Burkitt, Dwight, Quigley, Wilson, Gray, Imlach **Luton Town 1** (Pacey) Baynham; McNally, Hawkes, Groves, Owen, Pacey, Bingham, Brown, Morton, Cummins, Gregory. May 2; 100,000; J Clough

1960 **Wolves 3** (McGrath og, Deeley 2) Finlayson; Showell, Harris, Clamp, Slater, Flowers, Deeley, Stobart, Murray, Broadbent, Horne **Blackburn 0** Leyland; Bray, Whelan, Clayton, Woods, McGrath, Bimpson, Dobing, Dougan, Douglas, McLeod. May 7; 100,000; K Howley

1961 **Tottenham 2** (Smith, Dyson) Brown; Baker, Henry, Blanchflower, Norman, Mackay, Jones, White, Smith, Allen, Dyson **Leicester 0** Banks; Chalmers, Norman, McLintock, King, Appleton, Riley, Walsh, McIlmoyle, Keyworth, Cheesebrough. May 6; 100,000; J Kelly

1962 **Tottenham 3** (Greaves, Smith, Blanchflower pen) Brown; Baker, Henry, Blanchflower, Norman, Mackay, Medwin, White, Smith, Greaves, Jones **Burnley 1** (Robson) Blacklaw; Angus, Elder, Adamson, Cummings, Miller, Connelly, McIlroy, Pointer, Robson, Harris. May 5; 100,000; J Finney

1963 **Manchester Utd 3** (Law, Herd 2) Gaskell; Dunne, Cantwell, Crerand, Foulkes, Setters, Giles, Quixall, Herd, Law, Charlton **Leicester 1** (Keyworth) Banks; Sjoberg, Norman, McLintock, King, Appleton, Riley, Cross, Keyworth, Gibson, Stringfellow. May 25; 100,000; K Aston

1964 **West Ham 3** (Sissons, Hurst, Boyce) Standen; Bond, Burkett, Bovington, Brown, Moore, Brabrook, Boyce, Byrne, Hurst, Sissons **Preston 2** (Holden, Dawson) Kelly; Ross, Lawton, Smith, Singleton, Kendall, Wilson, Ashworth, Dawson, Spavin, Holden. May 2; 100,000; A Holland

1965 **Liverpool 2** (Hunt, St John) Lawrence; Lawler, Byrne, Strong, Yeats, Stevenson, Callaghan, Hunt, St John, Smith, Thompson **Leeds 1** (Bremner) Sprake; Reaney, Bell, Bremner, Charlton, Hunter, Giles, Storrie, Peacock, Collins, Johanneson. May 1; 100,000; W Clements. aet

1966 **Everton 3** (Trebilcock 2, Temple) West; Wright, Wilson, Gabriel, Labone, Harris, Scott, Trebilcock, Young, Harvey, Temple **Sheffield Wed 2** (McCalliog, Ford) Springett; Smith, Megson, Eustace, Ellis, Young, Pugh, Fantham, McCalliog, Ford, Quinn. May 14; 100,000; JK Taylor

1967 **Tottenham 2** (Robertson, Saul) Jennings; Kinnear, Knowles, Mullery, England, Mackay, Robertson, Greaves, Gilzean, Venables, Saul. Unused sub: Jones **Chelsea 1** (Tambling) Bonetti; Allan Harris, McCreadie, Hollins, Hinton, Ron Harris, Cooke, Baldwin, Hateley, Tambling, Boyle. Unused sub: Kirkup. May 20; 100,000; K Dagnall

1968 **WBA 1** (Astle) John Osborne; Fraser, Williams, Brown, Talbut, Kaye, Lovett, Collard, Astle Hope, Clark Sub: Clarke rep Kaye 91 **Everton 0** West; Wright, Wilson, Kendall, Labone, Harvey, Husband, Ball, Royle, Hurst, Morrissey. Unused sub: Kenyon. May 18; 100,000; L Callaghan. aet

1969 **Manchester City 1** (Young) Dowd; Book, Pardoe, Doyle, Booth, Oakes, Summerbee, Bell, Lee, Young, Coleman. Unused sub: Connor **Leicester 0** Shilton; Rodrigues, Nish, Roberts, Woollett, Cross, Fern, Gibson, Lochhead, Clarke, Glover. Sub: Manley rep Glover 70. April 26; 100,000; G McCabe

1970 **Chelsea 2** (Houseman, Hutchinson) Bonetti; Webb, McCreadie, Hollins, Dempsey, R Harris, Baldwin, Houseman, Osgood, Hutchinson, Cooke. Sub: Hinton rep Harris 91 **Leeds 2** (Charlton, Jones) Sprake; Madeley, Cooper, Bremner, Charlton, Hunter, Lorimer, Clarke, Jones, Giles, Gray Unused sub: Bates. April 11; 100,000; E Jennings. aet **Replay – Chelsea 2** (Osgood, Webb) Bonetti; Webb, McCreadie, Hollins, Dempsey, R Harris, Baldwin, Houseman, Osgood, Hutchinson, Cooke. Sub: Hinton rep Osgood 105 **Leeds 1** (Jones) Harvey; Madeley, Cooper, Bremner, Charlton, Hunter, Lorimer, Clarke, Jones, Giles, Gray Unused sub: Bates. April 29; 62,078; E Jennings. aet

173

1971   **Arsenal 2** (Kelly, George) Wilson; Rice, McNab, Storey, McLintock Simpson, Armstrong, Graham, Radford, Kennedy, George. Sub: Kelly rep Storey 70 **Liverpool 1** (Heighway) Clemence; Lawler, Lindsay, Smith, Lloyd, Hughes, Callaghan, Evans, Heighway, Toshack, Hall. Sub: Thompson rep Evans 70. May 8; 100,000; N Burtenshaw. aet

1972   **Leeds 1** (Clarke) Harvey; Reaney, Madeley, Bremner, Charlton, Hunter, Lorimer, Clarke, Jones, Giles, Gray. Unused sub: Bates **Arsenal 0** Barnett; Rice, McNab, Storey, McLintock, Simpson, Armstrong, Ball, George, Radford, Graham. Sub: Kennedy rep Radford 80. May 6; 100,000; DW Smith

1973   **Sunderland 1** (Porterfield) Montgomery; Malone, Guthrie, Horswill, Watson, Pitt, Kerr, Hughes, Halom, Porterfield, Tueart. Unused sub: Young **Leeds 0** Harvey; Reaney, Cherry, Bremner, Madeley, Hunter, Lorimer, Clarke, Jones, Giles, Gray. Sub: Yorath rep Gray 75. May 5; 100,000; K Burns

1974   **Liverpool 3** (Keegan 2, Heighway) Clemence; Smith, Lindsay, Thompson, Cormack, Hughes, Keegan, Hall, Heighway, Toshack, Callaghan. Unused sub: Lawler **Newcastle 0** McFaul; Clark, Kennedy, McDermott, Howard, Moncur, Smith, Cassidy, Macdonald, Tudor, Hibbitt. Sub: Gibb rep Smith 70. May 4; 100,000; GC Kew

1975   **West Ham 2** (Taylor 2) Day; McDowell, Taylor, Lock, Lampard, Bonds, Paddon, Brooking, Jennings, Taylor, Holland. Unused sub: Gould **Fulham 0** Mellor; Cutbush, Lacy, Moore, Fraser, Mullery, Conway, Slough, Mitchell, Busby, Barrett. Unused sub: Lloyd. May 3; 100,000; P Partridge

1976   **Southampton 1** (Stokes) Turner; Rodrigues, Peach, Holmes, Blyth, Steele, Gilchrist, Channon, Osgood, McCalliog, Stokes. Unused sub: Fisher **Manchester Utd 0** Stepney; Forsyth, Houston, Daly, Greenhoff, Buchan, Coppell, McIlroy, Pearson, Macari, Hill. Sub: McCreery rep Hill 66. May 1; 100,000; C Thomas

1977   **Manchester Utd 2** (Pearson, J Greenhoff) Stepney; Nicholl, Albiston, McIlroy, B Greenhoff, Buchan, Coppell, J Greenhoff, Pearson, Macari, Hill. Sub: McCreery rep Hill 81 **Liverpool 1** (Case) Clemence; Neal, Jones, Smith, Kennedy, Hughes, Keegan, Case, Heighway, Johnson, McDermott. Sub: Callaghan rep Johnson 64. May 21; 100,000; R Matthewson

1978   **Ipswich Town 1** (Osborne) Cooper; Burley, Mills, Talbot, Hunter, Beattie, Osborne, Wark, Mariner, Geddis, Woods. Sub: Lambert rep Osborne 79 **Arsenal 0** Jennings; Rice, Nelson, Price, Young, O'Leary, Brady, Hudson, Macdonald, Stapleton, Sunderland. Sub: Rix rep Brady 65. May 6; 100,000; D Nippard

1979   **Arsenal 3** (Talbot, Stapleton, Sunderland) Jennings; Rice, Nelson, Talbot, O'Leary, Young, Brady, Sunderland, Stapleton, Price, Rix. Sub: Walford rep Rix 83 **Manchester Utd 2** (McQueen, McIlroy) Bailey; Nicholl, Albiston, McIlroy, McQueen, Buchan, Coppell, J Greenhoff, Jordan, Macari, Thomas. Unused sub: Greenhoff. May 12; 100,000; R Challis

1980   **West Ham 1** (Brooking) Parkes; Stewart, Lampard, Bonds, Martin, Devonshire, Allen, Pearson, Cross, Brooking, Pike. Unused sub: Brush **Arsenal 0** Jennings; Rice, Devine, Talbot, O'Leary, Young, Brady, Sunderland, Stapleton, Price, Rix. Sub: Nelson rep Devine 61. May 10; 100,000; G Courtney

1981   **Tottenham 1** (Hutchinson og) Aleksic; Hughton, Miller, Roberts, Perryman, Villa, Ardiles, Archibald, Galvin, Hoddle, Crooks. Sub: Brooke rep Villa 68. **Manchester City 1** (Hutchinson) Corrigan; Ranson, McDonald, Reid, Power, Caton, Bennett, Gow, Mackenzie, Hutchison Reeves. Sub: Henry rep Hutchison 82. May 9; 100,000; K Hackett. aet **Replay – Tottenham 3** (Villa 2, Crooks) Aleksic; Hughton, Miller, Roberts, Perryman, Villa, Ardiles, Archibald, Galvin, Hoddle, Crooks. Unused sub: Brooke **Manchester City 2** (Mackenzie, Reeves pen) Corrigan; Ranson, McDonald, Reid, Power, Caton, Bennett, Gow, Mackenzie, Hutchison Reeves. Sub: Tueart rep McDonald 79. May 14; 92,000; K Hackett

1982   **Tottenham 1** (Hoddle) Clemence; Hughton, Miller, Price, Hazard, Perryman, Roberts, Archibald, Galvin, Hoddle, Crooks. Sub: Brooke rep Hazard 104 **Queens Park Rangers 1** (Fenwick) Hucker; Fenwick, Gillard, Waddock, Hazell, Roeder, Currie, Flanagan, Allen, Stainrod, Gregory. Sub: Micklewhite rep Allen 50. May 22; 100,000; C White. aet **Replay – Tottenham 1** (Hoddle pen) Clemence; Hughton, Miller, Price, Hazard, Perryman, Roberts, Archibald, Galvin, Hoddle, Crooks. Sub: Brooke rep Hazard 67 **Queens Park Rangers 0** Hucker; Fenwick, Gillard, Waddock, Hazell, Neill, Currie, Flanagan, Micklewhite, Stainrod, Gregory. Sub: Burke rep Micklewhite 84. May 27; 90,000; C White

1983 Manchester Utd 2 (Stapleton, Wilkins) Bailey; Duxbury, Moran, McQueen, Albiston, Davies, Wilkins, Robson, Muhren, Stapleton, Whiteside. Unused sub: Grimes **Brighton 2** (Smith, Stevens) Moseley; Ramsey, Gary A Stevens, Pearce, Gatting, Smillie, Case, Grealish, Howlett, Robinson, Smith. Sub: Ryan rep Ramsey 56. May 21; 100,000; AW Grey, aet **Replay – Manchester Utd 4** (Robson 2, Whiteside, Muhren pen) Bailey; Duxbury, Moran, McQueen, Albiston, Davies, Wilkins, Robson, Muhren, Stapleton, Whiteside. Unused sub: Grimes **Brighton 0** Moseley; Gary A Stevens, Pearce, Foster, Gatting, Smillie, Case, Grealish, Howlett, Robinson, Smith. Sub: Ryan rep Howlett 74. May 26; 100,000; AW Grey

1984 Everton 2 (Sharp, Gray) Southall; Gary M Stevens, Bailey, Ratcliffe, Mountfield, Reid, Steven, Heath, Sharp, Gray, Richardson. Unused sub: Harper **Watford 0** Sherwood; Bardsley, Price, Taylor, Terry, Sinnott, Callaghan, Johnston, Reilly, Jackett, Barnes. Sub: Atkinson rep Price 58. May 19; 100,000; J Hunting

1985 Manchester Utd 1 (Whiteside) Bailey; Gidman, Albiston, Whiteside, McGrath, Moran, Robson, Strachan, Hughes, Stapleton, Olsen. Sub: Duxbury rep Albiston 91. Moran sent off 77. **Everton 0** Southall; Gary M Stevens, Van den Hauwe, Ratcliffe, Mountfield, Reid, Steven, Sharp, Gray, Bracewell, Sheedy. Unused sub: Harper. May 18; 100,000; P Willis. aet

1986 Liverpool 3 (Rush 2, Johnston) Grobbelaar; Lawrenson, Beglin, Nicol, Whelan, Hansen, Dalglish, Johnston, Rush, Molby, MacDonald. Unused sub: McMahon **Everton 1** (Lineker) Mimms; Gary M Stevens, Van den Hauwe, Ratcliffe, Mountfield, Reid, Steven, Lineker, Sharp, Bracewell, Sheedy. Sub: Heath rep Stevens 65. May 10; 98,000; A Robinson

1987 Coventry City 3 (Bennett, Houchen, Mabbutt og) Ogrizovic; Phillips, Downs, McGrath, Kilcline, Peake, Bennett, Gynn, Regis, Houchen, Pickering. Sub: Rodger rep Kilcline 88. Unused sub: Sedgley **Tottenham 2** (Allen, Mabbutt) Clemence; Hughton Thomas, Hodge, Gough, Mabbutt, C Allen, P Allen, Waddle, Hoddle, Ardiles. Subs: Gary A Stevens rep Ardiles 91; Claesen rep Hughton 97. May 16; 98,000; N Midgley. aet

1988 Wimbledon 1 (Sanchez) Beasant; Goodyear, Phelan, Jones, Young, Thorn, Gibson Cork, Fashanu, Sanchez, Wise. Subs: Cunningham rep Cork 56; Scales rep Gibson 63 **Liverpool 0** Grobbelaar; Gillespie, Ablett, Nicol, Spackman, Hansen, Beardsley, Aldridge, Houghton, Barnes, McMahon. Subs: Johnston rep Aldridge 63; Molby rep Spackman 72. May 14; 98,203; B Hill

1989 Liverpool 3 (Aldridge, Rush 2) Grobbelaar; Ablett, Staunton, Nichol, Whelan, Hansen, Beardsley, Aldridge Houghton, Barnes, McMahon. Subs: Rush rep Aldridge 72; Venison rep Staunton 91 **Everton 2** (McCall 2) Southall; McDonald, Van den Hauwe, Ratcliffe, Watson, Bracewell, Nevin, Trevor Steven, Cottee, Sharp, Sheedy. Subs: McCall rep Bracewell 58; Wilson rep Sheedy 77. May 20; 82,500; J Worrall. aet

1990 Manchester Utd 3 (Robson, Hughes 2) Leighton; Ince, Martin, Bruce, Phelan, Pallister, Robson, Webb, McClair, Hughes, Wallace. Subs: Blackmore rep Martin 88; Robins rep Pallister 93. **Crystal Palace 3** (O'Reilly, Wright 2) Martyn; Pemberton, Shaw, Gray, O'Reilly, Thorn, Barber, Thomas, Bright, Salako, Pardew. Subs: Wright rep Barber 69; Madden rep Gray 117. May 12; 80,000; A Gunn. aet **Replay – Manchester Utd 1** (Martin) Sealey; Ince, Martin, Bruce, Phelan, Pallister, Robson, Webb, McClair, Hughes, Wallace. Unused subs: Robins, Blackmore **Crystal Palace 0** Martyn; Pemberton, Shaw, Gray, O'Reilly, Thorn, Barber, Thomas, Bright, Salako, Pardew. Subs: Wright rep Barber 64; Madden rep Salako 79. May 17; 80,000; A Gunn

1991 Tottenham 2 (Stewart, Walker og) Thorstvedt; Edinburgh, Van den Hauwe, Sedgley, Howells, Mabbutt, Stewart, Gascoigne, Samways, Lineker, Allen. Subs: Nayim rep Gascoigne 18; Walsh rep Samways 82. **Nottingham Forest 1** (Pearce) Crossley; Charles, Pearce, Walker, Chettle, Keane, Crosby, Parker, Clough, Glover, Woan. Subs: Hodge rep Woan 62; Laws rep Glover 108. May 18; 80,000; R Milford. aet

1992 Liverpool 2 (Thomas, Rush) Grobbelaar; Jones, Burrows, Nicol, Molby, Wright, Saunders, Houghton, Rush, McManaman, Thomas. Unused subs: Marsh, Walters **Sunderland 0** Norman; Owers, Ball, Bennett, Rogan, Rush, Bracewell, Davenport, Armstrong, Byrne, Atkinson. Subs: Hardyman rep Rush 69; Hawke rep Armstrong 77. May 9; 80,000; P Don

1993 Arsenal 1 (Wright) Seaman; Dixon, Winterburn, Linighan, Adams, Jensen, Davis, Parlour, Merson, Campbell, Wright. Subs: Smith rep Parlour 66; O'Leary rep Wright 90. **Sheffield Wed 1** (Hirst) Woods; Nilsson Worthington, Palmer, Hirst, Anderson, Waddle, Warhurst, Bright, Sheridan, Harkes. Subs: Hyde

rep Anderson 85; Bart-Williams rep Waddle 112. May 15; 79,347; K Barratt. aet **Replay – Arsenal 2** (Wright, Linighan) Seaman; Dixon, Winterburn, Linighan, Adams, Jensen, Davis, Smith, Merson, Campbell, Wright. Sub: O'Leary rep Wright 81. Unused sub: Selley **Sheffield Wed 1** (Waddle) Woods; Nilsson, Worthington, Palmer, Hirst, Wilson, Waddle, Warhurst, Bright, Sheridan, Harkes. Subs: Hyde rep Wilson 62; Bart-Williams rep Nilsson 118. May 20; 62,267; K Barratt. aet

1994 Manchester Utd 4 (Cantona 2 [2pens], Hughes, McClair) Schmeichel; Parker, Bruce, Pallister, Irwin, Kanchelskis, Keane, Ince, Giggs, Cantona, Hughes. Subs: Sharpe rep Irwin 84; McClair rep Kanchelskis 84. Unused sub: Walsh (gk) **Chelsea 0** Kharine; Clarke, Sinclair, Kjeldberg, Johnsen, Burley, Spencer, Newton, Stein, Peacock, Wise Substitutions Hoddle rep Burley 65; Cascarino rep Stein 78. Unused sub: Kevin Hitchcock (gk) May 14; 79,634; D Elleray

1995 Everton 1 (Rideout) Southall; Jackson, Hinchcliffe, Ablett, Watson, Parkinson, Unsworth, Horne, Stuart, Rideout, Limpar. Subs: Ferguson rep Rideout 51; Amokachi rep Limpar 69. Unused sub: Kearton (gk) **Manchester Utd 0** Schmeichel; Neville, Irwin, Bruce, Sharpe, Pallister, Keane, Ince, Brian McClair, Hughes, Butt. Subs: Giggs rep Bruce 46; Scholes rep Sharpe 72. Unused sub: Gary Walsh (gk) May 20; 79,592; G Ashby

1996 Manchester Utd 1 (Cantona) Schmeichel; Irwin, P Neville, May, Keane, Pallister, Cantona, Beckham, Cole, Butt, Giggs. Subs: Scholes rep Cole 65; G Neville rep Beckham 89. Unused sub: Sharpe **Liverpool 0** James; McAteer, Scales, Wright, Babb, Jones, McManaman, Barnes, Redknapp, Collymore, Fowler. Subs: Rush rep Collymore 74; Thomas rep Jones 85. Unused sub: Warner (gk) May 11; 79,007; D Gallagher

1997 Chelsea 2 (Di Matteo, Newton) Grodas; Petrescu, Minto, Sinclair, Lebouef, Clarke, Zola, Di Matteo, Newton, Hughes, Wise. Sub: Vialli rep Zola 89. Unused subs: Hitchcock (gk), Myers **Middlesbrough 0** Roberts; Blackmore, Fleming, Stamp, Pearson, Festa, Emerson, Mustoe, Ravanelli, Juninho, Hignett. Subs: Beck rep Ravanelli 24; Vickers rep Mustoe 29; Kinder, rep Hignett 74. May 17; 79,160; S Lodge

1998 Arsenal 2 (Overmars, Anelka) Seaman; Dixon, Winterburn, Vieira, Keown, Adams, Parlour, Anelka, Petit, Wreh, Overmars. Sub: Platt rep Wreh 63. Unused subs: Manninger (gk); Bould, Wright, Grimandi **Newcastle 0** Given; Pistone, Pearce, Batty, Dabizas, Howey, Lee, Barton, Shearer, Ketsbaia, Speed. Subs: Andersson rep Pearce 72; Watson rep Barton 77; Barnes rep Ketsbaia 85. Unused subs: Hislop (gk); Albert. May 16; 79,183; P Durkin

1999 Manchester Utd 2 (Sheringham, Scholes) Schmeichel; G Neville, Johnsen, May, P Neville, Beckham, Scholes, Keane, Giggs, Cole, Solskjaer. Subs: Sheringham rep Keane 9; Yorke rep Cole 61; Stam rep Scholes 77. Unused subs: Blomqvist, Van Der Gouw **Newcastle 0** Harper; Griffin, Charvet, Dabizas, Domi, Lee, Hamann, Speed, Solano, Ketsbaia, Shearer. Subs: Ferguson rep Hamann 46; Maric rep Solano 68; Glass rep Ketsbaia 79. Unused subs: Given (gk); Barton. May 22; 79,101; P Jones

2000 Chelsea 1 (Di Matteo) de Goey; Melchiot Desailly, Lebouef, Babayaro, Di Matteo, Wise, Deschamps, Poyet, Weah, Zola. Subs: Flo rep Weah 87; Morris rep Zola 90. Unused subs: Cudicini (gk), Terry , Harley **Aston Villa 0** James; Ehiogu, Southgate, Barry, Delaney, Taylor, Boateng, Merson, Wright, Dublin, Carbone. Subs: Stone rep Taylor 79; Joachim rep Carbone 79; Hendrie rep Wright 88. Unused subs: Enckelman (gk); Samuel May 20; 78,217; G Poll

2001 Liverpool 2 (Owen 2) Westerveld; Babbel, Henchoz, Hyypia, Carragher, Murphy, Hamann, Gerrard, Smicer, Heskey, Owen. Subs: McAllister rep Hamann 60; Fowler rep Smicer 77; Berger rep Murphy 77. Unused subs: Arphexad (gk); Vignal **Arsenal 1** (Ljungberg) Seaman; Dixon, Keown, Adams, Cole, Ljungberg, Grimandi, Vieira, Pires, Henry, Wiltord Subs: Parlour rep Wiltord 76; Kanu rep Ljungberg 85; Bergkamp rep Dixon 90. Unused subs: Manninger (gk); Lauren. May 12; 72,500; S Dunn

2002 Arsenal 2 (Parlour, Ljungberg) Seaman; Lauren, Campbell, Adams, Cole, Parlour, Wiltord, Vieira, Ljungberg, Bergkamp, Henry Subs: Edu rep Bergkamp 72; Kanu rep Henry 81; Keown rep Wiltord 90. Unused subs: Wright (gk); Dixon **Chelsea 0** Cudicini; Melchiot, Desailly, Gallas, Babayaro, Gronkjaer, Lampard, Petit, Le Saux, Floyd Hasselbaink, Gudjohnsen. Subs: Terry rep Babayaro 46; Zola rep Hasselbaink 68; Zenden rep Melchiot 77. Unused subs: de Goey (gk); Jokanovic. May 4; 73,963; M Riley

2003 Arsenal 1 (Pires) Seaman; Lauren, Luzhny, Keown, Cole, Ljungberg, Parlour, Gilberto, Pires, Bergkamp, Henry. Sub: Wiltord rep Bergkamp 77. Unused subs: Taylor (gk); Kanu, Toure, van Bronckhorst **Southampton 0** Niemi; Baird, Svensson, Lundekvam, Bridge, Telfer, Svensson, Oakley, Marsden, Beattie, Ormerod. Subs: Jones rep Niemi 66; Fernandes rep Baird 87; Tessem rep Svensson 75. Unused subs: Williams, Higginbotham. May 17; 73,726; G Barber

2004 **Manchester Utd 3** (Van Nistelrooy [2, 1 pen], Ronaldo) Howard; G Neville, Brown, Silvestre, O'Shea, Fletcher, Keane, Ronaldo, Scholes, Giggs, Van Nistelrooy. Subs: Carroll rep Howard, Butt rep Fletcher, Solskjaer rep Ronaldo 84. Unused subs: P Neville, Djemba-Djemba **Millwall 0** Marshall; Elliott, Lawrence, Ward, Ryan, Wise, Ifill, Cahill, Livermore, Sweeney, Harris. Subs: Cogan rep Ryan, McCammon rep Harris 74 Weston rep Wise 88. Unused subs: Gueret (gk); Dunne. May 22; 71,350; J Winter

2005 **Arsenal 0** Lehmann; Lauren, Toure, Senderos, Cole, Fabregas, Gilberto, Vieira, Pires, Reyes, Bergkamp Subs: Ljungberg rep Bergkamp 65, Van Persie rep Fabregas 86, Edu rep Pires 105. Unused subs: Almunia (gk); Campbell. Reyes sent off 90. **Manchester Utd 0** Carroll; Brown, Ferdinand, Silvestre, O'Shea, Fletcher, Keane, Scholes, Rooney, Van Nistelrooy, Ronaldo. Subs: Fortune rep O'Shea 77, Giggs rep Fletcher 91. Unused subs: Howard (gk); G Neville, Smith. **Arsenal** (Lauren, Ljungberg, van Persie, Cole, Vieira) beat Manchester Utd (van Nistelrooy, Scholes [missed], Ronaldo, Rooney, Keane) 5-4 on penalties

2006 **Liverpool 3** (Gerrard 2, Cisse) Reina; Finnan, Carragher, Hyypiä, Riise, Gerrard, Xabi, Sissoko, Kewell, Cisse, Crouch. Subs: Morientes rep Kewell 48, Kromkamp rep Alonso 67, Hamman rep Crouch 71. Unused subs: Dudek (gk); Traoré **West Ham 3** (Ashton, Konchesky, Carragher (og)) Hislop; Scaloni, Ferdinand, Gabbidon, Konchesky, Benayoun, Fletcher, Reo-Coker, Etherington, Ashton, Harewood. Subs: Zamora rep Ashton 71, Dailly rep Fletcher, Sheringham rep Etherington 85. Unused subs: Walker (gk); Collins. **Liverpool** (Hamann, Hyypiä [missed], Gerrard, Riise) beat **West Ham** (Zamora [missed], Sheringham, Konchesky [missed], Ferdinand [missed]) 3-1 on penalties. May 13; 71,140; A Wiley

2007 **Chelsea 1** (Drogba) Cech, Ferreira, Essien, Terry, Bridge, Mikel, Makelele, Lampard, Wright-Phillips, Drogba, J Cole Subs: Robben rep J Cole 45, Kalou rep Wright-Phillips 93, A Cole rep Robben 108. Unused subs: Cudicini (gk); Diarra. **Manchester Utd 0** Van der Sar, Brown, Ferdinand, Vidic, Heinze, Fletcher, Scholes, Carrick, Ronaldo, Rooney, Giggs Subs: Smith rep Fletcher 92, O'Shea rep Carrick, Solskjaer rep Giggs 112. Unused subs: Kuszczak (gk); Evra. May 19; 89,826; S Bennett

2008 **Portsmouth 1** (Kanu) James; Johnson, Campbell, Distin, Hreidarsson, Utaka, Muntari, Mendes, Diarra, Kranjcar, Kanu. Subs: Nugent rep Utaka 69, Diop rep Mendes 78, Baros rep Kanu 87. Unused subs: Ashdown (gk); Pamarot. **Cardiff 0** Enckelman; McNaughton, Johnson, Loovens, Capaldi, Whittingham, Rae, McPhail, Ledley, Hasselbaink, Parry. Subs: Ramsey rep Whittingham 62, Thompson rep Hasselbaink 70, Sinclair rep Rae 87. Unused subs: Oakes (gk); Purse. May 17; 89,874; M Dean

2009 Chelsea 2 (Drogba, Lampard), Cech; Bosingwa, Alex, Terry, A Cole, Essien, Mikel, Lampard, Drogba, Anelka, Malouda. Subs: Ballack rep Essien 61. Unused subs: Hilario (gk), Ivanovic, Di Santo, Kalou, Belletti, Mancienne. **Everton** 1 (Saha) Howard; Hibbert, Yobo, Lescott, Baines, Osman, Neville, Cahill, Pienaar, Fellaini, Saha. Subs: Jacobsen rep Hibbert 46, Vaughan rep Saha 77, Gosling rep Osman 83. Unused subs: Nash, Castillo, Rodwell, Baxter. May 30; 89,391; H Webb

2010 Chelsea 1 (Drogba) Cech; Ivanovic, Alex, Terry, A Cole, Lampard, Ballack, Malouda, Kalou, Drogba, Anelka. Subs: Belletti rep Ballack 44, J Cole rep Kalou 71, Sturridge rep Anelka 90. Unused subs: Hilario (gk), Zhirkov, Paulo Ferreira, Matic. **Portsmouth 0** James; Finnan, Mokoena, Rocha, Mullins, Dindane, Brown, Diop, Boateng, O'Hara, Piquionne. Subs: Utaka rep Boateng 73, Belhadj rep Mullins 81, Kanu rep Diop 81. Unused subs: Ashdown (gk), Vanden Borre, Hughes, Ben Haim. May 15; 88,335; C Foy

2011 Manchester City 1 (Y Toure) Hart; Richards, Kompany, Lescott, Kolarov, De Jong, Barry, Silva, Y Toure, Balotelli, Tevez. Subs: Johnson rep Barry73, Zabaleta rep Tevez 87, Vieira rep Silva 90. Unused subs: Given (gk), Boyata, Milner, Dzeko. **Stoke 0** Sorensen; Wilkinson, Shawcross, Huth, Wilson, Pennant, Whelan, Delap, Etherington, Walters, Jones. Subs: Whitehead rep Etherington 62, Carew rep Delap 80, Pugh rep Whelan 84. Unused subs: Nash (gk), Collins, Faye, Diao. May 14; 88,643; M Atkinson

2012 Chelsea 2 (Ramires, Drogba) Cech; Bosingwa, Ivanovic, Terry, Cole, Mikel, Lampard, Ramires, Mata, Kalou, Drogba. Subs: Meireles rep Ramires76, Malouda rep Mata 90. Unused subs: Turnbull (gk), Paulo Ferreira, Essien, Torres, Sturridge. **Liverpool 1** (Carroll) Reina; Johnson, Skrtel, Agger, Luis Enrique, Spearing, Bellamy, Henderson, Gerrard, Downing, Suarez. Subs Carroll rep Spearing 55, Kuyt rep Bellamy 78. Unused subs: Doni (gk), Carragher, Kelly, Shelvey, Rodriguez. May 5; 89,102; P Dowd

2013 Wigan 1 (Watson) Robles; Boyce, Alcaraz, Scharner, McCarthy, McArthur, McManaman, Maloney, Gomez, Espinoza, Kone. Subs: Watson rep Gomez 81. Unused subs: Al Habsi (gk), Caldwell, Golobart, Fyvie, Henriquez, Di Santo. **Manchester City 0** Hart, Zabaleta, Kompany,

Nastasic, Clichy, Toure, Barry, Silva, Tevez, Nasri, Aguero. Subs: Milner rep Nasri 54, Rodwell rep Tevez 69, Dzeko rep Barry 90. Unused subs: Pantilimon (gk), Lescott, Kolarov, Garcia. Sent off Zabaleta (84). May 11; 86,254; A Marriner

VENUES

Kennington Oval 1872; **Lillie Bridge** 1873; **Kennington Oval** 1874 – 1892 (1886 replay at the **Racecourse Ground, Derby**); **Fallowfield**, Manchester, 1893; **Goodison Park** 1894; **Crystal Palace** 1895 – 1915 (1901 replay at **Burnden Park**; 1910 replay at **Goodison Park**; 1912 replay at **Bramall Lane**); **Old Trafford** 1915; **Stamford Bridge** 1920 – 1922; **Wembley** 1923 – 2000 (1970 replay at **Old Trafford**; all replays after 1981 at **Wembley**); **Millennium Stadium** 2001 – 2006; **Wembley** 2007 – 2014

SUMMARY OF FA CUP WINS

Manchester Utd............ 11	Wolves............................4	Cardiff 1
Arsenal........................ 11	Sheffield Wed 3	Charlton 1
Tottenham...................... 8	West Ham 3	Clapham Rov.................... 1
Aston Villa 7	Bury 2	Coventry.......................... 1
Liverpool........................ 7	Nottm Forest 2	Derby............................... 1
Chelsea 7	Old Etonians 2	Huddersfield.................... 1
Blackburn Rov................ 6	Portsmouth 2	Ipswich............................ 1
Newcastle 6	Preston 2	Leeds 1
Everton 5	Sunderland 2	Notts Co........................... 1
Manchester City............. 5	Barnsley..........................1	Old Carthusians 1
The Wanderers 5	Blackburn Olympic...........1	Oxford University 1
WBA.............................. 5	Blackpool.........................1	Royal Engineers................ 1
Bolton 4	Bradford City 1	Southampton.................... 1
Sheffield Utd.................. 4	Burnley 1	Wigan 1
		Wimbledon....................... 1

APPEARANCES IN FINALS

(Figures do not include replays)

Arsenal........................ 18	The Wanderers* 5	Queen's Park (Glas)........... 2
Manchester Utd............. 18	West Ham 5	Blackburn Olympic* 1
Liverpool....................... 14	Derby...............................4	Bradford City* 1
Everton.......................... 13	Leeds 4	Brighton............................ 1
Newcastle...................... 13	Leicester..........................4	Bristol City 1
Chelsea 11	Oxford University 4	Coventry* 1
Aston Villa 10	Royal Engineers...............4	Crystal Palace................... 1
Manchester City............. 10	Southampton....................4	Fulham............................. 1
WBA.............................. 10	Sunderland 4	Hull.................................. 1
Tottenham....................... 9	Blackpool.........................3	Ipswich* 1
Blackburn Rov................. 8	Burnley 3	Luton 1
Wolves........................... 8	Cardiff 3	Middlesbrough.................. 1
Bolton 7	Nottm Forest 3	Millwall............................ 1
Preston 7	Barnsley...........................2	Old Carthusians*.............. 1
Old Etonians 6	Birmingham 2	QPR 1
Sheffield Utd.................. 6	Bury*...............................2	Stoke 1
Sheffield Wed................. 6	Charlton...........................2	Watford 1
Huddersfield 5	Clapham Rov....................2	Wigan 1
Portsmouth 5	Notts Co 2	Wimbledon* 1
(* Denotes undefeated)		

APPEARANCES IN SEMI-FINALS

(Figures do not include replays)

Manchester Utd 27, Arsenal 27, Everton 25, Liverpool 23, Chelsea 21, Aston Villa 20, WBA 20, Tottenham 19, Blackburn 18, Newcastle 17, Sheffield Wed 16, Bolton 14, Sheffield Utd 14, Wolves 14, Derby 13, Manchester City 12, Nottm Forest 12, Sunderland 12, Southampton 11, Preston 10, Birmingham 9, Burnley 8, Leeds 8, Huddersfield 7, Leicester 7, Portsmouth 7, West Ham 7, Fulham 6, Old Etonians 6, Oxford University 6, Millwall 5, Notts Co 5, The Wanderers 5, Watford 5, Cardiff 4, Luton 4, Queen's Park (Glasgow) 4, Royal Engineers 4, Stoke 4, Barnsley 3, Blackpool 3, Clapham Rov 3, *Crystal Palace 3, Ipswich Town 3, Middlesbrough 3, Norwich 3, Old Carthusians 3, Oldham 3, The Swifts 3, Blackburn Olympic 2, Bristol City 2, Bury 2, Charlton 2, Grimsby Town 2, Hull 2, Swansea 2, Swindon 2, Wigan 2, Wimbledon 2, Bradford City 1, Brighton 1, Cambridge University 1, Chesterfield 1, Coventry 1, Crewe 1, Darwen 1, Derby Junction 1, Marlow 1, Old Harrovians 1, Orient 1, Plymouth Argyle 1, Port Vale 1, QPR 1, Rangers (Glasgow) 1, Reading 1, Shropshire Wand 1, Wycombe 1, York 1 (*A previous and different Crystal Palace club also reached the semi-final in season 1871–72)

THE THINGS THEY SAY...

'I don't know how many people have been to Qatar in June, but I have and you can't play a football tournament there, even if all the stadiums had air-conditioning. FIFA have two choices. They can either move the time of the event or the location' – **Greg Dyke**, chairman of the FA, calling on the world governing body to switch the 2022 World Cup because of the extreme heat.

'The dream come true would be to manage Liverpool' – **Steven Gerrard**, looks ahead to when his playing days at Anfield are over.

'It's a nightmare, one of the worst days I have ever had in football' – **Wayne Rooney** after Manchester United's 3-0 home defeat by Liverpool.

'There's my goal of the month prize gone' – **Jack Wilshere**, Arsenal midfielder, sees his outstanding strike against Norwich outshone by Pajtim Kasami's 28-yard volley for Fulham at Crystal Palace.

'I have now been made aware of the health risks associated with the practice and accept that my actions were of poor judgement. I hope this will in no way influence or encourage others into putting their own health at risk' – **Kyle Walker**, Tottenham and England full-back, apologising after a newspaper photograph showed him inhaling nitrous oxide – laughing gas.

'If he was playing for Rochdale or somebody, they'd throw the book at him. But because he's an England player and we need him, it looks like nothing will happen' – **Harry Redknapp**, Queens Park Rangers manager, accuses the FA of hypocrisy for taking no action against Kyle Walker.

'I remember nothing about it. I asked the doc "who scored?" and he said "you". – **Romelu Lukaku** after being concussed scoring the winner for Everton against West Ham.

'He won't watch Match of the Day, that's for sure – **Paul Lambert**, Aston Villa manager, after Villa supporter Prince William watched a dour goalless draw with Sunderland.

'I saw him in the tunnel and thought "It's Jack and the Beanstalk this" – **Alex Bruce**, Hull defender, on the prospect of marking Stoke's 6ft 7in striker Peter Crouch.

FIRST TROPHY FOR CITY MANAGER MANUEL PELLEGRINI

THIRD ROUND	FOURTH ROUND	FIFTH ROUND	SEMI-FINALS	FINAL
*Manchester City......5	Manchester City......†2	Manchester City......3		
Wigan.......0				
			*Manchester City......6:3	
*Newcastle 2	*Newcastle 0			Manchester City.......3
Leeds.......0				
		*Leicester.......1		
*Leicester.......2	*Leicester 4			
Derby.......1				
	Fulham.......3			
*Fulham.......2				
Everton.......1				
		*Tottenham 1		
*Aston Villa.......0	*Tottenham ....†B2			
Tottenham.......4				
			West Ham 0:0	
*Hull.......1	Hull.......2			
Huddersfield 0				
		West Ham 2		
*Burnley 2	*Burnley 0			
Nottm Forest.......1				
	West Ham 2			
*West Ham 3				
Cardiff.......2				
		*Stoke.......0		
*Birmingham 3	*Birmingham 4			
Swansea.......1				
			Manchester Utd.......1:2	
*Tranmere.......0	Stoke.......†C4			
Stoke.......2				

```
*Manchester Utd ....... 1
 Liverpool ............ 0
                              *Manchester Utd ...... 4
                               Norwich .............. 0
*Watford .............. 2
 Norwich .............. †3
                                                            Manchester Utd ...... 2
*WBA .................. 1                                    Chelsea ............. 1
 Arsenal .............. †A1
                              *Arsenal ............. 0                                   Manchester Utd ...... 2
                               Chelsea ............. 2                                   *Sunderland ........ 2†D1
*Swindon .............. 0
 Chelsea .............. 2
                                                            *Sunderland ......... †2                     Sunderland ....... 1

*Southampton .......... 2
 Bristol City ......... 0
                               Southampton ......... 1
                              *Sunderland .......... 2
 Peterborough ......... 0
*Sunderland ........... 2
```

*Drawn at home; in semi-finals, †first leg; A – Arsenal won 4-3 on pens; B – Tottenham won 8-7 on pens; C – Stoke won 4-2 on pens; D – Sunderland won 2-1 on pens

FIRST ROUND: Barnsley 0 Scunthorpe 0 (aet, Barnsley won 5-4 on pens); Birmingham 3 Plymouth 2 (aet); Bournemouth 1 Portsmouth 0; Brentford 3 Dag & Red 2; Brighton 1 Newport 3 (aet); Bristol Rov 1 Watford 3; Bury 3 Crewe 2; Carlisle 3 Blackburn 3 (aet, Carlisle won 4-3 on pens); Charlton 4 Oxford 0; Cheltenham 4 Crawley 3 (aet); Colchester 1 Peterborough 5; Doncaster 1 Rochdale 0; Exeter 0 QPR 2; Gillingham 0 Bristol City 2; Leeds 2 Chesterfield 1; Leyton Orient 3 Coventry 2; Middlesbrough 1 Accrington 0; Millwall 2 AFC Wimbledon 1; Morecambe 1 Wolves 0; Northampton 1 MK Dons 2; Nottm Forest 3 Hartlepool 1; Notts Co 3 Fleetwood 1; Oldham 0 Derby 1; Port Vale 1 Walsall 2; Preston 1 Blackpool 0; Rotherham 2 Sheffield Wed 1; Sheffield Utd 1 Burton 2; Shrewsbury 1 Bolton 3; Southend 0 Yeovil 1; Stevenage 2 Ipswich 0; Swindon 1 Torquay 0; Tranmere 2 Mansfield 0; Wycombe 1 Leicester 2; York 0 Burnley 4

SECOND ROUND: Accrington 0 Cardiff 2; Aston Villa 3 Rotherham 0; Barnsley 1 Southampton 5; Bristol City 2 Crystal Palace 1; Burnley 2 Preston 0; Burton 2 Fulham 2 (aet, Fulham won 5-4 on pens); Carlisle 2 Leicester 5; Derby 5 Brentford 0; Doncaster 1 Leeds 3; Everton 2 Stevenage 1 (aet); Huddersfield 3 Charlton 2; Leyton Orient 0 Hull 1 (aet); Liverpool 4 Notts Co 2 (aet); Morecambe 0 Newcastle 2; Nottm Forest 2 Millwall 1 (aet); Norwich 6 Bury 3; Peterborough 6 Reading 0; QPR 0 Swindon 2; Stoke 3 Walsall 1; Sunderland 4 MK Dons 2; Tranmere 1 Bolton 1 (aet, Tranmere won 4-2 on pens); Watford 2 Bournemouth 0; WBA 3 Newport 0; West Ham 2 Cheltenham 1; Yeovil 3 Birmingham 3 (aet, Birmingham won 3-2 on pens)

CAPITAL ONE CUP FINAL

MANCHESTER CITY 3 SUNDERLAND 1
Wembley (84,697); Sunday, March 2 2014

Manchester City (4-4-2): Pantilimon, Zabaleta, Kompany (capt), Demichelis, Kolarov, Nasri, Toure, Fernandinho, Silva (Garcia, 77), Dzeko (Negredo 87), Aguero 6 (Jesus Navas 58). **Subs not used**: Hart, Lescott, Clichy, Milner. **Scorers**: Toure (55), Nasri (56), Jesus Navas (90). **Booked**: Negredo. **Manager**: Manuel Pellegrini
Sunderland (4-2-3-1): Mannone, Bardsley, Brown, O'Shea (capt), Alonso, Cattermole (Giaccherini 77), Ki Sung-Yueng, Larsson (Fletcher 60), Johnson (Gardner 60), Colback, Borini. **Subs not used**: Ustari, Celustka, Vergini, Scocco. **Scorer**: Borini (10). **Booked**: Alonso.
Manager: Gus Poyet
Referee: M Atkinson (Yorks). **Half-time**: 0-1

Wembley finals have delivered many memorable goals. Stan Mortensen, Ricky Villa, Norman Whiteside, Roberto Di Matteo and Steven Gerrard are among the players whose strikes matched the importance of the occasion and were instrumental in their teams' victories. But rarely has the stadium – old and new – witnessed two of such quality in such quick succession as those from Yaya Toure and Samir Nasri which put Manchester City on course for the 2014 League Cup. Toure curled his shot precisely into the top corner from 30 yards. Ninety seconds later, Nasri capped a man-of-the-match performance by finding the net with the outside of his right boot from just inside the penalty box. Substitute Jesus Navas added a third in the 90th minute to complete his side's comeback after they trailed to the opportunism of Fabio Borini, who brushed aside Vincent Kompany's challenge to put Sunderland ahead in the tenth minute. City thus confirmed their status as strong favourites to provide manager Manuel Pellegrini with his first trophy of significance in Europe. Overall, they were good value for their third success in the competition after victories in 1970 and 1976. But there were times in the first-half when the underdogs looked capable of matching the upset which brought Wigan the FA Cup at City's expense the previous season. Had Borini, on loan from Liverpool, accepted a second chance when breaking clear, they could well have done so. Instead, Kompany made amends for his earlier lapse with a crucial challenge and Gus Poyet's side were left with the consolation of having played a full part in one of the best finals of recent seasons. On the way, they had accounted for Southampton, Chelsea and Manchester United, an achievement which looked beyond them during the troubled early weeks of the season under Paolo Di Canio.

HOW THEY REACHED THE FINAL

MANCHESTER CITY
Round 3: 5-0 home to Wigan (Jovetic 2, Dzeko, Toure, Jesus Navas)
Round 4: 2-0 away to Newcastle (Negredo, Dzeko) – aet
Round 5: 3-1 away to Leicester (Dzeko 2, Kolarov)
Semi-finals: v West Ham – first leg, 6-0 home (Negredo 3, Dzeko 2, Toure); second leg, 3-0 away (Negredo 2, Aguero)

SUNDERLAND
Round 2: 4-2 home to MK Dons (Wickham 2, Altidore, Johnson)
Round 3: 2-0 home to Peterborough (Giaccherini, Roberge)
Round 4: 2-1 home to Southampton (Bardsley, Larsson)
Round 5: 2-1 home to Chelsea (Borini, Ki Sung-Yueng) – aet
Semi-finals: v Manchester Utd – first leg, 2-1 home (Giggs og, Borini pen); second leg, 1-2 away (Bardsley) – aet, agg 3-3, won 2-1 on pens

LEAGUE CUP – COMPLETE RESULTS

LEAGUE CUP FINALS

1961*	Aston Villa beat Rotherham 3-2 on agg (0-2a, 3-0h)
1962	Norwich beat Rochdale 4-0 on agg (3-0a, 1-0h)
1963	Birmingham beat Aston Villa 3-1 o agg (3-1h, 0-0a)
1964	Leicester beat Stoke 4-3 on agg (1-1a, 3-2h)
1965	Chelsea beat Leicester 3-2 on agg (3-2h, 0-0a)
1966	WBA beat West Ham 5-3 on agg (1-2a, 4-1h)

AT WEMBLEY

1967	QPR beat WBA (3-2)
1968	Leeds beat Arsenal (1-0)
1969*	Swindon beat Arsenal (3-1)
1970*	Man City beat WBA (2-1)
1971	Tottenham beat Aston Villa (2-0)
1972	Stoke beat Chelsea (2-1)
1973	Tottenham beat Norwich (1-0)
1974	Wolves beat Man City (2-1)
1975	Aston Villa beat Norwich (1-0)
1976	Man City beat Newcastle (2-1)
1977†*	Aston Villa beat Everton (3-2 after 0-0 and 1-1 draws)
1978††	Nottm Forest beat Liverpool (1-0 after 0-0 draw)
1979	Nottm Forest beat Southampton (3-2)
1980	Wolves beat Nottm Forest (1-0)
1981†††	Liverpool beat West Ham (2-1 after 1-1 draw)

MILK CUP

1982*	Liverpool beat Tottenham (3-1)
1983*	Liverpool beat Man Utd (2-1)
1984**	Liverpool beat Everton (1-0 after *0-0 draw)
1985	Norwich beat Sunderland (1-0)
1986	Oxford Utd beat QPR (3-0)

LITTLEWOODS CUP

1987	Arsenal beat Liverpool (2-1)
1988	Luton beat Arsenal (3-2)
1989	Nottm Forest beat Luton (3-1)
1990	Nottm Forest beat Oldham (1-0)

RUMBELOWS CUP

1991	Sheffield Wed beat Man Utd (1-0)
1992	Man Utd beat Nottm Forest (1-0)

COCA-COLA CUP

1993	Arsenal beat Sheffield Wed (2-1)
1994	Aston Villa beat Man Utd (3-1)
1995	Liverpool beat Bolton (2-1)
1996	Aston Villa beat Leeds (3-0)
1997***	Leicester beat Middlesbrough (*1-0 after *1-1 draw)
1998	Chelsea beat Middlesbrough (2-0)

WORTHINGTON CUP (at Millennium Stadium from 2001)

1999	Tottenham beat Leicester (1-0)
2000	Leicester beat Tranmere (2-1)
2001	Liverpool beat Birmingham (5-4 on pens after *1-1 draw)
2002	Blackburn beat Tottenham (2-1)
2003	Liverpool beat Man Utd (2-0)

CARLING CUP (at Wembley from 2008)

2004	Middlesbrough beat Bolton (2-1)
2005*	Chelsea beat Liverpool (3-2)
2006	Man Utd beat Wigan (4-0)
2007	Chelsea beat Arsenal (2-1)
2008*	Tottenham beat Chelsea (2-1)
2009	Man Utd beat Tottenham (4-1 on pens after *0-0 draw)
2010	Man Utd beat Aston Villa (2-1)
2011	Birmingham beat Arsenal (2-1)
2012	Liverpool beat Cardiff (3-2 on pens after *2-2 draw)

CAPITAL ONE CUP (at Wembley from 2013)

2013	Swansea beat Bradford (5-0)
2014	Manchester City beat Sunderland (3-1)

* After extra time. † First replay at Hillsborough, second replay at Old Trafford. †† Replayed at Old Trafford. ††† Replayed at Villa Park. ** Replayed at Maine Road. *** Replayed at Hillsborough

SUMMARY OF LEAGUE CUP WINNERS

Liverpool 8	Arsenal......................2	Oxford Utd 1
Aston Villa 5	Birmingham 2	QPR............................1
Chelsea 4	Norwich 2	Sheffield Wed 1
Nottm Forest............4	Wolves 2	Stoke 1
Tottenham 4	Blackburn 2	Swansea.....................1
Manchester Utd............4	Leeds. 1	Swindon 1
Leicester.....................3	Luton 1	WBA 1
Manchester City 3	Middlesbrough 1	

LEAGUE CUP FINAL APPEARANCES

11 Liverpool; **8** Aston Villa, Manchester Utd; **7** Arsenal, Tottenham; **6** Chelsea, Nottm Forest; **5** Leicester; **4** Manchester City, Norwich; **3** Birmingham, Middlesbrough, WBA; **2** Bolton, Everton, Leeds, Luton, QPR, Sheffield Wed, Stoke, Sunderland, West Ham, Wolves; **1** Blackburn, Bradford, Cardiff, Newcastle, Oldham, Oxford Utd, Rochdale, Rotherham, Southampton, Swansea, Swindon, Tranmere, Wigan (Figures do not include replays).

LEAGUE CUP SEMI-FINAL APPEARANCES

14 Arsenal, Aston Villa, Liverpool, Tottenham; **13** Manchester Utd **11** Chelsea; **9** West Ham; **8** Manchester City; **6** Blackburn, Nottm Forest, **5** Birmingham, Leeds, Leicester, Middlesbrough, Norwich; **4** Bolton, Burnley, Crystal Palace, Everton, Ipswich, Sheffield Wed, Sunderland, WBA; **3**, QPR, Swindon, Wolves; **2** Bristol City, Cardiff, Coventry, Derby, Luton, Oxford Utd, Plymouth, Southampton, Stoke City, Tranmere, Watford, Wimbledon; **1** Blackpool, Bradford, Bury, Carlisle, Chester, Huddersfield, Newcastle, Oldham, Peterborough, Rochdale, Rotherham, Sheffield Utd, Shrewsbury, Stockport, Swansea, Walsall, Wigan, Wycombe
(Figures do not include replays).

OTHER COMPETITIONS 2013–14

FA COMMUNITY SHIELD 0

Manchester United 2 Wigan Athletic 0
Wembley (80,235); Sunday, August 11 2013

Manchester Utd (4-3-3): De Gea, Rafael (Smalling 15), Vidic, Jones, Evra, Giggs (Anderson 66), Carrick, Cleverley, Welbeck (Kagawa 83), Van Persie (Januzaj 83), Zaha (Valencia 60). **Subs not used:** Lindegaard, Evans. **Scorer:** Van Persie (6, 59). **Booked:** Cleverley. **Manager:** David Moyes
Wigan (4-5-1): Carson, Boyce, Barnett, Perch, Crainey, Watson (Gomez 71), McArthur (McCann 60), McCarthy (Dicko 86), McClean (McManaman 62), Maloney (Espinoza 71), Holt (Fortune 60). **Sub not used:** Nicholls. **Booked:** McArthur, Espinoza. **Manager:** Owen Coyle
Referee: M Clattenburg (Co Durham). **Half-time:** 1-0

JOHNSTONE'S PAINT TROPHY

FIRST ROUND

Northern: Crewe 1 Accrington 0; Hartlepool 5 Bradford 0; Notts Co 1 Burton 0; Port Vale 2 Bury 1; Scunthorpe 0 Sheffield Utd 0 (Sheffield Utd won 5-3 on pens); Shrewsbury 1 Oldham 4; Tranmere 1 Fleetwood 2; Wolves 2 Walsall 2 (Wolves won 4-2 on pens)
Southern: Brentford 5 Wimbledon 3; Bristol City 2 Bristol Rov 1; Cheltenham 3 Plymouth 3 (Plymouth won 5-4 on pens); Dag & Red 4 Colchester 1; Exeter 0 Wycombe 2; Gillingham 1 Leyton Orient 3; MK Dons 2 Northampton 0; Torquay 0 Portsmouth 0 (Portsmouth won 5-3 on pens)

SECOND ROUND

Northern: Fleetwood 4 Crewe 0; Mansfield 0 Chesterfield 1; Morecambe 0 Carlisle 0 (Carlisle won 4-3 on pens); Port Vale 0 Rochdale 1; Preston 0 Oldham 2; Sheffield Utd 0 Hartlepool 1; Wolves 0 Notts Co 0 (Notts Co won 3-1 on pens); York 0 Rotherham 3

Southern: Crawley 2 Newport 3; Leyton Orient 0 Coventry 0 (Leyton Orient won 4-2 on pens); Oxford 1 Portsmouth 2; Peterborough 2 Brentford 1; Southend 2 Dag & Red 5; Stevenage 2 MK Dons 1; Swindon 3 Plymouth 1; Wycombe 2 Bristol City 1

THIRD ROUND

Northern: Chesterfield 3 Rochdale 0; Fleetwood 2 Carlisle 0; Hartlepool 1 Rotherham 2; Oldham 5 Notts Co 1

Southern: Newport 3 Portsmouth 0; Peterborough 1 Dag & Red 0; Stevenage 3 Leyton Orient 2; Swindon 2 Wycombe 1

SEMI-FINALS

Northern: Fleetwood 2 Rotherham 1; Oldham 1 Chesterfield 1 (Chesterfield won 6-5 on pens)

Southern: Newport 0 Peterborough 3; Swindon 1 Stevenage 1 (Swindon won 3-1 on pens)

AREA FINALS

Northern first leg: Fleetwood 1 (Ball 45) Chesterfield 3 (Evatt 21, Morsy 24, Ryan 65). Att: 3,508. **Second leg:** Chesterfield 0 Fleetwood 1 (Parkin 90). Att: 6,358 (Chesterfield won 3-2 on agg)

Southern first leg: Peterborough 2 (Branco 10 og, Vassell 14) Swindon 2 (Ranger 31, Brisley 45 og). Att: 3,312. **Second leg:** Swindon 1 (Pritchard 34) Peterborough 1 (Assombalonga 75). Att: 6,825 (agg: 3-3, Peterborough won 4-3 on pens)

FINAL

Chesterfield 1 Peterborough United 3
Wembley (35,662); Sunday, March 30 2014

Chesterfield (4-4-2): Lee, Darikwa, Evatt (capt), Cooper, Humphreys, Ryan, Morsy, O'Shea (Bennett 72), Banks (Hird 11, Richards 78), Roberts, Doyle. **Subs not used:** Dunbavin, Talbot. **Booked:** Humphreys, Roberts, Darikwa, Cooper. **Scorer:** Doyle (53). **Manager:** Paul Cook

Peterborough United (4-4-1-1): Olejnik, Little, Bostwick, Brisley (Alcock 72), Knight-Percival, McCann (Payne 67), Swanson, Rowe (capt), Newell, McQuoid (Isgrove 83), Assombalonga. **Subs not used:** Day, Ntlhe. **Scorers:** McQuoid (7), Brisley (38), Assombalonga (78 pen). **Booked:** Swanson. **Sent off:** Newell (68). **Manager:** Darren Ferguson

Referee: A D'Urso (Essex). **Half-time:** 0-2

FA CARLSBERG TROPHY

FIRST ROUND

Aldershot 1 Weston-super-Mare 1; Alfreton 0 Nuneaton 1; Altrincham 1 Leek 2; Arlesey 1 Whitehawk 5; Basingstoke 0 Havant 0; Bradford PA 2 Kidderminster 1; Braintree 3 Welling 0; Bury Town 0 Eastleigh 3; Chester 1 Barrow 2; Chorley 2 Curzon Ashton 1; Coalville 1 Grimsby 1; Dartford 1 Forest Green 1; Daventry 0 Maidenhead 1; East Thurrock 1 Dover 1; Ebbsfleet 3 Gloucester 0; Gateshead 4 Hednesford 1; Gosport 1 Concord 0; Halifax 0 Guiseley 1; Hayes 0 Barnet 1; Hendon 1 Whitstable 2; Hereford 0 Woking 3; Hungerford 2 Chesham 0; Hyde 1 North Ferriby 0; Leamington 0 Northwich 0; Lincoln 5 Stalybridge 1; Salisbury 0 Cambridge Utd 1; Southport 1 Boston 0; Staines 0 Luton 0; Tamworth 2 Macclesfield 0; Tonbridge 0 St Albans 0; Worcester 0 Telford 0; Wrexham 2 Gresley 1. **Replays:** Dover 3 East Thurrock 1; Forest Green 1 Dartford 0; Grimsby 3 Coalville 0; Havant 1 Basingstoke 0; Luton 2 Staines 0; Northwich 0 Leamington 1; St Albans 4 Tonbridge 0; Telford 0 Worcester 3; Weston-super-Mare 2 Aldershot 5

SECOND ROUND

Aldershot 4 Worcester 1; Barnet 1 Grimsby 2; Barrow 0 Maidenhead 2; Braintree 1 Lincoln 3; Chorley 0 Forest Green 0; Dover 2 Leamington 0; Eastleigh 2 Gateshead 0; Gosport 0

Nuneaton 0; Guiseley 3 Bradford PA 0; Leek 0 Hungerford 1; Luton 2 Wrexham 0; North Ferriby 4 Woking 0; St Albans 1 Cambridge Utd 2; Tamworth 2 Boston 0; Whitehawk 1 Havant 1; Whitstable 1 Ebbsfleet 2. **Replays:** Forest Green 0 Chorley 0 (aet, Chorley won 3-1 on pens); Havant 3 Whitehawk 1; Nuneaton 0 Gosport 0 (aet, Gosport won 4-3 on pens)

THIRD ROUND
Aldershot 3 Guiseley 0; Cambridge Utd 2 Luton 2; Eastleigh 3 Dover 2; Grimsby 2 Maidenhead 1; Havant 1 Ebbsfleet 0; Hungerford 0 Gosport 1; Lincoln 0 North Ferriby 4; Tamworth 1 Chorley 1. **Replays:** Chorley 2 Tamworth 2 (aet, Tamworth won 6-5 on pens); Luton 0 Cambridge Utd 1

FOURTH ROUND
Eastleigh 0 Cambridge Utd 1; Grimsby 4 Tamworth 1; Havant 4 Aldershot 1; North Ferriby 1 Gosport 2

SEMI-FINALS, FIRST LEG
Cambridge Utd 2 (Bird 21, 56) Grimsby 1 (John-Lewis 90). Att: 3,264. Havant 1 (Ciardini 59) Gosport 1 (Sills 47). Att: 1,314

SEMI-FINALS, SECONE LEG
Gosport 2 (Sills 45, 60) Havant 0. Att: 2,901 (Gosport won 3-1 on agg). Grimsby 1 (Neilson 42) Cambridge Utd 1 (Bird 8). Att: 3,931 (Cambridge Utd won 3-2 on agg)

FINAL

Cambridge United 4 Gosport Borough 0
Wembley (18,120); Sunday, March 23 2014
Cambridge United (4-3-3): Norris, Tait, Miller (capt), Coulson (Bonner 87), Taylor, Berry, Champion, Hughes (Arnold 73), Gillies (Pugh 61), Bird, Donaldson. **Subs not used:** Roberts, Austin. **Scorers:** Bird (38), Donaldson (50, 59), Berry (78 pen). **Manager:** Richard Money
Gosport Borough (4-4-2): Ashmore, Molyneaux, Forbes, Pearce, Poache, Carmichael, Brown (capt), Smith (Woodward 58), Gosney (Wooden 72), Sills (Williams 58), Bennett. **Subs not used:** Wilde, Scott. **Booked:** Pearce. **Manager:** Alex Pike
Referee: C Pawson (Yorks). **Half-time:** 1-0

FINALS – RESULTS

Associated Members' Cup
1984   (Hull) Bournemouth 2 Hull 1

Freight Rover Trophy – Wembley
1985   Wigan 3 Brentford 1
1986   Bristol City 3 Bolton 0
1987   Mansfield 1 Bristol City 1
            (aet; Mansfield won 5-4 on pens)

Sherpa Van Trophy – Wembley
1988   Wolves 2 Burnley 0
1989   Bolton 4 Torquay 1

Leyland Daf Cup – Wembley
1990   Tranmere 2 Bristol Rov 1
1991   Birmingham 3 Tranmere 2

Autoglass Trophy – Wembley
1992   Stoke 1 Stockport 0
1993   Port Vale 2 Stockport 1
1994   Huddersfield 1 Swansea 1
            (aet; Swansea won 3-1 on pens)

Auto Windscreens Shield – Wembley
1995   Birmingham 1 Carlisle 0
            (Birmingham won in sudden-death overtime)
1996   Rotherham 2 Shrewsbury 1
1997   Carlisle 0 Colchester 0
            (aet; Carlisle won 4-3 on pens)
1998   Grimsby 2 Bournemouth 1
            (Grimsby won with golden goal in extra-time)
1999   Wigan 1 Millwall 0
2000   Stoke 2 Bristol City 1

LDV Vans Trophy – Millennium Stadium
2001   Port Vale 2 Brentford 1
2002   Blackpool 4 Cambridge Utd 1
2003   Bristol City 2 Carlisle 0
2004   Blackpool 2 Southend 0
2005   Wrexham 2 Southend 0

Football League Trophy – Millennium Stadium
2006   Swansea 2 Carlisle 1

Johnstone's Paint Trophy – Wembley

2007	Doncaster 3 Bristol Rov 2 (aet) (Millennium Stadium)
2008	MK Dons 2 Grimsby 0
2009	Luton 3 Scunthorpe 2 (aet)
2010	Southampton 4 Carlisle 1
2011	Carlisle 1 Brentford 0
2012	Chesterfield 2 Swindon 0
2013	Crewe 2 Southend 0
2014	Peterborough 3 Chesterfield 1

OTHER LEAGUE CLUBS' CUP COMPETITIONS

FINALS – AT WEMBLEY

Full Members' Cup (Discontinued after 1992)

1985–86	Chelsea 5 Man City 4
1986–87	Blackburn 1 Charlton 0

Simod Cup

1987–88	Reading 4 Luton 1
1988–89	Nottm Forest 4 Everton 3

Zenith Data Systems Cup

1989–90	Chelsea 1 Middlesbrough 0
1990–91	Crystal Palace 4 Everton 1
1991–92	Nottm Forest 3 Southampton 2

Anglo-Italian Cup (Discontinued after 1996
* Home club)

1970	*Napoli 0 Swindon 3
1971	*Bologna 1 Blackpool 2 (aet)
1972	*AS Roma 3 Blackpool 1
1973	*Fiorentina 1 Newcastle 2
1993	Derby 1 Cremonese 3 (at Wembley)
1994	Notts Co 0 Brescia 1 (at Wembley)
1995	Ascoli 1 Notts Co 2 (at Wembley)
1996	Port Vale 2 Genoa 5 (at Wembley)

FA Vase

At Wembley (until 2000 and from 2007)

1975	Hoddesdon 2 Epsom & Ewell 1
1976	Billericay 1 Stamford 0*
1977	Billericay 2 Sheffield 1 (replay Nottingham after a 1-1 at Wembley)
1978	Blue Star 2 Barton Rov 1
1979	Billericay 4 Almondsbury Greenway 1
1980	Stamford 2 Guisborough Town 0
1981	Whickham 3 Willenhall 2*
1982	Forest Green 3 Rainworth MF Welfare 0
1983	VS Rugby 1 Halesowen 0
1984	Stansted 3 Stamford 2
1985	Halesowen 3 Fleetwood 1
1986	Halesowen 3 Southall 0
1987	St Helens 3 Warrington 2
1988	Colne Dynamoes 1 Emley 0*
1989	Tamworth 3 Sudbury 0 (replay Peterborough after a 1-1 at Wembley)
1990	Yeading 1 Bridlington 0 (replay Leeds after 0-0 at Wembley)
1991	Guiseley 3 Gresley Rov 1 (replay Bramall Lane Sheffield after a 4-4

	at Wembley)
1992	Wimborne 5 Guiseley 3
1993	Bridlington 1 Tiverton 0
1994	Diss 2 Taunton 1*
1995	Arlesey 2 Oxford City 1
1996	Brigg Town 3 Clitheroe 0
1997	Whitby Town 3 North Ferriby 0
1998	Tiverton 1 Tow Law 0
1999	Tiverton 1 Bedlington 0
2000	Deal 1 Chippenham 0
2001	Taunton 2 Berkhamsted 1 (Villa Park)
2002	Whitley Bay 1 Tiptree 0* (Villa Park)
2003	Brigg 2 AFC Sudbury 1 (Upton Park)
2004	Winchester 2 AFC Sudbury 0 (St Andrews)
2005	Didcot 3 AFC Sudbury 2 (White Hart Lane)
2006	Nantwich 3 Hillingdon 2 (St Andrews)
2007	Truro 3 AFC Totton 1
2008	Kirkham & Wesham (Fylde) 2 Lowestoft 1
2009	Whitley Bay 2 Glossop 0
2010	Whitley Bay 6 Wroxham 1
2011	Whitley Bay 3 Coalville 2
2012	Dunston 2 West Auckland 0
2013	Spennymoor 2 Tunbridge Wells 1
2014	Sholing 1 West Auckland 0

* After extra-time

FA Trophy Finals
At Wembley

1970	Macclesfield 2 Telford 0
1971	Telford 3 Hillingdon 2
1972	Stafford 3 Barnet 0
1973	Scarborough 2 Wigan 1*
1974	Morecambe 2 Dartford 1
1975	Matlock 4 Scarborough 0
1976	Scarborough 3 Stafford 2*
1977	Scarborough 2 Dag & Red 1
1978	Altrincham 3 Leatherhead 1
1979	Stafford 2 Kettering 0
1980	Dag & Red 2 Mossley 1
1981	Bishop's Stortford 1 Sutton 0
1982	Enfield 1 Altrincham 0*
1983	Telford 2 Northwich 1
1984	Northwich 2 Bangor 1 (replay Stoke

	after a 1-1 at Wembley)	
1985	Wealdstone 2 Boston 1	
1986	Altrincham 1 Runcorn 0	
1987	Kidderminster 2 Burton 1	
	(replay WBA after a 0-0 at Wembley)	
1988	Enfield 3 Telford 2 (replay WBA after a 0-0 at Wembley)	
1989	Telford 1 Macclesfield 0*	
1990	Barrow 3 Leek 0	
1991	Wycombe 2 Kidderminster 1	
1992	Colchester 3 Witton 1	
1993	Wycombe 4 Runcorn 1	
1994	Woking 2 Runcorn 1	
1995	Woking 2 Kidderminster 1	
1996	Macclesfield 3 Northwich 1	
1997	Woking 1 Dag & Red & Redbridge 0*	
1998	Cheltenham 1 Southport 0	
1999	Kingstonian 1 Forest Green 0	
2000	Kingstonian 3 Kettering 2	

At Villa Park

2001	Canvey 1 Forest Green 0
2002	Yeovil 2 Stevenage 0
2003	Burscough 2 Tamworth 1
2004	Hednesford 3 Canvey 2
2005	Grays 1 Hucknall 1* (Grays won 6-5 on pens)

At Upton Park

2006	Grays 2 Woking 0

At Wembley

2007	Stevenage 3 Kidderminster 2
2008	Ebbsfleet 1 Torquay 0
2009	Stevenage 2 York 0
2010	Barrow 2 Stevenage 1*
2011	Darlington 1 Mansfield 0 *
2012	York 2 Newport 0
2013	Wrexham 1 Grimsby 1 *Wrexham won 4-1 on pens)
2014	Cambridge Utd 4 Gosport 0

(*After extra-time)

FA Youth Cup Winners

Year	Winners	Runners-up	Agg
1953	Man Utd	Wolves	9-3
1954	Man Utd	Wolves	5-4
1955	Man Utd	WBA	7-1
1956	Man Utd	Chesterfield	4-3
1957	Man Utd	West Ham	8-2
1958	Wolves	Chelsea	7-6
1959	Blackburn	West Ham	2-1
1960	Chelsea	Preston	5-2
1961	Chelsea	Everton	5-3
1962	Newcastle	Wolves	2-1
1963	West Ham	Liverpool	6-5
1964	Man Utd	Swindon	5-2
1965	Everton	Arsenal	3-2
1966	Arsenal	Sunderland	5-3
1967	Sunderland	Birmingham	2-0
1968	Burnley	Coventry	3-2
1969	Sunderland	WBA	6-3
1970	Tottenham	Coventry	4-3
1971	Arsenal	Cardiff	2-0
1972	Aston Villa	Liverpool	5-2
1973	Ipswich	Bristol City	4-1
1974	Tottenham	Huddersfield	2-1
1975	Ipswich	West Ham	5-1
1976	WBA	Wolves	5-0
1977	Crystal Palace	Everton	1-0
1978	Crystal Palace	Aston Villa	*1-0
1979	Millwall	Man City	2-0
1980	Aston Villa	Man City	3-2
1981	West Ham	Tottenham	2-1
1982	Watford	Man Utd	7-6
1983	Norwich	Everton	6-5
1984	Everton	Stoke	4-2
1985	Newcastle	Watford	4-1
1986	Man City	Man Utd	3-1
1987	Coventry	Charlton	2-1
1988	Arsenal	Doncaster	6-1
1989	Watford	Man City	2-1
1990	Tottenham	Middlesbrough	3-2
1991	Millwall	Sheffield Wed	3-0
1992	Man Utd	Crystal Palace	6-3
1993	Leeds	Man Utd	4-1
1994	Arsenal	Millwall	5-3
1995	Man Utd	Tottenham	†2-2
1996	Liverpool	West Ham	4-1
1997	Leeds	Crystal Palace	3-1
1998	Everton	Blackburn	5-3
1999	West Ham	Coventry	9-0
2000	Arsenal	Coventry	5-1
2001	Arsenal	Blackburn	6-3
2002	Aston Villa	Everton	4-2
2003	Man Utd	Middlesbrough	3-1
2004	Middlesbrough	Aston Villa	4-0
2005	Ipswich	Southampton	3-2
2006	Liverpool	Man City	3-2
2007	Liverpool	Man Utd	††2-2
2008	Man City	Chelsea	4-2
2009	Arsenal	Liverpool	6-2
2010	Chelsea	Aston Villa	3-2
2011	Man Utd	Sheffield Utd	6-3
2012	Chelsea	Blackburn	4-1
2013	Norwich	Chelsea	4-2
2014	Chelsea	Fulham	7-6

(*One match only; †Manchester Utd won 4-3 on pens, ††Liverpool won 4-3 on pens)

WELSH CUP FINAL
New Saints 3 (Draper 73 pen, 78, Wilde 87) Aberystwyth 2 (Venables 10, 12 pen) –
Racecourse Ground, Wrexham. Att: 1,273

FA VASE FINAL
Sholing (Southampton) 1 (McLean 71) West Auckland 0 – Wembley. Att: 5,431

FA WOMEN'S CUP FINAL
Arsenal 2 (Smith 15, Kinga 61) Everton 0 -stadiummk, Milton Keynes. Att: 15,098

FA SUNDAY CUP FINAL
Humbledon Plains Farm (Sunderland) 5 (Davison 3, Croft, Winn) Oyster Martyrs (Liverpool) 2
(Swatton, Rainford) – Ewood, Park Blackburn

FA COMMUNITY SHIELD

CHARITY/COMMUNITY SHIELD RESULTS (POST WAR)
[CHARITY SHIELD]

Year	Winners	Runners-up	Score
1948	Arsenal	Manchester Utd	4-3
1949	Portsmouth	Wolves	*1-1
1950	England World Cup XI	FA Canadian Tour Team	4-2
1951	Tottenham	Newcastle	2-1
1952	Manchester Utd	Newcastle	4-2
1953	Arsenal	Blackpool	3-1
1954	Wolves	WBA	*4-4
1955	Chelsea	Newcastle	3-0
1956	Manchester Utd	Manchester City	1-0
1957	Manchester Utd	Aston Villa	4-0
1958	Bolton	Wolves	4-1
1959	Wolves	Nottm Forest	3-1
1960	Burnley	Wolves	*2-2
1961	Tottenham	FA XI	3-2
1962	Tottenham	Ipswich Town	5-1
1963	Everton	Manchester Utd	4-0
1964	Liverpool	West Ham	*2-2
1965	Manchester Utd	Liverpool	*2-2
1966	Liverpool	Everton	1-0
1967	Manchester Utd	Tottenham	*3-3
1968	Manchester City	WBA	6-1
1969	Leeds	Manchester City	2-1
1970	Everton	Chelsea	2-1
1971	Leicester	Liverpool	1-0
1972	Manchester City	Aston Villa	1-0
1973	Burnley	Manchester City	1-0
1974	Liverpool	Leeds	1-1
	(Liverpool won 6-5 on penalties)		
1975	Derby Co	West Ham	2-0
1976	Liverpool	Southampton	1-0
1977	Liverpool	Manchester Utd	*0-0
1978	Nottm Forest	Ipswich	5-0

1979	Liverpool	Arsenal	3-1
1980	Liverpool	West Ham	1-0
1981	Aston Villa	Tottenham	*2-2
1982	Liverpool	Tottenham	1-0
1983	Manchester Utd	Liverpool	2-0
1984	Everton	Liverpool	1-0
1985	Everton	Manchester Utd	2-0
1986	Everton	Liverpool	*1-1
1987	Everton	Coventry	1-0
1988	Liverpool	Wimbledon	2-1
1989	Liverpool	Arsenal	1-0
1990	Liverpool	Manchester Utd	*1-1
1991	Arsenal	Tottenham	*0-0
1992	Leeds	Liverpool	4-3
1993	Manchester Utd	Arsenal	1-1

(Manchester Utd won 5-4 on penalties)

1994	Manchester Utd	Blackburn	2-0
1995	Everton	Blackburn	1-0
1996	Manchester Utd	Newcastle	4-0
1997	Manchester Utd	Chelsea	1-1

(Manchester Utd won 4-2 on penalties)

1998	Arsenal	Manchester Utd	3-0
1999	Arsenal	Manchester Utd	2-1
2000	Chelsea	Manchester Utd	2-0
2001	Liverpool	Manchester Utd	2-1

COMMUNITY SHIELD

Year	Winners	Runners-up	Score
2002	Arsenal	Liverpool	1-0
2003	Manchester Utd	Arsenal	1-1

(Manchester Utd won 4-3 on penalties)

2004	Arsenal	Manchester Utd	3-1
2005	Chelsea	Arsenal	2-1
2006	Liverpool	Chelsea	2-1
2007	Manchester Utd	Chelsea	1-1

(Manchester Utd won 3-0 on penalties)

| 2008 | Manchester Utd | Portsmouth | 0-0 |

(Manchester Utd won 3-1 on pens)

| 2009 | Chelsea | Manchester Utd | 2-2 |

(Chelsea won 4-1 on pens)

2010	Manchester Utd	Chelsea	3-1
2011	Manchester Utd	Manchester City	3-2
2012	Manchester City	Chelsea	3-2
2013	Manchester Utd	Wigan	2-0

(Fixture played at Wembley 1974–2000 and from 2007); Millennium Stadium 2001–06; Villa Park 2012) * Trophy shared

FOOTBALL'S CHANGING HOMES

AFC Wimbledon are a step closer to returning to the club's 'spiritual' home in Plough Lane. An independent report for Merton Council has confirmed that Wimbledon greyhound track can be used for a new stadium, a decision which means the club are able to proceed with an application for planning permission for the site. 'There is still a long way to go and a lot of hard work to be done,' said AFC chief executive Erik Samuelson. 'But this is a significant moment in our plans and we can now move to the next stage of the process.' The original club had to leave their old ground – now a residential development – in 1991 after publication of the Taylor Report which, in the wake of the Hillsborough disaster, recommended all-seater stadiums. They shared Selhurst Park with Crystal Palace, then moved to Milton Keynes as MK Dons. The new club, founded in 2002 by supporters, worked their way up from the Combined Counties League and returned to the Football League in 2011, playing home games at Kingsmeadow in Kingston upon Thames. AFC believe they have now outgrown that venue and want to build a new 11,000-capacity home.

Queens Park Rangers have unveiled plans for a 40,000-seater stadium in north-west London. It would be part of the major regeneration of an area of industrial and railway land at Old Oak, two-and-a- half-miles from Loftus Road. Clubs officials hope to submit planning permission in early 2015. The proposals for the site include new homes, commercial space, hotel, cinemas and restaurants. **Tottenham** say it is 'feasible' that a move to a new 58,000-capacity stadium next to White Hart Lane could take place by mid-2017. The club anticipate putting out a tender for construction by the end of the year. They have outgrown the present 36,000-capacity ground and lost out to West Ham in a bid to move to the Olympic Stadium. The development is also part of a regeneration scheme for the area, with the club having purchased 18 acres of land over the past decade and relocated 72 businesses.

While **Liverpool** pursue plans to redevelop Anfield and boost capacity to almost 59,000, neighbours Everton have been looking for a site for a new 50,000-seater stadium. **Manchester City** received the go-ahead from local councillors to increase the capacity of the Etihad from 48,000 to about 62,000. A third tier is to be added to the North and South stands, with the completion date set for the 2015-16 season. The stadium will then be the second biggest in the Premier League, behind Manchester United's Old Trafford. **Brentford**, newly promoted to the Championship, have been granted permission to build their new 20,000-seater ground between Kew Bridge and the M4. The news came ahead of a vital game last season against promotion rivals Leyton Orient, which they won to move a step closer to finishing runners-up in League One. Another promoted club, **Scunthorpe** from League Two, want to build a new £18m ground, capacity 12,000, close to Glanford Park, their home since 1988.

Work is under way on a £40m, two-year redevelopment of **Bristol City**'s Ashton Gate which involves knocking down and rebuilding two stands, refurbishing the other two and increasing capacity from 21,000 to 27,000. The first stage has involved laying a new pitch – part turf and part artificial fibres. **Watford** are replacing the old East stand at Vicarage Road with a 2,600-seater structure which will also accommodate dressing rooms and administrative offices. Boundary Park at **Oldham**, now renamed SportsDirect Park, has a new look, with a stand being built on the open north side of the ground. At London Road **Peterborough**, a new stand is under construction at the Moy's End. Workmen have also been busy on redeveloping the East and West stands at Sixfields, **Northampton**.

The **Scottish FA** are considering a number of proposals for Hampden Park, with the lease on the national stadium expiring in 2020. They include exercising an option to renew it, acquiring the freehold from current owners Queen's Park FC – and moving international matches and cup finals to stadiums like Celtic Park, Ibrox and Murrayfield. This summer, Hampden has been temporarily converted to an athletics arena for the Commonwealth Games in Glasgow.

SCOTTISH TABLES 2013–2014

PREMIERSHIP

		P	W	D	L	F	A	W	D	L	F	A	GD	PTS
1	Celtic	38	16	3	0	50	10	15	3	1	52	15	77	99
2	Motherwell	38	13	2	4	39	29	9	2	8	25	31	4	70
3	Aberdeen	38	10	3	5	20	13	10	5	5	33	25	15	68
4	Dundee Utd	38	11	2	6	40	23	5	8	6	25	27	15	58
5	Inverness	38	8	6	5	26	16	8	3	8	18	28	0	57
6	St Johnstone	38	10	4	5	35	16	5	4	10	13	26	6	53
7	Ross	38	8	2	9	25	29	3	5	11	19	33	-18	40
8	St Mirren	38	7	7	5	23	20	3	2	14	16	38	-19	39
9	Kilmarnock	38	7	3	9	25	30	4	3	12	20	36	-21	39
10	Partick	38	2	8	9	21	37	6	6	7	25	28	-19	38
11	Hibernian*	38	4	7	9	20	29	4	4	10	11	22	-20	35
12	Hearts	38	6	3	10	21	29	4	5	10	24	36	-20	23

*Also relegated. League split after 33 games – teams staying in top six and bottom six regardless of points. Celtic into Champions League second qualifying round; Motherwell and St Johnstone into Europa League second qualifying round; Aberdeen into first qualifying round

Play-offs (on agg) – **Quarter-final:** Falkirk 4 Queen of South 3 (aet). **Semi-final:** Hamilton 2 Falkirk 1. **Final:** Hamilton 2 Hibernian 2 (aet, Hamilton won 4-3 on pens)

Player of Year: Kris Commons (Celtic). **Manager of Year:** Derek McInnes (Aberdeen)

PFA Team of Year: Forster (Celtic), Shinnie (Inverness), Van Dijk (Celtic), Reynolds (Aberdeen), Robertson (Dundee Utd), Armstrong (Dundee Utd), Pawlett (Aberdeen), Commons (Celtic), May (St Johnstone), Boyd (Kilmarnock), Ciftci (Dundee Utd)

Leading scorers (all competitions): 32 Commons (Celtic); 27 May (St Johnstone); 22 Boyd (Kilmarnock), McKay (Inverness), Sutton (Motherwell); 21 Stokes (Celtic); 17 Ciftci (Dundee Utd); 16 Thompson (St Mirren); 14 McGinn (Aberdeen); 11 Ainsworth (Motherwell), Doolan (Partick), Paterson (Hearts)

CHAMPIONSHIP

		P	W	D	L	F	A	W	D	L	F	A	GD	PTS
1	Dundee	36	11	4	3	27	9	10	2	6	27	17	28	69
2	Hamilton*	36	12	3	3	43	21	7	7	4	25	20	27	67
3	Falkirk	36	12	4	2	38	13	7	5	6	21	20	26	66
4	Queen of South	36	9	4	5	28	17	7	3	8	25	22	14	55
5	Dumbarton	36	7	5	6	33	28	8	1	9	32	36	1	51
6	Livingston	36	7	4	7	27	24	6	3	9	24	32	-5	46
7	Raith	36	7	4	7	29	33	4	5	9	19	28	-13	42
8	Alloa	36	7	1	10	15	24	4	6	8	19	27	-17	40
9	Cowdenbeath	36	7	3	8	32	30	4	4	10	18	42	-22	40
10	Morton	36	5	6	7	20	23	1	2	15	12	48	-39	26

*Also promoted

Play-offs (on agg) – **Semi-finals:** Cowdenbeath 5 Ayr 2; Dunfermline 4 Stranraer 2, aet. **Final:** Cowdenbeath 4 Dunfermline 1

Player of Year: Kane Hemmings (Cowdenbeath)

PFA Team of the Year: McGovern (Falkirk), McGinn (Dumbarton), Vaulks (Falkirk), Kingsley (Falkirk), Gordon (Hamilton), Andreu (Hamilton), Millar (Falkirk), Crawford (Hamilton), Hemmings (Cowdenbeath), Loy (Falkirk), MacDonald (Dundee)

Leading league scorers: 20 Loy (Falkirk); 18 Hemmings (Cowdenbeath); 17 MacDonald (Dundee), McNulty (Livingston); 13 Andreu (Hamilton), Keatings (Hamilton), Russell (Queen of South); 12 Antoine-Curier (Hamilton), Reilly (Queen of South), Stewart (Cowdenbeath)

LEAGUE ONE

		P	W	D	L	F	A	W	D	L	F	A	GD	PTS
1	Rangers	36	16	2	0	60	12	17	1	0	46	6	88	102
2	Dunfermline	36	9	4	5	33	23	10	2	6	35	31	14	63
3	Stranraer	36	9	4	5	30	22	5	5	8	27	35	0	51
4	Ayr	36	8	3	7	39	33	6	4	8	26	33	-1	49
5	Stenhousemuir	36	5	8	5	30	31	7	4	7	27	35	-9	48
6	Airdrie	36	9	2	7	27	26	3	7	8	20	31	-10	45
7	Forfar	36	6	4	8	27	24	6	3	9	28	38	-7	43
8	Brechin	36	7	4	7	32	34	5	2	11	25	37	-14	42
9	East Fife*	36	5	2	11	15	33	4	3	11	16	36	-38	32
10	Arbroath	36	6	1	11	28	36	3	3	12	24	39	-23	31

*Also relegated

Play-offs (on agg) – **Semi-finals**: East Fife 2 Clyde 2, aet, East Fife won 7-6 on pens; Stirling Alb 8 Annan 4. **Final**: Stirling Alb 3 East Fife 2

Player of Year: Lee Wallace (Rangers)

PFA Team of Year: Bell (Rangers), Williamson (Dunfermline), McCulloch (Rangers), Morris (Dunfermline), Wallace (Rangers), Stirling (Stranraer), Geggan (Dunfermline), Law (Rangers), Moffat (Ayr), Daly (Rangers), Swankie (Forfar)

Leading league scorers: 26 Moffat (Ayr); 18 Daly (Rangers); 17 McCulloch (Rangers); 14 Longworth (Stranraer); 13 Grehan (Stranraer); 12 Cook (Arbroath), Hilson (Forfar), Jackson (Brechin), Trouten (Brechin)

LEAGUE TWO

		P	W	D	L	F	A	W	D	L	F	A	GD	PTS
1	Peterhead	36	11	6	1	37	16	12	1	5	37	22	36	76
2	Annan	36	10	3	5	34	23	9	3	6	35	26	20	63
3	Stirling Alb*	36	9	6	3	34	22	7	4	7	26	28	10	58
4	Clyde	36	9	3	6	29	24	8	3	7	21	24	2	57
5	Berwick	36	10	2	6	38	22	6	8	25	27	14	52
6	Montrose	36	7	4	7	21	24	5	6	7	23	32	-12	46
7	Albion	36	10	2	6	23	20	2	6	10	18	34	-13	44
8	East Stirling	36	6	6	6	26	28	6	2	10	19	31	-14	44
9	Elgin	36	6	3	9	37	33	3	6	9	25	40	-11	36
	Queen's Park	36	2	5	11	17	36	3	4	11	19	32	-32	24

*Also promoted

Player of Year: Rory McAllister (Peterhead)

PFA Team of Year: Smith (Peterhead), Jacobs (Berwick), Noble (Peterhead), Dunlop (Albion), MacDonald (Clyde), Spittal (Queen's Park), Anderson (Queen's Park), Currie (Berwick), MacKay (Annan), McAllister (Peterhead), Rodgers (Peterhead)

Leading scorers: 32 McAllister (Peterhead); 17 Currie (Berwick); 15 Gunn (Elgin), Lavery (Berwick), White (Stirling Alb); 14 Sutherland (Elgin); 13 Mackay (Annan); 12 Todd (Annan); 11 McCluskey (Clyde)

193

SCOTTISH LEAGUE RESULTS 2013–2014

PREMIERSHIP

	Aberdeen	Celtic	Dundee Utd	Hearts	Hibernian	Inverness	Kilmarnock	Motherwell	Partick	Ross Co	St Johnstone	St Mirren
Aberdeen	–	0-2 / 2-1	1-0 / 1-1	1-3	1-0	1-0 / 0-1	2-1 / 2-1	0-1 / 0-1	4-0	1-0	0-0 / 1-0 / 1-1	2-0
Celtic	3-1 / 5-2	–	1-1 / 3-1	2-0	1-0	2-2 / 5-0 / 6-0	4-0	2-0 / 3-0	1-0	2-1 / 1-1	2-1 / 3-0	1-0 / 3-0
Dundee Utd	1-2 / 1-3	0-1 / 0-2	–	4-1	2-2	0-1 / 2-1	1-0 / 3-2	2-2 / 3-1 / 5-1	4-1	1-0	4-0 / 0-1	4-0 / 3-2
Hearts	2-1 / 1-1	1-3 / 0-2	0-0 / 1-2	–	1-0 / 2-0	0-2	0-4 / 5-0	0-1	0-2 / 2-4	2-2 / 2-0	0-2	0-2 / 2-1
Hibernian	0-2 / 0-2	1-1 / 0-4	1-1 / 1-3	2-1 / 1-2	–	0-2	3-0 / 0-1	0-1 / 3-3	1-1 / 1-1	0-0 / 2-1	0-0	2-0 / 2-3
Inverness	3-4 / 0-0	0-1	1-1 / 1-1	2-0 / 0-0	3-0 / 0-0	–	2-1	2-0 / 1-2	1-2 / 1-0	1-2	1-0 / 2-0	3-0 / 2-2
Kilmarnock	0-1	2-5 / 0-3	1-4	2-0 / 4-2	1-2 / 1-1	1-2 / 2-0	–	0-2	2-1 / 1-2	2-0 / 2-2	0-0 / 1-2	2-1 / 1-0
Motherwell	1-3 / 2-2	0-5 / 3-3	0-4 / 4-1	2-1	1-0	2-0 / 2-1	2-1 / 1-2	–	1-0 / 4-3	3-1 / 2-1	4-0 / 2-1	3-0
Partick	0-3 / 3-1	1-2 / 1-5	0-0 / 1-1	1-1 / 2-4	0-1 / 3-1	0-0	1-1 / 1-1	1-5	–	3-3 / 2-3	0-1	0-3 / 1-1
Ross Co	1-0 / 1-1	1-4	2-4 / 3-0	2-1 / 1-2	0-2 / 1-0	0-3 / 1-2	1-2 / 2-1	1-2	1-3 / 1-1	–	1-0	3-0 / 2-1
St Johnstone	0-2	0-1 / 3-3	3-0 / 2-0	1-0 / 3-3	1-2 / 2-0	4-0 / 0-1	3-1	2-0 / 3-0	1-1 / 1-1	4-0 / 0-1	–	2-0
St Mirren	1-1 / 0-1	0-4	4-1	1-1 / 1-1	0-0 / 2-0	0-0	1-1 / 2-0	0-1 / 3-2	1-2 / 0-0	2-1 / 1-0	4-3 / 0-1	–

CHAMPIONSHIP

	Alloa	Cowdenbeath	Dumbarton	Dundee	Falkirk	Hamilton	Livingston	Morton	Queen of South	Raith
Alloa	–	3-1	1-2	0-1	0-0	1-0	1-0	2-0	0-3	1-0
	–	0-1	1-5	0-3	3-0	0-3	0-3	2-0	0-1	0-1
Cowdenbeath	0-2	–	3-2	0-2	1-0	2-4	2-3	5-1	0-2	3-4
	2-2	–	2-4	2-0	0-2	1-1	4-0	3-0	1-1	1-0
Dumbarton	1-1	0-0	–	1-4	1-1	2-1	1-2	3-1	0-1	2-4
	4-1	5-1	–	0-1	2-1	4-1	2-2	2-0	0-3	3-3
Dundee	1-0	1-2	3-0	–	1-1	0-0	3-0	3-1	2-1	2-0
	1-1	4-0	2-1	–	0-1	1-0	0-1	2-0	1-0	0-0
Falkirk	0-0	4-0	1-2	3-1	–	1-2	4-1	3-1	2-1	3-1
	3-1	5-0	2-0	2-0	–	0-0	1-1	1-1	1-0	2-1
Hamilton	0-1	1-0	4-1	0-3	2-0	–	2-0	1-0	2-0	1-1
	2-1	3-4	3-3	1-1	3-1	–	2-0	10-2	3-1	3-2
Livingston	3-2	5-1	1-3	2-1	0-3	0-0	–	2-2	3-3	3-0
	2-0	1-0	1-2	0-2	0-1	1-1	–	0-1	1-2	2-0
Morton	0-2	2-0	2-0	1-2	0-2	1-1	1-5	–	0-2	1-1
	0-1	1-1	3-0	1-0	1-1	3-4	2-0	–	1-1	0-0
Queen of South	0-0	1 1	1 2	4-3	2-0	0-1	2-2	2-0	–	0-1
	3-1	2-1	3-1	0-1	1-2	1-1	2-0	3-0	–	1-0
Raith	4-2	3-3	2-1	0-0	1-1	0-1	1-0	2-1	2-1	–
	1-1	1-2	1-3	0-2	2-4	2-4	2-4	2-1	3-2	–

LEAGUE ONE

	Airdree	Arbroath	Ayr	Brechin	Dunferline	East Fife	Forfar	Rangers	Stenhousemuir	Stranraer
Airdree	–	2-1	0-1	3-1	0-3	1-3	0-2	0-6	0-1	3-2
	–	2-0	3-0	2-1	2-0	2-1	5-1	0-1	1-1	1-1
Arbroath	3-2	–	0-3	2-1	0-3	2-2	3-0	0-3	3-4	1-2
	0-1	–	2-3	0-1	1-2	2-1	2-3	1-2	2-1	4-2
Ayr	2-2	2-0	–	2-2	2-4	2-0	2-0	0-2	4-3	3-6
	3-0	2-1	–	1-3	1-1	4-1	2-3	0-2	2-3	5-0
Brechin	4-3	3-1	1-1	–	1-1	2-0	2-1	3-4	0-1	1-1
	1-1	2-4	2-1	–	3-2	3-0	1-5	1-2	1-3	1-3
Dunfermline	2-1	2-3	5-1	3-1	–	1-2	1-1	0-4	3-2	3-1
	0-1	3-0	3-0	2-1	–	1-2	0-0	1-1	0-0	3-2
East Fife	1-0	2-1	1-4	1-3	0-1	–	1-3	0-4	1-0	1-2
	0-0	1-0	0-5	1-2	1-3	–	2-1	0-1	1-2	1-1
Forfar	3-3	1-1	0-1	2-0	4-0	2-0	–	0-1	1-2	1-2
	1-1	0-2	4-2	1-1	2-4	1-2	–	0-2	3-0	1-0
Rangers	2-0	5-1	3-0	4-1	3-1	5-0	6-1	–	8-0	1-1
	3-0	3-2	2-1	2-1	2-0	2-0	3-0	–	3-3	3-0
Stenhousemuir	1-1	3-2	1-1	3-2	4-5	1-1	1-1	0-2	–	1-0
	1-2	2-2	1-1	4-2	1-2	1-1	4-1	0-4	–	1-1
Stranraer	3-1	3-2	1-1	3-0	1-2	2-0	0-4	0-3	1-0	–
	1-1	1-1	4-0	1-2	3-1	2-0	3-1	0-2	1-1	–

LEAGUE TWO

	Albion	Annan	Berwick	Clyde	East Stirling	Elgin	Montrose	Peterhead	Queen's Park	Stirling Alb
Albion	–	2-0	0-2	3-0	3-2	0-0	0-2	1-2	2-1	2-1
	–	0-2	0-3	1-0	2-1	5-2	1-0	0-0	1-0	0-2
Annan	1-1	–	3-2	1-2	1-2	2-1	2-1	2-0	3-2	4-4
	2-0	–	4-0	0-1	2-3	2-0	1-0	2-1	1-1	1-2
Berwick	2-1	4-2	–	0-1	2-0	2-3	1-1	1-3	4-0	1-1
	3-1	1-4	–	3-0	1-0	2-3	5-0	1-2	1-0	4-0
Clyde	2-2	2-1	1-0	–	1-2	2-1	0-3	1-3	3-0	2-1
	4-0	0-3	3-3	–	1-0	4-0	1-1	0-2	1-2	1-0
East Stirling	1-4	1-1	1-0	0-1	–	3-0	2-2	1-4	1-1	2-2
	1-1	2-1	1-1	2-4	–	3-0	1-2	2-0	1-4	1-0
Elgin	1-2	2-3	2-0	1-0	0-1	–	3-3	2-4	3-2	4-0
	1-1	2-3	1-3	3-1	5-0	–	2-3	2-3	1-1	2-3
Montrose	2-1	0-2	1-1	0-2	2-0	3-3	–	2-1	1-2	1-2
	2-1	2-1	0-0	0-2	2-0	0-3	–	2-3	1-0	0-0
Peterhead	1-1	2-2	1-1	1-1	1-1	2-2	3-0	–	2-1	3-1
	2-0	3-1	3-0	2-0	4-0	2-1	4-0	–	1-0	0-4
Queen's Park	1-1	2-5	0-4	1-1	1-3	3-3	0-1	0-5	–	0-2
	4-0	0-1	1-3	1-3	0-0	2-0	1-1	0-2	–	0-1
Stirling Alb	2-1	0-2	3-1	1-1	1-3	1-1	3-1	2-0	3-0	–
	2-0	1-1	2-1	4-1	2-1	2-2	2-2	1-2	2-2	–

HOW CELTIC WON A THIRD SUCCESSIVE TITLE

AUGUST 2013

3	Celtic 2 (Stokes 28, 88) Ross 1 (Maatsen 3). Att: 45,705
17	Aberdeen 0 Celtic 2 (Commons 45 pen, Forrest 87). Att: 20,017
24	Celtic 2 (Mulgrew 42, Matthews 82) Inverness 2 (Doran 14, Foran 35). Att: 45,160
31	Dundee Utd 0 Celtic 1 (Stokes 87). Att: 10,586

SEPTEMBER 2013

14	Hearts 1 (Holt 58) Celtic 3 (Commons 19 pen, Stokes 65, Pukki 86). Att: 15,928
21	Celtic 2 (Pukki 11, Mulgrew 26) St Johnstone 1 (Caddis 81). Att: 45,220
28	Kilmarnock 2 (Clingan 35, Clohessy 42) Celtic 5 (Commons 20, Samaras 24, 27, 88, Balde 90). Att: 6,149

OCTOBER 2013

5	Celtic 2 (Stokes 21, Commons 49) Motherwell 0. Att: 46,608
19	Hibernian 1 (Heffernan 18) Celtic 1 (Forrest 77). Att: 14,220
26	Partick 1 (Doolan 67) Celtic 2 (Samaras 34, Balde 75). Att: 7,978

NOVEMBER 2013

2	Celtic 1 (Mulgrew 90) Dundee Utd 1 (Armstrong 38). Att: 47,386
9	Ross Co 1 (Sproule 68) Celtic 4 (Van Dijk 41, 53, Ledley 70, 73). Att: 5,982
23	Celtic 3 (Commons 36, 90, Boerrigter 90) Aberdeen 1 (McGinn 45). Att: 49,683

DECEMBER 2013

6	Motherwell 0 Celtic 5 (Commons 44, 76, Ambrose 54, Stokes 78, Atajic 90). Att: 9,117
14	Celtic 1 (Pukki 29) Hibernian 0. Att: 46,065
21	Celtic 2 (Commons 64, Forrest 90) Hearts 0. Att: 46,058
26	St Johnstone 0 Celtic 1 (Van Dijk 5). Att: 7,034
29	Inverness 0 Celtic 1 (Commons 3). Att: 6,384

JANUARY 2014

1	Celtic 1 (Ledley 39) Partick 0. Att: 52,670
5	St Mirren 0 Celtic 4 (Mulgrew 53, Stokes 58, Commons 70, 72). Att: 5,778
18	Celtic 3 (Commons 5, 39 pen, McManus 69 og) Motherwell 0. Att: 47,489
26	Hibernian 0 Celtic 4 (Commons 9, 90 pen, Van Dijk 77, Pukki 83). Att: 12,542
29	Celtic 4 (Ledley 11, Ashcroft 21 og, Mulgrew 68, Balde 90) Kilmarnock 0. Att: 44,271

FEBRUARY 2014

2	Celtic 1 (Commons 6) St Mirren 0. Att: 45,014
16	Celtic 3 (Stokes 16, 64, 66) St Johnstone 0. Att: 45,239
22	Hearts 0 Celtic 2 (Griffiths 58, Pukki 90). Att: 15,801
25	Aberdeen 2 (Hayes 41, Rooney 45) Celtic 1 (Forrest 62). Att: 16,634

MARCH 2014

1	Celtic 5 (Griffiths 12, 57, 86, Mulgrew 22, Commons 78) Inverness 0. Att: 46,552
14	Kilmarnock 0 Celtic 3 (Commons 57, 59, 86). Att: 7,495
22	Celtic 3 (Johansen 44, Griffiths 61, Stokes 90) St Mirren 0. Att: 46,536
26	Partick 1 (Elliott 85) Celtic 5 (Stokes 4, 90, Henderson 49, Johansen 53, Commons 90). Att: 7,549 (clinched title)
29	Celtic 1 (Commons 35) Ross Co 1 (De Leeuw 16). Att: 49,270

APRIL 2014

5	Dundee Utd 0 Celtic 2 (Samaras 5, Stokes 24). Att: 11,033
19	Motherwell 3 (Sutton 5, 90, Francis-Angol 44) Celtic 3 (Stokes 45, Samaras 56, Griffiths 86). Att: 7,493
27	Celtic 6 (Stokes 34, 45, 54 pen, Griffiths 68, Pukki 78, Ambrose 78) Inverness 0. Att: 45,712

MAY 2014

3	Celtic 5 (Brown 25, 44, Stokes 53, Commons 69, 87) Aberdeen 2 (McGinn 28, Logan 56). Att: 47,468
7	St Johnstone 3 (Clancy 9, Brown 84, O'Halloran 86) Celtic 3 (Commons 53 pen, Pukki 74, Van Dijk 77. Att: 4,624
11	Celtic 3 (Stokes 64, Samaras 76 pen, Commons 82) Dundee Utd 1 (Twardzik 79 og). Att: 52,400

SCOTTISH HONOURS LIST

PREMIER DIVISION

	First	Pts	Second	Pts	Third	Pts
1975–6	Rangers	54	Celtic	48	Hibernian	43
1976–7	Celtic	55	Rangers	46	Aberdeen	43
1977–8	Rangers	55	Aberdeen	53	Dundee Utd	40
1978–9	Celtic	48	Rangers	45	Dundee Utd	44
1979–80	Aberdeen	48	Celtic	47	St Mirren	42
1980–81	Celtic	56	Aberdeen	49	Rangers	44
1981–2	Celtic	55	Aberdeen	53	Rangers	43
1982–3	Dundee Utd	56	Celtic	55	Aberdeen	55
1983–4	Aberdeen	57	Celtic	50	Dundee Utd	47
1984–5	Aberdeen	59	Celtic	52	Dundee Utd	47
1985–6	*Celtic	50	Hearts	50	Dundee Utd	47
1986–7	Rangers	69	Celtic	63	Dundee Utd	60
1987–8	Celtic	72	Hearts	62	Rangers	60
1988–9	Rangers	56	Aberdeen	50	Celtic	46
1989–90	Rangers	51	Aberdeen	44	Hearts	44
1990–1	Rangers	55	Aberdeen	53	Celtic	41
1991–2	Rangers	72	Hearts	63	Celtic	62
1992–3	Rangers	73	Aberdeen	64	Celtic	60
1993–4	Rangers	58	Aberdeen	55	Motherwell	54
1994–5	Rangers	69	Motherwell	54	Hibernian	53
1995–6	Rangers	87	Celtic	83	Aberdeen	55
1996–7	Rangers	80	Celtic	75	Dundee Utd	60
1997–8	Celtic	74	Rangers	72	Hearts	67

PREMIER LEAGUE

	First	Pts	Second	Pts	Third	Pts
1998–99	Rangers	77	Celtic	71	St Johnstone	57
1999–2000	Rangers	90	Celtic	69	Hearts	54
2000–01	Celtic	97	Rangers	82	Hibernian	66
2001–02	Celtic	103	Rangers	85	Livingston	58
2002–03	*Rangers	97	Celtic	97	Hearts	63
2003–04	Celtic	98	Rangers	81	Hearts	68
2004–05	Rangers	93	Celtic	92	Hibernian	61
2005–06	Celtic	91	Hearts	74	Rangers	73
2006–07	Celtic	84	Rangers	72	Aberdeen	65
2007–08	Celtic	89	Rangers	86	Motherwell	60
2008–09	Rangers	86	Celtic	82	Hearts	59
2009–10	Rangers	87	Celtic	81	Dundee Utd	63
2010–11	Rangers	93	Celtic	92	Hearts	63
2011–12	Celtic	93	**Rangers	73	Motherwell	62
2012–13	Celtic	79	Motherwell	63	St Johnstone	56

Maximum points: 72 except 1986–8, 1991–4 (88), 1994–2000 (108), 2001–10 (114)
* Won on goal difference. **Deducted 10 pts for administration

PREMIERSHIP

	First	Pts	Second	Pts	Third	Pts
2013–14	Celtic	99	Motherwell	70	Aberdeen	68

FIRST DIVISION (Scottish Championship until 1975–76)

	First	Pts	Second	Pts	Third	Pts
1890–1a	††Dumbarton	29	Rangers	29	Celtic	24
1891–2b	Dumbarton	37	Celtic	35	Hearts	30
1892–3a	Celtic	29	Rangers	28	St Mirren	23
1893–4a	Celtic	29	Hearts	26	St Bernard's	22
1894–5a	Hearts	31	Celtic	26	Rangers	21
1895–6a	Celtic	30	Rangers	26	Hibernian	24
1896–7a	Hearts	28	Hibernian	26	Rangers	25
1897–8a	Celtic	33	Rangers	29	Hibernian	22
1898–9a	Rangers	36	Hearts	26	Celtic	24
1899–1900a	Rangers	32	Celtic	25	Hibernian	24
1900–1c	Rangers	35	Celtic	29	Hibernian	25
1901–2a	Rangers	28	Celtic	26	Hearts	22
1902–3b	Hibernian	37	Dundee	31	Rangers	29
1903–4d	Third Lanark	43	Hearts	39	Rangers	38
1904–5a	†Celtic	41	Rangers	41	Third Lanark	35
1905–6a	Celtic	46	Hearts	39	Rangers	38
1906–7f	Celtic	55	Dundee	48	Rangers	45
1907–8f	Celtic	55	Falkirk	51	Rangers	50
1908–9f	Celtic	51	Dundee	50	Clyde	48
1909–10f	Celtic	54	Falkirk	52	Rangers	49
1910–11f	Rangers	52	Aberdeen	48	Falkirk	44
1911–12f	Rangers	51	Celtic	45	Clyde	42
1912–13f	Rangers	53	Celtic	49	Hearts	41
1913–14g	Celtic	65	Rangers	59	Hearts	54
1914–15g	Celtic	65	Hearts	61	Rangers	50
1915–16g	Celtic	67	Rangers	56	Morton	51
1916–17g	Celtic	64	Morton	54	Rangers	53
1917–18f	Rangers	56	Celtic	55	Kilmarnock	43
1918–19f	Celtic	58	Rangers	57	Morton	47
1919–20h	Rangers	71	Celtic	68	Motherwell	57
1920–1h	Rangers	76	Celtic	66	Hearts	56
1921–2h	Celtic	67	Rangers	66	Raith	56
1922–3g	Rangers	55	Airdrieonians	50	Celtic	40

Season	First		Second		Third	
1923–4g	Rangers	59	Airdrieonians	50	Celtic	41
1924–5g	Rangers	60	Airdrieonians	57	Hibernian	52
1925–6g	Celtic	58	Airdrieonians	50	Hearts	50
1926–7g	Rangers	56	Motherwell	51	Celtic	49
1927–8g	Rangers	60	Celtic	55	Motherwell	55
1928–9g	Rangers	67	Celtic	51	Motherwell	50
1929–30g	Rangers	60	Motherwell	55	Aberdeen	53
1930–1g	Rangers	60	Celtic	58	Motherwell	56
1931–2g	Motherwell	66	Rangers	61	Celtic	48
1932–3g	Rangers	62	Motherwell	59	Hearts	50
1933–4g	Rangers	66	Motherwell	62	Celtic	47
1934–5g	Rangers	55	Celtic	52	Hearts	50
1935–6g	Celtic	68	Rangers	61	Aberdeen	61
1936–7g	Rangers	61	Aberdeen	54	Celtic	52
1937–8g	Celtic	61	Hearts	58	Rangers	49
1938–9f	Rangers	59	Celtic	48	Aberdeen	46
1946–7f	Rangers	46	Hibernian	44	Aberdeen	39
1947–8g	Hibernian	48	Rangers	46	Partick	46
1948–9i	Rangers	46	Dundee	45	Hibernian	39
1949–50i	Rangers	50	Hibernian	49	Hearts	43
1950–1i	Hibernian	48	Rangers	38	Dundee	38
1951–2i	Hibernian	45	Rangers	41	East Fife	37
1952–3i	*Rangers	43	Hibernian	43	East Fife	39
1953–4i	Celtic	43	Hearts	38	Partick	35
1954–5f	Aberdeen	49	Celtic	46	Rangers	41
1955–6f	Rangers	52	Aberdeen	46	Hearts	45
1956–7f	Rangers	55	Hearts	53	Kilmarnock	42
1957–8f	Hearts	62	Rangers	49	Celtic	46
1958–9f	Rangers	50	Hearts	48	Motherwell	44
1959–60f	Hearts	54	Kilmarnock	50	Rangers	42
1960–1f	Rangers	51	Kilmarnock	50	Third Lanark	42
1961–2f	Dundee	54	Rangers	51	Celtic	46
1962–3f	Rangers	57	Kilmarnock	48	Partick	46
1963–4f	Rangers	55	Kilmarnock	49	Celtic	47
1964–5f	*Kilmarnock	50	Hearts	50	Dunfermline	49
1965–6f	Celtic	57	Rangers	55	Kilmarnock	45
1966–7f	Celtic	58	Rangers	55	Clyde	46
1967–8f	Celtic	63	Rangers	61	Hibernian	45
1968–9f	Celtic	54	Rangers	49	Dunfermline	45
1969–70f	Celtic	57	Rangers	45	Hibernian	44
1970–1f	Celtic	56	Aberdeen	54	St Johnstone	44
1971–2f	Celtic	60	Aberdeen	50	Rangers	44
1972–3f	Celtic	57	Rangers	56	Hibernian	45
1973–4f	Celtic	53	Hibernian	49	Rangers	48
1974–5f	Rangers	56	Hibernian	49	Celtic	45

*Won on goal average †Won .... on deciding match ††Title shared. Competition suspended 1940–46 (Second World War)

SCOTTISH CHAMPIONSHIP WINS

Rangers	*54	Hibernian	4	Kilmarnock	1
Celtic	45	Dumbarton	*2	Motherwell	1
Aberdeen	4	Dundee	1	Third Lanark	1
Hearts	4	Dundee Utd	1	(* Incl 1 shared)	

FIRST DIVISION (Since formation of Premier Division)

	First	Pts	Second	Pts	Third	Pts
1975–6d	Partick	41	Kilmarnock	35	Montrose	30
1976–7j	St Mirren	62	Clydebank	58	Dundee	51
1977–8j	*Morton	58	Hearts	58	Dundee	57
1978–9j	Dundee	55	Kilmarnock	54	Clydebank	54

	First		Second		Third	
1979–80j	Hearts	53	Airdrieonians	51	Ayr	44
1980–1j	Hibernian	57	Dundee	52	St Johnstone	51
1981–2j	Motherwell	61	Kilmarnock	51	Hearts	50
1982–3j	St Johnstone	55	Hearts	54	Clydebank	50
1983–4j	Morton	54	Dumbarton	51	Partick	46
1984–5j	Motherwell	50	Clydebank	48	Falkirk	45
1985–6j	Hamilton	56	Falkirk	45	Kilmarnock	44
1986–7k	Morton	57	Dunfermline	56	Dumbarton	53
1987–8k	Hamilton	56	Meadowbank	52	Clydebank	49
1988–9j	Dunfermline	54	Falkirk	52	Clydebank	48
1989–90j	St Johnstone	58	Airdrieonians	54	Clydebank	44
1990–1j	Falkirk	54	Airdrieonians	53	Dundee	52
1991–2k	Dundee	58	Partick	57	Hamilton	57
1992–3k	Raith	65	Kilmarnock	54	Dunfermline	52
1993–4k	Falkirk	66	Dunfermline	65	Airdrieonians	54
1994–5l	Raith	69	Dunfermline	68	Dundee	68
1995–6l	Dunfermline	71	Dundee Utd	67	Morton	67
1996–7l	St Johnstone	80	Airdrieonians	60	Dundee	58
1997–8l	Dundee	70	Falkirk	65	Raith	60
1998–9l	Hibernian	89	Falkirk	66	Ayr	62
1999–2000l	St Mirren	76	Dunfermline	71	Falkirk	68
2000–01l	Livingston	76	Ayr	69	Falkirk	56
2001–02l	Partick	66	Airdie	56	Ayr	52
2002–03l	Falkirk	81	Clyde	72	St Johnstone	67
2003–04l	Inverness	70	Clyde	69	St Johnstone	57
2004–05l	Falkirk	75	St Mirren	60	Clyde	60
2005–06l	St Mirren	76	St Johnstone	66	Hamilton	59
2006–07l	Gretna	66	St Johnstone	65	Dundee	53
2007–08l	Hamilton	76	Dundee	69	St Johnstone	58
2008–09l	St Johnstone	65	Partick	55	Dunfermline	51
2009–10l	Inverness	73	Dundee	61	Dunfermline	58
2010–11l	Dunfermline	70	Raith	60	Falkirk	58
2011–12l	Ross	79	Dundee	55	Falkirk	52
2012–13l	Partick	78	Morton	67	Falkirk	53

CHAMPIONSHIP

	First	Pts	Second	Pts	Third	Pts
2013–14l	Dundee	69	Hamilton	67	Falkirk	66

Maximum points: a, 36; b, 44; c, 40; d, 52; e, 60; f, 68; g, 76; h, 84; i, 60; j, 78; k, 88; l, 108   *Won on goal difference

SECOND DIVISION

	First	Pts	Second	Pts	Third	Pts
1921–2a	Alloa	60	Cowdenbeath	47	Armadale	45
1922–3a	Queen's Park	57	Clydebank	52	St Johnstone	50
1923–4a	St Johnstone	56	Cowdenbeath	55	Bathgate	44
1924–5a	Dundee Utd	50	Clydebank	48	Clyde	47
1925–6a	Dunfermline	59	Clyde	53	Ayr	52
1926–7a	Bo'ness	56	Raith	49	Clydebank	45
1927–8a	Ayr	54	Third Lanark	45	King's Park	44
1928–9b	Dundee Utd	51	Morton	50	Arbroath	47
1929–30a	*Leith Athletic	57	East Fife	57	Albion	54
1930–1a	Third Lanark	61	Dundee Utd	50	Dunfermline	47
1931–2a	*E Stirling	55	St Johnstone	55	Stenhousemuir	46
1932–3c	Hibernian	55	Queen of South	49	Dunfermline	47
1933–4c	Albion	45	Dunfermline	44	Arbroath	44
1934–5c	Third Lanark	52	Arbroath	50	St Bernard's	47
1935–6c	Falkirk	59	St Mirren	52	Morton	48

	First	Pts	Second	Pts	Third	Pts
1936–7c	Ayr	54	Morton	51	St Bernard's	48
1937–8c	Raith	59	Albion	48	Airdrieonians	47
1938–9c	Cowdenbeath	60	Alloa	48	East Fife	48
1946–7d	Dundee Utd	45	Airdrieonians	42	East Fife	31
1947–8e	East Fife	53	Albion	42	Hamilton	40
1948–9e	*Raith	42	Stirling	42	Airdrieonians	41
1949–50e	Morton	47	Airdrieonians	44	St Johnstone	36
1950–1e	*Queen of South	45	Stirling	45	Ayr	36
1951–2e	Clyde	44	Falkirk	43	Ayr	39
1952–3	E Stirling	44	Hamilton	43	Queen's Park	37
1953–4e	Motherwell	45	Kilmarnock	42	Third Lanark	36
1954–5e	Airdrieonians	46	Dunfermline	42	Hamilton	39
1955–6b	Queen's Park	54	Ayr	51	St Johnstone	49
1956–7b	Clyde	64	Third Lanark	51	Cowdenbeath	45
1957–8b	Stirling	55	Dunfermline	53	Arbroath	47
1958–9b	Ayr	60	Arbroath	51	Stenhousemuir	46
1959–60b	St Johnstone	53	Dundee Utd	50	Queen of South	49
1960–1b	Stirling	55	Falkirk	54	Stenhousemuir	50
1961–2b	Clyde	54	Queen of South	53	Morton	44
1962–3b	St Johnstone	53	E Stirling	49	Morton	48
1963–4b	Morton	67	Clyde	53	Arbroath	46
1964–5b	Stirling	59	Hamilton	50	Queen of South	45
1965–6b	Ayr	53	Airdrieonians	50	Queen of South	47
1966–7b	Morton	69	Raith	58	Arbroath	57
1967–8b	St Mirren	62	Arbroath	53	East Fife	49
1968–9b	Motherwell	64	Ayr	53	East Fife	48
1969–70b	Falkirk	56	Cowdenbeath	55	Queen of South	50
1970–1b	Partick	56	East Fife	51	Arbroath	46
1971–2b	*Dumbarton	52	Arbroath	52	Stirling	50
1972–3b	Clyde	56	Dunfermline	52	Raith	47
1973–4b	Airdrieonians	60	Kilmarnock	58	Hamilton	55
1974–5b	Falkirk	54	Queen of South	53	Montrose	53

SECOND DIVISION (MODERN)

	First	Pts	Second	Pts	Third	Pts
1975–6d	*Clydebank	40	Raith	40	Alloa	35
1976–7f	Stirling	55	Alloa	51	Dunfermline	50
1977–8f	*Clyde	53	Raith	53	Dunfermline	48
1978–9f	Berwick	54	Dunfermline	52	Falkirk	50
1979–80f	Falkirk	50	E Stirling	49	Forfar	46
1980–1f	Queen's Park	50	Queen of South	46	Cowdenbeath	45
1981–2f	Clyde	59	Alloa	50	Arbroath	46
1982–3f	Brechin	55	Meadowbank	54	Arbroath	49
1983–4f	Forfar	63	East Fife	47	Berwick	43
1984–5f	Montrose	53	Alloa	50	Dunfermline	49
1985–6f	Dunfermline	57	Queen of South	55	Meadowbank	49
1986–7f	Meadowbank	55	Raith	52	Stirling	52
1987–8f	Ayr	61	St Johnstone	59	Queen's Park	51
1988–9f	Albion	50	Alloa	45	Brechin	43
1989–90f	Brechin	49	Kilmarnock	48	Stirling	47
1990–1f	Stirling	54	Montrose	46	Cowdenbeath	45
1991–2f	Dumbarton	52	Cowdenbeath	51	Alloa	50
1992–3f	Clyde	54	Brechin	53	Stranraer	53
1993–4f	Stranraer	56	Berwick	48	Stenhousemuir	47
1994–5g	Morton	64	Dumbarton	60	Stirling	58
1995–6g	Stirling	81	East Fife	67	Berwick	60
1996–7g	Ayr	77	Hamilton	74	Livingston	64
1997–8g	Stranraer	61	Clydebank	60	Livingston	59
1998–9g	Livingston	77	Inverness	72	Clyde	53

	First		Second		Third	
1999–2000g	Clyde	65	Alloa	64	Ross Co	62
2000–01g	Partick	75	Arbroath	58	Berwick	54
2001–02g	Queen of South	67	Alloa	59	Forfar Athletic	53
2002–03g	Raith	59	Brechin	55	Airdrie	54
2003–04g	Airdrie	70	Hamilton	62	Dumbarton	60
2004–05g	Brechin	72	Stranraer	63	Morton	62
2005–06g	Gretna	88	Morton	70	Peterhead	57
2006–07g	Morton	77	Stirling	69	Raith	62
2007–08g	Ross	73	Airdrie	66	Raith	60
2008–09g	Raith	76	Ayr	74	Brechin	62
2009–10g	*Stirling	65	Alloa	65	Cowdenbeath	59
2010–11g	Livingston	82	*Ayr	59	Forfar	59
2011–12g	Cowdenbeath	71	Arbroath	63	Dumbarton	58
2012–13g	Queen of South	92	Alloa	67	Brechin	61

LEAGUE ONE

	First	Pts	Second	Pts	Third	Pts
2013–14g	Rangers	102	Dunfermline	63	Stranraer	51

Maximum points: a, 76; b, 72; c, 68; d, 52; e, 60; f, 78; g, 108 *Won on goal average/goal difference

THIRD DIVISION (MODERN)

1994–5	Forfar	80	Montrose	67	Ross Co	60
1995–6	Livingston	72	Brechin	63	Caledonian Th	57
1996–7	Inverness	76	Forfar	67	Ross Co	77
1997–8	Alloa	76	Arbroath	68	Ross Co	67
1998–9	Ross Co	77	Stenhousemuir	64	Brechin	59
1999–2000	Queen's Park	69	Berwick	66	Forfar	61
2000–01	*Hamilton	76	Cowdenbeath	76	Brechin	72
2001–02	Brechin	73	Dumbarton	61	Albion	59
2002–03	Morton	72	East Fife	71	Albion	70
2003–04	Stranraer	79	Stirling	77	Gretna	68
2004–05	Gretna	98	Peterhead	78	Cowdenbeath	51
2005–06	*Cowdenbeath	76	Berwick	76	Stenhousemuir	73
2006–07	Berwick	75	Arbroath	70	Queen's Park	68
2007–08	East Fife	88	Stranraer	65	Montrose	59
2008–09	Dumbarton	67	Cowdenbeath	63	East Stirling	61
2009–10	Livingston	78	Forfar	63	East Stirling	61
2010–11	Arbroath	66	Albion	61	Queen's Park	59
2011–12	Alloa	77	Queen's Park	63	Stranraer	58
2012–13	Rangers	83	Peterhead	59	Queen's Park	56

LEAGUE TWO

	First	Pts	Second	Pts	Third	Pts
2013–14	Peterhead	76	Annan	63	Stirling	58

Maximum points: 108 * Won on goal difference

RELEGATED FROM PREMIER DIVISION/PREMIER LEAGUE/PREMIERSHIP

1975–6	Dundee, St Johnstone		1985–6	No relegation
1976–7	Kilmarnock, Hearts		1986–7	Clydebank, Hamilton
1977–8	Ayr, Clydebank		1987–8	Falkirk, Dunfermline, Morton
1978–9	Hearts, Motherwell		1988–9	Hamilton
1979–80	Dundee, Hibernian		1989–90	Dundee
1980–1	Kilmarnock, Hearts		1990–1	No relegation
1981–2	Partick, Airdrieonians		1991–2	St Mirren, Dunfermline
1982–3	Morton, Kilmarnock		1992–3	Falkirk, Airdrieonians
1983–4	St Johnstone, Motherwell		1993–4	St J'stone, Raith, Dundee
1984–5	Dumbarton, Morton		1994–5	Dundee Utd

1995–6	Falkirk, Partick
1996–7	Raith
1997–8	Hibernian
1998–9	Dunfermline
1999–2000	No relegation
2000–01	St Mirren
2001–02	St Johnstone
2002–03	No relegation
2003–04	Partick
2004–05	Dundee
2005–06	Livingston

2006–07	Dunfermline
2007–08	Gretna
2008–09	Inverness
2009–10	Falkirk
2010–11	Hamilton
2011–12	Dunfermline, *Rangers
2012–13	Dundee
2013–14	Hibernian, **Hearts

*Following administration, liquidation and new club formed

**Deducted 15 points for administration

RELEGATED FROM FIRST DIVISION/CHAMPIONSHIP

1975–6	Dunfermline, Clyde
1976–7	Raith, Falkirk
1977–8	Alloa, East Fife
1978–9	Montrose, Queen of South
1979–80	Arbroath, Clyde
1980–1	Stirling, Berwick
1981–2	E Stirling, Queen of South
1982–3	Dunfermline, Queen's Park
1983–4	Raith, Alloa
1984–5	Meadowbank, St Johnstone
1985–6	Ayr, Alloa
1986–7	Brechin, Montrose
1987–8	East Fife, Dumbarton
1988–9	Kilmarnock, Queen of South
1989–90	Albion, Alloa
1990–1	Clyde, Brechin
1991–2	Montrose, Forfar
1992–3	Meadowbank, Cowdenbeath
1993–4	Dumbarton, Stirling, Clyde, Morton, Brechin
1994–5	Ayr, Stranraer

1995–6	Hamilton, Dumbarton
1996–7	Clydebank, East Fife
1997–8	Partick, Stirling
1998–9	Hamilton, Stranraer
1999–2000	Clydebank
2000–01	Morton, Alloa
2001–02	Raith
2002–03	Alloa Athletic, Arbroath
2003–04	Ayr, Brechin
2004–05	Partick, Raith
2005–06	Brechin, Stranraer
2006–07	Airdrie Utd, Ross Co
2007–08	Stirling
2008–09	*Livingston, Clyde
2009–10	Airdrie, Ayr
2010–11	Cowdenbeath, Stirling
2011–12	Ayr, Queen of South
2012–13	Dunfermline, Airdrie
2013–14	Morton

*relegated to Division Three for breaching insolvency rules

RELEGATED FROM SECOND DIVISION/LEAGUE ONE

1993–4	Alloa, Forfar, E Stirling, Montrose, Queen's Park, Arbroath, Albion, Cowdenbeath
1994–5	Meadowbank, Brechin
1995–6	Forfar, Montrose
1996–7	Dumbarton, Berwick
1997–8	Stenhousemuir, Brechin
1998–9	East Fife, Forfar
1999–2000	Hamilton
2000–01	Queen's Park, Stirling
2001–02	Morton

2002–03	Stranraer, Cowdenbeath
2003–04	East Fife, Stenhousemuir
2004–05	Arbroath, Berwick
2005–06	Dumbarton
2006–07	Stranraer, Forfar
2007–08	Cowdenbeath, Berwick
2008–09	Queen's Park, Stranraer
2009–10	Arbroath, Clyde
2010–11	Alloa, Peterhead
2011–12	Stirling
2012–13	Albion
2013–14	East Fife, Arbroath

PREMIERSHIP 2013–2014

(appearances and scorers)

ABERDEEN

Anderson R 27 (3)	Magennis J 1 (17)	Shaughnessy J.......... 20 (6)
Considine A.................21	McGinn N 35 (1)	Smith C.................. 8 (10)
Flood W 31 (2)	McManus D............ - (3)	Storie C.................. - (1)
Hayes J.................. 28 (3)	Murray C................. - (2)	Tate A.................... 5 (2)
Hector M 18 (2)	Pawlett P.............. 33 (2)	Vernon S.............. 14 (11)
Jack R....................34	Reynolds M.................37	Weaver N 1 (1)
Langfield J....................37	Robertson C 5 (3)	Wylde G.................. 3 (5)
Logan S....................13	Robson B.............. 20 (8)	Zola C.................. 11 (9)
Low N.................... 3 (9)	Rooney A....................13	

League goals (53): McGinn 13, Rooney 7, Vernon 6, Pawlett 5, Robson 4, Flood 3, Zola 3, Hayes 2, Jack 2, Reynolds 2, Anderson 1, Hector 1, Logan 1, Low 1, Magennis 1, Wylde 1
Scottish Cup goals (5): Anderson 1, Considine 1, McGinn 1, Pawlett 1, Rooney 1. **Communities Cup goals** (11): Hayes 3, Vernon 3, Considine 1, Pawlett 1, Rooney 1, Shaughnessy 1, Smith 1
Average home league attendance: 12,918

CELTIC

Ambrose E 37 (1)	Henderson L 4 (4)	O'Connell E....................1
Atajic B .... - (3)	Herron J 1	Pukki T.................. 13 (12)
Balde A 3 (17)	Izaguirre E....................34	Rogic T.................. 1 (2)
Biton N.................... 8 (7)	Johansen S 13 (3)	Samaras G 10 (10)
Boerrigter D 5 (10)	Kayal B.................... 7 (6)	Stokes A 30 (3)
Brown S.................. 37 (1)	Ledley J.................. 18 (2)	Twardzik F 1
Commons K 32 (2)	Lustig M 9 (7)	Watt T 1 (1)
Fisher D.................. 10 (2)	Matthews A 21 (2)	Zaluska L....................1
Forrest J 10 (6)	McGeouch D .... - (1)	Van Dijk V 35 (1)
Forster F....................37	Mouyokolo S 1 (1)	
Griffiths L 11 (2)	Mulgrew C.................. 27 (1)	

League goals (102): Commons 27, Stokes 20, Griffiths 7, Pukki 7, Samaras 7, Mulgrew 6, Van Dijk 5, Forrest 4, Ledley 4, Balde 3, Ambrose 2, Brown 2, Johansen 2, Atajic 1, Boerrigter 1, Henderson 1, Matthews 1, Opponents 2
Scottish Cup goals (8): Commons 3, Brown 2, Ledley 1, Lustig 1, Stokes 1. **Communities Cup goals**: None. **Champions League goals** (12): Samaras 4, Forrest 3, Commons 2, Ambrose 1, Kayal 1, Lustig 1
Average home league attendance: 47,079

DUNDEE UNITED

Armstrong S 32 (4)	Fraser S....................- (1)	Oyenuga K .... - (1)
Butcher C....................6	Gauld R 21 (10)	Paton P 36 (1)
Cierzniak R....................37	Gomis M.............. 5 (11)	Rankin J....................35
Ciftci N.............. 27 (5)	Good C....................4	Robertson A....................36
Connolly A .... - (2)	Goodwillie D.............. 9 (10)	Smith S.................. - (2)
Dillon S 22 (1)	Graham B 11 (19)	Souttar J.................. 21 (1)
Dow R 16 (10)	Gunning G 26 (1)	Watson K 24 (1)
El Alagui F 4 (9)	Mackay-Steven G....... 27 (8)	Wilson M 14
Erskine C.................. 4 (4)	McCallum M 1	

League goals (65): Ciftci 11, Armstrong 8, Mackay-Steven 7, Gauld 6, Graham 6, Dow 3, El Alagui 3, Goodwillie 3, Gunning 3, Robertson 3, Watson 3, Paton 2, Rankin 2, Dillon 1, Erskine

1, Good 1, Souttar 1, Opponents 1
Scottish Cup goals (15): Ciftci 4, Armstrong 3, Mackay-Steven 3, Robertson 2, Gauld 1, Graham 1, Gunning 1. **Communites Cup goals** (8): Goodwillie 3, Ciftci 2, Dow 1, Gauld 1, Watson 1
Average home league attendance: 7,547

HEART OF MIDLOTHIAN

Carrick D 14 (11)	McGhee J 14 (3)	Ridgers M 1
Hamill J................... 34 (1)	McGowan D....................37	Robinson S 31 (5)
Holt J 18 (5)	McHattie K 35	Smith D................. 18 (14)
King B...................... 7 (25)	McKay B................... 23 (5)	Stevenson R............. 25 (1)
King A...............................2	Nicholson S 15 (10)	Tapping C 13 (6)
MacDonald J..................37	Oliver G 1 (7)	Walker J................... 21 (5)
McCallum P 4 (2)	Paterson C 36 (1)	Wilson D.........................32

League goals (45): Paterson 11, Stevenson 7, Carrick 6, Hamill 5, Wilson 4, King B 3, Walker 3, Nicholson 2, Holt 1, McGhee 1, Robinson 1, Smith 1
Scottish Cup goals: None. **Communities Cup goals** (7): Hamill 4, McHattie 1, Stevenson 1, Wilson 1
Average home league attendance: 14,123

HIBERNIAN

Boateng D.................. 1 (2)	Haynes D 7 (2)	Stanton S 15 (13)
Cairney P 14 (4)	Heffernan P 13 (6)	Stevenson R............. 33 (2)
Caldwell R .... - (3)	Horribine D .... - (1)	Taiwo T 17 (4)
Collins J 27 (9)	Maybury A....................14	Thomson K 15 (3)
Craig L 31 (3)	McGivern R 31 (2)	Tudur Jones O 8 (6)
Cummings J 9 (7)	McPake J 1 (2)	Vine R 4 (6)
Forster J 26	Mullen F 3	Watmore D 4 (5)
Handling D 10 (9)	Murdoch S 1	Williams B 37
Hanlon P....................28	Nelson M 32 (1)	Zoubir A 3 (10)
Harris A................... 10 (5)	Robertson S 24	

League goals (31): Collins 6, Craig 6, Forster 4, Heffernan 4, Nelson 2, Stanton 2, Cairney 1, Hanlon 1, Haynes 1, Robertson 1, Stevenson 1, Taiwo 1, Whatmore 1. **Play-off – goals** (2): Cummings (2)
Scottish Cup goals (3): Handling 1, Nelson 1, Stanton 1. **Communities Cup goals** (5): Craig 3, Zoubir 1, Opponents 1. **Europa League goals**: None
Average home league attendance: 11,027

Agdestein T............... - (13)	Foran R 23 (1)	Tansey G................... 15 (1)
Brill D 37	Greenhalgh B 1 (5)	Tremarco C............... 20 (1)
Christie R 3 (12)	McKay B........................38	Vincent J 19 (2)
Devine D.................... 8 (5)	Meekings J....................34	Warren G 34
Doran A...........................33	Polworth L 7 (12)	Watkins M.............. 15 (11)
Draper R 33 (1)	Raven D............. 25 (1)	Williams D 11 (9)
Esson R 1	Ross N 25 (8)	
Evans A .... - (2)	Shinnie G 36	

INVERNESS CALEDONIAN THISTLE

League goals (44): McKay 18, Doran 5, Foran 4, Christie 3, Shinnie 3, Tansey 2, Warren 2, Draper 1, Polworth 1, Raven 1, Ross 1, Vincent 1, Watkins 1, Williams 1
Scottish Cup goals (8): Doran 3, McKay 3, Ross 2. **Communities Cup goals** (5): Draper 1, McKay 1, Ross 1, Tansey 1, Warren 1
Average home league attendance: 3,558

KILMARNOCK

Ashcroft L............. 23 (2)	Gardyne M 17 (6)	Muirhead R............ 10 (11)
Barbour R 6 (1)	Gros W 4 (10)	Nicholson B 14 (9)
Barr D 12	Heffernan P 4	O'Hara M 11 (3)
Bouzid I...................4	Irvine J 25 (2)	Pascali M.................. 29 (2)
Boyd K 35 (1)	Jacobs K........................5	Rabiu 6 (4)
Clingan S............... 13 (5)	Johnston C............. 15 (6)	Samson C 38
Clohessy S...............24	Kiltie G................. 3 (2)	Silva D 1 (2)
Eremenko A 9 (4)	Maksimenko V.................8	Slater C 20 (2)
Fisher G.....................1	McKenzie R 28 (5)	Stewart M 1 (3)
Fowler J 6 (3)	McKeown R.............. 6 (3)	Tesselaar J 36
Gabriel R 2	Moberg-Karlsson D...... 2 (2)	Winchester J .... - (4)

League goals (45): Boyd 22, McKenzie 4, Johnston 3, Clohessy 2, Muirhead 2, Nicholson 2, Ashcroft 1, Barr 1, Clingan 1, Eremenko 1, Gardyne 1, Irvine 1, Maksimenko 1, Slater 1, Opponents 2
Scottish Cup goals (2): Barr 1, Johnston 1. **Communities Cup goals:** None
Average home league attendance: 4,250

MOTHERWELL

Ainsworth L............. 22 (7)	Kerr F 10 (9)	Nielsen G...................19
Anier H.................. 19 (14)	Lasley K 37	Ramsden S.................18
Cadden C................... - (3)	Lawson P................. 5 (12)	Reid C 13 (1)
Carswell S 24 (3)	Leitch J 6 (3)	Shirkie D .... - (1)
Cummins A 1 (2)	McFadden J 21 (6)	Sutton J 37 (1)
Francis-Angol Z 21 (12)	McHugh R 3 (5)	Twardzik D 5
Hammell S....................34	McManus S...................37	Vigurs I 33 (3)
Hollis L.......................14	Moore C................. 3 (15)	
Hutchinson S 35	Murray E.................... 1 (2)	

League goals (64): Sutton 22, Ainsworth 11, Anier 9, McFadden 4, McManus 4, Vigurs 4, Francis-Angol 3, Lasley 2, Hutchinson 1, McHugh 1, Moore 1, Reid 1, Opponents 1
Scottish Cup goals: None. **Communities Cup goals** (2): McFadden 1, McHugh 1. **Europa League goals:** None
Average home league attendance: 5,175

PARTICK THISTLE

Baird J 2 (11)	Fox S...........................21	Moncur G.................... - (2)
Balatoni C.....................31	Fraser G 18 (1)	Muirhead A............. 18 (2)
Bannigan S....................33	Gabriel 15 (2)	O'Donnell S............. 23 (4)
Buaben P 9 (2)	Gallacher P............. 17 (1)	Osbourne I............. 11 (1)
Craigen J 26 (5)	Higginbotham K 33 (3)	Sinclair A.......................36
Doolan K................. 22 (14)	Lawless S 17 (11)	Taylor L 17 (3)
Elliott C 11 (19)	Lindsay L .... - (1)	Welsh S 10
Erskine C 14 (1)	Mair L 17	Wilson D .... - (1)
Forbes R 1 (15)	McMillan J.....................16	

League goals (46): Doolan 11, Higginbotham 8, Taylor 7, Lawless 4, Muirhead 3, Erskine 2, Fraser 2, Mair 2, Sinclair 2, Balatoni 1, Elliott 1, Forbes 1, McMillan 1, Moncur 1
Scottish Cup goals: None. **Communities Cup goals** (6): Elliott 2, Balatoni 1, Lawless 1, Muirhead 1, O'Donnell 1
Average home league attendance: 5,001

ROSS COUNTY

Arquin Y 14 (2)	Gordon B 25 (3)	Munro G 5 (1)
Boyd S 27 (1)	Ikonomou E................15	Mustafi O 2 (5)
Brittain R.....................34	Kettlewell S 22 (3)	Quinn R 20 (9)
Brown M.....................28	Kiss F.........................17	Ross S.......................5 (5)
Carey G 31 (5)	Klok M 4 (2)	Saunders S 4 (8)
Cikos E.......................14	Kovacevic M...............13	Slew J 17 (3)
Cooper A 5 (12)	Luckassen K 9 (5)	Songo'o Y 17
De Leeuw M 19 (14)	Maatsen D 2 (8)	Sproule I 7 (3)
Fraser M 10	McLean B 25 (1)	Tidser M 15 (1)
Glen G 4 (11)	Micic B.................. 8 (1)	

League goals (44): De Leeuw 9, Brittain 7, Kiss 6, Arquin 4, Carey 3, Songo'o 3, Kettlewell 2, Quinn 2, Sproule 2, Boyd 1, Cooper 1, Gordon 1, Maatsen 1, Saunders 1, Slew 1
Scottish Cup goals: None. **Communities Cup goals** (2): Brittain 1, Mustafi 1
Average home league attendance: 3,787

ST JOHNSTONE

Anderson S 29	Edwards G 4 (9)	McDonald G 26 (3)
Banks S.........................4	Fallon R 1 (7)	Millar C 26 (6)
Brown S 2 (2)	Hasselbaink N 20 (10)	Miller G 18 (7)
Caddis L .... - (8)	Iwelumo C.................. - (6)	OHalloran M.............. 9 (5)
Clancy T 3 (1)	Jahic S 3 (2)	Scobbie T 18 (3)
Cregg P 13 (7)	Kane C .... - (2)	Thomson C.................. - (1)
Croft L 10 (9)	MacKay D 36	Wotherspoon D 32 (6)
Davidson M 18 (3)	MacLean S 18 (3)	Wright F 25 (1)
Dunne J 13	Mannus A 34	
Easton B 22 (1)	May S 34 (4)	

League goals (48): May 20, MacLean 8, Hasselbaink 5, Mackay 3, Anderson 2, Brown 1, Caddis 1, Clancy 1, Davidson 1, Fallon 1, Miller 1, O'Halloran 1, Wotherspoon 1, Wright 1, Opponents 1
Scottish Cup goals (13): May 4, Anderson 2, MacLean 1, Dunne 1, Hasselbaink 1, Jahic 1, McDonald 1, O'Halloran 1, Wright 1. **Communities Cup goals** (4): May 2, Edwards 1, McDonald 1. **Europa League goals** (3): MacLean 1, May 1, Wright 1
Average home league attendance: 3,806

ST MIRREN

Bahoken S 2 (3)	Harkins G 7 (8)	McLean K 28 (2)
Brady A .... - (1)	Kello M.........................21	Naismith J 26 (1)
Campbell A 7 (4)	Kelly S 32 (1)	Newton C 36 (1)
Caprice J .... - (6)	Magennis J 7 (6)	Reilly T 1 (7)
Cornell D 5	Mair L 5 (1)	Robertson J .... - (1)
Dilo C 12 (1)	McAusland M 30 (2)	Teale G 6 (10)
Djemba-Djemba E...........2	McGinn J 31 (4)	Thompson S 37
Goodwin J 31 (1)	McGowan P 33 (3)	Wylde G 6 (11)
Grainger D 10 (3)	McGregor D 35	Van Zanten D 8 (8)

League goals (39): Thompson 13, McLean 6, McGowan 4, Newton 4, McGinn 3, Campbell 2, Naismith 2, Wylde 2, Harkins 1, Kelly 1, Opponents 1
Scottish Cup goals (6): Thompson 2, Harkins 1, Kelly 1, McLean 1, Newton 1, **Communities Cup goals** (1): Thompson 1
Average home league attendance: 4,511

ABERDEEN WIN FIRST TROPHY FOR 19 YEARS

SECOND ROUND	THIRD ROUND	FOURTH ROUND	SEMI-FINALS	FINAL
*Aberdeen ......†A0	Aberdeen 5	Aberdeen 2	Aberdeen 4	Aberdeen ......†E0
Alloa 0				
*Falkirk 2	*Falkirk 0			
Dunfermline 1				
*Airdrie 0	*Livingston 1	*Motherwell 0		
Livingston 2				
Bye	Motherwell 2			
Bye				
*Morton 4	*Celtic 0	*Morton 0	St Johnstone 0	
Montrose 0				
*Kilmarnock 0	Morton ......†1			
Hamilton 1				
Bye	*Hamilton 0	St Johnstone 1		
Bye				
*Stranraer 3	St Johnstone 3			
Ross 2				
*Raith 1	*Hibernian 5	*Hibernian 0	Hearts 2	
Hearts ......†B1				
	Stranraer 3			
	*Hearts ......†C3	Hearts 1		

*Queen of South .... †2
St Mirren 1

Queen of South 3

*Dumbarton 2
Dundee Utd 3

*Dundee Utd 4

Dundee Utd 1

*Partick .... †3
Cowdenbeath 1

Partick 1

Inverness .... †D2

*Dundee .... †2
Forfar 1

*Dundee 0

Inverness 1

Bye

*Inverness .... †2

Inverness 0

*Drawn at home; †after extra-time; A – Aberdeen won 6-5 on pens; B – Hearts won 5-4 on pens; C – Hearts won 4-2 on pens; D – Inverness won 4-2 on pens; E – Aberdeen won 4-2 on pens; semi-finals: Aberdeen v St Johnstone at Tynecastle, Hearts v Inverness at Easter Road

FIRST ROUND: Airdrie 4 Stenhousemuir 3; Arbroath 0 Montrose 1; Berwick 0 Cowdenbeath 5; Dumbarton 1 Albion 0; East Fife 2 Morton 6 (aet); East Stirling 0 Dunfermline 2; Elgin 1 Livingston 3; Falkirk 3 Clyde 0; Forfar 2 Rangers 1 (aet); Partick 2 Ayr 1; Peterhead 0 Alloa 2; Queen of South 3 Annan 0; Raith 6 Queen's Park 0; Stirling Alb 0 Hamilton 3; Stranraer 4 Brechin 3

SCOTTISH COMMUNITIES LEAGUE CUP FINAL

ABERDEEN 0 INVERNESS CALEDONIAN THISTLE 0
(aet, Aberdeen won 4-2 on pens)
Celtic Park (51,143); Sunday, March 16 2014

Aberdeen (4-4-2): Langfield, Logan, Anderson (capt), Reynolds, Considine (Vernon 109), Robson, Jack, Flood, Hayes (Smith 5, Low 70), McGinn, Rooney. **Subs not used:** Weaver, Tate. **Manager:** Derek McInnes

Inverness Caledonian Thistle (4-4-1-1): Brill, Raven, Devine, Meekings, Shinnie, Watkins (Ross 80), Draper, Tansey, Vincent (Doran 62), Foran (capt) (Christie 99), McKay. **Subs not used:** Esson, Tremarco. **Booked:** Foran, Shinnie, Draper. **Manager:** John Hughes

Referee: S McLean

Penalty shoot-out (Inverness first): McKay saved, Robson 0-1, Tansey missed, Low 0-2, Ross 1-2, Vernon 1-3, Doran 2-3, Rooney 2-4

SCOTTISH LEAGUE CUP FINALS

1946	Aberdeen beat Rangers (3-2)
1947	Rangers beat Aberdeen (4-0)
1948	East Fife beat Falkirk (4-1 after 0-0 draw)
1949	Rangers beat Raith Rov (2-0)
1950	East Fife beat Dunfermline Athletic (3-0)
1951	Motherwell beat Hibernian (3-0)
1952	Dundee beat Rangers (3-2)
1953	Dundee beat Kilmarnock (2-0)
1954	East Fife beat Partick (3-2)
1955	Hearts beat Motherwell (4-2)
1956	Aberdeen beat St Mirren (2-1)
1957	Celtic beat Partick (3-0 after 0-0 draw)
1958	Celtic beat Rangers (7-1)
1959	Hearts beat Partick (5-1)
1960	Hearts beat Third Lanark (2-1)
1961	Rangers beat Kilmarnock (2-0)
1962	Rangers beat Hearts (3-1 after 1-1 draw)
1963	Hearts beat Kilmarnock (1-0)
1964	Rangers beat Morton (5-0)
1965	Rangers beat Celtic (2-1)
1966	Celtic beat Rangers (2-1)
1967	Celtic beat Rangers (1-0)
1968	Celtic beat Dundee (5-3)
1969	Celtic beat Hibernian (6-2)
1970	Celtic beat St Johnstone (1-0)
1971	Rangers beat Celtic (1-0)
1972	Partick beat Celtic (4-1)
1973	Hibernian beat Celtic (2-1)
1974	Dundee beat Celtic (1-0)
1975	Celtic beat Hibernian (6-3)
1976	Rangers beat Celtic (1-0)
1977†	Aberdeen beat Celtic (2-1)
1978†	Rangers beat Celtic (2-1)
1979	Rangers beat Aberdeen (2-1)
1980	Dundee Utd beat Aberdeen (3-0 after 0-0 draw)
1981	Dundee Utd beat Dundee (3-0)
1982	Rangers beat Dundee Utd (2-1)
1983	Celtic beat Rangers (2-1)
1984†	Rangers beat Celtic (3-2)
1985	Rangers beat Dundee Utd (1-0)
1986	Aberdeen beat Hibernian (3-0)
1987	Rangers beat Celtic (2-1)
1988†	Rangers beat Aberdeen (5-3 on pens after 3-3 draw)
1989	Rangers beat Aberdeen (3-2)
1990†	Aberdeen beat Rangers (2-1)
1991†	Rangers beat Celtic (2-1)
1992	Hibernian beat Dunfermline Athletic (2-0)
1993†	Rangers beat Aberdeen (2-1)
1994	Rangers beat Hibernian (2-1)
1995	Raith Rov beat Celtic (6-5 on pens after 2-2 draw)
1996	Aberdeen beat Dundee (2-0)
1997	Rangers beat Hearts (4-3)

1998	Celtic beat Dundee Utd (3-0)
1999	Rangers beat St Johnstone (2-1)
2000	Celtic beat Aberdeen (2-0)
2001	Celtic beat Kilmarnock (3-0)
2002	Rangers beat Ayr (4-0)
2003	Rangers beat Celtic (2-1)
2004	Livingston beat Hibernian (2-0)
2005	Rangers beat Motherwell (5-1)
2006	Celtic beat Dunfermline Athletic (3-0)
2007	Hibernian beat Kilmarnock (5-1)
2008	Rangers beat Dundee Utd (3-2 on pens after 2-2 draw)
2009†	Celtic beat Rangers (2-0)
2010	Rangers beat St Mirren (1-0)
2011†	Rangers beat Celtic (2-1)
2012	Kilmarnock beat Celtic (1-0)
2013	St Mirren beat Hearts (3-2)
2014	Aberdeen beat Inverness Caledonian Thistle (4-2 on pens after 0-0 draw)

(† After extra time; Skol Cup 1985-93, Coca-Cola Cup 1995-97, Co-operative Insurance Cup 1999 onwards)

SUMMARY OF SCOTTISH LEAGUE CUP WINNERS

Rangers	27	East Fife	3	Motherwell	1
Celtic	14	Hibernian	3	Partick	1
Aberdeen	7	Dundee Utd	2	Raith Rov	1
Hearts	4	Kilmarnock	2	St Mirren	1
Dundee	3	Livington	1		

RAMSDENS CUP 2013–14

First round (north-east): Cowdenbeath 1 Dunfermline 3; Elgin 2 Montrose 0; Forfar 2 East Fife 1; Formartine 2 East Stirling 0; Peterhead 2 Brechin 1; Raith 2 Stirling Alb 1; Albion 0 Rangers 4; Stenhousemuir 4 Arbroath 4 (aet, Stenhousemuir won 3-2 on pens)
First round (south-west): Airdrie 2 Hamilton 1; Annan 1 Morton 0; Berwick 3 Livingston 2 (aet); Clyde 1 Falkirk 2; Queen of South 4 Spartans 0; Queen's Park 1 Ayr 2; Stranraer 4 Dumbarton 2; Alloa 0 Dundee 1
Second round: Airdrie 0 Queen of South 2; Ayr 1 Falkirk 2; Dundee 3 Forfar 1 (aet); Dunfermline 0 Raith 2; Formartine 5 Elgin 1; Peterhead 1 Stenhousemuir 3 (aet); Rangers 2 Berwick 0; Stranraer 2 Annan 3
Third round: Annan 4 Formartine 0; Dundee 1 Stenhousemuir 1 (aet, Stenhousemuir won 5-4 on pens); Queen of South 0 Rangers 3 Raith 1 Falkirk 0
Semi-finals: Raith 3 Annan 0; Stenhousemuir 0 Rangers 1

FINAL

RAITH ROVERS 1 RANGERS 0 (aet)
Easter Road (19,983); Sunday, April 6 2014

Raith Rovers (4-4-2): Robinson, Thomson (capt), Watson, Hill, Booth, Anderson, Moon (Mullen 77), Fox, Cardle (Spence 90), Baird, Elliot (P Smith 85). **Subs not used**: Laidlaw, Donaldson. **Scorer**: Baird (117). **Booked**: Fox, Elliot, Cardle, Anderson, Mullen. **Manager**: Grant Murray.
Rangers (4-4-2): Bell, Foster, McCulloch (capt), Mohsni, Wallace (Faure 65), Aird, Black, Hutton (Clark 61), S Smith (Gallagher 111), Daly, Law. **Subs not used**: Simonsen, Shiels.
Booked: Clark, Faure, Black, S Smith. **Manager**: Ally McCoist
Referee: K Clancy. **Half-time**: 0-0

FIRST SCOTTISH CUP SUCCESS FOR ST JOHNSTONE

FOURTH ROUND	FIFTH ROUND	SIXTH ROUND	SEMI-FINALS	FINAL
*St Johnstone ... 2	St Johnstone ... 4	St Johnstone ... 3	St Johnstone ... 2	St Johnstone ... 2
Livingston ... 0				
Brechin ... 1:3	*Forfar ... 0			
Forfar ... 1:1A3				
*Ross ... 0	*Hibernian ... 2	*Raith ... 1		
Hibernian ... 1				
*Dundee ... 0	Raith ... 3			
Raith ... 1				
*Hearts ... 0	*Celtic ... 1	*Aberdeen ... 1	Aberdeen ... 1	
Celtic ... 7				
*Partick ... 0	Aberdeen ... 2			
Aberdeen ... 1				
*Alloa ... 3	*Alloa ... 0	Dumbarton ... 0		
Stirling Alb ... 2				
*Berwick ... 1	Dumbarton ... 1			
Dumbarton ... 3				
*Falkirk ... 0	*Rangers ... 4	*Rangers ... 1:2	Rangers ... 1	
Rangers ... 2				
*Ayr ... 1:0	Dunfermline ... 0			
Dunfermline ... 1:1				
*Albion ... 1	*Albion ... 2	Albion ... 1:0		
Motherwell ... 0				
*Stenhousemuir ... 3	Stenhousemuir ... 0			
Fraserburgh ... 0				

*Clyde	1:1		
Stranraer	1:4		Dundee Utd 0

*Inverness	4	*Stranraer 2:0	
Morton	0		

*Queen of South.	2:0	*Inverness 0	
St Mirren	2:3		Dundee Utd 3

	Inverness 2:2	
	St Mirren 1	Dundee Utd 5

Kilmarnock	2	Dundee Utd 5	
*Dundee Utd.	5	*Dundee Utd. 2	

Drawn at home. †After extra-time. A – Forfar won 4-3 on pens. Both semi-finals at Ibrox Park.

FIRST ROUND: Brora 1 Vale of Laithen 0; Coldstream 0 Wick 6; Deveronvale 5 Clachnacuddin 0; Edinburgh Univ 0 Spartans 2; Forres 4 Keith 5; Fort William 0 Newton Stewart 0; Fraserburgh 4 Civil Service 0; Gala 3 Glasgow Univ 1; Girvan 1 Auchinleck 5; Golspie 0 Edinburgh City 4; Hawick 0 St Cuthbert 1; Huntly 3 Preston 4; Inverurie 3 Burntisland 0; Linlithgow 2 Nairn 0; Lossiemouth 0 Culter 0; Selkirk 1 Turriff 3; Threave 3 Rothes 0; Wigtown 3 Buckie 4. **Replays:** Newton Stewart 3 Fort William 1; Culter 3 Lossiemouth 1

SECOND ROUND: Albion 1 Spartans 0; Auchinleck 4 St Cuthbert 0; Berwick 2 Peterhead 1; Brora 1 Cove 1; Buckie 0 Annan 0; Dalbeattie 0 Montrose 1; Deveronvale 2 Linlithgow 2; East Stirling 6 T'reave 0; Edinburgh City 4 Fraserburgh 4; Formartine 0 Inverurie 2; Gala 0 Clyde 3; Keith 0 Elgin 4; Newton Stewart 0 Culter 6; Queen's Park 2 Preston 2; Stirling Alb 2 Whitehill 2; Turriff 4 Wick 2 **Replays:** Annan 4 Buckie 0; Cove 0 Brora 3; Fraserburgh 2 Edinburgh City 0; Linlithgow 1 Deveronvale 3; Preston 1 Queen's Park 2; Whitehill 1 Stirling Alb 2

THIRD ROUND: Albion 1 Devercnvale 0; Alloa 3 Inverurie 0; Arbroath 0 Brechin 2; Ayr 3 Queen's Park 0; Clyde 2 Brora 1; Culter 1 Berwick 1; Dumbarton 2 Cowdenbeath 1; East Stirling 0 Raith 2; Elgin 3 Dunfermline 5; Forfar 2 East Fife 1; Fraserburgh 2 Montrose 1; Queen of South 1 Hamilton 0; Rangers 3 Airdrie 0; Stenhousemuir 2 Annan 2; Stranraer 2 Auchinleck 2; Turriff 0 Stirling Alb 3. **Replays:** Annan 2 Stenhousemuir 4 (aet); Auchinleck 2 Stranraer 3; Berwick 3 Culter 1

WILLIAM HILL SCOTTISH CUP FINAL

ST JOHNSTONE 2 DUNDEE UNITED 0
Celtic Park (47,345); Saturday, May 17 2014

St Johnstone (4-4-2): Mannus, Mackay (capt), Wright, Anderson, Easton, Millar, Wotherspoon (McDonald 85), Dunne, O'Halloran (Croft 73), MacLean, May. **Scorers:** Anderson (45), MacLean (84). **Booked:** MacLean, Dunne, May. **Manager:** Tommy Wright. **Subs not used:** Banks, Cregg, Hasselbaink, Miller, wellumo. **Manager:** Tommy Wright

Dundee Utd (4-4-2): Cierzniak, Watson, Dillon (capt), Gunning, Robertson, Paton (Graham 77), Rankin, Dow, Armstrong, Mackay-Steven (Gauld 64), Ciftci. **Subs not used:** McCallum, Wilson, Souttar, Gomis, El Alagui. **Booked:** Paton, Gunning, Ciftci. **Manager:** Jackie McNamara

Referee: C Thomson

SCOTTISH FA CUP FINALS

1874	Queen's Park beat Clydesdale (2-0)
1875	Queen's Park beat Renton (3-0)
1876	Queen's Park beat Third Lanark (2-0 after 1-1 draw)
1877	Vale of Leven beat Rangers (3-2 after 0-0, 1-1 draws)
1878	Vale of Leven beat Third Lanark (1-0)
1879	Vale of Leven awarded Cup (Rangers withdrew after 1-1 draw)
1880	Queen's Park beat Thornliebank (3-0)
1881	Queen's Park beat Dumbarton (3-1)
1882	Queen's Park beat Dumbarton (4-1 after 2-2 draw)
1883	Dumbarton beat Vale of Leven (2-1 after 2-2 draw)
1884	Queen's Park awarded Cup (Vale of Leven withdrew from Final)
1885	Renton beat Vale of Leven (3-1 after 0-0 draw)
1886	Queen's Park beat Renton (3-1)
1887	Hibernian beat Dumbarton (2-1)
1888	Renton beat Cambuslang (6-1)
1889	Third Lanark beat Celtic (2-1)
1890	Queen's Park beat Vale of Leven (2-1 after 1-1 draw)
1891	Hearts beat Dumbarton (1-0)
1892	Celtic beat Queen's Park (5-1)
1893	Queen's Park beat Celtic (2-1)
1894	Rangers beat Celtic (3-1)
1895	St Bernard's beat Renton (2-1)
1896	Hearts beat Hibernian (3-1)
1897	Rangers beat Dumbarton (5-1)
1898	Rangers beat Kilmarnock (2-0)
1899	Celtic beat Rangers (2-0)
1900	Celtic beat Queen's Park (4-3)
1901	Hearts beat Celtic (4-3)
1902	Hibernian beat Celtic (1-0)
1903	Rangers beat Hearts (2-0 after 0-0, 1-1 draws)
1904	Celtic beat Rangers (3-2)
1905	Third Lanark beat Rangers (3-1 after 0-0 draw)
1906	Hearts beat Third Lanark (1-0)
1907	Celtic beat Hearts (3-0)
1908	Celtic beat St Mirren (5-1)
1909	Cup withheld because of riot after two drawn games in final between Celtic and Rangers (2-2, 1-1)
1910	Dundee beat Clyde (2-1 after 2-2, 0-0 draws)
1911	Celtic beat Hamilton (2-0 after 0-0 draw)
1912	Celtic beat Clyde (2-0)
1913	Falkirk beat Raith (2-0)
1914	Celtic beat Hibernian (4-1 after 0-0 draw)
1915–19	No competition (World War 1)
1920	Kilmarnock beat Albion (3-2)
1921	Partick beat Rangers (1-0)
1922	Morton beat Rangers (1-0)
1923	Celtic beat Hibernian (1-0)
1924	Airdrieonians beat Hibernian (2-0)
1925	Celtic beat Dundee (2-1)
1926	St Mirren beat Celtic (2-0)
1927	Celtic beat East Fife (3-1)
1928	Rangers beat Celtic (4-0)
1929	Kilmarnock beat Rangers (2-0)
1930	Rangers beat Partick (2-1 after 0-0 draw)

1931	Celtic beat Motherwell (4-2 after 2-2 draw)
1932	Rangers beat Kilmarnock (3-0 after 1-1 draw)
1933	Celtic beat Motherwell (1-0)
1934	Rangers beat St Mirren (5-0)
1935	Rangers beat Hamilton (2-1)
1936	Rangers beat Third Lanark (1-0)
1937	Celtic beat Aberdeen (2-1)
1938	East Fife beat Kilmarnock (4-2 after 1-1 draw)
1939	Clyde beat Motherwell (4-0)
1940–6	No competition (World War 2)
1947	Aberdeen beat Hibernian (2-1)
1948†	Rangers beat Morton (1-0 after 1-1 draw)
1949	Rangers beat Clyde (4-1)
1950	Rangers beat East Fife (3-0)
1951	Celtic beat Motherwell (1-0)
1952	Motherwell beat Dundee (4-0)
1953	Rangers beat Aberdeen (1-0 after 1-1 draw)
1954	Celtic beat Aberdeen (2-1)
1955	Clyde beat Celtic (1-0 after 1-1 draw)
1956	Hearts beat Celtic (3-1)
1957†	Falkirk beat Kilmarnock (2-1 after 1-1 draw)
1958	Clyde beat Hibernian (1-0)
1959	St Mirren beat Aberdeen (3-1)
1960	Rangers beat Kilmarnock (2-0)
1961	Dunfermline beat Celtic (2-0 after 0-0 draw)
1962	Rangers beat St Mirren (2-0)
1963	Rangers beat Celtic (3-0 after 1-1 draw)
1964	Rangers beat Dundee (3-1)
1965	Celtic beat Dunfermline (3-2)
1966	Rangers beat Celtic (1-0 after 0-0 draw)
1967	Celtic beat Aberdeen (2-0)
1968	Dunfermline beat Hearts (3-1)
1969	Celtic beat Rangers (4-0)
1970	Aberdeen beat Celtic (3-1)
1971	Celtic beat Rangers (2-1 after 1-1 draw)
1972	Celtic beat Hibernian (6-1)
1973	Rangers beat Celtic (3-2)
1974	Celtic beat Dundee Utd (3-0)
1975	Celtic beat Airdrieonians (3-1)
1976	Rangers beat Hearts (3-1)
1977	Celtic beat Rangers (1-0)
1978	Rangers beat Aberdeen (2-1)
1979†	Rangers beat Hibernian (3-2 after two 0-0 draws)
1980†	Celtic beat Rangers (1-0)
1981	Rangers beat Dundee Utd (4-1 after 0-0 draw)
1982†	Aberdeen beat Rangers (4-1)
1983†	Aberdeen beat Rangers (1-0)
1984†	Aberdeen beat Celtic (2-1)
1985	Celtic beat Dundee Utd (2-1)
1986	Aberdeen beat Hearts (3-0)
1987†	St Mirren beat Dundee Utd (1-0)
1988	Celtic beat Dundee Utd (2-1)
1989	Celtic beat Rangers (1-0)
1990†	Aberdeen beat Celtic (9-8 on pens after 0-0 draw)
1991†	Motherwell beat Dundee Utd (4-3)
1992	Rangers beat Airdrieonians (2-1)

1993	Rangers beat Aberdeen (2-1)
1994	Dundee Utd beat Rangers (1-0)
1995	Celtic beat Airdrieonians (1-0)
1996	Rangers beat Hearts (5-1)
1997	Kilmarnock beat Falkirk (1-0)
1998	Hearts beat Rangers (2-1)
1999	Rangers beat Celtic (1-0)
2000	Rangers beat Aberdeen (4-0)
2001	Celtic beat Hibernian (3-0)
2002	Rangers beat Celtic (3-2)
2003	Rangers beat Dundee (1-0)
2004	Celtic beat Dunfermline (3-1)
2005	Celtic beat Dundee Utd (1-0)
2006†	Hearts beat Gretna (4-2 on pens after 1-1 draw)
2007	Celtic beat Dunfermline (1-0)
2008	Rangers beat Queen of the South (3-2)
2009	Rangers beat Falkirk (1-0)
2010	Dundee Utd beat Ross Co (3-0)
2011	Celtic beat Motherwell (3-0)
2012	Hearts beat Hibernian (5-1)
2013	Celtic beat Hibernian (3-0)
2014	St Johnstone beat Dundee Utd (2-0)

† After extra time

SUMMARY OF SCOTTISH CUP WINNERS

Celtic 36, Rangers 33, Queen's Park 10, Hearts 8, Aberdeen 7, Clyde 3, Kilmarnock 3, St Mirren 3, Vale of Leven 3, Dundee Utd 2, Dunfermline 2, Falkirk 2, Hibernian 2, Motherwell 2, Renton 2, Third Lanark 2, Airdrieonians 1, Dumbarton 1, Dundee 1, East Fife 1, Morton 1, Partick 1, St Bernard's 1, St Johnstone 1

THE THINGS THEY SAY...

'The only people who should play for England are English people. If you live in England for five years it doesn't make you English' – **Jack Wilshere**, Arsenal's international midfielder.

'They test the border to see how far they can go. If the referees are consistent, they will stop it' – **Arsene Wenger**, Arsenal manager, calls for all players caught swearing to be shown a red card.

'I do understand the pressures they are under. But when you look at the constant protesting on the touchline, the harassing of the fourth official and comments afterwards, it doesn't do anyone or the game any good. It is a terrible example for their players, let alone the general public. It is time managers assumed a much greater level of responsibility for their behaviour' – **David Bernstein**, former FA chairman.

'People talk about the dreaded vote of confidence. But what we say is what we mean. Sam was doing nothing wrong, other than having an injury list which was pretty devastating' – **David Gold** on the backing for manager Sam Allardyce from himself and joint club owner David Sullivan after West Ham conceded 22 goals in six matches.

'It's a great competition and we've got to try as a nation to keep it that way by filling stadiums' – **Tony Pulis**, Crystal Palace manager, on declining FA Cup attendances.

'If I was the invisible man for a day, I'd hang around the QPR dressing room to hear what the players say about me' – **Harry Redknapp**, Loftus Road manager.

SKRILL PREMIER LEAGUE 2013–2014

		P	W	D	L	F	A	W	D	L	F	A	GD	PTS
			Home					**Away**						
1	Luton	46	18	3	2	64	16	12	8	3	38	19	67	101
2	Cambridge*	46	16	4	3	49	14	7	9	7	23	21	37	82
3	Gateshead	46	12	7	4	42	24	10	6	7	30	26	22	79
4	Grimsby	46	11	7	5	40	26	11	5	7	25	20	19	78
5	Halifax	46	16	6	1	55	19	6	5	12	30	39	27	77
6	Braintree	46	12	4	7	27	18	9	7	7	30	21	18	74
7	Kidderminster	46	15	4	4	45	22	5	8	10	21	37	7	72
8	Barnet	46	11	6	6	30	26	8	7	8	28	27	5	70
9	Woking	46	11	4	8	32	30	9	4	10	34	39	-3	68
10	Forest Green	46	13	4	6	47	22	6	4	13	33	44	14	67
11	Alfreton ††	46	13	6	4	45	33	8	1	14	24	41	-5	67
12	Salisbury ***	46	13	6	4	34	21	6	4	13	24	42	-5	67
13	Nuneaton	46	12	4	7	29	25	6	8	9	25	35	-6	66
14	Lincoln	46	10	7	6	30	19	7	7	9	30	40	1	65
15	Macclesfield	46	11	5	7	35	27	7	2	14	27	36	-1	61
16	Welling	46	10	5	8	31	24	6	7	10	28	37	-2	60
17	Wrexham	46	11	5	7	31	21	5	6	12	30	40	0	59
18	Southport	46	13	5	5	33	23	1	6	16	20	48	-18	53
19	Aldershot †	46	11	6	6	48	32	5	7	11	21	30	7	51
20	Hereford**	46	9	6	8	24	24	4	6	13	20	39	-19	51
21	Chester	46	5	12	6	26	30	7	3	13	23	40	-21	51
22	Dartford	46	8	3	12	32	35	4	5	14	17	39	-25	44
23	Tamworth	46	6	7	10	25	31	4	2	17	18	50	-38	39
24	Hyde FC	46	0	3	20	18	57	1	4	18	20	62	-81	10

*also promoted. ** expelled from Conference – failing to play debts; *** demoted to Conference South – failing to pay debts; † deducted 10 pts for adminstration; †† deducted 3 pts for ineligible player.

Leading scorers: 30 Gray (Luton); 29 Gregory (Halifax); 24 Williams (Aldershot); 19 Norwood (Forest Green); 18 Akinde (Alfreton), Boden (Macclesfield), Tomlinson (Lincoln); 17 Benson (Luton), Moult (Nuneaton), Rendell (Woking). **Manager of Year**: John Still (Luton)

Team of Year: Tyler (Luton), McNulty (Luton), Miller (Cambridge), Wells (Braintree), Pearson (Grimsby), Disley (Grimsby), Gutteridge (Luton), Berry (Cambridge), Gray (Luton), Gregory (Halifax), Norwood (Forest Green)

CHAMPIONS

1979–80	Altrincham	1992–93*	Wycombe	2005–06*	Accrington
1980–81	Altrincham	1993–94	Kidderminster	2006–07*	Dagenham
1981–82	Runcorn	1994–95	Macclesfield	2007–08*	Aldershot
1982–83	Enfield	1995–96	Stevenage	2008–09*	Burton
1983–84	Maidstone	1996–97*	Macclesfield	2009–10*	Stevenage
1984–85	Wealdstone	1997–98*	Halifax	2010–11*	Crawley
1985–86	Enfield	1998–99*	Cheltenham	2011–2012*	Fleetwood
1986–87*	Scarborough	1999–2000*	Kidderminster	2012–13*	Mansfield
1987–88*	Lincoln	2000–01*	Rushden	2013–14*	Luton
1988–89*	Maidstone	2001–02*	Boston	*Promoted to Football League
1989–90*	Darlington	2002–03*	Yeovil	Conference – Record
1990–91*	Barnet	2003–04*	Chester	attendance: 11,065 Oxford v
1991–92*	Colchester	2004–05*	Barnet	Woking, December 26, 2006

SKRILL PREMIER LEAGUE RESULTS 2013–2014

Home \ Away	Aldershot	Alfreton	Barnet	Braintree	Cambridge	Chester	Dartford	Forest Green	Gateshead	Grimsby	Halifax	Hereford	Hyde	K'minster	Lincoln	Luton	Macclesfield	Nuneaton	Salisbury	Southport	Tamworth	Welling	Woking	Wrexham
Aldershot	–	2-3	3-3	2-1	0-1	2-0	3-0	2-2	2-2	0-3	1-2	1-2	1-0	0-0	2-3	3-3	1-0	2-2	3-2	5-1	6-0	3-1	2-1	2-0
Alfreton	1-4	–	3-1	1-1	1-1	0-1	2-1	2-0	2-1	3-3	2-1	2-1	0-1	3-1	1-1	0-5	2-0	3-0	0-0	2-1	4-2	2-2	3-1	1-0
Barnet	1-3	3-1	–	1-1	2-2	0-1	2-1	0-0	3-2	0-0	1-0	1-0	3-1	2-1	1-1	1-0	3-3	2-3	0-0	2-1	1-1	0-0	1-1	1-0
Braintree	1-0	1-1	1-1	–	1-0	0-1	1-0	1-2	2-1	0-0	1-0	1-0	0-0	0-1	0-2	0-1	3-2	1-1	0-0	0-0	3-4	0-2	0-3	1-1
Cambridge	4-0	1-1	2-2	1-0	–	0-1	1-1	1-2	1-2	1-2	2-1	1-1	2-1	5-1	3-3	1-1	3-0	2-0	3-1	3-1	2-0	2-1	2-0	3-0
Chester	1-1	0-1	0-1	3-0	0-1	–	0-0	1-4	3-3	1-0	1-1	2-0	3-2	5-1	3-3	1-2	3-2	1-1	2-2	3-1	2-0	0-0	0-2	0-0
Dartford	1-1	0-2	2-1	1-0	2-1	0-0	–	1-0	1-0	1-0	1-1	1-1	2-1	5-1	2-0	0-1	3-1	2-0	3-0	3-0	0-2	2-0	0-0	1-5
Forest Green	4-0	2-1	2-1	0-1	2-1	1-2	1-0	–	1-0	1-0	1-1	1-1	4-3	0-0	5-1	2-0	4-1	1-4	0-1	2-0	2-0	1-2	3-4	1-1
Gateshead	0-0	3-1	3-2	2-1	1-1	3-1	1-1	3-3	–	2-1	2-1	4-0	4-0	1-1	4-1	0-0	2-3	2-1	2-2	1-0	1-2	3-0	2-2	3-1
Grimsby	1-1	2-1	2-0	0-0	1-2	1-0	1-0	4-0	0-1	–	1-2	1-1	1-0	1-1	3-1	2-0	1-1	1-0	2-1	0-2	1-0	1-2	0-2	0-2
Halifax	0-2	3-1	0-1	2-2	5-1	4-3	2-0	2-0	1-0	1-2	–	2-1	8-0	1-1	3-1	0-1	2-1	2-2	5-1	1-0	2-3	1-1	2-2	2-1
Hereford	2-2	2-1	1-0	1-0	2-1	1-1	2-0	0-2	1-1	1-1	1-1	–	4-0	3-1	1-0	0-0	2-3	1-0	4-0	3-1	1-2	3-0	2-2	2-1
Hyde	0-0	3-0	3-1	0-0	7-2	3-2	4-0	4-3	8-0	1-0	1-0	4-0	–	1-3	3-4	0-1	0-3	3-0	1-1	0-3	0-3	3-2	0-1	0-2
K'minster	0-1	3-1	2-1	3-0	5-1	5-1	3-0	3-0	1-1	1-1	3-1	1-1	2-1	–	4-1	0-2	1-1	1-1	1-1	1-1	1-0	2-1	3-2	2-5
Lincoln	1-0	4-1	2-3	3-0	3-3	1-2	2-2	1-2	4-1	0-1	5-1	4-1	3-4	4-1	–	2-2	1-2	2-1	2-1	0-0	1-0	1-0	0-2	3-1
Luton	1-1	3-3	1-0	3-0	1-1	1-2	0-1	2-0	0-0	1-2	2-0	0-0	0-1	0-2	2-2	–	1-0	0-1	1-2	0-1	1-2	0-5	0-2	2-0
Macclesfield	1-0	2-0	3-3	3-2	3-0	3-2	3-1	4-1	2-3	1-1	2-1	2-3	0-3	1-1	1-2	1-0	–	1-0	3-2	2-2	1-1	2-0	2-0	1-2
Nuneaton	1-0	3-0	2-3	1-1	2-0	1-1	2-0	1-4	2-1	1-0	2-2	1-0	3-0	1-1	2-1	0-1	1-0	–	2-1	3-1	1-1	3-0	2-2	1-2
Salisbury	1-0	0-0	0-0	0-0	3-1	2-2	3-0	0-1	2-2	2-1	5-1	4-0	1-1	1-1	2-1	1-2	3-2	2-1	–	4-1	1-2	0-0	1-3	1-1
Southport	1-0	2-1	2-1	0-0	3-1	3-1	3-0	2-0	1-0	0-2	1-0	3-1	0-3	1-1	0-0	0-1	2-2	3-1	4-1	–	4-1	4-3	2-4	3-2
Tamworth	1-0	1-1	1-1	3-4	2-0	2-0	0-2	2-0	1-2	1-0	2-3	1-2	0-3	1-0	1-0	1-2	1-1	1-1	1-2	4-1	–	1-1	2-4	1-1
Welling	1-0	1-2	0-0	0-2	2-1	0-0	2-0	1-2	3-0	1-2	1-1	3-0	3-2	2-1	1-0	0-5	2-0	3-0	0-0	4-3	1-1	–	3-0	2-4
Woking	1-2	2-1	1-1	0-3	2-0	0-2	0-0	2-0	3-4	1-2	2-2	0-2	3-2	0-1	2-0	0-2	2-0	2-2	1-3	2-0	2-0	3-0	–	2-0
Wrexham	2-1	2-3	1-0	2-3	3-0	0-0	1-2	2-1	3-2	0-1	1-1	1-1	0-0	0-0	0-1	0-0	1-2	0-0	1-1	2-0	2-0	2-4	2-0	–

SKRILL NORTH

		Home					Away						
		P	W	D	L	F	A	W	D	L	F	A	GD	PTS
1	Telford	42	16	2	3	46	20	9	8	4	36	33	29	85
2	North Ferriby	42	13	6	2	47	25	11	4	6	33	26	29	82
3	Altrincham *	42	13	5	3	47	21	11	4	6	48	30	44	81
4	Hednesford	42	14	3	4	52	27	10	3	8	35	38	22	78
5	Guiseley	42	14	2	5	35	20	9	7	5	43	36	22	78
6	Boston	42	15	4	2	54	21	5	8	8	31	39	25	72
7	Brackley	42	8	8	5	30	23	9	8	4	36	22	21	67
8	Solihull	42	7	9	5	29	27	10	5	6	34	25	11	65
9	Harrogate **	42	12	6	3	47	24	7	3	11	28	35	16	63
10	Bradford PA	42	7	7	7	36	36	8	5	8	30	34	-4	57
11	Barrow	42	6	8	7	20	28	8	6	7	30	28	-6	56
12	Colwyn Bay	42	5	9	7	26	32	9	4	8	37	35	-4	55
13	Leamington	42	10	3	8	26	19	3	10	8	28	34	1	52
14	Stockport	42	9	7	5	40	27	3	7	11	18	30	1	50
15	Worcester	42	8	6	7	26	22	5	5	11	14	31	-13	50
16	Gainsborough	42	8	4	9	41	40	5	2	14	26	46	-19	45
17	Gloucester	42	7	6	8	36	34	4	5	12	28	43	-13	45
18	Vauxhall	42	9	3	9	27	36	3	5	13	16	38	-31	44
19	Stalybridge	42	6	6	9	34	45	4	3	14	23	43	-31	39
20	Oxford City	42	7	6	8	29	26	2	7	12	21	44	-20	37
21	Histon	42	5	5	11	23	37	2	6	13	19	39	-34	32
22	Workington	42	6	5	10	25	38	0	5	16	14	47	-46	28

* Also promoted. ** 3pts deducted. Play-off Final: Altrincham 2 Guiseley 1 (aet)

SKRILL SOUTH

		Home					Away						
		P	W	D	L	F	A	W	D	L	F	A	GD	PTS
1	Eastleigh	42	17	2	2	40	16	9	6	6	31	24	31	86
2	Sutton	42	15	3	3	44	16	8	9	4	33	23	38	81
3	Bromley	42	15	2	4	54	26	10	3	8	28	24	32	80
4	Ebbsfleet	42	13	5	3	34	14	8	6	7	33	26	27	74
5	Dover *	42	7	6	8	22	19	13	3	5	41	19	25	69
6	Havant	42	13	2	6	36	23	6	10	5	21	20	14	69
7	Bath	42	11	6	4	38	26	7	6	8	26	26	12	66
8	Staines	42	13	5	3	33	22	5	4	12	23	35	-1	63
9	Concord	42	7	5	9	33	34	10	5	6	25	25	-1	61
10	Eastbourne	42	10	5	6	34	27	6	5	10	21	32	-4	58
11	Weston-S-Mare	42	11	4	6	31	25	5	5	11	19	30	-5	57
12	Gosport	42	9	4	8	25	22	7	3	11	21	29	-5	55
13	Boreham Wood	42	6	7	8	36	34	8	4	9	29	21	10	53
14	Basingstoke	42	8	5	8	26	22	7	3	11	29	34	-1	53
15	Bishop's St	42	8	7	6	31	27	5	6	10	32	41	-5	52
16	Farnborough	42	11	2	8	37	29	4	3	14	25	49	-16	50
17	Chelmsford	42	10	4	7	32	30	4	3	14	25	47	-20	49
18	Maidenhead	42	5	4	12	23	35	7	6	8	32	34	-14	46
19	Whitehawk	42	5	8	8	25	34	7	2	12	31	37	-15	46
20	Hayes	42	6	3	12	23	25	7	3	11	22	27	-7	45
21	Tonbridge	42	6	8	7	24	30	3	5	13	19	47	-34	40
22	Dorchester	42	4	5	12	18	45	4	2	15	15	49	-61	31

* Also promoted. Play-off Final: Ebbsfleet 0 Dover 1

OTHER LEAGUES 2013–14

CORBETT SPORTS WELSH PREMIER LEAGUE

	P	W	D	L	F	A	GD	Pts
New Saints	32	22	7	3	87	20	67	73
Airbus*	32	17	9	6	56	34	22	59
Carmarthen	32	14	6	12	54	51	3	48
Bangor	32	14	6	12	47	50	-3	48
Newtown	32	12	6	14	46	58	-12	42
Rhyl	32	11	5	16	43	49	-6	38
Aberystwyth**	32	15	9	8	72	48	24	51
Bala	32	13	6	13	61	45	16	45
Port Tablot	32	10	8	14	45	53	-8	38
Connah's Quay	32	10	8	14	47	65	-18	38
Prestatyn	32	9	8	15	42	47	-5	35
Afan Lido	32	3	6	23	21	100	-79	15

League split after 22 games, with teams staying in top six and bottom six regardless of results won. *1 point deducted; **3 points deducted. Cup Final: Carmarthen 0 Bala 0 (aet). Carmarthen won 3-1 on pens

RYMAN PREMIER LEAGUE

	P	W	D	L	F	A	GD	Pts
Wealdstone	46	28	12	6	99	43	56	96
Kingstonian	46	25	10	11	80	44	36	85
Bognor Regis	46	26	7	13	95	65	30	85
Lowestoft*	46	24	12	10	76	40	36	84
Hornchurch	46	24	11	11	83	53	30	83
Dulwich Hamlet	46	25	7	14	96	65	31	82
Maidstone	46	23	12	11	92	57	35	81
Hendon	46	21	7	18	84	69	15	70
Leiston	46	19	10	17	73	71	2	67
Billericay	46	19	9	18	66	64	2	66
Margate	46	18	10	18	70	67	3	64
Hampton	46	18	10	18	72	70	2	64
Canvey Is	46	17	11	18	65	65	0	62
Grays	46	17	10	19	74	82	-8	61
Bury	46	17	9	20	60	65	-5	60
Lewes	46	14	17	15	67	67	0	59
Met Police	46	15	13	18	58	59	-1	58
Harrow	46	15	13	18	66	72	-6	58
Enfield	46	13	12	21	64	90	-26	51
E Thurrock	46	13	10	23	66	84	-18	49
Wingate	46	14	7	25	57	84	-27	49
Thamesmead	46	12	10	24	61	90	-29	46
Carshalton	46	8	6	32	40	101	-61	30
Cray	46	7	5	34	40	137	-97	26

*Also promoted. Play-off Final: Lowestoft 3 Hornchurch 0

EVOSTICK NORTH PREMIER LEAGUE

	P	W	D	L	F	A	GD	Pts
Chorley	46	29	10	7	107	39	68	97
FC United	46	29	9	8	108	52	56	96
Fylde*	46	28	9	9	97	41	56	93
Worksop	46	27	7	12	120	87	33	88
Ashton	46	24	8	14	92	62	30	80
Skelmersdale	46	24	5	17	92	79	13	77
Rushall	46	21	12	13	79	65	14	75
Blyth	46	20	12	14	79	78	1	72
Whitby	46	18	16	12	82	64	18	70
Trafford	46	20	8	18	77	73	4	68
King's Lynn	46	20	8	18	76	77	-1	68
Matlock	46	18	13	15	61	53	8	67
Buxton	46	16	14	16	63	60	3	62
Barwell	46	17	11	18	62	67	-5	62
Grantham	46	17	10	19	77	78	-1	61
Witton	46	17	9	20	77	80	-3	60
Ilkeston	46	17	8	21	81	77	4	59
Stamford	46	17	7	22	75	85	-10	58
Nantwich	46	14	14	18	77	71	6	56
Marine	46	13	14	19	68	76	-8	53
Frickley	46	12	13	21	62	80	-18	49
Stafford	46	9	8	29	56	112	-56	35
Stocksbridge	46	5	8	33	60	130	-70	23
Droylsden	46	2	3	41	40	182	-142	9

*Also promoted. Play-off Final: Fylde 1 Ashton 1 (aet, Fylde won 4-3 on pens)

CALOR SOUTH PREMIER LEAGUE

	P	W	D	L	F	A	GD	Pts
Hemel Hempstead	44	32	6	6	128	38	90	102
Chesham	44	29	5	10	102	47	55	92
Cambridge City	44	27	7	10	95	49	46	88
St Albans*	44	25	10	9	89	49	40	85
Stourbridge	44	26	6	12	114	54	60	84
Hungerford	44	26	6	12	83	45	38	84
Poole **	44	25	10	9	82	48	34	82
Bideford	44	18	13	13	75	64	11	67
Biggleswade	44	16	16	12	85	61	24	64
Redditch	44	20	3	21	68	85	-17	63
Corby	44	18	6	20	65	68	-3	60
Weymouth	44	18	6	20	69	80	-11	60
Hitchin	44	16	11	17	63	52	11	59
Frome	44	16	9	19	63	74	-11	57
Arlesey	44	15	10	19	68	79	-11	55
St Neots	44	15	9	20	74	76	-2	54
Truro	44	15	9	20	68	84	-16	54
Chippenham	44	14	6	24	59	87	-28	48
Banbury	44	14	5	25	64	116	-52	47
Burnham	44	12	8	24	60	91	-31	44
Totton	44	10	7	27	58	119	-61	37
Bedford	44	6	6	32	46	114	-68	24
Bashley	44	4	4	36	33	131	-98	16

*Also promoted. ** 3pts deducted. Play-off Final: St Albans 3 Chesham 1.

PRESS AND JOURNAL HIGHLAND LEAGUE

	P	W	D	L	F	A	GD	Pts
Brora	34	31	2	1	123	16	107	95
Inverurie	34	23	6	5	97	39	58	75
Nairn	34	24	3	7	86	39	47	75
Formartine	34	22	6	6	88	36	52	72
Fraserburgh	34	23	2	9	89	44	45	71
Deveronvale	34	20	5	9	64	43	21	65
Cove	34	16	7	11	91	62	29	55
Wick	34	15	8	11	83	54	29	53
Forres	34	15	7	12	68	50	18	52
Buckie	34	13	10	11	54	48	6	49
Clachnacuddin	34	13	7	14	67	64	3	46
Turriff	34	13	5	16	60	57	3	44
Huntly	34	9	8	17	55	82	-27	35
Keith	34	9	2	23	50	98	-48	29
Lossiemouth	34	4	8	22	34	93	-59	20
Strathspey	34	3	3	28	28	116	-88	12
Rothes	34	3	3	28	36	136	-100	12
Fort William	34	1	6	27	35	131	-96	9

Cup Final: Clachnacuddin 3 Buckie 3 (aet, Clachnacuddin won 4-3 on pens)

BARCLAYS UNDER-21 PREMIER LEAGUE

	P	W	D	L	F	A	GD	Pts
Chelsea	21	13	5	3	49	26	23	44
Liverpool	21	13	3	5	55	30	25	42
Manchester Utd	21	11	6	4	34	18	16	39
Manchester City	21	12	2	7	50	28	22	38
Fulham	21	11	5	5	38	30	8	38
Leicester	21	11	4	6	37	30	7	37
Southampton	21	11	3	7	35	30	5	36
Sunderland	21	10	5	6	39	32	7	35
West Ham	21	10	3	8	34	32	2	33
Norwich	21	9	4	8	34	29	5	31
Everton	21	8	6	7	28	29	-1	30
Tottenham	21	8	4	9	40	43	-3	28
Bolton	21	8	3	10	40	47	-7	27
Arsenal	21	7	5	9	35	41	-6	26
Aston Villa	21	8	2	11	36	43	-7	26
WBA	21	8	1	12	35	43	-8	25
Reading	21	7	3	11	36	43	-7	24
Stoke	21	6	4	11	26	34	-8	22
Middlesbrough	21	6	2	13	25	37	-12	20
Wolves	21	6	2	13	26	41	-15	20
Newcastle	21	4	5	12	37	54	-17	17
Blackburn	21	3	5	13	18	47	-29	14

Play-off Final: Manchester Utd 1 Chelsea 2

IRISH FOOTBALL 2013–14

AIRTRICITY LEAGUE OF IRELAND

PREMIER DIVISION

	P	W	D	L	F	A	Pts
St Patrick's Ath	33	21	8	4	56	20	71
Dundalk	33	21	5	7	55	30	68
Sligo Rov	33	19	9	5	53	22	66
Derry City	33	17	5	11	57	39	56
Shamrock Rov	33	13	13	7	43	28	52
Cork City	33	13	7	13	47	50	46
Limerick	33	11	9	13	38	56	42
Drogheda Utd	33	8	14	11	44	46	38
UCD	33	8	6	19	45	73	30
Bohemians	33	7	8	18	27	47	29
Bray Wdrs	33	7	6	20	33	66	27
Shelbourne	33	5	6	22	25	56	21

Leading scorer: 18 Rory Patterson (Derry City). **Player of Year:** Killian Brennan (St Patrick's Ath).
Young Player of Year: Richie Towell (Dundalk). **Goalkeeper of Year:** Brendan Clarke (St Patrick's Ath). **Personality of Year:** Liam Buckley (St Patrick's Ath)

FIRST DIVISION

	P	W	D	L	F	A	Pts
Athlone Town	28	16	7	5	42	22	55
Longford Town	28	15	-5	8	55	34	50
Mervue Utd	28	14	7	7	46	31	49
Waterford Utd	28	14	5	9	40	24	47
Wexford Youths	28	10	3	15	28	47	33
Finn Harps	28	8	7	13	31	42	31
Cobh Ramblers	28	8	7	13	42	54	31
Salthill Devon	28	4	5	19	23	54	17

Leading scorer: 24 David O'Sullivan (Longford Town). **Player of Year:** Philip Gorman (Athlone Town)

FAI FORD CUP FINAL

Sligo Rov 3 (North 2, Elding) **Drogheda Utd** 2 (O'Connor, R Brennan). Aviva Stadium, Dublin, November 3, 2013
Sligo Rov: Rogers, Keane, Peers, Henderson (McMillan), Davoren, Ndo, Ventre, Cretaro (North), Djilali, Greene (Gaynor), Elding
Drogheda Utd: Schlingermann, Daly, McNally, Prendergast, Grimes, Byrne (Hynes), Cassidy, O'Connor (Rusk), R Brennan, G Brennan, O'Brien
Referee: P Tuite (Dublin)

EA SPORTS LEAGUE CUP FINAL

Shamrock Rov 2 (McCabe pen, Stewart) **Drogheda Utd** 0. Tallaght Stadium, Dublin, September 21, 2013

SETANTA SPORTS CUP FINAL

Sligo Rov 1 (O'Conor) **Dundalk** 0. Tallaght Stadium, Dublin, May 10, 2014

DANSKE BANK PREMIERSHIP

	P	W	D	L	F	A	Pts
Cliftonville	38	26	7	5	88	39	85
Linfield	38	24	7	7	81	46	79
Crusaders	38	18	12	8	67	42	66
Portadown	38	18	8	12	77	53	62
Glentoran	38	16	11	11	54	42	59
Glenavon	38	15	6	17	75	79	51
Ballymena Utd	38	13	8	17	48	59	47
Dungannon Swifts	38	12	8	18	49	66	44
Coleraine	38	10	12	16	51	61	42
Ballinamallard Utd	38	10	9	19	35	70	39
Warrenpoint Town	38	10	6	22	43	72	36
Ards	38	6	6	26	44	83	24

Leading scorer: 27 Joe Gormley (Cliftonville). **Player of Year**: Joe Gormley. **Young Player of Year**: Rhys Marshall (Glenavon). **Manager of Year**: Tommy Breslin (Cliftonville)

BELFAST TELEGRAPH CHAMPIONSHIP – DIVISION 1

	P	W	D	L	F	A	Pts
Institute	26	15	9	2	72	35	54
Bangor	26	16	5	5	65	39	53
Knockbreda	26	14	4	8	57	36	46
Dundela	26	14	4	8	65	47	46
Carrick Rgrs	26	14	4	8	52	34	46
HW Welders	26	11	8	7	46	34	41
Ballyclare Comrades	26	10	4	12	53	50	34
Loughall	26	9	6	11	48	56	33
Larne	26	9	5	12	32	47	32
Lisburn Distillery	26	8	7	11	43	49	31
Donegal Celtic	26	8	5	13	41	55	29
Dergview	26	6	8	12	30	46	26
Coagh Utd	26	5	6	15	38	74	21
Limavady Utd	26	4	3	19	19	59	15

Leading scorer: 29 Miguel Chines (Knockbreda). **Player of Year**: Michael McCrudden (Institute)

MARIE CURIE IRISH CUP FINAL

Glenavon 2 (Neill, Patton) **Ballymena Utd** 1 (Jenkins). Windsor Park, May 3, 2014
Glenavon: McGrath, Marshall, Lindsay, McKeown, Singleton, McGrory, McCabe, Martyn, Neill (Patton), Bates (Hamilton), Mulvenna (Murphy). Sent off: McKeown
Ballymena Utd: Shanahan, Ervin (Taggart), Munster (Stewart), Taylor, McBride, Kane, Thompson, Jenkins, Cushley, Boyce (Davidson), Teggart. Sent off: Thompson, Kane
Referee: R Crangle (Belfast)

LEAGUE CUP FINAL

Cliftonville 0 **Crusaders** 0 – aet, Cliftonville won 3-2 on pens. Solitude, Belfast, January 25, 2014

PADDY POWER COUNTY ANTRIM SHIELD FINAL

Linfield 0 **Crusaders** 0 – aet, Linfield won 4-1 on pens. Ballymena Showgrounds, March 4, 2014

UEFA CHAMPIONS LEAGUE 2013–14

FIRST QUALIFYING ROUND, ON AGGREGATE

Shirak 3 Tre Penne 1; Streymur 7 Lusitanos 3

SECOND QUALIFYING ROUND, FIRST LEG

Cliftonville 0 Celtic 3 (Lustig 25, Samaras 31, Forrest 84). Att: 5,442. **New Saints** 1 (Fraughan 12) Legia Warsaw 3 (Kucharczyk 48, Saganowski 58, Kosecki 75). Att: 2,925. **Sligo** 0 Molde 1 (Chukwa 43). Att: 3,840

SECOND QUALIFYING ROUND, SECOND LEG

Celtic 2 (Ambrose 16, Samaras 70) **Cliftonville** 0. Att: 29,758 (**Celtic** won 5-0 on agg). Legia Warsaw 1 (Dvalishvili 54) **New Saints** 0. Att: 11,712 (Legia Warsaw won 4-1 on agg). Molde 2 (Linnes 6, Coly 73) **Sligo** 0. Att: 5,765 (Molde won 3-0 on agg)

SECOND QUALIFYING ROUND, ON AGGREGATE

Dinamo Tbilisi 9 Streymur 2; Dinamo Zagreb 6 Fola Esch 0; Elfsborg 11 Daugava 1; Hafnarfjardar 3 Ekranas 1; Ludogorets 4 Slovan Bratislava 2; Maccabi Tel Aviv 4 Gyor 1; Maribor 2 Birkirkara 0; Nomme Kalju 2 HJK Helsinki 1; Partizan 1 Shirak 1 (Partizan won on away goal); Plzen 6 Zeljeznicar 4 Shakhtyor Karagandy 2 Bate Borisov 0; Sherriff Tiraspol 6 Sutjeska 1; Skenderbeu 1 Neftchi 0 (aet); Steaua Bucharest 5 Vardar Skopje 1

THIRD QUALIFYING ROUND, FIRST LEG

Celtic 1 (Commons 76) Elfsborg 0. Att: 40,153

THIRD QUALIFYING ROUND, SECOND LEG

Elfsborg 0 **Celtic** 0. Att: 9,040 (**Celtic** won 1-0 on agg)

THIRD QUALIFYING ROUND, ON AGGREGATE

Austria Vienna 1 Hafnarfjardar 0; Basle 4 Maccabi Tel Aviv 3; Dinamo Zagreb 4 Sherriff Tiraspol 0; Fenerbahce 4 Salzburg 2; Legia Warsaw 1 Molde 1 (Legia Warsaw won on away goal); Ludogorets 3 Partizan 1; Lyon 2 Grasshoppers 0; Maribor 1 Apoel Nicosia 1 (Maribor won on away goal); Metalist Kharkiv 3 PAOK Salonika 1 (Metalist Kharkiv disqualified over match fixing); Plzen 10 Nomme Kalju 2; PSV 5 Zulte-Waregem 0; Shakhtyor Karagandy 5 Skenderbeu 3; Steaua Bucharest 3 Dinamo Tbilisi 1; Zenit St Petersburg 6 Nordsjaelland 0

PLAY-OFF ROUND, FIRST LEG

Fenerbahce 0 **Arsenal** 3 (Gibbs 51, Ramsey 64, Giroud 77 pen). Att: 40,375. Shakhtyor Karangandy 2 (Finonchenko 12, Khizhnichenko 77) **Celtic** 0. Att: 20,000

PLAY-OFF ROUND, SECOND LEG

Arsenal 2 (Ramsey 25, 72) Fenerbahce 0. Att: 56,271 (Arsenal won 5-0 on agg). **Celtic** 3 (Commons 45, Samaras 48, Forrest 90) Shakhtyor Karagandy 0. Att: 50,063 (Celtic won 3-2 on agg)

PLAY-OFF ROUND, ON AGGREGATE

AC Milan 4 PSV 1; Austria Vienna 4 Dinamo Zagreb 3; Basle 6 Ludogorets 2; Plzen 4 Maribor

1; Real Sociedad 4 Lyon 0; Schalke 4 PAOK Salonika 3; Steaua Bucharest 3 Legia Warsaw 3 (Steaua Bucharest won on away goals); Zenit St Petersburg 8 Pacos Ferreira 3

GROUP A

September 17, 2013
Manchester Utd 4 (Rooney 22, 70, Van Persie 59, Valencia 79) **Bayer Leverkusen** 2 (Rolfes 54, Toprak 88). Att: 75,811
Manchester Utd (4-4-2): De Gea, Smalling, Ferdinand, Vidic, Evra, Valencia, Carrick, Fellaini (Cleverey 80), Kagawa (Young 70), Rooney (Hernandez 86), Van Persie. **Booked:** Van Persie
Real Sociedad 0 **Shakhtar Donetsk** 2 (Teixeira 65, 87). Att: 27,902

October 2, 2013
Bayer Leverkusen 2 (Rolfes 45, Hegeler 90) **Real Sociedad** 1 (Vela 51). Att: 27,462
Shakhtar Donetsk 1 (Taison 76) **Manchester Utd** 1 (Welbeck 18). Att: 51,555
Manchester Utd (4-4-2): De Gea, Rafael, Smalling, Vidic, Evra, Valencia, Carrick, Fellaini (Giggs 66), Cleverley, Welbeck (Jones 90), Van Persie. **Booked:** Fellaini, Vidic

October 23, 2013
Bayer Leverkusen 4 (Kiessling 23, 72, Rolfes 51 pen, Sam 57) **Shakhtar Donetsk** 0. Att: 25,184
Manchester Utd 1 (Martinez 2 og) **Real Sociedad** 0. Att: 74,654
Manchester Utd (4-4-2): Dea Gea, Rafael (Smalling 59), Jones, Evans, Evra, Valencia, Carrick, Giggs, Kagawa, Hernandez (Young 80), Rooney. **Booked:** Rafael, Kagawa

November 5, 2013
Real Sociedad 0 **Manchester Utd** 0. Att: 30,998
Manchester Utd (4-4-1-1): De Gea, Smalling, Ferdinand, Vidic, Evra, Valencia, Fellaini, Giggs, Kagawa (Jones 90), Rooney (Young 62), Hernandez (Van Persie 62). **Booked:** Fellaini, Evra. **Sent off:** Fellaini (90)
Shakhtar Donetsk 0 **Bayer Leverkusen** 0. Att: 50,115

November 27, 2013
Bayer Leverkusen 0 **Manchester Utd** 5 (Valencia 22, Spahic 30og, Evans 66, Smalling 77, Nani 88). Att: 29,412
Manchester Utd (4-2-3-1): De Gea, Smalling, Ferdinand, Evans, Evra (Buttner 70), Jones, Giggs, Valencia (Young 80), Kagawa, Nani, Rooney (Anderson 80)
Shakhtar Donetsk 4 (Luiz Adriano 37, Teixeira 48, Douglas Costa 68, 87) **Real Sociedad** 0. Att: 44,348

December 10, 2013
Manchester Utd 1 (Jones 67) **Shakhtar Donetsk** 0. Att: 74,506
Manchester Utd (4-2-3-1): De Gea, Rafael, Ferdinand, Evans, Buttner (Valencia 88), Jones, Giggs (Cleverley 63), Young (Van Persie 63), Kagawa, Januzaj, Rooney. **Booked:** Buttner, Cleverley
Real Sociedad 0 **Bayer Leverkusen** 1 (Toprak 49). Att: 23,408

FINAL TABLE

	P	W	D	L	F	A	Pts
Manchester Utd Q	6	4	2	0	12	3	14
Bayer Leverkusen Q	6	3	1	2	9	10	10
Shakhtar Donetsk	6	2	2	2	7	6	8
Real Sociedad	6	0	1	5	1	10	1

GROUP B

September 17, 2013
Copenhagen 1 (Jorgensen 14) **Juventus** 1 (Quagliarella 54). Att: 36,524
Galatasaray 1 (Bulut 84) **Real Madrid** 6 (Isco 33, Benzema 54, 81, Ronaldo 63, 66, 90). Att: 47,669

October 2, 2013
Juventus 2 (Vidal 78 pen, Quagliarella 87) **Galatasaray** 2 (Drogba 36, Bulut 88). Att: 33,466
Real Madrid 4 (Ronaldo 21, 66, Di Maria 71, 90) **Copenhagen** 0. Att: 69,347

October 23, 2013
Galatasaray 3 (Felipe Melo 10, Sneijder 38, Drogba 45) **Copenhagen** 1 (Claudemir 88). Att: 42,798
Real Madrid 2 (Ronaldo 4, 28 pen) **Juventus** 1 (Llorente 23). Att: 77,856

November 5, 2013
Copenhagen 1 (Braaten 6) **Galatasaray** 0. Att: 36,204
Juventus 2 (Vidal 42 pen, Llorente 65) **Real Madrid** 2 (Ronaldo 52, Bale 60). Att: 40,696

November 27, 2013
Juventus 3 (Vidal 29 pen, 61 pen, 63) **Copenhagen** 1 (Mellberg 56). Att: 39,506
Real Madrid 4 (Bale 37, Arbeloa 51, Di Maria 63, Isco 80) **Galatasaray** 1 (Bulut 38). Att: 67,728

December 10, 2013
Copenhagen 0 **Real Madrid** 2 (Modric 25, Ronaldo 48). Att: 37,241

December 11, 2013
Galatasaray 1 (Sneijder 85) **Juventus** 0. Att: 37,375

FINAL TABLE

	P	W	D	L	F	A	Pts
Real Madrid Q	6	5	1	0	20	5	16
Galatasaray Q	6	2	1	3	8	14	7
Juventus	6	1	3	2	9	9	6
Copenhagen	6	1	1	4	4	13	4

GROUP C

September 17, 2013
Benfica 2 (Djuricic 4, Luisao 30) **Anderlecht** 0. Att: 29,393
Olympiacos 1 (Weiss 25) **Paris SG** 4 (Cavani 20, Thiago Motta 68, 73, Marquinhos 86). Att: 31,253

October 2, 2013
Anderlecht 0 **Olympiacos** 3 (Mitroglou 17, 56, 72). Att: 15,918
Paris SG 3 (Ibrahimovic 5, 30, Marquinhos 25) **Benfica** 0. Att: 44,732

October 23, 2013
Anderlecht 0 **Paris SG** 5 (Ibrahimovic 17, 22, 36, 62, Cavani 52). Att: 18,465
Benfica 1 (Cardozo 83) **Olympiacos** 1 (Dominguez 29). Att: 38,149

November 5, 2013
Olympiacos 1 (Manolas 13) **Benfica** 0. Att: 31,461

Paris SG 1 (Ibrahimovic 70) **Anderlecht** 1 (De Zeeuw 68). Att: 43,091
November 27, 2013
Anderlecht 2 (Mbemba 18, Bruno 76) **Benfica** 3 (Matic 34, Mbemba 53 og, Rodrigo 90). Att: 16,780
Paris SG 2 (Ibrahimovic 7, Cavani 90) **Olympiacos** 1 (Manolas 80). Att: 44,446

December 10, 2013
Benfica 2 (Lima 45 pen, Gaitan 58) **Paris SG** 1 (Cavani 37). Att: 30,089
Olympiacos 3 (Saviola 33, 58, Dominquez 90 pen) **Anderlecht** 1 (Kljestan 39). Att: 31,444

FINAL TABLE

	P	W	D	L	F	A	Pts
Paris SG Q	6	4	1	1	16	5	13
Olympiacos Q	6	3	1	2	10	8	10
Benfica	6	3	1	2	8	8	10
Anderlecht	6	0	1	5	4	17	1

GROUP D

September 17, 2013
Bayern Munich 3 (Alaba 3, Mandzukic 41, Robben 68) **CSKA Moscow** 0. Att: 68,000
Plzen 0 **Manchester City** 3 (Dzeko 48, Toure 53, Aguero 58). Att: 11,281
Manchester City (4-2-3-1): Hart, Zabaleta, Kompany, Nastasic, Kolarov, Fernandinho, Toure (Garcia 80), Jesus Navas (Milner 67), Aguero, Nasri, Dzeko (Negredo 82). **Booked:** Kolarov, Fernandinho

October 2, 2013
CSKA Moscow 3 (Tosic 19, Honda 29, Reznik 78 og) **Plzen** 2 (Rajtoral 4, Bakos 90). Att: 6,135
Manchester City 1 (Negredo 80) **Bayern Munich** 3 (Ribery 7, Muller 56, Robben 60). Att: 45,201
Manchester City (4-2-3-1): Hart, Richards, Kompany, Nastasic, Clichy, Fernandinho, Toure, Jesus Navas, Aguero (Silva 70), Nasri (Milner 70), Dzeko (Negredo 56). **Booked:** Aguero, Nasri

October 23, 2013
Bayern Munich 5 (Ribery 25 pen, 61, Alaba 37, Schweinsteiger 64, Gotze 90) **Plzen** 0. Att: 68,000
CSKA Moscow 1 (Tosic 32) **Manchester City** 2 (Aguero 34, 42). Att: 14,000
Manchester City (4-4-2): Hart, Zabaleta, Garcia, Nastasic, Kolarov, Jesus Navas, Toure, Fernandinho, Silva (Nasri 79), Aguero (Clichy 89), Negredo (Dzeko 72). **Booked:** Toure, Zabaleta

November 5, 2013
Manchester City 5 (Aguero 3 pen, 20, Negredo 30, 51, 90) **CSKA Moscow** 2 (Doumbia 45, 71 pen). Att: 38,512
Manchester City (4-2-3-1): Pantilimon, Zabaleta, Demichelis, Nastasic, Clichy, Fernandinho Toure (Milner 46), Nasri (Jesus Navas 76), Aguero, Silva (Kolarov 66), Negredo. **Booked:** Toure
Plzen 0 **Bayern Munich** 1 (Mandzukic 66). Att: 11,360

November 27, 2013
CSKA Moscow 1 (Honda 62 pen) **Bayern Munich** 3 (Robben 17, Gotze 56, Muller 65 pen). Att: 14,000
Manchester City 4 (Aguero 33 pen, Nasri 66, Negredo 78, Dzeko 89) **Plzen** 2 (Horava 43, Tecl 69). Att: 37,742
Manchester City (4-4-2): Hart, Richards, Demichelis, Lescott, Kolarov, Milner, Garcia, Fernandinho (Toure 65), Nasri (Negredo 75), Aguero (Jesus Navas 46), Dzeko. **Booked:** Milner, Demichelis, Toure

December 10, 2013
Bayern Munich 2 (Muller 5, Gotze 12) **Manchester City** 3 (Silva 28, Kolarov 59 pen, Milner 62). Att: 68,000
Manchester City (4-2-3-1): Hart, Richards (Zabaleta 16), Demichelis, Lescott, Kolarov, Garcia, Fernandinho, Jesus Navas, Silva (Negredo 73), Milner, Dzeko (Rodwell 83). **Booked:** Dzeko, Milner, Fernandinho, Zabaleta
Plzen 2 (Kolar 77, Wagner 90) **CSKA Moscow** 1 (Musa 65). Att: 11,205

FINAL TABLE

	P	W	D	L	F	A	Pts
Bayern Munich Q	6	5	0	1	17	5	15
Manchester City Q	6	5	0	1	18	10	15
Plzen	6	1	0	5	6	17	3
CSKA Moscow	6	1	0	5	8	17	3

GROUP E

September 18, 2013
Chelsea 1 (Oscar 45) **Basle** 2 (Salah 71, Streller 82). Att: 40,358
Chelsea (4-2-3-1): Cech, Ivanovic, Luiz, Cahill, Cole, Lampard (Ba 75), Van Ginkel (Mikel 75), Willian (Mata 66), Oscar, Hazard, Eto'o. **Booked:** Van Ginkel
Schalke 3 (Uchida 67, Boateng 78, Draxler 85) **Steaua Bucharest** 0. Att: 49,358

October 1, 2013
Basle 0 **Schalke** 1 (Draxler 54). Att: 33,251
Steaua Bucharest 0 **Chelsea** 4 (Ramires 19, 55, Georgievski 44 og, Lampard 90). Att: 36,713
Chelsea (4-2-3-1): Cech, Ivanovic, Terry, Luiz, Cole, Ramires, Lampard, Oscar (Azpilicueta 79), Mata (Willian 81), Schurrle, Torres (Eto'o 71). **Booked:** Lampard, Cole

October 22, 2013
Schalke 0 **Chelsea** 3 (Torres 5, 69, Hazard 87). Att: 54,442
Chelsea (4-2-3-1): Cech, Ivanovic, Cahill, Terry, Azpilicueta, Ramires, Lampard, Hazard (Eto'o 88), Oscar (Luiz 84), Schurrle (Mikel 72), Torres. **Booked:** Cahill
Steaua Bucharest 1 (Tatu 88), **Basle** 1 (Diaz 48). Att: 23,899

November 6, 2013
Basle 1 (Sio 90) **Steaua Bucharest** 1 (Piovaccari 17). Att: 30,704
Chelsea 3 (Eto'o 31, 54, Ba 83) **Schalke** 0. Att: 41,194
Chelsea (4-2-3-1): Cech, Ivanovic, Cahill, Terry, Azpilicueta, Ramires, Mikel, Willian, Oscar (Lampard 81), Schurrle (De Bruyne 78), Eto'o (Ba 77)

November 26, 2013
Basle 1 (Salah 87) **Chelsea** 0. Att: 35,208
Chelsea (4-2-3-1): Cech, Ivanovic, Cahill, Terry, Azpilicueta, Ramires, Mikel, Lampard, Oscar (Hazard 55), Willian, Eto'o (Torres 41). **Booked:** Mikel, Ramires
Steaua Bucharest 0 **Schalke** 0. Att: 50,633

December 11, 2013
Chelsea 1 (Ba 11) **Steaua Bucharest** 0. Att: 41,181
Chelsea (4-2-3-1): Schwarzer, Ivanovic, Luiz, Terry, Cole, Lampard, Mikel (Ramires 67), Willian (De Bruyne 80), Oscar (Schurrle 70), Hazard, Ba. **Booked:** Mikel, Ivanovic
Schalke 2 (Draxler 51, Matip 57) **Basle** 0. Att: 52,093

FINAL TABLE

	P	W	D	L	F	A	Pts
Chelsea Q	6	4	0	2	12	3	12
Schalke Q	6	3	1	2	6	6	10
Basle	6	2	2	2	5	6	8
Steaua Bucharest	6	0	3	3	2	10	3

GROUP F

September 18, 2013
Marseille 1 (Ayew 90 pen) **Arsenal** 2 (Walcott 65, Ramsey 84). Att: 38,380
Arsenal (4-2-3-1): Szczesny, Sagna, Mertesacker, Koscielny, Gibbs, Flamini (Myaichi 90), Ramsey, Walcott (Monreal 77), Wilshere, Ozil, Giroud. **Booked:** Ramsey
Napoli 2 (Higuain 29, Insigne 67) **Borussia Dortmund** 1 (Zuniga 88 og). Att: 55,766

October 1, 2013
Arsenal 2 (Ozil 8, Giroud 15) **Napoli** 0. Att: 59,536
Arsenal (4-2-3-1): Szczesny, Sagna, Mertesacker, Koscielny, Gibbs, Flamini, Arteta, Ramsey (Monreal 89), Ozil, Rosicky (Wilshere 62), Giroud
Borussia Dortmund 3 (Lewandowski 19, 80 pen, Reus 52) **Marseille** 0. Att: 65,829

October 22, 2013
Arsenal 1 (Giroud 41) **Borussia Dortmund** 2 (Mkhitaryan 16, Lewandowski 62). Att: 60,011
Arsenal (4-2-3-1): Szczesny, Sagna, Mertesacker, Koscielny, Gibbs, Arteta, Ramsey (Bendtner 87), Wilshere (Cazorla 57), Ozil, Rosicky (Gnabry 89), Giroud. **Booked:** Rosicky, Ozil
Marseille 1 (Ayew 86) **Napoli** 2 (Callejon 42, Zapata 67). Att: 39,790

November 6, 2013
Borussia Dortmund 0 **Arsenal** 1 (Ramsey 62). Att: 65,829
Arsenal (4-2-3-1): Szczesny, Sagna, Mertesacker, Koscielny, Gibbs, Arteta, Ramsey, Rosicky (Vermaelen 90), Ozil, Cazorla (Monreal 75), Giroud (Bendtner 90). **Booked:** Arteta
Napoli 3 (Inler 22, Higuain 25, 75) **Marseille** 2 (Ayew 10, Thauvin 64). Att: 39,148

November 26, 2013
Arsenal 2 (Wilshere 1, 65) **Marseille** 0. Att: 59,912
Arsenal (4-2-3-1): Szczesny, Sagna, Mertesacker, Koscielny, Monreal, Flamini, Ramsey, Wilshere (Walcott 75), Ozil (Arteta 82), Rosicky (Cazorla 75), Giroud
Borussia Dortmund 3 (Reus 10 pen, Blaszcykowski 60, Aubameyang 78) **Napoli** 1 (Insigne 71). Att: 65,829

December 11, 2013
Marseille 1 (Diawara 14) **Borussia Dortmund** 2 (Lewandowski 4, Grosskreutz 86). Att: 36,655
Napoli 2 (Higuain 73, Callejon 90) **Arsenal** 0. Att: 34,027
Arsenal (4-2-3-1): Szczesny, Jenkinson, Mertesacker, Koscielny, Gibbs, Flamini, Arteta, Rosicky (Monreal 74), Ozil, Cazorla (Ramsey 68), Giroud. **Booked:** Arteta, Giroud, Ramsey. **Sent off:** Arteta (76)

FINAL TABLE

		P	W	D	L	F	A	Pts
Borussia Dortmund	Q	6	4	0	2	11	6	12
Arsenal	Q	6	4	0	2	8	5	12
Napoli		6	4	0	2	10	9	12
Marseille		6	0	0	6	5	14	0

GROUP G

September 18, 2013
Atletico Madrid 3 (Miranda 40, Turan 64, Baptistao 80) **Zenit St Petersburg** 1 (Hulk 58). Att: 33,855
Austria Vienna 0 **Porto** 1 (Gonzalez 55). Att: 37,500

October 1, 2013
Porto 1 (Martinez 16) **Atletico Madrid** 2 (Godin 58, Turan 87). Att: 33,989
Zenit St Petersburg 0 **Austria Vienna** 0. Att: 18,785

October 22, 2013
Austria Vienna 0 **Atletico Madrid** 3 (Raul Garcia 8, Diego Costa 20, 53). Att: 45,675
Porto 0 **Zenit St Petersburg** 1 (Kerzhakov 86). Att: 31,109

November 6, 2013
Atletico Madrid 4 (Miranda 11, Raul Garcia 25, Filipe Luis 45, Diego Costa 82) **Austria Vienna**
0. Att: 29,841
Zenit St Petersburg 1 (Hulk 28) **Porto** 1 (Gonzalez 23). Att: 17,786

November 26, 2013
Porto 1 (Martinez 49) **Austria Vienna** 1 (Kienast 11). Att: 24,809
Zenit St Petersburg 1 (Alderweireld 74 og) **Atletico Madrid** 1 (Adrian 53). Att: 17,885

December 11, 2013
Atletico Madrid 2 (Raul Garcia, Diego Costa 37) **Porto** 0. Att: 24,629
Austria Vienna 4 (Hosiner 44, 52, Jun 48, Kienast 90) **Zenit St Petersburg** 1 (Kerzhakov 35).
Att: 37,500

FINAL TABLE

	P	W	D	L	F	A	Pts
Atletico Madrid Q	6	5	1	0	15	3	16
Zenit St Petersburg Q	6	1	3	2	5	9	6
Porto	6	1	2	3	4	7	5
Austria Vienna	6	1	2	3	5	10	5

GROUP H

September 18, 2013
AC Milan 2 (Izaguirre 82 og, Muntari 85) **Celtic** 0. Att: 54,623
Celtic (4-4-1-1): Forster, Lustig, Ambrose, Van Dijk, Izaguirre, Matthews (Boerrigter 75), Brown,
Mulgrew (Biton 89), Samaras, Commons (Pukki 77), Stokes. **Booked:** Ambrose, Mulgrew, Brown
Barcelona 4 (Messi 21, 55, 75, Pique 69) **Ajax** 0. Att: 79,412

October 1, 2013
Ajax 1 (Denswil 90) **AC Milan** 1 (Balotelli 90 pen). Att: 57,692
Celtic 0 **Barcelona** 1 (Fabregas 76). Att: 58,128
Celtic (4-4-1-1): Forster, Lustig (Forrest 70), Ambrose, Van Dijk, Izaguirre, Matthews, Brown,
Mulgrew, Samaras, Commons (Pukki 86), Stokes (Kayal 70). **Booked:** Lustig, Samaras,
Izaguirre. **Sent off:** Brown (59)

October 22, 2013
AC Milan 1 (Robinho 10) **Barcelona** 1 (Messi 23). Att: 74,487
Celtic 2 (Forrest 45 pen, Kayal 54) **Ajax** 1 (Schone 90). Att: 58,719
Celtic (4-4-2): Forster, Lustig (Biton 77), Ambrose, Van Dijk, Izaguirre, Forrest, Kayal (Ledley
70), Mulgrew, Samaras, Stokes, Pukki (Balde 86). **Booked:** Van Dijk. **Sent off:** Biton (88)

November 6, 2013
Ajax 1 (Schone 51) **Celtic** 0. Att: 59,908
Celtic (4-4-1-1): Forster, Lustig, Ambrose, Van Dijk, Izaguirre, Forrest, Kayal (Ledley 77),
Mulgrew, Samaras, Commons (Pukki 81), Stokes (Boerrigter 73). **Booked:** Samaras, Izaguirre
Barcelona 3 (Messi 30 pen, 83, Busquets 39) **AC Milan** 1 (Pique 45 og). Att: 80,517

November 26, 2013
Ajax 2 (Serero 19, Hoesen 42) **Barcelona** 1 (Xavi 49 pen). Att: 53,000
Celtic 0 **AC Milan** 3 (Kaka 12, Zapata 49, Balotelli 59). Att: 58,619
Celtic (4-2-3-1): Forster, Lustig, Ambrose, Van Dijk, Izaguirre, Kayal (Ledley 30), Mulgrew, Forrest (Rogic 79), Commons (Stokes 65), Boerrigter, Samaras. **Booked:** Commons, Van Dijk, Izaguirre

December 11, 2013
AC Milan 0 **Ajax** 0. Att: 61,744
Barcelona 6 (Pique 7, Pedro 39, Neymar 44, 48, 58, Tello 72) **Celtic** 1 (Samaras 89). Att: 54,342
Celtic (4-5-1): Forrest, Lustig, Ambrose, Van Dijk, Matthews (Stokes 82), Brown, Biton (Commons 69), Ledley, Boerrigter, Samaras, Pukki (Mulgrew 46). **Booked:** Brown, Matthews

FINAL TABLE

	P	W	D	L	F	A	Pts
Barcelona Q	6	4	1	1	16	5	13
AC Milan Q	6	2	3	1	8	5	9
Ajax	6	2	2	2	5	8	8
Celtic	6	1	0	5	3	14	3

ROUND OF 16, FIRST LEG

February 18, 2014
Bayer Leverkusen 0 **Paris SG** 4 (Matuidi 3, Ibrahimovic 39 pen, 42, Cabaye 88). Att: 29,412
Manchester City 0 **Barcelona** 2 (Messi 54 pen, Dani Alves 90). Att: 46,030
Manchester City (4-4-1-1): Hart, Zabaleta, Kompany, Demichelis, Clichy, Jesus Navas (Nasri 57), Toure, Fernandinho, Kolarov (Lescott 57), Silva, Negredo (Dzeko 74). **Booked:** Negredo, Kolarov. **Sent off:** Demichelis (53)

February 19, 2014
AC Milan 0 **Atletico Madrid** 1 (Diego Costa 83). Att: 65,890
Arsenal 0 **Bayern Munich** 2 (Kroos 54, Muller 88). Att: 59,911
Arsenal (4-2-3-1): Szczesny, Sagna, Mertesacker, Koscielny, Gibbs (Monreal 31), Flamini, Wilshere, Oxlade-Chamberlain (Rosicky 74), Ozil, Cazorla (Fabianksi 38), Sanogo. **Booked:** Sanogo, Rosicky. **Sent off:** Szczesny (37)

February 25, 2014
Olympiacos 2 (Dominguez 38, Campbell 54) **Manchester Utd** 0. Att: 29,815
Manchester Utd (4-2-3-1): De Gea, Smalling, Ferdinand, Vidic, Evra, Cleverley (Kagawa 66), Carrick, Valencia (Welbeck 60), Rooney, Young, Van Persie. **Booked:** Evra, Ferdinand
Zenit St Petersburg 2 (Shatov 58, Hulk 70 pen) **Borussia Dortmund** 4 (Mkhitaryan 4, Reus 5, Lewandowski 61, 71). Att: 15,099

February 26, 2014
Galatasaray 1 (Chedjou 64) **Chelsea** 1 (Torres 9). Att: 49,914
Chelsea (4-2-3-1): Cech, Ivanovic, Cahill, Terry, Azpilicueta, Ramires, Lampard, Willian, Hazard (Oscar 90), Schurrle (Mikel 67), Torres (Eto'o 68). **Booked:** Terry, Schurrle, Ramires, Cech
Schalke 1 (Huntelaar 90) **Real Madrid** 6 (Benzema 13, 57, Bale 21, 69, Ronaldo 52, 89). Att: 54,442

ROUND OF 16, SECOND LEG

March 11, 2014
Atletico Madrid 4 (Diego Costa 3, 85, Turan 40, Raul Garcia 71) **AC Milan** 1 (Kaka 27). Att:

49,186 (Atletico Madrid won 5-1 on agg)
Bayern Munich 1 (Schweinsteiger 55) **Arsenal** 1 (Podolski 57). Att: 68,000 (Bayern Munich won 3-1 on agg)
Arsenal (4-2-3-1): Fabianski, Sagna, Mertesaker, Koscielny, Vermaelen, Arteta (Gnabry 77), Oxlade-Chamberlain (Flamini 84), Cazorla, Ozil (Rosicky 46), Podolski, Giroud. **Booked:** Podolski, Arteta, Vermaelen

March 12, 2014
Barcelona 2 (Messi 67, Dani Alves 90) **Manchester City** 1 (Kompany 89). Att: 85,957 (Barcelona won 4-1 on agg)
Manchester City (4-2-3-1): Hart, Zabaleta, Kompany, Lescott, Kolarov, Fernandinho, Milner, Silva (Negredo 72), Toure, Nasri (Jesus Navas 74), Aguero (Dzeko 46). **Booked:** Fernandinho, Kolarov, Zabaleta, Kompany. **Sent off:** Zabaleta (78)
Paris SG 2 (Marquinhos 13, Lavezzi 53) **Bayer Leverkusen** 1 (Sam 6). Att: 45,596 (Paris SG won 6-1 on agg)

March 18, 2014
Chelsea 2 (Eto'o 4, Cahill 43) **Galatasaray** 0. Att: 38,038 (Chelsea won 3-1 on agg)
Chelsea (4-2-3-1): Cech, Ivanovic, Cahill, Terry, Azpilicueta, Ramires, Lampard, Hazard, Oscar (Schurrle 82), Willian (Kalas 90), Eto'o (Torres 85). **Booked:** Oscar, Ivanovic
Real Madrid 3 (Ronaldo 22, 74, Morata 76) **Schalke** 1 (Hoogland 31). Att: 65,148 (Real Madrid won 9-2 on agg)

March 19, 2014
Borussia Dortmund 1 (Kehl 39) **Zenit St Petersburg** 2 (Hulk 16, Rondon 73). Att: 65,829 (Borussia Dortmund won 5-4 on agg)
Manchester Utd 3 (Van Persie 25 pen, 45, 52) **Olympiacos** 0. Att: 74,662 (Manchester Utd won 3-2 on agg)
Manchester Utd (4-2-3-1): De Gea, Rafael, Jones, Ferdinand, Evra, Carrick, Giggs, Welbeck (Fletcher 82), Rooney, Valencia (Young 77), Van Persie (Fellaini 90). **Booked:** Carrick, Evra, Ferdinand

QUARTER FINALS, FIRST LEG

April 1, 2014
Barcelona 1 (Neymar 71) **Atletico Madrid** 1 (Diego 57). Att: 79,941
Manchester Utd 1 (Vidic 58) **Bayern Munich** 1 (Schweinsteiger 66). Att: 75,199
Manchester Utd (4-2-3-1): De Gea, Jones, Ferdinand, Vidic, Buttner (Young 74), Carrick, Fellaini, Valencia, Giggs (Kagawa 46), Rooney, Welbeck (Hernandez 85). **Booked:** Valencia

April 2, 2014
Paris SG 3 (Lavezzi 4, Luiz 62 og, Pastore 90) **Chelsea** 1 (Hazard 27 pen). Att: 45,517
Chelsea (4-2-3-1): Cech, Ivanovic, Cahill, Terry, Azpilicueta, Ramires, Luiz, Willian, Oscar (Lampard 74), Hazard, Schurrle (Torres 59). **Booked:** Ramires, Willian, Luiz
Real Madrid 3 (Bale 3, Isco 27, Ronaldo 57) **Borussia Dortmund** 0. Att: 70,089

QUARTER-FINALS, SECOND LEG

April 8, 2014
Borussia Dortmund 2 (Reus 24, 37) **Real Madrid** 0. Att: 65,829 (Real Madrid won 3-2 on agg)
Chelsea 2 (Schurrle 32, Ba 87) **Paris SG** 0. Att: 38,080 (agg 3-3, Chelsea won on away goal)
Chelsea (4-2-3-1): Cech, Ivanovic, Cahill, Terry, Azpilicueta, Lampard (Ba 66), Luiz, Willian, Oscar (Torres 81), Hazard (Schurrle 18), Eto'o. **Booked:** Willian, Lampard, Ivanovic, Luiz

April 9, 2014
Atletico Madrid 1 (Koke 6) **Barcelona** 0. Att: 53,592 (Atletico Madrid won 2-1 on agg)
Bayern Munich 3 (Mandzukic 59, Muller 67, Robben 76) **Manchester Utd** 1 (Evra 57). Att: 67,300 (Bayern Munich won 4-2 on agg)
Manchester Utd (4-4-1-1): De Gea, Jones, Smalling, Vidic, Evra, Valencia, Fletcher (Hernandez 75), Carrick, Kagawa, Welbeck (Januzaj 81) Rooney. **Booked**: Vidic Evra

SEMI-FINALS, FIRST LEG

April 22, 2014
Atletico Madrid 0 **Chelsea** 0. Att: 52,560
Chelsea (4-3-3): Cech (Schwarzer 18), Azpilicueta, Cahill, Terry (Schurrle 73), Cole, Mikel, Luiz, Lampard, Ramires, Torres, Willian (Ba 90). **Booked**: Lampard, Mikel, Ba

April 23, 2014
Real Madrid 1 (Benzema 19) **Bayern Munich** 0. Att: 80,354

SEMI-FINALS, SECOND LEG

Bayern Munich 0 **Real Madrid** 4 (Sergio Ramos 16, 20, Ronaldo 34, 90). Att: 68,000 (Real Madrid won 5-0 on aggregate
Chelsea 1 (Torres 36) **Atletico Madrid** 3 (Adrian 44, Diego Costa 60, Turan 72). Att: 37,918 (Atletico Madrid won 3-1 on agg)
Chelsea (4-2-3-1): Schwarzer, Ivanovic, Cahill, Terry, Cole (Eto'o 54), Ramires, Luiz, Azpilicueta, Willian (Schurrle 77), Hazard, Torres (Ba 67). **Booked**: Cahill

FINAL

REAL MADRID 4 ATLETICO MADRID 1 (aet)
Estadio da Luz, Lisbon (60,976); Saturday, May 24 2014

Real Madrid (4-3-3): Casillas (capt), Carvajal, Varane, Sergio Ramos, Fabio Coentrao (Marcelo 59), Modric, Khedira (Isco 59), Di Maria, Bale, Benzema (Morata 79), Ronaldo. **Subs not used**: Diego Lopez, Pepe, Arbeloa, Illarramendi. **Scorers**: Sergio Ramos (90), Bale (110), Marcelo (118), Ronaldo (120 pen). **Booked**: Sergio Ramos, Khedira, Marcelo, Ronaldo, Varane. **Coach**: Carlo Ancelotti
Atletico Madrid (4-4-2): Courtois, Janfran, Miranda, Godin, Filipe Luis (Alderweireld 83), Raul Garcia (Sosa 66), Tiago, Gabi (capt), Koke, Diego Costa (Adrian 9), Villa. **Subs not used**: Aranzubia, Mario Suarez, Rodriguez, Diego. **Scorer**: Godin (36). **Booked**: Raul Garcia, Miranda, Villa, Juanfran, Koke, Gabi, Godin. **Coach**: Diego Simeone
Referee: B Kuipers (Holland). **Half-time**: 0-1

Leading scorers (from group stage): 17 Ronaldo (Real Madrid); 10 Ibrahimovic (Paris SG); 8 Diego Costa (Atletico Madrid), Messi (Barcelona); 6 Aguero (Manchester City), Bale (Real Madrid), Lewandowski (Borussia Dortmund)

FINAL FACTS AND FIGURES

● Atletico Madrid were also on the brink of victory in their only other appearance in the final, against Bayern Munich in 1974. They took the lead in extra-time through Luis Aragones and held it until the last minute when Hans-Georg Schwarzenbeck equalised. With no penalty shoot-outs in those days, the teams returned two days later for the replay at the Heysel Stadium in Brusssels, where Bayern won 4-0.

● This was Real Madrid 's tenth success. They won the first five tournaments, under the European Cup banner, and this was their 13th final.

- Gareth Bale became the fourth British player to help a foreign club win the final after Paul Lambert (Borussia Dortmund) in 1997, Steve McManaman (Real Madrid) in 2000 and 2002 and Owen Hargreaves (Bayern Munich) in 2001.

- Bale will return home for the European Super Cup match against Europa League winners Sevilla at Cardiff City Stadium on August 12.

- Carlo Ancelotti joined Bob Paisley as a three-time winner, Paisley having led Liverpool to the trophy in 1977, 1978 and 1981.

- This was the first final of Europe's top club competition to be played in Lisbon since 1967 when Celtic beat Inter Milan 2-1 to become the first British side to win it.

EUROPEAN CUP/CHAMPIONS LEAGUE FINALS

1956	Real Madrid 4, Reims 3 (Paris)
1957	Real Madrid 2, Fiorentina 0 (Madrid)
1958†	Real Madrid 3, AC Milan 2 (Brussels)
1959	Real Madrid 2, Reims 0 (Stuttgart)
1960	Real Madrid 7, Eintracht Frankfurt 3 (Glasgow)
1961	Benfica 3, Barcelona 2 (Berne)
1962	Benfica 5, Real Madrid 3 (Amsterdam)
1963	AC Milan 2, Benfica 1 (Wembley)
1964	Inter Milan 3, Real Madrid 1 (Vienna)
1965	Inter Milan 1, Benfica 0 (Milan)
1966	Real Madrid 2, Partizan Belgrade 1 (Brussels)
1967	Celtic 2, Inter Milan 1 (Lisbon)
1968†	Manchester Utd 4, Benfica 1 (Wembley)
1969	AC Milan 4, Ajax 1 (Madrid)
1970†	Feyenoord 2, Celtic 1 (Milan)
1971	Ajax 2, Panathinaikos 0 (Wembley)
1972	Ajax 2, Inter Milan 0 (Rotterdam)
1973	Ajax 1, Juventus 0 (Belgrade)
1974	Bayern Munich 4, Atletico Madrid 0 (replay Brussels, after a 1-1 draw, Brussels)
1975	Bayern Munich 2, Leeds Utd 0 (Paris)
1976	Bayern Munich 1, St. Etienne 0 (Glasgow)
1977	Liverpool 3, Borussia Moenchengladbach 1 (Rome)
1978	Liverpool 1, Brugge 0 (Wembley)
1979	Nott'm. Forest 1, Malmo 0 (Munich)
1980	Nott'm. Forest 1, Hamburg 0 (Madrid)
1981	Liverpool 1, Real Madrid 0 (Paris)
1982	Aston Villa 1, Bayern Munich 0 (Rotterdam)
1983	SV Hamburg 1, Juventus 0 (Athens)
1984†	Liverpool 1, AS Roma 1 (Liverpool won 4-2 on penalties) (Rome)
1985	Juventus 1, Liverpool 0 (Brussels)
1986†	Steaua Bucharest 0, Barcelona 0 (Steaua won 2-0 on penalties) (Seville)
1987	Porto 2, Bayern Munich 1 (Vienna)
1988†	PSV Eindhoven 0, Benfica 0 (PSV won 6-5 on penalties) (Stuttgart)
1989	AC Milan 4, Steaua Bucharest 0 (Barcelona)
1990	AC Milan 1, Benfica 0 (Vienna)
1991†	Red Star Belgrade 0, Marseille 0 (Red Star won 5-3 on penalties) (Bari)
1992	Barcelona 1, Sampdoria 0 (Wembley)
1993	Marseille 1, AC Milan 0 (Munich)
1994	AC Milan 4, Barcelona 0 (Athens)
1995	Ajax 1, AC Milan 0 (Vienna)
1996†	Juventus 1, Ajax 1 (Juventus won 4-2 on penalties) (Rome)
1997	Borussia Dortmund 3, Juventus 1 (Munich)
1998	Real Madrid 1, Juventus 0 (Amsterdam)
1999	Manchester Utd 2, Bayern Munich 1 (Barcelona)

2000	Real Madrid 3, Valencia 0 (Paris)
2001	Bayern Munich 1, Valencia 1 (Bayern Munich won 5-4 on penalties) (Milan)
2002	Real Madrid 2, Bayer Leverkusen 1 (Glasgow)
2003†	AC Milan 0, Juventus 0 (AC Milan won 3-2 on penalties) (Manchester)
2004	FC Porto 3, Monaco 0 (Gelsenkirchen)
2005†	Liverpool 3, AC Milan 3 (Liverpool won 3-2 on penalties) (Istanbul)
2006	Barcelona 2, Arsenal 1 (Paris)
2007	AC Milan 2, Liverpool 1 (Athens)
2008†	Manchester Utd 1, Chelsea 1 (Manchester Utd won 6-5 on penalties) (Moscow)
2009	Barcelona 2 Manchester Utd 0 (Rome)
2010	Inter Milan 2 Bayern Munich 0 (Madrid)
2011	Barcelona 3 Manchester Utd 1 (Wembley)
2012†	Chelsea 1 Bayern Munich 1 (Chelsea won 4-3 on pens) (Munich)
2013	Bayern Munich 3 Borussia Dortmund 1 (Wembley)
2014†	Real Madrid 4 Atletico Madrid 1 (Lisbon)

(† After extra time)
● Champions League since 1993

UEFA EUROPA LEAGUE 2013–14

FIRST QUALIFYING ROUND, FIRST LEG

Airbus 1 (Budrys 81) Ventspils 1 (Paulius 49). Att: 1,451. **Bala** 1 (Sheridan 5) Levadia 0. Att: 1,247. **Crusaders** 1 (Owens 23) Rosenborg 2 (Chibuike 45, Svenssoon 79). Att: 948. **Drogheda** 0 Malmo 0. Att: 1,496. Fuglafjordur 0 **Linfield** 2 (Waterworth 69, Lowry 75). Att: 411. **Prestatyn** 1 (Parkinson 45) Liepajas 2 (Kalns 16, Sadcins 62). Att: 1,017. Reykjavik 0 **Glentoran** 0. Att: 967. Zalgiris 2 (Komolov 24, Bilinski 71) **St Patrick's** 2 (Byrne 56, O'Brien 88). Att: 4,200

FIRST QUALIFYING ROUND, SECOND LEG

Glentoran 0 Reykjavik 3 (Martin 24, Saevarsson 65, 90). Att: 1,700 (Reykjavik won 3-0 on agg). Levadia 3 (Hunt 7, 22, 51) **Bala** 1 (Jones 90). Att: 2,567 (Levadia won 3-2 on agg). Liepajas 1 (Afanasjevs 18) **Prestatyn** 2 (Stephens 78, Gibson 90). Att: 2,500 (aet, agg 3-3, Prestatyn won 4-3 on pens). **Linfield** 3 (Gault 41, Mulgrew 56, Lowry 61) Fuglafjordur 0. Att: 1,600 (Linfield won 5-0 on agg). Malmo 2 (Forsberg 45, Kron 90) **Drogheda** 0. Att: 5,689 (Malmo won 2-0 on agg). Rosenborg 7 (Hoiland 16, Chibuike 36, 51, Dockal 58, Mikkelsen 61, Sorloth 73, Svenssoon 90) **Crusaders** 2 (Leeman 50, Owens 69). Att: 4,003 (Rosenberg won 9-3 on agg). **St Patrick's** 1 (Brennan 85 pen) Zalgiris 2 (Kuklys 45, Bilinski 52). Att: 2,700 (Zalgiris won 4-3 on agg). Ventspils 0 **Airbus** 0. Att: 1,100 (agg 1-1, Ventspils won on away goal)

FIRST QUALIFYING ROUND, ON AGGREGATE

Aktobe 4 Gandzasar 2; Astra 3 Domzale 0; Breidablik 4 FC Santa Coloma 0; Botev 6 Astana 0; Chikhura 1 Vaduz 1 (Chikhura won on away goal); Dacia 3 Teuta 3 (Dacia won on away goal); Differdange 3 Laci 1; Dinamo Minsk 8 Kruoja 0; Gefle 8 Trans Narva 1; Honved 13 Celik 1; IBV 2 Torshavn 1; Inter Baku 3 Mariehamn 1; Irtysh 2 Levski Sofia 0; Jeunesse Esch 3 TPS 2; Khazar 2 Sliema 1; Kukesi 1 Flora 1 (Kukesi won on away goal); Milsami 1 Dudelange 0; Mladost 2 Videoton 2 (Mladost won on away goals); Pyunik 2 Teteks 1; Qarabag 2 Metalurg Skopje 0; Rudar 2 Mika 1; Sarajevo 3 Libertas 1; Skonto 1 FC Tiraspol 1 (aet, Skonto won 4-2 on pens); Tromso 3 Celije 2; Turnovo 4 Suduva 4 (aet, Turnovo won 5-4 on pens); Valletta 4 Fiorita 0; Vikingur 2 Turku 1; Vojvodina 7 Hibernians 3; Zilina 6 Kutaisi 3; Zrinjski 4 UE Santa Coloma 1

SECOND QUALIFYING ROUND, FIRST LEG

Malmo 2 (Hamad 11, Eriksson 13) **Hibernian** 0. Att: 8,628. Rijeka 5 (Benko 19, 24, 60,

Jugovic 68, Zlomislic 86) **Prestatyn** 0. Att: 6,660. Rosenborg 0 **St Johnstone** 1 (Wright 19).
Att: 5,952. Trabzonspor 4 (Mierzejewski 11, Henrique 17, Molloy 40 og, Kacar 53) **Derry** 2
(McDaid 25, Kavanagh 33). Att: 17,213. Xanthi 0 **Linfield** 1 (Burns 26). Att: 2,117

SECOND QUALIFYING ROUND, SECOND LEG

Derry 0 Trabzonspor 3 (Henrique 57, 83, Ozdemir 90). Att: 2,150 (Trabzonspor won 7-2 on
agg). **Hibernian** 0 Malmo 7 (Eriksson 21, Forsberg 26, Halsti 30, Albornoz 41, Rantie 61,
Hamad 65, Kron 72). Att: 16,018 (Malmo won 9-0 on agg). **Linfield** 1 (Gault 100) Xanthi
2 (Marcelinho 28, 106). Att: 2,494 (aet, agg 2-2, Xanthi won on away goals); **Prestatyn**
0 Rijeka 3 (Mocinic 37, Boras 41, Mujanovic 67). Att: 930 (Rijeka won 8-0 on agg). **St
Johnstone** 1 (May 21) Rosenborg 1 (Soderlund 4). Att: 7,850 (St Johnstone won 2-1 on agg)

SECOND QUALIFYING ROUND, ON AGGREGATE

Aktobe 2 Hodd 1; Astra 3 Omonia 2; Botev 3 Zrinjski 1; Breidablik 1 Sturm Graz 0;
Chernomorets 3 Dacia 2; Crvena Zvezda 2 Vestmannaey 0; Differdange 5 Utrecht 4; Dila
Gori 3 Aalborg 0; Dinamo Minsk 4 Lokomotiva 4 (Dinamo Minsk won on away goals); FC
Minsk 3 Valletta 1; Gefle 4 Anorthosis 3; Hacken 3 Sparta Prague 2; Hajduk Split 3 Turnovo
2; Hapoel Tel-Aviv 6 Beroe 3; Kukesi 3 Sarajevo 2; Lech Poznan 5 Honka 2; Liberec 2
Skonto 2 (Liberec won on away goals); Maccabi Haifa 10 Khazar 0; Milsami 2 Shakhter 2
(aet, Milsami won 4-2 on pens); Mladost 3 Inter Bratis 2; Pandurii 4 Levadia 0; Petrolul 7
Vikingur 0; Qarabag 4 Gliwice 3 (aet); Rubin Kazan 4 Jagodina 2; Siroki 4 Irtysh 3; Slask
Wroclaw 6 Rudar 2; Standard Liege 6 Reykjavik 2; Stromsgodset 5 Debrecen 2; Trencin 2
Gothenburg 1; Tromso 2 Inter Baku 1; Thun 5 Chikhura 1; Ventspils 5 Jeunesse Esch 1;
Vojvodina 5 Honved 1; Zalgiris 3 Pyunik 1; Zilina 3 Ljubljana 3 (Zilina won on away goals)

THIRD QUALIFYING ROUND, FIRST LEG

FC Minsk 0 **St Johnstone** 1 (MacLean 69). Att: 2,900. **Motherwell** 0 Kuban 2 (Popov 52,
78). Att: 6,748. **Swansea** 4 (Michu 37, Bony 55, 60, Pozuelo 86) Malmo 0. Att: 16,176

THIRD QUALIFYING ROUND, SECOND LEG

Kuban 1 (McManus 50 og) **Motherwell** 0. Att: 31,754 (Kuban won 3-0 on agg); Malmo 0
Swansea 0. Att: 11,538 (Swansea won 4-0 on agg). **St Johnstone** 0 FC Minsk 1 (Rnic 75).
Att: 8,594 (aet, agg 1-1, FC Minsk won 3-2 on pens)

THIRD QUALIFYING ROUND, ON AGGREGATE

Aktobe 1 Breidablik 1 (aet, Aktobe won 2-1 on pens); Astra 5 Trencin 3; Chernomorets
3 Crvena Zvezda 1; Dila Gori 2 Hajduk Split 0; Estoril 1 Ramat Gan 0; Jablonec 5
Stromsgodset 2; Kukesi 2 Donets 1; Liberec 4 Zurich 2; Maccabi Haifa 3 Ventspils 0;
Pandurii 3 Hapoel Tel-Aviv 2; Petrolul 3 Vitesse Arnhem 2; Qarabag 3 Gefle 0; Rapid
Vienna 4 Asteras 2; Rijeka 3 Zilina 2; Rubin Kazan 4 Randers 1; Sevilla 9 Mladost 1; Slask
Wroclaw 4 Bruges 3; Standard Liege 4 Xanthi 2; St Etienne 6 Milsami 0; Stuttgart 1 Botev
1 (Stuttgart won on away goal); Thun 3 Hacken 1; Trabzonspor 1 Dinamo Minsk 0; Tromso 1
Differdange 1 (aet, Tromso won 4-3 on pens); Udinese 7 Siroki 0; Vojvodina 5 Bursaspor 2;
Zalgiris 2 Lech Poznan 2 (Zalgiris won on away goal)

PLAY-OFF ROUND, FIRST LEG

Dinamo Tbilisi 0 **Tottenham** 5 (Townsend 12, Paulinho 44, Soldado 58, 67, Rose 64). Att:
22,500; **Swansea** 5 (Routledge 14, 25, Michu 22, Pecanha 58 og, Pozuelo 70) Petrolul 1
(Grozav 87). Att: 12,590

PLAY-OFF ROUND, SECOND LEG

Petrolul 2 (Pirso 73, Younes 83) **Swansea** 1 (Lamah 74). Att: 12,880 (Swansea won 6-3 on agg). **Tottenham** 3 (Defoe 40, 45, Holtby 69) Dinamo Tbilisi 0. Att: 26,189 (Tottenham won 8-0 on agg)

PLAY-OFF ROUND, ON AGGREGATE

Alkmaar 3 Atromitos 3 (Alkmaar won on away goals); Apollon Limassol 2 Nice 1; Besiktas 3 Tromso 2; Chernomorets 1 Skenderbeu 1 (aet, Chernomorets won 7-6 on pens); Dnipro 5 Nomme Kalju 1; Dynamo Kiev 8 Aktobe 3; Eintracht Frankfurt 4 Qarabag 1; Elfsborg 2 Nordsjaelland 1; Esbjerg 5 St Etienne 3; Estoril 4 Pasching 1; Fiorentina 2 Grasshoppers 2 (Fiorentina won on away goals); Genk 7 Hafnarfjardar 2; Kuban 3 Feyenoord 1; Liberec 4 Udinese 2; Maccabi Haifa 3 Astra 1; Pandurii 2 Braga 1; Rapid Vienna 4 Dila Gori 0; Real Betis 8 Jablonec 1; Rijeka 4 Stuttgart 3; Rubin Kazan 5 Molde 0; Salzburg 7 Zalgiris 0; Sevilla 9 Slask Wroclaw 1; Sheriff Tiraspol 3 Vojvodina 2; Standard Liege 5 FC Minsk 1; St Gallen 5 Spartak Moscow 3; Thun 3 Partizan 1; Trabzonspor 5 Kukesi 1; Zulte-Waregem 3 Apoel Nicosia 2

GROUP A

Match-day 1: St Gallen 2 (Karanovic 56, Mathys 77) Kuban 0. Att: 16,500. Valencia 0 **Swansea** 3 (Bony 14, Michu 58, De Guzman 62). Att: 32,305
Match-day 2: Kuban 0 Valencia 2 (Alcacer 73, Feghouli 81). Att: 29,300. **Swansea** 1 (Routledge 52) St Gallen 0. Att: 15,397
Match-day 3: **Swansea** 1 (Michu 68) Kuban 1 (Cisse 90 pen). Att: 14,964. Valencia 5 (Alcacer 12, Fede 21, 30, Costa 33, Canales 71) St Gallen 1 (Nater 74). Att: 26,645
Match-day 4: Kuban 1 (Balde 90) **Swansea** 1 (Bony 9). Att: 27,843. St Gallen 2 (Besle 38, Karanovic 65) Valencia 3 (Piatti 30, 75, Canales 85). Att: 16,951
Match-day 5: Kuban 4 (Melgarejo 3, 72, Ignatiev 55, Kabore 90) St Gallen 0. Att: 19,032. **Swansea** 0 Valencia 1 (Parejo 21). Att: 17,896
Match-day 6: St Gallen 1 (Mathys 80) **Swansea** 0. Att: 15,298. Valencia 1 (Alcacer 67) Kuban 1 (Melgarejo 85). Att: 14,581

FINAL TABLE

	P	W	D	L	F	A	PTS
Valencia Q	6	4	1	1	12	7	13
Swansea Q	6	2	2	2	6	4	8
Kuban	6	1	3	2	7	7	6
St Gallen	6	2	0	4	6	13	6

GROUP B

Match-day 1: Dinamo Zagreb 1 (Fernandes 43) Chernomorets 2 (Antonov 62, Dja Djedje 65). Att: 3,500. PSV 0 Ludogorets 2 (Bezjak 60, Misidjan 75). Att: 11,000
Match-day 2: Chernomorets 0 PSV 2 (Depay 13, Jozefzoon 20). Att: 33,839. Ludogorets 3 (Quixada 11, Misidjan 34, Dyakov 61) Dinamo Zagreb 0. Att: 4,919
Match-day 3: Chernomorets 0 Ludogorets 1 (Zlatinski 45). Att: 20,082. Dinamo Zagreb 0 PSV 0. Played behind closed doors – previous fans' racist behaviour
Match-day 4: Ludogorets 1 (Quixada 47) Chernomorets 1 (Gai 65). Att: 6,113. PSV 2 (Maher 29, Toivonen 57) Dinamo Zagreb 0. Att: 10,500
Match-day 5: Chernomorets 2 (Antonov 78, Didenko 90) Dinamo Zagreb 1 (Beciraj 20). Att: 14,182. Ludogorets 2 (Bezjak 38, 79) PSV 0. Att: 3,012
Match-day 6: Dinamo Zagreb 1 (Cop 45) Ludogorets 2 (Abalo 27, Bezjak 72). Att: 3,120. PSV 0 Chernomorets 1 (Dja Djedje 59). Att: 11,500

	P	W	D	L	F	A	Pts
Ludogorets Q	6	5	1	0	11	2	16
Chernomorets Q	6	3	1	2	6	6	10
PSV	6	2	1	3	4	5	7
Dinamo Zagreb	6	0	1	5	3	11	1

GROUP C

Match-day 1: Salzburg 4 (Alan 36, Soriano 45 pen, 69, 79) Elfsborg 0. Att: 7,879. Standard Liege 1 (Mujangi Bia 73) Esbjerg 2 (Van Buren 63, Bakenga 90). Att: 11,871
Match-day 2: Elfsborg 1 (Claesson 23) Standard Liege 1 (Mujangi Bia 62). Att: 3,778. Esbjerg 1 (Pate Diouf 89) Salzburg 2 (Alan 6, 38). Att: 11,298
Match-day 3: Elfsborg 1 (Jonsson 69) Esbjerg 2 (Andreasen 6, 66). Att: 3,142. Salzburg 2 (Soriano 53, Ramalho 85) Standard Liege 1 (Mujangi Bia 88 pen). Att: 14,856
Match-day 4: Esbjerg 1 (Rohden 71 og) Elfsborg 0. Att: 10,049. Standard Liege 1 (M'Poku 55) Salzburg 3 (Svento 42, Kampl 45, Alan 58). Att: 12,005
Match-day 5: Esbjerg 2 (Van Buren 18, 79) Standard Liege 1 (De Camargo 53). Att: 9,184. Elfsborg 0 Salzburg 1 (Meilinger 39). Att: 2,456
Match-day 6: Salzburg 3 (Mane 20, 63, Kampl 58) Esbjerg 0. Att: 6,890. Standard Liege 1 (Mbombo 31) Elfsborg 3 (Nilsson 41, 45, Beckmann 52). Att: 6,466

	P	W	D	L	F	A	Pts
Salzburg Q	6	6	0	0	15	3	18
Esbjerg Q	6	4	0	2	8	8	12
Elfsborg	6	1	1	4	5	10	4
Standard Liege	6	0	1	5	6	13	1

GROUP D

Match-day 1: Maribor 2 (Milec 35, Fajic 74) Rubin Kazan 5 (Karadeniz 23, Marcano 27, Eremenko 69, Rondon 90, Ryazantsev 90). Att: 7,500. Zulte-Waregem 0 **Wigan** 0. Att: 8,000
Match-day 2: Rubin Kazan 4 (Duplus 60 og, Karadeniz 74, Ryazantsev 81, Natkho 89) Zulte-Waregem 0. Att: 4,057. **Wigan** 3 (Powell 22, 90, Watson 33) Maribor 1 (Tavares 60). Att: 12,753
Match-day 3: **Wigan** 1 (Powell 39) Rubin Kazan 1 (Prudnikov 15). Att: 14,723. Zulte-Waregem 1 (De Fauw 13) Maribor 3 (Crnic 21, Mertelj 34, Mezga 49). Att: 5,023
Match-day 4: Rubin Kazan 1 (Kuzmin 22) **Wigan** 0. Att: 5,579. Maribor 0 Zulte-Waregem 1 (Hazard 30 pen). Att: 8,500
Match-day 5: Rubin Kazan 1 (Natkho 43) Maribor 1 (Mezga 87). Att: 2,754. **Wigan** 1 (Barnett 7) Zulte-Waregem 2 (Hazard 37, Malanda 88). Att: 15,503
Match-day 6: Maribor 2 (Mezga 43, Filipovic 59) **Wigan** 1 (Gomez 41 pen). Att: 9,035. Zulte-Waregem 0 Rubin Kazan 2 (Natkho 79 pen, Rondon 86). Att: 6,083

	P	W	D	L	F	A	Pts
Rubin Kazan Q	6	4	2	0	14	4	14
Maribor Q	6	2	1	3	9	12	7
Zulte-Waregem	6	2	1	3	4	10	7
Wigan	6	1	2	3	6	7	5

GROUP E

Match-day 1: Fiorentina 3 (Gonzalo 30, Santos Ryder 67, Rossi 76) Pacos Ferreira 0. Att: 15,000. Pandurii 0 Dnipro 1 (Rotan 38). Att: 7,577

Match-day 2: Dnipro 1 (Seleznyov 57 pen) Fiorentina 2 (Gonzalo 53 pen, Ambrosini 73).
Att: 25,837. Pacos Ferreira 1 (Miguel 49) Pandurii 1 (Momcilovic 5). Att: 1,314
Match-day 3: Fiorentina 3 (Joaquin 26, Santos Ryder 34, Cuadrado 69) Pandurii 0. Att:
14,834. Pacos Ferreira 0 Dnipro 2 (Rotan 83, Konoplyanka 86). Att: 1,137
Match-day 4: Dnipro 2 (Matheus 44, Konoplyanka 66) Pacos Ferreira 0. Att: 14,039.
Pandurii 1 (Pereira 32) Fiorentina 2 (Santos Ryder 86, Valero 90). Att: 11,750
Match-day 5: Dnipro 4 (Kalinic 13, Zozulya 56, Shakhov 86, Kravchenko 89) Pandurii 1
(Pereira 70 pen). Att: 5,157. Pacos Ferreira 0 Fiorentina 0. Att: 1,347
Match-day 6: Fiorentina 2 (Joaquin 42, Cuadrado 77) Dnipro 1 (Konoplyanka 13). Att:
12,486. Pandurii 0 Pacos Ferreira 0. Att: 1,213

FINAL TABLE

	P	W	D	L	F	A	Pts
Fiorentina Q	6	5	1	0	12	3	16
Dnipro Q	6	4	0	2	11	5	12
Pacos Ferreira	6	0	3	3	1	8	3
Pandurii	6	0	2	4	3	11	2

GROUP F

Match-day 1: Eintracht Frankfurt 3 (Kadlec 4, Russ 16, Djakpa 52) Bordeaux 0. Att:
44,000. Maccabi Tel Aviv 0 Apoel Nicosia 0. Att: 11,772
Match-day 2: Apoel Nicosia 0 Eintracht Frankfurt 3 (Alexandrou 27 og, Lakic 57, Jung 67).
Att: 13,729. Bordeaux 1 (Jussie 48) Maccabi Tel Aviv 2 (Itzhaki 71, Micha 79). Att: 7,329
Match-day 3: Bordeaux 2 (Sane 24, Henrique 89) Apoel Nicosia 1 (Goncalves 45). Att:
10,404. Eintracht Frankfurt 2 (Kadlec 12, Meier 53) Maccabi Tel Aviv 0. Att: 40,800
Match-day 4: Apoel Nicosia 2 (Alexandrou 13, Morais 54) Bordeaux 1 (Sane 45). Att:
11,853. Maccabi Tel Aviv 4 (Zahavi 14, 90 pen, Itzhaki 30, 35) Eintracht Frankfurt 2 (Lakic
64, Meier 67 pen). Att: 13,232
Match-day 5: Apoel Nicosia 0 Maccabi Tel Aviv 0. Att: 13,052. Bordeaux 0 Eintracht
Frankfurt 1 (Lanig 81). Att: 19,013
Match-day 6: Eintracht Frankfurt 2 (Schrock 67, Djakpa 77) Apoel Nicosia 0. Att: 32,400.
Maccabi Tel Aviv 1 (Zahavi 74 pen) Bordeaux 0. Att: 11,742

FINAL TABLE

	P	W	D	L	F	A	Pts
Eintracht Frankfurt Q	6	5	0	1	13	4	15
Maccabi Tel Aviv Q	6	3	2	1	7	5	11
Apoel Nicosia	6	1	2	3	3	8	5
Bordeaux	6	1	0	5	4	10	3

GROUP G

Match-day 1: Dyamo Kiev 0 Genk 1 (Gorius 62). Att: 30,345. Thun 1 (Schneuwly 35) Rapid
Vienna 0. Att: 7,022
Match-day 2: Genk 2 (Gorius 55, Vossen 63) Thun 1 (Martinez 90). Att: 11,559. Rapid
Vienna 2 (Burgstaller 53, Trimmel 90) Dynamo Kiev 2 (Yarmolenko 30, Dibon 34 og). Att:
34,800
Match-day 3: Dynamo Kiev 3 (Yarmolenko 35, Mbokani 59, Gusev 78) Thun 0. Att: 26,042.
Genk 1 (Gorius 20) Rapid Vienna 1 (Sabitzer 82). Att: 14,142
Match-day 4: Thun 0 Dynamo Kiev 2 (Schenkel 29 og, Yarmolenko 68). Att: 6,523. Rapid
Vienna 2 (Boyd 40, 45) Genk 2 (Mbodj 29 pen, Buffel 60). Att: 34,300
Match-day 5: Genk 3 (Vossen 17 pen, Kumordzi 37, De Ceulaer 40) Dynamo Kiev 1
(Yarmolenko 9). Att: 13,337. Rapid Vienna 2 (Boyd 17, Boskovic 64) Thun 1 (Sadik 61). Att:
34,300

Match-day 6: Dynamo Kiev 3 (Lens 22, Gusev 28, Veloso 71) Rapid Vienna 1 (Boyd 6). Att: 18,762. Thun 0 Genk 1 (Vossen 31). Att: 5,185

FINAL TABLE

	P	W	D	L	F	A	Pts
Genk Q	6	4	2	0	10	5	14
Dynamo Kiev Q	6	3	1	2	11	7	10
Rapid Vienna	6	1	3	2	8	10	6
Thun	6	1	0	5	3	10	3

GROUP H

Match-day 1: Estoril 1 (Bruno Miguel 61) Sevilla 2 (Vitolo 59, Gameiro 77). Att: 4,154. Freiburg 2 (Schuster 23, Mehmedi 35) Liberec 2 (Kalitvintsev 66, Rabusic 73). Att: 14,100
Match-day 2: Liberec 2 (Sural 15, Kovac 63) Estoril 1 (Leal 45). Att: 7,500. Sevilla 2 (Perotti 63 pen, Bacca 90) Freiburg 0. Att: 17,041
Match-day 3: Freiburg 1 (Darida 11) Estoril 1 (Seba 53). Att: 14,500. Liberec 1 (Rabusic 20) Sevilla 1 (Vitolo 88). Att: 7,700
Match-day 4: Estoril 0 Freiburg 0. Att: 2,014. Sevilla 1 (Perotti 29) Liberec 1 (Pavelka 71). Att: 15,178
Match-day 5: Sevilla 1 (Gameiro 7) Estoril 1 (Fernandes 90). Att: 12,557. Liberec 1 (Rybalka 81) Freiburg 2 (Ginter 23, Coquelin 73). Att: 8,800
Match-day 6: Estoril 1 (Seba 82) Liberec 2 (Sural 18, Rabusic 70). Att: 1,247. Freiburg 0 Sevilla 2 (Iborra 40, Rusescu 90). Att: 17,000

FINAL TABLE

	P	W	D	L	F	A	Pts
Sevilla Q	6	3	3	0	9	4	12
Liberec Q	6	2	3	1	9	8	9
Freiburg	6	1	3	2	5	8	6
Estoril	6	0	3	3	5	8	3

GROUP I

Match-day 1: Guimaraes 4 (Ba 36, Plange 48, Maazou 68 pen, Andre 81) Rijeka 0. Att: 9,754. Real Betis 0 Lyon 0. Att: 22,463
Match-day 2: Lyon 1 (Gonalons 53) Guimaraes 1 (Maazou 39). Att: 30,061. Rijeka 1 (Benko 10) Real Betis 1 (Mabwati 14). Att: 7,313
Match-day 3: Lyon 1 (Grenier 67) Rijeka 0. Att: 30,461. Real Betis 1 (Vadillo 50) Guimaraes 0. Att: 17,100
Match-day 4: Rijeka 1 (Kramaric 21) Lyon 1 (Plea 14). Att: 7,300. Guimaraes 0 Real Betis 1 (Jesus Chuli 90). Att: 22,602
Match-day 5: Lyon 1 (Gomis 66) Real Betis 0. Att: 24,112. Rijeka 0 Guimaraes 0. Att: 7,138
Match-day 6: Real Betis 0 Rijeka 0. Att: 14,556. Guimaraes 1 (Crivellaro 11) Lyon 2 (Gomis 63 pen, Ferri 65). Att: 5,845

FINAL TABLE

	P	W	D	L	F	A	Pts
Lyon Q	6	3	3	0	6	3	12
Real Betis Q	6	2	3	1	3	2	9
Guimaraes	6	1	2	3	6	5	5
Rijeka	6	0	4	2	2	7	4

GROUP J

Match-day 1: Apollon Limassol 1 (Sangoy 18 pen) Trabzonspor 2 (Malouda 20, Erdogan 86). Att: 10,204. Lazio 1 (Hernanes 53) Legia Warsaw 0. Att: 11,769
Match-day 2: Legia Warsaw 0 Apollon Limassol 1 (Sangoy 56). Player behind closed doors – previous racist incidents. Trabzonspor 3 (Erdogan 12, Mierzejewski 22, Henrique 35) Lazio 3 (Onazi 29, Floccari 84, 85). Att: 13,002
Match-day 3: Apollon Limassol 0 Lazio 0. Att: 8,943. Trabzonspor 2 (Janko 7, Adin 83) Legia Warsaw 0. Att: 12,871
Match-day 4: Lazio 2 (Floccari 14, 37) Apollon Limassol 1 (Papoulis 39). Att: 6,498. Legia Warsaw 0 Trabzonspor 2 (Dosa Junior 72 og, Adin 79). Att: 14,088
Match-day 5: Legia Warsaw 0 Lazio 2 (Perea 24, Anderson 57). Att: 12,000. Trabzonspor 4 (Adin 23, 61, 83, Aydogdu 25) Apollon Limassol 2 (Gneki Guie 68, Sangoy 80 pen). Att: 11,151
Match-day 6: Apollon Limassol 0 Legia Warsaw 2 (Jodlowice 8, Brzyski 63). Att: 1,681. Lazio 0 Trabzonspor 0. Att: 7,732

FINAL TABLE

	P	W	D	L	F	A	Pts
Trabzonspor Q	6	4	2	0	13	6	14
Lazio Q	6	3	3	0	8	4	12
Apollon Limassol	6	1	1	4	5	10	4
Legia Warsaw	6	1	0	5	2	8	3

GROUP K

Match-day 1: Sheriff Tiraspol 0 Anzhi Makhachkala 0. Att: 8,882. **Tottenham** 3 (Defoe 21, 29, Eriksen 86) Tromso 0. Att: 26,581
Match-day 2: Anzhi Makhachkala 0 **Tottenham** 2 (Defoe 34, Chadli 39). Att: 5,662. Tromso 1 (Ondrasek 65) Sheriff Tiraspol 1 (Ricardinho 87). Att: 3,710
Match-day 3: Anzhi Makhachkala 1 (Burmistrov 19) Tromso 0. Att: 2,797. Sheriff Tiraspol 0 **Tottenham** 2 (Vertonghen 12, Defoe 75). Att: 11,725
Match-day 4: **Tottenham** 2 (Lamela 60, Defoe 67 pen) Sheriff Tiraspol 1 (Isa 72). Att: 32,225. Tromso 0 Anzhi Makhachkala 1 (Mkrtchyan 90). Att: 3,673
Match-day 5: Anzhi Makhachkala 1 (Epureanu 58) Sheriff Tiraspol 1 (Isa 52). Att: 2,760. Tromso 0 **Tottenham** 2 (Cauevic 63 og, Dembele 75). Att: 5,868
Match-day 6: Sheriff Tiraspol 2 (Cadu 4, Isa 36) Tromso 0. Att: 1,211. **Tottenham** 4 (Soldado 7, 16 pen, 70, Holtby 54) Anzhi Makhachkala 1 (Ewerton 44). Att: 23,101

FINAL TABLE

	P	W	D	L	F	A	Pts
Tottenham Q	6	6	0	0	15	2	18
Anzhi Makhachkala Q	6	2	2	2	4	7	8
Sheriff Tiraspol	6	1	3	2	5	6	6
Tromso	6	0	1	5	1	10	1

GROUP L

Match-day 1: Maccabi Haifa 0 Alkmaar 1 (Gudmundsson 71). Att: 10,000. PAOK Salonika 2 (Athanasiadis 75, Vukic 90) Shakhter Karagandy 1 (Canas 50 pen). Played behind closed doors – previous crowd trouble
Match-day 2: Alkmaar 1 (Gouweleeuw 82) PAOK Salonika 1 (Salpigidis 90). Att: 10,761. Shakhter Karagandy 2 (Finonchenko 40, Tarasov 45) Maccabi Haifa 2 (Ezra 54, Turgeman 78). Att: 19,000
Match-day 3: PAOK Salonika 3 (Vitor 35, Ninis 40, Salpigidis 66) Maccabi Haifa 2

(Ndlovu 14, Golasa 22). Att: 14,211. Shakhter Karagandy 1 (Finonchenko 11) Alkmaar 1
(Gudmundsson 26). Att: 19,000.
Match-day 4: Alkmaar 1 (Ortiz 55) Shakhter Karagandy 0. Att: 9,778. Maccabi Haifa 0
PAOK Salonika 0. Att: 10,000
Match-day 5: Alkmaar 2 (Gudelj 37, Gudmundsson 90) Maccabi Haifa 0. Att: 11,211.
Shakhter Karagandy 0 PAOK Salonika 2 (Dzidic 54 og, Kitsiou 90). Att: 7,556.
Match-day 6: Maccabi Haifa 2 (Gozlan 73, Abuhazira 81) Shakhter Karagandy 1 (Canas 44
pen). Att: 2,100. PAOK Salonika 2 (Lucas 38 pen, Pozoglou 90) Alkmaar 2 (Lam 31, Gorter
71 pen). Att: 11,211

FINAL TABLE

	P	W	D	L	F	A	Pts
Alkmaar Q	6	3	3	0	8	4	12
PAOK Salonika Q	6	3	3	0	10	6	12
Maccabi Haifa	6	1	2	3	6	9	5
Shakhter Karagandy	6	0	2	4	5	10	2

ROUND OF 32, FIRST LEG

Ajax 0 Salzburg 3 (Soriano 14 pen, 35, Mane 21). Att: 51,240. Anzhi Makhachkala 0
Genk 0. Att: 3,168. Chernomorets 0 Lyon 0. Att: 28,456. Dnipro 1 (Konoplyanka 81 pen)
Tottenham 0. Att: 22,356
Dynamo Kiev 0 Valencia 2 (Vargas 80, Feghouli 90). Att: 3,711. Esbjerg 1 (Pusic 10)
Fiorentina 3 (Matri 8, Ilicic 15, Aquilani 37 pen). Att: 11,033. Juventus 2 (Osvaldo 15,
Pogba 90) Trabzonspor 0. Att: 35,436. Lazio 0 Ludogorets 1 (Bezjak 45). Att: 7,459
Liberec 0 Alkmaar 1 (Viergever 89). Att: 6,719. PAOK Salonika 0 Benfica 1 (Lima 59).
Att: 24,670. Plzen 1 (Tecl 62) Shakhtar Donetsk 1 (Luiz Adriano 66). Att: 11,179. Porto 2
(Quaresma 45, Varela 68) Eintracht Frankfurt 2 (Joselu 72, Sandro 78 og). Att: 25,107
Maccabi Tel Aviv 0 Basle 0. Att: 13,519. Maribor 2 (Tavares 33, Vrsic 81) Sevilla 2 (Gameiro
47, Fazio 71). Att: 12,700. Real Betis 1 (Villa 4) Rubin Kazan 1 (Eremenko 74 pen). Att:
11,825. **Swansea** 0 Napoli 0. Att: 19,567

ROUND OF 32, SECOND LEG

Alkmaar 1 (Viergever 19) Liberec 1 (Budnik 71). Att: 10,166 (Alkmaar won 2-1 on agg).
Basle 3 (Stocker 18, Streller 60, 71) Maccabi Tel Aviv 0. Att: 15,212 (Basle won 3-0 on
agg). Benfica 3 (Gaitan 70, Lima 79 pen, Markovic 80) PAOK Salonika 0. Att: 31,058
(Benfica won 4-0 on agg)
Eintracht Frankfurt 3 (Aigner 37, Meier 52, 76) Porto 3 (Mangala 58, 71, Gilhas 86). Att:
48,000 (Agg 5-5, Porto won on away goals). Fiorentina 1 (Ilicic 47) Esbjerg 1 (Vestergaard
90). Att: 13,815 (Fiorentina won 4-2 on agg). Genk 0 Anzhi Makhachkala 2 (Tshimanga 64
og, Aliyev 71). Att: 10,176 (Anzhi Makhachkala won 2-0 on agg)
Ludogorets 3 (Bezjak 67, Zlatinski 78, Quixada 89) Lazio 3 (Keita 1, Perea 54, Klose 83).
Att: 28,742 (Ludogorets won 4-3 on agg). Lyon 1 (Lacazette 80) Chernomorets 0. Att:
25,039 (Lyon won 1-0 on agg). Napoli 3 (Insigne 17, Higuain 78, Inler 90) **Swansea** 1 (De
Guzman 30). Att: 31,121 (Napoli won 3-1 on agg)
Rubin Kazan 0 Real Betis 2 (Nono 45, Castro 64). Att: 5,102 (Real Betis won 3-1 on agg).
Salzburg 3 (Van der Hoorn 56 og, Mane 66, Soriano 77) Ajax 1 (Klaassen 82). Att: 29,320
(Salzburg won 6-1 on agg). Sevilla 2 (Reyes 42, Gameiro 59) Maribor 1 (Vrsic 90). Att:
21,562 (Sevilla won 4-3 on agg)
Shakhtar Donetsk 1 (Luiz Adriano 89) Plzen 2 (Kolar 29, Petrzela 33). Att: 36,729 (Plzen
won 3-2 on agg). **Tottenham** 3 (Eriksen 56, Adebayor 65, 69) Dnipro 1 (Zozulya 48). Att:
34,815 (Tottenham won 3-2 on agg). Trabzonspor 0 Juventus 2 (Vidal 19, Osvaldo 34). Att:
20,686 (Juventus won 4-0 on agg). Valencia 0 Dynamo Kiev 0. Att: 26,261 (Valencia won
2-0 on agg)

ROUND OF 16, FIRST LEG

Alkmaar 1 (Johannsson 29 pen) Anzhi Makhachkala 0. Att: 9,653. Basle 0 Salzburg 0. Att: 17,027. Ludogorets 0 Valencia 3 (Barragan 5, Fede 34, Senderos 59). Att: 41,085. Juventus 1 (Vidal 3) Fiorentina 1 (Gomez 79). Att: 39,610
Lyon 4 (Fofana 12, 70, Lacazette 53, Mvuemba 61) Plzen 1 (Horava 3). Att: 28,248. Porto 1 (Martinez 57) Napoli 0. Att: 25,250. Sevilla 0 Real Betis 2 (Baptistao 15, Sevilla 77). Att: 35,506. **Tottenham** 1 (Eriksen 63) Benfica 3 (Rodrigo 29, Luisao 58, 84). Att: 34,283

ROUND OF 16, SECOND LEG

Anzhi Makhachkala 0 Alkmaar 0. Att: 3,168 (Alkmaar won 1-0 on agg), Benfica 2 (Garay 34, Lima 90 pen) **Tottenham** 2 (Chadli 78, 79). Att: 40,000 (Benfica won 5-3 on agg). Fiorentina 0 Juventus 0. Att: 30,000 (Juventus won 2-1 on agg). Napoli 2 (Pandev 21, Zapata 90) Porto 2 (Ghilas 69, Quaresma 76). Att: 60,000 (Porto won 3-2 on agg) Plzen 2 (Kolar 60, Tecl 62) Lyon 1 (Gomis 45). Att: 10,352 (Lyon won 5-3 on agg). Real Betis 0 Sevilla 2 (Reyes 20, Bacca 75). Att: 38,799 (aet, agg 2-2, Sevilla won 4-3 on pens). Salzburg 1 (Soriano 22) Basle 2 (Streller 51, Sauro 60). Att: 29,320 (Basle won 2-1 on agg). Valencia 1 (Alcacer 59) Ludogorets 0. Att: 25,000 (Valencia won 4-0 on agg)

QUARTER-FINALS, FIRST LEG

Alkmaar 0 Benfica 1 (Salvio 49). Att: 16,906. Basle 3 (Delgado 34, 38, Stocker 90) Valencia 0. Played behind closed doors, previous crowd trouble. Porto 1 (Mangala 31) Sevilla 0. Att: 31,222. Lyon 0 Juventus 1 (Bonucci 85). Att: 37,084

QUARTER-FINALS, SECOND LEG

Benfica 2 (Rodrigo 39, 72) Alkmaar 0. Att: 35,723 (Benfica won 3-0 on agg). Juventus 2 (Pirlo 4, Umtiti 68 og) Lyon 1 (Briand 18). Att: 40,710 (Juventus won 3-1 on agg). Sevilla 4 (Rakitic 5 pen, Vitolo 26, Bacca 30, Gameiro 79) Porto 1 (Quaresma 90). Att: 31,422 (Sevilla won 4-2 on agg). Valencia 5 (Alcacer 38, 70, 113, Vargas 43, Bernat 118) Basle 0. Att: 33,152 (aet, Valencia won 5-3 on agg)

SEMI-FINALS, FIRST LEG

Benfica 2 (Garay 2, Lima (84) Juventus 1 (Tevez 73). Att: 55,779. Sevilla 2 (Mbia 33, Bacca 36) Valencia 0. Att: 33,496

SEMI-FINALS, SECOND LEG

Juventus 0 Benfica 0: Att: 40,775 (Benfica won 2-1 on agg). Valencia 3 (Feghouli 14, Beto 26 og, Mathieu 69) Sevilla 1 (Mbia 90). Att: 48,000 (agg 3-3, Sevilla won on away goal)

FINAL

SEVILLA 0 BENFICA 0 (aet, Sevilla won 4-2 on pens)
Juventus Stadium, Turin (33,120): Wednesday, May 14 2014

Sevilla (4-2-3-1): Beto, Coke, Pareja, Fazio, Alberto Moreno, Mbia, Daniel Carrico, Reyes (Marin 78) (Gameiro 104), Rakitic (capt), Vitolo (Diogo Figueiras 110), Bacca. **Subs not used:** Javi Varas, Fernando Navarro, Iborra, Trochowski. **Booked:** Fazio, Alberto Moreno, Coke. **Coach:** Unai Emery
Benfica (4-3-2-1): Oblak, Maxi Pereira, Luisao (capt), Garay, Siqueira (Cardozo 99), Ruben Amorim, Gomes, Gaitan (Ivan Calvaleiro 119), Sulejmani (Andre Ammeida 25) Rodrigo, Lima. **Subs not used:** Artur Moraes, Steven Vitoria, Djuricic, Jardel. **Booked:** Siqueria, Andre Almeida. **Coach:** Jorge Jesus
Referee: F Brych (Germany)

Leading scorers (from group stage): 8 Soriano (Salzburg); 7 Alcacer (Valencia); 6 Bezjak (Ludogorets); 5 Defoe (Tottenham), Gameiro (Sevilla), Adin (Trabzonspor); 4 Lima (Benfica), Bacca (Sevilla)

CLUB WORLD CUP – MOROCCO 2013

QUALIFYING MATCHES

Guangzhou Evergrande (China) 2 (Elkeson 49, Conca 67) Al Ahly (Egypt) O. Marrakech (34,579). Raja Casablanca (Morocco) 2 (Chtibi 25, Guehi 95) Monterrey (Mexico) 1 (Basanta 53) – aet, Agadir (26,529)

SEMI-FINALS

Guangzhou Evergrande O Bayern Munich 3 (Ribery 40, Mandzukic 44, Gotze 47). Agadir (27,311). Raja Casablanca 3 (Iajour 51, Moutouali 84, Mabide 90) Atletico Mineiro (Brazil) 1 (Gaucho 64). Marrakech (35,219)

FINAL
BAYERN MUNICH 2 RAJA CASABLANCA 0
Marrakech (37,774); Saturday, December 21 2013

Bayern Munich (4-1-4-1): Neuer, Rafinha, Boateng, Dante, Alaba, Lahm (capt), Shaqiri (Gotze 80), Thiago Alcantara, Kroos (Javi Martinez 60), Ribery, Muller (Mandzukic 76). **Subs not used**: Starke, Raeder, Van Buyten, Pizarro, Kirchhoff, Weiser, Contento, Hojbjerg, Green. **Scorers**: Dante (7), Thiago Alcantara (22). **Coach**: Pep Guardiola
Raja Casablanca (4-2-3-1): Askri, El Hachimi, Benlamalem, Oulhaj, Karrouchy, Guehi, Erraki, Chtibi, Moutouali (capt), Hafidi (Kachani 88), Iajour (Soulaimani 78). **Subs not used**: El Had, Zaari, Rahmani, Kanda, Eddine, Salhi, Kouchame, Dardouri, Coulibaly. **Booked**: Oulhaj, Soulaimani. **Coach**: Faouzi Benzarti
Referee: S Ricci (Brazil). **Half-time**: 2-0

EUROPEAN SUPER CUP

BAYERN MUNICH 2 CHELSEA 2
(aet, Bayern Munich won 5-4 on pens)
Prague (17,686); Friday, August 30 2013

Bayern Munich (4-1-4-1): Neuer, Rafinha (Javi Martinez 56), Boateng, Dante, Alaba, Lahm (capt), Robben (Shaqiri 95), Muller (Gotze 71), Kroos, Ribery, Mandzukic. **Subs not used**: Starke, Van Buyten, Contento, Pizarro. **Scorers**: Ribery (47), Martinez (120). **Booked**: Ribery, Boateng. **Coach**: Pep Guardiola
Chelsea (4-2-3-1): Cech, Ivanovic, Cahill, Luiz, Cole, Ramires, Lampard (capt), Hazard (Terry 113), Oscar, Schurrle (Mikel 87), Torres (Lukaku 97). **Subs not used**: Schwarzer, Azpilicueta, Essien, Mata. **Scorers**: Torres (8), Hazard (93). **Booked**: Cahill, Ramires, Luiz, Torres, Lukaku, Cole, Ivanovic. **Sent off**: Ramires (85). **Manager**: Jose Mourinho
Penalty shoot-out: 1-0 (Alaba), 1-1 (Luiz), 2-1 (Kroos), 2-2 (Oscar), 3-2 (Lahm), 3-3 (Lampard), 4-3 (Ribery), 4-4 (Cole), 5-4 (Shaqiri), 5-4 (Lukaku saved)
Referee: J Eriksson (Sweden). **Half-time**: 0-1

UEFA CUP FINALS

1972   Tottenham beat Wolves 3-2 on agg (2-1a, 1-1h)
1973   Liverpool beat Borussia Moenchengladbach 3-2 on agg (3-0h, 0-2a)

1974	Feyenoord beat Tottenham 4-2 on agg (2-2a, 2-0h)
1975	Borussia Moenchengladbach beat Twente Enschede 5-1 on agg (0-0h, 5-1a)
1976	Liverpool beat Brugge 4-3 on agg (3-2h, 1-1a)
1977	Juventus beat Atletico Bilbao on away goals after 2-2 agg (1-0h, 1-2a)
1978	PSV Eindhoven beat Bastia 3-0 on agg (0-0a, 3-0h)
1979	Borussia Moenchengladbach beat Red Star Belgrade 2-1 on agg (1-1a, 1-0h)
1980	Eintracht Frankfurt beat Borussia Moenchengladbach on away goals after 3-3 agg (2-3a, 1-0h)
1981	Ipswich Town beat AZ 67 Alkmaar 5-4 on agg (3-0h, 2-4a)
1982	IFK Gothenburg beat SV Hamburg 4-0 on agg (1-0h, 3-0a)
1983	Anderlecht beat Benfica 2-1 on agg (1-0h, 1-1a)
1984	Tottenham beat Anderlecht 4-3 on penalties after 2-2 agg (1-1a, 1-1h)
1985	Real Madrid beat Videoton 3-1 on agg (3-0a, 0-1h)
1986	Real Madrid beat Cologne 5-3 on agg (5-1h, 0-2a)
1987	IFK Gothenburg beat Dundee Utd 2-1 on agg (1-0h, 1-1a)
1988	Bayer Leverkusen beat Espanol 3-2 on penalties after 3-3 agg (0-3a, 3-0h)
1989	Napoli beat VfB Stuttgart 5-4 on agg (2-1h, 3-3a)
1990	Juventus beat Fiorentina 3-1 on agg (3-1h, 0-0a)
1991	Inter Milan beat AS Roma 2-1 on agg (2-0h, 0-1a)
1992	Ajax beat Torino on away goals after 2-2 agg (2-2a, 0-0h)
1993	Juventus beat Borussia Dortmund 6-1 on agg (3-1a, 3-0h)
1994	Inter Milan beat Salzburg 2-0 on agg (1-0a, 1-0h)
1995	Parma beat Juventus 2-1 on agg (1-0h, 1-1a)
1996	Bayern Munich beat Bordeaux 5-1 on agg (2-0h, 3-1a)
1997	FC Schalke beat Inter Milan 4-1 on penalties after 1-1 agg (1-0h, 0-1a)
1998	Inter Milan beat Lazio 3-0 (one match) – Paris
1999	Parma beat Marseille 3-0 (one match) – Moscow
2000	Galatasaray beat Arsenal 4-1 on penalties after 0-0 (one match) – Copenhagen
2001	Liverpool beat Alaves 5-4 on golden goal (one match) – Dortmund
2002	Feyenoord beat Borussia Dortmund 3-2 (one match) – Rotterdam
2003	FC Porto beat Celtic 3-2 on silver goal (one match) – Seville
2004	Valencia beat Marseille 2-0 (one match) – Gothenburg
2005	CSKA Moscow beat Sporting Lisbon 3-1 (one match) – Lisbon
2006	Sevilla beat Middlesbrough 4-0 (one match) – Eindhoven
2007	Sevilla beat Espanyol 3-1 on penalties after 2-2 (one match) – Hampden Park
2008	Zenit St Petersburg beat Rangers 2-0 (one match) – City of Manchester Stadium
2009†	Shakhtar Donetsk beat Werder Bremen 2-1 (one match) – Istanbul

EUROPA LEAGUE FINALS

2010†	Atletico Madrid beat Fulham 2-1 (one match) – Hamburg
2011	Porto beat Braga 1-0 (one match) – Dublin
2012	Atletico Madrid beat Athletic Bilbao 3-0 (one match) – Bucharest
2013	Chelsea beat Benfica 2-1 (one match) – Amsterdam
2014	Sevilla beat Benfica 4-2 on penalties after 0-0 (one match) – Turin

(† After extra-time)

FAIRS CUP FINALS

(As UEFA Cup previously known)

1958	Barcelona beat London 8-2 on agg (2-2a, 6-0h)
1960	Barcelona beat Birmingham 4-1 on agg (0-0a, 4-1h)
1961	AS Roma beat Birmingham City 4-2 on agg (2-2a, 2-0h)
1962	Valencia beat Barcelona 7-3 on agg (6-2h, 1-1a)

1963	Valencia beat Dynamo Zagreb 4-1 on agg (2-1a, 2-0h)
1964	Real Zaragoza beat Valencia 2-1 (Barcelona)
1965	Ferencvaros beat Juventus 1-0 (Turin)
1966	Barcelona beat Real Zaragoza 4-3 on agg (0-1h, 4-2a)
1967	Dinamo Zagreb beat Leeds Utd 2-0 on agg (2-0h, 0-0a)
1968	Leeds Utd beat Ferencvaros 1-0 on agg (1-0h, 0-0a)
1969	Newcastle Utd beat Ujpest Dozsa 6-2 on agg (3-0h, 3-2a)
1970	Arsenal beat Anderlecht 4-3 on agg (1-3a, 3-0h)
1971	Leeds Utd beat Juventus on away goals after 3-3 agg (2-2a, 1-1h)

CUP-WINNERS' CUP FINALS

1961	Fiorentina beat Rangers 4-1 on agg (2-0 Glasgow first leg, 2-1 Florence second leg)
1962	Atletico Madrid beat Fiorentina 3-0 (replay Stuttgart, after a 1-1 draw, Glasgow)
1963	Tottenham beat Atletico Madrid 5-1 (Rotterdam)
1964	Sporting Lisbon beat MTK Budapest 1-0 (replay Antwerp, after a 3-3 draw, Brussels)
1965	West Ham Utd beat Munich 1860 2-0 (Wembley)
1966†	Borussia Dortmund beat Liverpool 2-1 (Glasgow)
1967†	Bayern Munich beat Rangers 1-0 (Nuremberg)
1968	AC Milan beat SV Hamburg 2-0 (Rotterdam)
1969	Slovan Bratislava beat Barcelona 3-2 (Basle)
1970	Manchester City beat Gornik Zabrze 2-1 (Vienna)
1971†	Chelsea beat Real Madrid 2-1 (replay Athens, after a 1-1 draw, Athens)
1972	Rangers beat Moscow Dynamo 3-2 (Barcelona)
1973	AC Milan beat Leeds Utd 1-0 (Salonika)
1974	Magdeburg beat AC Milan 2-0 (Rotterdam)
1975	Dynamo Kiev beat Ferencvaros 3-0 (Basle)
1976	Anderlecht beat West Ham Utd 4-2 (Brussels)
1977	SV Hamburg beat Anderlecht 2-0 (Amsterdam)
1978	Anderlecht beat Austria WAC 4-0 (Paris)
1979†	Barcelona beat Fortuna Dusseldorf 4-3 (Basle)
1980†	Valencia beat Arsenal 5-4 on penalties after a 0-0 draw (Brussels)
1981	Dynamo Tbilisi beat Carl Zeiss Jena 2-1 (Dusseldorf)
1982	Barcelona beat Standard Liege 2-1 (Barcelona)
1983†	Aberdeen beat Real Madrid 2-1 (Gothenburg)
1984	Juventus beat Porto 2-1 (Basle)
1985	Everton beat Rapid Vienna 3-1 (Rotterdam)
1986	Dynamo Kiev beat Atletico Madrid 3-0 (Lyon)
1987	Ajax beat Lokomotiv Leipzig 1-0 (Athens)
1988	Mechelen beat Ajax 1-0 (Strasbourg)
1989	Barcelona beat Sampdoria 2-0 (Berne)
1990	Sampdoria beat Anderlecht 2-0 (Gothenburg)
1991	Manchester Utd beat Barcelona 2-1 (Rotterdam)
1992	Werder Bremen beat Monaco 2-0 (Lisbon)
1993	Parma beat Royal Antwerp 3-1 (Wembley)
1994	Arsenal beat Parma 1-0 (Copenhagen)
1995†	Real Zaragoza beat Arsenal 2-1 (Paris)
1996	Paris St Germain beat Rapid Vienna 1-0 (Brussels)
1997	Barcelona beat Paris St Germain 1-0 (Rotterdam)
1998	Chelsea beat VfB Stuttgart 1-0 (Stockholm)
1999	Lazio beat Real Mallorca 2-1 (Villa Park, Birmingham)

(† After extra time)

INTER-CONTINENTAL CUP

Year	Winners	Runners-up	Score
1960	Real Madrid (Spa)	Penarol (Uru)	0-0 5-1
1961	Penarol (Uru)	Benfica (Por)	0-1 2-1 5-0
1962	Santos (Bra)	Benfica (Por)	3-2 5-2
1963	Santos (Bra)	AC Milan (Ita)	2-4 4-2 1-0
1964	Inter Milan (Ita)	Independiente (Arg)	0-1 2-0 1-0
1965	Inter Milan (Ita)	Independiente (Arg)	3-0 0-0
1966	Penarol (Uru)	Real Madrid (Spa)	2-0 2-0
1967	Racing (Arg)	Celtic (Sco)	0-1 2-1 1-0
1968	Estudiantes (Arg)	Manchester Utd (Eng)	1-0 1-1
1969	AC Milan (Ita)	Estudiantes (Arg)	3-0 1-2
1970	Feyenoord (Hol)	Estudiantes (Arg)	2-2 1-0
1971	Nacional (Uru)	Panathanaikos (Gre)	* 1-1 2-1
1972	Ajax (Hol)	Independiente (Arg)	1-1 3-0
1973	Independiente (Arg)	Juventus* (Ita)	1-0 #
1974	Atletico Madrid (Spa)*	Independiente (Arg)	0-1 2-0
1975	Not played		
1976	Bayern Munich (WGer)	Cruzeiro (Bra)	2-0 0-0
1977	Boca Juniors (Arg)	Borussia Mönchengladbach* (WGer)	2-2 3-0
1978	Not played		
1979	Olimpia Asuncion (Par)	Malmö* (Swe)	1-0 2-1
1980	Nacional (Arg)	Nott'm Forest (Eng)	1-0
1981	Flamengo (Bra)	Liverpool (Eng)	3 0
1982	Penarol (Uru)	Aston Villa (Eng)	2-0
1983	Porto Alegre (Bra)	SV Hamburg (WGer)	2-1
1984	Independiente (Arg)	Liverpool (Eng)	1-0
1985	Juventus (Ita)	Argentinos Juniors (Arg)	2-2 (aet)
	(Juventus won 4-2 on penalties)		
1986	River Plate (Arg)	Steaua Bucharest (Rom)	1-0
1987	Porto (Por)	Penarol (Arg)	2-1 (aet)
1988	Nacional (Uru)	PSV Eindhoven (Hol)	1-1 (aet)
	(Nacional won 7-6 on penalties)		
1989	AC Milan (Ita)	Nacional (Col)	1-0 (aet)
1990	AC Milan (Ita)	Olimpia Asuncion (Par)	3-0
1991	Red Star (Yug)	Colo Colo (Chi)	3-0
1992	Sao Paulo (Bra)	Barcelona (Spa)	2-1
1993	Sao Paulo (Bra)	AC Milan (Ita)	3-2
1994	Velez Sarsfield (Arg)	AC Milan (Ita)	2-0
1995	Ajax (Hol)	Gremio (Bra)	0-0 (aet)
	(Ajax won 4-3 on penalties)		
1996	Juventus (Ita)	River Plate (Arg)	1-0
1997	Borussia Dortmund (Ger)	Cruzeiro (Arg)	2-0
1998	Real Madrid (Spa)	Vasco da Gama (Bra)	2-1
1999	Manchester Utd (Eng)	Palmeiras (Bra)	1-0
2000	Boca Juniors (Arg)	Real Madrid (Spa)	2-1
2001	Bayern Munich (Ger)	Boca Juniors (Arg)	1-0
2002	Real Madrid (Spa)	Olimpia Ascuncion (Par)	2-0
2003	Boca Juniors (Arg)	AC Milan (Ita)	1-1
	(Boca Juniors won 3-1 on penalties)		
2004	FC Porto (Por)	Caldas (Col)	0-0
	(FC Porto won 8-7 on penalties)		

Played as a single match in Japan since 1980
* European Cup runners-up # One match only
Summary: 43 contests; South America 22 wins, Europe 23 wins

CLUB WORLD CHAMPIONSHIP

2005	Sao Paulo beat Liverpool	1-0
2006	Internacional (Bra) beat Barcelona	1-0
2007	AC Milan beat Boca Juniors (Arg)	4-2

CLUB WORLD CUP

2008	Manchester Utd beat Liga de Quito	1-0
2009	Barcelona beat Estudiantes	2-1 (aet)
2010	Inter Milan beat TP Mazembe	3-0
2011	Barcelona beat Santos	4-0
2012	Corinthians beat Chelsea	1-0
2013	Bayern Munich beat Raja Casablanca	2-0

THE THINGS THEY SAY...

'It was handbags at half-mast' – **Alan Pardew**, Newcastle manager, on a touch-line clash between rival coaching staff during the match against Southampton.

'It was a piece of humour, an instant reaction. If you want a strait-laced suit you can have a strait-laced suit. Or you can have someone like me' – **Greg Dyke**, FA chairman, on his cut-throat gesture after England were drawn in a tough World Cup group with Italy, Uruguay and Costa Rica.

'I wouldn't trust the FA to show me a good manager if their lives depended on it' – **Harry Redknapp**, who was not interviewed for the England job which went to Roy Hodgson, criticises the governing body in his autobiography.

'He is someone you can compare with the best young Brazilian, Dutch and Spanish players. I've never seen an English player with that sort of mentality' – **Roberto Martinez**, Everton manager, on his midfielder Ross Barkley.

'He was one of the finest players I had the privilege to play against. Not only that, he was a true sportsman, as he proved in applauding Alex Stepney for his save in the 1968 European Cup Final' – **Sir Bobby Charlton** on the death of the legendary Eusebio.

'I would have changed all 11 players at half-time if I'd been able to' – **Manuel Pellegrini**, Manchester City manager, after his side were 2-0 down at home to Watford in the FA Cup before rallying to win 4-2.

''This is football from the 19th century' – **Jose Mourinho**, Chelsea manager, after West Ham's defensive display earned a goalless draw at Stamford Bridge.

'He can't take it because we've outwitted him' – **Sam Allardyce**, West Ham manager.

'They brought on two England internationals. That shows the strength in depth they have. I was going to bring on my assistant' – **Sean Dyche**, Burnley manager, after a 4-3 FA Cup defeat by Southampton.

EUROPEAN TABLES 2013–2014

FRANCE – LIGUE 1

	P	W	D	L	F	A	GD	Pts
Paris SG	38	27	8	3	84	23	61	89
Monaco	38	23	11	4	63	31	32	80
Lille	38	20	11	7	46	26	20	71
St Etienne	38	20	9	9	56	34	22	69
Lyon	38	17	10	11	56	44	12	61
Marseille	38	16	12	10	53	40	13	60
Bordeaux	38	13	14	11	49	43	6	53
Lorient	38	13	10	15	48	53	-5	49
Toulouse	38	12	13	13	46	53	-7	49
Bastia	38	12	11	15	42	56	-14	49
Reims	38	12	12	14	44	55	-11	48
Rennes	38	11	13	15	47	45	2	46
Nantes	38	12	11	15	38	43	-5	46
Evian	38	11	11	16	39	51	-12	44
Montpellier	38	8	18	12	45	53	-8	42
Guingamp	38	11	9	18	34	42	-8	42
Nice	38	12	6	20	30	45	-15	42
Sochaux	38	10	10	18	37	61	-24	40
Valenciennes	38	7	8	23	37	65	-28	29
Ajaccio	38	4	11	23	37	72	-35	23

Leading league scorers: 26 Ibrahimovic (Paris SG); 16 Aboubakar (Lorient), Ben Yedder (Toulouse), Cavani (Paris SG), Gignac (Marseille), Kalou (Lille); 15 Lacazette (Lyon); 14 Cabella (Montpellier), Gomis (Lyon)

Cup Final: Guingamp 2 (Martins-Pereira 37, Yatabare 46) Rennes 0

HOLLAND - EREDIVISIE

	P	W	D	L	F	A	GD	Pts
Ajax	34	20	11	3	69	28	41	71
Feyenoord	34	20	7	7	76	40	36	67
Twente	34	17	12	5	72	37	35	63
PSV	34	18	5	11	60	45	15	59
Heerenveen	34	16	9	9	72	51	21	57
Vitesse Arnhem	34	15	10	9	65	51	14	55
Groningen	34	14	9	11	57	55	2	51
Alkmaar	34	13	8	13	54	50	4	47
Den Haag	34	12	7	15	45	64	-19	43
Utrecht	34	11	8	15	46	65	-19	41
Zwolle	34	9	13	12	47	49	- 2	40
Cambuur	34	10	9	15	40	50	-10	39
Go Ahead	34	10	8	16	45	69	-24	38
Heracles	34	10	7	17	45	59	-14	37
Breda	34	8	11	15	43	54	-11	35
Waalwijk	34	7	11	16	44	64	-20	32
Nijmegen	34	5	15	14	54	82	-28	30
Roda JC	34	7	8	19	44	69	-25	29

Leading league scorers: 29 Finnbogason (Heerenveen); 23 Pelle (Feyenoord); 17 Johannsson (Alkmaar); 16 Tadic (Twente); 14 Castaignos (Twente), Higdon (Nijmegen); 13 Locadia (PSV); 12 Depay (PSV), Immers (Feyenoord), Toornstra (Utrecht)

Cup Final: Zwolle 5 (Thomas 8, 12, Fernandez 22, 34, Van Polen 50) Ajax 1 (Van Rhijn 3)

GERMANY – BUNDESLIGA

	P	W	D	L	F	A	GD	Pts
Bayern Munich	34	29	3	2	94	23	71	90
Borussia Dortmund	34	22	5	7	80	38	42	71
Schalke	34	19	7	8	63	43	20	64
Bayer Leverkusen	34	19	4	11	60	41	19	61
Wolfsburg	34	18	6	10	63	50	13	60
Borussia M'gladbach	34	16	7	11	59	43	16	55
Mainz	34	16	5	13	52	54	-2	53
Augsburg	34	15	7	12	47	47	0	52
Hoffenheim	34	11	11	12	72	70	2	44
Hannover	34	12	6	16	46	59	-13	42
Hertha Berlin	34	11	8	15	40	48	-8	41
Werder Bremen	34	10	9	15	42	66	-24	39
Eintracht Frankfurt	34	9	9	16	40	57	-17	36
Freiburg	34	9	9	16	43	61	-18	36
Stuttgart	34	8	8	18	49	62	-13	32
Hamburg	34	7	6	21	51	75	-24	27
Nurnberg	34	5	11	18	37	70	-33	26
Braunschweig	34	6	7	21	29	60	-31	25

Leading league scorers: 20 Lewandowski (Borussia Dortmund); 18 Mandzukic (Bayern Munich); 17 Drmic (Nurnberg); 16 Firmino (Hoffenheim), Reus (Borussia Dortmund), Ramos (Hertha Berlin); 15 Kiessling (Bayer Leverkusen), Okazaki (Mainz), Raffael (Borussia M'gladbach); 14 Olic (Wolfsburg)
Cup Final: Bayern Munich 2 (Robben 107, Muller 120) Borussia Dortmund 0 - aet

ITALY – SERIE A

	P	W	D	L	F	A	GD	Pts
Juventus	38	33	3	2	80	23	57	102
Roma	38	26	7	5	72	25	47	85
Napoli	38	23	9	6	77	39	38	78
Fiorentina	38	19	8	11	65	44	21	65
Inter Milan	38	15	15	8	62	39	23	60
Parma	38	15	13	10	58	46	12	58
Torino	38	15	12	11	58	48	10	57
AC Milan	38	16	9	13	57	49	8	57
Lazio	38	15	11	12	54	54	0	56
Verona	38	16	6	16	62	68	-6	54
Atalanta	38	15	5	18	43	51	-8	50
Sampdoria	38	12	9	17	48	62	-14	45
Udinese	38	12	8	18	46	57	-11	44
Genoa	38	11	11	16	41	50	-9	44
Cagliari	38	9	12	17	34	53	-19	39
Chievo	38	10	6	22	34	54	-20	36
Sassuolo	38	9	7	22	43	72	-29	34
Catania	38	8	8	22	34	66	-32	32
Bologna	38	5	14	19	28	58	-30	29
Livorno	38	6	7	25	39	77	-38	25

Leading league scorers: 22 Immobile (Torino); 21 Toni (Verona); 19 Tevez (Juventus); 17 Higuain (Napoli), Palacio (Inter Milan); 16 Berardi (Sassuolo), Di Natale (Udinese), Llorente (Juventus), Rossi (Fiorentina); 15 Callejon (Napoli), Gilardino (Genoa), Paulinho (Livorno)
Cup Final: Napoli 3 (Insigne 11, 17, Mertens 90) Fiorentina 1 (Vargas 28)

PORTUGAL – PRIMEIRA LIGA

	P	W	D	L	F	A	GD	Pts
Benfica	30	23	5	2	58	18	40	74
Sporting	30	20	7	3	54	20	34	67
Porto	30	19	4	7	57	25	32	61
Estoril	30	15	9	6	42	26	16	54
Nacional	30	11	12	7	43	35	8	45
Maritimo	30	11	8	11	40	44	-4	41
Setubal	30	10	9	11	41	41	0	39
Acedemica	20	9	10	11	25	35	-10	37
Braga	30	10	7	13	39	37	2	37
Guimaraes	30	10	5	15	30	35	-5	35
Rio Ave	30	8	8	14	21	35	-14	32
Arouca	30	8	7	15	28	42	-14	31
Gil Vicente	30	8	7	15	23	37	-14	31
Belenenses	30	6	10	14	19	33	-14	28
Pacos Ferreira	30	6	6	18	28	59	-31	24
Olhanense	30	6	6	18	21	49	-28	24

Leading league scorers: 20 Martinez (Porto); 16 Derley (Maritimo); 15 Martins (Setubal); 14 Lima (Benfica); 13 Montero (Sporting); 12 Rondon (Nacional); 11 Bebe (Pacos Ferreira), Evandro (Estoril), Rodrigo (Benfica)
Cup Final: Benfica 1 (Gaitan 20) Rio Ave 0

SPAIN – LA LIGA

	P	W	D	L	F	A	GD	Pts
Atletico Madrid	38	28	6	4	77	26	51	90
Barcelona	38	27	6	5	100	33	67	87
Real Madrid	38	27	6	5	104	38	66	87
Athletic Bilbao	38	20	10	8	66	39	27	70
Sevilla	38	18	9	11	69	52	17	63
Villarreal	38	17	8	13	60	44	16	59
Real Sociedad	38	16	11	11	62	55	7	59
Valencia	38	13	10	15	51	53	-2	49
Celta Vigo	38	14	7	17	49	54	-5	49
Levante	38	12	12	14	35	43	-8	48
Malaga	38	12	9	17	39	46	-7	45
Rayo Vallecano	38	13	4	21	46	80	-34	43
Getafe	38	11	9	18	35	54	-19	42
Espanyol	38	11	9	18	41	51	-10	42
Granada	38	12	5	21	32	56	-24	41
Elche	38	9	13	16	30	50	-20	40
Almeria	38	11	7	20	43	71	-28	40
Osasuna	38	10	9	19	32	62	-30	39
Real Valladolid	38	7	15	16	38	60	-22	36
Real Betis	38	6	7	25	36	78	-42	25

Leading league scorers: 31 Ronaldo (Real Madrid); 28 Diego Costa (Atletico Madrid), Messi (Barcelona); 19 Sanchez (Barcelona); 17 Benzema (Real Madrid), Griezmann (Real Sociedad); 16 Aduriz (Athletic Bilbao), Vela (Real Sociedad); 15 Bale (Real Madrid), Gameiro (Sevilla), Guerra (Real Valladolid), Pedro (Barcelona)
Cup Final: Real Madrid 2 (Di Maria 11, Bale 85) Barcelona 1 (Bartra 68)

BRITISH & IRISH INTERNATIONALS 2013–2014

* denotes new cap

WORLD CUP 2014 QUALIFYING

NORTHERN IRELAND 1 RUSSIA 0
Group F: Windsor Park (11,805); Wednesday, August 14 2013

Northern Ireland (4-4-2): Carroll (Olympiacos), McAuley (WBA), Hughes (Fulham), Cathcart (Blackpool), Lafferty (Burnley), Ferguson (Newcastle), McGinn (Aberdeen) (Evans, Blackburn 82), Davis (Southampton), Norwood (Huddersfield), Ward (Derby), Paterson (Huddersfield) (Grigg, Brentford 86). **Scorer**: Paterson (43). **Booked**: Lafferty, Paterson
Russia (4-5-1): Akinfeev, Anyukov, Ignashevich, Berezutskiy, Dzagoev (Cheryshev 46) (Samedov 52), Shirokov, Denisov, Bystrov, Fayzulin, Kombarov, Kerzhakov (Dzyuba 46).
Booked: Berezutskiy
Referee: T Hagen (Norway). **Half-time**: 1-0

ENGLAND 4 MOLDOVA 0
Group H: Wembley (61,607); Friday, September 6 2013

England (4-2-3-1): Hart (Manchester City), Walker (Tottenham), Cahill (Chelsea), Jagielka (Everton), Cole (Chelsea), Baines, Everton 46), Gerrard (Liverpool), Lampard (Chelsea), Walcott (Arsenal), Wilshere (Arsenal) (*Barkley, Everton 60),Welbeck (Manchester Utd), Lambert (Southampton) (Milner, Manchester City 70). **Scorers**: Gerrard (12), Lambert (26), Welbeck (45, 50). **Booked**: Welbeck
Moldova (4-3-2-1): Namasco, Bordiyan, Epureano, Armas, Golovatenco, Antoniuc, Gheorghiev (Pascenco 84), Bulgaru (Suvorov 57), Ionita (Onica 19), Dedov, Sidorenco
Referee: I Kruzliak (Slovakia). **Half-time**: 3-0

SCOTLAND 0 BELGIUM 2
Group A: Hampden Park (40,284); Friday, September 6 2013

Scotland (4-2-3-1): Marshall (Cardiff), Hutton (Aston Villa), Martin (Norwich), Hanley (Blackburn), Whittaker (Norwich), Brown (Celtic), Mulgrew (Celtic), Forrest (Celtic) (McCormack, Leeds 86), Maloney (Wigan), Snodgrass (Norwich) (*Anya, Watford 58), Griffiths (Wolves) (Rhodes, Blackburn 68). **Booked**: Snodgrass
Belgium (4-2-3-1): Courtois, Alderweireld, Van Buyten, Lombaerts (Pocognoli 76), Vertonghen, Witsel, Defour (Dembele 87), De Bruyne, Fellaini (Mirallas 67), Chadli, Benteke.
Scorers: Defour (38), Mirallas (88). **Booked** Fellaini, Lombaerts
Referee: P Tagliavento (Italy). **Half-time**: 0-1

MACEDONIA 2 WALES 1
Group A: Skopje (18,000); Friday, September 6 2013

Macedonia (4-2-3-1): Pacovski, Ristovski, Noveski, Sikov, Georgievski (Lazevski 77), Tasevski, Gligorov, Trickovski, Pandev, Ibraimi (Trajkovski 60), Kostovski (Mojsov 86).
Scorers: Trickovski (21), Trajkovski (80). **Booked**: Gligorov, Pandev, Kostovski, Ibraimi
Wales (4-4-1-1): Myhill (WBA), Gunter (Reading), Ricketts (Wolves), A Williams (Swansea), Davies (Swansea), Collison (West Ham) (Matthews, Celtic 80), Ledley (Celtic), Vaughan (Sunderland) (Vokes, Burnley 86), J Williams (Crystal Palace) (Crofts, Brighton 62), Ramsey (Arsenal), Bellamy (Cardiff). **Scorer**: Ramsey (39 pen). **Booked**: Vaughan, Bellamy, A Williams, Crofts
Referee: S Kever (Switzerland). **Half-time**: 1-1

NORTHERN IRELAND 2 PORTUGAL 4
Group F: Windsor Park (12,001); Friday, September 6 2013

Northern Ireland (4-4-2): Carroll (Olympiacos), Hodson (MK Dons), McAuley (WBA), J Evans (Manchester Utd), Brunt (WBA), Ferguson (Newcastle) (Baird, unatt 76), McGinn (Aberdeen) (Lafferty, Palermo 66), Davis (Southampton), Norwood (Huddersfield), Ward (Derby) (C Evans, Blackburn), Paterson (Huddersfield). **Scorers**: McAuley (36), Ward (52). **Booked**: Davis, Brunt, Carroll, Norwood. **Sent off**: Brunt (61), Lafferty (80)

Portugal (4-3-3): Rui Patricio, Joao Pereira, Bruno Alves, Pepe, Fabio Coentrao, Joao Moutinho, Miguel, Raul Meireles (Nani 52), Vierinha (Nelson 64), Helder Postiga, Ronaldo (Amorim 90). **Scorers**: Bruno Alves (21), Ronaldo (68, 77, 83). **Booked**: Pepe, Ronaldo, Fabio Coentrao. **Sent off**: Helder Postiga (43)
Referee: D Makkelie (Holland). **Half-time**: 1-1

REPUBLIC OF IRELAND 1 SWEDEN 2
Group C: Aviva Stadium (49,500); Friday, September 6 2013
Republic of Ireland (4-4-2): Forde (Millwall), Coleman (Everton), Dunne (QPR), O'Shea (Sunderland), Wilson (Stoke), Walters (Stoke) (Cox, Nottm Forest 68), Whelan (Stoke), McCarthy (Everton), McClean (Wigan) (*Pilkington, Norwich 74), Keane (LA Galaxy), Long (WBA). **Scorer**: Keane (21). **Booked**: Dunne, Whelan
Sweden (4-4-2): Isaksson, Lustig (Johansson 65), Nilsson, Antonsson, M Olsson, Larsson, Ekdal, Svensson (Wernblom 68), Kacaniklic, Elmander (J Olsson 90), Ibrahimovic. **Scorers**: Elmander (33), Svensson (57). **Booked**: Ekdal
Referee: D Skomina (Slovenia). **Half-time**: 1-1

UKRAINE 0 ENGLAND 0
Group H: Kiev (69,890); Tuesday, September 10 2013
Ukraine (4-1-4-1): Piatov, Fedetskiy, Khacheridi, Kucher, Shevechuk, Stepanenko, Yarmolenko (Khomchenovskiy 90), Halovskiy, Gusev (Bezus 67), Konoplyanka, Zozulya (Seleznyov 90). **Booked**: Kucher
England (4-2-3-1): Hart (Manchester City), Walker (Tottenham), Cahill (Chelsea), Jagielka (Everton), Cole (Chelsea), Gerrard (Liverpool), Lampard (Chelsea), Walcott (Arsenal) (Cleverley, Manchester Utd 87), Wilshere (Arsenal) (Young, Manchester Utd 67), Milner (Manchester City), Lambert (Southampton). **Booked**: Walker
Referee: P Proenca (Portugal)
(Frank Lampard's 100th cap)

MACEDONIA 1 SCOTLAND 2
Group A: Skopje (14,093); Tuesday, September 10 2013
Macedonia (4-4-2): Pacovski, Georgievski, Ristovski, Noveski, Sikov, Trickovski, Babunski (Tasevski 41), Jakovic (Kostovski 82), Pandev, Trajkovski (Ivanovski 56), Stepanovic. **Scorer**: Kostovski (83). **Booked**: Stepanovic, Sikov
Scotland (4-2-3-1): Marshall (Cardiff) (Gilks, Blackpool 46), Hutton (Aston Villa), Martin (Norwich), Hanley (Blackburn), Whittaker (Norwich) (Wallace, Rangers 79), Brown (Celtic), Mulgrew (Celtic), Bannan (Crystal Palace) (McArthur, Wigan 77), Maloney (Wigan), Anya (Watford), Naismith (Everton). **Scorers**: Anya (59), Maloney (88). **Booked**: Mulgrew, Whittaker, Anya
Referee: F Fautrel (France). **Half-time**: 0-0

WALES 0 SERBIA 3
Group A: Cardiff City Stadium (10,923); Tuesday, September 10 2013
Wales (4-2-3-1): Myhill (WBA), Gunter (Reading), Gabbidon (Crystal Palace), Davies (Swansea), Matthews (Celtic), Ledley (Celtic) (Robson-Kanu, Reading 75), Crofts (Brighton) (Vaughan, Sunderland 58), King (Leicester) (Bale, Real Madrid 58), Ramsey (Arsenal), Bellamy (Cardiff), Vokes (Burnley). **Booked**: Crofts
Serbia (4-2-3-1): Stojkovic, Ivanovic, Bisevac, Nastasic, Kolarov, Fejsa (Petrovic 90), Radovanovic (Milivojevic 67), Tadic (Krstcic 88), Duricic, Markovic, Djordevic. **Scorers**: Djordevic (9), Kolarov (38), Markovic (55). **Booked**: Fejsa
Referee: S Marciniak (Poland). **Half-time**: 0-2

LUXEMBOURG 3 NORTHERN IRELAND 2
Group F: Josy Barthel (1,114); Tuesday, September 10 2013
Luxembourg (4-4-2): Joubert, Laterza, Mutsch, Philipps, Janisch, Gerson, Jans, Bensi, Da Mota (Bukvic 89), Turpel (Luisi 68), Joachim. **Scorers**: Joachim (45), Bensi (78), Janisch (87). **Booked**: Joachim

Northern Ireland (4-4-2): Carroll (Olympiacos), Hodson (MK Dons), McAuley (WBA), Evans (Manchester Utd), Lafferty (Burnley) (Grigg, Brentford 80), Ferguson (Newcastle) (McKay, Inverness 60), McGinn (Aberdeen) (O'Connor, Rotherham 35), Davis (Southampton), Norwood (Huddersfield), Ward (Derby), Paterson (Huddersfield). **Scorers**: Paterson (14), McAuley(82). **Booked**: McAuley
Referee: R Malek (Poland). **Half-time**: 1-1

AUSTRIA 1 REPUBLIC OF IRELAND 0
Group C: Vienna (48,545); Tuesday, September 10 2013
Austria (4-4-2): Almer, Garics, Dragovic, Fuchs, Prodi, Alaba, Baumgartlinger, Burgstaller (Arnautovic 60), Kavlak (Leitgeb 46), Weimann (Janko 73), Harnik. **Scorer**: Alaba (84)
Republic of Ireland (4-4-2): Forde (Millwall), Coleman (Everton), Dunne (QPR), O'Shea (Sunderland) (Clark, Aston Villa 49) Wilson (Stoke), Walters (Stoke) Green (Leeds), McCarthy (Everton), Pilkington (Norwich) (McClean, Wigan 73), Keane (LA Galaxy) Long (WBA) (Sammon, Derby 81). **Booked**: O'Shea, Dunne
Referee: O Benqucrenca (Portugal). **Half-time**: 0-0
(Giovanni Trapattoni's last game as Republic of Ireland manager)

ENGLAND 4 MONTENEGRO 1
Group H: Wembey (83,807); Friday, October 11 2013
England (4-2-3-1): Hart (Manchester City), Walker (Tottenham), Cahill (Chelsea), Jagielka (Everton), Baines (Everton), Gerrard (Liverpool) (Milner, Manchester City 87), Lampard (Chelsea) (Carrick, Manchester Utd 65), *Townsend (Tottenham) (Wilshere, Arsenal 80), Rooney (Manchester Utd), Welbeck (Manchester Utd), Sturridge (Liverpool). **Scorers**: Rooney (49), Boskovic (62 og), Townsend (78), Sturridge (90 pen). **Booked**: Walker
Montenegro (4-4-2): Poleksic, Pavicevic (Beciraj 57), Kecojevic, Savic, Jovanovic, Zverotic, Drincic, Boskovic, Volkov (Vukcevic 72), Damjanovic, Jovetic (Kasalica 81). **Scorer**: Damjanovic (72). **Booked**: Pavicevic, Volkov
Referee: A Undiano (Spain). **Half-time**: 0-0

WALES 1 MACEDONIA 0
Group A: Cardiff City Stadium (11,257); Friday, October 11 2013
Wales (4-2-3-1): Hennessey (Wolves), Taylor (Swansea), Collins (West Ham), Gunter (Reading), *John (Cardiff), Vaughan (Sunderland), King (Leicester), Robson-Kanu (Reading), Ramsey (Arsenal), Bellamy (Cardiff), Church (Charlton) (Easter, Millwall 90). **Scorer**: Church (67). **Booked**: John, Taylor, Hennessey
Macedonia (4-3-3): Pacovski, Ristovski, Sikov, Noveski, Alioski, Stepanovic (Tasevski 75), Demiri (Kostovski 85), Rangjeolivic, Ibraimi, Pandev, Ivanovski (Trajkovski 80). **Booked**: Sikov
Referee: S Baliyan (Armenia). **Half-time**: 0-0

AZERBAIJAN 2 NORTHERN IRELAND 0
Group F: Baku (10,100); Friday, October 11 2013
Azerbaijan (4-4-2): Agayev, Shukurov, Ramaldanov, Sadygov, Allahverdiyev, Garayev, Amirguliyev, Abdullayev (Ozkara 82), Aliyev, Nadirov (Huseynov 46, Dadasov (Guseynov 90). **Scorers**: Dadasov (58), Shukurov (90). **Booked**: Ramaldanov
Northern Ireland (3-5-2): Carroll (Olympiacos), Cathcart (Blackpool), Evans (Manchester Utd), McAuley (WBA), Hodson (MK Dons) (McGinn, Aberdeen 66), Norwood (Huddersfield), Davis (Southampton), Brunt (WBA) (McKay, Inverness 74), Ferguson (Newcastle), Paterson (Huddersfield), Ward (Derby) (Grigg, Brentford 84). **Booked**: Norwood. **Sent off**: Evans (90)
Referee: A De Marco (Italy). **Half-time**: 0-0

GERMANY 3 REPUBLIC OF IRELAND 0
Group C: Cologne (46,237); Friday, October 11 2013
Germany (4-2-3-1): Neuer, Jansen, Mertesacker, Boateng, Lahm, Khedira (Kruse 82), Schweinsteiger, Kroos, Ozil, Schurrle (Gotze 86), Muller (Sam 88). **Scorers**: Khedira (12), Schurrle (58), Ozil (90). **Booked**: Khedira
Republic of Ireland (4-5-1): Forde (Millwall), Coleman (Everton), Clark (Aston Villa), Delaney (Crystal Palace), Kelly (Reading), Whelan (Stoke), Gibson (Everton), McCarthy (Everton),

Wilson (Stoke), Doyle (Wolves), Stokes (Celtic). **Booked**: Stokes
Referee: S Gumienny (Belgium). **Half-time**: 1-0

ENGLAND 2 POLAND 0
Group H: Wembley (85,186); Tuesday, October 15 2013
England (4-2-3-1): Hart (Manchester City), Smalling (Manchester Utd), Cahill (Chelsea), Jagielka (Everton), Baines (Everton), Gerrard (Liverpool), Carrick (Manchester Utd) (Lampard, Chelsea 71), Townsend (Tottenham) (Milner, Manchester City 86), Rooney (Manchester Utd), Welbeck (Manchester Utd), Sturridge (Liverpool) (Wilshere, Arsenal, 82).
Scorers: Rooney (41), Gerrard (88). **Booked**: Lampard, Rooney
Poland (4-5-1): Szczesny, Celeban, Jedrzejczyk, Glik, Wojtkowiak, Krychowiak, M Lewandowski (Kilch 46), Blaszczykowski, Mierzejewski (Zielinski 75), Sobota (Peszko 65), R Lewandowski. **Booked**: Jedrzejczyk
Referee: D Skomina (Slovenia). **Half-time**: 1-0

SCOTLAND 2 CROATIA 0
Group A: Hampden Park (30,172); Tuesday, October 15 2013
Scotland (4-4-1-1): McGregor (Hull), Hutton (Aston Villa), Martin (Norwich), Hanley (Blackburn), Mulgrew (Celtic), Bannan (Crystal Palace) (Burke, Birmingham 89), Brown (Celtic), Morrison (WBA), Anya (Watford) (Dorrans, WBA), Snodgrass (Norwich) (McArthur, Wigan 82), Naismith (Everton). **Scorers**: Snodgrass (28), Naismith (73). **Booked**: Morrison
Croatia (4-4-2): Pletikosa, Vida, Corluka, Lovren, Strinic, Srna, Vukojevic, Modric, Kranjcar (Perisic 69). Kalinic (Eduardo 59), Mandzukic (Jelavic 80). **Booked**: Vukojevic
Referee: O Hategan (Romania). **Half-time**: 1-0

BELGIUM 1 WALES 1
Group A: Brussels (45,410); Tuesday, October 15 2013
Belgium (4-1-4-1): Courtois, Alderweireld, Van Buyten (Vertonghen 73), Vermaelen, Pocognoli, Witsel, De Bruyne, Dembele, Chadli (Hazard 58), Mirallas (Bakkali 78), Lukaku.
Scorer: De Bruyne (64)
Wales (4-1-4-1): Hennessey (Wolves), Richards (Swansea), Gunter (Reading), Collins (West Ham) (*J Wilson, Bristol City 56), Taylor (Swansea), Ramsey (Arsenal), Vaughan (Sunderland), Robson Kanu (Reading) (*H Wilson, Liverpool 87), King (Leicester), Bellamy (Cardiff), Church (Charlton) (Vokes, Burnley 70). **Scorer**: Ramsey (88). **Booked**: Collins, Bellamy
Referee: S Karasev (Russia). **Half-time**: 0-0

ISRAEL 1 NORTHERN IRELAND 1
Group F: Ramat Gan (12,785); Tuesday, October 15 2013
Israel (4-2-3-1): Aouate, Meshumar, Ben Haim (Keinan 46), Melikson, Natcho, Zahavi (Ben Chaim 71), Ben Basat, Rafaelov (Shechter 79), Yeini, Davidzdze, Tibi. **Scorer**: Ben Basat (43).
Northern Ireland (4-2-3-1): Carroll (Olympiacos), Hodson (MK Dons), Lafferty (Burnley) (Ferguson, Newcastle 78), Baird (Reading), McArdle (Bradford), Cathcart (Blackpool), Evans (Blackburn) (Brunt, WBA 24), Clingan (Kilmarnock), Paterson (Huddersfield), Davis (Southampton), McGinn (Aberdeen) (Ward, Derby 65). **Scorer**: Davis (73). **Booked**: Cathcart
Referee: L Duhamel (France). **Half-time**: 1-0

REPUBLIC OF IRELAND 3 KAZAKHSTAN 1
Group C: Aviva Stadium (21,700); Tuesday, October 15 2013
Republic of Ireland (4-2-3-1): Forde (Millwall), Coleman (Everton), Dunne (QPR), O'Shea (Sunderland), Wilson (Stoke), Gibson (Everton) (Whelan, Stoke 37), McCarthy (Everton), Doyle (Wolves), Reid (Nottm Forest) (McGeady, Spartak Moscow 75), Stokes (Celtic) (Hoolahan (Norwich 86), Keane (LA Galaxy). **Scorers**: Keane (17 pen), O'Shea (27), Shomko (78 og).
Kazakhstan (4-1-4-1): Sidelnikov, Engel, Gurman, Dmitrenko, Kislitsyn (Finonchenko 32), Karpovich (Shabalin 84), Baizhanov, Korobkin, Chshyotkin (Yurin 62), Shomko, Khizhnichenko. **Scorer**: Shomko (13). **Booked**: Kislitsyn
Referee: V Direktorenko (Latvia). **Half-time**: 2-1

INTERNATIONAL FRIENDLIES

ENGLAND 3 SCOTLAND 2
Wembley (80,485); Wednesday, August 14 2013

England (4-3-3): Hart (Manchester City), Walker (Tottenham), Cahill (Chelsea), Jagielka (Everton) (Jones, Manchester Utd 84), Baines (Everton), Cleverley (Manchester Utd) (Milner, Manchester City 67), Gerrard (Liverpool) (Oxlade-Chamberlain, Arsenal 62), Wilshere (Arsenal) (Lampard, Chelsea 46), Walcott (Arsenal) (Zaha, Manchester Utd 75), Rooney (Manchester Utd) (*Lambert Southampton 67), Welbeck (Manchester Utd). **Scorers:** Walcott (29), Welbeck (53), Lambert (70). **Booked:** Walker, Walcott

Scotland (4-4-1-1): McGregor (Hull), Hutton (Aston Villa), Martin (Norwich), Hanley (Blackburn), Whittaker (Norwich), Snodgrass (Norwich), Conway, Cardiff 66), Morrison (WBA) (Rhodes, Blackburn 82), Brown (Celtic), Forrest (Celtic) (Mulgrew, Celtic 67), Maloney (Wigan) (Naismith (Everton 86), Miller (Vancouver) (Griffiths (Wolves 73). **Scorers:** Morrison (11), Miller (49). **Booked:** Snodgrass

Referee: F Brych (Germany). **Half-time:** 1-1

WALES 0 REPUBLIC OF IRELAND 0
Cardiff City Stadium (20,000); Wednesday, August 14 2013

Wales (4-4-1-1): Myhill (WBA), Gunter (Reading), Ricketts (Wolves), A Williams (Swansea), B Davies (Swansea), Collison (West Ham) (C Davies, Bolton 82), Ledley (Celtic) (King, Leicester 59), Allen (Liverpool) (Crofts, Brighton 86), Robson-Kanu (Reading) (Taylor, Swansea 74), J Williams (Crystal Palace), Bellamy (Cardiff) (Vokes, Burnley 59). **Booked:** A Williams

Republic of Ireland (4-4-1-1): Westwood (Sunderland), Coleman (Everton), Clark (Aston Villa), O'Shea (Sunderland) (O'Dea, Metalurh Donetsk 59), Wilson (Stoke), Walters (Stoke) (Sammon, Derby 84), McCarthy (Wigan), Whelan (Stoke) (Green, Leeds 59), Brady (Hull) (McClean, Wigan 46), Hoolahan (Norwich) (*Madden, Yeovil 69), Long (WBA) (Keogh, Millwall 74). **Booked:** Long

Referee: P Kralovec (Czech Republic)

ENGLAND 0 CHILE 2
Wembley (62,963); Friday, November 15 2013

England (4-3-2-1): *Forster (Celtic), Johnson (Liverpool), Cahill (Chelsea), Jones (Manchester Utd) (Smalling, Manchester Utd 56), Baines (Everton), Milner (Manchester City) (Defoe, Tottenham 66), Lampard (Chelsea) (Henderson, Liverpool 70), Wilshere (Arsenal) (Cleverley, Manchester Utd 70), *Lallana (Southampton) (Barkley, Everton 77), *Rodriguez (Southampton) (Townsend, Tottenham 56), Rooney (Manchester Utd). **Booked:** Cahill, Smalling

Chile (4-1-3-2): Bravo, Isla (Jara 60), Medel, Gonzalez, Mena, Diaz, Aranguiz (Gutierrez 46), Vargas (Munoz 71), Fernandez (Carmona 46), Beausejour (Fuenzalida 82), Sanchez. **Scorer:** Sanchez (7, 90). **Booked:** Beausejour, Jara, Mena

Referee: F Meyer (Germany). **Half-time:** 0-1

SCOTLAND 0 USA 0
Hampden Park (21,079); Friday, November 15 2013

Scotland (4-2-3-1): Marshall (Cardiff), Hutton (Aston Villa), *Greer (Brighton), Hanley (Blackburn), Whittaker (Norwich) (Wallace, Rangers 69), Brown (Celtic), Mulgrew (Celtic), Bannan (Crystal Palace) (Naismith, Everton 81), Snodgrass (Norwich) (McCormack, Leeds 69), Conway (Cardiff) (*Mackay-Steven, Dundee Utd 84), Fletcher (Sunderland)

USA (4-2-3-1): Howard, Evans (Lichaj 72), Cameron, Gonzalez, Beasley, Bradley, Jones (Diskerud 62), Bedoya (Wondolowski 81), Kljestan (Johannsson 62), Johnson (Shea 62), Altidore (Boyd 90)

Referee: M Oliver (England)

TURKEY 1 NORTHERN IRELAND 0
Adana (14,000); Friday, November 15 2013

Turkey (4-2-3-1): Zengin, Gonul (Camdal 72), Erkin, Ozyakup (Yilmaz 46), Kaya, Gulum, Buyuk (Ucan 67), Topal, Erding (Tore 77), Kisa (Sahan 83), Turan (Dogan 89). **Scorer**: Erding (45)

Northern Ireland (3-5-2): Carroll (Olympiacos) (Mannus, St Johnstone 46), Hughes (Fulham), Baird (Reading), Evans (Manchester Utd), Hodson (MK Dons), Norwood (Huddersfield), Davis (Southampton), Clingan (Kilmarnock) (McKay, Inverness 75), Lafferty (Burnley) (McGivern, Hibernian 76), Paterson (Huddersfield), McGinn (Aberdeen) (*Steele, New York Bulls 67). **Booked**: Norwood

Referee: B Nijhuis (Holland). **Half-time**: 1-0

REPUBLIC OF IRELAND 3 LATVIA 0
Aviva Stadium (37,100); Friday, November 15 2013

Republic of Ireland (4-4-1-1): Westwood (Sunderland), Coleman (Everton), Wilson (Stoke), O'Shea (Sunderland), Ward (Wolves), McGeady (Spartak Moscow) (Reid, Nottm Forest 73) Whelan (Stoke) (Green, Leeds 80), McCarthy (Everton) (Doyle, Wolves 80), McClean (Wigan) (Stokes, Celtic 80), Hoolahan (Norwich) (Long, WBA 73), Keane (LA Galaxy) (Walters, Stoke 73). **Scorers**: Keane (22), McGeady (67), Long (79)

Latvia (4-1-3-2): Vanins, Gabovs, Bulvitis, Gorkss, Maksimenko, Rode, Rugins (Fertovs 27), Laizans (Sinelnikovs 73), Lazdins, Sabala (Turkovs 62), Verpakovskis. **Booked**: Gabovs, Bulvitis, Rode

Referee: A Ekberg (Sweden). **Half-time**: 1-0
(Martin O'Neill's first game as Republic of Ireland manager)

WALES 1 FINLAND 1
Cardiff City Stadium (11,809); Saturday, November 16 2013

Wales (4-3-2-1): Hennessey (Wolves), Gunter (Reading) (Richards, Swansea 72), Williams (Swansea). Ricketts (Wolves), Taylor (Swansea) (Davies, Swansea 72), Allen (Liverpool) (Tudur Jones, Hibernian 90), Ledley (Celtic), King (Leicester), Robson-Kanu (Reading) (Cotterill, Doncaster 84), Bale (Real Madrid), Church (Charlton) (Vokes, Burnley 62) **Scorer**: King (58). **Booked**: King

Finland (4-5-1): Hradecky, Arkivuo (Lampi 45, Raitala 70), Moisander (Pasanen 62), Ojala (Toivio 46), Uronen, Riski, Schuller (Hetemaj 70), Sparv, Ring, Eremenko, Pukki (Hamalainen 62). **Scorer** Riski (90). **Booked**: Sparv

Referee: S Delferieri (Belgium). **Half-time**: 0-0

ENGLAND 0 GERMANY 1
Wembley (85,934); Tuesday, November 19 2013

England (4-2-3-1): Hart (Manchester City), Walker (Tottenham), Smalling (Manchester Utd), Jagielka (Everton), Cole (Chelsea) (Gibbs, Arsenal 53), Gerrard (Liverpool) (Henderson, Liverpool 56), Cleverley (Manchester Utd) (Wilshere, Arsenal 64), Lallana (Southampton) (Lambert, Southampton 76), Townsend (Tottenham), Rooney (Manchester Utd) (Barkley, Everton 71), Sturridge (Liverpool)

Germany (4-2-3-1): Weidenfeller, Westermann (Draxler 67), Mertesacker, Boateng (Hummels 46, Howedes 65), Schmelzer (Jansen 46), S Bender, L Bender, Gotze, Kroos, Reus (Schurrle 46), Kruse (Sam 82). **Scorer**: Mertesacker (39)

Referee: S Lannoy (France). **Half-time**: 0-1

NORWAY 0 SCOTLAND 1
Molde (9,750): Tuesday, November 19 2013

Norway (4-4-2): Nyland, Elabdellaoui (Linnes 60), Reginiussen (Strandberg 64), Forren, Hogli, Skjelbred (Daehli 67), Eikrem (Konradsen 80), Jenssen, Gamst Pedersen (Elyounoussi 86), Kamara (Abdellaoue 46), Pedersen. **Booked**: Linnes, Forren

Scotland (4-2-3-1): Marshall (Cardiff), Hutton (Aston Villa), Martin (Norwich), Greer

(Brighton), Whittaker (Norwich), Brown (Celtic), Adam (Stoke) (McArthur, Wigan 64), Bryson (Derby) (Bannan, Crystal Palace 46), Snodgrass (Norwich), Anya (Watford) (Conway, Cardiff 51), Naismith (Everton) (Berra, Ipswich 90). **Scorer:** Brown (61). **Booked:** Adam
Referee: M Strombergsson (Sweden). **Half-time:** 0-0

POLAND 0 REPUBLIC OF IRELAND 0
Poznan (31,094); Tuesday, November 19 2013
Poland (4-1-4-1): Szczesny, Celeban, Szukala, Kowalczyk, Marciniak, Pazdan, Sobota (Brzyski 81), Maczynski (Jedlowiec 59), Blaszczykowski (Robak 89), Cwielong (Olkowski 81), Lewandowski (Teodorczyk 59). **Booked:** Pazdan
Republic of Ireland (4-4-2): Forde (Millwall), Kelly (Reading), St Ledger (Leicester) (O'Shea, Sunderland 32), Wilson (Stoke) (Whelan, Stoke 76), Ward (Wolves), Walters (Stoke), Green (Leeds), McCarthy (Everton) (Pearce, Reading 62), McGeady (Spartak Moscow) (McClean, Wigan 63), Stokes (Celtic) (Doyle, Wolves 68), Long (WBA) (Hoolahan, Norwich 76).
Booked: O'Shea
Referee: R Turtz (Slovakia)

ENGLAND 1 DENMARK 0
Wembley (68,573); Wednesday, March 5 2014
England (4-2-3-1): Hart (Manchester City), Johnson (Liverpool), Cahill (Chelsea), Smalling (Manchester Utd), Cole (Chelsea) (*Shaw, Southampton 46), Henderson (Liverpool) (Oxlade-Chamberlain, Arsenal 77), Gerrard (Liverpool), Sterling (Liverpool) (Townsend, Tottenham 86), Rooney (Manchester Utd) (Welbeck, Manchester Utd 60), Wilshere (Arsenal) (Lallana, Southampton 58), Sturridge (Liverpool) (Milner, Manchester City 87). **Scorer:** Sturridge (82).
Denmark (4-2-3-1): Schmeichel, Jacobsen (Juelsgard 46), Kjaer (Bjelland 62), Agger, Ankerssen, Kvist, Poulsen (Olsen 81), Larsen (Kusk 46), Sloth (Zimling 62), Krohn-Dehli, Bendtner (Rasmussen 62). **Booked:** Sloth, Rasmussen
Referee: K Blom (Holland). **Half-time:** 0-0

POLAND 0 SCOTLAND 1
Warsaw (41,652); Wednesday, March 5 2014
Poland (4-2-3-1): Szczesny, Pisczczek, Szukala, Glik, Brzyski (Komorowski 90), Klich (Teodorczyk 82), Krychowiak (Judlowiec 88), Sobota, Obraniak (Robak 74), Peszko (Polanski 74), Milik. **Booked:** Peszko
Scotland (4-2-3-1): Marshall (Cardiff), Hutton (Aston Villa) (Bardsley, Sunderland 67), Martin (Norwich), Greer (Brighton), Mulgrew (Celtic), Brown (Celtic), Morrison (WBA) (D Fletcher, Manchester Utd 46), Bannan (Crystal Palace) (*Robertson, Dundee Utd 67), McCormack (Leeds) (Adam, Stoke 76), Anya (Watford) (Burke, Birmingham 90), S Fletcher (Sunderland) (Naismith, Everton 46). **Scorer:** Brown (77). **Booked:** Brown, Hutton, Naismith
Referee: A Bieri (Switzerland). **Half-time:** 0-0

WALES 3 ICELAND 1
Cardiff City Stadium (13,219); Wednesday, March 5 2014
Wales (4-2-3-1): Hennessey (Crystal Palace), Gunter (Reading), Collins (West Ham) (Gabbidon, Crystal Palace 46), A Williams (Swansea) (Ricketts, Wolves 64), Taylor (Swansea), *Huws (Manchester City), Allen (Liverpool), Robson-Kanu (Reading) (Davies, Swansea 88), King (Leicester) (Collison, West Ham 76), Bale (Real Madrid) (J Williams, Crystal Palace 72), Vokes (Burnley). **Scorers:** Collins (12), Vokes (64), Bale (70)
Iceland (4-4-2): Halldorsson, Skulason (Jonsson 84), T Bjarnason, R Sigurdsson (B Bjarnason 46), Arnason, Gudmundsson, G Sigurdsson, Gunnarsson, Hallfredsson, Sigthorsson (Sverrisson 76), Finnbogason (Ottesen 46). **Scorer:** Gudmundsson (26).
Booked: Jonsson
Referee: E Saar (Estonia). **Half-time:** 1-1

CYPRUS 0 NORTHERN IRELAND 0
Nicosia (500); Wednesday, March 5 2014
Cyprus (4-3-3): Georgallides, Charis Kyriakou, Junior, Merkis, Antoniades, Nicolaou (Artymatas 58), Laban (Charalambos Kyriakou 66), Makrides (Charalambides 63), Christofi (Makris 85), Aloneftis (Efrem 50), Mitidis (Papathanasiou 77). **Booked**: Laban
Northern Ireland (4-4-2): Mannus (St Johnstone) (Carroll, Olympiacos 46), Cathcart (Blackpool), McAuley (WBA), Bruce (Hull), McGivern (Hibernian), Davis (Southampton), Norwood (Huddersfield) (McCourt, Barnsley 74), McGinn (Aberdeen) (Ferguson, Newcastle 73), Brunt (WBA), Ward (Derby) (McKay, Inverness 63) (McArdle, Bradford 80), Paterson (Huddersfield) (Lafferty, Palermo 46). **Booked**: Ward. **Sent off**: McAuley (76)
Referee: L Liany (Israel)

REPUBLIC OF IRELAND 1 SERBIA 2
Aviva Stadium (37,243); Wednesday, March 5 2014
Republic of Ireland (4-4-1-1): Forde (Millwall), Coleman (Everton), Keogh (Derby), Wilson (Stoke), Ward (Wolves) (Clark Aston Villa 63), McGeady (Everton) (Murphy, Ipswich 72), McCarthy (Everton) (Meyler, Sunderland 63), Whelan (Stoke) (Quinn, Hull 80), Hoolahan (Norwich) (Pilkington, Norwich 64), McClean (Wigan), Long (Hull) (Walters, Stoke 72).
Scorer: Long (8). **Booked**: Hoolahan
Serbia (4-2-3-1): Stojkovic, Rukavina (Gudelj 89), Ivanovic, Bisevac, Kolarov, Fejsa, Matic, Basta (Tosic 59), Tadic (Ljajic 80), Markovic (Sulejmani 75), Djordjevic (Scepovic 86).
Scorers: McCarthy (48 og), Djordjevic (60). **Booked**: Ivanovic, Matic
Referee: V Kassai (Hungary). **Half-time**: 1-0

REPUBLIC OF IRELAND 1 TURKEY 2
Aviva Stadium (15,000); Sunday, May 25 2014
Republic of Ireland (4-1-4-1): *Elliot (Newcastle), Coleman (Everton), O'Shea (Sunderland), Delaney (Crystal Palace) (Meyler, Hull 66), Ward (Wolves), McGeady (Everton) (Murphy, Ipswich 66), Whelan (Stoke) (Quinn, Hull 82), Wilson (Stoke), McClean (Wigan), Hoolahan (Norwich), Long (Hull) (Walters, Stoke 66). **Scorer**: Walters (78)
Turkey (4-1-4-1): Kivrak, Gonul, Toprak, Balta, Erkin, Inan (Ozyakup 21), Ozek (Camdal 70), Sahin (Dogan 84), Kisa (Tufan 46), Calhanoglu (Adin 63), Erdinc (Pektemek 81). **Scorers**: Ozek (17), Camdal (75). **Booked**: Gonul
Referee: R Buquet (France). **Half-time**: 0-1

SCOTLAND 2 NIGERIA 2
Craven Cottage (24,000); Wednesday, May 28 2014
Scotland (4-2-3-1): McGregor (Hull), Hutton (Aston Villa), Greer (Brighton), Hanley (Blackburn), Robertson (Dundee Utd) (*Forsyth, Derby 76), Brown (Celtic), Mulgrew (Celtic), Maloney (Wigan), Morrison (WBA) (Boyd, Hull 63), Anya (Watford) (Whittaker, Norwich 84), Naismith (Everton) (*Martin, Derby 46). **Scorers**: Mulgrew (10), Egwuekwe (54 og). **Booked**: Brown
Nigeria (4-4-2): Ejide, Elderson, Kunle (Ambrose 75), Yobo, Egwuekwe, Uzoenyi (Moses 62), Obi (Igiebor 54), Gabriel, Babatunde (Oduamadi 66), Ameobi (Nwofor 61), Uchebo (Odemwingie 54). **Scorers**: Uchebo (41), Nwofor (90)
Referee: L Probert (England). **Half-time**: 1-1

ENGLAND 3 PERU 0
Wembley (83,578); Friday, May 30 2014
England (4-2-3-1): Hart (Manchester City), Johnson (Liverpool), Cahill (Chelsea), Jagielka (Everton) (Smalling, Manchester Utd 73), Baines (Everton) (*Stones, Everton 75), Gerrard (Liverpool) (Wilshere, Arsenal 64), Henderson (Liverpool), Lallana (Southampton) (Milner, Manchester City 73), Rooney (Manchester Utd) (Sterling, Liverpool 66), Welbeck (Manchester Utd), Sturridge (Liverpool) (Barkley, Everton 82). **Scorers**: Sturridge (32), Cahill (65), Jagielka

(70). **Booked**: Gerrard
Peru (4-3-2-1): Fernandez, Advincula (Velarde 78), Ramos (Riojas 68), Rodriguez, Callens, Ballon, Cruzado, Yotun, Deza (Ruidiaz 66), Carrillo (Flores 86), Ramirez (Hurtado 60).
Booked: Cruzado
Referee: V Kassai (Hungary). **Half-time**: 1-0

URUGUAY 1 NORTHERN IRELAND 0
Montevideo (45,000); Friday, May 30 2014
Uruguay (4-4-2): Muslera, Pereira, Lugano, Coates (Giminez 46), Caceres (Pereira 73), Rodrigues, Gargano (Perez 74), Arevalo, Ramirez (Lodeiro 65), Cavani (Hernandez 65), Forlan (Stuani 46). **Scorer**: Stuani (62). **Booked**: Gargano
Northern Ireland (4-4-1-1): Carroll (Olympiacos), Evans (Blackburn) (C McLaughlin, Fleetwood 87), Hughes (Queens Park Rangers), Baird (Burnley), *McCullough (Doncaster), McGinn (Aberdeen) (Magennis, Aberdeen 61), Clingan (Kilmarnock) (*Paton, Dundee Utd 74), Davis (Southampton), Ferguson (Newcastle) (Lafferty, Burnley 81), Norwood (Huddersfield) (Steele, New York Bulls 86), McKay (Inverness) (* R McLaughlin, Liverpool 81). **Booked**: Norwood, Clingan
Referee: L Vuaden (Brazil). **Half-time**: 0-0

REPUBLIC OF IRELAND 0 ITALY 0
Craven Cottage (22,879); Saturday, May 31 2014
Republic of Ireland (4-2-3-1): Forde (Millwall), Coleman (Everton), O'Shea (Sunderland), Pearce (Reading), Ward (Brighton), Hendrick (Derby), Meyler (Hull) (Green, Leeds 85), McGeady (Everton), Hoolahan (Norwich) (Quinn, Hull 67), Pilkington (Norwich) (McClean, Wigan 58), Long (Hull) (Cox, Nottm Forest 73)
Italy (4-1-3-2): Sirigu, Darmian (Abate 88), Paletta, Bonucci, De Sciglio, Motta (De Rossi 62), Verratti, Marchisio, Montolivo (Aquilani 15) (Parolo 37), Immobile (Cassano 56), Rossi (Cerci 71)
Referee: M Oliver (England)

ENGLAND 2 ECUADOR 2
Miami (21,534); Wednesday, June 4 2014
England (4-2-3-1): Foster (WBA), Milner (Manchester City), Jones (Manchester Utd), Smalling (Manchester Utd), Shaw (Southampton) (Stones, Everton 74), Lampard (Chelsea), Wilshere (Arsenal) (Lallana, Southampton 86), Oxlade-Chamberlain (Arsenal) (*Flanagan, Liverpool 63), Barkley (Everton) (Welbeck, Manchester Utd 84), Rooney (Manchester Utd) (Sterling, Liverpool 65), Lambert (Liverpool) (Henderson, Liverpool 84). **Scorers**: Rooney (29), Lambert (51). **Sent off**: Sterling (79)
Ecuador (4-4-2): Banguera, Paredes (Archilier 89), Guagua, Erazo, Ayovi, A Valencia, Noboa (Mendez 49), Montero (Arroyo 68), E Valencia (Ibarra 83), Gruezo (Saritama 89), Caicedo (Rojas 46). **Scorers**: E Valencia (8), Arroyo (70). **Sent off**: A Valencia (79)
Referee: J Marrufo (USA). **Half-time**: 1-1

HOLLAND 2 WALES 0
Amsterdam (51,000); Wednesday, June 4, 2014
Holland (4-3-1-2): Cillessen, Janmaat, De Vrij, Vlaar, Martins, Fer (Wijnaldum 46), De Jong (Huntelaar 78), Blind, Sneijder, Robben, Van Persie (Lens 46). **Scorers**: Robben (32), Lens (76)
Wales (4-5-1): Hennessey (Crystal Palace), Gunter (Reading), Gabbidon (Crystal Palace), *Chester (Hull), Taylor (Swansea) (*Dummett, Newcastle 83), Allen (Liverpool), Ledley (Crystal Palace) (Huws, Manchester City 62), King (Leicester) (Vaughan, Sunderland 77), J Williams (Crystal Palace) (*G Williams, Fulham 70), Robson-Kanu (Reading) (John, Cardiff 60), Church (Charlton) (Easter, Millwall 67)
Referee: B Yildirim (Turkey). **Half-time**: 1-0

CHILE 2 NORTHERN IRELAND 0
Valparaiso (20,000); Thursday, June 5 2014

Chile (3-4-3): Herrera, Medel (Vidal 77), Silva, Rojas, Isla, Diaz (Gutierrez 85), Carmona (Aranguiz 59), Mena, Orellana (Sanchez 59), Valdivia (Pinilla 77), Paredes (Vargas 61). **Scorers**: Vargas (79), Pinilla (82). **Booked**: Medel, Diaz

Northern Ireland (4-4-1-1): Carroll (Olympiacos), Evans (Blackburn) (*Donnelly, Fulham 89), C McLaughlin (Fleetwood), McCullough (Doncaster), Hughes (QPR), R McLaughlin (Liverpool) (McGinn, Aberdeen 70), Norwood (Huddersfield) (Steele, New York Bulls 88), Davis (Southampton), Ferguson (Newcastle) (Lafferty, Burnley 77), Clingan (Kilmarnock), McKay (Inverness) (Magennis, Aberdeen 63). **Booked**: Magennis

Referee: C Amarilla (Paraguay). **Half-time**: 0-0

ENGLAND 0 HONDURAS 0
Miami (18,000); Saturday, June 7 2014

England (4-2-3-1): Hart (Manchester City) (Forster, Celtic 75), Johnson (Liverpool), Cahill (Chelsea), Jagielka (Everton), Baines (Everton), Gerrard (Liverpool) (Wilshere, Arsenal 46), Henderson (Liverpool) (Lampard, Chelsea 83), Lallana (Southampton), Rooney (Barkley, Everton 46), Welbeck (Manchester Utd) (Lambert, Liverpool 78), Sturridge (Liverpool). **Booked**: Lallana, Cahill, Baines

Honduras (4-4-2): Valladares, Beckeles, Bernandez, Figueroa, Izaguirre (Martinez 90), Chavez (Najar 61), Garrido (Claros 46), W Palacios, Espinoza (Garcia 87), Bengtson (J Palacios 75), Costly (Delgado 69). **Booked**: Garrido, Izaguirre, Bernandez, Beckeles. **Sent off**: Beckeles (65)

Referee: R Salazar (USA)

REPUBLIC OF IRELAND 1 COSTA RICA 1
Chester, USA (7,000); Saturday, June 7 2014

Republic of Ireland (4-4-2): Forde (Millwall), Kelly (Reading), Keogh (Derby), *Duffy (Everton), Wilson (Stoke) (McClean, Wigan 40), Whelan (Stoke), Green (Leeds) (Hendrick, Derby 65, Pilkington (Norwich) (McGeady, Everton 65), Quinn (Hull) (Cox, Nottm Forest 83), Keane (LA Galaxy) (Hoolahan, Norwich 83), Doyle (Wolves) (Long, Hull 65). **Scorer**: Doyle (17). **Booked**: Doyle, Whelan, Forde, McClean

Costa Rica (4-4-2): Navas (Pemberton 46), Mora, Gonzalez, Duarte, Umana, Diaz, Borges, Cubero, Ruiz (Bolanos 74), Urena (Brenes 78), Campbell (Calvo 86). **Scorer**: Borges (63 pen). **Booked**: Gonzalez. **Sent off**: Gonzalez (41)

Referee: R Castro (Honduras). **Half-time**: 1-0

REPUBLIC OF IRELAND 1 PORTUGAL 5
East Rutherford, USA (40,000); Wednesday, June 11

Republic of Ireland: Forde (Millwall), Kelly (Reading) (Doyle Wolves 76), Keogh (Derby), Pearce (Reading), Ward (Wolves) (Quinn, Hull 67), Hendrick (Derby), Meyler (Sunderland), McGeady (Everton) (Cox, Nottm Forest 76), McClean (Wigan) (Pilkington, Norwich 67), Hoolahan (Norwich) (Keane, LA Galaxy 63), Walters (Stoke) (Long, Hull 63). **Scorer**: McClean (52). **Booked**: McClean, Pearce

Portugal (4-3-3): Rui Patricio, Ruben Amorim (Miguel Veloso 81), Neto (Pepe 65), Ricardo Costa, Fabio Coentrao, Joao Moutinho, William Carvalho, Raul Meireles (Andre Almeida 66) Varela (Vieirinha 73), Hugo Almeida (Helder Postiga 66), Ronaldo (Nani 65). **Scorers**: Hugo Almeida (2, 37), Keogh (20 og), Vieirinha (77), Fabio Coentrao (83)

Referee: B Toledo (USA). **Half-time**: 0-3

OTHER BRITISH & IRISH INTERNATIONAL RESULTS

ENGLAND

v ALBANIA

		E	A
1989	Tirana (WC)	2	0
1989	Wembley (WC)	5	0
2001	Tirana (WC)	3	1
2001	Newcastle (WC)	2	0

v ALGERIA

		E	A
2010	Cape Town (WC)	0	0

v ANDORRA

		E	A
2006	Old Trafford (EC)	5	0
2007	Barcelona (EC)	3	0
2008	Barcelona (WC)	2	0
2009	Wembley (WC)	6	0

v ARGENTINA

		E	A
1951	Wembley	2	1
1953*	Buenos Aires	0	0
1962	Rancagua (WC)	3	1
1964	Rio de Janeiro	0	1
1966	Wembley (WC)	1	0
1974	Wembley	2	2
1977	Buenos Aires	1	1
1980	Wembley	3	1
1986	Mexico City (WC)	1	2
1991	Wembley	2	2
1998†	St Etienne (WC)	2	2
2000	Wembley	0	0
2002	Sapporo (WC)	1	0
2005	Geneva	3	2

(*Abandoned after 21 mins – rain)
(† England lost 3-4 on pens)

v AUSTRALIA

		E	A
1980	Sydney	2	1
1983	Sydney	0	0
1983	Brisbane	1	0
1983	Melbourne	1	1
1991	Sydney	1	0
2003	West Ham	1	3

v AUSTRIA

		E	A
1908	Vienna	6	1
1908	Vienna	11	1
1909	Vienna	8	1
1930	Vienna	0	0
1932	Stamford Bridge	4	3
1936	Vienna	1	2
1951	Wembley	2	2
1952	Wembley	3	2
1958	Boras (WC)	2	2
1961	Vienna	1	3
1962	Wembley	3	1
1965	Wembley	2	3
1967	Vienna	1	0
1973	Wembley	7	0

		E	A
1979	Vienna	3	4
2004	Vienna (WC)	2	2
2005	Old Trafford (WC)	1	0
2007	Vienna	1	0

v AZERBAIJAN

		E	A
2004	Baku (WC)	1	0
2005	Newcastle (WC)	2	0

v BELARUS

		E	B
2008	Minsk (WC)	3	1
2009	Wembley (WC)	3	0

v BELGIUM

		E	B
1921	Brussels	2	0
1923	Highbury	6	1
1923	Antwerp	2	2
1924	West Bromwich	4	0
1926	Antwerp	5	3
1927	Brussels	9	1
1928	Antwerp	3	1
1929	Brussels	5	1
1931	Brussels	4	1
1936	Brussels	2	3
1947	Brussels	5	2
1950	Brussels	4	1
1952	Wembley	5	0
1954	Basle (WC)	4	4
1964	Wembley	2	2
1970	Brussels	3	1
1980	Turin (EC)	1	1
1990	Bologna (WC)	1	0
1998*	Casablanca	0	0
1999	Sunderland	2	1
2012	Wembley	1	0

(*England lost 3-4 on pens)

v BOHEMIA

		E	B
1908	Prague	4	0

v BRAZIL

		E	B
1956	Wembley	4	2
1958	Gothenburg (WC)	0	0
1959	Rio de Janeiro	0	2
1962	Vina del Mar (WC)	1	3
1963	Wembley	1	1
1964	Rio de Janeiro	1	5
1969	Rio de Janeiro	1	2
1970	Guadalajara (WC)	0	1
1976	Los Angeles	0	1
1977	Rio de Janeiro	0	0
1978	Wembley	1	1
1981	Wembley	0	1
1984	Rio de Janeiro	2	0
1987	Wembley	1	1
1990	Wembley	1	0
1992	Wembley	1	1
1993	Washington	1	1
1995	Wembley	1	3
1997	Paris (TF)	0	1

		E	
2000	Wembley	1	1
2002	Shizuoka (WC)	1	2
2007	Wembley	1	1
2009	Doha	0	1
2013	Wembley	2	1
2013	Rio de Janeiro	2	2

v BULGARIA

		E	B
1962	Rancagua (WC)	0	0
1968	Wembley	1	1
1974	Sofia	1	0
1979	Sofia (EC)	3	0
1979	Wembley (EC)	2	0
1996	Wembley	1	0
1998	Wembley (EC)	0	0
1999	Sofia (EC)	1	1
2010	Wembley (EC)	4	0
2011	Sofia (EC)	3	0

v CAMEROON

		E	C
1990	Naples (WC)	3	2
1991	Wembley	2	0
1997	Wembley	2	0
2002	Kobe (Japan)	2	2

v CANADA

		E	C
1986	Vancouver	1	0

v CHILE

		E	C
1950	Rio de Janeiro (WC)	2	0
1953	Santiago	2	1
1984	Santiago	0	0
1989	Wembley	0	0
1998	Wembley	0	2
2013	Wembley	0	2

v CHINA

		E	C
1996	Beijing	3	0

v CIS
(formerly Soviet Union)

		E	CIS
1992	Moscow	2	2

v COLOMBIA

		E	C
1970	Bogota	4	0
1988	Wembley	1	1
1995	Wembley	0	0
1998	Lens (WC)	2	0
2005	New York	3	2

v COSTA RICA

		E	CR
2014	Belo Horizonte (WC)	0	0

v CROATIA

		E	C
1995	Wembley	0	0
2003	Ipswich	3	1
2004	Lisbon (EC)	4	2
2006	Zagreb (EC)	0	2
2007	Wembley (EC)	2	3
2008	Zagreb (WC)	4	1
2009	Wembley (WC)	5	1

v CYPRUS

		E	C
1975	Wembley (EC)	5	0
1975	Limassol (EC)	1	0

v CZECH REPUBLIC

		E	C
1998	Wembley	2	0
2008	Wembley	2	2

v CZECHOSLOVAKIA

		E	C
1934	Prague	1	2
1937	White Hart Lane	5	4
1963	Bratislava	4	2
1966	Wembley	0	0
1970	Guadalajara (WC)	1	0
1973	Prague	1	1
1974	Wembley (EC)	3	0
1975*	Bratislava (EC)	1	2
1978	Wembley (EC)	1	0
1982	Bilbao (WC)	2	0
1990	Wembley	4	2
1992	Prague	2	2

(* Aband 0-0, 17 mins prev day – fog)

v DENMARK

		E	D
1948	Copenhagen	0	0
1955	Copenhagen	5	1
1956	W'hampton (WC)	5	2
1957	Copenhagen (WC)	4	1
1966	Copenhagen	2	0
1978	Copenhagen (EC)	4	3
1979	Wembley (EC)	1	0
1982	Copenhagen (EC)	2	2
1983	Wembley (EC)	0	1
1988	Wembley	1	0
1989	Copenhagen	1	1
1990	Wembley	1	0
1992	Malmo (EC)	0	0
1994	Wembley	1	0
2002	Niigata (WC)	3	0
2003	Old Trafford	2	3
2005	Copenhagen	1	4
2011	Copenhagen	2	1
2014	Wembley	1	0

v EAST GERMANY

		E	EG
1963	Leipzig	2	1
1970	Wembley	3	1
1974	Leipzig	1	1
1984	Wembley	1	0

v ECUADOR

		E	Ec
1970	Quito	2	0
2006	Stuttgart (WC)	1	0
2014	Miami	2	2

v EGYPT

		E	Eg
1986	Cairo	4	0
1990	Cagliari (WC)	1	0
2010	Wembley	3	1

v ESTONIA

		E	Est
2007	Tallinn (EC)	3	0
2007	Wembley (EC)	3	0

v FIFA

		E	F
1938	Highbury	3	0
1953	Wembley	4	4
1963	Wembley	2	1

v FINLAND

		E	F
1937	Helsinki	8	0
1956	Helsinki	5	1
1966	Helsinki	3	0
1976	Helsinki (WC)	4	1
1976	Wembley (WC)	2	1
1982	Helsinki	4	1
1984	Wembley (WC)	5	0
1985	Helsinki (WC)	1	1
1992	Helsinki	2	1
2000	Helsinki (WC)	0	0
2001	Liverpool (WC)	2	1

v FRANCE

		E	F
1923	Paris	4	1
1924	Paris	3	1
1925	Paris	3	2
1927	Paris	6	0
1928	Paris	5	1
1929	Paris	4	1
1931	Paris	2	5
1933	White Hart Lane	4	1
1938	Paris	4	2
1947	Highbury	3	0
1949	Paris	3	1
1951	Highbury	2	2
1955	Paris	0	1
1957	Wembley	4	0
1962	Hillsborough (EC)	1	1
1963	Paris (EC)	2	5
1966	Wembley (WC)	2	0
1969	Wembley	5	0
1982	Bilbao (WC)	3	1
1984	Paris	0	2
1992	Wembley	2	0
1992	Malmo (EC)	0	0
1997	Montpellier (TF)	1	0
1999	Wembley	0	2
2000	Paris	1	1
2004	Lisbon (EC)	1	2
2008	Paris	0	1
2010	Wembley	1	2
2012	Donetsk (EC)	1	1

v GEORGIA

		E	G
1996	Tbilisi (WC)	2	0
1997	Wembley (WC)	2	0

v GERMANY/WEST GERMANY

		E	G
1930	Berlin	3	3
1935	White Hart Lane	3	0
1938	Berlin	6	3
1954	Wembley	3	1
1956	Berlin	3	1
1965	Nuremberg	1	0
1966	Wembley	1	0
1966	Wembley (WCF)	4	2
1968	Hanover	0	1
1970	Leon (WC)	2	3
1972	Wembley (EC)	1	3
1972	Berlin (EC)	0	0
1975	Wembley	2	0
1978	Munich	1	2
1982	Madrid (WC)	0	0
1982	Wembley	1	2
1985	Mexico City	3	0
1987	Dusseldorf	1	3
1990*	Turin (WC)	1	1
1991	Wembley	0	1
1993	Detroit	1	2
1996†	Wembley (EC)	1	1
2000	Charleroi (EC)	1	0
2000	Wembley (WC)	0	1
2001	Munich (WC)	5	1
2007	Wembley	1	2
2008	Berlin	2	1
2010	Bloemfontein (WC)	1	4
2012	Donetsk (EC)	1	1
2013	Wembley	0	1

(*England lost 3-4 on pens)
(† England lost 5-6 on pens)

v GHANA

		E	G
2011	Wembley	1	1

v GREECE

		E	G
1971	Wembley (EC)	3	0
1971	Athens (EC)	2	0
1982	Salonika (EC)	3	0
1983	Wembley (EC)	0	0
1989	Athens	2	1
1994	Wembley	5	0
2001	Athens (WC)	2	0
2001	Old Trafford (WC)	2	2
2006	Old Trafford	4	0

v HOLLAND

		E	H
1935	Amsterdam	1	0
1946	Huddersfield	8	2
1964	Amsterdam	1	1
1969	Amsterdam	1	0
1970	Wembley	0	0
1977	Wembley	0	2
1982	Wembley	2	0
1988	Wembley	2	2
1988	Dusseldorf (EC)	1	3
1990	Cagliari (WC)	0	0
1993	Wembley (WC)	2	2
1993	Rotterdam (WC)	0	2
1996	Wembley (EC)	4	1
2001	White Hart Lane	0	2
2002	Amsterdam	1	1
2005	Villa Park	0	0
2006	Amsterdam	1	1
2009	Amsterdam	2	2
2012	Wembley	2	3

v HONDURAS

		E	H
2014	Miami	0	0

v HUNGARY

		E	H
1908	Budapest	7	0
1909	Budapest	4	2
1909	Budapest	8	2
1934	Budapest	1	2
1936	Highbury	6	2
1953	Wembley	3	6
1954	Budapest	1	7
1960	Budapest	0	2
1962	Rancagua (WC)	1	2
1965	Wembley	1	0
1978	Wembley	4	1
1981	Budapest (WC)	3	1
1981	Wembley (WC)	1	0
1983	Wembley (EC)	2	0
1983	Budapest (EC)	3	0
1988	Budapest	0	0
1990	Wembley	1	0
1992	Budapest	1	0
1996	Wembley	3	0
1999	Budapest	1	1
2006	Old Trafford	3	1
2010	Wembley	2	1

v ICELAND

		E	I
1982	Reykjavik	1	1
2004	City of Manchester	6	1

v ISRAEL

		E	I
1986	Tel Aviv	2	1
1988	Tel Aviv	0	0
2006	Tel Aviv (EC)	0	0
2007	Wembley (EC)	3	0

v ITALY

		E	I
1933	Rome	1	1
1934	Highbury	3	2
1939	Milan	2	2
1948	Turin	4	0
1949	White Hart Lane	2	0
1952	Florence	1	1
1959	Wembley	2	2
1961	Rome	3	2
1973	Turin	0	2
1973	Wembley	0	1
1976	New York	3	2
1976	Rome (WC)	0	2
1977	Wembley (WC)	2	0
1980	Turin (EC)	0	1
1985	Mexico City	1	2
1989	Wembley	0	0
1990	Bari (WC)	1	2
1996	Wembley (WC)	0	1
1997	Nantes (TF)	2	0
1997	Rome (WC)	0	0
2000	Turin	0	1
2002	Leeds	1	2
2012*	Kiev (EC)	0	0
2012	Berne	1	2
2014	Manaus (WC)	1	2

(*England lost 2-4 on pens)

v JAMAICA

		E	J
2006	Old Trafford	6	0

v JAPAN

		E	J
1995	Wembley	2	1
2004	City of Manchester	1	1
2010	Graz	2	1

v KAZAKHSTAN

		E	K
2008	Wembley (WC)	5	1
2009	Almaty (WC)	4	0

v KUWAIT

		E	K
1982	Bilbao (WC)	1	0

v LIECHTENSTEIN

		E	L
2003	Vaduz (EC)	2	0
2003	Old Trafford (EC)	2	0

v LUXEMBOURG

		E	L
1927	Luxembourg	5	2
1960	Luxembourg (WC)	9	0
1961	Highbury (WC)	4	1
1977	Wembley (WC)	5	0
1977	Luxembourg (WC)	2	0
1982	Wembley (EC)	9	0
1983	Luxembourg (EC)	4	0
1998	Luxembourg (EC)	3	0
1999	Wembley (EC)	6	0

v MACEDONIA

		E	M
2002	Southampton (EC)	2	2
2003	Skopje (EC)	2	1
2006	Skopje (EC)	1	0
2006	Old Trafford (EC)	0	0

v MALAYSIA

		E	M
1991	Kuala Lumpur	4	2

v MALTA

		E	M
1971	Valletta (EC)	1	0
1971	Wembley (EC)	5	0
2000	Valletta	2	1

v MEXICO

		E	M
1959	Mexico City	1	2
1961	Wembley	8	0
1966	Wembley (WC)	2	0
1969	Mexico City	0	0
1985	Mexico City	0	1
1986	Los Angeles	3	0
1997	Wembley	2	0
2001	Derby	4	0
2010	Wembley	3	1

v MOLDOVA

		E	M
1996	Kishinev	3	0
1997	Wembley (WC)	4	0
2012	Chisinu (WC)	5	0
2013	Wembley (WC)	4	0

v MONTENEGRO

		E	M
2010	Wembley (EC)	0	0
2011	Podgorica (EC)	2	2
2013	Podgorica (WC)	1	1
2013	Wembley (WC)	4	1

v MOROCCO

		E	M
1986	Monterrey (WC)	0	0
1998	Casablanca	1	0

v NEW ZEALAND

		E	NZ
1991	Auckland	1	0
1991	Wellington	2	0

v NIGERIA

		E	NZ
1994	Wembley	1	0
2002	Osaka (WC)	0	0

v NORWAY

		E	NZ
1937	Oslo	6	0
1938	Newcastle	4	0
1949	Oslo	4	1
1966	Oslo	6	1
1980	Wembley (WC)	4	0
1981	Oslo (WC)	1	2
1992	Wembley (WC)	1	1
1993	Oslo (WC)	0	2
1994	Wembley	0	0
1995	Oslo	0	0
2012	Oslo	1	0

v PARAGUAY

		E	P
1986	Mexico City (WC)	3	0
2002	Anfield	4	0
2006	Frankfurt (WC)	1	0

v PERU

		E	P
1959	Lima	1	4
1961	Lima	4	0
2014	Wembley	3	0

v POLAND

		E	P
1966	Goodison Park	1	1
1966	Chorzow	1	0
1973	Chorzow (WC)	0	2
1973	Wembley (WC)	1	1
1986	Monterrey (WC)	3	0
1989	Wembley (WC)	3	0
1989	Katowice (WC)	0	0
1990	Wembley (EC)	2	0
1991	Poznan (EC)	1	1
1993	Chorzow (WC)	1	1
1993	Wembley (WC)	3	0
1996	Wembley (WC)	2	1
1997	Katowice (WC)	2	0
1999	Wembley (EC)	3	1
1999	Warsaw (EC)	0	0
2004	Katowice (WC)	2	1
2005	Old Trafford (WC)	2	1
2012	Warsaw (WC)	1	1
2013	Wembley (WC)	2	0

v PORTUGAL

		E	P
1947	Lisbon	10	0
1950	Lisbon	5	3
1951	Goodison Park	5	2
1955	Oporto	1	3
1958	Wembley	2	1
1961	Lisbon (WC)	1	1
1961	Wembley (WC)	2	0
1964	Lisbon	4	3
1964	Sao Paulo	1	1
1966	Wembley (WC)	2	1
1969	Wembley	1	0
1974	Lisbon	0	0
1974	Wembley (EC)	0	0
1975	Lisbon (EC)	1	1
1986	Monterrey (WC)	0	1
1995	Wembley	1	1
1998	Wembley	3	0
2000	Eindhoven (EC)	2	3
2002	Villa Park	1	1
2004	Faro	1	1
2004*	Lisbon (EC)	2	2
2006†	Gelsenkirchen (WC)	0	0

(† England lost 1–3 on pens)
(*England lost 5–6 on pens)

v REPUBLIC OF IRELAND

		E	RoI
1946	Dublin	1	0
1949	Goodison Park	0	2
1957	Wembley (WC)	5	1
1957	Dublin (WC)	1	1
1964	Dublin	3	1
1977	Wembley	1	1
1978	Dublin (EC)	1	1
1980	Wembley (EC)	2	0
1985	Wembley	2	1
1988	Stuttgart (EC)	0	1
1990	Cagliari (WC)	1	1
1990	Dublin (EC)	1	1
1991	Wembley (EC)	1	1
1995*	Dublin	0	1
2013	Wembley	1	1

(*Abandoned 27 mins – crowd riot)

v ROMANIA

		E	R
1939	Bucharest	2	0
1968	Bucharest	0	0
1969	Wembley	1	1
1970	Guadalajara (WC)	1	0
1980	Bucharest (WC)	1	2
1981	Wembley (WC)	0	0
1985	Bucharest (WC)	0	0
1985	Wembley (WC)	1	1
1994	Wembley	1	1
1998	Toulouse (WC)	1	2
2000	Charleroi (EC)	2	3

v RUSSIA

		E	R
2007	Wembley (EC)	3	0
2007	Moscow (EC)	1	2

v SAN MARINO

		E	SM

1992	Wembley (WC)	6	0
1993	Bologna (WC)	7	1
2012	Wembley (WC)	5	0
2013	Serravalle (WC)	8	0

v SAUDI ARABIA

		E	SA
1988	Riyadh	1	1
1998	Wembley	0	0

v SERBIA-MONTENEGRO

		E	S-M
2003	Leicester	2	1

v SLOVAKIA

		E	S
2002	Bratislava (EC)	2	1
2003	Middlesbrough (EC)	2	1
2009	Wembley	4	0

v SLOVENIA

		E	S
2009	Wembley	2	1
2010	Port Elizabeth (WC)	1	0

v SOUTH AFRICA

		E	SA
1997	Old Trafford	2	1
2003	Durban	2	1

v SOUTH KOREA

		E	SK
2002	Seoguipo	1	1

v SOVIET UNION (see also CIS)

		E	SU
1958	Moscow	1	1
1958	Gothenburg (WC)	2	2
1958	Gothenburg (WC)	0	1
1958	Wembley	5	0
1967	Wembley	2	2
1968	Rome (EC)	2	0
1973	Moscow	2	1
1984	Wembley	0	2
1986	Tbilisi	1	0
1988	Frankfurt (EC)	1	3
1991	Wembley	3	1

v SPAIN

		E	S
1929	Madrid	3	4
1931	Highbury	7	1
1950	Rio de Janeiro (WC)	0	1
1955	Madrid	1	1
1955	Wembley	4	1
1960	Madrid	0	3
1960	Wembley	4	2
1965	Madrid	2	0
1967	Wembley	2	0
1968	Wembley (EC)	1	0
1968	Madrid (EC)	2	1
1980	Barcelona	2	0
1980	Naples (EC)	2	1
1981	Wembley	1	2
1982	Madrid (WC)	0	0
1987	Madrid	4	2
1992	Santander	0	1
1996*	Wembley (EC)	0	0
2001	Villa Park	3	0
2004	Madrid	0	1

2007	Old Trafford	0	1
2009	Seville	0	2
2011	Wembley	1	0
(*England won 4-2 on pens)			

v SWEDEN

		E	S
1923	Stockholm	4	2
1923	Stockholm	3	1
1937	Stockholm	4	0
1948	Highbury	4	2
1949	Stockholm	1	3
1956	Stockholm	0	0
1959	Wembley	2	3
1965	Gothenburg	2	1
1968	Wembley	3	1
1979	Stockholm	0	0
1986	Stockholm	0	1
1988	Wembley (WC)	0	0
1989	Stockholm (WC)	0	0
1992	Stockholm (EC)	1	2
1995	Leeds	3	3
1998	Stockholm (EC)	1	2
1999	Wembley (EC)	0	0
2001	Old Trafford	1	1
2002	Saitama (WC)	1	1
2004	Gothenburg	0	1
2006	Cologne (WC)	2	2
2011	Wembley	1	0
2012	Kiev (EC)	3	2
2012	Stockholm	2	4

v SWITZERLAND

		E	S
1933	Berne	4	0
1938	Zurich	1	2
1947	Zurich	0	1
1949	Highbury	6	0
1952	Zurich	3	0
1954	Berne (WC)	2	0
1962	Wembley	3	1
1963	Basle	8	1
1971	Basle (EC)	3	2
1971	Wembley (EC)	1	1
1975	Basle	2	1
1977	Wembley	0	0
1980	Wembley (WC)	2	1
1981	Basle (WC)	1	2
1988	Lausanne	1	0
1995	Wembley	3	1
1996	Wembley (EC)	1	1
1998	Berne	1	1
2004	Coimbra (EC)	3	0
2008	Wembley	2	1
2010	Basle (EC)	3	1
2011	Wembley (EC)	2	2

v TRINIDAD & TOBAGO

		E	T
2006	Nuremberg (WC)	2	0
2008	Port of Spain	3	0

v TUNISIA

		E	T
1990	Tunis	1	1
1998	Marseille (WC)	2	0

v TURKEY

		E	T
1984	Istanbul (WC)	8	0
1985	Wembley (WC)	5	0
1987	Izmir (EC)	0	0
1987	Wembley (EC)	8	0
1991	Izmir (EC)	1	0
1991	Wembley (EC)	1	0
1992	Wembley (WC)	4	0
1993	Izmir (WC)	2	0
2003	Sunderland (EC)	2	0
2003	Istanbul (EC)	0	0

v UKRAINE

		E	U
2000	Wembley	2	0
2004	Newcastle	3	0
2009	Wembley (WC)	2	1
2009	Dnipropetrovski (WC)	0	1
2012	Donetsk (EC)	1	0
2012	Wembley (WC)	1	1
2013	Kiev (WC)	0	0

v URUGUAY

		E	U
1953	Montevideo	1	2
1954	Basle (WC)	2	4
1964	Wembley	2	1
1966	Wembley (WC)	0	0
1969	Montevideo	2	1
1977	Montevideo	0	0
1984	Montevideo	0	2
1990	Wembley	1	2

1995	Wembley	0	0
2006	Anfield	2	1
2014	Sao Paulo (WC)	1	2

v USA

		E	USA
1950	Belo Horizonte (WC)	0	1
1953	New York	6	3
1959	Los Angeles	8	1
1964	New York	10	0
1985	Los Angeles	5	0
1993	Boston	0	2
1994	Wembley	2	0
2005	Chicago	2	1
2008	Wembley	2	0
2010	Rustenburg (WC)	1	1

v YUGOSLAVIA

		E	Y
1939	Belgrade	1	2
1950	Highbury	2	2
1954	Belgrade	0	1
1956	Wembley	3	0
1958	Belgrade	0	5
1960	Wembley	3	3
1965	Belgrade	1	1
1966	Wembley	2	0
1968	Florence (EC)	0	1
1972	Wembley	1	1
1974	Belgrade	2	2
1986	Wembley (EC)	2	0
1987	Belgrade (EC)	4	1
1989	Wembley	2	1

ENGLAND'S RECORD

England's first international was a 0-0 draw against Scotland in Glasgow, on the West of Scotland cricket ground, Partick, on November 30, 1872 Their complete record at the start of 2014–15 is:

P	W	D	L	F	A
934	527	229	178	2060	933

ENGLAND'S 'B' TEAM RESULTS

England scores first

1937	Stockholm	4	0	1950	Italy (A)	0	5
1948	Highbury	4	2	1950	Holland (H)	1	0
1949	Stockholm	1	3	1950	Holland (A)	0	3
1956	Stockholm	0	0	1950	Luxembourg (A)	2	1
1959	Wembley	2	3	1950	Switzerland (H)	5	0
1965	Gothenburg	2	1	1952	Holland (A)	1	0
1968	Wembley	3	1	1952	France (A)	1	7
1979	Stockholm	0	0	1953	Scotland (A)	2	2
1986	Stockholm	0	1	1954	Scotland (H)	1	1
1988	Wembley (WC)	0	0	1954	Germany (A)	4	0
1989	Stockholm (WC)	0	0	1954	Yugoslavia (A)	1	2
1992	Stockholm (EC)	1	2	1954	Switzerland (A)	0	2
1995	Leeds	3	3	1955	Germany (H)	1	1
1998	Stockholm (EC)	1	2	1955	Yugoslavia (H)	5	1
1999	Wembley (EC)	0	0	1956	Switzerland (H)	4	1
2001	Old Trafford	1	1	1956	Scotland (A)	2	2
2002	Saitama (WC)	1	1	1957	Scotland (H)	4	1
2004	Gothenburg	0	1	1978	W Germany (A)	2	1
2006	Cologne (WC)	2	2	1978	Czechoslovakia (A)	1	0
1949	Finland (A)	4	0	1978	Singapore (A)	8	0
1949	Holland (A)	4	0	1978	Malaysia (A)	1	1

1978	N Zealand (A)	4	0	1990	Rep of Ireland (A)	1	4
1978	N Zealand (A)	3	1	1990	Czechoslovakia (H)	2	0
1978	N Zealand (A)	4	0	1990	Algeria (A)	0	0
1979	Austria (A)	1	0	1991	Wales (A)	1	0
1979	N Zealand (H)	4	1	1991	Iceland (H)	1	0
1980	USA (H)	1	0	1991	Switzerland (H)	2	1
1980	Spain (H)	1	0	1991	Spanish XI (A)	1	0
1980	Australia (H)	1	0	1992	France (A)	3	0
1981	Spain (A)	2	3	1992	Czechoslovakia (A)	1	0
1984	N Zealand (H)	2	0	1992	CIS (A)	1	0
1987	Malta (A)	2	0	1994	N Ireland (H)	4	2
1989	Switzerland (A)	2	0	1995	Rep of Ireland (H)	2	0
1989	Iceland (A) .	2	0	1998	Chile (H)	1	2
1989	Norway (A)	1	0	1998	Russia (H)	4	1
1989	Italy (H)	1	1	2006	Belarus (H)	1	2
1989	Yugoslavia (H)	2	1	2007	Albania	3	1

GREAT BRITAIN v REST OF EUROPE (FIFA)

		GB	RofE			GB	RofE
1947	Glasgow	6	1	1955	Belfast	1	4

SCOTLAND

v ARGENTINA

		S	A
1977	Buenos Aires	1	1
1979	Glasgow	1	3
1990	Glasgow	1	0
2008	Glasgow	0	1

v AUSTRALIA

		S	A
1985*	Glasgow (WC)	2	0
1985*	Melbourne (WC)	0	0
1996	Glasgow	1	0
2000	Glasgow	0	2
2012	Edinburgh	3	1
(* World Cup play-off)			

v AUSTRIA

		S	A
1931	Vienna	0	5
1933	Glasgow	2	2
1937	Vienna	1	1
1950	Glasgow	0	1
1951	Vienna	0	4
1954	Zurich (WC)	0	1
1955	Vienna	4	1
1956	Glasgow	1	1
1960	Vienna	1	4
1963*	Glasgow	4	1
1968	Glasgow (WC)	2	1
1969	Vienna (WC)	0	2
1978	Vienna (EC)	2	3
1979	Glasgow (EC)	1	1
1994	Vienna	2	1
1996	Vienna (WC)	0	0
1997	Glasgow (WC)	2	0
(* Abandoned after 79 minutes)			
2003	Glasgow	0	2
2005	Graz	2	2
2007	Vienna	1	0

v BELARUS

		S	B
1997	Minsk (WC)	1	0
1997	Aberdeen (WC)	4	1
2005	Minsk (WC)	0	0
2005	Glasgow (WC)	0	1

v BELGIUM

		S	B
1947	Brussels	1	2
1948	Glasgow	2	0
1951	Brussels	5	0
1971	Liege (EC)	0	3
1971	Aberdeen (EC)	1	0
1974	Brugge	1	2
1979	Brussels (EC)	0	2
1979	Glasgow (EC)	1	3
1982	Brussels (EC)	2	3
1983	Glasgow (EC)	1	1
1987	Brussels (EC)	1	4
1987	Glasgow (EC)	2	0
2001	Glasgow (WC)	2	2
2001	Brussels (WC)	0	2
2012	Brussels (WC)	0	2
2013	Glasgow (WC)	0	2

v BOSNIA

		S	B
1999	Sarajevo (EC)	2	1
1999	Glasgow (EC)	1	0

v BRAZIL

		S	B
1966	Glasgow	1	1
1972	Rio de Janeiro	0	1
1973	Glasgow	0	1
1974	Frankfurt (WC)	0	0
1977	Rio de Janeiro	0	2
1982	Seville (WC)	1	4
1987	Glasgow	0	2
1990	Turin (WC)	0	1

| 1998 | St Denis (WC) | 1 | 2 |
| 2011 | Arsenal | 0 | 2 |

v BULGARIA

		S	B
1978	Glasgow	2	1
1986	Glasgow (EC)	0	0
1987	Sofia (EC)	1	0
1990	Sofia (EC)	1	1
1991	Glasgow (EC)	1	1
2006	Kobe	5	1

v CANADA

		S	C
1983	Vancouver	2	0
1983	Edmonton	3	0
1983	Toronto	2	0
1992	Toronto	3	1
2002	Edinburgh	3	1

v CHILE

		S	C
1977	Santiago	4	2
1989	Glasgow	2	0

v CIS (formerly Soviet Union)

		S	C
1992	Norrkoping (EC)	3	0

v COLOMBIA

		S	C
1988	Glasgow	0	0
1996	Miami	0	1
1998	New York	2	2

v COSTA RICA

		S	C
1990	Genoa (WC)	0	1

v CROATIA

		S	C
2000	Zagreb (WC)	1	1
2001	Glasgow (WC)	0	0
2008	Glasgow	1	1
2013	Zagreb (WC)	1	0
2013	Glasgow (WC)	2	0

v CYPRUS

		S	C
1968	Nicosia (WC)	5	0
1969	Glasgow (WC)	8	0
1989	Limassol (WC)	3	2
1989	Glasgow (WC)	2	1
2011	Larnaca	2	1

v CZECH REPUBLIC

		S	C
1999	Glasgow (EC)	1	2
1999	Prague (EC)	2	3
2008	Prague	1	3
2010	Glasgow	1	0
2010	Prague (EC)	0	1
2011	Glasgow (EC)	2	2

v CZECHOSLOVAKIA

		S	C
1937	Prague	3	1
1937	Glasgow	5	0
1961	Bratislava (WC)	0	4
1961	Glasgow (WC)	3	2
1961*	Brussels (WC)	2	4

1972	Porto Alegre	0	0
1973	Glasgow (WC)	2	1
1973	Bratislava (WC)	0	1
1976	Prague (WC)	0	2
1977	Glasgow (WC)	3	1
(*World Cup play-off)			

v DENMARK

		S	D
1951	Glasgow	3	1
1952	Copenhagen	2	1
1968	Copenhagen	1	0
1970	Glasgow (EC)	1	0
1971	Copenhagen (EC)	0	1
1972	Copenhagen (WC)	4	1
1972	Glasgow (WC)	2	0
1975	Copenhagen (EC)	1	0
1975	Glasgow (EC)	3	1
1986	Neza (WC)	0	1
1996	Copenhagen	0	2
1998	Glasgow	0	1
2002	Glasgow	0	1
2004	Copenhagen	0	1
2011	Glasgow	2	1

v EAST GERMANY

		S	EG
1974	Glasgow	3	0
1977	East Berlin	0	1
1982	Glasgow (EC)	2	0
1983	Halle (EC)	1	2
1986	Glasgow	0	0
1990	Glasgow	0	1

v ECUADOR

		S	E
1995	Toyama, Japan	2	1

v EGYPT

		S	E
1990	Aberdeen	1	3

v ESTONIA

		S	E
1993	Tallinn (WC)	3	0
1993	Aberdeen	3	1
1996	Tallinn (WC)	*No result	
1997	Monaco (WC)	0	0
1997	Kilmarnock (WC)	2	0
1998	Edinburgh (EC)	3	2
1999	Tallinn (EC)	0	0
(* Estonia absent)			
2004	Tallinn	1	0
2013	Aberdeen	1	0

v FAROE ISLANDS

		S	F
1994	Glasgow (EC)	5	1
1995	Toftir (EC)	2	0
1998	Aberdeen (EC)	2	1
1999	Toftir (EC)	1	1
2002	Toftir (EC)	2	2
2003	Glasgow (EC)	3	1
2006	Glasgow (EC)	6	0
2007	Toftir (EC)	2	0
2010	Aberdeen	3	0

v FINLAND

		S	F
1954	Helsinki	2	1
1964	Glasgow (WC)	3	1
1965	Helsinki (WC)	2	1
1976	Glasgow	6	0
1992	Glasgow	1	1
1994	Helsinki (EC)	2	0
1995	Glasgow (EC)	1	0
1998	Edinburgh	1	1

v FRANCE

		S	F
1930	Paris	2	0
1932	Paris	3	1
1948	Paris	0	3
1949	Glasgow	2	0
1950	Paris	1	0
1951	Glasgow	1	0
1958	Orebro (WC)	1	2
1984	Marseilles	0	2
1989	Glasgow (WC)	2	0
1990	Paris (WC)	0	3
1997	St Etienne	1	2
2000	Glasgow	0	2
2002	Paris	0	5
2006	Glasgow (EC)	1	0
2007	Paris (EC)	1	0

v GEORGIA

		S	G
2007	Glasgow (EC)	2	1
2007	Tbilisi (EC)	0	2

v GERMANY/WEST GERMANY

		S	G
1929	Berlin	1	1
1936	Glasgow	2	0
1957	Stuttgart	3	1
1959	Glasgow	3	2
1964	Hanover	2	2
1969	Glasgow (WC)	1	1
1969	Hamburg (WC)	2	3
1973	Glasgow	1	1
1974	Frankfurt	1	2
1986	Queretaro (WC)	1	2
1992	Norrkoping (EC)	0	2
1993	Glasgow	0	1
1999	Bremen	1	0
2003	Glasgow (EC)	1	1
2003	Dortmund (EC)	1	2

v GREECE

		S	G
1994	Athens (EC)	0	1
1995	Glasgow	1	0

v HOLLAND

		S	H
1929	Amsterdam	2	0
1938	Amsterdam	3	1
1959	Amsterdam	2	1
1966	Glasgow	0	3
1968	Amsterdam	0	0
1971	Amsterdam	1	2
1978	Mendoza (WC)	3	2
1982	Glasgow	2	1
1986	Eindhoven	0	0
1992	Gothenburg (EC)	0	1
1994	Glasgow	0	1
1994	Utrecht	1	3
1996	Birmingham (EC)	0	0
2000	Arnhem	0	0
2003*	Glasgow (EC)	1	0
2003*	Amsterdam (EC)	0	6
2009	Amsterdam (WC)	0	3
2009	Glasgow (WC)	0	1

(*Qual Round play-off)

v HUNGARY

		S	H
1938	Glasgow	3	1
1955	Glasgow	2	4
1955	Budapest	1	3
1958	Glasgow	1	1
1960	Budapest	3	3
1980	Budapest	1	3
1987	Glasgow	2	0
2004	Glasgow	0	3

v ICELAND

		S	I
1984	Glasgow (WC)	3	0
1985	Reykjavik (WC)	1	0
2002	Reykjavik (EC)	2	0
2003	Glasgow (EC)	2	1
2008	Reykjavik (WC)	2	1
2009	Glasgow (WC)	2	1

v IRAN

		S	I
1978	Cordoba (WC)	1	1

v ISRAEL

		S	I
1981	Tel Aviv (WC)	1	0
1981	Glasgow (WC)	3	1
1986	Tel Aviv	1	0

v ITALY

		S	I
1931	Rome	0	3
1965	Glasgow (WC)	1	0
1965	Naples (WC)	0	3
1988	Perugia	0	2
1992	Glasgow (WC)	0	0
1993	Rome (WC)	1	3
2005	Milan (WC)	0	2
2005	Glasgow (WC)	1	1
2007	Bari (EC)	0	2
2007	Glasgow (EC)	1	2

v JAPAN

		S	J
1995	Hiroshima	0	0
2006	Saitama	0	0
2009	Yokohama	0	2

v LATVIA

		S	L
1996	Riga (WC)	2	0
1997	Glasgow (WC)	2	0
2000	Riga (WC)	1	0
2001	Glasgow (WC)	2	1

v LIECHTENSTEIN

		S	L
2010	Glasgow (EC)	2	1

		S	L
2011	Vaduz (EC)	1	0

v LITHUANIA

		S	L
1998	Vilnius (EC)	0	0
1999	Glasgow (EC)	3	0
2003	Kaunus (EC)	0	1
2003	Glasgow (EC)	1	0
2006	Kaunas (EC)	2	1
2007	Glasgow (EC)	3	1
2010	Kaunas (EC)	0	0
2011	Glasgow (EC)	1	0

v LUXEMBOURG

		S	L
1947	Luxembourg	6	0
1986	Glasgow (EC)	3	0
1987	Esch (EC)	0	0
2012	Josy Barthel	2	1

v MACEDONIA

		S	M
2008	Skopje (WC)	0	1
2009	Glasgow (WC)	2	0
2012	Glasgow (WC)	1	1
2013	Skopje (WC)	2	1

v MALTA

		S	M
1988	Valletta	1	1
1990	Valletta	2	1
1993	Glasgow (WC)	3	0
1993	Valletta (WC)	2	0
1997	Valletta	3	2

v MOLDOVA

		S	M
2004	Chisinau (WC)	1	1
2005	Glasgow (WC)	2	0

v MOROCCO

		S	M
1998	St Etienne (WC)	0	3

v NEW ZEALAND

		S	NZ
1982	Malaga (WC)	5	2
2003	Edinburgh	1	1

v NIGERIA

		S	N
2002	Aberdeen	1	2
2014	Fulham	2	2

v NORWAY

		S	N
1929	Bergen	7	3
1954	Glasgow	1	0
1954	Oslo	1	1
1963	Bergen	3	4
1963	Glasgow	6	1
1974	Oslo	2	1
1978	Glasgow (EC)	3	2
1979	Oslo (EC)	4	0
1988	Oslo (WC)	2	1
1989	Glasgow (WC)	1	1
1992	Oslo	0	0
1998	Bordeaux (WC)	1	1
2003	Oslo	0	0
2004	Glasgow (WC)	0	1
2005	Oslo (WC)	2	1
2008	Glasgow (WC)	0	0
2009	Oslo (WC)	0	4
2013	Molde	1	0

v PARAGUAY

		S	P
1958	Norrkoping (WC)	2	3

v PERU

		S	P
1972	Glasgow	2	0
1978	Cordoba (WC)	1	3
1979	Glasgow	1	1

v POLAND

		S	P
1958	Warsaw	2	1
1960	Glasgow	2	3
1965	Chorzow (WC)	1	1
1965	Glasgow (WC)	1	2
1980	Poznan	0	1
1990	Glasgow	1	1
2001	Bydgoszcz	1	1
2014	Warsaw	1	0

v PORTUGAL

		S	P
1950	Lisbon	2	2
1955	Glasgow	3	0
1959	Lisbon	0	1
1966	Glasgow	0	1
1971	Lisbon (EC)	0	2
1971	Glasgow (EC)	2	1
1975	Glasgow	1	0
1978	Lisbon (EC)	0	1
1980	Glasgow (EC)	4	1
1980	Glasgow (WC)	0	0
1981	Lisbon (WC)	1	2
1992	Glasgow (WC)	0	0
1993	Lisbon (WC)	0	5
2002	Braga	0	2

v REPUBLIC OF IRELAND

		S	RoI
1961	Glasgow (WC)	4	1
1961	Dublin (WC)	3	0
1963	Dublin	0	1
1969	Dublin	1	1
1986	Dublin (EC)	0	0
1987	Glasgow (EC)	0	1
2000	Dublin	2	1
2003	Glasgow (EC)	0	2
2011	Dublin (CC)	0	1

v ROMANIA

		S	R
1975	Bucharest (EC)	1	1
1975	Glasgow (EC)	1	1
1986	Glasgow	3	0
1990	Glasgow (EC)	2	1
1991	Bucharest (EC)	0	1
2004	Glasgow	1	2

v RUSSIA

		S	R
1994	Glasgow (EC)	1	1
1995	Moscow (EC)	0	0

v SAN MARINO

		S	SM
1991	Serravalle (EC)	2	0
1991	Glasgow (EC)	4	0

1995	Serravalle (EC)	2	0
1995	Glasgow (EC)	5	0
2000	Serravalle (WC)	2	0
2001	Glasgow (WC)	4	0

v SAUDI ARABIA

		S	SA
1988	Riyadh	2	2

v SERBIA

		S	Se
2012	Glasgow (WC)	0	0
2013	Novi Sad (WC)	0	2

v SLOVENIA

		S	SL
2004	Glasgow (WC)	0	0
2005	Celje (WC)	3	0
2012	Koper	1	1

v SOUTH AFRICA

		S	SA
2002	Hong Kong	0	2
2007	Aberdeen	1	0

v SOUTH KOREA

		S	SK
2002	Busan	1	4

v SOVIET UNION (see also CIS and RUSSIA)

		S	SU
1967	Glasgow	0	2
1971	Moscow	0	1
1982	Malaga (WC)	2	2
1991	Glasgow	0	1

v SPAIN

		S	Sp
1957	Glasgow (WC)	4	2
1957	Madrid (WC)	1	4
1963	Madrid	6	2
1965	Glasgow	0	0
1975	Glasgow (EC)	1	2
1975	Valencia (EC)	1	1
1982	Valencia	0	3
1985	Glasgow (WC)	3	1
1985	Seville (WC)	0	1
1988	Madrid	0	0
2004*	Valencia	1	1

(*Abandoned after 59 mins – floodlight failure)

2010	Glasgow (EC)	2	3
2011	Alicante (EC)	1	3

v SWEDEN

		S	Swe
1952	Stockholm	1	3
1953	Glasgow	1	2
1975	Gothenburg	1	1
1977	Glasgow	3	1
1980	Stockholm (WC)	1	0
1981	Glasgow (WC)	2	0
1990	Genoa (WC)	2	1
1995	Solna	0	2
1996	Glasgow (WC)	1	0
1997	Gothenburg (WC)	1	2

2004	Edinburgh	1	4
2010	Stockholm	0	3

v SWITZERLAND

		S	Sw
1931	Geneva	3	2
1948	Berne	1	2
1950	Glasgow	3	1
1957	Basle (WC)	2	1
1957	Glasgow (WC)	3	2
1973	Berne	0	1
1976	Glasgow	1	0
1982	Berne (EC)	0	2
1983	Glasgow (EC)	2	2
1990	Glasgow (EC)	2	1
1991	Berne (EC)	2	2
1992	Berne (WC)	1	3
1993	Aberdeen (WC)	1	1
1996	Birmingham (EC)	1	0
2006	Glasgow	1	3

v TRINIDAD & TOBAGO

		S	T
2004	Hibernian	4	1

v TURKEY

		S	T
1960	Ankara	2	4

v UKRAINE

		S	U
2006	Kiev (EC)	0	2
2007	Glasgow (EC)	3	1

v USA

		S	USA
1952	Glasgow	6	0
1992	Denver	1	0
1996	New Britain, Conn	1	2
1998	Washington	0	0
2005	Glasgow	1	1
2012	Jacksonville	1	5
2013	Glasgow	0	0

v URUGUAY

		S	U
1954	Basle (WC)	0	7
1962	Glasgow	2	3
1983	Glasgow	2	0
1986	Neza (WC)	0	0

v YUGOSLAVIA

		S	Y
1955	Belgrade	2	2
1956	Glasgow	2	0
1958	Vaasteras (WC)	1	1
1972	Belo Horizonte	2	2
1974	Frankfurt (WC)	1	1
1984	Glasgow	6	1
1988	Glasgow (WC)	1	1
1989	Zagreb (WC)	1	3

v ZAIRE

		S	Z
1974	Dortmund (WC)	2	0

WALES

v ALBANIA

		W	A
1994	Cardiff (EC)	2	0
1995	Tirana (EC)	1	1

v ARGENTINA

		W	A
1992	Gifu (Japan)	0	1
2002	Cardiff	1	1

v ARMENIA

		W	A
2001	Yerevan (WC)	2	2
2001	Cardiff (WC)	0	0

v AUSTRALIA

		W	A
2011	Cardiff	1	2

v AUSTRIA

		W	A
1954	Vienna	0	2
1955	Wrexham	1	2
1975	Vienna (EC)	1	2
1975	Wrexham (EC)	1	0
1992	Vienna	1	1
2005	Cardiff	0	2
2005	Vienna	0	1
2013	Swansea	2	1

v AZERBAIJAN

		W	A
2002	Baku (EC)	2	0
2003	Cardiff (EC)	4	0
2004	Baku (WC)	1	1
2005	Cardiff (WC)	2	0
2008	Cardiff (WC)	1	0
2009	Baku (WC)	1	0

v BELARUS

		W	B
1998	Cardiff (EC)	3	2
1999	Minsk (EC)	2	1
2000	Minsk (WC)	1	2
2001	Cardiff (WC)	1	0

v BELGIUM

		W	B
1949	Liege	1	3
1949	Cardiff	5	1
1990	Cardiff (EC)	3	1
1991	Brussels (EC)	1	1
1992	Brussels (WC)	0	2
1993	Cardiff (WC)	2	0
1997	Cardiff (WC)	1	2
1997	Brussels (WC)	2	3
2012	Cardiff (WC)	0	2
2013	Brussels (WC)	1	1

v BOSNIA-HERZEGOVINA

		W	B-H
2003	Cardiff	2	2
2012	Llanelli	0	2

v BRAZIL

		W	B
1958	Gothenburg (WC)	0	1
1962	Rio de Janeiro	1	3
1962	Sao Paulo	1	3
1966	Rio de Janeiro	1	3
1966	Belo Horizonte	0	1
1983	Cardiff	1	1
1991	Cardiff	1	0
1997	Brasilia	0	3
2000	Cardiff	0	3
2006	White Hart Lane	0	2

v BULGARIA

		W	B
1983	Wrexham (EC)	1	0
1983	Sofia (EC)	0	1
1994	Cardiff (EC)	0	3
1995	Sofia (EC)	1	3
2006	Swansea	0	0
2007	Bourgas	1	0
2010	Cardiff (EC)	0	1
2011	Sofia (EC)	1	0

v CANADA

		W	C
1986	Toronto	0	2
1986	Vancouver	3	0
2004	Wrexham	1	0

v CHILE

		W	C
1966	Santiago	0	2

v COSTA RICA

		W	C
1990	Cardiff	1	0
2012	Cardiff	0	1

v CROATIA

		W	C
2002	Varazdin	1	1
2010	Osijek	0	2
2012	Osijek (WC)	0	2
2013	Swansea (WC)	1	2

v CYPRUS

		W	C
1992	Limassol (WC)	1	0
1993	Cardiff (WC)	2	0
2005	Limassol	0	1
2006	Cardiff (EC)	3	1
2007	Nicosia (EC)	1	3

v CZECHOSLOVAKIA (see also RCS)

		W	C
1957	Cardiff (WC)	1	0
1957	Prague (WC)	0	2
1971	Swansea (EC)	1	3
1971	Prague (EC)	0	1
1977	Wrexham (WC)	3	0
1977	Prague (WC)	0	1
1980	Cardiff (WC)	1	0
1981	Prague (WC)	0	2
1987	Wrexham (EC)	1	1
1987	Prague (EC)	0	2

v CZECH REPUBLIC

		W	CR
2002	Cardiff	0	0
2006	Teplice (EC)	1	2
2007	Cardiff (EC)	0	0

v DENMARK

		W	D
1964	Copenhagen (WC)	0	1
1965	Wrexham (WC)	4	2
1987	Cardiff (EC)	1	0
1987	Copenhagen (EC)	0	1
1990	Copenhagen	0	1
1998	Copenhagen (EC)	2	1
1999	Anfield (EC)	0	2
2008	Copenhagen	1	0

v EAST GERMANY

		W	EG
1957	Leipzig (WC)	1	2
1957	Cardiff (WC)	4	1

| 1969 | Dresden (WC) | 1 | 2 |
| 1969 | Cardiff (WC) | 1 | 3 |

v ESTONIA

		W	E
1994	Tallinn	2	1
2009	Llanelli	1	0

v FAROE ISLANDS

		W	FI
1992	Cardiff (WC)	6	0
1993	Toftir (WC)	3	0

v FINLAND

		W	F
1971	Helsinki (EC)	1	0
1971	Swansea (EC)	3	0
1986	Helsinki (EC)	1	1
1987	Wrexham (EC)	4	0
1988	Swansea (WC)	2	2
1989	Helsinki (WC)	0	1
2000	Cardiff	1	2
2002	Helsinki (EC)	2	0
2003	Cardiff (EC)	1	1
2009	Cardiff (WC)	0	2
2009	Helsinki (WC)	1	2
2013	Cardiff	1	1

v FRANCE

		W	F
1933	Paris	1	1
1939	Paris	1	2
1953	Paris	1	6
1982	Toulouse	1	0

v GEORGIA

		W	G
1994	Tbilisi (EC)	0	5
1995	Cardiff (EC)	0	1
2008	Swansea	1	2

v GERMANY/WEST GERMANY

		W	G
1968	Cardiff	1	1
1969	Frankfurt	1	1
1977	Cardiff	0	2
1977	Dortmund	1	1
1979	Wrexham (EC)	0	2
1979	Cologne (EC)	1	5
1989	Cardiff (WC)	0	0
1989	Cologne (WC)	1	2
1991	Cardiff (EC)	1	0
1991	Nuremberg (EC)	1	4
1995	Dusseldorf (EC)	1	1
1995	Cardiff (EC)	1	2
2002	Cardiff	1	0
2007	Cardiff (EC)	0	2
2007	Frankfurt (EC)	0	0
2008	Moenchengladbach (WC)	0	1
2009	Cardiff (WC)	0	2

v GREECE

		W	G
1964	Athens (WC)	0	2
1965	Cardiff (WC)	4	1

v HOLLAND

		W	H
1988	Amsterdam (WC)	0	1
1989	Wrexham (WC)	1	2

1992	Utrecht	0	4
1996	Cardiff (WC)	1	3
1996	Eindhoven (WC)	1	7
2008	Rotterdam	0	2
2014	Amsterdam	0	2

v HUNGARY

		W	H
1958	Sanviken (WC)	1	1
1958	Stockholm (WC)	2	1
1961	Budapest	2	3
1963	Budapest (EC)	1	3
1963	Cardiff (EC)	1	1
1974	Cardiff (EC)	2	0
1975	Budapest (EC)	2	1
1986	Cardiff	0	3
2004	Budapest	2	1
2005	Cardiff	2	0

v ICELAND

		W	I
1980	Reykjavik (WC)	4	0
1981	Swansea (WC)	2	2
1984	Reykjavik (WC)	0	1
1984	Cardiff (WC)	2	1
1991	Cardiff	1	0
2008	Reykjavik	1	0
2014	Cardiff	3	1

v IRAN

		W	I
1978	Tehran	1	0

v ISRAEL

		W	I
1958	Tel Aviv (WC)	2	0
1958	Cardiff (WC)	2	0
1984	Tel Aviv	0	0
1989	Tel Aviv	3	3

v ITALY

		W	I
1965	Florence	1	4
1968	Cardiff (WC)	0	1
1969	Rome (WC)	1	4
1988	Brescia	1	0
1996	Terni	0	3
1998	Anfield (EC)	0	2
1999	Bologna (EC)	0	4
2002	Cardiff (EC)	2	1
2003	Milan (EC)	0	4

v JAMAICA

		W	J
1998	Cardiff	0	0

v JAPAN

		W	J
1992	Matsuyama	1	0

v KUWAIT

		W	K
1977	Wrexham	0	0
1977	Kuwait City	0	0

v LATVIA

		W	L
2004	Riga	2	0

v LIECHTENSTEIN

		W	L
2006	Wrexham	4	0
2008	Cardiff (WC)	2	0

2009 Vaduz (WC) 2 0

v LUXEMBOURG

		W	L
1974	Swansea (EC)	5	0
1975	Luxembourg (EC)	3	1
1990	Luxembourg (EC)	1	0
1991	Luxembourg (EC)	1	0
2008	Luxembourg	2	0
2010	Llanelli	5	1

v MACEDONIA

		W	M
2013	Skopje (WC)	1	2
2013	Cardiff (WC)	1	0

v MALTA

		W	M
1978	Wrexham (EC)	7	0
1979	Valletta (EC)	2	0
1988	Valletta	3	2
1998	Valletta	3	0

v MEXICO

		W	M
1958	Stockholm (WC)	1	1
1962	Mexico City	1	2
2012	New York	0	2

v MOLDOVA

		W	M
1994	Kishinev (EC)	2	3
1995	Cardiff (EC)	1	0

v MONTENEGRO

		W	M
2009	Podgorica	1	2
2010	Podgorica (EC)	0	1
2011	Cardiff (EC)	2	1

v NEW ZEALAND

		W	NZ
2007	Wrexham	2	2

v NORWAY

		W	N
1982	Swansea (EC)	1	0
1983	Oslo (EC)	0	0
1984	Trondheim	0	1
1985	Wrexham	1	1
1985	Bergen	2	4
1994	Cardiff	1	3
2000	Cardiff (WC)	1	1
2001	Oslo (WC)	2	3
2004	Oslo	0	0
2008	Wrexham	3	0
2011	Cardiff	4	1

v PARAGUAY

		W	P
2006	Cardiff	0	0

v POLAND

		W	P
1973	Cardiff (WC)	2	0
1973	Katowice (WC)	0	3
1991	Radom	0	0
2000	Warsaw (WC)	0	0
2001	Cardiff (WC)	1	2
2004	Cardiff (WC)	2	3

2005 Warsaw (WC) 0 1
2009 Vila-Real (Por) 0 1

v PORTUGAL

		W	P
1949	Lisbon	2	3
1951	Cardiff	2	1
2000	Chaves	0	3

v QATAR

		W	Q
2000	Doha	1	0

v RCS (formerly Czechoslovakia)

		W	RCS
1993	Ostrava (WC)	1	1
1993	Cardiff (WC)	2	2

v REPUBLIC OF IRELAND

		W	RI
1960	Dublin	3	2
1979	Swansea	2	1
1981	Dublin	3	1
1986	Dublin	1	0
1990	Dublin	0	1
1991	Wrexham	0	3
1992	Dublin	1	0
1993	Dublin	1	2
1997	Cardiff	0	0
2007	Dublin (EC)	0	1
2007	Cardiff (EC)	2	2
2011	Dublin (CC)	0	3
2013	Cardiff	0	0

v REST OF UNITED KINGDOM

		W	UK
1951	Cardiff	3	2
1969	Cardiff	0	1

v ROMANIA

		W	R
1970	Cardiff (EC)	0	0
1971	Bucharest (EC)	0	2
1983	Wrexham	5	0
1992	Bucharest (WC)	1	5
1993	Cardiff (WC)	1	2

v RUSSIA (See also Soviet Union)

		W	R
2003*	Moscow (EC)	0	0
2003*	Cardiff (EC)	0	1
2008	Moscow (WC)	1	2
2009	Cardiff (WC)	1	3

(*Qual Round play-offs)

v SAN MARINO

		W	SM
1996	Serravalle (WC)	5	0
1996	Cardiff (WC)	6	0
2007	Cardiff (EC)	3	0
2007	Serravalle (EC)	2	1

v SAUDI ARABIA

		W	SA
1986	Dahran	2	1

v SERBIA

		W	S
2012	Novi Sad (WC)	1	6
2013	Cardiff (WC)	0	3

v SERBIA & MONTENEGRO

		W	S
2003	Belgrade (EC)	0	1
2003	Cardiff (EC)	2	3

v SLOVAKIA

		W	S
2006	Cardiff (EC)	1	5
2007	Trnava (EC)	5	2

v SLOVENIA

		W	S
2005	Swansea	0	0

v SOVIET UNION (See also Russia)

		W	SU
1965	Moscow (WC)	1	2
1965	Cardiff (WC)	2	1
1981	Wrexham (WC)	0	0
1981	Tbilisi (WC)	0	3
1987	Swansea	0	0

v SPAIN

		W	S
1961	Cardiff (WC)	1	2
1961	Madrid (WC)	1	1
1982	Valencia	1	1
1984	Seville (WC)	0	3
1985	Wrexham (WC)	3	0

v SWEDEN

		W	S
1958	Stockholm (WC)	0	0
1988	Stockholm	1	4
1989	Wrexham	0	2
1990	Stockholm	2	4
1994	Wrexham	0	2
2010	Swansea	0	1

v SWITZERLAND

		W	S
1949	Berne	0	4
1951	Wrexham	3	2
1996	Lugano	0	2

1999	Zurich (EC)	0	2
1999	Wrexham (EC)	0	2
2010	Basle (EC)	1	4
2011	Swansea (EC)	2	0

v TRINIDAD & TOBAGO

		W	T
2006	Graz	2	1

v TUNISIA

		W	T
1998	Tunis	0	4

v TURKEY

		W	T
1978	Wrexham (EC)	1	0
1979	Izmir (EC)	0	1
1980	Cardiff (WC)	4	0
1981	Ankara (WC)	1	0
1996	Cardiff (WC)	0	0
1997	Istanbul (WC)	4	6

v UKRAINE

		W	U
2001	Cardiff (WC)	1	1
2001	Kiev (WC)	1	1

v URUGUAY

		W	U
1986	Wrexham	0	0

v USA

		W	USA
2003	San Jose	0	2

v YUGOSLAVIA

		W	Y
1953	Belgrade	2	5
1954	Cardiff	1	3
1976	Zagreb (EC)	0	2
1976	Cardiff (EC)	1	1
1982	Titograd (EC)	4	4
1983	Cardiff (EC)	1	1
1988	Swansea	1	2

NORTHERN IRELAND

v ALBANIA

		NI	A
1965	Belfast (WC)	4	1
1965	Tirana (WC)	1	1
1983	Tirana (EC)	0	0
1983	Belfast (EC)	1	0
1992	Belfast (WC)	3	0
1993	Tirana (WC)	2	1
1996	Belfast (WC)	2	0
1997	Zurich (WC)	0	1
2010	Tirana	0	1

v ALGERIA

		NI	A
1986	Guadalajara (WC)	1	1

v ARGENTINA

		NI	A
1958	Halmstad (WC)	1	3

v ARMENIA

		NI	A
1996	Belfast (WC)	1	1
1997	Yerevan (WC)	0	0

2003	Yerevan (EC)	0	1
2003	Belfast (EC)	0	1

v AUSTRALIA

		NI	A
1980	Sydney	2	1
1980	Melbourne	1	1
1980	Adelaide	2	1

v AUSTRIA

		NI	A
1982	Madrid (WC)	2	2
1982	Vienna (EC)	0	2
1983	Belfast (EC)	3	1
1990	Vienna (EC)	0	0
1991	Belfast (EC)	2	1
1994	Vienna (EC)	2	1
1995	Belfast (EC)	5	3
2004	Belfast (WC)	3	3
2005	Vienna (WC)	0	2

v AZERBAIJAN

		NI	A
2004	Baku (WC)	0	0

		NI	
2005	Belfast (WC)	2	0
2012	Belfast (WC)	1	1
2013	Baku (WC)	0	2

v BARBADOS

		NI	B
2004	Bridgetown	1	1

v BELGIUM

		NI	B
1976	Liege (WC)	0	2
1977	Belfast (WC)	3	0
1997	Belfast	3	0

v BRAZIL

		NI	B
1986	Guadalajara (WC)	0	3

v BULGARIA

		NI	B
1972	Sofia (WC)	0	3
1973	Sheffield (WC)	0	0
1978	Sofia (EC)	2	0
1979	Belfast (EC)	2	0
2001	Sofia (WC)	3	4
2001	Belfast (WC)	0	1
2008	Belfast	0	1

v CANADA

		NI	C
1995	Edmonton	0	2
1999	Belfast	1	1
2005	Belfast	0	1

v CHILE

		NI	C
1989	Belfast	0	1
1995	Edmonton, Canada	0	2
2010	Chillan	0	1
2014	Valparaiso	0	2

v COLOMBIA

		NI	C
1994	Boston, USA	0	2

v CYPRUS

		NI	C
1971	Nicosia (EC)	3	0
1971	Belfast (EC)	5	0
1973	Nicosia (WC)	0	1
1973	Fulham (WC)	3	0
2002	Belfast	0	0
2014	Nicosia	0	0

v CZECHOSLOVAKIA/CZECH REP

		NI	C
1958	Halmstad (WC)	1	0
1958	Malmo (WC)	2	1
2001	Belfast (WC)	0	1
2001	Teplice (WC)	1	3
2008	Belfast (WC)	0	0
2009	Prague (WC)	0	0

v DENMARK

		NI	D
1978	Belfast (EC)	2	1
1979	Copenhagen (EC)	0	4
1986	Belfast	1	1
1990	Belfast (EC)	1	1
1991	Odense (EC)	1	2
1992	Belfast (WC)	0	1
1993	Copenhagen (WC)	0	1
2000	Belfast (WC)	1	1
2001	Copenhagen (WC)	1	1
2006	Copenhagen (EC)	0	0
2007	Belfast (EC)	2	1

v ESTONIA

		NI	E
2004	Tallinn	1	0
2006	Belfast	1	0
2011	Tallinn (EC)	1	4
2011	Belfast (EC)	1	2

v FAROE ISLANDS

		NI	Fl
1991	Belfast (EC)	1	1
1991	Landskrona, Sw (EC)	5	0
2010	Toftir (EC)	1	1
2011	Belfast (EC)	4	0

v FINLAND

		NI	F
1984	Pori (WC)	0	1
1984	Belfast (WC)	2	1
1998	Belfast (EC)	1	0
1999	Helsinki (EC)	1	4
2003	Belfast	0	1
2006	Helsinki	2	1
2012	Belfast	3	3

v FRANCE

		NI	F
1951	Belfast	2	2
1952	Paris	1	3
1958	Norrkoping (WC)	0	4
1982	Paris	0	4
1982	Madrid (WC)	1	4
1986	Paris	0	0
1988	Belfast	0	0
1999	Belfast	0	1

v GEORGIA

		NI	G
2008	Belfast	4	1

v GERMANY/WEST GERMANY

		NI	G
1958	Malmo (WC)	2	2
1960	Belfast (WC)	3	4
1961	Berlin (WC)	1	2
1966	Belfast	0	2
1977	Cologne	0	5
1982	Belfast (EC)	1	0
1983	Hamburg (EC)	1	0
1992	Bremen	1	1
1996	Belfast	1	1
1997	Nuremberg (WC)	1	1
1997	Belfast (WC)	1	3
1999	Belfast (EC)	0	3
1999	Dortmund (EC)	0	4
2005	Belfast	1	4

v GREECE

		NI	G
1961	Athens (WC)	1	2
1961	Belfast (WC)	2	0
1988	Athens	2	3
2003	Belfast (EC)	0	2
2003	Athens (EC)	0	1

v HOLLAND

		NI	H
1962	Rotterdam	0	4
1965	Belfast (WC)	2	1
1965	Rotterdam (WC)	0	0
1976	Rotterdam (WC)	2	2
1977	Belfast (WC)	0	1
2012	Amsterdam	0	6

v HONDURAS

		NI	H
1982	Zaragoza (WC)	1	1

v HUNGARY

		NI	H
1988	Budapest (WC)	0	1
1989	Belfast (WC)	1	2
2000	Belfast	0	1
2008	Belfast	0	2

v ICELAND

		NI	I
1977	Reykjavik (WC)	0	1
1977	Belfast (WC)	2	0
2000	Reykjavik (WC)	0	1
2001	Belfast (WC)	3	0
2006	Belfast (EC)	0	3
2007	Reykjavik (EC)	1	2

v ISRAEL

		NI	I
1968	Jaffa	3	2
1976	Tel Aviv	1	1
1980	Tel Aviv (WC)	0	0
1981	Belfast (WC)	1	0
1984	Belfast	3	0
1987	Tel Aviv	1	1
2009	Belfast	1	1
2013	Belfast (WC)	0	2
2013	Ramat Gan (WC)	1	1

v ITALY

		NI	I
1957	Rome (WC)	0	1
1957	Belfast	2	2
1958	Belfast (WC)	2	1
1961	Bologna	2	3
1997	Palermo	0	2
2003	Campobasso	0	2
2009	Pisa	0	3
2010	Belfast (EC)	0	0
2011	Pescara (EC)	0	3

v LATVIA

		NI	L
1993	Riga (WC)	2	1
1993	Belfast (WC)	2	0
1995	Riga (EC)	1	0
1995	Belfast (EC)	1	2
2006	Belfast (EC)	1	0
2007	Riga (EC)	0	1

v LIECHTENSTEIN

		NI	L
1994	Belfast (EC)	4	1
1995	Eschen (EC)	4	0
2002	Vaduz	0	0
2007	Vaduz (EC)	4	1
2007	Belfast (EC)	3	1

v LITHUANIA

		NI	L
1992	Belfast (WC)	2	2

v LUXEMBOURG

		NI	L
2000	Luxembourg	3	1
2012	Belfast (WC)	1	1
2013	Luxembourg (WC)	2	3

v MALTA

		NI	M
1988	Belfast (WC)	3	0
1989	Valletta (WC)	2	0
2000	Ta'Qali	3	0
2000	Belfast (WC)	1	0
2001	Valletta (WC)	1	0
2005	Valletta	1	1
2013	Ta'Qali	0	0

v MEXICO

		NI	M
1966	Belfast	4	1
1994	Miami	0	3

v MOLDOVA

		NI	M
1998	Belfast (EC)	2	2
1999	Kishinev (EC)	0	0

v MONTENEGRO

		W	M
2010	Podgorica	0	2

v MOROCCO

		NI	M
1986	Belfast	2	1
2010	Belfast	1	1

v NORWAY

		NI	N
1974	Oslo (EC)	1	2
1975	Belfast (EC)	3	0
1990	Belfast	2	3
1996	Belfast	0	2
2001	Belfast	0	4
2004	Belfast	1	4
2012	Belfast	0	3

v POLAND

		NI	P
1962	Katowice (EC)	2	0
1962	Belfast (EC)	2	0
1988	Belfast	1	1
1991	Belfast	3	1
2002	Limassol (Cyprus)	1	4
2004	Belfast (WC)	0	3
2005	Warsaw (WC)	0	1
2009	Belfast (WC)	3	2
2009	Chorzow (WC)	1	1

v PORTUGAL

		NI	P
1957	Lisbon (WC)	1	1
1957	Belfast (WC)	3	0
1973	Coventry (WC)	1	1
1973	Lisbon (WC)	1	1
1980	Lisbon (WC)	0	1
1981	Belfast (WC)	1	0

		NI	
1994	Belfast (EC)	1	2
1995	Oporto (EC)	1	1
1997	Belfast (WC)	0	0
1997	Lisbon (WC)	0	1
2005	Belfast	1	1
2012	Porto (WC)	1	1
2013	Belfast (WC)	2	4

v REPUBLIC OF IRELAND

		NI	RI
1978	Dublin (EC)	0	0
1979	Belfast (EC)	1	0
1988	Belfast (WC)	0	0
1989	Dublin (WC)	0	3
1993	Dublin (WC)	0	3
1993	Belfast (WC)	1	1
1994	Belfast (EC)	0	4
1995	Dublin (EC)	1	1
1999	Dublin	1	0
2011	Dublin (CC)	0	5

v ROMANIA

		NI	R
1984	Belfast (WC)	3	2
1985	Bucharest (WC)	1	0
1994	Belfast	2	0
2006	Chicago	0	2

v RUSSIA

		NI	R
2012	Moscow (WC)	0	2
2013	Belfast (WC)	1	0

v SAN MARINO

		NI	SM
2008	Belfast (WC)	4	0
2009	Serravalle (WC)	3	0

v SERBIA & MONTENEGRO

		NI	S
2004	Belfast	1	1

v SERBIA

		NI	S
2009	Belfast	0	1
2011	Belgrade (EC)	1	2
2011	Belfast (EC)	0	1

v SLOVAKIA

		NI	S
1998	Belfast	1	0
2008	Bratislava (WC)	1	2
2009	Belfast (WC)	0	2

v SLOVENIA

		NI	S
2008	Maribor (WC)	0	2
2009	Belfast (WC)	1	0
2010	Maribor (EC)	1	0
2011	Belfast (EC)	0	0

v SOVIET UNION

		NI	SU
1969	Belfast (WC)	0	0
1969	Moscow (WC)	0	2
1971	Moscow (EC)	0	1
1971	Belfast (EC)	1	1

v SPAIN

		NI	S
1958	Madrid	2	6
1963	Bilbao	1	1
1963	Belfast	0	1
1970	Seville (EC)	0	3
1972	Hull (EC)	1	1
1982	Valencia (WC)	1	0
1985	Palma, Majorca	0	0
1986	Guadalajara (WC)	1	2
1988	Seville (WC)	0	4
1989	Belfast (WC)	0	2
1992	Belfast (WC)	0	0
1993	Seville (WC)	1	3
1998	Santander	1	4
2002	Belfast	0	5
2002	Albacete (EC)	0	3
2003	Belfast (EC)	0	0
2006	Belfast (EC)	3	2
2007	Las Palmas (EC)	0	1

v ST KITTS & NEVIS

		NI	SK
2004	Basseterre	2	0

v SWEDEN

		NI	S
1974	Solna (EC)	2	0
1975	Belfast (EC)	1	2
1980	Belfast (WC)	3	0
1981	Stockholm (WC)	0	1
1996	Belfast	1	2
2007	Belfast (EC)	2	1
2007	Stockholm (EC)	1	1

v SWITZERLAND

		NI	S
1964	Belfast (WC)	1	0
1964	Lausanne (WC)	1	2
1998	Belfast	1	0
2004	Zurich	0	0
2010	Basle (EC)	1	4

v THAILAND

		NI	T
1997	Bangkok	0	0

v TRINIDAD & TOBAGO

		NI	T
2004	Port of Spain	3	0

v TURKEY

		NI	T
1968	Belfast (WC)	4	1
1968	Istanbul (WC)	3	0
1983	Belfast (EC)	2	1
1983	Ankara (EC)	0	1
1985	Belfast (WC)	2	0
1985	Izmir (WC)	0	0
1986	Izmir (EC)	0	0
1987	Belfast (EC)	1	0
1998	Istanbul (EC)	0	3
1999	Belfast (EC)	0	3
2010	Connecticut	0	2
2013	Adana	0	1

v UKRAINE

		NI	U
1996	Belfast (WC)	0	1
1997	Kiev (WC)	1	2
2002	Belfast (EC)	0	0
2003	Donetsk (EC)	0	0

v URUGUAY

		NI	U
1964	Belfast	3	0
1990	Belfast	1	0
2006	New Jersey	0	1
2014	Montevideo	0	1

v YUGOSLAVIA

		NI	Y
1975	Belfast (EC)	1	0

1975	Belgrade (EC)	0	1
1982	Zaragoza (WC)	0	0
1987	Belfast (EC)	1	2
1987	Sarajevo (EC)	0	3
1990	Belfast (EC)	0	2
1991	Belgrade (EC)	1	4
2000	Belfast	1	2

REPUBLIC OF IRELAND

v ALBANIA

		RI	A
1992	Dublin (WC)	2	0
1993	Tirana (WC)	2	1
2003	Tirana (EC)	0	0
2003	Dublin (EC)	2	1

v ALGERIA

		RI	A
1982	Algiers	0	2
2010	Dublin	3	0

v ANDORRA

		RI	A
2001	Barcelona (WC)	3	0
2001	Dublin (WC)	3	1
2010	Dublin (EC)	3	1
2011	La Vella (EC)	2	0

v ARGENTINA

		RI	A
1951	Dublin	0	1
1979*	Dublin	0	0
1980	Dublin	0	1
1998	Dublin	0	2
2010	Dublin	0	1
(*Not regarded as full Int)			

v ARMENIA

		RI	A
2010	Yerevan (EC)	1	0
2011	Dublin (EC)	2	1

v AUSTRALIA

		RI	A
2003	Dublin	2	1
2009	Limerick	0	3

v AUSTRIA

		RI	A
1952	Vienna	0	6
1953	Dublin	4	0
1958	Vienna	1	3
1962	Dublin	2	3
1963	Vienna (EC)	0	0
1963	Dublin (EC)	3	2
1966	Vienna	0	1
1968	Dublin	2	2
1971	Dublin (EC)	1	4
1971	Linz (EC)	0	6
1995	Dublin (EC)	1	3
1995	Vienna (EC)	1	3
2013	Dublin (WC)	2	2
2013	Vienna (WC)	0	1

v BELGIUM

		RI	B
1928	Liege	4	2
1929	Dublin	4	0
1930	Brussels	3	1
1934	Dublin (WC)	4	4
1949	Dublin	0	2
1950	Brussels	1	5
1965	Dublin	0	2
1966	Liege	3	2
1980	Dublin (WC)	1	1
1981	Brussels (WC)	0	1
1986	Brussels (EC)	2	2
1987	Dublin (EC)	0	0
1997*	Dublin (WC)	1	1
1997*	Brussels (WC)	1	2
(*World Cup play-off)			

v BOLIVIA

		RI	B
1994	Dublin	1	0
1996	East Rutherford, NJ	3	0
2007	Boston	1	1

v BOSNIA HERZEGOVINA

		RI	B-H
2012	Dublin	1	0

v BRAZIL

		RI	B
1974	Rio de Janeiro	1	2
1982	Uberlandia	0	7
1987	Dublin	1	0
2004	Dublin	0	0
2008	Dublin	0	1
2010	Arsenal	0	2

v BULGARIA

		RI	B
1977	Sofia (WC)	1	2
1977	Dublin (WC)	0	0
1979	Sofia (EC)	0	1
1979	Dublin (EC)	3	0
1987	Sofia (EC)	1	2
1987	Dublin (EC)	2	0
2004	Dublin	1	1
2009	Dublin (WC)	1	1
2009	Sofia (WC)	1	1

v CAMEROON

		RI	C
2002	Niigata (WC)	1	1

v CANADA

		RI	C
2003	Dublin	3	0

v CHILE

		RI	C
1960	Dublin	2	0
1972	Recife	1	2

1953	Dublin (WC)	4	0
1954	Luxembourg (WC)	1	0
1987	Luxembourg (EC)	2	0
1987	Luxembourg (EC)	2	1

v MACEDONIA

		RI	M
1996	Dublin (WC)	3	0
1997	Skopje (WC)	2	3
1999	Dublin (EC)	1	0
1999	Skopje (EC)	1	1
2011	Dublin (EC)	2	1
2011	Skopje (EC)	2	0

v MALTA

		RI	M
1983	Valletta (EC)	1	0
1983	Dublin (EC)	8	0
1989	Dublin (WC)	2	0
1989	Valletta (WC)	2	0
1990	Valletta	3	0
1998	Dublin (EC)	1	0
1999	Valletta (EC)	3	2

v MEXICO

		RI	M
1984	Dublin	0	0
1994	Orlando (WC)	1	2
1996	New Jersey	2	2
1998	Dublin	0	0
2000	Chicago	2	2

v MONTENEGRO

		RI	M
2008	Podgorica (WC)	0	0
2009	Dublin (WC)	0	0

v MOROCCO

		RI	M
1990	Dublin	1	0

v NIGERIA

		RI	N
2002	Dublin	1	2
2004	Charlton	0	3
2009	Fulham	1	1

v NORWAY

		RI	N
1937	Oslo (WC)	2	3
1937	Dublin (WC)	3	3
1950	Dublin	2	2
1951	Oslo	3	2
1954	Dublin	2	1
1955	Oslo	3	1
1960	Dublin	3	1
1964	Oslo	4	1
1973	Oslo	1	1
1976	Dublin	3	0
1978	Oslo	0	0
1984	Oslo (WC)	0	1
1985	Dublin (WC)	0	0
1988	Oslo	0	0
1994	New York (WC)	0	0
2003	Dublin	1	0
2008	Oslo	1	1
2010	Dublin	1	2

v OMAN

		RI	O
2012	Fulham	4	1

v PARAGUAY

		RI	P

1999	Dublin	2	0
2010	Dublin	2	1

v POLAND

		RI	P
1938	Warsaw	0	6
1938	Dublin	3	2
1958	Katowice	2	2
1958	Dublin	2	2
1964	Cracow	1	3
1964	Dublin	3	2
1968	Dublin	2	2
1968	Katowice	0	1
1970	Dublin	1	2
1970	Poznan	0	2
1973	Wroclaw	0	2
1973	Dublin	1	0
1976	Poznan	2	0
1977	Dublin	0	0
1978	Lodz	0	3
1981	Bydgoszcz	0	3
1984	Dublin	0	0
1986	Warsaw	0	1
1988	Dublin	3	1
1991	Dublin (EC)	0	0
1991	Poznan (EC)	3	3
2004	Bydgoszcz	0	0
2008	Dublin	2	3
2013	Dublin	2	0
2013	Poznan	0	0

v PORTUGAL

		RI	P
1946	Lisbon	1	3
1947	Dublin	0	2
1948	Lisbon	0	2
1949	Dublin	1	0
1972	Recife	1	2
1992	Boston, USA	2	0
1995	Dublin (EC)	1	0
1995	Lisbon (EC)	0	3
1996	Dublin	0	1
2000	Lisbon (WC)	1	1
2001	Dublin (WC)	1	1
2005	Dublin	1	0
2014	East Rutherford, USA	1	5

v ROMANIA

		RI	R
1988	Dublin	2	0
1990*	Genoa	0	0
1997	Bucharest (WC)	0	1
1997	Dublin (WC)	1	1
2004	Dublin	1	0

(*Rep won 5-4 on pens)

v RUSSIA (See also Soviet Union)

		RI	R
1994	Dublin	0	0
1996	Dublin	0	2
2002	Dublin	2	0
2002	Moscow (EC)	2	4
2003	Dublin (EC)	1	1
2010	Dublin (EC)	2	3
2011	Moscow (EC)	0	0

v SAN MARINO

		RI	SM
2006	Dublin (EC)	5	0

		RI	
2007	Rimini (EC)	2	1

v SAUDI ARABIA

		RI	SA
2002	Yokohama (WC)	3	0

v SERBIA

		RI	S
2008	Dublin	1	1
2012	Belgrade	0	0
2014	Dublin	1	2

v SLOVAKIA

		RI	S
2007	Dublin (EC)	1	0
2007	Bratislava (EC)	2	2
2010	Zilina (EC)	1	1
2011	Dublin (EC)	0	0

v SOUTH AFRICA

		RI	SA
2000	New Jersey	2	1
2009	Limerick	1	0

v SOVIET UNION (See also Russia)

		RI	SU
1972	Dublin (WC)	1	2
1973	Moscow (WC)	0	1
1974	Dublin (EC)	3	0
1975	Kiev (EC)	1	2
1984	Dublin (WC)	1	0
1985	Moscow (WC)	0	2
1988	Hanover (EC)	1	1
1990	Dublin	1	0

v SPAIN

		RI	S
1931	Barcelona	1	1
1931	Dublin	0	5
1946	Madrid	1	0
1947	Dublin	3	2
1948	Barcelona	1	2
1949	Dublin	1	4
1952	Madrid	0	6
1955	Dublin	2	2
1964	Seville (EC)	1	5
1964	Dublin (EC)	0	2
1965	Dublin (WC)	1	0
1965	Seville (WC)	1	4
1965	Paris (WC)	0	1
1966	Dublin (EC)	0	0
1966	Valencia (EC)	0	2
1977	Dublin	0	1
1982	Dublin (EC)	3	3
1983	Zaragoza (EC)	0	2
1985	Cork	0	0
1988	Seville (WC)	0	2
1989	Dublin (WC)	1	0
1992	Seville (WC)	0	0
1993	Dublin (WC)	1	3
2002*	Suwon (WC)	1	1
(*Rep lost 3-2 on pens)			
2012	Gdansk (EC)	0	4
2013	New York	0	2

v SWEDEN

		RI	S
1949	Stockholm (WC)	1	3
1949	Dublin (WC)	1	3
1959	Dublin	3	2
1960	Malmo	1	4

		RI	
1970	Dublin (EC)	1	1
1970	Malmo (EC)	0	1
1999	Dublin	2	0
2006	Dublin	3	0
2013	Stockholm (WC)	0	0
2013	Dublin (WC)	1	2

v SWITZERLAND

		RI	S
1935	Basle	0	1
1936	Dublin	1	0
1937	Berne	1	0
1938	Dublin	4	0
1948	Dublin	0	1
1975	Dublin (EC)	2	1
1975	Berne (EC)	0	1
1980	Dublin	2	0
1985	Dublin (WC)	3	0
1985	Berne (WC)	0	0
1992	Dublin	2	1
2002	Dublin (EC)	1	2
2003	Basle (EC)	0	2
2004	Basle (WC)	1	1
2005	Dublin (WC)	0	0

v TRINIDAD & TOBAGO

		RI	T&T
1982	Port of Spain	1	2

v TUNISIA

		RI	T
1988	Dublin	4	0

v TURKEY

		RI	T
1966	Dublin (EC)	2	1
1967	Ankara (EC)	1	2
1974	Izmir (EC)	1	1
1975	Dublin (EC)	4	0
1976	Ankara	3	3
1978	Dublin	4	2
1990	Izmir	0	0
1990	Dublin (EC)	5	0
1991	Istanbul (EC)	3	1
1999	Dublin (EC)	1	1
1999	Bursa (EC)	0	0
2003	Dublin	2	2
2014	Dublin	1	2

v URUGUAY

		RI	U
1974	Montevideo	0	2
1986	Dublin	1	1
2011	Dublin	2	3

v USA

		RI	USA
1979	Dublin	3	2
1991	Boston	1	1
1992	Dublin	4	1
1992	Washington	1	3
1996	Boston	1	2
2000	Foxboro	1	1
2002	Dublin	2	1

v YUGOSLAVIA

		RI	Y
1955	Dublin	1	4
1988	Dublin	2	0
1998	Belgrade (EC)	0	1
1999	Dublin (EC)	2	1

BRITISH AND IRISH INTERNATIONAL APPEARANCES SINCE THE WAR (1946–2014)

(As at start of season 2014–15; in year shown 2014 = season 2013–14
*Also a pre-war International player. Totals include appearances as substitute)

ENGLAND

Agbonlahor G (Aston Villa, 2009–10)	3
A'Court A (Liverpool, 1958–59)	5
Adams T (Arsenal, 1987–2001)	66
Allen A (Stoke, 1960)	3
Allen C (QPR, Tottenham, 1984–88)	5
Allen R (WBA, 1952–55)	5
Anderson S (Sunderland, 1962)	2
Anderson V (Nottm Forest, Arsenal, Manchester Utd, 1979–88)	30
Anderton D (Tottenham, 1994–2002)	30
Angus J (Burnley, 1961)	1
Armfield J (Blackpool, 1959–66)	43
Armstrong D (Middlesbrough, Southampton, 1980–4)	3
Armstrong K (Chelsea, 1955)	1
Ashton D (West Ham, 2008)	1
Astall G (Birmingham, 1956)	2
Astle J (WBA, 1969–70)	5
Aston J (Manchester Utd, 1949–51)	17
Atyeo J (Bristol City, 1956–57)	6
Bailey G (Manchester Utd, 1985)	2
Bailey M (Charlton, 1964–5)	2
Baily E (Tottenham, 1950–3)	9
Baines L (Everton, 2010–14)	26
Baker J (Hibs, Arsenal, 1960–6)	8
Ball A (Blackpool, Everton, Arsenal, 1965–75)	72
Ball M (Everton, 2001)	1
Banks G (Leicester, Stoke, 1963–72)	73
Banks T (Bolton, 1958–59)	6
Bardsley D (QPR, 1993)	2
Barham M (Norwich, 1983)	2
Barkley, R (Everton, 2014)	9
Barlow R (WBA, 1955)	1
Barmby N (Tottenham, Middlesbrough, Everton, Liverpool, 1995–2002)	23
Barnes J (Watford, Liverpool, 1983–96)	79
Barnes P (Manchester City, WBA, Leeds, 1978–82)	22
Barrass M (Bolton, 1952–53)	3
Barrett E (Oldham, Aston Villa, 1991–93)	3
Barry G (Aston Villa, Manchester City, 2000–12)	53
Barton J (Manchester City, 2007)	1
Barton W (Wimbledon, Newcastle, 1995)	3
Batty D (Leeds, Blackburn, Newcastle, Leeds, 1991–2000)	42
Baynham R (Luton, 1956)	3
Beardsley P (Newcastle, Liverpool, Newcastle, 1986–96)	59
Beasant D (Chelsea, 1990)	2
Beattie J (Southampton, 2003–04)	5
Beattie K (Ipswich, 1975–58)	9

Beckham D (Manchester Utd, Real Madrid, LA Galaxy, AC Milan 1997–2010)	115
Bell C (Manchester City, 1968–76)	48
Bent D (Charlton, Tottenham Sunderland, Aston Villa, 2006–12)	13
Bentley D (Blackburn, 2008–09)	7
Bentley R (Chelsea, 1949–55)	12
Berry J (Manchester Utd, 1953–56)	4
Bertrand R (Chelsea, 2013)	2
Birtles G (Nottm Forest, 1980–81)	3
Blissett L (Watford, AC Milan, 1983–84)	14
Blockley J (Arsenal, 1973)	1
Blunstone F (Chelsea, 1955–57)	5
Bonetti P (Chelsea, 1966–70)	7
Bothroyd J (Cardiff, 2011)	1
Bould S (Arsenal, 1994)	2
Bowles S (QPR, 1974–77)	5
Bowyer L (Leeds, 2003)	1
Boyer P (Norwich, 1976)	1
Brabrook P (Chelsea, 1958–60)	3
Bracewell P (Everton, 1985–86)	3
Bradford G (Bristol Rov, 1956)	1
Bradley W (Manchester Utd, 1959)	3
Bridge W (Southampton, Chelsea, Manchester City 2002–10)	36
Bridges B (Chelsea, 1965–66)	4
Broadbent P (Wolves, 1958–60)	7
Broadis I (Manchester City, Newcastle, 1952–54)	14
Brooking T (West Ham, 1974–82)	47
Brooks J (Tottenham, 1957)	3
Brown A (WBA, 1971)	1
Brown K (West Ham, 1960)	1
Brown W (Manchester Utd, 1999–2010)	23
Bull S (Wolves, 1989–91)	13
Butcher T (Ipswich, Rangers, 1980–90)	77
Butland J (Birmingham, 2013)	1
Butt N (Manchester Utd, Newcastle, 1997–2005)	39
Byrne G (Liverpool, 1963–66)	2
Byrne J (Crystal Palace, West Ham, 1962–65)	11
Byrne R (Manchester Utd, 1954–58)	33
Cahill G (Bolton, Chelsea, 2011–14)	27
Callaghan I (Liverpool, 1966–78)	4
Campbell F (Sunderland, 2012)	1
Campbell S (Tottenham, Arsenal, Portsmouth, 1996–2008)	73
Carragher J (Liverpool, 1999–2010)	38
Carrick M (West Ham, Tottenham, Manchester Utd, 2001–14)	31
Carroll A (Newcastle, Liverpool 2011–13)	9
Carson S (Liverpool, Aston Villa WBA, Bursaspor 2008–12)	4

*Carter H (Derby, 1947) 7
Caulker S (Tottenham, 2013) 1
Chamberlain M (Stoke, 1983–85) 8
Channon M (Southampton, Manchester
  City, 1973–78) 46
Charles G (Nottm Forest, 1991) 2
Charlton, J (Leeds, 1965–70) 35
Charlton, R (Manchester Utd, 1958–70) 106
Charnley R (Blackpool, 1963) 1
Cherry T (Leeds, 1976–80) 27
Chilton A (Manchester Utd, 1951–52) 2
Chivers M (Tottenham, 1971–74) 24
Clamp E (Wolves, 1958) 4
Clapton D (Arsenal, 1959) 1
Clarke A (Leeds, 1970–6) 19
Clarke H (Tottenham, 1954) 1
Clayton R (Blackburn, 1956–60) 35
Clemence R (Liverpool, Tottenham,
  1973–84) 61
Clement D (QPR, 1976–7) 5
Cleverley T (Manchester Utd, 2013–14) 13
Clough B (Middlesbrough, 1960) 2
Clough N (Nottm Forest, Liverpool,
  1989–93) 14
Coates R (Burnley, Tottenham, 1970–71) 4
Cockburn H (Manchester Utd,
  1947–52) 13
Cohen G (Fulham, 1964–68) 37
Cole Andy (Manchester Utd, 1995–2002) 15
Cole Ashley (Arsenal, Chelsea, 2001–14) 107
Cole C (West Ham, 2009–10) 7
Cole J (West Ham, Chelsea, 2001–10) 56
Collymore S (Nottm Forest, Aston Villa,
  1995–97) 3
Compton L (Arsenal, 1951) 2
Connelly J (Burnley, Manchester Utd,
  1960–66) 20
Cooper C (Nottm Forest, 1995) 2
Cooper T (Leeds, 1969–75) 20
Coppell S (Manchester Utd, 1978–83) 42
Corrigan J (Manchester City, 1976–82) 9
Cottee T (West Ham, Everton, 1987–89) 7
Cowans G (Aston Villa, Bari, Aston Villa,
  1983–91) 10
Crawford R (Ipswich, 1962) 2
Crouch P (Southampton, Liverpool,
  Portsmouth, Tottenham, 2005–11) 42
Crowe C (Wolves, 1963) 1
Cunningham L (WBA, Real Madrid,
  1979–81) 6
Curle K (Manchester City, 1992) 3
Currie A (Sheffield Utd, Leeds, 1972–79) 17

Daley T (Aston Villa, 1992) 7
Davenport P (Nottm Forest, 1985) 1
Davies K (Bolton, 2011) 1
Dawson M (Tottenham 2011) 4
Deane B (Sheffield Utd, 1991–93) 3
Deeley N (Wolves, 1959) 2
Defoe J (Tottenham, Portsmouth,
  Tottenham, 2004–14) 55
Devonshire A (West Ham, 1980–84) 8

Dickinson J (Portsmouth, 1949–57) 48
Ditchburn E (Tottenham, 1949–57) 6
Dixon K (Chelsea, 1985–87) 8
Dixon L (Arsenal, 1990–99) 22
Dobson M (Burnley, Everton, 1974–75) 5
Dorigo T (Chelsea, Leeds, 1990–94) 15
Douglas B (Blackburn, 1959–63) 36
Downing S (Middlesbrough, Aston Villa,
  Liverpool 2005–12) 34
Doyle M (Manchester City, 1976–77) 5
Dublin D (Coventry, Aston Villa, 1998–99) 4
Dunn D (Blackburn, 2003) 1
Duxbury, M (Manchester Utd, 1984–85) 10
Dyer K (Newcastle, West Ham, 2000–08) 33

Eastham G (Arsenal, 1963–66) 19
Eckersley W (Blackburn, 1950–54) 17
Edwards, D (Manchester Utd, 1955–58) 18
Ehiogu U (Aston Villa, Middlesbrough,
  1996–2002) 4
Ellerington W (Southampton, 1949) 2
Elliott W (Burnley, 1952–53) 5

Fantham J (Sheffield Wed, 1962) 1
Fashanu J (Wimbledon, 1989) 2
Fenwick T (QPR, 1984–88) 20
Ferdinand L (QPR, Newcastle,
  Tottenham, 1993–98) 17
Ferdinand R (West Ham, Leeds,
  Manchester Utd, 1997–2011) 81
Finney T (Preston, 1947–59) 76
Flanagan J (Liverpool, 2014) 1
Flowers R (Wolves, 1955–66) 49
Flowers T (Southampton, Blackburn,
  1993–98) 11
Forster, F (Celtic, 2014) 2
Foster B (Manchester Utd,
  Birmingham, WBA, 2007–14) 8
Foster S (Brighton, 1982) 3
Foulkes W (Manchester Utd, 1955) 1
Fowler R (Liverpool, Leeds, 1996–2002) 26
Francis G (QPR, 1975–76) 12
Francis T (Birmingham, Nottm Forest,
  Man City, Sampdoria, 1977–86) 52
Franklin N (Stoke, 1947–50) 27
Froggatt J (Portsmouth, 1950–53) 13
Froggatt R (Sheffield Wed, 1953) 4

Gardner A (Tottenham, 2004) 1
Garrett T (Blackpool, 1952–54) 3
Gascoigne P (Tottenham, Lazio,
  Rangers, Middlesbrough, 1989–98) 57
Gates E (Ipswich, 1981) 2
George C (Derby, 1977) 1
Gerrard S (Liverpool, 2000–14) 114
Gibbs K (Arsenal, 2011–14) 3
Gidman J (Aston Villa, 1977) 1
Gillard I (QPR, 1975–76) 3
Goddard P (West Ham, 1982) 1
Grainger C (Sheffield Utd, Sunderland,
  1956–57) 7
Gray A (Crystal Palace, 1992) 1

Lloyd L (Liverpool, Nottm Forest, 1971–80) 4
Lofthouse N (Bolton, 1951–59) 33
Lowe E (Aston Villa, 1947) 3

Mabbutt G (Tottenham, 1983–92) 16
Macdonald M (Newcastle, 1972–76) 14
Madeley P (Leeds, 1971–77) 24
Mannion W (Middlesbrough, 1947–52) 26
Mariner P (Ipswich, Arsenal, 1977–85) 35
Marsh R (QPR, Manchester City, 1972–73) 9
Martin A (West Ham, 1981–87) 17
Martyn N (Crystal Palace, Leeds, 1992–2002) 23
Marwood B (Arsenal, 1989) 1
Matthews R (Coventry, 1956–57) 5
*Matthews S (Stoke, Blackpool, 1947–57) 37
McCann G (Sunderland, 2001) 1
McDermott T (Liverpool, 1978–82) 25
McDonald C (Burnley, 1958–59) 8
McFarland R (Derby, 1971–77) 28
McGarry W (Huddersfield, 1954–56) 4
McGuinness W (Manchester Utd, 1959) 2
McMahon S (Liverpool, 1988–91) 17
McManaman S (Liverpool, Real Madrid, 1995–2002) 37
McNab R (Arsenal, 1969) 4
McNeil M (Middlesbrough, 1961–62) 9
Meadows J (Manchester City, 1955) 1
Medley L (Tottenham, 1951–52) 6
Melia J (Liverpool, 1963) 2
Merrick G (Birmingham, 1952–54) 23
Merson P (Arsenal, Middlesbrough, Aston Villa, 1992–99) 21
Metcalfe V (Huddersfield, 1951) 2
Milburn J (Newcastle, 1949–56) 13
Miller B (Burnley, 1961) 1
Mills D (Leeds, 2001–04) 19
Mills M (Ipswich, 1973–82) 42
Milne G (Liverpool, 1963–65) 14
Milner J (Aston Villa, Manchester City, 2010–14) 48
Milton A (Arsenal, 1952) 1
Moore R (West Ham, 1962–74) 108
Morley A (Aston Villa, 1982–83) 6
Morris J (Derby, 1949–50) 3
Mortensen S (Blackpool, 1947–54) 25
Mozley B (Derby, 1950) 3
Mullen J (Wolves, 1947–54) 12
Mullery A (Tottenham, 1965–72) 35
Murphy D (Liverpool, 2002–04) 9

Neal P (Liverpool, 1976–84) 50
Neville G (Manchester Utd, 1995–2009) 85
Neville P (Manchester Utd, Everton, 1996–2008) 59
Newton K (Blackburn, Everton, 1966–70) 27
Nicholls J (WBA, 1954) 2
Nicholson W (Tottenham, 1951) 1
Nish D (Derby, 1973–74) 5
Norman M (Tottenham, 1962–5) 23
Nugent D (Preston, 2007) 1

O'Grady M (Huddersfield, Leeds, 1963–9) 2

Osgood P (Chelsea, 1970–74) 4
Osman L (Everton, 2013) 2
Osman R (Ipswich, 1980–84) 11
Owen M (Liverpool, Real Madrid, Newcastle, 1998–2008) 89
Owen S (Luton, 1954) 3
Oxlade–Chamberlain A (Arsenal, 2012–14) 15

Paine T (Southampton, 1963–66) 19
Pallister G (Middlesbrough, Manchester Utd 1988–97) 22
Palmer C (Sheffield Wed, 1992–94) 18
Parker P (QPR, Manchester Utd, 1989–94) 19
Parker S (Charlton, Chelsea, Newcastle, West Ham, Tottenham, 2004–13) 18
Parkes P (QPR, 1974) 1
Parlour R (Arsenal, 1999–2001) 10
Parry R (Bolton, 1960) 2
Peacock A (Middlesbrough, Leeds, 1962–66) 6
Pearce S (Nottm Forest, West Ham, 1987–2000) 78
Pearson Stan (Manchester Utd, 1948–52) 8
Pearson Stuart (Manchester Utd, 1976–78) 15
Pegg D (Manchester Utd, 1957) 1
Pejic M (Stoke, 1974) 4
Perry W (Blackpool, 1956) 3
Perryman S (Tottenham, 1982) 1
Peters M (West Ham, Tottenham, 1966–74) 67
Phelan M (Manchester Utd, 1990) 1
Phillips K (Sunderland, 1999–2002) 8
Phillips L (Portsmouth, 1952–55) 3
Pickering F (Everton, 1964–65) 3
Pickering N (Sunderland, 1983) 1
Pilkington B (Burnley, 1955) 1
Platt D (Aston Villa, Bari, Juventus, Sampdoria, Arsenal, 1990–96) 62
Pointer R (Burnley, 1962) 3
Powell C (Charlton, 2001–02) 5
Pye J (Wolves, 1950) 1

Quixall A (Sheffield Wed, 1954–55) 5

Radford J (Arsenal, 1969–72) 2
Ramsey A (Southampton, Tottenham, 1949–54) 32
Reaney P (Leeds, 1969–71) 3
Redknapp J (Liverpool, 1996–2000) 17
Reeves K (Norwich, Manchester City, 1980) 2
Regis C (WBA, Coventry, 1982–88) 5
Reid P (Everton, 1985–88) 13
Revie D (Manchester City, 1955–57) 6
Richards, J (Wolves, 1973) 1
Richards M (Manchester City, 2007–12) 13
Richardson K (Aston Villa, 1994) 1
Richardson K (Manchester Utd 2005–07) 8
Rickaby S (WBA, 1954) 1
Ricketts M (Bolton, 2002) 1
Rimmer J (Arsenal, 1976) 1
Ripley S (Blackburn, 1994–97) 2

Rix G (Arsenal, 1981–84)	17
Robb J (Tottenham, 1954)	1
Roberts G (Tottenham, 1983–84)	6
Robinson P (Leeds, Tottenham, 2003–08)	41
Robson B (WBA, Manchester Utd, 1980–92)	90
Robson R (WBA, 1958–62)	20
Rocastle D (Arsenal, 1989–92)	14
Rodriguez J (Southampton, 2014)	1
Rodwell J (Everton, Manchester City, 2012–13)	3
Rooney W (Everton, Manchester Utd, 2003–14)	95
Rowley J (Manchester Utd, 1949–52)	6
Royle J (Everton, Manchester City, 1971–77)	6
Ruddock N (Liverpool, 1995)	1
Ruddy J (Norwich, 2013)	1
Sadler D (Manchester Utd, 1968–71)	4
Salako J (Crystal Palace, 1991–92)	5
Sansom K (Crystal Palace, Arsenal, 1979–88)	86
Scales J (Liverpool, 1995)	3
Scholes P (Manchester Utd, 1997–2004)	66
Scott L (Arsenal, 1947–49)	17
Seaman D (QPR, Arsenal, 1989–2003)	75
Sewell J (Sheffield Wed, 1952–54)	6
Shackleton L (Sunderland, 1949–55)	5
Sharpe L (Manchester Utd, 1991–94)	8
Shaw G (Sheffield Utd, 1959–63)	5
Shaw L (Southampton, 2014)	3
Shawcross, R (Stoke, 2013)	1
Shearer A (Southampton, Blackburn, Newcastle, 1992–2000)	63
Shellito K (Chelsea, 1963)	1
Shelvey J (Liverpool, 2013)	1
Sheringham E (Tottenham, Manchester Utd, Tottenham, 1993–2002)	51
Sherwood T (Tottenham, 1999)	3
Shilton P (Leicester, Stoke, Nottm Forest, Southampton, Derby, 1971–90)	125
Shimwell E (Blackpool, 1949)	1
Shorey N (Reading, 2007)	2
Sillett P (Chelsea, 1955)	3
Sinclair T (West Ham, Manchester City, 2002–04)	12
Sinton A (QPR, Sheffield Wed, 1992–94)	12
Slater W (Wolves, 1955–60)	12
Smalling C (Manchester Utd, 2012–14)	13
Smith A (Arsenal, 1989–92)	13
Smith A (Leeds, Manchester Utd, Newcastle, 2001–08)	19
Smith L (Arsenal, 1951–53)	6
Smith R (Tottenham, 1961–64)	15
Smith T (Birmingham, 1960)	2
Smith T (Liverpool, 1971)	1
Southgate G (Aston Villa, Middlesbrough, 1996–2004)	57
Spink N (Aston Villa, 1983)	1
Springett R (Sheffield Wed, 1960–66)	33
Staniforth R (Huddersfield, 1954–55)	8
Statham D (WBA, 1983)	3
Stein B (Luton, 1984)	1
Stepney A (Manchester Utd, 1968)	1
Sterland M (Sheffield Wed, 1989)	1
Sterling R (Liverpool, 2013–14)	7
Steven T (Everton, Rangers, Marseille, 1985–92)	36
Stevens G (Everton, Rangers, 1985–92)	46
Stevens G (Tottenham, 1985–86)	7
Stewart P (Tottenham, 1992)	3
Stiles N (Manchester Utd, 1965–70)	28
Stone S (Nottm Forest, 1996)	9
Stones J (Everton, 2014)	2
Storey P (Arsenal, 1971–73)	19
Storey-Moore I (Nottm Forest, 1970)	1
Streten B (Luton, 1950)	1
Sturridge D (Chelsea, Liverpool, 2012–14)	15
Summerbee M (Manchester City, 1968–73)	8
Sunderland, A (Arsenal, 1980)	1
Sutton C (Blackburn, 1997)	1
Swan P (Sheffield Wed, 1960–62)	19
Swift F (Manchester City, 1947–79)	19
Talbot B (Ipswich, Arsenal, 1977–80)	6
Tambling R (Chelsea, 1963–66)	3
Taylor E (Blackpool, 1954)	1
Taylor J (Fulham, 1951)	2
Taylor P (Liverpool, 1948)	3
Taylor P (Crystal Palace, 1976)	4
Taylor T (Manchester Utd, 1953–58)	19
Temple D (Everton, 1965)	1
Terry J (Chelsea, 2003–13)	78
Thomas D (QPR, 1975–76)	8
Thomas D (Coventry, 1983)	2
Thomas G (Crystal Palace, 1991–92)	9
Thomas M (Arsenal, 1989–90)	2
Thompson A (Celtic, 2004)	1
Thompson Peter (Liverpool, 1964–70)	16
Thompson Phil (Liverpool, 1976–83)	42
Thompson T (Aston Villa, Preston, 1952–57)	2
Thomson R (Wolves, 1964–65)	8
Todd C (Derby, 1972–77)	27
Towers A (Sunderland, 1978)	3
Townsend A (Tottenham, 2014)	5
Tueart D (Manchester City, 1975–77)	6
Ufton D (Charlton, 1954)	1
Unsworth D (Everton, 1995)	1
Upson M (Birmingham, West Ham, 2003–10)	21
Vassell D (Aston Villa, 2002–04)	22
Venables T (Chelsea, 1965)	2
Venison B (Newcastle, 1995)	2
Viljoen C (Ipswich, 1975)	2
Viollet D (Manchester Utd, 1960)	2
Waddle C (Newcastle, Tottenham, Marseille, 1985–92)	62
Waiters A (Blackpool, 1964–65)	5
Walcott T (Arsenal, 2006–14)	36

Walker D (Nottm Forest, Sampdoria,
Sheffield Wed, 1989–94) 59
Walker I (Tottenham, Leicester,
1996–2004) 4
Walker K (Tottenham, 2012–14) 10
Wallace D (Southampton, 1986) 1
Walsh P (Luton, 1983–4) 5
Walters M (Rangers, 1991) 1
Ward P (Brighton, 1980) 1
Ward T (Derby, 1948) 2
Warnock S (Blackburn, Aston Villa, 2008–11) 2
Watson D (Sunderland, Manchester City,
Werder Bremen, Southampton,
Stoke, 1974–82) 65
Watson D (Norwich, Everton, 1984–8) 12
Watson W (Sunderland, 1950–1) 4
Webb N (Nottm Forest, Manchester
Utd, 1988–92) 26
Welbeck D (Manchester Utd, 2011–14) 26
Weller K (Leicester, 1974) 4
West G (Everton, 1969) 3
Wheeler J (Bolton, 1955) 1
White D (Manchester City, 1993) 1
Whitworth S (Leicester, 1975–76) 7
Whymark T (Ipswich, 1978) 1
Wignall F (Nottm Forest, 1965) 2
Wilcox J (Blackburn, Leeds, 1996–2000) 3
Wilkins R (Chelsea, Manchester Utd,
AC Milan, 1976–87) 84
Williams B (Wolves, 1949–56) 24
Williams S (Southampton, 1983–85) 6
Willis A (Tottenham, 1952) 1

Wilshaw D (Wolves, 1954–57) 12
Wilshere J (Arsenal, 2011–14) 20
Wilson R (Huddersfield, Everton,
1960–8) 63
Winterburn N (Arsenal, 1990–93) 2
Wise D (Chelsea, 1991–2001) 21
Withe P (Aston Villa, 1981–85) 11
Wood R (Manchester Utd, 1955–56) 3
Woodcock A (Nottm Forest, Cologne,
Arsenal, 1977–86) 42
Woodgate J (Leeds, Newcastle, Middlesbrough,
Tottenham, 1999–2008) 8
Woods C (Norwich, Rangers,
Sheffield Wed, 1984–93) 43
Worthington F (Leicester, 1974–75) 8
Wright I (Crystal Palace, Arsenal, West Ham,
1991–99) 33
Wright M (Southampton, Derby,
Liverpool, 1984–96) 45
Wright R (Ipswich, Arsenal, 2000–02) 2
Wright T (Everton, 1968–70) 11
Wright W (Wolves, 1947–59) 105
Wright–Phillips S (Manchester City,
Chelsea, Manchester City, 2005–11) 36

Young A (Aston Villa, Manchester Utd, 2008–14) 30
Young G (Sheffield Wed, 1965) 1
Young L (Charlton, 2005) 7

Zaha W (Manchester Utd, 2013–14) 2
Zamora R (Fulham, 2011–12) 2

SCOTLAND

Adam C (Rangers, Blackpool, Liverpool,
Stoke, 2007–14) 25
Aird J (Burnley, 1954) 4
Aitken G (East Fife, 1949–54) 8
Aitken R (Celtic, Newcastle, St Mirren,
1980–92) 57
Albiston A (Manchester Utd, 1982–6) 14
Alexander G (Preston, Burnley, 2002–10) 40
Alexander N (Cardiff, 2006) 3
Allan T (Dundee, 1974) 2
Anderson J (Leicester, 1954) 1
Anderson R (Aberdeen, Sunderland,
2003–08) 11
Anya I (Watford, 2014) 6
Archibald S (Aberdeen, Tottenham,
Barcelona, 1980–86) 27
Auld B (Celtic, 1959–60) 3

Baird H (Airdrie, 1956) 1
Baird S (Rangers, 1957–58) 7
Bannan B (Aston Villa, Crystal Palace, 2011–14) 17
Bannon E (Dundee Utd, 1980–86) 11
Bardsley P (Sunderland, 2011–14) 13
Barr D (Falkirk, 2009) 1
Bauld W (Hearts, 1950) 3
Baxter J (Rangers, Sunderland, 1961–68) 34
Beattie C (Celtic, WBA, 2006–08) 7
Bell C (Kilmarnock, 2011) 1

Bell W (Leeds, 1966) 2
Bernard P (Oldham, 1995) 2
Berra C (Hearts, Wolves, Ipswich, 2008–14) 28
Bett J (Rangers, Lokeren, Aberdeen, 1982–90) 26
Black E (Metz, 1988) 2
Black I (Southampton, 1948) 1
Black I (Rangers, 2013) 1
Blacklaw A (Burnley, 1963–66) 3
Blackley J (Hibs, 1974–77) 7
Blair J (Blackpool, 1947) 1
Blyth J (Coventry, 1978) 2
Bone J (Norwich, 1972–73) 2
Booth S (Aberdeen, Borussia Dortmund,
Twente Enschede 1993–2002) 22
Bowman D (Dundee Utd, 1992–94) 6
Boyd G (Peterborough, Hull, 2013–14) 2
Boyd K (Rangers, Middlesbrough, 2006–11) 18
Boyd T (Motherwell, Chelsea, Celtic,
1991–2002) 72
Brand R (Rangers, 1961–62) 8
Brazil A (Ipswich, Tottenham, 1980–83) 13
Bremner D (Hibs, 1976) 1
Bremner W (Leeds, 1965–76) 54
Brennan F (Newcastle, 1947–54) 7
Bridcutt L (Brighton, 2013) 1
Broadfoot K (Rangers, 2009–11) 4
Brogan J (Celtic, 1971) 4
Brown A (East Fife, Blackpool, 1950–54) 13

Brown H (Partick, 1947) — 3
Brown J (Sheffield Utd, 1975) — 1
Brown R (Rangers, 1947–52) — 3
Brown S (Hibs, Celtic, 2007–14) — 38
Brown W (Dundee, Tottenham, 1958–66) — 28
Brownlie J (Hibs, 1971–76) — 7
Bryson C (Kilmarnock, Derby, 2011–14) — 2
Buchan M (Aberdeen, Manchester Utd, 1972–8) — 34
Buckley P (Aberdeen, 1954–55) — 3
Burchill M (Celtic, 2000) — 6
Burke C (Rangers, Birmingham, 2006–14) — 7
Burley C (Chelsea, Celtic, Derby, 1995–2003) — 46
Burley G (Ipswich, 1979–82) — 11
Burns F (Manchester Utd, 1970) — 1
Burns K (Birmingham, Nottm Forest, 1974–81) — 20
Burns T (Celtic, 1981–88) — 8

Calderwood C (Tottenham, Aston Villa, 1995–2000) — 36
Caldow E (Rangers, 1957–63) — 40
Caldwell G (Newcastle, Sunderland, Hibs, Wigan, 2002–13) — 55
Caldwell S (Newcastle, Sunderland, Celtic, Wigan, 2001–11) — 12
Callaghan T (Dunfermline, 1970) — 2
Cameron C (Hearts, Wolves, 1999–2005) — 28
Campbell R (Falkirk, Chelsea, 1947–50) — 5
Campbell W (Morton, 1947–48) — 5
Canero P (Leicester, 2004) — 1
Carr W (Coventry, 1970–73) — 6
Chalmers S (Celtic, 1965–67) — 5
Clark J (Celtic, 1966–67) — 4
Clark R (Aberdeen, 1968–73) — 17
Clarke S (Chelsea, 1988–94) — 6
Clarkson D (Motherwell, 2008–09) — 2
Collins J (Hibs, Celtic, Monaco, Everton, 1988–2000) — 58
Collins R (Celtic, Everton, Leeds, 1951–65) — 31
Colquhoun E (Sheffield Utd, 1972–73) — 9
Colquhoun J (Hearts, 1988) — 2
Combe J (Hibs, 1948) — 3
Commons K (Derby, Celtic, 2009–13) — 12
Conn A (Hearts, 1956) — 1
Conn A (Tottenham, 1975) — 2
Connachan E (Dunfermline, 1962) — 2
Connelly G (Celtic, 1974) — 2
Connolly J (Everton, 1973) — 1
Connor R (Dundee, Aberdeen, 1986–91) — 4
Conway C (Dundee Utd, Cardiff, 2010–14) — 7
Cooke C (Dundee, Chelsea, 1966–75) — 16
Cooper D (Rangers, Motherwell, 1980–90) — 22
Cormack P (Hibs, 1966–72) — 9
Cowan J (Morton, 1948–52) — 25
Cowie D (Dundee, 1953–58) — 20
Cowie D (Watford, 2010–12) — 10

Cox C (Hearts, 1948) — 1
Cox S (Rangers, 1948–54) — 25
Craig JP (Celtic, 1968) — 1
Craig J (Celtic, 1977) — 1
Craig T (Newcastle, 1976) — 1
Crainey S (Celtic, Southampton, Blackpool, 2002–12) — 12
Crawford S (Raith, Dunfermline, Plymouth Argyle, 1995–2005) — 25
Crerand P (Celtic, Manchester Utd, 1961–66) — 16
Cropley A (Hibs, 1972) — 2
Cruickshank J (Hearts, 1964–76) — 6
Cullen M (Luton, 1956) — 1
Cumming J (Hearts, 1955–60) — 9
Cummings W (Chelsea, 2002) — 1
Cunningham W (Preston, 1954–55) — 8
Curran H (Wolves, 1970–71) — 5

Dailly C (Derby, Blackburn, West Ham, 1997–2008) — 67
Dalglish K (Celtic, Liverpool, 1972–87) — 102
Davidson C (Blackburn, Leicester, Preston, 1999–2010) — 19
Davidson M (St Johnstone, 2013) — 1*
Davidson J (Partick, 1954–55) — 8
Dawson A (Rangers, 1980–83) — 5
Deans J (Celtic, 1975) — 2
*Delaney J (Manchester Utd, 1947–48) — 4
Devlin P (Birmingham, 2003–04) — 10
Dick J (West Ham, 1959) — 1
Dickov P (Manchester City, Leicester, Blackburn, 2001–05) — 10
Dickson W (Kilmarnock, 1970–71) — 5
Dixon P (Huddersfield, 2013) — 3
Dobie S (WBA, 2002–03) — 6
Docherty T (Preston, Arsenal, 1952–59) — 25
Dodds D (Dundee Utd, 1984) — 2
Dodds W (Aberdeen, Dundee Utd, Rangers, 1997–2002) — 26
Donachie W (Manchester City, 1972–79) — 35
Donnelly S (Celtic, 1997–99) — 10
Dorrans G (WBA, 2010–14) — 10
Dougall C (Birmingham, 1947) — 1
Dougan R (Hearts, 1950) — 1
Douglas R (Celtic, Leicester, 2002–06) — 19
Doyle J (Ayr, 1976) — 1
Duncan A (Hibs, 1975–76) — 6
Duncan D (East Fife, 1948) — 3
Duncanson J (Rangers, 1947) — 1
Durie G (Chelsea, Tottenham, Rangers, 1988–98) — 43
Durrant I (Rangers, Kilmarnock, 1988–2000) — 20

Elliott M (Leicester, 1997–2002) — 18
Evans A (Aston Villa, 1982) — 4
Evans R (Celtic, Chelsea, 1949–60) — 48
Ewing T (Partick, 1958) — 2
Farm G (Blackpool, 1953–59) — 10
Ferguson B (Rangers, Blackburn, Rangers, 1999–2009) — 45

Imlach S (Nottm Forest, 1958) 4
Irvine B (Aberdeen, 1991–94) 9
Iwelumo C (Wolves, Burnley, 2009–11) 4

Jackson C (Rangers, 1975–77) 21
Jackson D (Hibs, Celtic, 1995–99) 29
Jardine A (Rangers, 1971–80) 38
Jarvie A (Airdrie, 1971) 3
Jess E (Aberdeen, Coventry, Aberdeen, 1993–99) 17
Johnston A (Sunderland, Rangers, Middlesbrough, 1999–2003) 18
Johnston M (Watford, Celtic, Nantes, Rangers, 1984–92) 38
Johnston W (Rangers, WBA, 1966–78) 21
Johnstone D (Rangers, 1973–80) 14
Johnstone J (Celtic, 1965–75) 23
Johnstone L (Clyde, 1948) 2
Johnstone R (Hibs, Manchester City, 1951–56) 17
Jordan J (Leeds, Manchester Utd, AC Milan, 1973–82) 52

Kelly H (Blackpool, 1952) 1
Kelly J (Barnsley, 1949) 2
Kelly L (Kilmarnock, 2013) 1
Kennedy J (Celtic, 1964–65) 6
Kennedy J (Celtic, 2004) 1
Kennedy S (Rangers, 1975) 5
Kennedy S (Aberdeen, 1978–82) 8
Kenneth G (Dundee Utd, 2011) 2
Kerr A (Partick, 1955) 2
Kerr B (Newcastle, 2003–04) 3
Kyle K (Sunderland, Kilmarnock, 2002–10) 10

Lambert P (Motherwell, Borussia Dortmund, Celtic, 1995–2003) 40
Law D (Huddersfield, Manchester City, Torino, Manchester Utd, 1959–74) 55
Lawrence T (Liverpool, 1963–69) 3
Leggat G (Aberdeen, Fulham, 1956–60) 18
Leighton J (Aberdeen, Manchester Utd, Hibs, Aberdeen, 1983–99) 91
Lennox R (Celtic, 1967–70) 10
Leslie L (Airdrie, 1961) 5
Levein C (Hearts, 1990–95) 16
Liddell W (Liverpool, 1947–55) 28
Linwood A (Clyde, 1950) 1
Little R (Rangers, 1953) 1
Logie J (Arsenal, 1953) 1
Long H (Clyde, 1947) 1
Lorimer P (Leeds, 1970–76) 21

Macari L (Celtic, Manchester Utd, 1972–78) 24
Macaulay A (Brentford, Arsenal, 1947–48) 7
MacDonald A (Rangers, 1976) 1
MacDougall E (Norwich, 1975–76) 7
Mackail-Smith C (Peterborough, Brighton 2011–12) 7
Mackay D (Hearts, Tottenham, 1957–66) 22
Mackay G (Hearts, 1988) 4

Mackay M (Norwich, 2004–05) 5
Mackay–Steven G (Dundee Utd, 2014) 1
Mackie J (QPR, 2011–13) 9
MacLeod J (Hibs, 1961) 4
MacLeod M (Celtic, Borussia Dortmund, Hibs, 1985–91) 20
Maguire C (Aberdeen, 2011) 2
Maloney S (Celtic, Aston Villa, Celtic, Wigan, 2006–14) 32
Malpas M (Dundee Utd, 1984–93) 55
Marshall D (Celtic, Cardiff, 2005–14) 11
Marshall G (Celtic, 1992) 1
Martin B (Motherwell, 1995) 2
Martin C (Derby, 2014) 1
Martin F (Aberdeen, 1954–55) 6
Martin N (Hibs, Sunderland, 1965–66) 3
Martin R (Norwich, 2011–14) 11
Martis J (Motherwell, 1961) 1
Mason J (Third Lanark 1949–51) 7
Masson D (QPR, Derby, 1976–78) 17
Mathers D (Partick, 1954) 1
Matteo D (Leeds, 2001–02) 6
McAllister B (Wimbledon, 1997) 3
McAllister G (Leicester, Leeds, Coventry, 1990–99) 57
McAllister J (Livingston, 2004) 1
McArthur J (Wigan, 2011–14) 15
McAvennie F (West Ham, Celtic, 1986–88) 5
McBride J (Celtic, 1967) 2
McCall S (Everton, Rangers, 1990–98) 40
McCalliog J (Sheffield Wed, Wolves, 1967–71) 5
McCann N (Hearts, Rangers, Southampton, 1999–2006) 26
McCann R (Motherwell, 1959–61) 5
McClair B (Celtic, Manchester Utd, 1987–93) 30
McCloy P (Rangers, 1973) 4
McCoist A (Rangers, Kilmarnock, 1986–99) 61
McColl I (Rangers, 1950–58) 14
McCormack R (Motherwell, Cardiff, Leeds, 2008–14) 11
McCreadie E (Chelsea, 1965–9) 23
McCulloch L (Wigan, Rangers, 2005–11) 18
McDonald J (Sunderland, 1956) 2
McEveley, J (Derby, 2008) 3
McFadden J (Motherwell, Everton, Birmingham, 2002–11) 48
McFarlane W (Hearts, 1947) 1
McGarr E (Aberdeen, 1970) 2
McGarvey F (Liverpool, Celtic, 1979–84) 7
McGhee M (Aberdeen, 1983–84) 4
McGinlay J (Bolton, 1995–97) 14
McGrain D (Celtic, 1973–82) 62
McGregor A (Rangers, Besiktas, Hull, 2007–14) 32
McGrory J (Kilmarnock, 1965–66) 3
McInally A (Aston Villa, Bayern Munich, 1989–90) 8
McInally J (Dundee Utd, 1987–93) 10
McInnes D (WBA, 2003) 2
McKay D (Celtic, 1959–62) 14

McKean R (Rangers, 1976)	1
McKenzie J (Partick, 1954–56)	9
McKimmie S (Aberdeen, 1989–96)	40
McKinlay T (Celtic, 1996–98)	22
McKinlay W (Dundee Utd, Blackburn, 1994–99)	29
McKinnon R (Rangers, 1966–71)	28
McKinnon R (Motherwell, 1994–95)	3
McLaren A (Preston, 1947–48)	4
McLaren A (Hearts, Rangers, 1992–96)	24
McLaren A (Kilmarnock, 2001)	1
McLean G (Dundee, 1968)	1
McLean T (Kilmarnock, Rangers, 1969–71)	6
McLeish A (Aberdeen, 1980–93)	77
McLintock F (Leicester, Arsenal, 1963–71)	9
McManus S (Celtic, Middlesbrough, 2007–11)	26
McMillan I (Airdrie, 1952–61)	6
McNamara J (Celtic, Wolves, 1997–2006)	33
McNamee D (Livingston, 2004–06)	4
McNaught W (Raith, 1951–55)	5
McNaughton K (Aberdeen, Cardiff, 2002–08)	4
McNeill W (Celtic, 1961–72)	29
McPhail J (Celtic, 1950–54)	5
McPherson D (Hearts, Rangers, 1989–93)	27
McQueen G (Leeds, Manchester Utd, 1974–81)	30
McStay P (Celtic, 1984–97)	76
McSwegan G (Hearts, 2000)	2
Millar J (Rangers, 1963)	2
Miller C (Dundee Utd, 2001)	1
Miller K (Rangers, Wolves, Celtic, Derby, Rangers, Bursaspor, Cardiff, Vancouver, 2001–14)	69
Miller L (Dundee Utd, Aberdeen 2006–10)	3
Miller W (Celtic, 1946–47)	6
Miller W (Aberdeen, 1975–90)	65
Mitchell R (Newcastle, 1951)	2
Mochan N (Celtic, 1954)	3
Moir W (Bolton, 1950)	1
Moncur R (Newcastle, 1968–72)	16
Morgan W (Burnley, Manchester Utd, 1968–74)	21
Morris H (East Fife, 1950)	1
Morrison J (WBA, 2008–14)	31
Mudie J (Blackpool, 1957–58)	17
Mulgrew C (Celtic, 2012–14)	13
Mulhall G (Aberdeen, Sunderland, 1960–64)	3
Munro F (Wolves, 1971–75)	9
Munro I (St Mirren, 1979–80)	7
Murdoch R (Celtic, 1966–70)	12
Murray I (Hibs, Rangers, 2003–06)	6
Murray J (Hearts, 1958)	5
Murray S (Aberdeen, 1972)	1
Murty G (Reading, 2004–08)	4

Naismith S (Kilmarnock, Rangers, Everton, 2007–14)	29
Narey D (Dundee Utd, 1977–89)	35
Naysmith G (Hearts, Everton, Sheffield Utd, 2000–09)	46
Neilson R (Hearts, 2007)	1
Nevin P (Chelsea, Everton, Tranmere, 1987–96)	28
Nicholas C (Celtic, Arsenal, Aberdeen 1983–89)	20
Nicholson B (Dunfermline, 2001–05)	3
Nicol S (Liverpool, 1985–92)	27
O'Connor G (Hibs, Lokomotiv Moscow, Birmingham, 2002–10)	16
O'Donnell P (Motherwell, 1994)	1
O'Hare J (Derby, 1970–72)	13
O'Neil B (Celtic, VfL Wolfsburg, Derby, Preston, 1996–2006)	7
O'Neil J (Hibs, 2001)	1
Ormond W (Hibs, 1954–59)	6
Orr T (Morton, 1952)	2
Parker A (Falkirk, Everton, 1955–56)	15
Parlane D (Rangers, 1973–77)	12
Paton A (Motherwell, 1952)	2
Pearson S (Motherwell, Celtic, Derby, 2004–07)	10
Pearson T (Newcastle, 1947)	2
Penman A (Dundee, 1966)	1
Pettigrew W (Motherwell, 1976–77)	5
Phillips M (Blackpool, 2012–13)	2
Plenderleith J (Manchester City, 1961)	1
Pressley S (Hearts, 2000–07)	32
Provan D (Rangers, 1964–66)	5
Provan D (Celtic, 1980–82)	10
Quashie N (Portsmouth, Southampton, WBA, 2004–07)	14
Quinn P (Motherwell, 1961–62)	9
Rae G (Dundee, Rangers, Cardiff, 2001–09)	14
Redpath W (Motherwell, 1949–52)	9
Reilly L (Hibs, 1949–57)	38
Rhodes J (Huddersfield, Blackburn, 2012–14)	11
Ring T (Clyde, 1953–58)	12
Rioch B (Derby, Everton, 1975–78)	24
Riordan D (Hibs, 2006–10)	3
Ritchie P (Hearts, Bolton, 1999–2000)	6
Ritchie W (Rangers, 1962)	1
Robb D (Aberdeen, 1971)	5
Robertson A (Clyde, 1955)	5
Robertson A (Dundee Utd, 2014)	2
Robertson D (Rangers, 1992–94)	3
Robertson H (Dundee, 1962)	1
Robertson J (Tottenham, 1964)	1
Robertson J (Nott'm Forest, Derby, 1978–84)	28
Robertson J (Hearts, 1991–96)	16
Robertson S (Dundee Utd, 2009–11)	2
Robinson R (Dundee, 1974–75)	4
Robson B (Celtic, Middlesbrough, 2008–12)	17

WALES

Baker W (Cardiff, 1948) — 1

Bale G (Southampton, Tottenham, Real Madrid, 2006–14) — 44

Barnard D (Barnsley, Bradford City, Barnsley, Grimsby, 1998–2004) — 22

Barnes W (Arsenal, 1948–55) — 22

Bellamy C (Norwich, Coventry, Newcastle, Blackburn, Liverpool, West Ham, Manchester City, Liverpool, Cardiff, 1998–2014) — 78

Berry G (Wolves, Stoke, 1979–83) — 5

Blackmore C (Manchester Utd, Middlesbrough, 1985–97) — 39

Blake D (Cardiff, Crystal Palace, 2011–13) — 14

Blake N (Sheffield Utd, Bolton, Blackburn, Wolves, 1994–2004) — 29

Bodin P (Swindon, Crystal Palace, Swindon, 1990–95) — 23

Bowen D (Arsenal, 1955–59) — 19

Bowen J (Swansea City, Birmingham, 1994–97) — 2

Bowen M (Tottenham, Norwich, West Ham, 1986–97) — 41

Boyle T (Crystal Palace, 1981) — 2

Bradley M (Walsall, 2010) — 1

Brown J (Gillingham, Blackburn, Aberdeen, 2006–12) — 3

Browning M (Bristol Rov, Huddersfield, 1996–97) — 5

Burgess R (Tottenham, 1947–54) — 32

Burton A (Norwich, Newcastle, 1963–72) — 9

Cartwright L (Coventry, Wrexham, 1974–79) 7

Charles Jeremy (Swansea City, QPR, Oxford Utd, 1981–87) — 19

Charles John (Leeds, Juventus, Cardiff, 1950–65) — 38

Charles M (Swansea City, Arsenal, Cardiff, 1955–63) — 31

Chester J (Hull, 2014) — 1

Church S (Reading, Nottm Forest, Charlton, 2009–14) — 26

Clarke R (Manchester City, 1949–56) — 22

Coleman C (Crystal Palace, Blackburn, Fulham, 1992–2002) — 32

Collins D (Sunderland, Stoke, 2005–11) — 12

Collins J (Cardiff, West Ham, Aston Villa, West Ham, 2004–14) — 44

Collison J (West Ham, 2008–14) — 17

Cornforth J (Swansea City, 1995) — 2

Cotterill D (Bristol City, Wigan, Sheffield Utd, Swansea, Doncaster, 2006–14) — 20

Coyne D (Tranmere, Grimsby, Leicester, Burnley, Tranmere, 1996–2008) — 16

Crofts A (Gillingham, Brighton, Norwich, Brighton, 2006–14) — 27

Crossley M (Nottm Forest, Middlesbrough, Fulham, 1997–2005) — 8

Crowe V (Aston Villa, 1959–63) — 16

Curtis A (Swansea City, Leeds, Southampton, Cardiff, 1976–87) — 35

Daniel R (Arsenal, Sunderland, 1951–57) — 21

Davies A (Manchester Utd, Newcastle, Swansea City, Bradford City, 1983–90) — 13

Davies A (Yeovil 2006) — 1

Davies B (Swansea, 2013–14) — 10

Davies C (Charlton, 1972) — 1

Davies C (Oxford, Verona, Oldham, Barnsley, Bolton, 2006–14) — 7

Davies D (Everton, Wrexham, Swansea City 1975–83) — 52

Davies ER (Newcastle, 1953–58) — 6

Davies G (Fulham, Chelsea, Manchester City, 1980–86) — 16

Davies RT (Norwich, Southampton, Portsmouth, 1964–74) — 29

Davies RW (Bolton, Newcastle, Man Utd, Man City, Blackpool, 1964–74) — 34

Davies S (Manchester Utd, 1996) — 1

Davies S (Tottenham, Everton, Fulham, 2001–10) — 58

Davis G (Wrexham, 1978) — 3

Deacy N (PSV Eindhoven, Beringen, 1977–79) — 12

Delaney M (Aston Villa, 2000–07) — 36

Derrett S (Cardiff, 1969–71) — 4

Dibble A (Luton, Manchester City, 1986–89) — 3

Dorman A (St Mirren, Crystal Palace, 2010–11) — 3

Dummett P (Newcastle, 2014) — 1

Duffy R (Portsmouth, 2006–08) — 13

Durban A (Derby, 1966–72) — 27

Dwyer P (Cardiff, 1978–80) — 10

Eardley N (Oldham, Blackpool, 2008–11) — 16

Earnshaw R (Cardiff, WBA, Norwich, Derby, Nottm Forest, Cardiff, 2002–13) — 59

Easter J (Wycombe, Crystal Palace, Millwall, 2007–14) — 12

Eastwood F (Wolves, Coventry, 2008–11) — 11

Edwards C (Swansea City, 1996) — 1

Edwards D (Luton, Wolves, 2008–13) — 26

Edwards, G (Birmingham, Cardiff, 1947–50) — 12

Edwards, I (Chester, Wrexham, 1978–80) — 4

Edwards, L (Charlton, 1957) — 2

Edwards, R (Bristol City, 1997–98) — 4

Edwards, R (Aston Villa, Wolves, 2003–07) — 15

Emmanuel W (Bristol City, 1973) — 2

England M (Blackburn, Tottenham, 1962–75) — 44

Evans B (Swansea City, Hereford, 1972–74) — 7

Evans C (Manchester City, Sheffield Utd, 2008–11) — 13

Evans I (Crystal Palace, 1976–78) — 13

Evans P (Brentford, Bradford City, 2002–03) — 2

Evans R (Swansea City, 1964) — 1

Evans S (Wrexham, 2007–09) — 7

Felgate D (Lincoln, 1984) — 1

Fletcher C (Bournemouth, West Ham,

Crystal Palace, 2004–09) 36

Flynn B (Burnley, Leeds, 1975–84) 66

Ford T (Swansea City, Sunderland,
Aston Villa, Cardiff, 1947–57) 38

Foulkes W (Newcastle, 1952–54) 11

Freestone R (Swansea City, 2000–03) 1

Gabbidon D (Cardiff, West Ham, QPR,
Crystal Palace, 2002–14) 49

Garner G (Leyton Orient, 2006) 1

Giggs R (Manchester Utd, 1992–2007) 64

Giles D (Swansea City, Crystal Palace,
1980–83) 12

Godfrey B (Preston, 1964–65) 3

Goss J (Norwich, 1991–96) 9

Green C (Birmingham, 1965–69) 15

Green R (Wolves, 1998) 2

Griffiths A (Wrexham, 1971–77) 17

Griffiths H (Swansea City, 1953) 1

Griffiths M (Leicester, 1947–54) 11

Gunter C (Cardiff, Tottenham, Nottm Forest,
Reading, 2007–14) 53

Hall G (Chelsea, 1988–92) 9

Harrington A (Cardiff, 1956–62) 11

Harris C (Leeds, 1976–82) 23

Harris W (Middlesbrough, 1954–58) 6

Hartson J (Arsenal, West Ham, Wimbledon,
Coventry, Celtic, 1995–2006) 51

Haworth S (Cardiff, Coventry, 1997–8) 5

Hennessey T (Birmingham, Nottm Forest,
Derby, 1962–73) 39

Hennessey W (Wolves, Crystal Palace, 2007–14) 43

Hewitt R (Cardiff, 1958) 5

Hill M (Ipswich, 1972) 2

Hockey T (Sheffield Utd, Norwich,
Aston Villa, 1972–74) 9

Hodges G (Wimbledon, Newcastle,
Watford, Sheffield Utd, 1984–96) 18

Holden A (Chester, 1984) 1

Hole B (Cardiff, Blackburn, Aston Villa,
Swansea City, 1963–71) 30

Hollins D (Newcastle, 1962–66) 11

Hopkins J (Fulham, Crystal Palace,
1983–90) 16

Hopkins M (Tottenham, 1956–63) 34

Horne B (Portsmouth, Southampton,
Everton, Birmingham, 1988–97) 59

Howells R (Cardiff, 1954) 2

Hughes C (Luton, Wimbledon, 1992–97) 8

Hughes I (Luton, 1951) 4

Hughes M (Manchester Utd, Barcelona,
Bayern Munich, Manchester Utd, Chelsea,
Southampton, 1984–99) 72

*Hughes W (Birmingham, 1947) 3

Hughes WA (Blackburn, 1949) 5

Humphreys J (Everton, 1947) 1

Huws E (Manchester City, 2014) 2

Jackett K (Watford, 1983–88) 31

James EG (Blackpool, 1966–71) 9

James L (Burnley, Derby, QPR, Swansea City,

Sunderland, 1972–83) 54

James R (Swansea, Stoke, QPR,
Leicester, Swansea, 1979–88) 47

Jarvis A (Hull, 1967) 3

Jenkins S (Swansea, Huddersfield,
1996–2002) 16

John D (Cardiff, 2014) 2

Johnson A (Nottm Forest, WBA,
1999–2005) 15

Johnson M (Swansea, 1964) 1

Jones A (Port Vale, Charlton, 1987–90) 6

Jones Barrie (Swansea, Plymouth Argyle,
Cardiff, 1963–9) 15

*Jones Bryn (Arsenal, 1947–9) 4

Jones C (Swansea, Tottenham,
Fulham, 1954–69) 59

Jones D (Norwich, 1976–80) 8

Jones E (Swansea, Tottenham, 1947–9) 4

Jones J (Liverpool, Wrexham, Chelsea,
Huddersfield, 1976–86) 72

Jones K (Aston Villa, 1950) 1

Jones L (Liverpool, Tranmere, 1997) 2

Jones M (Leeds, Leicester, 2000–03) 13

Jones M (Wrexham, 2007–08) 2

Jones P (Stockport, Southampton, Wolves,
Millwall, QPR, 1997–2007) 50

Jones R (Sheffield Wed, 1994) 1

*Jones TG (Everton, 1946–49) 13

Jones V (Wimbledon, 1995–97) 9

Jones W (Bristol Rov, 1971) 1

Kelsey J (Arsenal, 1954–62) 41

King A (Leicester, 2009–14) 25

King J (Swansea, 1955) 1

Kinsey N (Norwich, Birmingham,
1951–56) 7

Knill A (Swansea, 1989) 1

Koumas J (Tranmere, WBA, Wigan,
2001–09) 34

Krzywicki R (WBA, Huddersfield,
1970–72) 8

Lambert R (Liverpool, 1947–9) 5

Law B (QPR, 1990) 1

Ledley J (Cardiff, Celtic, Crystal Palace,
2006–14) 51

Lee C (Ipswich, 1965) 2

Leek K (Leicester, Newcastle, Birmingham,
Northampton, 1961–65) 13

Legg A (Birmingham, Cardiff,
1996–2001) 6

Lever A (Leicester, 1953) 1

Lewis D (Swansea, 1983) 1

Llewellyn C (Norwich, Wrexham,
1998–2007) 6

Lloyd B (Wrexham, 1976) 3

Lovell S (Crystal Palace, Millwall,
1982–86) 6

Lowndes S (Newport, Millwall, Brighton,
Barnsley, 1983–88) 10

Lowrie G (Coventry, Newcastle, 1948–49) 4

Lucas M (Leyton Orient, 1962–63) 4

Lucas W (Swansea, 1949–51) 7
Lynch J (Huddersfield, 2013) 1

MacDonald, S (Swansea, 2011) 1
Maguire G (Portsmouth, 1990–92) 7
Mahoney J (Stoke, Middlesbrough,
Swansea, 1968–83) 51
Mardon P (WBA, 1996) 1
Margetson M (Cardiff, 2004) 1
Marriott A (Wrexham, 1996–98) 5
Marustik C (Swansea, 1982–83) 6
Matthews A (Cardiff, Celtic, 2011–14) 12
Medwin T (Swansea, Tottenham,
1953–63) 29
Melville A (Swansea, Oxford Utd,
Sunderland, Fulham, West Ham,
1990–2005) 65
Mielczarek R (Rotherham, 1971) 1
Millington A (WBA, Peterborough,
Swansea, 1963–72) 21
Moore G (Cardiff, Chelsea, Manchester Utd,
Northampton, Charlton, 1960–71) 21
Morgan C (MK Dons, Peterborough,
Preston, 2007–11) 23
Morison S (Millwall, Norwich, 2011–13) 20
Morris W (Burnley, 1947–52) 5
Myhill B (Hull, WBA, 2008–14) 20

Nardiello D (Coventry, 1978) 2
Nardiello D (Barnsley, QPR, 2007–08) 3
Neilson A (Newcastle, Southampton,
1992–97) 5
Nicholas P (Crystal Palace, Arsenal,
Crystal Palace, Luton, Aberdeen, Chelsea,
Watford, 1979–92) 73
Niedzwiecki E (Chelsea, 1985–88) 2
Nogan L (Watford, Reading, 1991–96) 2
Norman T (Hull, 1986–88) 5
Nurse M (Swansea, Middlesbrough,
1960–63) 12
Nyatanga L (Derby, Bristol City, 2006–11) 34

O'Sullivan P (Brighton, 1973–78) 3
Oster J (Everton, Sunderland,
1997–2005) 13

Page M (Birmingham, 1971–79) 28
Page R (Watford, Sheffield Utd, Cardiff,
Coventry, 1997–2006) 41
Palmer D (Swansea, 1957) 3
Parry J (Swansea, 1951) 1
Parry P (Cardiff, 2004–07) 11
Partridge D (Motherwell, Bristol City,
2005–06) 7
Pascoe C (Swansea, Sunderland,
1984–92) 10
Paul R (Swansea, Manchester City,
1949–56) 33
Pembridge M (Luton, Derby, Sheffield Wed,
Benfica, Everton, Fulham,
1992–2005) 54
Perry J (Cardiff, 1994) 1

Phillips D (Plymouth Argyle,
Manchester City, Coventry, Norwich,
Nottm Forest, 1984–96) 62
Phillips J (Chelsea, 1973–78) 4
Phillips L (Cardiff, Aston Villa, Swansea,
Charlton, 1971–82) 58
Pipe D (Coventry, 2003) 1
Pontin K (Cardiff, 1980) 2
Powell A (Leeds, Everton, Birmingham,
1947–51) 8
Powell D (Wrexham, Sheffield Utd, 1968–71) 11
Powell I (QPR, Aston Villa, 1947–51) 8
Price L (Ipswich, Derby, Crystal Palace,
2006–13) 11
Price P (Luton, Tottenham, 1980–84) , 25
Pring K (Rotherham, 1966–67) 3
Pritchard H (Bristol City, 1985) 1

Ramsey A (Arsenal, 2009–14) 30
Rankmore F (Peterborough, 1966) 1
Ratcliffe K (Everton, Cardiff, 1981–93) 59
Ready K (QPR, 1997–98) 5
Reece G (Sheffield Utd, Cardiff,
1966–75) 29
Reed W (Ipswich, 1955) 2
Rees A (Birmingham, 1984) 1
Rees J (Luton, 1992) 1
Rees R (Coventry, WBA, Nottm Forest,
1965–72) 39
Rees W (Cardiff, Tottenham, 1949–50) 4
Ribeiro C (Bristol City, 2010–11) 2
Richards A (Swansea, 2012–14) 4
Richards J (Swansea, 2012) 1
Richards, S (Cardiff, 1947) 1
Ricketts S (Swansea, Hull, Bolton,
Wolves, 2005–14) 52
Roberts A (QPR, 1993) 1
Roberts D (Oxford Utd, Hull, 1973–78) 17
Roberts G (Tranmere, 2000–06) 8
Roberts I (Watford, Huddersfield, Leicester,
Norwich, 1990–2002) 15
Roberts J (Arsenal, Birmingham,
1971–76) 21
Roberts J (Bolton, 1949) 1
Roberts M (QPR, 1997) 1
Roberts N (Wrexham, Wigan, 2000–04) 4
Roberts P (Portsmouth, 1974) 4
Roberts S (Wrexham, 2005) 1
Robinson C (Wolves, Portsmouth, Sunderland,
Norwich, Toronto 2000–08) 46
Robinson J (Charlton, 1996–2002) 30
Robson-Kanu H (Reading, 2010–14) 21
Rodrigues P (Cardiff, Leicester, City
Sheffield Wed, 1965–74) 40
Rouse V (Crystal Palace, 1959) 1
Rowley T (Tranmere, 1959) 1
Rush I (Liverpool, Juventus, Liverpool,
1980–96) 73

Saunders D (Brighton, Oxford Utd,
Derby, Liverpool, Aston Villa, Galatasaray,
Nottm Forest, Sheffield Utd, Benfica,

Bradford City, 1986–2001) 75

Savage R (Crewe, Leicester,
Birmingham, 1996–2005) 39

Sayer R (Cardiff, 1977–8) 7

Scrine F (Swansea, 1950) 2

Sear C (Manchester City, 1963) 1

Sherwood A (Cardiff, Newport,
1947–57) 41

Shortt W (Plymouth Argyle, 1947–53) 12

Showers D (Cardiff, 1975) 2

Sidlow C (Liverpool, 1947–50) 7

Slatter N (Bristol Rov, Oxford Utd,
1983–89) 22

Smallman D (Wrexham, Everton, 1974–6) 7

Southall N (Everton, 1982–97) 92

Speed G (Leeds, Everton, Newcastle,
1990–2004) 85

Sprake G (Leeds, Birmingham,
1964–75) 37

Stansfield F (Cardiff, 1949) 1

Stevenson B (Leeds, Birmingham,
1978–82) 15

Stevenson N (Swansea, 1982–83) 4

Stitfall R (Cardiff, 1953–57) 2

Stock B (Doncaster, 2010–11) 3

Sullivan D (Cardiff, 1953–60) 17

Symons K (Portsmouth, Manchester City,
Fulham, Crystal Palace, 1992–2004) 37

Tapscott D (Arsenal, Cardiff, 1954–59) 14

Taylor D (Crystal Palace, Sheffield Utd,
Burnley, Nottm Forest, 1996–2005) 15

Taylor N (Wrexham, Swansea, 2010–14) 16

Thatcher B (Leicester, Manchester City,
2004–05) 7

Thomas D (Swansea, 1957–58) 2

Thomas M (Wrexham, Manchester Utd,
Everton, Brighton, Stoke, Chelsea, WBA,
1977–86) 51

Thomas M (Newcastle, 1987) 1

Thomas R (Swindon, Derby, Cardiff,
1967–78) 50

Thomas S (Fulham, 1948–49) 4

Toshack J (Cardiff, Liverpool,
Swansea, 1969–80) 40

Trollope P (Derby, Fulham,

Northampton, 1997–2003) 9

Tudur Jones O (Swansea, Norwich,
Hibs, 2008–14) 7

Van den Hauwe P (Everton, 1985–89) 13

Vaughan D (Crewe, Real Sociedad, Blackpool,
Sunderland, 2003–14) 38

Vaughan N (Newport, Cardiff, 1983–85) 10

Vearncombe G (Cardiff, 1958–61) 2

Vernon R (Blackburn, Everton, Stoke,
1957–68) 32

Villars A (Cardiff, 1974) 3

Vokes S (Wolves, Burnley, 2008–14) 31

Walley T (Watford, 1971) 1

Walsh I (Crystal Palace, 1980–82) 18

Ward D (Bristol Rov, Cardiff, 1959–62) 2

Ward D (Notts Co, Nottm Forest, 2000–04) 5

Webster C (Manchester Utd, 1957–58) 4

Weston R (Arsenal, Cardiff, 2000–05) 7

Williams A (Stockport, Swansea, 2008–14) 45

Williams A (Reading, Wolves, Reading,
1994–2003) 13

Williams A (Southampton, 1997–98) 2

Williams D (Norwich, 1986–87) 5

Williams G (Cardiff, 1951) 1

Williams G (Derby, Ipswich, 1988–96) 13

Williams G (West Ham, 2006) 2

Williams G (Fulham, 2014) 1

Williams GE (WBA, 1960–69) 26

Williams GG (Swansea, 1961–62) 5

Williams HJ (Swansea, 1965–72) 3

Williams HT (Newport, Leeds, 1949–50) 4

Williams J (Crystal Palace, 2013–14) 6

Williams S (WBA, Southampton,
1954–66) 43

Wilson H (Liverpool, 2014) 1

Wilson J (Oldham, 2014) 1

Witcomb D (WBA, Sheffield Wed, 1947) 3

Woosnam P (Leyton Orient, West Ham,
Aston Villa, 1959–63) 17

Yorath T (Leeds, Coventry, Tottenham,
Vancouver Whitecaps 1970–81) 59

Young E (Wimbledon, Crystal Palace,
Wolves, 1990–96) 21

Aherne T (Belfast Celtic, Luton, 1947–50) 4

NORTHERN IRELAND

Anderson T (Manchester Utd, Swindon,
Peterborough, 1973–79) 22

Armstrong G (Tottenham, Watford, Real
Mallorca, WBA, 1977–86) 63

Baird C (Southampton, Fulham,
Burnley 2003–14) 66

Barr H (Linfield, Coventry, 1962–63) 3

Barton A (Preston, 2011) 1

Best G (Manchester Utd, Fulham,
1964–77) 37

Bingham W (Sunderland, Luton,
Everton, Port Vale, 1951–64) 56

Black K (Luton, Nottm Forest,

1988–94) 30

Blair R (Oldham, 1975–76) 5

Blanchflower RD (Barnsley, Aston Villa,
Tottenham, 1950–63) 56

Blanchflower J (Manchester Utd, 1954–58) 12

Blayney A (Doncaster, Linfield, 2006–11) 5

Bowler G (Hull, 1950) 3

Boyce L (Werder Bremen, 2011) 4

Braithwaite R (Linfield, Middlesbrough,
1962–65) 10

Braniff K (Portadown, 2010) 2

Brennan R (Luton, Birmingham, Fulham,
1949–51) 5

Briggs W (Manchester Utd, Swansea,

Burnley, Oxford Utd, 1993–2001) 25

Gregg H (Doncaster, Manchester Utd, 1954–64) 25

Griffin D (St Johnstone, Dundee Utd, Stockport, 1996–2004) 29

Grigg W (Walsall, Brentford, 2012–14) 5

Hamill R (Glentoran, 1999) 1

Hamilton B (Linfield, Ipswich, Everton, Millwall, Swindon, 1969–80) 50

Hamilton G (Glentoran, Portadown, 2003–08) 5

Hamilton W (QPR, Burnley, Oxford Utd, 1978–86) 41

Harkin J (Southport, Shrewsbury, 1968–70) 5

Harvey M (Sunderland, 1961–71) 34

Hatton S (Linfield, 1963) 2

Healy D (Manchester Utd, Preston, Leeds, Fulham, Sunderland, Rangers, Bury, 2000–13) 95

Healy F (Coleraine, Glentoran, 1982–83) 4

Hegan D (WBA, Wolves, 1970–73) 7

Hill C (Sheffield Utd, Leicester, Trelleborg, Northampton, 1990–99) 27

Hill J (Norwich, Everton, 1959–64) 7

Hinton E (Fulham, Millwall, 1947–51) 7

Hodson L (Watford, MK Dons, 2011–14) 14

Holmes S (Wrexham, 2002) 1

Horlock K (Swindon, Manchester City, 1995–2003) 32

Hughes A (Newcastle, Aston Villa, Fulham, QPR, 1997–2014) 90

Hughes J (Lincoln, 2006) 2

Hughes M (Oldham, 2006) 1

Hughes M (Manchester City, Strasbourg, West Ham, Wimbledon, Crystal Palace, 1992–2005) 71

Hughes P (Bury, 1987) 3

Hughes W (Bolton, 1951) 1

Humphries W (Ards, Coventry, Swansea, 1962–65) 14

Hunter A (Blackburn, Ipswich, 1970–80) 53

Hunter B (Wrexham, Reading, 1995–2000) 15

Hunter V (Coleraine, 1962) 2

Ingham M (Sunderland, Wrexham, 2005–07) 3

Irvine R (Linfield, Stoke, 1962–5) 8

Irvine W (Burnley, Preston, Brighton, 1963–72) 23

Jackson T (Everton, Nottm Forest, Manchester Utd, 1969–77) 35

Jamison J (Glentoran, 1976) 1

Jenkins I (Chester, Dundee Utd, 1997–2000) 6

Jennings P (Watford, Tottenham, Arsenal, Tottenham, 1964–86) 119

Johnson D (Blackburn, Birmingham, 1999–2010) 56

Johnston W (Glenavon, Oldham, 1962–66) 2

Jones J (Glenavon, 1956–57) 3

Jones S (Crewe, Burnley, 2003–08) 29

Keane T (Swansea, 1949) 1

Kee P (Oxford Utd, Ards, 1990–95) 9

Keith R (Newcastle, 1958–62) 23

Kelly H (Fulham, Southampton, 1950–51) 4

Kelly P (Barnsley, 1950) 1

Kennedy P (Watford, Wigan, 1999–2004) 20

Kirk A (Hearts, Boston, Northampton, Dunfermline, 2000–10) 11

Lafferty D (Burnley, 2012–14) 10

Lafferty K (Burnley, Rangers, Sion, Palermo, 2006–14) 37

Lawrie J (Port Vale, 2009–10) 3

Lawther W (Sunderland, Blackburn, 1960–62) 4

Lennon N (Crewe, Leicester, Celtic, 1994–2002) 40

Little A (Rangers, 2009–13) 9

Lockhart N (Linfield, Coventry, Aston Villa, 1947–56) 8

Lomas S (Manchester City, West Ham, 1994–2003) 45

Lutton B (Wolves, West Ham, 1970–4) 6

Magennis J (Cardiff, Aberdeen, 2010–14) 7

Magill E (Arsenal, Brighton, 1962–66) 26

Magilton J (Oxford Utd, Southampton, Sheffield Wed, Ipswich, 1991–2002) 52

Mannus A (Linfield, St Johnstone, 2004–14) 7

Martin C (Glentoran, Leeds, Aston Villa, 1947–50) 6

McAdams W (Manchester City, Bolton, Leeds, 1954–62) 15

*McAlinden J (Portsmouth, Southend, 1947–49) 2

McArdle R (Rochdale, Aberdeen, Bradford, 2010–14) 7

McAuley G (Lincoln, Leicester, Ipswich, WBA, 2005–14) 47

McBride S (Glenavon, 1991–92) 4

McCabe J (Leeds, 1949–54) 6

McCann G (West Ham, Cheltenham, Barnsley, Scunthorpe, Peterborough, 2002–12) 39

McCarthy J (Port Vale, Birmingham, 1996–2001) 18

McCartney G (Sunderland, West Ham) Sunderland 2002–10) 34

McCavana T (Coleraine, 1954–55) 3

McCleary J (Cliftonville, 1955) 1

McClelland J (Arsenal, Fulham, 1961–67) 6

McClelland J (Mansfield, Rangers, Watford, Leeds, 1980–90) 53

McCourt F (Manchester City, 1952–53) 6

McCourt P (Rochdale, Celtic, Barnsley, 2002–14) 14

McCoy R (Coleraine, 1987) 1

McCreery D (Manchester Utd, QPR, Tulsa, Newcastle, 1976–90) 67

McCrory S (Southend, 1958) 1

McCullough L (Doncaster, 2014) 2
McCullough W (Arsenal, Millwall, 1961–67) 10
McCurdy C (Linfield, 1980) 1
McDonald A (QPR, 1986–96) 52
McElhinney G (Bolton, 1984–85) 6
McEvilly L (Rochdale, 2002) 1
McFaul W (Linfield, Newcastle, 1967–74) 6
McGarry J (Cliftonville, 1951) 3
McGaughey M (Linfield, 1985) 1
McGibbon P (Manchester Utd, Wigan, 1995–2000) 7
McGinn N (Derry, Celtic, Aberdeen, 2009–14) 31
McGivern R (Manchester City, Hibs, 2009–14) 21
McGovern, M (Ross Co, 2010) 1
McGrath C (Tottenham, Manchester 1974–79) 21
McIlroy J (Burnley, Stoke, 1952–66) 55
McIlroy S (Manchester Utd, Stoke, Manchester City, 1972–87) 88
McKay A (Inverness, 2013–14) 7
McKeag W (Glentoran, 1968) 2
McKenna J (Huddersfield, 1950–52) 7
McKenzie R (Airdrie, 1967) 1
McKinney W (Falkirk, 1966) 1
McKnight A (Celtic, West Ham, 1988–89) 10
McLaughlin C (Preston, Fleetwood 2012–14) 3
McLaughlin J (Shrewsbury, Swansea, 1962–66) 12
McLaughlin R (Liverpool, 2014) 2
McLean B (Motherwell, 2006) 1
McMahon G (Tottenham, Stoke, 1995–98) 17
McMichael A (Newcastle, 1950–60) 40
McMillan S (Manchester Utd, 1963) 2
McMordie A (Middlesbrough, 1969–73) 21
McMorran E (Belfast Celtic, Barnsley, Doncaster, 1947–57) 15
McNally B (Shrewsbury, 1987–88) 5
McPake J (Coventry, 2012) 1
McParland P (Aston Villa, Wolves, 1954–62) 34
McQuoid J (Millwall, 2011–12) 5
McVeigh P (Tottenham, Norwich, 1999–2005) 20
Montgomery F (Coleraine, 1955) 1
Moore C (Glentoran, 1949) 1
Moreland V (Derby, 1979–80) 6
Morgan S (Port Vale, Aston Villa, Brighton, Sparta Rotterdam, 1972–99) 18
Morrow S (Arsenal, QPR, 1990–2000) 39
Mulgrew J (Linfield, 2010) 2
Mullan G (Glentoran, 1983) 5
Mulryne P (Manchester Utd, Norwich, 1997–2005) 26
Murdock C (Preston, Hibs, Crewe, Rotherham, 2000–06) 34

Napier R (Bolton, 1966) 1
Neill T (Arsenal, Hull, 1961–73) 59
Nelson S (Arsenal, Brighton, 1970–82) 51
Nicholl C (Aston Villa, Southampton, Grimsby, 1975–83) 51
Nicholl J (Manchester Utd, Toronto, Sunderland, Rangers, WBA, 1976–86) 73
Nicholson J (Manchester Utd, Huddersfield, 1961–72) 41
Nolan I (Sheffield Wed, Bradford City, Wigan, 1997–2002) 18
Norwood O (Manchester Utd, Huddersfield, 2011–14) 16

O'Boyle G (Dunfermline, St Johnstone, 1994–99) 13
O'Connor M (Crewe, Scunthorpe, Rotherham, 2008–14) 11
O'Doherty A (Coleraine, 1970) 2
O'Driscoll J (Swansea, 1949) 3
O'Kane W (Nottm Forest, 1970–75) 20
O'Neill C (Motherwell, 1989–91) 3
O'Neill J (Sunderland, 1962) 1
O'Neill J (Leicester, 1980–86) 39
O'Neill M (Distillery, Nottm Forest, Norwich, Manchester City, Notts Co, 1972–85) 64
O'Neill M (Newcastle, Dundee Utd, Hibs, Coventry, 1989–97) 31
Owens J (Crusaders, 2011) 1

Parke J (Linfield, Hibs, Sunderland, 1964–68) 14
Paterson M (Scunthorpe, Burnley, Huddersfield, 2008–14) 22
Paton P (Dundee Utd, 2014) 1
Patterson D (Crystal Palace, Luton, Dundee Utd, 1994–99) 17
Patterson R (Coleraine, Plymouth, 2010–11) 5
Peacock R (Celtic, Coleraine, 1952–62) 31
Penney S (Brighton, 1985–89) 17
Platt J (Middlesbrough, Ballymena, Coleraine, 1976–86) 23
Quinn J (Blackburn, Swindon, Leicester, Bradford City, West Ham, Bournemouth, Reading, 1985–96) 46
Quinn SJ (Blackpool, WBA, Willem 11, Sheffield Wed, Peterborough, Northampton, 1996–2007) 50

Rafferty W (Wolves, 1980) 1
Ramsey P (Leicester, 1984–89) 14
Rice P (Arsenal, 1969–80) 49
Robinson S (Bournemouth, Luton, 1997–2008) 7
Rogan A (Celtic, Sunderland, Millwall, 1988–97) 17
Ross W (Newcastle, 1969) 1
Rowland K (West Ham, QPR, 1994–99) 19
Russell A (Linfield, 1947) 1
Ryan R (WBA, 1950) 1

Sanchez L (Wimbledon, 1987–89) 3
Scott J (Grimsby, 1958) 2

Scott P (Everton, York, Aldershot, 1976–79) 10
Sharkey P (Ipswich, 1976) 1
Shields J (Southampton, 1957) 1
Shiels D (Hibs, Doncaster, Kilmarnock, Rangers, 2006–13) 14
Simpson W (Rangers, 1951–59) 12
Sloan D (Oxford Utd, 1969–71) 2
Sloan J (Arsenal, 1947) 1
Sloan T (Manchester Utd, 1979) 3
Smith A (Glentoran, Preston, 2003–05) 18
Smyth S (Wolves, Stoke, 1948–52) 9
Smyth W (Distillery, 1949–54) 4
Sonner D (Ipswich, Sheffield Wed, Birmingham, Nottm Forest, Peterborough, 1997–2005) 13
Spence D (Bury, Blackpool, Southend, 1975–82) 27
Sproule I (Hibs, 2006–08) 11
*Stevenson A (Everton, 1947–48) 3
Steele J (New York Bulls, 2014) 3
Stewart A (Glentoran, Derby, 1967–69) 7
Stewart D (Hull, 1978) 1
Stewart I (QPR, Newcastle, 1982–87) 31
Stewart T (Linfield, 1961) 1

Taggart G (Barnsley, Bolton, Leicester, 1990–2003) 51
Taylor M (Fulham, Birmingham, 1999–2012) 88
Thompson J (Watford, 2011) 2
Thompson P (Linfield, 2006–08) 7
Todd S (Burnley, Sheffield Wed, 1966–71) 11
Toner C (Leyton Orient, 2003) 2
Trainor D (Crusaders, 1967) 1
Tuffey J (Partick, Inverness, 2009–11) 8

Tully C (Celtic, 1949–59) 10

Uprichard W (Swindon, Portsmouth, 1952–59) 18

Vernon J (Belfast Celtic, WBA, 1947–52) 17
Walker J (Doncaster, 1955) 1
Walsh D (WBA, 1947–50) 9
Walsh W (Manchester City, 1948–49) 5
Ward J (Derby, 2012–14) 10
Watson P (Distillery, 1971) 1
Webb S (Ross Co, 2006–07) 4
Welsh E (Carlisle, 1966–67) 4
Whiteside N (Manchester Utd, Everton, 1982–90) 38
Whitley Jeff (Manchester City, Sunderland, Cardiff, 1997–2006) 20
Whitley Jim (Manchester City, 1998–2000) 3
Williams M (Chesterfield, Watford, Wimbledon, Stoke, Wimbledon, MK Dons, 1999–2005) 36
Williams P (WBA, 1991) 1
Wilson D (Brighton, Luton, Sheffield Wed, 1987–92) 24
Wilson K (Ipswich, Chelsea, Notts Co, Walsall, 1987–95) 42
Wilson S (Glenavon, Falkirk, Dundee, 1962–68) 12
Winchester C (Oldham, 2011) 1
Wood T (Walsall, 1996) 1
Worthington N (Sheffield Wed, Leeds, Stoke, 1984–97) 66
Wright T (Newcastle, Nottm Forest, Reading, Manchester City, 1989–2000) 31

REPUBLIC OF IRELAND

Aherne T (Belfast Celtic, Luton, 1946–54) 16
Aldridge J (Oxford Utd, Liverpool, Real Sociedad, Tranmere, 1986–97) 69
Ambrose P (Shamrock R, 1955–64) 5
Anderson J (Preston, Newcastle, 1980–89) 16
Andrews K (Blackburn, WBA, 2009–13) 35

Babb P (Coventry, Liverpool, Sunderland, 1994–2003) 35
Bailham E (Shamrock R, 1964) 1
Barber E (Bohemians, Birmingham, 1966) 2
Barrett G (Arsenal, Coventry, 2003–05) 6
Beglin J (Liverpool, 1984–87) 15
Bennett A (Reading, 2007) 2
Best L (Coventry, 2009–10) 7
Braddish S (Dundalk, 1978) 2
Branagan K (Bolton, 1997) 1
Bonner P (Celtic, 1981–96) 80
Brady L (Arsenal, Juventus, Sampdoria, Inter-Milan, Ascoli, West Ham, 1975–90) 72

Brady R (QPR, 1964) 6
Brady, R (Manchester Utd, Hull, 2013–14) 6
Breen G (Birmingham, Coventry, West Ham, Sunderland, 1996–2006) 63
*Breen T (Shamrock R, 1947) 3
Brennan F (Drumcondra, 1965) 1
Brennan S (Manchester Utd, Waterford, 1965–71) 19
Browne W (Bohemians, 1964) 3
Bruce A (Ipswich, 2007–09) 2
Buckley L (Shamrock R, Waregem, 1984–85) 2
Burke F (Cork Ath, 1952) 1
Butler P (Sunderland, 2000) 1
Butler T (Sunderland, 2003) 2
Byrne A (Southampton, 1970–74) 14
Byrne J (Shelbourne, 2004–06) 2
Byrne J (QPR, Le Havre, Brighton, Sunderland, Millwall, 1985–93) 23
Byrne P (Shamrock R, 1984–86) 8

Campbell A (Santander, 1985) 3
Campbell N (St Patrick's Ath,

Forde D (Millwall, 2011–14) 19

Gallagher C (Celtic, 1967) 2
Gallagher M (Hibs, 1954) 1
Galvin A (Tottenham, Sheffield Wed,
  Swindon, 1983–90) 29
Gamble J (Cork City, 2007) 2
Gannon E (Notts Co, Sheffield Wed,
  Shelbourne, 1949–55) 14
Gannon M (Shelbourne, 1972) 1
Gavin J (Norwich, Tottenham,
  Norwich, 1950–57) 7
Gibbons A (St Patrick's Ath, 1952–56) 4
Gibson D (Manchester Utd, Everton, 2008–14) 21
Gilbert R (Shamrock R, 1966) 1
Giles C (Doncaster, 1951) 1
Giles J (Manchester Utd, Leeds,
  WBA, Shamrock R, 1960–79) 59
Given S (Blackburn, Newcastle,
  Manchester City, Aston Villa 1996–2012) 125
Givens D (Manchester Utd, Luton, QPR,
  Birmingham, Neuchatel, 1969–82) 56
Gleeson S (Wolves, 2007) 2
Glynn D (Drumcondra, 1952–55) 2
Godwin T (Shamrock R, Leicester,
  Bournemouth, 1949–58) 13
Goodman J (Wimbledon, 1997) 4
Goodwin J (Stockport, 2003) 1
*Gorman W (Brentford, 1947) 2
Grealish A (Orient Luton, Brighton, WBA,
  1976–86) 45
Green P (Derby, Leeds, 2010–14) 22
Gregg E (Bohemians, 1978–80) 8
Grimes A (Manchester Utd, Coventry,
  Luton, 1978–88) 18

Hale A (Aston Villa, Doncaster,
  Waterford, 1962–72) 14
Hamilton T (Shamrock R, 1959) 2
Hand E (Portsmouth, 1969–76) 20
Harte I (Leeds, Levante, 1996–2007) 64
Hartnett J (Middlesbrough, 1949–54) 2
Haverty J (Arsenal, Blackburn, Millwall,
  Celtic, Bristol Rov, Shelbourne,
  1956–67) 32
Hayes A (Southampton, 1979) 1
*Hayes W (Huddersfield, 1947) 2
Hayes W (Limerick, 1949) 1
Healey R (Cardiff, 1977–80) 2
Healy C (Celtic, Sunderland, 2002–04) 13
Heighway S (Liverpool, Minnesota,
  1971–82) 34
Henderson B (Drumcondra, 1948) 2
Henderson W (Brighton, Preston,
  2006–08) 6
Hendrick J (Derby, 2013–14) 7
Hennessy J (Shelbourne, St Patrick's Ath,
  1956–69) 5
Herrick J (Cork Hibs, Shamrock R,
  1972–73) 3
Higgins J (Birmingham, 1951) 1
Holland M (Ipswich, Charlton, 2000–06) 49

Holmes J (Coventry, Tottenham,
  Vancouver W'caps, 1971–81) 30
Hoolahan W (Blackpool, Norwich, 2008–14) 15
Houghton R (Oxford Utd, Liverpool,
  Aston Villa, Crystal Palace, Reading,
  1986–97) 73
Howlett G (Brighton, 1984) 1
Hughton C (Tottenham, West Ham,
  1980–92) 53
Hunt N (Reading, 2009) 2
Hunt S (Reading, Hull, Wolves, 2007–12) 39
Hurley C (Millwall, Sunderland, Bolton,
  1957–69) 40

Ireland S (Manchester City, 2006–08) 6
Irwin D (Manchester Utd, 1991–2000) 56
Kavanagh G (Stoke, Cardiff, Wigan,
  1998–2007) 16
Keane Robbie (Wolves, Coventry, Inter Milan,
  Leeds, Tottenham, Liverpool, Tottenham,
  LA Galaxy, 1998–2014) 133
Keane Roy (Nottm Forest, Manchester Utd,
  1991–2006) 67
Keane T (Swansea, 1949) 4
Kearin M (Shamrock R, 1972) 1
Kearns F (West Ham, 1954) 1
Kearns M (Oxford Utd, Walsall,
  Wolves, 1970–80) 18
Kelly A (Sheffield Utd, Blackburn,
  1993–2002) 34
Kelly D (Walsall, West Ham, Leicester,
  Newcastle, Wolves, Sunderland,
  Tranmere, 1988–98) 26
Kelly G (Leeds, 1994–2003) 52
Kelly JA (Drumcondra, Preston,
  1957–73) 47
Kelly M (Portsmouth, 1988–91) 4
Kelly N (Nottm Forest, 1954) 1
Kelly P (Wolves, 1961–62) 5
Kelly S (Tottenham, Birmingham, Fulham,
  Reading, 2006–14) 39
Kenna J (Blackburn, 1995–2000) 27
Kennedy M (Portsmouth, 1986) 2
Kennedy M (Liverpool, Wimbledon,
  Manchester City, Wolves, 1996–2004) 34
Kenny P (Sheffield Utd, 2004–07) 7
Keogh A (Wolves, Millwall, 2007–14) 30
Keogh J (Shamrock R, 1966) 1
Keogh R (Derby, 2013–14) 5
Keogh S (Shamrock R, 1959) 1
Kernaghan A (Middlesbrough,
  Manchester City, 1993–96) 22
Kiely D (Charlton, WBA, 2000–09) 11
Kiernan F (Shamrock R, Southampton,
  1951–2) 5
Kilbane K (WBA, Sunderland, Everton,
  Wigan, Hull, 1997–2011) 110
Kinnear J (Tottenham, Brighton,
  1967–76) 26
Kinsella M (Charlton, Aston Villa,
  WBA, 1998–2004) 48

INTERNATIONAL GOALSCORERS 1946–2014

(start of season 2014–15)

ENGLAND

Charlton R	49
Lineker	48
Greaves	44
Owen	40
Rooney	40
Finney	30
Lofthouse	30
Shearer	30
Lampard Frank jnr	29
Platt	27
Robson B	26
Hurst	24
Mortensen	23
Crouch	22
Channon	21
Gerrard	21
Keegan	21
Peters	20
Defoe	19
Haynes	18
Hunt R	18
Beckham	17
Lawton	16
Taylor T	16
Woodcock	16
Scholes	14
Chivers	13
Mariner	13
Smith R	13
Francis T	12
Barnes J	11
Douglas	11
Mannion	11
Sheringham	11
Clarke A	10
Cole J	10
Flowers R	10
Gascoigne	10
Lee F	10
Milburn	10
Wilshaw	10
Beardsley	9
Bell	9
Bentley	9
Hateley	9
Wright I	9
Ball	8
Broadis	8
Byrne J	8
Hoddle	8
Kevan	8
Welbeck	8

Anderton	7
Connelly	7
Coppell	7
Fowler	7
Heskey	7
Paine	7
Young A	7
Charlton J	6
Johnson D	6
Macdonald	6
Mullen	6
Rowley	6
Terry	6
Vassell	6
Waddle	6
Wright-Phillips S	6
Adams	5
Atyeo	5
Baily	5
Brooking	5
Carter	5
Edwards	5
Ferdinand L	5
Hitchens	5
Latchford	5
Neal	5
Pearce	5
Pearson Stan	5
Pearson Stuart	5
Pickering F	5
Sturridge	5
Barmby	4
Barnes P	4
Bent	4
Bull	4
Dixon K	4
Hassall	4
Revie	4
Robson R	4
Steven	4
Walcott	4
Watson Dave (Sunderland)	4
Webb	4
Baker	3
Barry	3
Blissett	3
Butcher	3
Cahill	3
Currie	3
Elliott	3
Ferdinand R	3
Francis G	3
Grainger	3

Kennedy R	3
Lambert	3
McDermott	3
McManaman	3
Matthews S	3
Merson	3
Morris	3
O'Grady	3
Oxlade-Chamberlain	3
Peacock	3
Ramsey	3
Sewell	3
Wilkins	3
Wright W	3
Allen R	2
Anderson	2
Bradley	2
Broadbent	2
Brooks	2
Carroll	2
Cowans	2
Eastham	2
Froggatt J	2
Froggatt R	2
Haines	2
Hancocks	2
Hunter	2
Ince	2
Jagielka	2
Johnson A	2
Keown	2
King	2
Lee R	2
Lee S	2
Moore	2
Perry	2
Pointer	2
Richardson	2
Royle	2
Smith A (1989–92)	2
Southgate	2
Stone	2
Taylor P	2
Tueart	2
Upson	2
Wignall	2
Worthington	2
A'Court	1
Astall	1
Baines	1
Beattie K	1
Bowles	1
Bradford	1

McManus	2
Mulgrew	2
Pettigrew	2
Ring	2
Robertson A	2
Shearer D	2
Aitken R	1
Anya	1
Bannon	1
Beattie	1
Bett	1
Bone	1
Boyd T	1
Brazil	1
Broadfoot	1
Buckley	1
Burns	1
Calderwood	1
Campbell R	1
Clarkson	1
Combe	1
Conn	1
Craig	1
Curran	1
Davidson	1
Dickov	1
Dobie	1
Docherty	1
Duncan M	1
Elliott	1
Fernie	1
Fletcher S	1
Freedman	1
Goodwillie	1
Gray F	1
Gemmell T	1
Hanley	1
Hartley	1
Henderson J	1
Holt	1
Howie	1
Hughes J	1
Hunter W	1
Hutchison T	1
Goodwillie	1
Jackson C	1
Jardine	1
Johnstone L	1
Kyle	1
Lambert	1
Linwood	1
Mackail-Smith	1
Mackay G	1
MacLeod	1
McAvennie	1
McCall	1

McCalliog	1
McArthur	1
McCulloch	1
McKenzie	1
McKimmie	1
McKinnon	1
McLean	1
McLintock	1
McSwegan	1
Miller W	1
Mitchell	1
Morgan	1
Mulhall	1
Murray J	1
Narey	1
Naysmith	1
Ormond	1
Orr	1
Parlane	1
Provan D	1
Quashie	1
Quinn	1
Ritchie P	1
Sharp	1
Stewart R	1
Thornton	1
Wallace I	1
Webster	1
Weir A	1
Weir D	1
Wilkie	1
Wilson Danny	1

WALES

Rush	28
Allchurch I	23
Ford	23
Saunders	22
Bellamy	19
Earnshaw	16
Hughes M	16
Charles John	15
Jones C	15
Hartson	14
Toshack	13
Bale	12
Giggs	12
James L	10
Koumas	10
Davies RT	9
James R	8
Ramsey	8
Vernon	8
Davies RW	7
Flynn	7
Speed	7
Walsh I	7

Charles M	6
Curtis A	6
Davies S	6
Griffiths A	6
Medwin	6
Pembridge	6
Vokes	6
Clarke R	5
Leek	5
Blake	4
Coleman	4
Deacy	4
Eastwood	4
Edwards I	4
Tapscott	4
Thomas M	4
Woosnam	4
Allen M.	3
Bodin	3
Bowen M	3
Collins J	3
Edwards D	3
England	3
Ledley	3
Melville	3
Palmer D	3
Rees R	3
Robinson J	3
Church	2
Davies G	2
Durban A	2
Dwyer	2
Edwards G	2
Evans C	2
Giles D	2
Godfrey	2
Griffiths M	2
Hodges	2
Horne	2
Jones Barrie	2
Jones Bryn	2
King	2
Lowrie	2
Nicholas	2
Phillips D	2
Reece G	2
Savage	2
Slatter	2
Symons	2
Yorath	2
Barnes	1
Blackmore	1
Blake.	1
Bowen D	1
Boyle T	1
Burgess R	1

Charles Jeremy 1
Cotterill 1
Evans I 1
Fletcher...................... 1
Foulkes....................... 1
Harris C 1
Hewitt R 1
Hockey 1
Jones A 1
Jones D 1
Jones J 1
Krzywicki 1
Llewellyn 1
Lovell 1
Mahoney...................... 1
Moore G 1
Morison 1
O'Sullivan 1
Parry 1
Paul 1
Powell A 1
Powell D 1
Price P 1
Roberts P 1
Robinson C 1
Robson-Kanu 1
Smallman 1
Taylor 1
Vaughan 1
Williams Adrian 1
Williams Ashley.............. 1
Williams GE 1
Williams GG 1
Young 1

N IRELAND

Healy 36
Clarke...................... 13
Armstrong 12
Quinn JM 12
Dowie 11
Bingham 10
Crossan J 10
McIlroy J 10
McParland 10
Best 9
Lafferty...................... 9
Whiteside 9
Dougan 8
Irvine W 8
O'Neill M (1972–85) 8
McAdams 7
Taggart G 7
Wilson S 7
Gray 6
McLaughlin 6
Nicholson J 6

Wilson K 6
Cush 5
Davis......................... 5
Feeney ((2002–9)) 5
Hamilton W 5
Hughes M 5
Magilton 5
McIlroy S 5
Simpson 5
Smyth S 5
Walsh D 5
Anderson T 4
Elliott 4
Hamilton B 4
McAuley 4
McCann 4
McGrath 4
McMorran 4
O'Neill M (1989–96) 4
Quinn SJ 4
Brotherston 3
Harvey M 3
Lockhart 3
Lomas 3
McDonald 3
McMordie 3
Morgan S 3
Mulryne...................... 3
Nicholl C 3
Paterson 3
Spence D 3
Tully 3
Blanchflower D 2
Casey 2
Clements 2
Doherty P 2
Finney 2
Gillespie 2
Harkin 2
Lennon 2
McCourt...................... 2
McMahon 2
Neill W 2
O'Neill J 2
Peacock...................... 2
Penney....................... 2
Stewart I 2
Whitley 2
Barr 1
Black 1
Blanchflower J 1
Brennan 1
Brunt 1
Campbell W 1
Caskey 1
Cassidy 1
Cochrane T 1

Crossan E 1
D'Arcy 1
Doherty L 1
Elder 1
Evans C 1
Evans J....................... 1
Ferguson S................... 1
Ferguson W 1
Ferris 1
Griffin 1
Hill C 1
Hughes 1
Humphries 1
Hunter A 1
Hunter B 1
Johnston 1
Jones J 1
Jones, S...................... 1
McCartney 1
McClelland (1961) 1
McCrory...................... 1
McCurdy 1
McGarry 1
McGinn 1
McVeigh 1
Moreland 1
Morrow 1
Murdock 1
Nelson 1
Nicholl J 1
O'Boyle....................... 1
O'Kane 1
Patterson D 1
Patterson R 1
Rowland 1
Shiels........................ 1
Sproule 1
Stevenson 1
Thompson 1
Walker 1
Ward 1
Welsh 1
Williams 1
Wilson D 1

REP OF IRELAND

Keane Robbie................ 62
Quinn N 21
Stapleton 20
Aldridge 19
Cascarino 19
Givens 19
Cantwell 14
Daly.......................... 13
Doyle........................ 13
Harte 11
Long.......................... 11

Brady L	9	Andrews	3	Anderson	1
Connolly	9	Carey J	3	Brady R	1
Duff	9	Coad	3	Carroll	1
Keane Roy	9	Conway	3	Clark	1
Kelly D	9	Fahey	3	Dempsey	1
Morrison	9	Farrell	3	Duffy	1
Sheedy	9	Fogarty	3	Elliott	1
Curtis	8	Haverty	3	Fitzgerald J	1
Dunne R	8	Kennedy Mark	3	Fullam J	1
Grealish	8	Kinsella	3	Galvin	1
Kilbane	8	McAteer	3	Gibson	1
McGrath P	8	McGeady	3	Glynn	1
Staunton	8	Ryan R	3	Green	1
Breen G	7	St Ledger S	3	Grimes	1
Fitzsimons	7	Waddock	3	Healy	1
Ringstead	7	Walsh M	3	Holmes	1
Townsend	7	Whelan R	3	Hoolahan	1
Coyne	6	Barrett	2	Hughton	1
Houghton	6	Conroy	2	Hunt	1
McEvoy	6	Dennehy	2	Gibson	1
Martin C	6	Eglington	2	Kavanagh	1
Moran	6	Fallon	2	Keogh R	1
Cummins	5	Finnan	2	Kernaghan	1
Fagan F	5	Fitzgerald P	2	Mancini	1
Giles	5	Foley	2	McCann	1
Holland	5	Gavin	2	McClean	1
Lawrenson	5	Hale	2	McPhail	1
Rogers	5	Hand	2	Miller	1
Sheridan	5	Hurley	2	Mooney	1
Treacy	5	Kelly G	2	Moroney	1
Walsh D	5	Keogh A	2	Mulligan	1
Walters	5	Lawrence	2	O'Brien A	1
Byrne J	4	Leech	2	O'Dea	1
Cox	4	McCarthy	2	O'Callaghan K	1
Doherty	4	McLoughlin	2	O'Keefe	1
Ireland	4	O'Connor	2	O'Leary	1
Irwin	4	O'Farrell	2	O'Neill F	1
McGee	4	O'Reilly J	2	Pearce	1
Martin M	4	O'Shea	2	Ryan G	1
O'Neill K	4	Whelan G	2	Slaven	1
Reid A	4	Reid S	2	Sloan	1
Robinson	4	Ward	2	Strahan	1
Tuohy	4	Ambrose	1	Waters	1

HOME INTERNATIONAL RESULTS

Note: In the results that follow, WC = World Cup, EC = European Championship, CC = Carling Cup
TF = Tournoi de France For Northern Ireland read Ireland before 1921

ENGLAND V SCOTLAND

Played 111; England 46; Scotland 41; drawn 24 Goals: England 195, Scotland 171

		E	S			E	S
				1879	The Oval	5	4
1872	Glasgow	0	0	1880	Glasgow	4	5
1873	The Oval	4	2	1881	The Oval	1	6
1874	Glasgow	1	2	1882	Glasgow	1	5
1875	The Oval	2	2	1883	Sheffield	2	3
1876	Glasgow	0	3	1884	Glasgow	0	1
1877	The Oval	1	3	1885	The Oval	1	1
1878	Glasgow	2	7	1886	Glasgow	1	1

Year	Venue			Year	Venue		
1887	Blackburn	2	3	1947	Wembley	1	1
1888	Glasgow	5	0	1948	Glasgow	2	0
1889	The Oval	2	3	1949	Wembley	1	3
1890	Glasgow	1	1	1950	Glasgow (WC)	1	0
1891	Blackburn	2	1	1951	Wembley	2	3
1892	Glasgow	4	1	1952	Glasgow	2	1
1893	Richmond	5	2	1953	Wembley	2	2
1894	Glasgow	2	2	1954	Glasgow (WC)	4	2
1895	Goodison Park	3	0	1955	Wembley	7	2
1896	Glasgow	1	2	1956	Glasgow	1	1
1897	Crystal Palace	1	2	1957	Wembley	2	1
1898	Glasgow	3	1	1958	Glasgow	4	0
1899	Birmingham	2	1	1959	Wembley	1	0
1900	Glasgow	1	4	1960	Glasgow	1	1
1901	Crystal Palace	2	2	1961	Wembley	9	3
1902	Birmingham	2	2	1962	Glasgow	0	2
1903	Sheffield	1	2	1963	Wembley	1	2
1904	Glasgow	1	0	1964	Glasgow	0	1
1905	Crystal Palace	1	0	1965	Wembley	2	2
1906	Glasgow	1	2	1966	Glasgow	4	3
1907	Newcastle	1	1	1967	Wembley (EC)	2	3
1908	Glasgow	1	1	1968	Glasgow (EC)	1	1
1909	Crystal Palace	2	0	1969	Wembley	4	1
1910	Glasgow	0	2	1970	Glasgow	0	0
1911	Goodison Park	1	1	1971	Wembley	3	1
1912	Glasgow	1	1	1972	Glasgow	1	0
1913	Stamford Bridge	1	0	1973	Glasgow	5	0
1914	Glasgow	1	3	1973	Wembley	1	0
1920	Sheffield	5	4	1974	Glasgow	0	2
1921	Glasgow	0	3	1975	Wembley	5	1
1922	Birmingham	0	1	1976	Glasgow	1	2
1923	Glasgow	2	2	1977	Wembley	1	2
1924	Wembley	1	1	1978	Glasgow	1	0
1925	Glasgow	0	2	1979	Wembley	3	1
1926	Manchester	0	1	1980	Glasgow	2	0
1927	Glasgow	2	1	1981	Wembley	0	1
1928	Wembley	1	5	1982	Glasgow	1	0
1929	Glasgow	0	1	1983	Wembley	2	0
1930	Wembley	5	2	1984	Glasgow	1	1
1931	Glasgow	0	2	1985	Glasgow	0	1
1932	Wembley	3	0	1986	Wembley	2	1
1933	Glasgow	1	2	1987	Glasgow	0	0
1934	Wembley	3	0	1988	Wembley	1	0
1935	Glasgow	0	2	1989	Glasgow	2	0
1936	Wembley	1	1	1996	Wembley (EC)	2	0
1937	Glasgow	1	3	1999	Glasgow (EC)	2	0
1938	Wembley	0	1	1999	Wembley (EC)	0	1
1939	Glasgow	2	1	2013	Wembley	3	2

ENGLAND v WALES

Played 101; England won 66; Wales 14; drawn 21; Goals: England 245 Wales 90

Year	Venue	E	W	Year	Venue	E	W
1879	The Oval	2	1	1890	Wrexham	3	1
1880	Wrexham	3	2	1891	Sunderland	4	1
1881	Blackburn	0	1	1892	Wrexham	2	0
1882	Wrexham	3	5	1893	Stoke	6	0
1883	The Oval	5	0	1894	Wrexham	5	1
1884	Wrexham	4	0	1895	Queens Club, London	1	1
1885	Blackburn	1	1	1896	Cardiff	9	1
1886	Wrexham	3	1	1897	Bramall Lane	4	0
1887	The Oval	4	0	1898	Wrexham	3	0
1888	Crewe	5	1	1899	Bristol	4	0
1889	Stoke	4	1	1900	Cardiff	1	1
				1901	Newcastle	6	0

1902	Wrexham	0	0
1903	Portsmouth	2	1
1904	Wrexham	2	2
1905	Anfield	3	1
1906	Cardiff	1	0
1907	Fulham	1	1
1908	Wrexham	7	1
1909	Nottingham	2	0
1910	Cardiff	1	0
1911	Millwall	3	0
1912	Wrexham	2	0
1913	Bristol	4	3
1914	Cardiff	2	0
1920	Highbury	1	2
1921	Cardiff	0	0
1922	Anfield	1	0
1923	Cardiff	2	2
1924	Blackburn	1	2
1925	Swansea	2	1
1926	Selhurst Park	1	3
1927	Wrexham	3	3
1927	Burnley	1	2
1928	Swansea	3	2
1929	Stamford Bridge	6	0
1930	Wrexham	4	0
1931	Anfield	3	1
1932	Wrexham	0	0
1933	Newcastle	1	2
1934	Cardiff	4	0
1935	Wolverhampton	1	2
1936	Cardiff	1	2
1937	Middlesbrough	2	1
1938	Cardiff	2	4
1946	Maine Road	3	0
1947	Cardiff	3	0
1948	Villa Park	1	0
1949	Cardiff (WC)	4	1
1950	Sunderland	4	2
1951	Cardiff	1	1
1952	Wembley	5	2
1953	Cardiff (WC)	4	1
1954	Wembley	3	2
1955	Cardiff	1	2
1956	Wembley	3	1
1957	Cardiff	4	0
1958	Villa Park	2	2
1959	Cardiff	1	1
1960	Wembley	5	1
1961	Cardiff	1	1
1962	Wembley	4	0
1963	Cardiff	4	0
1964	Wembley	2	1
1965	Cardiff	0	0
1966	Wembley (EC)	5	1
1967	Cardiff (EC)	3	0
1969	Wembley	2	1
1970	Cardiff	1	1
1971	Wembley	0	0
1972	Cardiff	3	0
1972	Cardiff (WC)	1	0
1973	Wembley (WC)	1	1
1973	Wembley	3	0
1974	Cardiff	2	0
1975	Wembley	2	2
1976	Wrexham	2	1
1976	Cardiff	1	0
1977	Wembley	0	1
1978	Cardiff	3	1
1979	Wembley	0	0
1980	Wrexham	1	4
1981	Wembley	0	0
1982	Cardiff	1	0
1983	Wembley	2	1
1984	Wrexham	0	1
2004	Old Trafford (WC)	2	0
2005	Cardiff (WC)	1	0
2011	Cardiff (EC)	2	0
2011	Wembley (EC)	1	0
		E	I

ENGLAND v N IRELAND

Played 98; England won 75; Ireland 7; drawn 16 Goals: England 323, Ireland 81

1882	Belfast	13	0
1883	Aigburth, Liverpool	7	0
1884	Belfast	8	1
1885	Whalley Range	4	0
1886	Belfast	6	1
1887	Bramall Lane	7	0
1888	Belfast	5	1
1889	Goodison Park	6	1
1890	Belfast	9	1
1891	Wolverhampton	6	1
1892	Belfast	2	0
1893	Perry Barr	6	1
1894	Belfast	2	2
1895	Derby	9	0
1896	Belfast	2	0
1897	Nottingham	6	0
1898	Belfast	3	2
1899	Sunderland	13	2
1900	Dublin	2	0
1901	Southampton	3	0
1902	Belfast	1	0
1903	Wolverhampton	4	0
1904	Belfast	3	1
1905	Middlesbrough	1	1
1906	Belfast	5	0
1907	Goodison Park	1	0
1908	Belfast	3	1
1909	Bradford PA	4	0
1910	Belfast	1	1
1911	Derby	2	1
1912	Dublin	6	1
1913	Belfast	1	2
1914	Middlesbrough	0	3
1919	Belfast	1	1
1920	Sunderland	2	0
1921	Belfast	1	1
1922	West Bromwich	2	0
1923	Belfast	1	2
1924	Goodison Park	3	1
1925	Belfast	0	0

1926	Anfield	3	3
1927	Belfast	0	2
1928	Goodison Park	2	1
1929	Belfast	3	0
1930	Bramall Lane	5	1
1931	Belfast	6	2
1932	Blackpool	1	0
1933	Belfast	3	0
1935	Goodison Park	2	1
1935	Belfast	3	1
1936	Stoke	3	1
1937	Belfast	5	1
1938	Old Trafford	7	0
1946	Belfast	7	2
1947	Goodison Park	2	2
1948	Belfast	6	2
1949	Maine Road (WC)	9	2
1950	Belfast	4	1
1951	Villa Park	2	0
1952	Belfast	2	2
1953	Goodison Park (WC)	3	1
1954	Belfast	2	0
1955	Wembley	3	0
1956	Belfast	1	1
1957	Wembley	2	3
1958	Belfast	3	3
1959	Wembley	2	1
1960	Belfast	5	2
1961	Wembley	1	1
1962	Belfast	3	1
1963	Wembley	8	3
1964	Belfast	4	3
1965	Wembley	2	1
1966	Belfast (EC)	2	0
1967	Wembley (EC)	2	0
1969	Belfast	3	1
1970	Wembley	3	1
1971	Belfast	1	0
1972	Wembley	0	1
1973	*Goodison Park	2	1
1974	Wembley	1	0
1975	Belfast	0	0
1976	Wembley	4	0
1977	Belfast	2	1
1978	Wembley	1	0
1979	Wembley (EC)	4	0
1979	Belfast	2	0
1979	Belfast (EC)	5	1
1980	Wembley	1	1
1982	Wembley	4	0
1983	Belfast	0	0
1984	Wembley	1	0
1985	Belfast (WC)	1	0
1985	Wembley (WC)	0	0
1986	Wembley (EC)	3	0
1987	Belfast (EC)	2	0
2005	Old Trafford (WC)	4	0
2005	Belfast (WC)	0	1

(*Switched from Belfast because of political situation)

SCOTLAND v WALES

Played 107; Scotland won 61; Wales 23; drawn 23; Goals: Scotland 243, Wales 124

		S	W
1876	Glasgow	4	0
1877	Wrexham	2	0
1878	Glasgow	9	0
1879	Wrexham	3	0
1880	Glasgow	5	1
1881	Wrexham	5	1
1882	Glasgow	5	0
1883	Wrexham	3	0
1884	Glasgow	4	1
1885	Wrexham	8	1
1886	Glasgow	4	1
1887	Wrexham	2	0
1888	Edinburgh	5	1
1889	Wrexham	0	0
1890	Paisley	5	0
1891	Wrexham	4	3
1892	Edinburgh	6	1
1893	Wrexham	8	0
1894	Kilmarnock	5	2
1895	Wrexham	2	2
1896	Dundee	4	0
1897	Wrexham	2	2
1898	Motherwell	5	2
1899	Wrexham	6	0
1900	Aberdeen	5	2
1901	Wrexham	1	1
1902	Greenock	5	1
1903	Cardiff	1	0
1904	Dundee	1	1
1905	Wrexham	1	3
1906	Edinburgh	0	2
1907	Wrexham	0	1
1908	Dundee	2	1
1909	Wrexham	2	3
1910	Kilmarnock	1	0
1911	Cardiff	2	2
1912	Tynecastle	1	0
1913	Wrexham	0	0
1914	Glasgow	0	0
1920	Cardiff	1	1
1921	Aberdeen	2	1
1922	Wrexham	1	2
1923	Paisley	2	0
1924	Cardiff	0	2
1925	Tynecastle	3	1
1926	Cardiff	3	0
1927	Glasgow	3	0
1928	Wrexham	2	2
1929	Glasgow	4	2
1930	Cardiff	4	2
1931	Glasgow	1	1
1932	Wrexham	3	2
1933	Edinburgh	2	5
1934	Cardiff	2	3
1935	Aberdeen	3	2
1936	Cardiff	1	1
1937	Dundee	1	2
1938	Cardiff	1	2
1939	Edinburgh	3	2

1946	Wrexham	1	3		1971	Cardiff	0	0
1947	Glasgow	1	2		1972	Glasgow	1	0
1948	Cardiff (WC)	3	1		1973	Wrexham	2	0
1949	Glasgow	2	0		1974	Glasgow	2	0
1950	Cardiff	3	1		1975	Cardiff	2	2
1951	Glasgow	0	1		1976	Glasgow	3	1
1952	Cardiff (WC)	2	1		1977	Glasgow (WC)	1	0
1953	Glasgow	3	3		1977	Wrexham	0	0
1954	Cardiff	1	0		1977	Anfield (WC)	2	0
1955	Glasgow	2	0		1978	Glasgow	1	1
1956	Cardiff	2	2		1979	Cardiff	0	3
1957	Glasgow	1	1		1980	Glasgow	1	0
1958	Cardiff	3	0		1981	Swansea	0	2
1959	Glasgow	1	1		1982	Glasgow	1	0
1960	Cardiff	0	2		1983	Cardiff	2	0
1961	Glasgow	2	0		1984	Glasgow	2	1
1962	Cardiff	3	2		1985	Glasgow (WC)	0	1
1963	Glasgow	2	1		1985	Cardiff (WC)	1	1
1964	Cardiff	2	3		1997	Kilmarnock	0	1
1965	Glasgow (EC)	4	1		2004	Cardiff	0	4
1966	Cardiff (EC)	1	1		2009	Cardiff	0	3
1967	Glasgow	3	2		2011	Dublin (CC)	3	1
1969	Wrexham	5	3		2012	Cardiff (WC)	1	2
1970	Glasgow	0	0		2013	Glasgow (WC	1	2

SCOTLAND v NORTHERN IRELAND
Played 95; Scotland won 63; Northern Ireland 15; drawn 17; Goals: Scotland 257, Northern Ireland 80

		S	I					
1884	Belfast	5	0		1922	Glasgow	2	1
1885	Glasgow	8	2		1923	Belfast	1	0
1886	Belfast	7	2		1924	Glasgow	2	0
1887	Belfast	4	1		1925	Belfast	3	0
1888	Belfast	10	2		1926	Glasgow	4	0
1889	Glasgow	7	0		1927	Belfast	2	0
1890	Belfast	4	1		1928	Glasgow	0	1
1891	Glasgow	2	1		1929	Belfast	7	3
1892	Belfast	3	2		1930	Glasgow	3	1
1893	Glasgow	6	1		1931	Belfast	0	0
1894	Belfast	2	1		1932	Glasgow	3	1
1895	Glasgow	3	1		1933	Belfast	4	0
1896	Belfast	3	3		1934	Glasgow	1	2
1897	Glasgow	5	1		1935	Belfast	1	2
1898	Belfast	3	0		1936	Edinburgh	2	1
1899	Glasgow	9	1		1937	Belfast	3	1
1900	Belfast	3	0		1938	Aberdeen	1	1
1901	Glasgow	11	0		1939	Glasgow	2	0
1902	Belfast	5	1		1946	Glasgow	0	0
1902	Belfast	3	0		1947	Belfast	0	2
1903	Glasgow	0	2		1948	Glasgow	3	2
1904	Dublin	1	1		1949	Belfast	8	2
1905	Glasgow	4	0		1950	Glasgow	6	1
1906	Dublin	1	0		1951	Belfast	3	0
1907	Glasgow	3	0		1952	Glasgow	1	1
1908	Dublin	5	0		1953	Belfast	3	1
1909	Glasgow	5	0		1954	Glasgow	2	2
1910	Belfast	0	1		1955	Belfast	1	2
1911	Glasgow	2	0		1956	Glasgow	1	0
1912	Belfast	4	1		1957	Belfast	1	1
1913	Dublin	2	1		1958	Glasgow	2	2
1914	Belfast	1	1		1959	Belfast	4	0
1920	Glasgow	3	0		1960	Glasgow	5	1
1921	Belfast	2	0		1961	Belfast	6	1
					1962	Glasgow	5	1

		W	L				W	L
1963	Belfast	1	2		1977	Glasgow	3	0
1964	Glasgow	3	2		1978	Glasgow	1	1
1965	Belfast	2	3		1979	Glasgow	1	1
1966	Glasgow	2	1		1980	Belfast	0	1
1967	Belfast	0	1		1981	Glasgow (WC)	1	1
1969	Glasgow	1	1		1981	Glasgow	2	0
1970	Belfast	1	0		1981	Belfast (WC)	0	0
1971	Glasgow	0	1		1982	Belfast	1	1
1972	Glasgow	2	0		1983	Glasgow	0	0
1973	Glasgow	1	2		1984	Belfast	0	2
1974	Glasgow	0	1		1992	Glasgow	1	0
1975	Glasgow	3	0		2008	Glasgow	0	0
1976	Glasgow	3	0		2011	Dublin (CC)	3	0

WALES v NORTHERN IRELAND

Played 95; Wales won 44; Northern Ireland won 27; drawn 24; Goals: Wales 189, Northern Ireland 131

		W	L				W	L
1882	Wrexham	7	1		1935	Wrexham	3	1
1883	Belfast	1	1		1936	Belfast	2	3
1884	Wrexham	6	0		1937	Wrexham	4	1
1885	Belfast	8	2		1938	Belfast	0	1
1886	Wrexham	5	0		1939	Wrexham	3	1
1887	Belfast	1	4		1947	Belfast	1	2
1888	Wrexham	11	0		1948	Wrexham	2	0
1889	Belfast	3	1		1949	Belfast	2	0
1890	Shrewsbury	5	2		1950	Wrexham (WC)	0	0
1891	Belfast	2	7		1951	Belfast	2	1
1892	Bangor	1	1		1952	Swansea	3	0
1893	Belfast	3	4		1953	Belfast	3	2
1894	Swansea	4	1		1954	Wrexham (WC)	1	2
1895	Belfast	2	2		1955	Belfast	3	2
1896	Wrexham	6	1		1956	Cardiff	1	1
1897	Belfast	3	4		1957	Belfast	0	0
1898	Llandudno	0	1		1958	Cardiff	1	1
1899	Belfast	0	1		1959	Belfast	1	4
1900	Llandudno	2	0		1960	Wrexham	3	2
1901	Belfast	1	0		1961	Belfast	5	1
1902	Cardiff	0	3		1962	Cardiff	4	0
1903	Belfast	0	2		1963	Belfast	4	1
1904	Bangor	0	1		1964	Swansea	2	3
1905	Belfast	2	2		1965	Belfast	5	0
1906	Wrexham	4	4		1966	Cardiff	1	4
1907	Belfast	3	2		1967	Belfast (EC)	0	0
1908	Aberdare	0	1		1968	Wrexham (EC)	2	0
1909	Belfast	3	2		1969	Belfast	0	0
1910	Wrexham	4	1		1970	Swansea	1	0
1911	Belfast	2	1		1971	Belfast	0	1
1912	Cardiff	2	3		1972	Wrexham	0	0
1913	Belfast	1	0		1973	*Goodison Park	0	1
1914	Wrexham	1	2		1974	Wrexham	1	0
1920	Belfast	2	2		1975	Belfast	0	1
1921	Swansea	2	1		1976	Swansea	1	0
1922	Belfast	1	1		1977	Belfast	1	1
1923	Wrexham	0	3		1978	Wrexham	1	0
1924	Belfast	1	0		1979	Belfast	1	1
1925	Wrexham	0	0		1980	Cardiff	0	1
1926	Belfast	0	3		1982	Wrexham	3	0
1927	Cardiff	2	2		1983	Belfast	1	0
1928	Belfast	2	1		1984	Swansea	1	1
1929	Wrexham	2	2		2004	Cardiff (WC)	2	2
1930	Belfast	0	7		2005	Belfast (WC)	3	2
1931	Wrexham	3	2		2007	Belfast	0	0
1932	Belfast	0	4		2008	Glasgow	0	0
1933	Wrexham	4	1		2011	Dublin (CC)	2	0
1934	Belfast	1	1					

(*Switched from Belfast because of political situation in N Ireland)

BRITISH AND IRISH UNDER-21 INTERNATIONALS 2013–14

EUROPEAN CHAMPIONSHIP 2015 – QUALIFYING

WALES 1 FINLAND 5
Group 1: BookPeople Stadium, Bangor (1,023); Wednesday, August 14 2013
Wales: Ward (Liverpool), Hewitt (Ipswich) (Fox, Charlton 46), Freeman (Derby), Lucas (Swansea), Walsh (Crawley), Tancock (Swansea), Bodin (Torquay) (Burns, Bristol City 46), Huws (Manchester City), Cassidy (Wolves), Lawrence (Manchester Utd) (Dawson, Leeds 68), Isgrove (Southampton). **Booked**: Freeman, Lucas
Scorers – Wales: Huws (48 pen). **Finland**: Kastrati (8), Vayrynen (12, 31, 59), Yaghoubi (40). **Half-time**: 0–4

FAROE ISLANDS 1 REPUBLIC OF IRELAND 4
Group 6: Toftir (349); Wednesday, August 14 2013
Republic of Ireland: McCarey (Wolves), Shaughnessy (Aberdeen), McGinty (Sheffield Utd), O'Connor (Blackburn), Duffy (Everton), Doherty (Wolves), Harriman (QPR) (Grealish, Aston Villa 90), Carruthers (Aston Villa), Murray (Watford) (Sutherland, QPR 90), Reilly (Birmingham), O'Brien (Millwall). **Booked**: O'Brien
Scorers – Faroe Islands: Sorensen (15). **Republic of Ireland**: Carruthers (24), Doherty (68, 89), O'Brien (90). **Half-time**: 1–1

ENGLAND 1 MOLDOVA 0
Group 1: Madejski Stadium, Reading (5,268); Thursday, September 5 2013
England: Butland (Stoke), Stones (Everton), Wisdom (Liverpool), M Keane (Manchester Utd), Shaw (Southampton), Chalobah (Chelsea), Ward-Prowse (Southampton) (Hughes, Derby 66), Zaha (Manchester Utd), Carroll (Tottenham), Redmond (Norwich) (Sammy Ameobi, Newcastle 75), Berahino (WBA) (Kane, Tottenham 86)
Scorer – England: Berahino (13). **Half-time**: 1–0

HOLLAND 4 SCOTLAND 0
Group 3: Nijmegen (5,700); Thursday, September 5 2013
Scotland: Archer (Tottenham), Jack (Aberdeen), McGhee (Hearts), Findlay (Celtic), Robertson (Aberdeen), Fyvie (Wigan) (Macleod, Rangers 77), McGeouch (Celtic), Holt (Hearts), Watt (Celtic) (May, St Johnstone 54), Armstrong (Dundee Utd), Fraser (Bournemouth) (Paterson (Hearts 77). **Booked**: Jack
Scorers – Holland: De Vilhena (52), Castaignos (69), Van der Hoorn (74), Drost (78). **Half-time**: 0–0

SAN MARINO 1 WALES 0
Group 1: Serravalle (221); Friday, September 6 2013
Wales: Ward (Liverpool), Freeman (Derby), Fox (Charlton), Evans (Wolves), Tancock (Swansea), Walsh (Crawley), Burns (Bristol City) (Bodin, Torquay 84), Huws (Manchester City) (Ogleby, Wrexham 66), Cassidy (Wolves) (Bradshaw, Shrewsbury 54), Lawrence (Manchester Utd), Isgrove (Southampton). **Booked**: Isgrove, Huws, Freeman, Burns
Scorers – San Marino: Biordi (21). **Half-time**: 1–0

FINLAND 1 ENGLAND 1
Group 1: Tampere (4,455); Monday, September 9 2013
England: Butland (Stoke), Stones (Everton), Wisdom (Liverpool), M Keane (Manchester Utd), Shaw (Southampton), Chalobah (Chelsea) (Kane, Tottenham 57), Ward-Prowse (Southampton), Carroll (Tottenham), Redmond (Norwich) (Sammy Ameobi, Newcastle 57), Zaha (Manchester Utd) (Dier, Sporting Lisbon 75), Berahino (WBA). **Booked**: Zaha, Berahino, Stones. **Sent off**: Wisdom (74)
Scorers – Finland: Yaghoubi (15). **England**: Berahino (67). **Half-time**: 1–0

BELGIUM 1 NORTHERN IRELAND 0
Group 9: Louvain (2,949); Monday, September 9 2013
Northern Ireland: Brennan (Kilmarnock), Donnelly (Swansea), Sharpe (Derby), Thompson (Watford), Sendles-White (QPR), Millar (Oldham) (Shields, Dagenham 46), Ball (Tottenham) (Reid, Exeter 81), Winchester (Oldham) (McElroy, Hull 63), Brobbel (Middlesbrough), Carson (Ipswich), Gray (Accrington). **Booked**: Carson, Ball, Sendles-White, Donnelly. **Sent off**: Donnelly (90)
Scorer – Belgium: Batshuayi (44). **Half-time**: 1-0

REPUBLIC OF IRELAND 0 GERMANY 4
Group 6: Showgrounds, Sligo (1,936); Monday, September 9 2013
Republic of Ireland: McCarey (Wolves), Harriman (QPR), Duffy (Everton), O'Connor (Blackburn), McGinty (Sheffield Utd), Doherty (Wolves), Carruthers (Aston Villa), Murray (Watford), Reilly (Birmingham) (Grealish, Aston Villa 78), Forde (Wolves) (Smith, Watford 46), O'Brien (Millwall) (Burke, Aston Villa 82). **Sent off**: Carruthers (61)
Scorers – Germany: Leitner (12), Volland (22, 24), Hofmann (83). **Half-time**: 0-3

MOLDOVA 0 WALES 0
Group 1: Tiraspol (523); Tuesday, September 10 2013
Wales: Roberts (Cheltenham), Hewitt (Ipswich), Fox (Charlton), Lucas (Swansea), Ray (Crewe), Walsh (Crawley), Burns (Bristol City) (Bodin, Torquay 73), Huws (Manchester City), Ogleby (Wrexham) (Bradshaw, Shrewsbury 79), Lawrence (Manchester Utd), Isgrove (Southampton). **Booked**: Huws, Ogleby, Walsh

SAN MARINO 0 ENGLAND 4
Group 1: Serravalle (245); Thursday, October 10 2013
England: Butland (Stoke), Stones (Everton), Dier (Sporting Lisbon), M Keane (Manchester Utd), Jenkinson (Arsenal), Carroll (Tottenham), Ward-Prowse (Southampton), Sterling (Liverpool) (Ings, Burnley 66), Morrison (West Ham) (Lingard, Manchester Utd 56), Ince (Blackpool) (Redmond, Norwich 72), Kane (Tottenham). **Booked**: Sterling
Scorers – England: Keane (5), Kane (45 pen, 66, 89). **Half-time**: 0-2

SCOTLAND 2 SLOVAKIA 1
Group 3: St Mirren Park, Paisley (2,014); Thursday, October 10 2013
Scotland: Archer (Tottenham), Jack (Aberdeen), McGhee (Hearts), Findlay (Celtic), C Robertson (Aberdeen), Fyvie (Wigan) (A Robertson, Dundee Utd 74), McGeouch (Celtic), Armstrong (Dundee Utd), McGregor (Celtic) (Paterson, Hearts 86), Macleod (Rangers) (Holt, Hearts 82), May (St Johnstone). **Booked**: Fyvie, McGhee, Paterson
Scorers – Scotland: Armstrong (30), May (35). **Slovakia**: Malec (68). **Half-time**: 2-0

WALES 2 LITHUANIA 0
Group 1: BookPeople Stadium, Bangor (403); Friday, October 11 2013
Wales: Roberts (Cheltenham), Freeman (Derby), Fox (Charlton), Lucas (Swansea), Ray (Crewe), Walsh (Crawley), Bodin (Torquay), Burns (Bristol City), Lawrence (Manchester Utd), Harrison (Bristol Rov) (Edwards, Swansea 79), Pritchard (Fulham). **Booked**: Harrison, Walsh, Lawrence
Scorer – Wales: Lawrence (23 pen, 41 pen). **Half-time**: 2-0

NORTHERN IRELAND 0 BELGIUM 1
Group 9: Mourneview Park, Lurgan (150); Friday, October 11, 2013
Northern Ireland: Brennan (Kilmarnock), McKeown (Kilmarnock), Sendles-White (QPR), McCullough (Doncaster), Sharpe (Derby) (Gorman, Leyton Orient 46), Gray (Accrington), Carson (York), Clucas (Bristol Rov), Winchester (Oldham), Tempest (Notts Co) (Millar, Oldham 54), Brobbel (Middlesbrough) (McCartan, Accrington 71). **Booked**: McCullough, Winchester, Carson, Sendles-White
Scorer – Belgium: Batshuayi (45). **Half-time**: 0-1

ROMANIA 0 REPUBLIC OF IRELAND 0
Group 6: Piatra Neamt (998); Friday, October 11 2013
Republic of Ireland: McCarey (Wolves), O'Connor (Blackburn), Williams (Bristol City), Duffy (Everton), McGinty (Sheffield Utd), Smith (Watford) (Sutherland, QPR 77), Doherty (Wolves), Murray (Watford), Reilly (Birmingham), Forde (Wolves), O'Brien (Millwall). **Booked**: Murray, Doherty, Smith

GEORGIA 2 SCOTLAND 1
Group 3: Tbilisi (1,934); Monday, October 14 2013
Scotland: Archer (Tottenham), Jack (Aberdeen), McGhee (Hearts), Findlay (Celtic), C Robertson (Aberdeen), Fyvie (Wigan) (Macleod, Rangers 72), McGeouch (Celtic) (A Robertson, Dundee Utd 72), Armstrong (Dundee Utd), Holt (Hearts) (Paterson, Hearts 60), McGregor (Celtic), May (St Johnstone). **Booked**: Fyvie, Findlay
Scorers – Georgia: Kazaishvili (39), Jigauri (70). **Scotland**: Macleod (81). **Half-time**: 1-0

ENGLAND 5 LITHUANIA 0
Group 1: Portman Road, Ipswich (17,069); Tuesday, October 15 2013
England: Butland (Stoke), Stones (Everton), Chalobah (Chelsea), M Keane (Manchester Utd), Robinson (Liverpool), Ward-Prowse (Southampton), Carroll (Tottenham) (Jenkinson, Arsenal 15), Zaha (Manchester Utd), Morrison (West Ham), Ince (Blackpool) (Redmond, Norwich 77), Berahino (WBA) (Powell, Manchester Utd 77).
Scorers – England: Morrison (2, 71), Ward-Prowse (27), Berahino (63, 76 pen). **Half-time**: 2-0

WALES 4 SAN MARINO 0
Group 1: BookPeople Stadium, Bangor (278); Tuesday, October 15 2013
Wales: Roberts (Cheltenham), Hewitt (Ipswich), Ray (Crewe), Tancock (Swansea), Fox (Charlton), Bodin (Torquay), O'Sullivan (Cardiff) (Ogleby, Wrexham 79), Lucas (Swansea), Lawrence (Manchester Utd), Harrison (Bristol Rov) (Edwards, Swansea 73), Burns (Bristol City) (Evans, Wolves 79). **Booked**: Hewitt, Harrison
Scorers – Wales: Harrison (44), Lucas (50), Burns (64), Bodin (84). **Half-time**: 1-0

SERBIA 3 NORTHERN IRELAND 1
Group 9: Gornji Milanovac; Tuesday, October 15 2013
(played behind closed doors, previous crowd trouble)
Northern Ireland: Brennan (Kilmarnock), Donnelly (Fulham), McKeown (Kilmarnock), McCullough (Doncaster), Sharpe (Derby), Morgan (Nottm Forest), Brobbel (Middlesbrough) (Conlan, Burnley 84), Winchester (Oldham) (Tempest, Notts Co 69), Gray (Accrington), McCartan (Accrington) (Gorman, Leyton Orient 62), Millar (Oldham). **Booked**: Morgan, McCartan
Scorers – Serbia: Morgan (63 og), Milunovic (64), Vita (74). **Northern Ireland**: Gray (54).
Half-time: 0-0

REPUBLIC OF IRELAND 0 ROMANIA 1
Group 6: Showgrounds, Sligo (370); Tuesday, October 15 2013
Republic of Ireland: McCarey (Wolves), O'Connor (Blackburn), Duffy (Everton), Williams (Bristol City), McGinty (Sheffield Utd), Carruthers (Aston Villa), Murray (Watford), Sutherland (QPR) (Hayhurst, Preston 70), Smith (Watford) (Reilly, Birmingham 79), O'Brien (Millwall) (Burke, Aston Villa 68), Forde (Wolves). **Booked**: Carruthers, Smith, Williams, McCarey
Scorer – Romania: Madalin (54). **Half-time**: 0-0

ENGLAND 3 FINLAND 0
Group 1: stadium mk, Milton Keynes (19,807); Thursday, November 14 2013
England: Butland (Stoke), Jenkinson (Arsenal), Stones (Everton), M Keane (Manchester Utd), Shaw (Southampton), Chalobah (Chelsea) (Hughes, Derby 64), Ward-Prowse (Southampton), Morrison (West Ham) (Lingard, Manchester Utd 83), Sterling (Liverpool) (Ince, Blackpool 65), Berahino (WBA), Zaha (Manchester Utd). **Booked**: Berahino
Scorers – England: Keane (21), Berahino (37, 90). **Half-time**: 2-0

SCOTLAND 1 GEORGIA 1
Group 3: St Mirren Park, Paisley (1,737): Thursday, November 14 2013
Scotland: Archer (Tottenham), Jack (Aberdeen), McGhee (Hearts), Findlay (Celtic), Robertson (Dundee Utd), Macleod (Rangers), Armstrong (Dundee Utd), Gauld (Dundee Utd), McGeouch (Celtic) (McLean, St Mirren 56), May (St Johnstone), McGregor (Celtic) (Paterson, Hearts 68). **Booked:** Jack
Scorers – Scotland: Paterson (84). **Georgia:** Chanturia (35). **Half-time:** 0-1

ITALY 3 NORTHERN IRELAND 0
Group 9: Reggio Emilia (14,026): Thursday, November 14 2013
Northern Ireland: Brennan (Kilmarnock), Thompson (Watford), McCullough (Doncaster), Sendles-White (QPR), McKeown (Kilmarnock), Donnelly (Fulham), Morgan (Nottm Forest) (Tempest, Notts Co 67) (Brobbel, Middlesbrough 72), Winchester (Oldham), Carson (York), Millar (Oldham), Gray (Accrington) (Lavery, Sheffield Wed 79)
Scorers – Italy: Viviani (26), Rozzi (86), Belotti (88). **Half-time:** 1-0

REPUBLIC OF IRELAND 5 FAROE ISLANDS 2
Group 6: Showgrounds, Sligo (320); Friday, November 15 2013
Republic of Ireland: McDermott (Sandnes), O'Connor (Blackburn), Duffy (Everton), Williams (Bristol City), Dunne, Blackpool 63), McGinty (Sheffield Utd), Carruthers (Aston Villa), Reilly (Birmingham), Murray (Watford) (O'Sullivan, Blackburn 74), Forde (Wolves), O'Brien (Millwall) (Hayhurst, Preston 82), Grealish (Aston Villa)
Scorers – Republic of Ireland: Carruthers (17), O'Brien (20, 42), Grealish (25), Forde (39). **Faroe Islands:** Zachariasen (26, 37). **Half-time:** 5-2

ENGLAND 9 SAN MARINO 0
Group 1: Greenhous Meadow Stadium, Shrewsbury (9,264); Tuesday, November 19 2013
England: Butland (Stoke) (Bond, Watford 46), Jenkinson (Arsenal), Stones (Everton) (Dier, Sporting Lisbon 62), M Keane (Manchester Utd), Robinson (Liverpool), Ward-Prowse (Southampton), Hughes (Derby), Ince (Blackpool) (Bamford, Chelsea 64), Lingard (Manchester Utd), Sterling (Liverpool), Ings (Burnley)
Scorers: Keane (12), Sterling (14, 59), Ings (18, 50), Ward-Prowse (24), Ince (40), Jenkinson (61), Hughes (77). **Half-time:** 5-0
(Record England Under-21 win)

NORTHERN IRELAND 1 CYPRUS 0
Group 9: Mourneview Park, Lurgan (300); Tuesday, November 19 2013
Northern Ireland: Brennan (Kilmarnock), Donnelly (Fulham), McCullough (Doncaster), Sendles-White (QPR), Conlan (Burnley), Tempest (Notts Co), Winchester (Oldham), Brobbel (Middlesbrough), Lavery (Sheffield Wed) (McCartan, Accrington 75), Carson (York) (McGeehan, Norwich 66), Millar (Oldham) (Gorman, Leyton Orient 66). **Booked:** Sendles-White, Brobbel, McGeehan
Scorer – Northern Ireland: Gorman (85). **Half-time:** 0-0

MONTENEGRO 0 REPUBLIC OF IRELAND 0
Group 6: Podgorica (1,000); Tuesday, November 19 2013
Republic of Ireland: McDermott (Sandnes), Harriman (QPR), Duffy (Everton), Williams (Bristol City), McGinty (Sheffield Utd), Carruthers (Aston Villa), Reilly (Birmingham), Murray (Watford), Forde (Wolves), O'Brien (Millwall), Grealish (Aston Villa). **Booked:** Williams

ENGLAND 1 WALES 0
Group 1: iPro Stadium, Derby (13,438); Wednesday, March 5 2014
England: Butland (Stoke), Jenkinson (Arsenal), Stones (Everton), Chalobah (Chelsea) (Moore, Leicester 74), Robinson (Liverpool), Carroll (Tottenham), Ward-Prowse (Southampton), Redmond (Norwich), Morrison (West Ham) (Hughes, Derby 71), Ince (Blackpool) Berahino (WBA) (Ings, Burnley 67)
Wales: Roberts (Cheltenham), Freeman (Derby), Walsh (Crawley), Tancock (Swansea), John (Cardiff), Pritchard (Fulham) (Williams, Fulham 83), Lucas (Swansea), Lawrence

(Manchester Utd), Isgrove (Southampton), Burns (Bristol City) (Ogleby, Wrexham 78),
O'Sullivan (Cardiff) (Evans, Wolves 66).
Scorer – England: Redmond (56). **Half-time:** 0-0

NORTHERN IRELAND 0 ITALY 2
Group 9: Mourneview Park, Lurgan (500); Wednesday, March 5 2014
Northern Ireland: Brennan (Kilmarnock), Conlan (Burnley), Donnelly (Fulham), Sendles-
White (QPR), McCullough (Doncaster), Clucas (Bristol Rov) (McNair, Manchester Utd, 77),
Winchester (Oldham), McGeehan (Norwich) (Nolan, Crewe 62), Brobbel (Middlesbrough),
Millar (Oldham) (Gray, Accrington 66), Lavery (Sheffield Wed). **Booked:** Brennan, Clucas
Scorers – Italy: Rugani (59), Trotta (89). **Half-time:** 0-0

REPUBLIC OF IRELAND 1 MONTENEGRO 2
Group 6: Tallaght Stadium, Dublin (1,302); Wednesday, March 5 2014
Republic of Ireland: McDermott (Sandnes), Doherty (Wolves), Egan (Sunderland), Duffy
(Everton), McGinty (Sheffield Utd), Hendrick (Derby), Smith (Watford), Grealish (Aston Villa),
Murray (Watford) (McAlinden, Wolves 78), Forde (Wolves) (McEvoy, Tottenham) 82), O'Brien
(Millwall) (Drennan, Aston Villa 78). **Booked:** McGinty, Smith. **Sent off:** McGinty (90)
Scorers – Republic of Ireland: Doherty (11). **Montenegro:** Djordjevic (75), Mugosa (77).
Half-time: 1-0

WALES 1 ENGLAND 3
Group 1: Liberty Stadium, Swansea (5,000); Monday, May 19 2014
Wales: Roberts (Cheltenham), Freeman (Derby) (Alfei, Swansea 46), Ray (Crewe), Walsh
(Crawley), John (Cardiff), Lucas (Swansea), Pritchard (Fulham) (O'Sullivan, Cardiff 42),
Edwards (Swansea), Evans (Wolves), Burns (Bristol City), Isgrove (Southampton) (Williams,
Fulham 39)
England: Butland (Stoke), Jenkinson (Arsenal), M Keane (Manchester Utd), Moore
(Leicester), Garbutt (Everton), Ince (Blackpool) (Kane, Tottenham 79) (Forster-Caskey,
Brighton 85), Chalobah (Chelsea), Ward-Prowse (Southampton), Redmond (Norwich),
Lingard (Manchester Utd), Ings (Burnley) (Berahino, WBA 56). **Booked:** Ward-Prowse,
Chalobah
Scorers – England: Redmond (18, 38, 90). **Wales:** Edwards (20). **Half-time:** 1-2

SCOTLAND 1 HOLLAND 6
Group 3: St Mirren Park, Paisley (3,002); Wednesday, May 28 2104
Scotland: Archer (Tottenham), Paterson (Hearts), McGhee (Hearts), Findlay (Celtic),
McHattie (Hearts), McGinn (St Mirren) (Slater, Kilmarnock 87), McLean (St Mirren),
Armstrong (Dundee Utd), Fraser (Bournemouth) (Scougall, Sheffield Utd 75), May (St
Johnstone), McGregor (Celtic) (McKenzie, Kilmarnock 60). **Booked:** McHattie
Scorers – Scotland: May (85). **Holland:** Promes (26, 40, 42), Rekik (50), Ziyech (76, 79).
Half-time: 0-3

QUALIFYING TABLES
(Group winners and four best runners-up to two-leg play-offs to determine seven finalists.
Czech Republic qualify as hosts)

GROUP 1

	P	W	D	L	F	A	Pts
England	8	7	1	0	27	2	22
Moldova	8	4	1	3	9	3	13
Finland	8	3	3	2	10	8	12
Wales	8	3	1	4	9	10	10
Lithuania	7	2	1	4	5	14	7
San Marino	9	1	1	7	2	25	4

GROUP 2

	P	W	D	L	F	A	Pts
Denmark	8	6	2	0	26	6	20
Russia	8	6	1	1	15	8	19
Slovenia	8	3	2	3	17	10	11
Estonia	8	2	2	4	6	14	8
Bulgaria	8	2	2	4	15	17	8
Andorra	8	0	1	7	1	25	1

GROUP 3

	P	W	D	L	F	A	Pts
Holland	5	4	1	0	19	3	13
Slovakia	6	4	1	1	17	6	13
Georgia	7	2	1	4	7	15	7
Scotland	6	2	1	3	8	14	7
Luxembourg	6	1	0	5	4	17	3

GROUP 4

	P	W	D	L	F	A	Pts
Spain	6	6	0	0	22	5	18
Austria	6	4	0	2	12	11	12
Albania	8	2	0	6	6	7	6
Bosnia-Herz	6	2	0	4	9	16	6
Hungary	6	2	0	4	8	11	6

GROUP 5

	P	W	D	L	F	A	Pts
Croatia	7	5	1	1	17	4	16
Switzerland	6	4	0	2	16	5	12
Ukraine	4	2	1	1	8	5	7
Latvia	5	2	0	3	8	10	6
Liechtenstein	6	0	0	6	1	26	0

GROUP 6

	P	W	D	L	F	A	Pts
Germany	6	4	2	0	15	5	14
Montenegro	6	3	2	1	9	6	11
Romania	6	2	3	1	10	8	9
Rep of Ireland	7	2	2	3	10	10	8
Faroe Is	7	0	1	6	8	23	1

GROUP 7

	P	W	D	L	F	A	Pts
Poland	7	5	0	2	16	7	15
Greece	6	4	0	2	17	6	12
Sweden	6	3	1	2	13	11	10
Turkey	6	3	1	2	10	7	10
Malta	7	0	0	7	2	27	0

GROUP 8

	P	W	D	L	F	A	Pts
Portugal	6	6	0	0	17	4	18
Israel	5	3	0	2	17	11	9
Norway	7	3	0	4	10	17	9
Azerbaijan	6	1	1	4	5	12	4
Macedonia	6	1	1	4	3	8	4

GROUP 9

	P	W	D	L	F	A	Pts
Serbia	6	4	1	1	12	6	13
Belgium	7	4	1	2	9	7	13
Italy	6	4	0	2	9	4	12
Cyprus	6	2	0	4	6	8	6
N Ireland	7	1	0	6	2	13	3

GROUP 10

	P	W	D	L	F	A	Pts
France	6	6	0	0	22	5	18
Iceland	6	4	0	2	15	10	12
Kazakhstan	7	3	0	4	7	13	9
Armenia	6	2	0	4	5	14	6
Belarus	7	1	0	6	5	12	3

TOULON TOURNAMENT

ENGLAND 3 QATAR 0
Toulon; Thursday, May 22 2014

England: Bond (Watford), Browning (Everton), Moore (Leicester), Gibson (Middlesbrough), Garbutt (Everton) (Smith, Liverpool 74), Ward-Prowse (Southampton) (Dier, Sporting Lisbon 69), McEachran (Chelsea) (Cousins, Charlton 59), March (Brighton), Forster-Caskey (Brighton), Obita (Reading), Berahino (WBA) (Woodrow, Fulham 59)
Scorers – England: Obita (30), Forster-Caskey (54), Cousins (90). **Half-time**: 1-0

ENGLAND 1 BRAZIL 2
St Raphael; Monday, May 26 2014

England: Butland (Stoke), Browning (Everton), M Keane (Manchester Utd), Moore (Leicester), Garbutt (Everton) (Smith, Liverpool 61), Ward-Prowse (Southampton), Chalobah (Chelsea), Redmond (Norwich), Forster-Caskey (Brighton) (Woodrow, Fulham 51), Cousins (Charlton) (March, Brighton 80), Berahino (WBA). **Booked**: Ward-Prowse
Scorers – England: Ward-Prowse (72). **Brazil**: Alisson (8), Silva (47). **Half-time**: 0-1

ENGLAND 1 SOUTH KOREA 1
Aubagne; Wednesday, May 28 2014

England: Bond (Watford), Dier (Sporting Lisbon) (Browning, Everton 66), M Keane (Manchester Utd), Gibson (Middlesbrough), Garbutt (Everton), Ward-Prowse (Southampton), Chalobah (Chelsea), Redmond (Norwich), Forster-Caskey (Brighton) (W Keane, Manchester Utd 64), Smith (Liverpool) (March, Brighton 41), Woodrow (Fulham). **Booked**: Bond
Scorers – England: Woodrow (2). **South Korea**: Chang Min Lee (54). **Half-time**: 1-0

ENGLAND 1 COLOMBIA 1
Toulon; Friday, May 30 2014

England: Butland (Stoke), Dier (Sporting Lisbon) (M Keane, Manchester Utd 32), Moore (Leicester), Gibson (Middlesbrough), Browning (Everton), McEachran (Chelsea) (Forster-Caskey, Brighton 19), Cousins (Charlton), March (Brighton), W Keane (Manchester Utd) (Chalobah, Chelsea 74), Obita (Reading), Woodrow (Fulham) (Redmond, Norwich 67).
Booked: Dier, March
Scorers – England: Woodrow (15). **Colombia**: Rodriguez (69). **Half-time**: 1-0

ENGLAND 0 PORTUGAL 1 (Play-off for third place)
Avignon; Sunday, June 1 2014

England: Butland (Stoke), Browning (Everton), Moore (Leicester), Gibson (Middlesbrough), Garbutt (Everton), Chalobah (Chelsea). Ward-Prowse (Southampton), Redmond (Norwich), Forster-Caskey (Brighton) (W Keane, Manchester Utd 65), Berahino (WBA), Woodrow (Fulham)
Scorer – Portugal: Horta (56). **Half-time**: 0-0

Final
Brazil 5 France 2

INTERNATIONAL FRIENDLIES

ENGLAND 6 SCOTLAND 0
Bramall Lane, Sheffield (26,942); Tuesday, August 13 2013

England: Butland (Stoke), Stones (Everton), Wisdom (Liverpool), M Keane (Manchester Utd), Robinson (Liverpool), Shelvey (Swansea) (Carroll, Tottenham 58), Hughes (Derby) (Dier, Sporting Lisbon 73), Chalobah (Chelsea) (Barkley, Everton 44), Redmond (Norwich) (Lingard (Manchester Utd 65), Wickham (Sunderland) (Kane, Tottenham 57), Sterling (Liverpool) (Sammy Ameobi, Newcastle, 65)
Scotland: Archer (Tottenham), Jack (Aberdeen) (Duffie, Falkirk 46), McKay (Hearts), Robertson (Aberdeen), McHattie (Hearts), Fyvie (Wigan), McGeouch (Celtic), Bannigan (Partick) (Macleod, Rangers 79), Feruz (Chelsea) (May, St Johnstone 62), Armstrong (Dundee Utd) (Smith, Hearts 62), Watt (Celtic) (Holt, Hearts 73). **Booked**: Fyvie
Scorers – England: Redmond (3), Sterling (38), Wickham (50), Barkley (55), Shelvey (56), Carroll (61). **Half-time**: 2-0

NORTHERN IRELAND 1 DENMARK 4
Stangmore Park, Dungannon (350); Wednesday, August 14 2013

Northern Ireland: Brennan (Kilmarnock) (Glendinning, Linfield 46), Sendles-White (QPR), McKeown (Kilmarnock) (Sharpe, Derby 65), Thompson (Watford), McCullough (Doncaster), Tempest (Notts Co) (Ball, Stevenage 75), Millar (Oldham) (Morgan, Nottm Forest 46), Carson (Ipswich), Brobbel (Middlesbrough) (Gorman, Leyton Orient 75), Gray (Accrington) (Lavery, Sheffield Wed 46), Donnelly (Swansea)
Scorers – Northern Ireland: Thompson (24). **Denmark**: Toutouh (17), Brock-Madsen (57, 62), Jensen (64). **Half-time**: 1-1

SCOTLAND 2 HUNGARY 2
Tannadice Park, Dundee (4,537); Wednesday, March 5 2014

Scotland: Archer (Tottenham) (Kettings, Blackpool 46), M Fraser (Celtic), Findlay (Celtic), Kelly (St Mirren) (Chalmers, Celtic 46), McGhee (Hearts), Armstrong (Dundee Utd) (Stanton, Hibernian 46), Slater (Kilmarnock) (Grimmer (Fulham, 57), McLean (St Mirren) (McGinn, St Mirren 58), McGregor (Celtic) Paterson (Hearts) (Herron, Celtic, 76), R Fraser (Bournemouth) (Handling, Hibernian 76)
Scorers – Scotland: McGregor (25), R Fraser (38). **Hungary**: Rado (68 pen, 87).
Half-time: 2-0

TRANSFER TRAIL

Player	From	To	Date	£
Gareth Bale	Tottenham	Real Madrid	8/13	85,300,000
Cristiano Ronaldo	Manchester Utd	Real Madrid	7/09	80,000,000
Luis Suarez	Liverpool	Barcelona	7/14	75,000,000
Fernando Torres	Liverpool	Chelsea	1/11	50,000,000
Mesut Ozil	Real Madrid	Arsenal	9/13	42,400,000
David Luiz	Chelsea	Paris SG	6/14	40,000,000
Sergio Aguero	Atletico Madrid	Manchester City	7/11	38,500,000
Juan Mata	Chelsea	Manchester Utd	1/14	37,100,000
Andy Carroll	Newcastle	Liverpool	1/11	35,000,000
Cesc Fabregas	Arsenal	Barcelona	8/11	35,000,000
Alexis Sanchez	Barcelona	Arsenal	7/14	35,000,000
Robinho	Real Madrid	Manchester City	9/08	32,500,000
Eden Hazard	Lille	Chelsea	6/12	32,000,000
Diego Costa	Atletico Madrid	Chelsea	7/14	32,000,000
Dimitar Berbatov	Tottenham	Manchester Utd	9/08	30,750,000
Andriy Shevchenko	AC Milan	Chelsea	5/06	30,800,000
Xabi Alonso	Liverpool	Real Madrid	8/09	30,000,000
Fernandinho	Shakhtar Donetsk	Manchester City	6/13	30,000,000
Willian	Anzhi Makhachkala	Chelsea	8/13	30,000,000
Luke Shaw	Southampton	Manchester Utd	6/14	30,000,000
Rio Ferdinand	Leeds	Manchester Utd	7/02	29,100,000
Ander Herrara	Athletic Bilbao	Manchester Utd	6/14	28,800,000
Juan Sebastian Veron	Lazio	Manchester Utd	7/01	28,100,000
Yaya Toure	Barcelona	Manchester City	7/10	28,000,000
Marouane Fellaini	Everton	Manchester Utd	9/13	27,500,000
Wayne Rooney	Everton	Manchester Utd	8/04	27,000,000
Edin Dzeko	Wolfsburg	Manchester City	1/11	27,000,000
Luka Modric	Tottenham	Real Madrid	8/12	27,000,000
Cesc Fabregas	Barcelona	Chelsea	6/14	27,000,000
Roberto Soldado	Valencia	Tottenham	8/13	26,000,000
Marc Overmars	Arsenal	Barcelona	7/00	25,000,000
Carlos Tevez	Manchester Utd	Manchester City	7/09	25,000,000
Emmanuel Adebayor	Arsenal	Manchester City	7/09	25,000,000
Samir Nasri	Arsenal	Manchester City	8/11	25,000,000
Oscar	Internacional	Chelsea	7/12	25,000,000
Adam Lallana	Southampton	Liverpool	7/14	25,000,000
Arjen Robben	Chelsea	Real Madrid	8/07	24,500,000
Michael Essien	Lyon	Chelsea	8/05	24,400,000
David Silva	Valencia	Manchester City	7/10	24,000,000
James Milner	Aston Villa	Manchester City	8/10	24,000,000
Mario Balotelli	Inter Milan	Manchester City	8/10	24,000,000
Darren Bent	Sunderland	Aston Villa	1/11	24,000,000
Robin van Persie	Arsenal	Manchester Utd	8/12	24,000,000
Juan Mata	Valencia	Chelsea	8/11	23,500,000
David Beckham	Manchester Utd	Real Madrid	7/03	23,300,000
Didier Drogba	Marseille	Chelsea	7/04	23,200,000
Luis Suarez	Ajax	Liverpool	1/11	22,700,000
Nicolas Anelka	Arsenal	Real Madrid	8/99	22,300,000
Fernando Torres	Atletico Madrid	Liverpool	7/07	22,000,000
Joleon Lescott	Everton	Manchester City	8/09	22,000,000
Stevan Jovetic	Fiorentina	Manchester City	7/13	22,000,000

David Luiz	Benfica	Chelsea	1/11	21,300,000
Shaun Wright-Phillips	Manchester City	Chelsea	7/05	21,000,000
Nemanja Matic	Benfica	Chelsea	01/14	21,000,000
Lassana Diarra	Portsmouth	Real Madrid	12/08	20,000,000
Alberto Aquilani	Roma	Liverpool	8/09	20,000,000
Stewart Downing	Aston Villa	Liverpool	7/11	20,000,000
Lazar Markovic	Benfica	Liverpool	7/14	20,000,000
Ricardo Carvalho	Porto	Chelsea	7/04	19,850,000
Mario Balotelli	Manchester City	AC Milan	1/13	19,500,000
Ruud van Nistelrooy	PSV Eindhoven	Manchester Utd	4/01	19,000,000
Robbie Keane	Tottenham	Liverpool	7/08	19,000,000
Michael Carrick	Tottenham	Manchester Utd	8/06	18,600,000
Javier Mascherano	Media Sports	Liverpool	2/08	18,600,000
Rio Ferdinand	West Ham	Leeds	11/00	18,000,000
Anderson	Porto	Manchester Utd	7/07	18,000,000
Jo	CSKA Moscow	Manchester City	6/08	18,000,000
Yuri Zhirkov	CSKA Moscow	Chelsea	7/09	18,000,000
Ramires	Benfica	Chelsea	8/10	18,000,000
Romelu Lukaku	Anderlecht	Chelsea	8/11	18,000,000
Andre Schurrle	Bayer Leverkusen	Chelsea	6/13	18,000,000
Mamadou Sakho	Paris SG	Liverpool	9/13	18,000,000
David De Gea	Atletico Madrid	Manchester Utd	6/11	17,800,000
Roque Santa Cruz	Blackburn	Manchester City	6/09	17,500,000
Jose Reyes	Sevilla	Arsenal	1/04	17,400,000
Javier Mascherano	Liverpool	Barcelona	8/10	17,250,000
Damien Duff	Blackburn	Chelsea	7/03	17,000,000
Owen Hargreaves	Bayern Munich	Manchester Utd	6/07	17,000,000
Glen Johnson	Portsmouth	Liverpool	6/09	17,000,000
Paulinho	Corinthians	Tottenham	7/13	17,000,000
Andrey Arshavin	Zenit St Petersburg	Arsenal	2/09	16,900,000
Hernan Crespo	Inter Milan	Chelsea	8/03	16,800,000
Claude Makelele	Real Madrid	Chelsea	9/03	16,600,000
Luka Modric	Dinamo Zagreb	Tottenham	6/08	16,600,000
Darren Bent	Charlton	Tottenham	6/07	16,500,000
Phil Jones	Blackburn	Manchester Utd	6/11	16,500,000
Santi Cazorla	Malaga	Arsenal	8/12	16,500,000
Jose Bosingwa	Porto	Chelsea	6/08	16,200,000
Michael Owen	Real Madrid	Newcastle	8/05	16,000,000
Thierry Henry	Arsenal	Barcelona	6/07	16,000,000
Aleksandar Kolarov	Lazio	Manchester City	7/10	16,000,000
Robinho	Manchester City	AC Milan	8/10	16,000,000
Jordan Henderson	Sunderland	Liverpool	6/11	16,000,000
Ashley Young	Aston Villa	Manchester Utd	6/11	16,000,000
Adrian Mutu	Parma	Chelsea	8/03	15,800,000
Samir Nasri	Marseille	Arsenal	7/08	15,800,000
Javi Garcia	Benfica	Manchester City	8/12	15,800,000
Jermain Defoe	Portsmouth	Tottenham	1/09	15,750,000
Antonio Valencia	Wigan	Manchester Utd	6/09	15,250,000

BRITISH RECORD TRANSFERS FROM FIRST £1,000 DEAL

Player	From	To	Date	£
Alf Common	Sunderland	Middlesbrough	2/1905	1,000
Syd Puddefoot	West Ham	Falkirk	2/22	5,000
Warney Cresswell	South Shields	Sunderland	3/22	5,500

Player	From	To	Date	£
Bob Kelly	Burnley	Sunderland	12/25	6,500
David Jack	Bolton	Arsenal	10/28	10,890
Bryn Jones	Wolves	Arsenal	8/38	14,500
Billy Steel	Morton	Derby	9/47	15,000
Tommy Lawton	Chelsea	Notts Co	11/47	20,000
Len Shackleton	Newcastle	Sunderland	2/48	20,500
Johnny Morris	Manchester Utd	Derby	2/49	24,000
Eddie Quigley	Sheffield Wed	Preston	12/49	26,500
Trevor Ford	Aston Villa	Sunderland	10/50	30,000
Jackie Sewell	Notts Co	Sheffield Wed	3/51	34,500
Eddie Firmani	Charlton	Sampdoria	7/55	35,000
John Charles	Leeds	Juventus	4/57	65,000
Denis Law	Manchester City	Torino	6/61	100,000
Denis Law	Torino	Manchester Utd	7/62	115,000
Allan Clarke	Fulham	Leicester	6/68	150,000
Allan Clarke	Leicester	Leeds	6/69	165,000
Martin Peters	West Ham	Tottenham	3/70	200,000
Alan Ball	Everton	Arsenal	12/71	220,000
David Nish	Leicester	Derby	8/72	250,000
Bob Latchford	Birmingham	Everton	2/74	350,000
Graeme Souness	Middlesbrough	Liverpool	1/78	352,000
Kevin Keegan	Liverpool	Hamburg	6/77	500,000
David Mills	Middlesbrough	WBA	1/79	516,000
Trevor Francis	Birmingham	Nottm Forest	2/79	1,180,000
Steve Daley	Wolves	Manchester City	9/79	1,450,000
Andy Gray	Aston Villa	Wolves	9/79	1,469,000
Bryan Robson	WBA	Manchester Utd	10/81	1,500,000
Ray Wilkins	Manchester Utd	AC Milan	5/84	1,500,000
Mark Hughes	Manchester Utd	Barcelona	5/86	2,300,000
Ian Rush	Liverpool	Juventus	6/87	3,200,000
Chris Waddle	Tottenham	Marseille	7/89	4,250,000
David Platt	Aston Villa	Bari	7/91	5,500,000
Paul Gascoigne	Tottenham	Lazio	6/92	5,500,000
Andy Cole	Newcastle	Manchester Utd	1/95	7,000,000
Dennis Bergkamp	Inter Milan	Arsenal	6/95	7,500,000
Stan Collymore	Nottm Forest	Liverpool	6/95	8,500,000
Alan Shearer	Blackburn	Newcastle	7/96	15,000,000
Nicolas Anelka	Arsenal	Real Madrid	8/99	22,500,000
Juan Sebastian Veron	Lazio	Manchester Utd	7/01	28,100,000
Rio Ferdinand	Leeds	Manchester Utd	7/02	29,100,000
Andriy Shevchenko	AC Milan	Chelsea	5/06	30,800,000
Robinho	Real Madrid	Manchester City	9/08	32,500,000
Cristiano Ronaldo	Manchester Utd	Real Madrid	7/09	80,000,000
Gareth Bale	Tottenham	Real Madrid	9/13	85,300,000

- World's first £1m transfer: GuiseppeSavoldi, Bologna to Napoli, July 1975

TOP FOREIGN SIGNINGS

Player	From	To	Date	£
Zlatan Ibrahimovic	Inter Milan	Barcelona	7/09	60.300,000
Kaka	AC Milan	Real Madrid	06/08	56,000,000
Edinson Cavani	Napoli	Paris SG	7/13	53,000,000
Radamel Falcao	Atletico Madrid	Monaco	6/13	51,000,000
Neymar	Santos	Barcelona	6/13	48,600,000
Zinedine Zidane	Juventus	Real Madrid	7/01	47,200,000

James Rodriguez	Porto	Monaco	5/13	38,500,000
Luis Figo	Barcelona	Real Madrid	7/00	37,200,000
Javier Pastore	Palermo	Paris SG	8/11	36,600,000
Karim Benzema	Lyon	Real Madrid	7/09	35,800,000
Hernan Crespo	Parma	Lazio	7/00	35,000,000
Radamel Falcao	Porto	Atletico Madrid	8/11	34,700,000
Gonzalo Higuain	Real Madrid	Napoli	7/13	34,500,000
David Villa	Valencia	Barcelona	5/10	34,000,000
Thiago Silva	AC Milan	Paris SG	7/12	34,000,000
Lucas Moura	Sao Paulo	Paris SG	1/13	34,000,000
Asier Illarramendi	Real Sociedad	Real Madrid	7/13	34,000,000
Ronaldo	Inter Milan	Real Madrid	8/02	33,000,000
Gianluigi Buffon	Parma	Juventus	7/01	32,600,000
Axel Witsel	Benfica	Zenit St Petersburg	8/12	32,500,000
Hulk	Porto	Zenit St Petersburg	8/12	32,000,000
Javi Martinez	Athletic Bilbao	Bayern Munich	8/12	31,600,000
Mario Gotze	Borussia Dortmund	Bayern Munich	6/13	31,500,000
Christian Vieri	Lazio	Inter Milan	6/99	31,000,000
Alessandro Nesta	Lazio	AC Milan	8/02	30,200,000
Willian	Shakhtar Donetsk	Anzhi Makhachkala	1/13	30,000,000

WORLD'S MOST EXPENSIVE TEENAGER
£30m: Luke Shaw, 18, Southampton to Manchester Utd, June 2014

WORLD RECORD FOR 16-YEAR-OLD
£12m: Theo Walcott, Southampton to Arsenal, Jan 2006

RECORD FEE BETWEEN SCOTTISH CLUBS
£4.4m: Scott Brown, Hibernian to Celtic, May 2007

RECORD NON-LEAGUE FEE
£1m: Jamie Vardy, Fleetwood to Leicester, May 2012

RECORD FEE BETWEEN NON-LEAGUE CLUBS
£275,000: Richard Brodie, York to Crawley, Aug 2010

MILESTONES OF SOCCER

1848: First code of rules compiled at Cambridge University.
1857: Sheffield FC, world's oldest football club, formed.
1862: Notts Co (oldest League club) formed.
1863: Football Association founded – their first rules of game agreed.
1871: FA Cup introduced.
1872: First official International: Scotland 0 England 0. Corner-kick introduced.
1873: Scottish FA formed; Scottish Cup introduced.
1874: Shinguards introduced.
1875: Crossbar introduced (replacing tape).
1876: FA of Wales formed.
1877: Welsh Cup introduced.
1878: Referee's whistle first used.
1880: Irish FA founded; Irish Cup introduced.
1883: Two-handed throw-in introduced.
1885: Record first-class score (Arbroath 36 Bon Accord 0 – Scottish Cup). Professionalism legalised.
1886: International Board formed.

1887: Record FA Cup score (Preston 26 Hyde 0).

1888: Football League founded by William McGregor. First matches on Sept 8.

1889 Preston win Cup and League (first club to complete Double).

1890: Scottish League and Irish League formed.

1891: Goal-nets introduced. Penalty-kick introduced.

1892: Inter-League games began. Football League Second Division formed.

1893: FA Amateur Cup launched.

1894: Southern League formed.

1895: FA Cup stolen from Birmingham shop window – never recovered.

1897: First Players' Union formed. Aston Villa win Cup and League.

1898: Promotion and relegation introduced.

1901: Maximum wage rule in force (£4 a week). Tottenham first professional club to take FA Cup south. First six-figure attendance (110,802) at FA Cup Final.

1902: Ibrox Park disaster (25 killed). Welsh League formed.

1904: FIFA founded (7 member countries).

1905: First £1,000 transfer (Alf Common, Sunderland to Middlesbrough).

1907: Players' Union revived.

1908: Transfer fee limit (£350) fixed in January and withdrawn in April.

1911: New FA Cup trophy – in use to 1991. Transfer deadline introduced.

1914: King George V first reigning monarch to attend FA Cup Final.

1916: Entertainment Tax introduced.

1919: League extended to 44 clubs.

1920: Third Division (South) formed.

1921: Third Division (North) formed.

1922: Scottish League (Div II) introduced.

1923: Beginning of football pools. First Wembley Cup Final.

1924: First International at Wembley (England 1 Scotland 1). Rule change allows goals to be scored direct from corner-kicks.

1925: New offside law.

1926: Huddersfield complete first League Championship hat-trick.

1927: First League match broadcast (radio): Arsenal v Sheffield United. First radio broadcast of Cup Final (winners Cardiff City). Charles Clegg, president of FA, becomes first knight of football.

1928: First £10,000 transfer – David Jack (Bolton to Arsenal). WR ('Dixie') Dean (Everton) creates League record – 60 goals in season. Britain withdraws from FIFA

1930: Uruguay first winners of World Cup.

1931: WBA win Cup and promotion.

1933: Players numbered for first time in Cup Final (1-22).

1934: Sir Frederick Wall retires as FA secretary; successor Stanley Rous. Death of Herbert Chapman (Arsenal manager).

1935: Arsenal equal Huddersfield's Championship hat-trick record. Official two referee trials.

1936: Joe Payne's 10-goal League record (Luton 12 Bristol Rov 0).

1937: British record attendance: 149,547 at Scotland v England match.

1938: First live TV transmission of FA Cup Final. Football League 50th Jubilee. New pitch marking – arc on edge of penalty-area. Laws of Game re-drafted by Stanley Rous. Arsenal pay record £14,500 fee for Bryn Jones (Wolves).

1939: Compulsory numbering of players in Football League. First six-figure attendance for League match (Rangers v Celtic 118,567). All normal competitions suspended for duration of Second World War.

1945: Scottish League Cup introduced.

1946: British associations rejoin FIFA. Bolton disaster (33 killed) during FA Cup tie with Stoke. Walter Winterbottom appointed England's first director of coaching.

1947: Great Britain beat Rest of Europe 6-1 at Hampden Park, Glasgow. First £20,000 transfer – Tommy Lawton, Chelsea to Notts Co

1949: Stanley Rous, secretary FA, knighted. England's first home defeat outside British Champ. (0-2 v Eire).

1950: Football League extended from 88 to 92 clubs. World record crowd (203,500) at World Cup Final, Brazil v Uruguay, in Rio. Scotland's first home defeat by foreign team (0-1 v Austria).

1951: White ball comes into official use.

1952: Newcastle first club to win FA Cup at Wembley in successive seasons.

1953: England's first Wembley defeat by foreign opponents (3-6 v Hungary).

1954: Hungary beat England 7-1 in Budapest.

1955: First FA Cup match under floodlights (prelim round replay): Kidderminster v Brierley Hill Alliance.

1956: First FA Cup ties under floodlights in competition proper. First League match by floodlight (Portsmouth v Newcastle). Real Madrid win the first European Cup.

1957: Last full Football League programme on Christmas Day. Entertainment Tax withdrawn.

1958: Manchester United air crash at Munich. League re-structured into four divisions.

1960: Record transfer fee £55,000 for Denis Law (Huddersfield to Manchester City). Wolves win Cup, miss Double and Championship hat-trick by one goal. For fifth time in ten years FA Cup Final team reduced to ten men by injury. FA recognise Sunday football. Football League Cup launched.

1961: Tottenham complete the first Championship–FA Cup double this century. Maximum wage (£20 a week) abolished in High Court challenge by George Eastham. First British £100-a-week wage paid (by Fulham to Johnny Haynes). First £100,000 British transfer – Denis Law, Manchester City to Torino. Sir Stanley Rous elected president of FIFA.

1962: Manchester United raise record British transfer fee to £115,000 for Denis Law.

1963: FA Centenary. Season extended to end of May due to severe winter. First pools panel. English "retain and transfer" system ruled illegal in High Court test case.

1964: Rangers' second great hat-trick – Scottish Cup, League Cup and League. Football League and Scottish League guaranteed £500,000 a year in new fixtures copyright agreement with Pools. First televised 'Match of the Day' (BBC2): Liverpool 3 Arsenal 2.

1965: Bribes scandal – ten players jailed (and banned for life by FA) for match-fixing 1960–63. Stanley Matthews knighted in farewell season. Arthur Rowley (Shrewsbury) retires with record of 434 League goals. Substitutes allowed for injured players in Football League matches (one per team).

1966: England win World Cup (Wembley).

1967: Alf Ramsey, England manager, knighted; OBE for captain Bobby Moore. Celtic become first British team to win European Cup. First substitutes allowed in FA Cup Final (Tottenham v Chelsea) but not used. Football League permit loan transfers (two per club).

1968: First FA Cup Final televised live in colour (BBC2 – WBA v Everton). Manchester United first English club to win European Cup.

1970: FIFA/UEFA approve penalty shoot-out in deadlocked ties.

1971: Arsenal win League Championship and FA Cup.

1973: Football League introduce 3-up, 3-down promotion/relegation between Divisions 1, 2 and 3 and 4-up, 4-down between Divisions 3 and 4.

1974: First FA Cup ties played on Sunday. League football played on Sunday for first time. Last FA Amateur Cup Final. Joao Havelange (Brazil) succeeds Sir Stanley Rous as FIFA president.

1975: Scottish Premier Division introduced.

1976: Football League introduce goal difference (replacing goal average) and red/yellow cards.

1977: Liverpool achieve the double of League Championship and European Cup. Don Revie defects to United Arab Emirates when England manager – successor Ron Greenwood.

1978: Freedom of contract for players accepted by Football League. PFA lifts ban on foreign players in English football. Football League introduce Transfer Tribunal. Viv Anderson (Nottm Forest) first black player to win a full England cap. Willie Johnston (Scotland)

sent home from World Cup Finals in Argentina after failing dope test.

1979: First all-British £500,000 transfer – David Mills, Middlesbrough to WBA. First British million pound transfer (Trevor Francis – Birmingham to Nottm Forest). Andy Gray moves from Aston Villa to Wolves for a record £1,469,000 fee.

1981: Tottenham win 100th FA Cup Final. Liverpool first British side to win European Cup three times. Three points for a win introduced by Football League. QPR install Football League's first artificial pitch. Death of Bill Shankly, manager–legend of Liverpool 1959–74. Record British transfer – Bryan Robson (WBA to Manchester United), £1,500,000.

1982: Aston Villa become sixth consecutive English winners of European Cup. Tottenham retain FA Cup – first club to do so since Tottenham 1961 and 1962. Football League Cup becomes the (sponsored) Milk Cup.

1983: Liverpool complete League Championship–Milk Cup double for second year running. Manager Bob Paisley retires. Aberdeen first club to do Cup-Winners' Cup and domestic Cup double. Football League clubs vote to keep own match receipts. Football League sponsored by Canon, Japanese camera and business equipment manufacturers – 3-year agreement starting 1983–4. Football League agree two-year contract for live TV coverage of ten matches per season (5 Friday night, BBC, 5 Sunday afternoon, ITV).

1984: One FA Cup tie in rounds 3, 4, 5 and 6 shown live on TV (Friday or Sunday). Aberdeen take Scottish Cup for third successive season, win Scottish Championship, too. Tottenham win UEFA Cup on penalty shoot-out. Liverpool win European Cup on penalty shoot-out to complete unique treble with Milk Cup and League title (as well as Championship hat-trick). N Ireland win the final British Championship. France win European Championship – their first honour. FA National Soccer School opens at Lilleshall. Britain's biggest score this century: Stirling Alb 20 Selkirk 0 (Scottish Cup).

1985: Bradford City fire disaster – 56 killed. First £1m receipts from match in Britain (FA Cup Final). Kevin Moran (Manchester United) first player to be sent off in FA Cup Final. Celtic win 100th Scottish FA Cup Final. European Cup Final horror (Liverpool v Juventus, riot in Brussels) 39 die. UEFA ban all English clubs indefinitely from European competitions. No TV coverage at start of League season – first time since 1963 (resumption delayed until January 1986). Sept: first ground-sharing in League history – Charlton Athletic move from The Valley to Selhurst Park (Crystal Palace).

1986: Liverpool complete League and Cup double in player-manager Kenny Dalglish's first season in charge. Swindon (4th Div Champions) set League points record (102). League approve reduction of First Division to 20 clubs by 1988. Everton chairman Philip Carter elected president of Football League. Death of Sir Stanley Rous (91). 100th edition of News of the World Football Annual. League Cup sponsored for next three years by Littlewoods (£2m). Football League voting majority (for rule changes) reduced from three-quarters to two-thirds. Wales move HQ from Wrexham to Cardiff after 110 years. Two substitutes in FA Cup and League (Littlewoods) Cup. Two-season League/TV deal (£6.2m):- BBC and ITV each show seven live League matches per season, League Cup semi-finals and Final. Football League sponsored by Today newspaper. Luton first club to ban all visiting supporters; as sequel are themselves banned from League Cup. Oldham and Preston install artificial pitches, making four in Football League (following QPR and Luton).

1987: League introduce play-off matches to decide final promotion/relegation places in all divisions. Re-election abolished – bottom club in Div 4 replaced by winners of GM Vauxhall Conference. Two substitutes approved for Football League 1987–8. Red and yellow disciplinary cards (scrapped 1981) re-introduced by League and FA Football League sponsored by Barclays. First Div reduced to 21 clubs.

1988: Football League Centenary. First Division reduced to 20 clubs.

1989: Soccer gets £74m TV deal: £44m over 4 years, ITV; £30m over 5 years, BBC/BSB. But it costs Philip Carter the League Presidency. Ted Croker retires as FA chief executive; successor Graham Kelly, from Football League. Hillsborough disaster: 95 die at FA Cup semi-final (Liverpool v Nottm Forest). Arsenal win closest-ever Championship with last

kick. Peter Shilton sets England record with 109 caps.

1990: Nottm Forest win last Littlewoods Cup Final. Both FA Cup semi-finals played on Sunday and televised live. Play-off finals move to Wembley; Swindon win place in Div 1, then relegated back to Div 2 (breach of financial regulations) – Sunderland promoted instead. England reach World Cup semi-final in Italy and win FIFA Fair Play Award. Peter Shilton retires as England goalkeeper with 125 caps (world record). Graham Taylor (Aston Villa) succeeds Bobby Robson as England manager. International Board amend offside law (player 'level' no longer offside). FIFA make "professional foul" a sending-off offence. English clubs back in Europe (Manchester United and Aston Villa) after 5-year exile.

1991: First FA Cup semi-final at Wembley (Tottenham 3 Arsenal 1). Bert Millichip (FA chairman) and Philip Carter (Everton chairman) knighted. End of artificial pitches in Div 1 (Luton, Oldham). Scottish League reverts to 12-12-14 format (as in 1987–8). Penalty shoot-out introduced to decide FA Cup ties level after one replay.

1992: FA launch Premier League (22 clubs). Football League reduced to three divisions (71 clubs). Record TV-sport deal: BSkyB/BBC to pay £304m for 5-year coverage of Premier League. ITV do £40m, 4-year deal with Football League. Channel 4 show Italian football live (Sundays). FIFA approve new back-pass rule (goalkeeper must not handle ball kicked to him by team-mate). New League of Wales formed. Record all-British transfer, £3.3m: Alan Shearer (Southampton to Blackburn). Charlton return to The Valley after 7-year absence.

1993: Barclays end 6-year sponsorship of Football League. For first time both FA Cup semi-finals at Wembley (Sat, Sun). Arsenal first club to complete League Cup/FA Cup double. Rangers pull off Scotland's domestic treble for fifth time. FA in record British sports sponsorship deal (£12m over 4 years) with brewers Bass for FA Carling Premiership, from Aug. Brian Clough retires after 18 years as Nottm Forest manager; as does Jim McLean (21 years manager of Dundee Utd). Football League agree 3-year, £3m sponsorship with Endsleigh Insurance. Premier League introduce squad numbers with players' names on shirts. Record British transfer: Duncan Ferguson, Dundee Utd to Rangers (£4m). Record English-club signing: Roy Keane, Nottm Forest to Manchester United (£3.75m). Graham Taylor resigns as England manager after World Cup exit (Nov). Death of Bobby Moore (51), England World Cup winning captain 1966.

1994: Death of Sir Matt Busby. Terry Venables appointed England coach. Manchester United complete the Double. Last artificial pitch in English football goes – Preston revert to grass, summer 1994. Bobby Charlton knighted. Scottish League format changes to four divisions of ten clubs. Record British transfer: Chris Sutton, Norwich to Blackburn (£5m). FA announce first sponsorship of FA Cup – Littlewoods Pools (4-year, £14m deal, plus £6m for Charity Shield). Death of Billy Wright.

1995: New record British transfer: Andy Cole, Newcastle to Manchester United (£7m). First England match abandoned through crowd trouble (v Republic of Ireland, Dublin). Blackburn Champions for first time since 1914. Premiership reduced to 20 clubs. British transfer record broken again: Stan Collymore, Nottm Forest to Liverpool (£8.5m). Starting season 1995–6, teams allowed to use 3 substitutes per match, not necessarily including a goalkeeper. European Court of Justice upholds Bosman ruling, barring transfer fees for players out of contract and removing limit on number of foreign players clubs can field.

1996: Death of Bob Paisley (77), ex-Liverpool, most successful manager in English Football. FA appoint Chelsea manager Glenn Hoddle to succeed Terry Venables as England coach after Euro 96. Manchester United first English club to achieve Double twice (and in 3 seasons). Football League completes £125m, 5-year TV deal with BSkyB starting 1996–7. England stage European Championship, reach semi-finals, lose on pens to tournament winners Germany. Keith Wiseman succeeds Sir Bert Millichip as FA Chairman. Linesmen become known as 'referees' assistants'. Alan Shearer football's first £15m player (Blackburn to Newcastle). Nigeria first African country to win Olympic soccer. Nationwide Building Society sponsor Football League in initial 3-year deal worth

£5.25m Peter Shilton first player to make 1000 League appearances.

1997: Howard Wilkinson appointed English football's first technical director. England's first home defeat in World Cup (0-1 v Italy). Ruud Gullit (Chelsea) first foreign coach to win FA Cup. Rangers equal Celtic's record of 9 successive League titles. Manchester United win Premier League for fourth time in 5 seasons. New record World Cup score: Iran 17, Maldives 0 (qualifying round). Season 1997–8 starts Premiership's record £36m, 4-year sponsorship extension with brewers Bass (Carling).

1998: In French manager Arsene Wenger's second season at Highbury, Arsenal become second English club to complete the Double twice. Chelsea also win two trophies under new player-manager Gianluca Vialli (Coca-Cola Cup, Cup Winners' Cup). In breakaway from Scottish League, top ten clubs form new Premiership under SFA, starting season 1998–9. Football League celebrates its 100th season, 1998–9. New FA Cup sponsors – French insurance giants AXA (25m, 4-year deal). League Cup becomes Worthington Cup in £23m, 5-year contract with brewers Bass. Nationwide Building Society's sponsorship of Football League extended to season 2000–1.

1999: FA buy Wembley Stadium (£103m) for £320m, plan rebuilding (Aug 2000–March 2003) as new national stadium (Lottery Sports fund contributes £110m) Scotland's new Premier League takes 3-week mid-season break in January. Sky screen Oxford Utd v Sunderland (Div 1) as first pay-per-view match on TV. FA sack England coach Glenn Hoddle; Fulham's Kevin Keegan replaces him at £1m a year until 2003. Sir Alf Ramsey, England's World-Cup-winning manager, dies aged 79. With effect 1999, FA Cup Final to be decided on day (via penalties, if necessary). Hampden Park re-opens for Scottish Cup Final after £63m refit. Alex Ferguson knighted after Manchester United complete Premiership, FA Cup, European Cup treble. Starting season 1999–2000, UEFA increase Champions League from 24 to 32 clubs. End of Cup-Winners' Cup (merged into 121-club UEFA Cup). FA allow holders Manchester United to withdraw from FA Cup to participate in FIFA's inaugural World Club Championship in Brazil in January. Chelsea first British club to field an all-foreign line-up – at Southampton (Prem). FA vote in favour of streamlined 14-man board of directors to replace its 92-member council.

2000: Scot Adam Crozier takes over as FA chief executive. Wales move to Cardiff's £125m Millennium Stadium (v Finland). Brent Council approve plans for new £475m Wembley Stadium (completion target spring 2003); demolition of old stadium to begin after England v Germany (World Cup qual.). Fulham Ladies become Britain's first female professional team. FA Premiership and Nationwide League to introduce (season 2000–01) rule whereby referees advance free-kick by 10 yards and caution player who shows dissent, delays kick or fails to retreat 10 yards. Scottish football increased to 42 League clubs in 2000–01 (12 in Premier League and 3 divisions of ten; Peterhead and Elgin elected from Highland League). France win European Championship – first time a major international tournament has been jointly hosted (Holland/ Belgium). England's £10m bid to stage 2006 World Cup fails; vote goes to Germany. England manager Kevin Keegan resigns after 1-0 World Cup defeat by Germany in Wembley's last International. Lazio's Swedish coach Sven-Goran Eriksson agrees to become England head coach.

2001: Scottish Premier League experiment with split into two 5-game mini leagues (6 clubs in each) after 33 matches completed. New transfer system agreed by FIFA/UEFA is ratified. Barclaycard begin £48m, 3-year sponsorship of the Premiership, and Nationwide's contract with the Football League is extended by a further 3 years (£12m). ITV, after winning auction against BBC's Match of the Day, begin £183m, 3-season contract for highlights of Premiership matches; BSkyB's live coverage (66 matches per season) for next 3 years will cost £1.1bn. BBC and BSkyB pay £400m (3-year contract) for live coverage of FA Cup and England home matches. ITV and Ondigital pay £315m to screen Nationwide League and Worthington Cup matches. In new charter for referees, top men can earn up to £60,000 a season in Premiership. Real Madrid break world transfer record, buying Zinedine Zidane from Juventus for £47.2m. FA introduce prize money, round by round, in FA Cup.

2002: Scotland appoint their first foreign manager, Germany's former national coach Bertie Vogts replacing Craig Brown. Collapse of ITV Digital deal, with Football League owed £178m, threatens lower-division clubs. Arsenal complete Premiership/FA Cup Double for second time in 5 seasons, third time in all. Newcastle manager Bobby Robson knighted in Queen's Jubilee Honours. New record British transfer and world record for defender, £29.1m Rio Ferdinand (Leeds to Manchester United). Transfer window introduced to British football. FA Charity Shield renamed FA Community Shield. After 2-year delay, demolition of Wembley Stadium begins. October: Adam Crozier, FA chief executive, resigns.

2003: FA Cup draw (from 4th Round) reverts to Monday lunchtime. Scottish Premier League decide to end mid-winter shut-down. Mark Palios appointed FA chief executive. For first time, two Football League clubs demoted (replaced by two from Conference). Ban lifted on loan transfers between Premiership clubs. July: David Beckham becomes record British export (Manchester United to Real Madrid, £23.3m). Biggest takeover in British football history − Russian oil magnate Roman Abramovich buys control of Chelsea for £150m Wimbledon leave rented home at Selhurst Park, become England's first franchised club in 68-mile move to Milton Keynes.

2004: Arsenal first club to win Premiership with unbeaten record and only the third in English football history to stay undefeated through League season. Trevor Brooking knighted in Queen's Birthday Honours. Wimbledon change name to Milton Keynes Dons. Greece beat hosts Portugal to win European Championship as biggest outsiders (80-1 at start) ever to succeed in major international tournament. New contracts − Premiership in £57m deal with Barclays, seasons 2004−07. Coca-Cola replace Nationwide as Football League sponsors (£15m over 3 years), rebranding Div 1 as Football League Championship, with 2nd and 3rd Divisions, becoming Leagues 1 and 2. All-time League record of 49 unbeaten Premiership matches set by Arsenal. Under new League rule, Wrexham forfeit 10 points for going into administration.

2005: Brian Barwick, controller of ITV Sport, becomes FA chief executive. Foreign managers take all major trophies for English clubs: Chelsea, in Centenary year, win Premiership (record 95 points) and League Cup in Jose Mourinho's first season; Arsene Wenger's Arsenal win FA Cup in Final's first penalty shoot-out; under new manager Rafael Benitez, Liverpool lift European Cup on penalties after trailing 0-3 in Champions League Final. Wigan, a League club only since 1978, promoted to Premiership. In new record British-club take-over, American tycoon Malcolm Glazer buys Manchester United for £790m Tributes are paid world-wide to George Best, who dies aged 59.

2006: Steve Staunton succeeds Brian Kerr as Republic of Ireland manager. Chelsea post record losses of £140m. Sven-Goran Eriksson agrees a settlement to step down as England coach. Steve McClaren replaces him. The Premier League announce a new 3-year TV deal worth £1.7 billion under which Sky lose their monopoly of coverage. Chelsea smash the British transfer record, paying £30.8m for Andriy Shevchenko. Clydesdale Bank replace Bank of Scotland as sponsor of the SPL.

2007: Michel Platini becomes the new president of UEFA. Walter Smith resigns as Scotland manager to return to Rangers and is replaced by Alex McLeish. The new £800m Wembley Stadium is finally completed. The BBC and Sky lose TV rights for England's home matches and FA Cup ties to ITV and Setanta. World Cup-winner Alan Ball dies aged 61. Lawrie Sanchez resigns as Northern Ireland manager to take over at Fulham. Nigel Worthington succeeds him. Lord Stevens names five clubs in his final report into alleged transfer irregularities. Steve McClaren is sacked after England fail to qualify for the European Championship Finals and is replaced by Fabio Capello. The Republic of Ireland's Steve Staunton also goes. Scotland's Alex McLeish resigns to become Birmingham manager.

2008: The Republic of Ireland follow England's lead in appointing an Italian coach − Giovanni Trapattoni. George Burley leaves Southampton to become Scotland manager. Manchester United beat Chelsea in the first all-English Champions League Final. Manchester City

smash the British transfer record when signing Robinho from Real Madrid for £32.5m.

2009: Sky secure the rights to five of the six Premier League packages from 2010–13 with a bid of £1.6bn. Reading's David Beckham breaks Bobby Moore's record number of caps for an England outfield player with his 109th appearance. A British league record for not conceding a goal ends on 1,311 minutes for Manchester United's Edwin van der Sar. AC Milan's Kaka moves to Real Madrid for a world record fee of £56m. Nine days later, Manchester United agree to sell Cristiano Ronaldo to Real for £80m. Sir Bobby Robson dies aged 76 after a long battle with cancer. Shay Given and Kevin Kilbane win their 100th caps for the Republic of Ireland. The Premier League vote for clubs to have eight home-grown players in their squads. George Burley is sacked as Scotland manager and replaced by Craig Levein.

2010: npower succeed Coca-Cola as sponsors of the Football League. Portsmouth become the first Premier League club to go into administration. Chelsea achieve the club's first League and FA Cup double. Lord Triesman resigns as chairman of the FA and of England's 2018 World Cup bid. John Toshack resigns as Wales manager and is replaced by former captain Gary Speed. England are humiliated in the vote for the 2018 World Cup which goes to Russia, with the 2022 tournament awarded to Qatar.

2011: Seven club managers are sacked in a week. The transfer record between British clubs is broken twice in a day, with Liverpool buying Newcastle's Andy Carroll for £35m and selling Fernando Torres to Chelsea for £50m. Vauxhall replace Nationwide as sponsors of England and the other home nations. John Terry is restored as England captain. Football League clubs vote to reduce the number of substitutes from seven to five. Nigel Worthington steps down as Northern Ireland manager and is succeeded by Michael O'Neill. Sir Alex Ferguson completes 25 years as Manchester United manager. Manchester City post record annual losses of nearly £195m. Huddersfield set a Football League record of 43 successive unbeaten league games. Football mourns Gary Speed after the Wales manager is found dead at his home.

2012: Chris Coleman is appointed the new Wales manager. Fabio Capello resigns as manager after John Terry is stripped of the England captaincy for the second time. Roy Hodgson takes over. Rangers are forced into liquidation by crippling debts and a newly-formed club are demoted from the Scottish Premier League to Division Three. Manchester City become champions for the first time since 1968 after the tightest finish to a Premier League season. Chelsea win a penalty shoot-out against Bayern Munich in the Champions League Final. Capital One replace Carling as League Cup sponsors. Steven Gerrard (England) and Damien Duff (Republic of Ireland) win their 100th caps. The FA's new £120m National Football Centre at Burton upon Trent is opened. Scotland manager Craig Levein is sacked.

2013: Gordon Strachan is appointed Scotland manager. FIFA and the Premier League announce the introduction of goal-line technology. Energy company npower end their sponsorship of the Football League and are succeeded by Sky Bet. Sir Alex Ferguson announces he is retiring after 26 years as Manchester United manager. Wigan become the first club to lift the FA Cup and be relegated in the same season. Chelsea win the Europa League. Ashley Cole and Frank Lampard win their 100th England caps. Robbie Keane becomes the most capped player in the British Isles on his 126th appearance for the Republic of Ireland. Scottish Football League clubs agree to merge with the Scottish Premier League. Greg Dyke succeeds David Bernstein as FA chairman. Real Madrid sign Tottenham's Gareth Bale for a world record £85.3m. Giovanni Trapatonni is replaced as Republic of Ireland manager by Martin O'Neill.

2014: Sir Tom Finney, one of the finest British players of all-time, dies aged 91. England experience their worst-ever World Cup, finishing bottom the group with a single point. Germany deliver one of the most remarkable scorelines in World Cup history – 7-1 against Brazil in the semi-finals. Manchester United announce a world-record kit sponsorship with adidas worth £750m.

FINAL WHISTLE – OBITUARIES 2013–14

JULY 2013

BERT TRAUTMANN, 89, will always be remembered for one of the most courageous performances in the history of the FA Cup. The Manchester City goalkeeper, hurt when diving at the feet of Birmingham's Peter Murphy in the 1956 final, complained of nothing more than a stiff neck while receiving attention. He played the final 17 minutes of City's 3-1 victory, but three days later x-rays revealed a broken neck, with the second vertebrae smashed and the third wedged against it. That same year, Trautmann became the first foreigner to be voted Footballer of the Year. He went on to make 545 appearances for the club and in 2004 was awarded an OBE for his work on improving Anglo-German relations. The former Nazi paratrooper was captured in the latter stages of the Second World War and sent to a prison camp in Lancashire. He settled in England, started his career with non-league St Helens and joined City in 1949. After retiring, he managed Stockport and worked for the German FA promoting the game in Africa and Asia.

PHIL WOOSNAM, 80, followed a successful playing career in English football by pioneering the game in the United States. He coached the Atlanta Chiefs and the national team, then spent 14 years as commissioner of the North American Soccer League from 1968. During that time he raised its profile by negotiating the league's first television contract and introducing international players like Pele and Franz Beckenbauer. Woosnam, an inside-forward who started out with Manchester City and Leyton Orient, was the Amateur Player of the Year in 1955 and the first of his 17 caps for Wales, against Scotland, came before his first professional contract with West Ham. The cousin of golfer Ian Woosnam, he went on to play for Aston Villa.

LAWRIE REILLY, 84, was the last surviving member of Hibernian's 'Famous Five' forward line, which also featured Gordon Smith, Willie Ormond, Bobby Johnstone and Eddie Turnbull. At 5ft 7in he was small for a centre-forward, but strength and pace made him a prolific scorer. The one-club man scored 238 times in 355 appearances after signing in 1945 and was leading marksman in seven successive seasons. The most productive was the 1952–53 campaign which yielded 46 goals, including six hat-tricks. Reilly won three league titles before a cartilage injury ended his career at 29. He was the Edinburgh club's most-capped player, with 38 international appearances and 22 goals – five of them against England. But he missed out on the World Cup. Scotland refused to send a team to Brazil in 1950, while a bout of pleurisy forced him out of the 1954 finals in Switzerland. Reilly was inducted into the Scottish FA Hall of Fame in 2005.

GEORGE SMITH, 92, signed for Manchester City in 1938, but had to wait eight years for his debut because of the War. He survived a 'friendly fire' incident when a bullet entered his elbow and exited his hand and the club harboured doubts about whether he could play with such a severe injury. Smith, however, wore a glove to hide the wound and in 1946 scored all four goals in a 4-1 win over Manchester United. The inside-forward netted 75 in 166 appearances before moving to Chesterfield and playing another 250 matches between 1951–58.

DAVIE WHITE, 80, was appointed assistant to Scot Symon at Rangers in 1967 and replaced him as manager later that year. He was unable to disturb Celtic's domination under Jock Stein during two years in charge, but revived his career at Dundee, where his team beat Celtic 1-0 in the 1973–74 League Cup Final and reached three Scottish Cup semi-finals. White left the club in 1977 after failing win promotion back to the Premier Division. His entire playing career had been as a wing-half for Clyde.

CHRISTIAN BENITEZ, 27, spent the 2009–10 season on loan with Birmingham, making 30 Premier League appearances and scoring three goals. The club decided not to sign him on a permanent basis and he returned to the Mexican side Santos Laguna. Benitez, who played 58 times for Ecuador, died of a heart attack shortly after joining the Qatari club El Jaish.

DJALMA SANTOS, 84, was regarded by many as the best full-back ever to have played international football. The Brazilian, a contemporary of Pele and Garrincha, was a World Cup winner in Sweden in 1958 and Chile four years later. He also played in the finals in Switzerland

in 1954 and England in 1966 and won 110 caps, 98 of them full internationals. At club level, he made nearly 500 appearances for the great Palmeiras side of the 1960s.

AUGUST 2013

DAVE WAGSTAFFE, 70, was regarded by Wolves fans – and many more beyond Molineux – as the finest left-winger never to play for England. He made 404 appearances for the club from 1964–76, was a key figure in the team that regained top-flight status in 1967 and played a leading role in his team reaching two finals. Wagstaffe scored in the second leg of the 1972 inaugural UEFA Cup, which Wolves lost 3-2 on aggregate to Tottenham. Two years later, they defeated Manchester City to lift the League Cup. He joined them from City, having come through the Maine Road youth system, and later had two spells with Blackburn, during which he became the first player in English football to receive a red card. He also played for Blackpool.

BARRY STOBART, 75, was a surprise selection by Wolves manager Stan Cullis for the 1960 FA Cup Final against Blackburn. Cullis preferred him to the more established Bobby Mason and the centre-forward justified his place by playing a key role in a 3-0 victory. He had made his debut for the club that same season by scoring in a 2–0 win over Manchester United at Old Trafford. But his first-team appearances were restricted, apart from the 1962–63 season when he scored 14 goals in 24 league and cup games. Stobart moved on to Manchester City, then Aston Villa, Shrewsbury and the South African side Durban. Returning to England, he made a second visit to Wembley as manager of Willenhall, who lost the 1981 FA Vase Final 3–2 to Whickham.

MALCOLM BARRASS, 88, made 357 appearances for Bolton between 1945–57, the most high-profile of which came in the 1953 FA Cup Final. His team led Blackpool 3-1, but lost 4-3 to the wing wizardry of Stanley Matthews and a hat-trick by Stan Mortensen. During his time at the club, Barrass won three England caps, against Wales, Northern Ireland and Scotland. He later played for Sheffield United and was player-coach at Wigan during their non-league days.

GERRY BAKER, 75, scored seven times for St Mirren on the way to the 1959 Scottish FA Cup Final and netted the third goal in their 3-1 win over Aberdeen. The following season, he made history by scoring ten in a 15-0 first round victory over Glasgow University. Remarkably, a year later, brother Joe scored nine for Hibernian in a second round tie they won 15-1 against Peebles. Gerry, two years older, joined the club from Motherwell and went on to play for Manchester City, Hibernian, Ipswich, Coventry and Brentford on loan before finishing his career in non-league football. He was born in New York State, had dual American and British citizenship, and won seven caps for the United States national team. Joe Baker, who also had spells with Arsenal and the Italian club Torino and gained eight England caps, died in 2003.

COLIN MCADAM, 61, joined Rangers from Partick Thistle in 1980 for £165,000 – a fee set by an independent tribunal. The striker, who could also play as a central defender, scored 32 goals in 99 games for the club and had the rare distinction of playing against brother Tom in an Old Firm game with Celtic. Nicknamed 'The Beast,' McAdam had two spells with Partick and also played for Dumbarton, Motherwell, Hearts and Adelaide, during his time in Australia.

WILF CARTER, 79, scored 148 goals in 275 appearances for Plymouth between 1957–64 and ranks second to Sammy Black on the club's all-time list. He joined the club from West Bromwich Albion, netted 32 goals in his first season and was leading marksman for the next five campaigns. Carter chalked up eight hat-tricks and in 1960 netted five times in a 6-4 win over Charlton in a Division Two game.

STEVE AIZLEWOOD, 60, was a Wales Under-23 international centre-half who made nearly 200 appearances for home-town club Newport. A club record fee of £13,500 took him to Swindon in 1976. Then, in 1979, in one of the first transfers to require the new Football League arbitration service, he moved to Portsmouth for £45,000. There, he helped the club to promotion from the Fourth Division in 1980 and to the Division Three title in 1983. Aizlewood's brother Mark also began his career at Newport, went on to play for Charlton, Leeds and Cardiff and won 39 senior Wales caps.

FRED MARTIN, 84, joined Aberdeen in 1946 as an inside-forward, switched to goalkeeping during national service and went on to play for club and country in that position. He was part of the side that became champions for the first time in 1955 and won the League Cup the following season by beating St Mirren 2-1. He was also on the losing team in three Scottish Cup Finals, against Rangers, Celtic and St Mirren. Martin, who made 206 appearances in 14 years at Pittodrie, won six Scotland caps, two of them at the 1954 World Cup Finals in Switzerland.

GILMAR, 83, was Brazil's World Cup-winning goalkeeper in Sweden in 1958 and Chile four years later. His third tournament was in England in 1966 when Brazil failed to qualify from their group. Gilmar, who won 104 caps, played his club football for Corinthians, then the great Santos side.

JOHNNY HAMILTON, 78, made 496 appearances and scored 157 goals for Hearts between 1955–67. The Scotland Under-23 international winger, who could operate on either flank, played in two League Championship-winning sides. He also appeared in four League Cup Finals, gaining three winning medals and scoring against Partick and Third Lanark. He went on to serve Watford and Berwick before returning to Tynecastle to coach the youth team from 1974–79.

KEITH SKILLEN, 65, joined Fourth Division Workington after scoring 29 goals for Northern Premier League side Netherfield in the 1972–73 season. The inside-forward spent two years at the club, had a brief spell with Hartlepool, then returned to Borough Park for a further season after Workington were voted out of the Football League and replaced by Wimbledon.

SEPTEMBER 2013

DON DONOVAN, 83, was the last survivor of Everton's return to the top flight in 1954. The right-back played every match for the team that finished second to Leicester in Division Two. Donovan joined the club from Irish junior football and won five international caps for the Republic. He went on to captain Grimsby to promotion from the Third Division in 1962, then managed Boston United. Son Terry also played for Grimsby and won two Irish caps after joining Aston Villa.

RON FENTON, 73, was an inside-forward with Burnley, West Bromwich Albion, Birmingham and Brentford between 1957–70. He then joined the coaching staff at Notts County and had two years as manager after Jimmy Sirrel left to take over at Sheffield United. When Fenton was replaced on Sirrel's return to Meadow Lane, he moved to moved across the Trent to Nottingham Forest, spending spent ten years on their coaching staff and a further six as assistant to manager Brian Clough.

BRIAN SMITH, 57, was one of the unsung members of a Bolton squad featuring high-profile players like Frank Worthington, Willie Morgan, Sam Allardyce and Peter Reid. His senior appearances were restricted, but the midfielder played a part in promoted Wanderers retaining top-flight status in the 1978–79 season, helped by two wins over Manchester United. Smith spent five years at the club before joining Blackpool, then playing for Bournemouth and Bury.

BARRY HANCOCK, 74, joined Port Vale as an amateur in 1954, signed professional forms in 1957 and spent nearly ten years at the club, much of the time as a reserve player. The inside-forward later served Crewe and non-league Stafford.

GERRIE MUHREN, 67, won three successive European Cup Finals with Ajax – against Panathinaikos, Inter Milan and Juventus – in the early 1970s. The midfielder player, capped ten times by Holland, was the older brother of Arnold Muhren, who had spells with Ipswich and Manchester United.

OCTOBER 2013

PETER BROADBENT, 80, ranked alongside Bert Williams, Billy Wright, Ron Flowers and Bill Slater as one of Wolves' greatest-ever players. The inside-forward was part of the team, managed by Stan Cullis, that won the League title in 1954, 1958 and 1959 and the FA Cup in 1960. The club also embarked on a series of trailblazing European floodlit friendlies against the best sides in the world, paving the way for what is now the Champions League. Broadbent, a £10,000 club

record signing from Brentford in 1951, made 497 appearances and scored 145 goals, won seven England caps and was part of the 1958 World Cup squad in Sweden. He left Molineux in 1965 to join Shrewsbury and also played for Aston Villa and Stockport.

MICK BUCKLEY, 59, was an England youth and Under-23 international who came through the ranks at Everton. The midfielder had his best season at Goodison Park in 1974–75 when making 33 starts as Billy Bingham's team finished fourth, three points behind champions Derby. Buckley joined Sunderland for £80,000 and played an important role in promotion to the First Division as runners-up to Leicester in the 1979–80 campaign. He went on to serve Hartlepool, Carlisle and Middlesbrough.

ERNIE MORGAN, 86, scored 21 goals in his first season with Gillingham after moving from Lincoln in 1953. In his second, the centre-forward broke the club record with 31, a record he still shares with Brian Yeo, who matched the tally in the 1973–74 campaign. Morgan netted 73 goals in 155 appearances for the club before a knee ligament injury ended his career. He later managed Dartford to the Southern League title and the FA Trophy Final against Morecambe (1-2) in 1974

NORRIE MARTIN, 74, joined Rangers in 1958 and spent 12 years at Ibrox. The goalkeeper made 126 appearances, but was dogged by injury and never gained a winner's medal. He twice fractured his skull and had to wait five years for a league debut. Martin's best season was in 1966–67 when he played 38 matches, seven of them in the European Cup Winners' Cup in which Rangers lost the final 1-0 to Bayern Munich. He was also in the side beaten 4-0 by Celtic in the 1969 Scottish Cup Final. Martin later played for East Fife, Queen of the South and Hamilton.

CHARLIE DICKSON, 79, was regarded by many as Dunfermline's greatest-ever player. The centre-forward netted twice on his debut in 1955 and went on to score 215 goals in 340 appearances in nine years at East End Park – still a club record. They included 11 hat-tricks, including a double hat-trick against St Mirren, and the second goal in a 2-0 victory over Celtic in the 1961 Scottish Cup Final replay. Dickson later played for Queen of the South.

HAROLD RUDMAN, 88, joined Burnley in 1942, made his debut in the War-time North Regional League and served the club for 15 years. The right-back played nine times in the Second Division promotion-winning side of 1946–47 when Burnley finished runners-up to Manchester City, but most of his appearances for the senior team came after he turned 30. He later played for Rochdale.

TONY ALEXANDER, 78, made his league debut for home-town club Reading at Watford a week after reaching 18 and scored for the first time in his first home game against Queens Park Rangers. The inside-forward's career was interrupted by national service and he found competition for places tough on returning to Elm Park. He was released in 1956 and joined Yeovil.

DAVID MACFARLANE, 46, came on as a substitute for Rangers in their 2-1 win over Celtic in the 1986 Scottish League Cup Final. The midfield player sent four years at Ibrox and also played for Kilmarnock, Dundee and Partick.

TOMMY MCCONVILLE, 67, was one of the most successful and popular Irish League players of his era. The defender won three titles and three FAI Cups with Dundalk, making a record 580 appearances in 21 years with his home-town club. He won another title with Waterford, also played for Shamrock Rovers and Finn Harps and was capped six times by the Republic between 1971–73.

RAY MIELCZAREK, 67, was a Wales Youth and Under-23 international who went on to win one senior cap against Finland in 1971. He started his club career with Wrexham and played in two losing Welsh Cup Final teams. The centre-half moved to Huddersfield for a £20,000 fee, then joined Rotherham for £10,000. He was forced to retire at 28 because of a cruciate ligament injury.

GEOFF SMITH, 85, was turned down by Bradford City after a trial in 1948, but was successful with a second one four years later. The goalkeeper went on to make 214 successive appearances before injury ended the run in 1958. He played a total of 270 games for his one and only club, keeping 70 clean sheets. Only Paul Tomlinson has a better record in City's history.

NOVEMBER 2013

BILL FOULKES, 81, survived the 1958 Munich Disaster, which claimed the lives of eight of Manchester United's 'Busby Babes,' and went on to make 688 appearances for the club – a total bettered only by Ryan Giggs and Sir Bobby Charlton. He played at right-back in the early part of a 19-year career at Old Trafford before becoming an uncompromising centre-half. Foulkes won four First Division titles – two of them after Munich – and the 1963 FA Cup when United defeated Leicester 3-1 in the final. But his finest hour came at 36 when he scored a late equaliser at the Bernabeu in a 3-3 draw with Real Madrid which took his side through to the 1968 European Cup Final at Wembley, where they beat Benfica 4-1. Foulkes, who won one England cap against Northern Ireland in 1954, retired from playing in 1970 and stayed on as a coach for a brief spell. Then he managed teams in the United States – Chicago, Tulsa and San Jose – and in Norway and Japan.

STUART WILLIAMS, 83, made his debut for Wales in 1954, won 43 caps over the next 11 years and was captain 14 times. At the 1958 World Cup in Sweden, a shot from Pele deflected off his foot into the net for the only goal of the quarter-final tie against Brazil. The full-back started his career with home-town club Wrexham, then spent 12 years with West Bromwich Albion. He helped them finish runners-up to League champions Wolves in 1954, but missed out on their FA Cup-winning team against Preston in the same season. Williams also played for Southampton, winning promotion to the First Division as runners-up to Manchester City in 1966. After retiring, he was on the staff at Albion and Aston Villa, coached in Iran and Norway and had a spell as assistant to long-serving Southampton manager Ted Bates.

NILTON SANTOS, 88, was the third member of Brazil's World Cup-winning side in Sweden in 1958 and Chile four years later to pass away in the space of four months. One of the pioneers of the attacking left-back position, he was also a member of the squad at the 1950 and 1954 tournaments. He made 84 international appearances and played 723 times for Botafogo, his only club.

SAMMY TAYLOR, 80, was a free-scoring left-winger who played alongside the great Tom Finney at Preston. He joined the club from Falkirk for £8,000 in 1955 and in six seasons at Deepdale netted 48 goals in 166 appearances. The first was against Manchester United at Old Trafford and his tally included hat-tricks against Chelsea, Birmingham and Portsmouth. Taylor later helped Carlisle to promotion from Division Four and also played for Southport.

RON DELLOW, 99, was the oldest surviving player for a number of clubs. The right-winger served Mansfield, Manchester City and Tranmere. He then joined Carlisle in 1939, but had to wait seven years for his debut because of the War, in which he flew 31 missions as a Lancaster bomber pilot and was twice forced to ditch into the North Sea. Dellow then coached several; Dutch sides, including Volendam where he gave a debut to 17-year-old Arnold Muhren, who went on to win trophies with Ipswich and Manchester United.

ELFED MORRIS, 71, joined Chester from Wrexham and was part of the forward line that scored 138 of the team's 141 goals in Fourth Division matches and cup ties during the 1964–65 season. The outside-left contributed 26 of them and attracted interest from Sheffield United and Birmingham. But he remained at the club for six years before ending his league career with Halifax.

DAVE CARR, 76, was an inside-forward who helped Workington gain promotion from Division Four in the 1963–64 season. He joined the club from Darlington and went on to sign for Watford. There, Carr made only ten appearances before his career was ended by a car accident which left him in a coma for five weeks and in hospital for 13 months.

ROGER BARTON, 67, was an England Under-18 winger who started his club career with Wolves in 1963. He was unable to break into the senior side at Molineux and moved on to play for Lincoln, then Barnsley.

JACKIE MORLEY, 79, was signed for Waterford by player-manager Martin Ferguson, brother of Sir Alex Ferguson, in 1967, and won four League of Ireland titles with the club – three of them in successive seasons. The centre-half also played for Cork Hibernians and had a spell with West Ham.

JIM MCCLUSKEY, 63, took up refereeing in 1976 after a knee injury ended his playing career and became one of Scotland's leading officials. He refereed ten domestic finals and had more than 40 international appointments. They included six European Championship qualifiers, the second leg of the 1994 UEFA Cup Final between Inter Milan and Salzburg and friendlies between England and Brazil and Germany against Italy. His last match before retiring at 50 was the 2000 Scottish Cup Final between Rangers and Aberdeen. He later served on the referees' committee of the Scottish FA and was a match observer for UEFA.

DECEMBER 2013

WAYNE HARRISON, 46, became the world's most expensive teenager when joining Liverpool from Oldham in 1985. Manager Joe Fagan paid £250,000 for the 17-year-old forward after watching him score twice in an FA Youth Cup tie between the two clubs. A series of injuries, including a near-fatal loss of blood when he fell through a greenhouse, meant the forward never fulfilled his potential. Harrison came back from that accident to score 17 goals in 28 games as Liverpool's reserve team won the Central League title in 1990. But torn cruciate knee ligaments forced his retirement at the age of 22. He died on Christmas Day from pancreatic problems.

RON NOADES, 76, took over Crystal Palace in 1981 and presided over one of the most successful periods in their history. Palace won promotion to the old First Division in 1989 and reached the FA Cup Final the following year, drawing 3-3 with Manchester United and losing the replay 1-0. In 1991, they finished third behind Arsenal and Liverpool and defeated Everton 4-1 in the Zenith Data Systems Cup Final. Noades then played a leading role in the formation of the Premier League in 1992. He sacked Attilio Lombardo in 1998 and took over as manager at Selhurst Park in an effort to avoid relegation, before selling out in the summer and buying Brentford. There, he installed himself as chairman and manager, winning the Third Division title at the first attempt. Noades sold the club in 2006.

DAVID COLEMAN, 87, was the renowned sports presenter whose football commentaries were part of his wide-ranging remit at the BBC. He covered six World Cups, including the 1970 finals in Mexico when his description of the wonder save by Gordon Banks from Pele's header in the England-Brazil tie was one of the most treasured. Coleman presented *Match of the Day, Grandstand, Sportsnight with Coleman, BBC Sports Review of the Year* and *A Question of Sport* during nearly 50 years with the Corporation. Most memorably, he presented 11 Olympic Games.

DAVID JONES, 73, was an England youth international who became Crewe's youngest scorer, aged 16 years and 144 days, when he netted against Gateshead in 1956. The inside-forward moved on to Birmingham, then joined Millwall, where he won a Fourth Division championship medal in 1962 and scored 75 goals in 179 appearances. Jones finished his career in South Africa, playing for Johannesburg and Durban.

PAUL COMSTIVE, 52, played 320 league games for seven clubs. They included Bolton, for whom he scored two goals direct from corners against Bournemouth on New Year's Day 1990. Two years earlier, the midfielder helped Burnley to the Sherpa Van Trophy Final at Wembley, where they lost 2-0 to Wolves. The midfielder also served Blackburn, Rochdale, Wigan, Wrexham and Chester, then had spells with non-league Southport and Morecambe.

JANUARY 2014

EUSEBIO, 71, was widely regarded as one of the finest players of all time, a prolific scorer with dazzling dribbling skills and blistering acceleration. Nicknamed the 'Black Pearl,' he was leading marksman with nine goals for Portugal at the 1966 World Cup in England, four of them coming in a 5-3 quarter-final win over North Korea at Goodison Park after his side trailed 3-0. Another image ingrained on his career was at the end of a 2-1 defeat by England in the semi-finals when he left the Wembley pitch in tears. Eusebio, who scored 41 goals in 64 appearances for his country, returned to Wembley in 1968 with Benfica, who were beaten 4-1 by Manchester United in the European Cup. He played in three other finals, scoring twice in a 5-3 victory over Real

Madrid, then losing to AC Milan and Inter Milan. There were 11 Portuguese League titles, five domestic Cup successes and the European Footballer of the Year award in 1965. After 15 years with Benfica, he played in the United States and Mexico, along with a spell with Beira Mar back in Portugal. After retiring, with 733 goals in 745 matches, he became an ambassador for Benfica and Portuguese football.

BOBBY COLLINS, 82, was just 5ft 3in tall and wore size-four boots. But he became a hugely influential player for teams on both sides of the Border in a career of more than 800 appearances and more than 200 goals. The skilful and combative inside-forward spent ten years with Celtic during which they won the league and cup double in 1954, a second Scottish Cup and two League Cups. Everton paid a club record £23,500 for his services in 1958 and Don Revie spent £25,000 bringing him to Leeds four years later. There, he won the Second Division title and was captaining the side in pursuit of the Double in 1965. But Leeds lost the title to Manchester United on goal average and were beaten 2-1 by Liverpool in the FA Cup Final. That season, he was named Footballer of the Year by the Football Writers' Association. Collins, who won 31 Scotland caps, suffered a broken thighbone in a Fairs Cup tie against Torino in 1966 and afterwards struggled to regain previous form. He went on to play for Bury, Morton, Oldham, Shamrock Rovers in Ireland and had a spell in Australia. After retiring, he managed Huddersfield, Hull and Barnsley and had two coaching spells back at Leeds.

BERT WILLIAMS, 93, was England's oldest living former international, a goalkeeper given the nickname 'The Cat' by journalists after an outstanding performance in the 2-0 win over Italy in 1949 and one which accompanied him throughout his career. Another of his 24 caps was in the 1950 World Cup in Brazil when England suffered an embarrassing 1-0 defeat by the United States. 'The hurt of that result will never go away,' he said in an interview many years later. Williams joined Wolves from Walsall after the Second World War and made 420 appearances in 14 seasons at Molineux, a club record for a goalkeeper which stood for 42 years. His side won the 1949 FA Cup Final, defeating Leicester 3-1, and became League champions in 1954, finishing four points ahead of West Bromwich Albion. In 2010, he was awarded an MBE for services to football and charity work.

IAN REDFORD, 53, joined Rangers from Dundee in 1980 for £210,000 – then a Scottish record fee – and won three trophies in six seasons at Ibrox. He scored the League Cup decider against Dundee United the following year, gained a second winner's medal in that competition against the same opponents and won one Scottish Cup, with United again the losing finalists. The Scottish Under-21 midfielder, regarded as one of the most talented players never to have won a senior cap for his country, made 247 appearances for Rangers before moving to Dundee United in 1985 and playing a key role in their progress to the UEFA Cup Final in 1987 when they were beaten 2-1 on aggregate by Gothenburg. Redford then served Ipswich, home-town club St Johnstone and Brechin as player-manager. He finished at Raith, where he won the League Cup again – his side beating Celtic on penalties – along with the First Division title.

BRIAN GIBBS, 77, was part of the Colchester team that reached the quarter-finals of the FA Cup in 1971 with a famous 3-2 victory over Don Revie's Leeds. In the same year, he helped them win the pre-season Watney Cup on penalties against West Bromwich Albion. Gibbs started a career spanning more than 500 games as an apprentice at Portsmouth, played for Bournemouth, then became a prolific marksman with Gillingham, where he was top scorer for five successive seasons. The inside-forward netted 110 goals in 284 appearances, 17 of them in the 1963-64 campaign when Gillingham won the Fourth Division title on goal average after finishing level with Carlisle on 60 points.

ROY WARHURST, 87, won the Second Division title with Birmingham in the 1954–55 season when they pipped Luton and Rotherham on goal average after all three team finished on 54 points. The following season, he was ruled out of the FA Cup Final against Manchester City after sustaining a thigh injury in the sixth round victory over Arsenal. Many thought his absence was a key factor in a 3-1 defeat. Warhurst, a tough-tackling wing-half, joined the club from Sheffield United for £8,000 and made 239 appearances over seven years. He moved to City for £10,000 in 1957, then played for Crewe and Oldham before retiring.

ANDY GRAVER, 86, joined Lincoln in 1950 after making a single appearance for Newcastle and became one of the most prolific marksmen in the lower divisions. He scored a club record 150 goals in 289 appearances, 36 of them in 35 games in the 1951–52 season when his side won the Third Division North title. Lincoln netted 121 goals in that campaign, with Graver's tally highlighted by six in a record 11-1 win over Crewe – two with his right foot, two with his left and two headers. In between three spells at Sincil Bank, the centre-forward moved to Leicester for £27,500 and later to Stoke for £12,000. His third ended in 1961 and after playing non-league football he was forced to retire in 1963 with a broken ankle. He later served the club as a youth coach and scout.

ERIC BARNES, 76, captained Crewe to a famous FA Cup victory during 12 years at the heart of their defence. Then in the Fourth Division, they defeated Chelsea 2-1 in a third round tie at Stamford Bridge in 1961 with goals from Barrie Wheatley and Billy Stark. The previous season, Crewe had lost 13-2 to Tottenham in a fourth round replay. Barnes made his debut in 1958 and went on to make 390 appearances for his only club, winning promotion from the basement division in 1963 and 1968. Each time, Crewe went straight back down.

ARTHUR BELLAMY, 71, joined Burnley at 17, came through the youth and reserve teams and made his senior debut against Manchester City at Maine Road in 1963. He scored in a 5-2 victory and in the opening game of the following season netted a hat-trick as defending champions Everton were beaten 4-3. The inside-forward played for ten seasons, making 250 appearances, then spent three years at Chesterfield. Bellamy returned to Turf Moor in coaching and assistant manager roles and also worked as head groundsman.

ALBERT McCANN, 72, played for Portsmouth for 12 years, making 372 appearances and scoring 98 goals. The inside-forward was top scorer with 16 in the 1967–68 season when his side finished fifth in Division Two. He joined the club in 1962 from Coventry for £8,000 and was previously with Luton.

OLIVER CONMY, 74, joined Peterborough from Huddersfield in 1964 and in his first season helped the club reach the quarter-finals of the FA Cup for the first time. The inside-forward went on to make 304 appearances in six seasons, during which he won five caps with the Republic of Ireland.

ALAN BLACKBURN, 78, was a prolific scorer for West Ham's youth team and helped the reserves win the Combination League title in the 1953–54 season. He made 17 appearances for the senior side before joining Halifax in 1958, then playing for non-league Margate.

JIM APPLEBY, 79, was a centre-half who joined Burnley in 1953 and spent five years at the club. He then played for Blackburn, Southport and Chester and managed Horden Colliery Welfare in his native north-east.

JOE O'MAHONEY, 65, made his debut for Limerick in 1966 and played 418 League of Ireland matches for his home-town club in a 20-year career. He was captain and an ever-present in the 1979–80 title-winning season, led the team to the FAI Cup in 1982 and also played in the side that won the trophy in 1971. Two years earlier, the central defender was on the bench for a World Cup qualifier against Czechoslovakia.

FEBRUARY 2014

SIR TOM FINNEY, 91, was one of the all-time greats of English football, a player of sublime skill for club and country, a prolific scorer and a man whose modesty and unassuming nature remained intact throughout his distinguished career. 'He would have been great in any team, in any match and in any age, even if he had been wearing an overcoat,' Bill Shankly, the legendary Liverpool manager and a one-time team-mate, said of him. Finney was born within a stone's throw of Preston's Deepdale ground and made his official debut for the club in 1946, having played previously in unofficial matches after signing before the start of the Second World War. Nicknamed the 'Preston Plumber' after completing an apprenticeship with the family business, he operated comfortably on either wing, or at centre-forward, made 473 appearances, the last of them in 1960, and netted 210 goals. Preston twice finished League Championship runners

up – to Arsenal on goal average and to Wolves. They were also beaten by West Bromwich Albion in the 1954 FA Cup Final. But Finney did win major individual honours – the first player to be named Footballer of the Year on two occasions and a recipient of a PFA Merit Award. He made a scoring debut for England against Northern Ireland under new manager Walter Winterbottom in 1946, netted four times in a 5-3 victory over Portugal in 1950 and his tally of 30 international goals ranks him alongside Alan Shearer and Nat Lofthouse in England's all-time list. His 76 caps, the last against the Soviet Union in 1958, embraced three World Cups – Brazil, Switzerland and Sweden. Finney maintained his links with Preston, serving as the club's president, and his legacy lives on – the stadium is located on Sir Tom Finney Way, his statue is outside and a stand is named after him. He was awarded an OBE in 1961 and knighted in 1998.

MARIO COLUNA, 78, captained Benfica to two European Cup triumphs and Portugal to the semi-finals of the 1966 World Cup in England, where they lost to Alf Ramsey's side. He was the creative force for club and country and the player behind many of the goals scored for both by Eusebio. Benfica defeated Barcelona 3-2 in 1961 and Real Madrid 5-3 a year later. They also lost finals to AC Milan, Inter Milan and, in 1968, to Manchester United at Wembley. Coluna won 57 caps and after retiring returned to his native Mozambique to become national coach.

TONY HATELEY, 72, was a much-travelled, free-scoring centre-forward who was twice involved in club record transfers. Chelsea paid Aston Villa £100,000 for his services in 1966, then sold him to Liverpool the following year for £96,000. When Hateley retired in 1974, his combined transfer fees of nearly £400,000 were a record in English football. Hateley started his career with Notts County, helping the club win promotion from Division Four in 1960. In his second spell there, County won the Division Four title in 1971. Hateley also played for Coventry, Birmingham and Oldham, making almost 500 appearances and averaging a goal every two games. One of them, against Leeds, took Chelsea to their first FA Cup Final which they lost 2-1 to Tottenham in 1967. He never played for England, but son Mark, also a centre-forward, won 32 caps during his time with Portsmouth, AC Milan, Monaco and Rangers. Grandson Tom, a midfielder, has played for Motherwell and Tranmere.

GORDON HARRIS, 73, scored on his Burnley debut against Leeds towards the end of the 1958–59 season and went on to make 313 appearances for the club, scoring 81 goals. The left-winger played twice in the following campaign when Burnley became champions, finishing a point ahead of Wolves and two clear of Tottenham. He then became a mainstay of the team and played in the 1962 FA Cup Final defeat by Tottenham. Harris, nicknamed 'Bomber,' won one England cap four years later, replacing the injured Bobby Charlton against Poland. He was in Alf Ramsey's squad of 40 for the World Cup, but did not make the manager's final choice. Sold to Sunderland for £70,000 in 1968, he had three years as a regular at Roker Park and ended his career with South Shields.

LEN CHALMERS, 77, hobbled through 70 minutes of Leicester's 2-0 defeat by Tottenham in the 1961 FA Cup Final after sustaining a leg injury in a challenge from Les Allen. With no substitutes in those days, the full-back had to soldier on in a left-wing position trying to make a nuisance of himself. Two years later, he missed out on a return to Wembley for the final against Manchester United (1-3), having lost his place to the up-and-coming John Sjoberg. Chalmers had made his debut for the club on the final day of the 1957–58 season when Leicester avoided relegation by winning at Birmingham. He spent ten years at Filbert Street before joining Notts County.

GORDON NUTT, 81, was in the Arsenal side beaten 5-4 by Manchester United at Highbury on February 1, 1958 – a match that took on a tragic significance. It was the last time that United's 'Busby Babes' were seen together in a domestic fixture. For five days later, the Munich air crash claimed the lives of eight players returning from a European Cup match in Belgrade. Nutt made 51 appearances for Arsenal, having previously been with Coventry and Cardiff. The winger later had spells with Southend and PSV Eindhoven, then played for Sydney and Manly after emigrating to Australia in 1965.

LUIS ARAGONES, 75, coached Spain to victory at the 2008 European Championship, paving the way for a golden era for his country in international football. He adopted the intricate short-passing game proving so successful for Barcelona at club level and further success followed,

under Vicente del Bosque, at the 2010 World Cup and Euro 2012. Aragones previously won trophies with Atletico Madrid, as well as coaching Barcelona, Real Betis, Espanyol, Sevilla Valencia and the Turkish side Fenerbahce. As a free-scoring forward, he won three La Liga titles with Atletico, had a spell with Real Madrid and won 13 caps for the national team.

RICHARD MOLLER NIELSEN, 76, coached Denmark to a surprise victory in the 1992 European Championship. They failed to qualify for the tournament in Sweden, but were invited to compete when war-torn Yugoslavia were excluded. In just over a week, Moller Nielsen put together his squad and lifted the trophy with a 2-0 victory over favourites Germany in the final. Denmark also defeated Argentina by the same scoreline in the 1995 Confederations Cup. The following year, they were knocked out of Euro 96 in England at the group stage. Moller Nielsen, who won two caps as a player, later coached the Finland and Israel national teams.

ANDY PATON, 91, was voted Motherwell's greatest player by supporters in a poll in 2006. The centre-half made more than 500 appearances in 15 seasons and won two Scotland caps, in addition to making three War-time appearances for his country. Paton, born into a footballing family with his three uncles playing professionally, captained Motherwell to their first major trophy in the 1950-51 season – a 3-0 win over Hibernian in the League Cup Final. The following season, they defeated Dundee 4-0 in the Scottish Cup Final. He left Fir Park in 1958 for Hamilton and later became their manager.

TOMMY DIXON, 84, had impressive scoring records with West Ham and Reading in the 1950s. The centre-forward netted 25 goals in 44 games while playing Second Division football at Upton Park. He then netted 76 in 143 matches for Reading, then in the Third Division South. Dixon, who started his career as an amateur at Newcastle, also had spells with Brighton, Workington and Barrow.

ARTHUR ROWLEY, 80, made his debut for Liverpool on the opening day of the 1952-53 season, lining up alongside Billy Liddell and Bob Paisley in a game in which Charlie Ashcroft saved a penalty from Preston's Tom Finney. The inside-left spent most of his time at Anfield in the reserves, later played for Wrexham and Crewe and finished his career with non-league Burscough and Chorley.

JOHN POPPITT, 91, was a right-back who joined Queens Park Rangers from Derby in 1950. He made 111 appearances for the club and finished his career in non-league football, playing into his 40s.

NIGEL WALKER, 54, was a winger who spent much of his career in the north-east. He turned professional with Newcastle, making 81 appearances in five years from 1977, played briefly for Sunderland, then served Hartlepool. In between, he had spells at Crewe, Blackpool, Chester and San Diego in the United States, before playing for Blyth Spartans while working as a teacher.

EDDIE HOLDING, 83, had two spells with Walsall in the early 1950s. He was mainly a right-back, but moved into the forward line when required and in his second spell scored a hat-trick against Brighton on Christmas Day 1953. Holding played briefly for Derby and also served Barrow.

JOHN LUMSDEN, 71, helped two teams to promotion from the old Fourth Division. After joining Workington as a centre-half from Aston Villa, where he was unable to make the breakthrough, he switched to full-back and was an ever-present in the side that went up in the 1963-64 season. Lumsden made 290 appearances for the Cumbrian club before joining Chesterfield, who were champions of the division in the 1969-70 campaign.

JIMMY JONES, 85, won three Northern Ireland caps during a record-breaking career with Glenavon. The centre-forward scored 74 goals in his home-town club's Double-winning season of 1956-57 – a total still unsurpassed in the Irish League. In all he netted 517 goals and was the league's leading marksman for ten successive seasons, gaining two more titles and two more cup successes. They followed his recovery from a career-threatening broken leg sustained during a riot at Windsor Park in 1948 while playing for Belfast Celtic against Linfield. He also had spells with Larne, Fulham and Portadown.

ALEX 'SANDY' RUSSELL, 91, gained one cap for Northern Ireland – in a 7-2 defeat by England at Windsor Park in the 1946-47 season. The stadium held happier memories at club level for

the goalkeeper, who spent 16 years there with Linfield and won four Irish League titles. After retiring, Russell continued his association as coach and trainer, then had the Spion Kop Stand renamed in his honour.

MARCH 2014

HILDERALDO BELLINI, 83, led Brazil to their first World Cup victory in Sweden in 1958. The central defender was also the first captain to raise the trophy above his head as a symbol of triumph – a gesture later immortalised with a statue of him in front of Rio's Maracana Stadium. Bellini was part of the squad that retained the trophy in Chile four years later, although he never played in that tournament, and won the last of his 51 caps at the 1966 finals in England. He played his club football with Vasco da Gama, Sao Paulo and Atletico Paranaense.

STAN RICKABY, 89, was the last link with the West Bromwich Albion team that went close to winning the Double in the 1953–54 season. Albion lifted the FA Cup, beating Preston 3-2, and were First Division runners-up to Wolves, having been hit by an injury crisis in the final weeks of the campaign. Rickaby, signed from Middlesbrough for £7,500, missed the Wembley final through injury, but collected a medal after playing in every previous round. The right-back made 205 appearances in five years at the club and gained one England cap, in a 3-1 win over Northern Ireland in 1953. After leaving, he was player-manager at Poole and also played for Weymouth.

CALVIN PALMER, 73, was a tough-tackling wing-half who joined Nottingham Forest from non-league football in 1958. He went on to make nearly 200 appearances for Stoke after a £30,000 transfer in 1963, then spent three years with Sunderland, who paid £70,000 for his services. Palmer later had spells with Crewe and Hereford, in between playing and coaching in South Africa.

BRYAN ORRITT, 77, was a Wales Under-23 international who played for Birmingham in two finals of the Inter-Cities Fairs Cup – forerunner of the UEFA Cup and Europa League. His side lost 4-1 on aggregate to Barcelona in 1960 and 4-2 on aggregate to Roma the following year. The wing-half, who started his career with Bangor City, left St Andrews in 1962 for Middlesbrough, becoming the club's first substitute following a change in Football League rules in 1965. Orritt emigrated to South Africa, made a brief return to Teesside in 1974 to study coaching techniques, then managed Southern Suburbs in Johannesburg and coached youngsters in Soweto.

FRED STANSFIELD, 96, was the oldest surviving Wales international and Cardiff player. The centre-half won one cap, against Scotland in 1948, finding out about a late call-up to the team when a message was posted on the screen of his local cinema where he was watching a film with his wife. The previous year he captained Cardiff to the Division Three South title and later played for and managed Newport.

JOHN CHRISTIE, 84, helped Walsall to back-to-back promotions. They won the Fourth Division title in the 1959–60 season and a year later were runners-up to Bury in Division Three. The goalkeeper previously made 217 appearances for Southampton after joining the club from Ayr.

BOB CHARLES, 72, was a schoolboy international goalkeeper who went on to play in the same England youth team as World Cup winners Geoff Hurst and Nobby Stiles. He had a brief career with home-town club Southampton, winning a Third Division championship medal in the 1959–60 season, then playing for Weymouth and Hastings.

ALEC GASKELL, 81, made a single appearance for Newcastle on Boxing Day 1953, deputising for the injured Jackie Milburn against Middlesbrough. The centre-forward spent the rest of his career in the lower reaches of the Football League, playing for Southport, Mansfield and Tranmere.

VINCE RADCLIFFE, 68, was a half-back who played for Portsmouth between 1963–67, initially as Jimmy Dickinson's understudy. He later served Peterborough, Rochdale and Kings Lynn, then joined Western Suburbs after emigrating to Australia.

DENNIS JACKSON, 82, joined Aston Villa from Hednesford in 1954, went on to play for Millwall, then returned to non-league football with Rugby. The full-back later managed the Villa Old Stars team.

KEN PLANT, 88, netted 55 goals in 119 appearances for Bury and continued to score regularly after joining Colchester for £3,000 in 1954. The centre-forward was on the mark 84 times in 197 matches and was the club's leading scorer in three seasons. He also played non-league football for Nuneaton and Atherstone.

WALTER GERRARD, 70, was involved in one of the biggest shocks in the history of the Scottish Cup. The centre-forward was part of the Berwick squad – although he did not feature in the game – that defeated Rangers 1-0 in a first round tie at Shielfield Park in 1967. He also played for East Stirlingshire and Clydebank before helping to pioneer professional football in Hong Kong.

APRIL 2014

SANDY JARDINE, 65, was one of the most decorated and respected players in Scottish football. In a 15-year career with Rangers, the full-back won three league titles, five Scottish Cups and five League Cups. He lifted the European Cup-Winners' Cup when they beat Moscow Dynamo 3-2 in the 1972 final and was named Player of the Year three years later. After making 674 appearances for the Ibrox club, Jardine played for Hearts for five years, reached 1,000 games and won another Player of the Year award at the age of 37. He gained 38 international caps and played in the 1974 and 1978 World Cup Finals. Later, he was joint manager at Tynecastle with former Rangers team-mate Alex MacDonald, missing out on the title on goal difference in 1986 when Hearts and Celtic both finished on 50 points.

DYLAN TOMBIDES, 20, signed for West Ham as a 14-year-old and made his debut in a League Cup tie against Wigan in September 2012. He was regarded as one of the most exciting young players to come out of Australia. The striker died of testicular cancer and the club decided to retire his No 38 squad number. Before kick-off of the home game against Crystal Palace, his father Jim and brother Taylor laid out his shirt in the centre circle. Supporters paid their tribute by applauding when 38 minutes showed on the stadium clock.

SANDY BROWN, 75, made 31 appearances in Everton's title-winning season of 1969–70 when they finished nine points clear of Leeds. He also contributed to their FA Cup success four years earlier, featuring in four ties en route to the Wembley game against Sheffield Wednesday which his team won 3-2. Brown, signed from Partick Thistle, was an uncompromising left-back who was at times deployed as a defensive midfielder by manager Harry Catterick. He made 253 appearances for the club and later played for Shrewsbury and Southport.

GORDON SMITH, 59, made a crucial impact as a substitute for Aston Villa in the second replay of the 1977 League Cup Final against Everton at Old Trafford. With the teams still deadlocked at 2-2, after drawing 0-0 at Wembley and 1-1 at Hillsborough, he came on to supply the cross for Brian Little to score the winner seconds from the end of extra-time. The Scotland Under-23 full-back joined Villa from St Johnstone for £80,000, moved on to Tottenham for £150,000, then helped Wolves win promotion from Division Two in 1983.

ANDY DAVIDSON, 81, was a one-club man who made a record 579 appearances for Hull in a career spanning 16 seasons. He joined in 1947 and remained until leaving his assistant manager's position in 1979. Davidson, used in several roles before settling into the right-back slot, was a key figure in their successful 1965–66 season which brought the Third Division title and a run to the quarter-finals of the FA Cup. After injury curtailed his playing career, he joined the coaching staff.

DAVE BLAKEY, 84, made a record 658 appearances for Chesterfield – his only team. The centre-half and captain played his first game in 1948 and retired at the end of the 1966–67 season. From September 1952 to November 1957 he was an ever-present, a run of 244 league games. Bill Shankly wanted to sign him for Liverpool, but he turned down the move for financial reasons. Blakey later became chief scout for Burnley, scouted for Leeds and was assistant manager to Billy Bremner at Doncaster.

FRANK KOPEL, 65, made 407 appearances for Dundee United and twice won the Scottish League Cup during ten years at the club. His team defeated Aberdeen 3-0 in a replay in the 1979–80 season and successfully defended the trophy by beating Dundee by the same scoreline.

Kopel, a full-back, was a losing finalist in the Scottish Cup against Celtic in 1974 and against Rangers in a replay in 1981. He started his career with Manchester United, moved to Blackburn and after leaving Tannadice finished his playing career with Arbroath, where he was also assistant manager.

TITO VILANOVA, 45, was appointed Barcelona's coach in June 2012 after Pep Guardiola stepped down to take a break from football. In his one season in charge, the club won La Liga, matching Real Madrid's 100 points in the previous campaign and setting a new scoring record of 115 goals in 38 games. He left the job in July 2013 to continue treatment for cancer.

ROLANDO UGOLINI, 89, joined Middlesbrough from Celtic for a £7,000 fee in 1948 and made 335 appearances for the club over eight seasons. The goalkeeper, born in Italy and raised in Glasgow, went on to play for Wrexham, Dundee United and, briefly, Berwick Rangers.

PETER ELLSON, 88, joined Crewe in 1949 and made 234 appearances during seven years with the club. The goalkeeper then played for Runcorn in the Cheshire League.

MAY 2014

STAN CROWTHER, 78, holds a unique place in FA Cup history – the only man to have been allowed to play for two clubs in the same season. He was in Aston Villa's team beaten by Stoke in a third round tie in 1958 and would normally have been cup-tied for the remainder of the campaign. But in the wake of the Munich Air Disaster, which claimed the lives of eight of Manchester United's 'Busby Babes,' the wing-half moved to Old Trafford for a fee of £18,000 and was given dispensation by the FA to turn out for them in the competition. The move was completed shortly before their fifth round match against Sheffield Wednesday and Crowther helped United reach the final. They were beaten 2-0 by Bolton, 12 months after he was a Wembley winner with Villa – against United. The England Under-23 international's stay proved a short one and he moved on to Chelsea, then Brighton and finally into non-league football.

CLIVE CLARK, 73, played in three cup finals for West Bromwich Albion in successive years. The diminutive winger was among the scorers when they lifted the League Cup in 1966 with a 5-3 aggregate win over West Ham, the last time the competition was decided over two legs. The following season, when he was leading scorer with 29 goals, they lost 3-2 to Queens Park Rangers. Albion then defeated Everton 1-0 in the 1968 FA Cup Final. Clark joined them from QPR for £20,000, then a club record, and made 353 appearances, scoring 98 goals, in eight years at The Hawthorns. He also played for Preston and Southport.

TERRY BELL, 69, was signed from non-league football by Hartlepool manager Brian Clough and converted from a midfield player into a forward. He was top scorer in the club's first promotion season, from Division Four in 1967–68, and spent four years at the Victoria Ground. An £8,000 transfer took him to Reading, where he was Player of the Year in the 1970–71 campaign. He later played for Aldershot.

MALCOLM GLAZER, 85, led the controversial takeover of Manchester United in 2005. His family's purchase of the club for £790m was funded largely by loans secured against its assets and met with widespread protests from supporters. The New York-born billionaire, who also owned the Tampa Bay Buccaneers American football team, never set foot in Old Trafford. He suffered a stroke in 2006 and sons Joel and Avram took over day-to-day running of the club.

GEOFF RICHARDS, 85, netted on his debut for West Bromwich Albion against Luton in 1946. He was 17 and at the time the club's youngest scorer. The winger spent most of his time in the reserves before having to give up league football because of a knee injury. Richards continued to play non-league and was player-manager at Hednesford.

TERRY FARMER, 82, scored York's Fourth Division promotion-winning goal against Aldershot in 1959. The centre-forward joined the club from Rotherham and later played non-league football at Scarborough, Buxton, Worksop and Retford.

JUNE 2014

JOHN FANTHAM, 75, scored 166 goals in 434 appearances for Sheffield Wednesday, making him the club's leading post-war marksman. He netted 23 of them during the 1960–61 season when his side finished second to Tottenham in the old First Division. The inside-forward was also an FA Cup runner-up, Wednesday losing the 1966 final 3-2 to Everton after leading 2-0. Fantham, who spent 13 years at Hillsborough, won one England cap – in a 4-1 win over Luxembourg in a World Cup qualifier at Highbury in 1961. He later played for Rotherham and Macclesfield before retiring in 1972.

BRIAN FARMER, 80, played for Birmingham in two finals of the Inter-Cities Fairs Cup – forerunner of the UEFA Cup. His side lost 4-1 on aggregate to Barcelona in 1960 and were beaten 4-2 over two legs by Roma the following year. In 1962, the full-back joined Bournemouth and after retiring was a scout and non-league coach.

DAVID TAYLOR, 60, became the first chief executive of the Scottish FA, succeeding long-serving secretary Jim Farry in 1999. During that time, he oversaw the appointments of Berti Vogts and Walter Smith as Scotland manager, He left in 2007 to work for UEFA, serving as general secretary and as an executive director.

WILLIE HARVEY, 84, was an inside-forward who spent seven seasons with Kilmarnock from 1951. He also had spells with Dunfermline, Bradford Park Avenue and Arbroath and later played for teams in Australia.

JIM BULLIONS, 90, was the youngest member, aged 22, of the Derby team that beat Charlton 4-1 in the 1946 FA Cup Final. The wing-half also played for Leeds and Shrewsbury before finishing his career in non-league football. Reg Harrison (91), who played outside-right at Wembley, is now the only survivor of that successful side.

JULY 2014

ALFREDO DI STEFANO, 88, was universally acclaimed as one of the greatest players of all-time – a pioneer of the deep-lying centre-forward role and a player equally as adept at creating goals as scoring them. He was on the mark in each of Real Madrid's successes in the first five European Cup-Finals, including a hat-trick against Eintracht Frankfurt in 1960 when Ferenc Puskas netted the team's other four goals in a 7-3 victory, watched by a crowd of 127,621 at Hampden Park. Born in Buenos Aires, Di Stefano won two Argentine titles with River Plate and four with Millonarios, of Colombia, then helped Real become champions eight times. He was twice voted European Player of the Year and scored 307 goals in 396 matches in 11 seasons at the club before leaving, at the age of 38, for two years with Espanyol. The man nicknamed 'Blond Arrow' played international football for three countries, although never at the World Cup. Di Stefano won six caps with Argentina and played four times for Colombia, the latter appearances not officially recognised by FIFA. The world governing body initially ruled he could not represent Spain, reversing that decision after he acquired citizenship, and 31 further internationals yielded 23 goals. A managerial career, including spells with River Plate, Boca Juniors and Valencia, brought further league and cup honours. But major success eluded him back at Real, including a 1983 defeat in the European Cup-Winners Cup Final by an Aberdeen side managed by Alex Ferguson. He became the club's honorary president in 2000, a position he held until his death, a few weeks after Real's tenth victory, against Atletico Madrid, in Europe's top club competition.

DANNY CANNING, 88, won the Third Division South title with two clubs. He was Cardiff's goalkeeper in the 1946-47 campaign and helped Swansea become champions two seasons later. Canning later played for Nottingham Forest.

RECORDS SECTION

GOALSCORING
(†Football League pre-1992–93)

Highest: Arbroath 36 Bon Accord (Aberdeen) 0 in Scottish Cup 1, Sep 12, 1885. On same day, also in Scottish Cup 1, Dundee Harp beat Aberdeen Rov 35-0.

Internationals: France 0 England 15 in Paris, 1906 (Amateur); Ireland 0 England 13 in Belfast Feb 18, 1882 (record in UK); England 9 Scotland 3 at Wembley, Apr 15, 1961; Biggest England win at Wembley: 9-0 v Luxembourg (Euro Champ), Dec 15, 1982.

Other record wins: Scotland: 11-0 v Ireland (Glasgow, Feb 23, 1901); **Northern Ireland:** 7-0 v Wales (Belfast, Feb 1, 1930); **Wales:** 11-0 v Ireland (Wrexham, Mar 3, 1888); **Rep of Ireland:** 8-0 v Malta (Euro Champ, Dublin, Nov 16, 1983).

Record international defeats: England: 1-7 v Hungary (Budapest, May 23, 1954); **Scotland:** 3-9 v England (Wembley, Apr 15, 1961); **Ireland:** 0-13 v England (Belfast, Feb 18, 1882); **Wales:** 0-9 v Scotland (Glasgow, Mar 23, 1878); **Rep of Ireland:** 0-7 v Brazil (Uberlandia, May 27, 1982).

World Cup: Qualifying round – Australia 31 American Samoa 0, world record international score (Apr 11, 2001); Australia 22 Tonga 0 (Apr 9, 2001); Iran 19 Guam 0 (Nov 25, 2000); Maldives 0 Iran 17 (Jun 2, 1997). **Finals – highest scores:** Hungary 10 El Salvador 1 (Spain, Jun 15, 1982); Hungary 9 S Korea 0 (Switzerland, Jun 17, 1954); Yugoslavia 9 Zaire 0 (W Germany, Jun 18, 1974).

European Championship: Qualifying round – **highest scorers:** San Marino 0 Germany 13 (Serravalle, Sep 6, 2006). **Finals – highest score:** Holland 6 Yugoslavia 1 (quarter-final, Rotterdam, Jun 25, 2000).

Biggest England U-21 win: 9-0 v San Marino (Shrewsbury, Nov 19, 2013).

FA Cup: Preston 26 Hyde 0 1st round, Oct 15, 1887.

League Cup: West Ham 10 Bury 0 (2nd round, 2nd leg, Oct 25, 1983); Liverpool 10 Fulham 0 (2nd round, 1st leg, Sep 23, 1986). **Record aggregates:** Liverpool 13 Fulham 2 (10-0h, 3-2a), Sep 23, Oct 7, 1986; West Ham 12 Bury 1 (2-1a, 10-0h), Oct 4, 25, 1983; Liverpool 11 Exeter 0 (5-0h, 6-0a), Oct 7, 28, 1981.

League Cup - most goals in one match: 12 Reading 5 Arsenal 7 aet (4th round, Oct 30, 2012).

Premier League (beginning 1992–93): Manchester Utd 9 Ipswich 0, Mar 4, 1995. Tottenham 9 Wigan 1, Nov 22, 2009. **Record away win:** Nottm Forest 1 Manchester Utd 8 Feb 6, 1999.

Highest aggregate scores in Premier League – 11: Portsmouth 7 Reading 4, Sep 29, 2007; **10:** Tottenham 6 Reading 4, Dec 29, 2007; Tottenham 9 Wigan 1, Nov 22, 2009; Manchester Utd 8 Arsenal 2, Aug 28, 2011; Arsenal 7 Newcastle 3, Dec 29, 2012; WBA 5 Manchester Utd 5, May 19, 2013; **9:** Norwich 4 Southampton 5, Apr 9, 1994; Manchester Utd 9 Ipswich 0, Mar 4, 1995; Southampton 6 Manchester Utd 3, Oct 26, 1996; Blackburn 7 Sheffield Wed 2, Aug 25, 1997; Nottm Forest 1 Manchester Utd 8 Feb 6, 1999; Tottenham 7 Southampton 2, Mar 11, 2000; Tottenham 4 Arsenal 5, Nov 13, 2004; Middlesbrough 8 Manchester City 1, May 11, 2008; Chelsea 7 Sunderland 2, Jan 16, 2010; Manchester City 6 Arsenal 3, Dec 14, 2013.

†Football League (First Division): Aston Villa 12 Accrington 2, Mar 12, 1892; Tottenham 10 Everton

354

4, Oct 11, 1958 (highest Div 1 aggregate that century); WBA 12 Darwen 0, Apr 4, 1892; Nottm Forest 12 Leicester Fosse 0, Apr 21, 1909. **Record away win:** Newcastle 1 Sunderland 9, Dec 5, 1908; Cardiff 1 Wolves 9, Sep 3, 1955; Wolves 0 WBA 8, Dec 27, 1893.

New First Division (beginning 1992–93): Bolton 7 Swindon 0, Mar 8, 1997; Sunderland 7 Oxford Utd 0, Sep 19, 1998. **Record away win:** Stoke 0 Birmingham 7, Jan 10, 1998; Oxford Utd 0 Birmingham 7, Dec 12, 1998. **Record aggregate:** Grimsby 6 Burnley 5, Oct 29, 2002; Burnley 4 Watford 7, Apr 5, 2003.

Championship (beginning 2004–05): WBA 7 Barnsley 0, May 6, 2007. **Record away wins:** Wolves 0 Southampton 6, Mar 31, 2007; Bristol City 0 Cardiff 6, Jan 26, 2010; Doncaster 0 Ipswich 6, Feb 15, 2011; Millwall 0 Birmingham 6, Jan 14, 2012; Barnsley 0 Charlton 6, Apr 13, 2013. **Record aggregate:** Leeds 4 Preston 6, Sep 29, 2010; Leeds 3 Nottm Forest 7, Mar 20, 2012.

†**Second Division:** Newcastle 13 Newport Co 0, Oct 5, 1946; Small Heath 12 Walsall Town Swifts 0, Dec 17, 1892; Darwen 12 Walsall 0, Dec 26, 1896; Woolwich Arsenal 12 Loughborough 0, Mar 12, 1900; Small Heath 12 Doncaster 0, Apr 11, 1903. **Record away win:** *Burslem Port Vale 0 Sheffield Utd 10, Dec 10, 1892. **Record aggregate:** Manchester City 11 Lincoln 3, Mar 23, 1895.

New Second Division (beginning 1992–93): Hartlepool 1 Plymouth Argyle 8, May 7, 1994; Hartlepool 8 Grimsby 1, Sep 12, 2003.

New League 1 (beginning 2004–05): Swansea 7 Bristol City 1, Sep 10, 2005; Nottm Forest 7 Swindon 1, Apr 19, 2008; Bristol City 6 Gillingham 0, Mar 18, 2006; Swindon 6 Port Vale 0, Apr 19, 2008; Norwich 1 Colchester 7, Aug 8, 2009; Huddersfield 7 Brighton 1, Aug 18, 2009; Huddersfield 6 Wycombe 0, Nov 14, 2009; Stockport 0 Huddersfield 6, Apr 24, 2010; Oldham 0 Southampton 6, Jan 11, 2011; Wycombe 0 Huddersfield 6, Jan 6, 2012; Yeovil 0 Stevenage 6, Apr 14, 2012. **Record aggregate:** Hartlepool 4 Wrexham 6, Mar 5, 2005; Wolves 6 Rotherham 4, Apr 18, 2014.

†**Third Division:** Gillingham 10 Chesterfield 0, Sep 5, 1987; Tranmere 9 Accrington 0, Apr 18, 1959; Brentford 9 Wrexham 0, Oct 15, 1963. **Record away win:** Halifax 0 Fulham 8, Sep 16, 1969. **Record aggregate:** Doncaster 7 Reading 5, Sep 25, 1982.

New Third Division (beginning 1992–93): Barnet 1 Peterborough 9, Sep 5, 1998. **Record aggregate:** Hull 7 Swansea 4, Aug 30, 1997.

New League 2 (beginning 2004–05): Peterborough 7 Brentford 0, Nov 24, 2007 Shrewsbury 7 Gillingham 0, Sep 13, 2008; Crewe 7 Barnet 0, Aug 21, 2010; Crewe 8 Cheltenham 1, Apr 2, 2011.

Record away win: Boston 0 Grimsby 6, Feb 3, 2007; Macclesfield 0 Darlington 6, Aug 30, 2008; Lincoln 0 Rotherham 6, Mar 25, 2011. **Record aggregate:** Burton 5 Cheltenham 6, Mar 13, 2010; Accrington 7 Gillingham 4, Oct 2, 2010.

†**Third Division (North):** Stockport 13 Halifax 0 (still joint biggest win in Football League – see Div 2) Jan 6, 1934; Tranmere 13 Oldham 4, Dec 26, 1935. (17 is highest Football League aggregate score). **Record away win:** Accrington 0 Barnsley 9, Feb 3, 1934.

†**Third Division (South):** Luton 12 Bristol Rov 0, Apr 13, 1936; Bristol City 9 Gillingham 4, Jan 15, 1927; Gillingham 9 Exeter 4, Jan 7, 1951. **Record away win:** Northampton 0 Walsall 8, Apr 8, 1947.

†**Fourth Division:** Oldham 11 Southport 0, Dec 26, 1962. **Record away win:** Crewe 1 Rotherham 8, Sep 8, 1973. **Record aggregate:** Hartlepool 0 Barrow 4, Apr 4, 1959; Crystal Palace 9 Accrington 2, Aug 20, 1960; Wrexham 10 Hartlepool 1, Mar 3, 1962; Oldham 11 Southport 0, Dec 26, 1962; Torquay 8 Newport 3, Oct 19, 1963; Shrewsbury 7 Doncaster 4, Feb 1, 1975; Barnet 4 Crewe 7, Aug 17, 1991.

Scottish Premier – Highest aggregate: 12: Motherwell 6 Hibernian 6, May 5, 2010; **11:** Celtic 8 Hamilton 3, Jan 3, 1987; Motherwell 5 Aberdeen 6, Oct 20, 1999. **Other highest team scores:** Aberdeen 8 Motherwell 0 (Mar 26, 1979); Hamilton 0 Celtic 8 (Nov 5, 1988); Celtic 9 Aberdeen 0 (Nov 6, 2010).

Scottish League Div 1: Celtic 11 Dundee 0, Oct 26, 1895. **Record away win:** Hibs 11 *Airdrie 1, Oct 24, 1959.

Scottish League Div 2: Airdrieonians 15 Dundee Wanderers 1, Dec 1, 1894 (biggest win in history of League football in Britain).

Record modern Scottish League aggregate: 12 – Brechin 5 Cowdenbeath 7, Div 2, Jan 18, 2003.

Record British score since 1900: Stirling 20 Selkirk 0 (Scottish Cup 1, Dec 8, 1984). Winger Davie Thompson (7 goals) was one of 9 Stirling players to score.

LEAGUE GOALS – BEST IN SEASON (Before restructure in 1992)

Div		Goals	Games
1	WR (Dixie) Dean, Everton, 1927–28	60	39
2	George Camsell, Middlesbrough, 1926–27	59	37
3(S)	Joe Payne, Luton, 1936–37	55	39
3(N)	Ted Harston, Mansfield, 1936–37	55	41
3	Derek Reeves, Southampton, 1959–60	39	46
4	Terry Bly, Peterborough, 1960–61	52	46

(Since restructure in 1992)

Div		Goals	Games
1	Guy Whittingham, Portsmouth, 1992–93	42	46
2	Jimmy Quinn, Reading, 1993–94	35	46
3	Andy Morrell, Wrexham, 2002–03	34	45

Premier League – BEST IN SEASON

Andy Cole **34 goals** (Newcastle – 40 games, 1993–94); Alan Shearer **34 goals** (Blackburn – 42 games, 1994–95).

FOOTBALL LEAGUE – BEST MATCH HAULS

(Before restructure in 1992)

Div	Goals	
1	Ted Drake (Arsenal), away to Aston Villa, Dec 14, 1935	7
	James Ross (Preston) v Stoke, Oct 6, 1888	7
2	*Neville (Tim) Coleman (Stoke) v Lincoln, Feb 23, 1957	7
	Tommy Briggs (Blackburn) v Bristol Rov, Feb 5, 1955	7
3(S)	Joe Payne (Luton) v Bristol Rov, Apr 13, 1936	10
3(N)	Robert ('Bunny') Bell (Tranmere) v Oldham, Dec 26, 1935 he also missed a penalty	9
3	Barrie Thomas (Scunthorpe) v Luton, Apr 24, 1965	5
	Keith East (Swindon) v Mansfield, Nov 20, 1965	5
	Steve Earle (Fulham) v Halifax, Sep 16, 1969	5
	Alf Wood (Shrewsbury) v Blackburn, Oct 2, 1971	5
	Tony Caldwell (Bolton) v Walsall, Sep 10, 1983	5
	Andy Jones (Port Vale) v Newport Co., May 4, 1987	5
4	Bert Lister (Oldham) v Southport, Dec 26, 1962	6

*Scored from the wing

(Since restructure in 1992)

Div Goals

1   **4 in match** – John Durnin (Oxford Utd v Luton, 1992–93); Guy Whittingham (Portsmouth v Bristol Rov 1992–93); Craig Russell (Sunderland v Millwall, 1995–96); David Connolly (Wolves at Bristol City 1998–99); Darren Byfield (Rotherham at Millwall, 2002–03); David Connolly (Wimbledon at Bradford City, 2002–03); Marlon Harewood (Nottm Forest v Stoke, 2002–03); Michael Chopra (Watford at Burnley, 2002–03); Robert Earnshaw (Cardiff v Gillingham, 2003–04).

2   **5 in match** – Paul Barnes (Burnley v Stockport, 1996–97); Robert Taylor (all 5, Gillingham at Burnley, 1998–99); Lee Jones (all 5, Wrexham v Cambridge Utd, 2001–02).

3   **5** in match – Tony Naylor (Crewe v Colchester, 1992–93); Steve Butler (Cambridge Utd v Exeter, 1993–4); Guiliano Grazioli (Peterborough at Barnet, 1998–99).

Champ   **4** in match – Garath McCleary (Nottm Forest at Leeds 2011–12); Nikola Zigic (Birmingham at Leeds 2011–12; Craig Davies (Barnsley at Birmingham 2012–13; Ross McCormack (Leeds at Charlton 2013–14), Jesse Lingard (Birmingham v Sheffield Wed 2013–14).

Lge 1   **4** in match – Jordan Rhodes (all 4, Huddersfield at Sheffield Wed, 2011–12)
    5 in match – Juan Ugarte (Wrexham at Hartlepool, 2004–05); Jordan Rhodes (Huddersfield at Wycombe, 2011–12).

Last player to score 6 in English League match: Geoff Hurst (West Ham 8 Sunderland 0, Div 1 Oct 19,1968.

PREMIER LEAGUE – BEST MATCH HAULS

5 goals in match: Andy Cole (Manchester Utd v Ipswich, Mar 4, 1995); Alan Shearer (Newcastle v Sheffield Wed, Sep 19, 1999); Jermain Defoe (Tottenham v Wigan, Nov 22, 2009); Dimitar Berbatov (Manchester Utd v Blackburn, Nov 27, 2010).

SCOTTISH LEAGUE

Div		Goals
Prem	Gary Hooper (Celtic) v Hearts, May 13, 2012	5
	Kris Boyd (Rangers) v Dundee Utd, Dec 30, 2009	5
	Kris Boyd (Kilmarnock) v Dundee Utd, Sep 25, 2004	5
	Kenny Miller (Rangers) v St Mirren, Nov 4, 2000	5
	Marco Negri (Rangers) v Dundee Utd, Aug. 23, 1997	5
	Paul Sturrock (Dundee Utd) v Morton, Nov 17, 1984	5
1	Jimmy McGrory (Celtic) v Dunfermline, Jan 14, 1928	8
1	Owen McNally (Arthurlie) v Armadale, Oct 1, 1927	8
2	Jim Dyet (King's Park) v Forfar, Jan 2, 1930 on his debut for the club	8
2	John Calder (Morton) v Raith, Apr 18, 1936	8
2	Norman Haywood (Raith) v Brechin, Aug. 20, 1937	8

SCOTTISH LEAGUE – BEST IN SEASON

Prem	Brian McClair (Celtic, 1986–87)	35
	Henrik Larsson (Celtic, 2000–01)	35
1	William McFadyen (Motherwell, 1931–32)	53
2	*Jimmy Smith (Ayr, 1927–28 – 38 appearances)	66
	(*British record)	

CUP FOOTBALL

Scottish Cup: John Petrie (Arbroath) v Bon Accord, at Arbroath, 1st round, Sep 12, 1885   13

FA Cup: Ted MacDougall (Bournemouth) v Margate, 1st round, Nov 20,1971   9

FA Cup Final: Billy Townley (Blackburn) v Sheffield Wed, at Kennington Oval, 1890; Jimmy Logan (Notts Co) v Bolton, at Everton, 1894; Stan Mortensen (Blackpool) v Bolton, at Wembley, 1953   3

League Cup: Frank Bunn (Oldham) v Scarborough (3rd round), Oct 25, 1989   6

Scottish League Cup: Jim Fraser (Ayr) v Dumbarton, Aug. 13, 1952; Jim Forrest (Rangers) v Stirling Albion, Aug. 17, 1966   5

Scottish Cup: Most goals in match since war: 10 by **Gerry Baker** (St Mirren) in 15-0 win (1st round) v Glasgow Univ, Jan 30, 1960; 9 by his brother **Joe Baker** (Hibernian) in 15-1 win (2nd round) v Peebles, Feb 11, 1961.

AGGREGATE LEAGUE SCORING RECORDS

Goals

*Arthur Rowley (1947–65, WBA, Fulham, Leicester, Shrewsbury) **434**

†Jimmy McGrory (1922–38, Celtic, Clydebank) **410**

Hughie Gallacher (1921–39, Airdrieonians, Newcastle, Chelsea, Derby,
   Notts Co, Grimsby, Gateshead) **387**

William ('Dixie') Dean (1923–37, Tranmere, Everton, Notts Co) **379**

Hugh Ferguson (1916–30, Motherwell, Cardiff, Dundee) **362**

● Jimmy Greaves (1957–71, Chelsea, Tottenham, West Ham) **357**

Steve Bloomer (1892–1914, Derby, Middlesbrough, Derby) **352**

George Camsell (1923–39, Durham City, Middlesbrough) **348**

Dave Halliday (1920–35, St Mirren, Dundee, Sunderland, Arsenal,
   Manchester City, Clapton Orient) **338**

John Aldridge (1979–98, Newport, Oxford Utd, Liverpool, Tranmere) **329**

Harry Bedford (1919–34, Nottm Forest, Blackpool, Derby, Newcastle,
   Sunderland, Bradford PA, Chesterfield **326**

John Atyeo (1951–66, Bristol City) **315**

Joe Smith (1908–29, Bolton, Stockport) **315**

Victor Watson (1920–36, West Ham, Southampton) **312**

Harry Johnson (1919–36, Sheffield Utd, Mansfield) **309**

Bob McPhail (1923–1939, Airdrie, Rangers) **306**

(*Rowley scored 4 for WBA, 27 for Fulham, 251 for Leicester, 152 for Shrewsbury.)

● **Greaves'** 357 is record top-division total (he also scored 9 League goals for AC Milan).
Aldridge also scored 33 League goals for Real Sociedad. †McGrory scored 397 for Celtic,
13 for Clydebank).

Most League goals for one club: 349 – Dixie Dean (Everton 1925–37); 326 – George Camsell
(Middlesbrough 1925–39); 315 – John Atyeo (Bristol City 1951–66); 306 – Vic Watson
(West Ham 1920–35); 291 – Steve Bloomer (Derby 1892–1906, 1910–14); 259 – Arthur
Chandler (Leicester 1923–35); 255 – Nat Lofthouse (Bolton 1946–61); 251 – Arthur
Rowley (Leicester 1950–58).

More than 500 goals: Jimmy McGrory (Celtic, Clydebank and Scotland) scored a total of **550**
goals in his first-class career (1922–38).

More than 1,000 goals: Brazil's **Pele** is reputedly the game's all-time highest scorer with **1,283**
goals in 1,365 matches (1956–77), but many of them were scored in friendlies for his club,
Santos. He scored his 1,000th goal, a penalty, against Vasco da Gama in the Maracana
Stadium, Rio, on Nov 19, 1969. ● Pele (born Oct 23, 1940) played regularly for Santos from
the age of 16. During his career, he was sent off only once. He played 95 'A' internationals
for Brazil and in their World Cup-winning teams in 1958 and 1970. † Pele (Edson Arantes
do Nascimento) was subsequently Brazil's Minister for Sport. He never played at Wembley,
apart from being filmed there scoring a goal for a commercial. Aged 57, Pele received
an 'honorary knighthood' (Knight Commander of the British Empire) from the Queen at
Buckingham Palace on Dec 3, 1997.

Romario (retired Apr, 2008, aged 42) scored more than 1,000 goals for Vasco da Gama,
Barcelona, PSV Eindhoven, Valencia and Brazil (56 in 73 internationals).

MOST LEAGUE GOALS IN SEASON: DEAN'S 60

WR ('Dixie') Dean, Everton centre-forward, created a League scoring record in 1927–28
with 60 in 39 First Division matches. He also scored three in FA Cup ties, and 19 in
representative games, totalling 82 for the season.

George Camsell, of Middlesbrough, previously held the record with 59 goals in 37 Second
Division matches in 1926–27, his total for the season being 75.

SHEARER'S RECORD 'FIRST'

Alan Shearer (Blackburn) is the only player to score more than 30 top-division goals in 3

successive seasons since the War: 31 in 1993–94, 34 in 1994–95, 31 in 1995–96.

Thierry Henry (Arsenal) is the first player to score more than 20 Premiership goals in five consecutive seasons (2002–06). **David Halliday** (Sunderland) topped 30 First Division goals in 4 consecutive seasons with totals of 38, 36, 36 and 49 from 1925–26 to 1928–29.

MOST GOALS IN A MATCH

Sep 12, 1885: John Petrie set the all-time British individual record for a first-class match when, in Arbroath's 36-0 win against Bon Accord (Scottish Cup 1), he scored **13.**

Apr 13, 1936: Joe Payne set the still-existing individual record on his debut as a centre-forward, for Luton v Bristol Rov (Div 3 South). In a 12-0 win he scored **10.**

ROWLEY'S ALL-TIME RECORD

Arthur Rowley is English football's top club scorer with a total of 464 goals for WBA, Fulham, Leicester and Shrewsbury (1947–65). There were 434 in the League, 26 FA Cup, 4 League Cup.

Jimmy Greaves is second with a total of 420 goals for Chelsea, AC Milan, Tottenham and West Ham, made up of 366 League, 35 FA Cup, 10 League Cup and 9 in Europe. He also scored nine goals for AC Milan.

John Aldridge retired as a player at the end of season 1997–98 with a career total of 329 League goals for Newport, Oxford Utd, Liverpool and Tranmere (1979–98). In all competitions for those clubs he scored 410 in 737 appearances. He also scored 45 in 63 games for Real Sociedad.

MOST GOALS IN INTERNATIONAL MATCHES

13 by **Archie Thompson** for Australia v American Samoa in World Cup (Oceania Group qualifier) at Coff's Harbour, New South Wales, Apr 11, 2001. Result: 31-0.

7 by **Stanley Harris** for England v France in Amateur International in Paris, Nov 1, 1906. Result: 15-0.

6 by **Nat Lofthouse** for Football League v Irish League, at Wolverhampton, Sep 24, 1952. Result: 7-1.

Joe Bambrick for Northern Ireland against Wales (7-0) in Belfast, Feb 1, 1930 – a record for a Home Nations International.

WC Jordan in Amateur International for England v France, at Park Royal, Mar 23, 1908. Result: 12-0.

Vivian Woodward for England v Holland in Amateur International, at Chelsea, Dec 11,1909. Result: 9-1.

5 by **Howard Vaughton** for England v Ireland (Belfast) Feb 18, 1882. Result: 13-0.

Steve Bloomer for England v Wales (Cardiff) Mar 16, 1896. Result: 9-1.

Hughie Gallacher for Scotland against Ireland (Belfast), Feb 23, 1929. Result: 7-3.

Willie Hall for England v Northern Ireland, at Old Trafford, Nov 16, 1938. Five in succession (first three in 3·5 mins – fastest international hat-trick). Result: 7-0.

Malcolm Macdonald for England v Cyprus (Wembley) Apr 16, 1975. Result: 5-0.

Hughie Gallacher for Scottish League against Irish League (Belfast) Nov 11, 1925. Result: 7-3.

Barney Battles for Scottish League against Irish League (Firhill Park, Glasgow) Oct 31, 1928. Result: 8-2.

Bobby Flavell for Scottish League against Irish League (Belfast) Apr 30, 1947. Result: 7-4.

Joe Bradford for Football League v Irish League (Everton) Sep 25, 1929. Result: 7-2.

Albert Stubbins for Football League v Irish League (Blackpool) Oct 18, 1950. Result: 6-3.

Brian Clough for Football League v Irish League (Belfast) Sep 23, 1959. Result: 5-0.

LAST ENGLAND PLAYER TO SCORE ...

3 goals: Jermain Defoe v Bulgaria (4-0), Euro Champ qual, Wembley, Sep 3, 2010.

4 goals: Ian Wright v San Marino (7-1), World Cup qual, Bologna, Nov 17, 1993.

5 goals: Malcolm Macdonald v Cyprus (5-0), Euro Champ qual, Wembley, Apr 16, 1975.

INTERNATIONAL TOP SHOTS

		Goals	Games
England	Bobby Charlton (1958–70)	49	106
N Ireland	David Healy (2000–13)	36	95
Scotland	Denis Law (1958–74)	30	55
	Kenny Dalglish (1971–86)	30	102
Wales	Ian Rush (1980–96)	28	73
Rep of Ire	Robbie Keane (1998–2014)	62	133

ENGLAND'S TOP MARKSMEN
(As at start of season 2014–15)

	Goals	Games
Bobby Charlton (1958–70)	49	106
Gary Lineker (1984–92)	48	80
Jimmy Greaves (1959–67)	44	57
Michael Owen (1998–2008)	40	89
Wayne Rooney (2003–14)	40	95
Tom Finney (1946–58)	30	76
Nat Lofthouse (1950–58)	30	33
Alan Shearer (1992–2000)	30	63
Vivian Woodward (1903–11)	29	23
Frank Lampard (2003–14)	29	106
Steve Bloomer (1895–1907)	28	23
David Platt (1989–96)	27	62
Bryan Robson (1979–91)	26	90
Geoff Hurst (1966–72)	24	49
Stan Mortensen (1947–53)	23	25
Tommy Lawton (1938–48)	22	23
Peter Crouch (2005–11)	22	42
Mike Channon (1972–77)	21	46
Kevin Keegan (1972–82)	21	63

CONSECUTIVE GOALS FOR ENGLAND

Steve Bloomer scored in **10** consecutive appearances (19 goals) between Mar 1895 and Mar 1899.

Jimmy Greaves scored 11 goals in five consecutive matches from the start of season 1960–61.

Paul Mariner scored in five consecutive appearances (7 goals) between Nov 1981 and Jun 1982.

Wayne Rooney scored in five consecutive appearances (6 goals) between Oct 2012 and Mar 2013.

ENGLAND'S TOP FINAL SERIES MARKSMAN

Gary Lineker with 6 goals at 1986 World Cup in Mexico.

ENGLAND TOP SCORERS IN COMPETITIVE INTERNATIONALS

Michael Owen 26 goals in 53 matches; **Gary Lineker** 22 in 39; **Alan Shearer** 20 in 31.

MOST ENGLAND GOALS IN SEASON

13 – **Jimmy Greaves** (1960–61 in 9 matches); 12 – **Dixie Dean** (1926–27 in 6 matches); 10 – **Gary Lineker** (1990–91 in 10 matches); 10 – **Wayne Rooney** – (2008–09 in 9 matches).

MOST ENGLAND HAT-TRICKS

Jimmy Greaves 6; **Gary Lineker** 5, **Bobby Charlton** 4, **Vivian Woodward** 4, **Stan Mortensen** 3.

MOST GOALS FOR ENGLAND U-21s

13 – Alan Shearer (11 apps) Francis Jeffers (13 apps).

GOLDEN GOAL DECIDERS

The Football League, in an experiment to avoid penalty shoot-outs, introduced a new golden goal system in the 1994–95 **Auto Windscreens Shield** to decide matches in the knock-out stages of the competition in which scores were level after 90 minutes. The first goal scored in overtime ended play.

Iain Dunn (Huddersfield) became the first player in British football to settle a match by this sudden-death method. His 107th-minute goal beat Lincoln 3-2 on Nov 30, 1994, and to mark his 'moment in history' he was presented with a golden football trophy.

The AWS Final of 1995 was decided when Paul Tait headed the only goal for Birmingham against Carlisle 13 minutes into overtime – the first time a match at Wembley had been decided by the 'golden goal' formula.

First major international tournament match to be decided by sudden death was the Final of the **1996 European Championship** at Wembley in which Germany beat Czech Rep 2-1 by **Oliver Bierhoff's** goal in the 95th minute.

In the **1998 World Cup Finals** (2nd round), host country France beat Paraguay 1-0 with **Laurent Blanc's** goal (114).

France won the **2000 European Championship** with golden goals in the semi-final, 2-1 v Portugal (Zinedine Zidane pen, 117), and in the Final, 2-1 v Italy (David Trezeguet, 103).

Galatasaray (Turkey) won the **European Super Cup** 2-1 against Real Madrid (Monaco, Aug 25, 2000) with a 103rd minute golden goal, a penalty.

Liverpool won the **UEFA Cup** 5-4 against Alaves with a 117th-min golden goal, an own goal, in the Final in Dortmund (May 19, 2001).

In the **2002 World Cup Finals**, 3 matches were decided by Golden Goals: in the 2nd round Senegal beat Sweden 2-1 (Henri Camara, 104) and South Korea beat Italy 2-1 (Ahn Jung-hwan, 117); in the quarter-final, Turkey beat Senegal 1-0 (Ilhan Mansiz, 94).

France won the 2003 **FIFA Confederations Cup Final** against Cameroon (Paris, Jun 29) with a 97th-minute golden goal by Thierry Henry.

Doncaster won promotion to Football League with a 110th-minute golden goal winner (3-2) in the Conference Play-off Final against Dagenham at Stoke (May 10, 2003).

Germany won the **Women's World Cup Final** 2-1 v Sweden (Los Angeles, Oct 12, 2003) with a 98th-minute golden goal.

GOLD TURNS TO SILVER

Starting with the 2003 Finals of the UEFA Cup and Champions League/European Cup, UEFA introduced a new rule by which a silver goal could decide the winners if the scores were level after 90 minutes.

Team leading after 15 minutes' extra time win match. If sides level, a second period of 15 minutes to be played. If still no winner, result to be decided by penalty shoot-out.

UEFA said the change was made because the golden goal put too much pressure on referees and prompted teams to play negative football.

Although both 2003 European Finals went to extra-time, neither was decided by a silver goal. The new rule applied in the 2004 European Championship Finals, and Greece won their semi-final against the Czech Republic in the 105th minute.

The **International Board** decided (Feb 28 2004) that the golden/silver goal rule was 'unfair' and that from July 1 competitive international matches level after extra-time would, when necessary, be settled on penalties.

PREMIER LEAGUE TOP SHOTS (1992–2014)

Alan Shearer	260	Nicolas Anelka	125
Andy Cole	187	Jermain Defoe	124
Thierry Henry	175	Dwight Yorke	123

Wayne Rooney	173	Ian Wright	113
Frank Lampard	171	Dion Dublin	111
Robbie Fowler	163	Steven Gerrard	111
Michael Owen	150	Emile Heskey	111
Les Ferdinand	149	Ryan Giggs	109
Teddy Sheringham	147	Paul Scholes	107
Robin van Persie	134	Darren Bent	106
Jimmy Floyd Haselbaink	127	Matthew Le Tissier	102
Robbie Keane	126	Didier Drogba	100

LEAGUE GOAL RECORDS

The highest goal-scoring aggregates in the Football League, Premier and Scottish League are as follows:

For

	Goals	Games	Club	Season
Prem	103	38	Chelsea	2009–10
Div 1	128	42	Aston Villa	1930–31
New Div 1	108	46	Manchester City	2001–02
New Champ	99	46	Reading	2005–06
Div 2	122	42	Middlesbrough	1926–27
New Div 2	89	46	Millwall	2000–01
New Lge 1	106	46	Peterborough	2010–11
Div 3(S)	127	42	Millwall	1927–28
Div 3(N)	128	42	Bradford City	1928–29
Div 3	111	46	QPR	1961–62
New Div 3	96	46	Luton	2001–02
New Lge 2	96	46	Notts Co	2009–10
Div 4	134	46	Peterborough	1960–61
Scot Prem	105	38	Celtic	2003–04
Scot L 1	132	34	Hearts	1957–58
Scot L 2	142	34	Raith Rov	1937–38
Scot L 3 (Modern)	130	36	Gretna	2004–05

Against

	Goals	Games	Club	Season
Prem	100	42	Swindon	1993–94
Div 1	125	42	Blackpool	1930–31
New Div 1	102	46	Stockport	2001–02
New Champ	86	46	Crewe	2004–05
Div 2	141	34	Darwen	1898–99
New Div 2	102	46	Chester	1992–93
New Lge 1	98	46	Stockport	2004–05
Div 3(S)	135	42	Merthyr T	1929–30
Div 3(N)	136	42	Nelson	1927–28
Div 3	123	46	Accrington Stanley	1959–60
New Div 3	113	46	Doncaster	1997–98
New Lge 2	96	46	Stockport	2010–11
Div 4	109	46	Hartlepool Utd	1959–60
Scot Prem	100	36	Morton	1984–85
Scot Prem	100	44	Morton	1987–88
Scot L 1	137	38	Leith A	1931–32
Scot L 2	146	38	Edinburgh City	1931–32
Scot L 3 (Modern)	118	36	East Stirling	2003–04

BEST DEFENSIVE RECORDS

*Denotes under old offside law

Div	Goals Agst	Games	Club	Season
Prem	15	38	Chelsea	2004–05
1	16	42	Liverpool	1978–79
1	*15	22	Preston	1888–89
New Div 1	28	46	Sunderland	1998–99
New Champ	30	46	Preston	2005–06
2	18	28	Liverpool	1893–94
2	*22	34	Sheffield Wed	1899–1900
2	24	42	Birmingham	1947–48
2	24	42	Crystal Palace	1978–79
New Div 2	25	46	Wigan	2002–03
New Lge 1	32	46	Nottm Forest	2007–08
3(S)	*21	42	Southampton	1921–22
3(S)	30	42	Cardiff	1946–47
3(N)	*21	38	Stockport	1921–22
3(N)	21	46	Port Vale	1953–54
3	30	46	Middlesbrough	1986–87
New Div 3	20	46	Gillingham	1995–96
New Lge 2	31	46	Notts Co	2009–10
4	25	46	Lincoln	1980–81

SCOTTISH LEAGUE

Div	Goals Agst	Games	Club	Season
Prem	18	38	Celtic	2001–02
1	*12	22	Dundee	1902–03
1	*14	38	Celtic	1913–14
2	20	38	Morton	1966–67
2	*29	38	Clydebank	1922–23
2	29	36	East Fife	1995–96
New Div 3	21	36	Brechin	1995–96

TOP SCORERS (LEAGUE ONLY)

		Goals	Div
2013–14	Luis Suarez (Liverpool)	31	Prem
2012–13	Tom Pope (Port Vale)	31	Lge 2
2011–12	Jordan Rhodes (Huddersfield)	36	Lge 1
2010–11	Clayton Donaldson (Crewe)	28	Lge 2
2009–10	Rickie Lambert (Southampton)	31	Lge 1
2008– 09	Simon Cox (Swindon)		
	Rickie Lambert (Bristol Rov)	29	Lge 1
2007–08	Cristiano Ronaldo (Manchester Utd)	31	Prem
2006–07	Billy Sharp (Scunthorpe)	30	Lge 1
2005–06	Thierry Henry (Arsenal)	27	Prem
2004–05	Stuart Elliott (Hull)	27	1
	Phil Jevons (Yeovil)	27	2
	Dean Windass (Bradford City)	27	1
2003–04	Thierry Henry (Arsenal)	30	Prem
2002–03	Andy Morrell (Wrexham)	34	3
2001–02	Shaun Goater (Manchester City)	28	1
	Bobby Zamora (Brighton)	28	2
2000–01	Bobby Zamora (Brighton)	28	3
1999–00	Kevin Phillips (Sunderland)	30	Prem

1998–99	Lee Hughes (WBA)	31	1
1997–98	Pierre van Hooijdonk (Nottm Forest)	29	1
	Kevin Phillips (Sunderland)	29	1
1996–97	Graeme Jones (Wigan)	31	3
1995–96	Alan Shearer (Blackburn)	31	Prem
1994–95	Alan Shearer (Blackburn)	34	Prem
1993–94	Jimmy Quinn (Reading)	35	2
1992–93	Guy Whittingham (Portsmouth)	42	1
1991–92	Ian Wright (Crystal Palace 5, Arsenal 24)	29	1
1990–91	Teddy Sheringham (Millwall)	33	2
1989–90	Mick Quinn (Newcastle)	32	2
1988–89	Steve Bull (Wolves)	37	3
1987–88	Steve Bull (Wolves)	34	4
1986–87	Clive Allen (Tottenham)	33	1
1985–86	Gary Lineker (Everton)	30	1
1984–85	Tommy Tynan (Plymouth Argyle)	31	3
	John Clayton (Tranmere)	31	4
1983–84	Trevor Senior (Reading)	36	4
1982–83	Luther Blissett (Watford)	27	1
1981–82	Keith Edwards (Hull 1, Sheffield Utd 35)	36	4
1980–81	Tony Kellow (Exeter)	25	3
1979–80	Clive Allen (Queens Park Rangers)	28	2
1978–79	Ross Jenkins (Watford)	29	3
1977–78	Steve Phillips (Brentford)	32	4
	Alan Curtis (Swansea City)	32	4
1976–77	Peter Ward (Brighton)	32	3
1975–76	Dixie McNeil (Hereford)	35	3
1974–75	Dixie McNeil (Hereford)	31	3
1973–74	Brian Yeo (Gillingham)	31	4
1972–73	Bryan (Pop) Robson (West Ham)	28	1
1971–72	Ted MacDougall (Bournemouth)	35	3
1970–71	Ted MacDougall (Bournemouth)	42	4
1969–70	Albert Kinsey (Wrexham)	27	4
1968–69	Jimmy Greaves (Tottenham)	27	1
1967–68	George Best (Manchester Utd)	28	1
	Ron Davies (Southampton)	28	1
1966–67	Ron Davies (Southampton)	37	1
1965–66	Kevin Hector (Bradford PA)	44	4
1964–65	Alick Jeffrey (Doncaster)	36	4
1963–64	Hugh McIlmoyle (Carlisle)	39	4
1962–63	Jimmy Greaves (Tottenham)	37	1
1961–62	Roger Hunt (Liverpool)	41	2
1960–61	Terry Bly (Peterborough)	52	4

100 LEAGUE GOALS IN SEASON

Manchester City, First Div Champions in 2001–02, scored 108 goals.

Bolton, First Div Champions in 1996–97, reached 100 goals, the first side to complete a century in League football since 103 by **Northampton** (Div 4 Champions) in 1986–87.

Last League Champions to reach 100 League goals: Chelsea (103 in 2009–10). Last century of goals in the top division: 111 by runners-up **Tottenham** in 1962–63.

Clubs to score a century of Premier League goals in season: **Chelsea** 103 in 2009–10, Manchester City (102) and Liverpool (101) in 2013–14.

Wolves topped 100 goals in four successive First Division seasons (1957–58, 1958–59, 1959–60, 1960–61).

In **1930–31,** the top three all scored a century of League goals: 1 Arsenal (127), 2 Aston Villa (128), 3 Sheffield Wed (102).
Latest team to score a century of League goals: Peterborough with 106 in 2010–11 (Lge 1).

100 GOALS AGAINST

Swindon, relegated with 100 goals against in 1993–94, were the first top-division club to concede a century of League goals since **Ipswich** (121) went down in 1964. Most goals conceded in the top division: 125 by **Blackpool** in 1930–31, but they avoided relegation.

MOST LEAGUE GOALS ON ONE DAY

A record of 209 goals in the four divisions of the Football League (43 matches) was set on **Jan 2, 1932:** 56 in Div 1, 53 in Div 2, 57 in Div 3 South and 43 in Div 3 North.
There were two 10-goal aggregates: Bradford City 9, Barnsley 1 in Div 2 and Coventry City 5, Fulham 5 in Div 3 South.
That total of 209 League goals on one day was equalled on **Feb 1, 1936** (44 matches): 46 in Div 1, 46 in Div 2, 49 in Div 3 South and 69 in Div 3 North. Two matches in the Northern Section produced 23 of the goals: Chester 12, York 0 and Crewe 5, Chesterfield 6.

MOST GOALS IN TOP DIV ON ONE DAY

This record has stood since **Dec 26, 1963,** when 66 goals were scored in the ten First Division matches played.

MOST PREMIER LEAGUE GOALS ON ONE DAY

47, in nine matches on **May 8, 1993** (last day of season). For the first time, all 20 clubs scored in the Premier League programme over the weekend of Nov 27-28, 2010.

FEWEST PREMIER LEAGUE GOALS IN ONE WEEK-END

10, in 10 matches on **Nov 24/25, 2001**.

FEWEST FIRST DIV GOALS ON ONE DAY

For full/near full programme: **Ten goals**, all by home clubs, in ten matches on Apr 28, 1923 (day of Wembley's first FA Cup Final).

SCORER OF LEAGUE'S FIRST GOAL

Kenny Davenport (2 mins) for Bolton v Derby, Sep 8, 1888.

SCORERS IN CONSECUTIVE TOP-DIVISION MATCHES

Stan Mortensen scored in 11 consecutive Division One games for Blackpool in season 1950–51. **Ruud van Nistelrooy** (Manchester Utd) scored 13 goals in last 8 games of season 2002–03 and in first 2 of 2003–04. Since the last war, 3 other players scored in 10 successive matches in the old First Division: **Billy McAdams** (Man City, 1957–58), **Ron Davies** (Southampton, 1966–67) and John Aldridge (Liverpool, May–Oct 1987).

SCORERS FOR 7 PREMIER LEAGUE CLUBS

Craig Bellamy (Coventry, Newcastle, Blackburn, Liverpool, West Ham, Manchester City, Cardiff).

SCORERS FOR 6 PREMIER LEAGUE CLUBS

Les Ferdinand (QPR, Newcastle, Tottenham, West Ham, Leicester, Bolton); **Andy Cole** (Newcastle, Manchester Utd, Blackburn, Fulham, Manchester City, Portsmouth); **Marcus Bent** (Crystal Palace, Ipswich, Leicester, Everton, Charlton, Wigan); **Nick Barmby** (Tottenham, Middlesbrough, Everton, Liverpool, Leeds, Hull); **Peter Crouch** (Tottenham, Aston Villa, Southampton, Liverpool, Portsmouth, Stoke); **Robbie Keane** (Coventry, Leeds, Tottenham, Liverpool, West Ham, Aston Villa); **Nicolas Anelka** (Arsenal, Liverpool, Manchester City, Bolton, Chelsea, WBA); **Darren Bent** (Ipswich, Charlton, Tottenham, Sunderland, Aston Villa, Fulham).

SCORERS FOR 5 PREMIER LEAGUE CLUBS

Stan Collymore (Nottm Forest, Liverpool, Aston Villa, Leicester, Bradford); **Mark Hughes** (Manchester Utd, Chelsea, Southampton, Everton, Blackburn); **Benito Carbone** (Sheffield Wed, Aston Villa, Bradford, Derby, Middlesbrough); **Ashley Ward** (Norwich, Derby, Barnsley, Blackburn Bradford); **Teddy Sheringham** (Nottm Forest, Tottenham, Manchester Utd, Portsmouth, West Ham); **Chris Sutton** (Norwich, Blackburn, Chelsea, Birmingham, Aston Villa).

SCORERS IN MOST CONSECUTIVE LEAGUE MATCHES

Arsenal broke the record by scoring in 55 successive Premiership fixtures: the last match in season 2000–01, then all 38 games in winning the title in 2001–02, and the first 16 in season 2002–03. The sequence ended with a 2-0 defeat away to Manchester Utd on December 7, 2002.
Chesterfield previously held the record, having scored in 46 consecutive matches in Div 3 (North), starting on Christmas Day, 1929 and ending on December 27, 1930.

SIX-OUT-OF-SIX HEADERS

When **Oxford Utd** beat Shrewsbury 6-0 (Div 2) on Apr 23, 1996, all six goals were headers.

ALL–ROUND MARKSMEN

Alan Cork scored in four divisions of the Football League and in the Premier League in his 18-season career with Wimbledon, Sheffield Utd and Fulham (1977–95).
Brett Ormerod scored in all four divisions (2, 1, Champ and Prem Lge) for Blackpool in two spells (1997–2002, 2008–11). **Grant Holt** (Sheffield Wed, Rochdale, Nottm Forest, Shrewsbury, Norwich) has scored in four Football League divisions and in the Premier League.

MOST CUP GOALS

FA Cup – most goals in one season: 20 by Jimmy Ross (Preston, runners-up 1887–88); 15 by **Alex (Sandy) Brown** (Tottenham, winners 1900–01).
Most FA Cup goals in individual careers: 49 by Harry Cursham (Notts Co 1877–89); this century: **44** by Ian Rush (39 for Liverpool, 4 for Chester, 1 for Newcastle 1979–98). **Denis Law** was the previous highest FA Cup scorer in the 20th century with 41 goals for Huddersfield Town, Manchester City and Manchester Utd (1957–74).
Most FA Cup Final goals by individual: 5 by Ian Rush for Liverpool (2 in 1986, 2 in 1989, 1 in 1992).

HOTTEST CUP HOT-SHOT

Geoff Hurst scored 21 cup goals in season 1965–66: 11 League Cup, 4 FA Cup and 2 Cup-Winners' Cup for West Ham, and 4 in the World Cup for England.

SCORERS IN EVERY ROUND

Twelve players have scored in every round of the FA Cup in one season, from opening to Final inclusive: **Archie Hunter** (Aston Villa, winners 1887); **Sandy Brown** (Tottenham, winners 1901); **Harry Hampton** (Aston Villa, winners 1905); **Harold Blackmore** (Bolton, winners 1929); **Ellis Rimmer** (Sheffield Wed, winners 1935); **Frank O'Donnell** (Preston, beaten 1937); **Stan Mortensen** (Blackpool, beaten 1948); **Jackie Milburn** (Newcastle, winners 1951); **Nat Lofthouse** (Bolton, beaten 1953); **Charlie Wayman** (Preston, beaten 1954); **Jeff Astle** (WBA, winners 1968); **Peter Osgood** (Chelsea, winners 1970).
Blackmore and the next seven completed their 'set' in the Final at Wembley; Osgood did so in the Final replay at Old Trafford.
Only player to score in every **Football League Cup** round possible in one season: **Tony Brown** for WBA, winners 1965–66, with 9 goals in 10 games (after bye in Round 1).

TEN IN A ROW

Dixie McNeill scored for Wrexham in ten successive FA Cup rounds (18 goals): 11 in Rounds 1-6, 1977–78; 3 in Rounds 3-4, 1978–79; 4 in Rounds 3-4, 1979–80.

Stan Mortensen (Blackpool) scored 25 goals in 16 FA Cup rounds out of 17 (1946–51).

TOP MATCH HAULS IN FA CUP

Ted MacDougall scored nine goals, a record for the competition proper, in the FA Cup first round on Nov 20, 1971, when Bournemouth beat Margate 11-0. On Nov 23, 1970 he had scored six in an 8-1 first round replay against Oxford City.

Other six-goal FA Cup scorers include **George Hilsdon** (Chelsea v Worksop, 9-1, 1907–08), **Ronnie Rooke** (Fulham v Bury, 6-0, 1938–39), **Harold Atkinson** (Tranmere v Ashington, 8-1, 1952–53), **George Best** (Manchester Utd v Northampton 1969–70, 8-2 away), **Duane Darby** (Hull v Whitby, 8-4, 1996–97).

Denis Law scored all six for Manchester City at Luton (6-2) in an FA Cup 4th round tie on Jan 28, 1961, but none of them counted – the match was abandoned (69 mins) because of a waterlogged pitch. He also scored City's goal when the match was played again, but they lost 3-1.

Tony Philliskirk scored **five** when Peterborough beat Kingstonian 9-1 in an FA Cup 1st round replay on Nov 25, 1992, but had them wiped from the records.

With the score at 3-0, the Kingstonian goalkeeper was concussed by a coin thrown from the crowd and unable to play on. The FA ordered the match to be replayed at Peterborough behind closed doors, and Kingstonian lost 1-0.

● Two players have scored **ten goals** in FA Cup preliminary round matches: **Chris Marron** for South Shields against Radcliffe in Sep 1947; **Paul Jackson** when Sheffield-based club Stocksbridge Park Steels beat Oldham Town 17-1 on Aug 31, 2002. He scored 5 in each half and all ten with his feet – goal times 6, 10, 22, 30, 34, 68, 73, 75, 79, 84 mins.

QUICKEST GOALS AND RAPID SCORING

A goal in **4 sec** was claimed by **Jim Fryatt**, for Bradford PA v Tranmere (Div 4, Apr 25, 1965), and by **Gerry Allen** for Whitstable v Danson (Kent League, Mar 3,1989). **Damian Mori** scored in **4 sec** for Adelaide v Sydney (Australian National League, December 6, 1995).

Goals after **6 sec** – **Albert Mundy** for Aldershot v Hartlepool, Oct 25, 1958; **Barrie Jones** for Notts Co v Torquay, Mar 31, 1962; **Keith Smith** for Crystal Palace v Derby, Dec 12, 1964.

9.6 sec by **John Hewitt** for Aberdeen at Motherwell, 3rd round, Jan 23, 1982 (fastest goal in Scottish Cup history).

Colin Cowperthwaite reputedly scored in **3.5 sec** for Barrow v Kettering (Alliance Premier League) on Dec 8, 1979, but the timing was unofficial.

Phil Starbuck for Huddersfield **3 sec** after entering the field as 54th min substitute at home to Wigan (Div 2) on Easter Monday, Apr 12, 1993. Corner was delayed, awaiting his arrival and he scored with a header.

Malcolm Macdonald after **5 sec** (officially timed) in Newcastle's 7-3 win in a pre-season friendly at St Johnstone on Jul 29, 1972.

World's fastest goal: 2.8 sec, direct from kick-off, Argentinian **Ricardo Olivera** for Rio Negro v Soriano (Uruguayan League), December 26, 1998.

Fastest international goal: 8.3 sec, Davide Gualtieri for San Marino v England (World Cup qual, Bologna, Nov 17, 1993).

Fastest England goals: 17 sec, Tommy Lawton v Portugal in Lisbon, May 25, 1947. **27 sec, Bryan Robson** v France in World Cup at Bilbao, Spain on Jun 16, 1982; **37 sec, Gareth Southgate** v South Africa in Durban, May 22, 2003; **30 sec, Jack Cock** v Ireland, Belfast, Oct 25, 1919; **30 sec, Bill Nicholson** v Portugal at Goodison Park, May 19, 1951. **38 sec, Bryan Robson** v Yugoslavia at Wembley, Dec 13, 1989; **42 sec, Gary Lineker** v Malaysia in Kuala Lumpur, Jun 12, 1991.

Fastest international goal by substitute: 5 sec, John Jensen for Denmark v Belgium (Euro Champ), Oct 12, 1994.

Fastest goal by England substitute: 10 sec, Teddy Sheringham v Greece (World Cup qualifier) at Old Trafford, Oct 6, 2001.

Fastest FA Cup goal: 4 sec, Gareth Morris (Ashton Utd) v Skelmersdale, 1st qual round, Sep 15, 2001.

Fastest FA Cup goal (comp proper): 9.7 sec, Jimmy Kebe for Reading v WBA, 5th Round, Feb 13, 2010.

Fastest FA Cup Final goal: 25 sec, Louis Saha for Everton v Chelsea at Wembley, May 30, 2009.

Fastest goal by substitute in FA Cup Final: 96 sec, Teddy Sheringham for Manchester Utd v Newcastle at Wembley, May 22, 1999.

Fastest League Cup Final goal: 45 sec, John Arne Riise for Liverpool v Chelsea, 2005.

Fastest goal on full League debut: 7.7 sec, Freddy Eastwood for Southend v Swansea (Lge 2), Oct 16, 2004. He went on to score hat-trick in 4-2 win.

Fastest goal in cup final: 4.07 sec, 14-year-old Owen Price for Ernest Bevin College, Tooting, beaten 3-1 by Barking Abbey in Heinz Ketchup Cup Final at Arsenal on May 18, 2000. Owen, on Tottenham's books, scored from inside his own half when the ball was played back to him from kick-off.

Fastest Premier League goals: 10 sec, Ledley King for Tottenham away to Bradford, Dec 9, 2000; **10.4 sec, Alan Shearer** for Newcastle v Manchester City, Jan 18, 2003: **11 sec, Mark Viduka** for Leeds v Charlton, Mar 17, 2001; **12.5 sec. James Beattie** for Southampton at Chelsea, Aug 28, 2004; **13 sec, Chris Sutton** for Blackburn at Everton, Apr 1, 1995; **13 sec, Dwight Yorke** for Aston Villa at Coventry, Sep 30, 1995; **13 sec Asmir Begovic** (goalkeeper) for Stoke v Southampton, Nov 2, 2013; **13 sec Jay Rodriguez** for Southampton at Chelsea, Dec 1, 2013.

Fastest top-division goal: 7 sec, Bobby Langton for Preston v Manchester City (Div 1), Aug 25, 1948.

Fastest goal in Champions League: 10 sec, Roy Makaay for Bayern Munich v Real Madrid (1st ko rd), Mar 7, 2007.

Fastest Premier League goal by substitute: 9 sec, Shaun Goater, Manchester City's equaliser away to Manchester Utd (1-1), Feb 9, 2003. In Dec, 2011, Wigan's **Ben Watson** was brought off the bench to take a penalty against Stoke and scored.

Fastest goal on Premier League debut: 36 sec, Thievy Bifouma on as sub for WBA away to Crystal Palace, Feb 8, 2014.

Fastest goal by goalkeeper in professional football: 13 sec, Asmir Begovic for Stoke v Southampton (Prem Lge), Nov 2, 2013.

Fastest goal in women's football: 7 sec, Angie Harriott for Launton v Thame (Southern League, Prem Div), season 1998–99.

Fastest hat-trick in League history: 2 min 20 sec, Bournemouth's 84th-minute substitute **James Hayter** in 6-0 home win v Wrexham (Div 2) on Feb 24, 2004 (goal times 86, 87, 88 mins).

Fastest First Division hat-tricks since war: Graham Leggat, 3 goals in 3 minutes (first half) when Fulham beat Ipswich 10-1 on Boxing Day, 1963; **Nigel Clough,** 3 goals in **4 minutes** (81, 82, 85 pen) when Nottm Forest beat QPR 4-0 on Dec 13, 1987.

Premier League – fastest hat-trick: 4 min 30 sec (26, 29, 31) by **Robbie Fowler** in Liverpool 3, Arsenal 0 on Aug 28, 1994.

Fastest international hat-trick: 3 min 15 sec, Masashi Nakayami for Japan in 9-0 win v Brunei in Macao (Asian Cup), Feb 16, 2000.

Fastest international hat-trick in British matches: 3.5 min, Willie Hall for England v N Ireland at Old Trafford, Manchester, Nov 16, 1938. (Hall scored 5 in 7-0 win); **4.5 min, Arif Erdem** for Turkey v N Ireland, European Championship, at Windsor Park, Belfast, on Sep 4, 1999.

Fastest FA Cup hat-tricks: In 3 min, Billy Best for Southend v Brentford (2nd round, Dec 7, 1968); **2 min 20 sec, Andy Locke** for Nantwich v Droylsden (1st Qual round, Sep 9, 1995).

Fastest Scottish hat-trick: 2 min 30 sec, Ian St John for Motherwell away to Hibernian (Scottish League Cup), Aug 15, 1959.

Fastest hat-trick of headers: Dixie Dean's 5 goals in Everton's 7-2 win at home to Chelsea (Div 1) on Nov 14, 1931 included 3 headers between **5th** and **15th-min.**

Fastest all-time hat-trick: Reported at 1 min 50 sec, Eduardo Maglioni for Independiente

against Gimnasia de la Plata in Argentina Div , Mar 18, 1973.

Scored first kick: Billy Foulkes (Newcastle) for Wales v England at Cardiff, Oct 20, 1951, in his first international match.

Preston scored six goals in **7 min** in record 26-0 FA Cup 1st round win v Hyde, Oct 15, 1887.

Notts Co scored six second-half goals in **12 min** (Tommy Lawton 3, Jackie Sewell 3) when beating Exeter 9-0 (Div 3 South) at Meadow Lane on Oct 16, 1948.

Arsenal scored six in **18 min** (71-89 mins) in 7-1 home win (Div 1) v Sheffield Wed, Feb 15, 1992.

Tranmere scored six in first **19 min** when beating Oldham 13-4 (Div 3 North), December 26, 1935.

Sunderland scored eight in **28 min** at Newcastle (9-1 Div 1), December 5, 1908. Newcastle went on to win the title.

Southend scored all seven goals in **29 min** in 7-0 win at home to Torquay (Leyland Daf Cup, Southern quarter-final), Feb 26, 1991. Score was 0-0 until 55th minute.

Plymouth scored five in first **18 min** in 7-0 home win v Chesterfield (Div 2), Jan 3, 2004.

Five in 20 min: Frank Keetley in Lincoln's 9-1 win over Halifax in Div 3 (North), Jan 16, 1932; **Brian Dear** for West Ham v WBA (6-1, Div 1) Apr 16, 1965. **Kevin Hector** for Bradford PA v Barnsley (7-2, Div 4), Nov 20, 1965.

Four in 5 min: John McIntyre for Blackburn v Everton (Div 1), Sep 16, 1922; **WG (Billy) Richardson** for WBA v West Ham (Div 1), Nov 7, 1931.

Three in 2'5 min: Jimmy Scarth for Gillingham v Leyton Orient (Div 3S), Nov 1, 1952.

Three in three minutes: Billy Lane for Watford v Clapton Orient (Div 3S), December 20, 1933; **Johnny Hartburn** for Leyton Orient v Shrewsbury (Div 3S), Jan 22, 1955; **Gary Roberts** for Brentford v Newport, (Freight Rover Trophy, South Final), May 17, 1985; **Gary Shaw** for Shrewsbury v Bradford City (Div 3), December 22, 1990.

Two in 9 sec: Jamie Bates with last kick of first half, Jermaine McSporran 9 sec into second half when Wycombe beat Peterborough 2-0 at home (Div 2) on Sep 23, 2000.

Premier League – fastest scoring: Four goals in 4 min 44 sec, Tottenham home to Southampton on Sunday, Feb 7, 1993.

Premiership – fast scoring away: When **Aston Villa** won 5-0 at Leicester (Jan 31, 2004), all goals scored in **18 second-half min** (50-68).

Four in 13 min by Premier League sub: Ole Gunnar Solskjaer for Manchester Utd away to Nottm Forest, Feb 6, 1999.

FASTEST GOALS IN WORLD CUP FINAL SERIES

10.8 sec, Hakan Sukur for Turkey against South Korea in 3rd/4th-place match at Taegu, Jun 29, 2002; **15 sec,** Vaclav Masek for Czechoslovakia v Mexico (in Vina, Chile, 1962); **27 sec, Bryan Robson** for England v France in Bilbao, Spain, 1982).

TOP MATCH SCORES SINCE WAR

By English clubs: 13-0 by Newcastle v Newport (Div 2, Oct 1946); 13-2 by Tottenham v Crewe (FA Cup 4th. Rd replay, Feb 1960); 13-0 by Chelsea v Jeunesse Hautcharage, Lux. (Cup-Winners' Cup 1st round, 2nd leg, Sep 1971).

By Scottish club: 20-0 by Stirling v Selkirk (E. of Scotland League) in Scottish Cup 1st round. (Dec 1984). That is the highest score in British first-class football since Preston beat Hyde 26-0 in FA Cup, Oct 1887.

MOST GOALS IN CALENDAR YEAR

88 by **Lionel Messi** in 2012 (76 Barcelona, 12 Argentina).

GOALS BY GOALKEEPERS

(Long clearances unless stated)

Pat Jennings for Tottenham v Manchester Utd (goalkeeper Alex Stepney), Aug 12, 1967 (FA Charity Shield).

Peter Shilton for Leicester v Southampton (Campbell Forsyth), Oct 14, 1967 (Div 1).

Ray Cashley for Bristol City v Hull (Jeff Wealands), Sep 18, 1973 (Div 2).

Steve Sherwood for Watford v Coventry (Raddy Avramovic), Jan 14, 1984 (Div 1).

Steve Ogrizovic for Coventry v Sheffield Wed (Martin Hodge), Oct 25, 1986 (Div 1).

Andy Goram for Hibernian v Morton (David Wylie), May 7, 1988 (Scot Prem Div).

Andy McLean, on Irish League debut, for Cliftonville v Linfield (George Dunlop), Aug 20, 1988.

Alan Paterson for Glentoran v Linfield (George Dunlop), Nov 30, 1988 (Irish League Cup Final – only instance of goalkeeper scoring winner in a senior cup final in UK).

Ray Charles for East Fife v Stranraer (Bernard Duffy), Feb 28, 1990 (Scot Div 2).

Iain Hesford for Maidstone v Hereford (Tony Elliott), Nov 2, 1991 (Div 4).

Chris Mackenzie for Hereford v Barnet (Mark Taylor), Aug 12, 1995 (Div 3).

Peter Schmeichel for Manchester Utd v Rotor Volgograd, Sep 26, 1995 (header, UEFA Cup 1).

Mark Bosnich (Aston Villa) for Australia v Solomon Islands, Jun 11, 1997 (penalty in World Cup qual – 13-0).

Peter Keen for Carlisle away to Blackpool (goalkeeper John Kennedy), Oct 24, 2000 (Div 3).

Steve Mildenhall for Notts Co v Mansfield (Kevin Pilkington), Aug 21, 2001 (free-kick inside own half, League Cup 1).

Peter Schmeichel for Aston Villa v Everton (Paul Gerrard), Oct 20, 2001 (volley, first goalkeeper to score in Premiership).

Mart Poom for Sunderland v Derby (Andy Oakes), Sep 20, 2003 (header, Div 1).

Brad Friedel for Blackburn v Charlton (Dean Kiely), Feb 21, 2004 (shot, Prem).

Paul Robinson for Leeds v Swindon (Rhys Evans), Sep 24, 2003 (header, League Cup 2).

Andy Lonergan for Preston v Leicester (Kevin Pressman), Oct 2, 2004 (Champ).

Gavin Ward for Tranmere v Leyton Orient (Glenn Morris), Sep 2, 2006 (free-kick Lge 1).

Mark Crossley for Sheffield Wed v Southampton (Kelvin Davis), Dec 23, 2006 (header, Champ).

Paul Robinson for Tottenham v Watford (Ben Foster), Mar 17, 2007 (Prem).

Adam Federici for Reading v Cardiff (Peter Enckelman), Dec 28, 2008 (shot, Champ).

Chris Weale for Yeovil v Hereford (Peter Gulacsi), Apr 21, 2009 (header, Lge 1).

Scott Flinders for Hartlepool v Bournemouth (Shwan Jalal), Apr 30, 2011 (header, Lge 1).

Iain Turner for Preston v Notts Co (Stuart Nelson), Aug 27 2011 (shot, Lge 1).

Tim Howard for Everton v Bolton (Adam Bogdan), Jan 4, 2012 (Prem).

Asmir Begovic for Stoke v Southampton (Artur Boruc), Nov 2, 2013 (Prem).

MORE GOALKEEPING HEADLINES

Arthur Wilkie, sustained a hand injury in Reading's Div 3 match against Halifax on Aug 31, 1962, then played as a forward and scored twice in a 4-2 win.

Alex Stepney was Manchester Utd's joint top scorer for two months in season 1973–74 with two penalties.

Alan Fettis scored twice for Hull in 1994–95 Div 2 season, as a substitute in 3-1 home win over Oxford Utd (Dec 17) and, when selected outfield, with last-minute winner (2-1) against Blackpool on May 6.

Roger Freestone scored for Swansea with a penalty at Oxford Utd (Div 2, Apr 30, 1995) and twice from the spot the following season against Shrewsbury (Aug 12) and Chesterfield (Aug 26).

Jimmy Glass, on loan from Swindon, kept Carlisle in the Football League on May 8, 1999. With ten seconds of stoppage-time left, he went upfield for a corner and scored the winner against Plymouth that sent Scarborough down to the Conference instead.

Paul Smith, Nottm Forest goalkeeper, was allowed to run through Leicester's defence unchallenged and score direct from the kick-off of a Carling Cup second round second match on Sep 18, 2007. It replicated the 1-0 score by which Forest had led at half-time when the original match was abandoned after Leicester defender Clive Clarke suffered a heart attack. Leicester won the tie 3-2.

Tony Roberts (Dagenham), is the only known goalkeeper to score from open play in the FA Cup, his last-minute goal at Basingstoke in the fourth qualifying round on Oct 27, 2001 earning a 2-2 draw. Dagenham won the replay 3-0 and went on to reach the third round proper.

The only known instance in first-class football in Britain of a goalkeeper scoring direct from a

goal-kick was in a First Division match at Roker Park on Apr 14, 1900. The kick by Manchester City's **Charlie Williams** was caught in a strong wind and Sunderland keeper J. E Doig fumbled the ball over his line.

Jose Luis Chilavert, Paraguay's international goalkeeper, scored a hat-trick of penalties when his club Velez Sarsfield beat Ferro Carril Oeste 6-1 in the Argentine League on Nov 28, 1999. In all, he scored 8 goals in 72 internationals. He also scored with a free-kick from just inside his own half for Velez Sarsfield against River Plate on Sep 20, 2000.

Most goals by a goalkeeper in a League season: 5 (all penalties) by **Arthur Birch** for Chesterfield (Div 3 North), 1923–24.

When Brazilian goalkeeper **Rogerio Ceni** (37) converted a free-kick for Sao Paulo's winner (2-1) v Corinthians in a championship match on Mar 27, 2011, it was his 100th goal (56 free-kicks, 44 pens) in a 20-season career.

OWN GOALS

Most by player in one season: 5 by **Robert Stuart** (Middlesbrough) in 1934–35.

Three in match by one team: Sheffield Wed's **Vince Kenny**, **Norman Curtis** and **Eddie Gannon** in 5-4 defeat at home to WBA (Div 1) on Dec 26, 1952; Rochdale's **George Underwood**, **Kenny Boyle** and **Danny Murphy** in 7-2 defeat at Carlisle (Div 3 North), Dec 25, 1954; Sunderland's **Stephen Wright** and **Michael Proctor** (2) in 24, 29, 32 minutes at home to Charlton (1-3, Prem).

Feb 1, 2003; Brighton's **Liam Bridcutt** (2) and **Lewis Dunk** in 6-1 FA Cup 5th rd defeat at Liverpool, Feb 19, 2012.

Two in match by one player: Chris Nicholl (Aston Villa) scored all 4 goals in 2-2 draw away to Leicester (Div 1), Mar 20, 1976; **Jamie Carragher** (Liverpool) in first half at home to Manchester Utd (2-3) in Premiership, Sep 11, 1999; **Jim Goodwin** (Stockport) in 1-4 defeat away to Plymouth (Div 2), Sep 23, 2002; **Michael Proctor** (Sunderland) in 1-3 defeat at home to Charlton (Premiership), Feb 1, 2003. **Jonathan Walters** (Stoke) headed the first 2 Chelsea goals in their 4-0 Premier League win at the Britannia Stadium, Jan 12, 2013. He also missed a penalty.

Fastest own goals: 8 sec by **Pat Kruse** of Torquay, for Cambridge Utd (Div 4), Jan 3, 1977; in First Division, **16 sec** by **Steve Bould** (Arsenal) away to Sheffield Wed, Feb 17, 1990.

Late own-goal man: Frank Sinclair (Leicester) put through his own goal in the 90th minute of Premiership matches away to Arsenal (L1-2) and at home to Chelsea (2-2) in Aug 1999.

Half an own goal each: Chelsea's second goal in a 3-1 home win against Leicester on December 18, 1954 was uniquely recorded as 'shared own goal'. Leicester defenders **Stan Milburn** and **Jack Froggatt**, both lunging at the ball in an attempt to clear, connected simultaneously and sent it rocketing into the net.

Match of 149 own goals: When Adama, Champions of Malagasy (formerly Madagascar) won a League match 149-0 on Oct 31, 2002, all 149 were own goals scored by opponents Stade Olympique De L'Emryne. They repeatedly put the ball in their own net in protest at a refereeing decision.

MOST SCORERS IN MATCH

Liverpool set a Football League record with **eight** scorers when beating Crystal Palace 9-0 (Div 1) on Sep 12, 1989. Marksmen were: Steve Nicol (7 and 88 mins), Steve McMahon (16), Ian Rush (45), Gary Gillespie (56), Peter Beardsley (61), John Aldridge (67 pen), John Barnes (79), Glenn Hysen (82).

Fifteen years earlier, **Liverpool** had gone one better with **nine** different scorers when they achieved their record win, 11-0 at home to Stromsgodset (Norway) in the Cup-Winners' Cup 1st round, 1st leg on Sep 17, 1974.

Eight players scored for **Swansea** when they beat Sliema, Malta, 12-0 in the Cup-Winners' Cup 1st round, 1st leg on Sep 15, 1982.

Nine Stirling players scored in the 20-0 win against Selkirk in the Scottish Cup 1st Round on December 8, 1984.

Premier League record: **Seven Chelsea** scorers in 8-0 home win over Aston Villa, Dec 23, 2012. An eighth player missed a penalty.

LONG SCORING RUNS

Tom Phillipson scored in 13 consecutive matches for Wolves (Div 2) in season 1926–27, which is still an English League record. **Bill Prendergast** scored in 13 successive League and Cup appearances for Chester (Div 3 North) in season 1938–39.

Dixie Dean scored in 12 consecutive games (23 goals) for Everton in Div 2 in 1930–31.

Danish striker **Finn Dossing** scored in 15 consecutive matches (Scottish record) for Dundee Utd (Div 1) in 1964–65.

50-GOAL PLAYERS

With **52** goals for **Wolves** in 1987–78 (34 League, 12 Sherpa Van Trophy, 3 Littlewoods Cup, 3 FA Cup), **Steve Bull** became the first player to score 50 in a season for a League club since **Terry Bly** for Div 4 newcomers Peterborough in 1960–61. Bly's 54 comprised 52 League goals and 2 in the FA Cup, and included 7 hat-tricks, still a post-war League record. Bull was again the country's top scorer with 50 goals in season 1988–89: 37 League, 2 Littlewoods Cup and 11 Sherpa Van Trophy. Between Bly and Bull, the highest individual scoring total for a season was 49 by two players: **Ted MacDougall** (Bournemouth 1970–71, 42 League, 7 FA Cup) and **Clive Allen** (Tottenham 1986–87, 33 League, 12 Littlewoods Cup, 4 FA Cup).

HOT SHOTS

Jimmy Greaves was top Div 1 scorer (League goals) six times in 11 seasons: 32 for Chelsea (1958–59), 41 for Chelsea (1960–61) and, for Tottenham, 37 in 1962–63, 35 in 1963–64, 29 in 1964–65 (joint top) and 27 in 1968–69.

Brian Clough (Middlesbrough) was leading scorer in Div 2 in three successive seasons: 40 goals in 1957–58, 42 in 1958–59 and 39 in 1959–60.

John Hickton (Middlesbrough) was top Div 2 scorer three times in four seasons: 24 goals in 1967–68, 24 in 1969–70 and 25 in 1970–71.

MOST HAT-TRICKS

Nine by George Camsell (Middlesbrough) in Div 2, 1926–27, is the record for one season. Most League hat-tricks in career: 37 by **Dixie Dean** for Tranmere and Everton (1924–38).

Most top division hat-tricks in a season since last War: six by **Jimmy Greaves** for Chelsea (1960–61). **Alan Shearer** scored five hat-tricks for Blackburn in the Premier League, season 1995–96.

Frank Osborne (Tottenham) scored three consecutive hat-tricks in Div 1 in Oct–Nov 1925, against Liverpool, Leicester (away) and West Ham.

Tom Jennings (Leeds) scored hat-tricks in three successive Div 1 matches (Sep–Oct, 1926): 3 goals v Arsenal, 4 at Liverpool, 4 v Blackburn. Leeds were relegated that season.

Jack Balmer (Liverpool) scored his three hat-tricks in a 17-year career in successive Div 1 matches (Nov 1946): 3 v Portsmouth, 4 at Derby, 3 v Arsenal. No other Liverpool player scored during that 10-goal sequence by Balmer.

Gilbert Alsop scored hat-tricks in three successive matches for Walsall in Div 3 South in Apr 1939: 3 at Swindon, 3 v Bristol City and 4 v Swindon.

Alf Lythgoe scored hat-tricks in three successive games for Stockport (Div 3 North) in Mar 1934: 3 v Darlington, 3 at Southport and 4 v Wrexham.

TRIPLE HAT-TRICKS

There have been at least three **instances of 3 hat-tricks being scored for one team in a Football League match**:

Apr 21, 1909: Enoch West, Billy Hooper and **Alfred Spouncer** for Nottm Forest (12-0 v Leicester Fosse, Div 1).

Mar 3, 1962: Ron Barnes, Wyn Davies and **Roy Ambler** in Wrexham's 10-1 win against Hartlepool (Div 4).

Nov 7, 1987: Tony Adcock, Paul Stewart and David White for Manchester City in 10-1 win at home to Huddersfield (Div 2).

For the first time in the Premiership, **three** hat-tricks were completed on one day (Sep 23, 1995): **Tony Yeboah** for Leeds at Wimbledon; **Alan Shearer** for Blackburn v Coventry; **Robbie Fowler** with 4 goals for Liverpool v Bolton.

In the FA Cup, **Jack Carr, George Elliott** and **Walter Tinsley** each scored 3 in Middlesbrough's 9-3 first round win against Goole in Jan, 1915. **Les Allen** scored 5, **Bobby Smith** 4 and **Cliff Jones** 3 when Tottenham beat Crewe 13-2 in a fourth-round replay in Feb 1960.

HAT-TRICKS v THREE 'KEEPERS

When West Ham beat Newcastle 8-1 (Div 1) on Apr 21, 1986 **Alvin Martin** scored 3 goals against different goalkeepers: Martin Thomas injured a shoulder and was replaced, in turn, by outfield players Chris Hedworth and Peter Beardsley.

Jock Dodds of Lincoln had done the same against West Ham on Dec 18, 1948, scoring past Ernie Gregory, Tommy Moroney and George Dick in 4-3 win.

David Herd (Manchester Utd) scored against Sunderland's Jim Montgomery, Charlie Hurley and Johnny Parke in 5-0 First Division home win on Nov 26, 1966.

Brian Clark, of Bournemouth, scored against Rotherham's Jim McDonagh, Conal Gilbert and Michael Leng twice in 7-2 win (Div 3) on Oct 10, 1972.

On Oct 16, 1993 (Div 3) **Chris Pike** (Hereford) scored a hat-trick in 5-0 win over Colchester, who became the first team in league history to have two keepers sent off in the same game.

On Dec 18, 2004 (Lge 1), in 6-1 defeat at Hull, Tranmere used **John Achterberg** and **Russell Howarth,** both retired injured, and defender **Theo Whitmore.**

On Mar 9, 2008, Manchester Utd had three keepers in their 0-1 FA Cup quarter-final defeat by Portsmouth. **Tomasz Kuszczak** came on at half-time for **Edwin van der Sar** but was sent off when conceding a penalty. **Rio Ferdinand** went in goal and was beaten by Sulley Muntari's spot-kick.

Derby used three keepers in a 4-1 defeat at Reading (Mar 10, 2010, Champ). **Saul Deeney,** who took over when **Stephen Bywater** was injured, was sent off for a foul and **Robbie Savage** replaced him.

EIGHT-DAY HAT-TRICK TREBLE

Joe Bradford, of Birmingham, scored three hat-tricks in eight days in Sep 1929–30 v Newcastle (won 5-1) on the 21st, 5 for the Football League v Irish League (7-2) on the 25th, and 3 in his club's 5-7 defeat away to Blackburn on the 28th.

PREMIERSHIP DOUBLE HAT-TRICK

Robert Pires and **Jermaine Pennant** each scored 3 goals in Arsenal's 6-1 win at home to Southampton (May 7, 2003).

TON UP – BOTH ENDS

Manchester City are the only club to score and concede a century of League goals in the same season. When finishing fifth in the 1957–58 season, they scored 104 and gave away 100.

TOURNAMENT TOP SHOTS

Most individual goals in a World Cup Final series: 13 by **Just Fontaine** for France, in Sweden 1958. Most in European Championship Finals: 9 by **Michel Platini** for France, in France 1984.

MOST GOALS ON CLUB DEBUT

Jim Dyet scored eight in King's Park's 12-2 win against Forfar (Scottish Div 2, Jan 2, 1930). **Len Shackleton** scored six times in Newcastle's 13-0 win v Newport (Div 2, Oct 5, 1946) in the week he joined them from Bradford Park Avenue.

MOST GOALS ON LEAGUE DEBUT

Five by **George Hilsdon,** for Chelsea (9-2) v Glossop, Div 2, Sep 1, 1906. **Alan Shearer,** with three goals for Southampton (4-2) v Arsenal, Apr 9, 1988, became, at 17, the youngest player to score a First Division hat-trick on his full debut.

FOUR-GOAL SUBSTITUTE

James Collins (Swindon), sub from 60th minute, scored 4 in 5-0 home win v Portsmouth (Lge 1) on Jan 1, 2013.

CLEAN-SHEET RECORDS

On the way to promotion from Div 3 in season 1995–96, Gillingham's ever-present goalkeeper **Jim Stannard** set a clean-sheet record. In 46 matches. He achieved 29 shut-outs (17 at home, 12 away), beating the 28 by **Ray Clemence** for Liverpool (42 matches in Div 1, 1978–79) and the previous best in a 46-match programme of 28 by Port Vale (Div 3 North, 1953–54). In conceding only 20 League goals in 1995–96, Gillingham created a defensive record for the lower divisions.

Chris Woods, Rangers' England goalkeeper, set a British record in season 1986–87 by going 1,196 minutes without conceding a goal. The sequence began in the UEFA Cup match against Borussia Moenchengladbach on Nov 26, 1986 and ended when Rangers were sensationally beaten 1-0 at home by Hamilton in the Scottish Cup 3rd round on Jan 31, 1987 with a 70th-minute goal by **Adrian Sprott.** The previous British record of 1,156 minutes without a goal conceded was held by Aberdeen goalkeeper **Bobby Clark** (season 1970–01).

Manchester Utd set a new Premier League clean-sheet record of 1,333 minutes (including 14 successive match shut-outs) in season 2008–09 (Nov 15–Feb 21). **Edwin van der Sar's** personal British league record of 1,311 minutes without conceding ended when United won 2-1 at Newcastle on Mar 4, 2009.

Most clean sheets in season in top English division: **28** by **Liverpool** (42 matches) in 1978–79; **25** by **Chelsea** (38 matches) in 2004–05.

There have been three instances of clubs keeping 11 consecutive clean sheets in the Football League: **Millwall** (Div 3 South, 1925–26), **York** (Div 3, 1973–74) and **Reading** (Div 4, 1978–79). In his sequence, Reading goalkeeper **Steve Death** set the existing League shut-out record of 1,103 minutes.

Sasa Ilic remained unbeaten for over 14 hours with 9 successive shut-outs (7 in Div 1, 2 in play-offs) to equal a Charlton club record in Apr/May 1998. He had 12 clean sheets in 17 first team games after winning promotion from the reserves with 6 successive clean sheets.

Sebastiano Rossi kept a clean sheet in 8 successive away matches for AC Milan (Nov 1993–Apr 1994).

A world record of 1,275 minutes without conceding a goal was set in 1990–01 by **Abel Resino,** the Atletico Madrid goalkeeper. He was finally beaten by Sporting Gijon's Enrique in Atletico's 3-1 win on Mar 19, 1991.

In international football, the record is held by **Dino Zoff** with a shut-out for Italy (Sep 1972 to Jun 1974) lasting 1,142 minutes.

LOW SCORING

Fewest goals by any club in season in Football League: 18 by **Loughborough** (Div 2, 34 matches, 1899–1900); in 38 matches 20 by **Derby** (Prem Lge, 2007–08); in 42 matches, 24 by **Watford** (Div 2, 1971–72) and by **Stoke** (Div 1, 1984–85)); in 46-match programme, 27 by **Stockport** (Div 3, 1969–70).

Arsenal were the lowest Premier League scorers in its opening season (1992–93) with 40 goals in 42 matches, but won both domestic cup competitions. In subsequent seasons the lowest Premier League scorers were **Ipswich** (35) in 1993–94, **Crystal Palace** (34) in 1994–95, **Manchester City** (33) in 1995–96 and **Leeds** (28) in 1996–97 until **Sunderland** set the Premiership's new fewest-goals record with only 21 in 2002–03. Then, in 2007–08, **Derby** scored just 20.

LONG TIME NO SCORE

The world international non-scoring record was set by **Northern Ireland** when they played 13 matches and 1,298 minutes without a goal. The sequence began against Poland on Feb 13, 2002 and ended 2 years and 5 days later when David Healy scored against Norway (1-4) in Belfast on Feb 18, 2004.

Longest non-scoring sequences in Football League: 11 matches by **Coventry** in 1919–20 (Div 2); 11 matches in 1992–93 (Div 2) by **Hartlepool,** who after beating Crystal Palace 1-0 in the FA Cup 3rd round on Jan 2, went 13 games and 2 months without scoring (11 League, 1 FA Cup, 1 Autoglass Trophy). The sequence ended after 1,227 blank minutes with a 1-1 draw at Blackpool (League) on Mar 6.

In the Premier League (Oct–Jan season 1994–95) **Crystal Palace** failed to score in nine consecutive matches.

The British non-scoring club record is held by **Stirling:** 14 consecutive matches (13 League, 1 Scottish Cup) and 1,292 minutes play, from Jan 31 1981 until Aug 8, 1981 (when they lost 4-1 to Falkirk in the League Cup).

In season 1971–72, **Mansfield** did not score in any of their first nine home games in Div 3. They were relegated on goal difference of minus two.

FA CUP CLEAN SHEETS

Most consecutive FA Cup matches without conceding a goal: 11 by **Bradford City.** The sequence spanned 8 rounds, from 3rd in 1910–11 to 4th. Round replay in 1911–12, and included winning the Cup in 1911.

GOALS THAT WERE WRONGLY GIVEN

Tottenham's last-minute winner at home to Huddersfield (Div 1) on Apr 2, 1952: Eddie Baily's corner-kick struck referee WR Barnes in the back, and the ball rebounded to Baily, who crossed for Len Duquemin to head into the net. Baily had infringed the Laws by playing the ball twice, and the result (1-0) stood. Those two points helped Spurs to finish Championship runners-up; Huddersfield were relegated.

The second goal (66 mins) in **Chelsea's** 2-1 home win v Ipswich (Div 1) on Sep 26, 1970: Alan Hudson's shot hit the stanchion on the outside of goal and the ball rebounded on to the pitch. But instead of the goal-kick, referee Roy Capey gave a goal, on a linesman's confirmation. TV pictures proved otherwise. The Football League quoted from the Laws of the Game: 'The referee's decision on all matters is final.'

When **Watford's** John Eustace and **Reading's** Noel Hunt challenged for a 13th minute corner at Vicarage Road on Sep 20, 2008, the ball was clearly diverted wide. But referee Stuart Attwell signalled for a goal on the instruction his assistant and it went down officially as a Eustace own goal. The Championship match ended 2-2.

Sunderland's 1-0 Premier League win over **Liverpool** on Oct 17, 2009 was decided by one of the most bizarre goals in football history when Darren Bent's shot struck a red beach ball thrown from the crowd and wrong footed goalkeeper Jose Reina. Referee Mike Jones wrongly allowed it to stand. The Laws of the Game state: 'An outside agent interfering with play should result in play being stopped and restarted with a drop ball.'

Blackburn's 59th minute equaliser (2-2) in 3-3 draw away to Wigan (Prem) on Nov 19, 2011 was illegal. Morten Gamst Pedersen played the ball to himself from a corner and crossed for Junior Hoilett to net.

The Republic of Ireland were deprived of the chance of a World Cup place in the second leg of their play-off with France on Nov 18, 2009. They were leading 1-0 in Paris when Thierry Henry blatantly handled before setting up William Gallas to equalise in extra-time and give his side a 2-1 aggregate victory. The FA of Ireland's call for a replay was rejected by FIFA.

• The most notorious goal in World Cup history was fisted in by Diego Maradona in **Argentina's** 2-1 quarter-final win over England in Mexico City on Jun 22, 1986.

ATTENDANCES

GREATEST WORLD CROWDS

World Cup, Maracana Stadium, Rio de Janeiro, Jul 16, 1950. Final match (Brazil v Uruguay) attendance 199,850; receipts £125,000.

Total attendance in three matches (including play-off) between Santos (Brazil) and AC Milan for the Inter-Continental Cup (World Club Championship) 1963, exceeded 375,000.

BRITISH RECORD CROWDS

Most to pay: 149,547, Scotland v England, at Hampden Park, Glasgow, Apr 17, 1937. This was the first all-ticket match in Scotland (receipts £24,000).

At Scottish FA Cup Final: 146,433, Celtic v Aberdeen, at Hampden Park, Apr 24, 1937. Estimated another 20,000 shut out.

For British club match (apart from a Cup Final): 143,470, Rangers v Hibernian, at Hampden Park, Mar 27, 1948 (Scottish Cup semi-final).

FA Cup Final: 126,047, Bolton v West Ham, Apr 28, 1923. Estimated 150,000 in ground at opening of Wembley Stadium.

New Wembley: 89,874, FA Cup Final, Cardiff v Portsmouth, May 17, 2008.

World Cup Qualifying ties: 120,000, Cameroon v Morocco, Yaounde, Nov 29, 1981; 107,580, Scotland v Poland, Hampden Park, Oct 13, 1965.

European Cup: 135,826, Celtic v Leeds (semi-final, 2nd leg) at Hampden Park, Apr 15, 1970.

European Cup Final: 127,621, Real Madrid v Eintracht Frankfurt, at Hampden Park, May 18, 1960.

European Cup-Winners' Cup Final: 100,000, West Ham v TSV Munich, at Wembley, May 19, 1965.

Scottish League: 118,567, Rangers v Celtic, Jan 2, 1939.

Scottish League Cup Final: 107,609, Celtic v Rangers, at Hampden Park, Oct 23, 1965.

Football League old format: First Div: 83,260, Manchester Utd v Arsenal, Jan 17, 1948 (at Maine Road); **Div 2** 70,302 Tottenham v Southampton, Feb 25, 1950; **Div 3S:** 51,621, Cardiff v Bristol City, Apr 7, 1947; **Div 3N:** 49,655, Hull v Rotherham, Dec 25, 1948; **Div 3:** 49,309, Sheffield Wed v Sheffield Utd, Dec 26, 1979; **Div 4:** 37,774, Crystal Palace v Millwall, Mar 31, 1961.

Premier League: 76,098, Manchester Utd v Blackburn, Mar 31, 2007.

Football League – New Div 1: 41,214, Sunderland v Stoke, Apr 25, 1998; **New Div2:** 32,471, Manchester City v York, May 8, 1999; **New Div 3:** 22,319, Hull v Hartlepool Utd, Dec 26, 2002. **New Champs:** 52,181, Newcastle v Ipswich, Apr 24, 2010; **New Lge 1:** 38,256, Leeds v Gillingham, May 3, 2008; **New Lge 2:** 17,250, MK Dons v Morecambe, May 3, 2008.

In English Provinces: 84,569, Manchester City v Stoke (FA Cup 6), Mar 3, 1934.

Record for Under-21 International: 55,700, England v Italy, first match at New Wembley, Mar 24, 2007.

Record for friendly match: 104,679, Rangers v Eintracht Frankfurt, at Hampden Park, Glasgow, Oct 17, 1961.

FA Youth Cup: 38,187, Arsenal v Manchester Utd, at Emirates Stadium, Mar 14, 2007.

Record Football League aggregate (season): 41,271,414 (1948–49) – 88 clubs.

Record Football League aggregate (single day): 1,269,934, December 27, 1949, previous day, 1,226,098.

Record average home League attendance for season: 75,691 by Manchester Utd in 2007–08.

Long-ago League attendance aggregates: 10,929,000 in 1906–07 (40 clubs); 28,132,933 in 1937–38 (88 clubs).

Last 1m crowd aggregate, League (single day): 1,007,200, December 27, 1971.

Record Amateur match attendance: 100,000 for FA Amateur Cup Final, Pegasus v Harwich & Parkeston at Wembley, Apr 11, 1953.

Record Cup-tie aggregate: 265,199, at two matches between Rangers and Morton, in Scottish Cup Final, 1947–48.

Abandoned match attendance records: In England – 63,480 at Newcastle v Swansea City FA Cup 3rd round, Jan 10, 1953, abandoned 8 mins (0-0), fog.

In Scotland: 94,596 at Scotland v Austria (4-1), Hampden Park, May 8, 1963. Referee Jim Finney ended play (79 minutes) after Austria had two players sent off and one carried off.

Colchester's record crowd (19,072) was for the FA Cup 1st round tie v Reading on Nov 27, 1948, abandoned 35 minutes (0-0), fog.

SMALLEST CROWDS

Smallest League attendances: 450 Rochdale v Cambridge Utd (Div 3, Feb 5, 1974); 469, Thames v Luton (Div 3 South, December 6, 1930).

Only 13 people paid to watch Stockport v Leicester (Div 2, May 7, 1921) at Old Trafford, but up to 2,000 stayed behind after Manchester Utd v Derby earlier in the day. Stockport's ground was closed.

Lowest Premier League crowd: 3,039 for Wimbledon v Everton, Jan 26, 1993 (smallest top-division attendance since War).

Lowest Saturday post-war top-division crowd: 3,231 for Wimbledon v Luton, Sep 7, 1991 (Div 1).

Lowest Football League crowds, new format – Div 1: 849 for Wimbledon v Rotherham, (Div 1) Oct 29, 2002 (smallest attendance in top two divisions since War); 1,054 Wimbledon v Wigan (Div 1), Sep 13, 2003 in club's last home match when sharing Selhurst Park; **Div 2:** 1,077, Hartlepool Utd v Cardiff, Mar 22, 1994; **Div 3:** 739, Doncaster v Barnet, Mar 3, 1998.

Lowest top-division crowd at a major ground since the war: 4,554 for Arsenal v Leeds (May 5, 1966) – fixture clashed with live TV coverage of Cup-Winners' Cup Final (Liverpool v Borussia Dortmund).

Smallest League Cup attendances: 612, Halifax v Tranmere (1st round, 2nd leg) Sep 6, 2000; 664, Wimbledon v Rotherham (3rd round), Nov 5, 2002.

Smallest League Cup attendance at top-division ground: 1,987 for Wimbledon v Bolton (2nd Round, 2nd Leg) Oct 6, 1992.

Smallest Wembley crowds for England matches: 15,628 v Chile (Rous Cup, May 23, 1989 – affected by Tube strike); 20,038 v Colombia (Friendly, Sep 6, 1995); 21,432 v Czech. (Friendly, Apr 25, 1990); 21,142 v Japan (Umbro Cup, Jun 3, 1995); 23,600 v Wales (British Championship, Feb 23, 1983); 23,659 v Greece (Friendly, May 17, 1994); 23,951 v East Germany (Friendly, Sep 12, 1984); 24,000 v N Ireland (British Championship, Apr 4, 1984); 25,756 v Colombia (Rous Cup, May 24, 1988); 25,837 v Denmark (Friendly, Sep 14, 1988).

Smallest international modern crowds: 221 for Poland v N Ireland (4-1, friendly) at Limassol, Cyprus, on Feb 13, 2002. Played at neutral venue at Poland's World Cup training base. 265 (all from N Ireland) at their Euro Champ qual against Serbia in Belgrade on Mar 25, 2011. Serbia ordered by UEFA to play behind closed doors because of previous crowd trouble.

Smallest international modern crowds at home: N Ireland: 2,500 v Chile (Belfast, May 26, 1989 – clashed with ITV live screening of Liverpool v Arsenal Championship decider); Scotland: 7,843 v N Ireland (Hampden Park, May 6, 1969); Wales: 2,315 v N Ireland (Wrexham, May 27, 1982).

Smallest attendance for post-war England match: 2,378 v San Marino (World Cup) at Bologna (Nov 17, 1993). Tie clashed with Italy v Portugal (World Cup) shown live on Italian TV.

Smallest paid attendance for British first-class match: 29 for Clydebank v East Stirling, CIS Scottish League Cup 1st round, Jul 31, 1999. Played at Morton's Cappielow Park ground, shared by Clydebank. Match clashed with the Tall Ships Race which attracted 200,000 to the area.

FA CUP CROWD RECORD (OUTSIDE FINAL)

The first FA Cup-tie shown on closed-circuit TV (5th round, Saturday, Mar 11, 1967, kick-off 7pm) drew a total of 105,000 spectators to Goodison Park and Anfield. At Goodison, 64,851 watched the match 'for real', while 40,149 saw the TV version on eight giant screens at Anfield. Everton beat Liverpool 1-0.

LOWEST SEMI-FINAL CROWD

The smallest FA Cup semi-final attendance since the War was 17,987 for the Manchester Utd–Crystal Palace replay at Villa Park on Apr 12, 1995. Palace supporters largely boycotted tie after a fan died in car-park clash outside pub in Walsall before first match.
Previous lowest: 25,963 for Wimbledon v Luton, at Tottenham on Apr 9, 1988.
Lowest quarter-final crowd since the war: 8,735 for Chesterfield v Wrexham on Mar 9, 1997.
Smallest FA Cup 3rd round attendances for matches between League clubs: 1,833 for Chester v Bournemouth (at Macclesfield) Jan 5, 1991; 1,966 for Aldershot v Oxford Utd, Jan 10, 1987.

PRE-WEMBLEY CUP FINAL CROWDS

AT CRYSTAL PALACE

1895 42,560	1902 48,036	1908 74,967
1896 48,036	Replay 33,050	1909 67,651
1897 65,891	1903 64,000	1910 76,980
1898 62,017	1904 61,734	1911 69,098
1899 73,833	1905 101,117	1912 54,434
1900 68,945	1906 75,609	1913 120,028
1901 110,802	1907 84,584	1914 72,778

AT OLD TRAFFORD

1915   50,000

AT STAMFORD BRIDGE

1920 50,018	1921 72,805	1922 53,000

INTERNATIONAL RECORDS

MOST APPEARANCES

Peter Shilton, England goalkeeper, then aged 40, retired from international football after the 1990 World Cup Finals with the European record number of caps – 125. Previous record (119) was set by **Pat Jennings,** Northern Ireland's goalkeeper from 1964–86, who retired on his 41st birthday during the 1986 World Cup in Mexico. Shilton's England career spanned 20 seasons from his debut against East Germany at Wembley on Nov 25, 1970.

Eight players have completed a century of appearances in full international matches for England. **Billy Wright** of Wolves, was the first, retiring in 1959 with a total of 105 caps. **Bobby Charlton,** of Manchester Utd, beat Wright's record in the World Cup match against West Germany in Leon, Mexico, in Jun 1970 and **Bobby Moore,** of West Ham, overtook Charlton's 106 caps against Italy in Turin, in Jun 1973. Moore played 108 times for England, a record that stood until **Shilton** reached 109 against Denmark in Copenhagen (Jun 7, 1989). In season 2008–09, **David Beckham** (LA Galaxy/AC Milan) overtook Moore as England's most-capped outfield player. In the vastly different selection processes of their eras, Moore played 108 full games for his country, whereas Beckham's total of 115 to the end of season 2009–10, included 58 part matches, 14 as substitute and 44 times substituted. **Steven Gerrard** won his 100th cap against Sweden in Stockholm on Nov 14, 2012 and **Ashley Cole** reached 100 appearances against Brazil at Wembley on Feb 6, 2013. **Frank Lampard** played his 100th game against Ukraine in Kiev (World Cup qual) on Sep 10, 2013.

Robbie Keane won his 126th Republic of Ireland cap, overtaking Shay Given's record, In a World Cup qualifier against the Faroe Islands on Jun 7, 2013. Keane scored all his team's three goals in a 3-0 win.

Kenny Dalglish became Scotland's first 100-cap international v Romania (Hampden Park, Mar 26, 1986).

World's most-capped player: Ahmed Hassan, 184 for Egypt (1995–2012).

Most-capped European player: Vitalijs Astafjevs, 167 for Latvia (1992–2010).
Most-capped European goalkeeper: Thomas Ravelli, 143 Internationals for Sweden (1981–97).
Gillian Coultard, (Doncaster Belles), England Women's captain, received a special presentation from Geoff Hurst to mark 100 caps when England beat Holland 1-0 at Upton Park on Oct 30, 1997. She made her international debut at 18 in May 1981, and retired at the end of season 1999–2000 with a record 119 caps (30 goals).

BRITAIN'S MOST-CAPPED PLAYERS

(As at start of season 2014–15)

England		Paul McStay	76	Mal Donaghy	91
Peter Shilton	125	Tommy Boyd	72	Aaron Hughes	90
David Beckham	115			Sammy McIlroy	88
Steven Gerrard	114	**Wales**		Maik Taylor	88
Bobby Moore	108	Neville Southall	92		
Ashley Cole	107	Gary Speed	85	**Republic of Ireland**	
Bobby Charlton	106	Craig Bellamy	78	Robbie Keane	133
Frank Lampard	106	Dean Saunders	75	Shay Given	125
Billy Wright	105	Peter Nicholas	73	Kevin Kilbane	110
		Ian Rush	73	Steve Staunton	102
Scotland				Damien Duff	100
Kenny Dalglish	102	**Northern Ireland**			
Jim Leighton	91	Pat Jennings	119		
Alex McLeish	77	David Healy	95		

MOST ENGLAND CAPS IN ROW

Most consecutive international appearances: 70 by **Billy Wright,** for England from Oct 1951 to May 1959. He played 105 of England's first 108 post-war matches.
England captains most times: Billy Wright and Bobby Moore, 90 each.
England captains – 4 in match (v Serbia & Montenegro at Leicester Jun 3, 2003): **Michael Owen** was captain for the first half and after the interval the armband passed to **Emile Heskey** (for 15 minutes), **Phil Neville** (26 minutes) and substitute **Jamie Carragher** (9 minutes, including time added).

MOST SUCCESSIVE ENGLAND WINS

10 (Jun 1908–Jun 1909. Modern: 8 (Oct 2005–Jun 2006).

ENGLAND'S LONGEST UNBEATEN RUN

19 matches (16 wins, 3 draws), Nov 1965–Nov 1966.

ENGLAND'S TALLEST

At **6ft 7in, Peter Crouch** became England's tallest-ever international when he made his debut against Colombia in New Jersey, USA on May 31, 2005.

MOST PLAYERS FROM ONE CLUB IN ENGLAND SIDES

Arsenal supplied seven men (a record) to the England team v Italy at Highbury on Nov 14, 1934. They were: Frank Moss, George Male, Eddie Hapgood, Wilf Copping, Ray Bowden, Ted Drake and Cliff Bastin. In addition, Arsenal's Tom Whittaker was England's trainer.
Since then until 2001, the most players from one club in an England team was six from **Liverpool** against Switzerland at Wembley in Sep 1977. The side also included a Liverpool old boy, Kevin Keegan (Hamburg).
Seven **Arsenal** men took part in the England – France (0-2) match at Wembley on Feb 10, 1999. Goalkeeper David Seaman and defenders Lee Dixon, Tony Adams and Martin Keown lined up for England. Nicolas Anelka (2 goals) and Emmanuel Petit started the match for

France and Patrick Vieira replaced Anelka.

Manchester Utd equalled Arsenal's 1934 record by providing England with seven players in the World Cup qualifier away to Albania on Mar 28, 2001. Five started the match – David Beckham (captain), Gary Neville, Paul Scholes, Nicky Butt and Andy Cole – and two went on as substitutes: Wes Brown and Teddy Sheringham.

INTERNATIONAL SUBS RECORDS

Malta substituted all 11 players in their 1-2 home defeat against England on Jun 3, 2000. Six substitutes by England took the total replacements in the match to 17, then an international record.

Most substitutions in match by **England:** 11 in second half by Sven-Goran Eriksson against Holland at Tottenham on Aug 15, 2001; 11 against Italy at Leeds on Mar 27, 2002; Italy sent on 8 players from the bench – the total of 19 substitutions was then a record for an England match; 11 against Australia at Upton Park on Feb 12, 2003 (entire England team changed at half-time); 11 against Iceland at City of Manchester Stadium on Jun 5, 2004.

Forty three players, a record for an England match, were used in the international against Serbia & Montenegro at Leicester on Jun 3, 2003. England sent on 10 substitutes in the second half and their opponents changed all 11 players.

The **Republic of Ireland** sent on 12 second-half substitutes, using 23 players in all, when they beat Russia 2-0 in a friendly international in Dublin on Feb 13, 2002.

First England substitute: Wolves winger **Jimmy Mullen** replaced injured Jackie Milburn (15 mins) away to Belgium on May 18, 1950. He scored in a 4-1 win.

ENGLAND'S WORLD CUP-WINNERS

At Wembley, Jul 30, 1966, 4-2 v West Germany (2-2 after 90 mins), scorers Hurst 3, Peters. Team: Banks; Cohen, Wilson, Stiles, Jack Charlton, Moore (capt), Ball, Hurst, Bobby Charlton, Hunt, Peters. Manager **Alf Ramsey** fielded that same eleven in six successive matches (an England record): the World Cup quarter-final, semi-final and Final, and the first three games of the following season. England wore red shirts in the Final and The Queen presented the Cup to Bobby Moore. The players each received a £1,000 bonus, plus £60 World Cup Final appearance money, all less tax, and Ramsey a £6,000 bonus from the FA The match was shown live on TV (in black and white).

England's non-playing reserves – there were no substitutes – also received the £1,000 bonus, but no medals. That remained the case until FIFA finally decided that non-playing members and staff of World Cup-winning squads should be given replica medals. England's 'forgotten heroes' received theirs at a reception in Downing Street on June 10, 2009 and were later guests of honour at the World Cup qualifier against Andorra at Wembley. The 11 reserves were: Springett, Bonetti, Armfield, Byrne, Flowers, Hunter, Paine, Connelly, Callaghan, Greaves, Eastham.

BRAZIL'S RECORD RUN

Brazil hold the record for the longest unbeaten sequence in international football: 45 matches from 1993–97. The previous record of 31 was held by Hungary between Jun 1950 and Jul 1954.

ENGLAND MATCHES ABANDONED

May 17, 1953 v **Argentina** (Friendly, Buenos Aires) after 23 mins (0-0) – rain.

Oct 29, 1975 v **Czechoslovakia** (Euro Champ qual, Bratislava) after 17 mins (0-0) – fog. Played next day.

Feb 15, 1995 v **Rep of Ireland** (Friendly, Dublin) after 27 mins (1-0) – crowd disturbance.

ENGLAND POSTPONEMENTS

Nov 21, 1979 v **Bulgaria** (Euro Champ qual, Wembley, postponed for 24 hours – fog; Aug 10, 2011 v **Holland** (friendly), Wembley, postponed after rioting in London.

Oct 16, 2012 v **Poland** (World Cup qual, Warsaw) postponed to next day – pitch waterlogged. The friendly against **Honduras** (Miami, Jun 7, 2014) was suspended midway through the first half for 44 minutes – thunderstorm.

ENGLAND UNDER COVER

England played indoors for the first time when they beat Argentina 1-0 in the World Cup at the Sapporo Dome, Japan, on Jun 7, 2002.

ALL-SEATED INTERNATIONALS

The first **all-seated crowd** (30,000) for a full international in Britain saw **Wales** and **West Germany** draw 0-0 at Cardiff Arms Park on May 31, 1989. The terraces were closed.

England's first all-seated international at Wembley was against Yugoslavia (2-1) on December 13, 1989 (attendance 34,796). The terracing behind the goals was closed for conversion to seating.

The first **full-house all-seated** international at Wembley was for England v Brazil (1-0) on Mar 28, 1990, when a capacity 80,000 crowd paid record British receipts of £1,200,000.

MOST NEW CAPS IN ENGLAND TEAM

6, by Sir Alf Ramsey (v Portugal, Apr 3, 1974) and by Sven-Goran Eriksson (v Australia, Feb 12, 2003; 5 at half-time when 11 changes made).

PLAYED FOR MORE THAN ONE COUNTRY

Multi-nationals in senior international football include: **Johnny Carey** (1938–53) – caps Rep of Ireland 29, N Ireland 7; **Ferenc Puskas** (1945–62) – caps Hungary 84, Spain 4; **Alfredo di Stefano** (1950–56) – caps Argentina 7, Spain 31; **Ladislav Kubala** (1948–58) – caps, Hungary 3, Czechoslovakia 11, Spain 19, only player to win full international honours with 3 countries. Kubala also played in a fourth international team, scoring twice for FIFA v England at Wembley in 1953. Eleven players, including **Carey**, appeared for both N Ireland and the Republic of Ireland in seasons directly after the last war.

Cecil Moore, capped by N Ireland in 1949 when with Glentoran, played for USA v England in 1953.

Hawley Edwards played for England v Scotland in 1874 and for Wales v Scotland in 1876.

Jack Reynolds (Distillery and WBA) played for both Ireland (5 times) and England (8) in the 1890s.

Bobby Evans (Sheffield Utd) had played 10 times for Wales when capped for England, in 1910–11. He was born in Chester of Welsh parents.

In recent years, several players have represented USSR and one or other of the breakaway republics. The same applies to Yugoslavia and its component states. **Josip Weber** played for Croatia in 1992 and made a 5-goal debut for Belgium in 1994.

THREE-GENERATION INTERNATIONAL FAMILY

When Bournemouth striker **Warren Feeney** was capped away to Liechtenstein on Mar 27, 2002, he became the third generation of his family to play for Northern Ireland. He followed in the footsteps of his grandfather James (capped twice in 1950) and father Warren snr. (1 in 1976).

FATHERS & SONS CAPPED BY ENGLAND

George Eastham senior (pre-war) and **George Eastham junior**; **Brian Clough** and **Nigel Clough**; **Frank Lampard snr** and **Frank Lampard jnr**; **Mark Chamberlain** and **Alex Oxlade-Chamberlain**.

FATHER & SON SAME-DAY CAPS

Iceland made father-and-son international history when they beat Estonia 3-0 in Tallin on Apr 24, 1996. **Arnor Gudjohnsen** (35) started the match and was replaced (62 mins) by his 17-year-old son Eidur.

LONGEST UNBEATEN START TO ENGLAND CAREER
Steven Gerrard, 21 matches (W16, D5) 2000–03.

SUCCESSIVE ENGLAND HAT-TRICKS
The last player to score a hat-trick in consecutive England matches was **Dixie Dean** on the summer tour in May 1927, against Belgium (9-1) and Luxembourg (5-2).

MOST GOALS BY PLAYER v ENGLAND
4 by **Zlatan Ibrahimovic** (Sweden 4 England 2, Stockholm, Nov 14, 2012).

POST-WAR HAT-TRICKS v ENGLAND
Nov 25, 1953, **Nandor Hidegkuti** (England 3, Hungary 6, Wembley); May 11, 1958, **Aleksandar Petakovic** (Yugoslavia 5, England 0, Belgrade); May 17, 1959, **Juan Seminario** (Peru 4, England 1, Lima); Jun 15, 1988, **Marco van Basten** (Holland 3, England 1, European Championship, Dusseldorf). Six other players scored hat-tricks against England (1878–1930).

NO-SAVE GOALKEEPERS
Chris Woods did not have one save to make when England beat San Marino 6-0 (World Cup) at Wembley on Feb 17, 1993. He touched the ball only six times.

Gordon Banks had a similar no-save experience when England beat Malta 5-0 (European Championship) at Wembley on May 12, 1971. Malta did not force a goal-kick or corner, and the four times Banks touched the ball were all from back passes.

Robert Green was also idle in the 6-0 World Cup qualifying win over Andorra at Wembley on Jun 10, 2009.

WORLD/EURO MEMBERS
FIFA has 209 member countries, **UEFA** 54

FIFA WORLD YOUTH CUP (UNDER-20)
Finals: 1977 (Tunis) Soviet Union 2 Mexico 2 (Soviet won 9-8 on pens.); **1979** (Tokyo) Argentina 3 Soviet Union 1; **1981** (Sydney) W Germany 4 Qatar 0; **1983** (Mexico City) Brazil 1 Argentina 0; **1985** (Moscow) Brazil 1 Spain 0; **1987** (Santiago) Yugoslavia 1 W Germany 1 (Yugoslavia won 5-4 on pens.); **1989** (Riyadh) Portugal 2 Nigeria 0; **1991** (Lisbon) Portugal 0 Brazil 0 (Portugal won 4-2 on pens.); **1993** (Sydney) Brazil 2 Ghana 1; **1995** (Qatar) Argentina 2 Brazil 0; **1997** (Kuala Lumpur) Argentina 2 Uruguay 1; **1999** (Lagos) Spain 4 Japan 0; **2001** (Buenos Aires) Argentina 3 Ghana 0; **2003** (Dubai) Brazil 1 Spain 0; **2005** (Utrecht) Argentina 2 Nigeria 1; **2007** (Toronto) Argentina 2 Czech Republic 1; **2009** (Cairo) Ghana 0 Brazil 0 (aet, Ghana won 4-3 on pens); **2011** (Bogota) Brazil 3 Portugal 2 (aet); **2013** (Istanbul) France 0 Uruguay 0 (aet, France won 4-1 on pens).

FAMOUS CLUB FEATS

Chelsea were Premiership winners in 2004–05, their centenary season with the highest points total (95) ever recorded by England Champions. They set these other records: Most Premiership wins in season (29); most clean sheets (25) and fewest goals conceded (15) in top-division history. They also won the League Cup in 2005.

Arsenal created an all-time English League record sequence of 49 unbeaten Premiership matches (W36, D13), spanning 3 seasons, from May 7, 2003 until losing 2-0 away to Manchester Utd on Oct 24, 2004. It included all 38 games in season 2003–04.

The Double: There have been 11 instances of a club winning the Football League/Premier League title and the FA Cup in the same season. **Manchester Utd** and **Arsenal** have each done so three times: **Preston** 1888–89; **Aston Villa** 1896–97; **Tottenham** 1960–61; **Arsenal** 1970–71, 1997–98, 2001–02; **Liverpool** 1985–86; **Manchester Utd** 1993–94, 1995–96, 1998–99; **Chelsea** 2009–10.

The Treble: Liverpool were the first English club to win three major competitions in one season when in 1983–84, Joe Fagan's first season as manager, they were League Champions, League Cup winners and European Cup winners.

Sir Alex Ferguson's **Manchester Utd** achieved an even more prestigious treble in 1998–99, completing the domestic double of Premiership and FA Cup and then winning the European Cup. In season 2008–09, they completed another major triple success – Premier League, Carling Cup and World Club Cup.

Liverpool completed a unique treble by an English club with three cup successes under Gerard Houllier in season 2000–01: the League Cup, FA Cup and UEFA Cup.

Liverpool the first English club to win five major trophies in one calendar year (Feb– Aug 2001): League Cup, FA Cup, UEFA Cup, Charity Shield, UEFA Super Cup.

As Champions in season 2001–02, **Arsenal** set a Premiership record by winning the last 13 matches. They were the first top-division club since Preston in the League's inaugural season (1888–89) to maintain an unbeaten away record.

(See Scottish section for treble feats by Rangers and Celtic).

Record Home Runs: Liverpool went 85 competitive first-team games unbeaten at home between losing 2-3 to Birmingham on Jan 21, 1978 and 1-2 to Leicester on Jan 31, 1981. They comprised 63 in the League, 9 League Cup, 7 in European competition and 6 FA Cup.

Chelsea hold the record unbeaten home League sequence of 86 matches (W62, D24) between losing 1-2 to Arsenal, Feb 21, 2004, and 0-1 to Liverpool, Oct 26, 2008.

Third to First: Charlton, in 1936, became the first club to advance from the Third to First Division in successive seasons. **Queens Park Rangers** were the second club to achieve the feat in 1968, and **Oxford Utd** did it in 1984 and 1985 as Champions of each division. Subsequently, **Derby** (1987), **Middlesbrough** (1988), **Sheffield Utd** (1990) and **Notts Co** (1991) climbed from Third Division to First in consecutive seasons.

Watford won successive promotions from the modern Second Division to the Premier League in 1997–98, 1998–99. **Manchester City** equalled the feat in 1998–99, 1999–2000. Norwich climbed from League 1 to the Premier League in seasons 2009–10, 2010–11. Southampton did the same in 2010–11 and 2011–12.

Fourth to First: Northampton , in 1965 became the first club to rise from the Fourth to the First Division. **Swansea** climbed from the Fourth Division to the First (three promotions in four seasons), 1977–78 to 1980–81. **Wimbledon** repeated the feat, 1982–83 to 1985–86 **Watford** did it in five seasons, 1977–8 to 1981–82. **Carlisle** climbed from Fourth Division to First, 1964–74.

Non-League to First: When **Wimbledon** finished third in the Second Division in 1986, they completed the phenomenal rise from non-League football (Southern League) to the First Division in nine years. Two years later they won the FA Cup.

Tottenham, in 1960–61, not only carried off the First Division Championship and the FA Cup for the first time that century but set up other records by opening with 11 successive wins, registering most First Division wins (31), most away wins in the League's history (16), and equalling Arsenal's First Division records of 66 points and 33 away points. They already held the Second Division record of 70 points (1919–20).

Arsenal, in 1993, became the first club to win both English domestic cup competitions (FA Cup and League Cup) in the same season. **Liverpool** repeated the feat in 2001. **Chelsea** did it in 2007.

Chelsea achieved the FA Cup/Champions League double in May 2012.

Preston, in season 1888–89, won the first League Championship without losing a match and the FA Cup without having a goal scored against them. Only other English clubs to remain unbeaten through a League season were **Liverpool** (Div 2 Champions in 1893–94) and **Arsenal** (Premiership Champions 2003–04).

Bury, in 1903, also won the FA Cup without conceding a goal.

Everton won Div 2, Div 1 and the FA Cup in successive seasons, 1930–31, 1931–32, 1932–33.

Wolves won the League Championship in 1958 and 1959 and the FA Cup in 1960.

Liverpool won the title in 1964, the FA Cup in 1965 and the title again in 1966. In 1978 they became the first British club to win the European Cup in successive seasons. Nottm Forest

repeated the feat in 1979 and 1980.

Liverpool won the League Championship six times in eight seasons (1976–83) under **Bob Paisley's** management.

Sir Alex Ferguson's **Manchester Utd** won the Premier League in 13 of its 21 seasons (1992–2013). They were runners-up five times and third three times.

Most Premiership wins in season: 29 by Chelsea in 2004–05, 2005–06.

Biggest points-winning margin by League Champions: 18 by **Manchester Utd** (1999–2000).

FA CUP/PROMOTION DOUBLE

WBA are the only club to achieve this feat in the same season (1930-31).

COVENTRY UNIQUE

Coventry are the only club to have played in the Premier League, all four previous divisions of the Football League, in both sections (North and South) of the old Third Division and in the modern Championship.

FAMOUS UPS & DOWNS

Sunderland: Relegated in 1958 after maintaining First Division status since their election to the Football League in 1890. They dropped into Division 3 for the first time in 1987.

Aston Villa: Relegated with Preston to the Third Division in 1970.

Arsenal up: When the League was extended in 1919, Woolwich Arsenal (sixth in Division Two in 1914–15, last season before the war) were elected to Division One. Arsenal have been in the top division ever since.

Tottenham down: At that same meeting in 1919 Chelsea (due for relegation) retained their place in Division One but the bottom club (Tottenham) had to go down to Division Two.

Preston and **Burnley down**: Preston, the first League Champions in season 1888–89, dropped into the Fourth Division in 1985. So did Burnley, also among the League's original members in 1888. In 1986, Preston had to apply for re-election.

Wolves' fall: Wolves, another of the Football League's original members, completed the fall from First Division to Fourth in successive seasons (1984–85–86).

Lincoln out: Lincoln became the first club to suffer automatic demotion from the Football League when they finished bottom of Div 4, on goal difference, in season 1986–87. They were replaced by Scarborough, champions of the GM Vauxhall Conference. Lincoln regained their place a year later.

Swindon up and down: In the 1990 play-offs, Swindon won promotion to the First Division for the first time, but remained in the Second Division because of financial irregularities.

MOST CHAMPIONSHIP WINS

Manchester Utd have been champions of England a record 20 times (7 Football League, 13 Premier League).

LONGEST CURRENT MEMBERS OF TOP DIVISION

Arsenal (since 1919), **Everton** (1954), **Liverpool** (1962), **Manchester Utd** (1975).

CHAMPIONS: FEWEST PLAYERS

Liverpool used only **14** players (five ever-present) when they won the League Championship in season 1965–66. **Aston Villa** also called on no more than 14 players to win the title in 1980–81, with seven ever-present.

UNBEATEN CHAMPIONS

Only two clubs have become Champions of England with an unbeaten record: **Preston** as the Football League's first winners in 1888–89 (22 matches) and **Arsenal**, Premiership winners in 2003–04 (38 matches).

LEAGUE HAT-TRICKS

Huddersfield created a record in 1924–25–26 by winning the League Championship three years in succession.

Arsenal equalled this hat-trick in 1933–34–35, **Liverpool** in 1982–83–84 and **Manchester Utd** in 1999–2000–01. Sir Alex Ferguson's side became the first to complete two hat-tricks (2007–08–09).

'SUPER DOUBLE' WINNERS

Since the War, there have been three instances of players appearing in and then managing FA Cup and Championship-winning teams:

Joe Mercer: Player in Arsenal Championship teams 1948, 1953 and in their 1950 FA Cup side; manager of Manchester City when they won Championship 1968, FA Cup 1969.

Kenny Dalglish: Player in Liverpool Championship-winning teams 1979, 1980, 1982, 1983, 1984, player-manager 1986, 1988, 1990: player-manager when Liverpool won FA Cup (to complete Double) 1986; manager of Blackburn, Champions 1995.

George Graham: Played in Arsenal's Double-winning team in 1971, and as manager took them to Championship success in 1989 and 1991 and the FA Cup – League Cup double in 1993.

ORIGINAL TWELVE

The original 12 members of the Football League (formed in 1888) were: **Accrington, Aston Villa, Blackburn, Bolton, Burnley, Derby, Everton, Notts Co, Preston, Stoke, WBA** and **Wolves.**

Results on the opening day (Sep 8, 1888): Bolton 3, Derby 6; Everton 2, Accrington 1; Preston 5, Burnley 2; Stoke 0, WBA 2; Wolves 1, Aston Villa 1. Preston had the biggest first-day crowd: 6,000. Blackburn and Notts Co did not play that day. They kicked off a week later (Sep 15) – Blackburn 5, Accrington 5; Everton 2, Notts Co 1.

Accrington FC resigned from the league in 1893 and later folded. A new club, Accrington Stanley, were members of the league from 1921 until 1962 when financial problems forced their demise. The current Accrington Stanley were formed in 1968 and gained league status in 2007.

FASTEST CLIMBS

Three promotions in four seasons by two clubs – **Swansea City**: 1978 third in Div 4; 1979 third in Div 3; 1981 third in Div 2; **Wimbledon**: 1983 Champions of Div 4; 1984 second in Div 3; 1986 third in Div 2.

MERSEYSIDE RECORD

Liverpool is the only city to have staged top-division football – through Everton and/or Liverpool – **in every season** since League football began in 1888.

EARLIEST PROMOTIONS TO TOP DIVISION POST-WAR

Mar 23, 1974, **Middlesbrough;** Mar 25, 2006, **Reading.**

EARLIEST RELEGATIONS POST-WAR

From top division: **QPR** went down from the old First Division on Mar 29, 1969; **Derby** went down from the Premier League on Mar 29, 2008, with 6 matches still to play. From modern First Division: **Stockport** on Mar 16, 2002, with 7 matches still to play; **Wimbledon** on Apr 6, 2004, with 7 matches to play.

LEAGUE RECORDS

DOUBLE CHAMPIONS

Nine men have played in and managed League Championship-winning teams:

Ted Drake Player – Arsenal 1934, 1935, 1938. Manager – Chelsea 1955.

Bill Nicholson Player – Tottenham 1951. Manager – Tottenham 1961.
Alf Ramsey Player – Tottenham 1951. Manager – Ipswich 1962.
Joe Mercer Player – Everton 1939, Arsenal 1948, 1953. Manager – Manchester City 1968.
Dave Mackay Player – Tottenham 1961. Manager – Derby 1975.
Bob Paisley Player – Liverpool 1947. Manager – Liverpool 1976, 1977, 1979, 1980, 1982, 1983.
Howard Kendall Player – Everton 1970. Manager – Everton 1985, 1987.
Kenny Dalglish Player – Liverpool 1979, 1980, 1982, 1983, 1984. Player-manager – Liverpool 1986, 1988, 1990. Manager – Blackburn 1995.
George Graham Player – Arsenal 1971. Manager – Arsenal 1989, 1991.

GIGGS RECORD COLLECTION

Ryan Giggs (Manchester Utd) has collected the most individual honours in English football with a total of 34 prizes to the end of season 2012–13. They comprise: 13 Premier League titles, 4 FA Cups, 3 League Cups, 2 European Cups, 1 UEFA Super Cup, 1 Inter-Continental Cup, 1 World Club Cup, 9 Charity Shields/Community Shields. One-club man Giggs played 24 seasons for United, making a record 963 appearances. He won 64 Wales caps and on retiring as a player, aged 40, in May 2014, became the club's assistant manager.

CANTONA'S FOUR-TIMER

Eric Cantona played in four successive Championship-winning teams: Marseille 1990–01, Leeds 1991–92, Manchester Utd 1992–93 and 1993–94.

ARRIVALS AND DEPARTURES

The following are the Football League arrivals and departures since 1923:

Year	In	Out
1923	Doncaster	Stalybridge Celtic
	New Brighton	
1927	Torquay	Aberdare Athletic
1928	Carlisle	Durham
1929	York	Ashington
1930	Thames	Merthyr Tydfil
1931	Mansfield	Newport Co
	Chester	Nelson
1932	Aldershot	Thames
	Newport Co	Wigan Borough
1938	Ipswich	Gillingham
1950	Colchester, Gillingham	
	Scunthorpe, Shrewsbury	
1951	Workington	New Brighton
1960	Peterborough	Gateshead
1962	Oxford Utd	Accrington (resigned)
1970	Cambridge Utd	Bradford PA
1972	Hereford	Barrow
1977	Wimbledon	Workington
1978	Wigan	Southport
1987	Scarborough	Lincoln
1988	Lincoln	Newport Co
1989	Maidstone	Darlington
1990	Darlington	Colchester
1991	Barnet	
1992	Colchester	Aldershot, Maidstone (resigned)
1993	Wycombe	Halifax
1997	Macclesfield	Hereford

1998	Halifax	Doncaster
1999	Cheltenham	Scarborough
2000	Kidderminster	Chester
2001	Rushden	Barnet
2002	Boston	Halifax
2003	Yeovil, Doncaster	Exeter, Shrewsbury
2004	Chester, Shrewsbury	Carlisle, York
2005	Barnet, Carlisle	Kidderminster, Cambridge Utd
2006	Accrington, Hereford	Oxford Utd, Rushden & Diamonds
2007	Dagenham, Morecambe	Torquay, Boston
2008	Aldershot, Exeter	Wrexham, Mansfield
2009	Burton, Torquay	Chester, Luton
2010	Stevenage, Oxford Utd	Grimsby, Darlington
2011	Crawley, AFC Wimbledon	Lincoln, Stockport
2012	Fleetwood, York	Hereford, Macclesfield
2013	Mansfield, Newport	Barnet, Aldershot
2014	Luton, Cambridge Utd	Bristol Rov, Torquay

Leeds City were expelled from Div 2 in Oct, 1919; Port Vale took over their fixtures.

EXTENSIONS TO FOOTBALL LEAGUE

Clubs	Season	Clubs	Season
12 to 14	1891–92	44 to 66†	1920–21
14 to 28*	1892–93	66 to 86†	1921–22
28 to 31	1893–94	86 to 88	1923–24
31 to 32	1894–95	88 to 92	1950–51
32 to 36	1898–99	92 to 93	1991–92
36 to 40	1905–06	(Reverted to 92 when Aldershot closed, Mar 1992)	

*Second Division formed. † Third Division (South) formed from Southern League clubs.

†Third Division (North) formed.

Football League reduced to 70 clubs and three divisions on the formation of the FA Premier League in 1992; increased to 72 season 1994–95, when Premier League reduced to 20 clubs.

RECORD RUNS

Arsenal hold the record unbeaten sequence in the English League – 49 Premiership matches (36 wins, 13 draws) from May 7, 2003 until Oct 24, 2004 when beaten 2-0 away to Manchester Utd. The record previously belonged to **Nottm Forest** – 42 First Division matches (21 wins, 21 draws) from Nov 19, 1977 until beaten 2-0 at Liverpool on December 9, 1978.

Huddersfield set a new Football League record of 43 League 1 matches unbeaten from Jan 1, 2011 until Nov 28, 2011 when losing 2-0 at Charlton.

Best debuts: Ipswich won the First Division at their first attempt in 1961–62.

Peterborough in their first season in the Football League (1960–01) not only won the Fourth Division but set the all-time scoring record for the League of 134 goals. **Hereford** were promoted from the Fourth Division in their first League season, 1972–73.

Wycombe were promoted from the Third Division (via the play-offs) in their first League season, 1993–94. **Stevenage** were promoted from League 2 (via the play-offs) in their first League season, 2010–11. **Crawley** gained automatic promotion in their first season in 2011–12.

Record winning sequence in a season: 14 consecutive League victories (all in Second Division): **Manchester Utd** 1904–05, **Bristol City** 1905–06 and **Preston** 1950–51.

Best winning start to League season: 13 successive victories in Div 3 by **Reading**, season 1985–86.

Best starts in 'old' First Division: 11 consecutive victories by **Tottenham** in 1960–61; 10 by **Manchester Utd** 1985–86. In 'new' First Division, 11 consecutive wins by **Newcastle** in 1992–93 and by **Fulham** in 2000–01.

Longest unbeaten sequence (all competitions): 40 by **Nottm Forest**, Mar–December 1978. It

comprised 21 wins, 19 draws (in 29 League matches, 6 League Cup, 4 European Cup, 1 Charity Shield).

Longest unbeaten starts to League season: 38 matches (26 wins, 12 draws) in **Arsenal's** undefeated Premiership season, 2003–04; 29 matches – **Leeds**, Div 1 1973–74 (19 wins, 10 draws); **Liverpool**, Div 1 1987–88 (22 wins, 7 draws).

Most consecutive League matches unbeaten in a season: 38 **Arsenal** Premiership season 2003–04 (see above); 33 **Reading** (25 wins, 8 draws) 2005–06.

Longest winning sequence in Div 1: 13 matches by **Tottenham** – last two of season 1959–60, first 11 of 1960–61.

Longest winning one-season sequences in League Championship: 13 matches by **Preston**, 1891–92; **Sunderland**, also 1891–92; **Arsenal** 2001–02.

Longest unbeaten home League sequence in top division: 86 matches (62 wins, 24 draws) by **Chelsea** (Mar 2004–Oct 2008).

League's longest winning sequence with clean sheets: 9 matches by **Stockport** (Lge 2, 2006–07 season).

Premier League – best starts to season: Arsenal, 38 games, 2003–04; Manchester City, 14 games, 2011–12.

Best winning start to Premiership season: 9 consecutive victories by **Chelsea** in 2005–06.

Premier League – most consecutive wins (two seasons): 14 by **Arsenal**, Feb–Aug, 2002. Single season: 13 by **Arsenal** (Feb–May, 2002).

Premier League – most consecutive home wins: 20 by **Manchester City** (last 5 season 2010–11, first 15 season 2011–12).

Most consecutive away League wins in top flight: 11 by **Chelsea** (3 at end 2007–08 season, 8 in 2008–09).

Premier League – longest unbeaten away run: 27 matches (W17, D10) by **Arsenal** (Apr 5, 2003–Sep 25, 2004).

Record home-win sequences: Bradford Park Avenue won 25 successive home games in Div 3 North – the last 18 in 1926–27 and the first 7 the following season. Longest run of home wins in the top division is 21 by **Liverpool** – the last 9 of 1971–72 and the first 12 of 1972-73.

British record for successive League wins: 25 by **Celtic** (Scottish Premier League), 2003–04.

WORST SEQUENCES

Derby experienced the longest run without a win in League history in season 2007–08 – 32 games from Sep 22 to the end of the campaign (25 lost, 7 drawn). They finished bottom by a 24-pt margin. The sequence increased to 36 matches (28 lost, 8 drawn) at the start of the following season.

Cambridge Utd had the previous worst of 31 in 1983–84 (21 lost, 10 drawn). They were bottom of Div 2.

Worst losing start to a League season : 12 consecutive defeats by **Manchester Utd** (Div 1), 1930–31.

Worst Premier League start: QPR 16 matches without win (7 draws, 9 defeats), 2012–13.

Premier League – most consecutive defeats: 20 **Sunderland** last 15 matches, 2002–03, first five matches 2005–06.

Longest non-winning start to League season: 25 matches (4 draws, 21 defeats) by **Newport**, Div 4. Worst no-win League starts since then: 16 matches by **Burnley** (9 draws, 7 defeats in Div 2, 1979–80); 16 by **Hull** (10 draws, 6 defeats in Div 2, 1989–90); 16 by **Sheffield Utd** (4 draws, 12 defeats in Div 1, 1990–91).

Most League defeats in season: 34 by **Doncaster** (Div 3) 1997–98.

Fewest League wins in season: 1 by **Loughborough** (Div 2, season 1899–1900). They lost 27, drew 6, goals 18-100 and dropped out of the League. (See also Scottish section). 1 by **Derby** (Prem Lge, 2007–08). They lost 29, drew 8, goals 20-89.

Most consecutive League defeats in season: 18 by **Darwen** (Div 1, 1898–99); 17 by **Rochdale** (Div 3 North, 1931–32).

Fewest home League wins in season: 1 by **Loughborough** (Div 2, 1899–1900), **Notts Co** (Div 1, 1904–05), **Woolwich Arsenal** (Div 1, 1912–13), **Blackpool** (Div 1, 1966–67), **Rochdale**

(Div 3, 1973–74), **Sunderland** (Prem Lge, 2005–06); **Derby** (Prem Lge, 2007–08).
Most home League defeats in season: 18 by **Cambridge Utd** (Div 3, 1984–85).
Away League defeats record: 24 in row by **Crewe** (Div 2) – all 15 in 1894–95 followed by 9 in 1895–96; by **Nelson** (Div 3 North) – 3 in Apr 1930 followed by all 21 in season 1930–31. They then dropped out of the League.
Biggest defeat in Champions' season: During **Newcastle's** title-winning season in 1908–09, they were beaten 9-1 at home by Sunderland on December 5.

WORST START BY EVENTUAL CHAMPIONS

Sunderland took only 2 points from their first 7 matches in season 1912–13 (2 draws, 5 defeats). They won 25 of the remaining 31 games to clinch their fifth League title.

DISMAL DERBY

Derby were relegated in season 2007–08 as the worst-ever team in the Premier League: fewest wins (1), fewest points (11); fewest goals (20), first club to go down in March (29th).

UNBEATEN LEAGUE SEASON

Only three clubs have completed an English League season unbeaten: **Preston** (22 matches in 1888–89, the League's first season), **Liverpool** (28 matches in Div 2, 1893–94) and **Arsenal** (38 matches in Premiership, 2003–04).

100 PER CENT HOME RECORDS

Six clubs have won every home League match in a season: **Sunderland** (13 matches)' in 1891–92 and four teams in the old Second Division: **Liverpool** (14) in 1893–94, **Bury** (15) in 1894–95, **Sheffield Wed** (17) in 1899–1900 and **Small Heath,** subsequently **Birmingham** (17) in 1902–03. The last club to do it, **Brentford,** won all 21 home games in Div 3 South in 1929–30. **Rotherham** just failed to equal that record in 1946–47. They won their first 20 home matches in Div 3 North, then drew the last 3-3 v Rochdale.

BEST HOME LEAGUE RECORDS IN TOP FLIGHT

Sunderland, 1891–92 (P13, W13); **Newcastle,** 1906–07 (P19, W18, D1); **Chelsea,** 2005–06 (P19, W18, D1); **Manchester Utd,** 2010–11 (P19, W18, D1); **Manchester City,** 2011–12 (P19, W18, D1).

MOST CONSECUTIVE CLEAN SHEETS

Premier League – 14: **Manchester Utd** (2008–09); **Football League** – 11: **Millwall** (Div 3 South 1925–26); **York** (Div 3 1973–74); **Reading** (Div 4, 1978–79).

WORST HOME RUNS

Most consecutive home League defeats: 14 **Rochdale** (Div 3 North) seasons 1931–32 and 1932–33; 10 **Birmingham** (Div 1) 1985–86; 9 **Darwen** (Div 2) 1897–98; 9 **Watford** (Div 2) 1971–72.
Between Nov 1958 and Oct 1959 **Portsmouth** drew 2 and lost 14 out of 16 consecutive home games.
West Ham did not win in the Premiership at Upton Park in season 2002–03 until the 13th home match on Jan 29.

MOST AWAY WINS IN SEASON

Doncaster won 18 of their 21 away League fixtures when winning Div 3 North in 1946–47.

AWAY WINS RECORD

Most consecutive away League wins: 11 **Chelsea** (Prem Lge) – 8 at start of 2008–09 after ending previous season with 3.

100 PER CENT HOME WINS ON ONE DAY

Div 1 – All 11 home teams won on Feb 13, 1926 and on Dec 10, 1955. **Div 2** – All 12 home teams won on Nov 26, 1988. **Div 3**, all 12 home teams won in the week-end programme of Oct 18–19, 1968.

NO HOME WINS IN DIV ON ONE DAY

Div 1 – 8 away wins, 3 draws in 11 matches on Sep 6, 1986. **Div 2** – 7 away wins, 4 draws in 11 matches on Dec 26, 1987. **Premier League** – 6 away wins, 5 draws in 11 matches on Dec 26, 1994.

The week-end **Premiership** programme on Dec 7–8–9, 1996 produced no home win in the ten games (4 aways, 6 draws). There was again no home victory (3 away wins, 7 draws) in the week-end **Premiership** fixtures on Sep 23–24, 2000.

MOST DRAWS IN A SEASON (FOOTBALL LEAGUE)

23 by **Norwich** (Div 1, 1978–79), **Exeter** (Div 4, 1986–87). **Cardiff** and **Hartlepool** (both Div 3, 1997–98). **Norwich** played 42 matches, the others 46.

MOST DRAWS IN PREMIER LEAGUE SEASON

18 (in 42 matches) by **Manchester City** (1993–94), **Sheffield Utd** (1993–94), **Southampton** (1994–95).

MOST DRAWS IN ONE DIV ON ONE DAY

On Sep 18, 1948 **nine** out of 11 First Division matches were drawn.

MOST DRAWS IN PREMIER DIV PROGRAMME

Over the week-ends of December 2–3–4, 1995, and Sep 23–24, 2000, **seven** out of the ten matches finished level.

FEWEST DRAWS IN SEASON

In 46 matches: 3 by **Reading** (Div 3 South, 1951–52); **Bradford Park Avenue** (Div 3 North, 1956–57); **Tranmere** (Div 4, 1984–85); **Southend** (Div 3, 2002–03); in 42 matches: 2 by **Reading** (Div 3 South, 1935–36); **Stockport** (Div 3 North, 1946–47); in 38 matches: 2 by **Sunderland** (Div 1, 1908–09).

HIGHEST-SCORING DRAWS IN LEAGUE

Leicester 6, **Arsenal** 6 (Div 1 Apr 21, 1930); **Charlton** 6, **Middlesbrough** 6 (Div 2. Oct 22, 1960)
Latest **6-6** draw in first-class football was between **Tranmere** and **Newcastle** in the Zenith Data Systems Cup 1st round on Oct 1, 1991. The score went from 3-3 at 90 minutes to 6-6 after extra time, and Tranmere won 3-2 on penalties. In Scotland: **Queen of the South** 6, **Falkirk** 6 (Div 1, Sep 20, 1947).
Most recent **5-5** draws in top division: **Southampton** v **Coventry** (Div 1, May 4, 1982); **QPR** v **Newcastle** (Div 1, Sep 22, 1984); **WBA** v **Manchester Utd** (Prem Lge, May 19, 2013).

DRAWS RECORDS

Most consecutive drawn matches in Football League: 8 by **Torquay** (Div 3, 1969–70), **Middlesbrough** (Div 2, 1970–71), **Peterborough** (Div 4, 1971–72), **Birmingham** (Div 3 (1990–91), **Southampton** (Champ, 2005–06), **Chesterfield** (Lge 1, 2005–06), **Swansea** (Champ, 2008–09).
Longest sequence of draws by the same score: six 1-1 results by **QPR** in season 1957–58. **Tranmere** became the first club to play **five consecutive 0-0 League draws**, in season 1997–98.

IDENTICAL RECORDS

There is only **one instance** of two clubs in one division finishing a season with identical records. In 1907–08, **Blackburn** and **Woolwich Arsenal** were bracketed equal 14th in the First

Division with these figures: P38, W12, D12, L14, Goals 51-63, Pts. 36.
The total of **1195 goals** scored in the Premier League in season 1993–94 was repeated in 1994–95.

DEAD LEVEL
Millwall's record in Division Two in season 1973–74 was P42, W14, D14, L14, F51, A51, Pts 42.

CHAMPIONS OF ALL DIVISIONS
Wolves, Burnley and **Preston** are the only clubs to have won titles in the old Divisions 1, 2, 3 and 4. Wolves also won the Third Division North and the new Championship.

POINTS DEDUCTIONS
2000–01: Chesterfield 9 for breach of transfer regulations and falsifying gate receipts.
2002–03: Boston 4 for contractual irregularities.
2004–05: Wrexham, Cambridge Utd 10 for administration.
2005–06: Rotherham 10 for administration.
2006–07: Leeds, Boston 10 for administration; **Bury** 1 for unregistered player.
2007–08: Leeds 15 over insolvency rules; **Bournemouth, Luton, Rotherham** 10 for administration.
2008–09: Luton 20 for failing Insolvency rules, 10 over payments to agents; **Bournemouth, Rotherham** 17 for breaking administration rules; **Southampton, Stockport** 10 for administration – **Southampton** with effect from season 2009–10 **Crystal Palace** 1 for ineligible player.
2009–10: Portsmouth 9, **Crystal Palace** 10 for administration; **Hartlepool** 3 for ineligible player.
2010–11: Plymouth 10 for administration; **Hereford** 3, **Torquay** 1, each for ineligible player
2011–12: Portsmouth and **Port Vale** both 10 for administration – Portsmouth from following season.
2013–14: Coventry 10 for administration; **AFC Wimbledon** 3 for ineligible player.

Among previous points penalties imposed:
Nov 1990: Arsenal 2, **Manchester Utd** 1 following mass players' brawl at Old Trafford.
Dec 1996: Brighton 2 for pitch invasions by fans.
Jan 1997: Middlesbrough 3 for refusing to play Premiership match at Blackburn because of injuries and illness.
Jun 1994: Tottenham 12 (reduced to 6) and banned from following season's FA Cup for making illegal payments to players. On appeal, points deduction annulled and club re-instated in Cup.

NIGHTMARE STARTS
Most goals conceded by a goalkeeper on League debut: 13 by **Steve Milton** when Halifax lost 13-0 at Stockport (Div 3 North) on Jan 6, 1934.
Post-war: 11 by Crewe's new goalkeeper **Dennis Murray** (Div 3 North) on Sep 29, 1951, when Lincoln won 11-1.

RELEGATION ODD SPOTS
None of the Barclays Premiership relegation places in season 2004–05 were decided until the last day (Sunday, May 15). **WBA** (bottom at kick-off) survived with a 2-0 home win against Portsmouth, and the three relegated clubs were **Southampton** (1-2 v Manchester Utd), **Norwich** (0-6 at Fulham) and **Crystal Palace** (2-2 at Charlton).
In season 1937–38, **Manchester City** were the highest-scoring team in the First Division with 80 goals (3 more than Champions Arsenal), but they finished in 21st place and were relegated – a year after winning the title. They scored more goals than they conceded (77).
That season produced the **closest relegation battle** in top-division history, with only 4 points spanning the bottom 11 clubs in Div 1. **WBA** went down with **Manchester City**.
Twelve years earlier, in 1925–26, City went down to Division 2 despite totalling 89 goals – still the most scored in any division by a relegated team. Manchester City also scored 31 FA Cup

goals that season, but lost the Final 1-0 to Bolton Wanderers.

Cardiff were relegated from Div 1 in season 1928–29, despite conceding fewest goals in the division (59). They also scored fewest (43).

On their way to relegation from the First Division in season 1984–85, **Stoke** twice lost ten matches in a row.

RELEGATION TREBLES

Two Football League clubs have been relegated three seasons in succession. **Bristol City** fell from First Division to Fourth in 1980–81–82 and **Wolves** did the same in 1984–85–86.

OLDEST CLUBS

Oldest Association Football Club is **Sheffield FC** (formed in 1857). The oldest Football League clubs are **Notts Co**, 1862; **Nottm Forest,** 1865; and **Sheffield Wed,** 1866.

FOUR DIVISIONS

In **May, 1957**, the Football League decided to re-group the two sections of the Third Division into Third and Fourth Divisions in **season 1958–59**.

The Football League was reduced to three divisions on the formation of the Premier League in **1992**.

In season 2004 05, under new sponsors Coca-Cola, the titles of First, Second and Third Divisions were changed to League Championship, League One and League Two.

THREE UP – THREE DOWN

The Football League annual general meeting of Jun 1973 agreed to adopt the promotion and relegation system of three up and three down.

The **new system** came into effect in **season 1973–74** and applied only to the first three divisions; four clubs were still relegated from the Third and four promoted from the Fourth.

It was the first change in the promotion and relegation system for the top two divisions in 81 years.

MOST LEAGUE APPEARANCES

Players with more than 700 English League apps (as at end of season 2012–13)

1005 Peter Shilton 1966–97 (286 Leicester, 110 Stoke, 202 Nottm Forest, 188 Southampton, 175 Derby, 34 Plymouth Argyle, 1 Bolton, 9 Leyton Orient).

931 Tony Ford 1975–2002 (423 Grimsby, 9 Sunderland, 112 Stoke, 114 WBA, 5 Bradford City, 76 Scunthorpe, 103 Mansfield, 89 Rochdale).

840 Graham Alexander 1991–2012 (159 Scunthorpe, 152 Luton, 372 Preston, 157 Burnley).

824 Terry Paine 1956–77 (713 Southampton, 111 Hereford).

795 Tommy Hutchison 1968–91 (165 Blackpool, 314 Coventry City, 46 Manchester City, 92 Burnley, 178 Swansea). In addition, 68 Scottish League apps for Alloa 1965–68, giving career League app total of 863.

790 Neil Redfearn 1982–2004 (35 Bolton, 100 Lincoln, 46 Doncaster, 57 Crystal Palace, 24 Watford, 62 Oldham, 292 Barnsley, 30 Charlton, 17 Bradford City, 22 Wigan, 42 Halifax, 54 Boston, 9 Rochdale).

782 Robbie James 1973–94 (484 Swansea, 48 Stoke, 87 QPR, 23 Leicester, 89 Bradford City, 51 Cardiff).

777 Alan Oakes 1959–84 (565 Manchester City, 211 Chester, 1 Port Vale).

773 Dave Beasant 1980–2003 (340 Wimbledon, 20 Newcastle, 6 Grimsby, 4 Wolves, 133 Chelsea, 88 Southampton, 139 Nottm F, 27 Portsmouth, 16 Brighton).

770 John Trollope 1960–80 (all for Swindon, record total for one club).

769 David James 1990–2012 (89 Watford, 214 Liverpool, 67 Aston Villa, 91 West Ham, 93 Manchester City, 134 Portsmouth, 81 Bristol City).

764 Jimmy Dickinson 1946–65 (all for Portsmouth).

761 Roy Sproson 1950–72 (all for Port Vale).

760	Mick Tait 1974–97 (64 Oxford Utd, 106 Carlisle, 33 Hull, 240 Portsmouth, 99 Reading, 79 Darlington, 139 Hartlepool Utd).
758	Billy Bonds 1964–88 (95 Charlton, 663 West Ham).
758	Ray Clemence 1966–88 (48 Scunthorpe, 470 Liverpool, 240 Tottenham).
757	Pat Jennings 1963–86 (48 Watford, 472 Tottenham, 237 Arsenal).
757	Frank Worthington 1966–88 (171 Huddersfield Town, 210 Leicester, 84 Bolton, 75 Birmingham, 32 Leeds, 19 Sunderland, 34 Southampton, 31 Brighton, 59 Tranmere, 23 Preston, 19 Stockport).
755	Wayne Allison 1986–2008 (84 Halifax, 7 Watford, 195 Bristol City, 103 Swindon, 76 Huddersfield, 102 Tranmere, 73 Sheffield Utd, 115 Chesterfield).
749	Ernie Moss 1968–88 (469 Chesterfield, 35 Peterborough, 57 Mansfield, 74 Port Vale, 11 Lincoln, 44 Doncaster, 26 Stockport, 23 Scarborough, 10 Rochdale).
746	Les Chapman 1966–88 (263 Oldham, 133 Huddersfield Town, 70 Stockport, 139 Bradford City, 88 Rochdale, 53 Preston).
744	Asa Hartford 1967–90 (214 WBA, 260 Manchester City, 3 Nottm Forest, 81 Everton, 28 Norwich, 81 Bolton, 45 Stockport, 7 Oldham, 25 Shrewsbury).
743	Alan Ball 1963–84 (146 Blackpool, 208 Everton, 177 Arsenal, 195 Southampton, 17 Bristol Rov).
743	John Hollins 1963–84 (465 Chelsea, 151 QPR, 127 Arsenal).
743	Phil Parkes 1968–91 (52 Walsall, 344 QPR, 344 West Ham, 3 Ipswich).
737	Steve Bruce 1979–99 (205 Gillingham, 141 Norwich, 309 Manchester Utd 72 Birmingham, 10 Sheffield Utd).
734	Teddy Sheringham 1983–2007 (220 Millwall, 5 Aldershot, 42 Nottm Forest, 104 Manchester Utd, 236 Tottenham, 32 Portsmouth, 76 West Ham, 19 Colchester)
732	Mick Mills 1966–88 (591 Ipswich, 103 Southampton, 38 Stoke).
731	Ian Callaghan 1959–81 (640 Liverpool, 76 Swansea, 15 Crewe).
731	David Seaman 1982–2003 (91 Peterborough, 75 Birmingham, 141 QPR, 405 Arsenal, 19 Manchester City).
725	Steve Perryman 1969–90 (655 Tottenham, 17 Oxford Utd, 53 Brentford).
722	Martin Peters 1961–81 (302 West Ham, 189 Tottenham, 207 Norwich, 24 Sheffield Utd).
718	Mike Channon 1966–86 (511 Southampton, 72 Manchester City, 4 Newcastle, 9 Bristol Rov, 88 Norwich, 34 Portsmouth).
716	Ron Harris 1961–83 (655 Chelsea, 61 Brentford).
716	Mike Summerbee 1959–79 (218 Swindon, 357 Manchester City, 51 Burnley, 3 Blackpool, 87 Stockport).
714	Glenn Cockerill 1976–98 (186 Lincoln, 26 Swindon, 62 Sheffield Utd, 387 Southampton, 90 Leyton Orient, 40 Fulham, 23 Brentford).
705	Keith Curle 1981–2003 (32 Bristol Rov, 16 Torquay, 121 Bristol City, 40 Reading, 93 Wimbledon, 171 Manchester City, 150 Wolves, 57 Sheffield Utd, 11 Barnsley, 14 Mansfield.
705	Phil Neal 1968–89 (186 Northampton, 455 Liverpool, 64 Bolton).
705	John Wile 1968–86 (205 Peterborough, 500 WBA).
701	Neville Southall 1980–2000 (39 Bury, 578 Everton, 9 Port Vale, 9 Southend, 12 Stoke, 53 Torquay, 1 Bradford City).

● **Stanley Matthews** made 701 League apps 1932–65 (322 Stoke, 379 Blackpool), incl. 3 for Stoke at start of 1939–40 before season abandoned (war).

● Goalkeeper **John Burridge** made a total of 771 League appearances in a 28-season career in English and Scottish football (1968–96). He played 691 games for 15 English clubs (Workington, Blackpool, Aston Villa, Southend, Crystal Palace, QPR, Wolves, Derby, Sheffield Utd, Southampton, Newcastle, Scarborough, Lincoln, Manchester City and Darlington) and 80 for 5 Scottish clubs (Hibernian, Aberdeen, Dumbarton, Falkirk and Queen of the South).

LONGEST LEAGUE APPEARANCE SEQUENCE

Harold Bell, centre-half of Tranmere, was ever-present for the first nine post-war seasons (1946–55), achieving a League record of 401 consecutive matches. Counting FA Cup and other games, his run of successive appearances totalled 459.

The longest League sequence since Bell's was 394 appearances by goalkeeper **Dave Beasant** for Wimbledon, Newcastle and Chelsea. His nine-year run began on Aug 29, 1981 and was ended by a broken finger sustained in Chelsea's League Cup-tie against Portsmouth on Oct 31, 1990. Beasant's 394 consecutive League games comprised 304 for Wimbledon (1981–88), 20 for Newcastle (1988–89) and 70 for Chelsea (1989–90).

Phil Neal made 366 consecutive First Division appearances for Liverpool between December 1974 and Sep 1983, a remarkable sequence for an outfield player in top-division football.

MOST CONSECUTIVE PREMIER LEAGUE APPEARANCES

310 by goalkeeper **Brad Friedel** (152 Blackburn, 114 Aston Villa, 44 Tottenham, May 2004–Oct 2012). He played in 8 **ever-present seasons** (2004–12, Blackburn 4, Villa 3, Tottenham 1).

EVER-PRESENT DEFENCE

The **entire defence** of **Huddersfield** played in all 42 Second Division matches in season 1952–53, namely, Bill Wheeler (goal), Ron Staniforth and Laurie Kelly (full-backs), Bill McGarry, Don McEvoy and Len Quested (half-backs). In addition, Vic Metcalfe played in all 42 League matches at outside-left.

FIRST SUBSTITUTE USED IN LEAGUE

Keith Peacock (Charlton), away to Bolton (Div 2) on Aug 21, 1965.

FROM PROMOTION TO CHAMPIONS

Clubs who have become Champions of England a year after winning promotion: **Liverpool** 1905, 1906; **Everton** 1931, 1932; **Tottenham** 1950, 1951, **Ipswich** 1961, 1962; **Nottm Forest** 1977, 1978. The first four were placed top in both seasons: Forest finished third and first.

PREMIERSHIP'S FIRST MULTI-NATIONAL LINE-UP

Chelsea made history on December 26, 1999 when starting their Premiership match at Southampton without a single British player in the side.

Fulham's Unique XI: In the Worthington Cup 3rd round at home to Bury on Nov 6, 2002, Fulham fielded 11 players of 11 different nationalities. Ten were full Internationals, with Lee Clark an England U–21 cap.

On Feb 14, 2005 **Arsenal** became the first English club to select an all-foreign match squad when Arsene Wenger named 16 non-British players at home to Crystal Palace (Premiership).

Fifteen nations were represented at Fratton Park on Dec 30, 2009 (Portsmouth 1 Arsenal 4) when, for the first time in Premier League history, not one Englishman started the match. The line-up comprised seven Frenchmen, two Algerians and one from each of 13 other countries.

Players from 22 nationalities (subs included) were involved in the Blackburn–WBA match at Ewood Park on Jan 23, 2011.

PREMIER LEAGUE'S FIRST ALL-ENGLAND LINE-UP

On Feb 27, 1999 **Aston Villa** (at home to Coventry) fielded the first all-English line up seen in the Premier League (starting 11 plus 3 subs).

ENTIRE HOME-GROWN TEAM

Crewe Alexandra's starting 11 in the 2-0 home win against Walsall (Lge 1) on Apr 27, 2013 all graduated from the club's academy.

THREE-NATION CHAMPIONS

David Beckham won a title in four countries: with Manchester Utd six times (1996–97–99–2000–01–03), Real Madrid (2007), LA Galaxy (2011 and Paris St Germain (2013).

Trevor Steven earned eight Championship medals in three countries: two with Everton (1985, 1987); five with Rangers (1990, 1991, 1993, 1994, 1995) and one with Marseille in 1992.

LEEDS NO WIN AWAY

Leeds, in 1992–93, provided the first instance of a club failing to win an away League match as reigning Champions.

PIONEERS IN 1888 AND 1992

Three clubs among the twelve who formed the Football League in 1888 were also founder members of the Premier League: **Aston Villa, Blackburn** and **Everton.**

CHAMPIONS (MODERN) WITH TWO CLUBS – PLAYERS

Francis Lee (Manchester City 1968, Derby 1975); **Ray Kennedy** (Arsenal 1971, Liverpool 1979, 1980, 1982); **Archie Gemmill** (Derby 1972, 1975, Nottm Forest 1978); **John McGovern** (Derby 1972, Nottm Forest 1978) **Larry Lloyd** (Liverpool 1973, Nottm Forest 1978); **Peter Withe** (Nottm Forest 1978, Aston Villa 1981); **John Lukic** (Arsenal 1989, Leeds 1992); **Kevin Richardson** (Everton 1985, Arsenal 1989); **Eric Cantona** (Leeds 1992, Manchester Utd 1993, 1994, 1996, 1997); **David Batty** (Leeds 1992, Blackburn 1995); **Bobby Mimms** (Everton 1987, Blackburn 1995); **Henning Berg** (Blackburn 1995, Manchester Utd 1999, 2000); **Nicolas Anelka** (Arsenal 1998, Chelsea 2010); **Ashley Cole** (Arsenal 2002, 2004, Chelsea 2010); **Gael Clichy** (Arsenal 2004, Manchester City 2012); **Kolo Toure** (Arsenal 2004, Manchester City 2012); **Carlos Tevez** (Manchester Utd 2008, 2009, Manchester City 2012).

TITLE TURNABOUTS

In Jan 1996, **Newcastle** led the Premier League by 13 points. They finished runners-up to Manchester Utd.

At Christmas 1997, **Arsenal** were 13 points behind leaders Manchester Utd and still 11 points behind at the beginning of Mar 1998. But a run of 10 wins took the title to Highbury.

On Mar 2, 2003, **Arsenal,** with 9 games left, went 8 points clear of Manchester Utd, who had a match in hand. United won the Championship by 5 points.

In Mar 2002, **Wolves** were in second (automatic promotion) place in Nationwide Div 1, 11 points ahead of WBA, who had 2 games in hand. They were overtaken by Albion on the run-in, finished third, then failed in the play-offs. A year later they won promotion to the Premiership via the play-offs.

CLUB CLOSURES

Four clubs have left the Football League in mid-season: **Leeds City** (expelled Oct 1919); **Wigan Borough** (Oct 1931, debts of £20,000); **Accrington Stanley** (Mar 1962, debts £62,000); **Aldershot** (Mar 1992, debts £1.2m). **Maidstone,** with debts of £650,000, closed Aug 1992, on the eve of the season.

FOUR-DIVISION MEN

In season 1986–87, goalkeeper **Eric Nixon,** became the first player to appear in **all four divisions** of the Football League **in one season.** He served two clubs in Div 1: Manchester City (5 League games) and Southampton (4); in Div 2 Bradford City (3); in Div 3 Carlisle (16); and in Div 4 Wolves (16). Total appearances: 44.

Harvey McCreadie, a teenage forward, played in four divisions over two seasons inside a calendar year – from Accrington (Div 3) to Luton (Div 1) in Jan 1960, to Div 2 with Luton later that season and to Wrexham (Div 4) in Nov.

Tony Cottee played in all four divisions in season 2000–01, for Leicester (Premiership), Norwich (Div 1), Barnet (Div 3, player-manager) and Millwall (Div 2).

FATHERS AND SONS

When player-manager **Ian** (39) and **Gary** (18) **Bowyer** appeared together in the **Hereford** side at Scunthorpe (Div 4, Apr 21, 1990), they provided the first instance of father and son playing in the same team in a Football League match for 39 years. Ian played as substitute, and Gary scored Hereford's injury-time equaliser in a 3-3 draw.

Alec (39) and **David** (17) **Herd** were among previous father-and-son duos in league football – for Stockport, 2-0 winners at Hartlepool (Div 3 North) on May 5, 1951.

When Preston won 2-1 at Bury in Div 3 on Jan 13, 1990, the opposing goalkeepers were brothers: **Alan Kelly** (21) for Preston and **Gary** (23) for Bury. Their father, **Alan** (who kept goal for Preston in the 1964 FA Cup Final and won 47 Rep of Ireland caps) flew from America to watch the sons he taught to keep goal line up on opposite sides.

Other examples: **Bill Dodgin Snr** (manager, Bristol Rov) faced son **Bill Jnr** (manager of Fulham) four times between 1969 and 1971. On Apr 16, 2013 (Lge 1), Oldham, under **Lee Johnson,** won 1-0 at home to Yeovil, managed by his father **Gary.**

George Eastham Snr (manager) and son **George Eastham Jnr** were inside-forward partners for Ards in the Irish League in season 1954–55.

FATHER AND SON REFEREE PLAY-OFF FINALS

Father and son refereed two of the 2009 Play-off Finals. **Clive Oliver,** 46, took charge of Shrewsbury v Gillingham (Lge 2) and **Michael Oliver,** 26, refereed Millwall v Scunthorpe (Lge 1) the following day.

FATHER AND SON BOTH CHAMPIONS

John Aston snr won a Championship medal with Manchester Utd in 1952 and **John Aston jnr** did so with the club in 1967. **Ian Wright** won the Premier League title with Arsenal in 1998 and **Shaun Wright-Phillips** won with Chelsea in 2006.

FATHER AND SON RIVAL MANAGERS

When **Bill Dodgin snr** took Bristol Rov to Fulham for an FA Cup 1st Round tie in Nov 1971, the opposing manager was his son, **Bill jnr.** Rovers won 2-1. Oldham's new manager, **Lee Johnson,** faced his father **Gary's** Yeovil in a Lge 1 match in April, 2013. Oldham won 1-0.

FATHER AND SON ON OPPOSITE SIDES

It happened for the first time in FA Cup history (1st Qual Round on Sep 14, 1996) when 21-year-old **Nick Scaife** (Bishop Auckland) faced his father **Bobby** (41), who played for Pickering. Both were in midfield. Home side Bishops won 3-1.

THREE BROTHERS IN SAME SIDE

Southampton provided the first instance for 65 years of three brothers appearing together in a Div 1 side when **Danny Wallace** (24) and his 19-year-old twin brothers **Rodney** and **Ray** played against Sheffield Wed on Oct 22, 1988. In all, they made 25 appearances together for Southampton until Sep 1989.

A previous instance in Div 1 was provided by the Middlesbrough trio, **William, John** and **George Carr** with 24 League appearances together from Jan 1920 to Oct 1923.

The **Tonner** brothers, **Sam, James** and **Jack,** played together in 13 Second Division matches for Clapton Orient in season 1919–20.

Brothers **David, Donald** and **Robert Jack** played together in Plymouth's League side in 1920.

TWIN TEAM-MATES (see also Wallace twins above)

Twin brothers **David** and **Peter Jackson** played together for three League clubs (Wrexham, Bradford City and Tranmere) from 1954–62. The **Morgan** twins, **Ian** and **Roger,** played regularly in the QPR forward line from 1964–68. WBA's **Adam** and **James Chambers,** 18, were the first twins to represent England (v Cameroon in World Youth Championship, Apr 1999). They first played together in Albion's senior team, aged 19, in the League Cup 2nd.

Round against Derby in Sep 2000. Brazilian identical twins **Rafael** and **Fabio Da Silva** (18) made first team debuts at full-back for Manchester Utd in season 2008–09. Swedish twins **Martin** and **Marcus Olsson** played together for Blackburn in season 2011–12. **Josh** and **Jacob Murphy**, 19, played for Norwich in season 2013–2014.

SIR TOM DOES THE HONOURS

Sir Tom Finney, England and Preston legend, opened the Football League's new headquarters on their return to Preston on Feb 23, 1999. Preston had been the League's original base for 70 years before the move to Lytham St Annes in 1959.

SHORTENED MATCHES

The 0-0 score in the **Bradford City v Lincoln** Third Division fixture on May 11, 1985, abandoned through fire after 40 minutes, was subsequently confirmed as a result. It is the shortest officially- completed League match on record, and was the fourth of only five instances in Football League history of the score of an unfinished match being allowed to stand.

The other occasions: **Middlesbrough 4, Oldham 1** (Div 1, Apr 3, 1915), abandoned after 55 minutes when Oldham defender Billy Cook refused to leave the field after being sent off; **Barrow 7, Gillingham 0** (Div 4, Oct 9, 1961), abandoned after 75 minutes because of bad light, the match having started late because of Gillingham's delayed arrival.

A crucial **Manchester** derby (Div 1) was abandoned after 85 minutes, and the result stood, on Apr 27, 1974, when a pitch invasion at Old Trafford followed the only goal, scored for City by Denis Law, which relegated United, Law's former club.

The only instance of a first-class match in England being abandoned **'through shortage of players'** occurred in the First Division at Bramall Lane on Mar 16, 2002. Referee Eddie Wolstenholme halted play after 82 minutes because **Sheffield Utd** were reduced to 6 players against **WBA.** They had had 3 men sent off (goalkeeper and 2 substitutes), and with all 3 substitutes used and 2 players injured, were left with fewer than the required minimum of 7 on the field. Promotion contenders WBA were leading 3-0, and the League ordered the result to stand.

The last 60 seconds of **Birmingham v Stoke** (Div 3, 1-1, on Feb 29, 1992) were played behind locked doors. The ground had been cleared after a pitch invasion.

A First Division fixture, **Sheffield Wed v Aston Villa** (Nov 26, 1898), was abandoned through bad light after 79 mins with Wednesday leading 3-1. The Football League ruled that the match should be completed, and the remaining 10.5 minutes were played four months later (Mar 13, 1899), when Wednesday added another goal to make the result 4-1.

FA CUP RECORDS
(See also Goalscoring section)

CHIEF WINNERS

11 Manchester Utd, Arsenal; **8** Tottenham; **7** Aston Villa, Chelsea, Liverpool; **6** Blackburn, Newcastle.

Three times in succession: The Wanderers (1876–77–78) and Blackburn (1884–85–86).

Trophy handed back: The FA Cup became the Wanderers' absolute property in 1878, but they handed it back to the Association on condition that it was not to be won outright by any club.

In successive years by professional clubs: Blackburn (1890 and 1891); Newcastle (1951 and 1952); Tottenham (1961 and 1962); Tottenham (1981 and 1982); Arsenal (2002 and 2003); Chelsea (2009–10).

Record Final-tie score: Bury 6, Derby 0 (1903).

Most FA Cup Final wins at Wembley: Manchester Utd 9, Arsenal 8, Chelsea 6, Tottenham 6, Liverpool 5, Newcastle 5.

SECOND DIVISION WINNERS

Notts Co (1894), **Wolves** (1908), **Barnsley** (1912), **WBA** (1931), **Sunderland** (1973), **Southampton** (1976), **West Ham** (1980). When **Tottenham** won the Cup in 1901 they were a Southern League club.

'OUTSIDE' SEMI-FINALISTS

Wycombe, in 2001, became the eighth team from outside the top two divisions to reach the semi-finals, following **Millwall** (1937), **Port Vale** (1954), **York** (1955), **Norwich** (1959), **Crystal Palace** (1976), **Plymouth** (1984) and **Chesterfield** (1997). None reached the Final.

FOURTH DIVISION QUARTER-FINALISTS

Oxford Utd (1964), **Colchester** (1971), **Bradford City** (1976), **Cambridge Utd** (1990).

FOURTH ROUND – NO REPLAYS

No replays were necessary in the 16 fourth round ties in January 2008 (7 home wins, 9 away). This had not happened for 51 years, since 8 home and 8 away wins in season 1956–57.

FIVE TROPHIES

The trophy which Arsenal won in 2014 was the fifth in FA Cup history. These were its predecessors:

1872–95: First Cup stolen from shop in Birmingham while held by Aston Villa. Never seen again.

1910: Second trophy presented to Lord Kinnaird on completing 21 years as FA president.

1911–91: Third trophy used until replaced ('battered and fragile') after 80 years' service.

1992–2013 Fourth FA Cup lasted 21 years – now retained at FA headquarters at Wembley Stadium.

Traditionally, the Cup stays with the holders until returned to the FA in March.

FINALISTS RELEGATED

Six clubs have reached the FA Cup Final and been relegated. The first five all lost at Wembley - **Manchester City** 1926, **Leicester** 1969, **Brighton** 1983, **Middlesbrough** 1997 and **Portsmouth** 2010. **Wigan,** Cup winners for the first time in 2013, were relegated from the Premier League three days later.

FA CUP – TOP SHOCKS

(2014 = season 2013–14; rounds shown in brackets; R = replay)

1922 (1)	Everton	0	Crystal Palace	6
1933 (3)	Walsall	2	Arsenal	0
1939 (F)	Portsmouth	4	Wolves	1
1948 (3)	Arsenal	0	Bradford PA	1
1948 (3)	Colchester	1	Huddersfield	0
1949 (4)	Yeovil	2	Sunderland	1
1955 (5)	York	2	Tottenham	1
1957 (4)	Wolves	0	Bournemouth	1
1957 (5)	Bournemouth	3	Tottenham	1
1958 (4)	Newcastle	1	Scunthorpe	3
1959 (3)	Norwich	3	Manchester Utd	0
1959 (3)	Worcester	2	Liverpool	1
1961 (3)	Chelsea	1	Crewe	2
1964 (3)	Newcastle	1	Bedford	2
1965 (4)	Peterborough	2	Arsenal	1
1971 (5)	Colchester	3	Leeds	2
1972 (3)	Hereford	2	Newcastle	1R

1973 (F)	Sunderland	1	Leeds	0
1975 (3)	Burnley	0	Wimbledon	1
1978 (F)	Ipswich	1	Arsenal	0
1980 (3)	Chelsea	0	Wigan	1
1980 (3)	Halifax	1	Manchester City	0
1980 (F)	West Ham	1	Arsenal	0
1981 (4)	Exeter	4	Newcastle	OR
1984 (3)	Bournemouth	2	Manchester Utd	0
1985 (4)	York	1	Arsenal	0
1986 (3)	Birmingham	1	Altrincham	2
1988 (F)	Wimbledon	1	Liverpool	0
1989 (3)	Sutton	2	Coventry	1
1991 (3)	WBA	2	Woking	4
1992 (3)	Wrexham	2	Arsenal	1
1994 (3)	Liverpool	0	Bristol City	1R
1994 (3)	Birmingham	1	Kidderminster	2
1997 (5)	Chesterfield	1	Nottm Forest	0
2001 (4)	Everton	0	Tranmere	3
2003 (3)	Shrewsbury	2	Everton	1
2005 (3)	Oldham	1	Manchester City	0
2008 (6)	Barnsley	1	Chelsea	0
2009 (2)	Histon	1	Leeds	0
2010 (4)	Liverpool	1	Reading	2R
2011 (3)	Stevenage	3	Newcastle	1
2012 (3)	Macclesfield	2	Cardiff	1
2013 (4)	Norwich	0	Luton	1
2013 (4)	Oldham	3	Liverpool	2
2013 (F)	Wigan	1	Manchester City	0
2014 (3)	Rochdale	2	Leeds	0

YEOVIL TOP GIANT-KILLERS

Yeovil's victories over Colchester and Blackpool in season 2000–01 gave them a total of 20 FA Cup wins against League opponents. They set another non-League record by reaching the third round 13 times.

This was Yeovil's triumphant (non-League) Cup record against League clubs: 1924–25 Bournemouth 3-2; 1934–35 Crystal Palace 3-0, Exeter 4-1; 1938–39 Brighton 2-1; 1948–49 Bury 3-1, Sunderland 2-1; 1958–59 Southend 1-0; 1960–61 Walsall 1-0; 1963–64 Southend 1-0, Crystal Palace 3-1; 1970–71 Bournemouth 1-0; 1972–73 Brentford 2-1; 1987–88 Cambridge Utd 1-0; 1991–92 Walsall 1-0; 1992–93 Torquay 5-2, Hereford 2-1; 1993–94 Fulham 1-0; 1998–99 Northampton 2-0; 2000–01 Colchester 5-1, Blackpool 1-0.

NON-LEAGUE BEST

Since League football began in 1888, three non-League clubs have reached the FA Cup Final. **Sheffield Wed** (Football Alliance) were runners-up in 1890, as were **Southampton** (Southern League) in 1900 and 1902. **Tottenham** won the Cup as a Southern League team in 1901.

Otherwise, the furthest progress by non-League clubs has been to the 5th round on 6 occasions: **Colchester** 1948, **Yeovil** 1949, **Blyth** 1978, **Telford** 1985, **Kidderminster** 1994, **Crawley** 2011.

Greatest number of non-League sides to reach the **3rd round** is **8** in 2009: **Barrow, Blyth, Eastwood, Forest Green, Histon, Kettering, Kidderminster** and **Torquay**.

Most to reach **Round 4: 3** in 1957 (**Rhyl, New Brighton, Peterborough**) and 1975 (**Leatherhead, Stafford** and **Wimbledon**).

Five non-League clubs reaching **round 3** in 2001 was a Conference record. They were **Chester, Yeovil, Dagenham, Morecambe** and **Kingstonian**.

In season 2002–03, Team Bath became the first University-based side to reach the FA Cup 1st Round since **Oxford University** (Finalists in 1880).

NON-LEAGUE 'LAST TIMES'

Last time no non-League club reached round 3: 1951. Last time only one did so: 1969 (**Kettering**).

TOP-DIVISION SCALPS

Victories in FA Cup by non-League clubs over top-division teams since 1900 include: 1900–01 (Final, replay): **Tottenham** 3 Sheffield Utd 1 (Tottenham then in Southern League); 1919–20 **Cardiff** 2, Oldham 0; Sheffield Wed 0, **Darlington** 2; 1923–24 **Corinthians** 1, Blackburn 0; 1947–48 **Colchester** 1, Huddersfield 0; 1948–9 **Yeovil** 2, Sunderland 1; 1971–72 **Hereford** 2, Newcastle 1; 1974–75 Burnley 0, **Wimbledon** 1; 1985–86 Birmingham 1, **Altrincham** 2; 1988–89 **Sutton** 2, Coventry 1; 2012–13 Norwich 0, **Luton** 1.

MOST WINNING MEDALS

Ashley Cole has won the trophy seven times, with (Arsenal 2002–03–05) and Chelsea (2007–09–10–12). **The Hon Arthur Kinnaird** (The Wanderers and Old Etonians), **Charles Wollaston** (The Wanderers) and **Jimmy Forrest** (Blackburn) each earned five winners' medals. Kinnaird, later president of the FA, played in nine of the first 12 FA Cup Finals, and was on the winning side three times for The Wanderers, in 1873 (captain), 1877, 1878 (captain), and twice as captain of Old Etonians (1879, 1882).

MANAGERS' MEDALS BACKDATED

In 2010, the FA agreed to award Cup Final medals to all living managers who took their teams to the Final before 1996 (when medals were first given to Wembley team bosses). Lawrie McMenemy had campaigned for the award since Southampton's victory in 1976.

MOST WINNERS' MEDALS AT WEMBLEY

4 – **Mark Hughes** (3 for Manchester Utd, 1 for Chelsea), **Petr Cech, Frank Lampard, John Terry, Didier Drogba, Ashley Cole** (all Chelsea).
3 – **Dick Pym** (3 clean sheets in Finals), **Bob Haworth, Jimmy Seddon, Harry Nuttall, Billy Butler** (all Bolton); **David Jack** (2 Bolton, 1 Arsenal); **Bob Cowell, Jack Milburn, Bobby Mitchell** (all Newcastle); **Dave Mackay** (Tottenham); **Frank Stapleton** (1 Arsenal, 2 Manchester Utd); **Bryan Robson** (3 times winning captain), **Arthur Albiston, Gary Pallister** (all Manchester Utd); **Bruce Grobbelaar, Steve Nicol, Ian Rush** (all Liverpool); **Roy Keane, Peter Schmeichel, Ryan Giggs** (all Manchester Utd); **Dennis Wise** (1 Wimbledon, 2 Chelsea).
Arsenal's **David Seaman** and **Ray Parlour** have each earned 4 winners' medals (2 at Wembley, 2 at Cardiff) as have Manchester Utd's **Roy Keane** and **Ryan Giggs** (3 at Wembley, 1 at Cardiff).

MOST WEMBLEY FINALS

Nine players appeared in five FA Cup Finals at Wembley, replays excluded:
- **Joe Hulme** (Arsenal: 1927 lost, 1930 won, 1932 lost, 1936 won; Huddersfield: 1938 lost).
- **Johnny Giles** (Manchester Utd: 1963 won; Leeds: 1965 lost, 1970 drew at Wembley, lost replay at Old Trafford, 1972 won, 1973 lost).
- **Pat Rice** (all for Arsenal: 1971 won, 1972 lost, 1978 lost, 1979 won, 1980 lost).
- **Frank Stapleton** (Arsenal: 1978 lost, 1979 won, 1980 lost; Manchester Utd: 1983 won, 1985 won).
- **Ray Clemence** (Liverpool: 1971 lost, 1974 won, 1977 lost; Tottenham: 1982 won, 1987 lost).
- **Mark Hughes** (Manchester Utd: 1985 won, 1990 won, 1994 won, 1995 lost; Chelsea: 1997 won).
- **John Barnes** (Watford: 1984 lost; Liverpool: 1988 lost, 1989 won, 1996 lost; Newcastle:

1998 sub, lost): – first player to lose Wembley FA Cup Finals with three different clubs.

- **Roy Keane** (Nottm Forest: 1991 lost; Manchester Utd: 1994 won, 1995 lost, 1996 won, 1999 won).
- **Ryan Giggs** (Manchester Utd: 1994 won, 1995 lost, 1996 won, 1999 won, 2007 lost).
- Clemence, Hughes and Stapleton also played in a replay, making six actual FA Cup Final appearances for each of them.
- **Glenn Hoddle** also made six appearances at Wembley: 5 for Tottenham (incl. 2 replays), in 1981 won, 1982 won and 1987 lost, and 1 for Chelsea as sub in 1994 lost.
- **Paul Bracewell** played in four FA Cup Finals without being on the winning side – for Everton 1985, 1986, 1989, Sunderland 1992.

MOST WEMBLEY/CARDIFF FINAL APPEARANCES

8 by **Ashley Cole** (Arsenal: 2001 lost; 2002 won; 2003 won; 2005 won; Chelsea: 2007 won; 2009 won; 2010 won, 2012 won).

7 by **Roy Keane** (Nottm Forest: 1991 lost; Manchester Utd: 1994 won; 1995 lost; 1996 won; 1999 won; 2004 won; 2005 lost).

7 by **Ryan Giggs** (Manchester Utd): 1994 won; 1995 lost; 1996 won; 1999 won; 2004 won; 2005 lost; 2007 lost.

6 by **Paul Scholes** (Manchester Utd): 1995 lost; 1996 won; 1999 won; 2004 won; 2005 lost; 2007 lost.

5 by **David Seaman** and **Ray Parlour** (Arsenal): 1993 won; 1998 lost; 2001 lost; 2002 won; 2003 won; **Dennis Wise** (Wimbledon 1988 won; Chelsea 1994 lost; 1997 won; 2000 lost; Millwall 2004 lost); Patrick Vieira (Arsenal): 1998 won; 2001 lost; 2002 won; 2005 won; (Manchester City) 2011 won.

BIGGEST FA CUP SCORE AT WEMBLEY

5-0 by Stoke v Bolton (semi-final, Apr 17, 2011.

WINNING GOALKEEPER-CAPTAINS

1988 **Dave Beasant** (Wimbledon); 2003 **David Seaman** (Arsenal).

MOST WINNING MANAGERS - FIVE TIMES

Sir Alex Ferguson (Manchester Utd 1990, 1994, 1996, 1999, 2004); Arsene Wenger (Arsenal 1998, 2002, 2003, 2005, 2014).

PLAYER-MANAGERS IN FINAL

Kenny Dalglish (Liverpool, 1986); **Glenn Hoddle** (Chelsea, 1994); **Dennis Wise** (Millwall, 2004).

DEBUTS IN FINAL

Alan Davies (Manchester Utd v Brighton, 1983); **Chris Baird** (Southampton v Arsenal, 2003); **Curtis Weston** (Millwall sub v Manchester Utd, 2004).

SEMI-FINALS AT WEMBLEY

1991 Tottenham 3 Arsenal 1; **1993** Sheffield Wed 2 Sheffield Utd 1, Arsenal 1 Tottenham 0; **1994** Chelsea 2 Luton 0, Manchester Utd 1 Oldham 1; **2000** Aston Villa beat Bolton 4-1 on pens (after 0-0), Chelsea 2 Newcastle 1; **2008** Portsmouth 1 WBA 0, Cardiff 1 Barnsley 0; **2009** Chelsea 2 Arsenal 1, Everton beat Manchester Utd 4-2 on pens (after 0-0); **2010** Chelsea 3 Aston Villa 0, Portsmouth 2 Tottenham 0; **2011** Manchester City 1 Manchester Utd 0, Stoke 5 Bolton 0; **2012** Liverpool 2 Everton 1, Chelsea 5 Tottenham 1; **2013** Wigan 2 Millwall 0, Manchester City 2 Chelsea 1; **2014** Arsenal beat Wigan 4-2 on pens (after 1-1), Hull 5 Sheffield Utd 3.

CHELSEA'S FA CUP MILESTONES

Their victory over Liverpool in the 2012 Final set the following records:
Captain **John Terry** first player to lift the trophy four times for one club; **Didier Drogba** first to

score in four Finals; **Ashley Cole** first to earn seven winner's medals (Arsenal 3, Chelsea 4); **Roberto Di Matteo** first to score for and manage the same winning club (player for Chelsea 1997, 2000, interim manager 2012).

Chelsea's four triumphs in six seasons (2007–12) the best winning sequence since Wanderers won five of the first seven competitions (1872–78) and Blackburn won five out of eight (1884–91).

FIRST ENTRANTS (1871–72)

Barnes, Civil Service, Crystal Palace, Clapham Rov, Donnington School (Spalding), Hampstead Heathens, Harrow Chequers, Hitchin, Maidenhead, Marlow, Queen's Park (Glasgow), Reigate Priory, Royal Engineers, Upton Park and Wanderers. Total 15.

FA CUP FIRSTS

Out of country: Cardiff, by defeating Arsenal 1-0 in the 1927 Final at Wembley, became the first and only club to take the FA Cup out of England.

All-English Winning XI: First club to win the FA Cup with all-English XI: Blackburn Olympic in 1883. Others since: WBA in 1888 and 1931, Bolton (1958), Manchester City (1969), West Ham (1964 and 1975).

Non-English Winning XI: Liverpool in 1986 (Mark Lawrenson, born Preston, was a Rep of Ireland player).

Won both Cups: Old Carthusians won the FA Cup in 1881 and the FA Amateur Cup in 1894 and 1897. Wimbledon won Amateur Cup in 1963, FA Cup in 1988.

MOST GAMES NEEDED TO WIN

Barnsley played a record 12 matches (20 hours' football) to win the FA Cup in season 1911–12. All six replays (one in round 1, three in round 4 and one in each of semi-final and Final) were brought about by goalless draws.

Arsenal played 11 FA Cup games when winning the trophy in 1979. Five of them were in the 3rd round against Sheffield Wed.

LONGEST TIES

6 matches: (11 hours): Alvechurch v Oxford City (4th qual round, 1971–72). Alvechurch won 1-0.

5 matches: (9 hours, 22 mins – record for competition proper): Stoke v Bury (3rd round, 1954–55). Stoke won 3-2.

5 matches: Chelsea v Burnley (4th round, 1955–56). Chelsea won 2-0.

5 matches: Hull v Darlington (2nd round, 1960–61). Hull won 3-0.

5 matches: Arsenal v Sheffield Wed (3rd round, 1978–79). Arsenal won 2-0.

Other marathons (qualifying comp, all 5 matches, 9 hours): Barrow v Gillingham (last qual round, 1924–25) – winners Barrow; Leyton v Ilford (3rd qual round, 1924–25) – winners Leyton; Falmouth v Bideford (3rd qual round, 1973–74) – winners Bideford.

End of Cup Final replays: The FA decided that, with effect from 1999, there would be no Cup Final replays. In the event of a draw after extra-time, the match would be decided on penalties. This happened for the first time in 2005, when Arsenal beat Manchester Utd 5-4 on penalties after a 0-0 draw. A year later, Liverpool beat West Ham 3-1 on penalties after a 3-3 draw.

FA Cup marathons ended in season 1991–92, when the penalty shoot-out was introduced to decide ties still level after one replay and extra-time.

In 1932–33 **Brighton** (Div 3 South) played 11 FA Cup games, including replays, and scored 43 goals, without getting past round 5. They forgot to claim exemption and had to play from 1st qual round.

LONGEST ROUND

The longest round in FA Cup history was the **3rd round** in **1962–63**. It took 66 days to complete, lasting from Jan 5 to Mar 11, and included 261 postponements because of bad weather.

LONGEST UNBEATEN RUN

23 matches by Blackburn In winning the Cup in three consecutive years (1884–05–06), they won 21 ties (one in a replay), and their first Cup defeat in four seasons was in a first round replay of the next competition.

RE-STAGED TIES

Sixth round, Mar 9, 1974: Newcastle 4, Nottm Forest 3. Match declared void by FA and ordered to be replayed following a pitch invasion after Newcastle had a player sent off. Forest claimed the hold-up caused the game to change its pattern. The tie went to two further matches at Goodison Park (0-0, then 1-0 to Newcastle).

Third round, Jan 5, 1985: Burton 1, Leicester 6 (at Derby). Burton goalkeeper Paul Evans was hit on the head by a missile thrown from the crowd and continued in a daze. The FA ordered the tie to be played again, behind closed doors at Coventry (Leicester won 1-0).

First round replay, Nov 25, 1992: Peterborough 9 (Tony Philliskirk 5), Kingstonian 1. Match expunged from records because, at 3-0 after 57 mins, Kingstonian were reduced to ten men when goalkeeper Adrian Blake was concussed by a 50 pence coin thrown from the crowd. The tie was re-staged on the same ground behind closed doors (Peterborough won 1-0).

Fifth round: Within an hour of holders Arsenal beating Sheffield Utd 2-1 at Highbury on Feb 13, 1999, the FA took the unprecedented step of declaring the match void because an unwritten rule of sportsmanship had been broken. With United's Lee Morris lying injured, their goalkeeper Alan Kelly kicked the ball into touch. Play resumed with Arsenal's Ray Parlour throwing it in the direction of Kelly, but Nwankwo Kanu took possession and centred for Marc Overmars to score the 'winning' goal. After four minutes of protests by manager Steve Bruce and his players, referee Peter Jones confirmed the goal. Both managers absolved Kanu of cheating but Arsenal's Arsene Wenger offered to replay the match. With the FA immediately approving, it was re-staged at Highbury ten days later (ticket prices halved) and Arsenal again won 2-1.

PRIZE FUND

The makeover of the FA Cup competition took off in 2001–02 with the introduction of round-by-round prize-money.

FA CUP FOLLIES

1999–2000 The FA broke with tradition by deciding the 3rd round be moved from its regular Jan date and staged before Christmas. Criticism was strong, gates poor and the 3rd round in 2000–01 reverted to the New Year. By allowing the holders Manchester Utd to withdraw from the 1999–2000 competition in order to play in FIFA's inaugural World Club Championship in Brazil in Jan, the FA were left with an odd number of clubs in the 3rd round. Their solution was a 'lucky losers' draw among clubs knocked out in round 2. Darlington, beaten at Gillingham, won it to re-enter the competition, then lost 2-1 away to Aston Villa.

HAT-TRICKS IN FINAL

There have been three in the history of the competition: **Billy Townley** (Blackburn, 1890), **Jimmy Logan** (Notts Co, 1894) and **Stan Mortensen** (Blackpool, 1953).

MOST APPEARANCES

88 by **Ian Callaghan** (79 for Liverpool, 7 for Swansea City, 2 for Crewe); **87** by **John Barnes** (31 for Watford, **51** for Liverpool, 5 for Newcastle); **86** by **Stanley Matthews** (37 for Stoke, 49 for Blackpool); **84** by **Bobby Charlton** (80 for Manchester Utd, 4 for Preston); **84** by **Pat Jennings** (3 for Watford, 43 for Tottenham, 38 for Arsenal); **84** by **Peter Shilton** for seven clubs (30 for Leicester, 7 for Stoke, **18** for Nottm Forest, 17 for Southampton, 10 for Derby, 1 for Plymouth Argyle, 1 for Leyton Orient); **82** by **David Seaman** (5 for Peterborough, 5 for Birmingham, 17 for QPR, 54 for Arsenal, 1 for Manchester City).

THREE-CLUB FINALISTS

Five players have appeared in the FA Cup Final for three clubs: **Harold Halse** for Manchester Utd (1909), Aston Villa (1913) and Chelsea (1915); **Ernie Taylor** for Newcastle (1951), Blackpool (1953) and Manchester Utd (1958); **John Barnes** for Watford (1984), Liverpool (1988, 1989, 1996) and Newcastle (1998); **Dennis Wise** for Wimbledon (1988), Chelsea (1994, 1997, 2000), Millwall (2004); **David James** for Liverpool (1996), Aston Villa (2000) and Portsmouth (2008, 2010).

CUP MAN WITH TWO CLUBS IN SAME SEASON

Stan Crowther, who played for Aston Villa against Manchester Utd in the 1957 FA Cup Final, appeared for both Villa and United in the 1957–58 competition. United signed him directly after the Munich air crash and, in the circumstances, he was given dispensation to play for them in the Cup, including the Final.

CAPTAIN'S CUP DOUBLE

Martin Buchan is the only player to have captained Scottish and English FA Cup-winning teams – Aberdeen in 1970 and Manchester Utd in 1977.

MEDALS BEFORE AND AFTER

Two players appeared in FA Cup Final teams before and after the Second World War: **Raich Carter** was twice a winner (Sunderland 1937, Derby 1946) and **Willie Fagan** twice on the losing side (Preston 1937, Liverpool 1950).

DELANEY'S COLLECTION

Scotland winger **Jimmy Delaney** uniquely earned Scottish, English, Northern Ireland and Republic of Ireland Cup medals. He was a winner with Celtic (1937), Manchester Utd (1948) and Derry City (1954) and a runner-up with Cork City (1956).

STARS WHO MISSED OUT

Internationals who never won an FA Cup winner's medal include: Tommy Lawton, Tom Finney, Johnny Haynes, Gordon Banks, George Best, Terry Butcher, Peter Shilton, Martin Peters, Nobby Stiles, Alan Ball, Malcolm Macdonald, Alan Shearer, Matthew Le Tissier, Stuart Pearce, Des Walker, Phil Neal, Ledley King.

CUP WINNERS AT NO COST

Not one member of **Bolton**'s 1958 FA Cup-winning team cost the club a transfer fee. Each joined the club for a £10 signing-on fee.

11-NATIONS LINE-UP

Liverpool fielded a team of 11 different nationalities in the FA Cup 3rd round at Yeovil on Jan 4, 2004.

HIGH-SCORING SEMI-FINALS

The **record team score** in FA Cup semi-finals is **6**: 1891–92 WBA 6, Nottm Forest 2; 1907–08 Newcastle 6, Fulham 0; 1933–34 Manchester City 6, Aston Villa 1.

Most goals in semi-finals (aggregate): 17 in 1892 (4 matches) and 1899 (5 matches). In modern times: 15 in 1958 (3 matches, including Manchester Utd 5, Fulham 3 – highest-scoring semi-final since last war); 16 in 1989–90 (Crystal Palace 4, Liverpool 3; Manchester Utd v Oldham 3-3, 2-1. All **16 goals** in those three matches were scored by **different players**.

Stoke's win against Bolton at Wembley in 2011 was the first 5-0 semi-final result since Wolves beat Grimsby at Old Trafford in 1939.

Last hat-trick in an FA Cup semi-final was scored by **Alex Dawson** for Manchester Utd in 5-3 replay win against Fulham at Highbury in 1958.

SEMI-FINAL VENUES

Villa Park has staged more such matches (55 including replays) than any other ground. Next is Hillsborough (33).

ONE IN A HUNDRED

The 2008 semi-finals included only one top-division club, Portsmouth, for the first time in 100 years – since Newcastle in 1908.

FOUR SPECIAL AWAYS

For the only time in FA Cup history, **all four quarter-finals** in season 1986–87 were won by the away team.

DRAWS RECORD

In season 1985–86, **seven** of the eight 5th round ties went to replays – a record for that stage of the competition.

LUCK OF THE DRAW

In the FA Cup on Jan 11, 1947, eight of **London**'s ten Football League clubs involved in the 3rd round were drawn at home (including Chelsea v Arsenal). Only Crystal Palace played outside the capital (at Newcastle).

In the 3rd round in Jan 1992, Charlton were the only London club drawn at home (against Barnet), but the venue of the Farnborough v West Ham tie was reversed on police instruction. So Upton Park staged Cup ties on successive days, with West Ham at home on the Saturday and Charlton (who shared the ground) on Sunday.

Arsenal were drawn away in every round on the way to reaching the Finals of 1971 and 1972. **Manchester Utd** won the Cup in 1990 without playing once at home.

The 1999 finalists, **Manchester Utd** and **Newcastle,** were both drawn at home every time in Rounds 3–6.

On their way to the semi-finals of both domestic Cup competitions in season 2002–03, **Sheffield Utd** were drawn at home ten times out of ten and won all ten matches – six in the League's Worthington Cup and four in the FA Cup.

On their way to winning the Cup in 2014, **Arsenal** did not play once outside London. Home draws in rounds 3, 4, 5 and 6 were followed by the semi-final at Wembley.

ALL TOP-DIVISION VICTIMS

The only instance of an FA Cup-winning club meeting top-division opponents in every round was provided by Manchester Utd in 1947–48. They beat Aston Villa, Liverpool, Charlton, Preston, then Derby in the semi-final and Blackpool in the Final.

In contrast, these clubs have reached the Final without playing top-division opponents on the way: West Ham (1923), Bolton (1926), Blackpool (1948), Bolton (1953), Millwall (2004).

WON CUP WITHOUT CONCEDING GOAL

1873 **The Wanderers** (1 match; as holders, exempt until Final); 1889 **Preston** (5 matches); 1903 **Bury** (5 matches). In 1966 **Everton** reached Final without conceding a goal (7 matches), then beat Sheffield Wed 3-2 at Wembley.

HOME ADVANTAGE

For the first time in FA Cup history, all eight ties in the 1992–93 5th round were won (no replays) by the **clubs drawn at home.** Only other instance of eight home wins at the last 16 stage was in 1889–90, in what was then the 2nd round.

NORTH-EAST WIPE-OUT

For the first time in 54 years, since the 4th round in Jan, 1957, the North-East's 'big three' were knocked out on the same date, Jan 8, 2011 (3rd round). All lost to lower-division

opponents – **Newcastle** 3-1 at Stevenage, **Sunderland** 2-1 at home to Notts County and **Middlesbrough** 2-1 at Burton.

FEWEST TOP-DIVISION CLUBS IN LAST 16 (5th ROUND)

5 in 1958; **6** in 1927, 1970, 1982; **7** in 1994, 2003; **8** in 2002, 2004.

SIXTH-ROUND ELITE

For the first time in FA Cup 6th round history, dating from 1926 when the format of the competition changed, all **eight quarter-finalists** in 1995–96 were from the top division.

SEMI-FINAL – DOUBLE DERBIES

There have been three instances of both FA Cup semi-finals in the same year being local derbies: **1950** Liverpool beat Everton 2-0 (Maine Road), Arsenal beat Chelsea 1-0 after 2-2 draw (both at Tottenham); **1993** Arsenal beat Tottenham 1-0 (Wembley), Sheffield Wed beat Sheffield Utd 2-1 (Wembley); **2012** Liverpool beat Everton 2-1 (Wembley), Chelsea beat Tottenham 5-1 (Wembley).

TOP CLUB DISTINCTION

Since the Football League began in 1888, there has never been an FA Cup Final in which **neither club** represented the top division.

CLUBS THROWN OUT

Bury expelled (Dec 2006) for fielding an ineligible player in 3-1 2nd rd replay win at Chester. **Droylsden** expelled for fielding a suspended player in 2-1 2nd rd replay win at home to Chesterfield (Dec 2008).

SPURS OUT – AND IN

Tottenham were banned, pre-season, from the 1994–95 competition because of financial irregularities, but were re-admitted on appeal and reached the semi-finals.

FATHER & SON FA CUP WINNERS

Peter Boyle (Sheffield Utd 1899, 1902) and **Tommy Boyle** (Sheffield Utd 1925); **Harry Johnson Snr** (Sheffield Utd 1899, 1902) and **Harry Johnson Jnr** (Sheffield Utd 1925); **Jimmy Dunn Snr** (Everton 1933) and **Jimmy Dunn Jnr** (Wolves 1949); **Alec Herd** (Manchester City 1934) and **David Herd** (Manchester Utd 1963); **Frank Lampard Snr** (West Ham 1975, 1980) and **Frank Lampard Jnr** (Chelsea 2007, 2009, 2010, 2012).

BROTHERS IN FA CUP FINAL TEAMS (modern times)

1950 **Denis and Leslie Compton** (Arsenal); 1952 **George and Ted Robledo** (Newcastle); 1967 **Ron and Allan Harris** (Chelsea); 1977 **Jimmy and Brian Greenhoff** (Manchester Utd); 1996 and 1999 **Gary and Phil Neville** (Manchester Utd).

FA CUP SPONSORS

Littlewoods Pools became the first sponsors of the FA Cup in season 1994–95 in a £14m, 4-year deal. French insurance giants **AXA** took over (season 1998–99) in a sponsorship worth £25m over 4 years. German energy company **E.ON** agreed a 4-year deal worth £32m from season 2006–07 and extended it for a year to 2011. American beer company **Budweiser** began a three-year sponsorship worth £24m in season 2011–12.

FIRST GOALKEEPER-SUBSTITUTE IN FINAL

Paul Jones (Southampton), who replaced injured Antti Niemi against Arsenal in 2003.

LEAGUE CUP RECORDS

(See also Goalscoring section)

Highest scores: West Ham 10-0 v Bury (2nd round, 2nd leg 1983–84; agg 12-1); Liverpool 10-0 v Fulham (2nd round, 1st leg 1986–87; agg 13-2).

Most League Cup goals (career): 49 Geoff Hurst (43 West Ham, 6 Stoke, 1960–75); 49 Ian Rush (48 Liverpool, 1 Newcastle, 1981–98).

Highest scorer (season): 12 Clive Allen (Tottenham 1986–87 in 9 apps).

Most goals in match: 6 Frank Bunn (Oldham v Scarborough, 3rd round, 1989–90).

Most winners' medals: 5 Ian Rush (Liverpool).

Most appearances in Final: 6 Kenny Dalglish (Liverpool 1978–87), Ian Rush (Liverpool 1981–95).

Biggest Final win: Swansea City 5 Bradford City 0 (2013).

League Cup sponsors: Milk Cup 1981–86, Littlewoods Cup 1987–90, Rumbelows Cup 1991–92, Coca-Cola Cup 1993–98. Worthington Cup 1999–2003, Carling Cup 2003–12; Capital One Cup from season 2012–13.

Up for the cup, then down: In 2011, Birmingham became only the second club to win a major trophy (the Carling Cup) and be relegated from the top division. It previously happened to Norwich in 1985 when they went down from the old First Division after winning the Milk Cup.

Liverpool's League Cup records: Winners a record 8 times. **Ian Rush** only player to win 5 times. Rush also first to play in 8 winning teams in Cup Finals **at Wembley**, all with Liverpool (FA Cup 1986–89–92; League Cup 1981–82–83–84–95).

Britain's first under-cover Cup Final: Worthington Cup Final between Blackburn and Tottenham at Cardiff's Millennium Stadium on Sunday, Feb 24, 2002. With rain forecast, the retractable roof was closed on the morning of the match.

DISCIPLINE

SENDINGS-OFF

Season 2003–04 set an **all-time record** of 504 players sent off in English domestic football competitions. There were 58 in the Premiership, 390 Nationwide League, 28 FA Cup (excluding non-League dismissals), 22 League Cup, 2 in Nationwide play-offs, 4 in LDV Vans Trophy.

Most sendings-off in Premier League programme (10 matches): 9 (8 Sat, 1 Sun, Oct 31–Nov 1, 2009).

The 58 Premiership red cards was 13 fewer than the record English **top-division** total of 71 in 2002–03. **Bolton** were the only club in the English divisions without a player sent off in any first-team competition that season.

Worst day for dismissals in English football was Boxing Day, 2007, with **20 red cards** (5 Premier League and 15 Coca-Cola League). Three players, Chelsea's Ashley Cole and Ricardo Carvalho and Aston Villa's Zat Knight were sent off in a 4-4 draw at Stamford Bridge. Luton had three men dismissed in their game at Bristol Rov, but still managed a 1-1 draw.

Previous worst day was Dec 13, 2003, with **19 red cards** (2 Premiership and the 17 Nationwide League).

In the entire first season of post-war League football (1946–47) only 12 players were sent off, followed by 14 in 1949–50, and the total League dismissals for the first nine seasons after the War was 104.

The worst pre-War total was 28 in each of seasons 1921–22 and 1922–23.

ENGLAND SENDINGS-OFF

In a total of 15 England dismissals, David Beckham and Wayne Rooney have been red-carded twice. Beckham and Steven Gerrard are the only England captains to be sent off and Robert Green the only goalkeeper.

Jun 5, 1968	**Alan Mullery**	v Yugoslavia (Florence, Euro Champ)
Jun 6, 1973	**Alan Ball**	v Poland (Chorzow, World Cup qual)

Jun 12, 1977	**Trevor Cherry**	v Argentina (Buenos Aires, friendly)
Jun 6, 1986	**Ray Wilkins**	v Morocco (Monterrey, World Cup Finals)
Jun 30, 1998	**David Beckham**	v Argentina (St Etienne, World Cup Finals)
Sep 5, 1998	**Paul Ince**	v Sweden (Stockholm, Euro Champ qual)
Jun 5, 1999	**Paul Scholes**	v Sweden (Wembley, Euro Champ qual)
Sep 8, 1999	**David Batty**	v Poland (Warsaw, Euro Champ qual)
Oct 16, 2002	**Alan Smith**	v Macedonia (Southampton, Euro Champ qual)
Oct 8, 2005	**David Beckham**	v Austria (Old Trafford, World Cup qual)
Jul 1, 2006	**Wayne Rooney**	v Portugal (Gelsenkirchen, World Cup Finals)
Oct 10, 2009	**Robert Green**	v Ukraine (Dnipropetrovsk, World Cup qual)
Oct 7, 2011	**Wayne Rooney**	v Montenegro (Podgorica, Euro Champ qual)
Sep 11, 2012	**Steven Gerrard**	v Ukraine (Wembley, World Cup qual)
Jun 4, 2014	**Raheem Sterling**	v Ecuador (Miami, friendly)

Other countries: Most recent sendings-off of players representing other Home Countries:
N Ireland – Gareth McAuley (Friendly v Cyprus, Nicosia, Mar 5, 2014).
Scotland – Robert Snodgrass (World Cup qual v Wales, Hampden Park, Mar 22, 2013).
Wales – Aaron Ramsey (World Cup qual v Scotland, Hampden Park, Mar 22, 2013).
Rep of Ireland– Keith Andrews (European Champ v Italy, Poznan, Jun 18, 2012).
England dismissals at other levels:
U-23: Stan Anderson (v Bulgaria, Sofia, May 19, 1957); **Alan Ball** (v Austria, Vienna, Jun 2, 1965); **Kevin Keegan** (v E Germany, Magdeburg, Jun 1, 1972); **Steve Perryman** (v Portugal, Lisbon, Nov 19, 1974).
U-21: Sammy Lee (v Hungary, Keszthely, Jun 5, 1981); **Mark Hateley** (v Scotland, Hampden Park, Apr 19, 1982); **Paul Elliott** (v Denmark, Maine Road, Manchester, Mar 26, 1986); **Tony Cottee** (v W Germany, Ludenscheid, Sep 8, 1987); **Julian Dicks** (v Mexico, Toulon, France, Jun 12, 1988); **Jason Dodd** (v Mexico, Toulon, May 29, 1991; 3 Mexico players also sent off in that match); **Matthew Jackson** (v France, Toulon, May 28, 1992); **Robbie Fowler** (v Austria, Kafkenberg, Oct 11, 1994); **Alan Thompson** (v Portugal, Oporto, Sep 2, 1995); **Terry Cooke** (v Portugal, Toulon, May 30, 1996); **Ben Thatcher** (v Italy, Rieti, Oct 10, 1997); **John Curtis** (v Greece, Heraklion, Nov 13, 1997); **Jody Morris** (v Luxembourg, Grevenmacher, Oct 13, 1998); **Stephen Wright** (v Germany, Derby, Oct 6, 2000); **Alan Smith** (v Finland, Valkeakoski, Oct 10, 2000); **Luke Young** and **John Terry** (v Greece, Athens, Jun 5, 2001); **Shola Ameobi** (v Portugal, Rio Maior, Mar 28, 2003); **Jermaine Pennant** (v Croatia, Upton Park, Aug 19, 2003); **Glen Johnson** (v Turkey, Istanbul, Oct 10, 2003); **Nigel Reo-Coker** (v Azerbaijan, Baku, Oct 12, 2004); **Glen Johnson** (v Spain, Henares, Nov 16, 2004); **Steven Taylor** (v Germany, Leverkusen, Oct 10, 2006); **Tom Huddlestone** (v Serbia & Montenegro, Nijmegen, Jun 17, 2007); **Tom Huddlestone** (v Wales, Villa Park, Oct 14, 2008); **Michael Mancienne** (v Finland, Halmstad, Jun 15, 2009); **Fraizer Campbell** (v Sweden, Gothenburg, Jun 26, 2009); **Ben Mee** (v Italy, Empoli, Feb 8, 2011); **Danny Rose** (v Serbia, Krusevac, Oct 16, 2012); **Andre Wisdom** (v Finland, Tampere, Sep 9, 2013).
England 'B' (1): **Neil Webb** (v Algeria, Algiers, Dec 11, 1990).

MOST DISMISSALS IN INTERNATIONAL MATCHES

19 (10 Chile, 9 Uruguay), Jun 25, 1975; **6** (2 Mexico, 4 Argentina), 1956; **6** (5 Ecuador, 1 Uruguay), Jan 4, 1977 (4 Ecuadorians sent off in 78th min, match abandoned, 1-1); **5** (Holland 3, Brazil 2), Jun 6, 1999 in Goianio, Brazil.

INTERNATIONAL STOPPED THROUGH DEPLETED SIDE

Portugal v Angola (5-1), friendly international in Lisbon on Nov 14, 2001, abandoned (68 mins) because Angola were down to 6 players (4 sent off, 1 carried off, no substitutes left).

MOST 'CARDS' IN WORLD CUP FINALS MATCH

20 in Portugal v Holland quarter-final, Nuremberg, Jun 25, 2006 (9 yellow, 2 red, Portugal; 7 yellow, 2 red, Holland).

FIVE OFF IN ONE MATCH

For the first time since League football began in 1888, five players were sent off in one match (two Chesterfield, three Plymouth) in Div 2 at Saltergate on **Feb 22, 1997**. Four were dismissed (two from each side) in a goalmouth brawl in the last minute. Five were sent off on Dec 2, 1997 (4 Bristol Rov, 1 Wigan) in Div 2 match at Wigan, four in the 45th minute. The third instance occurred at Exeter on **Nov 23, 2002** in Div 3 (three Exeter, two Cambridge United) all in the last minute. On **Mar 27, 2012** (Lge 2) three Bradford players and two from Crawley were shown red cards in the dressing rooms after a brawl at the final whistle at Valley Parade.

Matches with **four** Football League club players being sent off in one match:

Jan 8, 1955: Crewe v Bradford City (Div 3 North), two players from each side.

Dec 13, 1986: Sheffield Utd (1 player) v Portsmouth (3) in Div 2.

Aug 18, 1987: Port Vale v Northampton (Littlewoods Cup 1st Round, 1st Leg), two players from each side.

Dec 12, 1987: Brentford v Mansfield (Div 3), two players from each side.

Sep 6, 1992: First instance in British first-class football of four players from one side being sent off in one match. Hereford's seven survivors, away to Northampton (Div 3), held out for a 1-1 draw.

Mar 1, 1977: Norwich v Huddersfield (Div 1), two from each side.

Oct 4, 1977: Shrewsbury (1 player), Rotherham (3) in Div 3.

Aug 22, 1998: Gillingham v Bristol Rov (Div 2), two from each side, all after injury-time brawl.

Mar 16, 2001: Bristol City v Millwall (Div 2), two from each side.

Aug 17, 2002: Lincoln (1 player), Carlisle (3) in Div 3.

Aug 26, 2002: Wycombe v QPR (Div 2), two from each side.

Nov 1, 2005: Burnley (1 player) v Millwall (3) in Championship.

Nov 24, 2007: Swindon v Bristol Rov (Lge 1), two from each side.

Mar 4, 2008: Hull v Burnley (Champ) two from each side.

Four Stranraer players were sent off away to Airdrie (Scottish Div 1) on Dec 3, 1994, and that Scottish record was equalled when four Hearts men were ordered off away to Rangers (Prem Div) on Sep 14, 1996. Albion had four players sent off (3 in last 8 mins) away to Queen's Park (Scottish Div 3) on Aug 23, 1997.

In the **Island Games** in Guernsey (Jul 2003), five players (all from Rhodes) were sent off against Guernsey for violent conduct and the match was abandoned by referee Wendy Toms.

Most dismissals one team, one match: Five players of America Tres Rios in first ten minutes after disputed goal by opponents Itaperuna in Brazilian cup match in Rio de Janeiro on Nov 23, 1991. Tie then abandoned and awarded to Itaperuna.

Eight dismissals in one match: Four on each side in South American Super Cup quarter-final (Gremio, Brazil v Penarol, Uruguay) in Oct 1993.

Five dismissals in one season – Dave Caldwell (2 with Chesterfield, 3 with Torquay) in 1987–88.

First instance of four dismissals in Scottish match: three Rangers players (all English – Terry Hurlock, Mark Walters, Mark Hateley) and Celtic's Peter Grant in Scottish Cup quarter-final at Parkhead on Mar 17, 1991 (Celtic won 2-0).

Four players (3 Hamilton, 1 Airdrie) were sent off in Scottish Div 1 match on Oct 30, 1993.

Four players (3 Ayr, 1 Stranraer) were sent off in Scottish Div 1 match on Aug 27, 1994.

In Scottish Cup first round replays on Dec 16, 1996, there were two instances of three players of one side sent off: Albion Rov (away to Forfar) and Huntly (away to Clyde).

FASTEST SENDINGS-OFF

World record – 10 sec: Giuseppe Lorenzo (Bologna) for striking opponent in Italian League match v Parma, Dec 9, 1990. Goalkeeper **Preston Edwards** (Ebbsfleet) for bringing down opponent and conceding penalty in Blue Square Premier League South match v Farnborough, Feb 5, 2011.

World record (non-professional) – 3 sec: David Pratt (Chippenham) at Bashley (British Gas Southern Premier League, Dec 27, 2008).

Domestic – **13 sec: Kevin Pressman** (Sheffield Wed goalkeeper at Wolves, Div 1, Sunday, Aug 14, 2000); **15 sec: Simon Rea** (Peterborough at Cardiff, Div 2, Nov 2, 2002). **19 sec: Mark Smith** (Crewe goalkeeper at Darlington, Div 3, Mar 12, 1994). **Premier League – 72 sec: Tim Flowers** (Blackburn goalkeeper v Leeds Utd, Feb 1, 1995).

In World Cup – **55 sec: Jose Batista** (Uruguay v Scotland at Neza, Mexico, Jun 13, 1986).

In European competition – **90 sec: Sergei Dirkach** (Dynamo Moscow v Ghent UEFA Cup 3rd round, 2nd leg, Dec 11, 1991).

Fastest FA Cup dismissal – **52 sec: Ian Culverhouse** (Swindon defender, deliberate hand-ball on goal-line, away to Everton, 3rd Round, Sunday Jan 5, 1997).

Fastest League Cup dismissal – **33 sec: Jason Crowe** (Arsenal substitute v Birmingham, 3rd Round, Oct 14, 1997). Also fastest sending off on debut.

Fastest Sending-off of substitute – **0 sec: Walter Boyd** (Swansea City) for striking opponent before ball in play after he went on (83 mins) at home to Darlington, Div 3, Nov 23, 1999. **15 secs: Keith Gillespie** (Sheffield Utd) for striking an opponent at Reading (Premiership), Jan 20, 2007. **90 sec: Andreas Johansson** (Wigan), without kicking a ball, for shirt-pulling (penalty) away to Arsenal (Premiership), May 7, 2006.

MOST SENDINGS-OFF IN CAREER

21	**Willie Johnston** , 1964–82 (Rangers 7, WBA 6, Vancouver Whitecaps 4, Hearts 3, Scotland 1)	
21	**Roy McDonough**, 1980–95 (13 in Football League – Birmingham, Walsall, Chelsea, Colchester, Southend, Exeter, Cambridge Utd plus 8 non-league)	
13	**Steve Walsh** (Wigan, Leicester, Norwich, Coventry)	
13	**Martin Keown** (Arsenal, Aston Villa, Everton)	
13	**Alan Smith** (Leeds, Manchester Utd, Newcastle, England U–21, England)	
12	**Dennis Wise** (Wimbledon, Chelsea, Leicester, Millwall)	
12	**Vinnie Jones** (Wimbledon, Leeds, Sheffield Utd, Chelsea, QPR)	
12	**Mark Dennis** (Birmingham, Southampton, QPR)	
12	**Roy Keane** (Manchester Utd, Rep of Ireland)	
10	**Patrick Vieira** (Arsenal)	
10	**Paul Scholes** (Manchester Utd, England)	

Most Premier League sendings-off: Patrick Vieira 9, Duncan Ferguson 8, Richard Dunne 8, Vinnie Jones 7, Roy Keane 7, Alan Smith 7. Lee Cattermole 7.

● **Carlton Palmer** holds the unique record of having been sent off with each of his five Premiership clubs: Sheffield Wed, Leeds, Southampton, Nottm Forest and Coventry.

FA CUP FINAL SENDINGS-OFF

Kevin Moran (Manchester Utd) v Everton, Wembley, 1985; **Jose Antonio Reyes** (Arsenal) v Manchester Utd, Cardiff, 2005; Pablo Zabaleta (Manchester City) v Wigan, Wembley 2013.

WEMBLEY SENDINGS-OFF

Aug 1948	**Branko Stankovic** (Yugoslavia) v Sweden, Olympic Games	
Jul 1966	**Antonio Rattin** (Argentina captain) v England, World cup quarter-final	
Aug 1974	**Billy Bremner** (Leeds) and **Kevin Keegan** (Liverpool), Charity Shield	
Mar 1977	**Gilbert Dresch** (Luxembourg) v England, World Cup	
May 1985	**Kevin Moran** (Manchester Utd) v Everton, FA Cup Final	
Apr 1993	**Lee Dixon** (Arsenal) v Tottenham, FA Cup semi-final	
May 1993	**Peter Swan** (Port Vale) v WBA, Div 2 Play-off Final	
Mar 1994	**Andrei Kanchelskis** (Manchester Utd) v Aston Villa, League Cup Final	
May 1994	**Mike Wallace, Chris Beaumont** (Stockport) v Burnley, Div 2 Play-off Final	
Jun 1995	**Tetsuji Hashiratani** (Japan) v England, Umbro Cup	
May 1997	**Brian Statham** (Brentford) v Crewe, Div 2 Play-off Final	
Apr 1998	**Capucho** (Portugal) v England, friendly	
Nov 1998	**Ray Parlour** (Arsenal) and **Tony Vareilles** (Lens), Champions League	
Mar 1999	**Justin Edinburgh** (Tottenham) v Leicester, League Cup Final	
Jun 1999	**Paul Scholes** (England) v Sweden, European Championship qual	

Feb 2000	**Clint Hill** (Tranmere) v Leicester, League Cup Final
Apr 2000	**Mark Delaney** (Aston Villa) v Bolton, FA Cup semi-final
May 2000	**Kevin Sharp** (Wigan) v Gillingham, Div 2 Play-off Final
Aug 2000	**Roy Keane** (Manchester Utd captain) v Chelsea, Charity Shield
May 2007	**Marc Tierney** (Shrewsbury) v Bristol Rov, Lge 2 Play-off Final
May 2007	**Matt Gill** (Exeter) v Morecambe, Conf Play-off Final
May 2009	**Jamie Ward** (Sheffield Utd) and **Lee Hendrie** (Sheffield Utd) v Burnley, Champ Play-off Final (Hendrie after final whistle)
May 2009	**Phil Bolland** (Cambridge Utd) v Torquay, Blue Square Prem Lge Play-off Final
May 2010	**Robin Hulbert** (Barrow) and **David Bridges** (Stevenage), FA Trophy Final
Apr 2011	**Paul Scholes** (Manchester Utd) v Manchester City, FA Cup semi-final
Apr 2011	**Toumani Diagouraga** (Brentford) v Carlisle, Johnstone's Paint Trophy Final
Sep 2012	**Steven Gerrard** (England) v Ukraine, World Cup qual
Feb 2013	**Matt Duke** (Bradford) v Swansea, League Cup Final
May 2013	**Pablo Zabaleta** (Manchester City) v Wigan, FA Cup Final
Mar 2014	**Joe Newell** (Peterborough) v Chesterfield, Johnstone's Paint Trophy Final
May 2014	**Gary O'Neil** (QPR) v Derby, Champ Play-off Final

WEMBLEY'S SUSPENDED CAPTAINS

Suspension prevented four **club captains** playing at Wembley in modern finals, in successive years. Three were in FA Cup Finals – **Glenn Roeder** (QPR, 1982), **Steve Foster** (Brighton, 1983), **Wilf Rostron** (Watford, 1984). Sunderland's **Shaun Elliott** was banned from the 1985 Milk Cup Final. Roeder was banned from QPR's 1982 Cup Final replay against Tottenham, and Foster was ruled out of the first match in Brighton's 1983 Final against Manchester Utd.

RED CARD FOR KICKING BALL-BOY

Chelsea's **Eden Hazard** was sent off (80 mins) in the League Cup semi-final, second leg at Swansea on Jan 23, 2013 for kicking a 17-year-old ball-boy who refused to hand over the ball that had gone out of play. The FA suspended Hazard for three matches.

BOOKINGS RECORDS

Most players of one Football League club booked in one match is **TEN** – members of the Mansfield team away to Crystal Palace in FA Cup third round, Jan 1963. Most yellow cards for one team in Premier League match – 8 for West Ham away to QPR, Oct 1, 2012.
Fastest bookings – 3 seconds after kick-off, **Vinnie Jones** (Chelsea, home to Sheffield Utd, FA Cup fifth round, Feb 15, 1992); 5 seconds after kick-off: **Vinnie Jones** (Sheffield Utd, away to Manchester Utd, Div 1, Jan 19, 1991). He was sent-off (54 mins) for second bookable offence.

FIGHTING TEAM-MATES

Charlton's **Mike Flanagan** and **Derek Hales** were sent off for fighting each other five minutes from end of FA Cup 3rd round tie at home to Southern League Maidstone on Jan 9, 1979.
Bradford City's **Andy Myers** and **Stuart McCall** had a fight during the 1-6 Premiership defeat at Leeds on Sunday, May 13, 2001.
On Sep 28, 1994 the Scottish FA suspended Hearts players **Graeme Hogg** and **Craig Levein** for ten matches for fighting each other in a pre-season 'friendly' v Raith.
Blackburn's England players **Graeme Le Saux** and **David Batty** clashed away to Spartak Moscow (Champions League) on Nov 22, 1995. Neither was sent off.
Newcastle United's England Internationals **Lee Bowyer** and **Kieron Dyer** were sent off for fighting each other at home to Aston Villa (Premiership on Apr 2, 2005).
Arsenal's **Emmanuel Adebayor** and **Nicklas Bendtner** clashed during the 5-1 Carling Cup semi-final 2nd leg defeat at Tottenham on Jan 22, 2008. Neither was sent off; each fined by their club.
Stoke's **Richardo Fuller** was sent off for slapping his captain, Andy Griffin, at West Ham in the Premier League on Dec 28, 2008.

FOOTBALL'S FIRST BETTING SCANDAL

A Football League investigation into the First Division match which ended Manchester Utd 2, Liverpool 0 at Old Trafford on Good Friday, Apr 2, 1915 proved that the result had been 'squared' by certain players betting on the outcome. Four members of each team were suspended for life, but some of the bans were lifted when League football resumed in 1919 in recognition of the players' war service.

PLAYERS JAILED

Ten professional footballers found guilty of conspiracy to fraud by 'fixing' matches for betting purposes were given prison sentences at Nottingham Assizes on Jan 26, 1965.
Jimmy Gauld (Mansfield), described as the central figure, was given four years. Among the others sentenced, **Tony Kay** (Sheffield Wed, Everton & England), **Peter Swan** (Sheffield Wed & England) and **David 'Bronco' Layne** (Sheffield Wed) were suspended from football for life by the FA.

DRUGS BANS

Abel Xavier (Middlesbrough) was the first Premiership player found to have taken a performance-enchancing drug. He was banned by UEFA for 18 months in Nov 2005 after testing positive for an anabolic steroid. The ban was reduced to a year in Jul 2006 by the Court of Arbitration for Sport. **Paddy Kenny** (Sheffield Utd goalkeeper) was suspended by an FA commission for 9 months from July, 2009 for failing a drugs test the previous May. Kolo Toure (Manchester City) received a 6-month ban in May 2011 for a doping offence. It was backdated to Mar 2.

LONG SUSPENSIONS

The longest suspension (8 months) in modern times for a player in British football was imposed on two Manchester Utd players. First was **Eric Cantona** following his attack on a spectator as he left the pitch after being sent off at Crystal Palace (Prem League) on Jan 25, 1995. The club immediately suspended him to the end of the season and fined him 2 weeks' wages (est £20,000). Then, on a disrepute charge, the FA fined him £10,000 (Feb 1995) and extended the ban to Sep 30 (which FIFA confirmed as world-wide). A subsequent 2-weeks' jail sentence on Cantona for assault was altered, on appeal, to 120 hours' community service, which took the form of coaching schoolboys in the Manchester area.
On **Dec 19, 2003** an FA Commission, held at Bolton, suspended **Rio Ferdinand** from football for 8 months (plus £50,000 fine) for failing to take a random drug test at the club's training ground on Sep 23. The ban operated from Jan 12, 2004.
Aug 1974: Kevin Keegan (Liverpool) and Billy Bremner (Leeds) both suspended for 10 matches and fined £500 after being sent off in FA Charity Shield at Wembley.
Jan 1988: Mark Dennis (QPR) given 8-match ban after 11th sending-off of his career.
Oct 1988: Paul Davis (Arsenal) banned for 9 matches for breaking the jaw of Southampton's Glenn Cockerill.
Oct 1998: Paolo Di Canio (Sheff Wed) banned for 11 matches and fined £10,000 for pushing referee Paul Alcock after being sent off at home to Arsenal (Prem), Sep 26.
Mar 2005: David Prutton (Southampton) banned for 10 matches (plus 1 for red card) and fined £6,000 by FA for shoving referee Alan Wiley when sent off at home to Arsenal (Prem), Feb 26.
Aug 2006: Ben Thatcher (Manchester City) banned for 8 matches for elbowing Pedro Mendes (Portsmouth).
Sep 2008: Joey Barton (Newcastle) banned for 12 matches (6 suspended) and fined £25,000 by FA for training ground assault on former Manchester City team-mate Ousmane Dabo.
May 2012: Joey Barton (QPR) suspended for 12 matches and fined £75,000 for violent conduct when sent off against Manchester City on final day of Premier League season.
Mar 2014: Joss Labadie (Torquay) banned for 10 matches and fined £2,000 for biting Chesterfield's Ollie Banks (Lge 2) on Feb 15, 2014.
Seven-month ban: Frank Barson, 37-year-old Watford centre-half, sent off at home to Fulham (Div 3 South) on Sep 29, 1928, was suspended by the FA for the remainder of the season.

Twelve-month ban: Oldham full-back **Billy Cook** was given a 12-month suspension for refusing to leave the field when sent off at Middlesbrough (Div 1), on Apr 3, 1915. The referee abandoned the match with 35 minutes still to play, and the score (4-1 to Middlesbrough) was ordered to stand.

Long Scottish bans: Sep 1954: Willie Woodburn, Rangers and Scotland centre-half, suspended for rest of career after fifth sending-off in 6 years.

Billy McLafferty, Stenhousemuir striker, was banned (Apr 14) for 8 and a half months, to Jan 1, 1993, and fined £250 for failing to appear at a disciplinary hearing after being sent off against Arbroath on Feb 1.

Twelve-match ban: On May 12, 1994 Scottish FA suspended Rangers forward **Duncan Ferguson** for 12 matches for violent conduct v Raith on Apr 16. On Oct 11, 1995, Ferguson (then with Everton) sent to jail for 3 months for the assault (served 44 days); Feb 1, 1996 Scottish judge quashed 7 matches that remained of SFA ban on Ferguson.

On Sep 29, 2001 the SFA imposed a **17-match suspension** on Forfar's former Scottish international **Dave Bowman** for persistent foul and abusive language when sent off against Stranraer on Sep 22. As his misconduct continued, he was shown **5 red cards** by the referee.

On Apr 3, 2009, captain **Barry Ferguson** and goalkeeper **Allan McGregor** were banned for life from playing for Scotland for gestures towards photographers while on the bench for a World Cup qualifier against Iceland.

On Dec 20, 2011 Liverpool and Uruguay striker **Luis Suarez** was given an 8-match ban and fined £40,000 by the FA for making 'racially offensive comments' to Patrice Evra of Manchester Utd (Prem Lge, Oct 15).

On Apr 25, 2013 **Luis Suarez** was given a 10-match suspension by the FA for 'violent conduct' – biting Chelsea defender Branislav Ivanovic, Prem Lge, Apr 21. The Liverpool player was also fined £200,000 by Liverpool. His ban covered the last 4 games of that season and the first 6 of 2013–14. On Jun 26, 2014, Suarez, while still a Liverpool player, received the most severe punishment in World Cup history – a four-month ban from 'all football activities' and £66,000 fine from FIFA for biting Giorgio Chiellini during Uruguay's group game against Italy.

TOP FINES

Clubs: £49,000,000 (World record) Manchester City: May 2014 for breaking UEFA Financial Fair Play rules (**£32,600,000** suspended subject to City meeting certain conditions over two seasons). **£5,500,000** West Ham: Apr 2007, for breaches of regulations involving 'dishonesty and deceit' over Argentine signings Carlos Tevez and Javier Mascherano; **£1,500,000** (increased from original £600,000) Tottenham: Dec 1994, financial irregularities; **£875,000** QPR: May 2011 for breaching rules when signing Argentine Alejandro Faurlin; **£300,000** (reduced to £75,000 on appeal) Chelsea: Jun 2005, illegal approach to Arsenal's Ashley Cole; **£175,000** Arsenal: Oct 2003, players' brawl v Manchester Utd; **£150,000** Leeds: Mar 2000, players' brawl v Tottenham; **£150,000** Tottenham: Mar 2000, players brawl v Leeds; **£115,000** West Ham: Aug 2009, crowd misconduct at Carling Cup; v Millwall; **£105,000** Chelsea: Jan 1991, irregular payments; **£100,000** Boston Utd: Jul 2002, contract irregularities; **£100,000** Arsenal and Chelsea: Mar 2007 for mass brawl after Carling Cup Final; **£100,000** (including suspended fine) Blackburn: Aug 2007, poor disciplinary record; **£100,000** Sunderland: May 2014, breaching agents' regulations; **£62,000** Macclesfield: Dec 2005, funding of a stand at club's ground.

Players: £220,000 (plus 4-match ban) John Terry (Chelsea): Sep 2012, racially abusing Anton Ferdinand (QPR); **£150,000** Roy Keane (Manchester Utd): Oct 2002, disrepute offence over autobiography; **£100,000** (reduced to £75,000 on appeal) Ashley Cole (Arsenal): Jun 2005, illegal approach by Chelsea; **£90,000** Ashley Cole (Chelsea): Oct 2012, offensive Tweet against FA; **£80,000 (plus 5-match ban)** Nicolas Anelka (WBA): Feb 2014, celebrating goal at West Ham with racially-offensive 'quenelle' gesture; **£75,000 (plus 12-match ban)** Joey Barton (QPR): May 2012, violent conduct v Manchester City; **£60,000 (plus 3-match ban)** John Obi Mikel (Chelsea): Dec 2012, abusing referee Mark Clattenburg after Prem Lge v Manchester Utd); **£60,000** Dexter Blackstock (Nottm Forest): May 2014,

breaching betting rules; **£50,000** Cameron Jerome (Stoke): Aug 2013, breaching FA betting rules; **£45,000** Patrick Vieira (Arsenal): Oct 1999, tunnel incidents v West Ham; **£45,000** Rio Ferdinand (Manchester Utd): Aug 2012, improper comments about Ashley Cole on Twitter; **£40,000** Lauren (Arsenal): Oct 2003, players' fracas v Manchester Utd; **£40,000 (plus 8-match ban)** Luis Suarez (Liverpool): Dec 2011, racially abusing Patrice Evra (Manchester Utd); **£40,000 (plus 3-match ban)** Dani Osvaldo (Southampton): Jan 2014, violent conduct, touchline Newcastle.

*In eight seasons with Arsenal (1996–2004) **Patrick Vieira** was fined a total of £122,000 by the FA for disciplinary offences.

Managers: £200,000 (reduced to £75,000 on appeal) Jose Mourinho (Chelsea): Jun 2005, illegal approach to Arsenal's Ashley Cole; **£60,000 (plus 7-match ban)** Alan Pardew (Newcastle): head-butting Hull player David Meyler (also fined £100,000 by club); **£33,000 (plus 3-match Euro ban)** Arsene Wenger (Arsenal): Mar 2012, criticising referee after Champions League defeat by AC Milan; **£30,000** Sir Alex Ferguson (Manchester Utd): Mar 2011 criticising referee Martin Atkinson v Chelsea; **£30,000 (plus 6-match ban, reduced to 4 on appeal)** Rui Faria (Chelsea assistant): May 2014, confronting match officials v Sunderland.

• Jonathan Barnett, Ashley Cole's agent was fined **£100,000** in Sep 2006 for his role in the 'tapping up' affair involving the player and Chelsea.

*£68,000 FA: May 2003, pitch invasions and racist chanting by fans during England v Turkey, Sunderland.

MANAGERS

INTERNATIONAL RECORDS

(As at start of season 2014–15)

	P	W	D	L	F	A
Roy Hodgson (England – appointed May 2012)	31	15	11	5	58	27
Gordon Strachan (Scotland – appointed Jan 2013	12	6	2	4	13	12
Chris Coleman (Wales – appointed Jan 2012)	17	5	3	9	15	29
Michael O'Neill (Northern Ireland – appointed Oct 2011)	18	1	7	10	12	33
Martin O'Neill (Republic of Ireland) - appointed Nov 2013)	6	1	3	2	6	5

FINAL RECORD

Giovanni Trapattoni (Republic of Ireland: May 2008–Sep 2013)	64	26	22	16	86	64

ENGLAND MANAGERS

		P	W	D	L
1946–62	**Walter Winterbottom**	139	78	33	28
1963–74	**Sir Alf Ramsey**	113	69	27	17
1974	**Joe Mercer**, caretaker	7	3	3	1
1974–77	**Don Revie**	29	14	8	7
1977–82	**Ron Greenwood**	55	33	12	10
1982–90	**Bobby Robson**	95	47	30	18
1990–93	**Graham Taylor**	38	18	13	7
1994–96	**Terry Venables**	23	11	11	1
1996–99	**Glenn Hoddle**	28	17	6	5
1999	**Howard Wilkinson**, caretaker	1	0	0	1
1999–2000	**Kevin Keegan**	18	7	7	4
2000	**Howard Wilkinson**, caretaker	1	0	1	0
2000	**Peter Taylor**, caretaker	1	0	0	1
2001–06	**Sven–Goran Eriksson**	67	40	17	10
2006–07	**Steve McClaren**	18	9	4	5
2007–12	**Fabio Capello**	42	28	8	6

INTERNATIONAL MANAGER CHANGES

England: Walter Winterbottom 1946–62 (initial coach); **Alf Ramsey** (Feb 1963–May 1974); **Joe Mercer** (caretaker May 1974); **Don Revie** (Jul 1974–Jul 1977); **Ron Greenwood** (Aug 1977–Jul 1982); **Bobby Robson** (Jul 1982–Jul 1990); **Graham Taylor** (Jul 1990–Nov 1993); **Terry Venables**, coach (Jan 1994–Jun 1996); **Glenn Hoddle**, coach (Jun 1996–Feb 1999); **Howard Wilkinson** (caretaker Feb 1999); **Kevin Keegan** coach (Feb 1999–Oct 2000); **Howard Wilkinson** (caretaker Oct 2000); **Peter Taylor** (caretaker Nov 2000); **Sven–Goran Eriksson** (Jan 2001–Aug 2006); **Steve McClaren** (Aug 2006–Nov 2007); **Fabio Capello** (Dec 2007–Feb 2012); **Roy Hodgson** (since May 2012).

Scotland (modern): Bobby Brown (Feb 1967–Jul 1971); **Tommy Docherty** (Sep 1971–Dec 1972); **Willie Ormond** (Jan 1973–May 1977); **Ally MacLeod** (May 1977–Sep 1978); **Jock Stein** (Oct 1978–Sep 1985); **Alex Ferguson** (caretaker Oct 1985–Jun 1986); **Andy Roxburgh**, coach (Jul 1986–Sep 1993); **Craig Brown** (Sep 1993–Oct 2001); **Berti Vogts** (Feb 2002–Oct 2004); **Walter Smith** (Dec 2004–Jan 2007); **Alex McLeish** (Jan 2007–Nov 2007); **George Burley** (Jan 2008–Nov 2009); **Craig Levein** (Dec 2009–Nov 2012); **Billy Stark** (caretaker Nov–Dec 2012); **Gordon Strachan** (since Jan 2013).

Northern Ireland (modern): Peter Doherty (1951–62); **Bertie Peacock** (1962–67); **Billy Bingham** (1967–Aug 1971); **Terry Neill** (Aug 1971–Mar 1975); **Dave Clements** (player-manager Mar 1975–1976); **Danny Blanchflower** (Jun 1976–Nov 1979); **Billy Bingham** (Feb 1980–Nov 1993); **Bryan Hamilton** Feb 1994–Feb 1998); **Lawrie McMenemy** (Feb 1998–Nov 1999); **Sammy McIlroy** (Jan 2000–Oct 2003); **Lawrie Sanchez** (Jan 2004–May 2007); **Nigel Worthington** (May 2007–Oct 2011); **Michael O'Neill** (since Oct 2011).

Wales (modern): Mike Smith (Jul 1974–Dec 1979); **Mike England** (Mar 1980–Feb 1988); **David Williams** (caretaker Mar 1988); **Terry Yorath** (Apr 1988–Nov 1993); **John Toshack** (Mar 1994, one match); **Mike Smith** (Mar 1994–Jun 1995); **Bobby Gould** (Aug 1995–Jun 1999); **Mark Hughes** (Aug 1999 – Oct 2004); **John Toshack** (Nov 2004–Sep 2010); Brian Flynn (caretaker Sep–Dec 2010); **Gary Speed** (Dec 2010–Nov 2011); **Chris Coleman** (since Jan 2012).

Republic of Ireland (modern): Liam Tuohy (Sep 1971–Nov 1972); **Johnny Giles** (Oct 1973–Apr 1980, initially player–manager); **Eoin Hand** (Jun 1980–Nov 1985); **Jack Charlton** (Feb 1986–Dec 1995); **Mick McCarthy** (Feb 1996–Oct 2002); **Brian Kerr** (Jan 2003–Oct 2005); **Steve Staunton** (Jan 2006–Oct 2007); **Giovanni Trapattoni** (May 2008–Sep 2013); **Martin O'Neill** (since Nov 2013).

WORLD CUP-WINNING MANAGERS

1930 Uruguay (Alberto Suppici); 1934 and 1938 Italy (Vittorio Pozzo); 1950 Uruguay (Juan Lopez Fontana); 1954 West Germany (Sepp Herberger); 1958 Brazil (Vicente Feola); 1962 Brazil (Aymore Moreira); 1966 England (Sir Alf Ramsey); 1970 Brazil (Mario Zagallo); 1974 West Germany (Helmut Schon); 1978 Argentina (Cesar Luis Menotti); 1982 Italy (Enzo Bearzot); 1986 Argentina (Carlos Bilardo); 1990 West Germany (Franz Beckenbauer); 1994 Brazil (Carlos Alberto Parreira); 1998 France (Aimee Etienne Jacquet); 2002 Brazil (Luiz Felipe Scolari); 2006 Italy (Marcello Lippi); 2010 Spain (Vicente Del Bosque); 2014 Germany (Joachim Low).

Each of the 20 winning teams had a manager/coach of that country's nationality.

YOUNGEST LEAGUE MANAGERS

Ivor Broadis, 23, appointed player-manager of Carlisle, Aug 1946; **Chris Brass**, 27, appointed player-manager of York, Jun 2003; **Terry Neill**, 28, appointed player manager of Hull, Jun 1970; **Graham Taylor**, 28, appointed manager of Lincoln, Dec 1972.

LONGEST-SERVING LEAGUE MANAGERS – ONE CLUB

Fred Everiss, secretary–manager of WBA for 46 years (1902–48); **George Ramsay**, secretary–manager of Aston Villa for 42 years (1884–1926); **John Addenbrooke**, Wolves, for 37 years (1885–1922). Since last war: **Sir Alex Ferguson** at Manchester Utd for 27 seasons (1986–2013); **Sir Matt Busby**, in charge of Manchester Utd for 25 seasons (1945–69, 1970–71;

Dario Gradi at Crewe for 26 years (1983–2007, 2009–11); **Jimmy Seed** at Charlton for 23 years (1933–56); **Brian Clough** at Nottm Forest for 18 years (1975–93); **Arsene Wenger** at Arsenal for 18 years (1996-to-date).

LAST ENGLISH MANAGER TO WIN CHAMPIONSHIP

Howard Wilkinson (Leeds), season 1991–92.

1,000-TIME MANAGERS

Only six have managed in more than **1,000 English League games**: Alec Stock, Brian Clough, Jim Smith, Graham Taylor, Dario Gradi and Sir Alex Ferguson.

Sir Matt Busby, Dave Bassett, Lennie Lawrence, Alan Buckley, Denis Smith, Joe Royle, Ron Atkinson, Brian Horton, Neil Warnock, Harry Redknapp, Graham Turner, Steve Coppell and Arsene Wenger have each managed more than **1,000 matches in all first class competitions**.

SHORT-TERM MANAGERS

Departed

3 days	Bill Lambton (Scunthorpe)	Apr 1959
7 days	Tim Ward (Exeter)	Mar 1953
7 days	Kevin Cullis (Swansea City)	Feb 1996
10 days	Dave Cowling (Doncaster)	Oct 1997
10 days	Peter Cormack (Cowdenbeath)	Dec 2000
13 days	Johnny Cochrane (Reading)	Apr 1939
13 days	Micky Adams (Swansea City)	Oct 1997
16 days	Jimmy McIlroy (Bolton)	Nov 1970
19 days	Martin Allen (Barnet)	Apr 2011
20 days	Paul Went (Leyton Orient)	Oct 1981
27 days	Malcolm Crosby (Oxford Utd)	Jan 1998
28 days	Tommy Docherty (QPR)	Dec 1968
28 days	Paul Hart (QPR)	Jan 2010
32 days	Steve Coppell (Manchester City)	Nov 1996
34 days	Niall Quinn (Sunderland)	Aug 2006
36 days	Steve Claridge (Millwall)	Jul 2005
39 days	Paul Gascoigne (Kettering)	Dec 2005
40 days	Alex McLeish (Nottm Forest)	Feb 2013
41 days	Steve Wicks (Lincoln)	Oct 1995
41 days	Les Reed (Charlton)	Dec 2006
44 days	Brian Clough (Leeds)	Sep 1974
44 days	Jock Stein (Leeds)	Oct 1978
48 days	John Toshack (Wales)	Mar 1994
48 days	David Platt (Sampdoria coach)	Feb 1999
49 days	Brian Little (Wolves)	Oct 1986
49 days	Terry Fenwick (Northampton)	Feb 2003
57 days	Henning Berg (Blackburn)	Dec 2012
61 days	Bill McGarry (Wolves)	Nov 1985

- In May 1984, Crystal Palace named **Dave Bassett** as manager, but he changed his mind four days later, without signing the contract, and returned to Wimbledon.
- In May 2007, **Leroy Rosenior** was reportedly appointed manager of Torquay after relegation and sacked ten minutes later when the club came under new ownership.
- **Brian Laws** lost his job at Scunthorpe on Mar 25, 2004 and was reinstated three weeks later.
- In an angry outburst after a play-off defeat in May 1992, Barnet chairman Stan Flashman sacked manager **Barry Fry** and re-instated him a day later.

EARLY-SEASON MANAGER SACKINGS

2012: Andy Thorn (Coventry) 8 days; John Sheridan (Chesterfield) 10 days; **2011:** Jim Jefferies

(Hearts) 9 days; **2010** Kevin Blackwell (Sheffield Utd) 8 days; **2009** Bryan Gunn (Norwich) 6 days; **2007:** Neil McDonald (Carlisle) 2 days; Martin Allen (Leicester) 18 days; **2004:** Paul Sturrock (Southampton) 9 days; **2004:** Sir Bobby Robson (Newcastle) 16 days; **2003:** Glenn Roeder (West Ham) 15 days; **2000:** Alan Buckley (Grimsby) 10 days; **1997:** Kerry Dixon (Doncaster) 12 days; **1996:** Sammy Chung (Doncaster) on morning of season's opening League match; **1996:** Alan Ball (Manchester City) 12 days; **1994:** Kenny Hibbitt (Walsall) and Kenny Swain (Wigan) 20 days; **1993:** Peter Reid (Manchester City) 12 days; **1991:** Don Mackay (Blackburn) 14 days; **1989:** Mick Jones (Peterborough) 12 days; **1980:** Bill McGarry (Newcastle) 13 days; **1979:** Dennis Butler (Port Vale) 12 days; **1977:** George Petchey (Leyton O) 13 days; **1977:** Willie Bell (Birmingham) 16 days; **1971:** Len Richley (Darlington) 12 days.

RECORD START FOR MANAGER

Russ Wilcox, appointed by Scunthorpe in Nov 2013, remained unbeaten in his first 28 league matches (14 won, 14 drawn) and took the club to promotion from League Two. It was the most successful start to a managerial career In English football, beating the record of 23 unbeaten games by Preston's William Sudell in 1889.

RECORD TOP DIVISION START

Arsenal were unbeaten in 17 league matches from the start of season 1947-48 under new manager **Tom Whittaker**.

SACKED, REINSTATED, FINISHED

Brian McDermott was sacked as Leeds manager on Jan 31, 2014. The following day, he was reinstated. At the end of the season, with the club under new ownership, he left by 'mutual consent.'

CARETAKER SUPREME

As Chelsea's season collapsed, Andre Villas-Boas was sacked in March 2012 after eight months as manager, 2012. Roberto Di Matteo was appointed caretaker and by the season's end his team had won the FA Cup and the Champions League.

MANAGER DOUBLES

Four managers have won the League Championship with different clubs: **Tom Watson**, secretary–manager with Sunderland (1892–93–95) and **Liverpool** (1901); **Herbert Chapman** with Huddersfield (1923–24, 1924–25) and Arsenal (1930–31, 1932–33); **Brian Clough** with Derby (1971–72) and Nottm Forest (1977–78); **Kenny Dalglish** with Liverpool (1985–86, 1987–88, 1989–90) and Blackburn (1994–95).

Managers to win the FA Cup with different clubs: **Billy Walker** (Sheffield Wed 1935, Nottm Forest 1959); **Herbert Chapman** (Huddersfield 1922, Arsenal 1930).

Kenny Dalglish (Liverpool) and **George Graham** (Arsenal) completed the Championship/FA Cup double as both player and manager with a single club. **Joe Mercer** won the title as a player with Everton, the title twice and FA Cup as a player with Arsenal and both competitions as manager of Manchester City.

CHAIRMAN–MANAGER

On Dec 20, 1988, after two years on the board, Dundee Utd manager **Jim McLean** was elected chairman, too. McLean, Scotland's longest–serving manager (appointed on Nov 24, 1971), resigned at end of season 1992–93 (remained chairman).

Ron Noades was chairman-manager of Brentford from Jul 1998–Mar 2001. **John Reames** did both jobs at Lincoln from Nov 1998–Apr 2000)

Niall Quinn did both jobs for five weeks in 2006 before appointing Roy Keane as manager of Sunderland.

TOP DIVISION PLAYER–MANAGERS

Les Allen (QPR 1968–69); **Johnny Giles** (WBA 1976–77); **Howard Kendall** (Everton 1981–82); **Kenny Dalglish** (Liverpool, 1985–90); **Trevor Francis** (QPR, 1988–89); **Terry Butcher** (Coventry, 1990–91), **Peter Reid** (Manchester City, 1990–93), **Trevor Francis** (Sheffield Wed, 1991–94), **Glenn Hoddle**, (Chelsea, 1993–95), **Bryan Robson** (Middlesbrough, 1994–97), **Ray Wilkins** (QPR, 1994–96), **Ruud Gullit** (Chelsea, 1996–98), **Gianluca Vialli** (Chelsea, 1998–2000).

FIRST FOREIGN MANAGER IN ENGLISH LEAGUE

Uruguayan **Danny Bergara** (Rochdale 1988–89).

COACHING KINGS OF EUROPE

When **Jose Mourinho** lifted the Champions League trophy with Inter Milan in 2010, he became only the third coach in European Cup history to win the world's greatest club prize with two different clubs. He had previously done it with Porto in 2004. The others to achieve this double were **Ernst Happel** with Feyenoord (1970) and Hamburg (1983) and **Ottmar Hitzfeld** with Borussia Dortmund (1997) and Bayern Munich (2001).

FOREIGN TRIUMPH

Former Dutch star **Ruud Gullit** became the first foreign manager to win a major English competition when Chelsea took the FA Cup in 1997.

Arsene Wenger and **Gerard Houllier** became the first foreign managers to receive recognition when they were awarded honorary OBEs in the Queen's Birthday Honours in Jun 2003 'for their contribution to English football and Franco–British relations'.

MANAGERS OF POST-WAR CHAMPIONS (*Double winners)

1947 George Kay (Liverpool); **1948** Tom Whittaker (Arsenal); **1949** Bob Jackson (Portsmouth). **1950** Bob Jackson (Portsmouth); **1951** Arthur Rowe (Tottenham); **1952** Matt Busby (Manchester Utd); **1953** Tom Whittaker (Arsenal); **1954** Stan Cullis (Wolves); **1955** Ted Drake (Chelsea); **1956** Matt Busby (Manchester Utd); **1957** Matt Busby (Manchester Utd); **1958** Stan Cullis (Wolves); **1959** Stan Cullis (Wolves).
1960 Harry Potts (Burnley); **1961** *Bill Nicholson (Tottenham); **1962** Alf Ramsey (Ipswich); **1963** Harry Catterick (Everton); **1964** Bill Shankly (Liverpool); **1965** Matt Busby (Manchester Utd); **1966** Bill Shankly (Liverpool); **1967** Matt Busby (Manchester Utd); **1968** Joe Mercer (Manchester City); **1969** Don Revie (Leeds).
1970 Harry Catterick (Everton); **1971** *Bertie Mee (Arsenal); **1972** Brian Clough (Derby); **1973** Bill Shankly (Liverpool); **1974** Don Revie (Leeds); **1975** Dave Mackay (Derby); **1976** Bob Paisley (Liverpool); **1977** Bob Paisley (Liverpool); **1978** Brian Clough (Nottm Forest); **1979** Bob Paisley (Liverpool).
1980 Bob Paisley (Liverpool); **1981** Ron Saunders (Aston Villa); **1982** Bob Paisley (Liverpool); **1983** Bob Paisley (Liverpool); **1984** Joe Fagan (Liverpool); **1985** Howard Kendall (Everton); **1986** *Kenny Dalglish (Liverpool – player/manager); **1987** Howard Kendall (Everton); **1988** Kenny Dalglish (Liverpool – player/manager); **1989** George Graham (Arsenal).
1990 Kenny Dalglish (Liverpool); **1991** George Graham (Arsenal); **1992** Howard Wilkinson (Leeds); **1993** Alex Ferguson (Manchester Utd); **1994** *Alex Ferguson (Manchester Utd); **1995** Kenny Dalglish (Blackburn); **1996** *Alex Ferguson (Manchester Utd); **1997** Alex Ferguson (Manchester Utd); **1998** *Arsene Wenger (Arsenal); **1999** *Alex Ferguson (Manchester Utd).
2000 Sir Alex Ferguson (Manchester Utd); **2001** Sir Alex Ferguson (Manchester Utd); **2002** *Arsene Wenger (Arsenal); **2003** Sir Alex Ferguson (Manchester Utd); **2004** Arsene Wenger (Arsenal); **2005** Jose Mourinho (Chelsea); **2006** Jose Mourinho (Chelsea); **2007** Sir Alex Ferguson (Manchester Utd); **2008** Sir Alex Ferguson (Manchester Utd); **2009** Sir Alex Ferguson (Manchester Utd); **2010** *Carlo Ancelotti (Chelsea); **2011** Sir Alex Ferguson (Manchester Utd); **2012** Roberto Mancini (Manchester City); **2013** Sir Alex Ferguson (Manchester Utd); **2014** Manuel Pellegrini (Manchester City).

WORLD NO 1 MANAGER

When **Sir Alex Ferguson**, 71, retired in May 2013, he ended the most successful managerial career in the game's history. He took Manchester United to a total of 38 prizes - 13 Premier League titles, 5 FA Cup triumphs, 4 League Cups, 10 Charity/Community Shields (1 shared), 2 Champions League wins, 1 Cup-Winners' Cup, 1 FIFA Club World Cup, 1 Inter-Continental Cup and 1 UEFA Super Cup. Having played centre-forward for Rangers, the Glaswegian managed 3 Scottish clubs, East Stirling, St Mirren and then Aberdeen, where he broke the Celtic/Rangers duopoly with 9 successes: 3 League Championships, 4 Scottish Cups, 1 League Cup and 1 UEFA Cup. Appointed at Old Trafford in November 1986, when replacing Ron Atkinson, he did not win a prize there until his fourth season (FA Cup 1990), but thereafter the club's trophy cabinet glittered with silverware. His total of 1,500 matches in charge ended with a 5-5 draw away to West Bromwich Albion. The longest-serving manager in the club's history, he constructed 4 triumphant teams. Sir Alex was knighted in 1999 and in 2012 he received the FIFA award for services to football. On retirement from management, he became a director and club ambassador. United maintained the dynasty of long-serving Scottish managers (Sir Matt Busby for 24 seasons) by appointing David Moyes, who had been in charge at Everton for 11 years.

MANAGERS' EURO TREBLES

Two managers have won the European Cup/Champions League three times. **Bob Paisley** did it with Liverpool (1977,78, 81).
Carlo Ancelotti's successes were with AC Milan in 2003 and 2007 and with Real Madrid in 2014.

MOURINHO'S RECORD

Jose Mourinho, who left Chelsea on September 19, 2007, was the most successful manager in the club's history. Appointed in June 2004 after taking Porto to successive Portuguese League titles, he won six trophies in three seasons at Stamford Bridge: Premiership in 2005 and 2006, League Cup in 2005 and 2007, FA Cup in 2007 and Community Shield in 2005. Under Mourinho, Chelsea were unbeaten at home in the Premier League with his record: P60 W46 D14 F123 A28. He won the Italian title with Inter Milan in 2009 and completed the treble of League, Cup and Champions League the following season before taking over at Real Madrid. There, in 2012, he achieved his seventh League title in ten years in four countries, Portugal, England, Italy and Spain.

RECORD MANAGER FEE

Chelsea paid Porto a record £13.25m compensation when they appointed **Andre Villas-Boas** as manager in June 2011. He lasted less than nine months at Stamford Bridge.

FATHER AND SON MANAGERS WITH SAME CLUB

Fulham: Bill Dodgin Snr 1949–53; Bill Dodgin Jnr 1968–72. **Brentford:** Bill Dodgin Snr 1953–57; Bill Dodgin Jnr 1976–80. **Bournemouth:** John Bond 1970–73; Kevin Bond 2006–08. **Derby:** Brian Clough 1967–73; Nigel Clough 2009.

SIR BOBBY'S HAT-TRICK

Sir Bobby Robson, born and brought up in County Durham, achieved a unique hat-trick when he received the Freedom of Durham in Dec 2008. He had already been awarded the Freedom of Ipswich and Newcastle. He died in July 2009 and had an express loco named after him on the East Coast to London line.

MANAGERS WITH MOST FA CUP SUCCESSES

5 Sir Alex Ferguson (Manchester Utd), Arsene Wenger (Arsenal); **3** Charles Foweraker (Bolton), John Nicholson (Sheffield Utd), Bill Nicholson (Tottenham).

RELEGATION 'DOUBLES'

Managers associated with two clubs relegated in same season: **John Bond** in 1985–86 (Swansea City and Birmingham); **Ron Saunders** in 1985–86 (WBA – and their reserve team – and Birmingham); **Bob Stokoe** in 1986–87 (Carlisle and Sunderland); **Billy McNeill** in 1986–87 (Manchester City and Aston Villa); **Dave Bassett** in 1987–88 (Watford and Sheffield Utd); **Mick Mills** in 1989–90 (Stoke and Colchester).

THREE FA CUP DEFEATS IN ONE SEASON

Manager **Michael Appleton** suffered three FA Cup defeats in season 2012-13, with Portsmouth (v Notts Co, 1st rd); Blackpool (v Fulham, 3rd rd); Blackburn (v Millwall, 6th rd).

WEMBLEY STADIUM

NEW WEMBLEY

A new era for English football began in March 2007 with the completion of the new national stadium. The 90,000-seater arena was hailed as one of the world's finest – but came at a price. Costs soared, the project fell well behind schedule and disputes involving the FA, builders Multiplex and the Government were rife. The old stadium, opened in 1923, cost £750,000. The new one, originally priced at £326m in 2000, ended up at around £800m. The first international after completion was an Under-21 match between England and Italy. The FA Cup Final returned to its spiritual home after being staged at the Millennium Stadium in Cardiff for six seasons. Then, England's senior team were back for a friendly against Brazil.

DROGBA'S WEMBLEY RECORD

Didier Drogba's FA Cup goal for Chelsea against Liverpool in May 2012 meant that he had scored in all his 8 competitive appearances for the club at Wembley. (7 wins, 1 defeat). They came in: 2007 FA Cup Final (1-0 v Manchester Utd); 2008 League Cup Final (1-2 v Tottenham); 2009 FA Cup semi-final (2-1 v Arsenal); 2009 FA Cup Final (2-1 v Everton); 2010 FA Cup semi-final (3-0 v Aston Villa); 2010 FA Cup Final (1-0 v Portsmouth); 2012 FA Cup semi-final (5-1 v Tottenham); 2012 FA Cup Final (2-1 v Liverpool).

INVASION DAY

Memorable scenes were witnessed at the first **FA Cup Final at Wembley**, Apr 28, 1923, between **Bolton** and **West Ham**. An accurate return of the attendance could not be made owing to thousands breaking in, but there were probably more than 200,000 spectators present. The match was delayed for 40 minutes by the crowd invading the pitch. Official attendance was 126,047. Gate receipts totalled £27,776. The two clubs and the FA each received £6,365 and the FA refunded £2,797 to ticket-holders who were unable to get to their seats. Cup Final admission has since been by ticket only.

REDUCED CAPACITY

Capacity of the all-seated Wembley Stadium was 78,000. The last 100,000 attendance was for the 1985 FA Cup Final between Manchester Utd and Everton. Crowd record for New Wembley: 89,874 for 2008 FA Cup Final (Portsmouth v Cardiff).

WEMBLEY'S FIRST UNDER LIGHTS

Nov 30, 1955 (England 4, Spain 1), when the floodlights were switched on after 73 minutes (afternoon match played in damp, foggy conditions).
First Wembley international played throughout under lights: England 8, N Ireland 3 on evening of Nov 20, 1963 (att: 55,000).

MOST WEMBLEY APPEARANCES

59 by **Tony Adams** (35 England, 24 Arsenal); 57 by Peter Shilton (52 England, 3 Nottm Forest, 1 Leicester, 1 Football League XI).

WEMBLEY HAT-TRICKS

Three players have scored hat-tricks in major finals at Wembley: **Stan Mortensen** for Blackpool v Bolton (FA Cup Final, 1953), **Geoff Hurst** for England v West Germany (World Cup Final, 1966) and **David Speedie** for Chelsea v Manchester City (Full Members Cup, 1985).

ENGLAND'S WEMBLEY DEFEATS

England have lost 24 matches to foreign opponents at Wembley:

Nov 1953	3-6 v Hungary	Sep 1991	0-1 v Germany
Oct 1959	2-3 v Sweden	Jun 1995	1-3 v Brazil
Oct 1965	2-3 v Austria	Feb 1997	0-1 v Italy
Apr 1972	1-3 v W Germany	Feb 1998	0-2 v Chile
Nov 1973	0-1 v Italy	Feb 1999	0-2 v France
Feb 1977	0-2 v Holland	Oct 2000	0-1 v Germany
Mar 1981	1-2 v Spain	Aug 2007	1-2 v Germany
May 1981	0-1 v Brazil	Nov 2007	2-3 v Croatia
Oct 1982	1-2 v W Germany	Nov 2010	1-2 v France
Sep 1983	0-1 v Denmark	Feb 2012	2-3 v Holland
Jun 1984	0-2 v Russia	Nov 2013	0-2 v Chile
May 1990	1-2 v Uruguay	Nov 2013	0-1 v Germany

A further defeat came in **Euro 96**. After drawing the semi-final with Germany 1-1, England went out 6-5 on penalties.

FASTEST GOALS AT WEMBLEY

In first-class matches: **25 sec** by Louis Saha for Everton in 2009 FA Cup Final against Chelsea; **38 sec** by Bryan Robson for England's against Yugoslavia in 1989; **42 sec** by **Roberto Di Matteo** for Chelsea in 1997 FA Cup Final v Middlesbrough; **44 sec** by **Bryan Robson** for England v Northern Ireland in 1982.

Fastest goal in **any** match at Wembley: **20 sec** by **Maurice Cox** for Cambridge University against Oxford in 1979.

FOUR WEMBLEY HEADERS

When **Wimbledon** beat Sutton 4-2 in the FA Amateur Cup Final at Wembley on May 4, 1963, Irish centre-forward **Eddie Reynolds** headed all four goals.

WEMBLEY ONE-SEASON DOUBLES

In 1989, **Nottm Forest** became the first club to win two Wembley Finals in the same season (Littlewoods Cup and Simod Cup).

In 1993, **Arsenal** made history there as the first club to win the League (Coca-Cola) Cup and the FA Cup in the same season. They beat Sheffield Wed 2-1 in both finals.

In 2012, **York** won twice at Wembley in nine days at the end of the season, beating Newport 2-0 in the FA Trophy Final and Luton 2-1 in the Conference Play-off Final to return to the Football League.

SUDDEN-DEATH DECIDERS

First Wembley Final decided on sudden death (first goal scored in overtime): Apr 23, 1995 – **Birmingham** beat Carlisle (1-0, Paul Tait 103 mins) to win Auto Windscreens Shield.

First instance of a golden goal deciding a major international tournament was at Wembley on Jun 30, 1996, when **Germany** beat the Czech Republic 2-1 in the European Championship Final with Oliver Bierhoff's goal in the 95th minute.

WEMBLEY'S MOST ONE-SIDED FINAL (in major domestic cups)

Swansea 5 Bradford 0 (League Cup, Feb 24, 2013).

FOOTBALL TRAGEDIES

DAYS OF TRAGEDY – CLUBS

Season 1988–89 brought the worst disaster in the history of British sport, with the death of 96 Liverpool supporters (200 injured) at the **FA Cup semi-final** against Nottm Forest at **Hillsborough, Sheffield**, on Saturday, Apr 15. The tragedy built up in the minutes preceding kick-off, when thousands surged into the ground at the Leppings Lane end. Many were crushed in the tunnel between entrance and terracing, but most of the victims were trapped inside the perimeter fencing behind the goal. The match was abandoned without score after six minutes' play. The dead included seven women and girls, two teenage sisters and two teenage brothers. The youngest victim was a boy of ten, the oldest 67-year-old Gerard Baron, whose brother Kevin played for Liverpool in the 1950 Cup Final. (*Total became 96 in Mar 1993, when Tony Bland died after being in a coma for nearly four years).

The two worst disasters in one season in British soccer history occurred at the end of 1984–85. On May 11, the last Saturday of the League season, 56 people (two of them visiting supporters) were burned to death – and more than 200 taken to hospital – when fire destroyed the main stand at the **Bradford City–Lincoln** match at Valley Parade.

The wooden, 77-year-old stand was full for City's last fixture before which, amid scenes of celebration, the club had been presented with the Third Division Championship trophy. The fire broke out just before half-time and, within five minutes, the entire stand was engulfed.

Heysel Tragedy

Eighteen days later, on May 29, at the European Cup Final between **Liverpool** and **Juventus** at the Heysel Stadium, Brussels, 39 spectators (31 of them Italian) were crushed or trampled to death and 437 injured. The disaster occurred an hour before the scheduled kick-off when Liverpool supporters charged a Juventus section of the crowd at one end of the stadium, and a retaining wall collapsed. The sequel was a 5-year ban by UEFA on English clubs generally in European competition, with a 6-year ban on Liverpool.

On May 26 1985 ten people were trampled to death and 29 seriously injured in a crowd panic on the way into the **Olympic Stadium, Mexico City** for the Mexican Cup Final between local clubs National University and America.

More than 100 people died and 300 were injured in a football disaster at **Nepal's national stadium** in Katmandu in Mar 1988. There was a stampede when a violent hailstorm broke over the capital. Spectators rushed for cover, but the stadium exits were locked, and hundreds were trampled in the crush.

In South Africa, on Jan 13 1991 40 black fans were trampled to death (50 injured) as they tried to escape from fighting that broke out at a match in the gold-mining town of Orkney, 80 miles from Johannesburg. The friendly, between top teams **Kaiser Chiefs** and **Orlando Pirates**, attracted a packed crowd of 20,000. Violence erupted after the referee allowed Kaiser Chiefs a disputed second-half goal to lead 1-0.

Disaster struck at the French Cup semi-final (May 5, 1992), with the death of 15 spectators and 1,300 injured when a temporary metal stand collapsed in the Corsican town of Bastia. The tie between Second Division **Bastia** and French Champions **Marseille** was cancelled. Monaco, who won the other semi-final, were allowed to compete in the next season's Cup-Winners' Cup.

A total of 318 died and 500 were seriously injured when the crowd rioted over a disallowed goal at the National Stadium in Lima, Peru, on May 24, 1964. **Peru** and **Argentina** were competing to play in the Olympic Games in Tokyo.

That remained **sport's heaviest death** toll until Oct 20, 1982, when (it was revealed only in Jul 1989) 340 Soviet fans were killed in Moscow's Lenin Stadium at the UEFA Cup second round first leg match between **Moscow Spartak** and **Haarlem** (Holland). They were crushed on an open stairway when a last-minute Spartak goal sent departing spectators surging back into the ground.

Among other crowd disasters abroad: Jun, 1968 – 74 died in Argentina. Panic broke out at the end of a goalless match between River Plate and Boca Juniors at Nunez, Buenos Aires, when Boca supporters threw lighted newspaper torches on to fans in the tiers below.

Feb 1974 – 49 killed in **Egypt** in crush of fans clamouring to see Zamalek play Dukla Prague.

Sep 1971 – 44 died in **Turkey**, when fighting among spectators over a disallowed goal (Kayseri v Siwas) led to a platform collapsing.

The then worst disaster in the history of British football, in terms of loss of life, occurred at Glasgow Rangers' ground at **Ibrox Park**, Jan 2 1971. Sixty-six people were trampled to death (100 injured) as they tumbled down Stairway 13 just before the end of the **Rangers v Celtic** New Year's match. That disaster led to the 1975 Safety of Sports Grounds legislation.

The Ibrox tragedy eclipsed even the Bolton disaster in which 33 were killed and about 500 injured when a wall and crowd barriers collapsed near a corner-flag at the **Bolton v Stoke** FA Cup sixth round tie on Mar 9 1946. The match was completed after half an hour's stoppage.

In a previous crowd disaster at **Ibrox** on Apr 5, 1902, part of the terracing collapsed during the Scotland v England international and 25 people were killed. The match, held up for 20 minutes, ended 1-1, but was never counted as an official international.

Eight leading players and three officials of **Manchester Utd** and eight newspaper representatives were among the 23 who perished in the air crash at **Munich** on Feb 6, 1958, during take-off following a European Cup-tie in Belgrade. The players were Roger Byrne, Geoffrey Bent, Eddie Colman, Duncan Edwards, Mark Jones, David Pegg, Tommy Taylor and Liam Whelan, and the officials were Walter Crickmer (secretary), Tom Curry (trainer) and Herbert Whalley (coach). The newspaper representatives were Alf Clarke, Don Davies, George Follows, Tom Jackson, Archie Ledbrooke, Henry Rose, Eric Thompson and Frank Swift (former England goalkeeper of Manchester City).

On May 14, 1949, the entire team of Italian Champions **Torino**, 8 of them Internationals, were killed when the aircraft taking them home from a match against Benfica in Lisbon crashed at Superga, near Turin. The total death toll of 28 included all the club's reserve players, the manager, trainer and coach.

On Feb 8, 1981, 24 spectators died and more than 100 were injured at a match in **Greece**. They were trampled as thousands of the 40,000 crowd tried to rush out of the stadium at Piraeus after Olympiacos beat AEK Athens 6-0.

On Nov 17, 1982, 24 people (12 of them children) were killed and 250 injured when fans stampeded at the end of a match at the Pascual Guerrero stadium in **Cali, Colombia**. Drunken spectators hurled fire crackers and broken bottles from the higher stands on to people below and started a rush to the exits.

On Dec 9, 1987, the 18-strong team squad of **Alianza Lima**, one of Peru's top clubs, were wiped out, together with 8 officials and several youth players, when a military aircraft taking them home from Puccalpa crashed into the sea off Ventillana, ten miles from Lima. The only survivor among 43 on board was a member of the crew.

On Apr 28, 1993, 18 members of **Zambia's international squad** and 5 ZFA officials died when the aircraft carrying them to a World Cup qualifying tie against Senegal crashed into the Atlantic soon after take-off from Libreville, Gabon.

On Oct 16 1996, 81 fans were crushed to death and 147 seriously injured in the '**Guatemala Disaster**' at the World Cup qualifier against Costa Rica in Mateo Flores stadium. The tragedy happened an hour before kick-off, allegedly caused by ticket forgery and overcrowding – 60,000 were reported in the 45,000-capacity ground – and safety problems related to perimeter fencing.

On Jul 9, 1996, 8 people died, 39 injured in riot after derby match between **Libya's two top clubs** in Tripoli. Al-Ahli had beaten Al-Ittihad 1-0 by a controversial goal.

On Apr 6, 1997, 5 spectators were crushed to death at **Nigeria's national stadium** in Lagos after the 2-1 World Cup qualifying victory over Guinea. Only two of five gates were reported open as the 40,000 crowd tried to leave the ground.

It was reported in the **Congo** (Oct 29, 1998) that a bolt of lightning struck a village match, killing all 11 members of the home team Benatshadi, but leaving the opposing players from Basangana unscathed. It was believed the surviving team wore better-insulated boots.

On Jan 10, 1999, eight fans died and 13 were injured in a stampede at **Egypt's Alexandria Stadium**. Some 25,000 spectators had pushed into the ground. Despite the tragedy, the cup-tie between Al-Ittihad and Al-Koroum was completed.

Three people suffocated and several were seriously injured when thousands of fans forced their way into **Liberia's national stadium** in Monrovia at a goalless World Cup qualifying match against Chad on Apr 23, 2000. The stadium (capacity 33,000) was reported 'heavily overcrowded'.

On Jul 9, 2000, 12 spectators died from crush injuries when police fired tear gas into the 50,000 crowd after South Africa scored their second goal in a World Cup group qualifier against Zimbabwe in **Harare**. A stampede broke out as fans scrambled to leave the national stadium. Players of both teams lay face down on the pitch as fumes swept over them. FIFA launched an investigation and decided that the result would stand, with South Africa leading 2-0 at the time of the 84th-minute abandonment.

On Apr 11, 2001, at one of the biggest matches of the South African season, 43 died and 155 were injured in a crush at **Ellis Park, Johannesburg**. After tearing down a fence, thousands of fans surged into a stadium already packed to its 60,000 capacity for the Premiership derby between top Soweto teams Kaizer Chiefs and Orlando Pirates. The match was abandoned at 1-1 after 33 minutes. In Jan 1991, 40 died in a crowd crush at a friendly between the same clubs at Orkney, 80 miles from Johannesburg.

On Apr 29, 2001, seven people were trampled to death and 51 injured when a riot broke out at a match between two of Congo's biggest clubs, Lupopo and Mazembe at **Lubumbashi**, southern Congo.

On May 6, 2001, two spectators were killed in Iran and hundreds were injured when a glass fibre roof collapsed at the over-crowded Mottaqi Stadium at Sari for the match between Pirouzi and Shemshak Noshahr.

On May 9, 2001, in Africa's worst football disaster, 123 died and 93 were injured in a stampede at the national stadium in **Accra, Ghana**. Home team Hearts of Oak were leading 2-1 against Asante Kotoko five minutes from time, when Asanti fans started hurling bottles on to the pitch. Police fired tear gas into the stands, and the crowd panicked in a rush for the exits, which were locked. It took the death toll at three big matches in Africa in Apr/May to 173.

On Aug 12, 2001, two players were killed by lightning and ten severely burned at a **Guatemala** Third Division match between Deportivo Culquimulilla and Pueblo Nuevo Vinas.

On Nov 1, 2002, two players died from injuries after lightning struck Deportivo Cali's training ground in **Colombia**.

On Mar 12 2004, five people were killed and more than 100 injured when spectators stampeded shortly before the Syrian Championship fixture between Al-Jihad and Al-Fatwa in **Qameshli**, Northern Syria. The match was cancelled.

On Oct 10, 2004, three spectators died in a crush at the African Zone World Cup qualifier between **Guinea** and **Morocco** (1-1) at Conakry, Guinea.

On Mar 25, 2005, five were killed as 100,000 left the Azadi Stadium, **Tehran**, after Iran's World Cup qualifying win (2-1) against Japan.

On Jun 2, 2007, 12 spectators were killed and 46 injured in a crush at the Chillabombwe Stadium, **Zambia**, after an African Nations Cup qualifier against Congo.

On Mar 29, 2009, 19 people died and 139 were injured after a wall collapsed at the Ivory Coast stadium in **Abidjan** before a World Cup qualifier against Malawi. The match went ahead, Ivory Coast winning 5-0 with two goals from Chelsea's Didier Drogba. The tragedy meant that, in 13 years, crowd disasters at club and internationals at ten different grounds across Africa had claimed the lives of 283 people.

On Jan 8, 2010, terrorists at **Cabinda**, Angola machine-gunned the Togo team buses travelling to the Africa Cup of Nations. They killed a driver, an assistant coach and a media officer and injured several players. The team were ordered by their Government to withdraw from the tournament.

On Oct 23, 2010, seven fans were trampled to death when thousands tried to force their way into the Nyayo National Stadium in **Nairobi** at a Kenya Premier League match between the

Gor Mahia and AFC Leopards clubs.

On Feb 1, 2012, 74 died and nearly 250 were injured in a crowd riot at the end of the Al-Masry v Al-Ahly match in **Port Said** – the worst disaster in Egyptian sport.

DAYS OF TRAGEDY – PERSONAL

Sam Wynne, Bury right-back, collapsed five minutes before half-time in the First Division match away to Sheffield Utd on Apr 30, 1927, and died in the dressing-room.

John Thomson, Celtic and Scotland goalkeeper, sustained a fractured skull when diving at an opponent's feet in the Rangers v Celtic League match on Sep 5, 1931, and died the same evening.

Sim Raleigh (Gillingham), injured in a clash of heads at home to Brighton (Div 3 South) on Dec 1, 1934, continued to play but collapsed in second half and died in hospital the same night.

James Thorpe, Sunderland goalkeeper, was injured during the First Division match at home to Chelsea on Feb 1, 1936 and died in a diabetic coma three days later.

Derek Dooley, Sheffield Wed centre-forward and top scorer in 1951–52 in the Football League with 46 goals in 30 matches, broke a leg in the League match at Preston on Feb 14, 1953, and, after complications set in, had to lose the limb by amputation.

John White, Tottenham's Scottish international forward, was killed by lightning on a golf course at Enfield, North London in Jul, 1964.

Tony Allden, Highgate centre-half, was struck by lightning during an Amateur Cup quarter-final with Enfield on Feb 25, 1967. He died the following day. Four other players were also struck but recovered.

Roy Harper died while refereeing the York v Halifax (Div 4) match on May 5, 1969.

Jim Finn collapsed and died from a heart attack while refereeing Exeter v Stockport (Div 4) on Sep 16, 1972.

Scotland manager **Jock Stein**, 62, collapsed and died at the end of the Wales-Scotland World Cup qualifying match (1-1) at Ninian Park, Cardiff on Sep 10, 1985.

David Longhurst, York forward, died after being carried off two minutes before half-time in the Fourth Division fixture at home to Lincoln on Sep 8, 1990. The match was abandoned (0-0). The inquest revealed that Longhurst suffered from a rare heart condition.

Mike North collapsed while refereeing Southend v Mansfield (Div 3) on Apr 16, 2001 and died shortly afterwards. The match was abandoned and re-staged on May 8, with the receipts donated to his family.

Marc-Vivien Foe, on his 63rd appearance in Cameroon's midfield, collapsed unchallenged in the centre circle after 72 minutes of the FIFA Confederations Cup semi-final against Colombia in Lyon, France, on Jun 26, 2003, and despite the efforts of the stadium medical staff he could not be revived. He had been on loan to Manchester City from Olympique Lyonnais in season 2002–03, and poignantly scored the club's last goal at Maine Road.

Paul Sykes, Folkestone Invicta (Ryman League) striker, died on the pitch during the Kent Senior Cup semi-final against Margate on Apr 12, 2005. He collapsed after an innocuous off-the-ball incident.

Craig Gowans, Falkirk apprentice, was killed at the club's training ground on Jul 8, 2005 when he came into contact with power lines.

Peter Wilson, Mansfield goalkeeping coach, died of a heart attack after collapsing during the warm-up of the League Two game away to Shrewsbury on Nov 19, 2005.

Matt Gadsby, Hinckley defender, collapsed and died while playing in a Conference North match at Harrogate on Sep 9, 2006.

Phil O'Donnell, 35-year-old Motherwell captain and Scotland midfield player, collapsed when about to be substituted near the end of the SPL home game against Dundee Utd on Dec 29, 2007 and died shortly afterwards in hospital.

GREAT SERVICE

'For services to Association Football', **Stanley Matthews** (Stoke, Blackpool and England), already a CBE, became the first professional footballer to receive a knighthood. This was bestowed in 1965, his last season. Before he retired and five days after his 50th birthday, he played for Stoke to set a record as the oldest First Division footballer (v Fulham, Feb 6, 1965).

Over a brilliant span of 33 years, he played in 886 first-class matches, including 54 full Internationals (plus 31 in war time), 701 League games (including 3 at start of season 1939–40, which was abandoned on the outbreak of war) and 86 FA Cup-ties, and scored 95 goals. He was never booked in his career.

Sir Stanley died on Feb 23, 2000, three weeks after his 85th birthday. His ashes were buried under the centre circle of Stoke's Britannia Stadium. After spending a number of years in Toronto, he made his home back in the Potteries in 1989, having previously returned to his home town, Hanley in Oct, 1987 to unveil a life-size bronze statue of himself. The inscription reads: 'Sir Stanley Matthews, CBE. Born Hanley, 1 Feb 1915.

His name is symbolic of the beauty of the game, his fame timeless and international, his sportsmanship and modesty universally acclaimed. A magical player, of the people, for the people.' On his home-coming in 1989, Sir Stanley was made President of Stoke, the club he joined as a boy 15 and served as a player for 20 years between 1931 and 1965, on either side of his spell with Blackpool.

In Jul 1992 FIFA honoured him with their 'Gold merit award' for outstanding services to the game.

Former England goalkeeper **Peter Shilton** has made more first-class appearances (1,387) than any other footballer in British history. He played his 1,000th. League game in Leyton Orient's 2-0 home win against Brighton on Dec 22, 1996 and made 9 appearances for Orient in his final season. He retired from international football after the 1990 World Cup in Italy with 125 caps, then a world record. Shilton kept a record 60 clean sheets for England.

Shilton's career spanned 32 seasons, 20 of them on the international stage. He made his League debut for Leicester in May 1966, two months before England won the World Cup.

His 1,387 first-class appearances comprise a record 1,005 in the Football League, 125 Internationals, 102 League Cup, 86 FA Cup, 13 for England U-23s, 4 for the Football League and 52 other matches (European Cup, UEFA Cup, World Club Championship, Charity Shield, European Super Cup, Full Members' Cup, Play-offs, Screen Sports Super Cup, Anglo-Italian Cup, Texaco Cup, Simod Cup, Zenith Data Systems Cup and Autoglass Trophy).

Shilton appeared 57 times at Wembley, 52 for England, 2 League Cup Finals, 1 FA Cup Final, 1 Charity Shield match, and 1 for the Football League. He passed a century of League appearances with each of his first five clubs: Leicester (286), Stoke (110), Nottm Forest (202), Southampton (188) and Derby (175) and subsequently played for Plymouth, Bolton and Leyton Orient.

He was awarded the MBE and OBE for services to football. At the Football League Awards ceremony in March 2013, he received the League's Contribution award.

Six other British footballers have made more than 1,000 first-class appearances:

Ray Clemence, formerly with Tottenham, Liverpool and England, retired through injury in season 1987–88 after a goalkeeping career of 1,119 matches starting in 1965–66.

Clemence played 50 times for his first club, Scunthorpe; 665 for Liverpool; 337 for Tottenham; his 67 representative games included 61 England caps.

A third great British goalkeeper, **Pat Jennings**, ended his career (1963–86) with a total of 1,098 first-class matches for Watford, Tottenham, Arsenal and N Ireland. They were made up of 757 in the Football League, 119 full Internationals, 84 FA Cup appearances, 72 League/Milk Cup, 55 European club matches, 2 Charity Shield, 3 Other Internationals, 1 Under-23 cap, 2 Texaco Cup, 2 Anglo-Italian Cup and 1 Super Cup. Jennings played his 119th and final international on his 41st birthday, Jun 12, 1986, against Brazil in Guadalajara in the Mexico World Cup.

Yet another outstanding 'keeper, **David Seaman**, passed the 1,000 appearances milestone for clubs and country in season 2002–03, reaching 1,004 when aged 39, he captained Arsenal to FA Cup triumph against Southampton.

With Arsenal, Seaman won 3 Championship medals, the FA Cup 4 times, the Double twice, the League Cup and Cup-Winners' Cup once each. After 13 seasons at Highbury, he joined Manchester City (Jun 2003) on a free transfer. He played 26 matches for City before a shoulder injury forced his retirement in Jan 2004, aged 40.

Seaman's 22-season career composed 1,046 first-class matches: 955 club apps (Peterborough 106, Birmingham 84, QPR 175, Arsenal 564, Manchester City 26); 75 senior caps for England, 6 'B' caps and 10 at U-21 level.

Defender **Graeme Armstrong**, 42-year-old commercial manager for an Edinburgh whisky company and part-time assistant-manager and captain of Scottish Third Division club Stenhousemuir, made the 1000th first team appearance of his career in the Scottish Cup 3rd Round against Rangers at Ibrox on Jan 23, 1999. He was presented with the Man of the Match award before kick-off.

Against East Stirling on Boxing Day, he had played his 864th League game, breaking the British record for an outfield player set by another Scot, Tommy Hutchison, with Alloa, Blackpool, Coventry, Manchester City, Burnley and Swansea City.

Armstrong's 24-year career, spent in the lower divisions of the Scottish League, began as a 1-match trialist with Meadowbank Thistle in 1975 and continued via Stirling Albion, Berwick Rangers, Meadowbank and, from 1992, Stenhousemuir.

Tony Ford became the first English outfield player to reach 1000 senior appearances in Rochdale's 1-0 win at Carlisle (Auto Windscreens Shield) on Mar 7, 2000. Grimsby-born, he began his 26-season midfield career with Grimsby and played for 7 other League clubs: Sunderland (loan), Stoke, WBA, Bradford City (loan), Scunthorpe, Mansfield and Rochdale. He retired, aged 42, in 2001 with a career record of 1072 appearances (121 goals) and his total of 931 League games is exceeded only by Peter Shilton's 1005.

On Apr 16, 2011, **Graham Alexander** reached 1,000 appearances when he came on as a sub for Burnley at home to Swansea. Alexander, 40, ended a 22-year career with the equaliser for Preston against Charlton (2-2, Lge 1) on Apr 28, 2012 – his 1,023rd appearance. He also played for Luton and Scunthorpe and was capped 40 times by Scotland.

KNIGHTS OF SOCCER

Players, managers and administrators who have been honoured for their services to football: **Charles Clegg** (1927), **Stanley Rous** (1949), **Stanley Matthews** (1965), **Alf Ramsey** (1967), **Matt Busby** (1968), **Walter Winterbottom** (1978) **Bert Millichip** (1991), **Bobby Charlton** (1994), **Tom Finney** (1998), **Geoff Hurst** (1998), **Alex Ferguson** (1999), **Bobby Robson** (2002), **Trevor Brooking** (2004), **Dave Richards** (2006), **Doug Ellis** (2011).

FOOTBALL IN STATUE

In recognition of **Brian Clough's** outstanding achievements as manager, a 9ft bronze statue was unveiled by his widow Barbara in Market Square, Nottingham on Nov 6, 2008. The bulk of the £60,000 cost was met by supporters of Forest, the club he led to back-to-back European Cup triumphs. There is also a statue of Clough in his home town, Middlesbrough, and at Derby's Pride Park stands a combined statue of the famous management team of Clough and Peter Taylor. Other leading managers and players have been honoured over the years. They include **Sir Matt Busby** (Manchester Utd), **Bill Shankly** (Liverpool), **Sir Alf Ramsey** and **Sir Bobby Robson** (Ipswich), **Stan Cullis** (Wolves), **Jackie Milburn** (Newcastle), **Bob Stokoe** (Sunderland), **Ted Bates** (Southampton), **Nat Lofthouse** (Bolton) and **Billy Bremner** (Leeds).

Bobby Moore, England's World Cup-winning captain, is immortalised by a statue at the new Wembley, where there is a bust of Sir Alf in the tunnel corridor. There are statues of **Sir Stanley Matthews** and **Sir Tom Finney** recognising their playing achievements with Stoke and Preston, and one honouring Manchester Utd's **Sir Bobby Charlton**, **George Best** and

Denis Law outside Old Trafford. At Upton Park, there is a combined statue of West Ham's World Cup-winning trio, **Bobby Moore**, **Sir Geoff Hurst** and **Martin Peters**. Similarly, Fulham legend **Johnny Haynes** and Charlton's greatest goalkeeper **Sam Bartram** are honoured. So, too, is Everton great **William Ralph 'Dixie' Dean** at Goodison Park. The original bust of **Herbert Chapman** remains on its plinth at Arsenal's former home at Highbury (now converted into apartments). A replica is in place at the Emirates Stadium, which also has a bust of the club's most successful manager, **Arsene Wenger**. A bust of **Derby's** record scorer, **Steve Bloomer**, is at Pride Park and there is one of Blackburn's former owner, **Jack Walker**, at Ewood Park. Chelsea honoured **Peter Osgood** in 2010 and Blackpool did the same for **Jimmy Armfield** the following year. 2011 also saw statues unveiled of **Herbert Chapman**, **Thierry Henry** and **Tony Adams**, as part of Arsenal's 125th anniversary, and of **Jimmy Hill** at Coventry. The following year, **Sir Bobby Robson** was honoured at Newcastle and **Sir Alex Ferguson** at Old Trafford. A 16ft statue of former Port Vale player and manager **Roy Sproson**, costing £96,000 and paid for by supporters, went up at Vale Park. In 2013, Arsenal commissioned a statue of **Dennis Bergkamp**, while Roy Hodgson unveiled a bust of **Sir Walter Winterbottom**, England's first manager (1946-62) at the National Football Centre at St George's Park on St George's Day, At Villa Park, there is a statue of **William McGregor**, founder of the Football League in 1888.

PENALTIES

The **penalty-kick** was introduced to the game, following a proposal to the Irish FA in 1890 by William McCrum, son of the High Sheriff for Co Omagh, and approved by the International Football Board on Jun 2, 1891.

First penalty scored in a first-class match in England was by John Heath, for Wolves v Accrington Stanley (5-0 in Div 1, Sep 14, 1891).

The greatest influence of the penalty has come since the 1970s, with the introduction of the shoot-out to settle deadlocked ties in various competitions.

Manchester Utd were the first club to win a competitive match in British football via a shoot-out (4-3 away to Hull, Watney Cup semi-final, Aug 5, 1970); in that penalty contest, George Best was the first player to score, Denis Law the first to miss.

The shoot-out was adopted by FIFA and UEFA the same year (1970).

In season 1991–92, penalty shoot-outs were introduced to decide FA Cup ties still level after one replay and extra time.

Wembley saw its first penalty contest in the 1974 Charity Shield. Since then many major matches across the world have been settled in this way, including:

1976	**European Championship Final (Belgrade):**	Czechoslovakia beat West Germany 5-3 (after 2-2)
1980	**Cup-Winners' Cup Final (Brussels):**	Valencia beat Arsenal 5-4 (after 0-0)
1984	**European Cup Final (Rome):**	Liverpool beat Roma 4-2 (after 1-1)
1984	**UEFA Cup Final:**	Tottenham (home) beat Anderlecht 4-3 (2-2 agg)
1986	**European Cup Final (Seville):**	Steaua Bucharest beat Barcelona 2-0 (after 0-0).
1987	**Freight Rover Trophy Final (Wembley):**	Mansfield beat Bristol City 5-4 (after 1-1)
1987	**Scottish League Cup Final (Hampden Park):**	Rangers beat Aberdeen 5-3 (after 3-3)
1988	**European Cup Final (Stuttgart):**	PSV Eindhoven beat Benfica 6-5 (after 0-0)
1988	**UEFA Cup Final:**	Bayer Leverkusen (home) beat Espanyol 3-2 after 3-3 (0-3a, 3-0h)
1990	**Scottish Cup Final (Hampden Park):**	Aberdeen beat Celtic 9-8 (after 0-0)
1991	**European Cup Final (Bari):**	Red Star Belgrade beat Marseille 5-3 (after 0-0)
1991	**Div 4 Play-off Final (Wembley):**	Torquay beat Blackpool 5-4 (after 2-2)
1992	**Div 4 Play-off Final (Wembley):**	Blackpool beat Scunthorpe 4-3 (after 1-1)
1993	**Div 3 Play-off Final(Wembley):**	York beat Crewe 5-3 (after 1-1)
1994	**Autoglass Trophy Final (Wembley):**	Swansea City beat Huddersfield 3-1 (after 1-1)

1994	**World Cup Final (Los Angeles):** Brazil beat Italy 3-2 (after 0-0)
1994	**Scottish League Cup Final (Ibrox Park):** Raith beat Celtic 6-5 (after 2-2)
1995	**Copa America Final (Montevideo):** Uruguay beat Brazil 5-3 (after 1-1)
1996	**European Cup Final (Rome):** Juventus beat Ajax 4-2 (after 1-1)
1996	**European U-21 Champ Final (Barcelona):** Italy beat Spain 4-2 (after 1-1)
1997	**Auto Windscreens Shield Final (Wembley):** Carlisle beat Colchester 4-3 (after 0-0)
1997	**UEFA Cup Final:** FC Schalke beat Inter Milan 4-1 (after 1-1 agg)
1998	**Div 1 Play-off Final (Wembley):** Charlton beat Sunderland 7-6 (after 4-4)
1999	**Div 2 Play-off Final (Wembley):** Manchester City beat Gillingham 3-1 (after 2-2)
1999	**Women's World Cup Final (Pasedena):** USA beat China 5-4 (after 0-0)
2000	**African Nations Cup Final (Lagos):** Cameroon beat Nigeria 4-3 (after 0-0)
2000	**UEFA Cup Final (Copenhagen):** Galatasaray beat Arsenal 4-1 (after 0-0)
2000	**Olympic Final (Sydney):** Cameroon beat Spain 5-3 (after 2-2)
2001	**League Cup Final (Millennium Stadium):** Liverpool beat Birmingham 5-4 (after 1-1)
2001	**Champions League Final (Milan):** Bayern Munich beat Valencia 5-4 (after 1-1)
2002	**Euro U-21 Champ Final (Basle):** Czech Republic beat France 3-1 (after 0-0)
2002	**Div 1 Play-off Final (Millennium Stadium):** Birmingham beat Norwich 4-2 (after 1-1)
2003	**Champions League Final (Old Trafford):** AC Milan beat Juventus 3-2 (after 0-0)
2004	**Div 3 Play-off Final (Millennium Stadium):** Huddersfield beat Mansfield 4-1 (after 0-0)
2004	**Copa America Final (Lima):** Brazil beat Argentina 4-2 (after 2-2)
2005	**FA Cup Final (Millennium Stadium):** Arsenal beat Manchester Utd 5-4 (after 0-0)
2005	**Champions League Final (Istanbul):** Liverpool beat AC Milan 3-2 (after 3-3)
2006	**African Cup of Nations Final (Cairo):** Egypt beat Ivory Coast 4-2 (after 0-0)
2006	**FA Cup Final (Millennium Stadium):** Liverpool beat West Ham 3-1 (after 3-3)
2006	**Scottish Cup Final (Hampden Park):** Hearts beat Gretna 4-2 (after 1-1)
2006	**Lge 1 Play-off Final (Millennium Stadium):** Barnsley beat Swansea City 4-3 (after 2-2)
2006	**World Cup Final (Berlin):** Italy beat France 5-3 (after 1-1)
2007	**UEFA Cup Final (Hampden Park):** Sevilla beat Espanyol 3-1 (after 2-2)
2008	**Champions League Final (Moscow):** Manchester Utd beat Chelsea 6-5 (after 1-1)
2008	**Scottish League Cup Final (Hampden Park):** Rangers beat Dundee Utd 3-2 (after 2-2)
2009	**League Cup Final (Wembley):** Manchester Utd beat Tottenham 4-1 (after 0-0)
2011	**Women's World Cup Final (Frankfurt):** Japan beat USA 3-1 (after 2-2)
2012	**League Cup Final (Wembley):** Liverpool beat Cardiff 3-2 (after 2-2)
2012	**Champions League Final (Munich):** Chelsea beat Bayern Munich 4-3 (after 1-1)
2012	**Lge 1 Play-off Final (Wembley):** Huddersfield beat Sheffield Utd 8-7 (after 0-0)
2012	**Africa Cup of Nations Final (Gabon):** Zambia beat Ivory Coast 8-7 (after 0-0)
2013	**FA Trophy Final (Wembley):** Wrexham beat Grimsby 4-1 (after 1-1)
2013	**European Super Cup (Prague):** Bayern Munich beat Chelsea 5-4 (after 2-2)
2014	**Scottish League Cup Final (Celtic Park):** Aberdeen beat Inverness 4-2 (after 0-0)
2014	**Lge 1 Play-off Final (Wembley):** Rotherham beat Leyton Orient 4-3 (after 2-2)
2014	**Europa Lge Final (Turin):** Sevilla beat Benfica 4-2 (after 0-0)

In South America in 1992, in a 26-shot competition, **Newell's Old Boys** beat America 11-10 in the Copa Libertadores.

Longest-recorded penalty contest in first-class matches was in Argentina in 1988 – from 44 shots, **Argentinos Juniors** beat Racing Club 20-19. Genclerbirligi beat Galatasaray 17-16 in a Turkish Cup-tie in 1996. Only one penalty was missed.

Highest-scoring shoot-outs in international football! **North Korea** beat Hong Kong 11-10 (after 3-3 draw) in an Asian Cup match in 1975; and **Ivory Coast** beat Ghana 11-10 (after 0-0 draw) in African Nations Cup Final, 1992.

Most penalties needed to settle an adult game in Britain: **44** in Norfolk Primary Cup 4th round replay, Dec 2000. Aston Village side **Freethorpe** beat Foulsham 20-19 (5 kicks missed). All 22 players took 2 penalties each, watched by a crowd of 20. The sides had drawn 2-2, 4-4 in a tie of 51 goals.

Penalty that took 24 days: That was how long elapsed between the award and the taking of a penalty in an Argentine Second Division match between **Atalanta** and Defensores in 2003. A riot ended the original match with 5 minutes left. The game resumed behind closed doors with the penalty that caused the abandonment. Lucas Ferreiro scored it to give Atalanta a 1-0 win.

INTERNATIONAL PENALTIES, MISSED

Four penalties out of five were missed when **Colombia** beat Argentina 3-0 in a Copa America group tie in Paraguay in Jul 1999. Martin Palmermo missed three for Argentina and Colombia's Hamilton Ricard had one spot-kick saved.

In the European Championship semi-final against Italy in Amsterdam on Jun 29, 2000, **Holland** missed five penalties – two in normal time, three in the penalty contest which Italy won 3-1 (after 0-0). Dutch captain Frank de Boer missed twice from the spot.

ENGLAND'S SHOOT-OUT RECORD

England have been beaten in seven out of nine penalty shoot-outs in major tournaments:

1990 (World Cup semi-final, Turin) 3-4 v West Germany after 1-1.
1996 (Euro Champ quarter-final, Wembley) 4-2 v Spain after 0-0.
1996 (Euro Champ semi-final, Wembley) 5-6 v Germany after 1-1.
1998 (World Cup 2nd round., St Etienne) 3-4 v Argentina after 2-2.
2004 (Euro Champ quarter-final, Lisbon) 5-6 v Portugal after 2-2.
2006 (World Cup quarter-final, Gelsenkirchen) 1-3 v Portugal after 0-0.
2007 (Euro U-21 Champ semi-final, Heerenveen) 12-13 v Holland after 1-1.
2009 (Euro U-21 Champ semi-final, Gothenburg) 5-4 v Sweden after 3-3.
2012 (Euro Champ quarter-final, Kiev) 2-4 v Italy after 0-0.

FA CUP SHOOT-OUTS

First penalty contest in the FA Cup took place in 1972. In the days of the play-off for third place, the match was delayed until the eve of the following season when losing semi-finalists Birmingham and Stoke met at St Andrew's on Aug 5. The score was 0-0 and Birmingham won 4-3 on penalties.

Highest-scoring: Preliminary round replay (Aug 30, 2005): Tunbridge Wells beat Littlehampton 16-15 after 40 spot-kicks (9 missed).

Competition proper: Macclesfield beat Forest Green 11-10 in 1st round replay (Nov 28, 2001) – 24 kicks.

Shoot-out abandoned: The FA Cup 1st round replay between Oxford City and Wycombe at Wycombe on Nov 9, 1999 was abandoned (1-1) after extra-time. As the penalty shoot-out was about to begin, a fire broke out under a stand. Wycombe won the second replay 1-0 at Oxford Utd's ground.

First FA Cup Final to be decided by shoot-out was in 2005 (May 21), when Arsenal beat Manchester Utd 5-4 on penalties at Cardiff's Millennium Stadium (0-0 after extra time). A year later (May 13) Liverpool beat West Ham 3-1 (3-3 after extra-time).

MARATHON SHOOT-OUT BETWEEN LEAGUE CLUBS

Highest recorded score in shoot-out between league clubs: Dagenham & Redbridge 14-13 against Leyton Orient (after 1-1) in Johnstone's Paint Trophy southern section on Sep 7, 2011

SHOOT-OUT RECORD WINNERS AND LOSERS

When **Bradford** beat Arsenal 3-2 on penalties in a League Cup fifth round tie, it was the club's ninth successive shoot-out victory in FA Cup, League Cup and Johnstone's Paint Trophy ties between Oct 2009 and Dec 2012.

Tottenham's 4-1 spot-kick failure against Basel in the last 16 of the Europa League was their seventh successive defeat in shoot-outs from Mar 1996 to Apr 2013 (FA Cup, League Cup, UEFA Cup, Europa League)

MISSED CUP FINAL PENALTIES

John Aldridge (Liverpool) became the first player to miss a penalty in an FA Cup Final at Wembley when Dave Beasant saved his shot in 1988 to help Wimbledon to a shock 1-0 win. Seven penalties before had been scored in the Final at Wembley.

Previously, **Charlie Wallace**, of Aston Villa, had failed from the spot in the 1913 Final against Sunderland at Crystal Palace, which his team won 1-0

Gary Lineker (Tottenham) had his penalty saved by Nottm Forest's Mark Crossley in the 1991 FA Cup Final.

For the first time, two spot-kicks were missed in an FA Cup Final. In 2010, Petr Cech saved from Portsmouth's **Kevin-Prince Boateng** while Chelsea's **Frank Lampard** put his kick wide.

Another miss at Wembley was by Arsenal's **Nigel Winterburn**, Luton's Andy Dibble saving his spot-kick in the 1988 Littlewoods Cup Final, when a goal would have put Arsenal 3-1 ahead. Instead, they lost 3-2.

Winterburn was the third player to fail with a League Cup Final penalty at Wembley, following **Ray Graydon** (Aston Villa) against Norwich in 1975 and **Clive Walker** (Sunderland), who shot wide in the 1985 Milk Cup Final, also against Norwich who won 1-0. Graydon had his penalty saved by Kevin Keelan, but scored from the rebound and won the cup for Aston Villa (1-0).

Derby's Martin Taylor saved a penalty from **Eligio Nicolini** in the Anglo-Italian Cup Final at Wembley on Mar 27, 1993, but Cremonese won 3-1.

LEAGUE PENALTIES RECORD

Most penalties in Football League match: Five – 4 to Crystal Palace (3 missed), 1 to Brighton (scored) in Div 2 match at Selhurst Park on Mar 27 (Easter Monday), 1989. Crystal Palace won 2-1. Three of the penalties were awarded in a 5-minute spell. The match also produced 5 bookings and a sending-off. Other teams missing 3 penalties in a match: Burnley v Grimsby (Div 2), Feb 13, 1909; Manchester City v Newcastle (Div 1), Jan 17, 1912.

HOTTEST MODERN SPOT-SHOTS

Matthew Le Tissier ended his career in season 2001–02 with the distinction of having netted 48 out of 49 first-team penalties for Southampton. He scored the last 27 after his only miss when Nottm Forest keeper Mark Crossley saved in a Premier League match at The Dell on Mar 24, 1993.

Graham Alexander scored 78 out of 84 penalties in a 22-year career (Scunthorpe, Luton, Preston twice and Burnley) which ended in 2012.

SPOT-KICK HAT-TRICKS

Right-back **Joe Willetts** scored three penalties when Hartlepool beat Darlington 6-1 (Div 3N) on Good Friday 1951.

Danish international **Jan Molby**'s only hat-trick in English football, for Liverpool in a 3-1 win at home to Coventry (Littlewoods Cup, 4th round replay, Nov 26, 1986) comprised three goals from the penalty spot.

It was the first such hat-trick in a major match for two years – since **Andy Blair** scored three penalties for Sheffield Wed against Luton (Milk Cup 4th round, Nov 20 1984).

Portsmouth's **Kevin Dillon** scored a penalty hat-trick in the Full Members Cup (2nd round) at home to Millwall (3-2) on Nov 4, 1986.

Alan Slough scored a hat-trick of penalties in an away game, but was on the losing side, when Peterborough were beaten 4-3 at Chester (Div 3, Apr 29, 1978).

Penalty hat-tricks in international football: **Dimitris Saravakos** (in 9 mins) for Greece v Egypt in 1990. He scored 5 goals in match. **Henrik Larsson**, among his 4 goals in Sweden's 6-0 home win v Moldova in World Cup qualifying match, Jun 6, 2001.

MOST PENALTY GOALS (LEAGUE) IN SEASON

13 out of 13 by **Francis Lee** for Manchester City (Div 1) in 1971–72. His goal total for the season was 33. In season 1988–89, **Graham Roberts** scored 12 League penalties for

Second Division Champions Chelsea. In season 2004–05, **Andrew Johnson** scored 11 Premiership penalties for Crystal Palace, who were relegated.

PENALTY-SAVE SEQUENCES

Ipswich goalkeeper **Paul Cooper** saved eight of the ten penalties he faced in 1979–80. **Roy Brown** (Notts Co) saved six in a row in season 1972–73.

Andy Lomas, goalkeeper for Chesham (Diadora League) claimed a record eighth **consecutive** penalty saves – three at the end of season 1991–92 and five in 1992–93.

Mark Bosnich (Aston Villa) saved five in two consecutive matches in 1993–94: three in Coca-Cola Cup semi-final penalty shoot–out v Tranmere (Feb 26), then two in Premiership at Tottenham (Mar 2).

MISSED PENALTIES SEQUENCE

Against Wolves in Div 2 on Sep 28, 1991, **Southend** missed their seventh successive penalty (five of them the previous season).

SCOTTISH RECORDS

(See also under 'Goals' & 'Discipline')

RANGERS' MANY RECORDS

Rangers' record-breaking feats include:

League Champions: 54 times (once joint holders) – world record.

Winning every match in Scottish League (18 games, 1898–99 season).

Major hat-tricks: Rangers have completed the domestic treble (League Championship, League Cup and Scottish FA Cup) a record seven times (1948–49, 1963–64, 1975–76, 1977–78, 1992–93, 1998–99, 2002–03).

League & Cup double: 17 times.

Nine successive Championships (1989–97). Four men played in all nine sides: Richard Gough, Ally McCoist, Ian Ferguson and Ian Durrant.

115 major trophies: Championships 54, Scottish Cup 33, League Cup 27, Cup-Winners' Cup 1.

CELTIC'S GRAND SLAM

Celtic's record in 1966–67 was the most successful by a British club in one season. They won the **Scottish League,** the **Scottish Cup,** the **Scottish League Cup** and became the first British club to win the **European Cup**. They also won the **Glasgow Cup**.

Celtic have three times achieved the Scottish treble (League Championship, League Cup and FA Cup), in 1966–67, 1968–69 and 2000–01 (in Martin O'Neill's first season as their manager). They became Scottish Champions for 2000–01 with a 1-0 home win against St Mirren on Apr 7 – the earliest the title had been clinched for 26 years, since Rangers' triumph on Mar 29, 1975. They have been champions 45 times.

They have won the Scottish Cup 36 times, and have completed the League and Cup double 15 times.

Celtic won nine consecutive Scottish League titles (1966–74) under Jock Stein.

They set a **British record** of 25 consecutive League wins in season 2003–04 (Aug 15 to Mar 14). They were unbeaten for 77 matches (all competitions) at Celtic Park from Aug 22, 2001, to Apr 21, 2004. They have won the Scottish Championship 43 times.

UNBEATEN SCOTTISH CHAMPIONS

Celtic and **Rangers** have each won the Scottish Championship with an unbeaten record: Celtic in 1897–98 (P18, W15, D3), Rangers in 1898–99 (P18, W18).

FORSTER'S SHUT-OUT RECORD

Celtic goalkeeper **Fraser Forster** set a record in Scottish top-flight football by not conceding a goal for 1,256 consecutive minutes in season 2013–14.

TRIO OF TOP CLUBS MISSING

Three of Scotland's leading clubs are missing from the 2014-15 Premiership season. With **Hearts** finishing bottom and **Rangers** still working their way back through the divisions after being demoted, they were joined in the second tier by **Hibernian**, who lost the play-off final on penalties to Hamilton.

SCOTTISH CUP HAT-TRICKS

Aberdeen's feat of winning the Scottish FA Cup in 1982–83–84 made them only the third club to achieve that particular hat-trick. **Queen's Park** did it twice (1874–75–76 and 1880–81–82), and **Rangers** have won the Scottish Cup three years in succession on three occasions: 1934–35–36, 1948–49–50 and 1962–63–64.

SCOTTISH CUP FINAL DISMISSALS

Five players have been sent off in the Scottish FA Cup Final: **Jock Buchanan** (Rangers v Kilmarnock, 1929); **Roy Aitken** (Celtic v Aberdeen, 1984); **Walter Kidd** (Hearts captain v Aberdeen, 1986); **Paul Hartley** (Hearts v Gretna, 2006); **Pa Kujabi** (Hibernian v Hearts, 2012).

RECORD SEQUENCES

Celtic hold Britain's League record of 62 matches undefeated, from Nov 13, 1915 to Apr 21, 1917, when Kilmarnock won 2-0 at Parkhead. They won 49, drew 13 (111 points) and scored 126 goals to 26.

Greenock Morton in 1963–64 accumulated 67 points out of 72 and scored 135 goals.

Queen's Park did not have a goal scored against them during the first seven seasons of their existence (1867–74, before the Scottish League was formed).

EARLIEST PROMOTIONS IN SCOTLAND

Dundee promoted from Div 2, Feb 1, 1947; **Greenock Morton** promoted from Div 2, Mar 2, 1964; **Gretna** promoted from Div 3, Mar 5, 2005.

WORST HOME SEQUENCE

After gaining promotion to Div 1 in 1992, **Cowdenbeath** went a record 38 consecutive home League matches without a win. They ended the sequence (drew 8, lost 30) when beating Arbroath 1-0 on Apr 2, 1994, watched by a crowd of 225.

ALLY'S RECORDS

Ally McCoist became the first player to complete 200 goals in the Premier Division when he scored Rangers' winner (2-1) at Falkirk on Dec 12, 1992. His first was against Celtic in Sep 1983, and he reached 100 against Dundee on Boxing Day 1987.

When McCoist scored twice at home to Hibernian (4-3) on Dec 7, 1996, he became Scotland's record post-war League marksman, beating Gordon Wallace's 264.

Originally with St Johnstone (1978–81), he spent two seasons with Sunderland (1981–83), then joined Rangers for £200,000 in Jun 1983.

In 15 seasons at Ibrox, he scored 355 goals for Rangers (250 League), and helped them win 10 Championships (9 in succession), 3 Scottish Cups and earned a record 9 League Cup winner's medals. He won the European Golden Boot in consecutive seasons (1991–92, 1992–93).

His 9 Premier League goals in three seasons for Kilmarnock gave him a career total of 281 Scottish League goals when he retired at the end of 2000–01. McCoist succeeded Walter Smith as manager of Rangers in May 2011.

SCOTLAND'S MOST SUCCESSFUL MANAGER

Bill Struth, 30 trophies for Rangers, 1920–54 (18 Championships, 10 Scottish Cups, 2 League Cups.

SMITH'S IBROX HONOURS

Walter Smith, who retired in May, 2011, won a total of 21 trophies in two spells as Rangers manager (10 League titles, 5 Scottish Cups, 6 League Cups).

RANGERS PUNISHED

In April 2012, **Rangers** (in administration) were fined £160,000 by the Scottish FA and given a 12-month transfer ban on charges relating to their finances. The ban was later overturned in court. The club had debts estimated at around £135m and on June 12, 2012 were forced into liquidation. A new company emerged, but Rangers were voted out of the Scottish Premier League and demoted to Division Three for the start of the 2012-13 season. Dundee, runners-up in Division One, replaced them in the top flight.

FIVE IN A MATCH

Paul Sturrock set an individual scoring record for the Scottish Premier Division with 5 goals in Dundee Utd's 7-0 win at home to Morton on Nov 17, 1984. **Marco Negri** equalled the feat with all 5 when Rangers beat Dundee Utd 5-1 at Ibrox (Premier Division) on Aug 23, 1997, and **Kenny Miller** scored 5 in Rangers' 7-1 win at home to St Mirren on Nov 4, 2000. **Kris Boyd** scored all Kilmarnock's goals in a 5-2 SPL win at home to Dundee Utd on Sep 25, 2004. **Boyd** scored another 5 when Rangers beat Dundee Utd 7-1 on Dec 30, 2009. That took his total of SPL goals to a record 160. **Gary Hooper** netted all Celtic's goals in 5-0 SPL win against Hearts on May 13, 2012

NEGRI'S TEN-TIMER

Marco Negri scored in Rangers' first ten League matches (23 goals) in season 1997–98, a Premier Division record. The previous best was 8 by **Ally MacLeod** for Hibernian in 1978.

DOUBLE SCOTTISH FINAL

Rangers v Celtic drew **129,643** and **120,073** people to the Scottish Cup Final and replay at Hampden Park, Glasgow, in 1963. Receipts for the two matches totalled £50,500.

MOST SCOTTISH CHAMPIONSHIP MEDALS

13 by **Sandy Archibald** (Rangers, 1918–34). Post-war record: 10 by **Bobby Lennox** (Celtic, 1966–79).

Alan Morton won **nine** Scottish Championship medals with Rangers in 1921–23–24–25–27–28–29–30–31. **Ally McCoist** played in the Rangers side that won nine successive League titles (1989–97).

Between 1927 and 1939 **Bob McPhail** helped Rangers win nine Championships, finish second twice and third once. He scored 236 League goals but was never top scorer in a single season.

TOP SCOTTISH LEAGUE SCORERS IN SEASON

Raith Rovers (Div 2) 142 goals in 1937–38; **Morton** (Div 2) 135 goals in 1963–64; **Hearts** (Div 1) 132 goals in 1957–58; **Falkirk** (Div 2) 132 goals in 1935–36; **Gretna** (Div 3) 130 goals in 2004–05.

SCOTTISH CUP – NO DECISION

The **Scottish FA** withheld their Cup and medals in 1908–09 after Rangers and Celtic played two drawn games in the Final. Spectators rioted.

FEWEST LEAGUE WINS IN SEASON

In modern times: 1 win by **Ayr** (34 matches, Div 1, 1966–67); **Forfar** (38 matches, Div 2, 1973–74); **Clydebank** (36 matches, Div 1, 1999–2000).

Vale of Leven provided the only instance of a British team failing to win a single match in a league season (Div 1, 18 games, 1891–92).

HAMPDEN'S £63M REDEVELOPMENT

On completion of redevelopment costing £63m **Hampden Park**, home of Scottish football and the oldest first-class stadium in the world, was re-opened full scale for the Rangers-Celtic Cup Final on May 29, 1999.

Work on the 'new Hampden' (capacity 52,000) began in 1992. The North and East stands were restructured (£12m); a new South stand and improved West stand cost £51m. The Millennium Commission contributed £23m and the Lottery Sports Fund provided a grant of £3.75m.

GRETNA'S RISE AND FALL

Gretna, who joined the Scottish League in 2002, won the Bell's Third, Second and First Division titles in successive seasons (2005–06–07). They also become the first team from the third tier to reach the Scottish Cup Final, taking Hearts to penalties (2006). But then it all turned sour. Businessman Brooks Mileson, who had financed this rise to the Premier League, withdrew his backing, causing the club to collapse. They went into administration, finished bottom of the SPL, were demoted to Division Three, then resigned from the League.

DEMISE OF AIRDRIE AND CLYDEBANK

In May 2002, First Division **Airdrieonians**, formed in 1878, went out of business. They had debts of £3m. Their place in the Scottish League was taken by **Gretna**, from the English Unibond League, who were voted into Div 3. Second Division **Clydebank** folded in Jul 2002 and were taken over by the new **Airdrie United** club.

FASTEST GOAL IN SPL

12.4 sec by **Anthony Stokes** for Hibernian in 4-1 home defeat by Rangers, Dec 27, 2009.

YOUNGEST SCORER IN SPL

Fraser Fyvie, aged 16 years and 306 days, for Aberdeen v Hearts (3-0) on Jan 27, 2010.

12 GOALS SHARED

There was a record aggregate score for the SPL on May 5, 2010, when **Motherwell** came from 6-2 down to draw 6-6 with **Hibernian**.

25-POINT DEDUCTION

Dundee were deducted 25 points by the Scottish Football League in November 2010 for going into administration for the second time. It left the club on minus 11 points, but they still managed to finish in mid-table in Division One.

GREAT SCOTS

In Feb 1988, the Scottish FA launched a national **Hall of Fame**, initially comprising the first 11 Scots to make 50 international appearances, to be joined by all future players to reach that number of caps. Each member receives a gold medal, invitation for life at all Scotland's home matches, and has his portrait hung at Scottish FA headquarters in Glasgow.

MORE CLUBS IN 2000

The **Scottish Premier League** increased from 10 to 12 clubs in season 2000–01. The **Scottish Football League** admitted two new clubs – Peterhead and Elgin City from the Highland League – to provide three divisions of 10 in 2000–01.

NOTABLE SCOTTISH 'FIRSTS'

- The father of League football was a Scot, **William McGregor**, a draper in Birmingham. The 12-club Football League kicked off in Sep 1888, and McGregor was its first president.

- **Hibernian** were the first British club to play in the European Cup, by invitation. They reached the semi-final when it began in 1955–56.
- **Celtic** were Britain's first winners of the European Cup, in 1967.
- Scotland's First Division became the **Premier Division** in season 1975–76.
- Football's **first international** was staged at the West of Scotland cricket ground, Partick, on Nov 30, 1872: Scotland 0, England 0.
- Scotland introduced its **League Cup** in 1945–46, the first season after the war. It was another 15 years before the Football League Cup was launched.
- Scotland pioneered the use in British football of **two subs** per team in League and Cup matches.
- The world's **record football score** belongs to Scotland: Arbroath 36, Bon Accord 0 (Scottish Cup 1st rd) on Sep 12, 1885.
- The Scottish FA introduced the penalty **shoot-out** to their Cup Final in 1990.
- On Jan 22, 1994 all six matches in the **Scottish Premier Division** ended as draws.
- Scotland's new Premier League introduced a **3-week shut-down** in Jan 1999 – first instance of British football adopting the winter break system that operates in a number of European countries. The SPL ended its New Year closure after 2003.
- **Rangers** made history at home to St Johnstone (Premier League, 0-0, Mar 4, 2000) when fielding a team entirely without Scottish players.

John Fleck, aged 16 years, 274 days, became the youngest player in a Scottish FA Cup Final when he came on as a substitute for Rangers in their 3-2 win over Queen of the South at Hampden Park on May 24, 2008

SCOTTISH CUP SHOCK RESULTS

1885–86	(1)	Arbroath 36 Bon Accord 0
1921–22	(F)	Morton 1 Rangers 0
1937–38	(F)	East Fife 4 Kilmarnock 2 (replay, after 1-1)
1960–61	(F)	Dunfermline 2 Celtic 0 (replay, after 0-0)
1966–67	(1)	Berwick 1 Rangers 0
1979–80	(3)	Hamilton 2 Keith 3
1984–85	(1)	Stirling 20 Selkirk 0
1984–85	(3)	Inverness 3 Kilmarnock 0
1986–87	(3)	Rangers 0 Hamilton 1
1994–95	(4)	Stenhousemuir 2 Aberdeen 0
1998–99	(3)	Aberdeen 0 Livingston 1
1999–2000	(3)	Celtic 1 Inverness 3
2003–04	(5)	Inverness 1 Celtic 0
2005–06	(3)	Clyde 2 Celtic 1
2008–09	(6)	St Mirren 1 Celtic 0
2009–10	(SF)	Ross Co 2 Celtic 0
2013–14	(4)	Albion 1 Motherwell 0

Scottish League (Coca-Cola) Cup Final
1994–95	Raith 2, Celtic 2 (Raith won 6-5 on pens)

MISCELLANEOUS

NATIONAL ASSOCIATIONS FORMED

FA	**1863**
FA of Wales	**1876**
Scottish FA	**1873**
Irish FA	**1904**
Federation of International Football Associations (FIFA)	**1904**

NATIONAL & INTERNATIONAL COMPETITIONS LAUNCHED

FA Cup	**1871**
Welsh Cup	**1877**
Scottish Cup	**1873**
Irish Cup	**1880**
Football League	**1888**
Premier League	**1992**
Scottish League	**1890**
Scottish Premier League	**1998**
Scottish League Cup	**1945**
Football League Cup	**1960**
Home International Championship	**1883–84**
World Cup	**1930**
European Championship	**1958**
European Cup	**1955**
Fairs/UEFA Cup	**1955**
Cup-Winners' Cup	**1960**
European Champions League	**1992**
Olympic Games Tournament, at Shepherd's Bush	**1908**

INNOVATIONS

Size of Ball: Fixed in **1872**.

Shinguards: Introduced and registered by Sam Weller Widdowson (Nottm Forest & England) in **1874**.

Referee's whistle: First used on Nottm Forest's ground in **1878**.

Professionalism: Legalised in England in the summer of **1885** as a result of agitation by Lancashire clubs.

Goal-nets: Invented and patented in **1890** by Mr JA Brodie of Liverpool. They were first used in the North v South match in Jan, **1891**.

Referees and linesmen: Replaced umpires and referees in Jan, **1891**.

Penalty-kick: Introduced at Irish FA's request in the season **1891–92**. The penalty law ordering the goalkeeper to remain on the goal-line came into force in Sep, **1905**, and the order to stand on his goal-line until the ball is kicked arrived in **1929–30**.

White ball: First came into official use in **1951**.

Floodlighting: First FA Cup-tie (replay), Kidderminster Harriers v Brierley Hill Alliance, **1955**. First Football League match: Portsmouth v Newcastle (Div 1), **1956**.

Heated pitch to beat frost tried by Everton at Goodison Park in **1958**.

First soccer closed-circuit TV: At Coventry ground in Oct **1965** (10,000 fans saw their team win at Cardiff, 120 miles away).

Substitutes (one per team) were first allowed in Football League matches at the start of season **1965–66**. Three substitutes (one a goalkeeper) allowed, two of which could be used, in Premier League matches, **1992–93**. The Football League introduced three substitutes for **1993–94**.

Three points for a win: Introduced by the Football League in **1981–82**, by FIFA in World Cup games in **1994**, and by the Scottish League in the same year.

Offside law amended, player 'level' no longer offside, and 'professional foul' made sending-off offence, **1990**.

Penalty shoot-outs introduced to decide FA Cup ties level after one replay and extra time, **1991–92**.

New back-pass rule: goalkeeper must not handle ball kicked to him by team-mate, **1992**.

Linesmen became 'referees' assistants', **1998**.

Goalkeepers not to hold ball longer than 6 seconds, **2000**.

Free-kicks advanced by ten yards against opponents failing to retreat, **2000**. This experimental rule in England was scrapped in 2005).

YOUNGEST AND OLDEST

Youngest Caps

Harry Wilson (Wales v Belgium, Oct 15, 2013)	**16 years 207 days**
Norman Whiteside (N Ireland v Yugoslavia, Jun 17, 1982)	**17 years 41 days**
Theo Walcott (England v Hungary, May 30, 2006)	**17 years 75 days**
Johnny Lambie (Scotland v Ireland, Mar 20, 1886)	**17 years 92 days**
Jimmy Holmes (Rep of Ireland v Austria, May 30, 1971)	**17 years 200 days**

Youngest England scorer: Wayne Rooney (17 years, 317 days) v Macedonia, Skopje, Sep 6, 2003.

Youngest England hat-trick scorer: Theo Walcott (19 years, 178 days) v Croatia, Zagreb, Sep 10, 2008.

Youngest England captains: Bobby Moore (v Czech., Bratislava, May 29, 1963), 22 years, 47 days; Michael Owen (v Paraguay, Anfield, Apr 17, 2002), 22 years, 117 days.

Youngest England goalkeeper: Jack Butland (19 years, 158 days) v Italy, Bern, Aug 15, 2012

Youngest England players to reach 50 caps: Michael Owen (23 years, 6 months) v Slovakia at Middlesbrough, Jun 11, 2003; Bobby Moore (25 years, 7 months) v Wales at Wembley, Nov 16, 1966.

Youngest player in World Cup Final: Pele (Brazil) aged 17 years, 237 days v Sweden in Stockholm, Jun 12, 1958.

Youngest player to appear in World Cup Finals: Norman Whiteside (N Ireland v Yugoslavia in Spain – Jun 17, 1982, age 17 years and 42 days.

Youngest First Division player: Derek Forster (Sunderland goalkeeper v Leicester, Aug 22, 1964) aged 15 years, 185 days.

Youngest First Division scorer: At 16 years and 57 days, schoolboy Jason Dozzell (substitute after 30 minutes for Ipswich at home to Coventry on Feb 4, 1984). Ipswich won 3-1 and Dozzell scored their third goal.

Youngest Premier League player: Matthew Briggs (Fulham sub at Middlesbrough, May 13, 2007) aged 16 years and 65 days.

Youngest Premier League scorer: James Vaughan (Everton, home to Crystal Palace, Apr 10, 2005), 16 years, 271 days.

Youngest Premier League captain: Lee Cattermole (Middlesbrough away to Fulham, May 7, 2006) aged 18 years, 47 days.

Youngest player sent off in Premier League: Wayne Rooney (Everton, away to Birmingham, Dec 26, 2002) aged 17 years, 59 days.

Youngest First Division hat-trick scorer: Alan Shearer, aged 17 years, 240 days, in Southampton's 4-2 home win v Arsenal (Apr 9, 1988) on his full debut. Previously, Jimmy Greaves (17 years, 309 days) with 4 goals for Chelsea at home to Portsmouth (7-4), Christmas Day, 1957.

Youngest to complete 100 Football League goals: Jimmy Greaves (20 years, 261 days) when he did so for Chelsea v Manchester City, Nov 19, 1960.

Youngest players in Football League: Reuben Noble-Lazarus (Barnsley 84th minute sub at Ipswich, Sep 30, 2008, Champ) aged 15 years, 45 days; Mason Bennett (Derby at Middlesbrough, Champ, Oct 22, 2011) aged 15 years, 99 days; Albert Geldard (Bradford PA v Millwall, Div 2, Sep 16, 1929) aged 15 years, 158 days; Ken Roberts (Wrexham v Bradford Park Avenue, Div 3 North, Sep 1, 1951) also 15 years, 158 days.

Youngest Football League scorer: Ronnie Dix (for Bristol Rov v Norwich, Div 3 South, Mar 3, 1928) aged 15 years, 180 days.

Youngest player in Scottish League: Goalkeeper Ronnie Simpson (Queens Park) aged 15 in 1946.

Youngest player in FA Cup: Andy Awford, Worcester City's England Schoolboy defender, aged 15 years, 88 days when he substituted in second half away to Boreham Wood (3rd qual round) on Oct 10, 1987.

Youngest player in FA Cup proper: Luke Freeman, Gillingham substitute striker (15 years, 233 days) away to Barnet in 1st round, Nov 10, 2007.

Youngest FA Cup scorer: Sean Cato (16 years, 25 days), second half sub in Barrow Town's 7-2 win away to Rothwell Town (prelim rd), Sep 3, 2011.

Youngest Wembley Cup Final captain: Barry Venison (Sunderland v Norwich, Milk Cup Final, Mar 24, 1985 – replacing suspended captain Shaun Elliott) – aged 20 years, 220 days.

Youngest FA Cup-winning captain: Bobby Moore (West Ham, 1964, v Preston), aged 23 years, 20 days.

Youngest FA Cup Final captain: David Nish aged 21 years and 212 days old when he captained Leicester against Manchester City at Wembley on Apr 26, 1969.

Youngest FA Cup Final player: Curtis Weston (Millwall sub last 3 mins v Manchester Utd, 2004) aged 17 years, 119 days.

Youngest FA Cup Final scorer: Norman Whiteside (Manchester Utd v Brighton, 1983 replay, Wembley), aged 18 years, 19 days.

Youngest FA Cup Final managers: Stan Cullis, Wolves (32) v Leicester, 1949; Steve Coppell, Crystal Palace (34) v Manchester Utd, 1990; Ruud Gullit, Chelsea (34) v Middlesbrough, 1997.

Youngest player in Football League Cup: Chris Coward (Stockport) sub v Sheffield Wed, 2nd Round, Aug 23, 2005, aged 16 years and 31 days.

Youngest Wembley scorer: Norman Whiteside (Manchester Utd v Liverpool, Milk Cup Final, Mar 26, 1983) aged 17 years, 324 days.

Youngest Wembley Cup Final goalkeeper: Chris Woods (18 years, 125 days) for Nottm Forest v Liverpool, League Cup Final on Mar 18, 1978.

Youngest Wembley FA Cup Final goalkeeper: Peter Shilton (19 years, 219 days) for Leicester v Manchester City, Apr 26, 1969.

Youngest senior international at Wembley: Salomon Olembe (sub for Cameroon v England, Nov 15, 1997), aged 16 years, 342 days.

Youngest winning manager at Wembley: Stan Cullis, aged 32 years, 187 days, as manager of Wolves, FA Cup winners on April 30 1949.

Youngest scorer in full international: Mohamed Kallon (Sierra Leone v Congo, African Nations Cup, Apr 22, 1995), reported as aged 15 years, 192 days.

Youngest English scorer in Champions League: Alex Oxlade-Chamberlain (Arsenal v Olympiacos, Sep 28, 2011) aged 18 years 1 month, 13 days

Youngest player sent off in World Cup Final series: Rigobert Song (Cameroon v Brazil, in USA, Jun 1994) aged 17 years, 358 days.

Youngest FA Cup Final referee: Kevin Howley, of Middlesbrough, aged 35 when in charge of Wolves v Blackburn, 1960.

Youngest player in England U-23 team: Duncan Edwards (v Italy, Bologna, Jan 20, 1954), aged 17 years, 112 days.

Youngest player in England U-21 team: Theo Walcott (v Moldova, Ipswich, Aug 15, 2006), aged 17 years, 152 days.

Youngest player in Scotland U-21 team: Christian Dailly (v Romania, Hampden Park, Sep 11, 1990), aged 16 years, 330 days.

Youngest player in senior football: Cameron Campbell Buchanan, Scottish-born outside right, aged 14 years, 57 days when he played for Wolves v WBA in War-time League match, Sep 26, 1942.

Youngest player in peace-time senior match: Eamon Collins (Blackpool v Kilmarnock, Anglo-Scottish Cup quarter-final 1st leg, Sep 9, 1980) aged 14 years, 323 days.

World's youngest player in top division match: Centre-forward Fernando Rafael Garcia, aged 13, played for 23 minutes for Peruvian club Juan Aurich in 3-1 win against Estudiantes on May 19, 2001.

Oldest player to appear in Football League: New Brighton manager Neil McBain (51 years, 120 days) as emergency goalkeeper away to Hartlepool (Div 3 North, Mar 15, 1947).

Other oldest post-war League players: Sir Stanley Matthews (Stoke, 1965, 50 years, 5 days); Peter Shilton (Leyton Orient 1997, 47 years, 126 days); Kevin Poole (Burton, 2010, 46 years, 291 days); Dave Beasant (Brighton 2003, 44 years, 46 days); Alf Wood (Coventry, 1958, 43 years, 199 days); Tommy Hutchison (Swansea City, 1991, 43 years, 172 days).

Oldest Football League debutant: Andy Cunningham, for Newcastle at Leicester (Div 1) on Feb

2, 1929, aged 38 years, 2 days.

Oldest post-war debut in English League: Defender David Donaldson (35 years, 7 months, 23 days) for Wimbledon on entry to Football League (Div 4) away to Halifax, Aug 20, 1977.

Oldest player to appear in First Division: Sir Stanley Matthews (Stoke v Fulham, Feb 6, 1965), aged 50 years, 5 days – on that his last League appearance, the only 50-year-old ever to play in the top division.

Oldest players in Premier League: Goalkeepers John Burridge (Manchester City v QPR, May 14, 1995), 43 years, 5 months, 11 days; Alec Chamberlain (Watford v Newcastle, May 13, 2007) 42 years, 11 months, 23 days; Steve Ogrizovic (Coventry v Sheffield Wed, May 6, 2000), 42 years, 7 months, 24 days; Brad Friedel (Tottenham v Newcastle, Nov 10, 2013) 42 years, 4 months, 22 days; Neville Southall (Bradford City v Leeds, Mar 12, 2000), 41 years, 5 months, 26 days. Outfield: Teddy Sheringham (West Ham v Manchester City, Dec 30, 2006), 40 years, 8 months, 28 days; Ryan Giggs (Manchester Utd v Hull, May 6, 2014), 40 years, 5 months, 7 days; Gordon Strachan (Coventry City v Derby, May 3, 1997), 40 years, 2 months, 24 days.

Oldest player for British professional club: John Ryan (owner-chairman of Conference club Doncaster, played as substitute for last minute in 4-2 win at Hereford on Apr 26, 2003), aged 52 years, 11 months, 3 weeks.

Oldest FA Cup Final player: Walter (Billy) Hampson (Newcastle v Aston Villa on Apr 26, 1924), aged 41 years, 257 days.

Oldest captain and goalkeeper in FA Cup Final: David James (Portsmouth v Chelsea, May 15, 2010) aged 39 years, 287 days.

Oldest FA Cup Final scorers: Bert Turner (Charlton v Derby, Apr 27, 1946) aged 36 years, 312 days. Scored for both sides. Teddy Sheringham (West Ham v Liverpool, May 13, 2006) aged 40 years, 41 days. Scored in penalty shoot-out.

Oldest FA Cup-winning team: Arsenal 1950 (average age 31 years, 2 months). Eight of the players were over 30, with the three oldest centre-half Leslie Compton 37, and skipper Joe Mercer and goalkeeper George Swindin, both 35.

Oldest World Cup-winning captain: Dino Zoff, Italy's goalkeeper v W Germany in 1982 Final, aged 40 years, 92 days.

Oldest player capped by England: Stanley Matthews (v Denmark, Copenhagen, May 15, 1957), aged 42 years, 103 days.

Oldest England scorer: Stanley Matthews (v N Ireland, Belfast, Oct 6, 1956), aged 41 years, 248 days.

Oldest British international player: Billy Meredith (Wales v England at Highbury, Mar 15, 1920), aged 45 years, 229 days.

Oldest 'new caps': Goalkeeper Alexander Morten, aged 41 years, 113 days when earning his only England Cap against Scotland on Mar 8, 1873; Arsenal centre-half Leslie Compton, at 38 years, 64 days when he made his England debut in 4-2 win against Wales at Sunderland on Nov 15, 1950. **For Scotland:** Goalkeeper Ronnie Simpson (Celtic) at 36 years, 186 days v England at Wembley, Apr 15, 1967.

Longest Football League career: This spanned 32 years and 10 months, by Stanley Matthews (Stoke, Blackpool, Stoke) from Mar 19, 1932 until Feb 6, 1965.

Shortest FA Cup-winning captain: 5ft 4in – Bobby Kerr (Sunderland v Leeds, 1973).

SHIRT NUMBERING

Numbering players in Football League matches was made compulsory in 1939. Players wore numbered shirts (1-22) in the FA Cup Final as an experiment in 1933 (Everton 1-11 v Manchester City 12-22).

Squad numbers for players were introduced by the Premier League at the start of season 1993–94. They were optional in the Football League until made compulsory in 1999–2000.

Names on shirts: For first time, players wore names as well as numbers on shirts in League Cup and FA Cup Finals, 1993.

SUBSTITUTES

In **1965**, the Football League, by 39 votes to 10, agreed that **one substitute** be allowed for an injured player at any time during a League match. First substitute used in Football League: Keith Peacock (Charlton), away to Bolton in Div 2, Aug 21, 1965.

Two substitutes per team were approved for the League (Littlewoods) Cup and FA Cup in season 1986–87 and two were permitted in the Football League for the first time in 1987–88.

Three substitutes (one a goalkeeper), two of which could be used, introduced by the Premier League for 1992–93. The Football League followed suit for 1993–94.

Three substitutes (one a goalkeeper) were allowed at the World Cup Finals for the first time at US '94.

Three substitutes (any position) introduced by Premier League and Football League in 1995–96.

Five named substitutes (three of which could be used) introduced in Premier League in 1996–97, in FA Cup in 1997–98, League Cup in 1998–99 and Football League in 1999–2000.

Seven named substitutes for Premier League, FA Cup and League Cup in 2008–09. Still only three to be used. Football League adopted this rule for 2009–10, reverted to five in 2011–12 and went back to seven for the 2012–13 season.

First substitute to score in FA Cup Final: Eddie Kelly (Arsenal v Liverpool, 1971). The **first recorded use** of a substitute was in 1889 (Wales v Scotland at Wrexham on Apr 15) when Sam Gillam arrived late – although he was a Wrexham player – and Allen Pugh (Rhostellyn) was allowed to keep goal until he turned up. The match ended 0-0.

When **Dickie Roose**, the Welsh goalkeeper, was injured against England at Wrexham, Mar 16, 1908, **Dai Davies** (Bolton) was allowed to take his place as substitute. Thus Wales used 12 players. England won 7-1.

END OF WAGE LIMIT

Freedom from the maximum wage system – in force since the formation of the Football League in 1888 – was secured by the Professional Footballers' Association in 1961. About this time Italian clubs renewed overtures for the transfer of British stars and Fulham's **Johnny Haynes** became the first British player to earn £100 a week.

THE BOSMAN RULING

On Dec 15, 1995 the **European Court of Justice** ruled that clubs had no right to transfer fees for out-of-contract players, and the outcome of the 'Bosman case' irrevocably changed football's player-club relationship. It began in 1990, when the contract of 26-year-old **Jean-Marc Bosman**, a midfield player with FC Liege, Belgium, expired. French club Dunkirk wanted him but were unwilling to pay the £500,000 transfer fee, so Bosman was compelled to remain with Liege. He responded with a lawsuit against his club and UEFA on the grounds of 'restriction of trade', and after five years at various court levels the European Court of Justice ruled not only in favour of Bosman but of all professional footballers.

The end of restrictive labour practices revolutionised the system. It led to a proliferation of transfers, rocketed the salaries of elite players who, backed by an increasing army of agents, found themselves in a vastly improved bargaining position as they moved from team to team, league to league, nation to nation. Removing the limit on the number of foreigners clubs could field brought an increasing ratio of such signings, not least in England and Scotland.

Bosman's one-man stand opened the way for footballers to become millionaires, but ended his own career. All he received for his legal conflict was 16 million Belgian francs (£312,000) in compensation, a testimonial of poor reward and martyrdom as the man who did most to change the face of football.

By 2011, he was living on Belgian state benefits, saying: 'I have made the world of football rich and shifted the power from clubs to players. Now I find myself with nothing.'

INTERNATIONAL SHOCK RESULTS

1950   USA 1 England 0 (World Cup).
1953   England 3 Hungary 6 (friendly).

1954	Hungary 7 England 1 (friendly)
1966	North Korea 1 Italy 0 (World Cup).
1982	Spain 0, Northern Ireland 1; Algeria 2, West Germany 1 (World Cup).
1990	Cameroon 1 Argentina 0; Scotland 0 Costa Rica 1; Sweden 1 Costa Rica 2 (World Cup).
1990	Faroe Islands 1 Austria 0 (European Champ qual).
1992	Denmark 2 Germany 0 (European Champ Final).
1993	USA 2 England 0 (US Cup tournament).
1993	Argentina 0 Colombia 5 (World Cup qual).
1993	France 2 Israel 3 (World Cup qual).
1994	Bulgaria 2 Germany 1 (World Cup).
1994	Moldova 3 Wales 2; Georgia 5 Wales 0 (European Champ qual).
1995	Belarus 1 Holland 0 (European Champ qual).
1996	Nigeria 4 Brazil 3 (Olympics).
1998	USA 1 Brazil 0 (Concacaf Gold Cup).
1998	Croatia 3 Germany 0 (World Cup).
2000	Scotland 0 Australia 2 (friendly).
2001	Australia 1 France 0; Australia 1, Brazil 0 (Confederations Cup).
2001	Honduras 2 Brazil 0 (Copa America).
2001	Germany 1 England 5 (World Cup qual).
2002	France 0 Senegal 1; South Korea 2 Italy 1 (World Cup).
2003:	England 1 Australia 3 (friendly).
2004:	Portugal 0 Greece 1 (European Champ Final).
2005:	Northern Ireland 1 England 0 (World Cup qual).
2014:	Holland 5 Spain 1 (World Cup).
2014:	Brazil 1 Germany 7 (World Cup).

GREAT RECOVERIES – DOMESTIC FOOTBALL

On Dec 21, 1957, **Charlton** were losing 5-1 against Huddersfield (Div 2) at The Valley with only 28 minutes left, and from the 15th minute, had been reduced to ten men by injury, but they won 7-6, with left-winger Johnny Summers scoring five goals. **Huddersfield** (managed by Bill Shankly) remain the only team to score six times in a League match and lose. On Boxing Day, 1927 in Div 3 South, **Northampton** won 6-5 at home to Luton after being 1-5 down at half-time. Season 2010–11 produced a Premier League record for **Newcastle**, who came from 4-0 down at home to Arsenal to draw 4-4. Previous instance of a team retrieving a four-goal deficit in the top division to draw was in 1984 when Newcastle trailed at QPR in a game which ended 5-5. In the 2012-13 League Cup, **Arsenal** were 0-4 down in a fourth round tie at Reading, levelled at 4-4 and went on to win 7-5 in extra-time.

MATCHES OFF

Worst day for postponements: Feb 9, 1963, when 57 League fixtures in England and Scotland were frozen off. Only 7 Football League matches took place, and the entire Scottish programme was wiped out.

Other weather-hit days:

Jan 12, 1963 and Feb 2, 1963 – on both those Saturdays, only 4 out of 44 Football League matches were played.

Jan 1, 1979 – 43 out of 46 Football League fixtures postponed.

Jan 17, 1987 – 37 of 45 scheduled Football League fixtures postponed; only 2 Scottish matches survived.

Feb 8–9, 1991 – only 4 of the week-end's 44 Barclays League matches survived the freeze-up (4 of the postponements were on Friday night). In addition, 11 Scottish League matches were off.

Jan 27, 1996 – 44 Cup and League matches in England and Scotland were frozen off.

On the weekend of Jan 9, 10, 11, 2010, 46 League and Cup matches in England and Scotland were victims of the weather. On the weekend of Dec 18-21, 2010, 49 matches were frozen off in England and Scotland.

Fewest matches left on one day by postponements was during the Second World War – Feb 3, 1940 when, because of snow, ice and fog only one out of 56 regional league fixtures took place. It resulted Plymouth Argyle 10, Bristol City 3.

The Scottish Cup second round tie between Inverness Thistle and Falkirk in season 1978–79 was **postponed 29 times** because of snow and ice. First put off on Jan 6, it was eventually played on Feb 22. Falkirk won 4-0.

Pools Panel's busiest days: Jan 17, 1987 and Feb 9, 1991 – on both dates they gave their verdict on 48 postponed coupon matches.

FEWEST 'GAMES OFF'

Season 1947–48 was the best since the war for English League fixtures being played to schedule. Only six were postponed.

LONGEST SEASON

The latest that League football has been played in a season was **Jun 7, 1947** (six weeks after the FA Cup Final). The season was extended because of mass postponements caused by bad weather in mid-winter.

The latest the FA Cup competition has ever been completed was in season 1981–82, when Tottenham beat QPR 1-0 in a Final replay at Wembley on May 27.

Worst winter hold-up was in season 1962–63. The Big Freeze began on Boxing Day and lasted until Mar, with nearly 500 first-class matches postponed. The FA Cup 3rd round was the longest on record – it began with only three out of 32 ties playable on Jan 5 and ended 66 days and 261 postponements later on Mar 11. The Lincoln–Coventry tie was put off 15 times. The Pools Panel was launched that winter, on Jan 26, 1963.

HOTTEST DAYS

The Nationwide League kicked off season 2003–04 on Aug 9 with pitch temperatures of 102 degrees recorded at Luton v Rushden and Bradford v Norwich. On the following day, there was a pitch temperature of 100 degrees for the Community Shield match between Manchester Utd and Arsenal at Cardiff's Millennium Stadium. Wembley's pitch-side thermometer registered 107 degrees for the 2009 Chelsea–Everton FA Cup Final.

FOOTBALL ASSOCIATION SECRETARIES/CHIEF EXECUTIVES

1863–66 Ebenezer Morley; 1866–68 **Robert Willis**; 1868–70 **RG Graham**; 1870–95 **Charles Alcock** (paid from 1887); 1895–1934 **Sir Frederick Wall**; 1934–62 **Sir Stanley Rous**; 1962–73 **Denis Follows** (latterly chief executive); 1973–89 **Ted Croker** (latterly chief executive); 1989–99 **Graham Kelly** (chief executive); 2000–02 **Adam Crozier** (chief executive); 2003–04 **Mark Palios** (chief executive); 2005–08: **Brian Barwick** (chief executive); 2009–10 **Ian Watmore** (chief executive); 2010 **Alex Horne** (general secretary).

FOOTBALL'S SPONSORS

Football League: Canon 1983–86; Today Newspaper 1986–87; Barclays 1987–93; Endsleigh Insurance 1993–96; Nationwide Building Society 1996–2004; Coca-Cola 2004–10; npower 2010–14; Sky Bet from 2014.

League Cup: Milk Cup 1982–86; Littlewoods 1987–90; Rumbelows 1991–92; Coca-Cola 1993–98; Worthington 1998–2003; Carling 2003–12; Capital One from 2012.

Premier League: Carling 1993–2001; Barclaycard 2001–04; Barclays from 2004.

FA Cup: Littlewoods 1994–98; AXA 1998–2002; E.ON 2006–11; Budweiser from 2011.

SOCCER HEADQUARTERS

Football Association: PO Box 1966, London SW1P 9EQ.

Premier League: 30 Gloucester Place, London W1U 8PL.

Football League: Edward VII Quay, Navigation Way, Preston PR2 2YF. London Office: 30 Gloucester Place, London W1U 8FL.

League Managers' Association: St Georges Park, Newborough Road, Burton on Trent DE13 9PD.
Professional Footballers' Association: 2 Oxford Court, Bishopsgate, Manchester M2 3WQ.
Scottish Football Association: Hampden Park, Glasgow G42 9AY.
Scottish Professional Football League: Hampden Park, Glasgow G42 9DE
Irish Football Association: 20 Windsor Avenue, Belfast BT9 6EG.
Irish Football League: Benmore House, 343-353 Lisburn Road, Belfast BT9 7EN.
League of Ireland: Sports Campus, Abbotstown, Dublin 15.
Football Association of Ireland: Sports Campus, Abbotstown, Dublin 15.
Welsh Football Association: 11/12 Neptune Court, Vanguard Way, Cardiff CF24 5PJ.
FIFA: P.O. Box 85, 8030 Zurich, Switzerland.
UEFA: Route de Geneve, CH-1260, Nyon, Geneva, Switzerland.

NEW HOMES OF SOCCER

Newly-constructed League grounds in England since the war: 1946 Hull (Boothferry Park); 1950 Port Vale (Vale Park); 1955 Southend (Roots Hall); 1988 Scunthorpe (Glanford Park); 1990 Walsall (Bescot Stadium); 1990 Wycombe (Adams Park); 1992 Chester (Deva Stadium); 1993 Millwall (New Den); 1994 Huddersfield (McAlpine Stadium); 1994 Northampton (Sixfields Stadium); 1995 Middlesbrough (Riverside Stadium); 1997 Bolton (Reebok Stadium); 1997 Derby (Pride Park); 1997 Stoke (Britannia Stadium); 1997 Sunderland (Stadium of Light); 1998 Reading (Madejski Stadium); 1999 Wigan (JJB Stadium); 2001 Southampton (St Mary's Stadium); 2001 Oxford Utd (Kassam Stadium); 2002 Leicester (Walkers Stadium); 2002 Hull (Kingston Communications Stadium); 2003 Manchester City (City of Manchester Stadium); 2003 Darlington (New Stadium); 2005 Coventry (Ricoh Arena); Swansea (Stadium of Swansea, Morfa); 2006 Arsenal (Emirates Stadium); 2007 Milton Keynes Dons (Stadium: MK); Shrewsbury (New Meadow); 2008 Colchester (Community Stadium); 2009 Cardiff City Stadium; 2010 Chesterfield (b2net Stadium), Morecambe (Globe Arena); 2011 Brighton (American Express Stadium); 2012 Rotherham (New York Stadium).

Bolton now Macron Stadium; Chesterfield now Proact Stadium; Derby now iPro Stadium; Huddersfield now John Smith's Stadium; Leicester now King Power Stadium; Manchester City now Etihad Stadium; Shrewsbury now Greenhous Meadow Stadium; Swansea now Liberty Stadium; Walsall now Banks's Stadium; Wigan now DW Stadium.

NATIONAL FOOTBALL CENTRE

The FA's new £120m centre at St George's Park, Burton upon Trent, was opened on Oct 9, 20012 by the Duke of Cambridge, president of the FA. The site covers 330 acres, has 12 full-size pitches (5 with undersoil heating and floodlighting). There are 5 gyms, a 90-seat lecture theatre, a hydrotherapy unit with swimming pool for the treatment of injuries and two hotels. It is the base for England teams, men and women, at all levels.

GROUND-SHARING

Manchester Utd played their home matches at **Manchester City's** Maine Road ground for 8 years after Old Trafford was bomb-damaged in Aug 1941. **Crystal Palace** and **Charlton** shared Selhurst Park (1985–91); **Bristol Rov** and **Bath City** (Twerton Park, Bath, 1986–96); **Partick Thistle** and **Clyde** (Firhill Park, Glasgow, 1986–91; in seasons 1990–01, 1991–92 **Chester** shared **Macclesfield's** ground (Moss Rose).

Crystal Palace and **Wimbledon** shared Selhurst Park, from season 1991–92, when **Charlton** (tenants) moved to rent Upton Park from **West Ham**, until 2003 when Wimbledon relocated to Milton Keynes. **Clyde** moved to Douglas Park, **Hamilton Academical's** home, in 1991–92. **Stirling Albion** shared Stenhousemuir's ground, Ochilview Park, in 1992–93. In 1993–94, **Clyde** shared **Partick's** home until moving to Cumbernauld. In 1994–95, **Celtic** shared Hampden Park with **Queen's Park** (while Celtic Park was redeveloped); **Hamilton** shared **Partick's** ground. **Airdrie** shared **Clyde's** Broadwood Stadium. **Bristol Rov** left **Bath City's** ground at the start of season 1996–97, sharing Bristol Rugby Club's Memorial Ground.

444

Clydebank shared **Dumbarton**'s Boghead Park from 1996–97 until renting **Greenock Morton**'s Cappielow Park in season 1999–2000. **Brighton** shared **Gillingham**'s ground in seasons 1997–98, 1998–99. **Fulham** shared **QPR**'s home at Loftus Road in seasons 2002–03, 2003–04, returning to Craven Cottage in Aug 2004. **Coventry** began playing their home games at Northampton in season 2013–14 while planning for a new stadium after moving out of the Ricoh Arena.

Inverness Caledonian Thistle moved to share **Aberdeen**'s Pittodrie Stadium in 2004–05 after being promoted to the SPL; **Gretna's** home matches on arrival in the SPL in 2007–08 were held at Motherwell and Livingston.

ARTIFICIAL TURF

QPR were the first British club to install an artificial pitch, in 1981. They were followed by **Luton** in 1985, and **Oldham** and **Preston** in **1986**. QPR reverted to grass in 1988, as did Luton and promoted Oldham in season 1991–92 (when artificial pitches were banned in Div 1). **Preston** were the last Football League club playing 'on plastic' in 1993–94, and their Deepdale ground was restored to grass for the start of 1994–95.

Stirling were the **first Scottish club** to play on plastic, in season 1987–88.

DOUBLE RUNNERS-UP

There have been nine instances of clubs finishing runner-up in **both the League Championship** and **FA Cup** in the same season: 1928 Huddersfield; 1932 Arsenal; 1939 Wolves; 1962 Burnley; 1965 and 1970 Leeds; 1986 Everton; 1995 Manchester Utd; 2001 Arsenal.

CORNER-KICK RECORDS

Not a single corner-kick was recorded when **Newcastle** drew 0-0 at home to **Portsmouth** (Div 1) on Dec 5, 1931.

The record for **most corners** in a match for one side is believed to be **Sheffield Utd's 28** to **West Ham's 1** in Div 2 at Bramall Lane on Oct 14, 1989. For all their pressure, Sheffield Utd lost 2-0.

Nottm Forest led **Southampton** 22-2 on corners (Premier League, Nov 28, 1992) but lost the match 1-2.

Tommy Higginson (Brentford, 1960s) once passed back to his own goalkeeper from a corner kick.

When **Wigan** won 4-0 at home to **Cardiff** (Div 2) on Feb 16, 2002, all four goals were headed in from corners taken by N Ireland international **Peter Kennedy**.

Steve Staunton (Rep of Ireland) is believed to be the only player to score direct from a corner in **two** Internationals.

In the 2012 Champions League Final, **Bayern Munich** forced 20 corners without scoring, while **Chelsea** scored from their only one.

SACKED AT HALF-TIME

Leyton Orient sacked **Terry Howard** on his 397th appearance for the club – at half-time in a Second Division home defeat against Blackpool (Feb 7, 1995) for 'an unacceptable performance'. He was fined two weeks' wages, given a free transfer and moved to Wycombe.

Bobby Gould resigned as **Peterborough**'s head coach at half-time in their 1-0 defeat in the LDV Vans Trophy 1st round at Bristol City on Sep 29, 2004.

Harald Schumacher, former Germany goalkeeper, was sacked as Fortuna Koln coach when they were two down at half-time against Waldhof Mannheim (Dec 15, 1999). They lost 5-1.

MOST GAMES BY 'KEEPER FOR ONE CLUB

Alan Knight made 683 League appearances for Portsmouth, over 23 seasons (1978–2000), a record for a goalkeeper at one club. The previous holder was Peter Bonetti with 600 League games for Chelsea (20 seasons, 1960–79).

PLAYED TWO GAMES ON SAME DAY

Jack Kelsey played full-length matches for both club and country on Wednesday Nov 26, 1958. In the afternoon he kept goal for Wales in a 2-2 draw against England at Villa Park, and he then drove to Highbury to help Arsenal win 3-1 in a prestigious floodlit friendly against Juventus.

On the same day, winger **Danny Clapton** played for England (against Wales and Kelsey) and then in part of Arsenal's match against Juventus.

On Nov 11, 1987, **Mark Hughes** played for Wales against Czechoslovakia (European Championship) in Prague, then flew to Munich and went on as substitute that night in a winning Bayern Munich team, to whom he was on loan from Barcelona.

On Feb 16, 1993 goalkeeper **Scott Howie** played in Scotland's 3-0 U-21 win v Malta at Tannadice Park, Dundee (ko 1.30pm) and the same evening played in Clyde's 2-1 home win v Queen of South (Div 2).

Ryman League **Hornchurch**, faced by end-of-season fixture congestion, played **two matches** on the same night (May 1, 2001). They lost 2-1 at home to Ware and drew 2-2 at Clapton.

RECORD LOSS

Manchester City made a record loss of £194.9m in the 2010–11 financial year.

FIRST 'MATCH OF THE DAY'

BBC TV (recorded highlights): Liverpool 3, Arsenal 2 on Aug 22, 1964. **First complete match to be televised:** Arsenal 3, Everton 2 on Aug 29, 1936. **First League match televised in colour:** Liverpool 2, West Ham 0 on Nov 15, 1969.

'MATCH OF THE DAY' – BIGGEST SCORES

Football League: Tottenham 9, Bristol Rov 0 (Div 2, 1977–78). **Premier League:** Nottm Forest 1, Manchester Utd 8 (1998–99); Portsmouth 7 Reading 4 (2007–08).

FIRST COMMENTARY ON RADIO

Arsenal 1 Sheffield Utd 1 (Div 1) broadcast on BBC, Jan 22, 1927.

OLYMPIC FOOTBALL WINNERS

1908 Great Britain (in London); **1912** Great Britain (Stockholm); **1920** Belgium (Antwerp); **1924** Uruguay (Paris); **1928** Uruguay (Amsterdam); **1932** No soccer in Los Angeles Olympics; **1936** Italy (Berlin); **1948** Sweden (London); **1952** Hungary (Helsinki); **1956** USSR (Melbourne); **1960** Yugoslavia (Rome); **1964** Hungary (Tokyo); **1968** Hungary (Mexico City); **1972** Poland (Munich); **1976** E Germany (Montreal); **1980** Czechoslovakia (Moscow); **1984** France (Los Angeles); **1988** USSR (Seoul); **1992** Spain (Barcelona); **1996** Nigeria (Atlanta); **2000** Cameroon (Sydney); **2004** Argentina (Athens); **2008** Argentina (Beijing); **2012** Mexico (Wembley).

Highest scorer in Final tournament: Ferenc Bene (Hungary) 12 goals, 1964.

Record crowd for Olympic Soccer Final: 108,800 (France v Brazil, Los Angeles 1984).

MOST AMATEUR CUP WINS

Bishop Auckland set the FA Amateur Cup record with 10 wins, and in 1957 became the only club to carry off the trophy in three successive seasons. The competition was discontinued after the Final on Apr 20, 1974. (Bishop's Stortford 4, Ilford 1, at Wembley).

FOOTBALL FOUNDATION

This was formed (May 2000) to replace the **Football Trust**, which had been in existence since 1975 as an initiative of the Pools companies to provide financial support at all levels, from schools football to safety and ground improvement work throughout the game.

SEVEN-FIGURE TESTIMONIALS

The first was **Sir Alex Ferguson**'s at Old Trafford on Oct 11, 1999, when a full-house of 54,842

saw a Rest of the World team beat Manchester Utd 4-2. United's manager pledged that a large percentage of the estimated £1m receipts would go to charity.

Estimated receipts of £1m and over came from testimonials for **Denis Irwin** (Manchester Utd) against Manchester City at Old Trafford on Aug 16, 2000 (45,158); **Tom Boyd** (Celtic) against Manchester Utd at Celtic Park on May 15, 2001 (57,000) and **Ryan Giggs** (Manchester Utd) against Celtic on Aug 1, 2001 (66,967).

Tony Adams' second testimonial (1-1 v Celtic on May 13, 2002) two nights after Arsenal completed the Double, was watched by 38,021 spectators at Highbury. Of £1m receipts, he donated £500,000 to Sporting Chance, the charity that helps sportsmen/women with drink, drug, gambling problems.

Sunderland and a Republic of Ireland XI drew 0-0 in front of 35,702 at the Stadium of Light on May 14, 2002. The beneficiary, **Niall Quinn**, donated his testimonial proceeds, estimated at £1m, to children's hospitals in Sunderland and Dublin, and to homeless children in Africa and Asia.

A record testimonial crowd of 69,591 for **Roy Keane** at Old Trafford on May 9, 2006 netted more than £2m for charities in Dublin, Cork and Manchester. Manchester Utd beat Celtic 1-0, with Keane playing for both teams.

Alan Shearer's testimonial on May 11, 2006, watched by a crowd of 52,275 at St James' Park, raised more than £1m. The club's record scorer, in his farewell match, came off the bench in stoppage time to score the penalty that gave Newcastle a 3-2 win over Celtic. Total proceeds from his testimonial events, £1.64m, were donated to 14 charities in the north-east.

Ole Gunnar Solskjaer, who retired after 12 years as a Manchester Utd player, had a crowd of 68,868, for his testimonial on Aug 2, 2008 (United 1 Espanyol 0). He donated the estimated receipts of £2m to charity, including the opening of a dozen schools In Africa.

Liverpool's **Jamie Carragher** had his testimonial against Everton (4-1) on Sep 4, 2010. It was watched by a crowd of 35,631 and raised an estimated £1m for his foundation, which supports community projects on Merseyside.

Gary Neville donated receipts of around £1m from his testimonial against Juventus (2-1) in front of 42,000 on May 24, 2011, to charities and building a Supporters' Centre near Old Trafford.

Paul Scholes had a crowd of 75,000 for his testimonial, Manchester United against New York Cosmos, on Aug 5, 2011. Receipts were £1.5m.

WHAT IT USED TO COST

Minimum admission to League football was one shilling in 1939 After the war, it was increased to 1s 3d in 1946; 1s 6d in 1951; 1s 9d in 1952; 2s in 1955; 2s 6d; in 1960; 4s in 1965; 5s in 1968; 6s in 1970; and 8s (40p) in 1972 After that, the fixed minimum charge was dropped.

Wembley's first Cup Final programme in 1923 cost three pence ($1^{1}/4$p in today's money). The programme for the 'farewell' FA Cup Final in May, 2000 was priced £10.

FA Cup Final ticket prices in 2011 reached record levels – £115, £85, £65 and £45.

WHAT THEY USED TO EARN

In the 1930s, First Division players were on £8 a week (£6 in close season) plus bonuses of £2 win, £1 draw. The maximum wage went up to £12 when football resumed post-war in 1946 and had reached £20 by the time the limit was abolished in 1961.

EUROPEAN TROPHY WINNERS

European Cup/Champions League: 10 Real Madrid; **7** AC Milan; **5** Liverpool, Bayern Munich; **4** Ajax, Barcelona; **3** Inter Milan, Manchester Utd; **2** Benfica, Juventus, Nottm Forest, Porto; **1** Aston Villa, Borussia Dortmund, Celtic, Chelsea, Feyenoord, Hamburg, Marseille, PSV Eindhoven, Red Star Belgrade, Steaua Bucharest

Cup-Winners' Cup: 4 Barcelona; **2** Anderlecht, Chelsea, Dynamo Kiev, AC Milan; **1** Aberdeen, Ajax, Arsenal, Atletico Madrid, Bayern Munich, Borussia Dortmund, Dynamo Tbilisi,

Everton, Fiorentina, Hamburg, Juventus, Lazio, Magdeburg, Manchester City, Manchester Utd, Mechelen, Paris St Germain, Parma, Rangers, Real Zaragoza, Sampdoria, Slovan Bratislava, Sporting Lisbon, Tottenham, Valencia, Werder Bremen, West Ham.

UEFA Cup: 3 Barcelona, Inter Milan, Juventus, Liverpool, Valencia; **2** Borussia Moenchengladbach, Feyenoord, Gothenburg, Leeds, Parma, Real Madrid, Sevilla, Tottenham; **1** Anderlecht, Ajax, Arsenal, Bayer Leverkusen, Bayern Munich, CSKA Moscow, Dynamo Zagreb, Eintracht Frankfurt, Ferencvaros, Galatasaray, Ipswich, Napoli, Newcastle, Porto, PSV Eindhoven, Real Zaragoza, Roma, Schalke, Shakhtar Donetsk, Zenit St Petersburg.

Europa League: 2 Atletico Madrid, **1** Chelsea, Porto, Sevilla.

- The Champions League was introduced into the European Cup in 1992–93 to counter the threat of a European Super League. The UEFA Cup became the Europa League, with a new format, in season 2009–10.

BRITAIN'S 34 TROPHIES IN EUROPE

Euro Cup/Champs Lge (13)	Cup-Winners' Cup (10)	Fairs/UEFA Cup/Europa Lge (11)
1967 Celtic	1963 Tottenham	1968 Leeds
1968 Manchester Utd	1965 West Ham	1969 Newcastle
1977 Liverpool	1970 Manchester City	1970 Arsenal
1978 Liverpool	1971 Chelsea	1971 Leeds
1979 Nottm Forest	1972 Rangers	1972 Tottenham
1980 Nottm Forest	1983 Aberdeen	1973 Liverpool
1981 Liverpool	1985 Everton	1976 Liverpool
1982 Aston Villa	1991 Manchester Utd	1981 Ipswich
1984 Liverpool	1994 Arsenal	1984 Tottenham
1999 Manchester Utd	1998 Chelsea	2001 Liverpool
2005 Liverpool		2013 Chelsea
2008 Manchester Utd		
2012 Chelsea		

ENGLAND'S EUROPEAN RECORD

Manchester Utd, Chelsea, Arsenal and Liverpool all reached the Champions League quarter-finals in season 2007–08 – the first time one country had provided four of the last eight. For the first time, England supplied both finalists in 2008 (Manchester Utd and Chelsea) and have provided three semi-finalists in 2007–08–09).

END OF CUP-WINNERS' CUP

The **European Cup-Winners' Cup**, inaugurated in 1960–61, terminated with the 1999 Final. The competition merged into a revamped **UEFA Cup**.

From its inception in 1955, the **European Cup** comprised only championship-winning clubs until 1998–99, when selected runners-up were introduced. Further expansion came in 1999–2000 with the inclusion of clubs finishing third in certain leagues and fourth in 2002.

EUROPEAN CLUB COMPETITIONS – SCORING RECORDS

European Cup – record aggregate: 18-0 by Benfica v Dudelange (Lux) (8-0a, 10-0h), prelim rd, 1965–66.

Record single-match score: 11-0 by Dinamo Bucharest v Crusaders (rd 1, 2nd leg, 1973-74 (agg 12-0).

Champions League – record single-match score: Liverpool 8-0 v Besiktas, Group A qual (Nov 6, 2007).

Highest match aggregate: 13 – Bayern Munich 12 Sporting Lisbon 1 (5-0 away, 7-1 at home, 1st ko rd, 2008–09)

Cup-Winners' Cup – *record aggregate: 21-0 by Chelsea v Jeunesse Hautcharage (Lux) (8-0a, 13-0h), 1st rd, 1971–72.

Record single-match score: 16-1 by Sporting Lisbon v Apoel Nicosia, 2nd round, 1st leg, 1963–64 (aggregate was 18-1).

UEFA Cup (prev Fairs Cup) – *Record aggregate: 21-0 by Feyenoord v US Rumelange (Lux) (9-0h, 12-0a), 1st round, 1972–73.

Record single-match score: 14-0 by Ajax Amsterdam v Red Boys (Lux) 1st rd, 2nd leg, 1984–85 (aggregate also 14-0).

Record British score in Europe: 13-0 by **Chelsea** at home to Jeunesse Hautcharage (Lux) in Cup-Winners' Cup 1st round, 2nd leg, 1971–72. Chelsea's overall 21-0 win in that tie is highest aggregate by British club in Europe.

Individual scoring record for European tie (over two legs): 10 goals (6 home, 4 away) by **Kiril Milanov** for Levski Spartak in 19-3 agg win Cup-Winners' Cup 1st round v Lahden Reipas, 1976–77. Next highest: **8 goals** by Jose Altafini for AC Milan v US Luxembourg (European Cup, prelim round, 1962–63, agg 14-0) and by **Peter Osgood** for Chelsea v Jeunesse Hautcharage (Cup-Winners' Cup, 1st round 1971–72, agg 21-0). Altafini and Osgood each scored 5 goals at home, 3 away.

Individual single-match scoring record in European competition: 6 by **Mascarenhas** for Sporting Lisbon in 16-1 Cup-Winner's Cup 2nd round, 1st leg win v Apoel, 1963–64; and by **Lothar Emmerich** for Borussia Dortmund in 8-0 CWC 1st round, 2nd leg win v Floriana 1965–66; and by Kiril Milanov for Levski Spartak in 12-2 CWC 1st round, 1st leg win v Lahden Reipas, 1976–77.

Most goals in single European campaign: 15 by Jurgen Klinsmann for Bayern Munich (UEFA Cup 1995–96).

Most goals by British player in European competition: 30 by Peter Lorimer (Leeds, in 9 campaigns).

Most individual goals in Champions League match: 5 by Lionel Messi (Barcelona) in 7-1 win at home to Bayer Leverkusen in round of 16 second leg, 2011–12.

Most European Cup goals by individual player: 49 by Alfredo di Stefano in 58 apps for Real Madrid (1955–64).

(*Joint record European aggregate)

First European treble: Clarence Seedorf became the first player to win the European Cup with three clubs: Ajax in 1995, Real Madrid in 1998 and AC Milan in 2003.

EUROPEAN FOOTBALL – BIG RECOVERIES

In the most astonishing Final in the history of the European Cup/Champions League, **Liverpool** became the first club to win it from a 3-0 deficit when they beat AC Milan 3-2 on penalties after a 3-3 draw in Istanbul on May 25, 2005. Liverpool's fifth triumph in the competition meant that they would keep the trophy.

The following season, **Middlesbrough** twice recovered from three-goal aggregate deficits in the **UEFA Cup**, beating Basel 4-3 in the quarter finals and Steaua Bucharest by the same scoreline in the semi-finals. In 2010, **Fulham** beat Juventus 5-4 after trailing 1-4 on aggregate in the second leg of their Europa League, Round of 16 match at Craven Cottage.

Two Scottish clubs have won a European tie from a 3-goal, first leg deficit: **Kilmarnock** 0-3, 5-1 v Eintracht Frankfurt (Fairs Cup 1st round, 1964–65); **Hibernian** 1-4, 5-0 v Napoli (Fairs Cup 2nd Round, 1967–68).

English clubs have three times gone out of the **UEFA Cup** after leading 3-0 from the first leg: 1975–76 (2nd Rd) **Ipswich** lost 3-4 on agg to Bruges; 1976–77 (quarter-final) **QPR** lost on penalties to AEK Athens after 3-3 agg; 1977–78 (3rd round) **Ipswich** lost on penalties to Barcelona after 3-3 agg.

On Oct 16, 2012, Sweden recovered from 0-4 down to draw 4-4 with Germany (World Cup qual) in Berlin.

● In the **1966 World Cup quarter-final** (Jul 23) at Goodison Park, North Korea led Portugal 3-0, but Eusebio scored 4 times to give **Portugal** a 5-3 win.

HEAVIEST ENGLISH-CLUB DEFEATS IN EUROPE

(Single-leg scores)

European Cup: Artmedia Bratislava 5, **Celtic** 0 (2nd qual round), Jul 2005 (agg 5-4); Ajax 5, **Liverpool** 1 (2nd round), Dec 1966 (agg 7-3); Real Madrid 5, **Derby** 1 (2nd round), Nov 1975 (agg 6-5).
Cup-Winners' Cup: Sporting Lisbon 5, **Manchester Utd** 0 (quarter-final), Mar 1964 (agg 6-4).
Fairs/UEFA Cup: Bayern Munich 6, **Coventry** 1 (2nd round), Oct 1970 (agg 7-3). **Combined London** team lost 6-0 (agg 8-2) in first Fairs Cup Final in 1958. Barcelona 5, **Chelsea** 0 in Fairs Cup semi-final play-off, 1966, in Barcelona (after 2-2 agg).

SHOCK ENGLISH CLUB DEFEATS

1968–69 (Eur Cup, 1st round): **Manchester City** beaten by Fenerbahce, 1-2 agg.
1971–72 (CWC, 2nd round): **Chelsea** beaten by Atvidaberg on away goals.
1993–94 (Eur Cup, 2nd round): **Manchester Utd** beaten by Galatasaray on away goals.
1994–95 (UEFA Cup, 1st round): **Blackburn** beaten by Trelleborgs, 2-3 agg.
2000–01 (UEFA Cup, 1st round): **Chelsea** beaten by St Gallen, Switz 1-2 agg.

PFA FAIR PLAY AWARD (Bobby Moore Trophy from 1993)

1988	Liverpool	2001	Hull
1989	Liverpool	2002	Crewe
1990	Liverpool	2003	Crewe
1991	Nottm Forest	2004	Crewe
1992	Portsmouth	2005	Crewe
1993	Norwich	2006	Crewe
1994	Crewe	2007	Crewe
1995	Crewe	2008	Crewe
1996	Crewe	2009	Stockport
1997	Crewe	2010	Rochdale
1998	Cambridge Utd	2011	Rochdale
1999	Grimsby	2012	Chesterfield
2000	Crewe	2013	Crewe

RECORD MEDAL SALES

West Ham bought (Jun 2000) the late **Bobby Moore**'s collection of medals and trophies for £1.8m at Christie's auction. It was put up for sale by his first wife Tina and included his World Cup-winner's medal.

A No. 6 duplicate red shirt made for England captain **Bobby Moore** for the 1966 World Cup Final fetched £44,000 at an auction at Wolves' ground in Sep, 1999. Moore kept the shirt he wore in that Final and gave the replica to England physio Harold Shepherdson.

Sir Geoff Hurst's 1966 World Cup-winning shirt fetched a record £91,750 at Christie's in Sep, 2000. His World Cup Final cap fetched £37,600 and his Man of the Match trophy £18,800. Proceeds totalling £274,410 from the 129 lots went to Hurst's three daughters and charities of his choice, including the Bobby Moore Imperial Cancer Research Fund.

In Aug, 2001, Sir Geoff sold his World Cup-winner's medal to his former club West Ham Utd (for their museum) at a reported £150,000.

'The **Billy Wright** Collection' – caps, medals and other memorabilia from his illustrious career – fetched over £100,000 at Christie's in Nov, 1996.

At the sale in Oct 1993, trophies, caps and medals earned by **Ray Kennedy**, former England, Arsenal and Liverpool player, fetched a then record total of £88,407. Kennedy, suffering from Parkinson's Disease, received £73,000 after commission. The PFA paid £31,080 for a total of 60 lots – including a record £16,000 for his 1977 European Cup winner's medal – to be exhibited at their Manchester museum. An anonymous English collector paid £17,000 for the medal and plaque commemorating Kennedy's part in the Arsenal Double in 1971.

Previous record for one player's medals, shirts etc collection: £30,000 (**Bill Foulkes**, Manchester Utd in 1992). The sale of **Dixie Dean**'s medals etc in 1991 realised £28,000.

In Mar, 2001, **Gordon Banks'** 1966 World Cup-winner's medal fetched a new record £124,750. TV's Nick Hancock, a Stoke fan, paid £23,500 for **Sir Stanley Matthews's** 1953 FA Cup-winner's medal. He also bought one of Matthews's England caps for £3,525 and paid £2,350 for a Stoke Div 2 Championship medal (1963).

Dave Mackay's 1961 League Championship and FA Cup winner's medals sold for £18,000 at Sotherby's. Tottenham bought them for their museum.

A selection of England World Cup-winning manager **Sir Alf Ramsey's** memorabilia – England caps, championship medals with Ipswich etc. – fetched more than £80,000 at Christie's. They were offered for sale by his family, and his former clubs Tottenham and Ipswich were among the buyers.

Ray Wilson's 1966 England World Cup-winning shirt fetched £80,750. Also in Mar, 2002, the No. 10 shirt worn by **Pele** in Brazil's World Cup triumph in 1970 was sold for a record £157,750 at Christies. It went to an anonymous telephone bidder.

In Oct, 2003, **George Best's** European Footballer of the Year (1968) trophy was sold to an anonymous British bidder for £167,250 at Bonham's. It was the then most expensive item of sporting memorabilia ever auctioned in Britain.

England captain **Bobby Moore's** 1970 World Cup shirt, which he swapped with Pele after Brazil's 1-0 win in Mexico, was sold for £60,000 at Christie's in Mar, 2004.

Sep, 2004: England shirt worn by tearful **Paul Gascoigne** in 1990 World Cup semi-final v Germany sold at Christie's for £28,680. At same auction, shirt worn by Brazil's **Pele** in 1958 World Cup Final in Sweden sold for £70,505.

May, 2005: The **second FA Cup** (which was presented to winning teams from 1896 to 1909) was bought for £420,000 at Christie's by Birmingham chairman David Gold, a world record for an item of football memorabilia. It was presented to the National Football Museum, Preston. At the same auction, the World Cup-winner's medal earned by England's **Alan Ball** in 1966 was sold for £164,800.

Oct, 2005: At auction at Bonham's, the medals and other memorabilia of Hungary and Real Madrid legend **Ferenc Puskas** were sold for £85,000 to help pay for hospital treatment.

Nov, 2006: A ball used in the 2006 World Cup Final and signed by the winning **Italy** team was sold for £1.2m (a world record for football memorabilia) at a charity auction in Qatar. It was bought by the Qatar Sports Academy.

Feb, 2010: A pair of boots worn by **Sir Stanley Matthews** in the 1953 FA Cup Final was sold at Bonham's for £38,400.

Oct, 2010: Trophies and memorabilia belonging to **George Best** were sold at Bonham's for £193,440. His 1968 European Cup winner's medal fetched £156,000.

Oct–Nov 2010: **Nobby Stiles** sold his 1966 World Cup winner's medal at an Edinburgh auction for a record £188,200. His old club, Manchester Utd, also paid £48,300 for his 1968 European Cup medal to go to the club's museum at Old Trafford. In London, the shirt worn by Stiles in the 1966 World Cup Final went for £75,000. A total of 45 items netted £424,438. **George Cohen** and **Martin Peters** had previously sold their medals from 1966.

Oct 2011: **Terry Paine** (who did not play in the Final) sold his 1966 World Cup medal for £27,500 at auction.

Mar 2013: **Norman Hunter** (Leeds and England) sold his honours' collection on line for nearly £100,000

Nov 2013: A collection of **Nat Lofthouse's** career memorabilia was sold at auction for £100,000. Bolton Council paid £75,000 for items including his 1958 FA Cup winner's medal to go on show at the local museum.

LONGEST UNBEATEN CUP RUN

Liverpool established the longest unbeaten Cup sequence by a Football League club: 25 successive rounds in the League/Milk Cup between semi-final defeat by Nottm Forest (1-2 agg) in 1980 and defeat at Tottenham (0-1) in the third round on Oct 31, 1984. During this period Liverpool won the tournament in four successive seasons, a feat no other Football League club has achieved in any competition.

NEAR £1M RECORD DAMAGES

A High Court judge in Newcastle (May 7, 1999) awarded Bradford City's 28-year-old striker **Gordon Watson** record damages for a football injury: £909,143. He had had his right leg fractured in two places by Huddersfield's Kevin Gray on Feb 1, 1997. Huddersfield were 'proven negligent for allowing their player to make a rushed tackle'. The award was calculated at £202,643 for loss of earnings, £730,500 for 'potential career earnings' if he had joined a Premiership club, plus £26,000 to cover medical treatment and care. Watson, awarded £50,000 in an earlier legal action, had a 6-inch plate inserted in the leg. He resumed playing for City in season 1998–99.

BIG HALF-TIME SCORES

Tottenham 10, Crewe 1 (FA Cup 4th round replay, Feb 3, 1960; result 13-2); Tranmere 8, Oldham 1 (Div 3N., Dec 26, 1935; result 13-4); **Chester City 8, York 0** (Div 3N., Feb 1, 1936; result 12-0; believed to be record half-time scores in League football).

Nine goals were scored in the first half – **Burnley 4, Watford 5** in Div 1 on Apr 5, 2003. Result: 4-7.

Stirling Albion led Selkirk 15-0 at half-time (result 20-0) in the Scottish Cup 1st round, Dec 8, 1984.

World record half-time score: **16-0** when **Australia** beat **American Samoa** 31-0 (another world record) in the World Cup Oceania qualifying group at Coff's Harbour, New South Wales, on Apr 11 2001.

• On Mar 4 1933 **Coventry** beat QPR (Div 3 South) 7-0, having led by that score at half-time. This repeated the half-time situation in Bristol City's 7-0 win over Grimsby on Dec 26, 1914.

TOP SECOND-HALF TEAM

Most goals scored by a team in one half of a League match is **11. Stockport** led Halifax 2-0 at half-time in Div 3 North on Jan 6 1934 and won 13-0.

FIVE NOT ENOUGH

Last team to score **5** in League match and lose: **Burton**, beaten 6-5 by Cheltenham (Lge 2, Mar 13, 2010).

LONG SERVICE WITH ONE CLUB

Bill Nicholson, OBE, was associated with Tottenham for 67 years – as a wing-half (1938–55), then the club's most successful manager (1958–74) with 8 major prizes, subsequently chief advisor and scout. He became club president, and an honorary freeman of the borough, had an executive suite named after him at the club, and the stretch of roadway from Tottenham High Road to the main gates has the nameplate Bill Nicholson Way. He died, aged 85, in Oct 2004.

Ted Bates, the Grand Old Man of Southampton with 66 years of unbroken service to the club, was awarded the Freedom of the City in Apr, 2001. He joined Saints as an inside-forward from Norwich in 1937, made 260 peace-time appearances for the club, became reserve-team trainer in 1953 and manager at The Dell for 18 years (1955–73), taking Southampton into the top division in 1966. He was subsequently chief executive, director and club president. He died in Oct 2003, aged 85.

Bob Paisley was associated with Liverpool for 57 years from 1939, when he joined them from Bishop Auckland, until he died in Feb 1996. He served as player, trainer, coach, assistant-manager, manager, director and vice-president. He was Liverpool's most successful manager, winning 13 major trophies for the club (1974–83).

Dario Gradi, MBE, stepped down after completing 24 seasons and more than 1,000 matches as manager of Crewe (appointed Jun 1983). Never a League player, he previously managed Wimbledon and Crystal Palace. At Crewe, his policy of finding and grooming young talent has earned the club more than £20m in transfer fees. He stayed with Crewe as technical director, and twice took charge of team affairs again following the departure of the managers who succeeded him, Steve Holland and Gudjon Thordarson.

Ronnie Moran, who joined Liverpool in as a player 1952, retired from the Anfield coaching staff

in season 1998–99.

Ernie Gregory served West Ham for 52 years as goalkeeper and coach. He joined them as boy of 14 from school in 1935, retired in May 1987.

Ryan Giggs played 24 seasons for Manchester Utd (1990-2014), then became assistant manager under Louis van Gaal.

Ted Sagar, Everton goalkeeper, 23 years at Goodison Park (1929 52, but only 16 League seasons because of war).

Alan Knight, goalkeeper, played 23 seasons (1977–2000) for his only club, Portsmouth.

Sam Bartram was recognised as one of the finest goalkeepers never to play for England, apart from unofficial wartime games. He was with Charlton from 1934–56

Jack Charlton, England World Cup winner, served Leeds from 1952–73.

Roy Sproson, defender, played 21 League seasons for his only club, Port Vale (1950–71).

TIGHT AT HOME

Fewest home goals conceded in League season (modern times): 4 by **Liverpool** (Div 1, 1978–9); 4 by **Manchester Utd** (Premier League, 1994–95) – both in 21 matches.

FOOTBALL POOLS

Littlewoods launched them in 1923 with a capital of £100. Coupons were first issued (4,000 of them) outside Manchester Utd's ground, the original 35 investors staking a total of £4 7s 6d (pay-out £2 12s).

Vernons joined Littlewoods as the leading promoters. The Treble Chance, leading to bonanza dividends, was introduced in 1946 and the Pools Panel began in Jan 1963, to counter mass fixture postponements caused by the Big Freeze winter.

But business was hard hit by the launch of the National Lottery in 1994. Dividends slumped, the work-force was drastically cut and in Jun 2000 the Liverpool-based Moores family sold Littlewoods Pools in a £161m deal. After 85 years, the name Littlewoods disappeared from Pools betting in Aug 2008. The New Football Pools was formed. Vernons and Zetters continued to operate under their own name in the ownership of Sportech. The record prize remains the £2,924,622 paid to a Worsley, Manchester, syndicate in Nov 1994.

Fixed odds football – record pay-out: £654,375 by Ladbrokes (May 1993) to Jim Wright, of Teignmouth, Devon. He placed a £1,000 each-way pre-season bet on the champions of the three Football League divisions – Newcastle (8–1), Stoke (6–1) and Cardiff (9–1).

Record match accumulators: £164,776 to £4 stake on 18 correct results, Oct 5, 6, 7, 2002. The bet, with Ladbrokes in Colchester, was made by Army chef Mark Simmons; £272,629 for £2.50 stake on 9 correct scores (6 English Prem Lge, 3 Spanish Cup) on Jan 5, 2011, by an anonymous punter at Ladbrokes in Berkshire.

TRANSFER WINDOW

This was introduced to Britain in Sep 2002 via FIFA regulations to bring uniformity across Europe (the rule previously applied in a number of other countries).

The transfer of contracted players is restricted to two periods: Jun 1–Aug 31 and Jan 1–31).

On appeal, Football League clubs continued to sign/sell players (excluding deals with Premiership clubs).

WORLD'S OLDEST FOOTBALL ANNUAL

Now in its 128th edition, this publication began as the 16-page Athletic News Football Supplement & Club Directory in 1887. From the long-established Athletic News, it became the Sunday Chronicle Annual in 1946, the Empire News in 1956, the News of the World & Empire News in 1961 and the News of the World Annual from 1965 until becoming the Nationwide Annual in 2008.

PREMIER LEAGUE CLUB DETAILS AND SQUADS 2014–15

(at time of going to press)

ARSENAL

Ground: Emirates Stadium, Highbury, London, N5 1BU
Telephone: 0207 704 4000. **Club nickname**: Gunners
Capacity: 60,432. **Colours**: Red and white. **Main sponsor**: Emirates
Record transfer fee: £42.4m to Real Madrid for Mesut Ozil, Sep 2013
Record fee received: £35m from Barcelona for Cesc Fabregas, Aug 2011
Record attendance: Highbury: 73,295 v Sunderland (Div 1) Mar 9, 1935. **Wembley**: 73,707 v Lens (Champ Lge) Nov 1998. **Emirates Stadium**: 60,161 v Manchester Utd (Prem Lge) Nov 3, 2007
League Championship: Winners 1930–31, 1932–33, 1933–34, 1934–35, 1937–38, 1947–48, 1952–53, 1970–71, 1988–89, 1990–91, 1997–98, 2001–02, 2003–04
FA Cup: Winners 1930, 1936, 1950, 1971, 1979, 1993, 1998, 2002, 2003, 2005, 2014
League Cup: Winners 1987, 1993
European competitions: Winners Fairs Cup 1969–70; Cup-Winners' Cup 1993–94
Finishing positions in Premier League: 1992–93 10th, 1993–94 4th, 1994–95 12th, 1995–96 5th, 1996–97 3rd, 1997–98 1st, 1998–99 2nd, 1999–2000 2nd, 2000–01 2nd, 2001–02 1st, 2002–03 2nd, 2003–04 1st, 2004–05 2nd, 2005–06 4th, 2006–07 4th, 2007–08 3rd, 2008–09 4th, 2009–10 3rd, 2010–11 4th, 2011–12 3rd, 2012–13 4th, 2013–14 4th
Biggest win: 12-0 v Loughborough (Div 2) Mar 12, 1900
Biggest defeat: 0-8 v Loughborough (Div 2) Dec 12, 1896
Highest League scorer in a season: Ted Drake 42 (1934–35)
Most League goals in aggregate: Thierry Henry 175 (1999–2007) (2012)
Longest unbeaten League sequence: 49 matches (2003–04)
Longest sequence without a League win: 23 matches (1912–13)
Most capped player: Thierry Henry (France) 81

Name	Height ft in	Previous club	Birthplace	Birthdate
Goalkeepers				
Martinez, Damian	6.4	Independiente	Mar del Plata, Arg	02.09.92
Szczesny, Wojciech	6.5	–	Warsaw, Pol	18.04.90
Defenders				
Debuchy, Mathieu	5.10	Newcastle	Fretin, Fr	28.07.85
Gibbs, Kieran	5.10	–	Lambeth	26.09.89
Jenkinson, Carl	6.1	Charlton	Harlow	08.02.92
Koscielny, Laurent	6.1	Lorient	Tulle, Fr	10.09.85
Mertesacker, Per	6.6	Werder Bremen	Hannover, Ger	29.09.84
Monreal, Nacho	5.10	Malaga	Pamplona, Sp	26.02.86
Vermaelen, Thomas	6.0	Ajax	Kapellen, Bel	14.11.85
Midfielders				
Arteta, Mikel	5.9	Everton	San Sebastian, Sp	28.03.82
Cazorla, Santi	5.6	Malaga	Llanera, Sp	13.12.84
Coquelin, Francis	5.10	–	Laval, Fr	13.05.91
Diaby, Abou	6.2	Auxerre	Paris, Fr	11.05.86
Flamini, Mathieu	5.10	AC Milan	Marseille, Fr	07.03.84
Ozil, Mesut	5.11	Real Madrid	Gelsenkirchen, Ger	15.10.88
Rosicky, Tomas	5.10	Borussia Dortmund	Prague, Cz	04.10.80
Ramsey, Aaron	5.11	Cardiff	Caerphilly	26.12.90
Wilshere, Jack	5.8	–	Stevenage	01.01.92

Zelalem, Gedion	5.11	Hertha Berlin	Berlin	26.01.97
Forwards				
Campbell, Joel	5.10	Saprissa	San Jose, CRica	26.06.92
Giroud, Olivier	6.4	Montpellier	Chambery, Fr	30.09.86
Gnabry, Serge	5.9	Stuttgart	Stuttgart, Ger	14.07.95
Miyaichi, Ryo	6.0	–	Aichi, Jap	14.12.92
Podolski, Lukas	6.0	Cologne	Gliwice, Pol	04.06.85
Oxlade-Chamberlain, Alex	5.11	Southampton	Portsmouth	15.08.93
Sanchez, Alexis	5.7	Barcelona	Tocopilla, Chil	19.12.88
Sanogo, Yaya	6.3	Auxerre	Massy, Fr	27.01.93
Walcott, Theo	5.8	Southampton	Newbury	16.03.89

ASTON VILLA

Ground: Villa Park, Trinity Road, Birmingham, B6 6HE
Telephone: 0871 423 8101. **Club nickname**: Villans
Capacity: 42,551. **Colours**: Claret and blue. **Main sponsor**: Dafabet
Record transfer fee: £24m to Sunderland for Darren Bent, Jan 2011
Record fee received: £24m from Manchester City for James Milner, Aug 2010
Record attendance: 76,588 v Derby (FA Cup 6) Mar 2, 1946
League Championship: Winners 1893–94, 1895–96, 1896–97, 1898–99, 1899–1900, 1909–10, 1980–81
FA Cup: Winners 1887, 1895, 1897, 1905, 1913, 1920, 1957
League Cup: Winners 1961, 1975, 1977, 1994, 1996
European competitions: Winners European Cup 1981–82; European Super Cup 1983
Finishing positions in Premier League: 1992–93 2nd, 1993–94 10th, 1994–95 18th, 1995–96 4th, 1996–97 5th, 1997–98 7th, 1998–99 6th, 1999–2000 6th, 2000–01 8th, 2001–02 8th, 2002–03 16th, 2003–04 6th, 2004–05 10th, 2005–06 16th, 2006–07 11th, 2007–08 6th, 2008–09 6th, 2009–10 6th, 2010–11 9th, 2011–12 16th, 2012–13 15th, 2013–14 15th
Biggest win: 12-2 v Accrington (Div 1) Mar 12, 1892; 11-1 v Charlton (Div 2) Nov 24, 1959; 10-0 v Sheffield Wed (Div 1) Oct 5, 1912, v Burnley (Div 1) Aug 29, 1925. Also: 13-0 v Wednesbury (FA Cup 1) Oct 30, 1886
Biggest defeat: 0-8 v Chelsea (Prem Lge) Dec 23, 2012
Highest League scorer in a season: 'Pongo' Waring 49 (1930–31)
Most League goals in aggregate: Harry Hampton 215 (1904–1915)
Longest unbeaten League sequence: 15 matches (1897, 1909–10 and 1949)
Longest sequence without a League win: 12 matches (1973–74 and 1986–87)
Most capped player: Steve Staunton (Republic of Ireland) 64

Goalkeepers				
Given, Shay	6.1	Manchester City	Lifford, Ire	20.04.76
Guzan, Brad	6.4	Chivas	Evergreen Park, US	09.09.84
Steer, Jed	6.3	Norwich	Norwich	23.09.92
Defenders				
Baker, Nathan	6.3	–	Worcester	23.04.91
Bennett, Joe	5.8	Middlesbrough	Rochdale	28.03.90
Clark, Ciaran	6.2	–	Harrow	26.09.89
Donacien, Janoi	6.0	Luton	St Lucia	03.11.93
Hutton, Alan	6.1	Tottenham	Glasgow	30.11.84
Lowton, Matthew	5.11	Sheffield Utd	Chesterfield	09.06.89
Luna, Antonio	5.10	Sevilla	Son Servera, Maj	17.03.91
Okore, Jores	6.0	Nordsjaelland	Abidjan Iv C	11.08.92
Senderos, Philippe	6.3	Valencia	Geneva, Swi	14.02.85
Stevens, Enda	6.0	Shamrock	Dublin, Ire	09.07.90

Vlaar, Ron	6.2	Feyenoord	Hensbroek, Hol	16.02.85

Midfielders

Bacuna, Leandro	6.2	Groningen	Groningen, Hol	21.08.91
Carruthers, Samir	5.8	Arsenal	Islington	04.04.93
Cole, Joe	5.9	West Ham	Islington	08.11.81
Delph, Fabian	5.9	Leeds	Bradford	05.05.91
El Ahmadi, Karim	5.10	Feyenoord	Enschede, Hol	27.01.85
Gardner, Gary	6.2	–	Solihull	29.06.92
Herd, Chris	5.8	–	Perth, Aus	04.04.89
Johnson, Daniel	5.8	Crystal Palace	Kingston	08.10.92
N'Zogbia, Charles	5.8	Wigan	Harfleur, Fr	28.05.86
Richardson, Kieran	5.10	Fulham	Greenwich	21.10.84
Tonev, Aleksandar	5.10	Lech Poznan	Elin Pelin, Bul	03.02.90
Westwood, Ashley	5.8	Crewe	Nantwich	01.04.90

Forwards

Agbonlahor, Gabriel	5.11	–	Birmingham	13.10.86
Bent, Darren	5.11	Sunderland	Wandsworth	06.02.84
Benteke, Christian	6.3	Genk	Kinshasa, DR Cong	03.12.90
Burke, Graham	5.11	–	Dublin	21.09.93
Robinson, Callum	5.10	–	Northampton	02.02.95
Kozak, Libor	6.4	Lazio	Opava, Cz	30.05.89
Weimann, Andreas	6.2	–	Vienna, Aut	05.08.91

BURNLEY

Ground: Turf Moor, Harry Potts Way, Burnley BB10 4BX
Telephone: 0871 221 1882. **Club nickname**: Clarets
Capacity: 21,940. **Colours**: Claret and blue. **Main sponsor**: Fun888
Record transfer fee: £3m to Hibernian for Steven Fletcher, Jul 2009
Record fee received: £6.5m from Wolves for Steven Fletcher, Jun 2010
Record attendance: 54,775 v Huddersfield (FA Cup 3) Feb 23, 1924
League Championship: Winners 1920–21, 1959–60
FA Cup: Winners 1914
League Cup: Semi-finals 1961, 1969, 1983, 2009
European competitions: European Cup quarter-finals 1960–61
Biggest win: 9-0 v Darwen (Div 1) Jan 9, 1892, v Crystal Palace (FA Cup 2) Feb 10, 1909, v New Brighton (FA Cup 4) Jan 26, 1957, v Penrith (FA Cup 1) Nov 17, 1984
Biggest defeat: 0-10 v Aston Villa (Div 1) Aug 29, 1925, v Sheffield Utd (Div 1) Jan 19, 1929
Highest League scorer in a season: George Beel 35 (1927–28)
Highest League goals in aggregate: George Beel 178 (1923–32)
Longest unbeaten League sequence: 30 matches (1920–21)
Longest sequence without a League win: 24 matches (1979)
Most capped player: Jimmy McIlroy (Northern Ireland) 51

Goalkeepers

Cisak, Alex	6.4	Oldham	Krakow, Pol	19.05.89
Gilks, Matt	6.1	Blackpool	Rochdale	04.06.82
Heaton, Tom	6.1	Bristol City	Chester	15.04.86

Defenders

Duff, Mike	6.1	Cheltenham	Belfast	11.01.78
Lafferty, Danny	6.1	Derry	Derry	01.04.89
Long, Kevin	6.2	Cork	Cork, Ire	18.08.90
Mee, Ben	5.11	Manchester City	Sale	23.09.89
O'Neill, Luke	6.0	Mansfield	Slough	20.08.91
Reid, Steven	6.1	WBA	Kingston	10.03.81
Shackell, Jason	6.4	Derby	Stevenage	27.09.83

Trippier, Kieran	5.10	Manchester City	Bury	19.09.90
Midfielders				
Arfield, Scott	5.10	Huddersfield	Livingston	01.11.88
Hewitt, Steven	5.7	–	Manchester	05.12.93
Howieson, Cameron	5.10	Mosgiel	Blenheim, NZ	22.12.94
Jones, David	5.10	Wigan	Southport	04.11.84
Kightly, Michael	5.11	Stoke	Basildon	24.01.86
Marney, Dean	5.11	Hull	Barking	31.01.84
Taylor, Matt	5.10	West Ham	Oxford	27.11.81
Wallace, Ross	5.6	Preston	Dundee	23.05.85
Forwards				
Barnes, Ashley	6.0	Brighton	Bath	31.10.89
Ings, Danny	5.10	Bournemouth	Winchester	16.03.92
Jutkiewicz, Lukas	6.1	Middlesbrough	Southampton	20.03.89
Sordell, Marvin	5.10	Bolton	Brent	17.02.91
Vokes, Sam	5.11	Wolves	Lymington	21.10.89

CHELSEA

Ground: Stamford Bridge Stadium, London SW6 1HS
Telephone: 0871 984 1955. **Club nickname**: Blues
Capacity: 42,055. **Colours**: Blue. **Main sponsor**: Samsung
Record transfer fee: £50m to Liverpool for Fernando Torres, Jan 2011
Record fee received: £40m from Paris SG for David Luiz, Jun 2014
Record attendance: 82,905 v Arsenal (Div 1) Oct 12, 1935
League Championship: Winners 1954–55, 2004–05, 2005–06, 2009–10
FA Cup: Winners 1970, 1997, 2000, 2007, 2009, 2010, 2012
League Cup: Winners 1965, 1998, 2005, 2007
European competitions: Winners Champions League 2011–12; Cup-Winners' Cup 1970–71, 1997–98; Europa League 2012–13; European Super Cup 1998
Finishing positions in Premier League: 1992–93 11th, 1993–94 14th, 1994–95 11th, 1995–96 11th, 1996–97 6th, 1997–98 4th, 1998–99 3rd, 1999–2000 5th, 2000–01 6th, 2001–02 6th, 2002–03 4th, 2003–04 2nd, 2004–05 1st, 2005–06 1st, 2006–07 2nd, 2007–08 2nd, 2008–09 3rd, 2009–10 1st, 2010–11 2nd, 2011–12 6th, 2012–13 3rd, 2013–14 3rd
Biggest win: 8-0 v Aston Villa (Prem Lge) Dec 23, 2012. Also: 13-0 v Jeunesse Hautcharage, (Cup-Winners' Cup 1) Sep 29, 1971
Biggest defeat: 1-8 v Wolves (Div 1) Sep 26, 1953; 0-7 v Leeds (Div 1) Oct 7, 1967, v Nottm Forest (Div 1) Apr 20, 1991
Highest League scorer in a season: Jimmy Greaves 41 (1960–61)
Most League goals in aggregate: Bobby Tambling 164 (1958–70)
Longest unbeaten League sequence: 40 matches (2004–05)
Longest sequence without a League win: 21 matches (1987–88)
Most capped player: Frank Lampard (England) 104

Goalkeepers				
Blackman, Jamal	6.6	–	Croydon	27.10.93
Cech, Petr	6.5	Rennes	Plzen, Cz	20.05.82
Schwarzer, Mark	6.4	Fulham	Sydney, Aus	06.10.72
Defenders				
Ake, Nathan	5.11	Feyenoord	The Hague, Hol	18.02.95
Azpilicueta, Cesar	5.10	Marseille	Pamplona, Sp	28.08.89
Bertrand, Ryan	5.10	–	Southwark	05.08.89
Cahill, Gary	6.2	Bolton	Sheffield	19.12.85
Filipe Luis	6.0	Atletico Madrid	Jaragua, Br	09.08.85
Ivanovic, Branislav	6.2	Lok Moscow	Mitrovica, Serb	22.02.84

Terry, John	6.1	–	Barking	07.12.80
Van Aanholt, Patrick	5.9	PSV	Hertogenbosch, Hol	29.08.90
Zouma, Kurt	6.3	St Etienne	Lyon, Fr	27.10.94
Midfielders				
Fabregas, Cesc	5.11	Barcelona	Arenys de Mar, Sp	04.05.87
Hazard, Eden	5.8	Lille	La Louviere, Bel	07.01.91
Marin, Marko	5.7	Werder Bremen	Bosanska, Bos	13.03.89
Matic, Nemanja	6.4	Benfica	Sabac, Serb	01.08.88
McEachran, Josh	5.10	–	Oxford	01.03.93
Mikel, John Obi	6.2	Lyn Oslo	Plato State, Nig	22.04.87
Moses, Victor	5.10	Wigan	Kaduna, Nig	12.12.90
Oscar	5.10	Internacional	Americana, Br	09.09.91
Pasalic, Mario	6.1	Hajduk Split	Mainz, Ger	09.02.95
Ramires	5.11	Benfica	Rio de Janeiro, Br	24.03.87
Romeu, Oriol	6.0	Barcelona	Ulldecona, Sp	24.09.91
Salah, Mohamed	5.9	Basle	El Gharbia, Egy	15.06.92
Van Ginkel, Marco	6.1	Vitesse Arnhem	Amersfoort, Hol	01.12.92
Willian	5.9	Anzhi Makhachkala	Ribeirao Pires, Br	09.08.88
Forwards				
Diego Costa	6.2	Atletico Madrid	Lagarto, Br	07.10.88
Kakuta, Gael	5.8	Lens	Lille, Fr	21.06.91
Lucas Piazon	6.0	Sao Paulo	Sao Paulo, Br	20.01.94
Lukaku, Romelu	6.3	Anderlecht	Antwerp, Bel	13.05.93
Schurrle, Andre	6.0	Bayer Leverkusen	Ludwigshafen, Ger	06.11.90
Torres, Fernando	6.1	Liverpool	Madrid, Sp	20.03.84

CRYSTAL PALACE

Ground: Selhurst Park, Whitehorse Lane, London SE25, 6PU
Telephone: 0208 768 6000. **Club nickname:** Eagles
Capacity: 26,309. **Colours:** Red and blue. **Main sponsor:** Neteller
Record transfer fee: £6m to Peterborough for Dwight Gayle, Jul 2013
Record fee received: £15m from Manchester Utd for Wilfried Zaha, Jan 2013
Record attendance: 51,482 v Burnley (Div 2), May 11, 1979
League Championship: 3rd 1990–91
FA Cup: Runners-up 1990
League Cup: Semi-finals 1993, 1995, 2001, 2012
Finishing positions in Premier League: 1992–93 20th, 1994–95 19th, 1997–98 20th, 2004–05 18th, 2013–14 11th
Biggest win: 9-0 v Barrow (Div 4) Oct 10, 1959
Biggest defeat: 0-9 v Liverpool (Div 1) Sep 12, 1989; 0-9 v Burnley (FA Cup 2 rep) Feb 10, 1909
Highest League scorer in a season: Peter Simpson 46 (1930–31)
Most League goals in aggregate: Peter Simpson 153 (1930–36)
Longest unbeaten League sequence: 18 matches (1969)
Longest sequence with a League win: 20 matches (1962)
Most capped player: Aki Riihilahti (Finland) 36

Goalkeepers				
Hennessey, Wayne	6.0	Wolves	Bangor, Wal	24.01.87
Kettings, Chris	6.4	Blackpool	Glasgow	25.10.92
Price, Lewis	6.3	Derby	Bournemouth	19.07.84
Speroni, Julian	6.1	Dundee	Buenos Aires, Arg	18.05.79
Defenders				
Dann, Scott	6.2	Blackburn	Liverpool	14.02.87
Delaney, Damien	6.2	Ipswich	Cork, Ire	29.07.81
Guedioura, Adlene	6.0	Wolves	La Roche, Fr	12.11.85

Hunt, Jack	5.9	Huddersfield	Leeds	06.12.90
Mariappa, Adrian	5.11	Reading	Harrow	03.10.86
McCarthy, Patrick	6.1	Charlton	Dublin, Ire	31.05.83
Ramage, Peter	6.1	QPR	Ashington	22.11.83
Ward, Joel	6.2	Portsmouth	Portsmouth	29.10.89
Midfielders				
Bannan, Barry	5.11	Aston Villa	Airdrie	01.12.89
Boateng, Hiram	5.10	–	Wandsworth	08.01.96
Bolasie, Yannick	6.2	Bristol City	Kinshasa, DR Cong	24.05.89
Campana, Jose	5.11	Sevilla	Seville, Sp	31.05.93
De Silva, Kyle	5.7	–	Croydon	29.11.93
Garvan, Owen	6.0	Ipswich	Dublin, Ire	29.01.88
Jedinak, Mile	6.3	Genclerbirligi	Sydney, Aus	03.08.84
Kebe, Jimmy	6.1	Reading	Vitry, Fr	19.01.84
Ledley, Joe	6.0	Celtic	Cardiff	23.01.87
O'Keefe, Stuart	5.8	Southend	Norwich	04.03.91
Puncheon, Jason	5.8	Southampton	Croydon	26.06.86
Thomas, Jerome	5.11	WBA	Wembley	23.03.83
Williams, Jonathan	5.7	–	Pembury	09.10.93
Forwards				
Dobbie, Stephen	5.8	Brighton	Glasgow	05.12.82
Gayle, Dwight	5.10	Peterborough	Walthamstow	20.10.90
Murray, Glenn	6.2	Brighton	Maryport	25.09.83

EVERTON

Ground: Goodison Park, Liverpool L4 4EL
Telephone: 0870 442 1878. **Club nickname**: Toffees
Capacity: 40,394. **Colours**: Blue and white. **Main sponsor**: Chang
Record transfer fee: £15m to Standard Liege for Marouane Fellaini, Aug 2008
Record fee received: £27m from Manchester Utd for Wayne Rooney, Aug 2004
Record attendance: 78,299 v Liverpool (Div 1) Sep 18, 1948
League Championship: Winners 1890–91, 1914–15, 1927–28, 1931–31, 1938–39, 1962–63, 1969–70, 1984–85, 1986–87
FA Cup: Winners 1906, 1933, 1966, 1984, 1995
League Cup: Runners-up 1977, 1984
European competitions: Winners Cup-Winners' Cup 1984–85
Finishing positions in Premier League: 1992–93 13th, 1993–94 17th, 1994–95 15th, 1995–96 6th 1996–97 15th 1997–98 17th 1998–99 14th, 1999–2000 13th, 2000–01 16th, 2001–02 15th, 2002–03 7th, 2003–04 17th, 2004–05 4th, 2005–06 11th, 2006–07 6th, 2007–08 5th, 2008–09 5th, 2009–10 8th, 20010–11 7th, 2011–12 7th, 2012–13 6th, 2013–14 5th
Biggest win: 9-1 v Manchester City (Div 1) Sep 3, 1906, v Plymouth (Div 2) Dec 27, 1930. Also: 11-2 v Derby (FA Cup 1) Jan 18, 1890
Biggest defeat: 0-7 v Portsmouth (Div 1) Sep 10, 1949, v Arsenal (Prem Lge) May 11, 2005
Highest League scorer in a season: Ralph 'Dixie' Dean 60 (1927–28)
Most League goals in aggregate: Ralph 'Dixie' Dean 349 (1925–37)
Longest unbeaten League sequence: 20 matches (1978)
Longest sequence without a League win: 14 matches (1937)
Most capped player: Neville Southall (Wales) 92

Goalkeepers
Howard, Tim	6.3	Manchester Utd	North Brunswick, US	03.06.79
Robles, Joel	6.5	Atletico Madrid	Getafe, Sp	17.06.90
Stanek, Jindrich	6.3	Sparta Prague	Strakonice, Cz	27.04.96

Defenders

Alcaraz, Antolin	6.2	Wigan	San Roque, Para	30.07.82
Baines, Leighton	5.7	Wigan	Liverpool	11.12.84
Browning, Tyias	5.11	–	Liverpool	27.05.94
Coleman, Seamus	5.10	Sligo	Donegal, Ire	11.10.88
Distin, Sylvain	6.4	Portsmouth	Paris, Fr	16.12.77
Duffy, Shane	6.4	–	Derry	01.01.92
Garbutt, Luke	5.10	Leeds	Harrogate	21.05.93
Hibbert, Tony	5.10	–	Liverpool	20.02.81
Jagielka, Phil	5.11	Sheffield Utd	Manchester	17.08.82
Stones, John	5.10	Barnsley	Barnsley	28.05.94

Midfielders

Barkley, Ross	6.2	–	Liverpool	05.12.93
Barry, Gareth	6.0	Manchester City	Hastings	23.02.81
Francisco Junior	5.5	Benfica	Guinea-Bissau	18.01.92
Gibson, Darron	5.9	Manchester Utd	Derry	25.10.87
Kennedy, Matthew	5.9	Kilmarnock	Dundonald	01.11.94
Lundstram, John	5.11	–	Liverpool	18.02.94
McCarthy, James	5.11	Wigan	Glasgow	12.11.90
McGeady, Aiden	5.11	Spartak Moscow	Paisley	04.04.86
Mirallas, Kevin	6.0	Olympiacos	Liege, Bel	05.10.87
Osman, Leon	5.8	–	Billinge	17.05.81
Oviedo, Bryan	5.8	Copenhagen	Ciudad, CRica	18.02.90
Pienaar, Steven	5.9	Tottenham	Johannesburg, SA	17.03.82

Forwards

Kone, Arouna	5.11	Wigan	Anyama Iv C	11.11.83
McAleny, Conor	5.10	–	Liverpool	12.08.92
Naismith, Steven	5.10	Rangers	Irvine	14.09.86

HULL CITY

Ground: Kingston Communications Stadium, Anlaby Road, Hull, HU3 6HU
Telephone: 01482 504600. **Club nickname**: Tigers
Capacity: 25,404. **Colours**: Amber and black. **Main sponsor**: Cash Converters
Record transfer fee: £7.5m to Everton for Nikica Jelavic, Jan 2014
Record fee received: £4m from Sunderland for Michael Turner, Aug 2009
Record attendance: Boothferry Park: 55,019 v Manchester Utd. (FA Cup 6) Feb 26, 1949;
Kingston Communications Stadium: 25,030 v Liverpool (Prem Lge) May 9, 2010; Also:
25,280 for England U21 v Holland, Feb 17, 2004
League Championship: 16th 2013–14
FA Cup: Runners-up 2014
League Cup: 4th rd 1974, 1976, 1978
Finishing positions in Premier League: 2008–09 17th, 2009–10 19th, 2013–14 16th
Biggest win: 11-1 v Carlisle (Div 3 N) Jan 14, 1939
Biggest defeat: 0-8 v Wolves (Div 2) Nov 4, 1911
Highest League scorer in a season: Bill McNaughton 39 (1932–33)
Most League goals in aggregate: Chris Chilton 195 (1960–71)
Longest unbeaten League sequence: 15 matches (1983)
Longest sequence without a League win: 27 matches (1989)
Most capped player: Theodore Whitmore (Jamaica) 28

Goalkeepers

Harper, Steve	6.2	Newcastle	Seaham	14.03.75
McGregor, Allan	6.0	Besiktas	Edinburgh	31.01.82

Defenders

Bruce, Alex	5.11	Leeds	Norwich	28.09.84

Chester, James	5.10	Manchester Utd	Warrington	23.01.89
Davies, Curtis	6.2	Birmingham	Waltham Forest	15.03.85
Figueroa, Maynor	5.11	Wigan	Juticalpa, Hond	02.05.83
McShane, Paul	6.0	Sunderland	Kilpeddar, Ire	06.01.86
Rosenior, Liam	5.10	Reading	Wandsworth	15.12.84
Midfielders				
Aluko, Sone	5.8	Rangers	Hounslow	19.02.89
Elmohamady, Ahmed	5.11	Sunderland	Basyoun, Egy	09.09.87
Huddlestone, Tom	6.1	Tottenham	Nottingham	28.12.86
Livermore, Jake	6.2	Tottenham	Enfield	14.11.89
Meyler, David	6.2	Sunderland	Cork, Ire	29.05.89
Quinn, Stephen	5.6	Sheffield Utd	Dublin, Ire	04.04.86
Snodgrass, Robert	6.0	Norwich	Glasgow	07.09.87
Forwards				
Boyd, George	5.10	Peterborough	Chatham	02.10.85
Brady, Robbie	5.10	Manchester Utd	Dublin, Ire	14.01.92
Ince, Tom	5.10	Blackpool	Stockport	30.01.92
Jelevic, Nikica	6.2	Everton	Capljina, Cro	27.08.85
Long, Shane	5.10	WBA	Gortnahoe, Ire	22.01.87
Sagbo, Yannick	6.0	Evian	Marseille, Fr	12.04.88

LEICESTER CITY

Ground: King Power Stadium, Filbert Way, Leicester, LE2 7FL
Telephone: 0844 815 6000. **Club nickname**: Foxes
Capacity: 32,312. **Colours**: Blue and white. **Main sponsor**: King Power
Record transfer fee: £5m to Wolves for Ade Akinbiyi, Jul 2000
Record fee received: £11m from Liverpoool for Emile Heskey, Mar 2000
Record attendance: Filbert Street: 47,298 v. Tottenham (FA Cup 5) Feb 18, 1928; King Power Stadium: 32,188 v Real Madrid (friendly) Jul 30, 2011
League Championship: Runners-up 1928–29
FA Cup: Runners-up 1949, 1961, 1963, 1969
League Cup: Winners 1964, 1997, 2000
European competitions: Cup-Winners' Cup rd 1 1961–62; UEFA Cup rd 1 1997–98, 2000–01
Finishing positions in Premier League: 1994–95 21st, 1996–97 9th, 1997–98 10th, 1998–99 10th, 1999–2000 8th, 2000–01 13th, 2001–02 20th, 2003–04 18th
Biggest win: 10-0 v Portsmouth (Div 1) Oct 20, 1928. Also: 13-0 v Notts Olympic (FA Cup) Oct 13, 1894
Biggest defeat (while Leicester Fosse): 0-12 v Nottm Forest (Div 1) Apr 21, 1909
Highest League scorer in a season: Arthur Rowley 44 (1956–57)
Most League goals in aggregate: Arthur Chandler 259 (1923–35)
Longest unbeaten League sequence: 23 matches (2008–09)
Longest sequence without a League win: 19 matches (1975)
Most capped player: John O'Neill (Northern Ireland) 39

Goalkeepers				
Hamer, Ben	6.4	Charlton	Taunton	20.11.87
Logan, Conrad	6.2	–	Ramelton, Ire	18.04.86
Schmeichel, Kasper	6.0	Leeds	Copenhagen, Den	05.11.86
Defenders				
Bakayogo, Zoumana	6.0	Tranmere	Paris, Fr	17.08.86
De Laet, Ritchie	6.1	Manchester Utd	Antwerp, Bel	28.11.88
Konchesky, Paul	5.10	Liverpool	Barking	15.05.81
Morgan, Wes	5.11	Nottm Forest	Nottingham	21.01.84
Moore, Liam	6.1	–	Leicester	31.01.93
Rowley, Louis	6.1	Manchester Utd	Nuneaton	21.04.95

Schlupp, Jeffrey	5.8	–	Hamburg, Ger	23.12.92
Upson, Matthew	6.1	Brighton	Eye	18.04.79
Wesilewski, Marcin	6.1	Anderlecht	Krakow, Pol	09.06.80
Midfielders				
Albrighton, Mark	6.1	Aston Villa	Tamworth	18.11.89
Drinkwater, Danny	5.10	Manchester Utd	Manchester	05.03.90
Hammond, Dean	6.0	Southampton	Hastings	07.03.83
James, Matty	5.10	Manchester Utd	Bacup	22.07.91
King, Andy	6.0	–	Maidenhead	29.10.88
Knockaert, Anthony	5.10	Guingamp	Roubaix, Fr	20.11.91
Mahrez, Riyad	5.11	Le Havre	Sarcelles, Fr	21.02.91
Forwards				
Barmby, Jack	5.11	Manchester Utd	Harlow	14.11.94
Nugent, David	5.11	Portsmouth	Liverpool	02.05.85
Taylor-Fletcher, Gary	6.0	Blackpool	Widnes	04.06.81
Vardy, Jamie	5.10	Fleetwood	Sheffield	11.01.87
Wood, Chris	6.3	WBA	Auckland, NZ	07.12.91

LIVERPOOL

Ground: Anfield, Liverpool L4 0TH
Telephone: 0151 263 2361. **Club nickname:** Reds or Pool
Capacity: 45,362. **Colours:** Red. **Main sponsor:** Standard Charter
Record transfer fee: £35m to Newcastle for Andy Carroll, Jan 2011
Record fee received: £75m from Barcelona for Luis Suarez, Jul 2014
Record attendance: 61,905 v Wolves, (FA Cup 4), Feb 2, 1952
League Championship: Winners 1900–01, 1905–06, 1921–22, 1922–23, 1946–47, 1963–64, 1965–66, 1972–73, 1975–76, 1976–77, 1978–79, 1979–80, 1981–82, 1982–83, 1983–84, 1985–86, 1987–88, 1989–90
FA Cup: Winners 1965, 1974, 1986, 1989, 1992, 2001, 2006
League Cup: Winners 1981, 1982, 1983, 1984, 1995, 2001, 2003, 2012
European competitions: Winners European Cup/Champions League 1976–77, 1977–78, 1980–81, 1983–84, 2004–05; UEFA Cup 1972–73, 1975–76, 2000–01; European Super Cup 1977, 2001, 2005
Finishing positions in Premier League: 1992–93 6th, 1993–94 8th, 1994–95 4th, 1995–96 3rd, 1996–97 4th, 1997–98 3rd, 1998–99 7th, 1999–2000 4th, 2000–01 3rd, 2001–02 2nd, 2002–03 5th, 2003–04 4th, 2004–05 5th, 2005–06 3rd, 2006–07 3rd, 2007–08 4th, 2008–09 2nd, 2009–10 7th, 2010–11 6th, 2011–12 8th, 2012–13 7th, 2013–14 2nd
Biggest win: 10-1 v Rotherham (Div 2) Feb 18, 1896. Also: 11-0 v Stromsgodset (Cup-Winners' Cup 1) Sep 17, 1974
Biggest defeat: 1-9 v Birmingham (Div 2) Dec 11, 1954
Highest League scorer in a season: Roger Hunt 41 (1961–62)
Most League goals in aggregate: Roger Hunt 245 (1959–69)
Longest unbeaten League sequence: 31 matches (1987–88)
Longest sequence without a League win: 14 matches (1953–54)
Most capped player: Steven Gerrard (England) 114

Goalkeepers				
Jones, Brad	6.3	Middlesbrough	Armadale, Aus	19.03.82
Mignolet, Simon	6.4	Sunderland	Sint-Truiden, Bel	06.08.88
Reina, Jose	6.2	Villarreal	Madrid, Sp	31.08.82
Defenders				
Agger, Daniel	6.3	Brondby	Hvidovre, Den	12.12.84
Coady, Conor	6.1	–	Liverpool	25.01.93
Coates, Sebastian	6.6	Nacional	Montevideo, Uru	07.10.90
Flanagan, Jon	5.11	–	Liverpool	01.01.93
Ilori, Tiago	6.3	Sporting	London	26.02.93

Johnson, Glen	5.11	Portsmouth	Greenwich	23.08.84
Jose Enrique	6.0	Newcastle	Valencia, Sp	23.01.86
Kelly, Martin	6.3	–	Whiston	27.04.90
McLaughlin, Ryan	5.11	–	Liverpool	21.01.93
Robinson, Jack	5.7	–	Warrington	01.09.93
Sakho, Mamadou	6.2	Paris SG	Paris, Fr	13.02.90
Skrtel, Martin	6.3	Zenit St Petersburg	Trencin, Slovak	15.12.84
Toure, Kolo	6.0	Manchester City	Bouake, Iv C	19.03.81
Wisdom, Andre	6.1		Leeds	09.05.93

Midfielders

Allen, Joe	5.7	Swansea	Carmarthen	14.03.90
Coutinho, Philippe	5.8	Inter Milan	Rio de Janeiro, Br	12.06.92
Emre Can	6.1	Bayer Leverkusen	Frankfurt	12.01.94
Gerrard, Steven	6.1	–	Whiston	30.05.80
Henderson, Jordan	5.10	Sunderland	Sunderland	17.06.90
Ibe, Jordon	5.7	Wycombe	Bermondsey	08.12.95
Lallana, Adam	5.10	Southampton	Bournemouth	10.05.88
Lucas Leiva	5.10	Gremio	Dourados, Br	09.01.87
Markovic, Lazar	5.9	Benfica	Cacak, Serb	02.03.94
Sterling, Raheem	5.7	–	Kingston, Jam	08.12.94
Teixeira, Joao Carlos	5.9	Sporting	Braga, Por	18.01.93

Forwards

Assaidi, Oussama	5.9	Heerenveen	Beni-Boughafer, Mor	15.08.88
Iago Aspas	5.10	Celta Vigo	Moana, Sp	01.08.87
Lambert, Rickie	5.10	Southampton	Liverpool	16.02.82
Sturridge, Daniel	6.2	Chelsea	Birmingham	01.09.89
Suso	5.8	Cadiz	Cadiz, Sp	19.11.93
Yesil, Samed	5.8	Bayer Leverkusen	Dusseldorf, Ger	25.05.94

MANCHESTER CITY

Ground: Etihad Stadium, Etihad Campus, Manchester M11 3FF
Telephone: 0870 062 1894. **Club nickname**: City
Capacity: 48,000. **Colours**: Sky blue and white. **Main sponsor**: Etihad
Record transfer fee: £38.5m to Atletico Madrid for Sergio Aguero, Jul 2011
Record fee received: £21m from Chelsea for Shaun Wright-Phillips, Jul 2005
Record attendance: Maine Road: 84,569 v Stoke (FA Cup 6) Mar 3, 1934 (British record for any game outside London or Glasgow). Etihad Stadium: 47,435 v QPR (Prem Lge) May 13, 2012. Also: 47,726 Zenit St Petersburg v Rangers (UEFA Cup Final) May 14, 2008
League Championship: Winners 1936–37, 1967–68, 2011–12, 2013–14
FA Cup: Winners 1904, 1934, 1956, 1969, 2011
League Cup: Winners 1970, 1976, 2014
European competitions: Winners Cup-Winners' Cup 1969–70
Finishing positions in Premier League: 1992–93 9th, 1993–94 16th, 1994–95 17th, 1995–96 18th, 2000–01: 18th, 2002–03 9th, 2003–04 16th, 2004–05 8th, 2005–06 15th, 2006–07 14th, 2007–08 9th, 2008–09 10th, 2009–10 5th, 2010–11 3rd, 2011–12 1st, 2012–13 2nd, 2013–14 1st
Biggest win: 10-1 Huddersfield (Div 2) Nov 7, 1987. Also: 10-1 v Swindon (FA Cup 4) Jan 29, 1930
Biggest defeat: 1-9 v Everton (Div 1) Sep 3, 1906
Highest League scorer in a season: Tommy Johnson 38 (1928–29)
Most League goals in aggregate: Tommy Johnson, 158 (1919–30)
Longest unbeaten League sequence: 22 matches (1946–47)
Longest sequence without a League win: 17 matches (1979–80)
Most capped player: Colin Bell (England) 48

Goalkeepers

Caballero, Willy	6.1	Malaga	Santa Elena, Arg	28.09.81
Hart, Joe	6.3	Shrewsbury	Shrewsbury	19.04.87
Wright, Richard	6.2	Ipswich	Ipswich	05.11.77

Defenders

Boyata, Dedryck	6.2	Brussels	Uccle, Bel	28.11.90
Clichy, Gael	5.11	Arsenal	Paris, Fr	26.07.85
Demichelis, Martin	6.0	At Madrid	Justiniano, Arg	20.12.80
Kompany, Vincent	6.4	Hamburg	Uccle, Bel	10.04.86
Kolarov, Aleksandar	6.2	Lazio	Belgrade, Serb	10.11.85
Nastasic, Matija	6.2	Fiorentina	Valjevo, Serb	28.03.93
Richards, Micah	5.11	–	Birmingham	24.06.88
Sagna, Bacary	5.9	Arsenal	Sens, Fr	14.02.83
Zabaleta, Pablo	5.10	Espanyol	Buenos Aires, Arg	16.01.85

Midfielders

Fernandinho	5.10	Shakhtar Donetsk	Londrina, Br	04.05.85
Fernando	6.0	Porto	Alto Paraiso, Br	25.07.87
Garcia, Javi	6.1	Benfica	Mula, Sp	08.02.87
Jesus Navas	5.8	Sevilla	Los Palacios, Sp	21.11.85
Milner, James	5.11	Aston Villa	Leeds	04.01.86
Nasri, Samir	5.10	Arsenal	Marseille, Fr	26.06.87
Rodwell, Jack	6.1	Everton	Birkdale	17.09.89
Silva, David	5.7	Valencia	Arguineguin, Sp	08.01.86
Toure, Yaya	6.3	Barcelona	Bouake, Iv C	13.05.83

Forwards

Aguero, Sergio	5.8	Atletico Madrid	Quilmes, Arg	02.06.88
Dzeko, Edin	6.4	Wolfsburg	Sarajevo, Bos	17.03.86
Guidetti, John	6.0	Brommapojkarna	Stockholm, Swe	15.04.92
Jovetic, Stevan	6.1	Fiorentina	Titograd, Mont	02.11.89
Negredo, Alvaro	6.1	Sevilla	Madrid, Sp	20.08.85

MANCHESTER UNITED

Ground: Old Trafford Stadium, Sir Matt Busby Way, Manchester, M16 ORA
Telephone: 0161 868 8000. **Club nickname:** Red Devils
Capacity: 75,811. **Colours:** Red and white. **Main sponsor:** Chevrolet
Record transfer fee: £37.1m to Chelsea for Juan Mata, Jan 2014
Record fee received: £80m from Real Madrid for Cristiano Ronaldo, Jun 2009
Record attendance: 75,811 v Blackburn (Prem Lge), Mar 31, 2007. Also: 76,962 Wolves v Grimsby (FA Cup semi-final) Mar 25, 1939. Crowd of 83,260 saw Manchester Utd v Arsenal (Div 1) Jan 17, 1948 at Maine Road – Old Trafford out of action through bomb damage
League Championship: Winners 1907–08, 1910–11, 1951–52, 1955–56, 1956–7, 1964–65, 1966–67, 1992–93, 1993–94, 1995–96, 1996–97, 1998–99, 1999–2000, 2000–01, 2002–03, 2006–07, 2007–08, 2008–09, 2010–11, 2012–13
FA Cup: Winners 1909, 1948, 1963, 1977, 1983, 1985, 1990, 1994, 1996, 1999, 2004
League Cup: Winners 1992, 2006, 2009
European competitions: Winners European Cup/Champions League 1967–68, 1998–99, 2007–08; Cup-Winners' Cup 1990–91; European Super Cup 1991
World Club Cup: Winners 2008
Finishing positions in Premier League: 1992–93 1st, 1993–94 1st, 1994–95 2nd, 1995–96 1st, 1996–97 1st, 1997–98 2nd, 1998–99 1st, 1999–2000 1st, 2000–01 1st, 2001–02 3rd, 2002–03 1st, 2003–04 3rd, 2004–05 3rd, 2005–06 2nd, 2006–07 1st, 2007–08 1st, 2000–09 1st, 2009–10 2nd, 2010–11 1st, 2011-12 2nd, 2012–13 1st, 2013–14 7th
Biggest win: As Newton Heath: 10-1 v Wolves (Div 1) Oct 15, 1892. As Manchester Utd: 9-0 v Ipswich (Prem Lge), Mar 4, 1995. Also: 10-0 v Anderlecht (European Cup prelim rd) Sep 26, 1956

Biggest defeat: 0-7v Blackburn (Div 1) Apr 10, 1926, v Aston Villa (Div 1) Dec 27, 1930, v Wolves (Div 2) 26 Dec, 1931
Highest League scorer in a season: Dennis Viollet 32 (1959–60)
Most League goals in aggregate: Bobby Charlton 199 (1956–73)
Longest unbeaten League sequence: 29 matches (1998–99)
Longest sequence without a League win: 16 matches (1930)
Most capped player: Bobby Charlton (England) 106

Goalkeepers

Amos, Ben	6.2	–	Macclesfield	10.04.90
De Gea, David	6.4	Atletico Madrid	Madrid, Sp	07.11.90
Johnstone, Sam	6.3	–	Preston	25.03.93
Lindegaard, Anders	6.4	Aalesund	Odense, Den	13.04.84

Defenders

Evans, Jonny	6.2	–	Belfast	03.01.88
Evra, Patrice	5.8	Monaco	Dakar, Sen	15.05.81
Jones, Phil	5.11	Blackburn	Blackburn	21.02.92
Keane, Michael	5.10	–	Stockport	11.01.93
Rafael	5.6	Fluminense	Petropolis, Br	09.07.90
Shaw, Luke	6.1	Southampton	Kingston	12.07.95
Smalling, Chris	6.1	Fulham	Greenwich	22.11.89
Varela, Guillermo	5.8	Penarol	Montevideo, Uru	24.03.93

Midfielders

Anderson	5.0	Porto	Alegre, Br	13.04.88
Bebe	6.3	Guimaraes	Agualva, Por	12.07.90
Carrick, Michael	6.0	Tottenham	Wallsend	28.07.81
Cleverley, Tom	5.10	–	Basingstoke	12.08.89
Fellaini, Marouane	6.4	Everton	Etterbeek, Bel	22.11.87
Fletcher, Darren	6.0	–	Edinburgh	01.02.84
Herrera, Ander	6.0	Athletic Bilbao	Bilbao, Sp	14.08.89
Januzaj, Adnan	5.11	Anderlecht	Brussels, Bel	05.02.95
Kagawa, Shinji	5.8	Borussia Dortmund	Kobe, Jap	17.03.89
Mata, Juan	5.7	Chelsea	Burgos, Sp	28.04.88
Nani	5.10	Sporting Lisbon	Amadora, Por	17.11.86
Valencia, Antonio	5.10	Wigan	Lago Agrio, Ec	04.08.85
Young, Ashley	5.10	Aston Villa	Stevenage	09.07.85
Zaha, Wilfried	5.10	Crystal Palace	Abidjan, Iv C	10.11.92

Forwards

Henriquez, Angelo	5.10	Universidad	Santiago, Chil	13.04.94
Hernandez, Javier	5.8	Chivas	Guadalajara, Mex	01.06.88
Powell, Nick	6.0	Crewe	Crewe	23.03.94
Rooney, Wayne	5.10	Everton	Liverpool	24.10.85
Van Persie, Robin	6.0	Arsenal	Rotterdam, Hol	06.08.83
Welbeck, Danny	5.10	–	Manchester	26.11.90

NEWCASTLE UNITED

Ground: St James' Park, Newcastle-upon-Tyne, NE1 4ST
Telephone: 0844 372 1892. **Club nickname**: Magpies
Capacity: 52,387. **Colours**: Black and white. **Main sponsor**: Wonga
Record transfer fee: £16m to Real Madrid for Michael Owen, Aug 2005
Record fee received: £35m from Liverpool for Andy Carroll, Jan 2011
Record attendance: 68,386 v Chelsea (Div 1) Sep 3, 1930
League Championship: Winners 1904–05, 1906–07, 1908–09, 1926–27
FA Cup: Winners 1910, 1924, 1932, 1951, 1952, 1955
League Cup: Runners-up 1976

European competitions: Winners Fairs Cup 1968–69; Anglo-Italian Cup 1972–73
Finishing positions in Premier League: 1993–94 3rd 1994–95 6th 1995–96 2nd 1996–97 2nd 1997–98 13th 1998–99 13th, 1999–2000 11th, 2000–01 11th, 2001–02 4th, 2002–03 3rd, 2003–04 5th, 2004–05 14th, 2005–06 7th, 2006–07 13th, 2007–08 12th; 2008–09 18th, 2010–11 12th, 2011–12 5th, 2012–13 16th, 2013–14 10th
Biggest win: 13-0 v Newport (Div 2) Oct 5, 1946
Biggest defeat: 0-9 v Burton (Div. 2) Apr 15, 1895
Highest League scorer in a season: Hughie Gallacher 36 (1926–27)
Most League goals in aggregate: Jackie Milburn 177 (1946–57)
Longest unbeaten League sequence: 14 matches (1950)
Longest sequence without a League win: 21 matches (1978)
Most capped player: Shay Given (Republic of Ireland) 83

Goalkeepers

Elliot, Rob	6.3	Charlton	Chatham	30.04.86
Krul, Tim	6.3	Den Haag	Den Haag, Hol	03.04.88

Defenders

Coloccini, Fabricio	6.0	Dep La Coruna	Cordoba, Arg	22.01.82
Dummett, Paul	6.0	–	Newcastle	26.09.91
Ferguson, Shane	5.11	–	Derry	12.07.91
Janmaat, Daryl	6.1	Feyenoord	Leidschendam, Hol	22.07.89
Haidara, Massadio	5.10	Nancy	Trappes, Fr	02.12.92
Santon, Davide	6.2	Inter Milan	Portomaggiore, It	02.01.91
Taylor, Ryan	5.8	Wigan	Liverpool	19.08.84
Taylor, Steven	6.2	–	Greenwich	23.01.86
Williamson, Mike	6.4	Portsmouth	Stoke	08.11.83
Yanga-Mbiwa, Mapou	6.0	Montpellier	Bangui, CARep	15.05.89

Midfielders

Anita, Vurnon	5.6	Ajax	Willemstad, Cur	04.04.89
Ben Arfa, Hatem	5.10	Marseille	Clamart, Fr	07.03.87
Bigirimana, Gael	5.10	Coventry	Bujumbura, Bur	22.10.93
Cabella, Remy	5.8	Montpellier	Ajaccio, Fr	08.03.90
Colback, Jack	5.10	Sunderland	Killingworth	24.10.89
De Jong, Siem	6.1	Ajax	Aigle, Swi	28.01.89
Gutierrez, Jonas	6.0	Real Mallorca	Saenz Pena, Arg	05.07.82
Marveaux, Sylvain	5.8	Rennes	Vannes, Fr	15.04.86
Obertan, Gabriel	6.2	Manchester Utd	Pantin, Fr	26.02.89
Sissoko, Moussa	6.2	Toulouse	Paris	16.08.89
Tiote, Cheick	5.11	Twente	Yamoussoukro, Iv C	21.06.86
Vuckic, Haris	6.2	Domzale	Ljubljana, Sloven	21.08.92

Forwards

Ameobi, Sammy	6.4	–	Newcastle	01.05.92
Ayoze Perez	5.11	Tenerife	Santa Cruz, Ten	23.07.93
Cisse, Papiss	6.0	Freiburg	Dakar, Sen	03.06.85
Gouffran, Yoan	5.10	Bordeaux	Villeneuve Georges, Fr	25.05.86
Riviere, Emmanuel	6.0	Monaco	Le Lamentin, Mart	03.03.90

QUEENS PARK RANGERS

Ground: Loftus Road Stadium, South Africa Road, London W12 7PA
Telephone: 0208 743 0262. **Club nickname:** Hoops
Capcity: 18,489. **Colours:** Blue and white. **Main sponsor:** Air Asia
Record transfer fee: £12.5m to Anzhi Makhachkala for Christopher Samba, Jan 2013
Record fee received: £12.5m from Anzhi Makhachkala for Christopher Samba, Jul 2013
Record attendance: 35,353 v Leeds (Div 1) 27 Apr, 1974
League Championship: Runners-up 1975–76

FA Cup: Runners-up 1982
League Cup: Winners 1967
European competitions: UEFA Cup quarter-finals 1976–77
Finishing positions in Premier League: 1992–93 5th, 1993–94 9th, 1994–95 8th, 1995–96 19th, 2011–12 17th, 2012–13 20th
Biggest win: 9-2 v Tranmere (Div 3) Dec 3, 1960. Also: 8-1 v Bristol Rov (FA Cup 1) Nov 27, 1937, v Crewe (Lge Cup 1) Oct 3, 1983
Biggest defeat: 1-8 v Mansfield (Div 3) Mar 15, 1965, v Manchester Utd (Div 1) Mar 19, 1969
Highest League scorer in a season: George Goddard 37 (1929–30)
Most League goals in aggregate: George Goddard 172 (1926–34)
Longest unbeaten League sequence: 20 matches (1972)
Longest sequence without a League win: 20 matches (1968–69)
Most capped player: Alan McDonald (Northern Ireland) 52

Goalkeepers

Green, Robert	6.2	West Ham	Chertsey	18.01.80
Murphy, Brian	6.0	Ipswich	Waterford, Ire	07.05.83

Defenders

Dunne, Richard	6.2	Aston Villa	Dublin, Ire	21.09.79
Ehmer, Max	6.2	–	Frankfurt, Ger	03.02.92
Ferdinand, Rio	6.2	Manchester Utd	Peckham	08.11.78
Harriman, Michael	5.6	–	Chichester	23.10.92
Hill, Clint	6.0	Crystal Palace	Liverpool	22.02.80
Onuoha, Nedum	6.2	Manchester City	Warri, Nig	12.11.86
Simpson, Danny	6.0	Newcastle	Salford	04.01.87
Traore, Armand	6.1	Arsenal	Paris, Fr	08.10.89
Yun Suk-Young	6.0	Chunnam	Suwon, S Kor	13.02.90

Midfielders

Barton, Joey	5.11	Newcastle	Huyton	02.09.82
Diakite, Samba	6.1	Nancy	Montfermeil, Fr	24.01.89
Faurlin, Alejandro	6.1	Instituto	Rosario, Arg	09.08.86
Granero, Esteban	5.11	Real Madrid	Madrid, Sp	02.08.87
Henry, Karl	6.1	Wolves	Wolverhampton	26.11.82
Hoilett, Junior	5.8	Blackburn	Ottawa, Can	05.06.90
Jenas, Jermaine	6.0	QPR	Nottingham	18.02.83
O'Neil, Gary	5.8	West Ham	Beckenham	18.05.83
Phillips, Matt	6.0	Blackpool	Aylesbury	13.03.91
Taarabt, Adel	5.11	Tottenham	Taza, Mor	24.05.89
Wright–Phillips, Shaun	5.6	Manchester City	Greenwich	25.10.81

Forwards

Austin, Charlie	6.2	Burnley	Hungerford	05.07.89
Remy, Loic	6.1	Marseille	Rilleux, Fr	02.01.87
Zamora, Bobby	6.0	Fulham	Barking	16.01.81

SOUTHAMPTON

Ground: St Mary's Stadium, Britannia Road, Southampton, SO14 5FP
Telephone: 0845 688 9448. **Club nickname**: Saints
Capacity: 32,689. **Colours**: Red and white. **Main sponsor**: Veho
Record transfer fee: £14.6m to Roma for Pablo Osvaldo, Aug 2013
Record fee received: £30m from Manchester Utd for Luke Shaw, Jun 2014
Record attendance: The Dell: 31,044 v Manchester Utd (Div 1) Oct 8, 1969; St Mary's: 32,363 v Coventry (Champ) Apr 28, 2012
League Championship: Runners-up 1983–84
FA Cup: Winners 1976
League Cup: Runners-up 1979

European competitions: Fairs Cup rd 3 1969–70; Cup-Winners' Cup rd 3 1976–77
Finishing positions in Premier League: 1992–93 18th, 1993–94 18th, 1994–5 10th, 1995–96 16th, 1996–97 16th, 1997–98 12th, 1998–99 17th, 1999–2000 15th, 2000–01 10th, 2001–02 11th, 2002–03 8th, 2003–04 12th, 2004–05 20th, 2012–13 14th, 2013–14 8th
Biggest win: 8-0 v Northampton (Div 3S) Dec 24, 1921
Biggest defeat: 0-8 v Tottenham (Div 2) Mar 28, 1936, v Everton (Div 1) Nov 20, 1971
Highest League scorer in a season: Derek Reeves 39 (1959–60)
Most League goals in aggregate: Mick Channon 185 (1966–82)
Longest unbeaten League sequence: 19 matches (1921)
Longest unbeaten League sequence: 20 matches (1969)
Most capped player: Peter Shilton (England) 49

Goalkeepers
Boruc, Artur	6.4	Fiorentina	Siedice, Pol	20.02.80
Davis, Kelvin	6.1	Sunderland	Bedford	29.09.76
Gazzaniga, Paulo	6.5	Gillingham	Murphy, Arg	02.01.92

Defenders
Clyne, Nathaniel	5.9	Crystal Palace	Stockwell	05.04.91
Fonte, Jose	6.2	Crystal Palace	Penafiel, Por	22.12.83
Hooiveld, Jos	6.4	Celtic	Zeijen, Hol	22.04.83
Lovren, Dejan	6.2	Lyon	Zenica, Bos	05.07.89
Stephens, Jack	6.1	Plymouth	Torpoint	27.01.94
Yoshida, Maya	6.2	Venlo	Nagasaki, Jap	24.08.88

Midfielders
Chambers, Calum	6.0	–	Petersfield	20.01.95
Cork, Jack	6.1	Chelsea	Carshalton	25.06.89
Davis, Steven	5.8	Rangers	Ballymena	01.01.85
Isgrove, Lloyd	5.10	–	Yeovil	12.01.93
Ramirez, Gaston	6.0	Bologna	Fray Bentos, Uru	02.12.90
Reed, Harrison	5.7	–	Worthing	27.01.95
Schneiderlin, Morgan	5.11	Strasbourg	Zellwiller, Fr	08.11.89
Tadic, Dusan	5.11	Twente	Backa Topola, Serb	20.11.88
Wanyama, Victor	6.2	Celtic	Nairobi, Ken	25.06.91
Ward-Prowse, James	5.8	–	Portsmouth	01.11.94

Forwards
Gallagher, Sam	6.4	–	Crediton	15.09.95
Mayuka, Emmanuel	5.9	Young Boys	Kabwe, Zim	21.11.90
Osvaldo, Dani	6.4	Roma	Buenos Aires, Arg	15.09.95
Pelle, Graziano	6.4	Feyenoord	San Cesario, It	15.07.85
Rodriguez, Jay	6.1	Burnley	Burnley	29.07.89

STOKE CITY

Ground: Britannia Stadium, Stanley Matthews Way, Stoke-on-Trent ST4 7EG
Telephone: 0871 663 2008. **Club nickname**: Potters
Capacity: 28,384. **Colours**: Red and white. **Main sponsor**: Bet 365
Record transfer fee: £10m to Tottenham for Peter Crouch, Aug 2012
Record fee received: £4.5m from Wolfsburg for Tuncay, Jan 2011
Record attendance: Victoria Ground: 51,380 v Arsenal (Div 1) Mar 29, 1937; Britannia Stadium: 28,218 v Everton (FA Cup 3) Jan 5, 2002
League Championship: 4th 1935–36, 1946–47
FA Cup: Runners-up 2011
League Cup: Winners 1972
European competitions: Europa League rd of 32 2011–12
Finishing positions in Premier League: 2008–09 12th, 2009–10 11th, 2010–11 13th, 2011–12 14th, 2012–13 13th, 2013–14 9th

Biggest win: 10-3 v WBA (Div 1) Feb 4, 1937
Biggest defeat: 0-10 v Preston (Div 1) Sep 14, 1889
Highest League scorer in a season: Freddie Steele 33 (1936–37)
Most League goals in aggregate: Freddie Steele 142 (1934–49)
Longest unbeaten League sequence: 25 matches (1992–93)
Longest sequence without a League win: 17 matches (1989)
Most capped player: Glenn Whelan (Republic of Ireland) 58

Goalkeepers

Bachmann, Daniel	6.3	Austria Vienna	Vienna, Aut	09.07.94
Begovic, Asmir	6.5	Portsmouth	Trebinje, Bos	20.06.87
Butland, Jack	6.4	Birmingham	Bristol	10.03.93
Sorensen, Thomas	6.5	Aston Villa	Federica, Den	12.06.76

Defenders

Bardsley, Phil	5.11	Sunderland	Salford	28.06.85
Cameron, Geoff	6.3	Houston	Attleboro, US	11.07.85
Huth, Robert	6.2	Middlesbrough	Berlin, Ger	18.08.84
Muniesa, Marc	5.11	Barcelona	Lloret de Mar, Sp	27.03.92
Pieters, Erik	6.1	PSV Eindhoven	Tiel, Hol	07.08.88
Shawcross, Ryan	6.3	Manchester Utd	Chester	04.10.87
Shotton, Ryan	6.3	–	Stoke	30.09.88
Teixeira, Dionatan	6.4	Banska Bystrica	Londrina, Br	24.07.92
Wheeler, Elliot	5.9	Portsmouth	Isle of Wight	19.12.93
Wilkinson, Andy	5.11	–	Stone	06.08.84
Wilson, Marc	6.2	Portsmouth	Belfast	17.08.87

Midfielders

Adam, Charlie	6.1	Liverpool	Dundee	10.12.85
Ireland, Stephen	5.8	Aston Villa	Cork, Ire	22.08.86
Ness, Jamie	5.10	Rangers	Irvine	02.03.91
N'Zonzi, Steven	6.3	Blackburn	La Garenne, Fr	15.12.88
Palacios, Wilson	6.0	Tottenham	La Ceiba, Hond	29.07.84
Shea, Brek	6.3	Dallas	College Station, US	28.02.90
Sidwell, Steve	5.10	Fulham	Wandsworth	14.12.82
Ward, Charlie	5.8	Aston Villa	Redditch	19.02.95
Whelan, Glenn	5.10	Sheffield Wed	Dublin, Ire	13.01.84

Forwards

Arnautovic, Marko	6.4	Werder Bremen	Vienna, Aut	19.04.89
Biram Diouf, Mame	6.1	Hannover	Dakar, Sen	16.12.87
Jerome, Cameron	6.1	Birmingham	Huddersfield	14.08.86
Crouch, Peter	6.7	Tottenham	Macclesfield	30.01.81
Odemwingie, Peter	6.0	Cardiff	Tashkent, Uzbek	15.07.81
Walters, Jon	6.0	Ipswich	Birkenhead	20.09.83

SUNDERLAND

Ground: Stadium of Light, Sunderland SR5 1SU
Telephone: 0191 551 5000. **Club nickname**: Black Cats
Capacity: 49,000. **Colours**: Red and white. **Main sponsor**: Bidvest
Record transfer fee: £13m to Rennes for Asamoah Gyan, Aug 2010
Record fee received: £24m from Aston Villa for Darren Bent, Jan 2011
Record attendance: Roker Park: 75,118 v Derby (FA Cup 6 rep) Mar 8, 1933. Stadium of Light: 48,353 v Liverpool (Prem Lge) Apr 13, 2002
League Championship: Winners 1891–92, 1892–93, 1894–95, 1901–02, 1912–13, 1935–36
FA Cup: Winners 1937, 1973
League Cup: Runners-up 1985
European competitions: Cup-Winners' Cup rd 2 1973–74

Finishing positions in Premier League: 1996–97 18th, 1999–2000 7th, 2000–01 7th, 2001–02 17th, 2002–03 20th, 2005–06 20th,2007–08 15th, 2008–09 16th, 2009–10 13th, 2010–11 10th, 2011–12 13th, 2012–13 17th, 2013–14 14th
Biggest win: 9-1 v Newcastle (Div 1) Dec 5, 1908. Also: 11-1 v Fairfield (FA Cup 1) Feb 2, 1895
Biggest defeat: 0-8 v Sheffield Wed (Div 1) Dec 26, 1911, v West Ham (Div 1) Oct 19, 1968, v Watford (Div 1) Sep 25, 1982
Highest League scorer in a season: Dave Halliday 43 (1928–29)
Most League goals in aggregate: Charlie Buchan 209 (1911–25)
Longest unbeaten League sequence: 19 matches (1998–99)
Longest sequence without a League win: 22 matches (2003–04)
Most capped player: Charlie Hurley (Republic of Ireland) 38

Goalkeepers

Mannone, Vito	6.3	Arsenal	Desio, It	02.03.88
Pantilimon, Costel	6.8	Manchester City	Bacau, Rom	01.02.87
Pickford, Jordan	6.1	–	Washington, Co Dur	07.03.94

Defenders

Brown, Wes	6.1	Manchester Utd	Manchester	13.10.79
Diakite, Modibo	6.4	Lazio	Bourgla-Reine, Fr	02.03.87
Jones, Billy	5.11	WBA	Shrewsbury	24.03.87
O'Shea, John	6.3	Manchester Utd	Waterford, Ire	30.04.81
Roberge, Valentin	6.2	Maritimo	Montreuil, Fr	09.06.87

Midfielders

Ba, El-Hadji	6.0	Le Havre	Paris, Fr	05.03.93
Bridcutt, Liam	5.9	Brighton	Reading	08.05.89
Cabral	5.10	Basel	Praia, Cape Verde	22.10.88
Cattermole, Lee	5.10	Wigan	Stockton	21.03.88
Giaccherini, Emanuele	5.8	Juventus	Bibbiena, It	05.05.85
Gomez, Jordi	5.10	Wigan	Barcelona, Sp	24.05.85
Johnson, Adam	5.9	Manchester City	Sunderland	14.07.87
Larsson, Sebastian	5.10	Birmingham	Eskiltuna, Swe	06.06.85
Mavrias, Charis	5.10	Panathinaikos	Zakynthos, Gre	21.02.94
Moberg Karlsson, David	5.11	Gothenburg	Mariestad, Swe	20.03.94
N'Diaye, Alfred	6.2	Bursaspor	Paris, Fr	06.03.90

Forwards

Altidore, Jozy	6.1	AZ Alkmaar	Livingston, US	06.11.89
Fletcher, Steven	6.1	Wolves	Shrewsbury	26.03.87
Graham, Danny	6.1	Swansea	Gateshead	12.08.85
Mandron, Mikael	6.3	–	Boulogne, Fr	11.10.94
Scocco, Ignacio	5.8	Internacional	Hughes, Arg	29.05.85
Watmore, Duncan	5.9	Altrincham	Cheadle Hulme	08.03.94
Wickham, Connor	6.3	Ipswich	Colchester	31.03.93

SWANSEA CITY

Ground: Liberty Stadium, Morfa, Swansea SA1 2FA
Telephone: 01792 616600. **Club nickname**: Swans
Capacity: 20,750. **Colours**: White. **Main sponsor**: GWFX
Record transfer fee: £12m to Vitesse Arnhem for Wilfried Bony, Jul 2013
Record fee received: £15m from Liverpool for Joe Allen, Aug 2012
Record attendance: Vetch Field: 32,796 v Arsenal (FA Cup 4) Feb 17, 1968; Liberty Stadium: 20,769 v Tottenham (Prem Lge) Jan 18, 2014
League Championship: 6th 1981–82
FA Cup: Semi-finals 1926, 1964
League Cup: Winners 2013
Finishing positions in Premier League: 2011–12 11th, 2012–13 9th, 2013–14 12th

European competitions: Cup-winners' Cup rd 2 1982–83; Europa Lge rd of 32 2013–14
Biggest win: 8-0 v Hartlepool (Div 4) Apr 1, 1978. Also: 12-0 v Sliema (Cup-winners' Cup rd 1, 1st leg), Sep 15, 1982
Biggest defeat: 0-8 v Liverpool (FA Cup 3) Jan 9, 1990, 0-8 v Monaco (Cup-winners' Cup rd 1, 2nd leg) Oct 1, 1991
Highest League scorer in a season: Cyril Pearce 35 (1931–32)
Most League goals in aggregate: Ivor Allchuch 166 (1949–58, 1965–68)
Longest unbeaten League sequence: 19 matches (1970–71)
Longest sequence without a League win: 15 matches (1989)
Most capped player: Ivor Allchurch (Wales) 42

Goalkeepers

Cornell, David	6.0	–	Swansea	28.03.91
Fabianski, Lukasz	6.3	Arsenal	Kostrzyn, Pol	18.04.85
Tremmel, Gerhard	6.3	Salzburg	Munich, Ger	16.11.78
Vorm, Michel	6.0	Utrecht	Nieuwegein, Hol	20.10.83

Defenders

Amat, Jordi	6.1	Espanyol	Canet de Mar, Sp	21.03.92
Bartley, Kyle	6.4	Arsenal	Stockport	22.05.91
Davies, Ben	5.6	–	Neath	24.04.93
Flores, Jose Manuel	6.2	Genoa	Cadiz, Sp	06.03.87
Kingsley, Stephen	5.10	Falkirk	Stirling	23.07.94
Rangel, Angel	5.11	Terrassa	Tortosa, Sp	28.10.82
Tate, Alan	6.1	Manchester Utd	Easington	02.09.82
Taylor, Neil	5.9	Wrexham	St Asaph	07.02.89
Tiendalli, Dwight	5.10	Twente	Paramaribo, Sur	21.10.85
Williams, Ashley	6.0	Stockport	Wolverhampton	23.08.84

Midfielders

Britton, Leon	5.5	Sheffield Utd	Merton	16.09.82
Canas, Jose	5.10	Real Betis	Jerez, Sp	27.05.87
Dyer, Nathan	5.10	Southampton	Trowbridge	29.11.87
Fulton, Jay	5.10	Falkirk	Bolton	04.04.94
Hernandez, Pablo	5.8	Valencia	Castellon, Sp	11.04.85
Ki Sung-Yueng	6.2	Celtic	Gwangju, S Kor	24.01.89
King, Adam	5.11	Hearts	Edinburgh	11.10.95
Pozuelo, Alejandro	5.8	Real Betis	Seville, Sp	20.09.91
Richards, Ashley	6.1	–	Swansea	12.04.91
Routledge, Wayne	5.7	Newcastle	Sidcup	07.01.85
Shelvey, Jonjo	6.0	Liverpool	Romford	27.02.92

Forwards

Bony, Wilfried	6.0	Vitesse Arnhem	Bingerville, Iv C	10.12.88
Donnelly, Rory	6.2	Cliftonville	Belfast	18.02.92
Emnes, Marvin	5.11	Middlesbrough	Rotterdam, Hol	27.05.88
Gomis, Bafetimbi	6.0	Lyon	La Seyne, Fr	06.08.85

TOTTENHAM HOTSPUR

Ground: White Hart Lane, Tottenham, London N17 0AP
Telephone: 0844 499 5000. **Club nickname**: Spurs
Capacity: 36,310. **Colours**: White. **MAIn sponsor**: AIA
Record transfer: £30m to Roma for Erik Lamela, Aug 2013
Record fee received: £85.3m from Real Madrid for Gareth Bale, Aug 2013
Record attendance: 75,038 v Sunderland (FA Cup 6) Mar 5, 1938
League Championship: Winners 1950–51, 1960–61
FA Cup: Winners 1901, 1921, 1961, 1962, 1967, 1981, 1982, 1991
League Cup: Winners 1971, 1973, 1999, 2008

European competitions: Winners Cup-Winners' Cup 1962–63; UEFA Cup 1971–72, 1983–84
Finishing positions in Premier League: 1992–93 8th, 1993–94 15th, 1994–95 7th, 1995–96 8th, 1996–97 10th, 1997–98 14th, 1998–99 11th, 1999–2000 10th, 2000–01 12th, 2001–02 9th, 2002–03 10th, 2003–04 14th, 2004–05 9th, 2005–06 5th, 2006–07 5th, 2007–08 11th, 2008–09 8th, 2009–10 4th, 2010–11 5th, 2011–12 4th, 2012–13 5th, 2013–14 6th
Biggest win: 9-0 v Bristol Rov (Div 2) Oct 22, 1977. Also: 13-2 v Crewe (FA Cup 4 replay) Feb 3, 1960
Biggest defeat: 0-7 v Liverpool (Div 1) Sep 2, 1979. Also: 0-8 v Cologne (Inter Toto Cup) Jul 22, 1995
Highest League scorer in a season: Jimmy Greaves 37 (1962–63)
Most League goals in aggregate: Jimmy Greaves 220 (1961–70)
Longest unbeaten League sequence: 22 matches (1949)
Longest sequence without a League win: 16 matches (1934–35)
Most capped player: Pat Jennings (Northern Ireland) 74

Goalkeepers

Archer, Jordan	6.3	–	Walthamstow	12.04.93
Friedel, Brad	6.3	Aston Villa	Lakewood, US	18.05.71
Lloris, Hugo	6.2	Lyon	Nice, Fr	26.12.86

Defenders

Assou–Ekotto, Benoit	5.10	Lens	Arras, Fr	24.03.84
Chiriches, Vlad	6.1	Steaua Bucharest	Bacau, Rom	14.11.89
Dawson, Michael	6.2	Nottm Forest	Northallerton	18.11.83
Fryers, Ezekiel	6.0	Standard Liege	Manchester	09.09.92
Kaboul, Younes	6.3	Portsmouth	St Julien, Fr	04.01.86
Naughton, Kyle	5.10	Sheffield Utd	Sheffield	11.11.88
Rose, Danny	5.8	Leeds	Doncaster	02.07.90
Vertonghen, Jan	6.2	Ajax	Sint-Niklaas, Bel	24.04.87
Walker, Kyle	5.10	Sheffield Utd	Sheffield	28.05.90

Midfielders

Bentaleb, Nabil	6.2	–	Lille, Fr	24.11.94
Carroll, Tom	5.10	–	Watford	28.05.92
Chadli, Nacer	6.2	Twente	Liege, Bel	02.08.89
Capoue, Etienne	6.2	Toulouse	Niort, Fr	11.07.88
Dembele, Mousa	6.1	Fulham	Wilrijk, Bel	16.07.87
Eriksen, Christian	5.10	Ajax	Middelfart, Den	14.02.92
Holtby, Lewis	5.10	Borussia M'gladbach	Erkelenz, Ger	18.09.90
Iago Falque	5.9	Juventus	Vigo, Sp	04.01.90
Lamela, Erik	6.0	Roma	Buenos Aires, Arg	04.03.92
Lennon, Aaron	5.5	Leeds	Leeds	16.04.87
Mason, Ryan	5.9	–	Enfield	13.06.91
Paulinho	6.0	Corinthians	Sao Paulo, Br	25.07.88
Sandro	6.2	Internacional	Riachinho, Br	15.03.89
Sigurdsson, Gylfi	6.1	Hoffenheim	Hafnarfjordur, Ice	08.09.89
Townsend, Andros	6.0	–	Leytonstone	16.07.91

Forwards

Adebayor, Emmanuel	6.3	Manchester City	Lome, Tog	24.12.84
Kane, Harry	6.2	–	Walthamstow	28.07.93
Soldado, Roberto	5.11	Valencia	Valencia, Sp	27.05.85

WEST BROMWICH ALBION

Ground: The Hawthorns, Halfords Lane, West Bromwich B71 4LF
Telephone: 0871 271 1100. **Club nickname**: Baggies
Capacity: 28,003. **Colours**: Blue and white. **Main sponsor**: QuickBooks

Record transfer fee: £10m to Dynamo Kiev for Brown Ideye, Jul 2014
Record fee received: £8.5m from Aston Villa for Curtis Davies, Jul 2008
Record attendance: 64,815 v Arsenal (FA Cup 6) Mar 6, 1937
League Championship: Winners 1919–20
FA Cup: Winners 1888, 1892, 1931, 1954, 1968
League Cup: Winners 1966
European competitions: Cup-Winners' Cup quarter-finals 1968–69; UEFA Cup quarter-finals 1978–79
Finishing positions in Premier League: 2002–03 19th, 2004–5 17th, 2005–6 19th; 2008–09 20th, 2010–11 11th, 2011–12 10th, 2012–13 8th, 2013–14 17th
Biggest win: 12-0 v Darwen (Div 1) Apr 4, 1892
Biggest defeat: 3-10 v Stoke (Div 1) Feb 4, 1937
Highest League scorer in a season: William Richardson 39 (1935–36)
Most League goals in aggregate: Tony Brown 218 (1963–79)
Longest unbeaten League sequence: 17 matches (1957)
Longest sequence without a League win: 14 matches (1995)
Most capped player: Chris Brunt (Northern Ireland) 36

Goalkeepers

Daniels, Luke	6.4	Manchester Utd	Bolton	05.01.88
Foster, Ben	6.2	Birmingham	Leamington	03.04.83
Myhill, Boaz	6.3	Hull	Modesto, US	09.11.82

Defenders

Baird, Chris	5.11	Burnley	Rasharkin	25.02.82
Daniels, Donervorn	6.1	–	Montserrat	24.11.93
Dawson, Craig	6.2	Rochdale	Rochdale	06.05.90
Lescott, Joleon	6.2	Manchester City	Birmingham	16.08.82
McAuley, Gareth	6.3	Ipswich	Larne	05.12.79
Olsson, Jonas	6.4	Nijmegen	Landskrona, Swe	10.03.83
O'Neil, Liam	5.11	Histon	Cambridge	31.07.93
Pocognoli, Sebastien	6.0	Hannover	Liege, Bel	01.08.87

Midfielders

Brunt, Chris	6.1	Sheffield Wed	Belfast	14.12.84
Dorrans, Graham	5.9	Livingston	Glasgow	05.05.87
Gardner, Craig	5.10	Sunderland	Solihull	25.11.86
Morrison, James	5.10	Middlesbrough	Darlington	25.05.86
Mulumbu, Youssouf	5.10	Paris SG	Kinshasa, DR Cong	25.01.87
Roofe, Kemar	5.10	–	Walsall	06.01.93
Sessegnon, Stephane	5.8	Sunderland	Allahe, Benin	01.06.84
Thorne, George	6.2	–	Chatham	04.01.93
Yacob, Claudio	5.11	Racing Club	Carcarana, Arg	18.07.87

Forwards

Anichebe, Victor	6.1	Everton	Lagos, Nig	23.04.88
Berahino, Saido	5.10	–	Burundi	04.08.93
Brown Ideye	5.11	Dynamo Kiev	Lagos, Nig	10.10.88
Nabi, Adil	5.8	–	Birmingham	28.02.94

WEST HAM UNITED

Ground: Boleyn Ground, Upton Park, London E13 9AZ
Telephone: 0208 548 2748. **Club nickname**: Hammers
Capacity: 35,547. **Colours**: Claret and blue. **Main sponsor**: Alpari
Record transfer fee: £15m to Liverpool for Andy Carroll, Jul 2013
Record fee received: £18m from Leeds for Rio Ferdinand, Nov 2000
Record attendance: 43,322 v Tottenham (Div 1) Oct 17, 1970
League Championship: 3rd 1985–86

FA Cup: Winners 1964, 1975, 1980
League Cup: Runners-up 1966, 1981
European competitions: Winners Cup-Winners' Cup 1964–65
Finishing positions in Premier League: 1993–94 13th, 1994–95 14th, 1995–96 10th, 1996–97 14th, 1997–98 8th, 1998–99 5th, 1999–2000 9th, 2000–01 15th, 2001–02 7th, 2002–03 18th, 2005–06 9th, 2006–07 15th, 2007–08 10th, 2008–09: 9th, 2009 10 17th, 2010–11 20th, 2012–13 10th, 2013–14 13th
Biggest win: 8-0 v Rotherham (Div 2) Mar 8, 1958, v Sunderland (Div 1) Oct 19, 1968. Also: 10-0 v Bury (League Cup 2) Oct 25, 1983
Biggest defeat: 0-7 v Barnsley (Div 2) Sep 1, 1919, v Everton (Div 1) Oct 22, 1927, v Sheffield Wed (Div 1) Nov 28, 1959
Highest League scorer in a season: Vic Watson 42 (1929–30)
Most League goals in aggregate: Vic Watson 298 (1920–35)
Longest unbeaten League sequence: 27 matches (1980–81)
Longest sequence without a League win: 17 matches (1976)
Most capped player: Bobby Moore (England) 108

Goalkeepers

Adrian	6.3	Real Betis	Seville, Sp	03.01.87
Henderson, Stephen	6.3	Portsmouth	Dublin, Ire	02.05.88
Jaaskelainen, Jussi	6.4	Bolton	Mikkeli, Fin	17.04.75

Defenders

Chambers, Leo	6.1	–	Brixton	05.08.95
Collins, James	6.2	Aston Villa	Newport	23.08.83
Cresswell, Aaron	5.7	Ipswich	Liverpool	15.12.89
Demel, Guy	6.3	Hamburg	Orsay, Fr	13.06.81
Kouyate, Cheikhou	6.4	Anderlecht	Dakar, Sen	21.12.89
O'Brien, Joey	6.2	Bolton	Dublin, Ire	17.02.86
Potts, Daniel	5.8	–	Romford	13.04.94
Reid, Winston	6.3	Midtjylland	Auckland, NZ	03.07.88
Tomkins, James	6.3	–	Basildon	29.03.89

Midfielders

Diame, Mohamed	6.1	Wigan	Creteil, Fr	14.06.87
Downing, Stewart	6.0	Liverpool	Middlesbrough	02.07.84
Jarvis, Matt	5.8	Wolves	Middlesbrough	22.05.86
Moncur, George	5.9	–	Swindon	18.08.93
Morrison, Ravel	5.10	Manchester Utd	Manchester	02.02.93
Noble, Mark	5.11	–	West Ham	08.05.87
Nolan, Kevin	6.1	Newcastle	Liverpool	24.06.82
Poyet, Diego	5.11	Charlton	Zaragoza, Sp	08.04.95
Turgott, Blair	6.0	–	Bromley	22.05.94
Whitehead, Danny	5.9	Stockport	Trafford	23.10.93

Forwards

Carroll, Andy	6.3	Liverpool	Gateshead	06.01.89
Cole, Carlton	6.3	Chelsea	Croydon	12.10.83
Lee, Elliot	5.11	–	Durham	16.12.94
Maiga, Modibo	6.1	Sochaux	Bamako, Mali	03.09.87
Valencia, Enner	5.11	Pachuca	Esmeraldas, Ec	04.11.89
Vaz Te, Ricardo	6.2	Barnsley	Lisbon, Por	01.10.86
Zarate, Mauro	5.10	Velez Sarsfield	Haedo, Arg	18.03.87

FOOTBALL LEAGUE PLAYING STAFFS 2014–15

(At time of going to press)

CHAMPIONSHIP

BIRMINGHAM CITY

Ground: St Andrew's, Birmingham B9 4NH
Telephone: 0844 557 1875. **Club nickname**: Blues
Colours: Blue and white. **Capacity**: 30,016
Record attendance: 66,844 v Everton (FA Cup 5) Feb 11, 1939

Goalkeepers

Doyle, Colin	6.5	–	Cork, Ire	12.08.85
Randolph, Darren	6.1	Motherwell	Bray, Ire	12.05.87
Townsend, Nick	5.11	–	Solihull	01.11.94

Defenders

Caddis, Paul	5.7	Swindon	Irvine	19.04.88
Eardley, Neal	5.11	Blackpool	Llandudno	06.11.88
Edgar, David	6.2	Burnley	Kitchener, Can	19.05.87
Gunning, Gavin	6.0	Dundee Utd	Dublin, Ire	26.01.91
Grounds, Jonathan	6.1	Oldham	Thornaby	02.02.88
Hall, Grant	6.3	Tottenham (loan)	Brighton	29.10.91
Hancox, Mitch	5.10	–	Solihull	09.11.93
Packwood, Will	6.3	–	Concord, US	21.05.93
Robinson, Paul	5.9	Bolton	Watford	14.12.78
Spector, Jonathan	6.1	West Ham	Arlington Heights, US	03.01.86

Midfielders

Adams, Charlee	5.11	–	Redbridge	16.02.95
Adeyemi, Tom	6.1	Norwich	Norwich	24.10.91
Brown, Reece	5.9	–	Dudley	03.03.96
Cotterill, David	5.9	Doncaster	Cardiff	04.12.87
Duffy, Mark	5.9	Doncaster	Liverpool	07.10.85
Gleeson, Stephen	6.2	MK Dons	Dublin, Ire	03.08.88
Gray, Demarai	5.10	–	Birmingham	28.06.96
Lee, Olly	5.11	Barnet	Havering	11.07.91
Reilly, Callum	6.1	–	Warrington	03.10.93
Shinnie, Andrew	5.11	Inverness	Aberdeen	17.07.89

Forwards

Donaldson, Clayton	6.1	Brentford	Bradford	07.02.84
Green, Matt	6.0	Mansfield	Bath	02.01.87
Novak, Lee	6.0	Huddersfield	Newcastle	28.09.88
Thomas, Wes	5.11	Rotherham	Barking	23.01.87

BLACKBURN ROVERS

Ground: Ewood Park, Blackburn BB2 4JF
Telephone: 0871 702 1875. **Club nickname**: Rovers
Colours: Blue and white. **Capacity**: 31,367
Record attendance: 62,522 v Bolton (FA Cup 6) Mar 2, 1929

Goalkeepers

Eastwood, Simon	6.2	Portsmouth	Luton	26.06.89
Kean, Jake	6.4	Derby	Derby	04.02.91
Robinson, Paul	6.2	Tottenham	Beverley	15.10.79

Defenders

Baptiste, Alex	5.11	Bolton (loan)	Sutton-in-Ashfield	31.01.86
Hanley, Grant	6.2	–	Dumfries	20.11.91
Henley, Adam	5.10	–	Knoxville, US	14.06.94
Kilgallon, Matt	6.1	Sunderland	York	08.01.84
Spurr, Tommy	6.1	Doncaster	Leeds	30.09.87
Songo'o, Yann	6.1	Sporting Kansas	Yaounde, Cam	19.11.91

Midfielders

Cairney, Tom	6.0	Hull	Nottingham	20.01.91
Conway, Craig	5.8	Cardiff	Irvine	02.05.85
Dunn, David	5.10	Birmingham	Great Harwood	27.12.79
Evans, Corry	5.11	Hull	Belfast	30.07.90
Lowe, Jason	6.0	–	Wigan	02.09.91
Marshall, Ben	6.0	Leicester	Salford	29.09.91
O'Sullivan, John	5.11	–	Dublin, Ire	18.09.93
Taylor, Chris	5.11	Millwall	Oldham	20.12.86
Williamson, Lee	5.10	Portsmouth	Derby	07.06.82

Forwards

Best, Leon	6.1	Newcastle	Nottingham	19.09.86
Brown, Chris	6.3	Doncaster	Doncaster	11.12.84
Gestede, Rudy	6.4	Cardiff	Nancy, Fr	10.10.88
King, Josh	5.11	Manchester Utd	Oslo, Nor	15.01.92
Rhodes, Jordan	6.1	Huddersfield	Oldham	05.02.90
Slew, Jordan	6.3	Sheffield Utd	Sheffield	07.09.92
Varney, Luke	5.11	Leeds	Leicester	28.09.82

BLACKPOOL

Ground: Bloomfield Road, Blackpool FY1 6JJ
Telephone: 0871 622 1953. **Club nickname**: Seasiders
Colours: Tangerine and white. **Capacity**: 16,750
Record attendance: 38,098 v Wolves (Div 1) Sep 17, 1955

Goalkeepers
Defenders

Dunne, Charles	6.1	Wycombe	Lambeth	13.02.93
MacKenzie, Gary	6.3	MK Dons	Lanark	15.10.85
McMahon, Tony	5.10	Sheffield Utd	Bishop Auckland	24.03.86

Midfielders

Perkins, David	5.6	Barnsley	Heysham	21.06.82

Forwards

Barkhuizen, Tom	5.11	–	Blackpool	04.07.93
Davies, Steve	6.1	Bristol City	Liverpool	29.12.87
Grant, Bobby	5.11	Rochdale	Litherland	01.07.90
Zenjov, Sergei	6.0	Karpaty Lviv	Parnu, Est	20.04.89

BOLTON WANDERERS

Ground: Macron Stadium, Burnden Way, Lostock, Bolton BL6 6JW
Telephone: 0844 871 2932. **Club nickname**: Trotters
Colours: White and navy. **Capacity**: 28,723
Record attendance: Burnden Park: 69,912 v Manchester City (FA Cup 5) Feb 18, 1933; Macron Stadium: 28,353 v Leicester (Prem Lge) Dec 28, 2003

Goalkeepers

Bogdan, Adam	6.4	Vasas	Budapest, Hun	27.09.87
Lonergan, Andy	6.4	Leeds	Preston	19.10.83

Defenders

Bolger, Cian	6.4	Leicester	Cellbridge, Ire	12.03.92
Dervite, Dorian	6.3	Charlton	Lille, Fr	25.07.88
McNaughton, Kevin	5.10	Cardiff (loan)	Dundee	28.08.82
Mills, Matt	6.3	Leicester	Swindon	14.07.86
Moxey, Dean	5.11	Crystal Palace	Exeter	14.01.86
Ream, Tim	6.1	NY Red Bulls	St Louis, US	05.10.87
Riley, Joe	6.0	–	Salford	13.10.91
Tierney, Marc	6.0	Norwich	Prestwich	23.08.85
Wheater, David	6.4	Middlesbrough	Redcar	14.02.87

Midfielders

Andrews, Keith	6.0	WBA	Dublin, Ire	13.09.80
Bastos, Yannick	5.10	Differdange	Luxembourg	30.05.93
Chung–Yong Lee	5.11	Seoul	Seoul, S Kor	02.07.88
Danns, Neil	5.9	Leicester	Liverpool	23.11.82
Davies, Mark	5.11	Wolves	Wolverhampton	18.02.88
Feeney, Liam	6.0	Millwall	Hammersmith	28.04.86
Holden, Stuart	5.10	Houston	Aberdeen	01.08.85
Iliev, Georg	6.0	–	Sofia, Bul	23.10.94
Lester, Chris	5.11	–	Salford	27.10.94
Medo, Mohamed	5.9	Partizan Belgrade	Bo, SLeone	16.11.87
Pratley, Darren	6.0	Swansea	Barking	22.04.85
Robinson, Andy	6.2	Southampton	Bournemouth	16.10.92
Spearing, Jay	5.7	Liverpool	Wallasey	25.11.88
Trotter, Liam	6.2	Millwall	Ipswich	24.08.88
Vela, Josh	5.11	–	Salford	14.12.93

Forwards

Beckford, Jermaine	6.2	Leicester	Ealing	09.12.83
Clough, Zach	5.8	–	Manchester	08.03.95
Davies, Craig	6.2	Barnsley	Burton	09.01.86
Eaves, Tom	6.4	Oldham	Liverpool	14.01.92
Hall, Robert	6.2	West Ham	Aylesbury	20.10.93
Odelusi, Sanmi	6.0	Reading	Dagenham	11.07.93
Wilkinson, Conor	6.3	–	Croydon	23.01.95
Youngs, Tom	5.9	–	Greenwich	06.09.94

BOURNEMOUTH

Ground: Goldsands Stadium, Dean Court, Bournemouth BH7 7AF
Telephone: 01202 726300. **Club nickname**: Cherries
Colours: Red and black. **Capacity**: 12,081
Record attendance: 28,799 v Manchester Utd (FA Cup 6) Mar 2, 1957

Goalkeepers

Camp, Lee	6.1	WBA	Derby	22.08.84
Flahavan, Darryl	5.11	Portsmouth	Southampton	28.11.78

Defenders

Addison, Miles	6.3	Derby	Newham	07.01.89
Cook, Steve	6.1	Brighton	Hastings	19.04.91
Elphick, Tommy	5.11	Bournemouth	Brighton	07.09.87
Francis, Simon	6.0	Charlton	Nottingham	16.02.85
Harte, Ian	5.10	Reading	Drogheda, Ire	31.08.77
Smith, Adam	5.11	Tottenham	Leystonstone	29.04.91
Ward, Elliott	6.1	Norwich	Harrow	19.01.85

Midfielders

Arter, Harry	5.9	Woking	Eltham	28.12.89

Daniels, Charlie	5.10	Leyton Orient	Harlow	07.09.86
Fraser, Ryan	5.4	Aberdeen	Aberdeen	24.02.94
Gosling, Dan	5.10	Newcastle	Brixham	02.02.90
MacDonald, Shaun	6.1	Swansea	Swansea	17.06.88
McDermott, Donal	5.9	Huddersfield	Ashbourne, Ire	19.10.89
McQuoid, Josh	5.10	Millwall	Southampton	15.12.89
O'Kane, Eunan	5.8	Torquay	Derry	10.07.90
Pugh, Marc	5.11	Hereford	Bacup	02.04.87
Ritchie, Matt	5.8	Swindon	Gosport	10.09.89
Stanislas, Junior	6.0	Burnley	Eltham	26.11.89
Forwards				
Kermogant, Yann	6.1	Charlton	Vannes, Fr	08.11.81
Pitman, Brett	6.0	Bristol City	St Helier, Jer	03.01.88
Rantie, Tokelo	5.9	Malmo	Parys, SA	08.09.90
Wilson, Callum	5.11	Coventry	Coventry	27.02.92

BRENTFORD

Ground: Griffin Park, Braemar Road, Brentford TW8 0NT
Telephone: 0845 345 6442. **Club nickname**: Bees
Colours: Red, white and black. **Capacity**: 12,763
Record attendance: 39,626 v Preston (FA Cup 6) Mar 5, 1938

Goalkeepers				
Bonham, Jack	6.3	Watford	Stevenage	14.09.93
Button, David	6.3	Charlton	Stevenage	27.02.89
Lee, Richard	5.11	Watford	Oxford	05.10.82
Defenders				
Bidwell, Jake	6.0	Everton	Southport	21.03.93
Calvet, Raphael	6.0	Auxerre	Auxerre, Fr	07.02.94
Craig, Tony	6.0	Millwall	Greenwich	20.04.85
Dean, Harlee	5.10	Southampton	Basingstoke	26.07.91
O'Connor, Kevin	5.11	–	Blackburn	24.02.82
Tarkowski, James	6.1	Oldham	Manchester	19.11.92
Midfielders				
Adams, Charlie	5.7	–	Hendon	16.05.94
Dallas, Stuart	6.0	Crusaders	Cookstown	19.04.91
Diagouraga, Toumani	6.3	Peterborough	Paris, Fr	09.06.87
Douglas, Jonathan	5.11	Swindon	Monaghan, Ire	22.11.81
Forshaw, Adam	6.1	Everton	Liverpool	08.10.91
Judge, Alan	6.0	Blackburn	Dublin, Ire	11.11.88
McCormack, Alan	5.8	Swindon	Dublin, Ire	10.01.84
Odubajo, Moses	5.10	Leyton Orient	Greenwich	28.07.93
Pritchard, Alex	5.7	Tottenham (loan)	Orsett	03.05.93
Reeves, Jake	5.7	–	Greenwich	30.05.93
Saunders, Sam	5.11	Dagenham	Greenwich	29.08.83
Tebar Ramiro, Marcos	6.1	Almeria	Madrid, Sp	07.02.86
Yennaris, Nico	5.9	Arsenal	Leytonstone	24.05.93
Forwards				
Gray, Andre	5.10	Luton	Wolverhampton	26.06.91

BRIGHTON AND HOVE ALBION

Ground: American Express Stadium, Village Way, Brighton BN1 9BL
Telephone: 01273 878288. **Club nickname**: Seagulls
Colours: Blue and white. **Capacity**: 30,250
Record attendance: Goldstone Ground: 36,747 v Fulham (Div 2) Dec 27, 1958; Withdean

Stadium: 8,729 v Manchester City (Carling Cup 2) Sep 23, 2008; American Express Stadium: 30,003 v Wolves (Champ) May 4, 2013

Goalkeepers

Ankergren, Casper	6.3	Leeds	Koge, Den	09.11.79

Defenders

Calderon, Inigo	5.11	Alaves	Vitoria, Sp	04.01.82
Chicksen, Adam	5.8	MK Dons	Milton Keynes	01.11.90
Dunk, Lewis	6.4	–	Brighton	21.11.91
Greer, Gordon	6.2	Swindon	Glasgow	14.12.80
Hughes, Aaron	6.1	QPR	Cookstown	08.11.79
Maksimenko, Vitalijs	6.1	Skonto Riga	Riga, Lat	08.12.90
Saltor, Bruno	5.11	Valencia	El Masnou, Sp	01.10.80

Midfielders

Agustien, Kemy	5.10	Swansea	Willemstad, Hol	20.08.86
Buckley, Will	6.0	Watford	Oldham	12.08.88
Crofts, Andrew	5.11	Norwich	Chatham	29.05.84
Forster-Caskey, Jake	5.10	–	Southend	25.04.94
Ince, Rohan	6.3	Chelsea	Whitechapel	08.11.92
LuaLua, Kazenga	5.11	Newcastle	Kinshasa, DR Cong	10.12.90
March, Solly	5.11	–	Eastbourne	20.07.94
Monakana, Jeffrey	5.11	Preston	Edmonton	05.11.93
Stephens, Dale	5.7	Charlton	Bolton	12.06.89
Toko, Nzuzi	5.8	Grasshoppers	Kinshasa, DR Cong	20.12.90

Forwards

O'Grady, Chris	6.1	Barnsley	Nottingham	25.01.86
Mackail-Smith, Craig	6.3	Peterborough	Watford	25.02.84
Ulloa, Leonardo	6.2	Almeria	General Roca, Arg	26.07.86

CARDIFF CITY

Ground: Cardiff City Stadium, Leckwith Road, Cardiff CF11 8AZ
Telephone: 0845 365 1115. **Club nickname**: Bluebirds
Colours: Red and black. **Capacity**: 28,000
Record attendance: Ninian Park: 62,634 Wales v England, Oct 17, 1959; Club: 57,893 v Arsenal (Div 1) Apr 22, 1953, Cardiff City Stadium: 28,018 v Liverpool (Prem Lge) Mar 22, 2014

Goalkeepers

Lewis, Joe	6.5	Peterborough	Broome	06.10.87
Marshall, David	6.3	Norwich	Glasgow	05.03.85
Moore, Simon	6.3	Brentford	Sandown	19.05.90

Defenders

Brayford, John	5.8	Derby	Stoke	29.12.87
Cala, Juan	6.2	Sevilla	Lebrija, Sp	26.11.89
Connolly, Matthew	6.2	QPR	Barnet	24.09.87
Fabio	5.6	Manchester Utd	Petropolis, Br	09.07.90
Hudson, Mark	6.3	Charlton	Guildford	30.03.82
John, Declan	5.10	–	Merthyr Tydfil	30.06.95
Theophile-Catherine, Kevin	6.0	Rennes	Saint-Brieuc, Fr	28.10.89
Turner, Ben	6.4	Coventry	Birmingham	21.08.88

Midfielders

Burgstaller, Guido	6.2	Rapid Vienna	Villach, Aut	29.04.89
Daehli, Mats	5.10	Molde	Oslo, Nor	02.03.95
Dikgacoi, Kagisho	5.11	Crystal Palace	Brandfort, SA	24.11.84
Eikrem, Magnus	5.8	Heerenveen	Molde, Nor	08.08.90
Gunnarsson, Aron	5.11	Coventry	Akureyri, Ice	22.04.89

Harris, Kadeem	5.9	Wycombe	Westminster	08.06.93
Kim Bo-Kyung	5.10	Cerezo Osaka	Gurye, S Kor	06.10.89
Kiss, Filip	6.1	Slovan Bratislava	Dunajska, Slovak	13.10.90
Medel, Gary	5.8	Sevilla	Santiago, Chil	03.08.87
Mutch, Jordon	5.9	Birmingham	Birmingham	02.12.91
Noone, Craig	6.3	Brighton	Fazackerley	17.11.87
Ralls, Joe	6.0	–	Aldershot	13.10.93
Whittingham, Peter	5.10	Aston Villa	Nuneaton	08.09.84
Forwards				
Guerra, Javi	5.11	Valladolid	Velez Malaga, Sp	15.03.82
Inge Berget, Jo	6.1	Molde	Oslo, Nor	11.09.90
Jones, Kenwyne	6.2	Stoke	Point Fortin, Trin	05.01.84
Le Fondre, Adam	5.9	Reading	Stockport	02.12.86
Macheda, Federico	6.0	Manchester Utd	Rome, It	22.08.91
Mason, Joe	5.10	Plymouth	Plymouth	13.05.91
Maynard, Nicky	5.11	West Ham	Winsford	11.12.86
Velikonja, Etien	5.10	Maribor	Sempeter, Sloven	26.12.88

CHARLTON ATHLETIC

Ground: The Valley, Floyd Road, London SE7 8BL
Telephone: 0208 333 4000. **Club nickname**: Addicks
Colours: Red and white. **Capacity**: 27,111
Record attendance: 75,031 v Aston Villa (FA Cup 5) Feb 12, 1938

Goalkeepers				
Pope, Nick	6.3	Bury Town	Cambridge	19.04.92
Defenders				
Ben Haim, Tal	6.0	Standard Liege	Rishon, Isr	31.03.82
Bikey, Andre	6.0	Panetolikos	Douala, Cam	08.01.85
Cousins, Jordan	5.10	–	Greenwich	06.03.94
Fox, Morgan	6.1	–	Chelmsford	21.09.93
Lennon, Harry	6.3	–	Barking	16.12.94
Morrison, Michael	6.1	Sheffield Wed	Bury St Edmunds	03.03.88
Nego, Loic	6.0	Ujpest	Paris, Fr	15.01.91
Solly, Chris	5.8	–	Rochester	20.01.90
Wiggins, Rhoys	5.9	Bournemouth	Hillingdon	04.11.87
Midfielders				
Buyens, Yoni	6.0	Standard Liege (loan)	Duffel, Bel	10.03.88
Gudmundsson, Johann Berg	6.1	Alkmaar	Reykjavik, Ice	27.10.90
Harriott, Callum	5.5	–	Norbury	04.03.94
Jackson, Johnnie	6.1	Notts Co	Camden	15.08.82
Moussa, Franck	5.8	Coventry	Brussels, Bel	24.07.89
Wilson, Lawrie	5.10	Stevenage	Collier Row	11.09.87
Forwards				
Ansah, Zak	5.10	Arsenal	Sidcup	04.05.94
Church, Simon	6.0	Reading	High Wycombe	10.12.88
Ghoochannejhad, Reza	5.11	Standard Liege	Mashhad, Iran	20.09.87
Parzyszek, Piotr	6.3	De Graafschap	Torun, Pol	08.09.93
Pigott, Joe	6.0	–	Maidstone	24.11.93
Tucudean, George	6.1	Standard Liege	Arad, Rom	30.04.91
Vetokele, Igor	5.9	Copenhagen	Luanda, Ang	23.03.92

DERBY COUNTY

Ground: iPro Stadium, Pride Park, Derby DE24 8XL
Telephone: 0871 472 1884. **Club nickname**: Rams

Colours: White and black. **Capacity**: 33,597
Record attendance: Baseball Ground: 41,826 v Tottenham (Div 1) Sep 20, 1969; iPro Stadium: 33,597 (England v Mexico) May 25, 2011; Club: 33,475 v Rangers (Ted McMinn testimonial) May 1, 2006

Goalkeepers

Grant, Lee	6.2	Burnley	Hemel Hempstead	27.01.83
Mitchell, Jonathan	5.11	Newcastle	Hartlepool	24.11.94
Roos, Kelle	6.5	Nuneaton	Rijkevoort, Hol	31.05.92

Defenders

Barker, Shaun	6.2	Blackpool	Nottingham	19.09.82
Buxton, Jake	5.11	Burton	Sutton-in-Ashfield	04.03.85
Christie, Cyrus	6.2	Coventry	Coventry	30.09.92
Forsyth, Craig	6.0	Watford	Carnoustie	24.02.89
Freeman, Kieron	6.1	Nottm Forest	Bestwood	21.03.92
Keogh, Richard	6.2	Coventry	Harlow	11.08.86
Naylor, Lee	5.10	Accrington	Bloxwich	19.03.80
Naylor, Tom	6.2	Mansfield	Sutton-in-Ashfield	28.06.91
O'Brien, Mark	5.11	Cherry Orchard	Dublin, Ire	20.11.92
Whitbread, Zak	6.2	Leicester	Houston, US	04.03.84

Midfielders

Alefe Santos	5.10	Bristol Rov	Sao Paulo	01.03.95
Bryson, Craig	5.8	Kilmarnock	Rutherglen	06.11.86
Bunjaku, Alban	6.0	Sevilla	Romford	20.05.94
Calero, Ivan	5.9	Atletico Madrid	Parla, Spain	21.04.95
Coutts, Paul	6.1	Preston	Aberdeen	22.07.88
Eustace, John	6.0	Watford	Solihull	03.11.79
Hendrick, Jeff	6.1	–	Dublin, Ire	31.01.92
Hughes, Will	6.1	–	Surrey	07.04.95
Thorne, George	6.2	WBA	Chatham	04.01.93

Forwards

Bennett, Mason	5.10	–	Langwith	15.07.96
Dawkins, Simon	5.10	Tottenham	Edgware	01.12.87
Martin, Chris	5.10	Norwich	Beccles	04.11.88
Russell, Johnny	5.10	Dundee Utd	Glasgow	08.04.90
Sammon, Conor	6.1	Wigan	Dublin, Ire	06.11.86
Ward, Jamie	5.5	Sheffield Utd	Birmingham	12.05.86

FULHAM

Ground: Craven Cottage, Stevenage Road, London SW6 6HH
Telephone: 0870 442 1222. **Club nickname**: Cottagers
Colours: White and black. **Capacity**: 25,700
Record attendance: 49,335 v Millwall (Div 2) Oct 8, 1938

Goalkeepers

Stockdale, David	6.3	Darlington	Leeds	28.09.85
Stekelenburg, Maarten	6.5	Roma	Haarlem, Hol	22.09.82

Defenders

Amorebieta, Fernando	6.4	Athletic Bilbao	Cantaura, Ven	29.03.85
Burn, Dan	6.7	Darlington	Blyth	09.05.92
Hoogland, Tim	6.0	Schalke	Marl, Ger	11.06.85
Hutchinson, Shaun	6.2	Motherwell	Newcastle	23.11.90
Stafylidis, Konstantinos	5.10	B Leverkusen (loan)	Thessaloniki, Gre	02.12.93
Voser, Kay	5.6	Basle	Baden, Swi	04.01.87
Zverotic, Elsad	5.10	Young Boys	Berane, Mont	31.10.86

Midfielders

Cole, Larnell	5.7	Manchester Utd	Manchester	09.03.93
Dejagah, Ashkan	6.0	Wolfsburg	Tehran, Iran	05.07.86
Kacaniklic, Alex	5.11	Liverpool	Helsingborg, Swe	13.08.91
Mesca	5.9	–	Bissau, Guin	06.05.93
Parker, Scott	5.7	Tottenham	Lambeth	13.10.80
Plumain, Ange-Freddy	6.0	Lens	Paris, Fr	02.03.95
Tunnicliffe, Ryan	6.0	Manchester Utd	Heywood	30.12.92

Forwards

David, Chris	5.8	–	Amsterdam, Hol	06.03.93
Dembele, Moussa	6.0	Paris SG	Pontoise, Fr	12.07.96
McCormack, Ross	5.10	Leeds	Glasgow	18.08.86
Mitroglou, Konstantinos	6.2	Olympiacos	Kavala, Gre	12.03.88
Rodallega, Hugo	6.0	Wigan	El Carmelo, Col	25.07.85
Ruiz, Bryan	6.2	Twente	Aljuela, C Rica	18.08.85
Taggart, Adam	6.0	Newcastle Jets	Perth, Aus	02.06.93
Trotta, Marcello	6.2	Manchester City	Santa Maria, C Verde	29.09.92
Woodrow, Cauley	6.1	Luton	Hemel Hempstead	02.12.94

HUDDERSFIELD TOWN

Ground: John Smith's Stadium, Huddersfield HD1 6PX
Telephone: 0870 444 4677. **Club nickname:** Terriers
Colours: Blue and white. **Capacity:** 24,500
Record attendance: Leeds Road: 67,037 v Arsenal (FA Cup 6) Feb 27, 1932;
John Smith's Stadium: 23,678 v Liverpool (FA Cup 3) Dec 12, 1999

Goalkeepers

Allinson, Lloyd	6.2	–	Rothwell	07.09.93
Murphy, Joe	6.2	Coventry	Dublin, Ire	21.08.81
Smithies, Alex	6.1	–	Huddersfield	25.03.90

Defenders

Carroll, Jake	6.0	St Patrick's	Dublin, Ire	11.08.91
Dixon, Paul	5.10	Dundee Utd	Aberdeen	22.11.86
Gerrard, Anthony	6.2	Cardiff	Liverpool	06.02.86
Lynch, Joel	6.1	Nottm Forest	Eastbourne	03.10.87
Peltier, Lee	5.10	Leeds	Liverpool	11.12.86
Smith, Tommy	6.1	Manchester City	Warrington	14.04.92
Wallace, Murray	6.2	Falkirk	Glasgow	10.01.93

Midfielders

Billing, Philip	6.4	–	Esbjerg, Den	11.06.96
Clayton, Adam	5.9	Leeds	Manchester	14.01.89
Crooks, Matt	6.0	–	Huddersfield	20.01.94
Gobern, Oscar	6.3	Southampton	Birmingham	26.01.91
Hammill, Adam	5.10	Wolves	Liverpool	25.01.88
Hogg, Jonathan	5.7	Watford	Middlesbrough	06.12.88
Holmes, Duane	5.8	–	Wakefield	06.11.94
Norwood, Oliver	5.11	Manchester Utd	Burnley	12.04.91
Sinnott, Jordan	5.11	–	Bradford	14.02.94
Tronstad, Sondre	5.8	IK Start	Norway	26.08.95
Ward, Daniel	5.11	Bolton	Bradford	09.12.90

Forwards

Bunn, Harry	5.9	Manchester City	Oldham	21.11.92
Carr, Daniel	6.0	Dulwich Hamlet	Lambeth	30.11.93
Lolley, Joe	5.10	Kidderminster	Redditch	25.08.92
Paterson, Martin	5.9	Burnley	Tunstall	13.05.87

Scannell, Sean	5.9	Crystal Palace	Croydon	21.03.89
Stead, Jon	6.3	Bristol City	Huddersfield	07.04.83
Vaughan, James	5.11	Norwich	Birmingham	14.07.88
Wells, Nahki	5.7	Bradford	Bermuda	01.06.90

IPSWICH TOWN

Ground: Portman Road, Ipswich IP1 2DA
Telephone: 01473 400500. **Club nickname**: Blues/Town
Colours: Blue and white. **Capacity**: 30,300
Record attendance: 38,010 v Leeds (FA Cup 6) Mar 8, 1975

Goalkeepers
| Bialkowski, Bartosz | 6.0 | Notts Co | Braniewo, Pol | 06.07.87 |
| Gerken, Dean | 6.2 | Bristol City | Southend | 04.08.85 |

Defenders
Berra, Christophe	6.1	Wolves	Edinburgh	31.01.85
Chambers, Luke	5.11	Nottm Forest	Kettering	29.08.85
Cresswell, Aaron	5.7	Tranmere	Liverpool	15.12.89
Hewitt, Elliott	5.11	Macclesfield	Bodelwyddan	30.05.94
Mings, Tyrone	6.3	Chippenham	Bath	13.03.93
Parr, Jonathan	6.0	Crystal Palace	Oslo, Nor	21.10.88
Smith, Tommy	6.1	–	Macclesfield	31.03.90
Veseli, Frederic	6.0	Manchester Utd	Renens, Swi	20.11.92

Midfielders
Anderson, Paul	5.9	Bristol City	Leicester	23.07.88
Henshall, Alex	5.10	Manchester City	Swindon	15.02.94
Hunt, Stephen	5.8	Wolves	Port Laoise, Ire	01.08.81
Hyam, Luke	5.10	–	Ipswich	24.10.91
Lawrence, Byron	5.10	–	Cambridge	12.03.96
Skuse, Cole	5.9	Bristol City	Bristol	29.03.86
Stewart, Cameron	5.8	Hull	Manchester	08.04.91
Tabb, Jay	5.7	Reading	Tooting	21.02.84
Wordsworth, Anthony	6.1	Colchester	Camden	03.01.89

Forwards
Marriott, Jack	5.9	–	Beverley	09.09.84
McGoldrick, David	6.1	Nottm Forest	Nottingham	29.11.87
Murphy, Daryl	6.2	Celtic	Waterford, Ire	15.03.83
Nouble, Frank	6.3	Wolves	Lewisham	24.09.91
Taylor, Paul	5.11	Peterborough	Liverpool	04.10.87

LEEDS UNITED

Ground: Elland Road, Leeds LS11 0ES
Telephone: 0871 334 1919. **Club nickname**: Whites
Colours: White. **Capacity**: 40,204
Record attendance: 57,892 v Sunderland (FA Cup 5 rep) Mar 15, 1967

Goalkeepers
Cairns, Alex	6.0	–	Doncaster	04.01.93
Kenny, Paddy	6.1	QPR	Halifax	17.05.78
Silvestri, Marco	6.3	Chievo	Castelnovo, It	02.03.91
Taylor, Stuart	6.5	Reading	Romford	28.11.80

Defenders
Berardi, Gaetano	5.11	Sampdoria	Sorengo, Swi	21.08.88
Byram, Sam	5.11	–	Thurrock	16.09.93
Lees, Tom	6.1	–	Warwick	18.11.90
Pearce, Jason	5.11	Portsmouth	Hillingdon	06.12.87

Name	Height	Previous Club	Birthplace	Date
Taylor, Charlie	5.9	–	York	18.09.93
Warnock, Stephen	5.10	Aston Villa	Ormskirk	12.12.81
White, Aidan	5.7	–	Leeds	10.10.91
Wootton, Scott	6.2	Manchester Utd	Birkenhead	12.09.91

Midfielders

Name	Height	Previous Club	Birthplace	Date
Austin, Rodolph	6.0	Brann	Clarendon, Jam	01.06.85
Bianchi, Tommaso	6.0	Sassuolo	Piombino, It	01.11.88
Dawson, Chris	5.6	–	Dewsbury	02.09.94
Mowatt, Alex	5.10	–	Doncaster	13.02.95
Murphy, Luke	6.2	Crewe	Alsager	21.10.89
Norris, David	5.8	Portsmouth	Peterborough	22.02.81
Thompson, Zac	5.10	Everton	Wigan	05.01.93
Tonge, Michael	5.11	Stoke	Manchester	07.04.83

Forwards

Name	Height	Previous Club	Birthplace	Date
Doukara, Souleymane	6.1	Catania (loan)	Meudon, Fr	29.09.91
Hunt, Noel	5.8	Reading	Waterford, Ire	26.12.82
Morison, Steve	6.2	Norwich	Enfield	29.08.83
Poleon, Dominic	5.9	Southend	Newham	07.09.93
Smith, Matt	6.6	Oldham	Birmingham	07.06.89

MIDDLESBROUGH

Ground: Riverside Stadium, Middlesbrough, TS3 6RS
Telephone: 0844 499 6789. **Club nickname**: Boro
Colours: Red. **Capacity**: 35,100
Record attendance: Ayresome Park: 53,536 v Newcastle (Div 1) Dec 27, 1949; Riverside Stadium: 34,836 v Norwich (Prem Lge) Dec 28, 2004; Also: 35,000 England v Slovakia Jun 11, 2003

Goalkeepers

Name	Height	Previous Club	Birthplace	Date
Konstantopoulos, Dimitrios	6.5	AEK Athens	Thessaloniki, Gre	29.11.79
Mejias, Tomas	6.5	Real Madrid	Madrid, Sp	30.01.89
Steele, Jason	6.2	–	Bishop Auckland	18.08.90

Defenders

Name	Height	Previous Club	Birthplace	Date
Ayala, Daniel	6.3	Norwich	El Saucejo, Sp	07.11.90
Friend, George	6.0	Doncaster	Barnstaple	19.10.87
Gibson, Ben	6.1	–	Nunthorpe	15.01.93
Hines, Seb	6.2	–	Wetherby	29.05.88
Reach, Adam	6.1	–	Gateshead	03.02.93
Williams, Rhys	6.1	Joondalup	Perth, Aus	07.07.88
Woodgate, Jonathan	6.2	Stoke	Middlesbrough	22.01.80

Midfielders

Name	Height	Previous Club	Birthplace	Date
Brobbel, Ryan	5.8	–	Hartlepool	05.03.93
Butterfield, Jacob	5.11	Norwich	Bradford	10.06.90
Halliday, Andrew	5.11	Livingston	Glasgow	18.10.91
Leadbitter, Grant	5.9	Ipswich	Chester-le-Street	07.01.86
Morris, Bryn	6.0	–	Hartlepool	25.04.96
Smallwood, Richard	5.11	–	Redcar	29.12.90
Whitehead, Dean	5.11	Stoke	Abingdon	12.01.82

Forwards

Name	Height	Previous Club	Birthplace	Date
Adomah, Albert	6.1	Bristol City	Lambeth	13.12.87
Carayol, Mustapha	5.10	Bristol Rov	Banjul, Gam	10.06.89
Kamara, Kei	6.3	Sporting Kansas	Kenema, SL	01.09.84
Kike	6.1	Real Murcia	Motilla del Palanca, Sp	25.11.89
Ledesma, Emmanuel	5.11	Walsall	Quilmes, Arg	24.05.88
Main, Curtis	5.10	Darlington	South Shields	20.06.92

| Tomlin, Lee | 5.11 | Peterborough | Leicester | 12.01.89 |
| Williams, Luke | 6.1 | – | Middlesbrough | 11.06.93 |

MILLWALL

Ground: The Den, Zampa Road, London SE16 3LN
Telephone: 0207 232 1222. **Club nickname**: Lions
Colours: Blue. **Capacity**: 19,734
Record attendance: The Den: 48,672 v Derby (FA Cup 5) Feb 20, 1937; New Den: 20,093 v Arsenal (FA Cup 3) Jan 10, 1994

Goalkeepers

| Bywater, Stephen | 6.2 | Sheffield Wed | Manchester | 07.06.81 |
| Forde, David | 6.2 | Cardiff | Galway, Ire | 20.12.79 |

Defenders

Beevers, Mark	6.4	Sheffield Wed	Barnsley	21.11.89
Dunne, Alan	5.10	–	Dublin, Ire	23.08.82
Hoyte, Justin	5.11	Middlesbrough	Leytonstone	20.11.84
Malone, Scott	6.2	Bournemouth	Rowley Regis	25.03.91
Robinson, Paul	6.1	–	Barnet	07.01.82
Shittu, Danny	6.3	QPR	Lagos, Nig	02.09.80
Webster, Byron	6.4	Yeovil	Leeds	31.03.87

Midfielders

Abdou, Nadjim	5.10	Plymouth	Martigues, Fr	13.07.84
Bailey, Nicky	5.10	Middlesbrough	Hammersmith	10.06.84
Chaplow, Richard	5.9	Southampton	Accrington	02.02.85
Edwards, Carlos	5.11	Ipswich	Port of Spain, Trin	24.10.78
Martin, Lee	5.10	Ipswich	Taunton	09.02.87
Upson, Ed	5.10	Yeovil	Bury St Edmunds	21.11.89
Williams, Shaun	6.0	MK Dons	Dublin, Ire	19.09.86
Woolford, Martyn	6.0	Bristol City	Pontefract	13.10.85
Wright, Josh	6.1	Scunthorpe	Tower Hamlets	06.11.89

Forwards

Easter, Jermaine	5.10	MK Dons	Cardiff	15.01.82
Fuller, Ricardo	6.3	Blackpool	Kingston, Jam	31.10.79
Gregory, Lee	6.2	Halifax	Sheffield	26.08.88
Marquis, John	6.1	–	Lewisham	16.05.92
McDonald, Scott	5.8	Middlesbrough	Melbourne, Aus	21.08.83

NORWICH CITY

Ground: Carrow Road, Norwich NR1 1JE
Telephone: 01603 760760. **Club nickname**: Canaries
Colours: Yellow and green. **Capacity**: 27,224
Record attendance: 43,984 v Leicester City (FA Cup 6), Mar 30, 1963

Goalkeepers

Bunn, Mark	6.0	Blackburn	Southgate	16.11.84
Rudd, Declan	6.3	–	Diss	16.01.91
Ruddy, John	6.4	Everton	St Ives, Cam	24.10.86

Defenders

Bassong, Sebastien	6.2	Tottenham	Paris, Fr	09.07.86
Bennett, Ryan	6.2	Peterborough	Orsett	06.03.90
Gafaiti, Adel	6.1	Rangers	Paris, Fr	13.09.94
Garrido, Javier	5.10	Lazio	Irun, Sp	15.03.85
Martin, Russell	6.0	Peterborough	Brighton	04.01.86
Olsson, Martin	5.10	Blackburn	Gavle, Swe	17.05.88
Turner, Michael	6.4	Sunderland	Lewisham	09.11.83

Whittaker, Steven	6.1	Rangers	Edinburgh	16.06.84
Midfielders				
Bennett, Elliott	5.9	Brighton	Telford	18.12.88
Fer, Leroy	6.2	Twente	Zoetermeer, Hol	05.01.90
Hoolahan, Wes	5.7	Blackpool	Dublin, Ire	10.08.83
Howson, Jonathan	5.11	Norwich	Leeds	21.05.88
Johnson, Bradley	6.0	Leeds	Hackney	28.04.87
Pilkington, Anthony	6.0	Huddersfield	Blackburn	06.06.88
Redmond, Nathan	5.8	Birmingham	Birmingham	06.03.94
Surman, Andrew	5.11	Wolves	Johannesburg, SA	20.08.86
Tettey, Alexander	5.11	Rennes	Accra, Gh	04.04.86
Forwards				
Becchio, Luciano	6.2	Leeds	Cordoba, Arg	28.12.83
Grabban, Lewis	6.0	Bournemouth	Croydon	12.01.88
Hooper, Gary	5.11	Celtic	Harlow	26.01.88
Lafferty, Kyle	6.4	Palermo	Enniskillen	16.09.87
Loza, Jamar	5.8	–	Kingston, Jam	10.05.94
Murphy, Jacob	5.10	–	Wembley	24.02.95
Murphy, Josh	5.9	–	Wembley	24.02.95
Van Wolfswinkel, Ricky	6.1	Sporting	Woudenberg, Hol	27.01.89

NOTTINGHAM FOREST

Ground: City Ground, Pavilion Road, Nottingham NG2 5FJ
Telephone: 0115 982 4444. **Club nickname**: Forest
Colours: Red and white. **Capacity**: 30,576
Record attendance: 49,946 v Manchester Utd (Div 1) Oct 28, 1967

Goalkeepers				
Darlow, Karl	6.1	Aston Villa	Northampton	08.10.90
De Vries, Dorus	6.0	Wolves	Beverwijk, Hol	29.12.80
Defenders				
Collins, Danny	6.0	Stoke	Chester	06.08.80
Fox, Danny	6.0	Southampton	Winsford	29.05.86
Halford, Greg	6.4	Portsmouth	Chelmsford	08.12.84
Harding, Dan	6.0	Southampton	Gloucester	23.12.83
Hobbs, Jack	6.3	Hull	Portsmouth	18.08.88
Laing, Louis	6.2	Sunderland	Newcastle	06.03.93
Lascelles, Jamaal	6.2	–	Derby	11.11.93
Lichaj, Eric	5.10	Aston Villa	Illinois, US	17.11.88
Mancienne, Michael	6.0	Hamburg	Feltham	08.01.88
Osborn, Ben	5.10	–	Derby	05.08.94
Riera, Roger	6.1	Barcelona	El Masnou, Sp	17.02.95
Wilson, Kevin	6.3	Celtic	Nottingham	03.09.85
Midfielders				
Cohen, Chris	5.11	Yeovil	Norwich	05.03.87
Lansbury, Henri	6.0	Arsenal	Enfield	12.10.90
Majewski, Radoslav	5.7	Polonia Warsaw	Pruszkow, Pol	
McLaughlin, Stephen	5.9	Derry	Donegal, Ire	14.06.90
Rees, Josh	5.9	–	Hemel Hempstead	04.10.93
Reid, Andy	5.7	Blackpool	Dublin	29.07.82
Vaughan, David	5.7	Sunderland	Rhuddlan	18.02.83
Forwards				
Cox, Simon	5.10	WBA	Reading	28.04.87
Blackstock, Dexter	6.2	Nottm Forest	Oxford	20.05.86
Fryatt, Matt	5.10	Hull	Nuneaton	05.03.86

Henderson, Darius	6.2	Millwall	Sutton	07.09.81
Mackie, Jamie	5.8	QPR	Dorking	22.09.85
Paterson, Jamie	5.9	Walsall	Coventry	20.12.91
Veldwijk, Lars	6.5	Excelsior	Uithoorn, Hol	21.08.91

READING

Ground: Madejski Stadium, Junction 11 M4, Reading RG2 OFL
Telephone: 0118 968 1100. **Club nickname**: Royals
Colours: Blue and white. **Capacity**: 24,200
Record attendance: Elm Park: 33,042 v Brentford (FA Cup 5) Feb 19, 1927; Madejski Stadium: 24,184 v Everton (Prem Lge) Nov 17, 2012

Goalkeepers
Andersen, Mikkel	6.5	Akademisk	Herlev, Den	17.12.88
Federici, Adam	6.2	Sardenga	Nowra, Aus	31.01.85
McCarthy, Alex	6.4	–	Guildford	03.12.89

Defenders
Cummings, Shaun	6.0	Chelsea	Hammersmith	28.02.89
Gunter, Chris	5.11	Nottm Forest	Newport	21.07.89
Hector, Michael	6.4	Thurrock	East Ham	19.07.92
Kelly, Stephen	5.11	Fulham	Dublin, Ire	06.09.83
Morrison, Sean	6.1	Swindon	Plymouth	08.01.91
Pearce, Alex	6.2	–	Wallingford	09.11.88
Sweeney, Pierce	6.0	Bray	Dublin, Ire	11.09.94

Midfielders
Akpan, Hope	6.0	Crawley	Liverpool	14.08.91
Drenthe, Royston	5.7	Vladikavkaz	Rotterdam, Hol	08.04.87
Edwards, Ryan	5.7	AIS	Sydney, Aus	17.11.93
Guthrie, Danny	5.9	Newcastle	Shrewsbury	18.04.87
Karacan, Jem	5.10	–	Catford	21.02.89
Obita, Jordan	5.11	–	Oxford	08.12.93
Robson-Kanu, Hal	6.0	–	Acton	21.05.89
Williams, Danny	6.0	Hoffenheim	Karlsruhe, Ger	08.03.89

Forwards
Blackman, Nick	5.10	Sheffield Utd	Whitefield	11.11.89
Pogrebnyak, Pavel	6.2	Fulham	Moscow, Rus	08.11.83
McCleary, Garath	5.11	Nottm Forest	Bromley	15.05.87
Samuel, Dominic	5.11	–	Southwark	01.04.94

ROTHERHAM UNITED

Ground: New York Stadium, New York Way, Rotherham S60 1AH
Telephone: 08444 140733. **Club nickname**: Millers
Colours: Red and white. **Capacity**: 12,000
Record attendance: Millmoor: 25,170 v Sheffield Wed (Div 2) Jan 26, 1952 and v Sheffield Wed (Div 2) Dec 13, 1952; **Don Valley Stadium**: 7,082 v Aldershot (Lge 2 play-off semi-final, 2nd leg) May 19, 2010; **New York Stadium**: 11,758 v Sheffield Utd (Lge 1) Sep 7, 2013

Goalkeepers
| Collin, Adam | 6.1 | Carlisle | Carlisle | 09.12.84 |
| Loach, Scott | 6.2 | Ipswich | Nottingham | 14.10.79 |

Defenders
Brindley, Richard	5.11	Chesterfield	Norwich	05.05.93
Broadfoot, Kirk	6.3	Blackpool	Irvine	08.08.84
Morgan, Craig	6.0	Preston	Flint	16.06.85
Richardson, Frazer	5.11	Middlesbrough	Rotherham	29.10.82
Rowe, Daniel	6.2	–	Billingham	24.10.95

Sadler, Mat	5.11	Crawley	Birmingham	26.02.85
Skarz, Joe	6.0	Bury	Huddersfield	13.07.89
Wood, Richard	6.3	Charlton	Ossett	05.07.85
Midfielders				
Arnason, Kari	6.3	Aberdeen	Gothenburg, Swe	13.10.82
Bradley, Mark	6.0	Walsall	Wordsley	14.01.88
Frecklington, Lee	5.8	Peterborough	Lincoln	08.09.85
Green, Paul	5.10	Leeds	Sheffield	10.04.83
Hall, Ryan	5.10	MK Dons	Dulwich	04.01.88
Newton, Conor	5.11	Newcastle	Newcastle	17.10.91
Pringle, Ben	6.1	Derby	Newcastle	27.05.89
Rose, Mitchell	5.9	–	Doncaster	04.07.94
Walker, Nicky	5.11	–	Rotherham	08.09.94
Worrall, David	6.0	Bury	Manchester	12.06.90
Forwards				
Agard, Kieran	5.10	Yeovil	Newham	10.10.89
Bowery, Jordan	6.1	Aston Villa	Nottingham	02.07.91
Brandy, Febian	5.7	Sheffield Utd	Manchester	04.02.89
Derbyshire, Matt	6.1	Nottm Forest	Blackburn	14.04.86
Revell, Alex	6.3	Leyton Orient	Cambridge	07.07.83

SHEFFIELD WEDNESDAY

Ground: Hillsborough, Sheffield, S6 1SW
Telephone: 0871 995 1867. **Club nickname**: Owls
Colours: Blue and white. **Capacity**: 39,814
Record attendance: 72,841 v Manchester City (FA Cup 5) Feb 17, 1934

Goalkeepers				
Kirkland, Chris	6.3	Wigan	Leicester	02.05.81
Westwood, Keiren	6.1	Sunderland	Manchester	23.10.84
Defenders				
Buxton, Lewis	6.1	Stoke	Newport, IOW	10.12.83
Floro, Rafael	5.10	Porto	Quarteira, Por	19.01.94
Hutchinson, Sam	6.0	Chelsea	Windsor	03.08.89
Loovens, Glenn	6.2	Zaragoza	Doetinchem, Hol	22.10.83
Mattock, Joe	6.0	WBA	Leicester	15.05.90
Onyewu, Oguchi	6.5	QPR	Washington, US	13.05.82
Zayatte, Kamil	6.2	Istanbul	Conakry, Gui	07.03.85
Midfielders				
Antonio, Michail	5.11	Reading	Wandsworth	28.03.90
Coke, Giles	6.0	Motherwell	Westminster	03.06.86
Corry, Paul	6.2	UCD	Dublin, Ire	03.02.91
Helan, Jeremy	5.11	Manchester City	Clichy, Fr	09.05.92
Lee, Kieran	6.1	Oldham	Tameside	22.06.88
Maghoma, Jacques	5.11	Burton	Lubumbashi, DR Cong	23.10.87
McCabe, Rhys	5.8	Rangers	Polbeth	24.07.92
Palmer, Liam	6.2	–	Worksop	19.09.91
Semedo, Jose	6.0	Charlton	Setubal, Por	11.01.85
Forwards				
Lavery, Caolan	5.11	Ipswich	Alberta, Can	22.10.92
Madine, Gary	6.4	Carlisle	Gateshead	24.08.90
Maguire, Chris	5.8	Derby	Bellshill	16.01.89
Nuhiu, Atdhe	6.6	Rapid Vienna	Prishtina, Kos	29.07.89

WATFORD

Ground: Vicarage Road Stadium, Vicarage Road, Watford WD18 OER
Telephone: 01923 223023. **Club nickname**: Hornets
Colours: Yellow and black. **Capacity**: 17,400
Record attendance: 34,099 v Manchester Utd (FA Cup 4 rep) Feb 3, 1969

Goalkeepers

Bond, Jonathan	6.3	–	Hemel Hempstead	19.05.93
Gomes, Heurelho	6.2	PSV Eindhoven	Joao Pinheiro, Br	15.12.81

Defenders

Angella, Gabriele	6.3	Udinese	Florence, It	28.04.89
Belkalem, Essaid	6.3	Granada	Mekla, Alg	01.01.89
Brown, Reece	6.2	Manchester Utd	Manchester	01.11.91
Cathcart, Craig	6.2	Blackpool	Belfast	06.02.89
Doyley, Lloyd	5.10	–	Whitechapel	01.12.82
Ekstrand, Joel	6.1	Udinese	Lund, Swe	04.02.89
Hoban, Tommie	6.2	–	Waltham Forest	24.01.94
Paredes, Juan Carlos	5.9	Granada	Esmeraldas, Ec	08.07.87
Pudil, Daniel	6.1	Granada	Prague, Cz	27.09.85
Tamas, Gabriel	6.2	Doncaster	Brasov (Rom)	09.11.83

Midfielders

Abdi, Almen	5.11	Udinese	Prizren, Kos	21.10.86
Anya, Ikechi	5.7	Granada	Glasgow	03.01.88
Battocchio, Cristian	5.8	Udinese	Rosario, Arg	10.02.92
Dyer, Lloyd	5.9	Leicester	Birmingham	13.09.82
Forestieri, Fernando	5.8	Udinese	Rosario, Arg	15.01.90
Iriney	5.10	Granada	Humaita, Br	23.04.81
McGugan, Lewis	5.10	Nottm Forest	Long Eaton	25.10.88
Murray, Sean	5.9	–	Abbots Langley	11.10.93
Smith, Connor	5.11	–	Mullingar, Ire	18.02.93
Tozser, Daniel	6.2	Parma (loan)	Szolnok, Hun	12.05.85

Forwards

Acuna, Javier	5.9	Udinese	Encarnacion, Par	23.06.88
Deeney, Troy	6.0	Walsall	Birmingham	29.06.88
Fabbrini, Diego	6.0	Udinese	Pisa, It	31.07.90
Ikpeazu, Uche	6.3	–	Harrow	28.02.95
Ranegie, Mathias	6.5	Udinese	Gothenburg, Swe	14.06.84
Vydra, Matej	5.11	Udinese (loan)	Chotebor, Cz	01.05.92

WIGAN ATHLETIC

Ground: DW Stadium, Robin Park, Wigan WN5 0UZ
Telephone: 01942 774000. **Club nickname**: Latics
Colours: Blue and white. **Capacity**: 25,023
Record attendance: Springfield Park: 27,526 v Hereford (FA Cup 2) Dec 12, 1953;
DW Stadium: 25,133 v Manchester Utd (Prem Lge) May 11, 2008

Goalkeepers

Al Habsi, Ali	6.5	Bolton	Muscat, Oman	30.12.81
Carson, Scott	6.3	Bursaspor	Whitehaven	03.09.85
Nicholls, Lee	6.3	–	Huyton	05.10.92

Defenders

Barnett, Leon	6.1	Norwich	Luton	30.11.85
Boyce, Emmerson	5.11	Crystal Palace	Aylesbury	24.09.79
Caldwell, Gary	5.11	Celtic	Stirling	12.04.82
Garcia, Juan Carlos	6.2	Olimpia	Tela, Hond	08.03.88

Kiernan, Rob	6.2	Watford	Rickmansworth	13.01.91
Perch, James	6.0	Newcastle	Mansfield	28.09.85
Ramis, Ivan	6.2	Real Mallorca	Sa Pobla, Sp	25.10.84
Rogne, Thomas	6.4	Celtic	Baerum, Nor	29.06.90
Tavernier, James	5.10	Newcastle	Bradford	31.10.91
Taylor, Andrew	5.10	Cardiff	Hartlepool	01.08.86
Taylor-Sinclair, Aaron	6.0	Partick	Aberdeen	08.04.91

Midfielders

Cowie, Don	5.11	Cardiff	Inverness	15.02.83
Espinoza, Roger	5.11	Sporting Kansas	Puerto Cortes, Hond	25.10.86
Fyvie, Fraser	5.8	Aberdeen	Aberdeen	27.03.93
Maloney, Shaun	5.7	Celtic	Miri, Malay	24.01.83
McArthur, James	5.7	Hamilton	Glasgow	07.10.87
McCann, Chris	6.1	Burnley	Dublin, Ire	21.07.87
McClean, James	5.11	Sunderland	Derry	22.04.89
Watson, Ben	5.10	Crystal Palace	Camberwell	09.07.85

Forwards

Fortune, Marc-Antoine	6.0	WBA	Cayenne, Fr Gui	02.07.81
Holt, Grant	6.0	Norwich	Carlisle	12.04.81
McManaman, Callum	5.11	Everton	Knowsley	25.04.91
Riera, Oriol	6.1	Osasuna	Vic, Sp	03.07.86
Waghorn, Martyn	5.10	Leicester	South Shields	23.01.90

WOLVERHAMPTON WANDERERS

Ground: Molineux Stadium, Waterloo Road, Wolverhampton WV1 4QR
Telephone: 0871 222 2220. **Club nickname**: Wolves
Colours: Gold and black. **Capacity**: 31,700
Record attendance: 61,315 v Liverpool (FA Cup 5) Feb 11, 1939

Goalkeepers

| Ikeme, Carl | 6.2 | – | Sutton Coldfield | 08.06.86 |
| McCarey, Aaron | 6.1 | – | Monaghan, Ire | 14.01.92 |

Defenders

Batth, Danny	6.3	–	Brierley Hill	21.09.90
Doherty, Matt	5.11	–	Dublin	16.01.92
Ebanks-Landell, Ethan	6.2	–	Smethwick	12.12.92
Elokobi, George	6.0	Colchester	Mamfe, Cam	31.01.86
Foley, Kevin	5.9	Luton	Luton	01.11.84
Golbourne, Scott	5.9	Barnsley	Bristol	29.02.88
Hause, Kortney	6.3	Wycombe	Redbridge	16.07.95
Iorfa, Dominic	6.2	–	Southend	08.07.95
Margreitter, Georg	6.2	Austria Vienna	Schruns, Aut	07.11.88
Ricketts, Sam	6.1	Bolton	Aylesbury	11.10.81
Stearman, Richard	6.2	Leicester	Wolverhampton	19.08.87
Ward, Stephen	5.11	Bohemians	Dublin, Ire	20.08.85

Midfielders

Boukari, Razak	5.11	Rennes	Lome, Tog	25.04.87
Davis, David	5.8	–	Smethwick	20.02.91
Doumbia, Tongo	6.3	Rennes	Vernon, Eure, Fr	06.08.89
Edwards, David	5.11	Luton	Pontesbury	03.02.85
Evans, Lee		Newport	Newport	24.07.94
Forde, Anthony	5.9	–	Ballingarry, Ire	16.11.93
Henry, James	6.1	Millwall	Reading	10.06.89
Jacobs, Michael	5.9	Derby	Rothwell	04.11.91
McDonald, Kevin	6.2	Sheffield Utd	Carnoustie	04.11.88

O'Hara, Jamie	5.11	Tottenham	Dartford	25.09.86
Price, Jack	5.7	–	Shrewsbury	19.12.92
Rowe, Tommy	5.11	Peterborough	Manchester	01.05.89
Sako, Bakary	5.11	St Etienne	Ivry-sur-Seine, Fr	26.04.88
Van La Parra, Rajiv	5.11	Heerenveen	Rotterdam, Hol	04.06.91
Forwards				
Clarke, Leon	6.2	Coventry	Wolverhampton	10.02.85
Dicko, Nouha	5.8	Wigan	Paris, Fr	14.05.92
Doyle, Kevin	5.11	Reading	Wexford, Ire	18.09.83
McAlinden, Liam	6.1	–	Cannock	26.09.93
Sigurdarson, Bjorn	6.1	Lillestrom	Akranes, Ice	26.02.91

LEAGUE ONE

BARNSLEY

Ground: Oakwell Stadium, Barnsley S71 1ET
Telephone: 01226 211211. **Club nickname:** Tykes
Colours: Red and white. **Capacity:** 23,009
Record attendance: 40,255 v Stoke (FA Cup 5) Feb 15, 1936

Goalkeepers				
Dibble, Christian	6.3	Bury	Wilmslow	11.05.94
Defenders				
Cranie, Martin	6.0	Coventry	Yeovil	26.09.83
Kennedy, Tom	5.11	Leicester	Bury	24.06.85
Mvoto, Jean-Ives	6.4	Oldham	Paris, Fr	06.09.88
Nyatanga, Lewin	6.2	Bristol City	Burton	18.08.88
Midfielders				
Cywka, Tomasz	5.11	Reading	Gliwice, Pol	27.06.88
Dawson, Stephen	5.6	Leyton Orient	Dublin, Ire	04.12.85
Digby, Paul	6.3	–	Sheffield	02.02.95
Hourihane, Conor	6.0	Plymouth	Cork, Ire	02.02.91
Jennings, Dale	5.10	Bayern Munich	Liverpool	21.12.92
Forwards				
Hemmings, Kane	6.1	Cowdenbeath	Burton	08.04.92
Noble-Lazarus, Reuben	5.11	–	Huddersfield	16.08.93
Rose, Danny	5.10	–	Barnsley	10.12.93

BRADFORD CITY

Ground: Coral Windows Stadium, Valley Parade, Bradford BD8 7DY
Telephone: 01274 773355. **Club nickname:** Bantams
Colours: Yellow and claret. **Capacity:** 25,136
Record attendance: 39,146 v Burnley (FA Cup 4) Mar 11, 1911

Goalkeepers				
McLaughlin, Jon	6.2	Harrogate	Edinburgh	09.09.87
Defenders				
Darby, Stephen	5.9	Liverpool	Liverpool	06.10.88
Davies, Andrew	6.2	Stoke	Stockton	17.12.84
McArdle, Rory	6.1	Aberdeen	Sheffield	01.05.87
Meredith, James	6.1	York	Albury, Aus	04.04.88
Sheehan, Alan	5.11	Notts Co	Athlone, Ire	14.09.86
Taylor, Matt	5.10	Charlton	Ormskirk	30.01.82
Midfielders				
Dolan, Matthew	5.9	Middlesbrough	Hartlepool	11.02.93

Doyle, Nathan	5.11	Barnsley	Derby	12.01.87
Kennedy, Jason	6.1	Rochdale	Roseworth	11.09.86
Knott, Billy	5.8	Sunderland	Canvey Is	28.11.92
Liddle, Gary	6.1	Notts Co	Middlesbrough	15.06.86
Yeates, Mark	5.9	Watford	Dublin, Ire	11.01.85
Forwards				
Clarke, Billy	5.9	Crawley	Cork, Ire	13.12.87
Clarkson, Lewis	5.8	Scarborough	Hull	08.11.93
De Vita, Raffaela	5.11	Swindon	Rome, It	23.09.87
Hanson, James	6.4	Guiseley	Bradford	09.11.87
McBurnie, Oliver	6.2	–	Leeds	04.06.96
Mclean, Aaron	5.7	Hull	Hammersmith	25.05.83

BRISTOL CITY

Ground: Ashton Gate, Bristol BS3 2EJ
Telephone: 0871 222 6666. **Club nickname**: Robins
Colours: Red and white. **Capacity**: 21,479
Record attendance: 43,335 v Preston (FA Cup 5) Feb 16, 1935

Goalkeepers				
Fielding, Frank	6.0	Derby	Blackburn	04.04.88
Parish, Elliot	6.2	Aston Villa	Towcester	20.05.90
Richards, David	5.11	Cardiff	Abergavenny	31.12.93
Defenders				
Ayling, Luke	6.1	Yeovil	Lambeth	25.08.91
Cunningham, Greg	6.0	Manchester City	Carnmore, Ire	31.01.91
El-Abd, Adam	6.0	Bristol City	Brighton	11.09.84
Flint, Aden	6.2	Swindon	Pinxton	11.07.89
Little, Mark	6.1	Peterborough	Worcester	20.08.88
Osborne, Karleigh	6.2	Millwall	Southall	19.03.83
Williams, Derrick	6.2	Aston Villa	Germany	17.01.93
Midfielders				
Bryan, Joe	5.7	–	Bristol	17.09.93
Elliott, Wade	5.10	Birmingham	Eastleigh	14.12.78
Freeman, Luke	5.10	Stevenage	Dartford	22.03.92
Pack, Marlon	6.2	Cheltenham	Portsmouth	25.03.91
Reid, Bobby	5.7	–	Bristol	02.02.93
Smith, Korey	6.0	Oldham	Hatfield	31.01.91
Wagstaff, Scott	5.11	Charlton	Maidstone	31.03.90
Wynter, Jordan	6.1	Arsenal	Goodmayes	24.11.93
Forwards				
Baldock, Sam	5.8	West Ham	Bedford	15.03.89
Burns, Wes	5.9	–	Cardiff	28.12.95
Emmanuel-Thomas, Jay	6.3	Ipswich	Forest Gate	27.12.90
Wilbraham, Aaron	6.3	Crystal Palace	Knutsford	21.10.79

CHESTERFIELD

Ground: Proact Stadium, Whittington Moor, Chesterfield S41 8NZ
Telephone: 01246 209765. **Club nickname**: Spireites
Colours: Blue and white. **Capacity**: 10,400
Record attendance: Saltergate: 30,561 v Tottenham (FA Cup 5) Feb 12, 1938; Proact Stadium: 10,089 v Rotherham (Lge 2) Mar 18, 2011

Goalkeepers				
Chapman, Aaron	6.8	Belper	Rotherham	29.05.90
Lee, Tommy	6.2	Macclesfield	Keighley	03.01.86

Defenders

Broadhead, Jack	6.3	–	Mansfield	02.10.94
Cooper, Liam	6.0	Hull	Hull	30.08.91
Evatt, Ian	6.3	Blackpool	Coventry	19.11.81
Hird Sam	6.0	Doncaster	Doncaster	07.09.87
Humphreys, Richie	5.11	Hartlepool	Sheffield	30.11.77
Jones, Daniel	6.2	Port Vale	Wordsley	23.12.86
Raglan, Charlie	6.0	FC United	Wythenshawe	28.04.93
Talbot, Drew	5.10	Luton	Barnsley	19.07.86

Midfielders

Banks, Ollie	6.3	FC United	Rotherham	21.09.92
Darikwa, Tendayi	6.2	–	Nottingham	13.12.91
Morsy, Sam	5.9	Port Vale	Wolverhampton	10.09.91
O'Shea, Jay	6.0	MK Dons	Dublin, Ire	10.08.88
Roberts, Gary	5.10	Swindon	Chester	18.03.84
Ryan, Jimmy	5.10	Scunthorpe	Maghull	06.09.88

Forwards

Doyle, Eoin	6.0	Hibernian	Dublin, Ire	12.03.88
Gardner, Dan	6.1	Halifax	Gorton	05.04.90
Gnanduillet, Armand	6.3	Poissy	Angers, Fr	13.02.92

COLCHESTER UNITED

Ground: Weston Homes Community Stadium, United Way, Colchester CO4 5HE
Telephone: 01206 755100. **Club nickname**: U's
Colours: Blue and white. **Capacity**: 10,105
Record attendance: Layer Road:19,072 v Reading (FA Cup 1) Nov 27, 1948;
Community Stadium: 10,064 v Norwich (Lge 1) Jan 16, 2010

Goalkeepers

Lewington, Chris	6.2	Dagenham	Sidcup	23.08.88
Walker, Sam	6.6	Chelsea	Gravesend	02.10.91

Defenders

Clohessy, Sean	5.10	Kilmarnock	Croydon	12.12.86
Eastman, Tom	6.3	Ipswich	Colchester	21.10.91
Gordon, Ben	5.9	Ross Co	Bradford	02.03.91
Okuonghae, Magnus	6.4	Dagenham	Croydon	16.02.86
Thompson, Josh	6.3	Portsmouth	Bolton	25.02.91
Wright, David	5.11	Crystal Palace	Warrington	01.05.80

Midfielders

Bean, Marcus	5.11	Brentford	Hammersmith	02.11.84
Eastmond, Craig	6.0	Arsenal	Battersea	09.12.90
Gilbey, Alex	6.0	–	Dagenham	09.12.94
Hubble, Conor	5.11	QPR	Chelmsford	29.11.94
Olufemi, Tosin	5.8	–	Hackney	13.05.94
Szmodics, Sammie	5.7	–	Colchester	24.09.95
Simmons, Jack	5.7	Ipswich	Basildon	25.11.94
Vose, Dominic	5.8	Barnet	Lambeth	23.11.93
Wright, Drey	5.9	–	Greenwich	30.04.95

Forwards

Bonne, Macauley	5.11	Ipswich	Ipswich	26.10.95
Holman, Dan	5.11	Braintree	Northampton	05.06.90
Ibehre, Jabo	6.2	MK Dons	Islington	28.01.83
Massey, Gavin	5.10	Watford	Watford	14.10.92
Sanchez Watt	5.11	Arsenal	Hackney	14.02.91
Sears, Freddie	5.10	West Ham	Hornchurch	27.11.89

COVENTRY CITY

Ground: Sixfields Stadium, Upton Way, Northampton NN5 5QA (Ground share with Northampton Town)
Club: Citibase, 101, Lockhurst Lane, Coventry CV6 5SF. **Telephone**: 02476 992326. **Club nickname**: Sky Blues
Colours: Sky blue. **Capacity**: 7,653
Record attendance: Highfield Road: 51,455 v Wolves (Div 2) Apr 29, 1967; Ricoh Arena: 31,407 v Chelsea (FA Cup 6), Mar 7 2009

Goalkeepers				
Allsop, Ryan	6.1	Bournmeouth (loan)	Birmingham	17.06.92
Burge, Lee	5.11	–	Hereford	09.01.93
Defenders				
Clarke, Jordan	6.0	–	Coventry	19.11.91
Haynes, Ryan	5.7	–	Northampton	27.09.95
Johnson, Reda	6.3	Sheffield Wed	Marseille, Fr	21.03.88
Phillips, Aaron	5.8	–	Warwick	20.11.93
Seaborne, Dan	6.0	Yeovil	Barnstaple	15.03.87
Urquhart, Stuart	6.2	Rangers	Glasgow	26.03.95
Webster, Andy	6.0	Hearts	Dundee	23.04.82
Willis, Jordan	5.11	–	Coventry	24.08.94
Midfielders				
Baker, Carl	6.2	Stockport	Whiston	26.12.82
Barton, Adam	5.10	Preston	Blackburn	07.01.91
Coulibaly, Mohamed	5.7	Bournemouth (loan)	Bakel, Sen	07.08.88
Fleck, John	5.7	Rangers	Glasgow	24.08.91
Garner, Louis	5.10	–	Manchester	31.10.94
Maddison, James	5.10	–	Coventry	23.11.96
O'Brien, Jim	6.0	Barnsley	Vale of Leven	28.09.87
Pugh, Danny	6.0	Leeds	Manchester	19.10.82
Swanson, Danny	5.7	Peterborough	Leith	28.12.86
Thomas, Conor	6.1	–	Coventry	29.10.93
Forwards				
Daniels, Billy	6.0	–	Bristol	03.07.94
Miller, Shaun	5.8	Sheffield Utd	Alsager	25.09.87
Thomas, George	5.8	–	Leicester	24.03.97

CRAWLEY TOWN

Ground: Checkatrade Stadium, Winfield Way, Crawley RH11 9RX
Telephone: 01293 410000. **Club nickname**: Reds
Colours: Red. **Capacity**: 5,996
Record attendance: 5,880 v Reading (FA Cup 3) Jan 5, 2013

Goalkeepers				
Jensen, Brian	6.1	Bury	Copenhagen, Den	08.06.75
Spiegel, Raphael	6.4	West Ham (loan)	Ruttenen, Swi	19.12.92
Defenders				
Bradley, Sonny	6.4	Portsmouth	Hull	13.09.91
Dickson, Ryan	5.10	Colchester	Saltash	14.12.86
Essam, Connor	6.0	Gillingham	Chatham	09.07.92
Leacock, Dean	6.3	Notts Co	Thornton Heath	10.06.84
Oyebanjo, Lanre	6.1	York	Hackney	27.04.90
Walsh, Joe	5.11	Swansea	Cardiff	13.05.92
Midfielders				
Edwards, Gwion	5.9	Swansea	Lampeter	01.03.93

Henderson, Conor	6.1	Hull	Sidcup	08.09.91
Simpson, Josh	5.9	Peterborough	Cambridge	06.03.87
Smith, Jimmy	6.1	Stevenage	Newham	07.01.87
Young, Lewis	5.9	Bury	Stevenage	27.09.89
Forwards				
Harrold, Matt	6.1	Bristol Rov	Leyton	25.07.84
McLeod, Izale	6.1	MK Dons	Birmingham	15.10.84
Tomlin, Gavin	5.10	Port Vale	Lewisham	21.08.83

CREWE ALEXANDRA

Ground: Alexandra Stadium, Gresty Road, Crewe CW2 6EB
Telephone: 01270 213014. **Club nickname**: Railwaymen
Colours: Red and white. **Capacity**: 10,066
Record attendance: 20,000 v Tottenham (FA Cup 4) Jan 30, 1960

Goalkeepers				
Garratt, Ben	6.1	–	Shrewsbury	25.04.93
Shearer, Scott	6.2	Rotherham	Glasgow	15.02.81
Defenders				
Audel, Thierry	6.2	Macclesfield	Nice, Fr	15.01.87
Davis, Harry	6.2	–	Burnley	24.09.91
Dugdale, Adam	6.3	Telford	Liverpool	13.09.87
Guthrie, Jon	5.10	–	Devizes	29.07.92
Ray, George	6.0	–	Warrington	13.10.93
Tootle, Matt	5.8	–	Knowsley	11.10.90
Turton, Oliver	5.11	–	Manchester	06.12.92
Midfielders				
Colclough, Ryan	6.0	–	Stoke	27.12.94
Grant, Anthony	5.10	Crewe	Lambeth	04.06.87
Inman, Brad	5.9	Newcastle	Adelaide, Aus	10.12.91
Molyneux, Lee	6.0	Accrington	Huyton	24.02.89
Nolan, Liam	5.9	Everton	Liverpool	20.09.94
Waters, Billy	5.9	–	Epsom	15.10.94
Forwards				
Clayton, Max	5.9	–	Crewe	09.08.94
Oliver, Vadaine	6.1	Lincoln	Sheffield	21.10.91
Pogba, Mathias	6.3	Wrexham	Paris, Fr	19.08.90

DONCASTER ROVERS

Ground: Keepmoat Stadium, Stadium Way, Doncaster DN4 5JW
Telephone: 01302 764664. **Club nickname**: Rovers
Colours: Red and white. **Capacity**: 15,231
Record attendance: Belle Vue: 37,149 v Hull (Div 3 N) Oct 2, 1948; Keepmoat Stadium: 15,001 v Leeds (Lge 1) Apr 1, 2008

Goalkeepers				
Maxted, Jonathan	6.0	–	Tadcaster	26.10.93
Turnbull, Ross	6.1	Chelsea	Bishop Auckland	04.01.85
Defenders				
Husband, James	5.11	–	Leeds	03.01.94
Jones, Rob	6.7	Sheffield Wed	Stockton	03.11.79
McCombe, Jamie	6.5	Huddersfield	Pontefract	01.01.83
McCullough, Luke	6.1	Manchester Utd	Portadown	15.02.94
Quinn, Paul	6.0	Cardiff	Wishaw	21.07.85
Wakefield, Liam	6.0	–	Doncaster	09.04.94

Midfielders

Bennett, Kyle	5.5	Bury	Telford	09.09.90
Coppinger, James	5.7	Exeter	Middlesbrough	10.01.81
De Val, Marc	5.11	Real Madrid	Blanes, Sp	15.02.90
Furman, Dean	6.0	Oldham	Cape Town, SA	22.06.88
Keegan, Paul	5.7	Bohemians	Dublin, Ire	05.07.84
Middleton, Harry	5.11	–	Doncaster	12.04.95
Wellens, Richie	5.9	Leicester	Manchester	26.03.80

Forwards

Forrester, Harry	5.10	Brentford	Milton Keynes	02.01.91
Peterson, Alex	6.0	–	Doncaster	17.10.94
Robinson, Theo	5.9	Derby	Birmingham	22.01.89

FLEETWOOD TOWN

Ground: Highbury Stadium, Park Avenue, Fleetwod FY7 6TX
Telephone: 01253 775080. **Club nickname**: Fishermen
Colours: Red and white. **Capacity**: 5,311
Record attendance: 5,194 v York (Lge 2 play-off semi-final, 2nd leg) May 16, 2014

Goalkeepers

Davies, Scott	6.0	Morecambe	Thornton Cleveleys	27.02.87
Lucas, David	6.1	Birmingham	Preston	23.11.77
Maxwell, Chris	6.2	Wrexham	St Asaph	30.07.90

Defenders

Andrew, Danny	5.11	Macclesfield	Holbeach	23.12.90
Brown, Junior	5.9	Northwich	Crewe	07.05.89
Cresswell, Ryan	6.2	Southend	Rotherham	22.12.87
Hogan, Liam	6.0	Halifax	Manchester	08.02.89
Jordan, Stephen	6.0	Dunfermline	Warrington	06.03.82
McLaughlin, Conor	6.0	Preston	Belfast	26.07.91
Morris, Josh	5.10	Blackburn (loan)	Preston	30.09.91
Pond, Nathan	6.2	Lancaster	Preston	05.01.85
Roberts, Mark	6.1	Stevenage	Northwich	16.10.83

Midfielders

Blair, Matty	5.10	York	Warwick	30.11.87
Evans, Gareth	6.0	Rotherham	Macclesfield	26.04.88
Hughes, Jeff	6.1	Notts Co	Larne	29.05.85
Murdoch, Stewart	6.0	Falkirk	Aberdeen	09.05.90
Sarcevic, Antoni	6.0	Chester	Manchester	13.03.92
Schumacher, Steven	6.0	Bury	Liverpool	30.04.84
Southern, Keith	5.10	Huddersfield	Gateshead	21.04.84

Forwards

Ball, David	6.0	Peterborough	Whitefield	14.12.89
Matt, Jamille	6.2	Kidderminster	Walsall	02.12.90
Proctor, Jamie	6.2	Crawley	Preston	25.03.92

GILLINGHAM

Ground: Priestfield Stadium, Redfern Avenue, Gillingham ME7 4DD
Telephone: 01634 300000. **Club nickname**: Gills
Colours: Blue and white. **Capacity**: 11,582
Record attendance: 23,002 v QPR. (FA Cup 3) Jan 10, 1948

Goalkeepers

Morris, Glenn	6.0	Aldershot	Woolwich	20.12.83
Nelson, Stuart	6.1	Notts Co	Stroud	17.09.81

Defenders

Barrett, Adam	5.10	Bournemouth	Dagenham	29.11.79

Davies, Callum	6.1	–	Chatham	08.02.93
Egan, John	6.2	Sunderland	Cork, Ire	20.10.92
Fish, Matt	5.10	Dover	Croydon	05.06.89
Hare, Josh	6.0	–	Canterbury	12.08.94
Legge, Leon	6.1	Brentford	Hastings	28.04.85
McKain, Devante	6.1	Fulham	Hammersmith	26.06.94
Morris, Aaron	6.0	Wimbledon	Rumney	30.12.89
Midfielders				
Dack, Bradley	5.8	–	Greenwich	31.12.93
Haysman, Kane	5.9	–	Tower Hamlets	29.12.94
Hessenthaler, Jake	5.10	–	Gravesend	20.04.90
Linganzi, Amine	6.2	Accrington	Algiers, Alg	16.11.89
Loft, Doug	6.0	Port Vale	Maidstone	25.12.86
Martin, Joe	6.0	Blackpool	Dagenham	29.11.89
McGlashan, Jermaine	5.7	Cheltenham	Croydon	14.04.88
Pritchard, Josh	6.0	Fulham	Stockport	23.09.92
Forwards				
Dickenson, Brennan	6.0	Brighton	Ashford, Surr	26.02.93
German, Antonio	6.1	Brentford	Harlesden	26.12.91
Kedwell, Danny	5.11	Wimbledon	Gillingham	03.08.83
McDonald, Cody	6.0	Coventry	Witham	30.05.86
Norris, Luke	6.1	Brentford	Stevenage	03.06.93

LEYTON ORIENT

Ground: Matchroom Stadium, Brisbane Road, London E10 5NE
Telephone: 0871 310 1881. **Club nickname**: O's
Colours: Red. **Capacity**: 9,271
Record attendance: 34,345 v West Ham (FA Cup 4) Jan 25, 1964

Goalkeepers				
Grainger, Charlie	6.2	–	Enfield	31.07.96
Legzdins, Adam	6.0	Derby	Stafford	23.11.86
Woods, Gary	6.1	Watford	Kettering	01.10.90
Defenders				
Baudry, Mathieu	6.2	Bournemouth	Le Havre, Fr	24.02.88
Clarke, Nathan	6.2	Huddersfield	Halifax	30.11.83
Cuthbert, Scott	6.2	Swindon	Alexandria, Sco	15.06.87
Omozusi, Elliot	5.11	Fulham	Hackney	15.12.88
Sawyer, Gary	6.0	Bristol Rov	Bideford	05.07.85
Vincelot, Romaine	5.10	Brighton	Poitiers, Fr	29.10.85
Midfielders				
Bartley, Marvin	5.11	Burnley	Reading	01.07.89
Cox, Dean	5.5	–	Brighton	12.08.87
James, Lloyd	5.11	Colchester	Bristol	16.02.88
Lee, Harry	5.11	–	Hackney	20.03.95
Pritchard, Bradley	6.1	Charlton	Harare, Zim	19.12.85
Forwards				
Batt, Shaun	6.2	Millwall	Luton	22.02.87
Dagnall, Chris	5.8	Barnsley	Liverpool	15.04.86
Lisbie, Kevin	5.10	Ipswich	Hackney	17.10.78
Mooney, David	6.2	Reading	Dublin, Ire	30.10.84

MILTON KEYNES DONS

Ground: stadiummk, Stadium Way West, Milton Keynes MK1 1ST
Telephone: 01908 622922. **Club nickname**: Dons

Colours: White. **Capacity**: 30,500
Record attendance: 20,516 v Wolves (Lge 1) Mar 29, 2014. Also: 20,222 England v Bulgaria (U-21 int) Nov 16, 2007

Goalkeepers

Burns, Charlie	6.2	–	Croydon	27.05.95
Martin, David	6.2	Liverpool	Romford	22.01.86
McLoughlin, Ian	6.3	Ipswich	Dublin, Ire	09.08.91

Defenders

Flanagan, Tom	6.2	–	Hammersmith	30.12.91
Galloway, Brendan	6.2	–	Zimbabwe	17.03.96
Hodson, Lee	5.11	Watford	Borehamwood	02.10.91
Kay, Antony	5.11	Huddersfield	Barnsley	21.10.82
Lewington, Dean	5.11	Wimbledon	Kingston	18.05.84
McFadzean, Kyle	6.1	Crawley	Sheffield	28.02.87

Midfielders

Alli, Dele	6.1	–	Milton Keynes	11.04.96
Baldock, George	5.9	–	Buckingham	26.01.93
Green, Danny	6.0	Charlton	Harlow	09.07.88
Potter, Darren	5.10	Sheffield Wed	Liverpool	21.12.84
Powell, Daniel	6.2	–	Luton	12.03.91
Randall, Mark	6.0	Ascoli	Milton Keynes	28.09.89
Reeves, Ben	5.10	Southampton	Verwood	19.11.91

Forwards

Bowditch, Dean	5.11	Yeovil	Bishop's Stortford	15.06.86
Grigg, Will	5.11	Brentford (loan)	Solihull	03.07.91
Hitchcock, Tom	5.11	QPR	Hemel Hempstead	01.10.92
Rasulo, Giorgio	5.10	–	Banbury	23.01.97

NOTTS COUNTY

Ground: Meadow Lane, Nottingham NG2 3HJ
Telephone: 0115 952 9000. **Club nickname**: Magpies
Colours: White and black. **Capacity**: 20,300
Record attendance: 47,310 v York (FA Cup 6) Mar 12, 1955

Goalkeepers

Spiess, Fabian	6.2		Germany	22.02.94

Defenders

Adams, Blair	5.9	Coventry	South Shields	08.09.91
Dumbuya, Mustapha	5.8	Crawley	SLeone	07.08.87
Hollis, Haydn	6.4	–	Selston	14.10.92

Midfielders

Dixon, Kyle	5.8	–	Nottingham	28.12.94
Haynes, Danny	5.11	Charlton	Peckham	19.01.88
Mullins, Hayden	6.0	Birmingham	Reading	27.03.79
Noble, Liam	5.8	Carlisle	Cramlington	08.05.91
Smith, Alan	5.10	MK Dons	Rothwell	28.10.80
Tempest, Greg	6.0	–	Nottingham	28.12.93
Thompson, Curtis	5.7	–	Nottingham	02.09.93
Wroe, Nicky	5.11	Preston	Sheffield	28.09.85
Ismail, Zeli	5.9	Wolves (loan)	Kukes, Alb	12.12.93

Forwards

Haynes, Danny	6.0	Charlton	Peckham	19.01.88
Murray, Ronan	5.8	Ipswich	Mayo, Ire	12.09.91
Spencer, Jimmy	6.1	Huddersfield	Leeds	13.12.91
Waite, Tyrell	5.11	Ilkeston	Derby	01.07.94

OLDHAM ATHLETIC

Ground: SportsDirect Park, Oldham OL1 2PA
Telephone: 0161 624 4972. **Club nickname**: Latics
Colours: Blue and white. **Capacity**: 10,638
Record attendance: 47,761 v Sheffield Wed (FA Cup 4) Jan 25, 1930

Goalkeepers

Rachubka, Paul	6.1	Leeds	San Luis Obispo, US	28.09.90

Defenders

Brown, Connor	5.9	Sheffield Utd	Sheffield	22.08.92
Kusunga, Genseric	6.1	Basle	Geneva, Swi	12.03.88
Lockwood, Adam	6.0	Guiseley	Wakefield	26.10.81
Mills, Joseph	5.9	Burnley	Swindon	30.10.89
Truelove, Jack	5.10	–	Burnley	27.12.95
Wilson, Brian	5.10	Colchester	Manchester	09.05.83
Wilson, James	6.2	Bristol City	Chepstow	26.02.89

Midfielders

Dayton, James	5.9	Kilmarnock	Enfield	12.12.88
Dieng, Timothee	6.2	Brest	Grenoble, Fr	09.04.92
Jones, Mike	6.0	Crawley	Birkenhead	15.08.87
Kelly, Liam	5.10	Bristol City	Milton Keynes	10.02.90
Mellor, David	5.9	Manchester Utd	Oldham	10.07.93
Winchester, Carl	6.0	Linfield	Belfast	12.04.93

Forwards

Bove, Jordan	5.9	–	Manchester	12.12.95
Clarke-Harris, Jonson	6.0	Coventry	Leicester	20.07.94
Philliskirk, Danny	5.10	Coventry	Oldham	10.04.91
Turner, Rhys	5.11	Stockport	Preston	22.07.95

PETERBOROUGH UNITED

Ground: London Road Stadium, Peterborough PE2 8AL
Telephone: 01733 563947. **Club nickname**: Posh
Colours: Blue and white. **Capacity**: 15,314
Record attendance: 30,096 v Swansea (FA Cup 5) Feb 20, 1965

Goalkeepers

Day, Joe	6.1	Rushden	Brighton	13.08.90
Olejnik, Bobby	6.0	Torquay	Vienna, Aut	26.11.86

Defenders

Baldwin, Jack	6.1	Hartlepool	Barking	30.06.93
Brisley, Shaun	6.2	Macclesfield	Macclesfield	06.05.90
Ntlhe, Kgosi	5.9	–	Pretoria, SA	21.02.94
Richens, Michael	5.10	Luton	Bedford	28.02.95
Santos, Ricardo	6.5	Thurrock	Almada, Port	18.06.95
Zakuani, Gabriel	6.1	Kalloni	Kinshasa, DR Congo	31.05.86

Midfielders

Anderson, Jermaine	5.11	–	Camden	16.05.96
Bostwick, Michael	6.1	Stevenage	Greenwich	17.05.88
Conlon, Tom	5.9	Newcastle Town	Stoke	03.02.96
Ferdinand, Kane	6.1	Southend	Newham	07.10.92
McCann, Grant	5.10	Scunthorpe	Belfast	14.04.80
Mendez-Laing, Nathaniel	5.10	Wolves	Birmingham	15.04.92
Newell, Joe	5.11	–	Tamworth	15.03.93
Oztumer, Erhun	5.3	Dulwich Hamlet	Greenwich	29.05.91
Payne, Jack	5.9	Gillingham	Gravesend	05.12.91

Taylor, Jon	5.11	Shrewsbury	Liverpool	20.07.92

Forwards

Ajose, Nicky	5.9	Manchester Utd	Bury	07.10.91
Assombalonga, Britt	5.10	Watford	Kinshasa, DR Cong	06.12.92
Barnett, Tyrone	6.3	Crawley	Stevenage	28.10.85
Washington, Conor	5.9	Newport	Chatham	18.05.92

PORT VALE

Ground: Vale Park, Hamil Road, Burslem, Stoke-on-Trent ST6 1AW
Telephone: 01782 655800. **Club nickname**: Valiants
Colours: Black and white. **Capacity**: 18,947
Record attendance: 49,768 v Aston Villa (FA Cup 5) Feb 20, 1960

Goalkeepers

Johnson, Sam	6.6	Stoke	Newcastle-under-Lyme	
01.12.92				
Neal, Chris	6.2	Shrewsbury	St Albans	23.10.85

Defenders

Dickinson, Carl	6.1	Watford	Swadlincote	31.03.87
Duffy, Richard	5.11	Exeter	Swansea	30.08.85
McGivern, Ryan	6.2	Hibernian	Newry	08.01.90
Robertson, Chris	6.3	Preston	Dundee	11.10.86
Yates, Adam	5.10	Morecambe	Stoke	28.05.83

Midfielders

Birchall, Chris	5.9	Columbus	Stafford	05.05.84
Brown, Michael	5.10	Leeds	Hartlepool	25.01.77
Daniel, Colin	5.11	Mansfield	Nottingham	15.02.88
Jennings, Steve	5.7	Tranmere	Liverpool	28.10.84
Lines, Chris	6.2	Sheffield Wed	Bristol	30.11.85
Lloyd, Ryan	5.10	–	Newcastle-u-Lyme	01.02.94
Marshall, Mark	5.7	Coventry	Manchester, Jam	05.05.87
Moore, Byron	6.0	Crewe	Stoke	24.08.88
O'Connor, Michael	6.1	Rotherham	Belfast	06.10.87

Forwards

Dodds, Louis	5.10	Leicester	Sheffield	08.10.86
Pope, Tom	6.3	Rotherham	Stoke	27.08.85
Williamson, Ben	5.11	Hyde	Lambeth	25.12.88

PRESTON NORTH END

Ground: Deepdale, Sir Tom Finney Way, Preston PR1 6RU
Telephone: 0844 856 1964. **Club nickname**: Lilywhites
Colours: White and navy. **Capacity**: 23,408
Record attendance: 42,684 v Arsenal (Div 1) Apr 23, 1938

Goalkeepers

James, Steven	6.0	–	Southport	19.12.94
Jones, Jamie	6.0	Leyton Orient	Kirkby	18.02.89
Stuckmann, Thorsten	6.6	Aachen	Gutersloh, Ger	17.03.81

Defenders

Buchanan, David	5.9	Tranmere	Rochdale	06.05.86
Clarke, Tom	5.11	Huddersfield	Halifax	21.12.87
Davies, Ben	5.11	–	Barrow	11.08.95
Huntington, Paul	6.2	Yeovil	Carlisle	17.09.87
Keane, Keith	5.9	Luton	Luton	20.11.86
King, Jack	6.0	Woking	Oxford	20.08.85
Laird, Scott	5.9	Stevenage	Taunton	15.05.88

Wiseman, Scott	6.0	Barnsley	Hull	13.12.85
Woods, Calum	5.11	Huddersfield	Liverpool	05.02.87
Wright, Bailey	5.10	VIS	Melbourne, Aus	28.07.92
Midfielders				
Browne, Alan	–	Cork	Cork, Ire	15.04.95
Brownhill, Josh	5.10	–	Warrington	19.12.95
Byrom, Joel	6.0	Stevenage	Oswaldtwistle	14.09.86
Hayhurst, Will	5.10	–	Blackburn	24.02.94
Holmes, Lee	5.8	Southampton	Mansfield	02.04.87
Humphrey, Chris	5.9	Motherwell	St Catherine, Jam	19.09.87
Kilkenny, Neil	5.8	Bristol City	Enfield	19.12.85
Reid, Kyel	5.11	Bradford	Deptford	26.11.87
Welsh, John	6.0	Tranmere	Liverpool	10.01.84
Forwards				
Davies, Kevin	6.0	Bolton	Sheffield	26.03.77
Gallagher, Paul	6.0	Leicester (loan)	Glasgow	09.08.84
Garner, Joe	5.10	Watford	Blackburn	12.04.88
Hugill, Jordan	6.0	Port Vale	Middlesbrough	04.06.92
Little, Andy	6.0	Rangers	Enniskillen	12.05.89

ROCHDALE

Ground: Spotland, Wilbutts Lane, Rochdale OL11 5DS
Telephone: 01706 644648. **Club nickname**: Dale
Colours: Blue and black. **Capacity**: 10,249
Record attendance: 24,231 v Notts Co (FA Cup 2) Dec 10, 1949

Goalkeepers				
Collis, Steve	6.3	Macclesfield	Harrow	18.03.81
Lillis, Josh	6.0	Scunthorpe	Derby	24.06.87
Defenders				
Bennett, Rhys	6.3	Bolton	Manchester	01.09.91
Eastham, Ashley	6.3	Blackpool	Preston	22.03.91
Lancashire, Olly	6.1	Aldershot	Basingstoke	13.12.88
McGinty, Sean	6.3	Sheffield Utd	Maidstone	11.08.93
O'Connor, D'Arcy	5.11	–	Oldham	21.12.94
Rafferty, Joe	6.0	Liverpool	Liverpool	06.10.93
Rose, Michael	5.11	Colchester	Salford	28.07.82
Tanser, Scott	6.0	–	Blackpool	23.10.94
Midfielders				
Allen, Jamie	5.11	–	Rochdale	29.01.95
Barry-Murphy, Brian	6.0	Bury	Cork, Ire	27.07.78
Done, Matt	5.10	Barnsley	Oswestry	22.07.88
Hery, Bastien	5.9	Sheffield Wed	Brou Chantereine, Fr	23.03.92
Lund, Matthew	6.0	Stoke	Manchester	21.11.90
Vincenti, Peter	6.2	Aldershot	St Peter, Jer	07.07.86
Forwards				
Bunney, Joe	5.10	–	Northwich	26.09.93
Donnelly, George	5.9	Macclesfield	Kirkby	28.05.88
Henderson, Ian	5.10	Colchester	Thetford	24.01.85
Hogan, Scott	5.11	Hyde	–	13.04.92
Logan, Joel	5.11	–	Manchester	25.01.95

SCUNTHORPE UNITED

Ground: Glanford Park, Doncaster Road, Scunthorpe DN15 8TD
Telephone: 0871 221 1899. **Club nickname**: Iron

Colours: Claret and blue. **Capacity**: 9,183
Record attendance: Old Show Ground: 23,935 v Portsmouth (FA Cup 4) Jan 30, 1954;
Glanford Park: 8,921 v Newcastle (Champ) Oct 20, 2009

Goalkeepers

Severn, James	6.3	Derby	Nottingham	10.10.91
Slocombe, Sam	6.0	Bottesford	Scunthorpe	05.06.88

Defenders

Boyce, Andrew	6.2	Lincoln	Doncaster	05.11.89
Canavan, Niall	6.3	–	Leeds	11.04.91
Dawson, Andy	5.9	Hull	Northallerton	20.10.78
Howe, Callum	6.2	–	Doncaster	09.04.94
Mirfin, David	6.1	Watford	Sheffield	18.04.85
Nolan, Eddie	6.1	Preston	Waterford, Ire	05.08.88
Waterfall, Luke	6.2	Gainsborough	Sheffield	30.07.90
Williams, Marcus	5.8	Sheffield Utd	Doncaster	08.04.86

Midfielders

Bishop, Neal	6.0	Blackpool	Stockton	07.08.81
Hawkridge, Terry	5.10	Gainsborough	Nottingham	23.02.90
Hornsey, Luke	5.10	–	Scunthorpe	02.10.94
McAllister, Sean	5.8	Cowdenbeath	Bolton	15.08.87
McSheffrey, Gary	5.8	Chesterfield	Coventry	13.08.72
Myrie-Williams, Jennison	6.0	Port Vale	Lambeth	17.05.88
Sparrow, Matt	5.10	Crawley	Wembley	03.10.81
Syers, David	5.10	Doncaster	Leeds	30.11.87

Forwards

Adelakun, Hakeeb	6.0	–	Hackney	11.06.96
Burton, Deon	5.10	Gillingham	Reading	25.10.76
Madden, Paddy	6.0	Yeovil	Dublin, Ire	04.03.90
Taylor, Lyle	6.2	Sheffield Utd	Greenwich	29.03.90
Winnall, Sam	5.11	Wolves	Wolverhampton	19.01.91

SHEFFIELD UNITED

Ground: Bramall Lane, Sheffield S2 4SU
Telephone: 0871 995 1899. **Club nickname**: Blades
Colours: Red and white. **Capacity**: 32,702
Record attendance: 68,287 v Leeds (FA Cup 5) Feb 15, 1936

Goalkeepers

Howard, Mark	6.1	Blackpool	Southwark	21.09.86
Long, George	6.4	–	Sheffield	05.11.93
Willis, George	5.11	–	Rotherham	30.07.95

Defenders

Alcock, Craig	5.8	Peterborough	Truro	08.12.87
Basham, Chris	5.11	Blackpool	Hebburn	18.02.88
Butler, Andy	6.0	Walsall	Doncaster	04.11.83
Collins, Neil	6.3	Leeds	Troon	02.09.83
Harris, Bob	5.8	Blackpool	Glasgow	28.08.87
Kennedy, Terry	5.10	–	Barnsley	14.11.93
Maguire, Harry	6.2	–	Sheffield	05.03.93
McGahey, Harrison	6.1	Blackpool	Preston	26.09.95

Midfielders

Baxter, Jose	5.10	Oldham	Bootle	07.02.92
Campbell-Ryce, Jamal	5.7	Notts Co	Lambeth	06.04.83
Cuvelier, Florent	6.0	Stoke	Brussels, Bel	12.09.92
Davies, Ben	5.7	Derby	Birmingham	27.05.81

Doyle, Michael	5.10	Coventry	Dublin, Ire	08.07.81
Flynn, Ryan	5.7	Falkirk	Edinburgh	04.09.88
McGinn, Stephen	5.10	Watford	Glasgow	02.12.88
Scougall, Stefan	5.7	Livingston	Edinburgh	07.12.92
Wallace, James	6.0	Tranmere	Fazackerley	19.12.91
Forwards				
De Girolano, Diego	5.10	–	Chesterfield	05.10.95
Eyre, Jake	5.11	–	Chester	02.11.95
Ironside, Joe	5.11	–	Middlesbrough	16.10.93
Marriott, Adam	5.10	Cambridge City	Brandon	14.04.91
McNulty, Mark	5.10	Livingston	Edinburgh	14.09.92
Murphy, Jamie	5.10	Motherwell	Glasgow	28.08.89
Porter, Chris	6.1	Derby	Wigan	12.12.83

SWINDON TOWN

Ground: County Ground, County Road, Swindon SN1 2ED
Telephone: 0871 423 6433. **Club nickname:** Robins
Colours: Red and white. **Capacity:** 15,728
Record attendance: 32,000 v Arsenal (FA Cup 3) Jan 15, 1972

Goalkeepers				
Belford, Tyrell	6.0	Liverpool	Nuneaton	06.05.94
Foderingham, Wes	6.1	Crystal Palace	Shepherd's Bush	14.01.91
Defenders				
Barthram, Jack	6.0	Tottenham	Newham	13.10.93
Byrne, Nathan	5.10	Tottenham	St Albans	05.06.92
Rossi Branco, Raphael	6.3	Whitehawk	Campinas, Br	25.07.90
Thompson, Nathan	5.10	–	Chester	22.04.91
Ward, Darren	6.3	Millwall	Kenton	13.09.78
Midfielders				
Gladwin, Ben	6.3	Marlow	Reading	08.06.92
Harley, Ryan	5.9	Brighton	Bristol	22.01.85
Kasim, Yaser	5.11	Brighton	Baghdad, Irq	16.05.91
Luongo, Massimo	5.10	Tottenham	Sydney, Aus	25.09.92
Reis, Tijane	5.9	Chaves	Canchungo, Guin-Bass	28.06.91
Rodgers, Anton	5.8	Oldham	Reading	26.01.93
Thompson, Louis	5.11	–	Bristol	19.12.94
Forwards				
Barker, George	5.8	Brighton	Portsmouth	26.09.91
Smith, Michael	6.4	Charlton	Wallsend	17.10.91
Waldron, Connor	5.11	–	Swindon	13.02.95

WALSALL

Ground: Banks's Stadium, Bescot Crescent, Walsall WS1 4SA
Telephone: 01922 622791. **Club nickname:** Saddlers
Colours: Red and white. **Capacity:** 11,300
Record attendance: Fellows Park: 25,453 v Newcastle (Div 2) Aug 29, 1961; Banks's Stadium: 11,049 v Rotherham (Div 1) May 10, 2004

Goalkeepers				
O'Donnell, Richard	6.2	Chesterfield	Sheffield	12.09.88
Defenders				
Benning, Malvind	5.10	–	Sandwell	02.11.93
Chambers, James	5.10	Doncaster	Sandwell	20.11.80
Downing, Paul	6.1	WBA	Taunton	26.10.91
Holden, Dean	6.1	Rochdale	Salford	15.09.79

O'Connor, James	5.10	Derby	Birmingham	20.11.84
Preston, Matt	6.0	–	Birmingham	16.03.95
Purkiss, Ben	6.2	Hereford	Sheffield	01.04.84
Taylor, Andy	5.11	Sheffield Utd	Blackburn	14.03.86
Midfielders				
Baxendale, James	5.8	Doncaster	Thorne	16.09.92
Chambers, Adam	5.10	Leyton Orient	Sandwell	20.11.80
Mantom, Sam	5.9	WBA	Stourbridge	20.02.92
Morris, Kieron	5.10	–	Hereford	03.06.94
Sawyers, Romaine	5.10	WBA	Birmingham	02.11.91
Forwards				
Bakayoko, Amadou	6.4	–	SLeone	01.01.96
Bradshaw, Tom	5.10	Shrewsbury	Shrewsbury	27.07.92
Cook, Jordan	5.9	Charlton	Sunderland	20.03.90

YEOVIL TOWN

Ground: Huish Park, Lufton Way, Yeovil BA22 8YF
Telephone: 01935 423662. **Club nickname:** Glovers
Colours: Green and white. **Capacity:** 9,565
Record attendance: 9,527 v Leeds (Lge 1) Apr 25, 2008

Goalkeepers				
Krysiak, Artur	6.4	Exeter	Lodz, Pol	11.08.89
Stewart, Gareth	6.0	Welling	Preston	03.02.80
Weale, Chris	6.2	Shrewsbury	Yeovil	09.02.82
Defenders				
Ayling, Luke	6.1	Arsenal	Lambeth	25.08.91
Edwards, Joe	5.8	Bristol City	Gloucester	31.10.90
Lanzoni, Matteo	6.3	Oldham	Como, It	18.07.88
Martin, Aaron	6.1	Birmingham	Newport, IOW	29.09.89
Moloney, Brendan	5.10	Bristol City	Beaufort, Ire	18.01.89
Nugent, Ben	6.1	Cardiff (loan)	Welwyn Garden City	29.11.92
Ofori-Twumasi, Nana	5.8	Northampton	Accra, Gh	15.05.90
Smith, Nathan	6.0	Chesterfield	Enfield	11.01.87
Sokolik, Jakub	6.2	Liverpool	Ostrava, Cz	28.08.93
Midfielders				
Berrett, James	5.10	Carlisle	Halifax	13.01.89
Davis, Liam	6.1	Oxford	Wandsworth	23.11.86
Dawson, Kevin	5.11	Shelbourne	Dublin, Ire	30.06.90
Foley, Sam	6.0	Newport	Upton-on-Severn	17.10.86
Grant, Joel	6.0	Wycombe	Hammersmith	27.08.87
Ralph, Nathan	5.9	Peterborough	Essex	14.02.93
Forwards				
Hayter, James	5.9	Doncaster	Sandown, IOW	09.04.79
Hoskins, Sam	5.9	Southampton	Dorchester	04.02.93
Leitch-Smith, Jay	5.11	Crewe	Crewe	06.03.90
Moore, Kieffer	6.5	Dorchester	Torquay	08.08.92

LEAGUE TWO

ACCRINGTON STANLEY

Ground: Store First Stadium, Livingstone Road, Accrington BB5 5BX
Telephone: 0871 434 1968. **Club nickname:** Stanley
Colours: Red and white. **Capacity:** 5,057

Record attendance: 4,368 v Colchester (FA Cup 3) Jan 3, 2004

Goalkeepers

Dawber, Andrew	6.0	–	Wigan	20.11.94

Defenders

Aldred, Tom	6.2	Colchester	Bolton	11.09.90
Atkinson, Rob	6.1	Fleetwood	North Ferriby	29.04.87
Buxton, Adam	6.1	Wigan	Liverpool	12.05.92
Hunt, Nicky	6.1	Rotherham	Westhoughton	03.09.83
Liddle, Michael	5.8	Sunderland	Hounslow	25.12.89
Winnard, Dean	5.9	Blackburn	Wigan	20.08.89

Midfielders

Hatfield, Will	5.8	Leeds	Dewsbury	10.10.91
Joyce, Luke	5.11	Carlisle	Bolton	09.07.87
Mingoia, Piero	5.7	Watford	Enfield	20.10.91
Windass, Josh	5.10	Huddersfield	Hull	09.01.94

Forwards

Bowerman, George	5.10	Woking	Wordsley	06.11.91
Carver, Marcus	5.11	–	Blackburn	22.10.93
Gray, James	5.10	Darlington	Yarm	26.06.92
McCartan, Shay	5.10	Burnley	Newry	18.05.94
Naismith, Kal	6.1	Rangers	Glasgow	18.02.92

AFC WIMBLEDON

Ground: Cherry Red Records Stadium, Kingston Road, Kingston upon Thames KT1 3PB
Telephone: 0208 547 3528. **Club nickname**: Dons
Colours: Blue. **Capacity**: 4,850
Record attendance: 4,749 v Exeter (Lge 2) Apr 23, 2013

Goalkeepers

Shea, James	5.11	Harrow	Islington	16.06.91
Worner, Ross	6.1	Aldershot	Hindhead	03.10.89

Defenders

Bennett, Alan	6.2	Cheltenham	Cork, Ire	04.10.81
Cooksley, Harry	6.1	Aldershot	Guildford	15.11.94
Frampton, Andy	5.11	Gillingham	Wimbledon	03.09.79
Fuller, Barry	5.10	Barnet	Ashford, Kent	25.09.84
Nicholson, Jake	6.0	Morton	Harrow	19.07.92
Smith, Jack	5.11	Millwall	Hemel Hempstead	14.11.83
Phillips, Mark	6.2	Southend	Lambeth	27.01.82

Midfielders

Arthur, Chris	5.10	Havant	Enfield	25.01.90
Bulman, Dannie	5.8	Crawley	Ashford, Sur	24.01.79
Francomb, George	6.0	Norwich	Hackney	08.09.91
Moore, Sammy	5.8	Dover	Deal	07.09.87
Pell, Harry	6.4	Hereford	Tilbury	21.10.91
Rigg, Sean	5.9	Oxford	Bristol	01.10.88
Sainte-Luce, Kevin	5.10	Cardiff	Paris, Fr	28.04.93

Forwards

Akinfenwa, Adebayo	6.1	Gillingham	West Ham	10.05.82
Azeez, Adebayo	6.0	Charlton	Sidcup	08.01.94
Tubbs, Matt	5.10	Bournemouth (loan)	Salisbury	15.07.84

BURTON ALBION

Ground: Pirelli Stadium, Princess Way, Burton upon Trent DE13 AR
Telephone: 01283 565938. **Club nickname**: Brewers

Colours: Yellow and black. Capacity: 6,912
Record attendance: 6,192 v Oxford Utd (Blue Square Prem Lge) Apr 17, 2009

Goalkeepers

Lyness, Dean	6.3	Kidderminster	Halesowen	20.07.91

Defenders

Cansdell-Sherriff, Shane	6.0	Preston	Sydney, Aus	10.11.82
Edwards, Phil	5.9	Rochdale	Bootle	08.11.85
Sharps, Ian	6.4	Rotherham	Warrington	23.10.80
Slade, Liam	6.3	–	Birmingham	14.05.95
Taft, George	6.3	Leicester	Leicester	29.07.93

Midfielders

Bell, Lee	5.11	Crewe	Crewe	26.01.83
Harness, Marcus	6.0	–	Coventry	01.08.94
MacDonald, Alex	5.7	Burnley	Chester	14.04.90
McCrory, Damien	6.2	Dagenham	Croom, Ire	23.02.90
McFadzean, Callum	5.11	Sheffield Utd (loan)	Sheffield	01.04.94
Mousinho, John	6.1	Preston	Isleworth	30.04.86
Palmer, Matt	5.10	–	Derby	01.08.93
Phillips, Jimmy	5.7	Stoke	Stoke	20.09.89
Weir, Robbie	5.9	Tranmere	Belfast	09.12.88

Forwards

Akins, Lucas	6.0	Stevenage	Huddersfield	25.02.89
Beavon, Stuart	5.10	Preston (loan)	Reading	05.05.84
Kee, Billy	5.9	Torquay	Leicester	01.12.90
Knowles, Dominic	5.9	Harrogate	Accrington	13.02.92
McGurk, Adam	5.10	Tranmere	Larne	24.01.89

BURY

Ground: J D Stadium, Gigg Lane, Bury BL9 9HR
Telephone: 08445 790009. Club nickname: Shakers
Colours: White and blue. Capacity: 11,640
Record attendance: 35,000 v Bolton (FA Cup 3) Jan 9, 1960

Goalkeepers

Jalal, Shwan	6.2	Bournemouth	Southampton	14.08.83
Lainton, Rob	6.2	Bolton	Ashton-under-Lyne	12.10.89

Defenders

Burke, James	5.11	Huddersfield	Shepley	16.04.94
Cameron, Nathan	6.2	Coventry	Birmingham	21.11.91
Hussey, Chris	6.0	Burton	Hammersmith	02.01.89
McNulty, Jim	6.0	Barnsley	Liverpool	13.02.85
Mills, Pablo	5.11	Rotherham	Birmingham	27.05.84
O'Brien, Keil	6.4	Chorley	–	29.06.92

Midfielders

Adams, Nicky	5.10	Rotherham	Bolton	16.10.86
Etuhu, Kelvin	6.1	Barnsley	Kano, Nig	30.05.88
Grimes, Ashley	6.0	Rochdale	Swinton	09.12.86
Jones, Craig	5.8	New Saints	Chester	20.03.87
Mayor, Danny	6.0	Sheffield Wed	Leyland	18.10.90
Procter, Andy	5.11	Preston	Blackburn	13.03.83
Sedgwick, Chris	6.0	Scunthorpe	Sheffield	28.04.80
Soares, Tom	6.0	Stoke	Reading	10.07.86
Tutte, Andrew	5.9	Rochdale	Liverpool	21.09.90

Forwards

Lowe, Ryan	5.11	Tranmere	Liverpool	18.09.78

Nardiello, Daniel	5.11	Rotherham	Coventry	22.10.82
Platt, Clive	6.4	Northampton	Wolverhampton	27.10.77
Walker, Regan	5.11	Manchester City	Manchester	04.06.96

CAMBRIDGE UNITED

Ground: Costings Abbey Stadium, Newmarket Road, Cambridge CB5 8LN
Telephone: 01223 566500. **Club nickname**: U's
Colours: Yellow and black. **Capacity**: 9,617
Record attendance: 14,000 v Chelsea (friendly) May 1, 1970

Goalkeepers
| Dunn, Chris | 6.3 | Yeovil | Brentwood | 23.10.87 |
| Norris, Will | 6.1 | Royston | Royston | 12.08.93 |

Defenders
Bonner, Tom	6.0	Dartford	Camden	06.02.88
Coulson, Josh	6.3	–	Cambridge	28.01.89
Miller, Ian	6.2	Grimsby	Colchester	23.11.83
Tait, Richard	5.11	Tamworth	Galashiels	02.12.89
Taylor, Greg	6.1	Luton	Bedford	15.01.90

Midfielders
Arnold, Nathan	5.7	Alfreton	Mansfield	26.07.87
Austin, Mitch	6.2	Stalybridge	Sydney, Aus	03.04.91
Berry, Luke	5.10	–	Bassingbourn	12.07.92
Chadwick, Luke	5.11	MK Dons	Cambridge	18.11.80
Champion, Tom	6.3	Dartford	Barnet	15.05.86
Donaldson, Ryan	5.9	Gateshead	Newcastle	01.05.91
Dunk, Harrison	6.0	Bromley	London	25.10.90
Hughes, Liam	6.4	Scunthorpe	Rotherham	10.08.92
Hunt, Johnny	5.11	Wrexham	Liverpool	23.08.90

Forwards
Appiah, Kwesi	5.11	Crystal Palace (loan)	Thamesmead	12.08.90
Cunnington, Adam	6.3	Tamworth	Leighton Buzzard	07.10.87
Elliott, Tom	6.3	Stockport	Leeds	09.11.90
Hurst Liam	5.10	Leicester	Leicester	02.09.94
Sam-Yorke, Delano	6.1	Basingstoke	–	20.01.89
Simpson, Robbie	6.1	Leyton Orient	Poole	15.03.85

CARLISLE UNITED

Ground: Brunton Park, Warwick Road, Carlisle CA1 1LL
Telephone: 01228 526237. **Club nickname**: Cumbrians
Colours: Blue and white. **Capacity**: 18,202
Record attendance: 27,500 v Birmingham City (FA Cup 3) Jan 5, 1957, v Middlesbrough (FA Cup 5) Jan 7, 1970

Goalkeepers
| Gillespie, Mark | 6.0 | – | Newcastle | 27.03.92 |
| Hanford, Dan | 6.3 | Floriana | Rochdale | 06.03.91 |

Defenders
Archibald-Henville, Troy	6.2	Swindon	Newham	04.11.88
Grainger, Danny	5.10	Dunfermline	Penrith	28.07.86
Meppen-Walter, Courtney	6.3	–	Bury	02.08.94
O'Hanlon, Sean	6.0	Hibernian	Liverpool	02.01.83

Midfielders
Brough, Patrick	6.3	–	Carlisle	20.02.96
Dempsey, Kyle	5.10	–	Maryport	17.09.95
Dicker, Gary	6.0	Crawley	Dublin, Ire	31.07.86

Gillies, Josh	5.10	Gateshead	Sunderland	12.06.90
Kearns, Danny	5.10	Peterborough	Belfast	26.08.91
Marrow, Alex	6.1	Blackburn	Tyldesley	21.01.90
Potts, Brad	6.2	–	Hexham	03.07.94
Robson, Matty	5.10	Hartlepool	Durham	23.01.85
Sweeney, Anthony	6.0	Hartlepool	Stockton	05.09.83
Symington, David	5.9	–	Workington	28.01.94
Thirlwell, Paul	5.11	Derby	Springwell	13.02.79
Forwards				
Amoo, David	5.10	Tranmere	Southwark	13.04.91
Beck, Mark	6.5	–	Sunderland	02.04.94
Paynter, Billy	6.0	Doncaster	Liverpool	13.07.84

CHELTENHAM TOWN

Ground: Abbey Business Stadium, Whaddon Road, Cheltenham GL52 5NA
Telephone: 01242 573558. **Club nickname**: Town
Colours: Red and black. **Capacity**: 7,066
Record attendance: 8,326 v Reading (FA Cup 1) Nov 17, 1956

Goalkeepers				
Carson, Trevor	6.0	Bury	Killyleagh	05.03.88
Defenders				
Black, Paul	6.0	Mansfield	Middleton	18.05.90
Bowen, James	5.11	-	Birmingham	04.02.96
Braham-Barrett, Craig	5.9	Macclesfield	Greenwich	01.09.88
Brown, Troy	5.10	Aldershot	Croydon	17.09.90
Elliott, Steve	6.2	Bristol Rov	Derby	29.10.78
Vaughan, Lee	5.7	Kidderminster	Castle Bromwich	17.07.86
Midfielders				
Hall, Asa	6.2	Shrewsbury	Sandwell	29.11.86
Hanks, Joe	6.1	–	Churchdown	02.03.95
Haworth, Andy	5.8	Notts Co	Lancaster	28.11.88
Kotwica, Zack	5.11	–	Gloucester	18.01.95
Powell, Adam	6.0	-	Worcester	30.09.95
Richards, Matt	5.9	Shrewsbury	Harlow	26.12.84
Taylor, Jason	6.1	Rotherham	Ashton-under-Lyne	28.01.87
Williams, Harry	5.11	–	Cheltenham	17.01.96
Forwards				
Dale, Bobbie	6.0	–	Worcester	25.11.95
Gornell, Terry	5.11	Rochdale	Liverpool	16.12.89
Harrison, Bryan	6.3	AFC Wimbledon	Wandsworth	15.06.87

DAGENHAM AND REDBRIDGE

Ground: Dagenham Stadium, Victoria Road, Dagenham RM10 7XL
Telephone: 0208 592 1549. **Club nickname**: Daggers
Colours: Red and blue. **Capacity**: 6,000
Record attendance: 5,949 v Ipswich (FA Cup 3), Jan 5, 2002

Goalkeepers				
Cousins, Mark	6.1	Colchester	Chelmsford	09.01.87
O'Brien, Liam	6.4	Brentford	Ruislip	30.11.91
Defenders				
Batt, Damian	5.10	Eastleigh	Welwyn Garden City	16.09.84
Connors, Jack	5.9	–	Brent	24.10.94
Doe, Scott	6.1	Weymouth	Reading	06.11.88
Gayle, Ian	5.11	–	Welling	23.10.92

Hoyte, Gavin	5.11	Arsenal	Waltham Forest	06.06.90
Partridge, Matt	6.2	Reading	Reading	24.10.94
Saah, Brian	6.1	Torquay	Rush Green	16.12.86
Midfielders				
Bingham, Billy	5.10	Crystal Palace	Greenwich	15.07.90
Elito, Medy	5.11	Colchester	Kinshasa, DR Cong	20.03.90
Howell, Luke	5.11	Lincoln	Cuckfield	05.01.87
Labadie, Joss	6.3	Torquay	Croydon	30.08.90
Ogogo, Abu	5.10	Arsenal	Epsom	03.11.89
Forwards				
Chambers, Ashley	5.10	Cambridge Utd	Leicester	01.03.90
Hines, Zavron	5.10	Bradford	Kingston, Jam	27.12.88
Murphy, Rhys	6.1	Telstar	Shoreham	06.11.90
Obafemi, Afolabi	6.2	Leyton Orient	London	25.11.94
Shields, Sean	5.7	St Albans	Enfield	20.01.92

EXETER CITY

Ground: St James Park, Stadium Way, Exeter EX4 6PX
Telephone: 01392 411243. **Club nickname**: Grecians
Colours: Red and white. **Capacity**: 8,830
Record attendance: 20,984 v Sunderland (FA Cup 6 replay) Mar 4, 1931

Goalkeepers				
Pym, Christy	5.11	–	Exeter	24.04.95
Defenders				
Baldwin, Pat	6.0	Southend	London	12.11.82
Bennett, Scott	5.10	–	Truro	30.11.90
Butterfield, Danny	5.9	Carlisle	Boston	21.11.79
Coles, Danny	6.1	Bristol Rov	Bristol	31.10.81
Moore-Taylor, Jordan	5.10	–	Exeter	21.01.94
Tillson, Jordan	6.0	Bristol Rov	Bath	05.03.93
Woodman, Craig	5.9	Brentford	Tiverton	22.12.82
Midfielders				
Davies, Arron	5.9	Northampton	Cardiff	22.06.84
Dawson, Aaron	5.11	–	Exeter	24.03.92
Keohane, Jimmy	5.11	Bristol City	Aylesbury	22.01.91
Oakley, Matt	5.10	Leicester	Peterborough	17.08.77
Sercombe, Liam	5.10	–	Exeter	25.04.90
Wheeler, David	5.11	Staines	Brighton	04.10.90
Forwards				
Nichols, Tom	5.10	–	Taunton	28.08.93
Reid, Jamie	5.11	–	Torquay	12.07.94

HARTLEPOOL UNITED

Ground: Victoria Park, Clarence Road, Hartlepool TS24 8BZ
Telephone: 01429 272584. **Club nickname**: Pool
Colours: Blue and white. **Capacity**: 7,787
Record attendance: 17,426 v Manchester Utd (FA Cup 3) Jan 5, 1957

Goalkeepers				
Flinders, Scott	6.4	Crystal Palace	Rotherham	12.06.86
Rafferty, Andy	5.11	Guisborough	Guisborough	27.05.88
Defenders				
Austin, Neil	5.10	Darlington	Barnsley	26.04.83
Bates, Matthew	5.10	Bradford	Stockton	10.12.86
Collins, Sam	6.2	Hull	Pontefract	05.06.77

Duckworth, Michael	5.11	Bradford PA	Germany	28.04.92
Holden, Darren	5.11	–	Krugersdorp, SA	27.08.93
Jones, Dan	6.0	–	Bishop Auckland	14.12.94
Parnaby, Stuart	5.10	Middlesbrough	Durham	19.07.82
Rowbotham, Josh	5.11	–	Stockton	07.01.93
Midfielders				
Compton, Jack	5.11	Colchester	Torquay	02.09.88
Franks, Jonathan	5.7	Middlesbrough	Stockton	08.04.90
Hawkins, Lewis	5.10	–	Hartlepool	15.06.93
Richards, Jordan	5.9	–	Sunderland	25.04.93
Walker, Brad	6.1	–	Billingham	25.04.96
Forwards				
Harewood, Marlon	6.1	Bristol City	Hampstead	25.08.79
James, Luke	5.11	–	Amble	04.11.94

LUTON TOWN

Ground: Kenilworth Stadium, Maple Road, Luton LU4 8AW
Telephone: 01582 411622. **Club nickname**: Hatters
Colours: Orange and black. **Capacity**: 10,226
Record attendance: 30,069 v Blackpool (FA Cup 6) Mar 4, 1959

Goalkeepers				
Justham, Elliot	6.3	East Thurrock	–	18.07.90
Tyler, Mark	5.11	Peterborough	Norwich	02.04.77
Defenders				
Connolly, Paul	6.1	Crawley	Liverpool	29.09.83
Fitzsimons, Danny	6.1	Histon	–	05.05.92
Franks, Fraser	6.0	Welling	Hammersmith	22.11.90
Griffiths, Scott	5.9	Peterborough	Westminster	27.11.85
Howells, Jake	5.9	–	Hemel Hempstead	18.04.91
Lacey, Alex	5.11	–	Milton Keynes	31.05.93
McNulty, Steve	6.1	Fleetwood	Liverpool	26.09.83
Parry, Andy	–	Southport	Liverpool	13.09.91
Wilkinson, Luke	6.2	Dagenham	Wells	02.12.91
Midfielders				
Angol, Lee	5.10	Wycombe	Carshalton	04.08.94
Drury, Andy	5.11	Crawley	Chatham	28.11.83
Guttridge Luke	5.8	Northampton	Barnstaple	27.03.82
Lawless, Alex	5.11	York	Tonypandy	05.02.83
Robinson, Matt	6.2	Leicester	Leicester	01.06.94
Smith, Jonathan	6.3	York	Preston	17.10.86
Stevenson, Jim	5.10	Histon	–	17.05.92
Whalley, Shaun	5.9	Southport	Whiston	07.08.87
Forwards				
Banton, Zane	5.6	–	Stevenage	06.09.96
Benson, Paul	6.2	Swindon	Southend	12.10.79
Cullen, Mark	5.9	Hull	Stakeford	21.04.02
Lafayette, Ross	6.2	Welling	London	11.04.87
Wall, Alex	5.11	Maidenhead	Thatcham	22.09.90

MANSFIELD TOWN

Ground: One Call Stadium, Quarry Lane, Mansfield NG18 5DA
Telephone: 01623 482482. **Club nickname**: Stags
Colours: Amber and blue. **Capacity**: 10,000
Record attendance: 24,467 v Nottm Forest (FA Cup 3) Jan 10, 1953

Goalkeepers
Defenders

Beevers, Lee	6.1	Walsall	Doncaster	04.12.83
Bell, Amari'i	5.11	Birmingham (loan)	Burton	05.05.94
Dempster, John	6.1	Crawley	Kettering	01.04.83
Jones, Luke	6.0	Stevenage	Blackburn	10.04.87
Riley, Martin	6.3	Wrexham	Wolverhampton	05.12.86
Sutton, Ritchie	6.0	Port Vale	Stoke	29.04.86
Tafazolli, Ryan	6.5	Cambridge City	Sutton	28.09.91

Midfielders

Bell, Fergus	6.0	Monza	Wandsworth	25.01.91
Clements, Chris	5.9	Hednesford	Birmingham	06.02.90
Clucas, Sam	6.2	Hereford	Lincoln	25.09.90
McGuire, Jamie	5.7	Fleetwood	Birkenhead	13.11.83
Murray, Adam	5.9	Luton	Birmingham	30.09.81
Thomas, Jack	5.9	–	Sutton-in-Ashfield	03.06.96

Forwards

Fisher, Alex	6.3	Monza	Westminster	30.06.90
Hearn, Liam	5.11	Grimsby	Nottingham	27.08.85
Palmer, Oliver	6.2	Havant	Epsom	21.01.92
Rhead, Matt	6.4	Corby	Stoke	31.05.84

MORECAMBE

Ground: Globe Arena, Christie Way, Westgate, Morecambe LA4 4TB
Telephone: 01524 411797. **Club nickname**: Shrimps
Colours: Red and white. **Capacity**: 6,476
Record attendance: Christie Park: 9,234 v Weymouth (FA Cup 3) Jan 6, 1962; Globe Arena: 5,003 v Burnley (League Cup 2) Aug 24, 2010

Goalkeepers

Arestidou, Andreas	6.1	Preston	Lambeth	06.12.89
Roche, Barry	6.4	Chesterfield	Dublin, Ire	06.04.82

Defenders

Beeley, Shaun	5.10	Fleetwood	Stockport	21.11.88
Doyle, Chris	5.11	–	Liverpool	17.02.95
Edwards, Ryan	5.11	Blackburn	Liverpool	07.10.93
Goodall, Alan	5.9	Fleetwood	Birkenhead	02.12.81
Hughes, Mark	6.3	Bury	Kirkby	09.12.86
McGowan, Aaron	5.9	–	Kirkby	24.07.96
Parrish, Andy	6.0	Bury	Bolton	22.06.88
Wilson, Laurence	5.10	Accrington	Liverpool	10.10.86
Wright, Andrew	6.1	Scunthorpe	Liverpool	15.01.85

Midfielders

Ellison, Kevin	6.0	Rotherham	Liverpool	23.02.79
Devitt, Jamie	5.10	Chesterfield	Dublin, Ire	06.07.90
Fleming, Andy	5.11	Wrexham	Liverpool	05.10.87
Kenyon, Alex	6.0	Stockport	Euxton	17.07.92
Marshall, Marcus	5.10	Bury	Hammersmith	07.10.89
Williams, Ryan	5.8	Rhyl	Birkenhead	08.04.91

Forwards

Amond, Padraig	5.11	Accrington	Carlow, Ire	15.04.88
Redshaw, Jack	5.6	Altrincham	Salford	20.11.90
Sampson, Jack	6.2	Bolton	Wigan	14.04.93

NEWPORT COUNTY

Ground: Rodney Parade, Newport NP19 0UU
Telephone: 01633 670690. **Club nickname**: Exiles
Colours: Amber and black. **Capacity**: 7,012
Record attendance: Somerton Park: 24,268 v Cardiff (Div 3S) Oct 16, 1937. Rodney Parade: 6,615 v Grimsby (Conf play-off semi-finals 2nd leg) Apr 28, 2013

Goalkeepers
Pidgeley, Lenny	6.4	Exeter	Twickenham	07.02.84
Stephens, Jamie	6.1	Liverpool	Wotton-under-Edge	24.08.93

Defenders
Feely, Kevin	6.2	Charlton	Kildare, Ire	30.08.92
Hughes, Andrew	5.11	Cardiff	Cardiff	05.06.92
Jackson, Ryan	5.9	Macclesfield	Streatham	31.07.90
Jones, Darren	6.1	AFC Wimbledon	Newport	26.08.83
Yakubu, Ismail	5.11	AFC Wimbledon	Kano, Nig	08.04.85

Midfielders
Byrne, Mark	5.9	Barnet	Dublin, Ire	09.11.88
Chapman, Adam	5.10	Oxford	Doncaster	29.11.89
Flynn, Michael	5.10	Bradford	Newport	17.10.80
Klukowski, Yan	6.1	Forest Green	Chippenham	01.01.87
Minshull, Lee	6.1	AFC Wimbledon	Chatham	11.11.85
Porter, Max	5.10	AFC Wimbledon	Havering	29.06.87
Sandell, Andy	5.11	Chippenham	Calne	08.09.83
Willmott, Robbie	5.9	Cambridge Utd	Harlow	16.05.90

Forwards
Crow, Danny	5.9	Luton	Great Yarmouth	26.01.86
Howe, Rene	6.0	Burton	Bedford	22.10.86
Jeffers, Shaun	6.1	Peterborough	Bedford	14.04.92
Jolley, Christian	6.0	AFC Wimbledon	Fleet	12.05.88
O'Connor, Aaron	5.10	Luton	Nottingham	09.08.83
Parker, Joe	5.10	Gloucester City	Gloucester	11.03.95
Zebroski, Chris	6.1	Eastleigh	Swindon	29.10.86

NORTHAMPTON TOWN

Ground: Sixfields Stadium, Upton Way, Northampton NN5 5QA
Telephone: 01604 683700. **Club nickname**: Cobblers
Colours: Claret and white. **Capacity**: 7,653
Record attendance: County Ground: 24,523 v Fulham (Div 1) Apr 23, 1966; Sixfields Stadium: 7,557 v Manchester City (Div 2) Sep 26, 1998

Goalkeepers
Duke, Matt	6.5	Bradford	Sheffield	16.06.77
Snedker, Dean	6.0	–	Northampton	17.11.94

Defenders
Alfei, Daniel	5.11	Swansea (loan)	Swansea	23.02.92
Collins, Lee	5.11	Barnsley	Telford	28.09.88
Diamond, Zander	6.2	Burton	Alexandria, Sco	03.12.85
Horwood, Evan	6.0	Tranmere	Hartlepool	10.03.86
Langmead, Kelvin	6.1	Peterborough	Coventry	23.03.85
Robertson, Gregor	6.0	Crewe	Edinburgh	19.01.84
Siddiqi, Kashif	5.9	Ventura	Hammersmith	25.01.86
Tozer, Ben	6.1	Newcastle	Plymouth	01.03.90

Midfielders
Carter, Darren	6.2	Cheltenham	Solihull	18.12.83

Hackett, Chris	6.0	Millwall	Oxford	01.03.83
Hornby, Lewis	5.10	–	Northampton	25.04.95
Morris, Ian	6.0	Torquay	Dublin, Ire	27.02.87
O'Toole, John-Joe	6.2	Bristol Rov	Harrow	30.09.88
Ravenhill, Ricky	5.10	Bradford	Doncaster	16.01.81
Forwards				
Mohamed, Kaid	5.11	Port Vale (loan)	Cardiff	23.07.84
Moyo, David	6.0	–	Harare, Zim	17.12.94
Nicholls, Alex	5.10	Walsall	Stourbridge	09.12.87
Richards, Marc	5.11	Chesterfield	Wolverhampton	08.07.82
Sinclair, Emile	6.0	Crawley	Leeds	29.12.87
Toney, Ivan	5.10	–	Northampton	16.03.96

OXFORD UNITED

Ground: Kassam Stadium, Grenoble Road, Oxford OX4 4XP
Telephone: 01865 337500. **Club nickname**: U's
Colours: Yellow. **Capacity**: 12,500
Record attendance: Manor Ground: 22,750 v Preston (FA Cup 6) Feb 29, 1964; Kassam Stadium: 12,243 v Leyton Orient (Lge 2) May 6, 2006

Goalkeepers				
Clarke, Ryan	6.3	Salisbury	Bristol	30.04.82
Crocombe, Max	6.4	Buckingham	Auckland, NZ	12.08.93
Defenders				
Hunt, David	5.11	Crawley	Dulwich	10.09.82
Long, Sam	5.10	–	Oxford	16.01.95
Meades, Jon	6.1	Bournemouth	Gloucester	02.03.92
Mullins, John	5.11	Rotherham	Hampstead	06.11.85
Newey, Tom	5.10	Scunthorpe	Sheffield	31.10.82
Raynes, Michael	6.3	Rotherham	Manchester	15.10.87
Whing, Andy	6.0	Leyton Orient	Birmingham	20.09.84
Wright, Jake	5.11	Brighton	Keighley	11.03.86
Midfielders				
Ashby, Josh	5.11	–	Oxford	03.05.96
Collins, Michael	6.0	Scunthorpe	Halifax	30.04.86
O'Dowda, Callum	5.11	–	Oxford	23.04.95
Potter, Alfie	5.7	Peterborough	Islington	09.01.89
Rose, Danny	5.8	Fleetwood	Bristol	21.02.88
Ruffels, Josh	5.10	Coventry	Oxford	23.10.93
Forwards				
Hylton, Danny	6.0	Rotherham	Camden	25.02.89
Kitson, Dave	6.3	Sheffield Utd	Hitchin	21.01.80
Marsh, Tyrone	5.11	–	Bedford	24.12.93

PLYMOUTH ARGYLE

Ground: Home Park, Plymouth PL2 3DQ
Telephone: 01752 562561. **Club nickname**: Pilgrims
Colours: Green and white. **Capacity**: 16,388
Record attendance: 43,596 v Aston Villa (Div 2) Oct 10, 1936

Goalkeepers				
Bittner, James	6.1	Salisbury	Devizes	02.02.82
McCormick, Luke	6.0	Oxford	Coventry	15.08.83
Defenders				
Bentley, Aaron	5.9	–	Plymouth	08.11.95

Blackman, Andre	6.0	Celtic	Lambeth	10.11.90
Hartley, Peter	6.2	Stevenage	Hartlepool	03.04.88
McHugh, Carl	5.11	Bradford	Toome, Ire	05.02.93
Nelson, Curtis	6.0	Stoke	Newcastle-under-Lyme	21.05.93
Purrington, Ben	5.9	–	Exeter	05.05.96

Midfielders

Allen, River	6.2	–	Plymouth	07.10.95
Banton, Jason	6.0	Crystal Palace	Tottenham	15.12.92
Blizzard, Dominic	6.2	Yeovil	High Wycombe	02.09.83
Cox, Lee	6.1	Swindon	Leicester	26.06.90
Mellor, Kelvin	6.2	Crewe	Crewe	25.01.91
Thomas, Nathan	5.10	Sunderland	Ingleby Barwick	27.09.94
Wotton, Paul	5.11	Yeovil	Plymouth	17.08.77

Forwards

Alessandra, Lewis	5.10	Morecambe	Heywood	08.02.89
Harvey, Tyler	6.1	–	Plymouth	29.06.95
Lecointe, Matt	5.10	–	Plymouth	28.10.94
Morgan, Marvin	6.4	Shrewsbury	Manchester	13.04.83
Reid, Reuben	6.0	Yeovil	Bristol	26.07.88
Smalley, Deane	6.0	Oxford	Chadderton	05.09.88

PORTSMOUTH

Ground: Fratton Park, Frogmore Road, Portsmouth, PO4 8RA
Telephone: 0239 273 1204. **Club nickname**: Pompey
Colours: Blue and white. **Capacity**: 20,700
Record attendance: 51,385 v Derby (FA Cup 6) Feb 26, 1949

Goalkeepers

| Jones, Paul | 6.3 | Crawley | Maidstone | 28.06.86 |
| Poke, Michael | 6.2 | Torquay | Ashford, Surr | 21.11.85 |

Defenders

Butler, Dan	5.9	-	Cowes	26.08.94
Chorley, Ben	6.3	Stevenage	Sidcup	30.09.82
Devera, Joe	6.2	Swindon	Southgate	06.02.87
Ertl, Johannes	6.2	Sheffield Utd	Graz, Aut	13.11.82
East, Danny	5.11	Hull	Beverley	26.12.91
Shorey, Nicky	5.9	Bristol City	Romford	19.02.81
Webster, Adam	6.3	–	Chichester	04.01.95
Whatmough, Jack	6.0	–	Gosport	19.08.96
Wynter, Alex	6.0	Crystal Palace (loan)	Beckenham	15.09.93

Midfielders

Atangana, Nigel	6.2	Havant	Corbeil-Essonnes, Fr	09.10.89
Barcham, Andy	5.10	Scunthorpe	Basildon	16.12.86
Dunne James	5.11	Stevenage	Farnborough	18.09.89
Fogden, Wes	5.9	Bournemouth	Havant	12.04.88
Hollands, Danny	5.11	Charlton	Ashford, Kent	06.11.85
Maloney, Jack	6.0	-	Ryde	08.12.94
Tarbuck, Bradley	5.10	-	Emsworth	06.11.95
Wallace, Jed	5.10	Farnborough	Reading	26.03.94

Forwards

Agyemang, Patrick	6.1	Stevenage	Walthamstow	29.09.81
Bird, Ryan	6.4	Burnham	Slough	15.11.87
Connolly, David	5.9	Southampton	Willesden	06.06.77
Craddock, Tom	5.11	Oxford	Darlington	14.10.86
Holmes, Ricky	6.2	Barnet	Uxbridge	19.06.87

Storey, Miles	5.11	Swindon (loan)	Sandwell	04.01.94
Taylor, Ryan	6.2	Bristol City	Rotherham	04.05.88
Westcarr, Craig	5.11	Walsall	Nottingham	29.01.85

SHREWSBURY TOWN

Ground: Greenhous Meadow Stadium, Oteley Road, Shrewsbury SY2 6ST
Telephone: 01743 289177. **Club nickname**: Shrews
Colours: Blue and yellow. **Capacity**: 9,875
Record attendance: Gay Meadow: 18,917 v Walsall (Div 3) Apr 26, 1961; Greenhous
Meadow: 9,510 v Wolves (Lge 1) Sep 21, 2013

Goalkeepers
| Halstead, Mark | 6.3 | Blackpool | Blackpool | 01.01.90 |
| Leutwiler, Jayson | 6.4 | Middlesbrough | Switzerland | 25.04.89 |

Defenders
Ellis, Mark	6.2	Crewe	Plymouth	30.09.88
Demetriou, Mickey	5.11	Kidderminster	Durrington	12.03.90
Gayle, Cameron	5.11	WBA	Birmingham	22.11.92
Grandison, Jermaine	6.4	Coventry	Birmingham	15.12.90
Goldson, Connor	6.3	–	Wolverhampton	18.12.92
Knight-Percival, Nat	6.0	Peterborough	Cambridge	31.03.87
Smith, Dominic	6.0	–	Shrewsbury	09.02.96

Midfielders
Caton, James	5.8	Blackpool	Widnes	04.01.94
Clark, Jordan	6.0	Barnsley	Hoyland	22.09.93
Lawrence, Liam	5.11	Barnsley	Retford	14.12.81
McAllister, David	5.11	Sheffield Utd	Dublin, Ire	29.12.88
Robinson, Andy	5.9	Tranmere	Birkenhead	03.11.79
Wesolowski, James	5.9	Oldham	Sydney, Aus	25.08.87
Wildig, Aaron	5.9	Cardiff	Hereford	15.04.92
Woods, Ryan	5.8	–	Norton Canes	13.12.93

Forwards
Akpa Akpro, Jean-Louis	6.0	Tranmere	Toulouse, Fr	04.01.85
Collins, James	6.2	Hibernian	Coventry	01.12.90
Vernon, Scott	6.1	Aberdeen	Manchester	13.12.83
Vincent, Ashley	6.0	Cheltenham	Birmingham	26.05.85

SOUTHEND UNITED

Ground: Roots Hall, Victoria Avenue, Southend SS2 6NQ
Telephone: 01702 304050. **Club nickname**: Shrimpers
Colours: Blue and white. **Capacity**: 12,392
Record attendance: 31,090 v Liverpool (FA Cup 3) Jan 10, 1979

Goalkeepers
| Bentley, Daniel | 6.2 | – | Basildon | 13.07.93 |
| Smith, Paul | 6.3 | Nottm Forest | Epsom | 17.12.79 |

Defenders
Coker, Ben	5.11	Colchester	Cambridge	01.07.90
Leonard, Ryan	6.1	Plymouth	Plymouth	24.05.92
Prosser, Luke	6.3	Port Vale	Enfield	28.05.88
Thompson, Adam	6.2	Watford	Harlow	28.09.92
White, John	6.0	Colchester	Colchester	25.07.86

Midfielders
Atkinson, Will	5.10	Bradford	Beverley	14.10.88
Clifford, Conor	5.8	Leicester	Dublin, Ire	01.10.91
Hurst, Kevan	6.0	Walsall	Chesterfield	27.08.85

Payne, Jack	5.6	–	Tower Hamlets	25.10.94
Pinnock, Mitch	5.10	–	Gravesend	12.12.94
Timlin, Michael	5.8	Swindon	Lambeth	19.03.85
Weston, Myles	5.11	Gillingham	Lewisham	12.03.88
Forwards				
Barnard, Lee	5.10	Southampton	Romford	18.07.84
Corr, Barry	6.3	Exeter	Newcastle, NI	02.04.85
Williams, Jason	6.0	–	Islington	15.11.95

STEVENAGE

Ground: Lamex Stadium, Broadhall Way, Stevenage SG2 8RH
Telephone: 01438 223223. **Club nickname:** Boro
Colours: White and red. **Capacity:** 6,920
Record attendance: 8,040 v Newcastle (FA Cup 4) January 25, 1998

Goalkeepers				
Beasant, Sam	6.5	Woking	Denham	08.04.88
Day, Chris	6.2	Millwall	Walthamstow	28.07.75
Defenders				
Ashton, Jon	6.2	Grays	Nuneaton	04.10.82
Charles, Darius	6.1	Ebbsfleet	Ealing	10.12.87
Dembele, Bira	6.3	Sedan	Villepinte, Fr	22.03.88
Henry, Ronnie	5.11	Luton	Hemel Hempstead	02.01.84
Johnson, Ryan	6.2	–	Birmingham	02.10.96
Wells, Dean	6.1	Braintree	Isleworth	25.05.85
Worley, Harry	6.4	Newport	Warrington	25.11.88
Midfielders				
Ball, Matt	5.10	Norwich	Welwyn Garden City	26.03.93
Beardsley, Chris	6.0	Preston	Derby	28.02.84
Bond, Andy	5.10	Chester	Wigan	16.03.86
Lee, Charlie	5.11	Gillingham	Whitechapel	05.01.87
Parrett, Dean	5.9	Tottenham	Hampstead	16.11.91
Walton, Simon	6.1	Hartlepool	Leeds	13.09.87
Whelpdale, Chris	6.0	Gillingham	Harold Wood	27.01.87
Forwards				
Deacon, Roarie	5.8	Sunderland	Wandsworth	12.10.91
Marriott, Adam	5.10	Cambridge City	Brandon	14.04.91
Zola, Calvin	6.3	Aberdeen	Kinshasa, DR Cong	31.12.84

TRANMERE ROVERS

Ground: Prenton Park, Prenton Road West, Birkenhead CH42 9PY
Telephone: 0871 221 2001. **Club nickname:** Rovers
Colours: White. **Capacity:** 16,587
Record attendance: 24,424 v Stoke (FA Cup 4) Feb 5, 1972

Goalkeepers				
Fon Williams, Owain	6.4	Rochdale	Caernarfon	17.03.87
Ramsbottom, Sam	6.1	–	Greasby	03.04.96
Defenders				
Boland, Antoine	5.9	Barnsley	Liverpool	30.12.94
Holmes, Danny	6.0	New Saints	Wirral	06.01.89
Holness, Marcus	6.0	Burton	Salford	08.12.88
Ridehalgh, Liam	5.10	Huddersfield	Halifax	20.04.91
Ihiekwe, Michael	6.1	Wolves	Liverpool	20.11.92
Midfielders				
Bell-Baggie, Abdulai	5.6	Salisbury	Sierra Leone	28.04.92

Gill, Matt	5.11	Exeter	Chatham	08.11.80
Kirby, Jake	5.9	–	Liverpool	09.05.94
Koumas, Jason	5.10	Wigan	Wrexham	25.09.79
Laird, Marc	6.1	Southend	Edinburgh	23.01.86
Power, Max	5.11	–	Birkenhead	27.07.93
Rowe, James	5.11	Forest Green	Oxford	21.10.91
Forwards				
Davies, Liam	6.0	–	Liverpool	02.07.96
Odejayi, Kayode	6.2	Rotherham	Ibadon, Nig	21.02.82
Richards, Elliot	5.10	Bristol Rov	New Tredegar	10.09.91
Stockton, Cole	6.1	–	Huyton	13.03.94

WYCOMBE WANDERERS

Ground: Adams Park, Hillbottom Road, High Wycombe HP12 4HJ
Telephone: 01494 472100. **Club nickname**: Chairboys
Colours: Light and dark blue. **Capacity**: 10,300
Record attendance: 10,000 v Chelsea (friendly) July 13, 2005

Goalkeepers

Horlock, Charlie	6.1			
Ingram, Matt	6.3	–	High Wycombe	18.12.93
Defenders				
Doherty, Gary	6.1	Charlton	Donegal, Ire	31.01.80
Fletcher, Tommy	6.0	Cheshunt	Hoddesdon	22.01.95
Jacobson, Joe	5.11	Shrewsbury	Cardiff	17.11.86
Jombati, Sido	6.1	Cheltenham	Lisbon, Por	20.08.87
Murphy, Peter	6.0	Accrington	Liverpool	13.02.90
Pierre, Aaron	6.1	Brentford	Souhall	17.02.93
Stewart, Anthony	6.0	–	Lambeth	18.09.92
Midfielders				
Bloomfield, Matt	5.8	Ipswich	Felixstowe	08.02.84
Kretzschmar, Max	5.9	–	Kingston	12.10.93
Lewis, Stuart	5.11	Dagenham	Welwyn Garden City	15.10.87
Scowen, Josh	5.10	–	Enfield	28.03.93
Wood, Sam	6.0	Brentford	Bexley	09.08.86
Forwards				
Cowan-Hall, Paris	5.8	Plymouth	Hillingdon	05.10.90
Craig, Steven	5.11	Partick	Blackburn, Scot	05.02.81
Hayes, Paul	6.0	Scunthorpe	Dagenham	20.09.83
McClure, Matt	5.10	Crystal Palace	Slough	17.11.91
Morias, Junior	5.8	–	Kingston, Jam	04.07.95

YORK CITY

Ground: Bootham Crescent, York, YO30 7AQ
Telephone: 01904 624447. **Club nickname**: Minstermen
Colours: Red and blue. **Capacity**: 7,872
Record attendance: 28,123 v Huddersfield (FA Cup 6) Mar 5, 1938

Goalkeepers

Ingham, Michael	6.4	Hereford	Preston	07.09.80
Mooney, Jason	6.9	Tranmere	Belfast	26.02.89
Defenders				
Ilesanmi, Femi	6.1	Dagenham	Southwark	18.04.91
Lowe, Keith	6.2	Cheltenham	Wolverhampton	13.09.85
McCombe, John	6.2	Mansfield	Pontefract	07.05.85
McCoy, Marvin	6.0	Wycombe	Waltham Forest	02.10.88

Parslow, Daniel	6.1	Cardiff	Rhymney	09.11.85
Straker, Antony	5.9	Southend	Ealing	23.09.88
Winfield, Dave	6.2	Shrewsbury	Aldershot	24.03.88
Midfielders				
Carson, Josh	5.9	Ipswich	Ballymena	03.06.93
Montrose, Lewis	6.2	Gillingham	Manchester	17.11.88
Murray, Cameron	5.7	Bradford	Halifax	21.03.95
Penn, Russell	6.0	Cheltenham	Wordsley	08.11.85
Platt, Tom	6.1	–	Pontefract	01.10.93
Summerfield, Luke	6.0	Shrewsbury	Ivybridge	06.12.87
Forwards				
Coulson, Michael	5.10	Grimsby	Scarborough	04.04.88
Fletcher, Wes	5.10	Burnley	Ormskirk	28.02.90
Hyde, Jake	6.1	Barnet	Maidenhead	01.07.90
Jarvis, Ryan	6.1	Torquay	Fakenham	11.07.86
Meikle, Lindon	5.10	Mansfield	Nottingham	21.03.88

SCOTTISH PREMIERSHIP SQUADS 2014–15

(at time of going to press)

ABERDEEN
Ground: Pittodrie Stadium, Pittodrie Street, Aberdeen AB24 5QH. **Capacity**: 20,897.
Telephone: 01224 650400. **Manager**: Derek McInnes. **Colours**: Red and white. **Nickname**:
Dons
Goalkeepers: Scott Brown, Jamie Langfield, Danny Rogers
Defenders: Russell Anderson, Andrew Considine, Shaleum Logan, Nicky Low, Mark Reynolds,
Clark Robertson, Joe Shaughnessy, Ash Taylor
Midfielders: Willo Flood, Jonny Hayes, Ryan Jack, Jamie Masson, Niall McGinn, Craig Murray,
Peter Pawlett, Barry Robson, Craig Storie, Scott Wright
Forwards: David Goodwillie, Declan McManus, Adam Rooney, Lawrence Shankland, Cameron
Smith

CELTIC
Ground: Celtic Park, Glasgow G40 3RE. **Capacity**: 60,355. **Telephone**: 0871 226 1888.
Manager: Ronny Deila. **Colours**: Green and white. **Nickname**: Bhoys
Goalkeepers: Fraser Forster, Craig Gordon, Lukasz Zaluska
Defenders: Efe Ambrose, Joe Chalmers, Darnell Fisher, Marcus Fraser, Emilio Izaguirre,
Mikael Lustig, Adam Matthews, Charlie Mulgrew, Lewis Toshney, Virgil van Dijk
Midfielders: Derk Boerrigter, Nir Biton, Scott Brown, Kris Commons, James Forrest, John Herron,
Jackson Irvine, Stefan Johansen, Beram Kayal, Dylan McGeouch, Tom Rogic, Filip Twardzik
Forwards: Bahrudin Atajic, Amido Balde, Holmbert Fridjonsson, Leigh Griffiths, Teemu Pukki,
Anthony Stokes, Tony Watt

DUNDEE
Ground: Dens Park, Sandeman Street, Dundee DD3 7JY. **Capacity**: 11,506. **Telephone**:
01382. 889966. **Manager**: Paul Hartley. **Colours**: Blue and white. **Nickname**: Dark Blues
Goalkeepers: Grant Adam, Scott Bain, Kyle Letheren
Defenders: Kyle Benedictus, Willie Dyer, Gary Irvine, Cammy Kerr, Paul McGinn, James
McPake
Midfielders: Iain Davidson, Simon Ferry, Gary Harkins, Jim McAlister, Kevin McBride, Nicky
Riley, Kevin Thomson
Forwards: Martin Boyle, Greg Stewart, Peter MacDonald, Paul McGowan, Phil Roberts, Craig
Wighton

DUNDEE UNITED

Ground: Tannadice Park, Tannadice Street, Dundee DD3 7JW. **Capacity**: 14,229. **Telephone**: 01382 833166. **Manager**: Jackie McNamara. **Colours**: Orange and black. **Nickname**: Terrors
Goalkeepers: Radoslaw Cierzniak, Marc McCallum
Defenders: Calum Butcher, Sean Dillon, Jaroslaw Fojut, Callum Morris, Andrew Robertson, John Souttar, Keith Watson, Mark Wilson
Midfielders: Stuart Armstrong, Aidan Connolly, Chris Erskine, Scott Fraser, Gary Mackay-Steven, Paul Paton, Darren Petrie, John Rankin, Blair Spittal, Scott Smith, Charlie Telfer
Forwards: Mario Bilate, Nadir Ciftci, Aidan Connolly, Ryan Dow, Michael Gardyne, Brian Graham, Jordan Moore, Kudus Oyenuga

HAMILTON ACADEMICAL

Ground: New Douglas Park, Hamilton ML3 OFT. **Capacity**: 6,078. **Telephone**: 01698 368652. **Manager**: Alex Neil. **Colours**: Red and white. **Nickname**: Accies
Goalkeepers: Blair Currie, Daniel Devine, Darren Hill, Michael McGovern
Defenders: Martin Canning, Michael Devlin, Ziggy Gordon, Stephen Hendrie, Kieran MacDonald, Scott McMann, Jesus Garcia Tena
Midfielders: Tony Andreu, Ali Crawford, Greg Docherty, Grant Gillespie, Doug Imrie, Darren Lyon, Jon Routledge, Louis Longridge, Alex Neil, Danny Redmond, Craig Watson
Forwards: Mickael Antoine-Curier, Eamonn Brophy, Darian MacKinnon, Jaison McGrath, Andy Ryan, Jason Scotland

INVERNESS CALEDONIAN THISTLE

Ground: Tulloch Caledonian Stadium, Stadium Road, Inverness IV1 1FF. **Capacity**: 7,800. **Telephone**: 01463 222880. **Manager**: John Hughes. **Colours**: Blue and red. **Nickname**: Caley Thistle
Goalkeepers: Dean Brill, Ryan Esson, Cameron Mackay
Defenders: Daniel Devine, Calum Howarth, Josh Meekings, David Raven, Graeme Shinnie, Carl Tremarco, Gary Warren
Midfielders: Jason Brown, Ryan Christie, Aaron Doran, Ross Draper, Liam Polworth, Nick Ross, Greg Tansey, James Vincent, Marley Watkins, Danny Williams
Forwards: Calum Ferguson, Richie Foran, Billy McKay, Alasdair Sutherland

KILMARNOCK

Ground: Rugby Park, Kilmarnock KA 1 2DP. **Capacity**: 18,128. **Telephone**: 01563 545300. **Manager**: Allan Johnston. **Colours**: Blue and white. **Nickname**: Killie
Goalkeepers: Conor Brennan, Craig Samson
Defenders: Lee Ashcroft, Ross Barbour, Sean Clohessy, Mark Connolly, Mark O'Hara
Midfielders: Paul Cairney, Sammy Clingan, Ross Davidson, Jamie Hamill, Manuel Pascali, Tope Obadeyi, Craig Slater
Forwards: Kris Boyd, Chris Johnston, Greg Kiltie, Josh Magennis, Lee Miller, Rory McKenzie, Robbie Muirhead

MOTHERWELL

Ground: Fir Park, Firpark Street, Motherwell ML1 2QN. **Capacity**: 13,677. **Telephone**: 01698 333333. **Manager**: Stuart McCall. **Colours**: Clarent and amber. **Nickname**: Well
Goalkeepers: Gunnar Neilsen, Dan Twardzik
Defenders: Zaine Francis-Angol, Adam Cummins, Steven Hammell, Fraser Kerr, Stephen McManus, Simon Ramsden, Craig Reid
Midfielders: Lionel Ainsworth, Stuart Carswell, Keith Lasley, Josh Law, Paul Lawson, Jack Leitch, Iain Vigurs
Forwards: Lee Erwin, Craig Moore, Robert McHugh, John Sutton

PARTICK THISTLE

Ground: Firhill Stadium, Firhill Road, Glasgow G20 7BA. **Capacity**: 10,102. **Telephone**: 0141 579 1971. **Manager**: Alan Archibald. **Colours**: Yellow, red and black. **Nickname**: Jags
Goalkeepers: Scott Fox, Paul Gallacher,
Defenders: Conrad Balatoni, Gabriel, Jordan McMillan, Aaron Muirhead, Stephen O'Donnell
Midfielders: Stuart Bannigan, James Craigen, Gary Fraser, Steve Lawless, Isaac Osbourne, Ryan Stevenson, Sean Welsh
Forwards: Kris Doolan, Christie Elliott, Kallum Higginbotham

ROSS COUNTY

Ground: Global Energy Stadium, Victoria Park, Jubilee Road, Dingwall IV15 9QZ. **Capacity**: 6,541. **Telephone**: 01349 860860. **Manager**: Derek Adams. **Colours**: Blue. **Nickname**: Staggies
Goalkeepers: Mark Brown, Antonio Reguero
Defenders: Tim Dreesen, Scott Boyd, Ben Frempah, Ross Mackillop, Steven Saunders
Midfielders: Jordi Balk, Richard Brittain, Joe Cardle, Graham Carey, Tony Dingwall, Scott Ferries,
Stuart Kettlewell, Marc Klok, Rocco Quinn
Forwards: Yoann Arquin, Liam Boyce, Melvin De Leeuw, Jake Jervis, Darren Maatsen, Kyle Macleod, Steven Ross

ST JOHNSTONE

Ground: McDiarmid Park, Crieff Road, Perth PH1 2SJ. **Capacity**: 10,696. **Telephone**: 01738 459090. **Manager**: Tommy Wright. **Colours**: Blue and white. **Nickname**: Saints
Goalkeepers: Steve Banks, Zander Clark, Alan Mannus
Defenders: Steven Anderson, Callum Davidson, Brian Easton, David Mackay, Gary Miller, Tom Scobbie, Frazer Wright
Midfielders: Scott Brown, Liam Caddis, Lee Croft, Murray Davidson, Gary McDonald, Chris Millar
Forwards: Steven MacLean, Stevie May, Michael O'Halloran, David Wotherspoon

ST MIRREN

Ground: St Mirren Park, Greenhill Road, Paisley PA3, 1RU. **Capacity**: 8,023. **Telephone**: 0141 889 2558. **Manager**: Tommy Craig. **Colours**: Black and white. **Nickname**: Buddies
Goalkeepers: Marian Kello, Mark Ridgers
Defenders: Sean Kelly, Ellis Plummer, Mark McAusland, Mohammed Yaqub, Jason Naismith, Mark Williams,
Midfielders: Adam Brown, Jim Goodwin, Declan Hughes, John McGinn, Kenny McLean, Gary Teale
Forwards: Ross Caldwell, James Marwood, Thomas Reilly, Steven Thompson, Gregg Wylde

ENGLISH FIXTURES 2014–2015
Premier League and Football League

Friday, 8 August
Championship
Blackburn v Cardiff

Saturday, 9 August
Championship
Brentford v Charlton
Brighton v Sheffield Wed
Derby v Rotherham
Huddersfield v Bournemouth
Ipswich v Fulham
Middlesbrough v Birmingham
Millwall v Leeds
Nottm Forest v Blackpool
Watford v Bolton
Wigan v Reading

League One
Barnsley v Crawley
Bradford v Coventry
Colchester v Oldham
Fleetwood v Crewe
Leyton Orient v Chesterfield
MK Dons v Gillingham
Port Vale v Walsall
Preston v Notts Co
Rochdale v Peterborough
Sheffield Utd v Bristol City
Swindon v Scunthorpe
Yeovil v Doncaster

League Two
Accrington v Southend
AFC Wimbledon v Shrewsbury
Bury v Cheltenham
Cambridge v Plymouth
Carlisle v Luton
Dag & Red v Morecambe
Exeter v Portsmouth
Newport v Wycombe
Northampton v Mansfield
Oxford v Burton
Stevenage v Hartlepool
Tranmere v York

Sunday, 10 August
Championship
Wolves v Norwich

Saturday, 16 August
Premier League
Arsenal v Crystal Palace
Leicester v Everton
Man Utd v Swansea
QPR v Hull
Stoke v Aston Villa
West Brom v Sunderland
West Ham v Tottenham

Championship
Birmingham v Brighton
Blackpool v Blackburn
Bolton v Nottm Forest
Bournemouth v Brentford
Cardiff v Huddersfield
Charlton v Wigan
Fulham v Millwall
Leeds v Middlesbrough
Norwich v Watford
Reading v Ipswich
Rotherham v Wolves
Sheffield Wed v Derby

League One
Bristol City v Colchester
Chesterfield v Rochdale
Coventry v Sheffield Utd
Crawley v Swindon
Crewe v Barnsley
Doncaster v Port Vale
Gillingham v Yeovil
Notts Co v Fleetwood
Oldham v Leyton Orient
Peterborough v MK Dons
Scunthorpe v Preston
Walsall v Bradford

League Two
Burton v Dag & Red
Cheltenham v Accrington
Hartlepool v Bury
Luton v AFC Wimbledon
Mansfield v Oxford
Morecambe v Newport
Plymouth v Exeter
Portsmouth v Cambridge
Shrewsbury v Tranmere
Southend v Stevenage
Wycombe v Carlisle
York v Northampton

Sunday, 17 August
Premier League
Liverpool v Southampton
Newcastle v Man City

Monday, 18 August
Premier League
Burnley v Chelsea

Tuesday, 19 August
Championship
Birmingham v Ipswich
Blackpool v Brentford
Bournemouth v Nottm Forest
Cardiff v Wigan
Charlton v Derby
Leeds v Brighton

Norwich v Blackburn
Rotherham v Watford
Sheffield Wed v Millwall
Bolton v Middlesbrough
Reading v Huddersfield

League One
Bristol City v Leyton Orient
Chesterfield v MK Dons
Coventry v Barnsley
Crawley v Bradford
Crewe v Rochdale
Doncaster v Preston
Gillingham v Swindon
Notts Co v Colchester
Oldham v Port Vale
Peterborough v Sheffield Utd
Scunthorpe v Fleetwood
Walsall v Yeovil

League Two
Burton v Exeter
Cheltenham v Carlisle
Hartlepool v Dag & Red
Luton v Bury
Mansfield v Newport
Morecambe v Oxford
Plymouth v Stevenage
Portsmouth v Northampton
Shrewsbury v Accrington
Southend v AFC Wimbledon
Wycombe v Tranmere
York v Cambridge

Wednesday, 20 August
Championship
Fulham v Wolves

Saturday, 23 August
Premier League
Aston Villa v Newcastle
Chelsea v Leicester
Crystal Palace v West Ham
Everton v Arsenal
Southampton v West Brom
Swansea v Burnley
Tottenham v QPR

Championship
Blackburn v Bournemouth
Brentford v Birmingham
Brighton v Bolton
Derby v Fulham
Huddersfield v Charlton
Middlesbrough v Sheffield Wed
Millwall v Rotherham
Nottm Forest v Reading
Watford v Leeds
Wigan v Blackpool
Wolves v Cardiff

League One
Barnsley v Gillingham
Bradford v Peterborough
Colchester v Doncaster
Fleetwood v Chesterfield
Leyton Orient v Walsall
MK Dons v Coventry
Port Vale v Notts Co
Preston v Oldham
Rochdale v Bristol City
Sheffield Utd v Crawley
Swindon v Crewe
Yeovil v Scunthorpe

League Two
Accrington v Luton
AFC Wimbledon v Hartlepool
Bury v Plymouth
Cambridge v Morecambe
Carlisle v Southend
Dag & Red v Mansfield
Exeter v York
Newport v Burton
Northampton v Shrewsbury
Oxford v Portsmouth
Stevenage v Wycombe
Tranmere v Cheltenham

Sunday, 24 August
Premier League
Hull v Stoke
Sunderland v Man Utd

Championship
Ipswich v Norwich

Monday, 25 August
Premier League
Man City v Liverpool

Saturday, 30 August
Premier League
Aston Villa v Hull
Burnley v Man Utd
Everton v Chelsea
Man City v Stoke
Newcastle v Crystal Palace
QPR v Sunderland
Swansea v West Brom
West Ham v Southampton

Championship
Brighton v Charlton
Derby v Ipswich
Fulham v Cardiff
Leeds v Bolton
Middlesbrough v Reading
Millwall v Blackpool
Norwich v Bournemouth
Rotherham v Brentford
Sheffield Wed v Nottm Forest
Watford v Huddersfield
Wigan v Birmingham
Wolves v Blackburn

League One
Colchester v Peterborough
Doncaster v Oldham
Fleetwood v Leyton Orient
Gillingham v Crewe
MK Dons v Crawley
Port Vale v Chesterfield
Preston v Sheffield Utd
Rochdale v Bradford
Scunthorpe v Walsall
Swindon v Coventry
Yeovil v Barnsley

League Two
AFC Wimbledon v Stevenage
Bury v Accrington
Cambridge v Carlisle
Cheltenham v Hartlepool
Mansfield v Burton
Northampton v Exeter
Oxford v Dag & Red
Plymouth v Southend
Portsmouth v Newport
Shrewsbury v Luton
Tranmere v Morecambe
York v Wycombe

Sunday, 31 August
Premier League
Leicester v Arsenal
Tottenham v Liverpool

League One
Notts Co v Bristol City

Saturday, 6 September
League One
Barnsley v Doncaster
Bradford v Yeovil
Bristol City v Scunthorpe
Chesterfield v Swindon
Coventry v Gillingham
Crawley v Rochdale
Crewe v Notts Co
Leyton Orient v Preston
Oldham v Fleetwood
Peterborough v Port Vale
Sheffield Utd v MK Dons
Walsall v Colchester

League Two
Accrington v Tranmere
Carlisle v AFC Wimbledon
Dag & Red v Northampton
Exeter v Mansfield
Hartlepool v Shrewsbury
Luton v Plymouth
Morecambe v Cheltenham
Southend v Oxford
Stevenage v York
Wycombe v Bury

Sunday, 7 September
League Two
Burton v Portsmouth

Monday, 8 September
League Two
Newport v Cambridge

Saturday, 13 September
Premier League
Arsenal v Man City
Chelsea v Swansea
Crystal Palace v Burnley
Liverpool v Aston Villa
Southampton v Newcastle
Stoke v Leicester
Sunderland v Tottenham
West Brom v Everton

Championship
Birmingham v Leeds
Blackburn v Wigan
Blackpool v Wolves
Bolton v Sheffield Wed
Bournemouth v Rotherham
Brentford v Brighton
Cardiff v Norwich
Charlton v Watford
Huddersfield v Middlesbrough
Ipswich v Millwall
Reading v Fulham

League One
Barnsley v MK Dons
Bradford v Swindon
Bristol City v Doncaster
Chesterfield v Scunthorpe
Coventry v Yeovil
Crawley v Fleetwood
Crewe v Port Vale
Leyton Orient v Colchester
Oldham v Gillingham
Peterborough v Notts Co
Sheffield Utd v Rochdale
Walsall v Preston

League Two
Accrington v AFC Wimbledon
Burton v York
Carlisle v Bury
Dag & Red v Cambridge
Exeter v Oxford
Hartlepool v Tranmere
Luton v Cheltenham
Morecambe v Plymouth
Newport v Northampton
Southend v Portsmouth
Stevenage v Shrewsbury
Wycombe v Mansfield

Sunday, 14 September
Premier League
Man Utd v QPR

Championship
Nottm Forest v Derby

Monday, 15 September
Premier League
Hull v West Ham

Tuesday, 16 September
Championship
Birmingham v Sheffield Wed
Blackpool v Watford
Bournemouth v Leeds
Brentford v Norwich
Cardiff v Middlesbrough
Charlton v Wolves
Huddersfield v Wigan
Ipswich v Brighton
Bolton v Rotherham
Reading v Millwall

League One
Colchester v Sheffield Utd
Doncaster v Crawley
Gillingham v Peterborough
MK Dons v Bradford
Notts Co v Leyton Orient
Port Vale v Bristol City
Preston v Chesterfield
Rochdale v Walsall
Scunthorpe v Coventry
Swindon v Oldham
Yeovil v Crewe

League Two
AFC Wimbledon v Burton
Bury v Stevenage
Cambridge v Exeter
Cheltenham v Southend
Mansfield v Morecambe
Northampton v Hartlepool
Oxford v Accrington
Plymouth v Wycombe
Portsmouth v Dag & Red
Shrewsbury v Carlisle
Tranmere v Newport
York v Luton

Wednesday, 17 September
Championship
Blackburn v Derby
Nottm Forest v Fulham

League One
Fleetwood v Barnsley

Saturday, 20 September
Premier League
Aston Villa v Arsenal
Burnley v Sunderland
Everton v Crystal Palace
Newcastle v Hull
QPR v Stoke
Swansea v Southampton

Tottenham v West Brom
West Ham v Liverpool

Championship
Brighton v Blackpool
Derby v Cardiff
Fulham v Blackburn
Leeds v Huddersfield
Middlesbrough v Brentford
Millwall v Nottm Forest
Norwich v Birmingham
Rotherham v Charlton
Sheffield Wed v Reading
Watford v Bournemouth
Wigan v Ipswich
Wolves v Bolton

League One
Colchester v Bradford
Doncaster v Chesterfield
Fleetwood v Bristol City
Gillingham v Walsall
MK Dons v Crewe
Notts Co v Oldham
Port Vale v Barnsley
Preston v Crawley
Rochdale v Coventry
Scunthorpe v Leyton Orient
Swindon v Sheffield Utd
Yeovil v Peterborough

League Two
AFC Wimbledon v Morecambe
Bury v Burton
Cambridge v Luton
Cheltenham v Dag & Red
Mansfield v Carlisle
Northampton v Accrington
Oxford v Stevenage
Plymouth v Hartlepool
Portsmouth v Wycombe
Shrewsbury v Newport
Tranmere v Exeter
York v Southend

Sunday, 21 September
Premier League
Leicester v Man Utd
Man City v Chelsea

Saturday, 27 September
Premier League
Arsenal v Tottenham
Chelsea v Aston Villa
Crystal Palace v Leicester
Hull v Man City
Liverpool v Everton
Man Utd v West Ham
Southampton v QPR
Sunderland v Swansea

Championship
Birmingham v Fulham

Blackburn v Watford
Blackpool v Norwich
Bolton v Derby
Bournemouth v Wigan
Brentford v Leeds
Cardiff v Sheffield Wed
Charlton v Middlesbrough
Huddersfield v Millwall
Ipswich v Rotherham
Nottm Forest v Brighton
Reading v Wolves

League One
Barnsley v Swindon
Bradford v Port Vale
Bristol City v MK Dons
Chesterfield v Notts Co
Coventry v Preston
Crawley v Yeovil
Crewe v Colchester
Leyton Orient v Rochdale
Oldham v Scunthorpe
Peterborough v Fleetwood
Sheffield Utd v Gillingham
Walsall v Doncaster

League Two
Accrington v Plymouth
Burton v Cheltenham
Carlisle v Tranmere
Dag & Red v York
Exeter v Bury
Hartlepool v Portsmouth
Luton v Oxford
Morecambe v Northampton
Newport v AFC Wimbledon
Southend v Shrewsbury
Stevenage v Mansfield
Wycombe v Cambridge

Sunday, 28 September
Premier League
West Brom v Burnley

Monday, 29 September
Premier League
Stoke v Newcastle

Tuesday, 30 September
Championship
Brighton v Cardiff
Derby v Bournemouth
Leeds v Reading
Middlesbrough v Blackpool
Millwall v Birmingham
Norwich v Charlton
Rotherham v Blackburn
Sheffield Wed v Ipswich
Watford v Brentford
Wigan v Nottm Forest
Wolves v Huddersfield

Wednesday, 1 October
Championship
Fulham v Bolton

Friday, 3 October
Championship
Blackpool v Cardiff

League Two
Burton v Cambridge
Dag & Red v Exeter

Saturday, 4 October
Premier League
Aston Villa v Man City
Hull v Crystal Palace
Leicester v Burnley
Liverpool v West Brom
Sunderland v Stoke
Swansea v Newcastle
Tottenham v Southampton

Championship
Blackburn v Huddersfield
Bolton v Bournemouth
Brentford v Reading
Charlton v Birmingham
Derby v Millwall
Leeds v Sheffield Wed
Middlesbrough v Fulham
Norwich v Rotherham
Watford v Brighton
Wolves v Wigan

League One
Bradford v Crewe
Chesterfield v Sheffield Utd
Coventry v Crawley
Fleetwood v Port Vale
Leyton Orient v Swindon
Notts Co v Gillingham
Peterborough v Oldham
Preston v Colchester
Rochdale v Barnsley
Scunthorpe v Doncaster
Walsall v Bristol City
Yeovil v MK Dons

League Two
Bury v Tranmere
Cheltenham v AFC Wimbledon
Hartlepool v Carlisle
Mansfield v Accrington
Oxford v Newport
Plymouth v Shrewsbury
Southend v Morecambe
Stevenage v Luton
Wycombe v Northampton
York v Portsmouth

Sunday, 5 October
Premier League
Chelsea v Arsenal
Man Utd v Everton

West Ham v QPR
Championship
Nottm Forest v Ipswich

Saturday, 11 October
League One
Barnsley v Bradford
Bristol City v Chesterfield
Colchester v Fleetwood
Crawley v Peterborough
Crewe v Coventry
Doncaster v Notts Co
Gillingham v Scunthorpe
MK Dons v Rochdale
Oldham v Walsall
Port Vale v Yeovil
Sheffield Utd v Leyton Orient
Swindon v Preston

League Two
Accrington v Dag & Red
AFC Wimbledon v Bury
Cambridge v Oxford
Carlisle v Stevenage
Exeter v Hartlepool
Luton v Southend
Morecambe v Wycombe
Newport v York
Northampton v Burton
Portsmouth v Mansfield
Shrewsbury v Cheltenham
Tranmere v Plymouth

Saturday, 18 October
Premier League
Arsenal v Hull
Burnley v West Ham
Crystal Palace v Chelsea
Everton v Aston Villa
Man City v Tottenham
Newcastle v Leicester
Southampton v Sunderland

Championship
Birmingham v Bolton
Bournemouth v Charlton
Brighton v Middlesbrough
Cardiff v Nottm Forest
Fulham v Norwich
Huddersfield v Blackpool
Ipswich v Blackburn
Millwall v Wolves
Reading v Derby
Rotherham v Leeds
Sheffield Wed v Watford
Wigan v Brentford

League One
Bradford v Sheffield Utd
Chesterfield v Oldham
Coventry v Bristol City
Fleetwood v Doncaster
Leyton Orient v MK Dons
Notts Co v Crawley

Peterborough v Barnsley
Preston v Port Vale
Rochdale v Gillingham
Scunthorpe v Colchester
Walsall v Crewe
Yeovil v Swindon

League Two
Burton v Morecambe
Bury v Portsmouth
Cheltenham v Northampton
Dag & Red v Newport
Hartlepool v Luton
Mansfield v Cambridge
Oxford v Tranmere
Plymouth v Carlisle
Southend v Exeter
Stevenage v Accrington
Wycombe v AFC Wimbledon
York v Shrewsbury

Sunday, 19 October
Premier League
QPR v Liverpool
Stoke v Swansea

Monday, 20 October
Premier League
West Brom v Man Utd
Tuesday, 21 October
Championship
Blackburn v Birmingham
Blackpool v Derby
Bournemouth v Reading
Brentford v Sheffield Wed
Cardiff v Ipswich
Charlton v Bolton
Huddersfield v Brighton
Norwich v Leeds
Rotherham v Fulham
Watford v Nottm Forest
Wigan v Millwall
Wolves v Middlesbrough

League One
Barnsley v Notts Co
Bristol City v Bradford
Colchester v Chesterfield
Crawley v Walsall
Crewe v Peterborough
Doncaster v Leyton Orient
Gillingham v Preston
MK Dons v Fleetwood
Oldham v Coventry
Port Vale v Scunthorpe
Sheffield Utd v Yeovil
Swindon v Rochdale

League Two
Accrington v Hartlepool
AFC Wimbledon v Plymouth
Cambridge v Cheltenham
Carlisle v Burton

Exeter v Wycombe
Luton v Dag & Red
Morecambe v York
Newport v Southend
Northampton v Oxford
Portsmouth v Stevenage
Shrewsbury v Bury
Tranmere v Mansfield

Saturday, 25 October
Premier League
Liverpool v Hull
Southampton v Stoke
Sunderland v Arsenal
Swansea v Leicester
Tottenham v Newcastle
West Brom v Crystal Palace
West Ham v Man City

Championship
Birmingham v Bournemouth
Bolton v Brentford
Brighton v Rotherham
Derby v Wigan
Fulham v Charlton
Ipswich v Huddersfield
Leeds v Wolves
Middlesbrough v Watford
Millwall v Cardiff
Nottm Forest v Blackburn
Reading v Blackpool
Sheffield Wed v Norwich

League One
Barnsley v Bristol City
Coventry v Peterborough
Crewe v Sheffield Utd
Doncaster v MK Dons
Gillingham v Crawley
Oldham v Bradford
Port Vale v Leyton Orient
Preston v Fleetwood
Scunthorpe v Notts Co
Swindon v Colchester
Walsall v Chesterfield
Yeovil v Rochdale

League Two
AFC Wimbledon v Tranmere
Cambridge v Hartlepool
Carlisle v Oxford
Luton v Northampton
Newport v Accrington
Plymouth v Cheltenham
Shrewsbury v Portsmouth
Southend v Bury
Stevenage v Burton
Wycombe v Dag & Red
York v Mansfield

Sunday, 26 October
Premier League
Burnley v Everton

Manchester Utd v Chelsea
League Two
Morecambe v Exeter

Monday, 27 October
Premier League
QPR v Aston Villa

Friday, 31 October
League Two
Accrington v Morecambe

Saturday, 1 November
Premier League
Arsenal v Burnley
Chelsea v QPR
Everton v Swansea
Hull v Southampton
Leicester v West Brom
Newcastle v Liverpool
Stoke v West Ham

Championship
Blackburn v Reading
Blackpool v Ipswich
Bournemouth v Brighton
Brentford v Derby
Cardiff v Leeds
Charlton v Sheffield Wed
Huddersfield v Nottm Forest
Norwich v Bolton
Rotherham v Middlesbrough
Watford v Millwall
Wigan v Fulham
Wolves v Birmingham

League One
Bradford v Doncaster
Bristol City v Oldham
Chesterfield v Yeovil
Colchester v Port Vale
Crawley v Crewe
Fleetwood v Gillingham
Leyton Orient v Coventry
MK Dons v Swindon
Notts Co v Walsall
Peterborough v Scunthorpe
Rochdale v Preston
Sheffield Utd v Barnsley

League Two
Burton v Plymouth
Bury v Cambridge
Cheltenham v York
Dag & Red v Shrewsbury
Exeter v Luton
Hartlepool v Newport
Mansfield v Southend
Northampton v AFC Wimbledon
Oxford v Wycombe
Portsmouth v Carlisle
Tranmere v Stevenage

Sunday, 2 November
Premier League
Aston Villa v Tottenham
Man City v Man Utd

Monday, 3 November
Premier League
Crystal Palace v Sunderland

Tuesday, 4 November
Championship
Birmingham v Watford
Brighton v Wigan
Derby v Huddersfield
Ipswich v Wolves
Leeds v Charlton
Middlesbrough v Norwich
Millwall v Blackburn
Sheffield Wed v Bournemouth
Bolton v Cardiff
Reading v Rotherham

Wednesday, 5 November
Championship
Fulham v Blackpool
Nottm Forest v Brentford

Saturday, 8 November
Premier League
Burnley v Hull
Liverpool v Chelsea
Man Utd v Crystal Palace
QPR v Man City
Southampton v Leicester
Sunderland v Everton
Tottenham v Stoke
West Ham v Aston Villa

Championship
Birmingham v Cardiff
Bolton v Wigan
Brighton v Blackburn
Derby v Wolves
Fulham v Huddersfield
Ipswich v Watford
Leeds v Blackpool
Middlesbrough v Bournemouth
Millwall v Brentford
Nottm Forest v Norwich
Reading v Charlton
Sheffield Wed v Rotherham

Sunday, 9 November
Premier League
Swansea v Arsenal
West Brom v Newcastle

Friday, 14 November
League One
Barnsley v Colchester

League Two
Cambridge v Northampton

Saturday, 15 November
League One
Coventry v Notts Co
Crewe v Chesterfield
Doncaster v Sheffield Utd
Gillingham v Leyton Orient
Oldham v Crawley
Port Vale v Rochdale
Preston v Bradford
Scunthorpe v MK Dons
Swindon v Bristol City
Walsall v Peterborough
Yeovil v Fleetwood

League Two
AFC Wimbledon v Dag & Red
Carlisle v Accrington
Luton v Tranmere
Morecambe v Bury
Plymouth v Portsmouth
Shrewsbury v Mansfield
Southend v Hartlepool
Stevenage v Cheltenham
Wycombe v Burton
York v Oxford

Sunday, 16 November
League Two
Newport v Exeter

Friday, 21 November
Championship
Cardiff v Reading

Saturday, 22 November
Premier League
Arsenal v Man Utd
Chelsea v West Brom
Everton v West Ham
Leicester v Sunderland
Man City v Swansea
Newcastle v QPR
Stoke v Burnley

Championship
Blackburn v Leeds
Blackpool v Bolton
Bournemouth v Ipswich
Brentford v Fulham
Charlton v Millwall
Huddersfield v Sheffield Wed
Norwich v Brighton
Rotherham v Birmingham
Watford v Derby
Wigan v Middlesbrough
Wolves v Nottm Forest

League One
Bradford v Gillingham
Bristol City v Preston

Chesterfield v Barnsley
Colchester v Coventry
Crawley v Scunthorpe
Fleetwood v Walsall
Leyton Orient v Crewe
MK Dons v Port Vale
Notts Co v Yeovil
Peterborough v Swindon
Rochdale v Doncaster
Sheffield Utd v Oldham

League Two
Accrington v Cambridge
Burton v Luton
Bury v Newport
Cheltenham v Wycombe
Dag & Red v Carlisle
Exeter v Shrewsbury
Hartlepool v York
Mansfield v Plymouth
Northampton v Stevenage
Oxford v AFC Wimbledon
Portsmouth v Morecambe
Tranmere v Southend

Sunday, 23 November
Premier League
Crystal Palace v Liverpool
Hull v Tottenham

Monday, 24 November
Premier League
Aston Villa v Southampton

Friday, 28 November
League One
Sheffield Utd v Notts Co

League Two
Accrington v Exeter

Saturday, 29 November
Premier League
Burnley v Aston Villa
Liverpool v Stoke
Man Utd v Hull
QPR v Leicester
Sunderland v Chelsea
Swansea v Crystal Palace
West Brom v Arsenal
West Ham v Newcastle

Championship
Birmingham v Nottm Forest
Bolton v Huddersfield
Bournemouth v Millwall
Brentford v Wolves
Brighton v Fulham
Charlton v Ipswich
Leeds v Derby
Middlesbrough v Blackburn
Norwich v Reading
Rotherham v Blackpool

Sheffield Wed v Wigan
Watford v Cardiff

League One
Barnsley v Scunthorpe
Bradford v Leyton Orient
Coventry v Walsall
Crawley v Chesterfield
Crewe v Doncaster
Gillingham v Port Vale
MK Dons v Colchester
Peterborough v Bristol City
Rochdale v Oldham
Swindon v Fleetwood
Yeovil v Preston

League Two
AFC Wimbledon v Cambridge
Bury v Dag & Red
Carlisle v Newport
Cheltenham v Oxford
Hartlepool v Wycombe
Luton v Mansfield
Plymouth v York
Shrewsbury v Burton
Southend v Northampton
Stevenage v Morecambe
Tranmere v Portsmouth

Sunday, 30 November
Premier League
Southampton v Man City
Tottenham v Everton

Tuesday, 2 December
Premier League
Arsenal v Southampton
Burnley v Newcastle
Leicester v Liverpool
Man Utd v Stoke
Swansea v QPR
Crystal Palace v Aston Villa
West Brom v West Ham

Wednesday, 3 December
Premier League
Chelsea v Tottenham
Everton v Hull
Sunderland v Man City

Saturday, 6 December
Premier League
Aston Villa v Leicester
Hull v West Brom
Liverpool v Sunderland
Man City v Everton
Newcastle v Chelsea
QPR v Burnley
Southampton v Man Utd
Stoke v Arsenal
Tottenham v Crystal Palace
West Ham v Swansea

Championship

Blackburn v Sheffield Wed
Blackpool v Birmingham
Cardiff v Rotherham
Derby v Brighton
Fulham v Watford
Huddersfield v Brentford
Ipswich v Leeds
Millwall v Middlesbrough
Nottm Forest v Charlton
Reading v Bolton
Wigan v Norwich
Wolves v Bournemouth

Saturday, 13 December

Premier League

Arsenal v Newcastle
Burnley v Southampton
Chelsea v Hull
Crystal Palace v Stoke
Everton v QPR
Leicester v Man City
Man Utd v Liverpool
Sunderland v West Ham
Swansea v Tottenham
West Brom v Aston Villa

Championship

Birmingham v Reading
Bolton v Ipswich
Bournemouth v Cardiff
Brentford v Blackburn
Brighton v Millwall
Charlton v Blackpool
Leeds v Fulham
Middlesbrough v Derby
Norwich v Huddersfield
Rotherham v Nottm Forest
Sheffield Wed v Wolves
Watford v Wigan

League One

Bristol City v Crawley
Chesterfield v Bradford
Colchester v Rochdale
Doncaster v Gillingham
Fleetwood v Sheffield Utd
Leyton Orient v Peterborough
Notts Co v Swindon
Oldham v Yeovil
Port Vale v Coventry
Preston v MK Dons
Scunthorpe v Crewe
Walsall v Barnsley

League Two

Burton v Hartlepool
Cambridge v Shrewsbury
Dag & Red v Tranmere
Exeter v Carlisle
Mansfield v Cheltenham
Morecambe v Luton
Newport v Stevenage

Northampton v Plymouth
Oxford v Bury
Portsmouth v Accrington
Wycombe v Southend
York v AFC Wimbledon

Friday, 19 December

League Two

Southend v Burton
Tranmere v Cambridge

Saturday, 20 December

Premier League

Aston Villa v Man Utd
Hull v Swansea
Liverpool v Arsenal
Man City v Crystal Palace
Newcastle v Sunderland
QPR v West Brom
Southampton v Everton
Stoke v Chelsea
Tottenham v Burnley
West Ham v Leicester

Championship

Blackburn v Charlton
Blackpool v Bournemouth
Cardiff v Brentford
Derby v Norwich
Fulham v Sheffield Wed
Huddersfield v Birmingham
Ipswich v Middlesbrough
Millwall v Bolton
Nottm Forest v Leeds
Reading v Watford
Wigan v Rotherham
Wolves v Brighton

League One

Barnsley v Leyton Orient
Bradford v Scunthorpe
Coventry v Fleetwood
Crawley v Port Vale
Crewe v Bristol City
Gillingham v Chesterfield
MK Dons v Oldham
Peterborough v Preston
Rochdale v Notts Co
Sheffield Utd v Walsall
Swindon v Doncaster
Yeovil v Colchester

League Two

Accrington v Wycombe
AFC Wimbledon v Mansfield
Bury v York
Carlisle v Northampton
Cheltenham v Portsmouth
Hartlepool v Oxford
Luton v Newport
Plymouth v Dag & Red
Shrewsbury v Morecambe
Stevenage v Exeter

Friday, 26 December

Premier League

Arsenal v QPR
Burnley v Liverpool
Chelsea v West Ham
Crystal Palace v Southampton
Everton v Stoke
Leicester v Tottenham
Man Utd v Newcastle
Sunderland v Hull
Swansea v Aston Villa
West Brom v Man City

Championship

Birmingham v Derby
Bolton v Blackburn
Bournemouth v Fulham
Brentford v Ipswich
Brighton v Reading
Charlton v Cardiff
Leeds v Wigan
Middlesbrough v Nottm Forest
Norwich v Millwall
Rotherham v Huddersfield
Sheffield Wed v Blackpool
Watford v Wolves

League One

Bristol City v Yeovil
Chesterfield v Peterborough
Colchester v Gillingham
Doncaster v Coventry
Fleetwood v Bradford
Leyton Orient v Crawley
Notts Co v MK Dons
Oldham v Crewe
Port Vale v Sheffield Utd
Preston v Barnsley
Scunthorpe v Rochdale
Walsall v Swindon

League Two

Burton v Tranmere
Cambridge v Southend
Dag & Red v Stevenage
Exeter v Cheltenham
Mansfield v Hartlepool
Morecambe v Carlisle
Newport v Plymouth
Northampton v Bury
Oxford v Shrewsbury
Portsmouth v AFC Wimbledon
Wycombe v Luton
York v Accrington

Sunday, 28 December

Premier League

Aston Villa v Sunderland
Hull v Leicester
Liverpool v Swansea
Man City v Burnley
Newcastle v Everton
QPR v Crystal Palace

Southampton v Chelsea
Stoke v West Brom
Tottenham v Man Utd
West Ham v Arsenal

Championship
Blackburn v Middlesbrough
Blackpool v Rotherham
Cardiff v Watford
Derby v Leeds
Huddersfield v Bolton
Millwall v Bournemouth
Nottm Forest v Birmingham
Reading v Norwich
Wolves v Brentford

League One
Bradford v Notts Co
Coventry v Chesterfield
Crawley v Colchester
Crewe v Preston
Gillingham v Bristol City
MK Dons v Walsall
Peterborough v Doncaster
Rochdale v Fleetwood
Sheffield Utd v Scunthorpe
Swindon v Port Vale
Yeovil v Leyton Orient

League Two
Accrington v Burton
AFC Wimbledon v Exeter
Bury v Mansfield
Carlisle v York
Cheltenham v Newport
Hartlepool v Morecambe
Luton v Portsmouth
Plymouth v Oxford
Shrewsbury v Wycombe
Southend v Dag & Red
Stevenage v Cambridge
Tranmere v Northampton

Monday, 29 December
Championship
Fulham v Brighton

League One
Barnsley v Oldham

Tuesday, 30 December
Championship
Ipswich v Charlton
Wigan v Sheffield Wed

Thursday, 1 January
Premier League
Aston Villa v Crystal Palace
Hull v Everton
Liverpool v Leicester
Man City v Sunderland
Newcastle v Burnley
QPR v Swansea

Southampton v Arsenal
Stoke v Man Utd
Tottenham v Chelsea
West Ham v West Brom

Saturday, 3 January
League One
Bristol City v Peterborough
Chesterfield v Crawley
Colchester v MK Dons
Doncaster v Crewe
Fleetwood v Swindon
Leyton Orient v Bradford
Notts Co v Sheffield Utd
Oldham v Rochdale
Port Vale v Gillingham
Preston v Yeovil
Scunthorpe v Barnsley
Walsall v Coventry

League Two
Burton v Shrewsbury
Cambridge v AFC Wimbledon
Dag & Red v Bury
Exeter v Accrington
Mansfield v Luton
Morecambe v Stevenage
Newport v Carlisle
Northampton v Southend
Oxford v Cheltenham
Portsmouth v Tranmere
Wycombe v Hartlepool
York v Plymouth

Friday, 9 January
League Two
Accrington v Bury

Saturday, 10 January
Premier League
Arsenal v Stoke
Burnley v QPR
Chelsea v Newcastle
Crystal Palace v Tottenham
Everton v Man City
Leicester v Aston Villa
Man Utd v Southampton
Sunderland v Liverpool
Swansea v West Ham
West Brom v Hull

Championship
Birmingham v Wigan
Blackpool v Millwall
Bolton v Leeds
Bournemouth v Norwich
Brentford v Rotherham
Cardiff v Fulham
Charlton v Brighton
Huddersfield v Watford
Ipswich v Derby
Nottm Forest v Sheffield Wed
Reading v Middlesbrough

League One
Barnsley v Yeovil
Bradford v Rochdale
Bristol City v Notts Co
Chesterfield v Port Vale
Coventry v Swindon
Crawley v MK Dons
Crewe v Gillingham
Leyton Orient v Fleetwood
Oldham v Doncaster
Peterborough v Colchester
Sheffield Utd v Preston
Walsall v Scunthorpe

League Two
Burton v Mansfield
Carlisle v Cambridge
Dag & Red v Oxford
Exeter v Northampton
Hartlepool v Cheltenham
Luton v Shrewsbury
Morecambe v Tranmere
Newport v Portsmouth
Southend v Plymouth
Stevenage v AFC Wimbledon
Wycombe v York

Sunday, 11 January
Championship
Blackburn v Wolves

Friday, 16 January
League Two
Cheltenham v Morecambe

Saturday, 17 January
Premier League
Aston Villa v Liverpool
Burnley v Crystal Palace
Everton v West Brom
Leicester v Stoke
Man City v Arsenal
Newcastle v Southampton
QPR v Man Utd
Swansea v Chelsea
Tottenham v Sunderland
West Ham v Hull

Championship
Brighton v Brentford
Derby v Nottm Forest
Fulham v Reading
Leeds v Birmingham
Middlesbrough v Huddersfield
Millwall v Ipswich
Norwich v Cardiff
Rotherham v Bournemouth
Sheffield Wed v Bolton
Watford v Charlton
Wigan v Blackburn
Wolves v Blackpool

League One
Colchester v Walsall
Doncaster v Barnsley
Fleetwood v Oldham
Gillingham v Coventry
MK Dons v Sheffield Utd
Notts Co v Crewe
Port Vale v Peterborough
Preston v Leyton Orient
Rochdale v Crawley
Scunthorpe v Bristol City
Swindon v Chesterfield
Yeovil v Bradford

League Two
AFC Wimbledon v Carlisle
Bury v Wycombe
Cambridge v Newport
Mansfield v Exeter
Northampton v Dag & Red
Oxford v Southend
Plymouth v Luton
Portsmouth v Burton
Shrewsbury v Hartlepool
Tranmere v Accrington
York v Stevenage

Saturday, 24 January
Championship
Brighton v Ipswich
Derby v Blackburn
Fulham v Nottm Forest
Leeds v Bournemouth
Middlesbrough v Cardiff
Millwall v Reading
Norwich v Brentford
Rotherham v Bolton
Sheffield Wed v Birmingham
Watford v Blackpool
Wigan v Huddersfield
Wolves v Charlton

League One
Colchester v Leyton Orient
Doncaster v Bristol City
Fleetwood v Crawley
Gillingham v Oldham
MK Dons v Barnsley
Notts Co v Peterborough
Port Vale v Crewe
Preston v Walsall
Rochdale v Sheffield Utd
Scunthorpe v Chesterfield
Swindon v Bradford
Yeovil v Coventry

League Two
AFC Wimbledon v Accrington
Bury v Carlisle
Cambridge v Dag & Red
Cheltenham v Luton
Mansfield v Wycombe
Northampton v Newport

Oxford v Exeter
Plymouth v Morecambe
Portsmouth v Southend
Shrewsbury v Stevenage
Tranmere v Hartlepool
York v Burton

Saturday, 31 January
Premier League
Arsenal v Aston Villa
Chelsea v Man City
Crystal Palace v Everton
Hull v Newcastle
Liverpool v West Ham
Man Utd v Leicester
Southampton v Swansea
Stoke v QPR
Sunderland v Burnley
West Brom v Tottenham

Championship
Birmingham v Norwich
Blackburn v Fulham
Blackpool v Brighton
Bolton v Wolves
Bournemouth v Watford
Brentford v Middlesbrough
Cardiff v Derby
Charlton v Rotherham
Huddersfield v Leeds
Ipswich v Wigan
Nottm Forest v Millwall
Reading v Sheffield Wed

League One
Barnsley v Port Vale
Bradford v Colchester
Bristol City v Fleetwood
Chesterfield v Doncaster
Coventry v Rochdale
Crawley v Preston
Crewe v MK Dons
Leyton Orient v Scunthorpe
Oldham v Notts Co
Peterborough v Yeovil
Sheffield Utd v Swindon
Walsall v Gillingham

League Two
Accrington v Northampton
Burton v Bury
Carlisle v Mansfield
Dag & Red v Cheltenham
Exeter v Tranmere
Hartlepool v Plymouth
Luton v Cambridge
Morecambe v AFC Wimbledon
Newport v Shrewsbury
Southend v York
Stevenage v Oxford
Wycombe v Portsmouth

Saturday, 7 February
Premier League
Aston Villa v Chelsea
Burnley v West Brom
Everton v Liverpool
Leicester v Crystal Palace
Man City v Hull
Newcastle v Stoke
QPR v Southampton
Swansea v Sunderland
Tottenham v Arsenal
West Ham v Man Utd

Championship
Brighton v Nottm Forest
Derby v Bolton
Fulham v Birmingham
Leeds v Brentford
Middlesbrough v Charlton
Millwall v Huddersfield
Norwich v Blackpool
Rotherham v Ipswich
Sheffield Wed v Cardiff
Watford v Blackburn
Wigan v Bournemouth
Wolves v Reading

League One
Colchester v Crewe
Doncaster v Walsall
Fleetwood v Peterborough
Gillingham v Sheffield Utd
MK Dons v Bristol City
Notts Co v Chesterfield
Port Vale v Bradford
Preston v Coventry
Rochdale v Leyton Orient
Scunthorpe v Oldham
Swindon v Barnsley
Yeovil v Crawley

League Two
AFC Wimbledon v Newport
Bury v Exeter
Cambridge v Wycombe
Cheltenham v Burton
Mansfield v Stevenage
Northampton v Morecambe
Oxford v Luton
Plymouth v Accrington
Portsmouth v Hartlepool
Shrewsbury v Southend
Tranmere v Carlisle
York v Dag & Red

Tuesday, 10 February
Premier League
Arsenal v Leicester
Hull v Aston Villa
Man Utd v Burnley
Southampton v West Ham
Crystal Palace v Newcastle

Liverpool v Tottenham
West Brom v Swansea

Championship
Birmingham v Millwall
Blackburn v Rotherham
Blackpool v Middlesbrough
Bournemouth v Derby
Brentford v Watford
Cardiff v Brighton
Charlton v Norwich
Huddersfield v Wolves
Ipswich v Sheffield Wed
Bolton v Fulham
Reading v Leeds

League One
Barnsley v Fleetwood
Bradford v MK Dons
Bristol City v Port Vale
Chesterfield v Preston
Coventry v Scunthorpe
Crawley v Doncaster
Crewe v Yeovil
Leyton Orient v Notts Co
Oldham v Swindon
Peterborough v Gillingham
Sheffield Utd v Colchester
Walsall v Rochdale

League Two
Accrington v Oxford
Burton v AFC Wimbledon
Carlisle v Shrewsbury
Dag & Red v Portsmouth
Exeter v Cambridge
Hartlepool v Northampton
Luton v York
Morecambe v Mansfield
Newport v Tranmere
Southend v Cheltenham
Stevenage v Bury
Wycombe v Plymouth

Wednesday, 11 February
Premier League
Chelsea v Everton
Stoke v Man City
Sunderland v QPR

Championship
Nottm Forest v Wigan

Saturday, 14 February
Championship
Birmingham v Middlesbrough
Blackpool v Nottm Forest
Bolton v Watford
Bournemouth v Huddersfield
Cardiff v Blackburn
Charlton v Brentford
Fulham v Ipswich
Leeds v Millwall

Norwich v Wolves
Reading v Wigan
Rotherham v Derby
Sheffield Wed v Brighton

League One
Bristol City v Sheffield Utd
Chesterfield v Leyton Orient
Coventry v Bradford
Crawley v Barnsley
Crewe v Fleetwood
Doncaster v Yeovil
Gillingham v MK Dons
Notts Co v Preston
Oldham v Colchester
Peterborough v Rochdale
Scunthorpe v Swindon
Walsall v Port Vale

League Two
Burton v Oxford
Cheltenham v Bury
Hartlepool v Stevenage
Luton v Carlisle
Mansfield v Northampton
Plymouth v Cambridge
Portsmouth v Exeter
Shrewsbury v AFC Wimbledon
Southend v Accrington
Wycombe v Newport
York v Tranmere

Sunday, 15 February
League Two
Morecambe v Dag & Red

Friday, 20 February
League Two
Accrington v Cheltenham

Saturday, 21 February
Premier League
Aston Villa v Stoke
Chelsea v Burnley
Crystal Palace v Arsenal
Everton v Leicester
Hull v QPR
Man City v Newcastle
Southampton v Liverpool
Sunderland v West Brom
Swansea v Man Utd
Tottenham v West Ham

Championship
Blackburn v Blackpool
Brentford v Bournemouth
Brighton v Birmingham
Derby v Sheffield Wed
Huddersfield v Cardiff
Ipswich v Reading
Middlesbrough v Leeds
Millwall v Fulham
Nottm Forest v Bolton

Watford v Norwich
Wigan v Charlton
Wolves v Rotherham

League One
Barnsley v Crewe
Bradford v Walsall
Colchester v Bristol City
Fleetwood v Notts Co
Leyton Orient v Oldham
MK Dons v Peterborough
Port Vale v Doncaster
Preston v Scunthorpe
Rochdale v Chesterfield
Sheffield Utd v Coventry
Swindon v Crawley
Yeovil v Gillingham

League Two
AFC Wimbledon v Luton
Bury v Hartlepool
Cambridge v Portsmouth
Carlisle v Wycombe
Dag & Red v Burton
Exeter v Plymouth
Newport v Morecambe
Northampton v York
Oxford v Mansfield
Stevenage v Southend
Tranmere v Shrewsbury

Tuesday, 24 February
Championship
Blackburn v Norwich
Brentford v Blackpool
Brighton v Leeds
Derby v Charlton
Huddersfield v Reading
Ipswich v Birmingham
Middlesbrough v Bolton
Millwall v Sheffield Wed
Watford v Rotherham
Wigan v Cardiff
Wolves v Fulham

Wednesday, 25 February
Championship
Nottm Forest v Bournemouth

Saturday, 28 February
Premier League
Arsenal v Everton
Burnley v Swansea
Leicester v Chelsea
Liverpool v Man City
Man Utd v Sunderland
Newcastle v Aston Villa
QPR v Tottenham
Stoke v Hull
West Brom v Southampton
West Ham v Crystal Palace

Championship
Birmingham v Brentford
Blackpool v Wigan
Bolton v Brighton
Bournemouth v Blackburn
Cardiff v Wolves
Charlton v Huddersfield
Fulham v Derby
Leeds v Watford
Norwich v Ipswich
Reading v Nottm Forest
Rotherham v Millwall
Sheffield Wed v Middlesbrough

League One
Bristol City v Rochdale
Chesterfield v Fleetwood
Coventry v MK Dons
Crawley v Sheffield Utd
Crewe v Swindon
Doncaster v Colchester
Gillingham v Barnsley
Notts Co v Port Vale
Oldham v Preston
Peterborough v Bradford
Scunthorpe v Yeovil
Walsall v Leyton Orient

League Two
Burton v Newport
Cheltenham v Tranmere
Hartlepool v AFC Wimbledon
Luton v Accrington
Mansfield v Dag & Red
Morecambe v Cambridge
Plymouth v Bury
Portsmouth v Oxford
Shrewsbury v Northampton
Southend v Carlisle
Wycombe v Stevenage
York v Exeter

Tuesday, 3 March
Premier League
Aston Villa v West Brom
Hull v Sunderland
QPR v Arsenal
Southampton v Crystal Palace
West Ham v Chelsea
Liverpool v Burnley

Championship
Birmingham v Blackpool
Bournemouth v Wolves
Brentford v Huddersfield
Brighton v Derby
Charlton v Nottm Forest
Leeds v Ipswich
Middlesbrough v Millwall
Norwich v Wigan
Rotherham v Cardiff
Watford v Fulham
Bolton v Reading

League One
Barnsley v Coventry
Bradford v Crawley
Colchester v Notts Co
Fleetwood v Scunthorpe
Leyton Orient v Bristol City
MK Dons v Chesterfield
Port Vale v Oldham
Preston v Doncaster
Rochdale v Crewe
Sheffield Utd v Peterborough
Swindon v Gillingham
Yeovil v Walsall

League Two
Accrington v Shrewsbury
AFC Wimbledon v Southend
Bury v Luton
Cambridge v York
Carlisle v Cheltenham
Dag & Red v Hartlepool
Exeter v Burton
Newport v Mansfield
Northampton v Portsmouth
Oxford v Morecambe
Stevenage v Plymouth
Tranmere v Wycombe

Wednesday, 4 March
Premier League
Man City v Leicester
Newcastle v Man Utd
Stoke v Everton
Tottenham v Swansea

Championship
Sheffield Wed v Blackburn

Saturday, 7 March
Championship
Blackburn v Bolton
Blackpool v Sheffield Wed
Cardiff v Charlton
Derby v Birmingham
Fulham v Bournemouth
Huddersfield v Rotherham
Ipswich v Brentford
Millwall v Norwich
Nottm Forest v Middlesbrough
Reading v Brighton
Wigan v Leeds
Wolves v Watford

League One
Barnsley v Walsall
Bradford v Chesterfield
Coventry v Port Vale
Crawley v Bristol City
Crewe v Scunthorpe
Gillingham v Doncaster
MK Dons v Preston
Peterborough v Leyton Orient
Rochdale v Colchester

Sheffield Utd v Fleetwood
Swindon v Notts Co
Yeovil v Oldham

League Two
Accrington v Portsmouth
AFC Wimbledon v York
Bury v Oxford
Carlisle v Exeter
Cheltenham v Mansfield
Hartlepool v Burton
Luton v Morecambe
Plymouth v Northampton
Shrewsbury v Cambridge
Southend v Wycombe
Stevenage v Newport
Tranmere v Dag & Red

Friday, 13 March
League Two
Newport v Cheltenham

Saturday, 14 March
Premier League
Arsenal v West Ham
Burnley v Man City
Chelsea v Southampton
Crystal Palace v QPR
Everton v Newcastle
Leicester v Hull
Man Utd v Tottenham
Sunderland v Aston Villa
Swansea v Liverpool
West Brom v Stoke

Championship
Birmingham v Huddersfield
Bolton v Millwall
Bournemouth v Blackpool
Brentford v Cardiff
Brighton v Wolves
Charlton v Blackburn
Leeds v Nottm Forest
Middlesbrough v Ipswich
Norwich v Derby
Rotherham v Wigan
Sheffield Wed v Fulham
Watford v Reading

League One
Bristol City v Gillingham
Chesterfield v Coventry
Colchester v Crawley
Doncaster v Peterborough
Fleetwood v Rochdale
Leyton Orient v Yeovil
Notts Co v Bradford
Oldham v Barnsley
Port Vale v Swindon
Preston v Crewe
Scunthorpe v Sheffield Utd
Walsall v MK Dons

League Two
Burton v Accrington
Cambridge v Stevenage
Dag & Red v Southend
Exeter v AFC Wimbledon
Mansfield v Bury
Morecambe v Hartlepool
Northampton v Tranmere
Oxford v Plymouth
Portsmouth v Luton
Wycombe v Shrewsbury
York v Carlisle

Tuesday, 17 March
Championship
Blackburn v Brentford
Blackpool v Charlton
Cardiff v Bournemouth
Derby v Middlesbrough
Huddersfield v Norwich
Ipswich v Bolton
Millwall v Brighton
Wigan v Watford
Wolves v Sheffield Wed
Reading v Birmingham

League One
Bristol City v Crewe
Chesterfield v Gillingham
Colchester v Yeovil
Doncaster v Swindon
Fleetwood v Coventry
Leyton Orient v Barnsley
Notts Co v Rochdale
Oldham v MK Dons
Port Vale v Crawley
Preston v Peterborough
Scunthorpe v Bradford
Walsall v Sheffield Utd

League Two
Cambridge v Tranmere
Dag & Red v Plymouth
Exeter v Stevenage
Mansfield v AFC Wimbledon
Morecambe v Shrewsbury
Newport v Luton
Northampton v Carlisle
Oxford v Hartlepool
Portsmouth v Cheltenham
Wycombe v Accrington
York v Bury

Wednesday, 18 March
Championship
Fulham v Leeds
Nottm Forest v Rotherham

League Two
Burton v Southend

Saturday, 21 March
Premier League

Aston Villa v Swansea
Hull v Chelsea
Liverpool v Man Utd
Man City v West Brom
Newcastle v Arsenal
QPR v Everton
Southampton v Burnley
Stoke v Crystal Palace
Tottenham v Leicester
West Ham v Sunderland

Championship
Blackburn v Brighton
Blackpool v Leeds
Bournemouth v Middlesbrough
Brentford v Millwall
Cardiff v Birmingham
Charlton v Reading
Huddersfield v Fulham
Norwich v Nottm Forest
Rotherham v Sheffield Wed
Watford v Ipswich
Wigan v Bolton
Wolves v Derby

League One
Barnsley v Preston
Bradford v Fleetwood
Coventry v Doncaster
Crawley v Leyton Orient
Crewe v Oldham
Gillingham v Colchester
MK Dons v Notts Co
Peterborough v Chesterfield
Rochdale v Scunthorpe
Sheffield Utd v Port Vale
Swindon v Walsall
Yeovil v Bristol City

League Two
Accrington v York
AFC Wimbledon v Portsmouth
Bury v Northampton
Carlisle v Morecambe
Cheltenham v Exeter
Hartlepool v Mansfield
Luton v Wycombe
Plymouth v Newport
Shrewsbury v Oxford
Southend v Cambridge
Stevenage v Dag & Red
Tranmere v Burton

Friday, 27 March
League Two
Accrington v Newport

Saturday, 28 March
League One
Bradford v Oldham
Bristol City v Barnsley
Chesterfield v Walsall
Colchester v Swindon
Crawley v Gillingham

Fleetwood v Preston
Leyton Orient v Port Vale
MK Dons v Doncaster
Notts Co v Scunthorpe
Peterborough v Coventry
Rochdale v Yeovil
Sheffield Utd v Crewe

League Two
Burton v Stevenage
Bury v Southend
Cheltenham v Plymouth
Dag & Red v Wycombe
Exeter v Morecambe
Hartlepool v Cambridge
Mansfield v York
Northampton v Luton
Oxford v Carlisle
Portsmouth v Shrewsbury
Tranmere v AFC Wimbledon

Friday, 3 April
Championship
Birmingham v Rotherham
Brighton v Norwich
Derby v Watford
Fulham v Brentford
Ipswich v Bournemouth
Millwall v Charlton
Nottm Forest v Wolves

League One
Coventry v Leyton Orient
Crewe v Crawley
Doncaster v Bradford
Gillingham v Fleetwood
Oldham v Bristol City
Port Vale v Colchester
Preston v Rochdale
Scunthorpe v Peterborough
Swindon v MK Dons
Walsall v Notts Co
Yeovil v Chesterfield

League Two
AFC Wimbledon v Northampton
Cambridge v Bury
Carlisle v Portsmouth
Luton v Exeter
Morecambe v Accrington
Newport v Hartlepool
Plymouth v Burton
Shrewsbury v Dag & Red
Southend v Mansfield
Stevenage v Tranmere
York v Cheltenham

Saturday, 4 April
Premier League
Arsenal v Liverpool
Burnley v Tottenham
Chelsea v Stoke
Crystal Palace v Man City
Everton v Southampton

Leicester v West Ham
Man Utd v Aston Villa
Sunderland v Newcastle
Swansea v Hull
West Brom v QPR

Championship
Bolton v Blackpool
Leeds v Blackburn
Middlesbrough v Wigan
Reading v Cardiff
Sheffield Wed v Huddersfield

League One
Barnsley v Sheffield Utd

League Two
Wycombe v Oxford

Monday, 6 April
Championship
Blackburn v Millwall
Blackpool v Reading
Bournemouth v Birmingham
Brentford v Nottm Forest
Cardiff v Bolton
Huddersfield v Ipswich
Norwich v Sheffield Wed
Rotherham v Brighton
Watford v Middlesbrough
Wigan v Derby
Wolves v Leeds

League One
Bradford v Preston
Bristol City v Swindon
Chesterfield v Crewe
Colchester v Barnsley
Crawley v Oldham
Fleetwood v Yeovil
Leyton Orient v Gillingham
MK Dons v Scunthorpe
Notts Co v Coventry
Peterborough v Walsall
Rochdale v Port Vale

League Two
Accrington v Carlisle
Burton v Wycombe
Bury v Morecambe
Cheltenham v Stevenage
Dag & Red v AFC Wimbledon
Exeter v Newport
Hartlepool v Southend
Mansfield v Shrewsbury
Northampton v Cambridge
Oxford v York
Portsmouth v Plymouth
Tranmere v Luton

Tuesday, 7 April
Championship
Charlton v Fulham

League One
Sheffield Utd v Doncaster

Friday, 10 April
Championship
Fulham v Wigan

Saturday, 11 April
Premier League
Burnley v Arsenal
Liverpool v Newcastle
Man Utd v Man City
QPR v Chelsea
Southampton v Hull
Sunderland v Crystal Palace
Swansea v Everton
Tottenham v Aston Villa
West Brom v Leicester
West Ham v Stoke

Championship
Birmingham v Wolves
Bolton v Norwich
Brighton v Bournemouth
Derby v Brentford
Ipswich v Blackpool
Leeds v Cardiff
Middlesbrough v Rotherham
Millwall v Watford
Nottm Forest v Huddersfield
Reading v Blackburn
Sheffield Wed v Charlton

League One
Barnsley v Chesterfield
Coventry v Colchester
Crewe v Leyton Orient
Doncaster v Rochdale
Gillingham v Bradford
Oldham v Sheffield Utd
Port Vale v MK Dons
Preston v Bristol City
Scunthorpe v Crawley
Swindon v Peterborough
Walsall v Fleetwood
Yeovil v Notts Co

League Two
AFC Wimbledon v Oxford
Cambridge v Accrington
Carlisle v Dag & Red
Luton v Burton
Morecambe v Portsmouth
Newport v Bury
Plymouth v Mansfield
Shrewsbury v Exeter
Southend v Tranmere
Stevenage v Northampton
Wycombe v Cheltenham
York v Hartlepool

Tuesday, 14 April
Championship
Birmingham v Blackburn
Brighton v Huddersfield
Derby v Blackpool
Ipswich v Cardiff
Leeds v Norwich
Middlesbrough v Wolves
Millwall v Wigan
Sheffield Wed v Brentford
Bolton v Charlton
Reading v Bournemouth

League One
Bradford v Bristol City
Chesterfield v Colchester
Coventry v Oldham
Fleetwood v MK Dons
Leyton Orient v Doncaster
Notts Co v Barnsley
Peterborough v Crewe
Preston v Gillingham
Rochdale v Swindon
Scunthorpe v Port Vale
Walsall v Crawley
Yeovil v Sheffield Utd

League Two
Bury v Shrewsbury
Cheltenham v Cambridge
Dag & Red v Luton
Hartlepool v Accrington
Mansfield v Tranmere
Oxford v Northampton
Plymouth v AFC Wimbledon
Southend v Newport
Stevenage v Portsmouth
Wycombe v Exeter
York v Morecambe

Wednesday, 15 April
Championship
Fulham v Rotherham
Nottm Forest v Watford

League Two
Burton v Carlisle

Friday, 17 April
League One
Port Vale v Preston

Saturday, 18 April
Premier League
Arsenal v Sunderland
Aston Villa v QPR
Chelsea v Man Utd
Crystal Palace v West Brom
Everton v Burnley
Hull v Liverpool
Leicester v Swansea
Man City v West Ham
Newcastle v Tottenham
Stoke v Southampton

Championship
Blackburn v Nottm Forest
Blackpool v Fulham
Bournemouth v Sheffield Wed
Brentford v Bolton
Cardiff v Millwall
Charlton v Leeds
Huddersfield v Derby
Norwich v Middlesbrough
Rotherham v Reading
Watford v Birmingham
Wigan v Brighton
Wolves v Ipswich

League One
Barnsley v Peterborough
Bristol City v Coventry
Colchester v Scunthorpe
Crawley v Notts Co
Crewe v Walsall
Doncaster v Fleetwood
Gillingham v Rochdale
MK Dons v Leyton Orient
Oldham v Chesterfield
Sheffield Utd v Bradford
Swindon v Yeovil

League Two
Accrington v Stevenage
AFC Wimbledon v Wycombe
Cambridge v Mansfield
Carlisle v Plymouth
Exeter v Southend
Luton v Hartlepool
Morecambe v Burton
Newport v Dag & Red
Northampton v Cheltenham
Portsmouth v Bury
Shrewsbury v York
Tranmere v Oxford

Saturday, 25 April
Premier League
Arsenal v Chelsea
Burnley v Leicester
Crystal Palace v Hull
Everton v Man Utd
Man City v Aston Villa
Newcastle v Swansea
QPR v West Ham
Southampton v Tottenham
Stoke v Sunderland
West Brom v Liverpool

Championship
Birmingham v Charlton
Bournemouth v Bolton
Brighton v Watford
Cardiff v Blackpool
Fulham v Middlesbrough
Huddersfield v Blackburn
Ipswich v Nottm Forest
Millwall v Derby

Reading v Brentford
Rotherham v Norwich
Sheffield Wed v Leeds
Wigan v Wolves

League One
Bradford v Barnsley
Chesterfield v Bristol City
Coventry v Crewe
Fleetwood v Colchester
Leyton Orient v Sheffield Utd
Notts Co v Doncaster
Peterborough v Crawley
Preston v Swindon
Rochdale v MK Dons
Scunthorpe v Gillingham
Walsall v Oldham
Yeovil v Port Vale

League Two
Burton v Northampton
Bury v AFC Wimbledon
Cheltenham v Shrewsbury
Dag & Red v Accrington
Hartlepool v Exeter
Mansfield v Portsmouth
Oxford v Cambridge
Plymouth v Tranmere
Southend v Luton
Stevenage v Carlisle
Wycombe v Morecambe
York v Newport

Saturday, 2nd May
Premier League
Aston Villa v Everton
Chelsea v Crystal Palace
Hull v Arsenal
Leicester v Newcastle
Liverpool v QPR
Man Utd v West Brom
Sunderland v Southampton
Swansea v Stoke
Tottenham v Man City
West Ham v Burnley

Championship
Blackburn v Ipswich
Blackpool v Huddersfield
Bolton v Birmingham
Brentford v Wigan
Charlton v Bournemouth
Derby v Reading
Leeds v Rotherham
Middlesbrough v Brighton
Norwich v Fulham
Nottm Forest v Cardiff
Watford v Sheffield Wed
Wolves v Millwall

League One
Barnsley v Rochdale
Bristol City v Walsall

Colchester v Preston
Crawley v Coventry
Crewe v Bradford
Doncaster v Scunthorpe
Gillingham v Notts Co
MK Dons v Yeovil
Oldham v Peterborough
Port Vale v Fleetwood
Sheffield Utd v Chesterfield
Swindon v Leyton Orient

League Two
Accrington v Mansfield
AFC Wimbledon v Cheltenham
Cambridge v Burton
Carlisle v Hartlepool
Exeter v Dag & Red
Luton v Stevenage
Morecambe v Southend
Newport v Oxford
Northampton v Wycombe
Portsmouth v York
Shrewsbury v Plymouth
Tranmere v Bury

Saturday, 9 May
Premier League
Arsenal v Swansea
Aston Villa v West Ham
Chelsea v Liverpool
Crystal Palace v Man Utd
Everton v Sunderland
Hull v Burnley
Leicester v Southampton
Man City v QPR
Newcastle v West Brom
Stoke v Tottenham

Saturday, 16 May
Premier League
Burnley v Stoke
Liverpool v Crystal Palace
Man Utd v Arsenal
QPR v Newcastle
Southampton v Aston Villa
Sunderland v Leicester
Swansea v Man City
Tottenham v Hull
West Brom v Chelsea
West Ham v Everton

Sunday, 24 May
Premier League
Arsenal v West Brom
Aston Villa v Burnley
Chelsea v Sunderland
Crystal Palace v Swansea
Everton v Tottenham
Hull v Man Utd
Leicester v QPR
Man City v Southampton
Newcastle v West Ham
Stoke v Liverpool

SCOTTISH FIXTURES 2014–2015
Premiership, Championship, League One and League Two

Saturday, 9 August
Premiership
Aberdeen v Dundee Utd
Celtic v Partick - Postponed
Dundee v Kilmarnock
Hamilton v Inverness
Motherwell v St Mirren
Ross Co v St Johnstone

Championship
Cowdenbeath v Falkirk
Hibernian v Livingston
Queen of South v Alloa
Raith Rov v Dumbarton

League One
Ayr v Morton
Dunfermline v Brechin
Peterhead v Stirling
Stenhousemuir v Airdrie
Stranraer v Forfar

League Two
Albion v Annan
Berwick v Arbroath
Elgin v East Fife
Montrose v East Stirling
Queen's Park v Clyde

Sunday, 10 August
Championship
Rangers v Hearts

Wednesday, 13 August
Premiership
Dundee Utd v Motherwell
Inverness v Dundee
Kilmarnock v Aberdeen
Partick v Ross Co
St Johnstone v Celtic
St Mirren v Hamilton

Friday, 15 August
Championship
Falkirk v Rangers

Saturday, 16 August
Premiership
Aberdeen v St Mirren
Celtic v Dundee Utd
Dundee v Partick
Hamilton v St Johnstone
Motherwell v Inverness
Ross Co v Kilmarnock

Championship
Alloa v Raith Rov
Dumbarton v Queen of South
Livingston v Cowdenbeath

League One
Airdrie v Peterhead
Brechin v Stenhousemuir
Forfar v Dunfermline
Morton v Stranraer
Stirling v Ayr
League Two
Annan v Queen's Park
Arbroath v Albion
Clyde v Montrose
East Fife v Berwick
East Stirling v Elgin

Sunday, 17 August
Championship
Hearts v Hibernian

Saturday, 23 August
Premiership
Dundee Utd v Ross Co
Inverness v Celtic
Kilmarnock v Motherwell
Partick v Hamilton
St Johnstone v Aberdeen
St Mirren v Dundee

Championship
Cowdenbeath v Alloa
Hibernian v Falkirk
Queen of South v Livingston
Raith Rov v Hearts
Rangers v Dumbarton

League One
Ayr v Forfar
Dunfermline v Airdrie
Peterhead v Morton
Stenhousemuir v Stirling
Stranraer v Brechin
League Two
Albion v East Fife
Berwick v East Stirling
Elgin v Clyde
Montrose v Annan
Queen's Park v Arbroath

Saturday, 30 August
Premiership
Aberdeen v Partick
Hamilton v Ross Co
Inverness v Kilmarnock
Motherwell v St Johnstone
St Mirren v Dundee Utd

Championship
Alloa v Hibernian
Cowdenbeath v Raith Rov
Dumbarton v Livingston
Hearts v Falkirk
Rangers v Queen of South

League One
Airdrie v Stirling
Brechin v Peterhead
Forfar v Morton
Stenhousemuir v Ayr
Stranraer v Dunfermline

League Two
Albion v Queen's Park
Annan v Elgin
Arbroath v Montrose
Clyde v Berwick
East Fife v East Stirling

Sunday, 31 August
Premiership
Dundee v Celtic

Saturday, 13 September
Premiership
Celtic v Aberdeen
Dundee Utd v Hamilton
Kilmarnock v St Mirren
Partick v Inverness
Ross Co v Motherwell
St Johnstone v Dundee

Championship
Dumbarton v Hearts
Falkirk v Queen of South
Hibernian v Cowdenbeath
Livingston v Alloa
Raith Rov v Rangers

League One
Ayr v Stranraer
Dunfermline v Stenhousemuir
Forfar v Peterhead
Morton v Airdrie
Stirling v Brechin

League Two
Annan v Berwick
Arbroath v East Fife
East Stirling v Clyde
Montrose v Albion
Queen's Park v Elgin

Saturday, 20 September
Premiership
Aberdeen v Ross Co
Celtic v Motherwell
Dundee v Dundee Utd
Hamilton v Kilmarnock
Inverness v St Johnstone
Partick v St Mirren

Championship
Alloa v Rangers
Falkirk v Dumbarton

Hearts v Cowdenbeath
Livingston v Raith Rov
Queen of South v Hibernian

League One
Airdrie v Stranraer
Brechin v Ayr
Morton v Dunfermline
Peterhead v Stenhousemuir
Stirling v Forfar

League Two
Berwick v Albion
Clyde v Arbroath
East Fife v Queen's Park
East Stirling v Annan
Elgin v Montrose

Saturday, 27 September
Premiership
Aberdeen v Inverness
Dundee Utd v St Johnstone
Kilmarnock v Partick
Motherwell v Hamilton
Ross Co v Dundee
St Mirren v Celtic

Championship
Cowdenbeath v Queen of South
Dumbarton v Alloa
Hearts v Livingston
Raith Rov v Falkirk
Rangers v Hibernian

League One
Ayr v Airdrie
Dunfermline v Peterhead
Forfar v Brechin
Stenhousemuir v Morton
Stranraer v Stirling

League Two
Albion v East Stirling
Arbroath v Elgin
Clyde v Annan
Montrose v East Fife
Queen's Park v Berwick

Saturday, 4 October
Premiership
Celtic v Hamilton
Dundee v Aberdeen
Inverness v Ross Co
Kilmarnock v Dundee Utd
Partick v Motherwell
St Johnstone v St Mirren

Championship
Dumbarton v Cowdenbeath
Falkirk v Alloa
Hibernian v Raith Rov
Livingston v Rangers
Queen of South v Hearts

League One
Airdrie v Forfar
Brechin v Morton
Peterhead v Ayr
Stenhousemuir v Stranraer
Stirling v Dunfermline

Friday, October 10
Championship
Raith Rov v Queen of South

Saturday, 11 October
Championship
Alloa v Hearts
Cowdenbeath v Rangers
Falkirk v Livingston
Hibernian v Dumbarton

League One
Airdrie v Brechin
Ayr v Dunfermline
Forfar v Stenhousemuir
Morton v Stirling
Stranraer v Peterhead

League Two
Annan v Arbroath
Berwick v Montrose
East Fife v Clyde
East Stirling v Queen's Park
Elgin v Albion

Saturday, 18 October
Premiership
Dundee Utd v Partick
Hamilton v Aberdeen
Motherwell v Dundee
Ross Co v Celtic
St Johnstone v Kilmarnock
St Mirren v Inverness

Championship
Alloa v Cowdenbeath
Hearts v Dumbarton
Livingston v Hibernian
Queen of South v Falkirk
Rangers v Raith Rov

League One
Brechin v Stranraer
Dunfermline v Forfar
Morton v Ayr
Peterhead v Airdrie
Stirling v Stenhousemuir

League Two
Albion v Clyde
Arbroath v East Stirling
Berwick v Elgin
East Fife v Annan
Queen's Park v Montrose

Saturday, 25 October
Premiership

Aberdeen v Motherwell
Celtic v Kilmarnock
Dundee v Hamilton
Inverness v Dundee Utd
Partick v St Johnstone
St Mirren v Ross Co

Championship
Dumbarton v Rangers
Falkirk v Cowdenbeath
Hibernian v Hearts
Livingston v Queen of South
Raith Rov v Alloa

League One
Ayr v Brechin
Dunfermline v Morton
Forfar v Stranraer
Stenhousemuir v Peterhead
Stirling v Airdrie

League Two
Albion v Berwick
Annan v East Stirling
Clyde v Elgin
Montrose v Arbroath
Queen's Park v East Fife

Saturday, 1 November
Premiership
Celtic v Inverness
Dundee Utd v St Mirren
Hamilton v Partick
Kilmarnock v Dundee
Ross Co v Aberdeen
St Johnstone v Motherwell

Saturday, 8 November
Premiership
Aberdeen v Celtic
Dundee v St Johnstone
Inverness v Hamilton
Kilmarnock v Ross Co
Motherwell v Dundee Utd
St Mirren v Partick

Championship
Alloa v Livingston
Cowdenbeath v Hibernian
Hearts v Raith Rov
Queen of South v Dumbarton
Rangers v Falkirk

League One
Airdrie v Stenhousemuir
Brechin v Stirling
Morton v Forfar
Peterhead v Dunfermline
Stranraer v Ayr

League Two
Arbroath v Queen's Park
East Fife v Albion

East Stirling v Berwick
Elgin v Annan
Montrose v Clyde

Saturday, 15 November
Championship
Falkirk v Hearts
Hibernian v Queen of South
Livingston v Dumbarton
Raith Rov v Cowdenbeath
Rangers v Alloa

League One
Airdrie v Morton
Ayr v Peterhead
Brechin v Forfar
Stenhousemuir v Dunfermline
Stirling v Stranraer

League Two
Albion v Arbroath
Annan v Montrose
Berwick v East Fife
Clyde v East Stirling
Elgin v Queen's Park

Saturday, 22 November
Premiership
Celtic v Dundee
Dundee Utd v Kilmarnock
Hamilton v St Mirren
Inverness v Motherwell
Partick v Aberdeen
St Johnstone v Ross Co

Championship
Alloa v Falkirk
Cowdenbeath v Livingston
Dumbarton v Hibernian
Hearts v Rangers
Queen of South v Raith Rov

League One
Dunfermline v Stirling
Forfar v Ayr
Morton v Stenhousemuir
Peterhead v Brechin
Stranraer v Airdrie

League Two
Arbroath v Clyde
Berwick v Annan
East Fife v Elgin
East Stirling v Montrose
Queen's Park v Albion

Saturday, 29 November
League Two
Annan v Albion
Clyde v Queen's Park
East Stirling v East Fife
Elgin v Arbroath
Montrose v Berwick

Saturday, 6 December
Premiership
Aberdeen v Hamilton
Dundee v Inverness
Motherwell v Celtic
Partick v Kilmarnock
Ross Co v Dundee Utd
St Mirren v St Johnstone

Championship
Alloa v Dumbarton
Falkirk v Hibernian
Hearts v Queen of South
Raith Rov v Livingston
Rangers v Cowdenbeath

League One
Brechin v Airdrie
Dunfermline v Ayr
Stenhousemuir v Forfar
Stirling v Peterhead
Stranraer v Morton

League Two
Albion v Elgin
Arbroath v Annan
Berwick v Clyde
East Fife v Montrose
Queen's Park v East Stirling

Saturday, 13 December
Premiership
Celtic v St Mirren
Dundee Utd v Aberdeen
Hamilton v Dundee
Inverness v Partick
Kilmarnock v St Johnstone
Motherwell v Ross Co

Championship
Cowdenbeath v Hearts
Dumbarton v Raith Rov
Hibernian v Alloa
Livingston v Falkirk
Queen of South v Rangers

League One
Airdrie v Dunfermline
Ayr v Stenhousemuir
Forfar v Stirling
Morton v Brechin
Peterhead v Stranraer

League Two
Annan v East Fife
Clyde v Albion
East Stirling v Arbroath
Elgin v Berwick
Montrose v Queen's Park

Saturday, 20 December
Premiership
Aberdeen v Kilmarnock

Dundee Utd v Celtic
Partick v Dundee
Ross Co v Hamilton
St Johnstone v Inverness
St Mirren v Motherwell

Championship
Dumbarton v Falkirk
Hearts v Alloa
Queen of South v Cowdenbeath
Raith Rov v Hibernian
Rangers v Livingston

League One
Ayr v Stirling
Dunfermline v Stranraer
Forfar v Airdrie
Morton v Peterhead
Stenhousemuir v Brechin

League Two
Albion v Montrose
Arbroath v Berwick
Clyde v East Fife
Elgin v East Stirling
Queen's Park v Annan

Saturday, 27 December
Premiership
Celtic v Ross Co
Dundee v St Mirren
Inverness v Aberdeen
Kilmarnock v Hamilton
Motherwell v Partick
St Johnstone v Dundee Utd

Championship
Alloa v Queen of South
Cowdenbeath v Dumbarton
Falkirk v Raith Rov
Hibernian v Rangers
Livingston v Hearts

League One
Airdrie v Ayr
Brechin v Dunfermline
Peterhead v Forfar
Stirling v Morton
Stranraer v Stenhousemuir

League Two
Annan v Clyde
Berwick v Queen's Park
East Fife v Arbroath
East Stirling v Albion
Montrose v Elgin

Thursday 1 January
Premiership
Aberdeen v St Johnstone
Dundee Utd v Dundee
Hamilton v Motherwell
Partick v Celtic

Ross Co v Inverness
St Mirren v Kilmarnock

Saturday, 3 January
Championship
Cowdenbeath v Raith Rov
Falkirk v Alloa
Hearts v Hibernian
Queen of South v Livingston
Rangers v Dumbarton

League One
Ayr v Stranraer
Dunfermline v Peterhead
Forfar v Brechin
Morton v Airdrie
Stenhousemuir v Stirling

League Two
Albion v Annan
Arbroath v Montrose
Berwick v East Stirling
Elgin v East Fife
Queen's Park v Clyde

Sunday, 4 January
Premiership
Dundee v Ross Co
Inverness v St Mirren
Kilmarnock v Celtic
Motherwell v Aberdeen
Partick v Dundee Utd
St Johnstone v Hamilton

Saturday, 10 January
Premiership
Celtic v St Johnstone
Dundee v Motherwell
Hamilton v Dundee Utd
Kilmarnock v Inverness
Ross Co v Partick
St Mirren v Aberdeen

Championship
Alloa v Rangers
Dumbarton v Hearts
Hibernian v Falkirk
Livingston v Cowdenbeath
Raith Rov v Queen of South

League One
Airdrie v Peterhead
Brechin v Ayr
Stenhousemuir v Morton
Stirling v Dunfermline
Stranraer v Forfar

League Two
Annan v Elgin
Arbroath v Albion
Clyde v Berwick
East Fife v Queen's Park
Montrose v East Stirling

Saturday, 17 January
Premiership
Aberdeen v Dundee
Dundee Utd v Inverness
Hamilton v Celtic
Motherwell v Kilmarnock
Ross Co v St Mirren
St Johnstone v Partick

Championship
Falkirk v Queen of South
Hibernian v Cowdenbeath
Livingston v Alloa
Raith Rov v Dumbarton
Rangers v Hearts

League One
Ayr v Morton
Dunfermline v Airdrie
Forfar v Stenhousemuir
Peterhead v Stirling
Stranraer v Brechin

League Two
Albion v East Fife
Berwick v Montrose
East Stirling v Annan
Elgin v Clyde
Queen's Park v Arbroath

Wednesday, 21 January
Premiership
Aberdeen v Ross Co
Celtic v Motherwell
Dundee v Kilmarnock
Inverness v St Johnstone
Partick v Hamilton
St Mirren v Dundee Utd

Saturday, 24 January
Premiership
Dundee Utd v Motherwell
Hamilton v Inverness
Kilmarnock v Partick
Ross Co v Celtic
St Johnstone v Aberdeen
St Mirren v Dundee

Championship
Alloa v Raith Rov
Cowdenbeath v Rangers
Dumbarton v Livingston
Hearts v Falkirk
Queen of South v Hibernian

League One
Airdrie v Stranraer
Brechin v Peterhead
Morton v Dunfermline
Stenhousemuir v Ayr
Stirling v Forfar

League Two
Annan v Berwick

Clyde v Arbroath
East Fife v East Stirling
Montrose v Albion
Queen's Park v Elgin

Saturday, 31 January
Premiership
Aberdeen v Dundee Utd
Celtic v Kilmarnock
Dundee v Hamilton
Inverness v Ross Co
Motherwell v St Johnstone
Partick v St Mirren

Championship
Alloa v Hearts
Cowdenbeath v Queen of South
Falkirk v Dumbarton
Hibernian v Raith Rov
Livingston v Rangers

League One
Airdrie v Brechin
Ayr v Dunfermline
Forfar v Morton
Peterhead v Stenhousemuir
Stranraer v Stirling

League Two
Albion v Queen's Park
Arbroath v East Fife
Berwick v Elgin
East Stirling v Clyde
Montrose v Annan

Saturday, 7 February
League One
Ayr v Airdrie
Dunfermline v Brechin
Forfar v Peterhead
Morton v Stirling
Stenhousemuir v Stranraer

League Two
Arbroath v East Stirling
Clyde v Annan
East Fife v Berwick
Elgin v Albion
Queen's Park v Montrose

Saturday, 14 February
Premiership
Dundee v Partick
Hamilton v Aberdeen
Kilmarnock v Dundee Utd
Ross Co v Motherwell
St Johnstone v Celtic
St Mirren v Inverness

Championship
Dumbarton v Cowdenbeath
Hearts v Livingston
Queen of South v Alloa

Raith Rov v Falkirk
Rangers v Hibernian

League One
Airdrie v Forfar
Brechin v Morton
Dunfermline v Stenhousemuir
Stirling v Ayr
Stranraer v Peterhead

League Two
Albion v Clyde
Annan v Queen's Park
Berwick v Arbroath
East Stirling v Elgin
Montrose v East Fife

Saturday, 21 February
Premiership
Aberdeen v St Mirren
Celtic v Hamilton
Dundee Utd v St Johnstone
Inverness v Kilmarnock
Motherwell v Dundee
Partick v Ross Co

Championship
Cowdenbeath v Alloa
Falkirk v Livingston
Hibernian v Dumbarton
Queen of South v Hearts
Raith Rov v Rangers

League One
Forfar v Dunfermline
Morton v Stranraer
Peterhead v Ayr
Stenhousemuir v Airdrie
Stirling v Brechin

League Two
Albion v East Stirling
Annan v Arbroath
East Fife v Clyde
Elgin v Montrose
Queen's Park v Berwick

Saturday, 28 February
Premiership
Celtic v Aberdeen
Dundee Utd v Partick
Motherwell v Inverness
Ross Co v Dundee
St Johnstone v Kilmarnock
St Mirren v Hamilton

Championship
Alloa v Hibernian
Dumbarton v Queen of South
Falkirk v Rangers
Hearts v Cowdenbeath
Livingston v Raith Rov

League One
Airdrie v Stirling
Ayr v Forfar
Brechin v Stenhousemuir
Peterhead v Morton
Stranraer v Dunfermline

League Two
Arbroath v Elgin
Berwick v Albion
Clyde v Montrose
East Fife v Annan
East Stirling v Queen's Park

Saturday, 7 March
Championship
Cowdenbeath v Falkirk
Dumbarton v Alloa
Hibernian v Livingston
Raith Rov v Hearts
Rangers v Queen of South

League One
Brechin v Airdrie
Dunfermline v Ayr
Morton v Forfar
Stenhousemuir v Peterhead
Stirling v Stranraer

League Two
Annan v Albion
Clyde v East Stirling
Elgin v Berwick
Montrose v Arbroath
Queen's Park v East Fife

Saturday, 14 March
Premiership
Aberdeen v Motherwell
Dundee v Celtic
Hamilton v Ross Co
Inverness v Dundee Utd
Kilmarnock v St Mirren
Partick v St Johnstone

Championship
Alloa v Falkirk
Cowdenbeath v Hibernian
Hearts v Dumbarton
Queen of South v Raith Rov
Rangers v Livingston

League One
Airdrie v Morton
Ayr v Stenhousemuir
Dunfermline v Stirling
Forfar v Stranraer
Peterhead v Brechin

League Two
Albion v Montrose
Arbroath v Clyde
Berwick v Annan

East Stirling v East Fife
Elgin v Queen's Park

Saturday, 21 March
Premiership
Celtic v Dundee Utd
Dundee v Aberdeen
Motherwell v Hamilton
Partick v Inverness
Ross Co v Kilmarnock
St Johnstone v St Mirren

Championship
Falkirk v Hearts
Hibernian v Rangers
Livingston v Dumbarton
Queen of South v Cowdenbeath
Raith Rov v Alloa

League One
Brechin v Forfar
Morton v Ayr
Stenhousemuir v Dunfermline
Stirling v Peterhead
Stranraer v Airdrie

League Two
Annan v East Stirling
Clyde v Elgin
East Fife v Arbroath
Montrose v Berwick
Queen's Park v Albion

Saturday, 28 March
Championship
Alloa v Livingston
Dumbarton v Falkirk
Hearts v Queen of South
Raith Rov v Hibernian
Rangers v Cowdenbeath

League One
Airdrie v Stenhousemuir
Ayr v Brechin
Dunfermline v Morton
Forfar v Stirling
Peterhead v Stranraer

League Two
Albion v Elgin
Annan v Clyde
Berwick v Queen's Park
East Fife v Montrose
East Stirling v Arbroath

Saturday, 4 April
Premiership
Aberdeen v Partick
Dundee Utd v Ross Co
Hamilton v St Johnstone
Inverness v Dundee
Kilmarnock v Motherwell
St Mirren v Celtic

Championship
Cowdenbeath v Dumbarton
Falkirk v Raith Rov
Hibernian v Queen of South
Livingston v Hearts
Rangers v Alloa

League One
Morton v Brechin
Peterhead v Dunfermline
Stenhousemuir v Forfar
Stirling v Airdrie
Stranraer v Ayr

League Two
Albion v Berwick
Arbroath v Annan
Clyde v East Fife
Elgin v East Stirling
Montrose v Queen's Park

Wednesday, 8 April
Premiership
Aberdeen v Inverness
Celtic v Partick
Dundee v Dundee Utd
Hamilton v Kilmarnock
Motherwell v St Mirren
Ross Co v St Johnstone

Championship
Dumbarton v Hibernian
Hearts v Alloa
Livingston v Falkirk
Queen of South v Rangers
Raith Rov v Cowdenbeath

Saturday, 11 April
Premiership
Dundee Utd v Hamilton
Inverness v Celtic
Kilmarnock v Aberdeen
Partick v Motherwell
St Johnstone v Dundee
St Mirren v Ross Co

Championship
Alloa v Dumbarton
Cowdenbeath v Livingston
Hibernian v Hearts
Queen of South v Falkirk
Rangers v Raith Rov

League One
Ayr v Peterhead
Brechin v Stirling
Dunfermline v Stranraer
Forfar v Airdrie
Morton v Stenhousemuir

League Two
Berwick v Clyde
East Fife v Albion
East Stirling v Montrose
Elgin v Arbroath
Queen's Park v Annan

Saturday, 18 April
Championship
Alloa v Queen of South
Dumbarton v Rangers
Falkirk v Cowdenbeath
Hearts v Raith Rov
Livingston v Hibernian

League One
Airdrie v Ayr
Brechin v Dunfermline
Peterhead v Forfar
Stirling v Morton
Stranraer v Stenhousemuir

League Two
Annan v East Fife
Arbroath v Queen's Park
Clyde v Albion
East Stirling v Berwick
Montrose v Elgin

Saturday, 25 April
Championship
Cowdenbeath v Hearts
Hibernian v Alloa
Queen of South v Dumbarton
Raith Rov v Livingston
Rangers v Falkirk

League One
Ayr v Stirling
Dunfermline v Forfar
Peterhead v Airdrie
Stenhousemuir v Brechin
Stranraer v Morton

League Two
Albion v Arbroath
Berwick v East Fife
Elgin v Annan
Montrose v Clyde
Queen's Park v East Stirling

Saturday, 2nd May
Championship
Alloa v Cowdenbeath
Dumbarton v Raith Rov
Falkirk v Hibernian
Hearts v Rangers
Livingston v Queen of South

League One
Airdrie v Dunfermline
Brechin v Stranraer
Forfar v Ayr
Morton v Peterhead
Stirling v Stenhousemuir

League Two
Annan v Montrose
Arbroath v Berwick
Clyde v Queen's Park
East Fife v Elgin
East Stirling v Albion

THE THINGS THEY SAY...

'The world changed and we had to change with it' – **Greg Dyke**, chairman of the FA, on the continuation of a 5.15pm kick-off for the FA Cup Final for commercial reasons.

'Success has many fathers, but Ron's role in the history of the Premier League was fundamental to its formation and the foundations of what it has become today' – **Richard Scudamore**, the league's chief executive, on the death of former Crystal Palace owner Ron Noades.

CONFERENCE FIXTURES 2014–2015

Saturday, 9 August
Aldershot v Altrincham
Alfreton v Woking
Bristol Rov v Grimsby
Chester v Barnet
Dartford v Wrexham
Dover v Halifax
Gateshead v Torquay
Lincoln v Kidderminster
Macclesfield v Braintree
Nuneaton v Eastleigh
Southport v Forest Green
Welling v AFC Telford

Tuesday, 12 August
AFC Telford v Macclesfield
Altrincham v Lincoln
Barnet v Bristol Rov
Braintree v Dover
Eastleigh v Aldershot
Halifax v Southport
Forest Green v Chester
Grimsby v Nuneaton
Kidderminster v Alfreton
Torquay v Welling
Woking v Dartford
Wrexham v Gateshead

Saturday, 16 August
AFC Telford v Aldershot
Altrincham v Bristol Rov
Barnet v Lincoln
Braintree v Chester
Eastleigh v Gateshead
Halifax v Welling
Forest Green v Alfreton
Grimsby v Dover
Kidderminster v Dartford
Torquay v Southport
Woking v Macclesfield
Wrexham v Nuneaton

Saturday, 23 August
Aldershot v Forest Green
Alfreton v Wrexham
Bristol Rov v AFC Telford
Chester v Halifax
Dartford v Torquay
Dover v Eastleigh
Gateshead v Grimsby
Lincoln v Braintree
Macclesfield v Kidderminster
Nuneaton v Barnet
Southport v Altrincham
Welling v Woking

Monday, 25 August
AFC Telford v Southport
Altrincham v Gateshead
Barnet v Dartford

Braintree v Nuneaton
Eastleigh v Welling
Halifax v Lincoln
Forest Green v Bristol Rov
Grimsby v Alfreton
Kidderminster v Chester
Torquay v Aldershot
Woking v Dover
Wrexham v Macclesfield

Saturday, 30 August
Aldershot v Grimsby
Alfreton v Braintree
Bristol Rov v Halifax
Dartford v AFC Telford
Dover v Kidderminster
Gateshead v Chester
Lincoln v Torquay
Macclesfield v Eastleigh
Nuneaton v Altrincham
Southport v Barnet
Welling v Forest Green
Wrexham v Woking

Saturday, 6 September
AFC Telford v Dover
Altrincham v Dartford
Barnet v Alfreton
Braintree v Bristol Rov
Chester v Macclesfield
Eastleigh v Southport
Halifax v Aldershot
Forest Green v Wrexham
Grimsby v Welling
Kidderminster v Gateshead
Torquay v Nuneaton
Woking v Lincoln

Tuesday, 9 September
Aldershot v Woking
Alfreton v Altrincham
Bristol Rov v Wrexham
Chester v Torquay
Dartford v Eastleigh
Dover v Barnet
Gateshead v AFC Telford
Lincoln v Grimsby
Macclesfield v Halifax
Nuneaton v Forest Green
Southport v Kidderminster
Welling v Braintree

Saturday, 13 September
AFC Telford v Barnet
Altrincham v Eastleigh
Braintree v Kidderminster
Dover v Macclesfield
Forest Green v Halifax
Gateshead v Dartford
Grimsby v Torquay

Lincoln v Bristol Rov
Nuneaton v Aldershot
Southport v Alfreton
Woking v Chester
Wrexham v Welling

Tuesday, 16 September
Aldershot v Braintree
Alfreton v AFC Telford
Barnet v Wrexham
Bristol Rov v Nuneaton
Chester v Southport
Dartford v Dover
Eastleigh v Forest Green
Halifax v Grimsby
Kidderminster v Altrincham
Macclesfield v Gateshead
Torquay v Woking
Welling v Lincoln

Saturday, 20 September
Aldershot v Lincoln
Alfreton v Nuneaton
Barnet v Altrincham
Bristol Rov v Woking
Chester v Wrexham
Dartford v Forest Green
Eastleigh v Braintree
Halifax v AFC Telford
Kidderminster v Grimsby
Macclesfield v Southport
Torquay v Dover
Welling v Gateshead

Saturday, 27 September
AFC Telford v Torquay
Altrincham v Welling
Braintree v Halifax
Dover v Alfreton
Forest Green v Barnet
Gateshead v Aldershot
Grimsby v Chester
Lincoln v Macclesfield
Nuneaton v Dartford
Southport v Bristol Rov
Woking v Kidderminster
Wrexham v Eastleigh

Tuesday, 30 September
AFC Telford v Chester
Alfreton v Halifax
Altrincham v Macclesfield
Braintree v Barnet
Dover v Aldershot
Eastleigh v Bristol Rov
Forest Green v Torquay
Grimsby v Southport
Lincoln v Gateshead
Welling v Dartford
Woking v Nuneaton

Wrexham v Kidderminster

Saturday, 4 October
Aldershot v Alfreton
Barnet v Eastleigh
Bristol Rov v Dover
Chester v Welling
Dartford v Grimsby
Halifax v Altrincham
Gateshead v Braintree
Kidderminster v AFC Telford
Macclesfield v Forest Green
Nuneaton v Lincoln
Southport v Woking
Torquay v Wrexham

Tuesday, 7 October
AFC Telford v Forest Green
Bristol Rov v Dartford
Chester v Aldershot
Halifax v Wrexham
Gateshead v Alfreton
Grimsby v Altrincham
Kidderminster v Welling
Macclesfield v Barnet
Nuneaton v Dover
Southport v Lincoln

Saturday, 11 October
Aldershot v Bristol Rov
Alfreton v Torquay
Altrincham v Woking
Barnet v Kidderminster
Braintree v Southport
Dartford v Macclesfield
Dover v Chester
Eastleigh v Halifax
Forest Green v Gateshead
Lincoln v AFC Telford
Welling v Nuneaton
Wrexham v Grimsby

Saturday, 18 October
Altrincham v Braintree
Bristol Rov v Forest Green
Chester v Alfreton
Dartford v Aldershot
Eastleigh v Nuneaton
Halifax v Kidderminster
Gateshead v Barnet
Lincoln v Wrexham
Macclesfield v Dover
Southport v Welling
Torquay v Grimsby
Woking v AFC Telford

Tuesday, 21 October
Barnet v Braintree

Saturday, 1 November
AFC Telford v Bristol Rov
Aldershot v Gateshead

Altrincham v Alfreton
Braintree v Woking
Eastleigh v Chester
Forest Green v Lincoln
Grimsby v Dartford
Kidderminster v Torquay
Nuneaton v Macclesfield
Southport v Dover
Welling v Barnet
Wrexham v Halifax

Tuesday, 4 November
Braintree v Grimsby
Lincoln v Altrincham

Tuesday, 11 November
AFC Telford v Altrincham
Alfreton v Bristol Rov
Barnet v Torquay
Dartford v Welling
Dover v Braintree
Forest Green v Eastleigh
Gateshead v Lincoln
Grimsby v Halifax
Kidderminster v Aldershot
Macclesfield v Chester
Woking v Wrexham

Saturday, 15 November
Aldershot v Nuneaton
Alfreton v Dover
Altrincham v Grimsby
Barnet v AFC Telford
Braintree v Wrexham
Bristol Rov v Kidderminster
Chester v Gateshead
Dartford v Southport
Eastleigh v Lincoln
Halifax v Woking
Torquay v Forest Green
Welling v Macclesfield

Saturday, 22 November
AFC Telford v Braintree
Aldershot v Eastleigh
Chester v Bristol Rov
Dover v Forest Green
Grimsby v Kidderminster
Lincoln v Dartford
Macclesfield v Alfreton
Nuneaton v Southport
Torquay v Gateshead
Welling v Halifax
Woking v Barnet
Wrexham v Altrincham

Tuesday, 25 November
Braintree v Welling
Bristol Rov v Barnet
Dartford v Chester
Dover v Nuneaton
Grimsby v Woking
Kidderminster v Wrexham

Macclesfield v Torquay
Southport v Aldershot

Saturday, 29 November
AFC Telford v Grimsby
Altrincham v Kidderminster
Barnet v Macclesfield
Bristol Rov v Welling
Halifax v Alfreton
Forest Green v Dartford
Gateshead v Dover
Lincoln v Southport
Nuneaton v Chester
Torquay v Eastleigh
Woking v Braintree
Wrexham v Aldershot

Tuesday, 2 December
Alfreton v Gateshead
Chester v AFC Telford
Dover v Torquay
Eastleigh v Dartford
Halifax v Forest Green
Kidderminster v Nuneaton
Woking v Altrincham
Wrexham v Bristol Rov

Saturday, 6 December
Aldershot v Kidderminster
Chester v Lincoln
Dartford v Halifax
Dover v Wrexham
Eastleigh v Grimsby
Forest Green v Altrincham
Gateshead v Woking
Macclesfield v AFC Telford
Nuneaton v Alfreton
Southport v Braintree
Torquay v Barnet
Welling v Bristol Rov

Tuesday, 9 December
AFC Telford v Welling
Aldershot v Macclesfield
Alfreton v Eastleigh
Forest Green v Woking
Gateshead v Southport
Lincoln v Nuneaton
Torquay v Halifax

Saturday, 20 December
AFC Telford v Eastleigh
Alfreton v Macclesfield
Altrincham v Dover
Barnet v Chester
Braintree v Torquay
Bristol Rov v Gateshead
Halifax v Nuneaton
Grimsby v Forest Green
Kidderminster v Lincoln
Welling v Aldershot
Woking v Southport
Wrexham v Dartford

Friday 26 December
Aldershot v Barnet
Chester v Altrincham
Dartford v Braintree
Dover v Welling
Eastleigh v Woking
Forest Green v Kidderminster
Gateshead v Halifax
Lincoln v Alfreton
Macclesfield v Grimsby
Nuneaton v AFC Telford
Southport v Wrexham
Torquay v Bristol Rov

Sunday, 28 December
AFC Telford v Gateshead
Alfreton v Dartford
Altrincham v Nuneaton
Barnet v Dover
Braintree v Eastleigh
Bristol Rov v Macclesfield
Halifax v Chester
Grimsby v Lincoln
Kidderminster v Southport
Welling v Torquay
Woking v Aldershot
Wrexham v Forest Green

Thursday 1 January
AFC Telford v Nuneaton
Alfreton v Lincoln
Altrincham v Chester
Barnet v Aldershot
Braintree v Dartford
Bristol Rov v Torquay
Halifax v Gateshead
Grimsby v Macclesfield
Kidderminster v Forest Green
Welling v Dover
Woking v Eastleigh
Wrexham v Southport

Sunday, 4 January
Aldershot v AFC Telford
Chester v Braintree
Dartford v Kidderminster
Dover v Grimsby
Eastleigh v Altrincham
Forest Green v Welling
Gateshead v Wrexham
Lincoln v Barnet

...nuary
...quay
...st Green
...gh
...cclesfield

Lincoln v Aldershot
Nuneaton v Gateshead
Southport v Chester
Welling v Alfreton
Woking v Bristol Rov
Wrexham v AFC Telford

Saturday, 24 January
AFC Telford v Halifax
Aldershot v Dover
Alfreton v Forest Green
Barnet v Southport
Bristol Rov v Braintree
Chester v Kidderminster
Dartford v Woking
Eastleigh v Wrexham
Gateshead v Welling
Macclesfield v Altrincham
Nuneaton v Grimsby
Torquay v Lincoln

Saturday, 31 January
Altrincham v Aldershot
Braintree v Macclesfield
Dartford v Bristol Rov
Halifax v Barnet
Forest Green v Nuneaton
Grimsby v AFC Telford
Kidderminster v Eastleigh
Lincoln v Dover
Southport v Gateshead
Welling v Chester
Woking v Alfreton
Wrexham v Torquay

Saturday, 7 February
Aldershot v Halifax
Alfreton v Southport
Barnet v Woking
Bristol Rov v Lincoln
Chester v Dartford
Dover v Altrincham
Eastleigh v AFC Telford
Forest Green v Grimsby
Gateshead v Kidderminster
Macclesfield v Welling
Nuneaton v Wrexham
Torquay v Braintree

Tuesday, 10 February
Southport v Eastleigh

Saturday, 14 February
AFC Telford v Dartford
Aldershot v Welling
Altrincham v Forest Green
Braintree v Alfreton
Eastleigh v Torquay
Halifax v Dover
Gateshead v Nuneaton
Grimsby v Bristol Rov
Kidderminster v Woking
Lincoln v Chester
Southport v Macclesfield
Wrexham v Barnet

Saturday, 21 February
Alfreton v Aldershot
Barnet v Grimsby
Bristol Rov v Altrincham
Chester v Eastleigh
Dartford v Gateshead
Dover v Southport
Halifax v Braintree
Forest Green v AFC Telford
Macclesfield v Lincoln
Nuneaton v Kidderminster
Welling v Wrexham
Woking v Torquay

Saturday, 28 February
AFC Telford v Alfreton
Aldershot v Dartford
Altrincham v Barnet
Eastleigh v Macclesfield
Forest Green v Southport
Gateshead v Bristol Rov
Grimsby v Braintree
Kidderminster v Halifax
Lincoln v Woking
Nuneaton v Welling
Torquay v Chester
Wrexham v Dover

Saturday, 7 March
Alfreton v Kidderminster
Barnet v Forest Green
Braintree v Gateshead
Bristol Rov v Eastleigh
Dover v Lincoln
Halifax v Dartford
Macclesfield v Aldershot
Southport v Nuneaton
Torquay v AFC Telford
Welling v Altrincham
Woking v Grimsby
Wrexham v Chester

Saturday, 14 March
AFC Telford v Woking
Aldershot v Southport
Altrincham v Wrexham
Chester v Grimsby
Dartford v Alfreton
Eastleigh v Barnet
Halifax v Bristol Rov
Forest Green v Braintree
Gateshead v Macclesfield
Kidderminster v Dover
Lincoln v Welling
Nuneaton v Torquay

Saturday, 21 March
Alfreton v Chester
Altrincham v Halifax
Barnet v Welling
Braintree v AFC Telford

Bristol Rov v Aldershot
Dover v Gateshead
Grimsby v Eastleigh
Macclesfield v Nuneaton
Southport v Dartford
Torquay v Kidderminster
Woking v Forest Green
Wrexham v Lincoln

Saturday, 28 March
Aldershot v Wrexham
Alfreton v Barnet
Chester v Woking
Dartford v Altrincham
Dover v AFC Telford
Gateshead v Eastleigh
Kidderminster v Braintree
Lincoln v Forest Green
Macclesfield v Bristol Rov
Nuneaton v Halifax
Southport v Torquay
Welling v Grimsby

Saturday, 4 April
AFC Telford v Kidderminster
Altrincham v Southport
Barnet v Nuneaton
Braintree v Lincoln
Bristol Rov v Chester
Eastleigh v Dover
Halifax v Macclesfield
Forest Green v Aldershot

Grimsby v Gateshead
Torquay v Dartford
Woking v Welling
Wrexham v Alfreton

Monday, 6 April
Aldershot v Torquay
Alfreton v Grimsby
Chester v Forest Green
Dartford v Barnet
Dover v Woking
Gateshead v Altrincham
Kidderminster v Bristol Rov
Lincoln v Halifax
Macclesfield v Wrexham
Nuneaton v Braintree
Southport v AFC Telford
Welling v Eastleigh

Saturday, 11 April
AFC Telford v Lincoln
Barnet v Halifax
Braintree v Aldershot
Bristol Rov v Southport
Chester v Dover
Dartford v Nuneaton
Eastleigh v Alfreton
Forest Green v Macclesfield
Grimsby v Wrexham
Torquay v Altrincham
Welling v Kidderminster
Woking v Gateshead

Saturday, 18 April
Aldershot v Chester
Alfreton v Welling
Altrincham v AFC Telford
Dover v Bristol Rov
Halifax v Torquay
Gateshead v Forest Green
Kidderminster v Barnet
Lincoln v Eastleigh
Macclesfield v Dartford
Nuneaton v Woking
Southport v Grimsby
Wrexham v Braintree

Saturday, 25 April
AFC Telford v Wrexham
Barnet v Gateshead
Braintree v Altrincham
Bristol Rov v Alfreton
Chester v Nuneaton
Dartford v Lincoln
Eastleigh v Kidderminster
Forest Green v Dover
Grimsby v Aldershot
Torquay v Macclesfield
Welling v Southport
Woking v Halifax

THE THINGS THEY SAY...

'I died a thousand deaths every time they crossed the half-way line' – **Roy Hodgson**, England manager, after a tense 2-0 victory over Poland took his side to the World Cup Finals.

'Joy is short-lived in this job. We have just had a successful period and although I wouldn't suggest we intend to rest on our laurels, I think we have earned the right to enjoy the fruits of our labours. Instead we get this. The players are as angry as I am' – **Roy Hodgson** denies an accusation of making a racist comment during his half-time team talk at Wembley.

'I'd still put my tenner on us. Why not?' – **Roy Hodgson** after being paired with Italy and Uruguay in their World Cup group.